ISBN 978-1-330-13379-8
PIBN 10034075

1 MONTH OF
FREE
READING

at
www.ForgottenBooks.com

By purchasing this book you are eligible for one month membership to ForgottenBooks.com, giving you unlimited access to our entire collection of over 1,000,000 titles via our web site and mobile apps.

To claim your free month visit: www.forgottenbooks.com/free34075

TO THE

QUEEN REGENT.

MADAM,

I Should never have entertained the leaſt Thought of preſenting to Your Majeſty the HISTORY OF THE INQUISITION, but that it afforded me an Opportunity of expreſſing my ſincere Joy, in that which is the common Happineſs of

A   theſe

thefe Nations; Your Majefty's juft Abhorrence of all the Frauds and Cruelties authorized and practifed by that infamous Tribunal, and Your generous Concern for the civil and religious Liberties of Mankind.

In the earlieft Part of Your Majefty's Life, when worldly Honours and Dignities muft have appeared with their greateft Charms, You became an illuftrious Example of Steadinefs in the Proteftant Faith. Your Refolution and Piety triumphed over the ftrongeft Temptations. God referved Your Majefty as a Blefling to the Kingdoms now under Your Guardianfhip. As a Reward of Your conftant Adherence to Truth and Virtue, he hath made You the beloved Queen of a free and powerful Nation, whofe Loyalty is the Effect of the moft voluntary Choice, and flows from the two ftrongeft Motives in the World, the Senfe both of their Intereft and Duty.

Under the Infpection of fuch a Queen and Mother, the *Britifh* Nation is in no Pain for the Royal Progeny, but looks on them with

2   Plea-

Pleafure, as the Sources of their future Happi-
nefs. Your Majefty's Example will infpire
them with Zeal for the Proteftant Religion,
and Your difinterefted Purfuit of Truth form
them into a Love of Liberty, and teach them
the true Notion and proper Ufe of it.

'Tis Your Majefty's happy Lot to live in an
Age, and be the Guardian of a Nation, in which
the Principles of all Religion undergo the moft
exact and critical Inquiry ; and 'tis the peculiar
Glory of His Majefty's Government, that all
Men are permitted to make fuch Inquiries with
Safety. As Superftition and Error can never
be effectually difcover'd and deftroy'd, nor Religion maintain its native Purity and Dignity
without the freeft Ufe of this invaluable Privilege, 'tis impoffible that the Ends of Government can require, or that true Religion can ever
prefcribe or juftify the leaft Invafion or Abridgment of it.

The Revelation of the Gofpel, fixed immovable upon its own Foundation of eternal Truth,
needs no Methods of Fraud and Violence for

its

its Support. The great Author of it appealed to the Reafon and Confciences of Men concerning the Proofs of his divine Miffion, and the Nature of the Doctrines he taught. His Apoftles after him claimed no Submiffion to their heavenly Dictates, without reafonable Convictions, founded in the Demonftration of the Spirit and of Truth. Happy had it been for the Chriftian Church, had the Examples of the Son of God and his Apoftles been, in this Refpect as well as others, counted worthy of Imitation!

Zeal for Religion, both in Princes and their Subjects, is unqueftionably a Duty. But Your Majefty underftands too well the great Obligations to Chriftian Charity, and feels too great a Pleafure in the Exercife of this facred Virtue, ever to fuffer Your own Zeal for Religion to lead You into a cruel perfecuting Warmth, or to encourage others in the ufe of any Methods for the Defence of Religion, which are not only contrary to the genuine Spirit and Defign of it, but in the Confequences deftructive of the Honour, Succefs, and even Being of it.

The

The Succeſſion of the illuſtrious Houſe of *Hanover* to the Throne of theſe Kingdoms, was a Bleſſing of long Expectation. The Severities which were exerciſed upon Proteſtant Diſſenters in former Reigns, upon the Account of Religion, made them caſt their Eyes upon that Auguſt Family. From thence, Madam, the Afflicted hoped for Relief: From thence the Sufferers for Conſcience-ſake expected, under God, their Salvation from the Yoak of Civil and Eccleſiaſtical Oppreſſion.

The Happineſs they both pray'd and longed for, but were allowed to ſee only afar off, we, their Poſterity, now enjoy. The all-merciful God hath abundantly anſwer'd their Prayers, and bleſſed us with the Fruits of their Expectations. When our Liberties were unrighteouſly invaded, and farther Difficulties and Sufferings were intended us, for our Fidelity to the preſent Royal Family, by an almoſt miraculous Providence, His late Majeſty came into our Relief, and will ever be remembered with Honour and

Gra-

Gratitude by us, as our Reftorer and Deliverer, and as the common Preferver of thefe Nations from that Deftruction which fo nearly threatened them.

His prefent Majefty, the Inheritor of His Royal Father's Virtues, as well as Kingdoms, will be reverenced for His impartial Protection of all His Subjects, for the Wifdom of His Counfels, the Steadinefs of His Meafures, and the glorious Succefs which hath crowned Them, in the Settlement of the different, and almoft contrary Interefts of *Europe*, and the Prefervation of the invaluable Bleffings of Peace.

Your Majefty will be admired for all thofe excellent Endowments, and amiable Virtues; which render You the greateft Ornament to publick and private Life. Your Regency of thefe Kingdoms, conducted with fuch Wifdom and Goodnefs, fhews You fit for the Weight of Government, and the Dignities of a Crown. Your Condefcenfion and Freedom in converfing
with

with Perfons of Learning and Virtue, difcovers Your Love of Truth, and Your Knowledge how to reconcile the Pleafures of Converfation and Friendfhip with the Reverence due to Majefty and Power. Your Love to true Religion, and Your Impartiality in fearching into the Nature of it, is the fulleft. Evidence that Your Majefty's Piety, as well as the Benevolence of Your natural Difpofition, muft neceffarily excite in Your Breaft a juft Averfion to all Methods of Violence for the Conviction and Converfion of others. Your Affection to the Proteftant Religion and Liberties in general, and Your fteady Regard to the Welfare of thefe Kingdoms in particular, indear Your Majefty to the prefent Generation, and will be fpoken of with Pleafure by thofe to come.

That God may long continue Your Majefty a Blefling in every Relation in which his Providence hath fixed You, and, after a full Enjoyment of the higheft Honour and Profperity, which this World can afford You, receive You to the more fubftantial and durable Bleffings of

the

D E D I C A T I O N.

the eternal World, is the fincere and fervent Prayer of,

May it pleafe Your Majefty,

Your Majefty's moft Obedient,

Moft Devoted, and

Moft Humble Servant,

SAMUEL CHANDLER.

PREFACE.

*T*HE *Introduction to* Mr. Limborch's *History of the Inquisition hath run out to such a Length, that I have but little Room for any Preface. That History needs nothing that I can say to recommend it. When it first came over to* England, *it was received with great Approbation by many of the principal Nobility and Clergy.* Mr. Lock, *that incomparable Judge of Men and Books, gives it the highest Character, and commends it for its Method and Perspicuity, and the Authorities by which it is so abundantly confirmed, and pronounces it a Work in its Kind absolutely perfect. He was particularly pleased that* Mr. Limborch *used the very Words of the Authors which he cites ; and, though this may make the reading of the History tedious to some, yet it was necessary, that the Inquisitors might be convicted by the*

B   *Testi-*

Teſtimony of their own Writers, of thoſe villanous Frauds and Cruelties, with which they are charged. In a Letter to Mr. Limborch himſelf, he tells him, that he had ſo fully expoſed their ſecret Arts of Wickedneſs and Cruelty, that, if they had any Remains of Humanity in them, they muſt be aſhamed of that horrid Tribunal, in which every Thing that was juſt and righteous was ſo monſtrouſly perverted; and that 'twas fit to be tranſlated into the vulgar Language of every Nation, that the meaneſt People might underſtand the Anti-chriſtian Practices of that execrable Court. The Papiſts were ſo apprehenſive of the Prejudices that might ariſe to their Cauſe by the Publication of this Book, that the Cardinals, Inquiſitors General at Rome, condemn'd it by an Edict, and forbad the reading it, under the ſevereſt Penalties.

Mr. Lock often mentions, in his Letters, ſeveral Additions which Mr. Limborch had prepared, and promiſed to tranſmit to him, that he might inſert them in their proper Places in the Margin. I know not whether he ever had the Pleaſure of ſeeing them; 'tis certain the Publick hath never hitherto been favour'd with them. When I firſt began my Tranſlation of the Hiſtory, the late ingenious Anthony Collins, Eſq; informed me, that he had ſome M. S. Papers of Mr. Limborch relating to it, and generouſly ſent them to me for my Peruſal. After this, I was informed by a worthy Friend, that there was a Gentleman in Holland who had a large Number of Corrections and Additions; and, upon my Application to him, he very kindly ordered them to be tranſcribed out of the Copy Mr. Limborch kept by him, which he had corrected and enlarged with his own Hand, and tranſmitted them to me from the Hague. His Name is Francis a Limborch, a worthy Relation of the learned Author's, to whom I take this Opportunity of returning my ſincere Thanks

2   *for*

for so valuable a Present. The Reader will find them included within these Hooks [ ]. I have added also a few marginal Notes, to explain some of the Terms made use of, and to confirm the History it self.

As to the Introduction, I thought it necessary to trace the History of Persecution from its first Beginnings, and thus to connect it with the Account of the Inquisition. Though it be long, it might have been greatly enlarged, especially with several remarkable Instances of it amongst the Pagans. *I cannot help inserting here one very extraordinary Passage from* Livy, *the* Roman *Historian, though it be a little out of its Place. He tells us *,*

" *That such a foreign Religion spread it self over the City, that* Lib. 25.
" *either Men or the Gods seemed entirely changed; that the* c. 10.
" Roman *Rites were not only forsaken in private, and within the*
" *Houses, but that even publickly, in the Forum and Capitol,*
" *great Numbers of Women flocked together, who neither sacrificed*
" *nor pray'd to the Gods, according to the manner of their Ancestors.*
" ——*This first excited the private Indignation of good Men, till*
" *at length it reached the Fathers, and became a publick Complaint.*
" *The Senate greatly blamed the Ædiles and capital Trium-*
" *virs, that they did not prohibit them, and when they endea-*

---

* Tanta religio, et ea magna ex parte externa, civitatem incessit, ut aut homines, aut Dii repente alii viderentur facti ; nec jam in secreto modo atq; intra parietes abolebantur Romani ritus, sed in publico etiam ac foro Capitalioq; mulierum turba erat, nec sacrificantium nec precantium Deos patrio more.——Primo secretæ bonorum indignationes exaudiebantur, deinde ad patres etiam, et ad publicam querimoniam excessit res. Incusati graviter ab Senatu Ædiles Triumviriq; capitales, quod non prohiberent : quum emovere eam multitudinem a foro, ac disjicere apparatus sacrorum conati.essent, haud procul afuit quin violarentur. Ubi potentius jam esse id malum apparuit quam ut minores per Magistratus sedaretur, M. Atilio, prætori urbis negotium ab Senatu datum est, ut his religionibus populum liberaret. Is et in concione Senatus consultum recitavit, et edixit, Ut quicumq; libros vaticinos precationesve, aut artem sacrificandi conscriptam haberet, eos libros omnes literasq; ad se ante Calendas Apriles deferret ; neu quis in publico sacrove loco, novo aut externo ritu sacrificaret.

" *voured*

" voured to drive away the Multitude from the Forum, and to
" throw down the Things they had provided for performing their
" sacred Rites, they were like to be torn in Pieces. And when
" the Evil grew too great to be cured by inferior Magistrates,
" the Senate order'd M. Atilius the Pretor of the City, to pre-
" vent the Peoples using these Religions." He accordingly publish'd this Decree of the Senate, that whoever had any Fortune-telling Books, or Prayers, or Ceremonies about Sacrifices written down, they should bring all such Books and
Writings to him, before the Calends of April, and that no
one should use any new or foreign Rite of sacrificing in
any publick or sacred Place.

Apud
Dion.
Cassium,
l. 52.
Mecenas, in his Advice to Augustus, says to him : Perform
divine Worship in all Things exactly according to the
Custom of your Ancestors, and compel others to do so
also ; and as to those who make any Innovations in Reli-
gion, hate and punish them ; and that not only for the
sake of the Gods, but because those who introduce new
Deities, excite others to make Changes in Civil Affairs.
Hence Conspiracies, Seditions, and Riots, Things very

Vit.Aug.
c. 93.
dangerous to Government. Accordingly Suetonius, in his
Life of this Prince, gives him this Character : " That tho' he
" religiously observed the ancient prescribed Ceremonies, yet he
" contemned all other foreign ones, and commended Caius, for
" that passing by Judæa, he would not pay his Devotions at Jeru-

Ibid.
c. 35.
" salem." He also, as the same Author tells us *, made a Law,
very much resembling our Test Act, by which he commanded,
that before any of the Senators should take their Places in

---

* Quo autem——religiosius Senatoria munera fungerentur, sanxit ut priusquam
consideret quisque, thure ac mero supplicaret apud aram ejus Dei, in cujus templo coi-
retur.

Council,

Council, they should offer Frankincense and Wine upon the Altar of that God in whose Temple they met.

These and other Passages that may be mention'd, abundantly prove that the Heathens were as much in Principle, and as really in Practice, Persecutors as the Christians ; and 'tis therefore very unfair and unreasonable to make it an Objection against Christianity, that so many of the Professors of it have, in all Ages, given into these ungodly and wicked Measures. If it proves any Thing, it will prove as much against natural Reason and Religion, as it doth against the Religion of Jesus. And if the Vices of Men, who have had no other Guide but the former, prove nothing against the Sufficiency and Goodness of them, Christians also may be very wicked Men, and yet the Religion they profess be a very excellent and divine one.

If any should ask, why I trouble the World with the Accounts of the Persecutions that Christians have raised against each other, at this Time, now that the Clergy of all Denominations seem to be entering into more moderate Measures ; I answer, to give the little Assistance I am able towards promoting a truly catholick and charitable Disposition ; there being, as I apprehend, no way so proper to expose the Doctrine and Practice of Persecution, as by a fair Representation of the unspeakable Mischiefs that have been occasioned by it ; nor any other Method so likely to render it the universal Abhorrence of Mankind, as to let them see, by past Examples, what Miseries they must expect, if God should ever, for our Sins, subject us again to the Yoak of Ecclesiastical Power ; which, wherever 'tis not kept under strict Restraint, will usurp upon the Authority and Dignity of Princes, and trample under Foot all the civil and religious Liberties of Mankind. 'Tis therefore highly incumbent upon all Persons in their several Stations ; 'tis what the Gentlemen of England,
who

who are born to *Eſtates* and *Honours,* and know the true *Value* of *Liberty* and *Property,* are more eſpe-cially concern'd in, to do all they can to prevent the *Encroachments* and gradual *Increaſes* of ſpiritual *Ty-ranny;* it being much more eaſy to do this, than to free themſelves from it, when once they have tamely ſubmitted to the *Uſurpations* of it.

If the perſecuting *Spirit* declines, 'tis far from being wholly extinguiſhed. The *Claims* of the *Church,* that now lie dormant, want nothing but a fair Op-portunity to revive. And for the *Truth* of this, I appeal to the late famous *Controverſy* about *Church Power* and *Authority.* May *God Almighty,* of his infinite *Mercy,* inſpire all *Ranks* and *Degrees* of *Men* with ſuch a *Love* to *Liberty,* and with ſuch a *Senſe* of the *Greatneſs* of their *Privilege,* in being free as to their *Conſciences, Religion, Perſons,* and *Eſtates,* as ſhall ſecure us from all *Attempts* to deprive us of it, or, at leaſt, as ſhall render all ſuch *Attempts* from warm deſigning *Bigots* wholly ineffectual.

'Tis, indeed, impoſſible to prevent all *Abuſes* of *Li-berty:* But theſe are infinitely more tolerable than the *Evils* that muſt neceſſarily flow from *Eccleſia-ſtical Tyranny,* which is deſtructive to *Knowledge, Learning, Piety* and *Virtue,* and every *Thing* that is dear and valuable to *Men* and *Chriſtians.* Even theſe *Abuſes* of *Liberty* have render'd many of the *Clergy* of the *Church* of England immortal, by their excel-lent *Defences* of the *Chriſtian Religion;* and I per-ſuade my ſelf that their *Lordſhips* of London, Dur-ham, Litchfield *and* Coventry, *had rather* he

remem-

remember'd and known to Posterity by Pastoral Letters, Defences of Christianity, *and* Vindications of Christ's Miracles, *than by that Rigidness and cruel Zeal for Uniformity in Opinions, and lifeless Ceremonies, by which many of their Predecessors have left an indelible Stain on their Names and Memories. May they go on thus to adorn their Episcopal Character; and, by being Examples of Christian Piety, Moderation, and Forbearance, influence the inferior Clergy to imitate them.*

I have nothing more to add, but to desire the Reader to over-look any lesser Faults that may have escaped me in the Introduction or Translation, and to ask my Subscribers Pardon for the long Delay of this Work. The ill State of my Health for many Months past, and my constant Engagements in Life, will be allowed as some Excuse by all equitable Persons. As to those who can make me no Allowance, all I can say to them is, that as this is the first Book that I have published by Subscription, so, according to my present Judgment, 'twill be the last. Such as it is, if it will do any Good, I shall be thankful to God, and not repent my own Labour.

London, Sept.
8, 1752.

SAMUEL CHANDLER.

A

A
L I S T
OF THE
SUBSCRIBERS.

A.

THE Reverend William Ayerſt, *D.D.*

Benjamin Avery, *L.L.D.*

The Rev. Mr. John Antleby

The Rev. Mr. John Archer

The Rev. Mr. Thomas Amory

Joſeph Andrews *Eſq;*

Robert Atwood *Eſq;*

Mr. Joſeph Adams

Mr. Thomas Aſhurſt

Mr. Allen

Mr. Abraham Atkyns

Mr. Edward Andrews

Mr. Daniel Adams

Mr. Thomas Aſtley

Mr. Samuel Avery

B.

The Right Honourable the Lord Viſcount Barrington

The Rev. Mr. Robert Billio

The Rev. Mr. Joſeph Billio, *2 Sets*

The Rev. Mr. John Bond

The Rev. Mr. John Barker

The Rev. Mr. Bale

The Rev. Mr. Samuel Bates

The Rev. Mr. George Benſon

The Rev. Mr. Joſhua Bays

The Rev. Mr. Joſeph Burroughs

Stamp Brooksbank *Eſq;*

Brook Bridges *Eſq;*

John Burton *Eſq;*

Nathaniel Braſſey *Eſq; 4 Sets*

James Brain *Eſq;*

Joſeph Bell *Eſq;*

Thomas

Thomas Bennet *Efq; of* Norton
Mr. Jonathan Bromley
Mr. John Bird
Mr. Levi Ball
Mr. William Bafnet
Mr. John Burkit
Mr. Simon Le Blanc
Mr. Benjamin Butcher
Mr. Samuel Bucknal, *Merchant*
George Bayley *of* Chichefter, *M. D.*
Mr. Thomas Browne
Mr. George Baker
Mr. Thomas Broadley, *Merchant*
Mr. Nehemiah Brooks
Mr. Richard Bulter
Mr. Humphry Bell
Mr. William Batt

C.

The Rev. Ruben Clark, *D. D.*
The Rev. Mr. William Crooke, *Prebendary of* Chichefter
The Rev. Mr. Samuel Clark
The Rev. Mr. Richard Choppin, *6 Sets*
The Rev. Mr. Edmund Calamy, *5 Sets*
Henry Cope *Efq;*
Benjamin Collier *Efq;*
Antony Collins *Efq;*
Mr. Thomas Coningham
Mr. Robert Cady
Mr. Samuel Craighead
Mr. John Cafwell
Mr. Paul Corbet
Mr. Jonathan Collier
Mr. Samuel Chandler *of* Portfmouth, *3 Sets*
Mr. John Carter, *Merchant*
Mr. Luke Cullimore, *Merchant*
Mr. John Copeland
Mr. John Chandler
Mr. John Cox
Mr. Cofeley *of* Briftol, *Bookfeller, 12 Sets*
Mr. Nehemiah Champion
Mr. Thomas Chinnall

D.

The Right Honourable James *Earl of* Derby, *L. P.*
John Dive *Efq; of* Queen-ftreet, Weftminfter
Humphry Davie *Efq;*
Benjamin Derby *Efq;*
The Rev. Mr. Jofeph. Denham
The Rev. Mr. Robert Dawfon
The Rev. Mr. Dodridge
Mr. James Deacon
Mr. Jofeph Dyer
Mr. Thomas Dyer
Mr. Rivers Dickenfon
Mr. Thomas Daville
Mr. Philip Dumouftier
Mr. Richard Dawfon
Mr. Benjamin Darling, *Merchant*
Mr. James Diggles
Mr. Michael Dean

E.

The Rev. John Evans, *D. D.*
The Rev. Jabez Earle, *D. D.*

F.

The Rev. Mr. Ebenezer Fletcher
The Rev. Mr. Samuel Fancourt
The Rev. Mr. William Ford
Mr. Philip Founareau
Mr. Thomas Fellows
Mr. Edward Forfter
Mr. Chriftopher Fowler
Mr. Thomas Fletcher, *2 Sets*
Mrs. Elizabeth Floyd
Mr. Bernard Frederick
Mr. James Figgins
Mr. Jofeph Fuller
Mr. Farr
Mr. Henry Faure
Mr. John Farringdon
Mr. Richard Ford, *Bookfeller, 5 Sets*

C   *The*

G.

The Rev. Benjamin Grofvenor, *D. D.*
The Rev. Mr. Philip Gibbs
The Rev. Mr. Edward Godwin
The Rev Mr. Thomas Green
The Rev. Mr. Henry Grove
The Rev. Mr. Grant
Thomas Gearing *Efq;*
Thomas Gordon *Efq;*
Mr. Robert Gibbs
Mr. John Grubb
Mr. Jofeph Gardner
John Gray, *M. D.*
Mr. Richard Godman, *Merchant*
Mr. Jofeph Gardner *of* Portfmouth
Capt. Simon Garbut
Mr. John Gough
Mr. William Goddard
Mr. John Goodchild
Mr. Thomas Gearing
Mrs. Elizabeth Gough

H.

Sir John Hartop, *Bart.*
The Rev. Samuel Holcomb, *D. D.*
The Rev. William Harris, *D. D.*
The Rev. Obadiah Hughes, *D. D.*
The Rev. Mr. John Horfeley
The Rev. Mr. John Hubbard
Robert Hucks *Efq;*
Henry Hall *Efq;*
John Halliday, *Gent.*
Mr James Hawkins
Mr. William Harrifon
Mr. John Hand
Mr. John Holmes
Mr. Haiftwell
Mr. Jafper Hale, *3 Sets*
Mr. Benjamin Hollis
Mr. Adam Holden
Mr. Humphry Hill
Mr. William Hoskyns
Mr. William Handley, *2 Sets*
Mr. Thomas Herne
Mr. Thomas Handley

Mr. William Hawkes
Mr. Hawkfworth
Mr. Peter Harvey
Mr. John Hollifter
Mr. Peter Hind
Mr. Samuel Hawkins
Mr. Farnham Haskell
Mr. George Houlme
Mr. Nathaniel Highmore
Mr. William Hoole
Mr. Richard Hett, *Bookfeller,* 14 *Sets*
Mr. Gavin Hamilton, *Bookfeller,* 7 *Sets*

J.

John Jacob *Efq;* 4 *Sets*
Stephen Jackfon *Efq;*
Mr. Benjamin James
Mr. Giles James, *L. P.*
Mr. John Jeffer
Mr. William Jeffries
Mr. Jofeph Jeffries
Mr. Jeremiah Immyns
Mr. Jofeph Ingram
Mr. Robert James

K.

John King *Efq;*
Samuel Kent *Efq;*

L.

The Rev. Samuel Lifle, *D. D.*
The Rev. Mr. Thomas Leaveﬂey
The Rev. Mr. Nathaniel Lardner
The Rev. Mr. Mofes Lowman
The Rev. Mr. Langford
Samuel Leﬃngham *Efq;*
Richard Lewen *Efq;*
Mr. John Lancafhire
Mr. Matthew Langley
Mr. Nicholas Langley
Mr. Benjamin Lehook
Mr. John Longuet

M.

The Rev. Ifaac Maddox, *D. D.*
The Rev. Mr. Lawrence Mace

The

The Rev. Mr. John Milner
The Rev. Mr. Daniel Markes
The Rev. Mr. John Moor
The Rev. Mr. Mash
The Rev. Mr. William May
The Rev. Mr. Murray
Henry Meriton *Esq;*
John Mitchel *Esq;*
Joseph Murden *Esq;*
Mr. Morgan Morse
Mr. Obadiah Marryat
Mr. John Morton
Mr. John Mount
Mrs. Moor
Mr. Joseph Mace
Mr. Samuel Morris
Mr. Gabriel Morley
Mr. John Mucklow
Mr. Anthony Malcher, *Merchant*
Mr. James Milnos, *Merchant*
Mr. William Man
Mr. Jasper Mauduit
Mr. William Mount, 7 *Sets*

N

The Rev. Mr. William Nash, *M. A.*
The Rev. Mr. Daniel Neal, *M. A.*
The Rev. Mr. John Norman
Mr. James Neave
Mr. Henry Newcomb
Mr. John Nicholson
Mr. *Alderman* Newnham *of* Portsmouth
Mr. William Newnham
Dr. Nettleton
Mr. —— Nicholson
Mr. John Noon, *Bookseller,* 7 *Sets*

O.

The Right Hon. Arthur Onflow, *Esq;*
  Speaker of the Honourable House of
  Commons, *L. P.*
Joshua Oldfield, *M. D.*
—— Oliver, *M. D. of the* Bath
Mr. Edmund Ogden
Mr. John Orr

P.

The Rev. Mr. John Phelps
The Rev. Mr. Samuel Price
The Rev. Mr. Thomas Priest
The Rev. Mr. John Partington
Archdale Palmer *Esq;*
John Palmer *Esq;*
Samuel Palmer *Esq;*
Thomas Palmer *Esq;*
David Polhill *Esq;*
Joshua Pembroke *Esq;*
Henry Plumtree, *M. D.*
Mr. Samuel Palmer
Mr. Thomas Partridge
Mr. Henry Palmer, *Merchant*
Mr. George Pell
Mr. Stephen Peters
Mr. Samuel Parish
Mr. Thomas Parish
Mr. Edward Clark Parish
Mr. John Peters
Mr. Thomas Palmer
Mr. Edward Petit
Mr. William Piercy
Mr. Thomas Penford
Mr. George Penfold
Mr. Edward Price
Mr. Michael Pope
Mr. John Peele, *Bookseller*

R.

Sir Thomas Roberts, *Bart.*
The Rev. Mr. James Read
The Rev. Mr. Henry Read
Samuel Read *Esq;*
Mathew Raper *Esq;*
Moses Raper *Esq;*
Dudley Ryder *Esq;*
Nathaniel Roffey *Esq;*
Mr. Richard Ryder
Mr. Gearing Roberts
Mr. Joseph Richman
Mr. John Richardson
Mr. William Rickman
Mr. Thomas Redman
Mrs. Reynolds.

Mr.

Mr. Daniel Radford
Mr. Benjamin Robinson
Mr. Samuel Randal
Mr. Robert Rogers
Mr. Richard Reynell

S.

The Rev. Bennet Stephenfon, *D. D.*
The Rev. —— Scott, *D. D.*
The Rev. Mr. George Smyth, *M. A.*
The Rev. Mr Joseph Sills
The Rev. Mr. John Southwell, 4 *Sets*
The Rev. Mr. Samuel Savage
The Rev. Mr. Sleigh
The Rev. Mr. Patrick Simpfon
The Rev. Mr. Nathaniel Sheiffield
The Rev. Mr. James Strong
The Rev. Mr. Arthur Shaliet
John Schrimfhire *Efq;*
Meyer Schæmberg, *M. D.*
Mr. Robert Sedgwick
Mr. Samuel Sedgwick
Mr. Jeremiah Smith
Mrs. Catharine Sharp
Mr. Shorey
Mr. Thomas Smith
Mr. John Smith
Mr. Samuel Stephenfon
Mr. Thomas Speidell
Mr. Joseph Selby
Mr. James Smith
Mr. Allen Smith
Mr. John Stansfield
Mr. Stephen Smith
Mr. John Staples

T.

The Rev. Edward Tenifon, *D. D.*
The Rev. Mr. Martin Thompkins
The Rev. Mr. John Tren
The Rev. Mr. Jeremiah Titcomb
St. Quintin Thompfon *Efq;*
John Tracy *Efq;*
Edmund Trench *Efq;*
Peter Temple *of* Bifhopftrow, *Gent.*
Mr. John Tatnell
Mr. John Tatlock

Mr. James Taylor
Mr. Harding Thompkins
Mr. John Towers
Mr. Henry Tatham
Mr. Peter Thornton, *Merchant*
Mr. Joseph Turner
Mr. Joseph Tindal
Mr. William Thornhil
Mr. Nathaniel Townfend
Mr. Samuel Travers, *Merchant*

W.

The Rev. Samuel Wright, *D. D.*
The Rev. Ifaac Watts, *D. D.*
The Rev. William Wifhart, *D. D.*
The Rev. Mr. James Watfon
The Rev. Mr. William Wallis
The Rev. Mr. Thomas Walker
The Rev. Mr. John Witter
The Rev. Mr. James Watkins
The Rev. Mr. Nathanael Whitlock
Wight Woolley *Efq;*
Arthur Woolley *Efq;*
Ifaac Welman *Efq;*
John Wowen *Efq;*
William Walter *Efq;*
James White, *Gent.*
Mr. James Weft
Mr. Watkinfon Wildman
Mr. Edward Walburge
Mr. Antony Walburge
Mr. George Willy, *jun.*
Mr. William Willy
Mr. Daniel Wilmott
Mrs. Mary Winnock
Mr. William Wildman
Mr. Thomas Walker
Mr. John Wefton *of* Greenwich
Mr. John Wainwright
Mr. Thomas Warren
Mr. Joel Watfon, *Merchant*
Mr. Winter
Mr. John Wells
Mr. Samuel Welton
Mr. Obadiah Weeks
Mr. Aaron Ward, *Bookfeller*

THE

THE
INTRODUCTION:
BEING THE
HISTORY
OF
PERSECUTION.

S Religion is a Matter of the higheſt Importance to every Man, there can be nothing which deſerves a more impartial Inquiry, or which ſhould be examined into with a more diſintereſted Freedom ; becauſe as far as our Acceptance with the Deity depends on the Knowledge and Practice of it, ſo far Religion is, and muſt be, to us a purely perſonal Thing, in which therefore we ought to be determined by nothing but the Evidence of Truth, and the rational Convictions of our own Mind and Conſcience. Without ſuch an Examination and Conviction we ſhall be in danger of being impoſed on by crafty and deſigning Men, who will not fail to make their Gain of the Ignorance and Credulity of thoſe they can deceive, nor ſcruple to recommend to them the worſt

Prin-

Principles and Superstitions, if they find them conducive or necessary to support their Pride, Ambition and Avarice. The History of almost all Ages and Nations is an abundant Proof of this Assertion.

God himself, who is the Object of all religious Worship, to whom we owe the most absolute Subjection, and whose Actions are all guided by the discerned Reason and fitness of Things, cannot, as I apprehend, consistent with his own most perfect Wisdom, require of his reasonable Creatures the explicite Belief of, or actual Assent to any Proposition which they do not, or cannot either wholly or partly understand; because 'tis requiring of them a real Impossibility, no Man being able to stretch his Faith beyond his Understanding, i. e. to see an Object that was never present to his Eyes, or to discern the Agreement or Disagreement of the different Parts of a Proposition, the Terms of which he hath never heard of, or cannot possibly understand. Neither can it be supposed that God can demand from us a Method of Worship of which we cannot discern some reason and fitness, because it would be to demand from us Worship without Understanding and Judgment, and without the Concurrence of the Heart and Conscience, i. e. a Kind of Worship different from, and exclusive of that, which in the Nature of Things is the most excellent and best, viz. the Exercise of those pure and rational Affections, and that Imitation of God by Purity of Heart, and the Practice of the Virtues of a good Life, in which the Power, Substance, and Efficacy of true Religion doth consist. If therefore nothing can or ought to be believed, but under the Direction of the Understanding, nor any Scheme of Religion and Worship to be received but what appears reasonable in it self, and worthy of God; the necessary Consequence is, that every Man is bound in Interest and Duty to make the best Use he can of his reasonable Powers, to examine without fear, all Principles before he receives them, and all Rites and Means of Religion and Worship before he submits to and complies with them. This is the common Privilege of human Nature, which no Man ought ever to part with himself, and of which he can't be deprived by others, without the greatest Injustice and Wickedness.

'Twill, I doubt not, appear evident beyond Contradiction, to all who impartially consider the History of past Ages and Nations, that where and whenever Men have been abridged, or wholly deprived of this Liberty, or have neglected to make the due and proper Use of it, or sacrificed their own private Judgments to the publick Conscience, or complimented the licensed spiritual Guides with the Direction of them, Ignorance and Superstition have proportionably prevailed; and that to these Causes have been owing those great Corruptions of Religion which have done so much Dishonour to God, and where-ever they have prevailed, been destructive to the Interests of true Piety and Virtue. So that instead of serving God with their Reason and Understanding, they have served their spiritual Leaders without either, and have been so far from rendring themselves acceptable to their Maker, that they have the more deeply, 'tis to be feared, incurred his Displeasure; because God can't but dislike the *Sacrifice of Fools*, and therefore of such who either neglect to

2   im-

improve the reasonable Powers he hath given them, or part with them in complaisance to the proud, ambitious, and ungodly Claims of others, which is one of the highest Instances of Folly that can possibly be mentioned.

I will not indeed deny, but that the appointing Persons, whose peculiar Office it should be to minister in the external Services of publick and social Worship, is, when under proper Regulations, of Advantage to the Decency and Order of Divine Service. But then I think it of the most pernicious Consequence to the Liberties of Mankind, and absolutely inconsistent with the true Prosperity of a Nation, as well as with the Interest and Success of rational Religion, to suffer such Ministers to become the Directors general of the Consciences and Faith of others, or publickly to assume, and exercise such a Power, as shall oblige others to submit to their Determinations without being convinced of their being wise and reasonable, and never to dispute their spiritual Decrees. The very Claim of such a Power is the highest Insolence, and an Affront to the common Sense and Reason of Mankind ; and where-ever 'tis usurped and allowed, the most abject Slavery both of Soul and Body is almost the unavoidable Consequence. For by such a Submission to spiritual Power the Mind and Conscience is actually enslaved, and by being thus render'd passive to the Priest, Men are naturally prepared for a servile Subjection to the Prince, and for becoming Slaves to the most arbitrary and tyrannical Government. And I believe it hath been generally found true by Experience, that the same Persons who have asserted their own Power over others in Matters of Religion and Conscience, have also asserted the absolute Power of the Civil Magistrate, and been the avowed Patrons of those admirable Doctrines of Passive-Obedience and Non-Resistance for the Subject. Our own Nation is sufficiently witness to the Truth of this.

'Tis therefore but too natural to suspect, that the secret Intention of all ghostly and spiritual Directors and Guides in decrying Reason, the noblest Gift of God, and without which even the Being of a God, and the Method of our Redemption by Jesus Christ, would be of no more significancy to us than to the Brutes that perish, is in reality the Advancement of their own Power and Authority over the Faith and Consciences of others, to which sound Reason is, and ever will be an Enemy. For though I readily allow the great Expediency and Need of Divine Revelation to assist us in our Inquiries into the Nature of Religion, and to give us a full View of the Principles and Practices of it ; yet a very small Share of Reason, without any supernatural Help, will suffice, if attended to, to let me know that my Soul is my own, and that I ought not to put my Conscience out to keeping to any Person whatsoever, because no Man can be answerable for it to the great God but my self ; and that therefore the Claim of Dominion, whoever makes it, either over mine or any others Conscience, is meer Imposture and Cheat, that hath nothing but Impudence or Folly to support it, and as truely visionary and romantick as the imaginary Power of Persons disorder'd in their Senses, and which would be of no more Significancy and Influence amongst Mankind than theirs, did not either the Views of ambitious Princes, or the Superstition and Folly of Bigots encourage and support it.

On thefe Accounts it is highly incumbent on all Nations, who enjoy the Bleffings of a limited Government, who would preferve their Conftitution, and
tranfmit it fafe to Pofterity, to be jealous of every Claim of fpiritual Power,
and not to enlarge the Authority and Jurifdiction of fpiritual Men, beyond
the Bounds of Reafon and Revelation. Let them have the freeft Indulgence to
do good, and fpread the Knowledge and Practice of true Religion, and promote Peace and Good-will amongft Mankind. Let them be applauded and
encouraged, and even rewarded, when they are Patterns of Virtue, and Examples of real Piety to their Flocks. Such Powers as thefe God and Man
would readily allow them, and as to any other I apprehend they have little right
to them, and am fure they have feldom made a wife or rational Ufe of them.
On the contrary, numberlefs have been the Confufions and Mifchiefs introduced into the World, and occafioned by the Ufurpers of fpiritual Authority.
In the Chriftian Church they have ever ufed it with Infolence, and generally
abufed it to Oppreffion and the worft of Cruelties. And though the Hiftory
of fuch Tranfactions can never be a very pleafing and grateful Tafk, yet I
think, on many Accounts it may be ufeful and inftructive; efpecially as it may
tend to give Men an Abhorrence of all the Methods of Perfecution, and put
them upon their Guard againft all thofe ungodly Pretenfions, by which Perfecution hath been introduced and fupported.

But how much foever the perfecuting Spirit hath prevailed amongft thofe who
have called themfelves Chriftians, yet certainly 'tis a great miftake to confine it
wholly to them. We have Inftances of Perfons, who were left to the Light of
Nature and Reafon, and never fufpected of being perverted by Revelation,
murthering and deftroying each other on the Account of Religion; and of fome
judicially condemned to Death for differing from the Orthodox, *i. e.* the eftablifhed Idolatry of their Country. And I doubt not, but that if we had as full
and particular an Account of the Tranfactions of the different religious Sects
and Parties amongft the Heathens, as we have of thofe amongft Chriftians, we
fhould find a great many more Inftances of this kind, than 'tis eafy or poffible
now to produce. However, there are fome very remarkable ones, which I
fhall not wholly omit.

SECT. I.

Of Perfecutions amongft the Heathens upon Account of Religion.

Cap. 5.
v. 6, &c.
THERE is a Paffage in the Book of *Judith* which intimates to us, that
the Anceftors of the *Jews* themfelves were perfecuted upon Account
of their Religion. *Achior*, Captain of the Sons of *Ammon*, gives *Holofernes* this
Account of the Origin of that Nation. *This People are defcended of the* Chaldeans;
and they fojourned heretofore in Mefopotamia, *becaufe they would not follow the Gods
of their Fathers which were in the Land of* Chaldea; *for they left the Way of their
Anceftors,*

Anceſtors, and· worſhipped the God of Heaven, the God whom they knew. So they caſt them out from the Face of their Gods, and they fled into Meſopotamia, *and ſojourned there many Days.* St. *Auſtin* and *Marſham* both take Notice of this Tra-^{De civit.} dition; which is farther confirmed by all the oriental Hiſtorians, who, as the ^{Dei, l. 16. c. 13.} learned Dr. *Hyde* tells us, unanimouſly affirm, that *Abraham* ſuffered many ^{Marſh.} Perſecutions upon the Account of his Oppoſition to the Idolatry of his Country; ^{Cron § 5.} and that he was particularly impriſoned for it by *Nimrod* in *Ur*. Some of the ^{De Relig.} eaſtern Writers alſo tell us, that he was thrown into the Fire, but that he was ^{Perſ. c. 2.} miraculouſly preſerved from being conſumed in it by God. This Tradition alſo the *Jews* believed, and is particularly mentioned by *Jonathan* in his *Targum* upon *Gen.* xi. 28. So early doth Perſecution ſeem to have begun againſt the Worſhippers of the true God.

Socrates, who in the Judgment of an Oracle was the wiſeſt Man living, was ^{Plat. in Apolog.} perſecuted by the *Athenians* on the Account of his Religion, and when paſt ſe-^{pro So-} venty Years of Age brought to a publick Trial and condemned. His Accuſa-^{crate.} tion was principally this, That he did unrighteouſly and curiouſly ſearch into ^{Diog.} the great Myſteries of Heaven and Earth; [a]that he corrupted the Youth, and ^{Laert. in} did not eſteem the Gods worſhipped by the City to be really Gods, and that he ^{vit. Soc.} introduced new Deities. This laſt part of his Accuſation was undoubtedly owing to his inculcating upon them more rational and excellent Conceptions of the Deity, than were allowed by the eſtabliſhed Creeds of his Country, and to his arguing againſt the Corruptions and Superſtitions which he ſaw univerſally practiſed by the *Greeks*. This was called corrupting the Youth who were his Scholars, and what, together with his ſuperior Wiſdom, raiſed him many Enemies amongſt all ſorts of People, who loaded him with Reproaches, and ſpread Reports concerning him greatly to his Diſadvantage, endeavouring thereby to prejudice the Minds of his very Judges againſt him. When he was brought to his Trial ſeveral of his Accuſers were never ſo much as named or diſcovered to him, ſo that as he himſelf complained, he was as it were fighting with a Shadow, when he was defending himſelf againſt his Adverſaries, becauſe he knew not whom he oppoſed, and had no one to anſwer him. However, he maintained his own Innocence with the nobleſt Reſolution and Courage; ſhewed he was far from corrupting the Youth, and openly declared that he believed the Being of a God. And as the Proof of this his Belief he bravely ſaid to his Judges, that though he was very ſenſible of his Danger from the Hatred and Malice of the People, yet that as he apprehended God himſelf had appointed him to teach his Philoſophy, ſo he ſhould grievouſly offend him ſhould he forſake his Station through fear of Death, or any other Evil; and that for ſuch a Diſobedience to the Deity they might more juſtly accuſe him as not believing there were any Gods: Adding, as though he had ſomewhat of the ſame bleſſed Spirit that afterwards reſted on the Apoſtles of Chriſt, that if they would diſmiſs him upon the Condition of not teaching his Philoſophy any more,

---

[a] Ἀδικεῖ Σωκρατης ους μεν η πολις νομιζει Θεις κ νομιζαν· ετερα ϑ καινα δαιμονια εισηγουμενℴ. Ἀδικει ϑ κ τus νεus διαφθειρων. Τιμημα θανατℴ.

b *I will obey God rather than you, and teach my Philosophy as long as I live.* However, notwithstanding the Goodnefs of his Caufe and Defence, he was condemned for Impiety and Atheifm, and ended his Life with a Draught of Poifon, dying a real Martyr for God, and the Purity of his Worfhip. Thus we fee that in the Ages of natural Reafon and Light, not to be orthodox, or to differ from the eftablifhed Religion, was the fame Thing as to be impious and atheiftical, and that one of the wifeft Men that ever lived was put to Death merely on account of his Religion.

I muft add, in Juftice to the Laity, that the Judges and Accufers of *Socrates* were not Priefts. *Melitus* was a Poet, *Anytus* an Artificer, and *Lycon* an Orator ; fo that the Profecution was truly Laick, and the Priefts don't appear to have had any Share in his Accufation, Condemnation, and Death. Nor, indeed, was their any Need of the Affiftance of Prieftcraft in this Affair, the Profecution of this excellent Man being perfectly agreeable to the Conftitution and Maxims of the *Athenian* Government ; which had, to ufe the Words of Dr Rogers a late Reverend Author, incorporated or made Religion a Part of the Laws of Vind. of the the civil Community. One of the *Attick* Laws was to this Effect : ` *Let it be* Civil Efta- *a perpetual Law, and binding at all Times, to worfhip our national Gods and Heroes* blifhment, *publickly, according to the Laws of our Anceftors.* So that no new Gods, nor new &c. Doctrines about old Gods, nor any new Rites of Worfhip, could be introduced by any Perfon whatfoever, without incurring the Penalty of this Law, which Cont. A- was Death. Thus *Jofephus* tells us, that 'twas prohibited by Law to teach pion. l. 2. new Gods, and that the Punifhment ordained againft thofe who fhould intro- c. 37. duce any fuch, was Death. Agreeably to this, the Orator *Ifocrates*, pleading Ifocrat. in the Grand Council of *Athens*, puts them in mind of the Cuftom and Practice Arcop. of their Anceftors : d *This was their principal Care to abolifh nothing they had received from their Fathers in Matters of Religion, nor to make any Addition to what they had eftablifhed.* And therefore, in his Advice to *Nicocles*, he exhorts him to e be *of the fame Religion with his Anceftors.* So that the Civil Eftablifhment of Religion in *Athens* was entirely exclufive, and no Toleration whatfoever al- Diog. lowed to thofe who differed from it. On this Account the Philofophers in ge- Laert. l. 5. neral were, by a publick Decree, banifhed from *Athens*, as teaching heterodox Theophr. Opinions, and corrupting the Youth in Matters of Religion, and by a Law, Athen. very much refembling the famous modern *Schifm Bill*, f prohibited from being l. 13. c. 9. Mafters and Teachers of Schools, without Leave of the Senate and People, even under Pain of Death. This Law, indeed, like the other, was but very fhort lived, and *Sophocles* the Author of it punifhed in a Fine of five Talents. *Lyfimachus* alfo banifhed them from his Kingdom. 'Tis evident from thefe Things, that according to the *Athenian* Conftitution, *Socrates* was legally condemned for not

b Πειϑομαι τῳ Θεω μᾱλλον η υμιν. Plat. Ibid. Act. 5. 29.

c Θεσμ Θ ειωνι Θ τοις Αιτιδα νεμοιδροις, κυει Θ τον απαντα χϱονον, Θεες τιμαϒ ϗ ηϱωας εϳχωεικε εν κοινω εμποινιμδις νομοις πατειοις.

d Εκεινο μονον ετεϱαν οπως μηδεν μητε των πατειων καταλυσωσι, μητ᾽ εξω των νομιζομϑων προϑησωσιν.

e Τα πεϱι τες Θεες ποιει μην ως οι πϱογονοι κατεδειξαν.

f Μηδενα των φιλοσοϱων σχολης αϕηγειϑαι, αν μη τη βελη ϗ τω δημω δοξη· ει δε μη, ϑανατον ειναι την ζημιαν.

believing

believing in the Gods of his Country, and presuming to have better Notions of the Deity than his Superiors. In like manner, a certain Woman, a Priestess, Jos. Ibid. was put to Death upon an Accusation of her introducing new Deities.

Diogenes Laertius tells us, that *Anaxagoras*, the Philosopher, was accused of In vit. Impiety, because he [g] affirmed, that *the Sun was a Globe of red hot Iron*; which Anax. was certainly great Heresy, because his Country worshipped him as a God. *Stilpo* was also banished his Country, as the same Writer tells us, because he l. 5. c. 38. denied [h] *Minerva to be a God, allowing her only to be a Goddess.* A very deep and curious Controversy this, and worthy the Cognizance of the Civil Magistrate. *Diagoras* was also condemned to Death, and a Talent decreed to him that Joseph. should kill him upon his Escape, being accused of deriding the Mysteries of Ibid. the Gods. *Protagoras* also would have suffered Death, had he not fled his Country, because he had written something about the Gods, that differed from the orthodox Opinions of the *Athenians.* Upon the same Account, Athen. *Theodorus*, called *Atheus*, was also put to Death. Ibid.

The *Lacedemonians* constantly expelled Foreigners, and would not suffer their Joseph. own Citizens to dwell in Foreign Parts, because they imagined that both the Ibid. § 36. one and the other tended to corrupt and weaken their own Laws ; nor would Athen. they suffer the teaching of Rhetorick or Philosophy, because of the Quar-l. 13. c. 9. rels and Disputes that attended it. The *Scythians*, who delighted in human Blood, and were, as *Josephus* says, little different from Beasts, yet were zea-Ibid. § 37. lously tenacious of their own Rites, and put *Anacharsis*, a very wise Person, to death, because he seemed to be very fond of the *Grecian* Rites and Cere- monies. *Herodotus* says, that he was shot through the Heart with an Arrow, Herodot. by *Saulius* their King, for sacrificing to the Mother of the Gods after the man-Melpom. ner of the *Grecians* ; and that *Scyles*, another of their Kings, was deposed by 109. Ed. them, for sacrificing to *Bacchus*, and using the *Grecian* Ceremonies of Reli-Hen. gion, and his Head afterwards cut off by *Octamasades*, who was chosen King Steph. in his room. *So rigid were they*, says the Historian, *in maintaining their own Customs, and so severe in punishing the Introducers of foreign Rites.* Many also Joseph. amongst the *Persians* were put to Death on the same Account. And, indeed, Ibid. 'twas almost the Practice of all Nations to punish those who disbelieved or de- rided their national Gods; as appears from *Timocles*, who, speaking of the Gods of the *Ægyptians*, says, *How shall the Ibis, or the Dog, preserve me ?* [i] And Athen. then adds, *Where is the Place that doth not immediately punish those who behave im-l. 7. c. 13. piously towards the Gods, such as are confessed to be Gods ?*

Juvenal [k] gives us a very tragical Account of some Disputes and Quarrels Satyr. 15. about Religion amongst the *Ægyptians*, who entertained an eternal Hatred

---

[g] Διοτι τον ηλιον μυδρον ελεγε διαπυρον.

[h] Μη ειναι αυτην Θεον, αλλα Θεαν.

[i] Οτι γαρ ες Θεους τους ομολογυμενους Θεους ατεβαντες κ διδοασιν ευθεως Δικην.

[k] Inter finitimos vetus atq; antiqua simultas,
    Immortale odium, & nunquam sanabile vulnus
    Ardet adhuc, Ombos & Tentyra. Summus utrinq;
    Inde furor vulgo, quod numina vicinorum
    Odit uterq; locus, cum solos credat habendos
    Esse deos quos ipse colit.————

and Enmity againſt each other, and eat and devoured one another, becauſe they did not all worſhip the ſame God.

Engliſh'd by
Mr. Dry-
den, &c.
Joſeph.
cont. Ap.
l. 2. § 6.

Ombos *and* Tentyr, *neighbouring Towns, of late,*
Broke into Outrage of deep feſter'd Hate.
Religious Spite and pious Spleen bred firſt
This Quarrel, which ſo long the Bigots nurſt.
Each calls the others God a ſenſeleſs Stock,
His own, Divine, tho' from the ſelf-ſame Block.
At firſt both Parties in Reproaches jar,
And make their Tongues the Trumpets of the War.
Words ſerve but to enflame the warlike Liſts,
Who wanting Weapons clutch their horny Fiſts.
Yet thus make ſhift t' exchange ſuch furious Blows,
Scarce one eſcapes with more than half a Noſe.
Some ſtand their Ground with half their Viſage gone,
But with the Remnant of a Face fight on.
Such transform'd Spectacles of Horror grow,
That not a Mother her own Son would know.
One Eye remaining, for the other Spies,
Which now on Earth a trampled Gelly lies.

All this religious Zeal hitherto is but mere Sport and childiſh Play, and therefore they piouſly proceed to farther Violences, to hurling of Stones, and throwing of Arrows, till one Party routs the other, and the Conquerors feaſt themſelves on the mangled Bodies of their divided Captives.

Yet hitherto both Parties think the Fray,
But Mockery of War, mere Childrens Play.
This whets their Rage, to ſearch for Stones ———
An Ombite *Wretch (by Headlong ſtrait betray'd,*
And falling down i'th' Rout) is Priſoner made.
Whoſe Fleſh torn off by Lumps the ravenous Foe
In Morſels cut, to make it farther go.
His Bones clean pick'd, his very Bones they gnaw ;
No Stomach's baulk'd, becauſe the Corps is raw.
T' had been loſt Time to dreſs him : Keen Deſire
Supplies the Want of Kettle, Spit, and Fire.

De Iſid. &
Oſir. p.
380. Ed.
Franc.

Plutarch *alſo relates*, that in his Time ſome of the Ægyptians who worſhipp'd a Dog, eat one of the Fiſhes, which others of the Ægyptians adored as their Deity ; and that upon this the Fiſh Eaters laid hold on the other's Dogs, and ſacrificed and eat them, and that this gave Occaſion to a bloody Battle, in which a great Number were deſtroy'd on both Sides.

Antiochus

Antiochus Epiphanes, tho' a very wicked Prince, yet was a great Zealot for his Religion, and endeavoured to propagate it by all the Methods of the most bloody Persecution. *Josephus* tells us, that after he had taken *Jerusalem,* and plunder'd the Temple, he caused an Altar to be built in it, upon which he sacrificed Swine, which were an Abomination to the *Jews,* and forbidden by their Laws. Not content with this, he compelled them to forsake the Worship of the true God, and to worship such as he accounted Deities; building Altars and Temples to them in all the Towns and Streets, and offering Swine upon them every Day. He commanded them to forbear circumcising their Children, grievously threatning such as should disobey his Orders. He also appointed Επισκοπυς, *Overseers,* to compel the *Jews* to come in, and do as he had ordered them. Such as rejected it, were continually persecuted, and put to Death, with the most grievous Tortures. He ordered them to be cruelly scourged, and their Bodies to be tore, and before they expired under their Tortures, to be crucified. The Women, and the Children which they circumcised, were, by his Command, hanged, the Children hanging from the Necks of their crucified Parents. Where-ever he found any of the sacred Books, or of the Law, he destroy'd them, undoubtedly to prevent the Propagation of heretical Opinions, and punished with Death such as kept them. The same Author tells us also, in his History of the *Maccabees,* that *Antiochus* put forth an Edict, whereby he made it Death for any to observe the *Jewish* Religion, and compelled them, by Tortures, to abjure it. The inhuman Barbarities he exercised upon *Eleazar* and the *Maccabees,* because they would not renounce their Religion, and sacrifice to his *Grecian* Gods, are not, in some Circumstances, to be parallel'd by any Histories of Persecution extant, and will ever render the Name and Memory of that illustrious Tyrant execrable and *infamous.* It was on the same religious Account that he banished ^{Athen.} the Philosophers from all Parts of his Kingdom, the Charge against them [l. 12. c. 12.] being, *their corrupting the Youth,* i. e. teaching them Notions of the Gods, different from the common orthodox Opinions which were established by Law, commanding *Phanias,* that such Youths as conversed with them should be hanged.

The ten Persecutions, as they are reckoned, of the Christians by the *Roman* Emperors, purely for their Religion, are standing Monuments of their religious Zeal, or rather of their outragious Fury against all who would not comply with the established Religion. Indeed, the very civil Constitution of *Rome* was founded upon persecuting Principles. *Tertullian* tells us, [i] *That* ^{Apol. c. 2.} *'twas an ancient Decree that no Emperor should consecrate a new God, unless he was approved by the Senate;* and one of the standing Laws of the Republick was to this Effect, as *Cicero* gives it, [k] *That no one should have separately new Gods,* ^{De Leg.} *nor worship privately foreign Gods, unless admitted by the Commonwealth.* This [l. 2.]

---

[i] Vetus erat decretum ne qui Deus ab imperatore consecraretur, nisi a Senatu probatus.

[k] Separatim nemo habessit deos neve novos, sed ne advenas, nisi publice adscitos, privatim colunto.

Law

Law he endeavours to vindicate by Reason and the Light of Nature, by adding, That *for Persons to worship their own, or new, or foreign Gods, would be to introduce Confusion and strange Ceremonies in Religion.* So true a Friend was this eminent *Roman*, and great Master of Reason, to Uniformity of Worship; and so little did he see the Equity, and indeed Necessity of an universal Toleration in Matters of Religion. Upon this Principle, after he had reasoned well against the false Notions of God that had obtained amongst his Countrymen, and the publick Superstitions of Religion, he concludes with what was enough to destroy the Force of all his Arguments, [l] *'Tis the Part of a wise Man to defend the Customs of his Ancestors, by retaining their sacred Rites and Ceremonies.* Thus narrow was the Foundation of the *Roman* Religion, and thus inconsistent the Sentiments of the wisest Heathens with all the Principles of Toleration and universal Liberty. It was no wonder therefore that Christianity, which was so perfectly contrary to the whole System of Pagan Theology, should be looked upon with an evil Eye, or that when the Number of Christians encreased, they should incur the Displeasure of the Civil Magistrate, and the Censure of the penal Laws that were in force against them.

De Leg. l. 2. c. 10.

De Divin. l. 2. fin.

The first publick Persecution of them by the *Romans* was begun by that Monster of Mankind, *Nero*; who, to clear himself of the Charge of burning *Rome*, endeavoured to fix the Crime on the Christians; and having thus falsly and tyrannically made them guilty, he put them to Death by various Methods of exquisite Cruelty. But though this was the Pretence for this Barbarity towards them, yet it evidently appears from undoubted Testimonies, that they were before hated upon Account of their Religion, and were therefore fitter Objects to fall a Sacrifice to the Resentment and Fury of the Tyrant. For *Tacitus* tells us, That *they were* [m] *hated for their Crimes.* And what these were, he afterwards sufficiently informs us, by calling their Religion [n] *an execrable Superstition.* In like manner *Suetonius*, in his Life of *Nero*, speaking of the Christians, says, [o] *They were a Set of Men who had embraced a new and accursed Superstition.* And therefore *Tacitus* farther informs us, That those who confessed themselves Christians, [p] *were condemned not so much for the Crime of burning the City, as for their being hated by all Mankind.* So that 'tis evident from these Accounts, that 'twas through popular Hatred of them for their Religion, that they were thus sacrificed to the Malice and Fury of *Nero*. Many of them he dressed up in the Skins of wild Beasts, that they might be devoured by Dogs. Others he crucified. Some he cloathed in Garments of Pitch and burnt them, that by their Flames he might supply the Absence of the Day-light.

Annal. l. 15. c. 44. Ibid. Cap. 16. Annal. l. 15. c. 44.

E. H. l. 3. c. 17, 18. The Persecution begun by *Nero* was revived, and carried on by *Domitian*, who put some to Death, and banish'd others upon Account of their Religion. *Eusebius* mentions *Flavia Domitilla*, Neice to *Flavius Clemens*, then Consul, as-

[l] Majorum Instituta tueri sacris Ceremoniisque retinendis, sapientis est.
[m] Per flagitia invisos.
[n] Exitiabilis superstitio.
[o] Genus Hominum, superstitionis novæ & maleficæ.
[p] Haud perinde in crimine incendii, quam odio humani generis convicti.

banished for this Reason to the Island *Pontia*. *Dion* the Historian's Account of this Affair is somewhat different. ^q " He tells us, That *Fabius Clemens* the " Consul, *Domitian*'s Cousin, who had married *Flavia Domitilla*, a near Re- " lation of *Domitian*, was put to Death by him, and *Domitilla* banished " to *Pandataria*, being both accused of Atheism ; and that on the same Ac- " count many who had embraced the *Jewish* Rites were likewise condemned, " some of whom were put to Death, and others had their Estates confisca- " ted." I think this Account can belong to no other but the Christians, whom *Dion* seems to have confounded with the *Jews* ; a Mistake into which he and others might naturally fall, because the first Christians were *Jews*, and came from the Land of *Judea*. The Crime with which these Persons were charged was Atheism ; the Crime commonly imputed to Christians, because they refused to worship the *Roman* Deities. And as there are no Proofs, that *Domitian* ever persecuted the *Jews* upon account of their Religion, nor any Intimation of this Nature in *Josephus*, who finished his Antiquities towards the latter end of *Domitian*'s Reign ; I think the Account of *Eusebius*, which he de-clares he took from Writers, who were far from being Friends to Christianity, is preferable to that of *Dion*'s ; and that therefore these Persecutions by *Domi-tian* were upon account of Christianity. However, they did not last long, for as *Eusebius* tells us, he put a Stop to them by an Edict in their favour. *Tertul-lian* also affirms the same, and adds, that he recalled those whom he had ba-nished. So that though this is reckon'd by Ecclesiastical Writers as the second Persecution, it doth not appear to have been general, or very severe. *Domi-tian* also expelled all the Philosophers from *Rome* and *Italy*.

Under *Trajan*, otherwise a most excellent Prince, began the third Persecu-tion, in the 14th Year of his Reign. In answer to a Letter of *Pliny* he ordered, ^r That *the Christians should not be sought after, but that if they were accused and convicted of being Christians they should be punished, such only excepted as should deny themselves to be Christians, and give an evident Proof of it by worshipping his Gods*. These were to receive Pardon upon this their Repentance, how much soever they might have been suspected before. From this imperial Rescript it is abundantly evident, that this Persecution of the Christians by *Trajan* was purely on the Score of their Religion, because he orders, that whosoever was accused and convicted of being a Christian should be punished with Death, unless he renounced his Profession, and sacrificed to the Gods. All that was re-quired, ^s says *Tertullian*, was *meerly to confess the Name, without any Cognizance being taken of any Crime*. *Pliny* himself, in his Letter to the Emperor, acquits them of every Thing of this Nature, and tells him, ^t That *all they acknowledged*

l. 67. in Domit.

E. H. L. 3. c 20. Apol. c. 5.

Suet. in vit. Domit. c. 10.

Apol. c. 2.

^q Ενεκληχθη ἡ αμφοιν εγκλημα αθεστητ Θ.
^r Conquirendi non sunt. Si deferantur & arguantur puniendi sunt ; ita tamen ut qui negaverit se Christianum esse, idq; reipsa manifestum fecerit, id est supplicando Diis nostris, quamvis suspectus in præteritum fuit, veniam ex pænitentia impetret.
^s Illud solum expectatur——confessio nominis, non examinatio criminis.
^t Adfirmabant autem hanc fuisse summam vel culpæ suæ, vel erroris, quod essent soliti stato die ante lucem convenire, carmenq; Christo, quasi Deo, dicere, secum invicem ; seq; sacramento, non in scelus aliquod astringere, sed ne furta, ne latrocinia, ne adulteria committerent.

was,

was, that their whole Crime or Error confifted in this, that at ftated Times they were ufed to meet before Day-light, and to fing an Hymn to Chrift as God, and that they bound themfelves by an Oath not to commit any Wickednefs, fuch as Thefts, Robberies, Adulteries, and the like. And to be affured of the Truth of this, he put two Maids to the Torture, and after examining them, found them guilty of nothing but *a wicked and unreafonable Superftition.* This is the nobleft Vindication of the Purity and Innocency of the Chriftian Affemblies, and abundantly juftifies the Account of *Eufebius* from *Hegefippus*, " *That the Church continued until thefe Times as a Virgin pure and uncorrupted*; and proves beyond all Contradiction, that the Perfecution raifed againft them was purely on a religious Account, and not for any Immoralities and Crimes againft the Laws, that could be proved againft the Chriftians, though their Enemies flandered them with the vileft, and hereby endeavoured to render them hateful to the whole World. *Why,* fays *Tertullian, doth a Chriftian fuffer, but for being of their Number? Hath any one proved Inceft, or Cruelty upon us, during this long fpace of Time? No; 'tis for our Innocence, Probity, Juftice, Chaftity, Faith, Veracity, and for the living God that we are burnt alive.* *Pliny* was forced to acquit them from every Thing but *an unreafonable Superftition,* i. e. their refolute Adherence to the Faith of Chrift. And yet though Innocent in all other refpects, when they were brought before his Tribunal he treated them in this unrighteous Manner: He only afked them, Whether they were Chriftians? If they confeffed it, he afked them the fame Queftion again and again, adding Threatnings to his Queftions. If they perfevered in their Confeffion he condemned them to Death, becaufe whatever their Confeffion might be, he was very fure, *that their Stubbornnefs and inflexible Obftinacy deferved Punifhment.* So that without being convicted of any Crime, but that of Conftancy in their Religion, this equitable Heathen, this rational Philofopher, this righteous Judge, condemns them to a cruel Death. And for this Conduct the Emperor, his Mafter, commends him. For in anfwer to *Pliny*'s Queftion, Whether he fhould go on to punifh the Name it felf, though chargeable with no Crimes, or the Crimes only which attended the Name? *Trajan* in his Refcript, after commending *Pliny,* orders, That if they were accufed and convicted of being Chriftians they fhould be put to Death, unlefs they renounced that Name, and facrificed to his Gods. *Tertullian* and *Athenagoras,* in their Apologies, very juftly inveigh with great Warmth againft this imperial Refcript; and indeed, a more fhameful Piece of Iniquity was never practifed in the darkeft Times of Popery. I hope alfo my Reader will obferve, that this was Lay-Perfecution, and owed its Rife to the religious Zeal of one of the beft of the *Roman* Emperors, and not only to the Contrivances of cruel and defigning Priefts; that it was juftified and carried on by a very famous and learned Philofopher, whofe Reafon taught him, that what he accounted Superftition, if incurable, was to be punifhed with Death; and that it was managed with great Fury and Barbarity, Multitudes of Perfons in the feveral Provinces being deftroyed merely on account of the Chriftian Name, by various and exquifite Methods of Cruelty.

E.H. L.3. c. 32.

Ad Scapul

" Αρα μεχρι των τοτε χρονων παρθενΘ καθαρα & αδιαφορΘ εμεινεν η εκκλησια.

2

The

The Refcript of *Adrian* his Succeffor to *Minutius Fundanus*, Pro-Conful of *Afia*, feems to have fomewhat abated the Fury of this Perfecution, though not wholly to have put an End to it. *Tertullian* tells us, that *Arrius Antoninus*, af- Ad Scap.² terwards Emperor, then Pro-Conful of *Afia*, when the Chriftians came in a Body before his Tribunal, order'd fome of them to be put to Death ; and faid to others, ˣ *You Wretches! If you will die ye have Precipicies and Halters.* He alfo fays, That feveral other Governors of Provinces punifhed fome few Chriftians, and difmiffed the reft ; fo that the Perfecution was not fo general, nor fevere as under *Trajan.*

Under *Antoninus Pius* the Chriftians were very cruelly treated in fome of the Provinces of *Afia*, which occafioned *Juftin Martyr* to write his firft Apology. It doth not however appear to have been done, either by the Order or Confent of this Emperor. On the contrary, he wrote Letters to the Cities of *Afia*, and particularly to thofe of *Lariffa*, *Theffalonica*, *Athens*, and all the *Greeks*, That they fhould create no new Troubles to them. 'Tis probable, that the *Afiatick* Cities perfecuted them by virtue of fome former imperial Edicts which don't appear ever to have been recalled ; and, perhaps, with the Connivance of *Antoninus Philofophus*, the Collegue and Succeffor of *Pius* in the Empire.

Under him began, as 'tis generally accounted, the fourth Perfecution, upon which *Juftin Martyr* wrote his fecond Apology, *Meliton* his, and *Athenagoras* E. H. l. 4. his Legation or Embaffy for the Chriftians. *Meliton*, as *Eufebius* relates it, c. 16. complains of it as *an almoft unheard of Thing, that pious Men were now perfecuted, and greatly diftreffed by new Decrees throughout Afia ; that moft impudent Informers, who were greedy of other Perfons Subftance, took Occafion from the imperial Edicts, to plunder others who were intirely innocent.* After this he humbly befeeches the Emperor, that he would not fuffer the Chriftians to be any longer ufed in fo cruel and unrighteous a Manner. *Juftin Martyr*, in the Account he gives of the Apol. 2da. Martyrdom of *Ptolemæus*, affures us, that the only Queftion afked him was, c. 42. Edit. *Whether he was a Chriftian?* And upon his confeffing that he was, he was im- Thirlb. mediately ordered to the Slaughter. *Lucius* was alfo put to Death for making the fame Confeffion, and afking *Urbicus* the Prefect, why he condemned *Ptolemy*, who was neither convicted of Adultery, Rape, Murther, Theft, Robbery, nor of any other Crime, but only for owning himfelf to be a Chriftian. From thefe Accounts 'tis abundantly evident, that it was ftill the very Name of a Chriftian that was made capital ; and that thefe Cruelties were committed by an Emperor who was a great Mafter of Reafon and Philofophy, not as Punifhments upon Offenders againft the Laws and publick Peace, but purely for the Sake of Religion and Confcience ; committed, to maintain and propagate Idolatry, which is contrary to all the Principles of Reafon and Philofophy, and upon Perfons of great Integrity and Virtue in Heart and Life, for their Adherence to the Worfhip of One God, which is the Foundation of all true Religion, and one of the plaineft and moft important Articles of it. The Tortures which the Perfecutors of the Chriftians applied, and the Cruelties they

ˣ Ω δειλοι, ει θελε]ε αποθνησκειν κρημυνες η βερχυς εχε]ε.

exercifed on them, enough, one would think, to have overcome the firm-eft human Refolution and Patience, could never extort from them a Con-feffion of that Guilt their Enemies would gladly have fixed on them. And yet Innocent as they were in all refpects, they were treated with the ut-moft Indignity, and deftroy'd by fuch Inventions of Cruelty, as were abhorrent to all the Principles of Humanity and Goodnefs. They were, indeed, accufed of Atheifm, *i. e.* for not believing in and worfhipping the fictitious Gods of the Heathens. This was the Cry of the Multitude againft *Polycarp : This is the Doctor of* Afia, *the Father of the Chriftians, the Subverter of our Gods, who teaches many that they muft not perform the facred Rites, nor worfhip our Deities.* This was the Reafon of the tumultuous Cry againft him, Αιρε τυς Αθεϫς, *Away with thefe Atheifts.* But would not one have imagined that Reafon and Philofophy fhould have informed the Emperor, that this kind of Atheifm was a real Vir-tue, and deferved to be encouraged and propagated amongft Mankind? No ; Reafon and Philofophy here failed him, and his blind Attachment to his Country Gods caufed him to fhed much innocent Blood, and to become the Deftroyer of the Saints of the Living God. At laft, indeed, the Emperor feems to have been fenfible of the great Injuftice of this Perfecution, and by an Edict ordered they fhould be no longer punifhed for being Chriftians.

I fhall not trouble my Reader with an Account of this Perfecution as carried on by *Severus, Decius, Gallus, Valerianus, Dioclefian,* and others of the *Roman* Emperors, but only obferve in general, that the moft exceffive and outragious Barbarities were made ufe of upon all who would not blafpheme Chrift, and of-fer Incenfe to the imperial Gods: They were publickly whipped; drawn by the Heels through the Streets of Cities, racked till every Bone of their Bodies was disjointed ; had their Teeth beat out ; their Nofes, Hands and Ears cut off ; fharp pointed Spears ran under their Nails ; were tortured with melted Lead thrown on their naked Bodies ; had their Eyes dug out ; their Limbs cut of ; were condemned to the Mines ; ground between Stones ; ftoned to Death ; burnt alive ; thrown Headlong from high Buildings ; beheaded ; fmothered in burning Lime-Kilns ; ran through the Body with fharp Spears ; deftroyed with Hunger, Thirft and Cold ; thrown to the wild Beafts ; broiled on Gridirons with flow Fires ; caft by Heaps into the Sea ; crucified ; fcraped to Death with fharp Shells ; torn in Pieces by the Boughs of Trees ; and, in a Word, deftroy'd by all the various Methods that the moft diabolical Subtlety and Mal ce could devife.

It muft indeed be confeffed, that under the latter Emperors who perfecuted the Chriftians, the Simplicity and Purity of the Chriftian Religion were greatly corrupted, and that Ambition, Pride and Luxury, had too generally prevail-ed both amongft the Paftors and People. *Cyprian,* who lived under the *Decian* Perfecution, writing concerning it to the Prefbyters and Deacons, fays, *It muft be owned and confeffed, that this outragious and heavy Calamity, which hath almoft devoured our Flock, and continues to devour it to this Day, hath hapned to us becaufe of our Sins, fince we keep not the Way of the Lord, nor obferve his heavenly Commands given to us for our Salvation. Though our Lord did the Will of his Father,*

yet

Marginal notes:

Eufeb. E. H. l. 4. c. 15.

Id. l. 4. c. 13.

Epift. xi. Ed. Fell.

yet we do not the Will of the Lord. Our principal Study is to get Money and Estates ; we follow after Pride ; we are at Leisure for nothing but Emulation and Quarrelling ; and have neglected the Simplicity of the Faith. We have renounced this World in Words only, and not in deed. Every one studies to please himself, and to displease others. After *Cyprian, Eusebius* the Historian gives a sad Account of the De- E. H. l. 8. generacy of Christians about the Time of the *Dioclesian* Persecution : He tells c. 1. us, *That through too much Liberty they grew negligent and slothful, envying and reproaching one another ; waging, as it were, civil Wars between themselves, Bishops quarrelling with Bishops, and the People divided into Parties : That Hypocrisy and Deceit were grown to the highest pitch of Wickedness ; that they were become so insensible, as not so much as to think of appeasing the Divine Anger, but that, like Atheists, they thought the World destitute of any providential Government and Care, and thus added one Crime to another ; that the Bishops themselves had thrown off all Care of Religion, were perpetually contending with one another, and did nothing but quarrel with, and threaten, and envy, and hate one another ; were full of Ambition, and tyrannically used their Power.* This was the deplorable State of the Christian Church, which God, as *Eusebius* well observes, first punished with a gentle Hand ; but when they grew harden'd and incurable in their Vices, he was pleased to let in the most grievous Persecutions upon them, under *Dioclesian*; which exceeded in Severity and Length all that had been before.

From these Accounts it evidently appears, that the Christian World alone is not chargeable with the Guilt of Persecution on the Score of Religion. 'Twas practised long before Christianity was in being, and first taught the Christians by the persecuting Heathens. The most eminent Philosophers espoused and vindicated persecuting Principles ; and Emperors, otherwise excellent and good, made no scruple of destroying Multitudes on a religious Account, such as *Trajan*, and *Aurelius Verus*. And I think I may farther add, that the Method of propagating Religion by Cruelty and Death, owes its Invention to *Lay Policy* and Craft ; and that how servilely soever the Priesthood hath thought fit to imitate them, yet that they have never exceeded them in Rigour and Severity. I can trace out the Footsteps but of very few Priests in the foregoing Accounts ; nor have I ever heard of more excessive Cruelties than those practised by *Antiochus*, the *Egyptian* Heretick Eaters, and the *Roman* Emperors. I may farther add on this important Article, that 'tis the Laity who have put it into the Power of the Priests to persecute, and rendered it worth their while to do it ; they have done it by the Authority of the civil Laws, as well as employed Lay Hands to execute the Drudgery of it. The Emoluments of Honours and Riches that have been annexed to the favourite Religion and Priesthood is the Establishment of civil Society, whereby Religion hath been made extremely profitable, and the Gains of Godliness worth contending for. Had the Laity been more sparing in their Grants, and their civil Constitutions formed upon the generous and equitable Principle of an universal Toleration, Persecution had never been heard of amongst Men. The Priests would have wanted not only the Power but the Inclination to persecute ; since few Persons have such an Attachment either to what they account Religion-

Religion or Truth, as to torment and deſtroy others for the ſake of it, unleſs tempted with the Views of worldly Ambition, Power and Grandure. Theſe Views will have the ſame Influence upon all bad Minds, whether of the Prieſt-hood or Laity, who, when they are determined at all Hazards to purſue them, will uſe all Methods, right or wrong, to accompliſh and ſecure them.

As therefore the Truth of Hiſtory obliges me to compliment the Laity with the Honour of this excellent Invention, for the Support and Propagation of Religion ; and as its Continuance in the World to this Day is owing to the Pro-tection and Authority of their Laws, and to certain political Ends and Purpo-ſes they have to ſerve thereby, the loading the Prieſthood only, or principal-ly, with the Infamy and Guilt of it, is a mean and groundleſs Scandal ; and to be perpetually objecting the Cruelties that have been practiſed by ſome who have called themſelves Chriſtians, on others for Conſcience ſake, as an Argu-ment againſt the Excellency of the Chriſtian Religion, or with a View to pre-judice others againſt it, is an Artifice unworthy a Perſon of common Un-derſtanding and Honeſty. Let all equally ſhare the Guilt, who are equally chargeable with it ; and let Principles be judged of by what they are in them-ſelves, and not by the Abuſes which bad Men may make of them : If any Ar-gument can be drawn from theſe, we may as well argue againſt the Truth and Excellency of Philoſophy, becauſe *Cicero* eſpouſed the Principles of Perſe-cution, and *Antoninus* the Philoſopher authorized all the Cruelties attending it. But the Queſtion in theſe Caſes is not, what one who calls himſelf a Philoſopher or a Chriſtian doth, but what true Philoſophy and genuine Chriſtianity lead to and teach ; and if Perſecution be the natural Effect of either of them, 'tis nei-ther in my Inclination or Intention to defend them. But I paſs from theſe Re-flections to the Hiſtory of Chriſtian Perſecutions.

SECT. II.

Of the Perſecutions amongſt Chriſtians upon Account of Religion.

IF any Perſon was to judge of the Nature and Spirit of the Chriſtian Reli-gion, by the Spirit and Conduct only of too many who have profeſſed to believe it in all Nations, and almoſt throughout all Ages of the Chriſtian Church, he could ſcarce fail to cenſure it as an Inſtitution unworthy the God of Order and Peace, ſubverſive of the Welfare and Happineſs of Societies, and deſigned to enrich and aggrandize a Few only, at the Expence of the Liberty, Reaſon, Conſciences, Subſtance, and Lives of others. For what Confuſions and Calamities, what Ruins and Deſolations, what Rapines and Murthers, have been introduced into the World, under the *pretended Authority* of Jeſus Chriſt, and ſupporting and propagating Chriſtianity ? What is the beſt part of our Eccleſiaſtical Hiſtory better than an Hiſtory of the Pride and Ambition, the Avarice and Tyranny, the Treachery and Cruelty of ſome, and of the

Per-

Perfecutions and dreadful Miferies of others? And what could an unprejudiced Perfon, acquainted with this melancholy Truth, and who had never feen the facred Records, nor informed himfelf from thence of the genuine Nature of Chriftianity, think, but that it was one of the worft Religions in the World, as tending to deftroy all the natural Sentiments of Humanity and Compaffion, and infpiring its Votaries with that *Wifdom which is from beneath*, and which *is earthly, fenfual and devilifh*? If this Charge could be juftly fixed upon the Religion of Chrift, it would be unworthy the Regard of every wife and good Man, and render it both the Intereft and Duty of every Nation in the World to reject it.

It muft be allowed by all who know any Thing of the Progrefs of the Chriftian Religion, that the firft Preachers and Propagators of it ufed none of thefe vile Methods to fupport and fpread it. Both their Doctrines and Lives deftroy every Sufpicion of this Nature; and yet in their Times the beginnings of this Spirit appeared: *Diotrephes loved the Preheminence*, and therefore would not own and receive the infpired Apoftle. We alfo read, that there were great Divifions and Schifms in the Church of *Corinth*, and that many grievous Diforders were caufed therein, by their ranking themfelves under different Leaders and Heads of Parties, one being for *Paul*, another for *Apollos*, and others for *Cephas*. Thefe Animofities were difficultly healed by the Apoftolick Authority; but do not however appear to have broken out into mutual Hatreds, to the open Difgrace of the Chriftian Name and Profeffion. The Primitive Chriftians feem for many Years generally to have maintained the warmeft Affection for each other, and to have diftinguifhed themfelves by their mutual Love, the great Characteriftick of the Difciples of Chrift. The Gofpels, and the Epiftles of the Apoftles all breath with this amiable Spirit, and abound with Exhortations to cultivate this God-like Difpofition. 'Tis reported of St. *John*, that in his extreme old Age at *Ephefus*, being carried into the Church by the Difciples, upon account of his great Weaknefs, he ufed to fay nothing elfe every Time he was brought there, but this remarkable Sentence, *Filioli diligite alterutrum*, *Little Children love one another*. And when fome of the Brethren were tired with hearing fo often the fame Thing, and afked him, Sir, Why do you always repeat this Sentence; he anfwered with a Spirit worthy an Apoftle, *Quia preceptum Domini eft. Et fi folum fiat, fufficit*. *'Tis the Command of the Lord, and the fulfilling of the Law*. Precepts of this kind fo frequently inculcated, could not but have a very good Influence in keeping alive the Spirit of Charity and mutual Love. And indeed the Primitive Chriftians were fo very remarkable for this Temper, that they were taken notice of on this very Account, and recommended even by their Enemies as Patterns of Beneficence and Kindnefs. {Hieron. in Gal. c. 6.}

But at length, in the fecond Century, the Spirit of Pride and Domination appeared publickly, and created great Diforders and Schifms amongft Chriftians. There had been a Controverfy of fome ftanding, on what Day *Eafter* fhould be celebrated. The *Afiatick* Churches thought that it ought to be kept on the fame Day on which the *Jews* held the Paffover, the fourteenth Day of *Nifan* their firft Month, on whatfoever Day of the Week it fhould fall out. The

d   Cuftom

Cuſtom of other Churches was different, who kept the Feſtival of *Eaſter* only
on that Lord's Day which was next after the fourteenth of the Moon. This
Controverſy appears at firſt View to be of no manner of Importance, as there
is no Command in the ſacred Writings to keep this Feſtival at all, much leſs
Euſeb. l. 5. ſpecifying the particular Day on which it ſhould be celebrated. *Euſebius* tells
c. 24. us from *Irenæus*, that *Polycarp* Biſhop of *Smyrna* came to *Anicetus* Biſhop of
Rome on account of this very Controverſy ; and that though they differed from
one another in this and ſome other leſſer Things, yet they embraced one another with a Kiſs of Peace ; *Polycarp* neither perſuading *Anicetus* to conform to
his Cuſtom, nor *Anicetus* breaking off Communion with *Polycarp*, for not complying with his. This was a Spirit and Conduct worthy theſe Chriſtian Biſhops : But *Victor* the *Roman* Prelate acted a more haughty and violent part ;
for after he had received the Letters of the *Aſiatick* Biſhops, giving their Reaſons for their own Practice, he immediately excommunicated all the Churches
of *Aſia*, and thoſe of the neighbouring Provinces, for Heterodoxy ; and by
his Letters declared all the Brethren unworthy of Communion. This Conduct
was greatly diſpleaſing to ſome other of the Biſhops, who exhorted him to
mind the Things that made for Peace, Unity, and Chriſtian Love. *Irenæus*
eſpecially, in the Name of all his Brethren, the Biſhops of *France*, blamed
him for thus cenſuring whole Churches of Chriſt, and puts him in mind of the
peaceable Spirit of ſeveral of his Predeceſſors, who did not break off Communion with their Brethren upon account of ſuch leſſer Differences as theſe. Indeed this Action of Pope *Victor* was a very inſolent Abuſe of Excommunication ; and is an abundant Proof that the Simplicity of the Chriſtian Faith was
greatly departed from, in that Heterodoxy and Orthodoxy were made to depend on Conformity or Non-Conformity to the Modes and Circumſtances of
certain Things, when there was no Shadow of any Order for the Things themſelves in the ſacred Writings ; and that the Luſt of Power, and the Spirit of
Pride, had too much poſſeſſed ſome of the Biſhops of the Chriſtian Church.
Euſeb. l. 5. The ſame *Victor* alſo excommunicated one *Theodoſius* for being unſound in the
c. 28. Doctrine of the Trinity.

'Tis no wonder that after this we ſhould find Matters growing worſe and
worſe. As the Primitive Chriſtians had any intervals from Perſecution they became more profligate in their Morals, and more quarrelſome in their Tempers. As the Revenues of the ſeveral Biſhops increaſed they grew more Ambitious, leſs capable of Contradiction, more haughty and arrogant in their Behaviour, more envious and revengeful in every part of their Conduct, and more
regardleſs of the Simplicity and Gravity of their Profeſſion and Character.
The Accounts I have before given of them from *Cyprian* and *Euſebius* before
Epiſt. 13. the *Diocleſian* Perſecution, to which I might add the later one of St. *Jerom*,
are very melancholy and affecting, and ſhew how vaſtly they were degenerated from the Piety and peaceable Spirit of many of their Predeceſſors, and how
ready they were to enter into the worſt Meaſures of Perſecution, could they
but have got the Opportunity and Power.

Under

Under *Conſtantine* the Emperor, when they were reſtored to full Liberty, their Churches rebuilt, and the imperial Edicts every where publiſhed in their Favour, they immediately began to diſcover what Spirit they were of; as ſoon as ever they had the Temptations of Honour and large Revenues before them. *Conſtantine's* Letters are full Proof of the Jealouſies and Animoſities that reigned amongſt them. In his Letters to *Miltiades* Biſhop of *Rome* he E. H. l. 10. tells him, that he had been informed that *Cæcilianus* Biſhop of *Carthage* had c. 5. been accuſed of many Crimes by ſome of his Collegues, Biſhops of *Africa*, and that it was very grievous to him to ſee ſo great a Number of People divided into Parties, and the Biſhops diſagreeing amongſt themſelves. And though the Ibid. Emperor was willing to reconcile them by a friendly Reference of the Controverſy to *Miltiades* and others, yet in ſpite of all his Endeavours they maintained their Quarrels, and factious Oppoſition to each other, and through ſecret Grudges and Hatred would not acquieſce in the Sentence of thoſe he had appointed to determine the Affair. So that as he complained to *Chreſtus* Biſhop of *Syracuſe*, thoſe who ought to have maintained a brotherly Affection and peaceable Diſpoſition towards each other, did in a ſcandalous and deteſtible Manner ſeparate from one another, and gave Occaſion to the common Enemies of Chriſtianity to deride and ſcoff at them. For this Reaſon he ſummoned a Council to meet at *Arles* in *France*, that after an impartial hearing of the ſeveral Parties, this Controverſy which had been carried on for a long while in a very intemperate Manner, might be brought to a Friendly and Chriſtian Compromiſe. *Euſebius* farther adds, that he not only called together Councils in the ſe- De Vit. veral Provinces upon account of the Quarrels that aroſe amongſt the Biſhops, Con. l. 1. but that he himſelf was preſent in them, and did all he could to promote Peace c. 44. amongſt them. However, all he could do had but little effect; and it muſt be owned that he himſelf greatly contributed to prevent it, by his large Endowment of Churches, by the Riches and Honours which he conferred on the Biſhops, and eſpecially by his authorizing them to ſit as Judges upon the Conſciences and Faith of others, by which he confirmed them in a worldly Spirit, the Spirit of Domination, Ambition, Pride and Avarice, which hath in all Ages proved fatal to the Peace and true Intereſt of the Chriſtian Church.

In the firſt Edict, given us at large by *Euſebius*, publiſhed in favour of the E. H. l. 10. Chriſtians, he acted the part of a wiſe, good, and impartial Governor, in c. 5. which, without mentioning any particular Sects, he gave full liberty to all Chriſtians, y and to all other Perſons whatſoever, of following that Religion which they thought beſt. But this Liberty was of no long Duration, and ſoon abridged in reference both to the Chriſtians and Heathens. For although in this firſt mentioned Edict he orders the Churches and Effects of the Chriſtians in general to be reſtored to them, yet in one immediately following he confines this Grant to the Catholick Church. After this, in a Letter to *Miltiades* Biſhop of *Rome*, complaining of the Differences fomented by the

---

y Ακολυθως τη ησυχια των ημετερων καιρων γινεςαι φανερον εςιν, οπως εξυσιαν εκαςΘ εχη τε ευσεβεςῃ κȷ τημελειν οποιον δ'αν βυληῃαι θεον.

African

African Bifhops, he lets him know, that he had fo great a Reverence for the Catholick Church, that he would not have him fuffer in any Place any Schifm or Difference whatfoever. In another to *Cæcilianus* Bifhop of *Carthage*, after giving him to underftand, that he had ordered *Urfus* to pay his Reverence three Thoufand Pieces; and *Heraclides* to difburfe to him whatever other Sums his Reverence fhould have occafion for, he orders him to complain of all Perfons who fhould go on to corrupt the People of the moft holy Catholick Church by any evil and falfe Doctrine, to *Anulinus* the Pro-Conful, and *Patricius*, to whom he had given Inftructions on this Affair, that if they perfevered in fuch Madnefs they might be punifhed according to his Orders. 'Tis eafy to guefs what the Catholick Faith and Church meant, *viz.* that which was approved by the Bifhops, who had the greateft Intereft in his Favour.

As to the Heathens, foon after the Settlement of the whole Empire under his Government, he fent into all the Provinces Chriftian Prefidents, forbidding them, and all other Officers of fuperior Dignity to facrifice, and confining to fuch of them as were Chriftians the Honours due to their Characters and Stations; hereby endeavouring to fupport the Kingdom of Chrift, which is not of this World, by Motives purely worldly, *viz.* the Profpects of temporal Preferments and Honours; and notwithftanding the excellent Law he had before publifhed, That every one fhould have free Exercife of his own Religion, and worfhip fuch Gods as they thought proper, he foon after prohibited the old Religion, *viz.* the Worfhip of Idols in Cities and Country; commanding that no Statues of the Gods fhould be erected, nor any Sacrifices offered upon their Altars. And yet notwithftanding this Abridgment of the Liberty of Religion, he declares in his Letters afterwards, written to all the feveral Governors of his Provinces, that though he wifhed the Ceremonies of the Temples, and the Power of Darknefs were wholly removed, he would force none, but that every one fhould have the Liberty of acting in Religion as he pleafed.

'Tis not to be wonder'd at, that the Perfons who advifed thefe Edicts to fupprefs the ancient Religion of the Heathens, fhould be againft tolerating any other amongft themfelves, who fhould prefume to differ from them in any Articles of the Chriftian Religion they had efpoufed; becaufe if erroneous and falfe Opinions in Religion, as fuch, are to be prohibited or punifhed by the Civil Power, there is equal Reafon for perfecuting a Chriftian, whofe Belief is wrong, and whofe Practice is erroneous, as for perfecuting Perfons of any other falfe Religion whatfoever; and the fame Temper and Principles that lead to the latter, will alfo lead to and juftify the former. And as the Civil Magiftrate, under the Direction of his Priefts, muft always judge for himfelf what is Truth and Error in Religion, his Laws for fupporting the one, and punifhing the other, muft always be in Confequence of this Judgment. And therefore if *Conftantine* and his Bifhops were right in prohibiting Heathenifm by Civil Laws, becaufe they believed it erroneous and falfe, *Dioclefian* and *Licinius*, and their Priefts, were equally right in prohibiting Chriftianity by Civil Laws, becaufe they believed it not only erroneous and falfe, but the higheft Impiety and Blafphemy againft their Gods, and even a Proof of Atheifm it felf. And by

by the same Rule every Christian, that hath Power, is in the right to perfecute his Christian Brother, whenever he believes him to be in the wrong. And
in truth, they seem generally to have acted upon this Principle; for which
Party soever of them could get uppermost was against all Toleration and Liberty for those who differed from them, and endeavoured by all Methods to
oppress and destroy them.

The Sentiments of the Primitive Christians, at least for near three Centuries,
in reference to the Deity of our Lord Jesus Christ, were, generally speaking,
pretty uniform; nor do there appear to have been any publick Quarrels
about this Article of the Christian Faith. Some few Persons indeed, differed Eusb.
from the commonly received Opinion. One *Theodotus* a Tanner, under the E. H. L 5.
Reign of *Commodus*, asserted Christ was a meer Man, and on this Account was c. 28.
excommunicated, with other of his Followers, by Pope *Victor*, who appears
to have been very liberal in his Censures against others. *Artemon* propagated
the same erroneous Opinion under *Severus*. *Beryllus* also, an *Arabian* Bishop Ibid. l. 6.
under *Gordian*, taught, That our Saviour had no proper personal Subsistence c. 33.
before his becoming Man, nor any proper Godhead of his own, but only the
Father's Godhead residing in him; but afterwards alter'd his Opinion, being
convinced of his Error by the Arguments of *Origen*. *Sabellius* also propagated l. 7. c. 27,
much the same Doctrine, denying also the real Personality of the Holy Ghost.
After him *Paulus Samosatenus*, Bishop of *Antioch*, and many of his Clergy, 28, 29.
publickly avowed the same Principles concerning Christ, and were excommunicated by a large Council of Bishops. But though these Excommunications
upon account of Differences in Opinion, prove that the Bishops had set up for
Judges of the Faith, and assumed a Power and Dominion over the Consciences
of others, yet as they had no civil Effects, and were not enforced by any penal
Laws, they were not attended with any publick Confusions, to the open Reproach of the Christian Church.

But when once Christianity was settled by the Laws of the Empire, and the
Bishops free to act as they pleased, without any fear of publick Enemies
to disturb and oppress them, they fell into more shameful and violent Quarrels,
upon account of their Differences concerning the Nature and Dignity of Christ.
The Controversy first began between *Alexander* Bishop of *Alexandria*, and *Arius* De vit.
one of his Presbyters, and soon spread it self into other Churches, enflaming Const. l. 2,
Bishops against Bishops, who out of a Pretence to support Divine Truth exci- c. 61.
ted Tumults, and entertained irreconcilable Hatreds towards one another. Soc. E. H.
These Divisions of the Prelates set the Christian People together by the Ears, l. 1, c. 6.
as they happened to favour their different Leaders and Heads of Parties; and
the Dispute was managed with such Violence, that it soon reached the whole
Christian World, and gave Occasion to the Heathens in several Places to ridicule the Christian Religion upon their publick Theatres. How different were Euseb. l 6,
the Tempers of the Bishops and Clergy of these Times from the excellent Spirit c. 45.
of *Dionysius* Bishop of *Alexandria*, in the Reign of *Decius*, who writing to *No-
vatus* upon account of the Disturbance he had raised in the Church of *Rome*,.
by the Severity of his Doctrine, in not admitting those who lapsed into Idolatry

in

in Times of Perfecution ever more to Communion, though they gave all the Marks of a true Repentance and Converfion, tells him, ² *One ought to fuffer any Thing in the World rather than divide the Church of God.*

Soc. E. H.
l. 1, c. 5. The Occafion of the *Arian* Controverfy was this. *Alexander* Bifhop of *Alexandria* fpeaking in a very warm Manner concerning the Trinity before the Prefbyters and Clergy of his Church, affirmed there was *an Unity in the Trinity,* and particularly that *the Son was Co-eternal and Confubftantial, and of the fame Dignity with the Father. Arius,* one of his Prefbyters, thought that the Bifhop, by this Doctrine, was introducing the *Sabellian* Herefy, and therefore oppofed him, arguing in this manner : ᵃ *If the Father begot the Son, he who was begotten muft have a beginning of his Exiftence ; and from hence, fays he, 'tis manifeft, that there was a Time when he was not ; the neceffary Confequence of which*

E H l. 1.
c. 15. he affirmed was this, *That he had his Subfiftence out of Things not exifting.* *Sozomen* adds farther, that he afferted, ᵇ *That by virtue of his Free-will the Son was capable of Vice as well as Virtue ; and that he was the mere Creature and Work of God.* The Bifhop being greatly difturbed by thefe Expreffions of *Arius,* upon account of the Novelty of them, and not able to bear fuch an Oppofition from one of his Prefbyters to his own Principles, commanded *Arius* to forbear the Ufe of them, and to embrace the Doctrine of the Confubftantiality and Co-eternity of the Father and the Son. But *Arius* was not thus to be convinced, efpecially as a great Number of the Bifhops and Clergy were of his Opinion, and fupported him ; and for this Reafon himfelf and the Clergy of his Party were excommunicated, and expelled the Church, in a Council of near an Hundred of the *Egyptian* and *Lybian* Bifhops met together for that purpofe, by the Bifhop, who in this cafe was both Party and Judge, the Enemy and Condemner of *Arius.* Upon this Treatment *Arius* and his Friends fent circular Letters to the feveral Bifhops of the Church, giving them an Account of their Faith, and defiring that if they found their Sentiments orthodox, they would write to *Alexander* in their Favour ; if they judged them wrong, they would give them Inftructions how to believe. Thus was the Difpute carried into the Chriftian Church, and the Bifhops being divided in their Opinions, fome of them wrote to *Alexander* not to admit *Arius* and his Party into Communion without renouncing their Principles, whilft others of them perfwaded him to act a different part. The Bifhop not only followed the Advice of the former, but wrote Letters to the feveral Bifhops not to communicate with any of them, nor to receive them if

Soc. E. H.
l. 1, c. 6. they fhould come to them, nor to credit *Eufebius,* nor any other Perfon that fhould write to them in their behalf, but to avoid them as the Enemies of God, and the Corrupters of the Souls of Men ; and not fo much as to falute them, or

Soz. l. 1.
c. 15. to have any Communion with them in their Crimes. *Eufebius,* who was Bifhop of *Nicomedia,* fent feveral Letters to *Alexander,* exhorting him to let the Controverfy peaceably drop, and to receive *Arius* into Communion ; but finding

---

ᶻ Εδει μὲν γὸ ᾗ πᾶν ὁτιῶν παθεῖν, ὑπὲρ τε μὴ διακνψαι την εκκλησιαν τε Θεε.

ᵃ Ει ο πατηρ εγεννησε τον υον, αρχην υπαρξεως εχει ο γεννηθεις. Και εκ τε̄]ς δηλ·ν, οτι ην ο]ε εκ ην ο υΘ· ακολεθει τε εξ αναγκης εξ εκ ον]ων εχειν αυ]ον την υποςασιν.

ᵇ Και αυτεξεσιο]ητι κακιας ᾗ αρετης δεκ]ικον υπαρχειν, ᾗ κτισμα ᾗ ποιημα, ᾗ αλλα πολλα.

him

him inflexible to all his repeated Entreaties, he got a Synod to meet in *Bithynia*, from whence they wrote Letters to the other Bishops, to engage them to receive the *Arians* to their Communion, and to persuade *Alexander* to do the same. But all their Endeavours proved ineffectual, and by these un-friendly Dealings the Parties grew more enraged against each other, and the Quarrel became incurable.

'Tis, I confess, not a little surprizing, that the whole Christian World should be put into such a Flame upon account of a Dispute of so very abstruse and metaphysical a Nature, as this really was in the Course and Management of it. *Alexander*'s Doctrine, as *Arius* represents it in his Letter to *Eusebius* of *Nicomedia*, was this, *God is always, and the Son always. The same Time the Fa-* _{Theod.} *ther, the same Time the Son. The Son co-exists with God unbegottenly, being ever* ^{E. H. l. 1.} *begotten, being unbegottenly begotten. That God was not before the Son, no not in Con-*^{c. 5.} *ception, or the least Point of Time, he being ever God, ever a Son. For the Son is out of God himself.* Nothing could be more inexcusable, than the tearing the Churches in pieces upon account of such high and subtle Points as these, ex-cept the Conduct of *Arius*, who on the other hand asserted, as *Alexander*, his Bishop, in his Letter to the Bishop of *Constantinople*, tells us, ^d *That there was a* ^{Id. l. 1.} *Time when there was no Son of God, and that he who before was not, afterwards* ^{c. 4.} *existed, being made, when soever he was made, just as any Man whatsoever, and that therefore he was of a mutable Nature, and equally receptive of Vice and Virtue, and other Things of the like kind.* If these were the Things taught, and publickly avowed by *Alexander* and *Arius*, as each represents the other's Principles, I perswade my self, that every sober Man will think they both deserved Censure, for thus leaving the plain Account of Scripture, introducing Terms of their own Invention into a Doctrine of pure Revelation, and at last censuring and writing one against another, and dividing the whole Church of Christ upon ac-count of them.

But 'tis no uncommon Thing for warm Disputants to mistake and misrepre-sent each other; and that this was the Case in the present Controversy, is, I think, evident beyond Dispute; *Alexander* and *Arius* describing each other's Opinions, not as they held them themselves, but according to the Consequen-ces each imagined to follow from them. Thus *Alexander* affirms in the afore-mentioned Letter, that *the Father ever was*, and thence infers what he thinks necessarily follows, that *the Son*, upon whose account he is called a Father, *must have ever been*, and yet expresly asserts the Son to be begotten, and that the Father alone is unbegotten. When *Arius* represents these Things to his Friend *Eusebius*, 'tis according to what he accounted the necessary Consequences of them, and not as they were really maintained by *Alexander*; and because

^c Ἀεὶ ὁ Θεὸς, ἀεὶ ὁ υἱός· ἅμα πατὴρ, ἅμα υἱός. συνυπάρχει ἀγεννήτως ὁ υἱὸς τῷ Θεῷ, ἀειγενής· ἐστιν, ἀγεννητογενής ἐστιν· οὐτε ἐπινοίᾳ οὐδὲ ἀτόμῳ τινὶ προάγει ὁ Θεὸς τὸ υἱὸ· ἀεὶ Θεὸς, ἀεὶ υἱός· ἐξ αὐτοῦ ἐστι τοῦ Θεὸ ὁ υἱός.

^d Ἦν ποτε ὅτε οὐκ ἦν ὁ υἱὸς τῶ Θεῶ, καὶ γέγονεν ὕστερον ὁ πρότερον μὴ ὑπάρχων, τοιοῦτο γενόμενος, ὅτε καὶ ποτε γέγονεν, οἷος καὶ πᾶς ἐστι πέφυκεν ἄνθρωπος· ὡς ἀκόλουθως καὶ φησιν αὐτὸν τρεπτῆς εἶναι φύσεως, ἀρετῆς τε καὶ κακίας ἐπιδεκτικόν.

he apprehended that the absolute Co-eternity of the Son with the Father was inconsistent with the Son's being begotten of him, he says that *Alexander* held he was *unbegottenly begotten*, or begotten and not begotten, thus making his own Consequences pass for the Bishop's Sentiments. On the other hand, *Arius* asserted, *The Son hath a beginning, and is from none of the Things that do exist* ; not meaning that he was not from Everlasting, before ever the Creation had a Being, or that he was created like other Beings absolutely out of nothing, or that like the rest of the Creation he was mutable in his Nature. *Arius* expresly declares the contrary in his Letter to *Eusebius*, his intimate Friend, from whom he had no reason to conceal his most secret Sentiments, and says, ^e *This is what*

Theod. l. H. l. 1. c. 5.

we have and do profess, That the Son is not unbegotten, nor in any manner a part of the unbegotten God, nor from any part of the material World, but that by the Will and Council of the Father he existed before all Times and Ages, perfect God, the only begotten and unchangeable, and that therefore before he was begotten or formed he was not, i. e. as he explains himself, ^f *There never was a Time when he was unbegotten.* His affirming therefore that the Son had a Beginning, was only saying, that he was in the whole of his Existence from the Father, as the Origin and Fountain of his Being and Deity, and not any Denial of his being from before all Times and Ages ; and his saying that he was no part of God, nor derived from Things that do exist, was not denying his Generation from God before all Ages, or his being compleatly God himself, or his being produced after a more excellent Manner than the Creatures, but that as he was always from God, so he was different both from him, and all other Beings, and a Sort of middle Nature between God and his Creatures ; whose beginning, as *Eusebius* of *Nicomedia* writes to *Paulinus* Bishop of *Tyre*, was ^g *not only inexplicable by Words,*

Id Ibid. c 6.

but unconceivable by the Understanding of Men, and by all other Beings superior to Men, and who was formed after the most perfect Likeness to the Nature and Power of God. This is the strongest Evidence that neither *Arius* nor his first Friends put the Son upon a Level with the Creatures, but that they were in many respects of the same Sentiments with those who condemned them. Thus *Alexander* declares the Son to be ^h *before all Ages. Arius* expresly says the same, that he was ⁱ *before all Times and Ages. Alexander* says, the *Father only is unbegotten. Arius, That there never was a Time when the Son was not begotten. Alexander,* that *the Subsistence of the Son is inexplicable even by Angels. Eusebius,* that *his beginning is inconceivable and inexplicable by Men and Angels. Alexander,* that *the Father was always a Father because of the Son. Arius,* that the Son was not before he was begotten, *i. e. That he was from before all Ages the begotten Son of God.*

---

^e Οτι ο υἱὸς ᾰκ ἐϛιν ἀγεννητὸς, ᾰδὲ μερὸς ἀγεννήτε καθ' ᾰδενα τρόπον, ᾰδὲ ἐξ ὑποκειμένε τινὸς. αλλ' ὅτι θελήματι ᾗ βελῆ ὑπέϛη πρὸ χρόνων ᾗ πρὸ αιωνων, πληρης Θεὸς, μονογενης, αναλλαιωτὸς ᾗ πριν γεννηθῆ——ᾰκ ην.

^f Αγεννητὸς γὸ ᾰκ ην.

^g Περι τελειαν ομοιότητα διαθεσεως τε ᾗ δυναμεως τε πεποιηκότα γεγονῶον· ᾰ την αρχην ᾰ λογω μονον αδιηγητον, αλλα ᾗ εννοια ᾰκ ανθρωπων μονον αλλα ᾗ των υπερ ανθρωπες παντων εναι ακαταληπτον πεπιϛευκαμῶ.

^h Προαιωνιὸς.

ⁱ Πρὸ χρονων ᾗ πρὸ αιωνων.

Arius

Arius again, [k] *That the Son was no part of God, nor from any Things that did exist.* Theod.
Alexander, That *the only begotten Nature was* [l] *a middle Nature, between the unbe-* E. H. l. 1.
gotten Father, and the Things created by him out of nothing. And yet notwithstand- c. 4.
ing all these Things, when *Alexander* gives an Account of the Principles of
Arius to the Bishops, he represents them in all the Consequences he thought fit
to draw from them, and charges him with holding, that the Son was made
like every other Creature absolutely out of nothing, and that therefore his Nature was mutable, and susceptive equally of Virtue and Vice ; with many
other invidious and unscriptural Doctrines, which *Arius* plainly appears not to
have maintained or taught.

But as 'tis the common Fate of religious Disputes to be managed with an
intemperate Heat, 'tis no wonder the Disputants should mistake each other, or
in their Warmth charge one another with Consequences which either they do
not see, or expresly deny. Whilst this is the Case the Controversy can never
be fairly managed, nor brought to a friendly and peaceable Issue. Many Methods were tried, but all in vain, to bring *Alexander* and *Arius* to a Reconciliation, the Emperor himself condescending to become a Mediator between
them.

The first Step he took to heal this Breach was right and prudent : He sent Eufeb. Vit.
his Letters to *Alexandria,* exhorting *Alexander* and *Arius* to lay aside their Dif- Conft. l. 1.
ferences, and become reconciled to each other. He tells them, That *after he* c. 63, &c.
*had diligently examined the Rise and Progress of this Affair, he found the Occasion of
the Difference to be very trifling, and not worthy such furious Contentions ; and that
therefore he promised himself that his Mediation between them for Peace would have
the desired Effect.* He tells *Alexander,* That *he required from his Presbyters a Declaration of their Sentiments concerning a silly, empty Question.* And *Arius,* That *he
had imprudently uttered what he should not have even thought of, or what at least he
ought to have kept secret in his own Breast ; and that therefore Questions about such
Things should not have been asked ; or if they had, should not have been answered ;
that they proceeded from an idle Itch of Disputation, and were in themselves of so high
and difficult a Nature, as that they could not be exactly comprehended, or suitably explained ;* and that to insist on such Points too much before the People, could
produce no other Effect, than to make some of them talk Blasphemy, and
others turn Schismaticks ; and that therefore *as they did not contend about any
essential Doctrine of the Gospel, nor introduce any new Heresy concerning the Worship
of God,* they should again communicate with each other ; and finally, that notwithstanding their Sentiments in these unnecessary and trifling Matters were
different from each other, they should acknowledge one another as Brethren,
and, laying aside their Hatreds, return to a firmer Friendship and Affection
than before.

But religious Hatreds are not so easily removed, and the Ecclesiastical
Combatants were too warmly engaged to follow this kind and wholesome Ad-

[k] Οτι κ μερϴ Θεκ εςιν, κδε εξ υποκειμϸν τινϴ.
[l] Μεσιʃευεσα παʃρϴ αγεννηʃα και των κʃιϸενʃων υπ' αυʃκ εξ κ ονʃων.

c

vice.

vice. The Bifhops of each fide had already interefted the People in their Quarrel, and heated them into fuch a Rage that they attacked and fought with, wounded and deftroyed each other, and acted with fuch Madnefs as to commit the greateft Impieties for the fake of Orthodoxy ; and arrived to that pitch of Infolence, as to offer great Indignities to the imperial Images. The old Controverfy about the Time of celebrating *Eafter* being now revived, added Fuel to the Flames, and render'd their Animofities too furious to be appeafed.

Conftantine being greatly difturbed upon this Account, fent Letters to the Bifhops of the feveral Provinces of the Empire to affemble together at *Nice* in *Bythinia*, and accordingly great Numbers of them came, *A. C.* 325. fome through hopes of Profit, and others out of Curiofity to fee fuch a Miracle as an Emperor, and many of them, as *Sozomen* informs us, to negotiate their own private Affairs, and to redrefs their Grievances, by accufing thofe who had injured them. The Number of them was three Hundred and eighteen, befides vaft Numbers of Prefbyters, Deacons, Acolythifts, and others. The Ecclefiaftical Hiftorians tell us, that in this vaft Collection of Bifhops fome were remarkable for their Gravity, Patience under Sufferings, Modefty, Integrity, Eloquence, and the like Virtues ; but yet they all agree that there were others of very different Characters. *Eufebius* tells us, fome came to the Council with
worldly Views of Gain ; and *Theodorit*, that others were fubtle and crafty, and of a quarrelling, malicious Temper, and actuated with a Spirit of Revenge. And indeed, this appeared immediately upon opening the Council ; for after the Emperor, who honoured this Affembly with his Prefence, had exhorted them to lay afide all their Differences, and to enter into Meafures of Union and Peace, inftead of applying themfelves to the Work for which they were convened, they began fhamefully to accufe each other before him, and raifed great Difturbances in the Council by their mutual Charges and Reproaches.
Sabinus, alfo, faith they were generally a Set of very ignorant Men, and deftitute of Knowledge and Learning. But as *Sabinus* was an Heretick of the *Macedonian* Sect, probably his Teftimony may be thought exceptionable ; and even fuppofing his Charge to be true, yet *Socrates* brings them off by telling us, that they were enlighten'd by God, and the Grace of his Holy Spirit, and fo could not poffibly err from the Truth. But as fome Men may poffibly queftion the Truth of their Infpiration, fo I think it appears but too plain, that an Affembly of Men, who met together with fuch different Views, were fo greatly prejudiced and inflamed againft each other, and are allowed, many of them, to be ignorant, till they received miraculous Illuminations from God, did not feem very likely to heal the Differences of the Church, or to examine with that Wifdom, Care and Impartiality, or to enter into thofe Meafures of Condefcenfion and Forbearance that were neceffary to lay a folid Foundation for Peace and Unity.

However, the Emperor brought them at laft to fome Temper, fo that they fell in good earneft to Creed-making, and drew up, and fubfcribed that, which from the Place where they were affembled was called the *Nicene*. By the Ac-

'counts of the Transactions in this Assembly, given by *Athanasius* himself, in his
Letter to the *African* Bishops, it appears, that they were determined to insert
into the Creed such Words as were most obnoxious to the Arians, and thus to
force them to a publick Separation from the Church. For when they resolved
to condemn some Expressions which the Arians were charged with making use
of, such as, *The Son was a Creature* ; *there was a Time when he was not*, and the
like ; and to establish the Use of others in their room, such as, *The Son was the
only begotten of God by Nature, the Word, the Power, the only Wisdom of the Father, and true God* ; the Arians immediately agreed to it : Upon this the Fathers made an Alteration, and explained the Words, *From God*, by the Son's
being of the Substance of God. And when the Arians consented also to this, the
Bishops farther added, to render the Creed more exceptionable, that *he was
Consubstantial, or of the same Substance with the Father*. And when the Arians
objected, that this Expression was wholly unscriptural, the Orthodox urged,
that though it was so, yet the Bishops that lived an Hundred and thirty Years
before them, made use of it. At last however all the Council subscribed the
Creed thus altered and amended, except five Bishops, who were displeased
with the Word *Consubstantial*, and made many Objections against it.

Eusebius, Bishop of *Cæsarea*, was also in doubt for a considerable Time,
whether he should set his Hand to it, and refused to do it, till the exceptionable Words had been fully debated amongst them, and he had obtained an Explication of them suitable to his own Sentiments. Thus when 'twas asserted by
the Creed, that *the Son was of the Father's Substance*, the negative Explication
agreed to by the Bishops was exactly the same Thing that was asserted by *Arius*, viz. that [m] *He was not a part of the Father's Substance*. Again, as the
Words, *begotten, not made*, were applied to the Son, they determined the
Meaning to be, that *the Son was produced after a different Manner than the Creatures which he made*, and was therefore of a more excellent Nature than any of
the Creatures, and that the Manner of his Generation could not be understood.
This was the very Doctrine of *Arius*, and *Eusebius* of *Nicomedia*, who declar'd,
that *as the Son was no part of God, so neither was he from any Thing created, and that
the Manner of his Generation was not to be described*. And as to the Word *Consubstantial* to the Father, it was agreed by the Council to mean no more, than that
*the Son had no Likeness with any created Beings, but was in all Things like to him that
begot him, and that he was not from any other Hypostasis or Substance but the Father's*.
Of this Sentiment also were *Arius*, and *Eusebius* his Friend, who maintained not
only his being of a more excellent Original than the Creatures, but that he was
formed *of an immutable and ineffable Substance and Nature, and after the most perfect
Likeness of the Nature and Power of him that formed him*. These were the Explications of these Terms agreed to by the Council, upon which *Eusebius* of *Cæsarea* subscribed them in the Creed ; and though some few of the Arian Bishops
refused to do it, yet it doth not appear to me, that it proceeded from their not
agreeing in the Sense of these Explications, but because they apprehended that

[m] Μεγ⊙ της ασιας αυτ.

e 2   the

the Words were very improper, and implied a great deal more than was pretended to be meant by them; and especially because an Anathema was added upon all who should presume not to believe in them and use them. *Eusebius* of *Cæsarea* gives a very extraordinary Reason for his subscribing this Anathema, *viz.* because *it forbids the Use of unscriptural Words, the introducing which he assigns as the Occasion of all the Differences and Disturbances which had troubled the Church.* But had he been consistent with himself, he ought never to have subscribed this Creed, for the very Reason he alledges why he did it; because the Anathema forbids only the unscriptural Words of *Arius*, such as, *He was made out of nothing; there was a Time when he was not,* and the like; but allowed and made sacred the unscriptural Expressions of the Orthodox, *viz. Of the Father's Substance,* and *Consubstantial,* and cut off from Christian Communion those who would not agree to them, though they were highly exceptionable to the Arian Party, and afterwards proved the Occasions of many cruel Persecutions and Evils.

In this publick Manner did the Bishops assert a Dominion over the Faith and Consciences of others, and assume a Power, not only to dictate to them what they should believe, but even to anathematize, and expel from the Christian Church, all who refused to submit to their Decisions, and own their Authority. For after they had carried their Creed, they proceeded to excommunicate *Arius* and his Followers, and banished *Arius* from *Alexandria.* They also condemned his Explication of his own Doctrine, and a certain Book, called *Thalia,* which he had written concerning it. After this they sent Letters to *Alexandria,* and to the Brethren in *Egypt, Lybia,* and *Pentapolis,* to acquaint them with their Decrees, and to inform them, that the Holy Synod had condemned the Opinions of *Arius,* and were so zealous in this Affair, that they had not patience so much as to hear his ungodly Doctrine and blasphemous Words, and that they had fully determined the Time for the Celebration of *Easter.* Finally, they exhort them to rejoice for the good Deeds they had done, and for that they had cut off all manner of Heresy, and to pray that their right Transactions might be established by Almighty God and our Lord Jesus Christ. When these Things were over, *Constantine* splendidly treated the Bishops, filled their Pockets, and sent them honourably home; advising them at parting to maintain Peace amongst themselves, and that none of them should envy another who might excel the rest in Wisdom and Eloquence, and that such should not carry themselves haughtily towards their Inferiors, but condescend to, and bear with their Weakness. A plain Demonstration that he saw into their Tempers, and was no Stranger to the Pride and Haughtiness that influenced some, and the Envy and Hatred that actuated others. After he had thus dismissed them he sent several Letters, recommending and enjoyning an universal Conformity to the Councils Decrees both in Ceremony and Doctrine, using, among other Things, this Argument for it, *That what they had decreed was the Will of God, and that the Agreement of so great a Number of such Bishops was by Inspiration of the Holy Ghost.*

Soc. l. 1. c. 9.

Euseb. de Vit. Const l. 3. c. 20

Soc. E. H. l. 1. c. 9.

'Tis-

'Tis natural here to obferve, that the Anathema's and Depofitions agreed on by this Council, and confirmed by the imperial Authority, were the beginning of all the Perfecutions that afterwards raged againft each Party in their Turns. As the Civil Power had now taken part in the Controverfies about Religion, by authorifing the Dominion of the Bifhops over the Confciences of others, enforcing their Ecclefiaftical Conftitutions, and commanding the univerfal Reception of that Faith they had decreed to be Orthodox, it was eafy to forefee that thofe who oppofed them would employ the fame Arts and Authority to eftablifh their own Faith and Power, and to opprefs their Enemies, the firft favourable Opportunity that prefented : And this the Event abundantly made good. And indeed how fhould it be otherwife ? For Doctrines that are determined merely by dint of Numbers, and the Awes of worldly Power, carry no manner of Conviction in them, and are not likely therefore to be believed on thefe Accounts by thofe who have once oppofed them. And as fuch Methods of deciding Controverfies equally fuit all Principles, the introducing them by any Party gives but too plaufible a Pretence to every Party, when uppermoft, to ufe them in its turn ; and though they may agree well enough with the Views of fpiritual Ambition, yet they can be of no Service in the World to the Intereft of true Religion, becaufe they are directly contrary to the Nature and Spirit of it ; and becaufe Arguments, which equally prove the Truth and Excellency of all Principles, cannot in the leaft prove the Truth of any.

If one may form a Judgment of the Perfons who compofed this Council, from the fmall Accounts we have left of them, they do not, I think, appear to have met fo much with a Defign impartially to debate on the Subjects in Controverfy, as to eftablifh their own Authority and Opinions, and opprefs their Enemies. For befides what hath been already obferved concerning their Temper and Qualifications, *Theodorit* informs us, that when thofe of the Arian Party propofed in writing to the Synod the Form of Faith they had drawn up, the Bifhops of the Orthodox fide no fooner read it but they gravely tore it in pieces, and called it a fpurious and falfe Confeffion ; and after they had filled the Place with Noife and Confufion, univerfally accufed them of betraying the Doctrine according to Godlinefs. Doth fuch a Method of Proceeding fuit very well with the Character of a Synod infpired, as the good Emperor declared, by the Holy Ghoft ? Is Truth and Error to be decided by Noife and Tumult ? Was this the Way to convince Gainfayers, and reconcile them to the Unity of the Faith? Or could it be imagined, that the diffatisfied Part of this venerable Affembly would acquiefce in the tyrannical Determination of fuch a Majority, and patiently fubmit to Excommunication, Depofition, and the Condemnation of their Opinions, almoft unheard, and altogether unexamin'd ? How juftly doth the Cenfure paffed by *Gregory Nazianzen* upon the Councils that were held in his Time agree to this famous one of *Nice*? If, fays he, *I muft fpeak the Truth, this is my Refolution, to avoid all Councils of the Bifhops, for I have not feen any good End anfwered by any Synod whatfoever ; for their love of Contention, and their luft of Power, are too great even for Words to exprefs.* The Emperor's Conduct to the Bifhops met at *Nice*, is full Proof of the former ; for when they were met in Council they

E. H.
l. 1. c. 7.

Vol. I
Epift. lv.
Edit. Col.

Eufeb. de
Vit. Conft.
imme. l. 3. c. 13.

immediately fell to wrangling and quarrelling, and were not to be appeafed and brought to Temper, till *Conftantine* interpofed, artfully perfuading fome, fhaming others into filence, and heaping Commendations on thofe Fathers that fpoke agreeable to his Sentiments. The Decifions they made concerning the Faith, and their Excommunications and Depofitions of thofe who differed from them, demonftrate alfo their affectation of Power and Dominion. But as they had great Reafon to believe, that their own Decrees would be wholly infignificant without the Interpofition of the imperial Authority to enforce them, they foon obtained their Defires, the Emperor readily confirming all they had determined, and injoining all Chriftians to fubmit themfelves to them.

His firft Letters to this purpofe were mild and gentle : But he was foon perfuaded into more violent Meafures ; for out of his great Zeal to extinguifh Herefy, he put forth publick Edicts againft the Authors and Maintainers of it ; and particularly againft the *Novatians, Valentinians, Marcionifts,* and others, whom after reproaching *with being Enemies of Truth, deftructive Counfellors, and with holding Opinions fuitable to their Crimes,* he deprives of the Liberty of meeting together for Worfhip, either in publick or private Places, and gives all their Oratories to the Orthodox Church. And with refpect to the Arians, he banifhed *Arius* himfelf, ordered all his Followers, as abfolute Enemies of Chrift, to be called *Porphyrians,* from *Porphyrius* an Heathen who wrote againft Chriftianity ; ordained that the Books written by them fhould be burnt, that there might be no Remains of their Doctrine left to Pofterity, and moft cruelly commanded, that if ever any one fhould dare to keep in his Poffeffion any Book written by *Arius,* and fhould not immediately burn it, he fhould be no fooner convicted of the Crime but he fhould fuffer Death.

Thus the Orthodox firft brought in the Punifhment of Herefy with Death, and perfuaded the Emperor to deftroy thofe whom they could not eafily convert. The Scriptures were now no longer the Rule and Standard of the Chriftian Faith. Orthodoxy and Herefy were from hence forward to be determined by the Decifions of Councils and Fathers, and Religion to be propagated no longer by the apoftolick Methods of Perfuafion, Forbearance, and the Virtues of an holy Life, but by imperial Edicts and Decrees ; and heretical Gainfayers not to be convinced, that they might be brought to the Acknowledgment of the Truth and be faved, but to be perfecuted and deftroyed. 'Tis no wonder, that after this there fhould be a continual Fluctuation of the publick Faith, juft as the prevailing Parties had the imperial Authority to fupport them, or that we fhould meet with little elfe in Ecclefiaftical Hiftory but Violence and Cruelties committed by Men who had left the Simplicity of the Chriftian Faith and Profeffion, enflaved themfelves to Ambition and Avarice, and had before them the enfnaring Views of temporal Grandure, high Preferments, and large Revenues. [n] *Since the Time that Avarice hath encreafed in the Churches,* fays St.

Eufeb. de Vit. Conft. c. 65.

Soz. l. 1. c. 21.

Soc. l. 1. c. 9.

Epift. xiii.

[n] Nunc autem ex quo in Ecclefiis crevit Avaritia, periit Lex de Sacerdote, & Vifio de Propheta. Singuli quiq; pro Potentia Epifcopalis nominis, quam fibi ipfi illicite abfq, Ecclefia vendicaverunt, totum quod Levitarum eft in Ufus fuos redigunt——Moriuntur Fame qui a ios fepelire mandantur, Pofcunt

St. *Jerom, the Law of the Priest, and the Vision of the Prophet hath failed. Whilst all contend for the Episcopal Power, which they unlawfully seize on without the Church's leave ; they apply to their own Uses all that belongs to the Levites. The miserable Priest begs in the Streets——They die with Hunger who are commanded to bury others. They ask for Pity who are commanded to pity others.——The Priests only care is to get Money——Hence Hatreds arise through the Avarice of the Priests ; hence the Bishops are accused by their Clergy ; hence the Quarrels of the Prelates ; hence the Causes of Desolations ; hence the Rise of their Wickedness.* Religion and Christianity seem indeed to be the least Thing that either the contending Parties had at heart, by the infamous Methods they took to establish themselves and ruin their Adversaries.

If one reads the Complaints of the Orthodox Writers against the Arians, one would think the Arians the most execrable Set of Men that ever lived, they being loaded with all the Crimes that can possibly be committed, and represented as bad, or even worse, than the Devil himself. But no wise Man will easily credit these Accounts, which the Orthodox give of their Enemies, because, as *Socrates* tells us, *This was the Practice of the Bishops towards all they* E. H. l. 1. *deposed, to accuse and pronounce them impious, but not to tell others the Reasons* c. 24. *why they accused them as such.* 'Twas enough for their Purpose to expose them to the publick Odium, and make them appear impious to the Multitude, that so they might get them expelled from their rich Sees, and be translated to them in their room. And this they did as frequently as they could, to the introducing infinite Calamities and Confusions into the Christian Church. And if the Writings of the Arians had not been prudently destroyed, I doubt not but we should have found as many Charges laid by them, with equal Justice, against the Orthodox, as the Orthodox have produced against them ; their very Suppression of the Arian Writings being a very strong Presumption against them, and the many imperial Edicts of *Constantine, Theodosius, Valentinian, Martian,* and others, against Hereticks, being an abundant Demonstration that they had a deep Share in the Guilt of Persecution.

Alexander, Bishop of *Alexandria,* in his Letter to the Bishop of *Constanti-* Theod. *nople,* complains that *Arius* and others, desirous of Power and Riches, did Day l. 1. c. 4, 5. and Night invent Calumnies, and were continually exciting Seditions and Persecutions against him ; and *Arius* in his turn, in his Letter to *Eusebius* of *Nicomedia,* with too much Justice charges Pope *Alexander* with violently persecuting and oppressing him upon account of what he called the Truth, and using every Method to ruin him, driving him out of the City as an atheistical Person, for not agreeing with him in his Sentiments about the Trinity. *Athanasius* also bitterly exclaims against the Cruelty of the Arians, in his Apology for his flight. *Whom have they not,* says he, *used with the greatest Indignity, that they have been* Vol. I. *able to lay hold of ? Who hath ever fallen into their Hands, that they have had any* P. 7-2.

Poscunt misericordiam, qui misereri aliis sunt precepti——Solus incubat Divitiis——Hinc propter Sacerdotum Avaritiam Odia consurgunt, hinc Episcopi accusantur a Clericis, hinc Principum Lites, hinc Desolationum Causæ, hinc Origo Criminis.

spite againft, whom they have not fo cruelly treated, as either to murther or to maim him? What Place is there where they have not left the Monuments of their Barbarity? What Church is there which doth not lament their Treachery againft their Bifhops? After this paffionate Exclamation he mentions feveral Bifhops they had banifhed or put to Death, and the Cruelties they made ufe of to force the Orthodox to renounce the Faith, and to fubfcribe to the Truth of the Arian Doctrines. But might it not have been afked, Who was it that firft brought in Excommunications, Depofitions, Banifhments, and Death, as the Punifhments of Herefy? Could not the Arians recriminate with Juftice? Were they not reproached as Atheifts, anathematized, expelled their Churches, exiled, and made liable to the Punifhment of Death by the Orthodox? Did not even they who complained of the Cruelty of the Arians in the moft moving Terms, create numberlefs Confufions and Slaughters by their violent Intrufions into the Sees of their Adverfaries? Was not *Athanafius* himfelf alfo accufed to the Emperor, by many Bifhops and Clergymen, who declared themfelves Orthodox, of being the Author of all the Seditions and Difturbances in the Church, by excluding great Multitudes from the publick Services of it ; of murthering fome, putting others in Chains, punifhing others with Stripes and Whippings, and of burning Churches? And if the Enemies of *Athanafius* endeavoured to ruin him by fuborned Witneffes and falfe Accufations, *Athanafius* himfelf ufed the fame Practices to deftroy his Adverfaries, and particularly *Eufebius* of *Nicomedia*, by fpiriting up a Woman to charge *Eufebius* with getting her with Child, the Falfhood of which was detected at the Council of *Tyre*. His very Ordination alfo to the Bifhop of *Alexandria*, was cenfured as clandeftine and illegal. Thefe Things being reported to *Conftantine*, he ordered a Synod to meet at *Cæfarea* in *Paleftine*, of which Place *Eufebius Pamphilus* was Bifhop, before whom *Athanafius* refufed to appear. But after the Council was removed to *Tyre* he was obliged by force to come thither, and commanded to anfwer to the feveral Crimes objected againft him. Some of them he cleared himfelf of, and as to others he defired more Time for his Vindication. At length, after many Seffions, both his Accufers, and the Multitude who were prefent in the Council, demanded his Depofition as an Impoftor, a violent Man, and unworthy the Priefthood. Upon this *Athanafius* fled from the Synod, after which they condemned him, and deprived him of his Bifhoprick, and ordered he fhould never more enter *Alexandria*, to prevent his exciting Tumults and Seditions. They alfo wrote to all the Bifhops to have no Communion with him, as one convicted of many Crimes, and as having convicted himfelf by his flight of many others, to which he had not anfwered. And for this their Procedure they affigned thefe Reafons, that he defpifed the Emperor's Orders, by not coming to *Cæfarea* ; that he came with a great Number of Perfons to *Tyre*, and excited Tumults and Difturbances in the Council, fometimes refufing to anfwer to the Crimes objected againft him, at other Times reviling all the Bifhops ; fometimes not obeying their Summons, and at others refufing to fubmit to their Judgment ; that he was fully and evidently convicted of breaking in pieces the facred Cup, by fix Bifhops who had been fent into *Egypt* to

Soz. l. 1.
c. 22.

Philoftorg.
Compen.
E. H. l. 8.
c. 11.

Soz. l. 2.
c. 25, 28.

-inquire out the Truth. *Athanafius*, however, appealed to *Conftantine*, and gave him fuch a Reprefentation of the Council's Tranfactions as greatly offended him. But when *Eufebius* and others laid the whole Matter before him, the Emperor entirely altered his Sentiments, confirmed his Depofition, and ba--nifhed him into *France*.

Indeed *Athanafius*, notwithftanding his fad Complaints under Perfecution, and his exprefly calling it a diabolical Invention, yet feems to be againft it only Ad Imp. when he and his own Party were perfecuted, but not againft perfecuting the Conft. Enemies of Orthodoxy. In his Letter to *Epictetus*, Bifhop of *Corinth*, he faith, I Apol. *wonder that your Piety hath born thefe Things (viz.* the Herefies he had before- P. 716. mentioned*) and that you did not immediately put thofe Hereticks under Reftraint, and* Vol. I. *propofe the true Faith to them ; that if they would not forbear to contradict they* p. 584. *might be declared Hereticks ; for 'tis not to be endured that thefe Things fhould be either faid or heard amongft Chriftians.* And in another Place he fays, *that they ought to* Orat. 1. *be had in univerfal Hatred for oppofing the Truth ;* and comforts himfelf, that the cont. Ar. Emperor, upon due Information, would put a Stop to their Wickednefs, and P. 304. that they would not be long liv'd. And to mention no more, *I therefore exhort* Vol. I. *you,* fays he, *let no one be deceived, but as though the Jewifh Impiety was prevailing* P. 291. *over the Faith of Chrift, be ye all zealous in the Lord. And let every one hold faft the Faith he hath received from the Fathers, which alfo the Fathers met together at Nice declared in Writing, and endure none of thofe who may attempt to make any Innovations therein.* 'Tis needlefs to produce more Inftances of this kind ; whofoever P. 292. gives himfelf the Trouble of looking over any of the Writings of this Father, will find in them the moft furious Invectives againft the *Arians*, and that he ftudioufly endeavours to reprefent them in fuch Colours, as might render them the Abhorrence of Mankind, and excite the World to their utter Extirpation.

I write not thefe Things out of any Averfion to the Memory, or peculiar Principles of *Athanafius* ; whether I agree with him, or differ from him in Opinion, I think my felf equally obliged to give impartially the true Account of him. And as this which I have given of him is drawn partly from Hiftory, and partly from his own Writings, I think I cannot be juftly charged with mifreprefenting him. To fpeak plainly, I think that *Athanafius* was a Man of an haughty and inflexible Temper, and more concerned for Victory and Power than for Truth, Religion or Peace. The Word *Confubftantial* that was inferted into the *Nicene* Creed, and the Anathema denounced againft all who would or Soz. l. 2. could not believe in it, furnifhed Matter for endlefs Debates. Thofe who were c. 18. againft it cenfured as Blafphemers thofe who ufed it ; and as denying the proper Subfiftence of the Son, and as falling into the Sabellian Herefy. The Confubftantialifts on the other fide reproached their Adverfaries as Heathens, and with bringing in the Polytheifm of the Gentiles. And though they equally denied the Confequences which their refpective Principles were charged with, yet as the Orthodox would not part with the Word *Confubftantial*, and the Arians could not agree to the Ufe of it, they continued their unchriftian Reproaches and Accufations of each other. *Athanafius* would yield to no Terms

f of

of Peace, nor receive any into Communion, who would not absolutely submit
to the Decisions of the Fathers of *Nice*. In his Letter to *Johannes* and *Antiochus* he exhorts them to hold fast the Confession of those Fathers, and *to reject
all who should speak more or less than was contained in it*. And in his first Oration against the Arians he declares in plain Terms, "That the expressing
" a Person's Sentiments in the Words of Scripture was no sufficient Proof of
" Orthodoxy, because the Devil himself used Scripture Words to cover his
" wicked Designs upon our Saviour ; and even farther, that Hereticks were
" not to be received, though they made use of the very Expressions of Or-
" thodoxy it self." With one of so suspicious and jealous a Nature there could
scarce be any possible Terms of Peace, it being extremely unlikely, that without
some kind Allowances, and mutual Abatements, so wide a Breach could ever
be compromised. Even the Attempts of *Constantine* himself to soften *Athanasius*, and reconcile him to his Brethren, had no other Influence upon him,
than to render him more imperious and obstinate ; for after *Arius* had given in
such a Confession of his Faith as satisfied the Emperor, and expresly denied
many of the Principles he had been charged with, and thereupon humbly desired the Emperor's Interposition, that he might be restored to the Communion of the Church ; *Athanasius*, out of Hatred to his Enemy, flatly denied
the Emperor's Request, and told him, that 'twas impossible for those who had
once rejected the Faith, and were anathematized, ever to be wholly restored.
This so provoked the Emperor, that he threaten'd to depose and banish him,
unless he submitted to his Order ; which he shortly after did, by sending him
into *France*, upon an Accusation of several Bishops, who, as *Socrates* intimates,
were worthy of Credit, That he had said he would stop the Corn that was yearly sent to *Constantinople* from the City of *Alexandria*. To such an Height of
Pride was this Bishop now arrived, as even to threaten the Sequestration of the
Revenues of the Empire. *Constantine* also apprehended, that this Step was necessary to the Peace of the Church, because *Athanasius* absolutely refused to
communicate with *Arius* and his Followers.

Soon after these Transactions *Arius* died, and the Manner of his Death, as it
was reported by the Orthodox, *Athanasius* thinks of it self sufficient fully to
condemn the Arian Heresy, and an evident Proof that it was hateful to God.
Nor did *Constantine* himself long survive him ; he was succeeded by his three
Sons, *Constantine*, *Constantius*, and *Constans*. *Constantine* the eldest recalled
Athanasius from Banishment, and restored him to his Bishoprick, upon which
Account there arose most grievous Quarrels and Seditions, many being killed, and many publickly whipped by *Athanasius*'s Order, according to the Accusations of his Enemies. *Constantius*, after his elder Brother's Death, convened a Synod at *Antioch* in *Syria*, where *Athanasius* was again deposed for these
Crimes, and *Gregory* put into the See of *Alexandria*. In this Council a new
Creed was drawn up, in which the Word *Consubstantial* was wholly omitted,
and the Expressions made use of so general, as that they might have been
equally agreed to by the Orthodox and Arians. In the Close of it several Anathema's were added, and particularly upon all who should teach or preach
                                                                        other-

Marginal notes:
Vol. I.
p. 951.

P. 291.

Soc. l. 1.
c. 27.

Id Ibid.
c. 35.

Ad Solit.
Vit. Agen.
Epist.
p. 809,
810.

Soc. l. 2.
c. 8.
Soz. l. 3.
c. 5.

Soz. l. 3.
c. 5.
Soc. l. 2.
c. 10.

otherwife than what this Council had received, becaufe, as they themfelves fay, *They did really believe and follow all Things delivered by the Holy Scriptures, both Prophets and Apoftles.* So that now the whole Chriftian World was under a fynodical Curfe, the oppofite Councils having damned one another, and all that differed from them. And 'if Councils, as fuch, have any Authority to anathematife all who will not fubmit to them, this Authority equally belongs to every Council ; and therefore 'twas but a natural Piece of Revenge, that as the Council of *Nice* had fent all the Arians to the Devil, the Arians, in their turn, fhould take the Orthodox along with them for Company, and thus repay one Anathema with another.

Conftantius himfelf was warmly on the Arian fide, and favoured the Bifhops of that Party only, and ejected *Paul* the Orthodox Bifhop from the See of *Conftantinople*, as a Perfon altogether unworthy of it, *Macedonius* being fubftitu- Soc. l. 3. ted in his room. *Macedonius* was in a different Scheme, or at leaft expreffed c. 4. himfelf in different Words both from the Orthodox and Arians, and affert- Athanaf. ed, That the Son was not Confubftantial but ὁμοιούσιος, not of the fame, but a Trin. V.1. like Subftance with the Father, and openly propagated this Opinion, after he p. 210. had thruft himfelf into the Bifhoprick of *Paul*. This the orthodox Party highly Soc. l. 2. refented, oppofing *Hermogenes*, whom *Conftantius* had fent to introduce him, c. 13. and in their Rage burnt down his Houfe, and drew him round the Streets by his Feet till they had murthered him. But notwithftanding the Emperor's Orders were thus oppofed, and his Officers killed by the orthodox Party, he treated them with great Lenity, and in this Inftance punifhed them much lefs than their Infolence and Fury deferved. Soon after this *Athanafius* and *Paul* c. 15. were reftored again to their refpective Sees ; and upon *Athanafius*'s entering *Alexandria* great Difturbances arofe, which were attended with the Deftruction of many Perfons, and *Athanafius* accufed of being the Author of all thofe Evils. Soon after *Paul*'s return to *Conftantinople* he was banifhed from thence again by the Emperor's Order, and *Macedonius* re-entered into Poffeffion of that See, upon which Occafion three Thoufand one Hundred and fifty Perfons were murthered, fome by the Soldiers, and others by being preffed to Death by the Croud. *Athanafius* alfo foon followed him into Banifhment, being accufed of Soc. l. 2. felling the Corn which *Conftantine* the Great had given for the Support of the c. 17. Poor of the Church of *Alexandria*, and putting the Money in his own Pocket ; and being therefore threaten'd by *Conftantius* with Death. But they were both a little while after recalled by *Conftans*, then banifhed again by *Conftantius* ; and *Paul*, as fome fay, murthered by his Enemies the Arians, as he was carrying into Exile ; though, as *Athanafius* himfelf owns, the Arians exprefly denied Ad Sol. it, and faid, that he died of fome Diftemper. *Macedonius* having thus gotten Vit. Ag. quiet Poffeffion of the See of *Conftantinople*, prevailed with the Emperor to P. 813. publifh a Law, by which thofe of the Confubftantial, or orthodox Party, were Soc. l. 2. driven not only out of the Churches but Cities too, and many of them compel- c. 27. led to communicate with the Arians by Stripes and Torments, by Profcriptions and Banifhments, and other violent Methods of Severity. Upon the Banifh- Ad Conft. ment of *Athanafius*, whom *Conftantius* in his Letter to the Citizens of *Alexan-* Apol. *dria* p. 695.

dria calls an Impoſtor, a Corrupter of Men's Souls, a Diſturber of the City, a perni-
cious Fellow, one convicted of the worſt Crimes, not to be expiated by his ſuffering
Death ten Times, George was put into the See of *Alexandria,* whom the Emperor, in the ſame Letter, ſtiles *a moſt venerable Perſon, and the moſt capable of all*

Cont. Ar. *Men to inſtruct them in heavenly Things* ; though *Athanaſius,* in his uſual Stile,
Orat. 1. calls him *an Idolater and Hangman, and one capable of all Violences, Rapines,*
p. 290. *and Murthers* ; and whom he actually charges with committing the moſt im-
l. 2, c. 25. pious Actions and outragious Cruelties. Thus, as *Socrates* obſerves, was the
Church torn in pieces by a Civil War for the ſake of *Athanaſius* and the Word
Conſubſtantial.

The Truth is, that the Chriſtian Clergy were now become the chief Incendiaries and Diſturbers of the Empire, and the Pride of the Biſhops, and the
Fury of the People on each ſide were grown to ſuch an Height; as that there
ſcarce ever was an Election or Reſtoration of a Biſhop in the larger Cities, but
it was attended with Slaughter and Blood. *Athanaſius* was ſeveral Times baniſhed and reſtored, at the Expence of Blood ; the Orthodox were depoſed,
and the Arians ſubſtituted in their room, with the Murther of Thouſands ; and
as the Controverſy was now no longer about the plain Doctrines of uncorrupted
Chriſtianity, but about Power and Dominion, high Preferments, large Reve-

Soc. l 2. nues, and ſecular Honours ; agreeably hereto, the Biſhops were introduced
c. 15, 16. into their Churches, and placed on their Thrones, by armed Soldiers, and
paid no Regard to the Eccleſiaſtical Rules, or the Lives of their Flocks, ſo
they could get Poſſeſſion, and keep out their Adverſaries: And when once
they were in, they treated thoſe who differ'd from them without Moderation
or Mercy, turning them out of their Churches, denying them the Liberty of
Worſhip, putting them under an Anathema, and perſecuting them with innumerable Methods of Cruelty ; as is evident from the Accounts given by the
Eccleſiaſtical Hiſtorians, of *Athanaſius, Macedonius, George,* and others, which
may be read at large in the forementioned Places. In a Word, they ſeemed
to treat one another with the ſame implacable Bitterneſs and Severity, as ever
their common Enemies, the Heathens, treated them, as though they thought
that Perſecution for Conſcience ſake had been the diſtinguiſhing Precept of the
Chriſtian Religion ; and that they could not more effectually recommend and
diſtinguiſh themſelves as the Diſciples of Chriſt, than by taring and devouring

Am. Mar. one another. This made *Julian,* the Emperor, ſay of them, *That he found by*
l. 22. c. 5. *Experience, that even Beaſts are not ſo cruel to Men, as the generality of Chriſtians*
were to one another.

This was the unhappy State of the Church in the Reign of *Conſtantius,* which
affords us little more than the Hiſtory of Councils and Creeds differing from,
and contrary to each other ; Biſhops depoſing, cenſuring, and anathematizing
their Adverſaries, and the Chriſtian People divided into Factions under their
reſpective Leaders, for the ſake of Words they underſtood nothing of the Senſe
of, and ſtriving for Victory even to Bloodſhed and Death. Upon the Succeſſion of *Julian* to the Empire, though the contending Parties could not unite
againſt the common Enemy, yet they were by the Emperor's Clemency and

Wiſdom

Wiſdom kept in tolerable Peace and Order. The Biſhops which had been ^{Soc. l. 3.} baniſhed by *Conſtantius* his Predeceſſor, he immediately recalled, ordered their ^{c. 1.} Effeɛts, which had been confiſcated, to be reſtored to them, and commanded that no one ſhould injure or hurt any Chriſtian whatſoever. And as *Ammianus Marcellinus*, an heathen Writer of thoſe Times, tells us, he cauſed the Chriſtian ^{l. 22. c. 5.} Biſhops and People, who were at variance with each other, to come into his Palace, and there admoniſhed them, that they ſhould every one profeſs their own Religion, without Hindrance or Fear, provided they did not diſturb the publick Peace by their Diviſions. This was an Inſtance of great Moderation and Generoſity, and a Pattern worthy the Imitation of all his Succeſſors.

In the beginning of *Julian*'s Reign ſome of the Inhabitants of *Alexandria*, ^{Soc. l. 3.} and, as was reported, the Friends of *Athanaſius*, by his Advice, raiſed a great ^{c. 2, 3, 4.} Tumult in the City, and murthered *George*, the Biſhop of the Place, by taring him ^{Philoſt.l.7.} ^{c. 2.} in pieces, and burning his Body ; upon which *Athanaſius* returned immediately from his Baniſhment, and took Poſſeſſion of his See, turning out the Arians from their Churches, and forcing them to hold their Aſſemblies in private and mean Places. *Julian*, with great Equity, ſeverely reproved the *Alexandrians* for this their Violence and Cruelty, telling them, that though *George* might have greatly injured them, yet they ought not to have revenged themſelves on him, but to have left him to the Juſtice of the Laws. *Athanaſius*, upon his Reſtoration, immediately convened a Synod at *Alexandria*, in which was firſt aſſerted the Divinity of the Holy Spirit, and his Conſubſtantiality with the Father and the Son. But his Power there was but ſhort ; for being accuſed to *Julian* ^{c. 13.} as the Deſtroyer of that City, and all *Egypt*, he ſaved himſelf by flight, but ſoon after ſecretly returned to *Alexandria*, where he lived in great privacy till ^{Theod.} the Storm was blown over by *Julian*'s Death, and the Succeſſion of *Jovian* to ^{l. 4. c. 2.} the Empire, who reſtored him to his See, in which he continued undiſturbed to his Death.

Although *Julian* behaved himſelf with great Moderation, upon his firſt Acceſſion to the imperial Dignity, towards the Chriſtians, as well as others, yet his Hatred to Chriſtianity ſoon appeared in many Inſtances. For though he did not, like the reſt of the Heathen Emperors, proceed to ſanguinary Laws, ^{Soc. l. 3.} yet he commanded, that the Children of Chriſtians ſhould not be inſtruɛted in ^{c. 14, &c.} the *Grecian* Language and Learning. By another Ediɛt he ordained, That no Chriſtian ſhould bear any Office in the Army, nor have any Concern in the Diſtribution and Management of the publick Revenues. He taxed very heavily, ^{Theod.} and demanded Contributions from all who would not ſacrifice, to ſupport the ^{l. 3. c. 6,} ^{&c.} vaſt Expences he was at in his Eaſtern Expeditions. And when the Governors of the Provinces took Occaſion from hence to oppreſs and plunder them, he diſmiſſed thoſe who complained with this ſcornful Anſwer, *Your God hath commanded you to ſuffer Perſecution* ! He alſo deprived the Clergy of all their Immunities, Honours, and Revenues, granted them by *Conſtantine*, abrogated the Laws made in their Favour, and ordered they ſhould be liſted amongſt the Number of Soldiers. He deſtroyed ſeveral of their Churches, and ſtripped them of their Treaſure and ſacred Veſſels. Some he puniſhed with Baniſhment,

ment, and others with Death, under pretence of their having pulled down fome of the Pagan Temples, and infulted himfelf.

The Truth is, that the Chriftian Bifhops and People fhewed fuch a turbulent and feditious Spirit, that 'twas no wonder that *Julian* fhould keep a jealous Eye over them, and though otherwife a Man of great Moderation, connive at the Severities his Officers fometimes practifed on them. Whether he would have proceeded to any farther Extremities againft them, had he returned Victorious from his *Perfian* Expedition, as *Theodorit* affirms he would, cannot, I l. 3. c. 21. think, be determined. He was certainly a Perfon of great Humanity in his natural Temper ; but how far his own Superftition, and the Imprudencies of the Chriftians, might have altered this Difpofition, 'tis impoffible to fay. Thus much is certain, that the Behaviour of the Chriftians towards him, was, in many Inftances, very blameable, and fuch as tended to irritate his Spirit, and awaken his Refentment. But whatever his Intentions were, he did not live to execute them, being flain in his *Perfian* Expedition.

Soc l. 3. He was fucceeded by *Jovian*, who was a Chriftian by Principle and Profef-
c 24, 25. fion. Upon his return from *Perfia* the Troubles of the Church immediately revived, the Bifhops and Heads of Parties crouding about him, each hoping that he would lift on their fide, and grant them Authority to opprefs their Ad-
Theod. verfaries. *Athanafius*, amongft others, writes to him in favour of the *Nicene*
l. 4. c. 4 Creed, and warns him againft the Blafphemies of the Arians ; and though he doth not directly urge him to perfecute them, yet he tells him, that 'tis neceffary to adhere to the Decifions of that Council concerning the Faith, and that their Creed was Divine and Apoftolical ; and that no Man ought to reafon or difpute againft it, as the Arians did. A Synod alfo of certain Bifhops met at *Antioch* in *Syria* ; and though feveral of them had been Oppofers of the *Nicene* Doctrine before, yet finding that this was the Faith efpoufed by *Jovian*, they with great Obfequioufnefs readily confirm'd it, and fubfcribed it, and in a flattering Letter fent it to him, reprefenting that this true and orthodox Faith was the great Center of Unity. The Followers alfo of *Macedonius*, who rejected the Word *Confubftantial*, and held the Son to be only *like to the Father*, moft humbly befought him, that fuch who afferted the Son to be unlike the Father might be driven from their Churches, and that they themfelves might be put into them in their room ; with the Bifhops Names fubfcribed to the Petition. But *Jovian*, though himfelf in the orthodox Doctrine, did not fuffer himfelf to be drawn into Meafures of Perfecution by the Arts of thefe temporizing Prelates, but difmiffed them civilly with this Anfwer : *I hate Contention, and love thofe only that ftudy Peace* ; declaring, that *he would trouble none upon account of their Faith, whatever it was ; and that he would favour and efteem fuch only who fhould fhew themfelves Leaders in reftoring the Peace of the Church.* *Themiftius* the Philofopher, in his Oration upon *Jovian*'s Confulate, commends him very juftly on this account, that he gave free Liberty to every one to worfhip God as he would, and defpifed the flattering Infinuations of thofe who would have perfuaded him to the Ufe of violent Methods, concerning whom he pleafantly, but with too much Truth, faid, *That he found by Experience, that they worfhip not God, but the Purple.* The

The two Emperors, *Valentinianus* and *Valens*, who succeeded *Jovian*, were of very different Tempers, and embraced different Parties in Religion. The former was of the Orthodox fide; and though he favoured those most who were of his own Sentiments, yet he gave no Difturbance to the Arians. On the contrary, *Valens*, his Brother, was of a rigid and fanguinary Difpofition, and feverely perfecuted all who differed from him. In the beginning of their Reign a Synod met in *Illyricum*, who again decreed the Confubftantiality of Father, Son, and Holy Ghoft. This the two Emperors declared in a Letter their Affent to, and ordered that this Doctrine fhould be preached. However, they both publifhed Laws for the Toleration of all Religions, even the Heathen and Arian. But *Valens* was foon prevailed on by the Arts of *Eudoxius*, Bifhop of *Conftantinople*, to forfake both his Principles of Religion and Moderation, and embracing the Arian Party, he cruelly perfecuted all thofe who were of the orthodox Party. The Conduct of the orthodox Synod met at *Lampfacus* was the firft Thing that enraged him; for having obtained of him leave to meet, for the Amendment and Settlement of the Faith, after two Months Confulta-tion they decreed the Doctrine of the Son's being like the Father as to his Ef-fence, to be Orthodox, and depofed all the Bifhops of the Arian Party. This highly exafperated *Valens*, who thereupon called a Council of Arian Bifhops, and commanded the Bifhops that compofed the Council at *Lampfacus* to em-brace the Opinions of *Eudoxius* the Arian, and upon their refufal immediately fent them into Banifhment, and gave their Churches to their Enemies, fparing only *Paulinus*, for the remarkable Sanctity of his Life. After this he enter'd into more violent Meafures, and caufed the Orthodox, fome of them to be whipped, others to be difgraced, others to be imprifoned, and others to be fined. He alfo put great Numbers to death, and particularly caufed eighty of them at once to be put on Board a Ship, and the Ship to be fired when it was failed out of the Harbour, where they miferably perifhed by the Water and the Flames. Thefe Perfecutions he continued to the End of his Reign, and was greatly affifted in them by the Bifhops of the Arian Party.

In the mean Time great Difturbances happened at *Rome*. *Liberius*, Bifhop of that City being dead, *Urfinus*, a Deacon of that Church, and *Damafus*, were both nominated to fucceed him. The Party of *Damafus* prevailed, and got him chofen and ordained. *Urfinus* being enraged that *Damafus* was prefer-red before him, fet up feparate Meetings, and at laft procured himfelf to be privately ordained by certain obfcure Bifhops. This occafioned great Difputes amongft the Citizens, which fhould obtain the Epifcopal Dignity, and the Matter was carried to fuch an Height, that great Numbers were murthered in the Quar-rel on both fides, no lefs than one Hundred thirty feven Perfons being deftroy'd in the Church it felf, according to *Ammianus*, who adds, ° *That 'twas no wonder to fee thofe who were ambitious of human Greatnefs, contending with fo much Heat*

Soc. l. 4.

c. 1.

Theod.
l. 4. c. 8.
Cod.
Theod.
tit. 16. l. 9.

Soc. l. 4.
c. 6.
Soz. l. 6.
c. 7.

Soc. Ibid.
c. 15, 16.
Theod.
l. 4. c. 22.

Soc. l. 4.
c. 29.

l. 27. c. 3.

° Cum id adepti, futuri fint ita fecuri, ut ditentur oblationibus Matronarum, procedantq, vehicu-lis infidentes, circumfpecte veftiti, epulas curantes profufas, adeo ut eorum convivia regales fupe-rent menfas.

and *Animofity for that Dignity, becaufe when they had obtained it, they were fure to be enriched by the Offerings of the Matrons, of appearing Abroad in great Splendor, of being admired for their coftly Coaches, fumptuous in their Feafts, out-doing Sovereign Princes in the Expences of their Tables.* For which Reafon *Prætextatus*, an Heathen, who was Prefect of the City the following Year, faid, *Make me Bifhop of* Rome *and I'll be a Chriftian too.*

Gratian, the Son of *Valentinian*, his Partner and Succeffor in the Empire, was of the orthodox Party, and after the Death of his Uncle *Valens* recalled thofe whom he had banifhed, and reftored them to their Sees. But as to the Arians, he fent *Sapores*, one of his Captains, to drive them, as wild Beafts, out of all their Churches. *Socrates* and *Sozomen* tell us, however, that by a Law he ordained, that Perfons of all Religions fhould meet, without fear, in their feveral Churches, and worfhip according to their own Way, the *Eunomians, Photinians* and *Manichees* excepted.

Theodofius, foon after his Advancement by *Gratian* to the Empire, difcovered a very warm Zeal for the orthodox Opinions ; for obferving that the City of *Conftantinople* was divided into different Sects, he wrote a Letter to them from *Theffalonica*, wherein he tells them, *That 'twas his Pleafure, that all his Subjects fhould be of the fame Religion with* Damafus *Bifhop of* Rome, *and* Peter *Bifhop of* Alexandria ; and that their Church only fhould be called Catholick, who worfhipped the Divine Trinity as equal in Honour ; and that thofe who were of another Opinion fhould be called Hereticks, become infamous, and be fubject to other Punifhments, He alfo forbid Affemblies and Difputations in the *Forum*, and made a Law for the Punifhment of thofe that fhould prefume to argue about the Effence and Nature of God. Upon his firft coming to *Conftantinople*, being very folicitous for the Peace and Increafe of the Church, he fent for *Demophilus* the Arian Bifhop, and afked him whether he would confent to the *Nicene* Faith, and thus accept the Peace he offered him ; adding, *If you refufe to do it I will drive you from your Churches.* And upon *Demophilus's* Refufal, the Emperor was as good as his Word, and turned him and all the Arians out of the City, after they had been in poffeffion of the Churches there for Forty Years. But being willing more effectually to extinguifh Herefy, he fummoned a Council of Bifhops of his own Perfuafion, *A. C.* 383. to meet together at *Conftantinople*, in order to confirm the *Nicene* Faith : The Number of them were one Hundred and fifty ; to thefe were added thirty fix of the *Macedonian* Party. And accordingly this Council, which is reckoned the fecond Oecumenical or general one, all of them, except the *Macedonians*, did decree that the *Nicene* Faith fhould be the Standard of Orthodoxy ; and that all Herefies fhould be condemned. They alfo made an Addition to that Creed, explaining the orthodox Doctrine of the Spirit againft *Macedonius*, viz. after the Words Holy Ghoft, they inferted, *The Lord, the Quickner, proceeding from the Father, whom with the Father and the Son we worfhip and glorify, and who fpake by the Prophets.* When the Council was ended the Emperor put forth two Edicts againft Hereticks ; by the firft prohibiting them from holding any Affemblies ; and by the fecond, forbidding them to meet in Fields or Villages, order-

Side notes:
Theod. l 5. c. 2.

Soz l. 7. c. 4 6.

Soc. l. 5. c. 7.

c. 8.

The fecond general Council, A. C. 383.

Cod. Theod. l. 11, 12.

ordering the Houfes where they met to be confifcated, and commanding that fuch who went to other Places to teach their Opinions, or perform their religious worfhip, fhould be forced to return to the Places where they dwelt, condemning all thofe Officers and Magiftrates of Cities who fhould not prevent fuch Affemblies. A little while after the Conclufion of this Council, finding that many Diforders were ftill occafioned through the Oppofition of the feveral Parties to one another, he convened the principal Perfons of each, and ordered them to deliver into his Hand a written Form of their Belief, which after he had received, he retired by himfelf, and earneftly prayed to God, that he would enable him to make Choice of the Truth. And when after this he had perufed the feveral Papers delivered to him, he tore them all in pieces, except that which contained the Doctrine of the indivifible Trinity, to which he intirely adhered. After this he publifhed a Law, by which he forbid Hereticks to worfhip or preach, or to ordain Bifhops or others, commanding fome to be banifhed, others to be rendered infamous, and to be deprived of the common Privileges of Citizens, with other grievous Penalties of the like nature. *Sozomen*, however, tells-us, that he did not put thefe Laws in execution, becaufe his Intention was not to punifh his Subjects, but to terrify them into the fame Opinions of God with himfelf, praifing at the fame time thofe who voluntarily embraced them. *Socrates* alfo confirms the fame, telling us, that he only banifhed *Eunomius* from *Conftantinople* for holding private Affemblies, and reading his Books to them, and thereby corrupting many with his Doctrine. But that as to others he gave them no Difturbance, nor forced them to communicate with him, but allowed them all their feveral Meetings, and to enjoy their own Opinions as to the Chriftian Faith. Some he permitted to build Churches without the Cities, and the *Novatians* to retain their Churches within, becaufe they held the fame Doctrines with himfelf.

Soz. l. 7.
c. 12.

Socrates l. 5. c. 20.

Arcadius and *Honorius*, the Sons and Succeffors of *Theodofius*, embraced the orthodox Religion and Party, and confirmed all the Decrees of the foregoing Emperors in their Favour. Soon after their Acceffion to the imperial Dignity, *Nectarius* Bifhop of *Conftantinople* died, and *John*, called for his Eloquence *Chryfoftom*, was ordained in his room : He was a Perfon of a very rigid and fevere Temper, an Enemy to Hereticks, and againft allowing them any Toleration. *Gaina*, one of the principal Officers of *Arcadius*, and who was a Chriftian of the Arian Perfwafion, defired of the Emperor one Church for himfelf and thofe of his Opinion, within the City. *Chryfoftom* being informed of it, immediately went to the Palace, taking with him all the Bifhops he could find at *Conftantinople*, and in the Prefence of the Emperor bitterly inveigh'd againft *Gaina*, who was himfelf at the Audience, and reproached him for his former Poverty, as alfo with Infolence and Ingratitude. Then he produced the Law that was made by *Theodofius*, by which Hereticks were forbidden to hold Affemblies within the Walls of the City ; and turning to the Emperor, perfwaded him to keep in force all the Laws againft Hereticks ; adding, that 'twas better voluntarily to quit the Empire, than to be guilty of the Impiety of betraying the Houfe of God. *Chryfoftom* carried his Point, and the Confequence of it was

Soz. l. 8.
c. 1, 2, 4.

an

an Infurrection of the *Goths* in the City of *Conftantinople*, which had like to have
ended in the Burning the imperial Palace, and the Murther of the Emperor,
and did actually end in the cutting off all the *Gothick* Soldiers, and the Burning
of their Church, with great Numbers of Perfons in it, who fled thither for

Soz. l. 8.
c. 6. Safety, and were locked in to prevent their efcape.   His violent Treatment of
feveral Bifhops, and the arbitrary Manner of his depofing them, and fubftituting others in their room, contrary to the Defires and Prayers of the People, is
but too full a Proof of his imperious Temper, and love of Power.   Not content with this, he turned his Eloquence againft the Emprefs *Eudoxia*, and in a
fet Oration inveighing againft bad Women, he expreffed himfelf in fuch a
Manner, as that both his Friends and Enemies believed that the Invective was
chiefly levelled againft her.   This fo enraged her, that fhe foon procured his
Depofition and Banifhment.   Being foon after reftored, he added new Provoca-
tions to the former, by rebuking the People for certain Diverfions they took
at a Place where the Statue of the Emprefs was erected.   This fhe took for an
Infult on her Perfon, and when *Chryfoftom* knew her Difpleafure on this Account, he ufed more fevere Expreffions againft her than before, faying, *Hero-
dias is enraged again ; fhe raifes frefh Difturbances ; and again defires the Head of*
John *in a Charger*.   On this and other Accounts he was depofed and banifhed
by a Synod convened for that purpofe, Bifhops being always to be had in
thofe Days eafily, to do what was defired or demanded of them by the Emperors.

Soz. l. 8.
c. 16. *Chryfoftom* died in his Banifhment, according to the Chriftian Wifh of *Epipha-
nius*, *I hope you'll not die Bifhop of* Conftantinople ; which *Chryfoftom* returned
with a Wifh of the fame good Temper, *I hope you'll not live to return to your
own City* ; fo deadly was the Hatred of thefe Saints and Fathers againft each
other.   After *Chryfoftom*'s Death his Favourers and Friends were treated with
great Severity, not indeed on the Account of Religion, but for other Crimes

Soc. l. 6.
c. 18. of Sedition they were charged with, and particularly, for burning down one of
the Churches in the City, the Flames of which fpread themfelves to the Senate
Houfe and entirely confumed it.

Under the fame Emperors the Donatifts gave fad Specimens of their Cruelty

Epift. 50.
ad Bon. & in *Africa* towards the Orthodox, as St. *Auftin* informs us.   They feized on *Maximianus*, one of the *African* Bifhops, as he was ftanding at the Altar, beat him

Fpift. 68.
ad Januar. unmercifully, and ran a Sword into his Body, leaving him for dead.   And a
little after he adds, That it would be tedious to recount the many horrible
Things they made the Bifhops and Clergy fuffer ; fome had their Eyes put
out ; one Bifhop had his Hands and Tongue cut off, and others were cruelly
deftroyed.   I forbear, fays *Auftin*, to mention their barbarous Murthers, and
demolifhing of Houfes, not private ones only, but the very Churches them-

Cod.
Theod.
l. 52. felves.   *Honorius* publifhed very fevere Edicts againft them, ordaining, That if
they did not, both Clergy and Laity, return to the Catholicks by fuch a Day,
they fhould be heavily fined, their Eftates fhould be confifcated, the Clergy
banifhed, and their Churches all given to the Catholicks.   Thefe Laws *Auftin*
commends as rightly and pioufly ordained, maintaining the Lawfulnefs of perfecuting Hereticks by all manner of Ways, Death only excepted.

Under

The INTRODUCTION.

Under the Reign of *Theodosius*, *Arcadius* his Son, those who were called Hereticks were grievously persecuted by the Orthodox. *Theodosius*, Bishop of Soc. l. 7. *Synnada* in *Phrygia*, expelled great Numbers of the Followers of *Macedonius* c. 3. from the City and Country round about, *Not from any Zeal for the true Faith*, as *Socrates* says, *but through Covetousness, and a Design to extort Money from them*. On this Account he used all his Endeavours to oppress them, and particularly *Agapetus* their Bishop, armed his Clergy against them, and accused them before the Tribunal of the Judges. And because he did not think the Governors of the Provinces sufficient to carry on this good Work of Persecution, he went to *Constantinople* to procure fresh Edicts against them; but by this means he lost his Bishoprick, the People refusing him Admission into the Church upon his return, and chusing *Agapetus*, whom he had persecuted, in his room.

Theophilus, Bishop of *Alexandria*, the great Enemy of *Chrysostom*, being l. 7. c. 7. dead, *Cyrill* was enthroned in his room, not without great Disturbance and Opposition from the People, and used his Power for the Oppression of Hereticks; for immediately upon his Advancement, he shut up all the Churches of the *Novatians* in that City, took away all their sacred Treasures, and stripped *Theopemptus* their Bishop, of every Thing that he had. Nor was this much to be l. 7. c. 13, wonder'd at, since, as *Socrates* observes, that from the Time of *Theophilus*, 14. *Cyrill*'s Predecessor, *The Bishop of* Alexandria *began to assume an Authority and Power above what belonged to the sacerdotal Order*. On this Account the great Men hated the Bishops, because they usurped to themselves a good part of that Power which belonged to the imperial Governors of Provinces; and particularly, *Cyrill* was hated by *Orestes*, Prefect of *Alexandria*, not only for this Reason, but because he was a continual Spy upon his Actions. At length their Hatred to each other publickly appeared. *Cyrill* took on him, without acquainting the Governor, or contrary to his leave, to deprive the *Jews* of all their Synagogues, and banished them from the City, and encouraged the Mob to plunder them of their Effects. This the Prefect highly resented, and refused the Bishop's Offers of Peace and Friendship. Upon this about fifty Monks came into the City for *Cyrill*'s Defence, and meeting the Prefect in his Chariot publickly insulted him, calling him Sacrificer and Pagan; adding many other injurious Reproaches. One of them, called *Ammonius*, wounded him in the Head with a Stone, which he flung at him with great Violence, and covered him all over with Blood; and being, according to the Laws, put by *Orestes* publickly to the Torture, he died through the Severity of it. St. *Cyrill* honourably received the Body into the Church, gave him the new Name of *Thaumasius*, or, *The Wonderful*, ordered him to be looked on as a Martyr, and lavishly extolled him in the Church, as a Person murthered for his Religion. This scandalous Procedure of *Cyrill*'s the Christians themselves were ashamed of, because 'twas publickly known, that the Monk was punished for his Insolence; and even St. *Cyrill* himself had the Modesty at last to use his Endeavours that the whole Affair might be entirely forgotten. The Murther also of *Hypatia* Id. Ibid. by *Cyrill*'s Friends and Clergy, merely out of Envy to her superior Skill in Phi- c. 15. losophy, brought him and his Church of *Alexandria* under great Infamy; for

as

as fhe was returning home from a Vifit, one *Peter* a Clergyman, with fome other Murtherers, feized on her, dragged her out of her Chariot, carried her to one of the Churches, ftripped her naked, fcraped her to Death with Shells, then tore her in pieces, and burnt her Body to Afhes.

Innocent alfo, Bifhop of *Rome*, grievoufly perfecuted the *Novatians*, and took from them many Churches ; and, as *Socrates* obferves, was the firft Bifhop of that See who difturbed them. *Celeftine* alfo, one of his Succeffors, imitated this Injuftice, and took from the *Novatians* the Remainder of their Churches, and forced them to hold their Affemblies in private ; *For the Bifhops of* Rome, *as well as thofe of* Alexandria, *had ufurped a tyrannical Power, which, as Priefts, they had no right to* ; and would not fuffer thofe who agreed with them in the Faith, as the *Novatians* did, to hold publick Affemblies, but drove them out of their Oratories, and plundered them of all their Subftance.

Neftorius, Bifhop of *Conftantinople*, immediately upon his Advancement, fhewed himfelf a violent Perfecutor ; for as foon as ever he was ordained, he addreffed himfelf to the Emperor before the whole Congregation, and faid, *Purge me, O Emperor, the Earth from Hereticks, and I will give thee in recompence the Kingdom of Heaven. Conquer with me the Hereticks, and I with thee will fubdue the* Perfians. And agreeable to his bloody Wifhes, the fifth Day after his Confecration, he endeavoured to demolifh the Church of the Arians, in which they were privately affembled for Prayer. The Arians in their Rage, feeing the Deftruction of it determined, fet Fire to it themfelves, and occafioned the Burning down the neighbouring Houfes ; and for this Reafon not only the Hereticks, but thofe of his own Perfuafion, diftinguifhed him by the Name of *Incendiary*. But he did not reft here, but tried all Tricks and Methods to deftroy Hereticks ; and by thefe Means endangered the Subverfion of *Conftantinople* it felf. He perfecuted the *Novatians*, through hatred of *Paul* their Bifhop for his eminent Piety. He grievoufly oppreffed thofe who were not Orthodox as to the Day of keeping *Eafter*, in *Afia*, *Lydia*, and *Caria*, and occafioned the Murthers of great Numbers on this Account, at *Miletus* and *Sardis*.

Few indeed of the Bifhops were free from this wicked Spirit. *Socrates*, however, tells us, that *Atticus* Bifhop of *Conftantinople* was a Perfon of great Piety and Prudence, and that he did not offer Violence to any of the Hereticks, but that after he had once attempted to terrify them, he behaved more mildly and gently to them afterwards. *Proclus* alfo, Bifhop of the fame City, who had been brought up under *Atticus*, was a careful Imitator of his Piety and Virtue, and exercifed rather greater Moderation than his Mafter, being gentle towards all Men, from a Perfwafion, that this was a much more proper Method than Violence to reduce Hereticks to the true Faith, and therefore he never made ufe of the imperial Power for this purpofe. And in this he imitated *Theodofius* the Emperor, who was not at all concerned or difpleafed that any fhould think differently of God from himfelf. However, the Number of Bifhops of this Temper was but fmall. Nothing pleafed the generality of them but Methods of Severity, and the utter Ruin and Extirpation of their Adverfaries.

Under

Under the Reign of this Emperor, the Arians also, in their Turn, used the Orthodox with no greater Moderation, than the Orthodox had used them. The *Vandals*, who were partly Pagans, and partly Arians, had seized on *Spain* and *Africa*, and exercised innumerable Cruelties on those who were not of the same Religion with themselves. *Trafimond* their General in *Spain*, and *Genferick* in *Africa*, used all possible Endeavours to propagate Arianism throughout all their Provinces. And the more effectually to accomplish this Design, they filled all Places with Slaughter and Blood, by the Advice of the Bishops of their Party, burning down Churches, and putting the orthodox Clergy to the most grievous and unheard of Tortures, to make them discover the Gold and Silver of their Churches, repeating these kind of Tortures several times, so that many actually died under them. *Genferick* seized on all the sacred Books he could find, that they might be deprived of the Means of defending their Opinions. By the Counsel of his Bishops, he ordered that none but Arians should be admitted to Court, or employ'd in any Offices about his Children, or so much as enjoy the Benefit of a Toleration. *Armogeftes*, *Mafculon*, and *Saturus*, three Officers of his Court, were inhumanly tortured to make them embrace Arianism ; and, upon their refusal, they were stripped of their Honours and Estates, and forced to protract a miserable Life in the utmost Poverty and Want. These and many more Instances of *Genferick's* Cruelty towards the Orthodox, during a long Reign of thirty eight Years, are related by *Victor*, *l. 1. in fine.*

During these Transactions, a new Controversy, of a very extraordinary and important Nature, arose in the Church, which, as the other had done before, occasioned many Disorders and Murthers, and gave Birth to the third general Council. *Nestorius*, the persecuting Bishop of *Constantinople*, altho' tolerably found in the Doctrine of the real Deity of the *Logos*, yet excepted against the Virgin *Mary's* being called Θεοτοκ©-, i. e. *Mother of God*, because, as he argued, *Mary was a Woman, and that therefore God could not be born of her* ; adding, *I cannot call him God, who once was not above two or three Months old* ; and therefore he substituted another Word in the room of it, calling her Χειστοτοκ©-, or *Mother of Christ*. By this Means, he seemed to maintain, not only the Distinction of the two Natures in Christ, for he allowed the proper Personality and Subsistence of the *Logos*, but that there were also two distinct Persons in Christ ; the one a mere Man, absolutely distinct from the Word, and the other God, as absolutely distinct from the human Nature. This caused great Disturbances in the City of *Constantinople*, and the Dispute was thought of such Consequence, as to need a Council to settle it. Accordingly *Theodosius* convened one at *Ephesus*, *A. C.* 434. of which *Cyrill* was President ; and as he hated *Nestorius*, he persuaded the Bishops of his own Party to decree, that the Virgin was, and should be, the Mother of God, and to anathematise all who should not confess her in this Character, nor own that the Word of God the Father was united substantially to the Flesh, making one Christ of two Natures, both God and Man together ; or who should ascribe what the Scriptures say of Christ, to two Persons or Subsistences, interpreting some of the Man,
exclusive

Evag. E. H. l. 1. c. 2. Soc. l. 7. c. 32, 34.

Third general Council, A. C. 434. Soc. Ibid. Evag. l. 1. c. 5.

exclufive of the Word; and others of the Word, exclufive of the human Nature; or who fhould prefume to call the Man Chrift Θεoφoϛ, *the Bearer, or the Receptable of God,* inftead of God; and haftily to depofe *Neftorius* five Days before the coming of *John* Bifhop of *Antioch,* with his fuffragran Bifhops. *John,* upon his Arrival at *Ephefus,* depofed *Cyrill,* in a Council of Bifhops held for that Purpofe, and accufed him of being the Author of all the Diforders occafioned by this Affair, and of having rafhly proceeded to the Depofition of *Neftorius. Cyrill* was foon abfolved by his own Council, and, in Revenge, depofed *John* of *Antioch,* and all the Bifhops of his Party. But they were both reconciled by the Emperor, and reftored each other to their refpective Sees, and, as the Effect of their Reconciliation, both fubfcribed to the Condemnation of *Neftorius,* who was fent into Banifhment, where, after fuffering great Hardfhips, he died miferably; being thus made to tafte thofe Sweets of Perfecution, he had fo liberally given to others, in the Time of his Power and

Evag. l. 1. c. 12. Profperity. The Emperor himfelf, though at firft he difapproved of this Council's Conduct, yet afterwards was perfuaded to ratify their Decrees, and publifhed a Law, by which all who embraced the Opinions of *Neftorius,* were, if Bifhops or Clergymen, ordered to be expelled the Churches; or if

Chal.Concil.Act.10. Frag. Epift. Edef. Epic. Laymen, to be anathematifed. This occafioned irreconcileable Hatreds amongft the Bifhops and People, who were fo enraged againft each other; that there was no paffing with any Safety from one Province or City to another, becaufe every one purfued his Neighbour as his Enemy, and, without any Fear of God, revenged themfelves on one another, under a Pretence of Ecclefiaftical Zeal.

Evag. l. 2. c. 1. *Marcian,* the Succeffor of *Theodofius* in the Empire, embraced the Orthodox Party and Opinions, and was very defirous to bring about an entire Uniformity in the Worfhip of God, and to eftablifh the fame Form of Doxologies amongft

Concil. Chalced. Act. 13. all Chriftians whatfoever. Agreeably to this his Temper, *Eufebius,* Bifhop of *Nicomedia,* addrefs'd him foon after his Promotion in thefe Words : *God hath juftly given you the Empire, that you fhould govern all for the univerfal Welfare, and for the Peace of his holy Church : And therefore, before and in all Things, take Care of the Principles of the orthodox and moft holy Faith, and extinguifh the Roarings of*

Evag. l. 2. c. 2. *the Hereticks, and bring to Light the Doctrines of Piety.* The Legates alfo of *Leo,* Bifhop of *Rome,* prefented him their Accufations againft *Diofcorus,* Bifhop of *Alexandria* ; as did alfo *Eufebius,* Bifhop of *Dorylæum,* befeeching the Emperor that thefe Things might be judged and determined by a Synod. *Marcian* confented, and ordered the Bifhops to meet firft at *Nice,* and afterwards

The fourth general Council, A.C. 454. l. 1. c. 9, 10. at *Chalcedon.* This was the fourth oecumenical or general Council, confifting of near fix hundred Prelates. The principal Caufe of their affembling was the Eutychian Herefy. *Eutyches,* a Prefbyter of *Conftantinople,* had afferted, in the Reign of *Theodofius, jun.* that *Jefus Chrift confifted of two Natures before his Union or Incarnation, but that after this he had one Nature only.* He alfo denied that *the Body of Chrift was of the fame Subftance with ours.* On this Account, he was depofed by a particular Council at *Conftantinople* by *Flavian,* Bifhop of that Place: But, upon his complaining to the Emperor that the

Acts

Acts of that Council were falsified by his Enemies, a second Synod of the neighbouring Bishops met in the same City, who, after examining those Acts, found them to be genuine, and confirmed the Sentence against *Eutyches*. But *Dioscorus*, Bishop of *Alexandria*, who was at Enmity with *Flavian* of *Constantinople*, obtained, from *Theodosius*, that a third Council should be held on this Affair, which accordingly met at *Ephesus*, which the Orthodox stigmatised by the Name of Ληϲεικη, the thieving Council, or Council of Thieves. *Dioscorus* was President of it, and, after an Examination of the Affair of *Eutyches*, his Sentence of Excommunication and Deposition was taken off, and himself restored to his Office and Dignity, the Bishops of *Constantinople*, *Antioch*, and others, being deposed in his stead. But the condemned Bishops, and the Legates from *Rome*, appealed from this Sentence to another Council, and prevailed with *Theodosius* to issue his Letters for the assembling one : But as he died before they could meet, the Honour of determining this Affair was reserved for his Successor *Marcian* ; and when the Fathers, in Obedience to his Summons, were convened at *Chalcedon*, the Emperor favoured them with his Presence ; and, in a Speech to them, told them, *That he had nothing more at Heart than to preserve the true and orthodox Christian Faith, safe and uncorrupted, and that therefore he proposed to them a Law, that no one should dare to dispute of the Person of Christ, otherwise than as it had been determined by the Council of* Nice. After this Address of the Emperor, the Fathers proceeded to their synodical Business, and, notwithstanding the Synod was divided, some of the Fathers piously crying out, *Damn* Dioscorus, *banish* Dioscorus, *banish the* Ægyptian, *banish the Heretick, Christ hath deposed* Dioscorus ; others, on the contrary, *Restore* Dioscorus *to the Council, restore* Dioscorus *to his Churches* ; yet, through the Authority of the Legates of *Rome*, Dioscorus was deposed for his Contempt of the sacred Canons, and for his Contumacy towards the holy universal Synod. After this, they proceeded to settle the Faith according to the *Nicene* Creed, the Opinions of the Fathers, and the Doctrine of *Athanasius*, *Cyrill*, *Cælestine*, *Hilarius*, *Basil*, *Gregory*, and *Leo* ; and decreed, that *Christ was truly God, and truly Man, consubstantial to the Father as to his Deity, and consubstantial to us as to his Humanity, and that he was to be confessed as consisting of two Natures without Mixture, Conversion of one into the other, and without Division or Separation ; and that it should not be lawful for any Persons to utter, or write, or compose, or think, or teach any other Faith whatsoever* ; and that if any should presume to do it, they should, if Bishops or Clergymen, be deposed ; and if Monks or Laicks, be anathematised. This procured a loud Acclamation : *God bless the Emperor, God bless the Empress. We believe as Pope* Leo *doth. Damn the Dividers and the Confounders. We believe as* Cyrill *did : Immortal be the Name of* Cyrill. *Thus the Orthodox believe* ; *and cursed be every one that doth not believe so too.* *Marcian* ratified their Decrees, and banished *Dioscorus*, and put forth an Edict, containing very severe Penalties against the *Eutychians* and *Apollinarists*, commanding that no one whatsoever, either of the Clergy or Laity, should publickly dispute about Religion, under Pain of Banishment, and Loss of all Honours, Dignities, Orders, &c. For this Reason, Pope *Leo*

Evag. l. 2. c. 4, 18.

Evag. l. 2. c. 5. *Hist. of the Inquisition*, l. 1. c. 3.

2   returns

Auguſt.
Epiſt. 75. returns him Thanks, that he had deſtroy'd theſe Hereſies, and exhorts him farther, that he would reform the See of *Alexandria*, and not only depoſe the heretical Clergy of *Conſtantinople* from their clerical Orders, but expel them from the City it ſelf.

Evag. l. 2.
c. 5. *Proterius* was ſubſtituted by this Council Biſhop of *Alexandria*, in the room of *Dioſcorus*; and, upon his taking Poſſeſſion of his Biſhoprick, the whole City was put into the utmoſt Confuſion, being divided, ſome for *Dioſcorus*, Niceph.
l. 15. c. 8 ſome for *Proterius*. The Mob aſſaulted with great Violence their Magiſtrates, and being oppoſed by the Soldiers, they put them to flight by a Shower of Stones; and as they betook themſelves to one of the Churches for Sanctuary, the Mob beſieged it, and burnt it to the Ground, with the Soldiers in it. The Emperor ſent two thouſand other Soldiers to quel this Diſturbance, who encreaſed the Miſeries of the poor Citizens, by offering the higheſt Indigni- Evag. l. 2.
c. 8. ties to their Wives and Daughters. And though they were for ſome Time kept in Awe, yet, upon *Marcian*'s Death, they broke out into greater Fury, ordained *Timotheus* Biſhop of the City, and murthered *Proterius*, by running him through with a Sword. After this, they hung him by a Rope, in a publick Place, by way of Deriſion, and then, after they had ignominiouſly drawn him round the whole City, they burnt him to Aſhes, and even fed on his very Bowels in the Fury of their Revenge. The Orthodox charged theſe Outrages upon the *Eutychians*; but *Zacharias*, the Hiſtorian, mentioned by *Evagrius*, ſays, *Proterius* himſelf was the Cauſe of them, and that he raiſed the greateſt Diſturbances in the City: And, indeed, the Clergy of *Alexandria*, in their Letter to *Leo*, the Emperor, concerning this Affair, acknowledge, that *Proterius* had depoſed *Timotheus*, with four or five Biſhops, and ſeveral Monks, for Hereſy, and obtained of the Emperor their actual Baniſhment. c. 5. Great Diſturbances happened alſo in *Paleſtine* on the ſame Account; the Monks who oppoſed the Council forcing *Juvenal*, Biſhop of *Jeruſalem*, to quit his See, and getting one *Theodoſius* ordained in his room. But the Emperor ſoon reſtored *Juvenal*, after whoſe Arrival the Tumults and Miſeries of the City greatly encreaſed, the different Parties acting by one another juſt as their Fury and Revenge inſpired them.

c. 9, 10. *Leo* ſucceeded *Marcian*, and ſent circular Letters to the ſeveral Biſhops, to make Enquiries concerning the Affairs of *Alexandria*, and the Council of *Chalcedon*. Moſt of the Biſhops adhered to the Decrees of thoſe Fathers, and agreed to depoſe *Timotheus*, who was ſent to bear *Dioſcorus* Company in Ba-niſhment.

Under *Zeno*, the Son-in-Law, and Succeſſor of *Leo*, *Hunnerick* the *Vandal* grievouſly perſecuted the Orthodox in *Africa*. In the Beginning of his Reign, he made a very equitable Propoſal, that he would allow them the Liberty of chooſing a Biſhop, and worſhipping according to their own Way, provided the Emperor would grant the Arians the ſame Liberty in *Conſtantinople*, and other Places. This the Orthodox would not agree to, chooſing rather to have their own Brethren perſecuted, than to allow Toleration to ſuch as differed from them. *Hunnerick* was greatly enraged by this Refuſal, and exer-ciſed

cifed great feverity towards all who would not profefs the Arian Faith, being
excited hereto by *Cyrill* one of his Bifhops, who was perpetually fuggefting to
him, that the Peace and Safety of his Kingdom could not be maintained, unlefs he extirpated all who differed from him as publick Nufances. This cruel
ecclefiaftical Advice was agreeable to the King's Temper, who immediately
put forth the moft fevere Edicts againft thofe who held the Doctrine of the
Confubftantiality, and turned all thofe Laws which had been made againft the
Arians, and other Hereticks, againft the Orthodox themfelves, it being, as
Hunnerick obferves in his Edict, *an Inftance of Virtue in a King, to turn evil
Counfels againft thofe who were the Authors of them.* But though the Perfecution
carried on by the Orthodox was no Vindication of *Hunnerick*'s Cruelty towards
them, yet I think they ought to have obferved the Juftice of divine Providence, in fuffering a wicked Prince to turn all thofe unrighteous Laws upon
themfelves, which, when they had Power on their fide, they had procured for
the Punifhment and Deftruction of others. A particular Account of the Cruelties exercifed by this Prince may be read at large in *Victor de Vandal Perfec.*
l. 3.

Zeno, though perfectly Orthodox in his Principles, yet was a very wicked
and profligate Prince, and rendered himfelf fo extremely hateful to his own
Family, by his Vices and Debaucheries, that *Bafilifcus*, Brother of *Verina*,
Mother of *Zeno*'s Emprefs, expelled him the Empire, and reigned in his ftead ;
and having found by Experience, that the Decrees of the Council of *Chalcedon* Evag. l. 3.
had occafioned many Difturbances, he by an Edict ordained, that the *Nicene* c. 4.
Creed alone fhould be ufed in all Churches, as being the only Rule of the pure
Faith, and fufficient to remove every Herefy, and perfectly to unite all the
Churches ; confirming at the fame Time the Decrees of the Councils of *Conftantinople* and *Ephefus*. But as to thofe of the Council of *Chalcedon* he ordered,
that as they had deftroyed the Unity and good Order of the Churches, and the
Peace of the whole World, they fhould be anathematized by all the Bifhops ;
and that where-ever any Copies of thofe Articles fhould be found they fhould
be immediately burnt. And that whofoever after this fhould attempt, either
by Difpute or Writing, or Teaching, at any Time, Manner or Place, to utter,
or fo much as name the Novelties that had been agreed on at *Chalcedon* contrary
to the Faith, fhould, as the Authors of Tumults and Seditions in the Churches
of God, and as Enemies to God and himfelf, be fubject to all the Penalties of
the Laws, and be depofed, if Bifhops or Clergymen ; and if Monks or
Laicks, be punifhed with Banifhment, and Confifcation of their Effects, and
even with Death it felf. Moft of the eaftern Bifhops fubfcribed thefe Letters l. 3. c. 5.
of *Bafilifcus* ; and being afterwards met in Council at *Ephefus*, they depofed
Acacius the orthodox Bifhop of *Conftantinople*, and many other Bifhops that
agreed with him. They alfo wrote to the Emperor to inform him, That *they
had voluntarily fubfcribed his Letters* ; and to perfuade him to adhere to them, or
that otherwife *the whole World would be fubverted, if the Decrees of the Synod of*
Chalcedon *fhould be re-eftablifhed, which had already produced innumerable Slaughters, and occafioned the fhedding of the Blood of the orthodox Chriftians.* But *Acacius*,

Biſhop of *Conſtantinople*, ſoon forced *Baſiliſcus* to alter his Meaſures, by raiſing up the Monks and Mob of the City againſt him; ſo that he recalled his former Letters, and ordered *Neſtorius* and *Eutyches*, with all their Followers, to be anathematized, and ſoon after he quitted the Empire to *Zeno*. Upon his

Evag. l. 3. ſ. 8, 9. Reſtoration he immediately reſcinded the Acts of *Baſiliſcus*, and expelled thoſe Biſhops from their Sees which had been ordained during his Abdication. In the mean Time the *Aſiatick* Biſhops, who in their Letter to *Baſiliſcus* had declared, that the Report of their *ſubſcribing involuntarily, and by force, was a Slander and a Lye*; yet upon this Turn of Affairs, in order to excuſe themſelves to *Acacius*, and to ingratiate themſelves with *Zeno*, affirm, *That they did it not voluntarily, but by force, ſwearing that they had always, and did now believe the Faith of the Synod of* Chalcedon. *Evagrius* leaves it in doubt, whether *Zacharias* defamed them, or whether the Biſhops lyed, when they affirmed that they ſubſcribed involuntarily, and againſt their Conſciences.

c. 13. ſ. 14. *Zeno* obſerving the Diſputes that had ariſen through the Decrees of the laſt Council, publiſhed his *Henoticon*, or his *uniting and pacifick Edict*, in which he confirmed the *Nicene, Conſtantinopolitan*, and *Epheſine* Councils, ordained that the *Nicene* Creed ſhould be the Standard of Orthodoxy, declared that neither himſelf nor the Churches have, or had, or would have any other Symbol or Doctrine but that, condemned *Neſtorius* and *Eutyches*, and their Followers; and ordered, that whoſoever had, or did think otherwiſe, either now or formerly, whether at *Chalcedon* or any other Synod, ſhould be anathematized. The Intention of the Emperor by this Edict, was plainly to reconcile the Friends and Oppoſers of the Synod of *Chalcedon*; for he condemned *Neſtorius* and *Eutyches*, as that Council had done, but did not anathematize thoſe who would not receive their Decrees, nor ſubmit to them as of equal Authority with thoſe of the three former Councils: But this Compromiſe was far from having the deſired effect.

c. 11, 12. During theſe Things ſeveral Changes happen'd in the Biſhoprick of *Alexandria*. *Timothy*, Biſhop of that Place being dead, one *Peter Mongus* was elected by the Biſhops Suffragans of that See, which ſo enraged *Zeno*, that he intended to have put him to Death, but changed it for Baniſhment, and *Timothy*, Succeſſor of *Proterius*, was ſubſtituted in his room. Upon *Timothy*'s Death *John*, a Preſbyter of that Church, obtained the Biſhoprick by Symony, and in Defiance of an Oath he had taken to *Zeno*, that he would never procure himſelf to be elected into that See. Upon this he was expelled, and *Mongus* reſtored by the Emperor's Order. *Mongus* immediately conſented, and ſubſcribed to the pacifick Edict, and received into Communion thoſe who had formerly been

c. 16. of a different Party. Soon after this he was accuſed by *Calenduo* Biſhop of *Antioch* for Adultery, and for having publickly anathematized the Synod of *Chal-*

c. 17. *cedon* at *Alexandria*; and though this latter Charge was true, yet he ſolemnly denied it in a Letter to *Acacius* Biſhop of *Conſtantinople*, turning with the Time, condemning and receiving it, juſt as it ſuited his Views, and ſerved his Intereſt.

c. 20, 21. But being at laſt accuſed before *Felix* Biſhop of *Rome*, he was pronounced an Heretick, excommunicated, and anathematized.

Anaſta-

Anaſtaſius, who ſucceeded *Zeno*, was himſelf a great Lover of Peace, and endeavoured to promote it, both amongſt the Clergy and Laity, and therefore ordered, that there ſhould be no Innovations in the Church whatſoever. But this Moderation was by no means pleaſing to the Monks and Biſhops. Some of them were great Sticklers for the Council of *Chalcedon*, and would not allow ſo much as a Syllable or a Letter of their Decrees to be altered, nor communicate with thoſe who did not receive them. Others were ſo far from ſubmitting to this Synod, and their Determinations, that they anathematized it ; whilſt others adhered to *Zeno's Henoticon*, and maintained Peace with one another, even though they were of different Judgment concerning the Nature of Chriſt. Hence the Church was divided into Factions, ſo that the Biſhops would not communicate with each other. Not only the Eaſtern Biſhops ſeparated from the Weſtern ; but thoſe of the ſame Provinces had Schiſms amongſt themſelves. The Emperor, to prevent as much as poſſible theſe Quarrels, baniſhed thoſe who were moſt remarkably troubleſome from their Sees, and particularly the Biſhops of *Conſtantinople* and *Antioch*, forbidding all Perſons to preach either for or againſt the Council of *Chalcedon*, in any Places where it had not been uſual to do it before ; that by allowing all Churches their ſeveral Cuſtoms, he might prevent any Diſturbances upon account of Innovations. But the Monks and Biſhops prevented all theſe Attempts for Peace, by forcing one another to make new Confeſſions and Subſcriptions, and by anathematizing all who differed from them as Hereticks; ſo that by their ſeditious and obſtinate Behaviour they occaſioned innumerable Quarrels and Murthers in the Empire. They alſo treated the Emperor himſelf with great Inſolence, and excommunicated him as an Enemy to the Synod of *Chalcedon*. *Macedonius*, Biſhop of *Conſtantinople*, and his Clergy, raiſed the Mob of that City againſt him, only for adding to one of their Hymns theſe Words, *Who was crucified for us*. And when for this Reaſon *Macedonius* was expelled his Biſhoprick, they urged on the People to ſuch an height of Fury as endangered the utter Deſtruction of the City ; for in their Rage they ſet Fire to ſeveral Places in it, cut off the Head of a Monk, crying out, he was *an Enemy of the Trinity* ; and were not to be appeaſed till the Emperor himſelf went amongſt them without his imperial Diadem, and brought them to Temper by proper Submiſſions and Perſuaſions. And though he had great Reaſon to be offended with the Biſhops for ſuch Uſage, yet he was of ſo human and tender a Diſpoſition, that though he ordered ſeveral of them to be depoſed for various Offences, yet apprehending that it could not be effected without Bloodſhed, he wrote to the Prefect of *Aſia*, *Not to do any Thing in the Affair, if it would occaſion the ſhedding a ſingle Drop of Blood*.

Under this Emperor *Symmachus* Biſhop of *Rome* expelled the *Manichees* from the City, and ordered their Books to be publickly burnt before the Doors of the Church.

Juſtin was more zealous for Orthodoxy than his Predeceſſor *Anaſtaſius*, and in the firſt Year of his Reign gave a very ſignal Proof of it. *Severus*, Biſhop of *Antioch*, was warm againſt the Council of *Chalcedon*, and continually anathematizing it in the Letters he wrote to ſeveral Biſhops ; and becauſe the People

Margin notes: Evag. l. 3. c. 30. — c. 31, 32. — c. 44. — c. 34. — Platin. — Evag. l. 3. c. 4, 9.

quarrel-

quarrelled on this Account, and divided into several Parties, *Justin* ordered the Bishop to be apprehended, and his Tongue to be cut out, and commanded that the Synod of *Chalcedon* should be preached up through all the Churches of the Empire. *Platina* also tells us, that he banished the Arians, and gave their Churches to the Orthodox. *Hormisda* also, Bishop of *Rome*, in imitation of his Predecessor *Symmachus*, banished the Remainder of the *Manichees*, and caused their Writings to be burnt.

In vit. Johan. 1. *Platin.*

Justinian, his Successor in the Empire, succeeded him also in his Zeal for the Council of *Chalcedon*, and banished the Bishops of *Constantinople* and *Antioch*, because they would not obey his Orders, and receive the Decrees of that Synod. He also published a Constitution, by which he anathematized them and all their Followers, and ordered, that whosoever should preach their Opinions should be subject to the most grievous Punishments. By this means nothing was openly preached in any of the Churches but this Council ; nor did any one dare to anathematize it. And whosoever were of a contrary Opinion, they were compelled by innumerable Methods to come into the Orthodox Faith. In the third Year of his Reign he published a Law, ordering that there should be no Pagans, nor Hereticks, but orthodox Christians only, allowing to Hereticks three Months only for their Conversion. By another he deprived Hereticks of the Right of Succession. By another he rendered them incapable of being Witnesses in any Trial against Christians. He prohibited them also from baptizing any Persons, and from transcribing heretical Books under the Penalty of having the Hand cut off. These Laws were principally owing to the Persuasions of the Bishops. Thus *Agapetus*, Bishop of *Rome*, who had condemned *Anthimus*, and deposed him from his See of *Constantinople*, persuaded *Justinian* to banish all those whom he had condemned for Heresy. *Pelagius* also desired, that Hereticks and Schismaticks might be punished by the secular Power, if they would not be converted. The Emperor was too ready to comply with this Advice. But notwithstanding all this Zeal for Orthodoxy, and the cruel Edicts published by him for the Extirpation of Heresy, he was infamously Covetous, sold the Provinces of the Empire to Plunderers and Oppressors, stripped the Wealthy of their Estates upon false Accusations and forged Crimes, and went Partners with common Whores in their Gains of Prostitution ; and what is worse, in the Estates of those whom those Wretches falsely accused of Rapes and Adultery. And yet, that he might appear as Pious as he was Orthodox, he built out of these Rapines and Plunders many stately and magnificent Churches ; many religious Houses for Monks and Nuns, and Hospitals for the Relief of the Aged and Infirm. *Evagrius* also charges him with more than bestial Cruelty in the Case of the *Venetians*, whom he not only allowed, but even by Rewards encouraged to murther their Enemies at Noon-day, in the very Heart of the City, to break open Houses, and plunder the Possessors of their Riches, forcing them to redeem their Lives at the Expence of all they had. And if any of his Officers punished them for these Violences, they were sure to be punished themselves with Infamy or Death. And that each side might taste of his Severities, he afterwards turned his

Evag. l. 3. c. 11.

Paul. Liacon. c. 16.

Cod. de Hæret.

Novel. 42. c. 1.

Platin.

Evag. l. 4. c. 30.

c. 32.

his Laws againſt the *Venetians*, putting great Numbers of them to Death, for thoſe very Murthers and Violences he had before encouraged and ſupported.

During his Reign, in the 24th Year of it, was held the fifth general Council at *Conſtantinople*, conſiſting of about 165 Fathers. The Occaſion of their Meeting was the Oppoſition that was made to the four former general Councils, and particularly the Writings of *Origen*, which *Euſtochius*, Biſhop of *Jeruſalem* accuſed, as full of many dangerous Errors. In the firſt Seſſions it was debated, Whether *thoſe who were dead were to be anathematized?* One *Eutychius* looked with Contempt on the Fathers for their Heſitation in ſo plain a Matter, and told them, that there needed no Deliberation about it ; for that King *Joſias* formerly did not only deſtroy the idolatrous Prieſts who were living, **but** dug alſo thoſe who had been dead long before out of their Graves. So clear a Determination of the Point, who could reſiſt? The Fathers immediately were convinced, and *Juſtinian* cauſed him to be conſecrated Biſhop of *Conſtantinople*, in the Room of *Menas*, juſt deceas'd, for this his Skill in Scripture and Caſuiſtry. The Conſequence was, that the Decrees of the four preceeding Councils were all confirmed ; thoſe who were condemned by them re-condemned and anathematized, particularly *Theodorus* Biſhop of *Mopſueſtia*, and *Ibas*, with their Writings, as favouring the Impieties of *Neſtorius* ; and finally, *Origen*, with all his deteſtible and execrable Principles, and all Perſons whatſoever who ſhould think, or ſpeak of them, or dare to defend them. After theſe Tranſactions the Synod ſent an Account of them to *Juſtinian*, whom they complimented with the Title of *the moſt Chriſtian King, and with having a Soul partaker of the heavenly Nobility.* And yet ſoon after theſe Flatteries his moſt Chriſtian Majeſty turned Heretick himſelf, and endeavoured with as much Zeal to propagate Hereſy as he had done Othodoxy before : He publiſhed an Edict, by which he ordained, That *the Body of Chriſt was incorruptible, and incapable even of natural and innocent Paſſions* ; *that before his Death he eat in the ſame manner as he did after his Reſurrection, receiving no Converſion or Change from his very Formation in the Womb, neither in his voluntary or natural Affections, nor after his Reſurrection.* But as he was endeavouring to force the Biſhops to receive his Creed, God was pleaſed, as *Evagrius* obſerves, to cut him off, and notwithſtanding *the heavenly Nobility of his Soul, he went,* as the ſame Author charitably ſuppoſes, *to the Devil.*

Hunnerick, the Arian King of the *Vandals*, treated the Orthodox in this Emperor's Reign with great Cruelty in *Africa*, becauſe they would not embrace the Principles of *Arius* ; ſome he burnt, and others he deſtroyed by different Kinds of Death ; he ordered the Tongues of ſeveral of them to be cut out, who afterwards made their Eſcape to *Conſtantinople*, where *Procopius*, if you will believe him, affirms he heard them ſpeak as diſtinctly as if their Tongues had remained in their Heads. *Juſtinian* himſelf mentions them in one of his Conſtitutions. Two of them however, who happen'd to be Whore-Maſters, loſt afterwards on this Account, the Uſe of their Speech, for this Reaſon, and the Honour and Grace of Martyrdom.

The Fifth
general
Council,
A. C. 551.

Evag. l. 4.
c. 38.

c. 39.

c. 41.

l. 5. c. 1.

l. 4. c. 14.

Juſtin

Juſtin the younger, who ſucceeded *Juſtinian*, publiſhed an Edict ſoon after his
Advancement, by which he ſent all Biſhops to their reſpective Sees, and to perform divine Worſhip according to the uſual Manner of their Churches, without
making any Innovations concerning the Faith. As to his perſonal Character,
he was extremely diſſolute, and debauched, and addicted to the moſt vile and
criminal Pleaſures. He was alſo ſordidly Covetous, and ſold the very Bi-
ſhopricks to the beſt Bidders, putting them up to publick Auction. Nor was
he leſs remarkable for his Cruelty : He had a near Relation of his own Name,
whom he treacherouſly murthered, and of whom he was ſo jealous, that he
could not be content till he and his Empreſs had trampled his Head under their
Feet. However, he was very Orthodox, and publiſhed a new Explication of
the Faith, which for Clearneſs and Subtlety exceeded all that went before it.
In this he profeſſes, That *he believed in Father, Son, and Holy Spirit, the Con-*
ſubſtantial Trinity, one Deity, or Nature, or Eſſence, in one Virtue, Power and
Energy, in three Hypoſtaſes or Perſons ; and that he adored the Unity in Trinity, and
the Trinity in Unity, having a moſt admirable Difference and Union ; the Unity ac-
cording to the Eſſence or Deity ; the Trinity according to the Properties, Hypoſtaſes or
Perſons ; for they are divided indiviſibly ; or if I may ſo ſpeak, they are joined toge-
ther ſeparately. The Godhead in the Three is One, and the Three are One, the Deity
being in them ; or to ſpeak more accurately, the Three are the Deity, God the Father,
God the Son, and God the Holy Ghoſt, each Perſon being conſidered by itſelf, the Mind
thus ſeparating Things inſeparable ; the Three being underſtood to be together God, be-
ing one in Operation and Nature. We believe alſo in one only begotten Son of God, the
Word ———— for the Holy Trinity receives no Addition of a fourth Perſon, even after
the Incarnation of God the Word, one of the holy Trinity. But our Lord Jeſus Chriſt
is one and the ſame, Conſubſtantial to God, even the Father, according to his Deity,
and Conſubſtantial to us according to his Manhood. He ſuffered in the Fleſh, but was
impaſſible in the Deity. For we do not own that God the Word who wrought the Mi-
racles was one, and he that ſuffered another ; but we confeſs that our Lord Jeſus
Chriſt, the Word of God, was one and the ſame, who was made Fleſh and became
perfect Man ; and that the Miracles and Sufferings were of one and the ſame : For it
was not a Man that gave himſelf for us, but God the Word himſelf, being made Man
without change ; ſo that when we confeſs our Lord Jeſus Chriſt to be one and the ſame,
compounded of each Nature, of the Godhead and Manhood, we do not introduce any
Confuſion or Mixture by the Union ———— for as God remains in the Manhood, ſo alſo
nevertheleſs doth the Man, being in the Excellency of the Deity, Emanuel being both
in one and the ſame, even one God and alſo Man. And when we confeſs him to be per-
fect in the Godhead, and perfect in the Manhood, of which he is compounded, we
don't introduce a Diviſion in part, or Section to his one compounded Perſon, but only
ſignify the Difference of the Natures, which is not taken away by the Union ; for the
divine Nature is not converted into the human, nor the human Nature changed into the
divine. But we ſay, that each being conſidered, or rather actually exiſting in the very
Definition or Reaſon of its proper Nature, conſtitute the Oneneſs in Perſon. Now this
Oneneſs as to Perſon ſignifies that God the Word, i. e. *one Perſon of the three Perſons*
of the Godhead was not united to a pre-exiſtent Man, but that he formed to himſelf in
the

the Womb of our holy Lady Mary, *glorious Mother of God, and ever a Virgin, and out of her, in his own Person, Flesh consubstantial to us, and liable to all the same Passions, without Sin, animated with a reasonable and intellectual Soul.* —— *For considering his inexplicable Oneness, we orthodoxly confess one Nature of God the Word made Flesh, and yet conceiving in our Minds the Difference of the Natures, we say they are two, not introducing any Manner of Division. For each Nature is in him, so that we confess him to be one and the same Christ, one Son, one Person, one Hypostasis, God and Man together. Moreover, we anathematize all who have, or do think otherwise, and judge them as cut off from the holy Catholick, and apostolick Church of God.* To this extraordinary Edict, all, says the Historian, gave their Consent, esteeming it to be very Orthodox, though they were not more united amongst themselves than before.

Under *Mauritius, John* Bishop of *Constantinople,* in a Council held at that City, stiled himself Oecumenical Bishop, by the Consent of the Fathers there assembled ; and the Emperor himself ordered *Gregory* to acknowledge him in that Character. *Gregory* absolutely refused it, and replied, that the Power of binding and loosing was delivered to *Peter* and his Sucessors, and not to the Bishops of *Constantinople* ; admonishing him to take care, that he did not provoke the Anger of God against himself, by raising Tumults in his Church. This Pope was the first who stiled himself, *Servus Servorum Dei,* Servant of the Servants of God ; and had such an Abhorrence of the Title of Universal Bishop, that he said, *I confidently affirm, that whosoever calls himself universal Priest is the Forerunner of Antichrist, by thus proudly exalting himself above others.*

But however modest *Gregory* was in refusing and condemning this arrogant Title, *Boniface* III. thought better of the Matter, and after great struggles, prevailed with *Phocas,* who murthered *Mauritius* the Emperor, to declare, that the See of the blessed Apostle *Peter,* which is the Head of all Churches, should be so called and accounted by all, and the Bishop of it Oecumenical or universal Bishop. The Church of *Constantinople* had claimed this Precedence and Dignity, and was sometimes favoured herein by the Emperors, who declared, that the first See ought to be in that Place which was the Head of the Empire. The *Roman* Pontiffs, on the other hand, affirmed, that *Rome,* of which *Constantinople* was but a Colony, ought to be esteemed the Head of the Empire, because the *Greeks* themselves, in their Writings, stile the Emperor, *Roman* Emperor, and the Inhabitants of *Constantinople* are called *Romans* and not *Greeks* ; not to mention, that *Peter,* the Prince of the Apostles, gave the Keys of the Kingdom of Heaven to his Successors, the Popes of *Rome.* On this Foundation was the Superiority of the Church of *Rome* to that of all other Churches built ; and *Phocas,* who was guilty of all Villanies, was one of the fittest Persons that could be found to gratify *Boniface* in this Request. *Boniface* also called a Council at *Rome,* where this Supremacy was confirmed, and by whom it was decreed, that Bishops should be chosen by the Clergy and People, approved by the Prince of the City, and ratified by the Pope with these Words, *Volumus & jubemus,* For this is our Will and Command. To reward *Phocas* for the Grant of the Primacy, he approved the Murther of *Mauritius,* and very

2   honour-

Platin in
vit. Greg.
l.

l. 6. Epist.
194.

Platin in
vit. Bonif.
III.

honourably received his Images, which he fent to *Rome*. And having thus wickedly poffeffed themfelves of this unrighteous Power, the Popes as wickedly ufed it, foon brought almoft the whole Chriftian World into fubjection to them, and became the Perfecutors General of the Church of God; proceeding from one Ufurpation to another, till at laft they brought Emperors, Kings and Princes into fubjection, forcing them to ratify their unrighteous Decrees, and to punifh, in the fevereft Manner, all that fhould prefume to oppofe and contradict them, till fhe became *drunken with the Blood of the Saints, and with the Blood of the Martyrs of Jefus.* Babylon *the great, the Mother of Harlots, and Abominations of the Earth.*

The Inquifition is the Mafter-piece of their Policy and Cruelty; and fuch an Invention for the Suppreffion of Religion and Truth, Liberty and Knowledge, Innocence and Virtue, as could proceed from no other Wifdom but that which is *earthly, fenfual, and devilifh.* And as the Hiftory of it, which I now prefent my Reader with in his own Language, gives the moft perfect Account of the Laws and Practices of this accurfed Tribunal, I fhall not enter into the Detail of popifh Perfecutions, efpecially as we have a full Account of thofe practifed amongft our felves in *Fox* and other Writers, who have done Juftice to this Subject. I fhall only add a few Things relating to the two other general Councils, as they are ftiled by Ecclefiaftical Hiftorians.

Plat.in vit. Honorii I. Under *Heraclius,* the Succeffor of *Phocas,* great Difturbances were raifed upon Account of what they called the Herefy of the *Monothelites,* i. e. thofe who held there were not two Wills, the Divine and Human, in Chrift, but only one fingle Will or Operation. The Emperor himfelf was of this Opinion, being perfuaded into it by *Pyrrhus* Patriarch of *Conftantinople,* and *Cyrus* Bifhop of *Alexandria.* And though he afterwards feems to have changed his Mind in this Point, yet in order to promote Peace, he put forth an Edict, forbidding Difputes or Quarrels, on either fide the Queftion. *Conftans,* his Grandfon, was at the fame Sentiment, and at the Inftigation of *Paul* Bifhop of *Conftantinople,* grievoufly perfecuted thofe who would not agree with him. Plat.in vit. Mart. *Martyn,* Pope of *Rome,* fent his Legates to the Emperor and Patriarch to forfake their Errors, and embrace the Truth; but his Holinefs was but little regarded, and after his Legates were imprifoned and whipped, they were fent into Banifhment. This greatly enraged *Martyn,* who convened a Synod at *Rome* of 150 Bifhops, who decreed, that whofoever fhould *not confefs two Wills, and two Operations united, the Divine and the Human, in one and the fame Chrift, fhould be anathema,* and that *Paul* Bifhop of *Conftantinople,* fhould be condemned and depofed. The Emperor highly refented this Conduct, and fent *Olympius Hexarch* into *Italy* to propagate the *Monothelite* Doctrine; and either to kill *Martyn,* or fend him Prifoner to *Conftantinople. Olympius* not being able to execute either Defign, *Theodorus* was fent in his room, who apprehended the Pope, put him in Chains, and got him conveyed to the Emperor, who after ignominioufly treating him, banifhed him to *Pontus,* where he died in great Act. 15,6. Conftant. Mifery and Want. The Bifhops of *Conftans*'s Party were greatly affiftant Tom.Con-cil. 2. to him in this Work of Perfecution, and fhewed more Rage againft their

Fellow-

Fellow - Chriftians, than they did againft the very Barbarians themfelves.

Conftantine, the Eldeft Son of *Conftans,* cut off his two younger Brothers No- *Tle Sixth*
fes, that they might not fhare the Empire with him ; but however happen- *general*
ed to be more Orthodox than his Predeceffors ; and by the Perfuafion of *Aga-* *Council,*
tho, Pope of *Rome,* convened the Sixth General Council at *Conftantinople,* *Piat.in vit.*
in which were prefent 289 Bifhops.   The Fathers of this holy Synod compli- *Agath.*
mented the Emperor with being *another David, raifed up by Chrift, their God,*
a Man after his own Heart ; who had not given Sleep to his Eyes, nor Slumber to
his Eye-lids, till he had gathered them together, to find out the perfeft Rule of Faith.
After this they condemned the Herefy of one Will in Chrift, and declared, *That*
they glorified two natural Wills and Operations, indivifibly, inconvertibly, without
Confufion, and infeparably in the fame Lord Jefus Chrift, our true God, i. e. *the di-*
vine Operation, and the human Operation.   So that now the Orthodox Faith
in Reference to Chrift was this ; That *he had two Natures, the divine and hu-*
man ; that thefe two Natures were united, without Confufion, into one fingle Perfon ;
and that in this one fingle Perfon, there were two diftinct Wills and Operations, the
human and divine.   Thus, at laft, 681 Years after Chrift, was the Orthodox
Faith, relating to his Deity, Humanity, Nature and Wills, decided and fettled by this Synod ; who, after having pronounced Anathemas againft the Living and Dead, ordered the Burning of heretical Books, and deprived feveral
Bifhops of their Sees ; procured an Edict from the Emperor, commanding all
to receive their Confeffion of Faith, and denouncing not only eternal, but corporal Punifhments to all Recufants, *viz.* If they were Bifhops, or Clergymen,
or Monks, they were to be banifhed.   If Laymen, of any Rank and Figure,
they were to forfeit their Eftates, and lofe their Honours.   If of the common
People, they were to be expelled the Royal City.   Thefe their definitive Sentences were concluded with the ufual Exclamation, of *God fave the Emperor,*
Long live the Orthodox Emperor ; down with the Hereticks ; curfed be Euty ches,
Macarius, *&c. The Trinity hath depofed them.*

The next Controverfy of Importance was relating to the Worfhip of Images.   The Refpect due to the Memories of the Apoftles and Martyrs of the
Chriftian Church, was gradually carried into great Superftition, and at
Length degenerated into downright Idolatry.   Not only Churches were dedicated to them, but their Images placed in them, and religious Adoration
paid to them.   *Platina* tells us, That amongft many other Ceremonies introduced by Pope *Sixtus* III. in the Fifth Century, he perfuaded *Valentinian* the
younger, Emperor of the *Weft,* to beautify and adorn the Churches, and to
place upon the Altar of St. *Peter,* a golden Image of our Saviour, enriched
with Jewels.   In the next Century the Images of the Saints were brought in,
and religious Worfhip paid to them.   This appears from a Letter of Pope
Gregory's, to the Bifhop of *Marfeilles,* who broke in Pieces certain Images, becaufe they had been fuperftitioufly adored.   *Gregory* tells him, *I commend you,* l. 9. Ind.t.
that through a pious Zeal, you would not fuffer that which is made with Hands to be Ep. 9.
adored ; but I blame you for breaking the Images in Pieces.   For 'tis one Thing to
adore a Picture, and another to learn by the Hiftory of the Picture, what is to be
i   *adored.*

l. 7. Jud 2.
Ep. 109.
Platin.
adored. And elfewhere he declares, That *Images and Pictures in Churches, were very ufeful for the Inftruction of the Ignorant, who could not read.* Sergius, after this, repaired the Images of the Apoftles. *John* VII. adorned a great many Churches with the Pictures and Images of the Saints. And at length, in the Reign of *Philippicus, Conftantine* the Pope, in a Synod held at *Rome,* decreed, That Images fhould be fixed up in the Churches, and have great Adoration paid them. He alfo condemned and excommunicated the Emperor himfelf for Herefy ; becaufe he erafed the Pictures of the Fathers, which had been painted on the Walls of the Church of St. *Sophia* at *Conftantinople* ; and commanded, that his Images fhould not be received into the Church ; that his Name fhould not be ufed in any publick or private Writings, nor his Effigies ftamped upon any kind of Money whatfoever.

This Superftition of bringing Images into Churches was warmly oppofed, and gave Occafion to many Difturbances and Murders. The Emperor *Leo Ifaurus* greatly difapproved this Practice, and publifhed an Edict, by which, he commanded all the Subjects of the *Roman* Empire, to deface all the Pictures, and to take away all the Statues of the Martyrs and Angels out of the Churches, in order to prevent Idolatry, threatning to punifh thofe who did not, as publick Plat.in vit.
Gregor.II. Enemies. Pope *Gregory* II. oppofed this Edict, and admonifhed all Catholicks, in no manner to obey it. This occafioned fuch a Tumult at *Ravenna* in *Italy,* between the Partifans of the Emperor and the Pope, as ended in the Murder of *Paul,* Exarch of *Italy,* and his Son ; which enraged the Emperor in an high Degree ; fo that he ordered all Perfons to bring to him all their Images of Wood, Brafs and Marble, which he publickly burnt ; punifhing with Death, all fuch as were found to conceal them. He alfo convened a Synod at *Conftantinople* ; where, after a careful and full Examination, it was unanimoufly agreed, that the Interceffion of the Saints was a meer Fable ; and the Worfhip of Images and Relicts was downright Idolatry, and contrary to the Word of God. And as *Germanus,* Patriarch of *Conftantinople,* favoured Images, the Emperor banifhed him, and fubftituted *Anaftatius,* who was of his own Sentiments, in his Room. *Gregory* III. in the Beginning of his Pontificate, Platin. affembled his Clergy, and by their unanimous Confent, depofed him on this Account, from the Empire, and put him under Excommunication ; and was the firft who withdrew the *Italians* from their Obedience to the Emperors of *Conftantinople,* calling in the Affiftance of *Charles* King of *France.* After this, he placed the Images of Chrift and his Apoftles in a more fumptuous Manner than they were before upon the Altar of St. *Peter,* and at his own Expence, made a golden Image of the Virgin *Mary,* holding Chrift in her Arms, for the Church of St. *Mary ad Præfepe.*

Conftantine Copronymus, Leo's Son and Succeffor in the Empire, inherited his Father's Zeal againft the Worfhip of Images, and called a Synod at *Conftantinople,* to determine the Controverfy. The Fathers being met together, to the Number of 330, after confidering the Doctrine of Scripture, and the Opinions of the Fathers, decreed, *That every Image, of whatfoever Materials made and formed by the Artift, fhould be caft out of the Chriftian Church as a ftrange and abominable Thing* ; adding an Anathema upon all who fhould make Images or
Pictures,

Pictures, or Representations of God, or of Christ, or of the Virgin Mary, *or of any of the Saints, condemning it as a vain and diabolical Invention ; deposing all Bishops, and subjecting the Monks and Laity, who should set up any of them in publick or private, to all the Penalties of the imperial Constitutions.* They also deposed *Constantine,* Patriarch of *Constantinople,* for opposing this Decree ; and the Emperor first banished him, and afterwards put him to Death ; and commanded, That this Council should be esteemed and received as the seventh oecumenical, or universal one. *Paul* I. Pope of *Rome,* sent his Legate to *Constantinople,* to admonish the Emperor to restore the sacred Images and Statues which he had destroy'd ; and threatened him with Excommunication upon his Refusal. But *Copronymus* slighted the Message, and treated the Legates with great Contempt, and used the Image Worshippers with a great deal of Severity. _{Platin in vit. Paul I.}

Constantine, Bishop of *Rome,* the Successor of *Paul,* seems also to have been an Enemy to Images, and was there tumultuously deposed, and *Stephen* III. substituted in his Room, who was a warm and furious Defender of them. He immediately assembled a Council in the *Lateran* Church, where the holy Fathers abrogated all *Constantine's* Decrees ; deposed all that had been ordained by him Bishops, made void all his Baptisms and Chrisms ; and as some Historians relate, after having beat him, and used him with great Indignity, made a Fire in the Church, and burnt him therein. After this, they annulled all the Decrees of the Synod of *Constantinople,* ordered the Restoration of Statues and Images, and anathematized that execrable and pernicious Synod, giving this excellent Reason for the Use of Images, *That if 'twas lawful for Emperors, and those who had deserved well of the Commonwealth, to have their Images erected, but not lawful to set up those of God ; the Condition of the immortal God would be worse than that of Men.* After this the Pope published the Acts of the Council, and pronounced an Anathema against all those who should oppose it. _{Id. in vit. Stephani.}

Thus the Mystery of this Iniquity worked, till at length, under the Reign of *Irene* and *Constantine* her Son, a Synod was packed up of such Bishops as were ready to make any Decrees that should be agreeable to the *Roman* Pontiff, and the Empress. They met at *Nice,* to the Number of about 350. In this venerable Assembly it was decreed, *That holy Images of the Cross should be consecrated, and put on the sacred Vessels and Vestments, and upon Walls and Boards, in private Houses and publick Ways ; and especially that there should be erected Images of the Lord God, our Saviour Jesus Christ, of our blessed Lady, the Mother of God, of the venerable Angels, and of all the Saints. And that whosoever should presume to think or teach otherwise, or to throw away any painted Books, or the Figure of the Cross, or any Image or Picture, or any genuine Relicts of the Martyrs, they should, if Bishops or Clergymen, be deposed, or if Monks or Laymen, be excommunicated.* Then they pronounced Anathemas upon all who should not receive Images, or who should apply what the Scriptures say against Idols, to the holy Images, or who should call them Idols, or who should wilfully communicate with those who rejected and despised them ; adding, according to Custom, *Long live* Constantine *and* Irene *his Mother. Damnation to all Hereticks. Damnation on the Council that roared against venerable Images. The holy Trinity hath deposed them.* _{The seventh general Council, A.C.}

Irene and *Constantine* approved and subscribed these Decrees, and the Consequence was, That Idols and Images were erected in all the Churches ; and those who were against them, treated with great Severity. This Council was held under the Popedom of *Hadrian* I. and thus, by the Intrigues of the Popes of *Rome*, Iniquity was established by a Law, and the Worship of Idols authorized and established in the Christian Church, though contrary to all the Principles of natural Religion, and the Nature and Design of the Christian Revelation.

In vit. Hadrian I.
'Tis true, that this Decision of the Council did not put an entire End to the Controversy. *Platina* tells us, That *Constantine* himself not long after annulled their Decrees, and removed his Mother from all Share in the Government. The Synod also of *Francfort*, held about six Years after, decreed that the Worship and Adoration of Images was impious ; condemned the Synod of *Nice*, which had established it, and ordered that it should not be called either the Seventh, or an universal Council. But as the *Roman* Pontiffs had engrossed almost all Power into their own Hands, all Opposition to Image Worship became ineffectual ; especially as they supported their Decrees by the Civil Power, and caused great Cruelties to be exercised towards all those who should dare dispute or contradict them.

For many Years the World groaned under this antichristian Yoke ; nor were any Methods of Fraud, Imposture and Barbarity left unpractised to support and perpetuate it. As the Clergy rid Lords of the Universe, they grew wanton and insolent in their Power ; and as they drained the Nations of their Wealth to support their own Grandure and Luxury, they degenerated into the worst and vilest set of Men that ever burdened the Earth. They were shamefully ignorant, and scandalously vicious ; well versed in the most exquisite Arts of Torture and Cruelty, and absolutely divested of all Bowels of Mercy and Compassion towards those, who even in the smallest Matters differed from the Dictates of their Superstition and Impiety. The infamous Practices of that accursed Tribunal, the Inquisition, the Wars against Hereticks in the Earldom of *Tholouse*, the Massacres of *Paris* and *Ireland*, the many Sacrifices they have made in *Great-Britain*, the Fires they have kindled, and the Flames they have lighted up in all Nations, where their Power hath been acknowledged, witness against them, and demonstrate them to be very Monsters of Mankind. So that one would really wonder, that the whole World hath not entered into a Combination, and risen in Arms against so execrable a Set of Men, and extirpated them as savage Beasts, from the Face of the whole Earth ; who, out of a Pretence of Religion, have defiled it with the Blood of innumerable Saints and Martyrs, and made use of the Name of the most holy Jesus, to countenance and sanctify the most abominable Impieties.

But it pleased God, in his good Providence, to take the Remedy and Cure of these Evils, into his own Hands ; and after several fruitless Attempts by Men, to bring about, at last, a Reformation of Religion, by his own Wisdom and Power. The History of this great Event hath been very particularly and faithfully given by many excellent Writers, to which I muft here refer my Readers; and it muft be owned, that the Perfons employ'd by Almighty God, to accomplifh this great Work, were, many of them, remarkable for their great Learning and exemplary Piety. I am fure I have no Inclination to detract from their Worth and Merit. One would indeed have imagined, that the Cruelties exercifed by the Papifts, upon all who oppofed their Superftitions in Worfhip, and their Corruptions in Doctrine, fhould have given the firft Reformers an utter Abhorrence of all Methods of Perfecution for Confcience fake, and have kept them from ever entering into any fuch Meafures themfelves. But it muft be confeffed, that however they differed from the Church of *Rome*, as to Doctrines and Difcipline, yet, that they too generally agreed with her, in the Methods to fupport, what they themfelves apprehended to be Truth and Orthodoxy; and were angry with the Papifts, not for perfecuting, but for perfecuting themfelves and their Followers; being really of opinion that Hereticks might be perfecuted, and, in fome Cafes, perfecuted to Death. And that this was their avowed Principle, they gave abundant Demonftration by their Practice.

Luther, the great Inftrument, under God, of the Reformation in *Germany,* Luther. was, as his Followers allow, naturally of a warm and violent Temper; but was however in his Judgment againft punifhing Hereticks with Death. Thus, in his Account of the State of the Popifh Church, as related by *Seckendorf,* he fays: *The true Church teaches the Word of God, but forces no one to it. If any one* l. 2. Sect. *will not believe it, fhe difmiffes him, and feparates her felf from him, according* 36. §. 83. *to the Command of Chrift, and the Example of* Paul *in the* Acts, *and leaves him to the Judgment of God: Whereas our Executioners, and moft cruel Tyrants, teach not the Word of God, but their own Articles, acting as they pleafe, and then adjudge thofe who refufe to believe their Articles, and obey their Decrees, to the Fires.* The fame Author gives us many other ftrong Paffages to the fame Purpofe. Particularly, in one of his Letters to *Lincus,* who afked his Opinion about the Punifhment of falfe Teachers, *Luther* fays: *I am very averfe to the fhedding of* Ibid. Sect. *Blood, even in the Cafe of fuch as deferve it: And I the more efpecially dread it in* 13. §. 43. *this Cafe, becaufe, as the Papifts and Jews, under this Pretence, have deftroy'd holy Prophets and innocent Men; fo I am afraid the fame would happen amongft our felves, if in one fingle Inftance it fhould be allow'd lawful for Seducers to be put to Death. I can therefore, by no Means, allow that falfe Teachers fhould be deftroy'd.* But as to all other Punifhments, *Luther* feems to have been of *Auftin's* Mind, and thought that they might be lawfully ufed. For after the before-mention'd Paffage, he adds, *'Tis fufficient that they fhould be banifhed.* And in another Ibid. Sect. Place, he allows, That *Hereticks may be corrected, and forced, at leaft, to filence,* 36. §. 83. *if they publickly deny any one of the Articles received by all Chriftians, and particularly that Chrift is God; affirming him to be a mere Man or Prophet. This,* fays he, *is not to force Men to the Faith, but to reftrain publick Blafphemy.* In another Place he goes farther, and fays, That *Hereticks are not, indeed, to be put* l. 3. Sect. *to Death, but may however be confined, and fhut up in fome certain Place, and put* 8. §. 28. *under Reftraint as Madmen.* As to the *Jews,* he was for treating them more
                                                    feverely,

l. 3. Sect.
27. § 3.

severely, and was of Opinion, that *their Synagogues should be levelled with the Ground, their Houses destroy'd, their Books of Prayer, and of the* Talmud, *and even those of the* Old Testament, *be taken from them, their Rabbi's be forbid to teach, and forced, by hard Labour, to get their Bread* ; *and if they would not submit to this, that they should be banished, as was formerly practised in* France *and* Spain.

l. 3. Sect.
32. § 125.
Germany.

This was the Moderation of this otherwise great and good Man, who was indeed against putting Hereticks to Death, but for almost all other Punishments that the civil Magistrate could inflict : And, agreeably to this Opinion, he persuaded the Electors of *Saxony*, not to tolerate, in their Dominion, the Followers of *Zuinglius*, in the Opinion of the Sacrament ; because he esteemed the real Presence an essential or fundamental Article of Faith ; nor to enter into any Terms of Union with them, for their common Safety and Defence, against the Endeavours of the Papists to destroy them. And accordingly, notwithstanding all the Endeavours of the *Landgrave* of *Hesse Cassel*, to get them included in the common League against the Papists, the Elector would never allow it, being vehemently dissuaded from it by *Luther*, *Melancton*, and

l. 2 Sect.
6. §. 11.

others of their Party, who alleged, *That they taught Articles contrary to those received in* Saxony ; *and that therefore there could be no Agreement of Heart with them.* In one of his Conferences with *Bucer*, he declared, That there could be no Union, unless *Zuinglius* and his Party should think and teach otherwise ; cursing all Phrases and Interpretations that tended to assert the figurative

Sect. 17.
§. 47.

Presence only, affirming, That *either those of his own Opinion, or those of* Zuinglius, *must be the Ministers of the Devil.* On this Account, though *Luther* was for treating *Zuinglius* and his Followers, with as much Christian Friendship as he could afford them, yet he would never own them for Brethren, but looked on them as Hereticks, and pressed the Electors of *Saxony* not to allow

l. 3. Sect
6. §. 15.
Sect. 13.
§. 41.
Ibid.

them in their Dominions. He also wrote to *Albert* Duke of *Prussia*, to persuade him to banish them his Territories. *Seckendorf* also tells us, That the *Lutheran* Lawyers of *Wittenburg*, condemned to Death one *Peter Pestelius*, for being a *Zuinglian* ; though this was disapproved by the Elector of *Saxony*. Several also of the Anabaptists were put to Death by the *Lutherans*, for their Obstinacy in propagating their Errors, contrary to the Judgment of the Landgrave of *Hesse Cassel*, who declared himself for more moderate Measures, and for uniting all sorts of Protestants amongst themselves.

Calvin.

John Calvin, another of the Reformers, and to whom the Christian World is, on many Accounts, under very great Obligations, was, however well known to be in Principle and Practice a Persecutor. So entirely was he in the persecuting Measures, that he wrote a Treatise in Defence of them, maintaining the Lawfulness of putting Hereticks to Death. And that by Hereticks, he meant such who differed from himself, is evident from his Treatment of *Castellio* and *Servetus*.

The former, not inferior to *Calvin* himself in Learning and Piety, had the Misfortune to differ from him in Judgment, in the Points of Predestination, Election, Free-will and Faith. This *Calvin* could not bear, and therefore
treated

greated *Caſtellio*, in ſo rude and cruel a Manner, as I believe his warmeſt Friends will be aſhamed to juſtify. In ſome of his Writings he calls him, *Blaſphemer, Reviler, malicious barking Dog, full of Ignorance, Beſtiality and Impudence, Impoſtor, a baſe Corrupter of the Sacred Writings, a Mocker of God, a Contemner of all Religion, an impudent Fellow, a filthy Dog, a Knave, an impious, leud, crooked minded Vagabond, beggerly Rogue.* At other Times he calls him *A Diſciple and Brother of Servetus, and an Heretick. Caſtellio*'s Reply to all theſe Flowers, is worthy the Patience and Moderation of a Chriſtian, and from his Slanderer he appeals to the righteous Judgment of God. But not content with theſe Invectives, *Calvin* farther accuſed him of three Crimes which *Caſtellio* particularly anſwers. The firſt was of Theft, in taking away ſome Wood, that belonged to another Perſon, to make a Fire to warm himſelf withal : This *Calvin* calls, *Curſed Gain, at another's Expence and Damage* ; whereas, in Truth, the Fact was this. *Caſtellio* was thrown into ſuch Circumſtances of Poverty by the Perſecutions of *Calvin* and his Friends, that he was ſcarce able to maintain himſelf. And as he dwelt near the Banks of the *Rhine*, he uſed, at leiſure Hours, to draw out of the River, with an Hook, the Wood that was brought down by the Waters of it. This Wood was no private Property, but every Man's that could catch it. *Caſtellio* took it in the Middle of the Day, and amongſt a great Number of Fiſhermen, and ſeveral of his own Acquaintance ; and was ſometimes paid Money for it by the Decree of the Senate. This the charitable *Calvin* magnifies into a Theft, and publiſhes to the World to paint out the Character of his Chriſtian Brother.

But his Accuſations ran farther yet ; and he calls God to witneſs, that whilſt he maintained *Caſtellio* in his Houſe, *he never ſaw any one more proud, or perfidious, or void of Humanity* ; *and 'twas well known he was an Impoſtor, of a peculiar Impudence, and one that took Pleaſure in ſcoffing at Piety, and that he delighted himſelf in laughing at the Principles of Religion.* Theſe Charges *Caſtellio* anſwers in ſuch a Manner, as was enough to put even Malice it ſelf to ſilence. For, notwithſtanding *Calvin*'s Appeal to God for the Truth of theſe Things, yet he himſelf, and two of his principal Friends, who were eminent Preachers in *Savoy*, preſſed *Caſtellio*, even contrary to his Inclination, to take the Charge of a School in *Stratſburg* : And therefore, as he ſays to *Calvin*, *With what Conſcience could you make me Maſter, if you knew me to be ſuch a Perſon, when I dwelt in your Houſe ? What Sort of Men muſt they be who would commit the Education of Children to ſuch a wicked Wretch as you appeal to God you knew me to be ?* But what is yet more to the Purpoſe, is, that after he had been Maſter of that School three Years, *Calvin* gave him a Teſtimonial, written and ſigned with his own Hand, as to the Integrity of his paſt Behaviour, affirming, amongſt other Things, That *he had behaved himſelf in ſuch a Manner, that he was, by the Conſent of all of them, appointed to the Paſtoral Office.* And in the Concluſion he adds, *Leſt any one ſhould ſuſpect any other Reaſon why Sebaſtian went from us, we teſtify to all whereſoever he may come, That he himſelf voluntarily left the School, and ſo behaved himſelf in it, as that we adjudged him worthy this ſacred Miniſtry.*

2

niftry. And that he was not actually received into it, was *non aliqua vitæ macula*, not owing to any Blemifh of his Life, nor to any impious Tenets that he held in Matters of Faith, but to this only caufe ; the Difference of our Opinions about *Solomon*'s Songs, and the Article of Chrift's Defcent into Hell. But how is this Teftimonial, that *Caftellio* had no *macula vitæ*, was unblameable as to his Life, reconcileable with the Appeal to God, that he was proud and perfidious, and void of Humanity, and a profeffed Scoffer at Religion, whilft he dwelt at *Calvin*'s Houfe? If this Charge was true, How came *Calvin* and his Friends to apppoint him Mafter of a School, and judge him worthy the facred Miniftry? Or if he was of fo bad Character once, and afterwards gave the Evidence of a fincere Repentance by an irreproachable Behaviour, what Equity or Juftice, what Humanity or Honour, was there in publifhing to the World Faults that had been repented of and forfaken? *Caftellio* folemnly protefts that he had never injured *Calvin*, and that the fole Reafon of his Difpleafure againft him was becaufe he differed from him in Opinion. On this Account he endeavoured to render him every where Impious, prohibited the Reading of his Books ; and, what is the laft Effort of Enmity, endeavoured to excite the civil Magiftrate againft him to put him to Death. But God was pleafed to protect this good Man from the Rage of his Enemies. He died at *Bafil*, in Peace, and received an honourable Burial, the juft Reward of his Piety, Learning, and Merit.

Bez. in vit.
Ca. vin. I may add to this Account, *Calvin*'s Treatment of one *Jerom Bolfec*, who from a Carmelite Monk had embraced the reformed Religion, but held the Doctrine of Free-will and Predeftination upon the Forefight of good Works. *Calvin* was prefent at a Sermon preached by him at *Geneva*, upon thefe Articles, and the Sermon being ended, publickly oppofed him in the Congregation. When the Affembly was difmiffed, poor *Bolfec* was immediately apprehended, and fent to Prifon, and foon after, by *Calvin*'s Counfel, banifhed for Sedition and *Pelagianifm* from the City, and forbid ever to come into it, or the Territories of it under Pain of being whipped, *A. C.* 1551.

Geneva. But *Calvin*'s Treatment of the unfortunate *Servetus* was yet more fevere. His Book entitled, *Reftitutio Chriftianifmi*, which he fent in *MS.* to *Calvin*, enraged him to that Degree, that he afterwards kept no Temper or Meafures with him, fo that as *Bolfec* and *Uytenbogaert* relate, in a Letter written by him to his Friends *Viret* and *Farel*, he tells them, That *if this Heretick* (Servetus) Biblioth.
Raifon.
Pour d'
Octobre,
&c. 1728
Art. VIII. *fhould ever fall into his Hands, he would take Care that he fhould lofe his Life.* Servetus his Imprifonment at *Vienne*, foon gave him an Opportunity to fhew his Zeal againft him: For, in Order to ftrengthen the Evidence againft him, *Calvin* fent to the Magiftrates of that City, the Letters and Writings which *Servetus* had fent to him at *Geneva*. This is evident from the Sentence it felf againft him, in which thofe Writings, as well as his printed Book, are exprefly mentioned as containing the Proofs of his Herefy. Whether *Calvin* fent them of his own Accord, or, at the Defire of the Magiftrates of *Vienne*, I fhall not prefume to determine. If of his own Accord, it was a bafe Officioufnefs, and if at the Requeft of thofe Magiftrates, it was a moft unaccountable Conduct in a

Proteftant, to fend Evidence to a Popifh Court, to put a Proteftant to Death ; efpecially confidering that *Servetus* could not differ more from *Calvin* than *Calvin* did from the Papifts, their common Adverfaries, and who certainly deferved as much to be burnt, in their Judgment, as *Servetus* did in *Calvin*'s.

Befides this, *Servetus* farther charges him with writing to one *William Trie* at *Lyons*, to furnifh the Magiftrates of that City with Matter of Accufation againft him. The Author of the *Bibliotheque* beforementioned, fays, this is a meer Romance, dreffed up by *Servetus*. I confefs it doth not appear to me in fo very romantick a Light, at leaft *Calvin*'s Vindication of himfelf from this Charge doth not feem to be altogether fufficient. He fays, '*Tis commonly reported, that I occafioned* Servetus *to be apprehended at* Vienne, *on which Account, 'tis faid by many, that I have acted difhonourably, in thus expofing him to the mortal Enemies of the Faith, as though I had thrown him into the Mouth of the Wolves. But, I befeech you, how came I, fo fuddenly, into fuch an Intimacy with the Pope's Officers ? 'Tis very likely, truly, that we fhould correfpond together by Letters ; and that thofe who agree with me, juft as* Belial *doth with* Jefus Chrift, *fhould enter into a Plot with their mortal Enemy, as with their Companion: This filly Calumny will fall to the Ground, when I fhall fay, in one Word, That there is nothing in it.* But how doth all this confute *Servetus*'s Charge ? For whatever Differences there might be between *Calvin* and the Papifts in fome Things, yet, why might he not write to the Papifts at *Vienne* to put *Servetus* to Death for what was equally counted Herefy by them both, and when they agreed as the moft intimate Friends and Companions in the Lawfulnefs of putting Hereticks to Death. What *Calvin* fays of the Abfurdity of an Intimacy and Confpiracy with him their mortal Enemy, is no Abfurdity at all. *Herod* and *Pontius Pilate*, tho' Enemies, agreed in the Condemnation of the Son of God. Befides, 'tis certain, that the Magiftrates at *Vienne* had *Servetus*'s Manufcripts fent to them from *Geneva*, either by *Calvin*, or the Magiftrates of that City ; and when *Servetus* was afterwards apprehended at *Geneva*, the Magiftrates there fent a Meffenger to *Vienne*, for a Copy of the Procefs that had been there carried on againft him, which that Meffenger received, and actually brought back to *Geneva*. So that nothing is more evident, than that there was an Intimacy and Confpiracy between the Proteftants of *Geneva* and the Papifts at *Vienne*, to take away the Life of poor *Servetus* ; and that, though they were mortal Enemies in other Things, and as far different from one another as Chrift and *Belial*, yet that they agreed harmonioufly in the Doctrine and Practice of Perfecution, and were one in the Defign and Endeavour of murthering this unhappy Phyfician. And though *Calvin* is pleafed magifterially to deny his having any Communication by Letters with the Papifts at *Vienne*, yet, I think, his Denial far from fufficient to remove the Sufpicion. He himfelf exprefly fays, that many Perfons blamed him for not acting honourably in that Affair ; and the Accufation was fupported by *Servetus*'s Complaint, and by what is a much ftronger Evidence, by the original Papers and Letters which *Servetus* had fent to *Calvin*, which were actually produced by the Judges at *Vienne*, and recited in the Sentence as part of the Foundation of his Condemnation. And as *Calvin*

k himfelf

himfelf never, as I can find, hath attempted to clear up thefe ftrong Circumftances, though he owed it to himfelf and his Friends, I think he can't well
be excufed from practifing the Death of *Servetus* at *Vienne*, and lending his
Affiftance to the bloody Papifts of that Place the more effectually to procure
his Condemnation.

But he had the good Fortune to make his Efcape from Imprifonment,
and was, *June* 17, 1553. condemned for Contumacy, and burnt in Effigie
by the Order of his Judges, having himfelf got fafe to *Geneva*, where
he was re-condemned, and actually burnt in Perfon, *October* 27. of the fame
Year, 1553. He had not been long in this City before *Calvin* fpirited up one
Nicholas de la Fountain, probably one of his Pupils, to make Information
againft him, wifely avoiding it himfelf, becaufe, according to the Laws of
Geneva, the Accufer muft fubmit to Imprifonment with the Party he accufes,
till the Crime appears to have a folid Foundation and Proof. Upon this Information *Servetus* was apprehended and imprifoned. *Calvin* ingenuoufly
owns[a], That this whole Affair was carried on at his Inftance and Advice;
and that, in order to bring *Servetus* to Reafon, he himfelf found out the Party
to accufe him, and begin the Procefs againft him. And therefore, though,
as the forementioned Author of the *Bibliotheque* for *Jan. &c.* 1729. obferves, the Action after its Commencement was carried on according to the
Courfe of Law; yet, as *Calvin* accufed him for Herefy, got him imprifon'd,
and began the criminal Procefs againft him, he is anfwerable for all the Confequences of his Trial, and was in reality the firft and principal Author of his
Death, efpecially as the penal Laws againft Hereticks feem at that Time to
have been in force at *Geneva*, fo that *Servetus* could not efcape the Fire upon his
Conviction of Herefy.

When he was in Gaol he was treated with the fame Rigor as if he had been
detained in one of the Prifons of the Inquifition. He was ftripped of all Means of
procuring himfelf the Conveniencies and Supplies he needed in his Confinement.
They took from him ninety feven Pieces of Gold, a gold Chain worth twenty
Crowns, fix gold Rings, and at laft put him into a deep Dungeon, where he
was almoft eaten up with Vermin. All this Cruelty was practifed upon a Proteftant, in the Proteftant City of *Geneva*. Befides this, he could never get a
Proctor or Advocate to affift him, or help him in pleading his Caufe, though
he requefted it, as being a Stranger, and ignorant of the Laws and Cuftoms
of the Country. *Calvin*, at the Requeft of the Judges, drew up certain Propofitions out of *Servetus*'s Books, reprefenting them as blafphemous, full of
Errors, and prophane Reveries, all repugnant to the Word of God, and to
the common Confent of the whole Church; and, indeed, appears to have
been acquainted with, and confulted in the whole Procefs, and to have ufed
all his Arts and Endeavours to prevent his coming off with Impunity.

---

[a] Unus ex Syndicis, me autore, in carcerem duci juffit. Epift. ad *Sultzer*. Quum agnitus fu-
iffet, retinendum putavi. *Nicholaus* meus ad capitale judicium ipfum vocavit. Epift. ad *Farrel*.

'Tis

'Tis but a poor and mean Excuse that *Calvin* makes for himself in this respect, when he says, *As to the Fact I will not deny, but that 'twas at my Prosecu-*Epist. ad
tion he was imprison'd — *But that after he was convicted of his Heresies I made no*Farrel.
Instances for his being put to Death. But what need of Instances? He had already accused him, got him imprison'd, prosecuted in a criminal Court for
the capital Crime of Heresy, and actually drew up forty Articles against him
for Heresy, Blasphemy, and false Doctrine. When he was convicted of these
Crimes the Law could not but take its Course, and his being burnt to Death
was the necessary Consequence of his Conviction. What occasion was there
then for *Calvin* to press his Execution, when the Laws themselves had adjudged him to the Flames? But even this Excuse, poor as it is, is not sincerely and honestly made. For *Calvin* was resolved to use all his Interest to
destroy him. In his Letter to *Farrel* he expresly says[b], *I hope, at least, they will
condemn him to Death, but not to the terrible one of being burnt.* And in another to
Sultzer[c], *Since the Papists, in order to vindicate their own Superstitions cruelly shed
innocent Blood, 'tis a Shame that Christian Magistrates should have no Courage at
all in the Defence of certain Truth.* —— *However, I will certify you of one Thing,
that the City Treasurer is rightly determined, that he shall not escape that End which
we wish him.* And in another to the Church at *Franckfort*[d], *The Author* (Ser-Epist. ad
vetus) *is put in Gaol by our Magistrates, and I hope he'll shortly suffer the Punish-*Farrel.
ment he deserves. There was but one way possible for him to escape, and that
was by bringing his Cause from the criminal Court, where he was prosecuted,
before the Council of the two Hundred. And this *Calvin* vigorously opposed,
and reflected on the Syndick himself for endeavouring it. He says, that he
pretended Illness for three Days, and then came into Court to save that Wretch
(*Servetus*) from Punishment, and was not ashamed to demand, that the Cognisance of the Affair should be referred to the two Hundred. However, he was una-
nimously condemned. Now, what great Difference is there between a Prosecu-
tor's endeavouring to prevent the only Method by which a Criminal can be
saved, and his actually pressing for his being put to Death? *Calvin* actually
did the former, and yet would fain persuade us he had no hand in the latter.
'Tis much of a Piece with this, his desiring that the Rigor of *Servetus*'s Death
might be mitigated; for as the Laws against Hereticks were in force at *Geneva*, the Tribunal that judged *Servetus* could not, after his Conviction of
Heresy, absolve him from Death, nor change the manner of it, as *Calvin*
says, he would have had it; and therefore his desiring that the Rigor of it
might be abated, looks too much like the Practise of the Inquisitors, who

---

[b] Spero capitale saltem fore Judicium : Pœnæ vero atro citatem remitti cupio.   Epist. ad *Farrel.*
Cras ad supplicium ducetur.   Genus mortis conati sumus mutare, sed frustra.   Altera Epist.
ad *Farrel.*
   [c] Quum tam acres sunt & animosi superstitionum suarum vindices Papistæ, ut atrociter sæviant
ad fundendum innoxium sanguinem, pudeat Christianos Magistratus in tuenda certa veritate nihil
prorsus habere animi. —— Tantum unius rei te admonitum volo, Quæstorem Urbis —— in hac causa
recto esse animo, ut saltem exitum quem optamus non fugiat.
   [d] Auctor ipse tenetur in carcere a Magistratu nostro, & propediem, ut spero, daturus est pœnas.

when they deliver over an Heretick to the secular Arm, beseech it so to mode-rate the Rigor of the Sentence, as not to endanger Life or Limb.

This was the Part that *Calvin* acted in the Affair of *Servetus*, which I have represented in the most impartial Manner, as it appears to me ; and am sorry I am not able to wipe off so foul a Stain from the Memory of this otherwise ex-cellent and learned Reformer. But when his Enemies charge him with acting meerly from Principles of Malice and Revenge in this matter, I think it an evident Abuse and Calumny. He was, in his own Judgment, for persecuting and destroying Hereticks, as appears from the Treatise he published in Vindi-cation of this Practice, entitled [e], *A Declaration for maintaining the true Faith, held by all Christians, concerning the Trinity of Persons in One only God, by* John Calvin, *against the detestable Errors of* Michael Servetus, *a* Spaniard. *In which 'tis al-so proved, that it is lawful to punish Hereticks ; and that this Wretch was justly executed in the City of* Geneva. Geneva, 1554. This Principle was maintain-ed by almost all the Fathers and Bishops of the Church since the three first Centuries, who esteemed Heresy as one of the worst of Impieties, and thought it the Duty of the civil Magistrate to employ their Power for the Suppression of it, and for the Support and Establishment of the orthodox Faith. And though the first Reformers abhorred the Cruelty of the Papists towards the Protestants, they had neverthelesse the same Abhorrence of what they counted Heresy that the Papists had, and agreed with them in the Lawfulness of sup-pressing it by the civil Power. So that *Calvin* acted in this Affair from a Prin-ciple, though a mistaken Principle of Conscience, and had the Encouragement and Approbation of the most learned and pious Reformers of the Times he lived in. *Melancton*, in a Letter to *Bullinger*, says, *I have read also what you have written concerning the Blasphemies of* Servetus, *and I approve your Piety and Judgment. I think also, that the Senate of* Geneva *hath done right, that they have put to Death that obstinate Person who would not cease to blaspheme ; and I wonder that there are any who disapprove that Severity.* He affirms the same also in another Letter to *Calvin* himself. *Bucer* also said publickly in his Sermon, that *he ought to have his Bowels pulled out, and be torn in pieces,* as *Calvin* relates it in his Letter to *Sultzer*. *Farrel* in a Letter to *Calvin* says, that *he deserved to die ten Thousand Deaths, that it would be a Piece of Cruelty, and an Injustice to Christ, and the Doctrine of Piety, for Magistrates not to take notice of the horrible Blasphe-mies of that wicked Heretick. And he hoped God would so order it, that as the Ma-gistrates of* Geneva *were very Praise-worthy for punishing Thieves and sacrilegious Persons, so they would behave themselves well in the Affair of* Servetus, *by putting him to Death, who had so long obstinately persisted in his Heresies, and destroy'd so many Persons by them.*

The Pastors of the Church at *Basil*, in their Letter to the Syndicks and Se-nate of *Geneva*, express their Joy for the Apprehension of *Servetus*, and advise

---

[e] Declaration pour maintenir le vraye Foy que tiennent tous Chretiens de la Trinite des Per-sonnes en un seul Dieu , par *Jean Calvin*, contre les Erreurs detestables de *Michael Servetus*, *Espag-nol*, ou il est aussi montre qu'il est licite de punir les Heretiques : & qu' a bon droict ces Meschant a ete execute par Justice en la ville de *Geneve*. A Geneve, 1554.

them firſt to *uſe all Endeavours to recover him* ; *but that if he perſiſted in his Per-*
verſeneſs, they ſhould puniſh him according to their Office, and the Power they had
received from God, to prevent his giving any Diſturbance to the Church, and leſt the
latter end ſhould be worſe than the firſt. The Miniſters of the Church of *Bern*
were of the ſame Opinion, and in their Letter to the Magiſtrates of *Geneva* ſay,.
We pray the Lord that he would give you the Spirit of Prudence, Counſel and Strength,
to remove this Plague from the Churches, both your *own and others*, and adviſe them
to neglect nothing that may be judged unworthy a Chriſtian Magiſtrate to omit. The
Miniſters of *Zurich* give much the ſame Advice, and thought that there was
need of a great deal of Diligence in the Affair ; *eſpecially as the reformed Churches*
were evil thought of, amongſt other Reaſons, for this, as being themſelves heretical,
and Favourers of Hereticks. But that, as the Providence of God had given them an
Opportunity of wiping off ſo evil a Suſpicion, and preventing the farther ſpreading of
ſo contagious a Poiſon, they did not doubt but their Excellencies would be careful to im-
prove it. Thoſe of *Scaffhuſen* ſubſcribed to the Judgment of thoſe of *Zurich*,
and declare, that they did not doubt, but that their Prudence would put a
ſtop to the Attempts of *Servetus*, leſt his Blaſphemies, as a Canker, ſhould
eat up the Members of Chriſt ; adding theſe remarkable Words, *That to endea-*
vour to oppoſe his Dreams by a train of Reaſoning, what would it be, but to grow mad
with a Madman.

Theſe Extracts, which are taken out of the Letters printed at the End of
Calvin's Inſtitutions, clearly demonſtrate, that he acted ſeriouſly and deliberately in the Affair of *Servetus*, and that he conſulted the neighbouring
Churches; and had their Opinion of the Lawfulneſs and Expediency of putting
him to Death for his Hereſies. And though it doth not wholly excuſe his
Fault, yet it ought in Juſtice to be allowed as an Abatement and Extenu-
ation of it ; and, I think, evidently proves, what his Enemies are very unwilling to allow, that he was not tranſported by Rage and Fury, and did not
act meerly from the Dictates of Envy and Malice, but from a miſtaken Zeal
againſt what he accounted Blaſphemy and Hereſy, and with the concurrent
Advice of his Brethren in the Miniſtry, and Fellow-Labourers in the great
Work of the Reformation. And I think his eminent Services to the Church
of God, both by his Preaching and Writings, ought, notwithſtanding all his
Failings, to ſecure to his Memory the Honour and Reſpect that is due to it.
For he deſerved well of all the reformed Churches, and was an eminent Inſtrument in the Hand of Providence, in promoting the great and glorious Work
of ſaving Men from the groſs Errors, Superſtitions, and Idolatries of the
Romiſh Church. And as I thought my ſelf obliged impartially to repreſent
theſe Things as they appear'd to me, I hope all who love to diſtinguiſh themſelves by *Calvin's* Name, will be careful not to imitate him in this great Ble-
miſh of his Life; which, in reality, hath tarniſh'd a Character, that would
otherwiſe have appeared amongſt the firſt and brighteſt of the Age he
lived in.

In the Year 1632. after *Calvin's* Death, one *Nicholas Anthoine* was condemned alſo by the Council of *Geneva* to be firſt hanged, and afterwards burnt,
becauſe,

because, that having forgotten the Fear of God, he had committed the Crime of Apostacy and High-Treason against God, by having opposed the Holy Trinity, denied our Lord and Saviour Jesus Christ, blasphemed his holy Name, renounced his Baptism, and the like.

Bern.
Beza in
vit. Calv.
B. Aret.
Hist. Val.
Gent.

Valentinus Gentilis, a Native of *Cosentia* in *Italy,* had the Misfortune also to fall into some heterodox Opinions concerning the Trinity, and held, that the Father alone was αυτοθεϴ, God of himself, αγεννηϴ, unbegotten, *Essentiator,* the giver of Essence to all other Beings; but that the Son was *Essentiatus,* of a derived Essence from the Father, and therefore not αυτοθεϴ, or God of himself, though at the same Time he allowed him to be truly God. He held much the same as to the Holy Ghost, making them Three eternal Spirits, distinguish'd by a gradual and due Subordination, reserving the Monarchy to the Father, whom he stiled the One only God. Being forced to fly his native Country on Account of his Religion he came to *Geneva,* where there was a Church of *Italian* Refugees, several of whom, such as *G. Blandrata,* a Physician, *Gribaldus* a Lawyer, and *Paulus Alciatus,* differ'd from the commonly received Notions of the Trinity. When their Heterodoxes came to be known at *Geneva,* they were cited before the Senators, Ministers, and Presbyters; and being heard in their own Defence, were refuted by *Calvin,* and all subscribed to the orthodox Faith. But *V. Gentilis* having after this endeavoured to propagate his own Opinions, he was again apprehended, and forced by *Calvin* and others to a publick Abjuration, and condemned *An.* 1558. to an exemplary Penance, *viz.* " That he should be stripped close " to his Shirt, then bare-foot and bare-headed should carry in his Hand a " lighted Torch, and beg God and the Court's Pardon on his Knees, by con- " fessing himself maliciously and wickedly to have spread Abroad a false and " heretical Doctrine; but that he did now from his Heart detest and abhor " those abominable, lying, and blasphemous Books, he had composed in its " Defence; in testimony of which he was to cast them, with his own Hands, " into the Flames, there to be burnt to Ashes. And for more ample Satis- " faction, he was enjoined to be led through all the Streets of *Geneva,* at the " sound of Trumpet, in his penitential Habit, and strictly commanded not " to depart the City without Permission." And this Penance he actually underwent. But having found means to make his Escape, he came at last to *Gaium,* a Prefecture, subject to the Canton of *Bern,* where he was seized and imprisoned by the Governor, who immediately sent an Account of his Apprehension to the Senate of *Bern,* who ordered him to be brought Prisoner to that City, where they put him in Gaol. After they had seized all his Books and Papers, they collected several Articles, with the Heads of an Indictment out of them to be preferred against him. Amongst others these were two, 1. *That he dissented from us and all the Orthodox in the Doctrine of the Trinity.* And, 2. *That his Writings contain'd many impious Blasphemies, concerning the Trinity.* And because he continued obstinate in his Opinions, notwithstanding the Endeavours of the Divines to convert him, he was condemned by the Senate, for his Blasphemies against the Son of God, and the glorious Mystery of the Trinity,

I   to

to be beheaded, which Sentence was executed on him in *September*, *Anno* 1566.

At *Bafil* alfo Herefy was a Crime punifhable with Death, fince the Refor-_{Bafil.} mation, as appears from the Treatment of the dead Body of *David George*, an Brandt enthufiaftical Anabaptift. Having left *Holland* he went to *Bafil*, and fettled Hift. Book there as one that was banifhed out of his Country for the fake of his Religion, 3. p. 77. propagating his own Doctrines by Letters, Books, and Meffengers in *Holland*. But his Errors being difcovered after his Death, he was taken out of his Grave, and together with his Books and Pictures burnt to Afhes, by order of the Magiftrates, at the Place of Execution, without the Walls of *Bafil*, *May* 13, 1559. His Opinions were firft extracted from the printed Books and Manufcript Papers found in his Houfe, and he declared an Arch-Heretick.

Zurich alfo furnifhes us with an Inftance of great Cruelty towards an Ana-Zurich. baptift. A fevere Edict was publifhed againft them, in which there was a Book 2. Penalty of a filver Mark, about four Shillings *Englifh* Money, fet upon all P. 57. fuch as fhould fuffer themfelves to be re-baptized, or fhould with-hold Baptifm from their Children. And it was further declared, That thofe who openly oppofed this Order, fhould be yet more feverely treated. Accordingly one *Felix* was drowned at *Zurich* upon the Sentence pronounced by *Zuinglius*, in thefe four Words, *Qui interum mergit, mergatur. He that redips let him be drowned.* This happen'd in the Year 1526. About the fame Time alfo, and fince, there were fome more of them put to Death. From the fame Place alfo *Ochinus* was banifhed, in his old Age, in the Depth of Winter, toge-Bez Epift. ther with his Children, becaufe he was an *Arian*, and defended Poligamy, I. if *Beza*'s Account of him be true.

Lubieniecius, a *Polifh* Unitarian, was through the Practices of the *Calvinifts*, Poland. banifhed with his Brethren from *Poland*, his native Country, and forced to Vit. Lub. leave feveral Proteftant Cities of *Germany*, to which he had fled for Refuge, praf. Hift. particularly *Stetin*, *Frederickftadt*, and *Hamburgh*, through the Practices of Polon. the *Lutheran* Divines, who were againft all Toleration. At *Hamburgh* he received the Orders of the Magiftrates of the City to depart the Place on his Death-bed; and when his dead Body was carried to *Altenau* to be interr'd, though the Preachers could not, as they endeavour'd, prevent his being buried in the Church, yet they did actually prevent the ufual funeral Honours being paid him. *John Sylvanus*, Superintendant of the Church of *Heidelberg*, was put to Death by order of *Frederick* Elector *Palatine*, *An.* 1571. being accufed Lub. Hift. of *Arianifm*. l. 2. c. 5.

If we pafs over into *Holland*, we fhall alfo find, that the Reformers there Holland. were moft of them in the Principles and Meafures of Perfecution, and managed their Differences with that Heat and Fury as gave great Advantages to the Papifts, their common Enemies. In the very Infancy of the Reformation the *Lutherans* and *Calvinifts* condemned each other for their fuppofed Heterodoxy in the Affair of the Sacrament, and looked upon compliance and mutual Toleration to be Things intolerable. Thefe Differences were kept up principally

by

by the Clergy of each Party. The Prince of *Orange*, and States of *Holland*, who were heartily inclined to the Reformation, were not for confining their Protection to any particular Set of Principles or Opinions, but for granting an univerfal Indulgence in all Matters of Religion, aiming at Peace and mutual Forbearance, and to open the Church as wide as poffible for all Chriftians of unblameable Lives; whereas the Clergy being biaffed by their Paffions and Inclinations for thofe Mafters, in whofe Writings they had been inftructed, endeavoured with all their Might to eftablifh and conciliate Authority to their refpective Opinions; aiming only at Decifions and Definitions, and fhutting up the Church by Limitations in many doubtful and difputable Articles; fo that the Difturbances which were raifed, and the Severities which were ufed upon the Account of Religion, proceeded from the Bigotry of the Clergy, contrary to the Defire and Intention of the civil Magiftrate.

Before the Minifters of the reformed Party were engaged in the Controverfy with *Arminius*, their Zeal was continually exerting it felf againft the Anabaptifts, whom they declared to be excommunicated and cut off from the Church, and endeavoured to convert by Violence and Force, prohibiting them from preaching under Fines, and banifhing them their Country, upon account of their Opinions. And the better to colour thefe Proceedings, fome of them wrote in defence of Perfecution; or which is the fame Thing, againft the Toleration of any Religion or Opinions different from their own; and for the better Support of Orthodoxy, they would have had the Synods ordain, that all Church Officers fhould renew their Subfcriptions to the Confeffion and Catechifm every Year, that hereby they might the better know who had changed their Sentiments, and differed from the received Faith. This Practice was perfectly agreeable to the *Geneva* Difcipline; *Calvin* himfelf, as hath been fhewn, being in Judgment for perfecuting Hereticks; and *Beza* having wrote a Treatife, *An.* 1600. to prove the Lawfulnefs of punifhing them. This Book was tranflated from the *Latin*, into the *Low Dutch* Language by *Bogerman*, afterwards Prefident of the Synod of *Dort*, and publifhed with a Dedication, and Recommendation of it to the Magiftrates. The Confequence of this was, that very fevere Placarts were publifhed againft the Anabaptifts in *Friefland* and *Groningen*, whereby they were forbidden to preach; and all Perfons prohibited from letting their Houfes and Grounds to them, under the Penalty of a large Fine, or Confinement to Bread and Water for fourteen Days. If they offended the third Time, they were to be banifhed the City, and the Jurifdiction thereof. Whofoever was difcovered to rebaptize any Perfon fhould forfeit twenty Dollars; and upon a fecond Conviction be put to Bread and Water, and then be banifhed. Unbaptifed Children were made incapable of inheriting; and if any married out of the reformed Church, he was declared incapable of inheriting any Eftate, and the Children made illegitimate.

But the Controverfy that made the greateft Noife, and produced the moft remarkable Effects, was that carried on between the *Calvinifts* and *Arminians*. *Jacobus Arminius*, one of the Profeffors of Divinity at *Leyden*, difputing in his turn about the Doctrine of Predeftination, advanced feveral Things differing
from

Brandt. Hift. V 2. l.17.

from the Opinions of *Calvin* on this Article, and was in a few Months after warmly oppofed by *Gomarus* his Collegue, who held, That *'twas appointed by an eternal Decree of God, who amongft Mankind fhall be faved, and who fhall be damned.* This was indeed the Sentiment of moft of the Clergy of the *United Provinces,* who therefore endeavoured to run down *Arminius* and his Doctrine with the greateft Zeal, in their private Converfations, publick Difputes, and in their very Sermons to their Congregations, charging him with Innovations, and of being a Follower of the ancient heretical Monk *Pelagius* ; whereas the Government was more inclinable to *Arminius*'s Scheme, as being lefs rigid in its Nature, and more intelligible by the People, and endeavoured all they could to prevent thefe Differences of the Clergy from breaking out into an open Quarrel, to the Difturbance of the publick Peace. But the Minifters of the Predeftinarian Party would enter into no Treaty for Peace : The Remonftrants were the Objects of their furious Zeal, whom they called *Mamalukes, Devils, and Plagues,* animating the Magiftrates to extirpate and deftroy them, and crying out from the Pulpits, *We muft go through thick and thin, without fearing to ftick in the Mire : We know what* Elijah *did to* Baal's *Priefts,* And when the Time drew near for the Election of new Magiftrates, they prayed to God for fuch Men, *as would be zealous even to Blood, though it were to coft the whole Trade of their Cities.* They alfo accufed them of keeping up a Correfpondence with the Jefuits and *Spaniards,* and of a Defign to betray their Country to them.

These Proceedings gave great Difturbance to the Magiftrates, efpecially as many of the Clergy took great Liberties with them, furioufly inveighing againft them in their Sermons as Enemies to the Church, and Perfecutors ; as Libertines and Free-Thinkers, who hated the fincere Minifters of God, and endeavoured to turn them out of their Office. This Conduct, together with their obftinate Refufal of all Meafures of Accommodation, and Peace with the Remonftrants, fo incenfed the Magiftrates, that in feveral Cities they fufpended fome of the warmeft and moft feditious of them, and prohibited them from the publick Exercifes of their minifterial Function ; particularly *Gezelius* of *Roterdam,* and afterwards *Rofæus,* Minifter at the *Hague,* for endeavouring to make a Schifm in the Church, and exhorting the People to break off Communion with their Brethren. Being thus difcarded, they affumed to themfelves the Name of the perfecuted Church, and met together in private Houfes, abfolutely refufing all Communion with the Remonftrant Minifters and Party, in fpite of all the Attempts made ufe of to reconcile and unite them.

What the Minifters of the Contraremonftrant Party aimed at, was the holding a national Council, which at length, after a long Oppofition, was agreed to in the Affembly of the *States General,* who appointed *Dort* for the Place of the Meeting. Prince *Maurice* of *Orange,* the Stadholder, effectually prepared Matters for holding the faid Affembly ; and as he declared himfelf openly for the Contraremonftrant Party, not for that he was of their Opinions in Religion, being rather inclined to thofe of *Arminius,* but becaufe he thought them the beft

Friends

Friends to his Family, he took Care that the Council fhould confift of fuch Perfons as were well affected to them.　In order to this his Excellency changed the Government of moft of the Towns of *Holland,* depofed thofe Magiftrates who were of the Remonftrant Perfuafion, or that favoured them in the Bufinefs of the Toleration, and filled up their Places with Contraremonftrants, or fuch as promoted their Interefts, making ufe of the Troops of the States to obviate all Oppofition.　The Confequence of this was the Imprifonment of feveral great Men of the Remonftrant Perfuafion, fuch as the Advocate *Oldenbarnevelt, Grotius* and others; and the Sufpenfion, or total Deprivation of a confiderable Number of the Remonftrant Clergy, fuch as *Vitenbogart* of the *Hague, Grovinckbovius* of *Roterdam, Grevius* and others, by particular Synods met together for that purpofe, and to prepare Things, and appoint Perfons for the enfuing national one at *Dort.*　The Perfons fixed on were generally the moft violent of the Contraremonftrant Party, and who had publickly declared, that they would not enter into Communion with thofe who differ'd from them, nor agree to any Terms of Moderation and Peace.　There were alfo feveral foreign Divines fummoned to this Council, who were moft of them in the *Calviniftick* Scheme, and profeffed Enemies to the *Arminians.*　The Lay Commiffioners alfo, who were chofen by the States, were moft of them very partial Contraremonftrants, and two or three of them, who feemed more impartial than the others, were hardly fuffered to fpeak; and if they did, were prefently fufpected, and reprefented by Letters fent to the States, and Prince *Maurice* at the *Hague,* as Perfons that favoured the Remonftrants, which was then confider'd as a Crime againft the Government, infomuch that by thefe Infinua-

*The Coun-*tions, they were in danger of being ftripped of all their Employments.　The
cil of Dort, firft Seffion and Opening of this venerable Affembly, was *Nov.* 13, 1618.
A.C *John Rogerman* was chofen Prefident of it; the fame worthy and moderate Di-
1618. vine, who had before tranflated into *Low Dutch Beza*'s Treatife, to prove the Lawfulnefs of punifhing Hereticks, with a Preface Recommendatory to the civil Magiftrate; chofen, not by the whole Synod, but by the Low Country Divines only, the Foreigners not being allowed any Share in the Election.

At the fifth Seffion the Remonftrants petitioned the Synod, That a competent Number of their Friends might have leave to appear before them, and that the Citation might be fent to the whole Body, and not to any fingle Perfon, to the End that they might be at liberty to fend fuch as they fhould judge beft qualified to defend their Caufe; and particularly infifted, that *Grovinckbovius* and *Goulart* might be of the Number.　One would have thought that fo equitable a Requeft fhould have been readily granted.　But they were told, that it could not be allowed that the Remonftrants fhould pafs for a diftinct Body, or make any Deputation of Perfons in their common Name to treat of their Affairs; and agreeably to this Declaration the Summons that were given out, were not fent to the Remonftrants as a Body or Part of the Synod, but to fuch particular Perfons as the Synod thought fit to chofe out of them; which was little lefs than citing them as Criminals before a Body of
Men,

Men, which chiefly confifted of their profeffed Adverfaries. When they firft Act. Syn.
appeared in the Synod, and *Epifcopius* in the Name of the reft of them, talked Dord. Seff.
of entring into a regular Conference about the Points in difference ; they were ¹¹.
immediately given to underftand, that no Conference was intended, but that
their only Bufinefs was to deliver their Sentiments, and humbly to wait for the
Judgment of the Council concerning them, *Epifcopius*, in the Name of his
Brethren, declared, that they did not own the Synod for their lawful Judges,
becaufe moft of that Body were their avowed Enemies, and Fomenters and Promoters of the unhappy Schifm amongft them ; upon which they were immediately reprimanded by the Prefident, for impeaching and arraigning their Authority, and prefuming to prefcribe Laws to thofe whom the *States General* had
appointed for their Judges. The Divines of *Geneva* added upon this Head,
*That if People obftinately refufed to fubmit to the lawful Determinations of the Church,
there then remained two Methods to be ufed againft them ; the one, that the civil Magiftrate might ftretch out his Arm of Compulfion ; the other, that the Church might
exert her Power, in order to feparate and cut off by a publick Sentence, thofe who
violated the Laws of God.* After many Debates on this Head, between the Synod and the Remonftrants, who adhered to their Refolution, of not owning
the Synod for their Judges, they were turned out of it by *Bogerman* the Prefident with great Infolence and Fury ; to the high Diffatisfaction of many of the
foreign Divines.

After the Holy Synod had thus rid themfelves of the Remonftrants, whofe
Learning and good Senfe would have rendered them exceeding troublefome to
this Affembly, they proceeded to fix the Faith ; and as they had no Oppofition
to fear, and were almoft all of one fide, at leaft in the main Points, they
agreed in their Articles and Canons ; and in their Sentence againft the Remonftrant Clergy who had been cited to appear before them; which was to this
Effect : " They befeeched and charged in the Name of Chrift, all and fingular
" the Minifters of the Churches throughout the united *Netherlands*, &c. that
" they forfake and abandon the well known five Articles of the Remonftrants,
" as being falfe, and no other than Secret Magazines of Errors ——— And
" whereas fome, who are gone out from amongft us, calling themfelves Re-
" monftrants, have out of private Views and Ends, unlawfully violated the
" Difcipline and Government of the Church ——— have not only trumped up
" old Errors, but hammered out new ones too ——— have blackened and ren-
" dered odious the eftablifhed Doctrine of the Church with impudent Slan-
" ders and Calumnies, without end or meafure, have filled all Places with
" Scandal, Difcord, Scruples, Troubles of Confcience ——— all which heinous
" Offences ought to be reftrained and punifhed in Clergymen with the fevereft
" Cenfures : Therefore this national Synod ——— being affured of its own
" Authority ——— doth hereby declare and determine, that thofe Minifters,
" who have acted in the Churches as Heads of Factions, and Teachers of Er-
" rors, are guilty, and convicted of having violated our Holy Religion,
" having made a Rent in the Unity of the Church, and given very great Scan-
" dal : And as for thofe who were cited before this Synod, that they are be-

" fides

" fides guilty of intolerable Difobedience ———— to the Commands of the
" venerable Synod : For all which Reafons the Synod doth in the firft Place,
" difcharge the aforefaid cited Perfons from all ecclefiaftical Adminiftrations,
" and deprive them of their Offices, judging them likewife unworthy of any
" academical Employment ——— And as for the reft of the Remonftrant Cler-
" gy, they are hereby recommended to the Provincial Synods, Claffes and
" Confiftories ——— who are to take the utmoft care ——— that the Patrons of
" Errors be prudently difcovered ; that all obftinate, clamorous, and factious
" Difturbers of the Church, under their Jurifdiction, be forthwith deprived
" of their ecclefiaftical and academical Offices —— And they the faid provin-
" cial Synods are therefore exhorted ——— to take a particular Care, that they
" admit none into the Miniftry who fhall refufe to fubfcribe, or promife to
" preach the Doctrine afferted in thefe Synodical Decrees ; and that they fuf-
" fer none to continue in the Miniftry, by whofe publick Diffent the Doctrine
" which hat . been fo unanimoufly approved by all the Members of this Synod,
" the Harmony of the Clergy, and the Peace of the Church, may be again
" difturbed ——— And they moft earneftly and humbly befeech their gracious
" God, that their High Mightineffes may fuffer and ordain this wholefome
" Doctrine, which the Synod hath faithfully expreffed ——— to be maintained
" alone, and in its Purity within their Provinces ——— and reftrain turbulent
" and unruly Spirits ——— and may likewife put in Execution the Sentence
" pronounced againft the above-mentioned Perfons ——— and ratify and con-
" firm the Decrees of the Synod by their Authority.

The States readily obliged them in this Chriftian and Charitable Requeft ; for
as foon as the Synod was concluded the old Advocate *Barnevelt* was beheaded, who
had been a zealous and hearty Friend to the Remonftrants and their Principles ;
and *Grotius* condemned to perpetual Imprifonment ; and becaufe the cited
Minifters would not promife wholly, and always to abftain from the Exercife
of their minifterial Functions, the States paffed a Refolution for the banifhing
of them, on pain if they did not fubmit to it, of being treated as Difturbers
of the publick Peace. And though they only begged a refpite of the Sentence for a few Days, to put their Affairs in order, and to provide themfelves with a little Money to fupport themfelves and Families in their Banifhment, even this was unmercifully denied them, and they were hurried away
next Morning by four a Clock, as though they had been Enemies to the
Religion and Liberties of their Country.

Such was the Effect of this famous Prefbyterian Synod, who behaved themfelves
as tyrannically towards their Brethren, as any prelatical Council whatfoever
could do ; and to the Honour of the Church of *England* it muft be faid, that they
owned their Synodical Power, and concurred by their Deputies, *Carleton* Bifhop
of *Landaff*, *Hall*, *Davenant*, and *Ward*, in condemning the Remonftrants, in
excommunicating and depriving them, and turning them out of their Churches,
and in eftablifhing both the Difcipline and Doctrines of *Geneva* in the *Netherlands*.
For after the Council was ended, the Remonftrants were every where driven out
of their Churches, and prohibited from holding any private Meetings, and many
of

of them baniſhed on this very account. The Reader will find a very particular Relation of theſe Tranſactions, in the learned *Gerard Brandt*'s Hiſtory of
the Reformation of the *Low Countries*, to which I muſt refer him.

If we look into our own Country we ſhall find numerous Proofs of the
ſame antichriſtian Spirit and Practice. Even our firſt Reformers, who had
ſeen the Flames which the Papiſts had kindled againſt their Brethren, yet
lighted Fires themſelves to conſume thoſe who differed from them. *Cranmer*'s
Hands were ſtained with the Blood of ſeveral. He had a Share in the Proſecution and Condemnation of that pious and excellent Martyr *John Lambert* ;
and conſented to the Death of *Ann Aſkew*, who were burnt for denying the corporal Preſence, which, though *Cranmer* then believed, he ſaw afterwards reaſon to deny. In the Year 1549. *Joan Bocher* was condemned for ſome enthu-
ſiaſtical Opinions about Chriſt, and delivered over to the ſecular Power.
The Sentence being returned to the Council, King *Edward* VI. was moved to
ſign a Warrant for her being burnt, but could not be prevailed with to do it.
Cranmer endeavoured to perſuade him by ſuch Arguments as rather ſilenced
than ſatisfied the young King. So he ſet his Hand to the Warrant with Tears
in his Eyes, ſaying to the Archbiſhop, that if he did wrong, ſince it was in
Submiſſion to his Authority, he ſhould anſwer for it to God. Though this
ſtruck *Cranmer* with Horror, yet he at laſt put the Sentence in Execution
againſt her. About two Years after one *George Van Pare*, a *Dutch* Man, was
accuſed before them, for ſaying, That God the Father was only God, and
that Chriſt was not very God. And though he was a Perſon of a very holy
Life, yet becauſe he would not abjure, he was condemned for Hereſy, and
burnt in *Smithfield*. The Archbiſhop himſelf was afterwards burnt for Hereſy,
which, as *Fox* obſerved, many looked on a juſt Retaliation from the Providence of God, for the cruel Severities he had uſed towards others.

The Controverſy about the Popiſh Habits was one of the firſt that aroſe
amongſt the *Engliſh* Reformers. *Cranmer* and *Ridley* were zealous for the Uſe
of them, whilſt other very pious and learned Divines were for laying them
aſide, as the Badges of Idolatry and Antichriſt. Amongſt theſe was Doctor
Hooper, nominated to the Biſhoprick of *Gloceſter* ; but becauſe he refuſed to be
conſecrated in the old Veſtments, he was, by Order of Council firſt ſilenced,
and then confined to his own Houſe ; and afterwards, by *Cranmer*'s Means,
committed to the *Fleet* Priſon, where he continued ſeveral Months.

In the beginning of Queen *Elizabeth*'s Reign, *A. C.* 1559. an Act paſſed
for the Uniformity of Common Prayer, and Service in the Church, and Adminiſtration of the Sacraments, by which the Queen and Biſhops were empow-
red to ordain ſuch Ceremonies in Worſhip, as they ſhould think for the Honour of God, and the Edification of his Church. This Act was rigorouſly
preſſed, and great Severities uſed to ſuch as could not comply with it. *Parker*
Archbiſhop of *Canterbury*, made the Clergy ſubſcribe to uſe the preſcribed
Rites and Habits, and cited before him many of the moſt famous Divines who
ſcrupled them, and would allow none to be preſented to Livings, or preferred
in the Church, without an intire Conformity. He ſummoned the whole Body
of

*Great-
Britain.*

Burnet's
Hiſt. Ref.
Vol. II. p.
106, 107.

*Queen
Elizabeth.*

of the *London* Paftors and Curates to appear before him at *Lambeth*, and immediately fufpended Thirty feven, who refufed to fubfcribe to the Unity of Apparel, and fignified to them, that within three Months they fhould be totally
deprived if they would not conform. So that many Churches were fhut up ;
and though the People were ready to mutiny for want of Minifters, yet the
Archbifhop was deaf to all their Complaints, and in his great Goodnefs and
Piety was refolved they fhould have no Sacraments or Sermons without the
Surplice and the Cap. And in order to prevent all Oppofition to Church
Tyranny, the *Star Chamber* publifhed a Decree for Sealing up the Prefs, and
prohibiting any Perfon to print or publifh any Book againft the Queen's In-
junctions, or againft the Meaning of them. This Decree was figned by the
Bifhops of *Canterbury* and *London*.

This rigid and fanatical Zeal for Habits and Ceremonies, caufed the Puritans to feparate from the Eftablifhed Church, and to hold private Affemblies
for Worfhip. But the Queen and her Prelates foon made them feel their Vengeance. Their Meetings were difturbed, and thofe who attended them apprehended, and fent in large Numbers, Men and Women, to *Bridewell*, for
Conviction. Others were cited into the *Spiritual Courts*, and not difchargod
till after long Attendance and great Charges. Subfcriptions to Articles of
Faith were violently preffed upon the Clergy, and about one Hundred of
them were deprived, *Anno* 1572. for refufing to fubmit to them. Some were
clofely imprifoned, and died in Gaol, through Poverty and Want. And that
ferious Piety, and Chriftian Knowledge might gain Ground, as well as Uniformity, the Bifhops, by order of the Queen, put down the Prophefyings of
the Clergy, *Anno* 1574. who were forbid to affemble, as they had done for
fome Years, to difcourfe with one another upon religious Subjects and Sermons ; and as fome ferious Perfons of the Laity were ufed to meet on Holy
Days, or after they had done work, to read the Scriptures, and to improve
themfelves in Chriftian Knowledge ; the Parfons of the Parifhes were fent for,
and ordered to fupprefs them. Eleven *Dutch* Men, who were Anabaptifts,
were condemned in the Confiftory of St. *Paul* to the Fire, for Herefy ; nine
of whom were banifhed, and two of them burnt alive in *Smithfield*. In the
Year 1583. *Copping* and *Thacker*, two Puritan Minifters, were hanged for
Non-Conformity. It would be endlefs to go through all the Severities
that were ufed in this Reign upon the Account of Religion. As the Queen.was
of a very high and arbitrary Temper, fhe preffed Uniformity with great
Violence, and found Bifhops enough, *Parker*, *Aylmer*, *Whitgift*, and others,
to juftify and promote her Meafures ; who either enter'd their Sees with perfecuting Principles, or embraced them foon after their Entrance, as beft be-
fitting the Ends of their Promotion. Silencings, Deprivations, Imprifonments,
Gibbets, and Stakes, upon the Account of Religion, were fome of the powerful Reafonings of thofe Times. The Bifhops rioted in Power, and many of
them abufed it to the moft cruel Oppreffions. The Cries of innocent Prifoners, widowed Wives, and ftarving Children, made no Impreffion on their
Hearts. Piety and Learning with them were void of Merit. Refufal of

2   Sub-

Subfcriptions, and Non-Conformity were Crimes never to be forgiven. A particular Account of thefe Things may be feen in Mr. *Neal's* excellent Hiftory of the Puritans, who hath done Juftice to that Subject. I fhall only add, That the Court of High-Commiffion eftablifhed in this Reign, by the Inftigation of *Whitgift*, Archbifhop of *Canterbury*, by which the Commiffioners were impowered to enquire into all Mifdemeanors, by all fuch Ways and Means as they could devife, and thought neceffary, to examine Perfons upon Oath, and to punifh thofe who refufed the Oath by Fine or Imprifonment, according to their Difcretion, was an high Stretch of the Prerogative, and had a very near Refemblance to the Courts of Inquifition, and the Cruelties that were practifed in it, and the exorbitant Fines that were levied by it in the two following Reigns, made it the univerfal Abhorrence of the Nation, fo that it was diffolved by Parliament, with a Claufe that no fuch Court fhould be erected for the future.

King *James* I. who was bred up in the Kirk of *Scotland*, which profeffed the Faith and Difcipline of thofe called Puritans in *England*; and though he bleffed God, *For honouring him to be King over fuch a Kirk, the fincereft Kirk in the World,* yet, upon his Acceffion to the *Englifh* Throne, foon fhewed his Averfion to the Conftitution of that Kirk; and to their Brethren, the Puritans in *England.* . Thefe were folicitous for a farther Reformation in the Church, which the Bifhops oppofed, inftilling this Maxim into the King, *No Bifhop no King*; which, as ftale and falfe a Maxim as it is, hath been lately trumpt up, and publickly recommended, in a Sermon on the 30th of *January.* In the Conference at *Hampton* Court his Majefty not only fided with the Bifhops, but affured the Puritan Minifters, who were fent for to it, that *he had not called the Affembly together for any Innovations, for that he acknowledged the Government Ecclefiaftical, as it then was, to have been approved by God himfelf*; giving them to underftand, that *if they did not conform, he would either hurry them out of the Kingdom, or elfe do worfe.* And thefe Reafonings of the King's were fo ftrong, that *Whitgift,* Archbifhop of *Canterbury*, with an impious and fordid Flattery faid, *He was verily perfuaded that the King fpoke by the Spirit of God.* 'Twas no wonder that the Bifhops, thus fupported by an infpired King, fhould get an eafy Victory over the Puritans, which poffibly they would not have done, had his Majefty been abfent, and the Aids of his Infpiration withdrawn, fince the Archbifhop did not pretend that himfelf or his Brethren had any fhare of it. But having thus gotten the Victory, they ftrove by many Methods of Violence to maintain it; and ufed fuch Severities towards the Non-Conformifts, that they were forced to feek Refuge in foreign Countries. The Truth is, this Conference at *Hampton* Court was never intended to fatisfy the Puritans, but as a Blind to introduce Epifcopacy into *Scotland*, and to fubvert the Conftitution and Eftablifhment of that Church.

His Majefty, in one of his Speeches to his Parliament, tells them, that *he was never violent and unreafonable in his Profeffion of Religion.* I believe all Mankind will now acquit him of any violent and unreafonable Attachment to the Proteftant Religion and Liberties. He added in the fame Speech, it may be queftion-

James I.

Wilfon.

Heylin's *Life of Whitgift,* Laud, p. 58.

queftioned, whether by Infpiration of the Spirit, *I acknowledge the* Roman *Church to be our Mother Church, although defiled with fome Infirmities and Corruptions.* And he did behave as a very dutiful Son of that Mother Church, by the many Favours he fhewed to the Papifts during his Reign, by his Proclamations for Uniformity in Religion, and encouraging and fupporting his Bifhops in their Perfecutions of fuch as differ'd from, or could not fubmit to them. *Bancroft,* promoted to the Archbifhoprick of *Canterbury,* was, as the

Wilfon. Hiftorian calls him, *A fturdy Piece,* a cruel and inflexible Perfecutor, treating
Life of the Non-Conformifts with the greateft Rigor and Severity ; and who, as *Hey-*
Laud, *lin* tells us, *was refolved to break them, if they would not bow.* He put the
p. 58. Canons and Conftitutions agreed on *A. C.* 1603. furioufly into Execution, and fuch as ftood out againft them, he either deprived or filenced. And

Wilfon. indeed, as the aforementioned Author fays, *Who could ftand againft a Man of fuch a Spirit, armed with Authority, having the Law on his Side, and the King to his Friend.* During his being Archbifhop he deprived, filenced, fufpended, and admonifhed, above three Hundred Minifters. The Violences he and his Brethren ufed in the High-Commiffion Courts, render'd it a publick Grievance.

Wilfon. *Every Man muft conform to the Epifcopal Way, and quit his Hold in Opinion or Safety. That Court was the Touchftone, to try whether Men were Metal for their Stamp ; and if they were not foft enough to take fuch Impreffions as were put upon them, they were made malleable there, or elfe they could not pafs current. This was the beginning of that Mifchief, which when it came to a full Ripenefs, made fuch a bloody Tincture in both Kingdoms, as never will be got out of the Bifhop's Lawn Sleeves.* But nothing difpleafed the fober Part of the Nation more, than the Publication of the Book of Sports, which the Bifhops procured from the King, and which came out with a Command, enjoining all Minifters to read it to their Parifhioners, and to approve of it ; and thofe who did not, were brought into the High-Commiffion, imprifoned, and fufpended ; this Book being only a Trap to catch fome confcientious Men, that they could not otherwife, with all their

Wilfon. Cunning, enfnare. *Thefe, and fuch like Machinations of the Bifhops,* fays my Author, *to maintain their temporal Greatnefs, Eafe, and Plenty, made the Stones in the Walls of their Palaces, and the Beam in the Timber afterwards cry out, moulder away, and come to nothing ;* and caufed their Light to go out *Offenfive to the Noftrils of the Rubbifh of the People.* Indeed many of the King's Bifhops, fuch as *Bancroft, Neal,* and *Laud,* who was a reputed Papift in *Oxford,* and a Man of a dangerous, turbulent Spirit, were fit for any Work ; and as they don't appear to have had any Principles of real Piety themfelves, they were the fitteft Tools that could be made ufe of to perfecute thofe who had. *Neal,* when he was Bifhop of *Litchfield* and *Coventry,* profecuted one *Edward Wightman,* for broaching erroneous Doctrine, and having canonically condemned him, got the King's Warrant for his Execution, and he was accordingly burnt in *Litchfield.* One *Legat* alfo, was profecuted and condemned for Herefy, by *King* Bifhop of *London,* and expired in the Flames of *Smithfield.* He denied the Divinity of our Saviour, according to the *Athanafian* Mode of explaining it ; but, as *Fuller* tells us, he was excellently fkilled in Scripture, and his

2   Con-

Converſation very unblameable. But as theſe Sacrifices were unacceptable to the People, the King preferred, that Hereticks hereafter, though condemn'd, ſhould ſilently and privately waſte themſelves away in Priſon, rather than to amuſe others with the Solemnity of a publick Execution.

In the Reign of the Royal Martyr, the Church was in the Height of her *Charles* I. Glory and Power ; though ſuch is the Fate of all human Things, that ſhe ſoon ſicken'd, languiſhed, and died. *Laud* carried all before him, and ruled the Church with a Rod of Iron ; and though he ſeems to have had too much Pride to ſubmit to the Pope of *Rome*, he acted the Part of a Pope himſelf, allowing himſelf, as *Heylin* tells us, to be addreſſed under the Titles of *Holineſs*, and *moſt holy Father*. The Things he ſeemed principally to have had at Heart, were the introducing an arbitrary Government into the State, the Suppreſſion and Extirpation of Nonconformity, and bringing the Church of *England*, in Rites and Ceremonies, to as near a Reſemblance as poſſibly he could, to the Church of *Rome*. This appears, by his protecting *Montague*, *Manwaring* and *Sibthorp*, who had infamouſly preach'd up the King's abſolute Power, and making the two former Biſhops of the Church ; by his perſecuting the Puritan Miniſters in the Star-Chamber and High Commiſſion Court, who, as *Heylin* tells us, *Laud* uſed to ſay, were as bad as the Papiſts, impriſoning and fining, and forcing many others to take Sanctuary in *New England* ; by his putting down and ſilencing all Lecturers throughout the ſeveral Dioceſes of the Kingdom, by his ſuſpending and ejecting ſuch as refuſed to read the Book of Sports, by his forcing the *French* and *Dutch* Churches to a Conformity with the Rites and Ceremonies of the Church of *England*, by his obliging the *Scots* to receive Epiſcopacy, a Liturgy and Canons, by his forming new Articles and eccleſiaſtical Conſtitutions for the *Engliſh* Clergy, and enjoining them a ſtrict Oath for the preventing of all Innovations ; by the many Popiſh Superſtitions he introduced into the publick Worſhip, ſuch as Altars, Tapers, Candles, Candleſticks, Copes, Hoods, Images, Pictures, Cringes, Bows, Conſecrations, and the like, and by the Lenity that was ſhewn throughout the whole of his Adminiſtration to the Papiſts themſelves, whilſt many worthy and learned Proteſtant Gentlemen and Divines were treated with the utmoſt Indignity and Barbarity ; ſome of them dying in Goal, and others being made to undergo the moſt cruel bodily Puniſhments, for daring to oppoſe the arbitrary and ſuperſtitious Proceedings of this furious and relentleſs Prelate. No Man of Compaſſion can read his Treatment of Dr. *Leighton* without being ſhocked and moved in the ſame tender Manner as the Houſe of Commons were, who ſeveral Times interrupted, by their Tears, the reading of the Doctor's Petition ; which I ſhall here preſent my Reader with entire, and leave him to form what Character he pleaſes of the Man, that could contrive and carry on ſuch a Scene of barbarous and execrable Cruelty.

To the Honourable and High Court of Parliament, The humble Petition of Alexander Leighton, *Prisoner in the* Fleet ;

Humbly Sheweth,

*H*O *W your much and long distressed Petitioner, on the* 17*th of* February *gone ten Years, was apprehended in* Black-Fryers, *coming from the Sermon, by a high Commission Warrant (to which no Subject's Body is liable) and thence, with a Multitude of Staves and Bills, was dragged along (and all the way reproached by the Name of* Jesuit *and Traitor) till they brought him to* London-house, *where he was shut up, and, by a strong Guard, kept (without Food) till seven of the Clock, till Dr.* Laud, *then Prelate of* London, *and Dr.* Corbet, *then of* Oxford, *returned from* Fulham house, *with a Troop attending. The Goaler of* Newgate *was sent for, who came with Irons, and with a strong Power of Halberts and Staves ; they carried your Petitioner through a blind hollow Way, without Pretence or Examination, and opening up a Gate into the Street (which some say, had not been opened since Queen* Mary's *Days) they thrust him into a loathsome and ruinous Dog-hole, full of Rats and Mice, which had no Light but a little Grate ; and the Roof being uncovered, the Snow and Rain beat in upon him, having no Bedding, nor Place to make a Fire, but the Ruins of an old smoaky Chimney ; where he had neither Meat nor Drink, from the* Tuesday *at Night, till the* Thursday *at Noon. In this woful Place, and doleful Plight, they kept him close, with two Doors shut upon him, for the Space of fifteen Weeks, suffering none to come at him, till at length, his Wife was only admitted.*

The fourth Day after his Commitment, the High Commission Pursevants came (under the Conduct of the Sheriffs of London) *to your Petitioner's House, and a mighty Multitude with them ; giving out, that they came to search for* Jesuits *Books. There those violent Fellows of Prey laid violent Hands upon your Petitioner's distressed Wife, with such barbarous Inhumanity as he is ashamed to express ; and so rifled, every Soul in the House, holding a bent Pistol to a Child's Breast of five Years old, threatning to kill him, if he would not tell where the Books were ; through which, the Child was so affrighted that he never cast it. They broke open Presses, Chests, Boxes, the Boards of the House, and every Thing they found in the Way, though they were willing to open all. They, and some of the Sheriffs Men, spoiled, robbed, and carried away all the Books and Manuscripts they found, with Houshold Stuff, your Petitioner's Apparel, Arms, and other Things ; so that they left nothing that liked them ; notwithstanding, your Petitioner's Wife told the Sheriffs, they might come to reckon for it. They carried also a great Number of divers of your Petitioner's Books, and other Things, from one Mr.* Archer's *House, as he will testify. Further, your Petitioner being denied the Copy of his Commitment, by the Goaler of* Newgate, *his Wife, with some Friends, repaired to the Sheriff, offering him bail, according to the Statute in that behalf ; which being shew'd by an Attorney at Law, the Sheriff replied, That he wished the Laws of the Land and Privileges of the Subject, had never been named in the Parliament, &c. Your Petitioner (having thus suffered in Body, Liberty, Family,*

Estate,

2

Eſtate, and Houſe) at the End of *fifteen Weeks was ſerved with a Subpœna, on In-formation laid againſt him by* Sir Robert Heath, *then his Majeſty's Attorney-General ; whoſe Dealing with your Priſoner was full of Cruelty and Deceit. In the mean Time it did more than appear, to four Phyſicians, that Poiſon had been given him in* Newgate ; *for his Hair and Skin came off in a Sickneſs (deadly to the Eye) in the Height whereof, as he did lie, cenſure was paſt againſt him in the Star Chamber, without hearing (which had not been heard of) notwithſtanding of a Certificate from four Phyſicians, and Affidavit made by an Attorney, of the Deſperateneſs of the Diſeaſe. But nothing would ſerve Dr.* Laud, *but the higheſt Cenſure that ever was paſt in that Court, to be put upon him ; and ſo it was to be inflicted with Knife, Fire, and Whip, at and upon the Pillory, with ten thouſand Pounds Fine ; which ſome of the Lords conceived ſhould never be inflicted, only it was impoſed (as on a dying Man) to terrify others. But the ſaid Doctor and his Combinants, cauſed the ſaid Cenſure to be executed the 26th Day of* November *following (with a Witneſs) for the Hang-man was armed with Strong-drink all the Night before, in Priſon, and, with threatning Words, to do it cruelly. Your Petitioner's Hands being tied to a Stake (beſides all other Torments) he received thirty ſix Stripes with a trible Cord ; after which, he ſtood almoſt two Hours on the Pillory, in cold Froſt and Snow, and ſuffered the reſt ; as cutting off the Ear, firing the Face, and ſlitting of the Noſe ; ſo that he was made a Theatre of Miſery to Men and Angels : And being ſo broken with his Sufferings that he was not able to go, the Warden of the* Fleet *would not ſuffer him to be carried in a Coach ; but he was forced to go by Water, to the further indangering of his Life ; returning to the Goal after much harſh and cruel Uſage, for the Space of eight Years, paying more for a Chamber then the Worth of it (having not a bit of Bread, nor drop of Water allowed.) The Clerk of the* Fleet, *to top up your Petitioner's Sufferings, ſent for him to his Office, and without Warrant, or Cauſe given by your Petitioner, ſet eight ſtrong Men-fellows upon him, who tore his Clothes, bruiſed his Body, ſo that he was never well, and carried him by Head and Heels, to that loathſome and common Goal, where, beſides the Filthineſs of the Place and Vileneſs of the Company, divers Contrivances were laid for taking away the Life of your Petitioner, as ſhall manifeſtly appear, if your Honours will be pleaſed to receive and peruſe a Schedal of that Subject.*

Now the Cauſe of all this harſh, cruel, and continued ill Uſage, unparalled yet upon any one ſince Britain *was bleſſed with Chriſtianity, was nothing but a Book written by your Petitioner, called* Pious Plea *againſt the Prelacy ; and that, by the Call of divers and many good Chriſtians in the Parliament Time, after divers Refuſals given by your Petitioner, who would not publiſh it being done, till it had the View and Approbation of the beſt in the City, Country, and Univerſity, and ſome of the Parliament it ſelf : In Witneſs whereof he had about 500 Hands ; for revealing of whoſe Names he was promiſed more Favours by* Sir Robert Heath *then he will ſpeak of : But denying to turn Accuſer of his Brethren he was threaten'd with a Storm, which he felt to the full ; wherein (through God's Mercy) he had lived ; though but lived, chuſing rather to lay his Neck to the Yoke for others, then to releaſe himſelf by others Sufferings.*

Further, the Petitioner was robbed of divers Goods, by one Lightborn, Graves, *and others, Officers and Servants of the* Fleet, *amounting towards the Value of thirty Pounds, for which* Lightborn *offered Composition (by a second Hand) upon the hearing of the Approach of Parliament; but your Petitioner (notwithstanding his Necessity) refused to hearken to any such illegal and dangerous way. To innumerate the rest of your Petitioner's heavy Pressures, would take up a Volume, with which he will not burden your Honours, till further Opportunity.*

And therefore, he humbly and heartily intreateth, that you would be graciously pleased to take this his Petition into your serious Thoughts, and to command Deliverance, that he may plead his own Cause, or rather Christ's and the States. As also to afford such Cost and Damages as he has suffer'd in Body, Estate, and Family, having been Prisoner (and that, many Times) in the most nasty Prisons, eleven Years, not suffered to breath in the open Air: To which, give him leave to add his great Sufferings in all those Particulars, some sixteen Years ago, for publishing a Book, called, The Looking-glass of Hly War.

Further, as the Cause is Christ's and the States, so your Petitioner conceiveth (under Correction) that the Subject of the Book will be the prime and main Matter of your Agitation, to whose Wisdom he hopeth the Book shall approve it self.

Also your Petitioner's wearing Age, going now in seventy two Years, together with the Sicknesses and Weakness of his long distressed Wife, require a speedy Deliverance.

Lastly, the Sons of Death, the Jesuits, *and* Jesuited, *have so long insulted in their own licentious Liberty, and over the Miseries of your Servant and others ; who, forbearing more Motives, craves Pardon for his Prolixity, being necessitated thereto from the Depth and Length of his Miseries. In all which he ceaseth not to pray, &c. and,*

Kisseth your Hands.

Prov. xxiv. 11.

Wilt thou not deliver them that are drawn unto Death, and those that are ready to be slain?

These and the like Violences of *Laud* and his Creatures drew down the just Vengeance of the Parliament on his Head, and involved the Church of *England* it self in his Ruin. Bishops and Common Prayer were now no more. The Church was formed after a quite different Model ; and the Presbyterian Discipline received and established ; both the Lords and Commons taking the solemn League and Covenant, which was intended for the utter abolishing prelatical Government. The Writers of the Church Party think this an everlasting Brand of Infamy upon the Presbyterians. But how doth this throw greater Infamy upon them, than the Subversion of Presbytery in *Scotland,* and the imposing Canons and Common Prayer on that Nation, doth on *Laud* and his Creatures? If the Alteration of the established Religion, in any Nation, be a Crime, in it self, 'tis so in every Nation ; and I doubt not but the *Scotch* Presbyterians think that that Archbishop, and the prelatical Party, acted as unjustly, illegally, and tyrannically, in introducing the *English* Form of Church Government and Worship into *Scotland,* contrary to their former Settlement, and the Inclination of almost the whole Nation, as the High-Church Party can do with respect to the
Presby-

Prefbyterians, for altering the Form of the Eftablifhment in *England:* And, indeed, the fame Arguments that will vindicate the Alterations made in *Scotland* by the King and the Bifhops, will vindicate thofe made in *England* by the Parliament and the Prefbyterians.

It would have been highly honourable to the Prefbyterian Party, had they *Presbyte,i.* ufed their Power, when in Poffeffion of it, with Moderation, and avoided all *ans.* thofe Methods of Perfecutions and Sufpenfions they had themfelves felt the Effects of in former Times. But to do them Juftice, they had no great Inclination for moderate Meafures. As foon as they came into the Church, all others muft out who would not comply, and fubmit to Sequeftrations and Imprifonments. The folemn League and Covenant was impofed and rigoroufly exacted of all People, as they would efcape the Brand and Penalty of Malignants. Many of the Epifcopal Clergy, both in the City and Country, were expelled their Livings, though by a Generofity, not afterwards imitated by them, Provifion was made for the Support of their Wives and Children. The Lord Mayor, Aldermen, and Common-Council-Men of *London,* prefented a Remonftrance to the Parliament, defiring a ftrict Courfe for fuppreffing all private and feparate Congregations ; that all Anabaptifts, Hereticks, &c. as not conformed to the publick Difcipline, may be declared and proceeded againft ; that all be requred to obey the Government fettled, or to be fettled, and that none difaffected to the Prefbyterian Government, be employ'd in any Place of publick Truft. An Ordinance of Parliament was made, by which every Minifter that fhould ufe the Common-Prayer in Church or Family, was to forfeit five Pounds for the firft Time, ten Pounds for the fecond, and to fuffer a Years Imprifonment for the third. Alfo every Minifter, for every Neglect of the Directory, was to pay forty Shillings ; and for every Contempt of it, by writing or preaching, to forfeit, at the Difcretion of thofe before whom he was convicted, any Sum not under five Pounds, nor above fifty Pounds. The Parliament alfo appointed Elderfhips to fufpend, at their Difcretion, fuch whom they fhould judge to be fcandalous, from the Sacrament, with a Liberty of Appeal to the claffical Elderfhip, &c. They fet up alfo arbitrary Rules about the Examination and Ordination of Minifters by *Triers,* who were to be found in Faith, and fuch as ufually received the Sacrament. And in thefe Things they were quicken'd by the *Scots,* who complained that Reformation moved fo flowly, and that Sects and Errors encreafed, and Endeavours were ufed for their Toleration. Great Reftraints alfo were put upon the Liberty of the Prefs, by feveral Ordinances made for that Purpofe. And to fay the truth, when they once got Prefbytery eftablifhed, they ufed the fame Methods of Sufpenfions, Sequeftrations and Fines that the prelatical Party had done before, though not with equal Severity ; and were as zealous for Uniformity in their own Covenant and Difcipline, as the Bifhops were for Hierarchy, Liturgy, and Ceremonies.

But the Triumphs of the Prefbytery and Covenant, were but fhort. Up- *Charles II.* on the Reftoration of the Royal Wanderer, *Charles* II. Prelacy immediately revived, and exerted it felf in its primitive Vigour and Severity. In his Ma-

2   jefty's

jefty's firſt Declaration to his loving Subjects, he was pleaſed to promiſe *a Liberty to tender Conſciences, and that no Man ſhould be diſquieted or called in Queſtion for Differences of Opinion in Matters of Religion; and that he would conſent to an Act of Parliament for the full granting that Indulgence.* But other Meaſures ſoon prevailed. In the ſecond Year after his Reſtoration, the Act of Uniformity was paſſed, by which all Miniſters were to read, and *publickly declare unfeigned Aſſent and Conſent to all and every Thing contained in, and preſcribed by the Book of Common Prayer,* before the Feaſt of St. *Bartholomew,* then enſuing, under the Penalty of immediate and abſolute Deprivation. The Conſequence of this Act was, that between two and three thouſand excellent Divines were turned out of their Churches; many of them, to ſay the leaſt, as eminent for Learning and Piety as the Biſhops, who were the great Promoters of this barbarous Act; and themſelves and Families, many of them, expoſed to the greateſt Diſtreſs and Poverty. This cruel Injuſtice obliged the ejected Miniſters, and their Friends, to ſet up ſeparate Congregations, and occaſioned ſuch a Diviſion from the eſtabliſhed Church, as will, I hope, ever remain, to witneſs againſt the Tyranny of thoſe Times, and the reverend Authors and Promoters of that Act, to maintain the Spirit and Practice of ſerious Religion, and as a publick Proteſtation for the civil and religious Liberties of Mankind, till Time ſhall be no more, or till the Church ſhall do her ſelf the Juſtice and Honour to open wide her Gates, for the Reception of all into her Communion and Miniſtry, who are not rendered incapable of either by Jeſus Chriſt, the great Shepherd and Biſhop of Souls. But however, Meaſures were then ſoon taken to diſturb their Meeting. In 1664. the Bill againſt frequenting Conventicles paſſed; the firſt Offence made puniſhable with five Pounds, or three Months Impriſonment; the ſecond Offence with ten Pounds, or ſix Months Impriſonment; and the third with Baniſhment to ſome of the foreign Plantations; ſham Plots, being father'd on the Diſſenters, to prepare the Way for theſe Severities. But ſome of the Biſhops, ſuch as *Sheldon, Ward, Wrenn,* &c. did not think theſe Hardſhips enough, and therefore, notwithſtanding the Devaſtations of the Plague, and tho' ſeveral of the ejected Miniſters ſhewed their Piety and Courage, in ſtaying and preaching in the City during the Fury of it, the five Mile Act was paſſed againſt them the next Year, at *Oxford*; by which, all the ſilenced Miniſters were obliged to take an Oath, that it was not lawful, on any Pretence whatſoever, to take Arms againſt the King, or any commiſſion'd by him; and that they would not, at any time, endeavour an Alteration in the Government of Church and State. Such who ſcrupled the Oath, were forbid to come within five Miles of any City or Parliament Burrough, or of the Church where they had been Miniſters, under Penalty of forty Pounds, or ſix Months Impriſonment, for every Offence. After theſe things, ſeveral Attempts were ſet on Foot for a Comprehenſion, but rendered ineffectual by the Practices of the Biſhops, and particularly by *Ward,* Biſhop of *Salisbury,* who had himſelf taken the ſolemn League and Covenant: But having forſaken his firſt Principles, 'tis no Wonder he became a bitter Perſecutor. In the Year 1670. another ſevere Act was paſſed againſt them, by which it was provided, that if any

Per-

Perfon, upwards of fixteen, fhould be prefent at any Conventicle, under Colour of exercifing Religion, in any other Manner than according to the Practice of the Church of *England*, where there were five Perfons or more, befides thofe of the faid Houfhold, the Offenders were to pay five Shillings for the firft Offence, and ten Shillings for the fecond, and the Preacher to forfeit twenty Pounds for the firft, and forty Pounds for the fecond Offence. And thofe who knowingly fuffered any fuch Conventicles in their Houfes, Barns, Yards, &c. were to forfeit twenty Pounds. The Effect of thefe Acts was, that great Numbers of Minifters and their People, were laid in Goals amongft Thieves and common Malefactors, where they fuffered the greateft Hardfhips and Indignities; their Effects were feized on, and themfelves and Families reduced to almoft Beggary and Famine. But at length, this very Parliament which had paffed thefe fevere Bills againft Proteftant Diffenters, began themfelves to be awakened, and juftly grew jealous of their Religion and Liberties, from the Encreafe of Popery : And therefore, to prevent all Dangers which might happen from Popifh Recufants, they paffed, in 1673. the Teft Act ; which hath fince been, contrary to the original Defign of the Law, turned againft the Proteftant Diffenters, and made ufe of to exclude them from the Enjoyment of thofe Rights and Privileges which they have a natural Claim to. In the Year 1680. a Bill paffed both Houfes of Parliament, for exempting his Majefty's Proteftant diffenting Subjects from certain Penalties ; but when the King came to the Houfe, to pafs the Bills, this Bill was taken from the Table, and never heard of more : And though this Parliament voted, that the Profecution of Proteftant Diffenters, upon the penal Laws, was grievous to the Subject, a weakening the Proteftant Intereft, an Encouragement to Popery, and dangerous to the Peace of the Kingdom ; yet they underwent a frefh Profecution, their Meetings were broken up, many Minifters imprifoned, and moft exorbitant Fines levied on them and their Hearers.

In the Beginning of King *James*'s Reign thefe rigorous Proceedings were James II. continued ; but as the Defign of that unhappy biggotted Prince was to fubvert the Religion and Laws of thefe Kingdoms, he publifhed, in the Year 1687. a Declaration for a general Liberty of Confcience to all Perfons, of what Perfuafion foever ; not out of any Regard or Affection to the Proteftant Diffenters, but for the promoting the Popifh Religion and Intereft. He alfo caufed an Order of Council to be paffed, that his Declaration of Indulgence fhould be read in all Churches and Chapels, in the Time of Divine Service, all over *England* and *Wales*. But though the Diffenters ufed the Liberty which was thus granted them, and had feveral Opportunities to have been revenged on their former Perfecutors ; yet they had too much Honour and Regard to the Proteftant Religion and Liberties, ever to fall in with the Meafures of the Court, or lend their Affiftance to introduce arbitrary Power and Popery. And as the Divines of the Church of *England*, when they faw King *James*'s furious Meafures to fubvert the whole Conftitution, threw off their ftiff and haughty Carriage towards the Diffenters, owned them for Brethren, put on the Appearance of the Spirit of Peace and Charity, and affured them, that no fuch rigorous
Methods

Methods fhould be ufed towards them for the future, Things that never entered into their Hearts whilft they were triumphant in Power, and which nothing but a fenfe of their own extreme Danger feems then to have extorted from them : The Diffenters, far from following their Refentments, readily entered into all Meafures with them for the common Safety, and were amongft the firft and heartieft Friends of the Revolution, under King *William* III. of glorious and immortal Memory.

WIL. III.   Soon after the Settlement of this Prince upon the Throne, an Act was paffed for exempting their Majefties Proteftant Subjects, diffenting from the Church of *England*, from the penal Laws ; and though the King, in a Speech to the two Houfes of Parliament, told them, That he hoped they would leave Room for the Admiffion of all Proteftants, that were willing and able to ferve him ; agreeable to which, a Claufe was ordered to be brought into the Houfe of Lords, to take away the neceffity of receiving the Sacrament to make Perfons capable of Offices ; yet his Majefty's gracious Intentions were fruftrated, and the Claufe rejected, by a great Majority. Another Claufe alfo that was afterwards added, That the receiving the Sacrament in tne Church of *England*, or in any other Proteftant Congregation, fhould be a fufficient Qualification, met with the fame Fate as the former : So that though the Diffenters were freed from the penal Laws, they were left under a Brand of Infamy, and render'd incapable of ferving their King and Country, and the Lord's Supper laid open to be proftituted by Law, to the moft abandon'd and profligate Sinners ; and an Inftitution defigned for the Union of all Chriftians, made the Teft of a Party, and the Means of their Separation from each other ; a Scandal that remains upon the Church of *England* to this Day. It is indeed but too plain, that when the eftablifhed Church faw it felf out of Danger, fhe forgot the Promifes of Moderation and Condefcention towards the Diffenters, who readily and openly declared their Willingnefs to yield to a Coalition. But as the Clergy had formed a Refolution of confenting to no Alterations in order to fuch an Union ; all the Attempts made to this Purpofe became wholly ineffectual. Indeed, their very Exemption from the penal Laws was envied them by many, and feveral Attempts were made to difturb and profecute them in this Reign, but were prevented from taking Effect by royal Injunctions.

Q. Ann.   Upon the Death of King *William*, and the Succeffion of Queen *Ann*, the Hatred of the Clergy towards the Diffenters, that had lurked in their Breafts, during the former Reign, immediately broke out. Several Sermons were preached to render them odious, and expofe them to the Fury of the Mob. A Bill was brought in and paffed by the Houfe of Commons, for preventing occafional Conformity, impofing an hundred Pounds Penalty upon every Perfon reforting to a Conventicle or Meeting, after his Admiffion into Offices, and five Pounds for every Days Continuance in fuch Offices, after having been prefent at fuch Conventicle. But upon fome Difagreement between the Lords and Commons, the Bill dropped for that Time. The fame Bill, with fome few Alterations, paffed the Houfe of Commons the two next Seffions, but was rejected by the Lords. During this Reign feveral Pamphlets were publifh'd,

con-

containing bitter Invectives against the Diffenters, and exciting the Government to extirpate and destroy them. Several Profecutions were also carried on against them for teaching Schools, &c. with great Eagernefs and Malice. In 1709. an open Rebellion broke out, when the Mob pulled down the Meeting-Houfes, and publickly burnt the Pews and Pulpits. *Sacheverell* was Trumpet to the Rebellion, by preaching Treafon and Perfecution, and the Parliament that cenfured him, was haftily diffolved. The Parliament that fucceeded, 1711. was of a true Tory Spirit and Complection, and in its fecond Seffion, paffed the Bill againft occafional Conformity. The next Parliament, which met in 1714. was of the fame Difpofition, and paffed a Bill to prevent the Growth of Schifm, by which the Diffenters were reftrained from teaching Schools, or from being Tutors to inftruct Pupils in any Family, without the Licenfe of the Archbifhop, or Bifhop of the Diocefe where they refided; and the Juftices of the Peace had Power given them finally to determine in all Cafes relating thereto. Another Bill was alfo intended to be brought in againft them, to incapacitate them for voting in Elections for Parliament Men, or being chofen Members of Parliament themfelves.

But before thefe unjuft Proceedings had their intended Effect, the Proteftant Succeffion, in his late Majefty King *George* I. took Place; Queen *Ann* dying on the firft of *Auguft*, the very Day on which the Schifm Bill was to have commenced; which, together with that to prevent occafional Conformity, were both repealed by the firft Parliament called together by that excellent Prince. And I cannot help thinking that if the Church of *England* had then confented to have fet the Diffenters intirely free, by repealing the Teft and Corporation Acts; it would have been much to its own Honour and Reputation, as well as a great Strength and Security to the national Intereft. But the Time was not then come. We ftill labour under the Oppreffion of thofe two Acts; and notwithftanding our Zeal for his Majefty's Perfon and Family, muft fit down as eafy as we can, with the Inclination to ferve him, whilft, by Law, we are denied the Opportunity and Power. {.mark}George I.

The Sentiments of his late Majefty, of glorious Memory, with refpect to Moderation, and the tolerating of Diffenters, were fo fully underftood by the whole Nation, as kept the Clergy in tolerable good Order, and from breaking out into many Outrages againft them. But a Controverfy that began amongft themfelves foon difcovered what Spirit many of them were of. The then Bifhop of *Bangor*, the now worthy and reverend Bifhop of *Salisbury*, happen'd, in a Sermon before his Majefty, to affert the fupreme Authority of Chrift as King in his own Kingdom; and that he had not delegated his Power, like temporal Lawgivers, during their Abfence from their Kingdoms to any Perfons, as his Deputies and Vicegerents. *Anno* 1717. He alfo publifhed his Prefervative, in which he advanced fome Pofitions contrary to temporal and fpiritual Tyranny, and in behalf of the civil and religious Liberties of Mankind. The Goodnefs of his Lordfhip's Intentions to ferve the Family of his prefent Majefty, the Intereft of his Country, and

n the

the Honour of the Church of God, might, methinks, have screen'd him from all scurrilous Abuses. But how numerous were his Adversaries, and how hard the Weapons with which they attacked him ! Not only the Dregs of the People and Clergy opened against him, but mighty Men, and Men of great Renown, from whom better Things might have been expected, enter'd the Lists with him ; and because the avowed Champions for spiritual Power, and the Division of the Kingdom between Christ Jesus and themselves. His Lordship of *Bangor* had this manifest Advantage upon the Face of the Argument. He pleaded for Christ's being King in his own Kingdom. His Adversaries pleaded for the Translation of his Kingdom to certain spiritual Viceroys. He for Liberty of private Judgment in Matters of Religion and Conscience. They for Dominion over the Faith and Consciences of others. He against all the Methods of Persecution. They for penal Laws, for Corporation and Test Acts, and the powerful Motives of positive and negative Discouragements. He, with the Spirit of Meekness, and of a Friend to Truth. They with Bitterness and Rancour, and an evident Regard to Interest and Party. However, the lower House of Convocation accused and prosecuted him for attempting the Subversion of all Government and Discipline in the Church of Christ, with a View, undoubtedly, of bringing him under a spiritual Censure, and with impeaching the regal Supremacy in Causes Ecclesiastical, to subject him to the Weight of a Civil one. Of the Bishop it must be said, to his everlasting Honour, that the Temper he discovered, under the Opposition he met with, and the Slanders that were thrown on him, was as much more amiable than that of his Adversaries ; as his Cause was better, his Writings and Principles more consistent, and his Arguments more conclusive and convincing. But notwithstanding these Advantages, his Lordship had great Reason to be thankful to God that the Civil Power supported and protected him, otherwise his Enemies would not, in all Probability, have been content with throwing Scandal upon his Character, but forced him to have parted with SOMETHING, and then delivered him unto Satan for the Punishment of his Flesh, and made him have felt the Weight of that Authority, which God made him the happy and honourable Instrument of opposing; especially if they were all of them of a certain good Archdeacon's Mind, who thought he deserved to have his Tongue cut out.

The Dissenters also have had their Quarrels and Controversies amongst themselves, and managed them with great Warmth and Eagerness of Temper. During their Persecution under King *Charles* II. and the common Danger of the Nation under his Brother *James*, they kept tolerably quiet; the Designs of the common Enemy to ruin them all, uniting them the more firmly amongst themselves. But after the Revolution, when they were secure from Oppression by the civil Power, they soon fell into eager Disputes about Justification and other Points of like Nature. The high flown orthodox Party would scarce own for their Brethren, those who were for Moderation in these Principles, or who differed in the least from their Doctrine concerning

cerning

cerning them. And when they could no longer produce Reafon and Scrip- Nelfon's
ture in their Defence, they, fome of them, made ufe of infamous Methods *Life of B.* Bull,
of Scandal, and endeavoured to blaft the Character of a reverend and wor- p. 275,
thy Divine Dr. *Williams*, in the moft defperate Manner ; becaufe they could 276.
no otherwife anfwer and refute his Arguments. But his Virtue ftood the
Shock of all their Attempts to defame it ; for after, about eight Weeks
fpent in an Enquiry into his Life, by a Committee of the united Minifters, which
received all Manner of Complaints and Accufations againft him ; it was declared at a general Meeting, as their unanimous Opinion, and repeated and a-
greed to in three feveral Meetings fucceffively, that he was intirely clear and
innocent of all that was laid to his Charge. Thus was he vindicated in the
ampleft Form, after the ftricteft Examination that could be made, and his
Adverfaries, who dealt in Defamation and Scandal, if not brought to Repentance, were yet put to Silence. It was almoft incredible how much he was
a Sufferer for his Oppofition to *Antinomianifm*, by a ftrong Party, who left nothing unattempted to crufh him, if it had been poffible. But as his Innocence appeared the brighter, after his Character had been thoroughly fifted,
he was, under God, greatly inftrumental in putting a Stop to thofe pernicious Opinions which his Oppofers propagated ; which ftruck at the very Ef-
fentials of all natural and revealed Religion. His *Gofpel Truth* remains a
Monument of his Honour, a Monument his Enemies were never able to
deftroy. However, nothing would ferve but his Exclufion from the Merchant's Lecture at *Pinners-Hall*. Three other worthy Divines, who had been
his Partners in that Service, bore him Company, and their Places were fupplied with four others, of unqueftionable Rigidnefs and Sterling Orthodoxy. Many Papers were drawn up on each Side, in order to an Accommodation ; fo that it looked, as Dr. *Calamy* tells us, as if the Creed making Age
was again revived. It was infifted, that *Arminianifm* fhould be renounced on
one Side, and *Antinomianifm* on the other. But all was in vain ; and the
Papers that were drawn up to compofe Matters created new Heats, inftead
of extinguifhing the old ones. Thefe Contentions were kept up for feveral
Years, till at laft, the Difputants grew weary, and the Controverfy thread-
bare, when it dropped of it felf.

The next Thing that divided them was the *Trinitarian* Controverfy, and
the Affair of Subfcription to human Creeds and Articles of Faith, as a Teft of
Orthodoxy. In the Year 1695. a great Conteft arofe about the Trinity, amongft
the Divines of the Church of *England*, who charged each other with *Trithe-
ifm* and *Sabellianifm* ; and according to the ecclefiaftical Manner of managing
Difputes, beftowed Invectives and fcurrilous Language very plentifully, upon each other. The Diffenters, in the Reign of his late Majefty, not only
unfortunately fell into the fame Debate, but carried it on, fome of them
at leaft, with equal want of Prudence and Temper. In the Weft of *England*,
where the Fire firft broke out, Moderation, Chriftian Forbearance, and
Charity, feemed to have been wholly extinguifhed. The Reverend and
Learned Mr. *James Peirce*, Minifter in the City of *Exeter*, was difmiffed from
his

his Congregation, upon a Charge of Herefy; and treated, by his Oppofers, with fhameful Rudenefs and Infolence. Other Congregations were alfo practifed with, to difcard their Paftors, upon the fame Sufpicion, who were accufed of impioufly *denying the Lord that bought them*, to render them odious to their Congregations, merely becaufe they could not come up to the unfcriptural Tefts of human Orthodoxy. And when feveral of the Minifters of *London* thought proper to interpofe, and try, if by Advices for Peace, they could not compofe the Differences of their Brethren in the Weft: This Chriftian Defign was as furioufly oppofed as if it had been a Combination to extirpate Chriftianity it felf; and a Propofal made in the Room of it, that the Article of the Church of *England*, and the Anfwer in the Affembly's Catechifm, relating to the Trinity, fhould be fubfcribed by all the Minifters, as a Declaration of their Faith, and a Teft of their Orthodoxy. This Propofal was confidered by many of the Minifters, not only as a Thing unreafonable in it felf, thus to make Inquifition into the Faith of others, but highly inconfiftent with the Character of Proteftants, diffenting from the national Eftablifhment; and diffenting from it for this Reafon amongft others, becaufe the eftablifhed Church exprefly claims *an Authority in Controverfies of Faith*. And therefore, after the Affair had been debated for a confiderable while, the Queftion was folemnly put, and the Propofal rejected by a Majority of Voices. This the Zealots were highly difpleafed with, and accordingly publickly proclaimed their Refentments from the Pulpits. Fafts were appointed folemnly to deplore, confefs, and pray againft the aboundings of Herefy; and their Sermons directly levelled againft the two great Evils of the Church, *Nonfubfcription* and *Arianifm*. Through the Goodnefs of God they had no Power to proceed farther: And when praying and preaching, in this Manner, began to grow tedious, and were, by Experience, found to prove ineffectual, to put a Stop to the Progrefs of the Caufe of Liberty, their Zeal immediately abated, the Cry of Herefy was feldomer heard, and the Alarum of the Church's being endangered by pernicious Errors, gradually ceafed; it being very obfervable, that though Herefy be ever, in its Nature, the fame Thing, yet that the Cry againft it is either more or lefs, according as the political Managers of it can find more or fewer Paffions to work on, or a greater or lefler Intereft to fubferve by it.

And thus have I brought the Hiftory of Perfecution down to our own Times. If Church Hiftory would have afforded me any Thing better, I affure my Reader he fhould have had it told with Pleafure. The Story, as it is, I have told with Grief. But 'tis Time to difmifs him from fo ungrateful an Entertainment, and fee what ufeful Reflections we can make on the Whole.

SECT.

SECT. III.

REMARKS *upon the* HISTORY *of* Chriſtian Perſecution.

I. 'TIS a Truth too evident to be denied, That the Clergy in general, throughout almoſt all the ſeveral Ages of the Chriſtian Church, have been deep and warm in the Meaſures of Perſecution; as though it had been a Doctrine expreſly inculcated in the ſacred Writings, and recommended by the Practice of our Saviour and his Apoſtles. Indeed, could ſuch a Charge as this have been juſtly fixed on the great Author of our Religion, or the Meſſengers he ſent into the World to propagate it; I think it would have been ſuch an Evidence of its having been dictated by weak, or wicked, or worldly minded Men, as nothing could poſſibly have diſproved. But that Chriſtianity might be free from every Imputation of this kind, God was pleaſed to ſend his Son into the World, without any of the Advantages of worldly Riches and Grandeur, and abſolutely to diſclaim all the Prerogatives of an earthly Kingdom. His diſtinguiſhing Character was that of *meek and lowly*; and the Methods by which he conquered and triumphed over his Enemies, and drew all Men to him, was *Patience and Conſtancy, even to the Death.* And when he ſent out his own Apoſtles, he ſent them out but poorly furniſhed, to all human Appearance, for their Journey; *without Staves, or Scrip, or* Luke ix. 3. *Bread, or Money,* to let them know that he had but little of this World to give them; and that their whole Dependance was on Providence. One Thing however he aſſured them of, that they ſhould be *delivered up to the* Matt. x. *Councils, and ſcourged in the Synagogues, and be hated of all Men for his ſake.* So 17. far was he from giving them a Power to perſecute, that he foretold them they muſt ſuffer Perſecution for his Name: This the Event abundantly juſtified. And how amiable was their Behaviour under it? How greatly did they recommend the Religion they taught by the Methods they took to propagate it? *The Arms of their Warfare were not carnal, but ſpiritual.* The Argument they uſed to convince thoſe they preached to, was the *Demonſtration of the Spirit, and of Power.* They approved *themſelves as the Miniſters of God, by much Patience, by Afflictions, Neceſſities, Diſtreſſes, Stripes, Impriſonments, Tumults, Labours, Watchings, Faſtings, Pureneſs, Knowledge, Long-ſuffering, Kindneſs, by the Holy Ghoſt, by Love unfeigned, by the Word of Truth, by the Power of God, and by the Armour of Righteouſneſs on the right Hand and on the left.* Oh how unlike were their Succeſſors to them in theſe Reſpects! How different their Methods to convince Gainſayers! Excommunications, Suſpenſions, Fines, Baniſhments, Impriſonments, Bonds, Scourges, Tortures and Death, were the powerful Arguments introduced into the Church, and recommended, practiſed and ſanctified by many of the pretended Fathers of it. Even thoſe whom Superſtition hath dignified by the Name of Saints, *Athanaſius, Chryſoſtom, Gregory, Cyril,* and others, grew wanton with Power, cruelly oppreſſed thoſe who
differed.

differed from them, and stained most of them their Characters with the Guilt
of Rapine and Murder. Their religious Quarrels were managed with
such an unrelenting, furious Zeal, as disturbed the imperial Government,
threw Kingdoms and Nations into Confusion, and turned the Church it self
into an Aceldama, or Field of Blood. Some few there have been who were
of a different Spirit, who not only abstained from persecuting Counsels and
Measures themselves, but with great Justice and Freedom censured them in
others. But as to your Saints and Fathers, your Patriarchs and Bishops,
your Councils and Synods, together with the Rabble of Monks, they were
most of them the Advisers, Abetters and Practicers of Persecution. They
knew not how to brook Opposition to their own Opinions and Power, branded all Doctrines different from their own, with the odious Name of Heresy,
and used all their Arts and Influence to oppress and destroy those who presumed to maintain them. And this they did with such Unanimity and Constancy, through a long Succession of many Ages, as would tempt a stander
by to think, that a Bishop or Clergyman, and a Persecutor, were the same
Thing, or meant the self same individual Character and Office in the Christian Church.

I am far from writing these Things with any Design to depreciate and
blacken the episcopal Order in general. 'Tis an Office of great Dignity
and Use, according to the original Design of its Institution. But when that
Design is forgotten, or wholly perverted ; when, instead of becoming *Overseers* of the Flock of Christ, the Bishops *tare and devour* it, and proudly usurp Dominion over the Consciences of Christians, when they ought to be content
with being Helpers of their Joy, I know no Reason why the Name should
be complimented, or the Character held sacred, when 'tis abused to Infolence, Oppression and Tyranny ; or why the venerable Names of Fathers and
Saints, should screen the Vices of the Bishops of former Ages, who, notwithstanding their writing in behalf of Christianity and Orthodoxy, brought
some of them the greatest Disgrace on the Christian Religion, by their wicked Practices, and exposed it to the severest Satyrs of its professed Enemies:
And for the Truth of this, I appeal to the foregoing History. If any Observations on their Conduct should affect the Temper and Principles of any
now living, they themselves only are answerable for it, and welcome to make
what Use and Application of them they please. Sure I am that the representing them in their true Light, reflects an Honour upon those reverend
and worthy Prelates, who maintain that Moderation and Humility, which is
essential to the true Dignity of the Episcopal Character, and who use no
other Methods of Conviction and Persuasion, but those truly Apostolical ones,
of sound Reasoning and exemplary Piety. May God grant a great Increase,
and a continual Succession of them in the Christian Church.

II. But as the Truth of History is not to be concealed; and as it can do
no Service to the Christian Cause to palliate the Faults of any Set of Christians whatsoever ; especially when all Parties have been more or less involved in the same Guilt ; I must observe farther, as an Aggravation of
                                                                    this

this Guilt, that the Things for which Chriſtians have perſecuted each other, have been generally Matters of no Importance in Religion, and oftentimes ſuch as have been directly contrary to the Nature of it. If my Reader would know upon what Accounts the Church hath been filled with Diviſions and Schiſms; why Excommunications and Anathemas have been ſo dreadfully toſſed about; what hath given Occaſion to ſuch a Multitude of Suſpenſions, Depoſitions and Expulſions; what hath excited the Clergy to ſuch numberleſs Violences, Rapines, Cruelties and Murders, he will probably be ſurprized to be informed, that 'tis nothing of any Conſequence or real Importance, nothing relating to the Subſtance and Life of pure and undefiled Religion; little beſides hard Words, technical Terms, and inexplicable Phraſes, Points of mere Speculation, abſtruſe Queſtions, and metaphyſical Notions; Rites and Ceremonies, Forms of human Invention, and certain Inſtitutions, that have had their Riſe and Foundation only in Superſtition. Theſe have been the great Engines of Diviſion; theſe the ſad Occaſions of Perſecution. Would it not excite ſometimes Laughter, and ſometimes Indignation, to read of a proud and imperious Prelate, excommunicating the whole Chriſtian Church, and ſending, by Wholeſale, to the Devil, all who did not agree with him in the preciſe Day of obſerving *Eaſter?* Eſpecially when there is ſo far from being any Direction given by Chriſt or his Apoſtles about the Day; that there is not a ſingle Word about the Feſtival it ſelf. And is it not an amazing Inſtance of Stupidity and Superſtition, that ſuch a paltry and whimſical Controverſy ſhould actually engage, for many Years, the whole Chriſtian World, and be debated with as much Warmth and Eagerneſs, as if all the Intereſts of the preſent and future State had been at Stake; as if Chriſt himſelf had been to be crucified afreſh, and his whole Goſpel to be ſubverted and deſtroy'd.

The *Arian* Controverſy, that made ſuch Havock in the Chriſtian Church, was, if I may be allowed to ſpeak it without Offence, in the Beginning only, about Words; though probably, ſome of *Arius* his Party went farther afterwards than *Arius* himſelf did at firſt. *Arius,* as hath been ſhewn, expreſly allowed the Son to be πρὸ χρονων καὶ πρὸ αιωνων, *before all Times and Ages,* πληρης Θεος, *perfect God,* αναλλαιατος, *unchangeable,* and begotten after the moſt perfect Likeneſs of the unbegotten Father. This, to me, appears to bid very fair for Orthodoxy, and was, I think, enough to have reconciled the Biſhop and his Presbyter, if there had not been ſome other Reaſons of the Animoſity between them. But when other Terms were invented, that were hard to be underſtood, and difficult to be explained; the original Controverſy ceaſed, and the Diſpute then was about the Meaning of thoſe Terms, and the Fitneſs of their Uſe in explaining the Divinity of the Son of God. *Arius* knew not how to reconcile the Biſhop's Words, αειγενης, *ever begotten;* with the Aſſertion, that the Son, συνυπαρχει αγεννητως τω Θεω, *coexiſts unbegottenly with God;* and thought it little leſs than a Contradiction to affirm, that he was αγεννητογενης, *unbegottenly begotten.* And as to the Word ομοουσιος, *Conſubſtantial, Arius* ſeems to have thought that it deſtroy'd the perſonal Subſiſtence of the

Son,

I

Son, and brought in the Doctrine of *Sabellius*; or elfe, that it implied, that the Son was μερος τε πατρος, *a Part of the Father*; and for this Reafon declined the Ufe of it. And, indeed, it doth not appear to me that the Council of *Nice* had themfelves any determinate and fixed Meaning to the Word, as, I think may be fairly inferred from the Debates of that Council, with *Eufebius*, Bifhop of *Cæfarea*, about that Term; which, though put into their Creed, in Oppofition to the *Arians*, was yet explained by them in fuch a Senfe as almoft any *Arian* could have, *bona fide*, fubfcribed. On the other hand, the Bifhop of *Alexandria* feems to have thought, that when *Arius* afferted that the Son exifted θελημαλι κι βυλη τε πατρος, *by the Will and Counfel of the Father*; it implied the Mutability of his Nature; and that, when he taught concerning the Son, οἱι ην οἱε ικ ην, *that there was a Time when he was not*; it inferred his being a temporary and not an eternal Being; though *Arius* exprefly denied both thefe Confequences. In fhort, it was a Controverfy upon this me-

Thud.
E H. l. 1.
c. 5.

taphyfical Queftion, *Whether or no God could generate or produce a Being, in Strictnefs of Speech, as eternal as himfelf?* or, *Whether God's generating the Son doth not neceffarily imply the Pre-exiftence of the Father, either* επινοια, *in Conception, or* ολογω τινι, *fome fmall imaginable Point of Time*, as *Arius* imagined, and the Bifhop denied. This was, in Fact, the State of this Controverfy. And did not the Emperor *Conftantine* give a juft Character of this Debate, when he declared the Occafion of the Difference to be very trifling; and that their Quarrels arofe from an idle itch of Difputation, fince they did not contend about any effential Doctrine of the Gofpel? Could thefe hard Words and inexplicable Points juftify the Clergy in their intemperate Zeal; and in their treating each other with the Rancour and Bitternefs of the moft implacable Enemies? What hath the Doctrine of real Godlinefs, what hath the Church of God to do with thefe Debates? Hath the Salvation of Mens Souls, and the Practice of Virtue any Dependance upon Mens receiving unfcriptural Words, in which they cannot believe, becaufe they cannot underftand them, and which, thofe who firft introduced them were not able to explain? If I know my own Heart, I would be far from giving up any plain and important Doctrine of the Gofpel. But will any Man cooly and foberly affirm, that nice and intricate Queftions, that depend upon metaphyfical Diftinctions, and run fo high as the moft minute fuppofeable Atome, or Point of Time, can be either plain or important Doctrines of the Gofpel? Oh Jefus! If thou be *the Son of the everlafting God, the Brightnefs of thy Father's Glory, and the exprefs Image of his Perfon*; if thou art the moft perfect Refemblance of his all perfect Goodnefs, that kind Benefactor, that God-like Friend to the human Race, which the faithful Records of thy Life declare thee to be, How can I believe the effential Doctrines of thy Gofpel to be thus wrapped up in Darknefs; or, that the Salvation of that Church, *which thou haft purchafed with thy Blood*, depends on fuch myfterious and inexplicable Conditions? If thy Gofpel reprefents thee right, furely thou muft be better pleafed with the humble, peaceable Chriftian, who, when honeftly fearching into the Glories of thy Nature, and willing to give thee all the Adoration thy great Father hath or-

I   dered

dered him to pay thee, falls into fome Errors, as the Confequence of human Weaknefs; than with that imperious and tyrannical Difciple, who divides thy Members, tares the Bowels of thy Church, and fpreads Confufion and Strife throughout thy Followers and Friends, even for the fake of Truths that lie remote from Mens Underftanding, and in which thou haft not thought proper to make the full, the plain Decifion. If Truth is not to be given up for the fake of Peace, I am fure Peace is not to be facrificed for the fake of fuch Truths; and if the Gofpel is a Rule worthy our Regard, the Clergy of thofe Times can never be excufed for the Contentions they raifed, and the Miferies they occafioned in the Chriftian World, upon Account of them.

The third and fourth General Councils feem to have met upon an Occafion of much the like Importance. The firft Council of *Nice*, determined the Son to be a diftinct Hypoftafis, or Perfon from, but of the fame Nature with the Father. The fecond at *Conftantinople*, added the Holy Ghoft to the fame Subftance of the Father, and made the fame individual Nature to belong equally and wholly, to Father, Son, and Holy Ghoft; thus making them three diftinct Perfons in one undivided Effence. But as they determined the Son to be truly Man, as well as truly God, the Bifhops brought a new Controverfy into the Church, and fell into furious Debates and Quarrels about his Perfonality. *Neftorius*, Bifhop of *Conftantinople*, with his Followers, maintained two diftinct Perfons in Chrift, agreeable to his two diftinct Natures. But Saint *Cyril*, the implacable Enemy of *Neftorius*, got a Council to decree, that the two Natures of God and Man being united together in our Lord, made one Perfon or Chrift, and to curfe all who fhould affirm that there were two diftinct Perfons or Subfiftences in him. 'Tis evident, that either *Cyril*, and his Council, muft have been in the wrong in this Decree, or the two former Councils of *Nice* and *Conftantinople* wrong in theirs; becaufe 'tis certain, that they decreed the Word PERSON to be ufed in two infinitely different Senfes. According to thofe of *Nice* and *Conftantinople*, one individual Nature or Effence contain'd three diftinct Perfons. According to *Cyril*'s Council, two Natures or Effences infinitely different, and as diftinct as thofe of God and Man, conftituted but one Perfon. Now how *one Nature fhould be three Perfons, and yet two Natures one Perfon*, will require the Skill even of Infallibility it felf to explain ; and as thefe Decrees are evidently contradictory to one another, I am afraid we muft allow, that the Holy Ghoft had no Hand in one or other of them. This fome of the Clergy very eafily obferved; and therefore, to maintain the Unity of the Perfon of Chrift, *Eutyches* and *Diofcorus* maintained, that though Chrift confifted of two Natures before his Incarnation, yet after that, he had but one Nature only. But this was condemned by the Council of *Chalcedon*, and the Contradictions of the former Councils declared all to be true, and render'd facred with the Stamp of Orthodoxy. This was alfo ratified by the fifth Council under *Juftinian*, who alfo pioufly and charitably raked into the Duft of poor *Origen*, and damned him for an Heretick. But ftill there was a Difficulty yet remaining, about the Perfon of Chrift : For as Chrift's being one Perfon did not deftroy

the

the Diftinction of his two Natures, it became a very important and warm Controverfy, Whether Chrift had any more than one Will, as he was but one Perfon in two Natures? or, Whether he had not two Wills, agreeable to his two diftinct Natures, united in one Perfon? This occafioned the calling the fixth General Council, who determined it for the two Wills; in which, according to my poor Judgment, they were very wrong. And had I had the Honour to have been of this venerable Affembly, I would have compleated the Myftery, by decreeing, that as Chrift had but one Perfon, he could have but one perfonal Will; but however, that as he had two Natures, he muft alfo have two natural Wills. I beg my Reader's Pardon for thus prefuming to offer my own Judgment, in Oppofition to the Decree of the holy Fathers; but at the fame Time, I cannot help fmiling at the Thought, of two or three hundred venerable Bifhops and Fathers thus trifling in Council, and folemnly playing at Queftions and Commands, to puzzle others, and divert themfelves. Were it not for the fatal Confequences that attended their Decifions, I fhould look on them as *Bifhops in Mafquerade*, met together only to ridicule the Order, or to fet the People a laughing at fo awkward a Mixture of Gravity and Folly. Surely the Reverend Clergy of thofe Days had but little to do amongft their Flocks, or but little Regard to the Nature and End of their Office. Had they been faithful to their Character, inftead of *doting about Queftions and Strifes of Words, whereof came Envy, Strife, Railings, evil Surmifings, perverfe Difputings of Men of corrupt Minds, and deftitute of the Truth, fuppofing that Gain is Godlinefs,* they would have confented to, and taught wholfome Words, even the Words of our Lord *Jefus Chrift, and the Doctrine which is according to Godlinefs.*

But this was not the Temper of the Times. It would have been indeed more tolerable, had the Clergy confined their Quarrels to themfelves, and quarrelled only about fpeculative Doctrines and harmlefs Contradictions. But to intereft the whole Chriftian World in thefe Contentions, and to excite furious Perfecutions for the Support of Doctrines and Practices, even oppofite to the Nature, and deftructive of the very End of Chriftianity, is equally monftrous and aftonifhing. And yet this is the Cafe of the feventh General Council, who decreed the Adoration of the Virgin *Mary*, of Angels, and of Saints, of Relicts, of Images and Pictures, and who thereby obfcured the Dignity, and corrupted the Simplicity of the Chriftian Worfhip and Doctrine. This the venerable Fathers of that Council did, and pronounced Anathemas againft all who would not come into their idolatrous Practices, and excited the Civil Power to opprefs and deftroy them.

III. Surely it could not be a Zeal for God and Chrift, and the Truth and Honour of Chriftianity, no real Love to Piety and Vertue, that prompted and lead them on to thefe Acts of Injuftice and Cruelty. Without any Breach of Charity, it may be afferted of moft, if not all of them, that 'twas their Pride, and their immoderate Love of Dominion, Grandeur and Riches, that influenced them to thefe unworthy and wicked Meafures. The Intereft of Religion and Truth, the Honour of God and the Church, is, I know, the ftale Pretence; but a Pretence, I.

am

am afraid, that hath but little Probability or Truth to support it. For what hath Religion to do with the Obfervation of Days? or, What could excite *Victor* to excommunicate fo many Churches about *Eafter*, but the Pride of his Heart, and to let the World fee, how large a Power he had to fend Souls to the Devil? How is the Honour of God promoted, by Speculations that have no Tendency to Godlinefs? Will any Man ferioufly affirm, that the ancient Difputes about υπιςασις, ϖςσωτον, ιδιοτητις, ουσις, ομοασιος, εμοιυσιος, and the reft of the hard Words that were invented, did any Honour to the Name of Chrift, or were of any Advantage to the Religion of his Gofpel? Or, can he believe that *Alexander, Arius, Athanafius, Macedonius,* and others, were influenced in all their Contentions and Quarrels, in all the Confufions they were the Authors of, and the Murders they occafioned, purely by religious Motives? Surely the Honour of Religion muft be promoted by other Means; and genuine Chriftianity may flourifh, and, indeed, would have flourifh'd much better, had thefe Difputes never been introduced into the Church; or, had they been managed with Moderation and Forbearance. But fuch was the Haughtinefs of the Clergy, fuch their Thirft of Dominion over the Confciences of others, fuch their Impatience of Contradiction, that nothing would content them but implicit Faith to their Creeds, abfolute Subjection to their Decrees, and Subfcription to their Articles without Examination or Conviction of their Truth; or for want of thefe, Anathemas, Depofitions, Banifhments and Death.

The Hiftory of all the Councils, and of almoft all the Bifhops that is left us, is a Demonftration of this fad Truth. What Council can be named, that did not affume a Power to explain, amend, fettle, and determine the Faith? That did not anathematife and depofe thofe who could not agree to their Decifions, and that did not excite the Emperors to opprefs and deftroy them? Was this the Humility and Condefcention of Servants and Minifters? Was not this lording it over the Heritage of God, feating themfelves in the Throne of the Son of God, and making themfelves owned as *Fathers and Mafters,* in Oppofition to the exprefs Command of Chrift to the contrary?

Clemens Romanus, in his firft Epiftle to the *Corinthians,* Cap. 44. tells us, That * *the Apoftles knew, by the Lord Jefus Chrift, that the Epifcopal Name and Office would be the Occafion of Contention in the Chriftian Church;* a † *noble Inftance,* fays the learned *Fell,* in his Remarks on the Place, *of the prophetick Spirit of the Apoftolick Age.* Formerly, he adds, that *Mens Ambition and evil Practices to ob-tain this Dignity, produced Schifms and Herefies.* And 'twas indeed no Wonder that fuch Diforders and Confufions fhould be occafioned, when the Bifhopricks were certain Steps, not only to Power and Dominion, but to the Emoluments and Advantages of Riches and Honours. Even long before the Time of *Conftantine,* the Clergy had got a very great Afcendant over the

Apud Co-tel. p.173. Edic. Am-ftel.

---

* Και οι αποςολοι ημων εγνωσαν δια τυ κυειυ ημων Ιησυ χειςυ, οτι εεις εςαι επι τυ ονοματος της επισκοπης.

† Luculenta praefenfo rerum——— quacq; propheticum Apoftolici ævi——— Spiritum proficetur. Olim fchifmata & hærefes fubinde ortæ, præ fatiga iftius defiderio & ambitu.

O 2　　　　　　　　　　　　　　　　　　　　　　　　　Laity,

Laity, and grew, many of them, rich, by the voluntary Oblations of the
People: But the Grants of that Emperor confirm'd them in a worldly Spirit,
and the Dignities and vaft Revenues that were annexed to many of the Sees,
gave Rife to infinite Evils and Difturbances. So they could but get Poffeffion of them, they cared not by what Means, whether by clandeftine Ordinations, fcandalous Symony, the Expulfion of the Poffeffors, or through
the Blood of their Enemies. How many Lives were loft at *Rome, Conftantinople, Alexandria* and *Antioch*, by the furious Contentions of the Bifhops of
thofe Sees; depofing one another, and forcibly entring upon Poffeffion?
Would *Athanafius*, and *Macedonius, Damafus*, and others, have given Occafion to fuch Tumults, and Murders, merely for Words and Creeds, had there
not been fomewnat more fubftantial to have been got by their Bifhopricks?
Would *Cyril* have perfecuted the *Novatians*, had it not been for the fake of their
Riches, of which he plunder'd them, foon after his Advancement to the See
of *Alexandria?* No. The Character given by the Hiftorian of *Theodofius*,
Bifhop of *Synada*, may be too truly applied to almoft all the reft of them;
who perfecuted the Followers of *Macedonius*, not from a Principle of Zeal
for the Faith, but through a covetous Temper, and the Love of Money.
This St. *Jerome* obferved with Grief, in the Paffage cited *p. 31.* of this Introduction, and *Ammianus Marcellinus*, an Heathen Writer, reproach'd them
with, in the Paffage cited *p. 39.*

IV. I think it will evidently follow, from this Account, that the Determinations of Councils, and the Decrees of Synods, as to Matters of Faith,
are of no manner of Authority, and can carry no Obligation upon any Chriftian whatfoever. I will not mention here one Reafon, which would be it
felf fufficient, if all others were wanting, *viz.* That they have no Power
given them in any Part of the Gofpel Revelation, to make thefe Decifions in
controverted Points, and to oblige others to fubfcribe them; and that therefore the Pretence to it is an Ufurpation of what belongs to the great God,
who only hath, and can have a Right to prefcribe to the Confciences of
Men. But to let this pafs, what one Council can be fixed upon, that will
appear to be compofed of fuch Perfons, as, upon an impartial Examination,
can be allowed to be fit for the Work of fettling the Faith, and determining all Controverfies relating to it? I mean in which the Majority of the
Members may, in Charity, be fuppofed to be difinterefted, wife, learned, peaceable and pious Men? Will any Man undertake to affirm this
of the Council of *Nice?* Can any Thing be more evident than that the
Members of that venerable Affembly, came, many of them, full of Paffion
and Refentment; that others of them were crafty and wicked, and others
ignorant and weak? Did their Meeting together in a Synod immediately
cure them of their Defire of Revenge, make the Wicked virtuous, or the
Ignorant wife? If not, their joint Decree, as a Synod, could really be of
no more Weight than their private Opinions; nor, perhaps, of fo much;
becaufe, 'tis well known, that the great Tranfactions of fuch Affemblies,
are generally managed and conducted by a few; and that Authority, Perfuafion,

fuafion, Profpect of Intereft, and other temporal Motives, are commonly made Ufe of to fecure a Majority. The Orthodox have taken Care to deſtroy all the Accounts given of this Council, by thofe of the oppofite Party ; and *Eufebius*, Biſhop of *Cafarea*, hath paffed it over in Silence; and only dropped two or three Hints, that are very far from being favourable to thofe reverend Fathers. In a Word, nothing can be collected from Friends or Enemies, to induce one to believe, that they had any of thofe Qualifications which were neceffary to fit them for the Province they had undertaken, of fettling the Peace of the Church by a fair, candid and impartial Determination of the Controverfy that divided it : So that the Emperor *Conſtantine*, and *Socrates* the Hiſtorian, took the moſt effectual Method to vindicate their Honour, by pronouncing them infpired by the Holy Ghoſt, which they had great need of, to make up the want of all other Qualifications.

The fecond General Council were plainly the Creatures of the Emperor *Theodofius*, all of his own Party, and convened to do as he bid them ; which they did, by confirming the *Nicene* Faith, and condemning all Herefies. The third General Council were the Creatures of *Cyril*, who was their Prefident, and the inveterate Enemy of *Neſtorius*, whom he condemned for Herefy, and was himfelf condemned for his Raſhnefs in this Affair, and excommunicated by the Biſhop of *Antioch*. The fourth met under the Awes of the Emperor *Marcian*, managed their Debates with Noife and Tumult, were formed into a Majority by the Intrigues of the Legates of *Rome* ; and fettled the Faith by the Opinions of *Athanafius*, *Cyril*, and others. I need not mention more ; the farther we go the worfe they will appear. Now may it not be asked, How came the few Biſhops, who met by Command of *Theodofius*, to be ſtiled an Oecumenical or General Council ? As they came to decree, as he decreed they ſhould, what Authority, with any wife Man, can their Decifions have ? As they were all of one Side, except thirty fix of the *Macedonian* Party, who were afterwards added ; what lefs could be expected ; but that they would decree themfelves Orthodox, eſtabliſh their own Creed, and anathematize all others for Hereticks ? And as to the next Council, I confefs I can pay no Refpect or Reverence to a Set of Clergy, met under the Direction and Influence of a Man of *Cyril's* Principles and Morals ; efpecially as the main Tranfaction of that Council was hurried on by a Defire of Revenge, and done before the Arrival of the Biſhop of *Antioch*, with his fuffragan Brethren, and condemned by him as foon as he was informed of it ; till at length the Power and Influence of the Emperor reconciled the two haughty Prelates ; made them reverfe their mutual Excommunications, decree the fame Doctrine, and join in pronouncing the fame Anathemas. Cannot any one difcern more of Refentment and Pride in their firſt Quarrel, than of a Regard to Truth and Peace ; and more of Complaifance to the Emperor than of Concern for the Honour of Chriſt in their after Reconciliation ? And as to the next Council, let any one but read over the Account given of it by *Evagrius* ; what horrible Confufions there were amongſt them ; how they threw about Anathemas and Curfes ; how they father'd their Violences

on

on Chrift; how they fettled the Faith by the Doctrines of *Athanafius, Cyril,* and other Fathers ; and if he can bring himfelf to pay any Reverence to their Decrees, I envy him not the Submiffion he pays them, nor the Rule by which he guides and determines his Belief.

I confefs I cannot read the Account of thefe Tranfactions, tneir afcribing their Anathemas and Curfes to Chrift and the Holy Trinity, and their Decifions as to the Faith, to the Holy Ghoft, without Indignation at the horrid Abufe of thofe facred Names. Their very Meeting to pronounce Damnation on their Adverfaries, and to form Creeds for the Confciences of others, is no lefs than a Demonftration that they had no Concurrence of the Son of God, no Influence of the Holy Spirit of God. The Faith was already fettled for them, and for all other Chriftians in the facred Writings, and needed no Decifion of Councils to explain and amend it. The very Attempt was Infolence and Ufurpation. Infallibility is a neceffary Qualification for an Office of fuch Importance. But what Promife is there made to Councils of this divine Gift ? or, if there fhould be any fuch Promife made to them ; yet the Method of their Debates, their fcandalous Arts to defame their Adverfaries, and the Contradictions they decreed for Truth and Gofpel, proves, to the fulleft Conviction, that they forfeited the Grace of it. And indeed, if *the Fruits of the Spirit are Love, Peace, Long-fuffering, Gentlenefs, Goodnefs, and Meeknefs,* there appeared few or no Signs of them in any of the Councils. The Soil was too rank and hot to produce them.

I wifh, for the Honour of the former Times, I could give a better Account of thefe Affemblies of the Clergy, and fee Reafon to believe my felf that they were, generally fpeaking, Men of Integrity, Wifdom, Candour, Moderation and Virtue. The Debates of fuch Men would have deferved Regard, and their Opinions would have challenged a proper Reverence. But even had this been the Cafe, their Opinions could have been no Rule to others, and how great a Veneration foever we might have had for their Characters, we ought, as Men and Chriftians, to have examined their Principles. There is one Rule fuperior to them and us, by which Chriftians are to try all Doctrines and Spirits ; the Decifion of which, is more facred than that of all human Wifdom and Authority, and every where, and in all Ages obligatory. But as the ancient Councils confifted of Men of quite other Difpofitions ; and as their Decifions in Matters of Faith were arbitrary and unwarranted ; and as thofe Decifions themfelves were generally owing to Court Practices, intriguing Statefmen, the Thirft of Revenge, the Management of a few crafty interefted Bifhops, to Noife and Tumult, the Profpects and Hopes of Promotions and Tranflations, and other the like Caufes ; the Reverence paid them by many Chriftians is truly furprizing ; and I cannot account for it any way but one, *viz.* that thofe who thus cry up their Authority, are in hopes of fucceeding them in their Power ; and therefore would feign perfuade others that their Decrees are facred and binding, to make way for the impofing of their own.

It

It would be well worth the while of fome of thefe Council-mongers to lay down fome proper Rules and Diftinctions, by which we may judge what Councils are to be received, and which to be rejected; and particularly why the four firft General Councils fhould be fubmitted to in Preference to all others. Councils have often decreed contrary to Councils, and the fame Bi-fhops have decreed different Things in different Councils; and even the third and fourth General Councils determined the Ufe of the Word P E R S O N, in an infinitely different Senfe from what the two firft did. Heretical Councils, as they are called, have been more in Number than fome Orthodox gene-ral ones, called by the fame imperial Authority, have claimed the fame Powers, pretended to the fame Influence of the Holy Ghoft, and pronounced the fame Anathemas againft Principles and Perfons. By what *Criteria* or certain Marks then muft we judge, which of thefe Councils are thieving, general, particular, orthodox, heretical, and which not? The Councils themfelves muft not be Judges in their own Caufe; for then we muft re-ceive, or reject them all. The Characters of the Bifhops that compofed them will not do, for their Characters feem equally amiable and Chriftian on each fide. The Nature of the Doctrine, *as decreed by them*, is far from being a fafe Rule; becaufe, if human Authority, or Church Power makes Truth in any Cafe, it makes it in every Cafe; and therefore, upon this Foot the Decrees at *Tyre* and *Ephefus*, are as truly binding as thofe at *Nice* and *Chalcedon*. Or, if we muft judge of the Councils by the Nature of the Doctrine, abftracted from all human Authority, thofe Councils can have no Authority at all. Every Man muft fit in Judgment over them, and try them by Reafon and Scripture, and reject and receive them, juft as he would do the Opinions of any other Perfons whatfoever. And, I humbly conceive, they fhould have no better Treatment, becaufe they de-ferve none.

V. If then the Decrees of Fathers and Councils, if the Decifions of human Authority in Matters of Religion, are of no avail, and carry with them no Obligation, it follows, that the impofing Subfcriptions to Creeds and Arti-cles of Faith, as Tefts of Orthodoxy, is a Thing unreafonable in it felf, as it hath proved of infinite ill Confequence in the Church of God.

I call it an *unreafonable Cuftom*, not only becaufe where there is no Power to make Creeds for others, there can be no Right to impofe them; but be-caufe no one good Reafon can be affigned for the Ufe and Continuance of this Practice. For, as my Lord Bifhop of *London* admirably well explains this Matter, *As long as Men are Men, and have different Degrees of Underftanding,* Bifhop of *and every one a Partiality to his own Conceptions, it is not to be expected that they* London, *fhould agree in any one entire Scheme, and every Part of it, in the Circumftances as* 2d Paft. *well as the Subftance, in the Manner of Things, as well as in the Things themfelves.* Let. p. 14, *The Queftion therefore is not in general about a Difference in Opinion, which, in* §5. *our prefent State, is unavoidable; but about the Weight and Importance of the Things wherein Chriftians differ, and the Things wherein they agree. And it will appear, that the feveral Denominations of Chriftians agree both in the Subftance of Religion, and in the necessary Inforcements of the Practice of it. That the World, and all Things in it, were created by God, and are under the Direction and Government of his all powerful Hand, and all seeing Eye; that there is an essential Difference between Good and Evil, Virtue and Vice; that there will be a State of future Rewards and Punishments according to our Behaviour in this Life; that Christ was a Teacher sent from God, and that his Apostles were divinely inspired; that all Christians are bound to declare and profess themselves to be his Disciples; that not only the Exercise of the several Virtues, but also a Belief in Christ is necessary in order to their obtaining the Pardon of Sin, the Favour of God, and eternal Life; that the Worship of God is to be performed chiefly by the Heart, in Prayers, Praises, and Thanksgivings; and, as to all other Points, that they are bound to live by the Rules which Christ and his Apostles have left them in the Holy Scriptures. Here then,* adds the learned Bishop, *is a fixed, certain, and uniform Rule of Faith and Practice, containing all the most necessary Points of Religion, established by a divine Sanction, embraced as such, by all Denominations of Christians, and in it self abundantly sufficient to preserve the Knowledge and Practice of Religion in the World. As to Points of greater Intricacy, and which require uncommon Degrees of Penetration and Knowledge; such indeed, have been Subjects of Dispute amongst Persons of Study and Learning in the several Ages of the Christian Church; but the People are not obliged to enter into them, so long as they do not touch the Foundations of Christianity, nor have an Influence upon Practice. In other Points it is sufficient that they believe the Doctrines, so far as they find, upon due Enquiry and Examination, according to their several Abilities and Opportunities, that God hath revealed them.* This incomparable Passage of this Reverend and truly Charitable Prelate, I have transcribed intire; because it will undoubtedly give a Sanction to my own Principles of universal Benevolence and Charity. His Lordship affirms, that *all Denominations of Christians* (he will allow me to mention a few of them; Socinians, Arians, Athanasians, Sabellians, Pelagians, Arminians, Calvinists, Episcopalians, Presbyterians, Independants, Anabaptists, &c.) *agree in the Substance of Religion, and in the necessary Enforcements of the Practice of it;* inasmuch as they do all believe firmly and sincerely, those Principles which his Lordship calls, with great Reason and Truth, *a fixed, certain, and uniform Rule of Faith and Practice, as containing all the most necessary Points of Religion, and in it self abundantly sufficient to preserve the Knowledge and Practice of Religion in the World.* My Inference from this noble Concession, for which all the Friends to Liberty, in Church and State, throughout *Great Britain,* will thank his Lordship, is this; that since all Denominations of Christians do, in his Lordship's Judgment, receive his fixed, certain, and uniform Rule of Faith, and embrace all the most necessary Points of Religion; to impose Subscriptions to Articles of Faith and human Creeds, must be a very unreasonable and needless Thing: For either such Articles and Creeds contain nothing more than this same Rule of Faith and Practice; and then all Subscriptions to them is Impertinent; because this is already received by all Denominations of Christians, and is abundantly sufficient, by the Bishop's own Allowance, to preserve the Knowledge and Practice of Religion in the World: Or such Articles and Creeds contain something more

than

than his Lordſhip's fixed Rule of Faith and Practice, ſomething more than all the moſt neceſſary Points of Religion, ſomething more than is ſufficient to preſerve the Knowledge and Practice of Religion in the World, *h. e.* ſome very unneceſſary Points of Religion ; ſomething on which the Preſervation of Religion doth not depend ; and of Conſequence, Subſcriptions to unneceſſary Articles of Faith, on which Religion doth not depend, can never be neceſſary to qualify any Perſon for a Miniſter of the Church of Chriſt, and therefore not for the Church of *England,* if that be Part of the Church of Chriſt. And this is the more unneceſſary, becauſe, as his Lordſhip farther well obſerves, *the People are not obliged to enter into them, ſo long as they do not touch the Foundations of Chriſtianity,* i. e. ſo far as his Lordſhip's certain, fix'd and uniform Rule, which contains all neceſſary Points of Religion, is not affected by them. And if the People are not obliged to enter into Points of great Intricacy and Diſpute, I humbly conceive, the Clergy cannot be obliged to preach them ; and that of Conſequence 'tis as abſurd to impoſe upon them Subſcriptions to ſuch Things, as to oblige them to ſubſcribe what they need not preach, nor any of their People believe.

Upon his Lordſhip's Principles, the impoſing Subſcriptions to the hard unſcriptural Expreſſions of the *Athanaſians* and *Arians,* by each Party in their Turns, and to the thirty nine Articles of the Church of *England,* muſt be a very unreaſonable and unchriſtian Thing ; becauſe, the Peculiarities to be ſubſcribed, do not one of them, enter into his ſpecified Points of Religion, and are not neceſſary to preſerve Religion in the World ; and after ſo publick a Declaration of Charity towards all Denominations of Chriſtians, and the Safety of Religion and the Church, upon the general Principles he hath laid down, there is no Reaſon to doubt but his Lordſhip will uſe that Power and Influence which God hath entruſted him with, to remove the Wall of Separation in the eſtabliſhed Church, in order to the uniting all differing Sects, all Denominations of Chriſtians, in one viſible Communion ; and that he will join in that moſt Chriſtian and Catholick Prayer of one of his own Brethren, though diſapproved of by another of narrower Principles, *Bleſ-* *Biſhop of* *ſed be they who have contributed to ſo good a Work.* Subſcriptions have ever been *Bangor's* *Anſwer to* a Grievance in the Church of God, and the firſt Introduction of them was *the Dean* owing to Pride, and the Claim of an unrighteous and ungodly Power. Nei- *of Wor-* ther the Warrant of Scripture, nor the Intereſt of Truth made them neceſſary. *ceſter.* 'Tis, I think, but by few, if any, pretended that the ſacred Writings coun- *Poſtſcript,* tenance this Practice. They do indeed abound with Directions and Exhor- *p. 107.* tations to *adhere ſtedfaſtly to the Faith, not to be moved from the Faith,* nor *toſſed about with every Wind of Doctrine.* But what is the Faith which we are to adhere to ? What the Faith eſtabliſhed and ſtamped for Orthodox by the Biſhops and Councils ? Ridiculous ! If this was the Caſe, our Faith muſt be as various as their Creeds, and as abſurd and contradictory as their Deciſions. No, The Faith we are to be grounded and ſettled in, is that *which was at once delivered to the Saints,* that which was preached by the Apoſtles to *Gentiles,* as well as *Jews ; the wholeſome Words we are to conſent to are the Words*

of

of our Lord Jesus Christ, and the Doctrine which is according to Godliness This all genuine Christians receive, out of regard to a much higher Authority than belongs to any Set of Men in the World ; and therefore the Sanction of Fathers and Councils in this Case, is as impertinent as a Man's pretending to give a Sanction to the Constitutions of the Great God. And as to all other Articles of Faith, neither they, nor any others, have any Commission to impose them on the Consciences of Men, and the Moment they attempt to do it, they cease to be Servants in the House of God, and act as the true and proper Lords of the Heritage.

But it may be said, That *the Church hath Power to determine in Controversies of Faith ; so as not to decree any thing against Scripture, nor to enforce any thing to be believed as necessary to Salvation besides it* ; i. e. I suppose the Church hath Power to guard the Truths of Scripture ; and in any Controversies about Doctrines, to determine what is or is not agreeable to Scripture, and to enforce the Reception of what they thus decree, by obliging others to subscribe to their Decisions. If this be the Case, then it necessarily follows, that their Determinations must be ever right, and constantly agreeable to the Doctrine of holy Writ ; and that they ought never to determine, but when they are in the Right, and are sure they are in the Right ; because, if the Matter be difficult in its Nature, or the Clergy have any Doubts and Scruples concerning it, or are liable to make false Decisions, they cannot, with any Reason, make a final Decision ; because 'tis possible they may decide on the wrong side of the Question ; and thus decree Falshood instead of Truth. And I presume there are but few who will claim, in Words, so extraordinary a Power as that of establishing Falshood in the room of Truth and Scripture. And even supposing their Decisions to be right, how will it follow that they have a Power to oblige others to submit to and subscribe them ? If by sound Reason and Argument they can convince the Consciences of others, they are sure of the Agreement of all such with them in Principle ; and upon this Foot Subscriptions are wholly useless ; and if they cannot convince them, 'tis a very unrighteous Thing to impose Subscriptions on them ; and a shameful Prevarication with God and Man for any to submit to them without it. Decisions made in Controversies of Faith, by the Clergy, carry in them no Force nor Evidence of Truth. Let their Office be ever so sacred, it doth not exempt them from human Frailties and Imperfections. They are as liable to Error and Mistake, to Prejudice and Passion, as any of the Laity whatsoever can be. How then can the Clergy have any Authority in Controversies of Faith, which the Laity have not ? That they have erred in their Decisions, and decreed Light to be Darkness, and Darkness Light ; that they have perplexed the Consciences of Men, and corrupted the Simplicity of the Faith in Christ, all their Councils and Synods are a notorious Proof. With what Justice or Modesty then can they pretend to a Power of obliging others to believe their Articles, or subscribe them ? If I was to speak the real Truth, it will be found, that those numerous Opinions which have been anathematised as Heretical, and which

2   have

have broken the Chriſtian World into Parties, have been generally invented, and broached, and propagated by the Clergy; witneſs *Arius, Macedonius, Neſto- rius, Eutyches, Dioſcorus,* and others; and therefore if we may judge by any Obſervations made on the Riſe of Hereſy, what is a proper Method to put a Stop to the Progreſs of it, it cannot be the Clergy's forming Articles of Faith, and forcing others to ſubſcribe them; becauſe this is the very Method by which they have eſtabliſhed and propagated it.

The Truth is, this Method of preventing Error will ſuit all Religions, and all Sorts of Principles whatſoever, and is that by which Error main- tains its Ground, and is indeed render'd impregnable. All the different Sorts of *Chriſtians, Papiſts* and *Proteſtants, Greeks, Lutherans, Calviniſts* and *Ar- minians,* cannot certainly be right in their diſcriminating Principles. And yet where ſhall we find any Clergy that don't pretend a Right to impoſe Subſcrip- tions, and who do not maintain theTruth of the Articles to which they make ſuch Subſcription neceſſary? Upon this Foot the Doctrines of the Council of *Trent,* the thirty nine Articles of the Church of *England,* and the Aſſemblies Confeſſion of Faith, are all of them equally true, Chriſtian and Sacred; for they are in dif- ferent Places embraced as Standards of Orthodoxy, and their Sacredneſs and Authority ſecur'd and maintain'd by the Subſcriptions of the Clergy to them: And therefore, I think it as little agreeable to Prudence as it is to Juſtice for Chriſtians to keep up a Practice that may be ſo eaſily, and hath been ſo of- ten turned into a Security for Hereſy, Superſtition and Idolatry; and eſpe- cially for Proteſtants to ware any longer theſe Marks of Slavery, which their Enemies, whenever they have Power, will not fail to make Uſe of, either to fetter their Conſciences, or diſtinguiſh them for the Burning.

But it may be ſaid that the Abuſe of Subſcriptions is no Argument againſt the Uſe of them; and that, as they are proper to diſcover what Mens Senti- ments are, they may be ſo far ſometimes a Guard and Security to the Truth. But as all Parties, who uſe them, will urge this Reaſon for them, that they are in Poſſeſſion of the Truth, and therefore willing to do all they can to ſe- cure and promote it; of Conſequence Subſcriptions to Articles of Faith can never be looked on properly as Guards to real Truth, but as Guards to cer- tain prevailing Principles, whether true or falſe. And even in this Caſe they are wholly Ineffectual. The Clergy of the Church of *England* are bound to ſubſcribe the thirty nine Articles, *i. e.* to the Truth of *Athanaſian* and *Calvi- niſtick* Principles. But hath this Subſcription anſwer'd its End? Do not the Clergy, who are all Subſcribers, and who often repeat their Subſcriptions, differ about theſe Heads as much as if they had never ſubſcribed at all? Men that have no Principles of Religion and Virtue, but enter the Church only with a View to the Benefices and Preferments of it, will ſubſcribe ten thou- ſand Times over, and to any Articles that can be given them, whether true or falſe. Thus the *Aſiatick* Biſhops ſubſcribed to the Condemnation of the Decrees of the Council of *Chalcedon,* and inform *Baſiliſcus* the Emperor that their Subſcriptions were voluntary. And yet when *Baſiliſcus* was depoſed, they immediately ſubſcribed to the Truth of thoſe Decrees, and ſwore their

firſt

firſt Subſcription was involuntary.   So that Subſcriptions cannot keep out any
Atheiſts, Infidels, or profligate Perſons.   And as to others, daily Experience
teaches us, that they either disbelieve the Articles they ſubſcribe, ſubſcribing them only as Articles of Peace; or elſe, that after they have ſubſcribed
them, they ſee Reaſon, upon a more mature Deliberation, to alter their
Minds, and change their original Opinions.   So that till Men can be brought
always to act upon Conſcience, never to ſubſcribe what they do not believe,
nor ever to alter their Judgment, as to the Articles they have ſubſcribed ; Subſcriptions are as impertinent and uſeleſs as they are unreaſonable, and can never anſwer the Purpoſes of thoſe who impoſe them.

But I apprehend farther, that this impoſing of Subſcriptions is *not only an
unreaſonable Cuſtom,* but attended with many very pernicious Conſequences.   It is
a great Hindrance to that Freedom and Impartiality of Inquiry which is the
unalterable Duty of every Man, and neceſſary to render his Religion reaſonable and acceptable.   For why ſhould any Perſon make any Inquiries
for his own Information, when his Betters have drawn up a Religion for
him, and thus kindly ſaved him the Labour and Pains ? And as his worldly
Intereſt may greatly depend on his doing as he is bid, and ſubſcribing as he
is ordered ; is it not reaſonable to think that the generality will contentedly
take every thing upon Truſt, and prudently refrain from creating to themſelves Scruples and Doubts, by nicely examining what they are to ſet their
Hands to, leaſt they ſhould miſs of Promotion for not being able to comply
with the Condition of it, or enjoy their Promotions with a diſſatisfied and
uneaſy Conſcience ?

Subſcriptions will, I own, ſometimes prove Marks of Diſtinction, and as
Walls of Separation : For though Men of Integrity and Conſcience may,
and oftentimes undoubtedly do ſubmit to them ; yet Men of no Principles,
or very looſe ones, worldly and ambitious Men, the Thoughtleſs and Ignorant, will moſt certainly do it, when they find it for their Intereſt.   The
Church that encloſes her ſelf with theſe Fences, leaves abundant Room for the
Entrance of Perſons of ſuch Characters.   To whom then doth ſhe refuſe
Admittance ? Why, if to any, it muſt be to Men who cannot bend their
Conſciences to their Intereſt ; who cannot believe, without Examination,
nor ſubſcribe any Articles of Faith as true, without underſtanding and believing them.   'Tis in the very Nature of Subſcriptions to exclude none but
theſe, and to diſtinguiſh ſuch only for Shame and Puniſhment.   Now how is
this conſiſtent with any Thing that is called Reaſon or Religion ? If there
could be found out any wiſe and reaſonable Methods to throw out of the
Chriſtian Church and Miniſtry, Men who are in their Hearts Unbelievers,
who abide in the Church only for the Revenues ſhe yields to them, who ſhift
their religious and political Principles, according to their Intereſt, who propagate Doctrines inconſiſtent with the Liberties of Mankind, and are ſcandalous
and immoral in their Lives ; if Subſcriptions could be made to anſwer theſe
Ends, and theſe only, and to throw Infamy upon ſuch Men, and upon ſuch
Men only ; no one would have any Thing to alledge againſt the Uſe of them.
                                                                Whereas,

Whereas, in Truth, Subfcriptions are the great Securities of fuch profligate Wretches, who, by complying with them, enter into the Church, and thereby fhare in all the temporal Advantages of it ; whilft the fcrupulous, confcientious Chriftian is the only one fhe excludes, who thinks the Word of God a more fure Rule of Faith than the Dictates of Men ; and that Subfcriptions are Things much too facred to be trifled with, or lightly fubmitted to.

They are indeed very great Snares to many Perfons, and Temptations to them too often to trefpafs upon the Rules of ftrict Honefty and Virtue. For when Mens Subfiftence and Advantages in the World depend on their fubfcribing to certain Articles of Faith, 'tis one of the moft powerful Arguments that can be, to engage them to comply with it. 'Tis poffible indeed they may have their Objections againft the Reafonablenefs and Truth of what they are to fubfcribe. But will not Intereft often lead them to overlook their Difficulties, to explain away the natural Meaning of Words, to put a different Senfe upon the Articles than what they will fairly bear, to take them in any Senfe, and to fubfcribe them in no Senfe only as Articles of Peace ? It muft be by fome fuch Evafions that *Arians* fubfcribe to *Athanafian* Creeds, and *Arminians* to Principles of rigid *Calvinifm*. This the Clergy have been again and again reproach'd with, even by the Enemies of Chriftianity. And I am forry to fay it, they have not been able to wipe off the Scandal from themfelves. I am far from faying or believing that all the Clergy make thefe evafive Subfcriptions : Thofe only that do fo give this Offence ; and if they are, in other Cafes, Men of Integrity and Confcience, they are Objects of great Compaffion. As far as my own Judgment is concerned, I think this Manner of Subfcribing to Creeds and Articles of Faith, is infamous in its Nature, and vindicable upon no Principles of Confcience and Honour. It tends to render the Clergy contemptible in the Eyes of the People, who will be apt to think that they have but little Reafon to regard the Sermons of Men, who have prevaricated in their Subfcriptions, and that they preach for the fame Reafon only that they fubfcribed, *viz.* their worldly Intereft. 'Tis of very pernicious Influence and Example, and in its Confequences leads to the Breach of all Faith amongft Mankind, and tends to the Subverfion of civil Society. For if the Clergy are known to prevaricate in fubfcribing to religious Tefts of Orthodoxy, is it not to be fear'd that others may learn from them to prevaricate in their Subfcriptions to civil Tefts of Loyalty ? And indeed, there is a great deal of Reafon to imagine, that if Men can tutor and twift their Confciences fo as to fubfcribe Articles of Faith, contrary to their own Perfuafion, and only as Articles of Peace, or a Qualification for a Living, they would fubfcribe for the fame Reafon to Popery or Mahometanifm ; for if this be a good Reafon for fubfcribing any Articles which I do not believe, 'tis a Reafon for fubfcribing all ; and therefore I humbly apprehend that a Practice, which gives fo much Occafion to fuch fcandalous Prevarications with God and Man, fhould be caft off as an infufferable Grievance, and as an Yoak upon the Necks of the Clergy, too heavy for them to bear.

Let

Let me add farther, that this Practice of impofing Subfcriptions, hath been the Occafion of innumerable Mifchiefs in the Church of God. 'Twas the common Cry of the Orthodox and *Arians,* and all other Hereticks, in their Turns of Power, *Either fubfcribe or depart from your Churches.* This enflamed the Clergy againft each other, and filled them with Hatred, Malice and Revenge. For as by impofing thefe Subfcriptions, Inquifition was made into the Confciences of others; the Refufal to fubmit to them was a certain Mark of Herefy and Reprobation; and the Confequence of this was the Infliction of all fpiritual and temporal Punifhments. 'Twas impoffible but that fuch Procedures fhould perpetuate the Schifms and Divifions of the Church, fince the Wrath of Man cannot work the Righteoufnefs of God, and fince Civil Punifhments have no Tendency to convince the Confcience, but only to enflame the Paffions againft the Advifers and Inflicters of them. And as ecclefiaftical Hiftory gives us fo dreadful an Account of the melancholy and tragical Effects of this Practice, one would think that no Nation, who knew the Worth of Liberty, no Chriftan Proteftant Church, that hath any Regard for the Peace of the Flock of Chrift, fhould ever be found to authorize and continue it.

VI. What Security then fhall we have left us for Truth and Orthodoxy, when our Subfcriptions are gone? Why, the facred Scriptures, thofe Oracles of the great God, and Freedom and Liberty to interpret and underftand them as we can; the Confequence of this would be great Integrity and Peace of Confcience, in the Enjoyment of our religious Principles, Union and Friendfhip amongft Chriftians, notwithftanding all their Differences in Judgment, and great Refpect and Honour to thofe faithful Paftors, that carefully feed the Flock of God, and lead them into Paftures of Righteoufnefs and Peace. We fhall lofe only the Incumbrances of Religion, our Bones of Contention, the Shackles of our Confciences, and the Snares to Honefty and Virtue; whilft all that is fubftantially good and valuable, all that is truly divine and heavenly, would remain to enrich and blefs us. The Clergy would indeed lofe their Power to do Mifchief; but would they not be happy in that Lofs, efpecially as they would be infinitely more likely to do good? They would be no longer looked on as Fathers and Dictators in the Faith; but ftill they might remain Ambaffadors for Chrift, befeeching Men, in Chrift's ftead, to become reconciled to God. And was all human Authority, in Matters of Faith, thus wholly laid afide, would not the Word of God have a freer Courfe, and be much more abundantly glorified? All Chriftians would look upon Scripture as the only Rule of their Faith and Practice, and therefore fearch it with greater Diligence and Care, and be much more likely to underftand the Mind of God therein. The main Things of Chriftianity, would unqueftionably be generally agreed to by all; and as to other Things, Points of Speculation, and difficult Queftions, if Chriftians differ'd about them, their Differences would be of no great Importance, and might be maintained, confiftent with Charity and Peace.

Indeed, a strict and constant Adherence to Scripture, as the only Judge in Controversies of Christian Faith, would be the most likely Method to introduce into the Church, a real Uniformity of Opinion as well as Practice. For if this was the Case, many Disputes would be wholly at an End, as having nothing to give Occasion to them in the sacred Writings; and all others would be greatly shorten'd, as hereby all foreign Terms, and human Phrases of Speech, by which the Questions that have been controverted amongst Christians, have been darken'd and perplexed, would be immediately laid aside, and the only Enquiry would be, What is the Sense of Scripture? What the Doctrine of Christ and his Apostles? This is a much more short and effectual Way of determining Controversies, than sending Men to *Nice* and *Chalcedon*, to Councils and Synods, to *Athanasius* or *Arius*, to *Calvin* or *Arminius*, or any other Persons whatsoever that can be mentioned, who at best deliver but their own Sense of Scripture, and are not to be regarded any farther than they agree with it. It was a Departure from this, as the great Standard of Faith, and corrupting the Simplicity of the Gospel Doctrine by hard unscriptural Words, that gave Occasion to the innumerable Controversies, that formerly troubled the Christian Church. Human Creeds were substituted in the Room of Scripture; and according as Circumstances differ'd, or new Opinions were broached, so were the Creeds corrected, amended and enlarged, till they became so full of Subtleties, Contradictions, and Nonsense, as must make every thoughtful Man read many of them with Contempt. The Controversy was not about Scripture Expressions, but about the Words of Men, not about the Sense of Scripture, but the Decrees of Councils, and the Opinions of *Athanasius*, *Leo*, *Cyril*, and the venerable Fathers. And upon this foot 'twas no Wonder their Disputes should be endless; since the Writings of all fallible Men must certainly be more obscure and intricate than the Writings of the infallible Spirit of Truth, who could be at no Loss about the Doctrines he dictated, nor for proper Words suitably to express them. 'Tis infinite, 'tis endless Labour, to consult all that the Fathers have written; and when we have consulted them, What one Controversy have they rationally decided? What one Christian Doctrine have they clearly and solidly explain'd? How few Texts of Scripture have they critically settled the Sense and Meaning of? How often do they differ from one another, and in how many Instances from themselves? Those who read them greatly differ in their Interpretation of them; and Men of the most contrary Sentiments, all claim them for their own. *Athanasius* and *Arians* appeal to the Fathers, and support their Principles by Quotations from them. And are these the venerable Gentlemen whose Writings are to be set up in Opposition to the Scripture, or set up as authoritative Judges of the Sense of Scripture? Are Creeds of their dictating to be submitted to as the only Criterion of Orthodoxy, or esteemed as Standards to distinguish between Truth and Error? Away with this Folly and Superstition! The Creeds of the Fathers and Councils are but human Creeds, that have all the Marks in them of human Frailty and Ignorance. The Creeds which are to be found in the Gospel, are the infallible Dictates of

the

the Spirit of the God of Truth, and as such, claim our Reverence and Submission ; and as the forming our Principles according to them, as far as we are able to understand them, makes us Christians in the Sight of God, it should be sufficient to every ones being owned as a Christian by others, without their using any inquisitory Forms of Trial, till they can produce their Commission from Heaven for the Use of them. This, as it is highly reasonable in it self, would do the highest Honour to the Christian Clergy ; who, instead of being reproach'd for Haughtiness and Pride, as Incendiaries and Plagues of Mankind, as the Sowers of Contention and Strife, and Disturbers of the Peace of the Church of God ; would be honoured for their Works sake, esteemed for their Characters, lov'd as Blessings to the World, heard with Pleasure, and successful in their Endeavours to recommend the Knowledge and Practice of Christianity.

VII. Were the Doctrines of the Gospel regarded as they should be, and the Precepts of the Christian Religion submitted to by all who profess to believe it, universal Benevolence would be the certain Effect, and eternal Peace and Union would reign amongst the Members of the Christian Church. For if there are any Commands of certain Clearness, any Precepts of evident Obligation in the Gospel, they are such as refer to the Exercise of Love, and the maintaining universal Charity. In our Saviour's admirable Discourse on the Mount, this was the excellent Doctrine he taught : *Blessed are the Meek, for they shall inherit the Earth. Blessed are the Merciful, for they shall obtain Mercy. Blessed are the Peace-makers, for they shall be called the Children of God.* And in another Place, describing the Nature of Religion in general, he tells us, that *the Love of God is the first Commandment, and that the second is like unto it ; Thou shalt love thy Neighbour as thy self.* This he enjoins upon his Disciples as his peculiar Command : *This is my Commandment, that ye love one another, as I have loved you ;* and recommends it to them as that whereby they were to be distinguished from all other Persons. *A new Commandment I give unto you, that ye love one another as I have loved you, that ye also love one another. By this shall all Men know that ye are my Disciples, if ye have Love one to another.* This was the more needful for them, considering that our Lord foreknew the grievous Persecutions that would befal them for his sake ; to encourage them under which, he pronounces them blest : *Blessed are they which are persecuted for Righteousness sake, for theirs is the Kingdom of Heaven* ; whilst, at the same time, he leaves a Brand of Infamy on Persecutors, and marks them out for the Vengeance of God : *Rejoice and be exceeding glad, for great is your Reward in Heaven ; for so persecuted they the Prophets that were before you. Woe unto you, for ye build the Sepulchres of the Prophets, and your Fathers killed them ; therefore, saith the Wisdom of God, I will send you Prophets and Apostles, and they will slay and persecute them, that the Blood of all the Prophets—— may be required of this Generation.* And, indeed, so far was our Lord from encouraging any persecuting Methods, that he rebuked and put a Stop to all the Appearances of them. Thus when his Disciples would have called down Fire from Heaven to consume the *Samaritans,*

Matt. v. 5, 7, 9

Matt. xxii. 35.

John xv. 12.

xiii. 34, 35.

Matt. v. 10.

Luke xi. 47, &c.

ritans, who refufed to receive him, he rebuked them, and faid, *Ye know not* Luke ix. *what manner of Spirit ye are of* ; *the Son of Man is not come to deftroy Mens Lives,* 55, 56. *but to fave them* ; and when one of thofe who were with Chrift cut off the Ear of one of the high Prieft's Servants, upon his laying Hands on him, he feverely reproved him ; *Put up again thy Sword into its Place* ; *for all they that take the* Matt. *Sword fhall perifh with the Sword.* And, in order to cure his Apoftles of their xxvi. 52. Ambition and Pride, and to prevent their claiming an undue Power, he gave them an Example of great Humility and Condefcention, in wafhing and wiping their Feet, and forbid them imitating the Gentiles, *by exercifing* xx. 25, *Dominion and Authority* ; *but whoever will be great amongft you, let him be your* &c. *Minifter* ; *and whofoever will be chief amongft you, let him be your Servant, even as the Son of Man came not to be minifter'd unto, but to minifter, and to give his Life a Ranfom for many.* And as the Jewifh Teachers took on them the Name of Rabbi, to denote their Power over the Confciences of thofe they inftructed, he commanded his Difciples, *Be ye not called Rabbi, for one is your Mafter, even* xxiii. 8, *Chrift, and all ye are Brethren* ; *and call no Man Father upon Earth, for one is your* &c. *Father, which is in Heaven.* *But he that is greateft amongft you, fhall be your Servant.* From thefe, and other Paffages of like Nature, it is very evident, that there is nothing in the Life of Jefus Chrift, that gives any Countenance to thefe wicked Methods of propagating and fupporting Religion, that fome of his pretended Followers have made ufe of, but the ftrongeft Directions to the contrary.

It is indeed objected, that Chrift fays, *Compel them to come in, that my Houfe* Luke xiv. *may be full :* But that this Compulfion means nothing more than Invitation and 23. Perfuafion, is evident, from the parallel Place of Scripture, where what St. Luke calls, *Compel them to come in,* is expreffed by, *Bid them to the Marriage,* i. e. Matt. xxii. endeavour, not by Force of Arms, but by Argument and Reafon, by Im- 9. portunity and Earneftnefs, and by fetting before Men the Promifes and Threatnings of the Gofpel, and thus addreffing your felves to their Hopes and Fears, to perfuade and compel them to embrace my Religion, and become the Subjects of my Kingdom ; and in this moral Senfe of Compulfion, the original Word is often ufed. But farther, 'tis, by a late Writer, reckon'd Chriftiani- very furprizing, that Chrift fhould fay, *Think not I am come to fend Peace,* J ty as old, *come not to fend Peace, but a Sword* ; *for I am come to fet a Man at Variance with* &c. p. 305. *his Father, and the Daughter againft her Mother,* &c. But how is this fo very 34, 35. furprizing ? or what Man of common Senfe can miftake the Meaning of the Words, who reads the whole Difcourfe ? In the former Part of it, 'tis exprefly declared, that the moft grievous Perfecutions fhould befall his Difci- ples for his fake ; that *Brother fhould deliver up Brother to Death, and the Father the Child* ; *and the Children fhall rife up againft their Parents, and caufe them to be put to Death.* Can any Man underftand this of an Intention in Chrift to fet People at Variance, when 'tis a Prediction only of what fhould be the Confequence of publifhing his Gofpel, through the Malice and Cruelty of its Oppofers ; a Prediction of what his Difciples were to fuffer, and not of what they were to make others to fuffer. And as to that Paf-

q

Luke xii. 49, 51. fage in *Luke, I am come to fend Fire on the Earth ; and what will I, if it be already kindled? Suppofe ye that I am come to give Peace on Earth? I tell you nay, but rather Divifion.* How is it explain'd by Chrift himfelf? Why, in the very next Words : *For from henceforth,* i. e. upon the Publication of my Religion and Gofpel, *there fhall be five in one Houfe divided, three againft two, and two againft three,* &c. Can any Man need Paraphrafe and Criticifm to explain thefe Paffages of any Thing, but of that Perfecution which fhould befall the Preachers and Believers of the Gofpel ? Or imagine it to be a prophetick Defcription of a Fire to be blown up by Chrift to confume others, when the whole Connection evidently refers it to a Fire, that the Oppofers of his Religion fhould blow up, to confume himfelf and Followers? Jefus knew 'twas fuch a Fire as would firft confume himfelf. *I am come to fend Fire on the Earth ; and what will I, if it be already kindled?* Or, as the Words fhould be tranflated, *How do I wifh it was already kindled?* How do I wifh it to break out on my own Perfon, that I might glorify God by my Sufferings and Death? For as it follows, *I have a Baptifm to be baptized with,* a Baptifm with my own Blood : *And how am I ftraiten'd till it be accomplifh'd!* After this Account of his own Sufferings, he foretells the fame fhould befall his Followers : *Suppofe ye that I am come to give Peace on Earth? I tell you, Nay, but rather Divifion,* i. e. as I my felf muft fuffer to bear Witnefs to the Truth, fo, after my Deceafe, fuch fhall be the unreafonable and furious Oppofition to my Gofpel, as fhall occafion Divifions amongft the neareft Relations, fome of whom fhall hate and perfecute the other for their embracing my Religion. And of Confequence *Chrift did not declare, in the moft exprefs Terms,* as the fore-

Ibid. mentioned Writer afferts, *That he came to do that which we muft fuppofe he came to hinder.* He did only declare, that he came to do what he was refolved not to hinder, *i. e.* to publifh fuch a Religion as his Enemies would put him to Death for, and as would occafion Divifions amongft the neareft Relations, through the unreafonable Hatred and Oppofition that fome would fhew to others upon Account of it. This Matter is elfewhere clearly expreffed

John xvi 1, 2, 3. by Chrift : *Thefe Things have I fpoken to you, that ye fhould not be offended. They fhall put you out of the Synagogues ; yea, the Time cometh, that whofoever killeth you, will think that he doth God Service. And thefe Things will they do unto you, becaufe they have not known the Father nor me,* i. e. have not underftood either natural Religion, or the Religion of my Gofpel.

There is therefore nothing in the Conduct or Doctrines of Jefus Chrift to countenance or encourage Perfecution. His Temper was benevolent, his Conduct merciful, and one governing Defign of all he faid, was to promote Meeknefs and Condefcenfion, univerfal Charity and Love. And in this all

Rom. xii. 9, 10. his Apoftles were careful Imitators of his Example : *Let Love,* faith St. *Paul, be without Diffimulation ; be kindly affectioned one to another with brotherly Love, in Honour, prefering one another. If it be poffible, as much as in you lies, live*

xiii. 10: *peaceably with all Men.* And the Love he recommended was fuch, *as worketh no ill to his Neighbour,* and which therefore he declares *to be the fulfilling of the Law.* And, leaft different Sentiments in leffer Matters fhould caufe Divifions viſions amongſt Christians, he commands, *to receive him that is weak in the* Rom. xiv. *Faith, not to doubtful Diſputations,* μη ἐις διακρισεις διαλογισμων, not to judge or [1]. to contend about Diſputations, or diſputable Things. Upon Account of ſuch Matters, he orders that none ſhould *deſpiſe or judge others, becauſe God* Rom. xiv. *had received them,* and becauſe every Man ought to be *fully perſuaded in his own* [3, 5.] *Mind,* and becauſe *the Kingdom of God was not Meat and Drink, but Righteouſneſs* 17. *and Peace, and Joy, in the Holy Ghoſt,* and becauſe every one was to *give an* 4. *Account of himſelf to God,* to whom alone, as his only Maſter, he was to ſtand or fall. From theſe ſubſtantial Reaſons, he infers, *We then that are ſtrong,* xv. 1. who have the moſt perfect Underſtanding of the Nature of Chriſtianity, and our Chriſtian Liberty, *ought to bear the Infirmities of the Weak, and not to* 5. *pleaſe our ſelves ;* and having pray'd for them, that the God of Patience and Conſolation would grant them to *be like minded one towards another, according to,* or after the Example of *Chriſt,* that, notwithſtanding the Strength of ſome, and the Weakneſs of others, they might, *with one Mind, and with one Mouth,* 6. *glorify God, even the Father of our Lord Jeſus Chriſt ;* he adds, as the Concluſion of his Argument, *Wherefore receive ye one another, as Chriſt alſo received* 7. *us to the Glory of God.*

In his Letters to the *Corinthians,* he diſcovers the ſame divine and aimiable 1 Cor. i. Spirit. In his firſt Epiſtle, he beſeeches them, *by the Name of the Lord Jeſus* 10, &c. *Chriſt, that they would all ſpeak the ſame Thing, and that there ſhould be no Schiſm amongſt them,* but that they ſhould be *perfectly joined together in the ſame Mind, and in the ſame Judgment,* i. e. that they ſhould all own and ſubmit to Chriſt, as their only Lord and Head, and not rank themſelves under different Leaders, as he had been informed they had done ; for that they were *the Body of* xii 27. *Chriſt,* and all of them his Members, and ought therefore to maintain that *Charity* to one another, *which ſuffereth long, and is kind, which envieth not,* xiii. 1, &c. *vaunteth not it ſelf, is not puffed up, doth not behave it ſelf unſeemly, ſeeketh not her own, is not edſily provoked, thinketh no Evil, rejoiceth not in Iniquity, but rejoiceth in the Truth, beareth all Things, believeth all Things, hopeth all Things, endureth all Things, which is greater and more excellent than Faith and Hope, which fails not in Heaven it ſelf,* where Faith and Hope ſhall be at an End ; and without which, though we could *ſpeak with the Tongue of Men and Angels, ſhould have the Gift of Prophecy, and underſtand all Myſteries, and all Knowledge, and could remove Mountains, yea, though we ſhould beſtow all our Goods to feed the Poor, and give our Bodies to be burned, we ſhould be only as ſounding Braſs, and as a tinkling Cymbal,* nothing in the Account of God, nothing as to any real Profit and Advantage that will accrue to us. And, in his ſecond Epiſtle, he takes his Leave 2 Cor. of them with this divine Exhortation, and glorious Encouragement: *Finally,* xiii. 11. *Brethren, farewell, be perfect, be of good Comfort, be of one Mind,* το αυτο φρονειτε, be affectionate and kindly diſpoſed to one another, as though you were influenced by one common Mind ; *Live in Peace, and the God of Love and Peace ſhall be with you.*

In his Epiſtle to the *Galatians,* he gives us a Catalogue of thoſe Works Gal v. of the Fleſh which exclude Men from the Kingdom of God, ſuch as Adul- 19, &c. tery,

tery, Fornication,—*Hatred, Variance, Emulation, Wrath, Strife, Seditions, He-*
refies, Envyings, and the like ; and then affures us, that *the Fruits of the Spirit*
are Love, Joy, Peace, Long-fuffering, Gentlenefs, Goodnefs, Faith, Meeknefs, and
Temperance, againft which there is no Law; and, after having laid down this as

Gal. vi. an effential Principle of Chriftianity, that *neither Circumcifion availeth any Thing,*
15. *nor Uncircumcifion, but a new Creature,* or, as 'tis expreffed in another Place,
Faith which works by Love ; he pronounces this truly apoftolick Benediction,
16. *As many as walk according to this Rule, Peace be on them, and Mercy, and upon*
the Ifrael *of God.*

The fame divine and excellent Strain runs through his Letter to the *Ephe-*
Eph. iv. *fians : I therefore, the Prifoner of the Lord, befeech you that ye walk worthy of the Vo-*
1, &c. *cation wherewith ye are called, with all Lowlinefs and Meeknefs, with Long-fuffering*
and Meeknefs, forbearing one another in Love, endeavouring to keep the Unity of the
Spirit in the Bond of Peace ; and the Term of this Union, which he lays down
is the Acknowledgment of one Catholick Church, one Spirit, one Lord and
Mediator, and *one God, even the Father of all, who is above all, through all, and*
31. *in all.* The contrary Vices of *Bitternefs, and Wrath, and Anger, and Clamour,*
32. *and evil fpeaking, and Malice, are to be put away,* as Things that *grieve the Holy*
Spirit of God : and we muft *be kind one to another, forgiving one another, even as*
v. 1, 2. *God, for Chrift's fake, hath forgiven us, and be Followers of God, by walking in*
Love, even as Chrift hath alfo loved us, and hath given himfelf for us.

His Exhortation to the *Philippians,* is in the moft moving Terms : *If there*
Phil. ii. *be any Confolation in Chrift, if any Comfort of Love, if any Fellowfhip of the Spirit,*
1, &c. *if any Bowels and Mercies, fulfil ye my Joy, that ye be like minded, having the fame*
Love, being of one Accord, of one Mind. Let nothing be done through Strife or Vain-
glory, but in lowlinefs of Mind let each efteem other better than themfelves.

In his Exhortation to the *Coloffians,* he warmly preffes our cultivating the
Coloff. iii. fame Difpofition, and abounding in the fame Practice : *Put of all thefe, Anger,*
3, &c. *Wrath, Malice ;—put on as the Elect of God, holy and beloved, Bowels of Mercies,*
Kindnefs, Humblenefs of Mind, Meeknefs, Long-fuffering, forbearing one another,
and forgiving one another, even as Chrift forgave us. And, above all thefe Things,
put on Charity, which is the Bond of Perfectnefs, and let the Peace of God rule in
your Hearts, to which alfo ye are called in one Body.

In his Directions to *Timothy,* he gives him this Summary of all practical
1 Tim. i Religion : *The End of the Commandment is Charity out of a pure Heart, and a good*
5, &c. *Confcience, and Faith unfeigned,* and he afcribes Mens turning afide to vain
jangling, to their having fwerved from this great Principle.

And, to mention no more Paffages on this Head, I fhall conclude this whole
Account with that amiable Defcription of the Wifdom, that is from above gi-.
ven by St. *James : The Wifdom that is from above, is pure and peaceable, and*
James iii. *gentle, and eafy to be intreated, full of good Fruits, without Partiality, and without*
14, &c. *Hypocrify. But if we have bitter Envying and Strife in our Hearts, we have nothing*
to glory in, but we lye againft the Truth, i. e. belye our Chriftian Profeffion ; for
whatever falfe Judgment we may pafs upon our felves, this *Wifdom defcendeth*
not from above, but is earthly, fenfual, devilifh ; for where *Envying and Strife is, there*
is Confufion, and every evil Work. .

I i

I have' thrown all thefe excellent Paffages of the facred Writings together, that it may appear in the moft convincing Light, that the Scriptures have nothing in them to countenance the Spirit, or any of the Methods of Perfecution, and to confront the melancholy Account I have given before of the Progrefs and Ravages caufed by this accurfed Evil. Good God, how have the Practices of Chriftians differed from the Precepts of Chriftianity ! Would one imagine that the Authors of thofe dreadful Mifchiefs and Confufions were the Bifhops and Minifters of the Chriftian Church? That they had ever read the Records of Chriftian Religion? Or if they had, that they ever believed them?

But it may be objected, that whatever may be the Precepts of the Chriftian Religion, yet the Conduct even of the Apoftles themfelves gives fome Countenance to the Spirit and Practice of Perfecution, and particularly the Conduct of St. *Paul* ; and that fuch Powers are given to the Guides and Bifhops of the Chriftian Church, as do either exprefly or virtually include in them a Right to perfecute. Let us briefly examine each of thefe Pretenfions.

As to the Practice of the Apoftles, *Beza* mentions two Inftances to vindicate the Punifhment of Hereticks. The firft is that of *Ananias* and *Sapphira*, ftruck dead by *Peter* ; and the other that of *Elymas* the Sorcerer, ftruck blind by *Paul*. But how impertinently are both thefe Inftances alledged ? Herefy was not the Thing punifhed in either of them. *Ananias* and *Sapphira* were ftruck dead for Hypocrify and Lying, and for confpiring, if it were poffible, to deceive God. *Elymas* was a *Jewifh* Sorcerer, and falfe Prophet, a fubtle mifchievous Fellow, an Enemy to Righteoufnefs and Virtue, who withftood the Apoftolick Authority, and endeavoured, by his Frauds, to prevent the Converfion of the Deputy to the Chriftian Faith. The two firft of thefe Perfons were punifhed with Death. By whom? What, by *Peter?* No, by the immediate Hand of God. *Peter* gave them a Reproof fuitable to their Wickednefs ; but as to the Punifhment, he was only the Mouth of God in declaring it, even of that God who knew the Hypocrify of their Hearts, and gave this fignal Inftance of his Abhorrence of it in the Infancy of the Chriftian Church, greatly to difcourage, and, if poffible, for the future, to prevent Mens thus dealing fraudulently and infincerely with God. And, I prefume, if God hath a Right to punifh Frauds and Cheats in another World, he hath a Right to do fo in this ; efpecially in the Inftance before us, which feems to have fomething very peculiar in it. *Peter* exprefly fays to *Sapphira*, *How is it that ye have agreed together to tempt the Spirit of the Lord?* What can this tempting of the Spirit of the Lord be, but an Agreement between *Ananias* and his Wife, to put this Fraud on the Apoftle, to fee whether or no he could difcover it by the Spirit he pretended to? This was a proper Challenge to the Spirit of God, which the Apoftles were endewed with, and a Combination to put the Apoftolick Character to the Trial. Had not the Cheat been difcovered, the Apoftle's Infpiration and Miffion would have been defervedly queftioned, and as the State of Chriftianity required that this divine Miffion fhould be abundantly eftablifhed, *Peter* lets them know that

De Hæret. a Magift. pun. p. 161, &c.

Acts v 9.

I₃ their.

their Hypocrify was difcover'd, and, to create the greater Regard and At-
tention to their Perfons and Meffage, God faw fit to punifh that Hypocrify
with Death.

Acts xiii.
6, &c.
As to *Elymas* the Sorcerer, this Inftance is as foreign and impertinent as
the other. *Sergius Paulus*, Proconful of *Cyprus*, had entertained at *Paphos* one
Barjefus a *Jew*, a Sorcerer; and hearing alfo that *Paul* and *Barnabas* were in
the City, he fent for them to hear the Doctrine they preached. Accordingly they endeavoured to inftruct the *Deputy* in the Chriftian Faith, but were
withftood by *Elymas*, who, by his Subtleties and Tricks, endeavoured to hinder his Converfion. St. *Paul* therefore, in order to confirm his own divine
Miffion, and to prevent the Deputy's being deceived by the Frauds and Sorceries of *Elymas*, after feverely rebuking him for his Sin, and Oppofition to
Chriftianity, tells him, not that the Proconful ought to put him in Jail, and
punifh him with the civil Sword, but that God himfelf would decide the
Controverfy, by ftriking the Sorcerer himfelf immediately blind, which accordingly came to pafs, to the full Conviction of the Proconful. Now what
is there in all this to vindicate Perfecution? God punifhes wicked Men for
Fraud and Sorcery, who knew their Hearts, and had a Right to punifh the
Iniquity of them. Therefore Men may punifh others for Opinions they think
to be true, and are confcientious in embracing, without knowing the Heart,
or being capable of difcovering any Infincerity in it. Or God may vindicate
the Character and Miffion of his own Meffengers, when wickedly oppofed
and denied, by immediate Judgments inflicted by himfelf on their Oppofers.
Therefore the Magiftrate may punifh and put to Death, without any Warrant from God, fuch who believe their Miffion, and are ready to fubmit to it,
as far as they underftand the Nature and Defign of it. Are thefe Confequences juft and rational? or would any Man have brought thefe Inftances
as Precedents for Perfecution, that was not refolved, at all Hazards, to defend and practife it?

1 Cor.v. 5.
Gal. i. 9
v. 12.
Rom. xvi.
17.
1 Cor.v. 9
But doth not St. *Paul* command to *deliver Perfons to Satan for the Deftruction
of the Flefh?* Doth he not *wifh that they were even cut off who trouble Chriftians,
and enjoin us to mark them which caufe Divifions and Offences, contrary to his Doctrine, and to avoid them, and not to eat with them?* Undoubtedly he doth. But
what can be reafonably infer'd from hence in favour of Perfecution, merely
for the fake of Opinions and Principles? In all thefe Inftances, the Things
cenfured are Immoralities and Vices. The Perfon who was deliver'd by
St. *Paul* to Satan, was guilty of a Crime not fo much as named by the *Gentiles*
themfelves, the inceftuous Marriage of his Father's Wife; and the Perfons we
are, as Chriftians, commanded not to keep company and eat with, are Men
of fcandalous Lives; fuch as Fornicators, or Covetous, or Idolaters, or
Railers, or Drunkards, or Extortioners, making a Profeffion of the Chriftian
Religion, or, in St. *Paul's* Phrafe, *called Brethren*; a wife and prudent Exhor-
ration in thofe Days efpecially, to prevent others from being corrupted by
fuch Examples, and any Infamy thrown on the Chriftian Name and Character.
As to hofe whom the Apoftle *wifhes cut off*, they were the perfecuting *Jews*,

who fpread Contention amongft Chriftians, and taught them to bite and devour one another, upon Account of Circumcifion, and fuch-like Trifles; Men that were the Plagues and Corrupters of the Society they belonged to. Men who caufed fuch Divifions, and who caufed them out of a Love to their own Belly, deferved to have a Mark fet upon them, and to be avoided by all who regarded their own Intereft, or the Peace of others.

What the Apoftle means by delivering to Satan, I am not able certainly to determine. It was not, I am fure, the putting the Perfon in Jail, or torturing his Body by an Executioner; nor fending him to the Devil by the Sword or the Fagot. One Thing included in it undoubtedly was, his Separation from the Chriftian Church: *Put away from amongft your felves that wicked* 1 Cor. v. *Perfon*, which probably was attended with fome bodily Diftemper, which, as it 13. came from God, had a Tendency to bring the Perfon to Confideration and Reflection. The immediate Defign of it was the Deftruction of the Flefh, to cure him of his Inceft, that, by Repentance and Reformation, his *Spirit might be faved in the Day of Chrift*; and the Power by which the Apoftle inflicted this Punifhment, was peculiar to himfelf, which God gave him *for Edification, and* 2 Cor. *not for Deftruction:* So that whatever is precifely meant by delivering to Satan, x. 8. it was the Punifhment of a notorious Sin; a Punifhment that carried the Marks of God's Hand, and was defign'd for the Perfon's Good, and was actually inftrumental to recover and fave him, 2 *Cor.* ii. But what Refemblance is there in all this to Perfecution, in which there is no Appearance of the Hand of God, nor any Marks but thofe of the Cruelty and Vengeance of Men; no Immorality punifhed, and, generally fpeaking, nothing that in its Nature deferves Punifhment, or but what deferves Encouragement and Applaufe. And 'tis very probable that this is what St. *Paul* means by his *wifhing thofe cut off* who difturbed the Peace of the *Galatian* Chriftians, by fpreading Divifions amongft them, and exciting Perfecutions againft them; though, I confefs, if St. *Paul* meant more, and pray'd to God that thofe obftinate and incorrigible Enemies to Chriftianity, who, for private Views of worldly Intereft, raifed perpetual Difturbances and Perfecutions where-ever they came, might receive the juft Punifhment of their Sins, and be hereby prevented from doing farther Mifchief, I don't fee how this would have been inconfiftent with Charity, or his own Character, as an infpired Apoftle.

It may poffibly be urged, that though the Things cenfured in thefe Places are Immoralities, yet that there are other Paffages which refer only to Principles, and that the Apoftle *Paul* fpeaks againft them with great Severity: As particularly, *If any Man preach any other Gofpel unto you, than that ye have re-* Gal. i. 5. *ceived, let him be accurfed* And again, *A Man that is an Heretick, after the firft* Tit. iii. *and fecond Admonition, reject.* As to the firft of thefe, nothing can be more 10. evident than that the Apoftle pronounces an Anathema only againft thofe who fubverted the Chriftian Religion, fuch who taught that it was infufficient to Salvation, without Circumcifion, and Submiffion to the *Jewifh* Law: As the Gofpel he taught, was what he had received from Chrift, he had, as an Apoftle, a Right to warn the Churches he wrote to againft corrupting the

2 Sim-

Simplicity of it, and to pronounce an Anathema, *i. e.* to declare, in the Name of his great Master, that all such false Teachers should be condemned who continued to do so; and this is the utmost that can be made of the Expression; and therefore this Place is as impertinently alledged in favour of Persecution, as it would be to alledge those Words of Christ: *He that believeth not, shall be condemned.* The Anathema pronounced, was the divine Vengeance, it was *Anathema Maranatha,* to take Place only when the Lord should come to Judgment, and not to be executed by human Vengeance.

As to Heresy, against which such dreadful Outcries have been raised, 'tis taken indifferently in a good or a bad Sense in the Scripture. In the bad Sense, it signifies, not an involuntary Error, or Mistake of Judgment, into which serious and honest Minds may fall, after a careful Enquiry into the Will of God, but a wilful criminal Corruption of the Truth for worldly Ends and Purposes. Thus'tis reckon'd, by St. *Paul* himself, amongst the Works of the Flesh, Gal. v. 20. such as Adultery, Fornication, Variance, Strifes, and the like, because Heresy is embraced for the sake of fleshly Lusts, and always ministers to the serving them. Thus St. *Peter, There were false Prophets also amongst the People, even as there shall* 2 Pet. ii. *be false Teachers amongst you, who privily shall bring in damnable Heresies, even deny-* 1, &c. *ing the Lord that bought them, and bring upon themselves swift Destruction; and many shall follow their pernicious Ways, by reason of whom the Way of Truth shall be* v. 10. *evil spoke of; and through Covetousness shall they, with feigned Words, make Merchandize of you;* whom he farther describes, *as walking after the Flesh in the Lust of Uncleanness,* and as given to almost all manner of Vices. This is *Heresy, and denying the Lord that bought us,* and the only Meaning of the Expression, as used by the Apostle; though it hath been applied by weak or designing Men, Tit. iii. to denote all such as don't believe their metaphysical Notion of the Trinity, 11. or the *Athanasian* Creed. Hence it is that St. *Paul* gives it, as the general Character of an Heretick, that *he is subverted,* viz. from the Christian Faith, *sinneth,* viz. by voluntarily embracing Errors, subversive of the Gospel, in favour of his Lusts, on which Account he is *self-condemn'd,* viz. by his own Conscience, both in the Principles he teaches, and the vile Uses to which he makes them serve: So that tho' sincere and honest Enquirers after Truth, Persons who fear God, and practise Righteousness, may be Hereticks in the Esteem of Men, for not understanding and believing their Peculiarities in Religion, yet they are not and cannot be Hereticks, according to the Scripture Description of Heresy, in the Notion of which there is always supposed a wicked Heart, causing Men wilfully to embrace and propagate such Principles as are subversive of the Gospel, in order to serve the Purposes of their Avarice, Ambition, and Lust. Such Heresy as this is unquestionably one of the worst of Crimes, and Hereticks of this kind are worthy to be rejected. It must be confessed, that Heresy hath been generally taken in another Sense, and to mean Opinions that differ from the established Orthodoxy, or from the Creeds of the Clergy, that are uppermost in Power; who have not only taken on them to reject such as have differ'd from them, from their Communion and Church, but to deprive them of Fortune, Liberty and Life. But as St. *Paul*'s Notion of Herefy entirely differs from what the Clergy have generally taught about it, theirs may be allowed to be a very irrational and abfurd Doctrine, and the Apoftle's remain a very wife and good one ; and though they have gone into all the Lengths of Wickednefs to punifh what they have ftigmatized with the Name of Herefy, they have had no apoftolick Example or Precept to countenance them ; Scripture Hereticks being only to be rejected from the Church, according to St. *Paul*, and as to any farther Punifhment, 'tis deferred till the Lord fhall come.

As to the Powers given to the Guides, or Overfeers, or Bifhops of the Church, I allow their Claims have been exceeding great. They have affumed to themfelves the Name of the *Church* and *Clergy*, hereby to diftinguifh themfelves from the Flock of Chrift. They have taken on them, as we have feen, to determine, mend, and alter the Faith, to make Creeds for others, and oblige them to fubfcribe them, and to act as though our Saviour had divefted himfelf of his own Rights, and given unto them *all Power in Heaven and Earth.* But thefe Claims have as little Foundation in the Gofpel as in Reafon. The Words *Clergy* and *Church*, are never once ufed in Scripture to denote the Bifhops or other Officers, but the Chriftian People. St. *Peter* advifes the Presbyters *to feed the Flock of God, and to exercife the Epifcopal Office* 1 Pet. v. *willingly,* [a] *not as lording it over the Heritages*, or Clergy of God. And St. [3.] *Paul*, writing to his *Ephefians*, and fpeaking of their Privileges as Chriftians, fays, that *by Chrift they were made God's peculiar Lot*, or Heritage, or [b] *Clergy.* In like manner, the Body of Chriftians in general, and particular Congregations in particular Places, are called the Church, but the Minifters of the Gofpel never in contradiftinction to them. 'Tis of all Believers that St. *Peter* gives that noble Defcription, that they are *a fpiritual Houfe, an holy Priefthood, to offer up fpiritual Sacrifices, a chofen Generation, a royal Priefthood, an holy Nation,* and a [c] *peculiar People*, or a People for his peculiar Heritage, or *purchafed Poffeffion*, as the Word is render'd, *Eph.* i. 14. So that to be the Church, the Clergy, and the facred Priefts of God, is an Honour common to all Chriftians in general by the Gofpel Charter. Thefe are not the Titles of a few only, who love to exalt themfelves above them.

Undoubtedly, the Order of the Chriftian Worfhip requires, that there fhould be proper Perfons to guide and regulate the Affairs of it. And accordingly St. *Paul* tells us, that *Chrift gave fome Apoftles, fome Prophets, fome* Eph. iv. *Evangelifts; and fome Paftors and Teachers*, different Officers, according to the 11. different State and Condition of his Church. To the Apoftles, extraordinary Powers were given, to fit them for the Service to which they were called ; and, to enable them to manage thefe Powers in a right Manner, they were under the peculiar Conduct of the Spirit of God. Thus our Saviour, after his Refurrection, breathed on his Difciples the Holy Ghoft, and faid, *Whofe foever Sins ye remit, they are remitted to them ; and whofe foever Sins ye retain,* John xx. 23.

[a] Μη ως καταχυειδοντες των κληρων.
[b] Εν ω κ εκληρωθημ⟨ε⟩ν.
[c] Λαⲟ⳽ εις περιποιησιν.

they

they are retained; a Commiſſion of the ſame import with that which he gave them before, *Matt.* xviii. 18. *Whatſoever ye ſhall bind on Earth, ſhall be bound in Heaven; and whatſoever ye ſhall looſe on Earth, ſhall be looſed in Heaven.* To *bind,* is to *retain Mens Sins*; and to *looſe,* is to *remit their Sins* And this Power the Apoſtles had ; and it was abſolutely neceſſary they ſhould have it, or they could never have ſpread his Religion in the World. But wherein did this binding and looſing, this retaining and remitting Sins, conſiſt? What, in their ſaying to this Man, I abſolve you from your Sins ; and to the other, I put you under the Sentence of Damnation? Would any conſiderate Man in the World have ever credited their Pretenſions to ſuch an extravagant Power? Or can one ſingle Inſtance be produced of the Apoſtles pretending to exerciſe it? No. Their Power of binding and looſing, of retaining and remitting Sins conſiſted in this, and in this principally, *viz.* their fixing the great Conditions of Mens future Salvation, and denouncing the Wrath of Almighty God againſt all, who, thro' wilful Obſtinacy, would not believe and obey the Goſpel. And the Commiſſion was given them in the moſt general Terms, *Whoſe ſoever Sins ye retain,* &c. not becauſe they were to go to particular Perſons, and peremptorily ſay, *You ſhall be ſaved, and you ſhall be damned,* but becauſe they were to preach the Goſpel to *Gentiles,* as well as *Jews,* and to fix thoſe Conditions of future Happineſs and Miſery, that ſhould conclude all the Nations of the Earth, to whom the Goſpel ſhould be preached. This was their proper Office and Work, as Apoſtles ; and, in order to this, they had the Spirit given them, to bring all Things that Chriſt had ſaid to their Remembrance, and to inſtruct them fully in the Nature and Doctrines of the Goſpel. And as they have declared the whole Counſel of God to the World, they have looſed and bound all Mankind, *even the very Biſhops and Paſtors of the Church, as well as others,* as they have fixed thoſe Conditions of Pardon and Mercy, of future Happineſs and Miſery for all Men, from which God will not recede, to the End of Time. This was a Power fit to be entruſted with Men under the Conduct of an unerring Spirit, and with them only; whereas the common Notion of ſacerdotal or prieſtly Abſolution, as it hath no Foundation in this Commiſſion to the Apoſtles, nor in any Paſſage of the ſacred Writings, is irrational and abſurd, and which the Prieſts have no more Power to give, than any other common Chriſtian whatſoever, no, nor than they have to make a new Goſpel.

I would add, that as the Apoſtles received this Commiſſion from Chriſt, they were bound to confine themſelves wholly to it, and not to exceed the Limits of it. They were his Servants who ſent them, and the Meſſage they received from him, that, and that only, were they to deliver to the World. Thus St. *Paul* ſays of himſelf, that *God had committed to him the Word of Reconciliation,* and that he was *an Ambaſſador for Chriſt* ; that *he preached not himſelf, but Chriſt Jeſus the Lord, and himſelf the Servant of others for Jeſus ſake.*; that he had *no Dominion over others Faith,* no Power to impoſe upon them arbitrary Things, or Articles of Faith, which he had not received from Chriſt; and that accordingly he *determined to know nothing but Chriſt, and him crucified,* i. e. to

2 Cor. v. 20.
iv. 5.
i. 24.

1 Cor. ii. 2.

2   preach

preach nothing but the pure and uncorrupted Doctrines of his Gospel; and that this was his great Comfort, that he had *not shunned to declare the Counsel of God.* If then the inspired Apostles were to confine themselves to what they received from God, and had no Power to make Articles of Faith, and fix Terms of Communion and Salvation, other than what they were immediately ordered to do by Christ, it is absolutely impossible that the Clergy can have that Power now; who have, as I apprehend, no immediate Commission from Christ, nor any direct Inspiration from his Holy Spirit. Nor is there any Thing in the Circumstances of the World to render such a Power desirable; because the Apostles have shewn us all Things that we need believe or practise as Christians, and commanded the Preachers of the Gospel to teach no other Doctrines but what they received from them. Hence St. *Peter's* Advice to the Elders, that they should *feed the Flock of God, not as lording it over* 1 Pet. v. 3. *the Heritage.* And St. *Paul,* in his Epistles to *Timothy,* instructing him in the Nature of the Gospel Doctrines and Duties, tells him, that *by putting the* 1 Tim. iv. *Brethren in Remembrance of these Things, he would approve himself a good Minister* 6. *of Jesus Christ,* and commands him to *take Heed to himself, and to the Doctrines* vi. 13, 14, he had taught him, *and to continue in them,* charging him, in *the Sight of God,* 20. *and before Christ Jesus, to keep the Commandment given him, that which was com-* 2 Tim. ii. *mitted to his Trust, without Spot, unrebukeable, till the Appearance of Christ Jesus.* 21 These were the Things to which *Timothy* was to confine himself, and to commit to others, that they might be continually preached in the Christian Church; and of Consequence 'tis the same Apostolick Doctrine that the Bishops, or Elders, or Ministers of the Church, are to instruct their Hearers in now, as far as they understand it, without mixing any Thing of their own with it, or of any other Persons whatsoever.

The great End and Design of the ministerial Office, is for the *perfecting* Acts xx. *of the Saints, and the edifying of the Body of Christ.* Hence *the Elders* are com-18. manded *to take Heed to themselves, and to the Flock over which the Holy Ghost had made them* BISHOPS, *to feed the Church of God.* They are likewise exhorted to *hold fast the faithful Word, as they had been taught, that by sound Doctrine they may be able to exhort and convince others.* They are to *give Attendance to Reading, Exhortation, and Doctrine,* and to put others in Remembrance of the great Truths of the Gospel, charging them, before the Lord, not to strive about unprofitable Words, but *to be gentle to all Men,* and *in Meekness to instruct even those who oppose.* They are to *contend earnestly for the Faith,* as well as other Christians, but then 'tis for *that Faith which was once delivered to the Saints;* and, even for this, *the Servant of the Lord is not, μαχεϑϑ, to fight.* He is not to 2 Tim. ii. use *carnal,* but *spiritual Weapons,* nor to put on any Armour, but that of 24. Righteousness on the Right Hand, and on the Left. They are to *speak the* Eph. iv. *Truth,* but it must be *in Love.* They should be *zealously affected,* but it should 15. be always *in a good Thing.* They must *stop the Mouths of unruly and vain Talkers,* Tit. i. 11. but it must be by *Uncorruptness of Doctrine, Gravity, Sincerity, and sound Speech,* ii. 8. *that cannot be condemned.* Upon these, and the like Accounts, they are said

r 2 to

to be *over us in the Lord*, to *rule us*, and to be *our Guides* ; Words that do not
imply any Dominion that they have over the Confciences of others, nor any
Right in them to prefcribe Articles of Faith and Terms of Communion for
others. This they are exprefly forbidden, and commanded to preach the
Word of God only, and pronounced accurfed if they teach any other Gofpel
than that which they have received from the Apoftles. And of Confequence
when we are bid *to obey* and *fubmit our felves* to them, it is meant then, and
then only when they *rule us in the Lord*, when they fpeak to us the Word of
God, and *labour in the Word and Doctrine.* In all other Cafes, they have no
Power, nor is there any Obedience due to them. They are to be refpected,
and to *be had in double Honour for their Work fake*, i. e. when they *preach not
themfelves, but Chrift Jefus the Lord*, and when their Faith and Converfation
is fuch, as to become worthy our Imitation. But if *they teach otherwife, and
confent not to the Words of our Lord Jefus, if they doat about Words whereof come
Envy, Strife and Railing, fuppofing that Gain is Godlinefs, from fuch we are commanded to withdraw our felves.* The Epifcopal Character, however otherwife
greatly venerable, then forfeits the Reverence due to it, and becomes contemptible.

So that there are no Powers or Privileges annexed to the Epifcopal or Minifterial Character in the facred Writings, that are in the leaft favourable
to the Caufe of Perfecution, or that countenance fo vile and detestable a
Practice. As to the Affair of Excommunication, by which the Clergy have
fet the World fo often in a Flame, there is nothing in the facred Records
that confines the Right of exercifing it to them, nor any Command ever to
exercife it, but towards notorious and fcandalous Offenders. The inceftuous *Corinthian* was delivered over to Satan by the Church in full Affembly,
on which Account his Punifhment or Cenfure is faid to be *by many*. And
though St. *Paul* bids *Titus* to *reject an Heretick*, he alfo bids the *Corinthians* to
put away that wicked Perfon from amongft them, which had brought fuch a Scandal upon their Church, and the *Theffalonians, to withdraw themfelves from every
Brother that fhould walk diforderly.* So that as the Clergy have no Right, from
the New Teftament, to determine in Controverfies of Faith, nor to create any
new Species of Herefy, fo neither have they any exclufive Right to cut off any
Perfons from the Body of the Church, much lefs to cut them off from it for
not fubmitting to their Creeds and Canons; and of Confequence no Power to
mark them out by this Act to the civil Magiftrate, as Objects of his Indignation and Vengeance.

I have been the longer on this Head, that I might fully vindicate the
Chriftian Revelation, from every Sufpicion of being favourable to Perfecution. Notwithftanding fome late Infinuations of this kind that have been
thrown out againft it by its profeffed Adverfaries, let but the Expreffions
of Scripture be interpreted with the fame Candour as any other Writings
are, and there will not be found a fingle Sentence to countenance this Doctrine and Practice. And therefore though Men of corrupt Minds, or weak
Judgments, have, for the fake of worldly Advantages, or through ftrong

*1 Cor. v.
4.
2 Cor. ii.
6.*

                                                              2   Preju-

Prejudices, entered into the Measures of Persecution under Pretence of vindicating the Christian Religion, yet as they have no Support and Foundation in the Gospel of Christ, the Gospel ought not to be reproached for this, or any other Faults of those who profess to believe it. Let Persecution be represented as a most detestable and impious Practice, and let Persecutors of every Denomination and Degree bear all the Reproaches they deserve, and be esteemed, as they ought to be, the Disturbers, Plagues and Curses of Mankind, and the Church of God; but let not the Religion of Jesus Christ suffer for their Crimes, nor share any Part of that Scandal, which is due only to those who have dishonoured their Character and Profession, and abused the most beneficent and kind Institution that ever appeared in the World.

It is in order to expose this shameful Practice, and render it the Abhorrence of all Mankind, that I have drawn up the foregoing Sheets, and, I presume, that no one who hath not put off Humanity it self can read them, without becoming Sentiments of Indignation. The true Use to be made of that History, is, not to think dishonourably of Christ and his Religion, not to contemn and despise his faithful Ministers, who, by Preaching and Practice, by Reason and Argument, endeavour to propagate Knowledge, Piety, Righteousness, Charity, and all the Virtues of private and social Life. The Blessing of the Almighty God be with them. The Grace of our Lord Jesus Christ succeed and prosper them. I say therefore, the Use of the foregoing History is to teach Men to adhere close to the Doctrines and Words of Christ and his Apostles, to argue for the Doctrines of the Gospel with Meekness and Charity, to introduce no new Terms of Salvation and Christian Communion, not to trouble the Christian Church with metaphysical Subtleties and abstruse Questions, that minister to Quarelling and Strife, not to pronounce Censures, Judgments, and Anathemas, upon such as may differ from us in speculative Truths, not to exclude Men from the Rights of civil Society, nor lay them under any negative or positive Discouragements for Conscience sake, or for their different Usages and Rites in the Externals of Christian Worship; but to remove those which are already laid, and which are as much a Scandal to the Authors and Continuers of them, as they are a Burthen to those who labour under them. These were the sole Views that influenced me to lay before my Reader the foregoing melancholy Account; not any Design to reflect on the Clergy in general, whose Office and Character I greatly reverence, and who, by acting according to the original Design of their Institution, would prove the most useful Set of Men in every Nation and Kingdom, and thereby secure to themselves all the Esteem they could reasonably desire in the present World, and, what is infinitely more valuable, the Approbation of their great Lord and Master in another.

F I N I S.

J

Lo

TO THE

Moſt Reverend Father in GOD,

J O H N,

Lord Arch-Biſhop of *Canterbury,*

Primate and Metropolitan of all *ENGLAND.*

May it pleaſe Your GRACE;

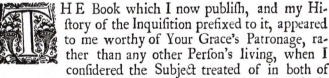 H E Book which I now publiſh, and my Hi-
ſtory of the Inquiſition prefixed to it, appeared
to me worthy of Your Grace's Patronage, rather than any other Perſon's living, when I
conſidered the Subject treated of in both of
them, and that high Station, which in theſe moſt difficult
Times You ſupport with the greateſt Honour and univerſal

*

verfal Applaufe of all good Men, for the common Advantage of the Reformed Churches.

The Book it felf contains the Sentences of the *Tholoufe* Inquifition, pronounced during the Space of fixteen Years, principally againft the *Albigenfes* and *Valdenfes*, about the Beginning of the Fourteenth Century. In thefe Sentences there are not only many curious Things, which greatly illuftrate the Hiftories of thofe Times, but the Inquifition it felf, and the Method of its Procedure, is reprefented by about one hundred Sentences pronounced by it, and held up as it were in a Glafs to be difcerned by all : From hence, even the Papacy it felf, which principally is fupported by Cruelty and Perfecution, may be more fully known, which, tho' covered with Sheeps Cloathing to deceive the Unwary, cherifhes a Wolf in its Bofom. My Hiftory of the Inquifition gives Light to the Book of Sentences. My Defign in it was to give a Reprefentation of that Tribunal, not in a falfe Difguife, nor deform'd by unnatural and hideous Colours, but in living and genuine ones ; I mean, to draw the Picture of that horrible Court, which makes its principal Boaft of the Title of Sanctity, to the Life, not from the Writings of thofe who feparate from the Church of *Rome*, but that there may be no Room for Calumny, from thofe of the Popifh Doctors, and even Inquifitors themfelves ; that hereby the vaft Power granted to the Inquifitors, the moft cruel Laws of it, and the injuft Method of Procedure, quite different from the Ufage of all other Courts, might appear to the whole World, and that hereby the Papacy it felf might be known to all Mankind to be what it really is. For indeed there is nothing that more evidently difcovers its Nature, than that immenfe and fupream Power, by which the Pope of

Rome, claiming to be the Vicâr of Chrift on Earth, makes himfelf the Judge of the Faith, and ufurps Dominion over the Confciences of the Faithful. And of this the Office of the Inquifition is the moft abundant Proof. For here the Pope, as fupream Legiflator, makes Laws, by which he endeavours to bind, under the moft fevere Penalties, all who wear the Name of Chrift, without excepting thofe of the higheft Rank, no not Princes and Kings, to obey and believe all Things, which are eftablifhed by the Canons of the Church of *Rome*. And as fupream Judge of the Faith, he erects himfelf a Tribunal, from the Judgment of which none of the Faithful are exempted : He fends his Inquifitors into all Provinces and Countries, who, as Judges delegated by him, exercife Judgment in his Name, and make all Magiftrates and Princes obedient to their Commands, as tho' they were the Commands of the Pope himfelf. And that it may appear that he fets himfelf up as God, he endeavours to fearch out the moft concealed Things, and, as far as he can, the very Thoughts of the Heart. He commands the moft private Affairs, tranfacted between the moft intimate Friends, to be informed of to the Inquifitors, if there appears to be the leaft Sufpicion of a wavering Faith, under this moft fevere Threatning, that if any one doth not immediately difcover what he hath heard and feen, he fhall be efteemed as an Accomplice in the Crime, and as an Hinderer of the holy Office of the Inquifition ; that by this Means, even from the fmalleft Proofs, he may form a Judgment of the very Thoughts, or by the moft cruel Tortures draw out a Confeffion of every Thing harbour'd in the Mind, or at leaft punifh the Action or Word that gave Occafion to the Sufpicion. And that it may more evidently appear, that this Tribunal is

* 2

erected

erected not for the Honour, but rather for the Reproach of Chrift, he ordains thofe Punifhments, and exercifes thofe Judgments, not againft the profane and impious Violaters of the Divine Laws, Thieves, Adulterers, Drunkards, Revilers, and the like, concerning whom the Scripture plainly pronounces, that they fhall not inherit the Kingdom of Heaven; but againft the Tranfgreffors of his Laws, which, without any Foundation in the Word of God, he hath, by an infolent Ufurpation of fpiritual Power, laid on the Church of God, as a Yoke to diftinguifh all who are fubject to him. So that if any one doth not obferve the leaft Ceremony he commands, or not believe what is ordered by him to be believed, altho' he is perfuaded by the clear Teftimony of the Word of God, that he ought to act and believe otherwife, or gives the leaft Proof of fuch a Belief, he can't efcape the cruel Hands of the Inquifitors. So that by thefe Fruits 'tis evident, he prefers his own Commandments to the Divine.

On the other hand, all who defire to preferve the Purity and Liberty of the Gofpel, every where highly efteem and honour Your Grace, who, as you prefide over the Church of *England* by far the moft Eminent of all the Reformed Churches, are for this Reafon, I had almoft faid, their common Defender. You by Methods and Counfels, directly contrary to the Papal Tyranny, labour with great Succefs to promote the Chriftian Doctrine and Faith, and to bring Men into the Way of Salvation. For, not to mention Your Grace's chafte and natural Eloquence in Preaching, fo agreeable to the Holy Scriptures, the Strength and Force of Your Judgment in Arguing, Your Learning, not for Oftentation, but Ufefulnefs, and thofe other excellent Qualifications, which formerly drew the

Hopes

Hopes and Eyes of all good Men upon You, and for
which You are now an Ornament to Your Profeſſion; the
great Goodneſs of Your Mind, ſo highly becoming an
Evangelical Paſtor, gives a happy Preſage to the Reformation, even now in Danger, and lately almoſt oppreſſed.
For ſuch is the Integrity of Your Life, ſuch the Simplicity and Candor of your Behaviour, ſuch Your Charity and
Benevolence to all, ſuch Your Wiſdom from long Experience, that You ſeem to have been choſen by Divine Providence, by Your Conduct to unite and ſtrengthen the
reformed Churches, to heal their Differences, and to advance and defend the Goſpel Liberty and Chriſtian Religion againſt the Attempts and ſavage Cruelty of the Papiſts.
For You not only approve, but are a Pattern of true Goſpel Charity. You oppoſe the Papal Tyranny and Barbarity, by Purity of Life and Gentleneſs of Diſpoſition, the
very Methods by which Chriſtianity formerly overcame
and deſtroyed Idolatry, and the Heathen Impiety and Tyranny, and by which it always will triumph over its Enemies. I could not therefore ſubmit this Work to any but
Your Grace's Protection, and perſuade my ſelf You will
with me judge it to be ſeaſonable; eſpecially in this State
of Affairs, in which the Papacy is endeavouring, eſpecially
in *England*, to erect it ſelf again, and uſurp the ſole Dominion; that in this Treatiſe all Men may ſee, as in a
Glaſs, its living and genuine Repreſentation, and never
ſuffer themſelves to be deceived by a falſe and diſguiſed
Appearance, but acknowledge it to be what it really is,
viz. an Aſſembly and Combination of cruel and bloody
Men, who affect and uſurp, where-ever they can, a Dominion over Conſcience, and thus erect a Kingdom oppoſite

fite to that of Chrift's : That by this Means, they may,
under Your Conduct and Government, as a truly fpiritual
Father, learn to abhor, and with all their Hearts, to deteft
that imperious Society, and oppofe the Propagation of it,
by Faith unfeigned, a Charity truly Chriftian, and by
Sanctity of Behaviour ; and that they may alfo confult the
Safety of the reformed Church, and efpecially learn from
thence to abhor all Cruelty and Punifhment towards Diffenters and erroneous Perfons, in other Refpects pious,
as thofe who know, that we muft all give an Account of
our Faith before the Tribunal of Chrift, the fupream
Lawgiver and Judge, and that it is not lawful for any
Men to give a Law to Confciences, or prefcribe the Rules
of Believing, becaufe this is in Reality to afcend the Tribunal of Chrift himfelf. Thus the Church will profper and
flourifh under Your Grace's Care; Enmities, Hatred
and Schifms, which have miferably divided it into Parties, will be deftroyed ; and if God, offended with us
for our Sins, fhall not vouchfafe to reftore to us thofe
golden Ages of the primitive Church, in which all the
Faithful were of one Heart and one Mind, yet that we
may all at leaft learn this from hence, not to rule over
another's Confcience, never to punifh an erroneous Chriftian for a mere harmlefs Miftake, never to put to Death
any one for an ingenuous Profeffion of his Faith, of which
he is ready to give an Account to God, but to refute their
Errors by the Force of Reafon, and the plain Teftimony
of Scripture, and in the mean while to wait with Gentlenefs and Patience for their Repentance, if peradventure
God fhould grant them to underftand their Errors, and
give them an Heart fincerely to embrace the Truth.

May

May the God of Peace, who brought again from the Dead that great Shepherd of the Sheep, our Lord Jefus Chrift, by the Blood of the everlafting Covenant, profper all your moft pious Endeavours for the Peace and Safety of the Church, and grant that You may happily reftore it when fallen, and fupport it when tottering, by the fame Aids, with which it firft grew, encreafed, and was eftablifhed. Thefe are the fincere and moft affectionate Prayers of, may it pleafe Your Grace,

Your G R A C E'*s*

Moft Humble and

Devoted Servant,

Philip a Limborch.

Mr. *LIMBORCH*'s

PREFACE

TO THE

READER.

WHEN *first I determined to publish the Book of the
Sentences of the* Tholouse *Inquisition, I had Reason
to think that it would be the same with others, as I
found it with my self, viz. that several Things in those
Sentences would not be very clear, unless the Nature of
the Inquisition, and Method of Proceeding in it, were,
in some Measure, understood; and therefore, I intended, for the Reader's Advantage, to prefix to it a Dissertation concerning the Inquisition: But, as I turned over the Authors who treated of this Affair,
I found such Plenty of Matter, that I laid by my first Design, and
resolved to write an entire History of the Inquisition. Whether I have
answered Expectation, the Reader must judge: I am sure I was
not wanting in the desire to serve him. The History it self I have
comprehended in Four Books; in which I have so fully explained every
Thing relating to the Inquisition, and that could clear up the Books of
Sentences, that I am perswaded the Reader will find no Obscurity left
when he peruses them. He will perceive, by the Laws and Bulls
every where published against Hereticks, why such a Punishment is
inflicted upon each Person, and the Crimes objected to the Criminals,
and why the Sentences are conceived in these and no other Words. And*
although

although the Punishments enjoyned Penitents, by way of wholesome Penances, are arbitrary, and left to the Pleasure of the Inquisitors, yet they are directed by some certain Laws and Customs ; so that, upon hearing the Crimes read objected to any Criminal, it may, from thence, be easily gathered to what Penance he is to be condemned, according to the Laws and Customs received in the Inquisition.

I have not, through an Attachment to any Party, written any Thing contrary to Truth. I have made use of Popish Authors, yea, Inquisitors themselves, and Counsellors of the Inquisition, who are so far from having written any Thing untrue, out of Hatred to the Inquisition, that they every where cry up the Sanctity of it, and, without End or Measure, inculcate its vast Advantage to the Church of Rome ; and therefore, whatever they write concerning the Inquisition, and Method of Proceeding before that Tribunal, I assured my self I might safely relate, without any Charge of Calumny on account of it. And, to cut off all Pretence for such a Charge, I thought proper to retain the very Words of the Popish Doctors, as they are extant in their own Books, without any Alteration, unless where, because of their Prolixness, I have abridged them ; and, even then, I have made use of their own Words, as far as the Nature of an Abridgment would allow ; so that he who reads my History, will read not so much my Words, as those of the Inquisitors themselves, and other Popish Doctors. I thought I should hereby greatly serve the Publick, by shewing what sort of Court that of the Inquisition is, the Papists and Inquisitors themselves being Witnesses. Amongst all the Authors I have quoted, R. Gonsalvius Montanus is the only one that was a Protestant ; and, as far as I can gather from his Book, was one of those, who, about the Death of the Emperor Charles V. gathered a Church for worshipping God in a purer Manner at Seville, upon discovering the grievous Errors and Superstitions of the Church of Rome, which was afterwards dispersed by that most cruel Inquisition, of which there were held Acts of Faith at Seville and Valladolid, An. 1559. But I have scarce any Thing from him but what is affirmed by other Authors ; he only supplies me with Instances fully to illustrate what others write concerning the Inquisition, the Laws of it, and Method of Proceeding. To him I may add James Usher, Archbishop of Armagh, from whose Treatise, De Successione, &c. I have borrowed some few Things. But, inasmuch as even these Things were taken from Popish Authors, of whom there are frequent

Quota-

PREFACE to the READER.

Quotations in that Treatise, what I have transcribed from thence, ought, in Justice, to have the same Authority with the Papists, as though I had quoted it from the very Authors, whose Words are made use of by that most learned Prelate.

The Reader may, perhaps, wonder at one Thing, that I have always called those Hereticks that have been proceeded against by the Inquisition : But, as I was relating the Popes Bulls, and the Decrees of Popish Councils, I could not help using the same Words I found in them. By an Heretick, therefore, I understand one condemned for Heresy by the Church of Rome. I could not rehearse their Decrees but in their own Words, and was therefore forced always to use them, unless I would have interrupted the Course of the History, by repeated and innumerable Alterations, and thereby rendered it less pleasing and acceptable. Let it therefore suffice, once for all, to say, that, by the Word Heretick, when I ever speak of the Inquisition against Hereticks, I do not mean one who is truly an Heretick, but accounted an Heretick by the Church of Rome, taking the Word in the Popish Sense of it. In the mean while, those who are Hereticks in their Account, are not so in mine ; and I sincerely believe, that those which the Church of Rome hath condemned for Heresy, have died, and gloriously endured the Punishment of Fire for the Testimony of Jesus Christ, and the maintaining a good Conscience. These few Things I thought proper to advise my kind Reader of, and hope he will pass a favourable Judgment. Sep. 13. An. CIƆIƆCXCII.

A

A CATALOGUE of the AUTHORS out of whose Writings the HISTORY of the INQUISITION is principally drawn.

Irectorium Inquifitorum Fr. Nicolai Eymerici Ord. Præd, cum Commentariis Francifci Pegnæ J. V. D. Romæ in ædibus populi Romani. MD-LXXXV. fol. Eymericus *was born at* Girona *in* Catalonia, *was a Predicant Monk, and flourished in the Papacy of* Urban V. *and* Gregory XI. *and in the Reign of* Peter IV. *King of* Aragon. *He was made Inquifitor General about the Year* 1358. *and fucceeded* Nicholas Rofell. *He was made a Cardinal* An. 1356. *He died* Jan. 4, 1393. *having executed the Office of the Holy Inquifition for forty four Years together.*

Pegna *was a* Spaniard, *of the Kingdom of* Aragon, *made Auditor of the* Roman *Rota, in the room of* Chriftopher Robufterius, Oct. 14, 1588. *He was advanced to the Deanery of the fame Court* June 9, 1604. *in the room of Cardinal* Jerom Pamphilii, *and died in that Deanery* Aug. 21, 1612.

Francifci Pegnæ Inftructio, feu Praxis Inquifitorum, cum annotationibus Cæfaris Carenæ. Lugduni 1669. poft Carenæ tractatum de Officio SS. Inquifitionis. fol.

Guidonis Fulcodii, quæftiones quindecim ad Inquifitores; cum annotationibus Cæfaris Carenæ, ibid. Fulcodius *was a Cardinal, and afterwards Pope, by the Name of* Clement IV.

Lucerna Inquifitorum Fr. Bernardi Comenfis, cum annot. Francifci Pegnæ, impreffa Romæ cum licentiâ Superiorum, ex officina Bartholomæi Graffi. 1584.

Jacobus Simancas de Catholicis Inftitutionibus. Simancas *was Bishop of* Badajox *in the Kingdom of* Portugal, *and Province of* Eftremadura.

Joannes à Royas, de hæreticis eorumque impiâ intentione & credulitate. Royas *was a Licentiate of the Canon and Civil Law, Inquifitor of heretical Pravity at* Valencia *in* Spain.

Zanchini Ugolini tractatus de hæreticis: cum Additionibus Fr. Camilli Campegii. Z. Ugolinus *was a Lawyer of* Rimini *in* Italy.

C. Campegius *was a Predicant Friar, and Inquifitor General in all the Territories of* Ferrara.

Conradus Brunus de hæreticis & fchifmaticis, lib. 6.

M

Forma procedendi contra hæreticos, feu inquifitos de hærefi, & in caufa hærefis. Autor creditur Joannes Calderinus.

Hi quinque autores exftant in Parte II. Tom. XI. tractatuum illuftrium Juris confultorum, quæ agit, de judiciis criminalibus S. Inquifitionis.

Ludovicus à Paramo, de Origine & Progreffu Officii Sanctæ Inquifitionis, ejufque dignitate & utilitate. Madriti, ex Typographiâ Regiâ. cɪɔ ɪɔ xcɪɪx. fol. Ludovicus à Paramo *was Archdeacon and Canon of* Leon, *a City in* Spain, *and Inquifitor of the Kingdom of* Sicily.

Antonii de Soufa, Aphorifmi Inquifitorum. Lugduni, apud Aniffon. 1669. 8. Soufa *was a* Portuguefe *of* Lisbon, *a Predicant Friar, Mafter of Divinity, and Counfellor to the King and the Tribunal of the fupream Holy Inquifition.*

Cæfaris Carenæ, tractatus de Officio Sanctiffimæ Inquifitionis, & modo procedendi in caufis fidei. Lugduni apud Aniffon. 1669. fol. Carena, *D. D. was Auditor of Cardinal* Camporeus, *Judge Confervator, Counfellor, and Advocate Fifcal of the Holy Office.*

Reignaldi Gonfalvii Montani Sanctæ Inquifitionis Hifpanicæ artes aliquot detectæ ac palam traductæ. Heidelbergæ 1567. 8.

Pauli Servitæ Hiftoria Inquifitionis, præfertim prout in Dominio Veneto obfervatur.

Relation de l'Inquifition de Goa. 12. à Paris 1687.

Memoires de la Cour d'Efpagne. 12. à la Haye. 1691.

Abrahami Bzovii Annalium Ecclefiafticorum Baronii Continuatio, Antwerpiæ 1617.

Annales Ecclefiaftici ex Tomis octo ad unum pluribus auctum redacti: Autore Odorico Raynaldo. Romæ ex Typographia Varefii. 1667. Raynaldus *was of* Trevifo, *Presbyter of the Congregation of the Oratory.*

Compendium Bullarii Flavii Cherubini. Lugduni apud Laurentium Durand, 1624. 4.

Lucæ Waddingi Annales Minorum, in quibus res omnes trium Ordinum Francifcanorum tractantur. Lugduni 1625. fol.

Jacobi Augufti Thuani Hiftoria fui temporis.

Jacobus Ufferius Archiepifcopus Armachanus de Succeffione Ecclefiarum in Occidentis præfertim partibus.

Liber Sententiarum Inquifitionis Tholofanæ.

Liber catenatus, MS. inter archiva Capituli S. Salvatoris, Trajecti ad Rhenum.

Gloffarium ad Scriptores mediæ & infimæ Latinitatis, Cæroli du Frefne Domini du Cange. Lutet. Paris. 1678. fol.

Dominici Macri Hierolexicon. Romæ 1677. fol.

2   T H E

THE CONTENTS.

BOOK I.

Of the Origin and Progress of the INQUISITION.

XXII. Of

The CONTENTS.

BOOK II.

Of the Minifters of the Office of the INQUISITION.

V O L. II.

B O O K III.

Of the Crimes belonging to the Tribunal of the INQUISITION.

B O O K IV.

Of the Manner of Proceeding before the TRIBUNAL of the INQUISITION.

THE

THE

HISTORY

OF THE

INQUISITION.

CHAP. I.

The Doctrine of JESUS CHRIST *forbids Perfecution on the Account of* RELIGION.

LTHOUGH the very Name of the INQUISITION was not fo much as heard of in the Chriftian Church, before the Thirteenth Century, yet having now fpread it felf almoft throughout the whole World, and become every where notorious; it is not to be wondered at, that there fhould be a general Curiofity in Mankind of more thoroughly underftanding it, and knowing by what Laws it is conducted, and what are the Methods of Proceeding therein. The Doctors of the *Romifh Church* give it the higheft Commendations, as the only and moft certain Means of extirpating Herefies, and an impregnable Support of the

B   Faith;

Faith; not invented by human Wifdom and Council, but given to Men by the immediate Influence of Heaven, whofe Tribunal breathes nothing but Holinefs, and to which they give fuch Titles as denote the moft perfect Sanctity. The Inquifition it felf is called the *Holy Office*; the Prifon of the Inquifition the *Holy Houfe*, fo that the very Name raifes it Refpect and Veneration: Yea, they go fo far as to compare it with the Sun; and affirm, that as it would be accounted ridiculous to commend and extol the Sun, it would be equally fo to pretend to praife the Inquifition. The Proteftants on the other hand reprefent it, not only as a cruel and bloody, but moft unjuft Tribunal; where, as the Laws by which other Tribunals are governed are difregarded, fo many Things, which every where elfe would be efteemed Unrighteous, are commended as Holy. And they are fo far from thinking that it is a proper Means of reftraining or punifhing the Guilty, (which is the principal Thing to be aim'd at by every Tribunal) that on the contrary, they believe it was invented for the Oppreffion of Truth, and the Defence of Superftition and Tyranny; where Perfons, let their Innocency appear as bright as the Sun at Noon-day, are treated as the moft vile and perfidious Wretches, and cruelly put to Death by the fevereft Tortures. I therefore thought it might be of Service to the World, to defcribe the Origine of this Tribunal; and againft whom, and by what Methods they generally proceed in it. In order to this, it is neceffary to look back, and deduce this whole Affair from the very Original.

The Chriftian Religion, taught by the infpired Apoftles, made its Progrefs in the World, and fhewed it felf to be of Divine Original by the Holinefs of its Precepts, the exceeding Greatnefs of its Promifes, and the many Miracles wrought in Confirmation of it; and, at laft, brought the whole World into its Obedience without the Affiftance of Carnal Weapons, or Temporal Power. Our Lord himfelf expected only a voluntary Obedience from Mankind; as he required only to be worfhipped in Spirit, and commanded every one that would be his Difciple to deny himfelf, which is the proper Work of the Mind and Soul, and cannot be effected by any external Violence whatfoever. Even God the Father himfelf heretofore, in order to reprefent the Nature of the Kingdom of his Son Jefus Chrift, fhewed it to *Daniel* under the Figure of the Son of Man, whilft the other Kingdoms of this World were denoted by the Images of wild Beafts; for no other Caufe undoubtedly, but to fhew the different Nature of Chrift's Kingdom from the Kingdoms of this World. Thefe are to be erected, enlarged, and preferved by Violence and Arms, and Meafures fierce and beftial; his, by Mildnefs, Gentlenefs, and the Weight of Arguments, in order to convince, and not offer Force to the Mind. The Precepts of the Gofpel breathe nothing but Charity and Love: Our Lord calls Charity his New Commandment, by which he would have all Men know and diftinguifh his Difciples. But there is nothing fo oppofite to Charity as the punifhing an erroneous Perfon, who believes he promotes the Divine Glory by his Error; and in Defence of it, is ready to undergo the moft cruel and fhameful Death.

Our

Our Saviour fent his Difciples like Sheep into the midft of Wolves, in order to bear Teftimony to the Gofpel by their Patience under Sufferings,
and hereby fpread the divine Savour of it through the World. It was
far from his Defign, that like Wolves they fhould tear and devour the Sheep;
or that they fhould violently compel thofe by the Terrors of Torments and
Death to embrace his Religion, whom they could not gain by the Force
of Arguments: Befides, all agree that Faith is the Gift of God, and therefore can never be produced by human Force; nor can God be prevailed on by external Violence to communicate this his excellent Gift. The
Mind is to be convinced by Arguments; the Tongue and bodily Members
may be forced by external Violence; but this can never extort from any one a
real Belief of that to be true, which he is perfwaded in his Mind is falfe: So
that nothing can be more directly oppofite to the Genius of Chriftianity,
than to perfecute the Erroneous; to expofe them under the infamous Name
of Hereticks to the Fury of the Mob, and punifh them with a cruel
Death.

Nor are we to think, that thefe gentle Means of propagating Chriftianity
were proper only for the Time of its firft Appearance, when the Church
was deftitute of the Civil Power; and by Reafon of its Oppofi-ion to the
prevailing Religions of the World, drew upon it felf the Anger and Fury
of the Princes of it; but that the Cafe is now alter'd, fince the Kings and
Rulers, upon their Converfion to the Faith, are obliged to fubject their
Scepters to Jefus Chrift: For the Change of Fortune makes no Change in his
Religion; nor can the Alteration of any worldly Affairs take away the Force
and Obligation of his Commands; for Chrift, by his Apoftles, preached one
Scheme of Doctrines to laft for ever. 'Tis true, that Kings are to fubmit their Scepters to Chrift, not by forcing Men with Punifhments, in Oppofition to his Commands, to profefs, contrary to their Confcience and real
Sentiments, what they believe to be falfe, and fo to fill his Church with Hy-
pocrites inftead of true Believers; but by ordaining equal and juft Laws,
agreeable to the Gofpel Precepts, for the Prefervation of the Publick
Tranquility; and that there may be nothing to obftruct the true fpiritual Worfhip of God, and the Salvation of Souls. This is that moft harmlefs, and yet moft powerful Method of propagating the Gofpel, agreeable to
its Nature and Genius, by which in the Beginning, it was fpread in a
fhort Time through the whole World, by a few weak and defencelefs Perfons,
inftructed only by the Divine Spirit, through the Weight of its Arguments,
and the Power of its Miracles; and by which it may be ftill propagated,
and preferved pure and uncorrupt, againft all the Attempts of Unbelievers
and Hereticks: For our Lord did not furnifh his Difciples with carnal Weapons to oppofe the Frauds, Impoftures, Violence and Perfecutions of the
World, but with fpiritual Weapons, which through God are powerful to
bring every Imagination into Captivity to the Obedience of Chrift, that
they might triumph over the World in the midft of Afflictions, by their
Innocence, Simplicity, Fortitude and Patience. So far indeed was he from
ordaining

ordaining Persecutions, as the Punishment of Error, that he commands his Church, when suffering Persecutions, to pray for those that persecute it. By this Means the Church in the Beginning was founded, and so wonderfully propagated throughout the whole World in its first and purest Ages.

CHAP. II.

The Opinion of the PRIMITIVE CHRISTIANS *concerning Persecution.*

AGREEABLE to this Practice was the universal and constant Doctrine of these Times; for the primitive Christians opposed with the greatest Vigour, all Cruelty and Persecution for the Sake of Religion. 'Tis true, indeed, that they condemned the Heathen for their Barbarities; and argued wholly for this, that Christians should have the free Exercise of their Religion granted them; but they us'd such Arguments, and Topicks of Reasoning, and even sometimes when treating of different Subjects, express'd themselves in such a manner, as plainly declares that they do equally condemn all Sort of Violence for the Sake of Religion, against all Persons whatsoever. Thus *Tertullian,* in his Apology, *c.* 24. says: *Take heed that this be not made use of to the Praise of Impiety,* viz. *to take away from Men the Liberty of Religion, and forbid them the Choice of their Deity ; so that it should be criminal for them to worship whom they would, and they should be compelled to worship whom they would not ; no one would accept of an involuntary Service, no not a Man.* And in the 28th Chap. *It plainly appears unjust, that Men possessed of Liberty and Choice, should be compelled against their Will to sacrifice. For in other Cases a willing Mind is required in the Performance of Divine Worship ; and it may justly be accounted ridiculous to force any Person to honour the Gods, whom he ought willingly for his own Sake to endeavour to appease.* And again, in his Book to *Scapula,* cap. 2. *Every one hath a natural Right and Power to worship according to his Perswasion, for no Man's Religion can be either hurtful or profitable to his Neighbour : Nor can it be a Part of Religion to compel Men to Religion, which ought to be voluntarily embraced, and not through Constraint ; since 'tis expected, that even your Sacrifices should be offered with a willing Mind ; so that if you compel us to sacrifice, think not to please your Gods ; for unless they delight in Strife, they will not desire unwilling Sacrifices : But God is not a Lover of Contention.* Cyprian also agrees with *Tertullian* his Master, in his 62d Letter to *Pomponius,* concerning Virgins, where, treating of the Excommunication of Offenders, he thus speaks: *God commanded, that those who would not obey his Priests, and those Judges, which Time after Time he appointed, should be slain. Such were cut off with the Sword during the Dispensation of the Circumcision in the Flesh. But now, since the spiritual Circumcision takes Place in all the faithful Servants of God, the Proud and Obstinate are to be slain*
with

with the spiritual Sword, by being cast out of the Church. And in his 51st Letter to *Maximus*, the Presbyter, disputing against those who separated themselves from the Church, he speaks to them in this manner : *Since upon your Deliverance from Prison, you became infected with an heretical and schismatical Opinion, so it was, that all your Glory remained in Prison behind you ; There you seemed to have left the Dignity of your Character, since you, the Soldiers of Christ, returned not to the Church when you came from your Imprisonment, who went into Imprisonment with the Commendation and Applauses of the Church ; for though there may be Tares in the Church, this ought to be no Obstruction to our Faith and Charity ; nor is their being in the Church any Reason for our Departure out of it : It should be our Care that we be found the true Wheat, that when the Master shall gather it into his Granaries, we may reap the Fruit of our Work and Labour.* The *Apostle, in his Epistle to the* Corinthians, *says*, That in a large House there are not only Vessels of Gold and Silver, but of Wood and Earth, some to Honour, and some to Dishonour. *Let us endeavour, as much as we can, to be found amongst those of Gold and Silver. 'Tis the sole Prerogative of the Lord to break the Earthen ones, to whom the Iron Rod is committed. The Servant cannot be greater than his Lord ; nor should any one arrogate to himself what the Father hath committed to the Son only,* viz. *to winnow and purge the Flower, and separate, by any human Judgment, the Chaff from the Wheat.* And in his 55th to *Cornelius :* Nor *let any one wonder that some should forsake the Servant appointed over them, when the Disciples left the Lord himself, though he wrought the greatest Signs and Wonders ; and proved by the Testimony of his Works, that he acted by the Power of his Father. And yet he did not reproach or grievously threaten them when they forsook him, but gently turned to his Apostles and said,* What, and will you forsake me also ? *Observing that sacred Law, of every one's being left to his own Liberty and Will, and making for himself his own Choice, whether of Life or Death.* And a little after, to the same Purpose : *As for our part, most dear Brother, we are in Conscience obliged to endeavour, that no one perish from the Church through our Default ; but if any one destroys himself, and will not repent and return to the Church, we who endeavoured their Salvation, shall be without Blame in the Day of Judgment ; and they only remain in Punishment, who would not be healed by our salutary Admonitions.* And since from these Passages, it plainly appears, that *Cyprian* taught, that all Force in Matters of Religion, is contrary to the Nature of Christianity ; I cannot but take Notice of the Dishonesty of *Bellarmine*, who in 'de Laicis. his 3d Book of Controversies, *c.* 21. brings in *Cyprian* as a Defender of the Murder of Hereticks ; who *having in his Book concerning Martyrdom, cited that Passage out of* Deut. xiii. *That the false Prophet shall be slain, adds, If this was to be done under the Old Testament, much more under the New.* But if we look to the Words immediately following, we shall find that *Cyprian's* Opinion was quite the reverse : For these are the Words of *Cyprian : If before the coming of Christ, the Commands of worshipping God, and forsaking Idols, were to be observed, how much rather are they to be observed since his Appearance ? who not only exhorted us by Words, but by his own Actions ; and who, after having endured all manner of Injuries and Reproaches, was crucified, that he might leave us an Example how*

how to suffer and die. So that he hath no Excuse who will not suffer on his own Account; for as he *suffered for the Sins of all, how much more ought every one to suffer for his own Sins?* If this Paſſage be read entire, it will appear, how very falſly *Bellarmine* hath applied it to the Defence of the Murder of Hereticks, which was only intended as an Exhortation to the patient ſuffering of Martyrdom.

Lactantius defends the ſame Doctrine in a nobler and plainer manner, *lib. 5. c. 20. There is no need of Compulſion and Violence, becauſe Religion cannot be forced, and Men muſt be made willing, not by Stripes, but Arguments. Let them draw the Sword of their Reaſon: If their Reaſons are good, let them produce them ; we are ready to hear, if they can teach ; if they are ſilent, we cannot believe them: If they pretend to force us, we cannot yield to them: Let them imitate us, or fairly debate the Caſe with us. 'Tis not our manner, as they object, to entice Men ; we teach, prove, and demonſtrate ; no one is kept amongſt us againſt his Will ; and he muſt be unacceptable to God, who wants Devotion and Faith ; and yet none forſake us, being preſerved by the ſole Evidence and Force of Truth.* And a little after: *Let them learn from this what Difference there is between Truth and Falſhood; in that they, though boaſting of their Eloquence, cannot perſwade ; yet Chriſtians, though unskilful and ignorant, can ; for the Thing it ſelf, and Truth pleads in their behalf. To what Purpoſe then is their Rage, but to expoſe more that Folly which they ſtrive to conceal? Slaughter and Piety are quite oppoſite to each other ; nor can Truth conſiſt with Violence, or Juſtice with Cruelty.* And a little after: *They are convinced that there is nothing more excellent than Religion, and therefore think that it ought to be defended with Force ; but they are miſtaken both in the Nature of Religion, and in the proper Methods to ſupport it ; for Religion is to be defended, not by Murder, but Perſwaſion ; not by Cruelty, but Patience ; not by Wickedneſs, but Faith. Thoſe are the Methods of bad Men, theſe of good ; and 'tis neceſſary that a religious Man ſhould be good, and not evil ; for if you attempt to defend Religion by Blood and Torments, and Evil, this is not to defend, but to violate and pollute it: For there is nothing ſhould be more free than the Choice of our Religion, in which, if the Conſent of the Worſhipper be wanting, it becomes entirely void and ineffectual. The true Way therefore of defending Religion is by Faith, a patient Suffering, and Dying for it: This renders it acceptable to God, and ſtrengthens its Authority and Influence.* This was that moſt harmleſs Perſwaſion of the Primitive Chriſtians, before the World had yet entered into the Church, and by its Pomp and Pride had perverted the Minds, and corrupted the Manners of its Profeſſors.

CHAP.

CHAP. III.

The Laws of the Emperors, *after the* Nicene Council, *againſt the* Arians *and other Hereticks.*

AFTER the Converſion of *Conſtantine* to the Chriſtian Religion, the Civil Power became veſted in the Hands of Chriſtians. This Change in their Circumſtances produced as great a Change in their Doctrine and Manners ; and the degenerate Poſterity, deviating from the Example of their Anceſtors, introduced into the Church Methods of Cruelty, not only equal to thoſe of the Heathen, but even greater than were ever practiſed by them. What gave the firſt Riſe to it was, the Diſpute between *Alexander*, Biſhop of *Alexandria*, and *Arius*, a Presbyter of the ſame Church : When the News of this was brought to *Conſtantine*, he firſt by Letters ſharply reproved them both : *Alexander* for being needleſly inquiſitive, and *Arius* for his imprudent Anſwers, *about an unneceſſary Queſtion, which aroſe from their want of being bet-* *Euſeb. in* *ter employ'd, and a contentious and factious Spirit* ; and ſeriouſly exhorts them *Life of* to mutual Peace in theſe Words amongſt others : *Since therefore the one hath* *Conſtant.* *been needleſly inquiſitive, and the other as imprudent in his Anſwers, you ought* l. 2. c. *mutually to pardon each other : And as you do not differ about any of the prin-* 69, 7 c. *cipal Requirements of the Chriſtian Law, nor pretend to introduce any new Opinion* Socrat. l. *into the Worſhip of God, but are in theſe Things of one and the ſame Mind, you* 1. c. 7. *ought to maintain Communion with one another.* But afterwards, with the Perſwaſion of the Biſhops, or out of ſome political View, he called the *Nicene Council*, that by their Authority the Opinion of *Arius* might be condemned. *Euſebius*, who was preſent at that Council, was able to give the beſt Account of it ; but he choſe rather that their Actions ſhould be for ever forgotten, and contented himſelf in a very few Words to declare the Iſſue of it : And if we add to the Account given by him, the ſomewhat larger one given by *Socrates*, it appears plain, that all who would not ſubſcribe to their Decrees, were condemned to Baniſhment , and there is no room to doubt, ſuch are the Frailties of human Nature; but that many through Fear were compelled to ſubſcribe: Some few indeed there were, who not at all terrified with the Fear of Baniſhment, went into Exile with *Arius*, whom the Synod had condemned, becauſe they would not conſent to his Condemnation. The Emperor himſelf put forth an Edict, by which he ordained, that all the Books written by *Arius* Socrat. l. ſhould be burnt, *condemning to Death every one that ſhould conceal any of* Arius's Socrat. l. *Books, and not commit them to the Flames.* He afterwards put forth a freſh Law 1. c. 9. againſt the Recuſants, by which he took from them their Places of Worſhip, *Euſeb. Life* and prohibited their Meeting not only in publick, but even in any private *of Conſtan.* Houſes whatſoever. 1. 3, c. 6 ;,

After they had thus proceeded to Methods of Severity, and civil Puniſhments were decreed againſt thoſe, whoſe Opinions the Council were pleaſed to condemn,

I

condemn, whom they expofed under the infamous Name of Hereticks, and render'd odious to the People, their Cruelty was not fatisfied with one Degree of Punifhment only; they went from one to another, that fo the Doctrine condemned by the Council might find none that fhould dare to defend it, and fo might at laft be totally extirpated. From pecuniary Mulcts, they proceeded to the Forfeiture of Goods, Banifhment, and at length to Slaughter and Blood; for fuch is the Nature of Cruelty, that it feldom confines it felf to the firft Beginnings; but when it is once let loofe, like an impetuous Torrent, it fpeads it felf every where, and from every Occafion grows more outragious and furious. This will appear moft plainly in the Account I am now giving of the Methods for the Reftraining and Punifhment of Hereticks.

For in the firft Place, Laws were made againft Hereticks, whereby they were prohibited from having Churches, holding Affemblies, the enjoying any Ecclefiaftical Preferments, the Confecration of Bifhops, the Ordination of Priefts, the making of Wills, the fucceeding to Inheritances, the fharing in any Charities, the Advancement to publick Offices, and ordaining fevere Punifhments againft thofe who did not obferve thefe Prefcriptions.

L. Omnes, And firft, it was determined who fhould be accounted Hereticks. *They are*
c. de Hæret. *comprehended under the Name of Hereticks, and are adjudged to the Punifhments pronounced againft fuch, who fhall be difcovered to differ, even in the leaft Point, from the Judgment and Practice of the Catholick Religion.* By the fame Law it is ordained, *That no one fhould dare, either to teach or learn thofe Things that fhall have*
Cunæi. *been decreed to be profane..* By the Law following, their Churches are taken from them, and they are prohibited to perform Holy Offices, either in private Houfes or Churches, under the Forfeiture of one hundred Pounds of Gold
Mani- upon all Contraveners. The following Law is yet more fevere, which takes
chæos. from them the Power of Giving, Buying, Selling, making Contracts or Wills, or inheriting their Parents Eftates, unlefs they renounce their heretical Pravity. There are many Laws extant concerning the Banifhment of Hereticks. *Theodofius* II. and *Valentinian* III. counting up thirty-two Sects, and their Followers, decree, *Let not thefe and the* Manicheans, *who are arifen to the Height of Impiety, have the Liberty of dwelling any where within the Dominions of the* Roman
L. Ariani, *Empire:* Let the Manicheans *be expelled from every City, and punifhed with*
c. de Hæret. *Death; for they are not to be fuffered to have any Dwelling on the Earth, left they fhould infect the very Elements themfelves.*

See alfo *L. Quicunque,* where the forementioned Penalties are not only repeated, but other kinds of Punifhments ordained againft them; which are all extant in the Law of the Emperor *Martian,* who renews the Punifhments ordained by the preceding Emperors againft the *Eutichians,* and which is recorded at the End of the Council of *Chalcedon,* and which will fuffice inftead of all other Inftances. By this Law the Emperor ordained, *That they fhould not have Power of difpofing their Eftates, and making a Will, nor of inheriting what others fhould leave them by Will. Neither let them receive Advantage by any Deed of Gift, but let whatfoever is given them, either by the Bounty of the Living, or the Will of*

2   *the*

the Dead, be immediately forfeited to our Treasury ; nor let them have the Power, by any Title or Deed of Gift, to transfer any Part of their own Estates to others. Neither shall it be lawful for them to have or ordain Bishops or Presbyters, or any other of the Clergy whatsoever ; as knowing that the Eutychians *and* Apollinarists, *who shall presume to confer the Names of Bishop or Presbyter, or any other sacred Office upon any one, as well as those who shall dare to retain them, shall be condemned to Banishment, and the Forfeiture of their Goods. And as to these who have been formerly Ministers in the Catholick Church, or Monks of the orthodox Faith, and forsaking the true and orthodox Worship of the Almighty God, have or shall embrace the Heresies and abominable Opinions of* Apollinarius *or* Eutyches, *let them be subject to all the Penalties ordained by this, or any foregoing Laws whatsoever against Hereticks, and banished from the* Roman Dominions, *according as former Laws have decreed against the* Manicheans. *Farther, let not any of the* Apollinarists, *or* Eutychians, *build Churches or Monasteries, or have Assemblies and Conventicles either by Day or Night ; nor let the Followers of this accursed Sect meet in any one's House or Tenement, or in a Monastery, nor in any other Place whatsoever : But if they do, and it shall appear to be with the Consent of the Owners of such Places, after a due Examination, let such Place or Tenement in which they meet be immediately forfeited to us ; or if it be a Monastery, let it be given to the orthodox Church of that City in whose Territory it is. But if so be they hold these unlawful Assemblies and Conventicles without the Knowledge of the Owner, but with the Privity of him who receives the Rents of it, the Tenant, Agent, or Steward of the Estate, let such Tenant, Agent, or Steward, or whoever shall receive them into any House or Tenement, or Monastery, and suffer them to hold such unlawful Assemblies and Conventicles, if he be of low and mean Condition, be publickly bastinado'd as a Punishment to himself, and as a Warning to others ; but if they are Persons of Repute, let them forfeit ten Pounds of Gold to our Treasury. Farther, let no* Apollinarist *or* Eutychian *ever hope for any military Preferment, except to be listed in the Foot Soldiers, or Garrisons : But if any of them shall be found in any other military Service, let them be immediately broke, and forbid all Access to the Palace, and not suffered to dwell in any other City, Town or Country, but that wherein they were born.*

. But if any of them are born in this august City, let them be banished from this most sacred Society, and from every Metropolitan City of our Provinces. Farther, let no Apollinarist, *or* Eutychian, *have the Power of calling Assemblies, publick or private, or gathering together any Companies, or disputing in any heretical manner ; or of defending their perverse and wicked Opinions ; nor let it be lawful for any one to speak or write, or publish any thing of their own, or the Writings of any others, contrary to the Decrees of the venerable Synod of* Chalcedon. *Let no one have any such Books, nor dare to keep any of the impious Performances of such Writers. And if any are found guilty of these Crimes, let them be condemned to perpetual Banishment ; and as for those, who through a Desire of Learning, shall hear others disputing of this wretched Heresy, 'tis our Pleasure that they forfeit ten Pounds of Gold to our Treasury, and let the Teacher of these unlawful Tenets be punished with Death. Let all such Books and Papers as contain any of the damnable Opinions*

C   *of of* Eutyches, or Apollinarius, *be burnt, that all the Remains of their impious Per-verseness may perish with the Flames ; for 'tis but just that there should be a proportionable Punishment to deter Men from these most outragious Impieties. And let all the Governors of our Provinces, and their Deputies, and the Magistrates of our Cities,. know, that if, through Neglect or Presumption, they shall suffer any Part of this most religious Edict to be violated, they shall be condemned to a Fine of ten Pounds of Gold, to be paid into our Treasury ; and shall incur the farther Penalty of being declared infamous.*

Given at *Constantinople,* in the Ides
   of *August,* and the Consulate of
   Constantius and *Rufus.*

At the same Time that they published these cruel Laws, the Authors of them would fain be thought to offer no Violence to Conscience. This same Emperor *Martian,* in another Epistle to the *Archimandrites* of *Jerusalem,* at the End of the Acts of the Synod of *Chalcedon,* says, *Such therefore is our Clemency, that we use no Force with any one, to compel him to subscribe or agree with us, if he be unwilling : For we would not by Terrors and Violence drive Men even into the Paths of Truth.* Who would not wonder that they should thus seek to colour over their Cruelties ? A Doctrine is forbidden to be learnt or taught, under the severest Penalties, which those ought to think themselves obliged to profess, who are perswaded of the Truth of it ; and those who do profess it, are for that Reason exposed to many Punishments ; and yet the Authors of such Punishments would still be thought to offer no Violence to Conscience. But I would fain know, for what End are all these Penalties against Hereticks ordained ? For no other surely, but that Men may be deterred by the Fear of them from meeting together, and openly professing themselves, or teaching others those Doctrines, which they think themselves obliged in Conscience both to profess and propagate ; and that being at length quite tired out by these Evils, they may join themselves to the established Churches, and at least profess to believe their received Opinions. But this is to offer Violence to Conscience, or to force Men, by the Fear of Punishments, not to profess what they believe, or to pretend to believe what they do not ; neither of which can be done, but in Opposition to the Voice and Dictates of Conscience.

Simanc. Tit. 46. §. 48. The Constitution of *Theodosius* was in much severer Terms, which is extant in the Code of *Theodosius, tit. de Judæis, l.* 1. *& lib.* 16. *tit.* 6. *l.* 75. in which we read thus : *Farther, we ordain, that whosoever shall perswade or force a Slave, or Freeman, to forsake the Worship of the Christian Religion, and join himself to any accursed Sect or Rite, let him be punished with the Loss of Fortune and Life.* And a little after : *Let him first incur the Forfeiture of his Goods, and afterwards be condemned to the Loss of Life, who by false Doctrine shall pervert any one from the Faith.* This Law so pleases *Simanca,* that he congratulates himself on its being made by an Emperor that was a *Spaniard* ; for after having
                                                            recited

recited it, he adds: *A Law truly worthy of an Emperor that was a* Spaniard, as though it was the Glory of *Spain* to exceed all Nations in Cruelty, and its Honour, even in former Ages, to have been as remarkable for using severer Methods of Punishments in this World to miserable Hereticks than others, as they now are for the Barbarities practised by the bloody Tribunal of the Inquisition. The Emperors *Honorius* and *Theodosius* also, *Cod. Ne Sanct. Baptisma iteretur, l. 2.* thus command: *If any one shall be discovered to have rebaptized any of the Ministers of the Catholick Party, let him be put to Death, both the Person guilty of this execrable Impiety (if he be of an Age capable of Guilt) and the Party seduced by him.*

And that there might be no Remains of the Opinions condemned by the Synod, and to prevent their being transmitted to Posterity ; it was prohibited by the severest Laws, either to keep or transcribe any of their Books. We have seen before the Law of *Constantine,* against all who should conceal any of *Arius*'s Books ; and another Edict of *Martian,* against the Books of *Eutyches. Theodosius* published such another Law against the Books of *Nestorius,* after he had been condemned in the Council of *Ephesus, l. Damnato, c. de Hæreticis* : *Let not any one dare to keep, or read, or transcribe the impious Books of the accursed and execrable* Nestorius, *written against the venerable orthodox Party, and the Decrees of the most holy Council of Prelates at* Ephesus ; *and we ordain that they be diligently sought after, and publickly burnt. Justinian* also forbids the transcribing any heretical Books, under the Penalty of having the Hand cut off. For after that *Anthimus* had been condemned in the fifth Synod, he made this Law against his Books. *Novel* 42. *cap.* 1. *We prohibit all to keep any of his Books: And as it is not lawful for any one to write, or have in his Possession the Books of* Nestorius, *according as the Emperors, our Predecessors, have thought fit in their Constitutions to ordain, with respect to the Sayings and Writings of* Porphyry *against Christianity ; so let nothing said or written by* Severus *remain in the Possession of any Christian ; but let them be abhorred as profane by the Catholick Church, and burnt by those that have them, unless they are willing to suffer the appointed Penalty. Let them not therefore be transcribed by the Notaries of any Sort, as knowing that the Punishment of those who shall write any of his Books, shall be the Loss of their Hand.* From these several Laws, *Conrad Brunus* infers, that the Schools of Hereticks are to be destroyed thus : " The Schools of Hereticks ^{Brun. l. 6.}
" are to be destroyed by these Means. Heretical Masters must be removed, ^{c. 5. §. 27,}
" the Scholars must be prohibited from coming to their Schools, the Places ^{&c.}
" they use to meet in must be appropriated to Ecclesiastical Purposes. The
" Masters are to be removed by being publickly put to Death ; the Pu-
" nishment ordained against Hereticks, who shall dare to teach unlawful Opi-
" nions, as *Valentinian* and *Martian* have enacted, *l. Quicunque, c. de Hæret.*
" The Scholars are to be prohibited from going to heretical Schools by a pe-
" cuniary Mulct, *viz.* under the Forfeiture of ten Pounds of Gold, according
" to the Constitution of the Emperor *Martian, d. l. Quicunque, §. Eos vero,*
" *c. de Hæret.* And in general, the Houses where heretical Assemblies and
" Conventicles are held, are to be forfeited to the King or Church ; but
" those

" thofe efpecially wherein their Errors and Herefies are taught ; according
" to the Conftitution of *Juftinian* againft *Anthimus, &c. Interdicimus autem, &c.*
Thus did the Chriftians imitate the Heathen Cruelty, by perfecuting thofe
that differed from them, and followed the Example of *Julian*, in deftroying
their Schools, which the Heathens themfelves condemned as barbarous and
cruel : For thus *Ammianus Marcellinus* declares, b. 25. *His Laws, abfolutely
commanding fome Things to be done, and forbidding others, were generally good, fome
few excepted ; among which was that cruel one, by which he prohibited the Chriftian Mafters of Rhetorick and Grammar to teach, to prevent any from forfaking
the Worfhip of the Gods :* But in Procefs of Time, under the Government of
the Popes, the Edicts of the Chriftians vaftly exceeded this Cruelty of *Julian.*

'Tis true, thefe were Laws made by the Civil Magiftrate, but that they
were publifhed with the Approbation of the Bifhops, no one can doubt, who
compares our Times with the Antient. The Bifhops could not bear that their
Decrees and Anathemas fhould be flighted as infignificant and harmlefs Flafhes.
They would fain have all condemned by their Sentence appear to others to
be juftly condemned ; and eagerly thirfted after the Mitres and Churches of
thofe, whofe Doctrines they were pleafed to anathematize ; and therefore,
in order to get Poffeffion of them, it was found neceffary to arm the fecular
Power, and to enact civil Laws againft them, that hereby they might ftrip
them of their Dignities, and drive them into Banifhment, in order to enter on
their vacant Sees. Nor let any one imagine, that the ancient Times were
more holy than ours ; the fame worldly Spirit that now influences our Synods,
governed the Councils of the ancient Bifhops : Even the Council of *Nice*, fo
much celebrated and extolled, is an abundant Proof of this. Such was the
fierce and reftlefs Spirit of the Bifhops there met together ; fo many and
bitter their Contentions, that, forgetting the principal Caufe of their meeting together, they meanly prefented Accufations againft each other to the Emperor, who, that he might put an End to their Quarrels, ordered the Accufations to be burnt ; and commanded them that they fhould immediately go
upon the Bufinefs for which they had been affembled. Who can believe, that
an Affembly of Men, inflamed with Paffion and mutual Hatred, and breathing nothing but Revenge, would reft contented, with having procured the
Condemnation only of their hated Enemies, and not rather ufe their utmoft
Endeavours to excite the Emperor to banifh thofe whom they had condemned ?

Hift. Ec. l.
7. c. 3. But not to rely on Conjectures, *Socrates* exprefly tells us : " That *Theodofius*
" Bifhop of *Synada* in the greater *Phrygia*, cruelly perfecuted the Hereticks
" of the *Macedonian* Sect, of which there was a great Number in that
" City ; driving them not only from the City, but from the very Country
" alfo ; *not according to the Cuftom of the orthodox Church, which ufes no Me-*
" *thods of Perfecution,* nor thro' Zeal for the true Faith ; but from a covetous
" Defire of enriching himfelf with the Spoils of the Hereticks. To this End
" he left no Means untried to ruin the Followers of *Macedonius*, arming his
" Clergy, and perfecuting them by innumerable fubtle Methods, and Tricks
" of Law. But his Malice was principally levelled againft their Bifhop *Aga-*
" *petus,*

" *petus*, whom he tired out with repeated Injuries.   And becaufe he did not
" think the Governors of the Provinces fufficient for the Punifhment of Here-
" ticks, he went to *Conftantinople* to folicite new Edicts from the Magiftrates.

Nor were the Bifhops of *Rome* afraid to implore the Affiftance of the Empe-*Simanca*
rors againft Hereticks.   Pope *Anaftafius* perfwaded the Judges to condemn the *t.t.* 49.
Manicheans to perpetual Banifhment, whom he could not bring over to the §. 14.
Catholick Faith ; left by their Contagion they fhould infect the holy Flock.
And *Leo* the Great, writing to *Leo* the Emperor, fays : *That the perverfe*
and enfnaring Difputations of the Hereticks would foon come to an End, if put un-
der Reftraint by the Imperial Power.   And in his 43d Epiftle to the fame Prince :
Vouchfafe, by your Regard for the Faith, to yield this Remedy to the Church ; that
Hereticks may not only be kept out of all holy Orders, but even expelled from every
City, that the holy People of God may be in no farther Danger of Infection from
thefe wicked Men.   And in his 45th Epiftle, he exhorts the Emprefs *Pulcheria,*
That fhe would banifh Eutyches *further from* Conftantinople, *that he might re-*
ceive no Comfort from thofe whom he had drawn over to his Impiety.

But further, when they had got into Poffeffion of the fupreme Power in
Rome, they were oftentimes the Authors of Perfecution themfelves.   Pope
Celeftine, as *Socrates* relates in his Ecclefiaftical Hiftory, *b.* 7. *c.* 11. " took
" from the *Novatians* their Churches in *Rome,* fo that *Rufticula,* their Bifhop,
" was forced to meet his Flock in private Houfes : For till this Time the
" *Novatians* flourifhed in *Rome,* were in Poffeffion of many Churches, and
" had large Congregations to fill them ; but they fell a Sacrifice to Envy,
" becaufe, *The Bifhops both of* Rome *and* Alexandria *had ufurped a tyrannical* (N. r.)
" *Power, exceeding all the Bounds of the Priefthood.*   For this Reafon, the Bifhops
" of *Rome* did not permit even thofe who agreed with themfelves in Opi-
" nion, to hold free and open Affemblies ; but though they praifed them for
" their Agreement with them in the Faith, yet deprived them of all the'r
" Subftance.   But the Bifhops of *Conftantinople* were however free from this
" wicked Spirit ; for they not only fuffered the *Novatians* to meet within the
" City, but even bore them a very fincere Affection."   But the Bifhops of
Rome, even when they had no Power at *Conftantinople,* yet by their perpetual Solicitations of the Emperors there, at laft extorted from them the Oppreffion of Hereticks.   Whilft *Juftinian* was Emperor, the Followers of *An-*
thimus and *Severus* held their publick Affemblies, although they had been
condemned and excommunicated by the Pope of *Rome.*   Wherefore the Bifhops
of the *Second Syria,* and the *Archimandrites* and *Monks,* fent Letters to *Agapetus,*
Bifhop of *Rome,* then at *Conftantinople,* in which they befought him to deliver
them from Hereticks.   The Bifhops thus : *Take from us fpeedily thefe evil Men,*
and offer up this acceptable Sacrifice to God and our Saviour, that we may have a
good Account to give in the future awful Judgment.   Preferve the Ecclefiaftical Dig-
nity free from all Fear, and the thrice repeated heretical Difturbance ; eftablifh our
Order ; and put our moft juft Emperor in Mind of thofe many and righteous Sentences
that were firft prónounced from the Apoftolick Chair ; ordaining, that thofe who
had their impious Writings fhould deliver them up, and commit them to the Flames,
in

in Imitation of those who were inflamed with Zeal to destroy the Writings of the Manicheans, *and those of the impious* Nestorius, *and the hardned* Eutyches, *and* Dioscorus *their Father and Protector : So will you deprive of all Hope those who vainly trust in them. We therefore pray, most holy Father, that you would put in Execution that Sentence against* Anthimus, *which is both God's and yours, that so all Offence may be removed from these little ones, that believe in the Lord, and from us all.* The Monks also making the same Request, in the Conclusion give this Reason for it : *For this Cause we have sent unto you to* Rome, *and have promised and even undertaken for your desired Return. We have received these Promises from the most pious Emperor, that what you shall canonically pronounce, he will piously execute, that all the World may be delivered from this present Disturbance by them. Agapetus* had passed his Sentence before this Request of the Bishops and Monks, and condemned *Anthimus,* and pronounced, that as he had been expelled from the Bishoprick of *Constantinople* before, so he should now be banished from that of *Trapezuntium,* and degraded from every priestly Office and Function. *But no sooner had he received these Letters of the Bishops and Monks, but he sent to* Justinian *the Emperor, that he would banish those whom he had condemned for Hereticks.* Baronius adds, *When he had done these Things, and thus performed all the Duties of his Office, the most holy* Agapetus *died, in order to receive his Reward now his Work was done :* As though it was such an heroick Action, to conclude his Life with exciting the Emperor to persecute those whom he had condemned for Hereticks, as merited the Reward of eternal Salvation. After the Death of *Agapetus,* the Monks renewed their bloody Petitions to the Emperor, and beseech'd him that he would banish those whom *Anacletus* had condemned as Hereticks : *For,* say they, *there is Reason to fear, most pious Emperor, lest for our long Delay, that of the People of* Israel *should happen to us, who have amongst us Men accursed from the Priesthood ;* who (because they had in the Midst of them Achan and Jonathan, who exposed themselves to a Curse, the one wilfully, the other through Ignorance) were in Danger of being entirely destroyed, though they knew not that they had the accursed Thing amongst them. *Despise not therefore, O ye most Christian Emperors, so great an Evil, but be filled with Zeal to promote the Knowledge of God and his Interest, fulfilling what is written :* A wise King scattereth the Wicked ; *that with* David *and* Josias, *and* Elias *and* Agapetus, *who were inspired with the noblest Zeal for God, you may have a Part in this World as they had, and bring all your Enemies under your Footstool ; and that he may grant you hereafter, with them, an eternal Kingdom, who hath promised, that he will give an hundred fold here, and hereafter Life eternal.* Not long after, *Anthimus* and his Followers were condemned by the Council of *Constantinople,* through the Intrigues of the *Roman* Legates ; and many Petitions were offered to the Emperor for the Banishment of those the Synod had condemned as Hereticks ; so that by the cursed Solicitations of the Ecclesiasticks, he was even forced to consent to their Persecution.

It must however be owned, that some of the Bishops were Enemies to Persecution ; and being of more moderate Sentiments, blamed those who defended and encouraged it. *Sulpitius Severus* tells us : *That* Idacius *and* Ithacius *foolishly*
applied

applied themfelves to the fecular Powers, that by their Sentence and Authority they would banifh the Hereticks from Cities, viz. Inftantius *and* Salvianus, Helpidius *and* Prifcillianus. And when afterward *Prifcillianus* appealed from the Synod of *Burdeaux* to the Emperor, the Bifhops *Idacius* and *Ithacius* followed him as his Accufers : But Martin, *then Bifhop of* Treves, *was continually foliciting* Itha-cius *to defift from his Accufation ; and prayed* Maximus *that he would abftain from the Blood of thofe unhappy Men ; that it was more than fufficient, that they were ad-judged Hereticks, and expelled the Churches by the Epifcopal Sentence ; and that it was a new and unheard-of Impiety, that the Civil Power fhould judge in the Af-fairs of the Church.* And the Interceffion of *Martin* prevailed fo far, *that whilft he continued at* Treves *all Procefs was ftopped ; and when he was about to go from thence, by a peculiar Influence, he obtained a Promife from* Maximus, *that nothing cruel fhould be inflicted upon the Accufed ;* although, after his De-parture, *Prifcillianus* was condemned to Death. The Reafon affigned by *Bel-larmine,* that thefe Bifhops were cenfured, *viz. becaufe they brought an Ecclefia-ftical Affair before the Emperor, and became Accufers in a Caufe of Blood,* is very frivolous. 'Tis true, that *Martin* blames *Ithacius* that he accufed *Prifcillian* before the Emperor's Tribunal ; and that, as *Sulpicius Severus* teftifies, not fo much from his Hatred of Herefy, as from a Defire of Revenge ; and there-fore *Martin* adds, that it was a new and unheard-of Impiety, that the fecu-lar Power fhould judge an Ecclefiaftical Caufe. But by this *Martin* plainly fhows, that fecular Punifhments ought never to be inflicted on religious Ac-counts, becaufe Matters of Faith do not come under the Cognizance of the fe-cular Tribunal ; and that the Progrefs of Herefy neither can nor ought to be prevented by the Blood of Hereticks ; and therefore he obtained a Promife from *Maximus* that nothing cruel fhould be inflicted on the Accufed. We ac-knowledge with *Bellarmine,* that a Bifhop ought not to be an Accufer in the Caufe of Blood ; but at the fame Time, cannot imagine, with what Juftice a Bi-fhop, who ought not to act the Part of an Accufer, may not only excommu-nicate Hereticks, but, as *Bellarmine* contends, deliver them over to the fecular Power, and even exhort the Judges to perform their Duty : For this is fome-thing more than to act the Part of an Accufer. An Accufer only labours to prove the Crime, that when proved, the Judge may pafs Sentence on it ; but when a Bifhop, by his own Sentence, pronounces any Perfon an Heretick, and delivers him over to the fecular Arm, he lays the Judge under a Neceffity of burning, without any farther Examination, the miferable Heretick. And if, thro' Compaffion, he feems willing to defer the Execution, the Bifhop exhorts, and even compels him, under the Penalty of Excommunication, to perform his Office. Who in fuch a Cafe will clear the Bifhop from the Guilt of the Blood and Murder of the Heretick ? Who doth not fee that the Bifhop is the fole Caufe ; and the Civil Magiftrate, who in all Things blindly fubmits to the Bifhop, is the Inftrument only of the Heretick's Death ; efpecially as it is un-lawful for him, under any Pretence, to refufe Obedience to the Bifhop's Or-ders ? If therefore 'tis unlawful for a Bifhop to turn Accufer in a Cafe of Blood ; much more unlawful is it for him to deliver thofe he condemns as He-reticks.

reticks to the fecular Arm, and prefs the Civil Power to put their Sentence in Execution. But to return from this Digreffion. *Martin* not content to blame *Ithacius*, after *Prifcillian* was put to Death, excommunicated him, and with him thofe who were the Authors of his Murther. The Fear of this Excommunication faved many, that had been thrown into Prifon, from Death. The Emperor, who favoured *Ithacius* and *Urfatus*, oftentimes preffed, and at laft commanded *Martin* that he fhould communicate with him; but could not prevail, till he had promifed to recal the Tribunes that had been fent into *Spain* to deftroy the Churches: Nor could he be at laft prevail'd with, notwithftanding the vigorous Endeavours of the Bifhops, to fubfcribe to his Confent to communicate with him; fo unjuft did it feem to him to punifh Men with Death for their Errors in Matters of Faith. Few indeed was the Number of thefe Bifhops, who had the Courage to oppofe this perfecuting Spirit; and therefore, generally fpeaking, the poor Hereticks were made to undergo all Sorts of the moft cruel Punifhments.

C H A P. IV.

The Arian *Perfecutions of the* Orthodox.

BUT neither did the *Arians*, when they had an Emperor of their own Party, refrain from any Sort of Cruelty, but perfecuted thofe, by whom they had been deprived, with a more implacable and bloody Hatred. The Perfecutions againft *Athanafius*, their principal Adverfary, are notorious to all. *Athanafius* himfelf, in his Letter to the Hermits, gives us many Inftances of their Cruelty, which is the Burthen of his Epiftle; and aggravated as far as Words can do it, *viz.* That they fcourged the Bifhops in *Egypt*, and bound them with cruel Chains; That they fent *Sarapammo* into Banifhment, and beat *Potammo* in fo barbarous a manner on his Back, that he was left for dead, and died foon after of his Bruifes and Pain; That they would not fuffer a dead Woman to be buried; That they ejected many Bifhops from their Sees, and fent them into Banifhment; and that they obtained an Edict from the Emperor, that the Bifhops fhould not only be banifhed from the Cities and Churches, but even punifhed with Death wherever they could be found. And he adds: *That fo dreadfully were Men terrified by them, that fome pretended to believe their Herefies; and others through Fear chofe rather to fly into Defarts than fall into their Hands.* In another Place he fays: *How many Bifhops were brought before Governors and Kings, and heard this Sentence from their Judges:* Either Subscribe, or depart from your Churches? *For the Emperor hath commanded you fhould be banifhed from your Churches. How many in every City fcattered themfelves up and down for fear of being accufed as the Bifhops Friends? For the Magiftrates were written to, and commanded upon*

P. 817.
P. 821.

P. 819.

Penalty

Penalty of a Fine, to compel the Bifhops of their refpective Cities to fubfcribe. In fine, all Places and Cities were filled with Terrors and Tumults ; for Violence was offered to the Bifhops, and the Judges faw the Mournings and Sighs of the People. And at length, after a tragical Account of the various Cruelties and Perfe-cutions of the *Arians,* he adds : *That they would not fuffer the Friends of thofe they* P. 859. *had flain, to bury their dead Bodies, but hid them in private Places, that hereby they might conceal their Murthers.* There are other Paffages to the fame Purpofe in the fame Epiftle.

In his firft Apology alfo for his Flight, he fpeaks to the fame Purpofe, and among other Things relates, that *Sebaftianus,* Captain of the Forces, at the Inftigation of *George* the Bifhop, *ordered Virgins to be brought to a flaming* P. 704. *Pile, and violently compelled them by Fire to declare their Profeffion of the* Arian *Faith ; and when he perceived their Courage was not to be thus fubdued, he ftripped their Bodies naked, and fo mangled their Faces with Blows, that it was a long while before their own Relations knew them again. He alfo apprehended forty Men, and miferably tore their Bodies by a new Method of Cruelty ; for he made Rods of the Palm Tree, retaining their Prickles, and with thefe beat them on their Backs, in fuch a barbarous manner, that fome, by Reafon of the Prickles fticking in their Flefh, were forced feveral Times to apply to the Phyficians for a Cure ; whilft others actually dy'd under the Torture. As for the others, as many as they apprehended,* they banifhed them, with the Virgins, into Great Hoafis, a Country in Egypt.

And that they might have fome Pretext to palliate their Perfecutions, *lib. 2.* *Victor,* in his Account of the Perfecutions of the *Vandals,* tells us, that the very Laws made by the Catholicks againft heretical Impiety, were now turned, and executed upon the Catholicks themfelves ; fo that what they once fuffered from the Catholicks, they made the Catholicks to fuffer in their Turn, now they had got the fecular Power on their Side.

Lucius, an *Arian* Bifhop, befides the Slaughters, Torments, Banifhments, *Brunus, l.* Hangings, Burnings, and other innumerable Cruelties he exercifed on the *2. c. 3.* Catholicks, laid wafte the Monafteries and Caves of the Monks. Almoft the fame Things are related of *Severus,* Bifhop of *Antioch. Victor* in his firft Book of the *Vandal* Perfecution, fays, that being infected with the *Arian* Herefy, they filled every Place with Fire and Slaughter, and burnt and demolifhed the Churches, Temples, and Monafteries ; and tortured the Bifhops and Priefts with various kinds of Cruelties, to force them to deliver up all the Gold and Silver they had of their own, or that belonged to their Churches ; and if they gave them any, they put them to yet more exquifite Tortures to force them to deliver up the whole, as imagining they had concealed a Part from them. They deprived the Catholicks up and down of their Churches, and commanded them to be fhut up. The fame *Victor* recounts the vari- *c. 6. §. 6.* ous Sorts of Cruelties wherewith the *Arians* perfecuted the Catholicks, viz. *c. 28. §.* that in *Africa* they were, by the *Vandals,* firft deprived of their Churches *4, 5.* and Houfes, then driven without the City-Walls, without Creature, Wea-pon, or Clothes ; and yet farther, by a publick Edict, it was commanded,

D that

that no one fhould entertain or feed them ; and if any one out of Compaffion did this, he was burnt, with his entire Family.

§. 8. §. 8.   *Hunerick,* the *Arian* King of the *Vandals* in *Africa,* among other Cruelties he exercifed on the Catholicks, threw an immenfe Multitude of them one upon another, like Heaps of Locufts, into ftrait and vile Places, where they had no Conveniency for eafing Nature, but were forced to do it amongft one another as they lay, fo that the Stench and Terror exceeded all other kinds of Punifhments. *Victor* relates thefe Things,, who himfelf was an Eye-witnefs to them.

l. 2.   The fame *Victor* relates other kinds of Cruelty practifed by *Hunerick*; but it would be too tedious to recount them all.   'Tis enough to add, that fome had their Tongues cut out, others their Hands, others their Feet chopt off ; others their Eyes dug out, and others were miferably flain through the Extremity of their Tortures.   See alfo *Hift. Tripart, b.* 5. *c.* 32. and *b.* 4. *c.* 39.

Auftin alfo, in his 50th Epiftle to *Boniface,* and in his 68th Epiftle, and in other Books which he wrote againft the *Donatifts,* recounts the various Cruelties of the *Donatifts* and *Circumcellians*; fo that the Chriftians feemed only to be employed in mutual Butcherings of one another ; and acted as though the whole Perfection of the Chriftian Life confifted, not in the Holinefs of their Manners, but in a bitter and imprudent Zeal ; fo that *Ammianus Marcellinus,* an Heathen Writer, defcribing thofe Times, relates of *Julian* the Emperor, *b.* 22. *That he ordered the Chriftian Bifhops and People that were at Variance with each other, to come into his Palace, and there admonifhed them, that they fhould every one profefs his own Religion, without Hindrance or Fear, whilft they did not difturb the publick Peace by their Divifions*; *which he did for this Reafon, becaufe as he knew their Liberty would increafe their Divifions, he might now have nothing to fear from their being an united People*; *having found by Experience, that even Beafts are not fo cruel to Men, as the Generality of Chriftians are to each other.*

The Ecclefiaftical Doctors give very pathetick and odious Defcriptions of the Perfecutions of the *Arians.*   'Tis abundantly plain from the Writings of the Orthodox, which now remain, that their Edicts were far from being vain and harmlefs Terrors.   And if we now had the Writings of the *Arians,* we fhould not probably find fofter Things related by them of the Orthodox, than the Orthodox in their Writings relate of the *Arians:*   But by reafon of the fevere Edicts againft keeping their Books, their Works are entirely deftroy'd ; and we have now no Remains of the Hiftory of thofe Times but what we find in the Writings of the Orthodox.   And though thefe were in fome Refpects great Men, yet their Actions and Writings abundantly teftify, that they were far from being free from human Paffions, Hatred, Anger, and the Study of Revenge ; efpecially when they had to do with their Adverfaries, and thofe who differed from them in Matters of Religion.   This hath been the Unhappinefs of all Times, that it is too generally true of Divines, what *Tom. 5. p.* *Erafmus* with Grief declared of the Divines of his own, *That the Behaviour of*
65.   *fome*

some of them is such, that they have brought a Reproach on this most holy Study it self, since those who have attained to the Height of this Profession, are sometimes more fierce than the Laity, more ambitious, easier provok'd, more virulent with their Tongues, and more unfit for all manner of Converse in Life, not only than unlearned Persons, but than they themselves would otherwise be ; so that some have imagined that the very Study of Divinity hath made them such: or, as he elsewhere says, *that their Behaviour is such, that Divinity hath been looked on as a Sort of Study that deprives Men of Sincerity and common Sense.* Let us not imagine, that these Things are not equally true of the ancient, as well as of the modern Divines. He that but dips into the Acts of the ancient Councils, and Ecclesiastical Remains, will evidently see, that they had the same Passions with those of our own Time, were equally precipitant in condemning, bitter in reproaching, and violent in persecuting those they call'd Hereticks. *Socrates* writes of the Bishops of his own Time, *That their manner was, to load with Reproaches, and pronounce impious all they deposed, without declaring the Causes of their Impiety.* Hist. Eccl. b. 1. c. 24. When they write against their Adversaries, their Stile is oftentimes bitter ; an Impotency of Mind that many have observed in the principal and most celebrated Authors. *Erasmus,* tho' he highly commends *Jerome,* hath several Times observed the same in him. In his Apology to *Martin Dorpius,* he thus writes of him : *Even* Jerome, *a Man so grave and pious, could not always govern himself ; he grows furiously hot against* Vigilantius, *immoderately insults* Jovinian, *and bitterly inveighs against* Ruffinus. In his Apology against *Sutor,* he goes farther, and says ; *That tho' his Memory is now deservedly accounted sacred by all, yet whilst he lived, he reviled, and railed at, and deceived others ; and was in his Turn reviled, and railed at, and deceived by others.* Hutter *gives no better a Character of* Jerome, *writing against the* Irenicum *of* Paræus, p. 14. *He that turns over the Writings of St.* Jerome *against* Jovinian, Vigilantius, *and* Ruffinus, *will be amaz'd to see in a Monk such a boiling and bitter Gall.* Upon which Account *Budæus* pleasantly writes to *Erasmus : Who knows, but that for this Reason he may be brought and scourged before the Tribunal of Christ ?* I don't mention these Things to blacken the Reputation of *Jerome,* but to shew by the Example of this otherwise great Man, how difficult it is to govern ones self in theological Debates, when we see Men, famous for their Piety, thus carried away by the Heat of Disputes. The Moderation of *Austin* is generally commended : But he that reads his Writings against the *Donatists,* must acknowledge, that in the Warmth of Disputation he oftentimes exceeds the Bounds of Moderation, and lays to their Charge every thing that came uppermost. *Athanasius*'s Epistle to the Monks is Proof enough of his ungovernable and angry Temper, in which we find nothing but foul and reproachful Language against the *Arians* ; a plain Proof of a violently disorder'd Mind. I question not but that he had weighty Reasons for his Anger and Hatred. But 'tis as certain, that when the Mind is disorder'd, tho' for the most just Cause, many Things are rashly thrown out, the Effect of Choler, and not agreeable to Truth : So that 'tis by no Means safe, hastily to credit, all that the an-

Tom. 9.
P. 3, 4.
Tom. 3.
p. 119.
Tom. 9.
p. 640.

Erasmi,
Tom, 3.
P. 156.

gry

gry Fathers have said of, or imputed to their Adversaries, especially as they
have taken Care to suppress their Writings. *Cunæus* very solidly and gravely

Præfat. in pronounces his Opinion of the *Greek* Fathers, *viz. The common People think,*
Juliani   *that he must be very criminal, who doth not believe, that Piety, the great Sup-*
Cæsares.   *port of Christianity, is always attended with Candour. For my own part, as I*
esteem them on many Accounts to be excellent and divine Men, so I know that
they have done ill designedly, and were of a very bitter Spirit. Not to mention
others, the Greek Fathers, thro' a national Vice, were always too violent on both
Sides. They had all of them a rolling Eloquence, admirable Learning, and a
Genius fit for every thing; and on these Accounts one may discern a Sharpness
and Eagerness breathing throughout all the Remains they have transmitted to Po-
sterity. As for those they were angry with, tho' great Men in themselves, and
worthy the highest Commendation, they blacken'd them as the vilest Persons; and
on the other hand, they were so lavish of their Praises on those they approved, that,
tho' they had little to deserve it, Posterity admires their Virtues, and even adores
a Stone of their Sepulchre as a God.   Not much different from this, is that Pas-

l.11.p.663 sage of *Melchior Canus,* in his *Common Places of Divinity: I cannot excuse*
Sozomen's *Lyes: For he was a Greek, which Nation is and ever was ad-*
dicted to lying.   And he was so fully convinced, that the most shameful Lyes
had crept into the Histories of his own Church, that he breaks out into

p.650. this Complaint: *I speak it rather with Grief, than as a Matter of Reproach,*
that Laertius *hath written the Lives of the Philosophers with greater Regard to*
Truth, than Christians have the Lives of their Saints; and that Suetonius's *Ac-*
count of the Cæsars *is written with greater Incorruptness and Integrity, than the*
Account which the Catholicks have given, I will not say of their Emperors, but
of their Martyrs, Virgins, and Confessors. The two former have not concealed the
real or suspected Vices of their best Philosophers or Princes, nor the Appearances
of Virtue in the worst; whereas ours, for the most part, either are governed by
their Passions, or industriously forge so many idle Stories, that I am not only ashamed
but tired of them. Such as these are so far from being useful to the Church of Christ,
that they greatly disserve its Interest. I forbear their Names, because here I blame
their Morals, and not their Learning, as to which the Censure might be more
free. As to Behaviour, one ought to be more cautious towards the Living, and
more respectful towards the Dead: But this is certain, that whoever mix Fable
and Falshood with Ecclesiastical History, can't be good and upright Men, and
their whole Account can be invented for no other Purpose, but to increase their
Gains, or to establish Error; of which the first is vile, the other pernicious.

p.654. And a little after, describing the Office of a good Historian, he says: *That*
he ought not to dare to say any thing false, or omit any thing true, that he may'nt
be suspected to write either out of Favour or Hatred. He adds: *Since these*
Things are necessary Marks of Honesty and Integrity, 'tis strange that Suetonius
should have observed them all, and almost all ours have entirely omitted them.
'Tis no difficult Matter to conjecture what their Candour and Fidelity is,
in relating the Actions of their Adversaries, and those whom they have
condemned for Hereticks, who have been so immoderate and false in their
                                                                    Commen-

Commendations of their Saints. *Canus* himfelf confeffes, that moft uf their Writers have been deftitute of every Qualification of a good Hiftorian. *Bellarmine*, in his *Marks of the Church*, fays: *The Catholicks are no where* cap. 16. *found to have praifed or approved either the Doctrine or Life of any Heathens or Hereticks.* So that it was a fufficient Reafon to write the worft Things of any Man, or to conceal and condemn to eternal Oblivion the beft and moft laudable Actions, if he had been pronounced an Heretick by the Church; and the Papifts now think it Reafon enough to give no Credit to any Perfon, if he doth not condemn, or if he praifes the Actions of thofe who have been declared Hereticks by the Church of *Rome*, and hath in any manner oppofed her. On this Principle, *Melchior Canus* gives his Reafons, why all p. 662. the Faithful of Chrift ought to explode the Hiftory of *Cario*. For, fays he, *in his Writings, he villifies and cruelly ufes fome of the Popes, who were the beft of Men, and commends and extols fome of the* German *Emperors, who were Rebels and Enemies to the Church of* Rome. *So that you may know the Lion by his Paw*, i. e. *a* Lutheran *by thofe he praifes or condemns.* If this Inference of *Canus* were true, 'tis neceffary, that he who would be owned for a Catholick, muft load all the Enemies of the Church of *Rome* with Infamy and Difgrace, and never blame the Catholicks, but praife and commend every thing they do. But if we read the Writings and Hiftories of the modern Papifts, we fhall find them filled with fo many Stories and evident Lyes, to which the publick Acts and Documents bear Witnefs, that one can fcarce find the fmalleft Footfteps of Truth in them, and may juftly affirm, that they wrote entirely for Gain, or the Eftablifhment of Error. And if their Power fhould rife again to the fame Height as it was in former Ages, fo that they fhould be able wholly to deftroy the Writings and Monuments of thofe who differ from them, and Perfons were to learn from their Writings only the Doctrines and Actions of the Reform'd and Proteftant, who doth not fee what wretched Accounts they would tranfmit to Pofterity, even lighter than Vanity it felf; which however could fcarce be convicted of Falfhood by proper Teftimonies, after they had thus deftroyed the contrary Documents? And therefore, as 'tis not fafe to form a Judgment of the Principles and Behaviour of the Reform'd and Proteftant from Popifh Writings only, fo we ought to be very cautious and backward of pronouncing concerning the Doctrines and Actions of thofe who were condemned for Hereticks, from the Writings and Hiftories of the Ancients, becaufe their Writings have been fo entirely fupprefs'd by the Induftry and Care of their Adverfaries, that there is fcarce one genuine Book of theirs remaining, wherein they have defcribed or defended their Doctrine or Manner of Proceeding. But 'tis Time to return from this Digreffion.

We have fhewn with what Bitternefs the Orthodox have perfecuted the *Arians* and *Donatifts*; nor did the *Arians* exercife lefs Cruelty againft the Orthodox, when they had an Emperor who favour'd their Party. But it muft be confefs'd this Cruelty was not always equal: For although the *Arians*

Arians are not to be excus'd in their barbarous Treatment of the Orthodox ; yet we read that sometimes it was greatly abated. *Socrates* in his Ecclesiastical History, *l.* 4. *c.* 32. relates of *Valens* the Emperor, *That he violently oppos'd those who professed the Doctrine of Consubstantiality, threatning
them every Day with severer Punishments* ; till Themistius *the Philosopher partly
mitigated his Rage, by an Oration, called* πρεσζωντικος, *in which he admonishes the
Emperor, that he should not so greatly wonder that there was such a Diversity of
Opinions amongst Christians* ; *for that it was but small if compared with the Number of the different Opinions amongst the* Greeks, *which were more than three hundred. This Variety of Opinions must necessarily cause Divisions* ; *but that God was
pleased with this Diversity of Sentiments, that all might learn the more to reverence
his Majesty from the Difficulty of understanding him. When the Philosopher had represented these and other Things of like Nature to him, the Emperor grew afterwards
more mild, though he did not entirely lay aside his Fury, punishing the Priests with
Banishment instead of Death.* But afterwards, as the same *Socrates* relates,
c. 35. being pressed with the *Gothick* War, he left off banishing the *Homou-
sians.* Farther, there were some amongst them who abstained from all Violence in Matters of Religion, and were willing to allow the free Exercise of it
to those who differed from them. *Grotius* gives them this Testimony : *Nor
is this a little to their Praise, that the* Vandals, *about the Times of* Hunnerick,
and Gundemond, *and the* Goths, *always abstained from offering Violence to the
Consciences of those subject to them, and permitted the Followers of the* Nicene *Faith
to believe and teach, and perform divine Worship as they pleased. The Ambassadors of the* Goths *said to* Belisarius, *that they never forced any one with Threatnings to change his Profession* ; *nor hinder'd the* Goths *themselves from believing the*
Nicene *Faith* ; *adding, that the* Goths *did not shew less Reverence towards the
sacred Places than the* Romans *themselves.* And a little after, *p.* 32. Theude-
rick, *King of the* Ostrogoths *and* Italy, *is highly extolled by* Eunodius, *the Catholick
Bishop of* Ticinum, *for his Piety and Worship of the true God. Such was his Regard even to the Religion he did not profess, that he always made the best Men Bishops.* Concerning which, his Nephew *Athalarick* thus writes : " 'Twas but
" just to obey the Will of so good a Prince, who in a Religion he did not be-
" lieve, acted with so wise Deliberation, as to choose such a Bishop, as made
" it appear that this was his governing Desire, to see the Religion of all Chur-
" ches flourish under good Priests." *Hence it came to pass, that he called a Synod
to put an End to a Schism that had arose, as* Paulus Warnefredi, *and* Zonaras *declare* : He annulled all *Simoniacal Ordinations, and desired the Catholick Bishops
to pray in his Behalf for the divine Assistance* ; *as may be seen in* Cassiodorus : *So
that I do not wonder that* Silverius, *Catholick Bishop of* Rome, *was suspected by
the* Greeks, *of favouring the Empire of the* Goths *rather than the* Greeks.
Procopius *furnishes us with this noble Instance of the Equity of the* Goths *in Religion.*

In like Manner the Orthodox Emperors did not always make Use of that
Severity which their Laws threaten'd against Hereticks, it being sometimes
their Intention only to terrify with the Fear of Punishments, and not to inflict

Proleg. ad
Procop.
Goth. &
Vandalic.
p. 31.

2   the

the Punishments themselves. *Sozomen* relates, that " *Theodosius* commanded *Ez. Hiß.*
" by a Law, that Hereticks should not assemble together, nor teach their *l. 7. c. 12.*
" Opinions, nor ordain Bishops or others. That some of them should be
" driven from their Cities and Lands ; others declar'd infamous, and denied
" the Privileges of the City which other Citizens enjoy'd ; and that he or-
" dained other grievous Penalties by his Laws, which he never executed :
" For he endeavour'd not to punish, but only terrify his Subjects, and thus
" to bring them into his own Sentiments of the Deity ; for he commended
" those who were willingly converted." The same Writer relates of *Va-*
lentinian, who enjoy'd the Empire with his Brother *Valens.* " They were *l. 6. c. 6.*
" both Christians by Religion ; but differ'd in their Opinions and Manners.
" For *Valens,* when baptiz'd by *Eudoxius* the Bishop, furiously followed the
" Doctrine of *Arius,* and was angry that he could not force all into his Senti-
" ments. But *Valentinian* embraced the *Nicene* Faith, and favour'd those who
" were of his Mind ; but never injur'd any who were of a different Opini-
" on." *Socrates* also, and *Sozomen* relate of *Gratian,* who govern'd the Empire *Hiß. Ec.*
with *Valentinian* the Younger, that he ordain'd by Law, *That all Persons of l. 5. c. 2.*
every Religion, without Exception, should meet in their Churches ; and that the l. 7. c. 1.
Eunomians, Photinians, *and* Manichees *only should be expelled from them. So-*
crates, after having recounted the various Sects of Hereticks, adds, *That the l. 5. c. 20.*
Emperor Theodofius *persecuted none of them except* Eunomius, *whom for gather-*
ing Assemblies, and reading over the Books he had written in private Houses at Conftantinople, *he sent into Banishment, because he corrupted many with his Doctrine :*
As to the rest he offer'd them no Injuries, nor forced them to communicate with himself ;
but permitted all to meet in their Conventicles, and to think as they pleased of the
Christian Faith. Some of them he suffer'd to build themselves Oratories without the
Cities, but the Novatians *to have their Churches within them, without fear ; be-*
cause they held the same Sentiments, in Matters of Faith, with himself. And he
relates of *Atticus,* Bishop of *Constantinople, That he did not only preserve his own l. 7. c. 2.*
People in the Faith, but even surpriz'd the very Hereticks by his wonderful Prudence ;
that he had no Inclination to persecute them, and that having once attempted to
terrify them, he always after shew'd himself more mild and gentle towards them.

CHAP. V.

The Opinion of some of the FATHERS *concerning the Persecution of*
DISSENTERS.

WHAT the Opinion of those ancient Doctors of the Church, whom
we call Fathers, was, we may learn from their Writings. *Atha-*
nasius, in his Epistle to the Hermits, speaks in this Manner of the *Arians,*
and thus paints out their Persecutions against the Orthodox : *That* Jewish *He- p. 82.*
resy

refy hath not only learnt to deny Chrift, but also to delight in Slaughters. But even this was not fufficient to fatisfy them. For as the Father of their Herefy goes about as a roaring Lion, feeking whom to devour ; fo thefe having Liberty to go up and down, run about, and whomfoever they happen to meet with, who either blame their Flight, or abhor their Herefy, inhumanly tare them with Scourges, or bind them with Chains, or banifh them from their native Country.   And a little after : *If it be a mean and difhoneft Thing, that fome Bifhops have chang'd their Opinion through Fear, how much more heinous and vile is their Wickednefs, who, as is the Cafe generally of thofe who miftruft the Goodnefs of their Caufe, have forced others againft their Will to renounce their Belief ? Thus alfo the Devil, becaufe he hath no Truth in him, invades Men with the Hatchet and Ax ; and thus violently breaks open the Doors of thofe that receive him. The Saviour, on the contrary, is gentle ; his Language is,* If any one will, let him follow me, and become my Difciple. *When he comes to any one, he doth not make ufe of Force, but knocks at the Door, and fays,* Open to me, my Sifter, my Spoufe. *If they open he enters ; if they refufe it he departs : For Truth is not to be preach'd by Swords, or Darts, or military Weapons ; but by Perfwafion and Advice. But what room is there for the Liberty of Perfwafion, where Men are awed by the imperial Authority ? And what fignifies Reafoning, when whoever oppofes is fure to be rewarded with Banifhment or Death ?* And after a great deal more, he thus inveighs againft the bloody *Arians : All their Endeavours abound with Slaughter and Impiety ; and fuch is the accurfed Craftinefs of their Temper and Behaviour, that they abufe and deceive Men by the Promifes of Honours, and Majeftracies, and Money, that fo when they cannot obtain the Conftitution of their Bifhoprick by lawful Means, they may give the more fimple fome Appearance of a right Inftitution. So that the very Name of* Heathen *is too good for them ; fo far are they from meriting the Name of* Chriftians, *and their Actions fo unlike thofe of Men, that they are perfectly favage and brutal. For fuch is their Cruelty and Barbarity, that they are more bloody than the very Executioners, and more vile than any other Hereticks, and greatly excelled, even by the* Heathens *themfelves : For I have heard from the Fathers, and I believe it true, that in the Perfecution under* Maximianus, *the Grandfather of* Conftantius, *the Heathens conceal'd our Chriftian Brethren when they were fought after, and were themfelves oftentimes fin'd and imprifon'd for no other Reafon, but becaufe they would not betray thofe that fled to them, thinking themfelves bound to protect them with the fame Fidelity as they would have expected themfelves ; not in the leaft afraid to expofe themfelves to Danger on that Account. But now thefe wonderful Inventors of a new Herefy, famous for nothing fo much as their Treachery, act quite the Reverfe ; for they feek out thofe that conceal themfelves, and lay Snares for thofe that harbour them ; and become of their own Accord, very Executioners ; accounting the Concealed and the Concealor equally their Enemy : So that they are naturally bloody, and Murtherers, and Rivals of the Wickednefs of* Judas. *'Tis indeed impoffible that any Words can fufficiently defcribe their Actions.*   What would not this Doctor have faid, had he feen the cruel Laws of the Inquifition brought into Ufe, by which 'tis not only a Crime to conceal an Heretick, but all who do not inform againft him are anathematiz'd as Favourers and Defenders of

Here-

p. 830.

p. 852.

Hereticks, and Hinderers of the Office of the Inquiſition, and condemned to other Puniſhments, according to the arbitrary Will of the Inquiſitors. He would unqueſtionably have complained that he wanted Words to deſcribe ſuch an execrable Cruelty.   For if what the *Arians* did was beyond Deſcription, how much leſs can any Words give a juſt Repreſentation of the Barbarity of the Inquiſitors, which is as much ſuperior to the Cruelty of the *Arians*, as theirs was, according to *Athanaſius*, to that of the Heathens.   But *Athanaſius* goes on : *Oh their new Hereſy ! Such are its Wickedneſſes and Impieties, that let the Devil be ever ſo bad, this will appear to be the Devil all over. Such a monſtrous Evil never roſe up before ; for thoſe who had any heretical Opinions, uſed to keep their Thoughts and Sentiments to themſelves.   But now* Euſebius *and* Arius, *like Serpents crawling out of their Dens, vomit openly the Poiſon of their impious Sect ; this taking the Liberty publickly to blaſpheme, and the other as publickly to defend his Blaſphemy : But this he could not defend till he had found an Emperor to ſupport his Blaſphemy.   On the other hand, the Fathers in a general Council, of about* 300 *Biſhops, condemn'd the Arian Hereſy, and ſhew'd that 'twas contrary to the Faith of the Church : But the Defenders of the Sect, ſeeing themſelves deſpis'd, and being able to alledge nothing agreeable to Reaſon, have invented a new Way, and attempted to ſupport themſelves by the ſecular Power ; in which one cannot help being amaz'd at their Inſolence and Wickedneſs ; and how much it exceeds all other Hereſies. For the Madneſs of other Hereſies conſiſts in perſwaſive Words, in order to deceive the Simple : And as for the Heathens, the Apoſtle tells us, they deceive Men by their Eloquence and Oratory, and ſubtle Speeches ; and the* Jews, *forgetting the Scriptures, contend about Fables and endleſs Genealogies : The* Manicheans *alſo, and* Valentinians, *and the other Hereticks, endeavour to ſupport their Trifles by adulterating and corrupting the ſacred Scriptures.   But the* Arians, *more perverſe than all the reſt, plainly declare all the other kindred Hereſies to be inferior to theirs, ſince they allow themſelves in much more impious Practices, and endeavour to rival all others, but eſpecially the* Jews *in their Wickedneſs and Villainies ; for as they immediately brought* Paul *before the Governors Tribunal, whom they could not convict of the Crimes objected to him ; ſo theſe, every Day deviſing freſh Tricks, uſe no other Arguments but the Power of the Judges ; and if any one but once contradicts them, he is immediately dragged before the Governor and Captain: And farther, other Hereſies being overcome by the Demonſtration of the Truth, ſhut their Mouths in Silence, and have nothing to do but to bluſh upon Conviction. But this new and execrable Hereſy when overcome with Reaſon, and put to ſhame by the Power of Truth, endeavours to bring Men over to its Intereſt by Violence, Stripes and Jails, when Words prove ineffectual to perſwade them ; and even by this ſhews it ſelf to be an Enemy to true Piety and the Worſhip of God: For 'tis the Property of true Religion, not to force but perſwade.   Thus our Lord, far from forcing Men, left them to the Liberty of their own Will,* commonly thus ſpeaking to all: If any one will come after me ; *and to his Diſciples :* And will you go away alſo ? *But what is more ſuitable to the Nature of ſuch an Hereſy as this, which is quite repugnant to true Religion, and in Rebellion to Chriſt, avows* Conſtantius *as the Author of its Impiety, hereby making*
       E   *him,*

him, as it were, an Antichrist; what more agreeable to its Nature than to act in Defiance to the Saviour ?

In his first Apology for his Flight, he speaks to the same Purpose. And in the first Place to prevent the *Arians* imputing these Persecutions to the Judges, and so pronouncing themselves innocent, he says: *What the Judges seem to do, they are the true Authors of ; or rather, they make themselves the Tools to execute the Sentence and Malice of the Judges.* And afterwards he shews from whom they learn'd these Persecutions. *Pray let them tell me, since whatever is said to them, they pretend is unworthy their Regard, whence they have learn'd the Doctrine of Persecution ? Surely they had it not from the Saints ; it therefore follows, that they must have received it from the Devil, whose Language is,* I will pursue and overtake. *It is the Command of God, and agreeable to the Practice of the Saints, that we should fly ; but to persecute is the Invention of the Devil, who being an Enemy to all, is desirous of exciting every where Persecution.* In this and the like Manner, *Athanasius,* whilst persecuted by the *Arians,* largely and pathetically argues, condemning Persecution of every Sort upon the Score of Religion, and freely pronouncing it the Invention of the Devil. And yet we do not find that this same *Athanasius* made the least Intercession with the Emperor *Constantine,* when the *Nicene* Synod was ended, to prevent the Banishment of *Arius* and his Followers ; no, nor one single Word to shew that he even disapprov'd of *Arius*'s Banishment ; through a too common Weakness of Mind, whereby Men are apt to think, that the same Thing done to them by others would be most unjust, that would not be unjust in them to do to others.

Hilarius against *Auxentius* the *Arian,* shews, with equal Eloquence, his Detestation of Cruelty towards Men differing in their religious Sentiments. *And first I cannot help pitying the Misfortune of our Age, and lamenting the absurd Opinions of the present Times ; according to which, human Arts must support the Cause of God, and the Church of Christ be defended by Methods of secular Ambition. I beseech you, O ye Bishops, who believe your selves to be such, what Helps did the Apostles make Use of in propagating the Gospel ? What Powers assisted them in preaching Christ, and converting all Nations from Idols to God ? Had they any of the Nobles from the Palaces joined with them, when they sung Hymns to God in Prison and in Chains, and after they had been cruelly scourged ? Did* Paul *gather the Church of Christ by Virtue of the Royal Edict, when he himself was made a Spectacle in the publick Theatre ? Was the Preaching of the Divine Truth protected by.* Nero, Vespasian *or* Decius, *which flourished by Means of their very Hatred towards us ? Had they not the Keys of the Kingdom of Heaven ? Surely they had, though they maintained themselves by their own Hands and Labours, met together in Garrets and secret Places, and travelled by Sea and Land over almost all the Nations, Towns and Cities of the Earth, in Opposition to the Edicts both of Senate and Kings ? Did not Mens Hatred of the Gospel manifest the Divine Power, in that the more Christ was forbidden to be preach'd, he was still the more preach'd in the World ? But now (O wretched Case !) earthly Suffrages are to recommend the Divine Faith ; and Christ is declared to be destitute of Power, since Ambition is become the Means of reconciling Men to his Name.*

p. 702.

p. 716.

Name. The Church now terrifies Men by Banishments and Jails, which was at first believed in by Means of Banishments and Jails: She now relies on the Dignity of her Communicants, though at first confecrated by the Terror of her Perfecutors: She now puts her Priests to flight; though she was at first propagated by the Flight of her Priests. She now glories that she is beloved of the World; though she could not belong to Christ, unless the World hated her. And in his first Book to *Constantine,* to the fame Purpose. *God rather chose to teach Men the Knowledge of himself than forcibly demand it; and by gaining Authority to his own Precepts, by wonderful heavenly Works, shew'd that he disdained a Mind compelled even to the Acknowledgment of himself. If such a Method as this was made Use of to propagate the true Faith, the Episcopal Doctrine should agree with it, and say, He is the God of the whole World, and needs not a constrained Obedience. He doth not require a forced Confession: He is not to be deceived, but engaged: He is to be worshiped, not for his own sake, but ours. I can accept him only that is willing; hear him only that prays, and heal him only that freely confesses him. He is to be fought with Simplicity of Mind, to be learn'd by humble Confession, to be loved with true Affection, to be reverenc'd with Fear, and his Favour to be secured by an honest Mind. But what strange Thing is this, that the Priests are forced by Chains and severe Penalties to fear God? The Priests are kept in Prison; the People are bound in Chains; Virgins are stripp'd naked, and their Bodies, consecrated to God, exposed by Way of Punishment to publick View, made an open Spectacle, and fitted for the Torture.*

Ambrose also taught the fame Doctrine. *The Apostles are not commanded t. take Rods in their Hands,* as Matthew writes. *What is a Rod but an Ensign of Power, and an Instrument of Vengeance to inflict Pain? And therefore the Disciples of an humble Master,* I say of an humble Master, for in his Humility his Judgment was taken from him, *can only perform the Duty he hath enjoyned them by Offices of Humility: For he sent Persons forth to sow the Faith, who should not force Men but teach them; nor exercise Power, but exalt the Doctrine of Humility.* And a little after he adds: *When the Apostles would have had Fire from Heaven, to consume the* Samaritans, *who would not receive our Lord Jesus into their City; he turned about and rebuked them, saying,* Ye know not what Spirit ye are of; for the Son of Man is not come to destroy Mens Lives, but to save them.

Gregory Narianzen evidently shews himself to be of the fame Sentiment, although he hath not handled this Argument professedly: For having observed that Men were not easily and at once, but slowly and gradually, brought off from Idolatry to the Law, and from the Law to the Gospel; and having consider'd the Reason of it, he thus speaks: *And why is it thus? Because we are to know, that Men are not to be driven by Force, but to be drawn by Perfwasion. For that which is forced is not lasting; this even the Waves teach us, when they are repelled by Violence; and the very Plants when bent contrary to their Nature. That which is voluntary is both more lasting and safe. This is agreeable to the Divine Equity; the other an Instance of Tyranny. So that he did not think it just even to do good to Men against their Will, or without their Con-*

E 2   *fent.*

Comment. in Luc. l.7. in c. 10.

sent. And in the Poem of his own Life, he speaks to the same Purpose:

> *Perswasion's much more just than Violence ;*
> *Fitter for us, and those whom we attempt*
> *To reconcile unto the Being Supream :*
> *What by Compulsion's done can never last.*
> *Like as the bending Bow, and Stream repell'd,*
> *The Force remov'd, by their own Power return*
> *To native Form and Place, scorning Restraint.*
> *That's only durable which is th' Effect*
> *Of free Consent and Choice. Love leads the Way,*
> *And steady keeps, by kind, yet powerful Influence.*

Optatus Milevitanus writing against *Parmenianus,* the *Donatist,* vindicates the Church from the Charge of persecuting Dissenters from it. For when *Parmenianus* objected to the Catholicks : *That cannot be called the Church, which feeds on cruel Dainties, and grows fat with the Flesh and Blood of the Saints :* *Optatus* thus answers him, *l.* 2. *The Church hath its proper Members ; the Bishops, Presbyters, Deacons, Ministers, and the Body of the Faithful. To which of these different Orders in the Church can you impute what you object ? Point out, if you can, by Name, any Minister or Deacon, or instance in any one Presbyter that hath been concerned in it, or any Bishops who have approved it. What one amongst us hath endeavoured to ensnare, or hath persecuted any Person ? Declare, if you can, and prove one single Instance of Persecution by us.* In this Passage he plainly acknowledges, that the Church ought not to feed on cruel Dainties, and denies that the *Donatists* can, with Truth, object this to his own Church ; though indeed, 'tis scarce to be believed, when one considers the Edicts of the Emperors against the *Donatists,* and other Hereticks. But he goes on, and largely shews, that the *Donatists* themselves had fed on these cruel Dainties, and feasted on Christian Blood ; and at length concludes : *See, your own Party have made good what you your self have confessed, that that cannot be the Church which feeds on cruel Dainties. Missionary Dragoons, and ordained Bishops are vastly different. What you have falsely laid to our Charge, hath been done by others, not by us ; and what you have owned to be unlawful to do, you your selves have acted.*

What was *Chrysostom's* Sentiment in this Affair, he himself sufficiently declares in his Sermon about Excommunication, where he thus inveighs against those, who pronounced others accursed : *I see Men, who understand not the genuine Sense, nor indeed any thing of the sacred Writings, who, to pass by other Things, I am not ashamed to own, are Furious, Triflers, Quarrelsome, who know not what they say, nor whereof they affirm ; bold and peremptory in this one Thing, ever determining Articles of Faith, and declaring accursed, Things they understand not. Upon this Account we are become the Scorn of the Enemies of our Faith, who look upon us as Persons that have no Regard for Virtue, and never learnt to do good. How*

am

am I afflicted and grieved for these Things? And afterwards, citing that Place of St. *Paul,* 2 Tim. ii. 24, 25, 26. *The Servant of the Lord must not strive, but be gentle,* &c. he goes on: *Entice him with the Bait of Compassion, and thus endeavour to draw him out from Destruction, that being thus delivered from the Infection of his former Error, he may live, and thou may'st deliver thy Soul. But if he obstinately refuses to hear, witness against him, lest thou become guilty; only let it be with Long-suffering and Gentleness, lest the Judge require his Soul at thy Hand. Let him not be hated, shunn'd, or persecuted, but exercise towards him a sincere and fervent Charity.* And at length he thus concludes: *Impious and heretical Principles are to be opposed and anathematized; but Men themselves are to be spared, and we must pray for their Salvation.* If this was his Opinion as to those who anathematised others only upon the Account of Heresy, how zealous would he have been against such, who, not content to pronounce Hereticks accursed, deliver them over to the secular Arm to be most cruelly punished?

He farther declares his Opinion, in his eighth Homily on the first of *Genesis*: *Hereticks may be compared to Persons in a Disease, and that are almost deprived of their Sight; for as the one cannot bear the Light of the Sun thro' the Weakness of their Eyes, and the other thro' Illness nauseate the most wholsome Food; so they being distemper'd in their Minds, and darkned in their Understanding, cannot endure to behold the Light of Truth. We ought therefore, in Discharge of our Duty, to hold out the helping Hand, and speak to them with great Meekness. For thus St. Paul hath advised, saying, That our Adversaries are to be instructed with Gentleness, if peradventure God may give them Repentance, to the Acknowledgment of the Truth, and that they may escape out of the Snare of the Devil, having been taken captive by him at his Will —— so that there is need of a double Measure of Gentleness and Forbearance, to deliver and bring them out of the Snares of the Devil.* But in his 47th Homily upon *Matt.* xiii. explaining the Parable of the Tares, he doth not condemn all Sorts of external Violence against Hereticks: *Wilt thou therefore that we go and gather them up? But the Lord forbad it, lest also ye pluck up the Wheat with the Tares; which he said to prevent Wars, and Effusion of Blood, and Slaughter. For if Hereticks were to be killed, a bloody and eternal War would spread it self thro' the World. And therefore he forbids it on a double Account; the one, that the Wheat might not be burnt; the other, that unless they were healed, they could not escape the severest Punishment. Therefore, if you would punish them, and not hurt the Corn, you must wait for the proper Time and Season. What then doth he mean when he says, lest also ye pluck up the Wheat? Undoubtedly this, that if you take up Arms, you must necessarily destroy many of the Saints with the Hereticks; or that even some of these may be changed into the true Wheat: If therefore you too hastily pluck them up, you will destroy all that good Wheat, which might have been produced out of the very Tares. But he doth not forbid us to confine, or shut the Mouths of Hereticks, or to hinder their Liberty of Speech, or synodical Assemblies, or prevent their Union, but only to murder and destroy them.*

St. *Jerome* is of the same Mind, who in his 62d Letter to *Theophilus* against *John of Jerusalem,* thus speaks: *The Church of Christ was founded on the bloody Sufferings*

and

*and Patience of its firſt Profeſſors, and not on their abuſing and injuring others :
It grew by Perſecutions, and triumphed by Martyrdoms.* For tho' he ſhews himſelf very ſevere againſt Hereticks, yet he was not for puniſhing them with
Death, but treating them with Gentleneſs. Thus in his Comment on *Hoſea* ii. 1.
You that believe in Chriſt, whether Jews *or* Gentiles, *ſay ye to the Branches that
are broken off, and the People that is caſt out, My People, for he is thy Brother ; and
my Siſter, for ſhe hath obtained Mercy. When the Fulneſs of the* Gentiles *ſhall come
in, then ſhall all* Iſrael *be ſaved. This is commanded us, that we ſhould not wholly
deſpair of Hereticks, but provoke them to Repentance, and with a brotherly Affection
wiſh their Salvation.* And explaining the Parable of the Tares, *Matt.* xiii. he
ſays : *Wherefore he who governs the Church ought not to ſleep, leſt thrò' his Negligence the Enemy ſhould ſow the Tares,* i. e. *heretical Opinions. But whereas 'tis
ſaid, leſt gathering the Tares, ye pluck up alſo the Corn, 'tis to ſhew us, that there
is a Place for Repentance, and that we ought not haſtily to cut off our Brother, becauſe it may happen, that he who To-day is infected with heretical Pravity, may repent To-morrow, and become a Defender of the Truth.* And in his Commentary on
the Epiſtle to the *Galatians,* ch. v. 9. *A little Leaven leavens the whole Lump,* among
other Things he hath this : *A Spark is to be extinguiſhed as ſoon as it appears,
and the Leaven not to be ſuffer'd to approach the Lump : Corrupted Fleſh is to be cut
off, and ſcaby Sheep to be driven from the Sheepfold, leſt the whole Houſe, Lump, Body
and Flock, ſhould be burn'd, leavened, corrupted, and periſh.* Arius at firſt was
but as a ſingle Spark, which, becauſe it was not immediately extinguiſhed, ſet on Fire
and ravaged the whole World.

CHAP. VI.

St. AUGUSTINE'S *Opinion concerning the Perſecution of* HERETICKS.

AUguſtine, in his former Writings, condemned all Violence upon the Account of Religion ; for, writing againſt the fundamental Epiſtle of *Mani-
chæus,* he begins with this Addreſs to the *Manichæans : The Servant of the Lord
ought not to ſtrive,* &c. *It is therefore our Buſineſs willingly to act this Part. God
gives that which is good to thoſe who willingly ask it of him. They only rage againſt
you, who know nothing of the Labour that is neceſſary to find out Truth, or the Difficulty of avoiding Errors. 'Tis they who rage againſt you, who know not how uncommon and difficult it is to overcome carnal Imaginations by the Calmneſs of a pious Mind.
'Tis they who rage againſt you, who are ignorant how hard it is to heal the Eye of the
inward Man, ſo that it can behold its Sun ; not that Sun whoſe celeſtial Body you
worſhip, and which irradiates the fleſhly Eyes of Men and Beaſts, but that of which
the Prophet writes,* The Sun of Righteouſneſs *is riſen on me ; and of which we
read in the Evangeliſt,* He was that true Light which enlightens every Man that
cometh into the World. *They rage againſt you, who know not that 'tis by many*

Sighs and Groans we must attain to a small Portion of the Knowledge of God. Lastly, they rage against you, who are not deceived with that Error, into which they see you are fallen. But as for my self, I, who after long and great Fluctuation, can at last perceive, what is that Sincerity which is free from all Mixture of vain Fable, cannot by any Means rage against you, whom I ought to bear with, as I was once borne with my self, and to treat you with the same Patience that my Friends exercised towards me, when I was a zealous and blind Espouser of your Error.

And again, in his Questions upon St. *Matthew*'s Gospel, *chap.* 12. when the good Corn sprung up and brought forth Fruit, then appear'd the Tares also: *For when the spiritual Man begins to discern all Things, he begins to discern Errors. His Servants* said to him, Wilt thou that we go and gather the Tares? *Are we to suppose that those are the Servants, whom he calls a little after Reapers, which in the Exposition of the Parable he expresly saith to be Angels? But who will dare affirm, that the Angels knew not who sowed the Tares, and then first discerned them, when they perceived the Fruit come forth? We ought rather to interpret it of faithful Men here, signified by the Name of Servants, whom he also calls the good Seed. Nor is it any Wonder that the same Persons should be called the good Seed, and the Servants of the Master, since Christ says of himself, that he is the Gate, and the Shepherd; for the same Thing is represented under many different Similitudes for different Reasons; and the rather here, because when he speaks to the Servants, he doth not say,* When the Harvest comes, I will say to you, Gather first the Tares: *But I will speak, says he, to the Reapers. From whence we may infer, that the gathering the Tares to burn them is the Business of others, and that no Son of the Church should imagine that 'tis an Office belonging to him. When therefore any Person begins to be spiritual, he perceives the Errors of the Hereticks, and judges and discerns every thing that he reads or hears to differ from the Rule of Truth. But until he grows more perfect in these spiritual Things, and ripens into Fruit as the Seed did, he may be surprized how so many Falshoods of the Hereticks should exist under the Christian Name. Hence it was that the Servants said,* Didst thou not sow good Seed in this Field? Whence then the Tares? *When at last he comes to* know, *that this is owing to the Subtlety of the Devil, who, far from being awed by the Authority of so great a Name, covers his own Falshoods under it, he may have an Inclination to destroy such Men out of the World, according as he hath Opportunity. But whether he ought to do this, and whether it be the Duty of Men, he consults the Justice of God, whether he hath commanded or permits it? Hence the Servants said,* Wilt thou that we go and gather them? *To which the Truth it self answered: The Condition of Man in this Life is not such, that it can certainly be known, what that Man may afterwards prove, who is now seen to be in a manifest Error; or how his Error may contribute to the Increase of the Good. And therefore such are not to be destroyed, lest whilst we endeavour to kill the evil, we kill also the good, or such as possibly may hereafter prove so; and lest we hereby prejudice the good, to whom the other may be, tho' unwillingly, useful. But the most proper Time for this is, at the End of all Things, when there will be no farther Opportunity of amending the Life, or of advancing in the Truth, by the Occasion and Comparison of other Mens Errors. And even then this is to be done not by Men, but by the Angels.* Hence
it

it was that the Maſter anſwers, No, *leſt gathering the Tares ye pull up alſo*
the Wheat. But in the Time of Harveſt I will ſay to the Reapers, &c. And
thus he render'd them the moſt patient and calm.

But afterwards, upon his ſharp and long Diſputes with the *Donatiſts,* tho' he
was ſo far of the ſame Mind, as that he was not willing to puniſh them with
Death, yet he ſo far altered his Opinion, as that he did not diſapprove of, but
was for actually inflicting all Puniſhments, which did not cut off the Hopes of
Repentance, *i. e.* all manner, Death only excepted ; that being terrified by
them, they might be compelled to embrace the orthodox Faith ; which he
hath ſhewn in a few Words, in his ſecond Book of *Retractations,* c. 5. *I have*
two Books entitled, Againſt the *Donatiſts : In the firſt I declared, that I did not*
approve that ſchiſmatical Perſons ſhould be compelled to Communion by any ſecular
Power. The Reaſon was, becauſe I had not then experienced what great Miſchief
would ariſe from their Impunity, nor how much Good Diſcipline would conduce to their
Converſion. He argues the ſame more largely in his 48th Letter to *Vincentius,*
on Account of the *Rogatian* Hereſy : *My firſt Opinion was, that none was to be*
forced to the Unity of Chriſt ; but that he was to be dealt with by Words, fought with
by Argument, overcome by Reaſon, leſt thoſe who once were open Hereticks ſhould be-
come feigned Catholicks. But I changed my Opinion, not from the Contradiction of
others, but from demonſtrative Examples. My own City was firſt alledged, which
tho' entirely in the Hereſy of Donatus, *was converted to the Catholick Unity by Fear of*
the Imperial Laws, and now ſo thoroughly deteſts their pernicious Animoſity, that one
would be apt to believe it had never been infected with it. Many other Cities were
particularly named to me, ſo that from hence I underſtood the Meaning of what is
written, Give Opportunity to a wiſe Man, and he will be wiſer. *For how ma-*
ny, to our certain Knowledge, were willing to become Catholicks, convinced by evident
Truth ; but yet deferred it through Fear of offending their Friends ? How many
were held in Subjection, not to Truth, in which you never had any Concern,
but to Obſtinacy of Habit, whereby was fulfilled in them that divine Paſſage, An
evil Servant will not grow better by Words ; even though he underſtand,
he will not obey. How many imagined that the Donatiſts *were the true Church,*
becauſe Security had render'd them proud, ſloathful and negligent in their Enquiries
after the Catholick Truth ? How many were prevented, by the falſe Reports of Slan-
derers, from entring into the Church ; who gave out that we placed I know not
what upon the Altar of God ? How many thought it indifferent to what Party a
Chriſtian belonged, and therefore continued Donatiſts, *becauſe they were born in that*
Sect, and no one forced them to forſake it, and return to the Catholick Faith ? Now
the Terror of thoſe Laws, by the Publication of which Kings ſerve the Lord with
Fear, was of ſuch Advantage to all theſe, that they ſay, ſome of them : This was what
we intended. Bleſſed be God, that hath given us the Occaſion of doing it now, and
prevented all farther Delays. Others ſay : This we knew to be true. But we
were under an unaccountable Prepoſſeſſion. Bleſſed be God, who hath broke our
Bonds in ſunder, and hath brought us to the Bond of Peace. Others ſay : We knew
not that the Truth was here, neither were we willing to learn it. But Fear made us
diligent in inquiring after it, being apprehenſive, that we ſhould loſe our temporal

2   *Enjoyments,*

Enjoyment, without gaining any eternal Blessings. Blessed be God, who by Fear hath cured us of our Negligence, so that thro' Terror we have enquired after, what in a State of Security we should never have been careful to have known. Others say: We were afraid to enter thro' false Reports, which we could not know to be false unless we entered. Neither should we have entered, unless we had been forced. Blessed be God, who hath taken away our Fear by the Rod, and given us to understand how vain and lying the Reports are, which have been raised of his Church. Hence we believe all those Things to be false, which the Authors of this Heresy have raised, since their Followers have spread much greater Falshoods. Others say: We thought it signified nothing of whatever Party we were Christians. But blessed be God, who hath brought us from the Schism, and shewn us that 'tis agreeable to the one God, that he should be worshipped in Unity. Should I therefore oppose my self to my Colleagues in preventing Methods so gainful to the Lord, and thereby hinder the gathering into the Sheepfold of Peace, where there is one Flock and one Shepherd, the stray'd Sheep of Christ, who now wander in the Mountains and Hills, i. e. in the Swellings of their Pride? Ought I to oppose such a Provision as this, for fear of your losing the Things you call your own, whilst if you were free from Fear, you would proscribe even Christ himself? Have you a Liberty of making Wills by the Roman Law, and ought you to destroy by infamous Charges the Will delivered by God to the Fathers, in which 'tis written, In thy Seed shall all Nations be blessed? *Should you be allowed to make free Contracts in buying and selling, and yet dare to divide amongst your selves what the betrayed Saviour bought for us? Is it just that your Donations to others should be valid, and should not what God hath given to his Children be firm, whom he hath called from the rising of the Sun to the setting of it? Can it be unjust to banish you from the Land of your Body, when you endeavour to banish Christ from the Kingdom of his Blood, from Sea to Sea, and from the River to the utmost Bounds of the World? No: Let the Kings of the Earth serve Christ, even by making Laws for Christ.*

From these Words of *Austin,* it appears clearer than the Light, that he approved of the Punishment ordained by Civil Laws against the Erroneous, as that they ought not to make Wills, nor buy and sell, nor receive Legacies, but that they should be sent into Banishment. And to shew that he thought this Punishment just upon the *Donatists* and *Rogatians,* he adds: *The Terror of temporal Powers, when it opposes the Truth, is a glorious Trial to the Good and Resolute, but a dangerous Temptation to the Weak. But when it inculcates the Truth upon the Erroneous and Schismatical, to ingenuous Minds it is an useful Admonition, but to the Foolish it proves an unprofitable Affliction.* There is no Power but what is of God, and he that resisteth the Power, resisteth the Ordinance of God: For Princes are not a Terror to them that do well, but to those who do ill. Wilt thou not therefore fear the Power? Do well, and thou shalt have Praise from it. *For if the Power favouring the Truth corrects any one, he who is made better by it hath Praise from it: Or if, in Opposition to the Truth, it rages against any one, he who is crowned Conqueror hath Praise from it. But as for thee, thou dost not well that thou should'st not fear the Power.* And to make this appear, he largely refutes his Opinion, and then thinks he hath evinced the

Justice

Juſtice of the Perſecution raiſed againſt them. And in the former Part of his Letter, he argues, that they ought to be compelled to return to the Church, not by Reaſon only, but by Terrors. *For*, ſays he, *if they ſhould be terrified, and not taught, it would ſeem to be the Exerciſe of an unjuſt Power over them; and if they were taught, and not terrified, their old Habits would harden them, and they would move more ſlowly into the Way of Salvation.*

The like may be read in his 50th Epiſtle, to *Boniface*, a military Man of *Cæſar*'s Retinue: *A Perſon in a raging Phrenzy can't bear the Phyſician, nor a libertine Son his Father; the one becauſe he is bound, the other becauſe he is chaſtiſed; both becauſe they are loved. But if they neglect them, and ſuffer them to periſh, 'tis a falſe and cruel Mildneſs; for if the Horſe and Mule, who have no Underſtanding, bite and ſtrike at thoſe who handle them to cure their Wounds, who yet, tho' they are of-tentimes in Danger, and ſometimes receive Miſchief, don't leave them, till by medi-cinal Smart and Pains they have made them ſound; how much leſs ought one Man to be given up by another, a Brother by his Brother, leſt he periſh eternally; when after Correction he might be brought to underſtand, how great a Benefit was conferred on him, even when he was complaining of ſuffering Perſecution. Therefore, as the Apoſtle ſays,* Let us do good to all as we have Opportunity; *let thoſe, that can, do it by Diſcourſes of the Catholick Precepts, others by the Laws of Catholick Princes, that all may be called to Salvation, and recovered from Deſtruction, partly by thoſe who obey divine Admonitions, and partly by thoſe who obey the Imperial Commands. When the Emperors make bad Laws in Favour of Falſhood againſt the Truth, true Be-lievers are approved, and thoſe who perſevere are crowned with Victory. But when they ordain good Laws for the Truth, in Oppoſition to Error, the Unruly are ter-rified, and the Wiſe amended. He therefore who refuſes to obey the Imperial Laws, when made againſt the Truth of God, acquires a great Reward: He who refuſes to obey, when made for Support of divine Truth, expoſes himſelf to moſt grievous Puniſhment. For in the Times of the Prophets all thoſe Kings are blamed, who did not forbid and aboliſh every thing contrary to the divine Precepts, and thoſe who did are highly commended. Even King* Nebuchadnezzar, *when he was a Servant of Idols, made an impious Law, that the Image ſhould be worſhipped. But thoſe who did not obey his wicked Conſtitution, acted piouſly and faithfully. And yet the ſame King, changed by a divine Miracle, made a pious and commendable Law for the Truth; that whoever ſhould blaſpheme the true God of* Shadrack, Meſhack, *and* Abednego, *ſhould be deſtroy'd with his whole Houſe. Thoſe who deſpiſed this Law, and deſervedly ſuffered the Penalty of it, might yet ſay, what theſe do, that they were righteous Perſons, becauſe perſecuted by the King's Law; which they might ſay as well, if they were as mad as thoſe who divide the Members of Chriſt, deſtroy the Sacraments of Chriſt, and yet glory in Perſecution: Becauſe they are forbidden to do theſe Things by the Imperial Laws made for the Unity of Chriſt, they vainly boaſt of their Innocence, and ſeek the Glory of Martyrdom from Men, which they cannot re-ceive from the Lord.* After which he ſubjoins a long Diſcourſe to prove, that all who ſuffer Perſecution are not Martyrs, but ſuch only who ſuffer for Righ-teouſneſs; and that all Perſecutors are not of the falſe Church. *For* Agar *ſuf-fered Perſecution from* Sarah; *and yet ſhe who perſecuted was holy, and ſhe who*

ſuffered

fuffered Perfecution unholy. And a little after : *If therefore we will acknowledge the Truth, 'that is an unjuft Perfecution, which the Wicked make on the Church of Chrift, and that a juft Perfecution which the Churches of Chrift make on the Wicked. So that the Church is bleffed which fuffers Perfecution for Righteoufnefs Sake, and they miferable who fuffer Perfecution for Unrighteoufnefs. Befides, the Church perfecutes, by Love ; they, by Rage ; fhe, that fhe may correct ; they, in order to overthrow ; fhe, that fhe may recal from Error ; they, to force others into it. She perfecutes and apprehends Enemies, to cure them of their Vanity, and that they may advance in the Truth ; they return Evil for Good, and becaufe we confult their eternal Salvation, endeavour to deprive us of our temporal Safety.* And afterwards : *'Tis an Inftance of Mercy to them, becaufe by thefe Imperial Laws, they are fnatched, tho' againft their Wills, from that Sect, where they have learnt their Errors from the Doctrines of Devils, that they may be healed by being accuftomed to found Doctrines and Manners in the Catholick Church. For many of thofe, whofe pious Fervour of Faith and Charity in the Unity of Chrift we now admire, give Thanks to God with great Gladnefs, that they are not now in the Error to think thefe evil Things good ; which Thanks they would never have given willingly, unlefs they had been forced unwillingly to depart from that accurfed Society.*

As to the Objection, that the Apoftles never defired fuch Methods from the Kings of the Earth, he anfwers ; That none of the Emperors then believed in Chrift, and therefore could not ferve him by making Laws for Godlinefs, againft Impiety. *But afterwards, when that began to be fulfilled, which is written,* All the Kings of the Earth fhall worfhip him, all Nations fhall ferve him, *what Perfon in his Wits could then thus addrefs himfelf to Kings ? It doth not concern you, who in your Dominions defends or oppofes the Church of our Lord, who will be religious or impious. May it not as well be faid, It is nothing to you, who in your Dominions is chaft or lewd ? For fince God hath given to all Men Freedom of Will, why fhould Adulteries be punifhed by Law, and Sacrileges permitted ? Is the Prefervation of the Soul's Fidelity to God of lefs Importance than a Woman's to her Husband ? Or becaufe thofe Things which are done, not from any Contempt of Religion, but merely thro' Ignorance, are to be more gently animad-* N. B. *verted on, are they therefore to be entirely neglected ? Who doubts whether it be better to draw Men to the Worfhip of God by Argument, than to compel them with the Fear of Punifhment or Pain ? But doth it follow, that becaufe thofe who are won by Reafon are the beft, that therefore others are to be wholly difregarded ? We can produce many Inftances to prove, of how great Advantage Compulfion by Fear and Pain hath been, they having been hereby render'd open to Inftruction, or excited to the Practice of what they have been taught.* And afterwards : *To what Purpofe do thefe Men cry out, Men are free either to believe, or not believe. To whom did Chrift ufe Violence ? Whom did he force ? I produce the Apoftle* Paul. *Let them own that Chrift firft forced, and afterwards taught him ; firft ftruck, and then comforted him. 'Tis wonderful to confider, how he, who, forced by bodily Punifhment, firft entered into the Gofpel, laboured in it more abundantly than all they, who by the Word only were called to the Belief of it. By how much greater his Fear was that forced his Love, by fo much the more perfect was his Love that caft out Fear. Why then fhould not the*

the Church compel her loſt Sons to return, ſince theſe loſt Sons have compelled others to their Deſtruction? Eſpecially as the holy Mother more kindly embraces thoſe, who, having been not ſo much compelled as ſeduced, are made to return by terrible tho' wholſome Laws, into her Boſom, and rejoices over them much more than over thoſe ſhe hath never loſt. What, doth it not belong to the Paſtoral Care, to recover thoſe Sheep, when found, to the Lord's Flock, by the Terror of Stripes, or even Pains, if they reſiſt, which having not been violently ſnatched away, have wandered from the Flock, thro' ſoft and gentle Perſwaſion? And a few Lines afterwards : _Becauſe they cannot ſhew that they are compelled to Evil, they argue, that they ought not to be compelled even to what is good. But we have ſhewn that_ Paul _was compelled by Chriſt, ſo that the Church imitates its Lord in compelling thoſe, firſt waiting before ſhe compels any, that the Preaching of the Prophets might be fulfilled with reſpect to the Faith of Kings and Nations. For to this Purpoſe may be underſtood that of bleſſed_ Paul, Having in a Readineſs to revenge all Diſobedience, when your Obedience is firſt fulfilled. _Hence alſo our Lord himſelf, firſt commands the Gueſts to be invited, and afterwards compelled to his great Supper. For when the Servants anſwered him,_ Lord, it is done as thou commandedſt ; and yet there is Room, _he ſaid,_ Go out into the High-ways and Hedges, and compel them to come in. _Now in thoſe who were firſt kindly brought in, is fulfilled the firſt Obedience ; in thoſe who are compelled the Diſobedience is revenged. For what is this,_ Compel them to come in ; _when 'tis firſt ſaid,_ Bring in ; _and the Anſwer was,_ It is done as thou haſt commanded, and yet there is Room? _If he would have it underſtood, of being compelled by the Terror of Miracles, thoſe were done in greateſt abundance, in Behalf of thoſe who were firſt called, eſpecially of thoſe of whom 'tis ſaid,_ The Jews ſeek Signs. The like may be read in his 204th Epiſtle to _Donatus,_ a _Donatiſt_ Preſbyter, in which he relates the various Cruelties of the _Donatiſts_ and _Circumcellians,_ and writes that many were reduced to the Unity of the Church, by the Laws made againſt them. After a long Account of this, he anſwers an Objection of the _Donatiſts,_ that the Catholicks coveted and took away their Goods, and ſhews the Falſhood of it. See alſo his 116th Epiſtle to the _Donatiſts._

From hence we may ſee that _Auſtin_ hath very fully taught, and endeavoured by many Arguments to prove, that Hereticks ought to be compelled to return to the Church by external Violence and the Fear of Puniſhments, tho' he was not willing that they ſhould be put to Death. Wherefore he not only writes to _Dulcitius_ the Tribune in his 60th Epiſtle : _Thou haſt not received by any Laws the Power of the Sword over them, nor do any of the Imperial Conſtitutions, which thou art intruſted with the Execution of,_ command thee to put them to Death. But in his 158th and 159th Epiſtle to _Marcellinus,_ and in his 160th to _Apringius,_ he largely intercedes to prevent their Death, and _that their Puniſhment might not reach ſo far._ And in his 127th Epiſtle to _Donatus,_ Proconſul of _Africa,_ he thus writes : _Since there are ſuch terrible Judges and Laws, to prevent their incurring the Puniſhment of the eternal Judgment, we would have them corrected, not deſtroyed: We would not that the neceſſary Diſcipline towards them ſhould be neglected, nor that they ſhould be puniſhed according to their Deſerts. Put ſuch a Reſtraint_

ſtraint

ſtraint on their Sins, as that there may be ſome to repent that they have ſinned. So that tho' he intercedes for them that they ſhould not be put to Death, yet the only Puniſhment he would have Hereticks exempted from is Death. Hence in his Epiſtle to *Creſconius* the Grammarian, *b. 3. c. 50.* he ſaith: *No good Men in the Catholick Church are pleaſed, that any one, even an Heretick, ſhould be puniſhed with Death.* But as to all other Methods of Perſecution, *Auſtin* is ſo far from being againſt them, that he recommends them, as a Remedy proper for the Extirpation of Hereſies. Hence in his firſt Book againſt *Gaudentius, c. 5.* he ſays: *God forbid that this ſhould be called perſecuting Men, when 'tis only a perſecuting their Vices, in order to deliver them from the Power of them ; juſt as the Phyſician treats his diſtemper'd Patient.*

This then is the ſo much admired Clemency of *Auſtin*, that he interceded with the Proconſuls, that the *Donatiſts* ſhould not be puniſhed with Death ; whilſt at the ſame Time he not only approved of all other Penalties except Death, ſuch as Baniſhment, the denying them Power to make Wills, to inherit their Patrimony, or to receive what was left them by others, of making Contracts, buying and ſelling, and the like ; but he himſelf accuſed them to the Proconſuls, that if they perſiſted in theſe Opinions, they might ſuffer theſe Puniſhments. Who doth not ſee, that under ſuch Circumſtances, Life is ſometimes worſe than Death ? And that, as *Arcadius* and *Honorius* decreed with reſpect to the Children of thoſe condemned for Treaſon, Life would be a Puniſhment, and Death a real Relief? 'Tis much more terrible to pine away in Poverty, Baniſhment, and other Miſeries, and then periſh by a lingering Death, than to be killed outright, tho' in a cruel and bloody manner. Yea ſometimes, ſuch hath been the Cruelty of Perſecutors, that they have denied thoſe they have perſecuted, Death, that they might not ſeem to give them the Honour of Martyrdom ; whilſt they have invented and exerciſed on them all manner of Miſeries and Tortures, that by the Weight and Length of their Puniſhments, they might force them to a Denial of their Faith. There is no need to produce many Proofs or Examples of this Nature, or to ſearch into Antiquity for Inſtances. I ſhall only produce two freſh ones, one of which now preſents it ſelf to us in *France.*. There we ſee that the miſerable Reform'd are not puniſh'd with Death, but given up to the licentious Abuſes of Soldiers, and that they have no End of their Troubles, unleſs they abjure the Reform'd Religion. And yet all the Reform'd unanimouſly agree, they never ſuffer'd a more grievous Perſecution. *Bohemia* will afford us another Inſtance of Perſons forced by the like Cruelty to Apoſtacy. We read in the Hiſtory of the *Bohemian* Perſecution, *c.* 99. that when the Vice Chamberlain of the Kingdom had ſolicited the Inhabitants of the City *Tuſta* in vain to Apoſtacy, and was complaining of their Obſtinacy in the Jeſuits College at *Prague*, one *Martyn de Huerda*, a *Spaniard*, was preſent, and laughed at it, and promiſed to accompliſh the Matter for 500 Pieces of Gold. " Taking with him ſome Bands " of Soldiers, he entered the City, and ſent them by Tens and Twenties to each " Senator, and gave them Liberty to plague them by every Method they could " invent ; and by this Means in a little while compelled them all to Apo-
" ſtacy,

" ſtacy, and then received his Reward from the Chamberlain. The ſame
" *Martyn,* when others had attempted, in vain, the Reformation, as they cal-
" led it, of the City *Kutteberge,* terrified the Citizens by the ſame Means,
" till at length they were ſo oppreſſed by Means of the Soldiery, and broken
" by their continu'd Perſecutions, that moſt of them complied with their Ene-
" mies, and ſubmitted their Necks to the Antichriſtian Yoke ; whilſt others,
" leaving every Thing behind them but their Wives and Children, went into
" Baniſhment." *c.* 93. The like Sort of Reformation we may read, *c.* 97.
made in the City *Zaterus. Cap.* 103. gives an Account of various Puniſhments inflicted, by the Cruelty of which many were forced to Apoſtacy,
though not one put to Death. Yea, there is an Account, §. 13. " That
" ſome, who begged rather to be put to Death, than compelled to Apo-
" ſtacy, were anſwer'd : Cæſar *did not thirſt after their Blood, but the Salva-*
" *tion of their Souls.* The like Requeſt made by others was received with
" Laughter. *Ho, Sirrah, Do you want the Honour of Martyrdom ? Ye*
" *Wretches, you are unworthy of having any Occaſion wherein to glory.*" From
theſe Examples 'tis clearer than Day, that ſome Perſecutions, though not
reaching to Death, may be more cruel than Death it ſelf. And though
poſſibly ſome Perſon may pretend a Sort of Gentleneſs in all this, yet let
him remember what *Bellarmine* juſtly writes, *De Laicis, l.* 3. *c.* 21. That *Au-*
ſtin excepts the Puniſhment of Death ; *not that he thought they did not deſerve*
it, but becauſe it became the Clemency of the Church ; and becauſe there were, as
yet, no imperial Laws : For the law Quicunque, C. de Hæretici, *was not made*
till a little after Auſtin's *Death, ordaining Hereticks to be put to Death.* By
which he plainly inſinuates, that he believed that if there had been any imperial Law, ordaining the Puniſhment of Death to Hereticks, *Auſtin* would
have approved of it ; for he immediately adds : *That it appears that* Auſtin
thought it juſt to kill Hereticks ; becauſe he ſhews, that if the Donatiſts *were*
put to Death, they would be juſtly puniſhed, l. 1. cont. Epiſt. Parmen. c. 7.
and elſewhere.

If any one will compare theſe Things with the former Opinion of *Auſtin,*
he may juſtly cry out, Oh how much is *Auſtin* changed from himſelf, who,
mindful of his own former Error, from which he was not recover'd, but by
the great Patience of his Friends, was againſt uſing Methods of Cruelty,
even towards the *Manichæans.* But now he approves of all Puniſhments
againſt the *Donatiſts,* Death only excepted, that they may be compelled into
the Catholick Church, even againſt their Wills, under a Pretence that at
laſt they may voluntarily remain in her Communion. Now he puts into the
Mouths of Perſons theſe forced ſtudied Speeches and Pretences, by which they
are taught to palliate their Return into the Church, which was in reality
wholly owing to Violence and the Fear of Puniſhment, as though it had
been voluntary, and the very Means of their Salvation. But let us ſup-
poſe, that they believe themſelves obliged by Virtue of a divine Command to
preach their Doctrine, leſt they ſhould diſobey God ; and that therefore they
ought to return into their own Country to propagate it : What would good
St.

St. *Auſtin* determine againſt them in ſuch a Caſe? Why, all his Arguments tend to this, that if they ſhould return, contrary to the imperial Edict, he ſhould not at all diſapprove a capital Puniſhment, if it was ſo appointed by the Laws.

And indeed, all who ſince *Auſtin* have taught that Hereticks are to be per-ſecuted, and even puniſhed with Death, have made Uſe of no Authority more than *Auſtin*'s; and to ſhew how highly they eſteem his Authority, they uſe his Arguments as the very ſtrongeſt, though in themſelves abſurd, and manifeſtly contrary to Scripture, to defend a Doctrine ſo abſolutely repug-nant to the Nature of Chriſtianity. From him they have borrowed the Di-ſtinction, that it is unlawful for Hereticks to perſecute the Church, but the Duty of the Church to perſecute Hereticks. This is now become the com-mon Exception of all the Murderers of Hereticks, with which every one armed with the ſecular Power, under a ſpecious Pretence, perſecutes and oppreſſes thoſe who differ from him: This is the principal Argument by which the Papiſts defend themſelves, when they would juſtify their own Perſecution of Hereticks, and condemn all others that perſecute them. And which is the Wonder, they commend as praiſe-worthy and heroical what is practiſed by their own Church againſt others, even when they condemn the ſame Things as cruel and inhumane in them; as though they were exempted from the common Law of Nature, of doing to others as they would be done by. *Conrad Brunus* complains of the Hereticks and Schiſmaticks, that the *Vandals* B. 2. c. 8. and *Donatiſts* in *Africa*, turned and executed all the Laws made againſt Here-§. 3. ticks upon the Catholicks. *Theſe,* ſays he, *the Hereticks alſo of our Time imitate*: In this indeed they are worſe than they; *becauſe they denied thoſe Laws were ever made againſt themſelves; whereas our modern Hereticks affirm they were made, and ought to be executed againſt the Catholicks, as may eaſily be ſeen from many of their Wri-tings.* In the ſame Book he complains: *That the Hereticks ſpare neither Age, nor Sex, nor Degree, nor Dignity; but rage promiſcuouſly againſt Children and grown Perſons, Women and Men, Virgins and Married, old Men and young.* He adds, *c.* 13. *'Tis cruel and moſt inhumane to abuſe the Dead: But this is peculiar to our Hereticks and Schiſmaticks. They conceal the Bodies of Biſhops and Presbyters, Wo-men and Virgins, whom they have barbarouſly killed, and deny them Burial. The Bodies of ſome they have taken out of their Graves, and caſt upon the Ground*; Trip. l. 2. *others have contemptuouſly ſcattered into the Air the Aſhes of thoſe whom they have*c. 3. *burnt, and thrown the Bodies of ſome into Rivers.* If any one conſiders the De-Pope Leo, cretals of the Popes, the Inſtructions of the Inquiſition, and the uſual Manner Ep. 73. of proceeding in it, in which there is no Diſtinction of Perſons; but all are ſubjected to the Inquiſition without Reſpect to Age, Sex or Dignity, which not only forbids the burying dead Hereticks, but annexes a Puniſhment to thoſe who bury them; and oftentimes commands their dead Bodies to be taken up, and to be either thrown upon Dunghills, or reduced to Aſhes, and their Aſhes ſcatter'd in the Air, as ſhall be hereafter more large-ly ſhewn: I ſay, if any one conſiders theſe Things, he might well think *Bru-nus* to be in jeſt; unleſs he was of *Auſtin*'s Opinion, that the Church might

do

do againſt Hereticks what it would not be lawful for Hereticks to do againſt the Church: Which Doctrine once allow'd, every one will decide for himſelf, that his is the true Church, and hence claim a Right of perſecuting others, and perſwade himſelf he doth not act unjuſtly, even though he would not allow others to act ſo by himſelf. Thus we ſee, that Chriſtians by this idle Doctrine, are deviated from their original Simplicity and Meekneſs; and that in the room of mutual Love, by which all the Faithful were of one Heart and one Soul, there have ſucceeded in the Church of Chriſt, not only Diſcords, Contentions, Hatreds and Enmities, but Slaughters, and the worſt of cruel Butcheries.

But ſurely they ought to conſider, that they cannot without Injuſtice, do to others what they think it would be unjuſt in others to do to them; and that therefore as they would not themſelves be perſecuted by others, it muſt be unjuſt in them cruelly to perſecute others, even though they think them Hereticks. For as *Salvian,* Presbyter of *Marſeilles,* admirably writes in his Treatiſe of the Government of God, *B.* 5. *p.* 150, 151. *They are Hereticks, but not willingly. They are Hereticks in our Account, but not in their own. For they judge themſelves to be ſo very good Catholicks, that they give us the infamous Name of Hereticks: So that juſt what we think of them, they think of us. We know they do an Injury to the only begotten Son of God, becauſe they affirm him to be leſs than the Father. They think we derogate from the Father's Honour, becauſe we make the Son equal to him. The Truth is with us; they imagine it to be with them: We truly honour God; they think that their Opinion is moſt honourable to God. They are defective in their Duty; but believe that this is the chief Duty of Religion. They are Impious; but think it to be true Piety: Though therefore they err, they err with an honeſt Mind, not from Hatred but real Affection to God, and believing that they honour and love the Lord. Though they have not true Faith, they eſteem even this to be the moſt perfect Love of God. How they ſhall be puniſh'd in the Day of Judgment for this Error in Opinion, no one knows but the Judge. And therefore I think God patiently bears with them, becauſe he ſees that though they do not believe aright, yet that they err from a real Love to Piety and Truth, &c.* But the Minds of Chriſtians have been perverted from this Branch of Equity through the Prevalence of Self-love; ſo that when they could prevail with the Civil Power to aſſiſt them, they have pronounced all that differed from them Hereticks, and then exerciſed all Kinds of Cruelty againſt them.

C H A P.

C H A P. VII.

The PERSECUTIONS *of the* POPES *against* HERETICKS.

IN the following Ages the Affairs of the Church were so manag'd under the Government of the Popes, and all Persons so strictly curbed by the Severity of the Laws, that they durst not even so much as whisper against the received Opinions of the Church. Besides this, so deep was the Ignorance that had spread it self over the World, that Men, without the least Regard to Knowledge and Learning, received with a blind Obedience every Thing that the Ecclesiasticks order'd them, however stupid and superstitious, without any Examination ; and if any one dared in the least to contradict them, he was sure immediately to be punish'd ; whereby the most absurd Opinions came to be establish'd by the Violence of the Popes. 'Twas at this Time that the Doctrine of Transubstantiation was introduced into the Church, now, in every Thing, subject to the Pope's Beck ; and how dangerous it was to oppose it, we may learn from the Instance of *Berengarius* of *Tours*, Archdeacon of *Angiers*, who, teaching that the Bread and Wine in the Supper, was only the Figure of the Body and Blood of the Lord, was condemn'd as an Heretick, by *Leo* IX. in a Synod at *Rome* and *Vercellæ*, in the Year 1050, and five Years after, *viz.* 1055. was forced to recant, and to subscribe with his own Hand to the Faith of the *Roman* Church, and confirm it with an Oath, by *Victor* II. in the Council of *Tours*. But as *Berengarius* his Recantation was forced ; and as he afterwards defended that Opinion, which in his Heart he believed, *Nicolaus* II. called a Council at the *Lateran*, *Anno* 1059. and there again condemn'd *Berengarius*, and compell'd him to make a solemn Abjuration, which *Berengarius* publickly read, and sign'd with his own Hand. This was that famous Abjuration, which begins, *Ego Berengarius*. Thus was the Truth suppressed by the Papal Violence. In the *East* also, *Anno* 1118. one *Basilius*, the Author of the Sect of the *Bongomili*, was publickly burnt for Heresy by the Command of *Alexius Comnenus* the Emperor, as *Baronius* relates, *Anno* 1118. §. 27.

In the mean Time the Power of the *Roman* Pontiff grew to a prodigious Height, and began to be very troublesome, even to the Emperors themselves ; for not content with the Ecclesiastical Power, they claimed also the Subjection of the Secular. But in the midst of this thick Darkness, some Glimmerings of Light broke forth through the great Mercy of God.

For after the Year of Christ, 1100. there arose various Disputes between the Emperors and Popes, about the Papal Power in secular Affairs, which, as they were managed with great Warmth, gave Occasion to many more strictly to examine that unbounded Power which the Popes of *Rome* claimed to themselves. Some of the Emperors bravely maintained their Rights against the Papal Encroachments, and were supported, not only by the Arms and Forces of Generals

G   and

and Princes, but by Bifhops and Divines, who ftrenuoufly wrote in their Defence.
This fpirited up many others to oppofe that unbounded Authority, which the
Popes affumed in Matters of Faith, who not only argued that they were capable of erring, as well as the other Bifhops, but actually pointed out and cenfured their many Errors and Abufes of their unlimited Power : All thefe the
Court of *Rome* branded with the infamous Name of Hereticks, and would
have made the Sacrifice to the publick Hatred.

They appeared firft in fome Parts of *Italy*, but principally in the *Milaneze*
and *Lombardy* : And becaufe they dwelt in different Cities, and had their particular Inftructors, the Papifts, to render them the more odious, have
reprefented them as different Sects, and afcribed to them as different Opinions, though others affirm they all held the fame Opinions, and were entirely
of the fame Sect. The Truth is, that from the oldeft Accounts of them
we fhall find, that they did not all hold the fame Tenets, and were not
of the fame Sect ; though neither their Opinions nor Sects were fo many and
different as the Papifts reprefent. The Principal of them were *Tanchelinus*,
Petrus de Bruis, *Petrus Abailardus*, *Arnaldus Brixianus*, whofe Opinion *Baronius* calls the Herefy of the Politicians, *Hendricus*, and others, who preached
partly in *Italy*, and partly in *France* about the Country of *Tholoufe* ; and becaufe afterwards the greater Number of them propagated their Opinions in
the Province of *Albigeois*, in *Languedoc*, and gather'd there large and numerous Churches, who openly profeffed their Faith ; they were ftiled *Albigenfes*.

CHAP. VIII.

Of the ALBIGENSES *and* VALDENSES.

ABOUT the fame Time the *Valdenfes*, or the poor Men of *Lyons*, appeared at *Lyons*, whofe Original hath been largely fhewn by the moft
Reverend and Learned *Ufher*, Archbifhop of *Armagh*, in his Book *De Succeffione*, &c. *ch.* viii. I fhall therefore only enquire, whether the *Valdenfes* and
Albigenfes were the fame People, according to the common Opinion of Proteftants, or different from one another. It cannot be doubted but that they
had fome Opinions in common. But there is nothing more evident, than
that there was amongft them a great Variety of Doctrines, and Difference of
Rites and Cuftoms, as appears from the Book of the Sentences of the Inquifition at *Tholoufe*, which I have publifh'd, in which are to be found many of the
Sentences pronounced againft the *Albigenfes* and *Valdenfes*, which difcover
fome very curious and uncommon Things, concerning their Doctrines and
Rites ; and which are fuch evident Proofs of their difference in Opinions and
Cuftoms, that from the reading of a few Lines, one may eafily know whe-

I   then

ther the Sentence pronounced was againſt the *Albigenſes* or *Valdenſes*; which manifeſt Difference hath induced me to believe that they were two diſtinct Sects; though I have hitherto been in the common Opinion, that they were but one. And that this may appear more clearly, I ſhall here give out of the Book of Sentences, the Doctrines common to both, and thoſe in which they differ'd, and deſcribe their particular Rites and Cuſtoms.

The Opinions common to them both were theſe : *Every Oath is unlawful* fol. 39. b. *and ſinful* ; and therefore they would never, upon any Occaſion, take an fol. 96. Oath.

Concerning *Penance and the Confeſſion of Sins :* The *Albigenſes* are ſaid to fol. 40. believe, *That Confeſſion made to the Prieſts of the Church of* Rome, *ſignifies nothing :* *That neither the Pope nor any other of the Church of* Rome *can abſolve any one from his Sins ; but that they have the Power of Abſolving from their Sins, all thoſe who become of their Sect, by the Impoſition of Hands.*

Almoſt the ſame Things are aſcribed to the *Valdenſes*, that they teach, *That they have Power from God only, even as the Apoſtles had, of confeſſing Men* fol. 96. *and Women of their Sins, who believe them, and are willing to confeſs to them : That they hear their Confeſſions, and enjoyn them Penance for their Sins ; although theſe who hear their Confeſſions, are not ordained by the Church, are not Prieſts or Clerks, but Laicks only ; and though they confeſs that they have not, in the leaſt, received this Power from the Church of* Rome. And farther, in moſt of the Sentences againſt the *Valdenſes*, we find, *That they confeſſed their Sins to one of the* Valdenſes, *and received Abſolution and Penance from him, and believed that the ſaid Confeſſion and Abſolution, and Penance, as much avail'd to the Salvation of the Soul, as though they had been confeſſed to a proper Prieſt.* But their Doctrine is beſt underſtood by the Sentence of *Hugueta,* the Wife of *John,* of *Vienna : That God only can abſolve from Sins ; and that he who receives Confeſſion, can only* fol. 147. *adviſe what a Man ought to do, and enjoin Penance ; and that a wiſe and prudent Perſon may do this, whether he be a Prieſt or not.*

As to the Church of *Rome,* the *Albigenſes* are ſaid to believe, *That there* fol. 40. *are two Churches, one merciful, viz. theirs and the Church of Chriſt ; which retains that Faith, in which every one, and without which no one can be ſaved : The other a cruel one, viz. The Church of* Rome, *which is the Mother of Fornications, the Temple of the Devil, and Synagogue of Satan ; and that no one can be ſaved in the Faith of that Church.* And elſewhere we read, *That no* fol. 3. *Man can be ſaved, that is not received by them, and unleſs he die of their Sect.*

The *Valdenſes* are ſaid to have taught almoſt the ſame Things : *That they* fol. 96. *are not ſubject to the Roman Pontiff, nor to the Prelates of the Church of* Rome : *That they cannot be excommunicated by the Pope, nor the other Prelates of that Church : That they ought not to obey the Pope, when he commands them to forſake and abjure their Sect, as condemned by the Church : That the Church of* Rome *ſins, and acts unlawfully and unjuſtly againſt them, becauſe it perſecutes and condemns them.* And that they farther taught, *That the Prelates of the Church of* Rome, fol. 128. b. *are blind Leaders of the Blind ; do not preſerve the Truth of the Goſpel, nor imitate the apoſtolick Poverty ; and that the very Church of* Rome *is an Houſe of Lies.*

The

The Opinions that are afcribed to the *Albigenfes*, but never to the *Valdenfes*,
fol. 40. are thefe: *That there are two Gods and Lords ; the one good, the other evil.
That the Creation of all Things, vifible and corporeal, was not from God our hea-
venly Father, and the Lord Jefus Chrift, but by the Devil and Satan, the evil
God, who is the God of this World, and the Maker and Prince of it:* Which
fol. 68. they exprefs elfewhere in this Manner: *That it was not God that caufed the
Earth to yield Seed and bring forth Fruit.* And elfewhere: *That the good
God made all Things invifible and incorruptible ; and that the evil Prince,* viz.
Lucifer, *made all Things vifible and corruptible, and even humane Bodies.*
fol. 120. *b.* And in another Place: *That there were two Gods, one good, the other bad ;
and that the bad God created all Things vifible.*

Since thefe Things are to be met with in the Sentence of *Petrus Auterias*,
one of their famons Doctors, I am apt to think, not only that fome of the
Manichæans, who were banifhed from *Afia*, and came into *Bulgaria*, and afterwards went into the Country of *Tholoufe*, lurked amongft them ; but that
they had, many of them at leaft, embraced the *Manichæan* Opinions. And
indeed, we ought not to conceal the Truth. For although they are to be
commended for having difcover'd many of the *Romifh* Errors in Doctrine,
and for their forfaking the Communion of that Church ; yet we ought ingenuoufly to own their Miftakes. And as their recommending to thofe they
received into their Communion, what they called the *Endura, i. e.* fafting
themfelves to Death, was certainly an Error in Practice ; fo that we need not
be afhamed to own that they fometimes erred in Matters of Faith. 'Tis rather to be wonder'd at, that in fo barbarous an Age, they fhould throw off
fo many Errors, than that they fhould retain fome.

But befides, they are faid alfo to have held the following Opinions.
fol. 40. That all the Sacraments of the Church of *Rome* are vain and unprofitable, viz. The Euchariſt, Baptifm, Confirmation, Order, and extreme Unction.
fol. 39. *b.* As to the Euchariſt, they are reported to have believed; *That there was
fol. 120. *b.* not the Body of Chriſt, and that there was nothing but meer Bread.*
fol. 120. *b.* As to the Baptifms: *That they condemned the Baptifm of Water, faying: That
a Man was to be faved by their laying on of Hands upon thofe who believed them ;*
fol. 68. *a.* *and that their Sins were to be remitted without Confeffion and Satisfaction: That
no Baptifm availed any Thing ; no, not their own.* We read alfo in the Sentence
of *Petrus Raymundus Dominicus de Borno,* that he heard *Peter Auterii* teach-
fol. 176. ing, amongft other Things, *That the Baptifm of Water, made by the Church,
was of no avail to Children ; becaufe they were fo far from confenting to it, that
they wept.*

fol. 3. As to extreme Unction: *That the Order of St. James, or extreme Unction
upon the Sick, made by material Oil, fignified nothing ; and that they prefer Impofition of Hands, which the Inquifitors call execrable.*
fol. 3. As to Orders: *That they reproach and condemn the Conftitution of the whole
Church of* Rome, *and deny all the Prelates of it the Power of Binding and Loofing ;
faying: That they cannot loofe or bind other Sinners, fince they themfelves are greater*
Sin-

Sinners ; *but that they can give to those they receive, the Holy Spirit, in order to their Salvation.*

As to Matrimony : *That it is always sinful, and cannot be without Sin* ; *and* fol. 40. *was never appointed by the good God.* Also : *That carnal Matrimony between* fol. 82. *b. a Man and Woman, is not true Matrimony, nor good, nor lawful, nor appointed by God* ; *but a quite different spiritual Matrimony.*

As to the Incarnation of Christ : *That the Lord did not take a real humane Bo-* fol. 40. *dy, nor real humane Flesh of our Nature* ; *and that he did not really arise with it, nor do other Things relating to our Salvation* ; *nor sit down at the Right-hand of the Father with it, but only with the Likeness of it.* They affirm also : *That the most holy Virgin* Mary*, the Mother of our Lord, neither is, nor was a carnal Wo-man, but their Church, which they say is true Penitence* ; *and that this is the Vir-*gin Mary. Or as we read elsewhere : *That God never enter'd into the Womb* fol. 82. *b. of the blessed Virgin* Mary ; *and that he only is the Mother, and Brother, and Sister of God, that keeps the Commands of God the Father.* Likewise, that *is was* fol. 120. *b. impossible for God to be incarnate* ; *because he never humbled himself so much, as to put himself in the Womb of Woman.*

Concerning the Resurrection of the Dead : They are charged *with denying* fol. 120. *b. the Resurrection of Bodies.* Or : *There will be no future Resurrection of humane* fol. 146. *Bodies* ; *and altho' the Souls of Men shall come to Judgment, they shall not come in their Bodies.* Which is elsewhere more distinctly explain'd : *That they imagine a* fol. 40. *Sort of spiritual Bodies, and a Sort of an inward Man* ; *in which Bodies Persons are hereafter to rise.* One of the *Albigenses* is said to have believed, that *when* fol. 146. *the Souls of wicked Men are gone out of their Bodies, before and after Judgment, they go through* los Bauffes, *and* los Tertres, *i. e. over Rocks and Precipices* ; *and that the Devil throws them headlong from the Rocks.* Also, *That the Souls of Men, even after their Separation from the Body, have Flesh and Bones, Hands and Feet, and all Members* ; *which though they are thrown by Devils headlong from the Rocks, and by this Means tormented, yet can never die.*

As to the Adoration of the Cross : *That no Man ought to adore the Cross* : fol. 68. Which in another Place is very odiously represented, viz. *That the Sign of the* fol. 3. *holy Cross, which the universal Church worships as the Emblem of our Salvation, and the Representation of our Lord's Passion, is a detestable Emblem of the Devil.* And the Reason of this is added elsewhere : *That the Cross of Christ ought not* fol. 176. *to be adored* ; *because no Man worships the Gallows upon which his Father was hanged.*

As to the humane Soul : *That Souls were Spirits banished from Heaven because* fol. 120. *b. of their Sins.*

These are said to be the Principles of the *Albigenses*; and they will all ap-pear in the Sentence pronounced against *Stephana de Proaudo,* which I shall here give at large, from the Book of the Sentences of the Inquisition at *Tho-louse.*

" In the Year of our Lord 1307; the 5th of the Nones of *March,* and first
" Sunday in *Lent,* We the before-mention'd Inquisitor and Vicars. Whereas
" it most evidently and lawfully appears to us, by thy wicked Assertions, that
" thou,

" thou *Stephana de Proaudo*, formerly Wife of *Peter Gilbert*, being infected
" with the peftiferous Doctrines of Hereticks, doft affert and confefs into-
" lerable and abominable Errors, contrary to the Catholick Faith of the ho-
" ly *Roman* Church, denying, with profane Lips, that the Incarnation of our
" Lord *Jefus Chrift* hath been or is from the Woman, and that there is to be
" a Refurrection of human Bodies, attributing the Creation of vifible Things
" to the Devil, whom thou afferteft to be the Prince of this World, thereby
" denying the Creation to be from the Almighty God. And thou doft re-
" proachfully difown, deny and condemn, acccording to the Error of hereti-
" cal Impiety, all the feven Sacraments of our Salvation, *viz.* Baptifm by
" corporal Water, and adminifter'd to Children. Likewife the Sacrament of
" the holy Body and Blood of our Lord *Jefus Chrift* from Bread and Wine up-
" on the Altar. And the Confeffion of Sins made to the Priefts of the *Roman*
" Church, to whom thou denyeft the Power of binding and loofing. Likewife
" the Sacrament of carnal Matrimony, which thou afferteft and affirmeft can-
" not be without Sin, according to the Doctrine of thofe Hereticks. Thou
" alfo reproacheft and blafphemeft our holy Orders, by preferring the damn-
" ed and profane Order of Hereticks. Thou fayeft that the Order of St.
" *James*, or extreme Unction of the Sick with material Oil, profits no-
" thing, preferring to it the execrable Impofition of Hands, which they
" call Spiritual Baptifm, or the Confolation, or Reception, and good End.
" Thou alfo approveft and commendeft, doft defend and fuftain, the Life,
" Sect and Faith of the faid Hereticks, and impioufly afferteft and declareft,
" that there is no Salvation to any unlefs he be received by them, and die in
" their Sect. Likewife thou afferteft and affirmeft, that the Sign of the holy
" Crofs, which the whole Church adores as the Sign of our Salvation, and a
" Reprefentation of our Saviour's Paffion, is the deteftable Sign of the
" Devil. Likewife thou reproacheft and condemneft the State of the
" whole *Roman* Church, and denieft the Power of binding and loofing in
" all the Prelates of the *Roman* Church, faying, that they cannot bind
" and loofe other Sinners, fince they are greater Sinners themfelves ;
" and thou afferteft that thofe Hereticks, whom thou calleft and affirm-
" eft to be good Men, can give the Holy Spirit for Salvation to thofe
" whom they receive, and fayeft that they are Imitators of the Apoftle, lead
" their Life, and are of their Sect, and fayeft and attefteft many other erro-
" neous and falfe Things, according to the Premiffes, as we our felves have
" heard them with our Ears feveral Times from thy own Mouth, in the Pre-
" fence of many Perfons. Likewife we have heard from thee, many others
" being prefent and hearing alfo, that thou haft feen and heard, in their turn,
" feven perfect Hereticks in *Tholoufe*, viz. *Peter Raimondi de Sancto Papulo*,
" and *Meffier Bernart de Monte Acuto*, and *Peter Auterii*, and *James* his Son,
" and *William Auterii*, Brother of the faid *Peter*, and *Aucelius* and *Andrew*,
" and haft feen an eighth Heretick in the Way, whom thou nameft *Philip*.
" Likewife thou haft confeffed before the faid Inquifitor, that thou haft ado-
" red the faid Heretick *James* after an heretical Manner. Upon all which Er-
" rors

" rors and Herefies thou haft been frequently admonifhed, and exhorted by
" Reafons and Authorities of holy Scripture, and befought by fweet Words in
" the Lord, as well by me the aforefaid Inquifitor, and the Vicars, as by many
" religious Perfons, Predicants and Minors, and other Orders, and by other
" good Men of the Clergy and Laity in the City of *Tholoufe*, and even by
" thy own Parents, that thou would'ft forfake the aforefaid Errors, and
" with a good and pure Heart would'ft return to holy Mother the Church
" of *Rome*, without which there is no Salvation, and wouldft abandon that
" deteftible heretical Sect, which leads Souls to Damnation, and infernal De-
" ftruction. But thou would'ft not hitherto acquiefce, nor, tho' long waited
" for, be converted to the Catholick Faith, but even yet perfevereft in thy
" faid Obftinacy with an harden'd Mind. Therefore with the Advice of good
" Men, fkilful in the Canon and Civil Law, and of many religious Perfons,
" that fuch a fcabbed Sheep may not infect the found Sheep of the Lord's
" Flock, having God before our Eyes, and not being able to bear fuch
" Blafphemy and Scandal to the Faith, and the Name of our Lord *Jefus*
" *Chrift*, and having peremptorily affigned to thee this prefent Day, to hear
" thy definitive Sentence, and laying the holy Gofpel before us, we do ad-
" judge thee to be an Heretick, and as fuch leave thee to the fecular
" Court.

These Opinions of the *Albigenfes* are not one of them afcrib'd to the *Valdenfes*,
who had quite different Tenets, which are never mentioned in the Sentences of
the *Albigenfes*. They are fuch as thefe:

That all Judgment is forbidden by God, and that of Confequence 'tis a Sin, and fol. 96.
contrary to what God hath forbidden, for any Judge to condemn any Man to Punifh-
ment or Death, in any Cafe, or for any Caufe whatfoever. And for this they apply
thefe Words of the Gofpel, Judge not that ye be not judged.

That the Indulgences given by the Prelates of the Church of Rome are of no avail; fol. 96.
That there is no Purgatory for Souls after this Life; and that the Prayers and
Vows of the Faithful for the Dead cannot profit them. This is elfewhere more
diftinctly explained: *That this Life is the only Purgatory and Place for Repen-* fol. 92.
tance for Sins; and that when the Soul goes from the Body, it goes either to Pa-
radife or Hell; and that therefore the Valdenfes *make no Prayers or Vows for the*
Dead, becaufe, fay they, thofe who are in Paradife do not need them, and thofe that
are in Hell cannot reap any Advantage by them.

That in the Church there are but three Orders, viz. of Bifhops, Priefts, and fol. 146. b.
Deacons. It is imputed to them alfo as a Crime, that tho' they were Laymen, fol. 128. b.
they preached from the Gofpels, Epiftles, and other Books of the holy Scriptures; whereas the Preaching and Expofition of the Scripture is entirely forbidden the Laity. All thefe Things will appear more plain from a Sentence
paffed on one of the *Valdenfes*, which I fhall here infert, out of the Book of the
Sentences of the *Tholoufe* Inqu. *fol.* 128.

" In the Name of our Lord *Jefus Chrift*, Amen. We the forefaid Inquifi-
" tors of heretical Pravity, and delegated Commiffaries of the venerable Per-
" fons, the Vicars General and Chapter of the Church of *Aix*, during the Va-
" cancy

" cancy of the See. Whereas it evidently and legally appears to us, as
" well by the Inquifition made in general againft all who are infected with
" heretical Pravity, and by the Publick Acts and Procefs of the faid Inquifi-
" tion, as well as by thy Anfwers, and Affertions, and proper Confeffions
" made in Judgment, that you *John Chauoat,* Son of *Peter Chauoat,* of the
" Village of *Mulfia,* near *Urgeletum,* in the Diocefe of *Befancon,* ufually dwel-
" ling at *Vienne* in the Diocefe of *Aix,* was long fince taken up, and have been
" found by Procefs, to be of the Sect and Herefy of thofe, who are called *Val-*
" *denfes,* or poor Men of *Lyons* ; which Sect and Herefy the holy *Roman*
" Church hath many Years ago condemned as heretical, and hath perfecuted
" and condemned the Followers and Profeffors of it as Hereticks ; which Sect
" thou haft held and maintained for nine Years paft, participating and com-
" municating with the *Valdenfes,* knowing them to be fuch, by eating and
" drinking according to their Manner, praying with them on your bended
" Knees, by hearing their Words and Preachings which they make in their
" Conventicles to their Believers, and by receiving them in thy Houfe, and
" alfo by often confeffing thy Sins to them, and humbly receiving from them
* *Meliora-* " Abfolution and Penance, which they call the * Amendment ; and whereas
mentum. " being apprehended, and at the Beginning, being judicially required, would'ft
" not fwear, but didft feveral Times refufe to abjure the faid Sect and Herefy,
" affirming that you believed it to be good, and that the Followers of it were
" good Men, and might be faved in it. And finally, whereas you have feign-
" edly and falfly faid with your Mouth, but not with your Heart, that you
" would depart from it, and abjure it, and haft in Word but not with the
" Heart judicially abjured it ; of which Feignednefs and Falfhood, and the
" Doublenefs of thy Heart there is legal Proof, by thofe Things which you
" have plainly and fully fince recognized, afferted and confeffed in Judgment.
" And farther, whereas you have manifefted your Treachery after your
" feigned tho' judicial Abjuration of the faid Sect and Herefy, by having de-
" nied, and ftill denying with an obftinate Mind, tho' oftentimes required in
" Judgment, to fwear that you would fpeak the Truth, and doft as before,
" and much more evidently, approve and commend the Errors and Herefies
" of the faid Sect, and afferteft, that the Followers of it are juft and good
" Men ; and that the Prelates of the *Roman* Church, and the Inquifitors
" of heretical Pravity, who perfecute them, do unjuftly and unrighteoufly,
" in apprehending and detaining them, becaufe unwilling to forfake the faid
" Sect, and by delivering them over to the fecular Power. Particularly,
" whereas the erroneous Followers and profane Profeffors of the Sect and He-
" refy of the *Valdenfes* hold and affirm, that they are not fubject to our Lord
" the Pope, or the *Roman* Pontiff, or to other Prelates of the Church of
" *Rome,* becaufe it unjuftly perfecutes and condemns them. *Item,* They
" affert that they cannot be excommunicated by the faid *Roman* Pontiff and
" Prelates, and that no one of them is to be obey'd, when they order and
" command the Followers and Profeffors of the faid Sect to defert and ab-
" jure it, altho' condemn'd as heretical by the *Roman* Church. *Item,* The

" forefaid Sect and Herefy, and Followers and Profeffors of the fame, hold
" and dogmatize, that every Oath, without Exception or Expofition, is pro-
" hibited of God, and is unlawful, and a Sin; and this we have heard from
" your own Mouth, that you fo believe and hold, by applying to this Pur-
" pofe the Words of the holy Gofpel, and of St. *James* the Apoftle, of not
" Swearing, tho' in a mad and miftaken Senfe: Whereas, according to the
" found Doctrine of the Saints, and Doctors of the Church, and Tradition
" of the faid Holy Catholick Church, 'tis not only lawful but neceffary to
" fwear for attefting the Truth in Judgment, and alfo by a Statute long
" fince publifhed againft the forefaid Error, 'tis appointed, that thofe who
" by a damnable Superftition refufe an Oath, and will not fwear, fhall be for
" this Reafon declared Hereticks, and fubjected to the Penalties ordered by
" the Canon. *Item,* Thou thy felf haft oftentimes, and before many of us,
" being canonically and judicially required to fwear for the Truth, wholly
" refufed to fwear, and yet refufeft it, afferting that you believe that 'tis
" prohibited by God, and unlawful, and a Sin to fwear at all. *Item,* From
" the fame Fountain of Error, and miftaken Underftanding, the forefaid Sect
" and Herefy afferts, that all Judgment is prohibited of God, and by Confe-
" quence that 'tis a Sin, and againft the divine Prohibition, that any Judge,
" in any Cafe, or for whatfoever Caufe, fhould judge any Man to bodily Pu-
" nifhment, or to Death; applying, without a proper Expofition, the Words
" of the holy Gofpel, where it is written, *Judge not, that ye be not judged*; Item,
" *Thou fhalt not kill,* not underftanding nor receiving them as the holy *Roman*
" Church underftands and delivers them to the Faithful, according to the
" Doctrine of the Fathers and Doctors, and canonical Sanctions; which faid
" Sanctions the faid Sect, departing from the right Path, neither receives nor
" accounts valid, but defpifes, renounces, and condemns. *Item,* Moft per-
" nicioufly erring about the Sacrament of true Penance, and the Keys of
" the Church; they fay, and teach, and hold, that they have Power from God,
" as the Apoftles had, of hearing the Confeffions of the Sins of all that are
" willing to confefs, and of abfolving and enjoining Penances: And they do
" hear the Confeffions of fuch, and enjoin thofe who confefs to them Pe-
" nances for their Sins, tho' they are not ordained Clerks or Priefts by any
" Bifhop of the *Roman* Church, but are mere Laicks, and confefs they have
" not any fuch Power from the *Roman* Church, but rather deny it, and in-
" deed have it not from God, nor from his Church, fince they are with-
" out the Church, and cut off from the Church, out of which there is no
" true Penance or Salvation. *Item,* Thou thy felf haft confeffed in Judg-
" ment, that long fince thou haft confeffed thy Sins feverally to four of
" the *Valdenfes,* viz. *John Moran, Peter de Cernone, John Brayffan,* and *Ste-*
" *phen Porcherii,* and haft received Penance from them, knowing them to be
" *Valdenfes,* and that they were not Priefts ordained by any Bifhop of the *Roman*
" Church. *Item,* The forefaid Sect and Herefy of the *Valdenfes* make a Jeft
" of the Indulgences which are granted by the Prelates of the Church, af-
" ferting that they are not valid. *Item,* It denies that there is after this Life

H   " any

" any Purgatory for Souls, and of Confequence that Prayers, and Alms,
" and Maffes, and other Vows of Piety, which are made by the Faithful
" for the Dead, can at all profit them. *Item,* Detracting from the Prelates of
" the Church of *Rome,* they deny and condemn their State, faying, that they
" are blind, and Leaders of the Blind, and that they do not preferve the Go-
" fpel Truth, nor follow the Apoftolick Poverty. They alfo obftinately
" and falfly affirm, that the Church of *Rome* is the Houfe of a Lye. *Item,*
" Comparing themfelves with the Apoftolical Life and Perfection, and equal-
" ling themfelves to them in Merit, they vainly glory in themfelves, boafting
" that they hold and preferve the Evangelick and Apoftolick Poverty. *Item,*
" Thefe and other Things, as well erroneous as mad, they privately dog-
" matize to their Believers in their Conventicles. *Item,* They preach from
" the Gofpels and Epiftles, and other facred Writings, which by expound-
" ing they corrupt, as Mafters of Errors, who know not how to be Difciples
" of the Truth, becaufe the Preaching and Expofition of the facred Scrip-
" tures is wholly forbidden to the Laity. *Item,* The faid Sect of the *Val-*
" *denfes* differs and difagrees in feveral Things, in Life and Manners, from
" the common Converfation of the Faithful, as is found and plainly appears
" by the Inquifition and Examination as well of the *Valdenfes* themfelves, as
" their Believers, and efpecially by the Confeffions of thofe who are con-
" verted by the Inquifitors from that Sect and Herefy. Moreover, thou
" *John* haft judicially before us and elfewhere, oftentimes approved and
" praifed the faid Sect and Herefy of the *Valdenfes,* and doft yet approve
" and commend it, nor wilt depart from it, nor abjure and forfake it, but
" rather perfevereft in it with an obftinate Mind, altho' by us and feveral
" other good Men thou haft been oftentimes invited to Converfion, and
" haft been canonically admonifhed and judicially required by us, that
" in Heart and Deed thou fhouldft turn from it, and with thy Mouth and
" Soul wholly abjure it. We therefore the forefaid Inquifitors, having God
" before our Eyes, *&c.* do declare and pronounce, and deliver you over to
" the fecular Court, as relapfed into the Herefy which you have before
" judicially abjured, and as an impenitent and obftinate Heretick, affectio-
" nately bewailing it, as the canonical Sanctions oblige us to do, to preferve
" your Life and Members untouched. Signed,

> (L. S.) William Juliani, *publick and*
>   *fworn Notary for the Office of*
>   *the Inquifition* ; *and* James
>   Mafquetius, *Notary of the*
>   *Inquifition.* (L. S.)

From thefe Inftances it appears, that the Opinions of the *Albigenfes* and
Valdenfes were different. However, 'tis not to be doubted, but that oftentimes their Enemies gave very vile and odious Accounts of the Doctrines they
held; as will appear by comparing the feveral Places in which they de-
                                                                          fcribe

scribe them. For the same Opinion, which in one Place appears extremely erroneous; in another, when 'tis more fully explained, and without Spite, is harmless enough; of which the single Instance of the Resurrection of the Dead is full Proof. For sometimes the *Albigenses* are accused, that *they deny the Resurrection of human Bodies*; as tho' they quite denied the Resurrection of the Dead; which yet in another Place is more distinctly explained thus, that *the Dead shall arise with spiritual Bodies*. And that their Opinions have been misrepresented elsewhere, there can be no Doubt, and it will appear upon a Comparison of the several Places, wherein they are recorded. But that the Opinions of the *Albigenses* and *Valdenses* were very different, cannot be denied. For if they had held the same, no Reason can be assigned, why different ones should have been ascribed to them. One would rather be inclined to believe, that as their Persecutors greedily sought after every Occasion to punish them, they would have fastened on every one of them all the heretical Opinions of the *Valdenses* and *Albigenses*; that so being burdened with numerous Crimes, the Inquisitors might seem to have the more just Pretence for condemning them.

For this very Cause it may be justly concluded, that many other of those impious Tenets that are ascribed by *Baronius*, *Bzovius*, and others, to the *Albigenses* and *Valdenses*, were invented out of mere Hatred to them, and to render them detestable to the People; especially that impious Opinion, which *Eymericus Direct. Inquis. Par. 2. Quæs.* 14. imputes to the *Valdenses: That 'tis better to satisfy a Man's Lust by any Act of Uncleanness whatsoever, than to be perpetually burning; and that (as they say and practise) 'tis lawful in the dark for Men and Women to lie promiscuously with one another, whensoever and as often as they have the Inclination and Desire.* For if this had been their Tenet, would there not have been one of that vast Number of Prisoners, that they condemned to such various Punishments, to be found, that was infected with it? Or, if it could have been proved upon them, was the Equity, Humanity and Compassion of the Inquisitors so very great, as to have concealed a Crime, that would have been condemned by the common Voice of Mankind, and exposed those that were guilty of it to the most severe Punishment and Death? Would they, by such a Method of acting, have given the World occasion to censure them for persecuting, and cruelly punishing Men merely for the Sake of holding Opinions different from the *Roman* Faith, tho' consistent with a due Regard to a good Conscience, when at the same Time they might have accused them of so horrid an Impiety? If they had been really such execrable Persons, their Crimes ought to have been publickly exposed; and thus they themselves would have sunk under the Weight of Infamy, and their Prosecutors would have been so far from being charged as bloody Inquisitors, that they would have deserved the universal Applause.

Hence we may learn what Credit is to be given to Popish Writers, when they give us an Account of the Opinions and Practices of those they call Hereticks. 'Tis their Way to charge all that separate from their Communion with Impurity and Lust, as tho' the only Cause of their leaving the Com-

munion

munion of the Church of *Rome*, was a difhonourable and vile Love of Wo‑
men ; and they have moft impudently dared to reproach with this Vice,
Perfons that have been remarkable for their Chaftity and Continence. In
the mean while, nothing is more notorious, than that their Monks and
Priefts, who are forbid the Remedy of a chafte and honourable Matrimony,
abandon themfelves without Shame to the moft impure Embraces, and infa‑
moufly wallow in carnal Pleafures. *Erafmus, Tom.* 9. *Page* 401. fays ; *There
is a certain* German *Bifhop, who declared publickly at a Feaft, that in one Year he
had brought to him* 11000 *Priefts that openly kept Whores:* For they pay annually a
certain Sum to the Bifhop. This was one of the hundred Grievances that the
German Nation propofed to the Pope's Nuncio at the Convention at *Norim‑
berg,* in the Years 1522 and 1523. Grievance 91. *That the Bifhops in moft Places,
and their Officials, not only fuffer the Priefts to keep Whores, fo they pay a certain
Sum of Money, but even force the chafter Priefts, who live without Whores, to pay
the Price of thofe that keep them ; alledging, that the Bifhop wants Money, and
that thofe Priefts who pay it may either remain fingle, or keep Whores as they
pleafe. How wicked a Thing this is, every one underftands.* The fame *Erafmus,*
in his Account of the Errors of *Bedda, Tom.* 9. *p.* 484. hath the following Paf‑
fage : *What Wonder if fome Nuns in the Age of St.* Auftin *are faid to have mar‑
ried, when in this Age there are faid to be fo many Monafteries that are nothing
better than publick Stews, and more that are private ones. Even in thofe where
the Rules are more ftrict, there are more that have the Veil than their Virginity.
This I relate with Grief, and I wifh it was not true.* And a little after : *I know
fome, that have buried in the Monafteries the Girls they have abufed, that the Affair
might be hufhed up.* And *p.* 569. *Bedda,* fays he, *cries out glorioufly, God for‑
bid, God forbid, that any Man fhould be admitted to the Dignity of the Prieft‑
hood, who doth not wholly deny himfelf carnal Embraces, tho' at this Day there
are fome to be found who keep fifty Whores, not to add any thing worfe.* And
p. 985. concerning the Prohibition of Flefh : *Amongft the Priefts, how fcarce
is the Number that live chafte ? I fpeak of thofe who keep publickly at home their
Whores, inftead of Wives ; for I will not mention the Myfteries of their more fe‑
cret Lufts : I fpeak of thofe Things only that are well known to every one.* But
the Inftance he gives, *p.* 1380. is yet more execrable : That a certain *Domi‑
nican* Profeffor of Divinity, whofe Name was *John,* mention'd to him at *Ant‑
werp,* in the Houfe of *Nicholas* of *Middlebourge,* a Phyfician, a Divine of *Lo‑
vain,* who told him, that he refufed to give Abfolution to a certain Con‑
feffor of the Nuns, becaufe he acknowledged he had lain with 200 of them. But
what need is there of producing Teftimonies out of particular Authors ? The
very Laws of the Inquifition, which ordain Punifhments for thofe Priefts,
who follicit not only Women, but, what is much worfe, even Boys, in the
Sacrament of Confeffion, are an undeniable Proof that thefe Crimes are too
frequent and common in that State of impure Celebacy. So that having their
own Minds infnared with the Lufts of the Flefh, and *their Eyes,* as the Scrip‑
ture expreffes it, *full of Adultery,* like the Generality of Mankind, they judge
of others by themfelves, and infinuate that the only, at leaft the chief Caufe
of

of forfaking the Church of *Rome*, is the immoderate Love of Women: Whereas, if they were not acted by the Principles of a good Confcience, but from a Defire of gratifying their luftful Inclination, they might with much more Safety abide in the Communion of the Church of *Rome*, where they have daily Occafions offered to them of fulfilling the Lufts of the Flefh: They have nothing to fear, even from the bloody Tribunals of the Inquifition, if they are but cautious, tho' they follicit Women in the very Sacrament of Confeffion. This for once to refute the Calumnies of the Papifts, who, whenever they are giving an Account of the Rife of any of thofe they call Hereticks, are perpetually repeating this Charge againft them. But to return to our Purpofe:

Befides the above-mentioned Differences of Doctrines between the *Albigenfes* and *Valdenfes*, they differed alfo in their Rites and Cuftoms. For at firft there were two Sorts of the *Albigenfes*. Some profeffed their Faith, and ufed their *fol.* 40. *a.* Cuftoms, and were called *Perfecti* feu *Confolati, Perfect* or *Comforted*. Others only enter'd into a Covenant with thefe perfect ones, which they call *La Con-venenfa, The Agreement*, that at the End of Life they would be received into *fol.* 15. *b.* their Sect. This Reception is often called *Heretication*, and was performed 61.*a.*70.*a.* after this manner to *Benedictus Molinerii* in a certain Illnefs that he laboured under: Bernard de Goch, *one of the* Albigenfes, *held the Hands of the fick Per-fol.* 120. *b. fon between his own, and held a certain Book over him, in which he read the Go-fpel of St.* John, In the Beginning was the Word, *and delivered to him a fine Thread, with which he was to be tied for Herefy*. The Rites adminifter'd to a fick Woman were fomewhat different: Petrus Auterii *faid in the Prefence of the fol.* 86. *a. fick Woman, Praife God; either inftructing the Woman to fay fo, or faying fo by himfelf. Then he laid his Hand upon the Woman, holding a certain Book, and p.* 43. *a. reading fome Words, but firft put a white Linen Cloth upon her, and after he had read in the Book*, Peter *and* Aurelius *made many Bows near her Bed*. For this Reception they were prepared by certain Abftinences, which I gather from the Sentence of *Peter Raymundus Dominicus de Borno*, who is faid to have feen *Peter Auterii* with *Peter Sancii*, who then kept thofe Fafts, which they are obliged to do, who are to be admitted to the Sect of the Hereticks.

This Admiffion was believed to fave the Soul of the Perfon admitted, and was called *Spiritual Baptifm, The Confolation, The Reception*, and *Good End*. So *fol.* 86. *a.* that they were believed to be fo fanctified by it, as that afterwards it was *fol.* 3. *a.* unlawful for them to be touched by a Woman. Thus we read in the Sen-tence of a Woman, whofe Father had been received amongft the *Albigenfes*; *fol.* 49. *That fhe was forbid by her Father to touch him, becaufe after his Reception no Woman ought to touch him, and from that Time fhe never did touch him*. And in another Woman's Sentence; *That 'twas unlawful for her to touch* Petrus *fol.* 68. *b.* Sancii, *and that fhe heard that 'twas reported amongft them, that they neither touch a Woman, nor fuffer themfelves to be touched by one*.

But inafmuch as it was poffible that the Perfon received might return to his former Pollutions, his Reception was delay'd to his laft Sicknefs, when there was no more Hopes of Recovery, that fo he might not lofe the Good he had.

had received ; for which Reafon fome were not admitted, tho' one of the *Albi-genfes* was prefent ; becaufe 'twas not believed they would immediately die.

fol 68.   Thus 'tis reported of *Petrus Sancii,* that being called *to hereticate a certain fick Woman, fhe was not then hereticated ; becaufe he did not think it proper upon Account of her not being weak enough.* And afterwards, though the Diftemper grew more violent, *Petrus Sancii* did not hereticate her, becaufe fhe recovered.

As for thofe who were received during their Illnefs, they were commanded to make Ufe of the *Endura,* i. e. Fafting ; and to haften their Death by the opening a Vein, and Bathing. Thus 'tis reported of a certain Woman ; That *fhe*

fol. 14. *b.*   *perfevered* in the Abftinence which they call the *Endura, many Days ; and haften'd her bodily Death, by lofing her Blood, frequent Bathing, and greedily taking a poifonous Draught of the Juice of wild Cucumbers, mixing with it broken Glafs, that*

fol. 46.   *by tearing of her Bowels fhe might fooner die.* Of another, 'tis faid, *That fhe was forbidden by her Mother-in-Law to give her little Daughter, that had been hereticated*

fol. 49.   *by Peter Sancii, any Milk to drink, by which it died.* Another confeffes, *That fhe had not feen her Father, fince his Heretication, eating or drinking any Thing but*

fol. 63.   *cold Water.* But one *Hugo,* who continued feveral Days in the *Endura,* did afterwards, by his Mother's Perfuafion, eat and recover. The fame Year *Peter Sancii* invited him *to enter into the* Endura, *and fo make a good End ; but he would not agree to it till he came to die.* The fame *Hugo* faw, *that* Sancius *procured and haften'd his own Death, by Bleeding, Bathing, and Cold.* Petrus Auterii

fol. 65. *b.*   is faid to have received another Woman ; *and after her Reception, to have forbid, that any Meat fhould be given to the faid hereticated fick Woman ; and there were two Women who attended her, that watched that there fhould be neither Meat nor Drink given her the whole Night, nor following Day, left fhe fhould lofe the Good fhe had received, and contradict the Order of* Peter Auterii ; *although the faid fick Woman defired that they would give her Meat.* But the third Day after, fhe eat and

fol. 82. *b.*   grew well. In the Sentence of *Peter Raymundus,* of the *Hugo's,* we read thefe Things concerning the *Endura. You voluntarily fhorten your own corporal Life, and inflict Death upon your felf ; becaufe you put your felf in that Abftinence, which the Hereticks call* Endura, *in which* Endura *you remained fix Days, without Meat or Drink, and wouldft not eat, neither yet wilt, though oftentimes invited to it.* However, all of them did not care to fubject themfelves to fo fevere a Law.

fol. 71.   For we read of a certain Woman, that fhe would not fuffer her fick Daughter, although near Death, to be received ; *becaufe then her faid Daughter muft be put*

fol. 30. *b. in the* Endura. There is alfo an Inftance of a Woman, who for fear fhe fhould be taken up by the Inquifitors, put her felf in the *Endura* ; and fending for a Chirurgeon, order'd him to open one of her Veins in a Bath : And after the Chirurgeon was gone, fhe unbound her Arm in the Bath, that fo the Blood running out more freely, fhe might fooner die. After this fhe bought Poifon in order to deftroy her felf. Afterwards fhe procured a Coblers Awl, which in that barbarous Age they call *Alzena,* intending to run it into her Side : But the Women difputing amongft themfelves, whether the Heart was on the right Side or the left, fhe at laft drunk up the Poifon, and died the Day after.

They

They had alſo a peculiar Manner of ſaluting each other, by embracing, *ſol. 59 b.* putting their Hands to both Sides, and turning their Head three Times to *ſol. 176. b.* each Shoulder, ſaying every Time, Praiſe the Lord : Which Manner of Sa-*ſol 120.b.* lutation ſeems to have been very common among them ; becauſe we find it *ſol. 9. b.* mentioned in the Sentences of many of them, and was performed ſometimes with bended Knees ; ſometimes by putting their Hands down, even to the Ground. Sometimes alſo this Cuſtom was inſiſted on : So we read of a certain *ſol. 91.* Perſon, *being required by the ſaid Heretick, to bend the Knee before him, and ſay, Praiſe ye the Lord ; he bent on his Knee, and ſaid before him, Praiſe ye the Lord. The Heretick anſwer'd ; May God bring you to a good End.* And of a certain Woman, *ſol. 89.* *That ſhe ſaw a certain Perſon bowing before* Peter Auterii, *in her aforeſaid Houſe ; and then ſhe was required to make her Amendment before the ſaid Heretick, as the other did. And then ſhe alſo began to bend the Knee before the ſaid Heretick, and knew not how to make the aforeſaid Amendment ; upon which, they who were preſent began to laugh, which made her bluſh and go away.* We read of another, that *ſol. 70.* he agreed with *Peter Auterii, That he would commend himſelf to him ; that he might pray to God for him ; and began to bow the Knee before him : And that* Peter Auterii *ſaid, Ye may not do it ; for this is not the Place ; and ſo ſent him away, that he might not bow the Knee before him, which he was willing and had began to do.* Nor was this Manner of Salutation required only from thoſe who were admitted, but alſo made Uſe of by thoſe who were called *Perfect* ; and admitted others, as often as they met one another. Thus we read in the Sentence of *ſol. 16.b.* Amelius de Perlis, *That he and* Peter Auterius *ſaluted each other with mutual Adoration before the Inquiſitors ; and that they both adored each other, after an heretical Manner, before them, by falling on their Faces on the Ground ; and ſaid that they were of the ſame Sect ; and acknowledged that they had elſewhere oftentimes adored one another after the ſame Manner.*

They faſted three Days a Week on Bread and Water. A certain ſick Man *ſol. 120. b.* was told, That *he muſt have no Food, unleſs he could repeat the* Pater Noſter. *ſol. 49.*

We read of the *Valdenſes,* that they had certain *Elders* (Majores) of their *ſol. 147.* Sect. Thus *John* of *Lorain* was called *Majoralis* of that Sect ; and *Chriſtian,* and *John of Chabley, Majores.*

'Tis reported of them alſo, That *they prayed on their Knees before and after Dinner, leaning on a Table.* This occurs in almoſt all the Sentences of the *Valdenſes.* 'Twas alſo cuſtomary with them to ſay Grace over their Meat ; becauſe *Perrin Faber* was accuſed, that *he eat and drank with the* Valdenſes, at *ſol. 109. b.* *the ſame Table that had been bleſſed by them.*

They uſed to compare themſelves with the Apoſtolical Life and Perfection ; and ſol. 128. b. boaſt that they were equal to them in Merit ; and that they preſerved and imitated the Evangelick and Apoſtolick Poverty ; upon which Account they obtained the Name of the *poor Men of* Lyons.

Beſides this, they had other Cuſtoms different from the common Way of *ſol. 128. b.* Living. Thus we read, That *the ſaid Sect of the* Valdenſes, *ſeparated and differed in other Things from the common Life and Manners of the Faithful.*

And

fol. 123.　　And laſtly, we read in the Sentence of *John Philibert*, a Preſbyter, *That the* Valdenſes *preach to their Believers ſometime after Supper, in the Night, out of the Goſpels and Epiſtles, in the vulgar Language.*

Since therefore there is ſo great a Diverſity in the Opinions and Cuſtoms of the *Albigenſes* and *Valdenſes*, 'tis very evident that they were two diſtinct Sects, both of them abhorring the Communion of the Church of *Rome* ; but in many Things differing from each other. This appears moſt plainly from theſe Acts ; for all thoſe that received Sentence, to Page 92. are *Albigenſes : Stephen Poncher* is the firſt of the *Valdenſes*, mentioned in the ſame Page. Page 96. follows the Sentence againſt *John Brayſſe*, the *Valdenſian.* After that, the *Albigenſes* and *Valdenſes* are condemned promiſcuouſly, but in ſuch a Manner, as that at firſt View, one may know one from the other. The principal Perſons of the *Albigenſes*, who received others, and are mentioned in the ſeveral Sentences, are *Petrus Auterii, James*, his Son ; and *William, Peter*'s Brother, *Petrus Raimundi de Sancto Papulo, Aimericus Barrotti, Amelius de Perlis, Andreas de Padris, Octavius, Petrus Sancii de Garda, Bernardus Andoyni de Monte Acuto*, and a great Number of others, mentioned *p.* 93, 101, 106, 123, 146. *b.* From hence I conclude, that they were not only two diſtinct Sects originally, but that they were not united into one Church afterwards, at leaſt, in the Year 1320. *i. e.* half an Age after their firſt Riſe.

Pegna *in Direct. par.* 2. *com.* 25.　　I cannot however deny, that *Ivonetus*, who lived about thoſe Times, attributes many Things to the *Valdenſes*, which in theſe Acts are aſcribed to the *Albigenſes*, viz. that they are divided into two Parties. *There are ſome*, ſays Ivonetus, *who are accounted Perfect : Theſe are properly called the poor Men of* Lyons. *All are not taken in under this Character, but are firſt inſtructed themſelves, a long while, that they may know how to teach others. Theſe Perfect declare that they have nothing of their own, neither Houſes nor Poſſeſſions, nor certain Dwellings. And if they had any Wives before, they put them away. They ſay they are the true Succeſſors of the Apoſtles, and are the Maſters and Confeſſors of others ; go viſiting about the Countries, and confirming their Diſciples in their Error : Theſe Diſciples bring them all Things neceſſary. Into whatever Place they come, they give Notice of their Arrival : They are met by great Numbers in ſome ſafe and ſecret Place, to ſee and hear them. They ſend them the beſt of Meat and Drink. They appoint Collections for Support of their Poor, their Maſters and Students, who have nothing of their own ; or elſe to inveigle others, who are drawn over to their Party by the Love of Money.* Moſt of theſe Things are aſcribed in theſe Acts, to the *Albigenſes* ; ſo that they ſometimes ſeem to have been confounded with one another.

On the other hand, *Pegna* and *Eymericus* ſeem to have acknowledged a Difference between them. For *Pegna*, upon *Eymericus*'s Directory of the Inquiſitors, *Par.* 2. *Comment.* 38. calls the *Sacrament of the* Albigenſes, Conſolamentum, *the Conſolation* ; and adds, that their other Sacrament was the Bleſſing of Bread. *This*, ſays he, *is a Sort of breaking Bread, which they daily uſe at Dinner and Supper :* 'Tis *performed after this Manner. When the* Puritans (ſo he calls the *Albigenſes*) *are come to the Table, they all ſay the Lord's Prayer ; in*

I　　　　　　　　　　　　　　　　　　　　　　　　　　　　　　*the*

the mean while, he who is the principal Person amongst them, either as to Riches or Dignity, takes in his Hand one or more Loaves, according to the Number of those that are present ; and saying, The Grace of our Lord Jesus Christ be with you all always *; he breaks the Loaf or Loaves, and distributes to all that sit down, whither they are Puritans, or only their Believers.' And in this they differ from the poor Men of* Lyons *; for they perform this Ceremony or Blessing, only once in a Year.*

Of the *Valdenses,* Eymericus *thus writes,* P. 3. Num. 112. *Those among them that are Perfect, put in the upper Part of the Shoe or Zabbata, a Sort of a Escutheon, as a Sign, from which they are called* Inzabbatati. *They have one among them, superior to the rest, whom they call* Majoralis *or* Elder, *to whom alone, and to no other, they yield Obedience. When they sit at Table they bless in this Manner :* He who blessed the five Barly Loaves and two Fishes, in the Desart, to his Disciples, bless this Table to us. *And when they rise, they repeat those Words of the Revelation ;* Blessing, and Honour, and Wisdom, and Thanks, and Glory, and Strength, be unto our God for ever and ever. *Amen. Always holding their Eyes and Hands lift up to Heaven.* This Account is agreeable to what we read of the *Valdenses,* in the Book of Sentences of the *Thoulouse* Inquisition, but much more explicite and distinct.

The same *Eymericus,* Num. 88, &c. charges these Hereticks, of his Time, with many Equivocations and Tricks, by which they endeavour to deceive the Inquisitors, when they interrogate them concerning their Faith, *viz. If they are asked,* Do you believe the Sacrament of Baptism necessary to Salvation *; they answer ;* I believe. *By which, they mean their own private Faith, and not their believing the Doctrine they are asked about :* Or, if it pleases God, I believe well *; meaning, that it is not pleasing to God, that they should believe as the Inquisitors would have them :* Or, by returning the Question. Sir, How do you believe ? *And when the Inquisitor answers,* I believe the Faith of the Church of Rome, *they reply,* I believe so *; meaning, that they believe the Inquisitor believes as he says ; not that they believe as he doth.* These and other like Things he affirms that he observed, during the Administration of his Office.

I have been the longer on this Account of the *Albigenses* and *Valdenses,* that every one may judge whether they were one or two different Sects. To speak my own Mind freely, they appear to me to have been two distinct ones ; and that they were entirely ignorant of many Tenets, that are now ascribed to them. Particularly the *Valdenses* seem to have been plain Men, of mean Capacities, unskilful and unexperienced ; and if their Opinions and Customs were to be examined without Prejudice, it would appear, that amongst all the modern Sects of Christians, they bare the greatest Resemblance to that of the *Memnonites.*

CHAP. IX.

Of the PERSECUTIONS *against the* ALBIGENSES *and* VALDENSES.

Baron.
§.18. *N.* 4.

IT was the entire Study and Endeavour of the Popes, to crush in its Infancy, every Doctrine that any way opposed their exorbitant Power. In the Year 1163. at the Synod of *Tours*, all the Bishops and Priests in the Country of *Tholouse*, were commanded *to take Care, and to forbid, under the Pain of Excommunication, every Person from presuming to give Reception, or the least Assistance to the Followers of this Heresy,* which first began in the Country of *Tholouse, whenever they should be discovered. Neither were they to have any Dealings with them in buying or selling ; that by being thus deprived of the common Assistances of Life, they might be compelled to repent of the Evil of their Way. Whosoever shall dare to contravene this Order, let him be excommunicated as a Partner with them in their Guilt. As many of them as. can be found, let them be imprisoned by the Catholick Princes, and punished with the Forfeiture of all their Substance.*

Pegna *in*
Eymeric.
p. 2. com.
39.
Bzovius,
a. 1199.
§. 38.

Some of the *Valdenses* coming into the neighbouring Kingdom of *Arragon,* King *Ildefonsus,* in the Year 1194. put forth, against them, a very severe and bloody Edict, by which *he banished them from his Kingdom, and all his Dominions,, as Enemies of the Cross of Christ, Prophaners of the Christian Religion, and publick Enemies to himself and Kingdom.* He adds: *If any, from this Day forwards, shall presume to receive into their Houses the aforesaid* Valdenses *and* Inzabbatati, *or other Hereticks, of whatsoever Profession they be, or. to hear in any Place their abominable Preachings, or to give them Food, or to do them any kind Office whatsoever ; let him know, that he shall incur the Indignation of Almighty God and Ours ; that. he shall forfeit all his Goods, without the Benefit of Appeal, and be punish'd as though guilty of High Treason, &c. Let it be farther observed, That if any Person, of high or low Condition, shall find any of the often before mentioned accursed Wretches, in any Part of our Dominions, who hath had three Days Notice of this our Edict, and who either intends not to depart at all, or not immediately, but who contumaciously stays, or travels about ; every Evil, Disgrace, and Suffering that he shall inflict on such Person, except Death or Maiming, will be very grateful and acceptable to us ; and he shall be so far from incurring any Punishment upon this Account,, that he shall be rather entitled to our Favour. However, we give these wicked Wretches Liberty till the Day after All Saints (though it may. seem contrary to Justice and Reason) by which they. must be either gone from our Dominions, or upon. their Departure out of them : But afterwards they shall be plunder'd, whipp'd and. beat, and treated with all Manner of Disgrace and Severity.*

Raynald.
a. 1199.
§. 23, 24.

Nor did they act with less Cruelty against Hereticks in *Orvieto. Peter Parentius,* the *Præfect,* declared, and that publickly, to a large Assembly, That whosoever, within an appointed Day, would come back to the Church,. which never shuts her Bosom to those who return, and obey the Commands of the Bishops, should obtain Pardon and Favour ; but that whosoever
should

should refuse to return by the prefixed Day, should be subject to the Punishment appointed by the Laws and Canons. But what this Favour was, is described in the publick Records of that Church, in these Words: *But the
Bishop inflamed against the Wickedness of the* Manichæans, *received, with a
pastoral Concern, the Confession of the Hereticks, returning from their Heresy to the
Catholick Unity, and presented them to the Præfect. Some of these he bound in
Iron Chains, others he caused to be publickly whipped, others he miserably banished
out of the City, others he fined, who were true Penitents on Account of the Money they
lost ; from others he took large Securities, and pulled down the Houses of many more:
So that the Governor of the City, walking after the Royal Pattern, turned aside
neither to the left Hand nor to the right.* To this Account *Raynaldus* adds, *These* §. 23.
Things did this new Phineas, *burning with an holy Zeal, for the Catholick Faith,
this Year in the Time of* Lent. But he was a little after killed by the Hereticks.

About the Year 1200, Pope *Innocent* III. wrote to several Archbishops Bzovius,
and Bishops in *Guienne*, and other Provinces of *France*, that they should ba- *a.* 1198.
nish the *Valdenses*, *Puritans*, and * *Paterines*, from their Territories ; and §. 6.
sends thither the Friars, *Reyner*, and *Guido* the Founder of the Order of Raynald.
Hospitallers, to convert Hereticks ; and commands the Bishops, that those who §. 37.
would not be converted should be banish'd ; and that they should humbly receive, and inviolably observe whatever Friar *Reyner* should ordain against
Hereticks, their Favourers and Defenders. He commanded also the Princes,
Earls, &c. That those Hereticks who should be excommunicated as impenitent by Friar *Reyner*, should be adjudged to Forfeiture of their Estates and
Banishment ; that if after this Interdict they should be found in their Dominions, they should proceed more severely against them, as became Christian Princes. He gave moreover full Power to *Reyner*, to compel the Princes
to this Work, under Pain of Excommunication, and Interdict of their Dominions, without Appeal ; and commands him not to delay to publish the Sentence of Excommunication against the Receivers of excommunicated Hereticks. And to conclude, he exhorts the People to give all Assistance, when
required, against Hereticks, to the Friars *Reyner* and *Guido*, and grants to all
who should stand by them faithfully and zealously, the same Indulgence of
Sins, which is used to be granted to those who visited the Threshold of St.
Peter or St. *James*. The next Year following he commands the Archbishops of Bzovius,
Aix and *Metz*, and others, with some Abbots, that they should examine the *a* 1199.
poor Men of *Lyons*, and others, concerning the Orthodox Faith ; and as they §. 21.
found the Matter, should give him full Information by Messenger or Letters ;
that being thus more fully informed by them, he might know the better how
to proceed against them. He made also the most severe Laws for the Extirpation of Heresy, which are contained in his Letters to the Citizens of *Viterbo*, Raynald.
some of whom had been infected with Heresy.   *a.* 1199.
                                                                           §. 27.

---

* Some of the Sectaries of the *Valdenses :* They called themselves *Paterines*, after the Example
of the Martyrs, who suffered Martyrdom for the Catholick Faith ; because they, like them,
were *expositos passionibus*, exposed to Sufferings. *Du Fresne Glossar. Med. & inf. Lat. in voce.*

CHAP. X.

Of DOMINICUS, *and the first Rise of the* Tholouse INQUISITION.

THUS far we have consider'd the Method of Proceeding against Hereticks, as committed to the Bishops, with whom the Government and
Care of the Churches were entrusted, according to the received Decrees of the
Church of *Rome.* But inasmuch as their Number did not seem sufficient to
that Court, or because they were too negligent in the Affair, and did not proceed with that Fury against Hereticks as the Pope would have had them;
therefore, that he might put a Stop to the encreasing Progress of Heresies,
and more effectually extinguish them, about the Year of our Lord, 1200.
he founded the Order of the *Dominicans* and *Franciscans,* that they might
preach against Heresies. *Dominick* and his Followers were sent into the
Country of *Tholouse,* where he preached, with great Vehemence, against the
Hereticks that were arisen there; from whence his Order hath obtained the
Name of *Preachers,* or *Predicants.* Father *Francis,* with his Disciples, batteled
it with the Hereticks of *Italy.* They were both commanded by the Pope, to
excite the Catholick Princes and People to extirpate Hereticks; and in all
Places to enquire out their Number and Quality, and also the Zeal of the
Catholicks and Bishops in their Extirpation; and to transmit a faithful Ac-
count to *Rome.* Hence they were called *Inquisitors.*
    It is evident that the first Inquisitors were *Dominican* Friars, or of the Or-
der of *Predicants;* but 'tis not so certain what Year the Inquisition it self was
first introduced. *Dominick,* as hath been said, was sent into the Country of
De Succes. *Tholouse,* * or *Gallia Narbonensis:* He, as *Bertrand* relates in his Account of the
Ecclef. in Affairs of *Tholouse,* whom *Usser* cites, first lodged in the House of a certain
Occidente, Nobleman, to whom belonged the House of the Inquisition at *Tholouse,* near
s. 9. §. 9. the Castle of *Narbonne;* and finding him sadly infected with Heresy, Father
Dominick, Inquisitor of the Faith, reduced him to the Path of Truth; upon
which, he devoted himself and his House, to St. *Dominick* and his Order: Which
House hath ever since belonged to the Inquisition, and the *Dominican* Order.
From hence we may gather, that *Dominick* was the first Inquisitor; and that
the Inquisition was first introduced into *Tholouse:* But as to the Year when, Writers differ; some referring it to the Year of Christ, 1212; others to 1208;
and others to 1215. This is certain, and agreed by all, that it began under
the Papacy of *Innocent* III. and that *Dominick* was appointed the first Inquisitor
in *Gallia Narbonensis:* But whether he received his Office of Inquisitor from
Arnaldus, Abbot of *Cisteaux,* Legate of the Apostolick See, in *France,* or immediately from the Pope, is disputed by the Popish Writers. Those who endeavour to reconcile the Difference, say that *Dominick* was first appointed

    * That Part of *France,* which anciently contained the Provinces of *Savoy, Dauphine, Provinces*
and *Languedoc.*

                                                                Inqui-

Inquifitor by the Legate, and afterwards confirmed by the Pope himfelf. *Ludovicus a Paramo* feems to be of the fame Opinion ; for he fays, that Fa- *lib.* 2. *tit.* ther *Dominick* firft difcourfed of his Defign, to introduce the Inquifition, to 1. *cap.* 1. the Abbot of *Cifteaux*, at that Time Apoftolick Legate in *France* ; and that *n.* 13. the Abbot appointed him Inquifitor, at the fame Time referring the Affair to the Pope. After this he was confirmed in the Office by a Cardinal Legate in that Kingdom ; and at length, after the Conclufion of the *Lateran* Council, *Ann.* 1216. he was made Inquifitor by Authority of the Pope's Letters, a Copy of which fome Authors affirm they have actually feen.

" When *Dominick* had received thefe Letters, upon a certain Day, in the *c.* 2. *n.* 4.
" Midft of a great Concourfe of People, he declared openly in his Sermon,
" in the Church of St. *Prullian*, that he was raifed to a new Office by the
" Pope ; adding, that he was refolved to defend, with his utmoft Vigour,
" the Doctrines of the Faith ; and that if the Spiritual and Ecclefiaftical
" Arms were not fufficient for this End, 'twas his fixed Purpofe to call in
" the Affiftance of the Secular Arm, to excite and compel the Catholick
" Princes to take Arms againft Hereticks, that the very Memory of them
" might be entirely deftroy'd." It evidently appears that *Dominick* was a bloody and cruel Man. This is more than obfcurely intimated by the *Dominican*, *Camillus Campegius*, Inquifitor General of *Ferrara*, who after having recited the Letters of *Dominick*, in which he declares the Penances he enjoin- *c.* 20. ed to *Pontius Rogerii*, adds : *I have the more willingly annexed to this Treatife of* Zauchini, *Punifhments thefe Letters of St.* Dominick *our Father, who firft exercifed the Office of Inquifitor, that all may be able to make a Comparifon between the ancient Severity made ufe of to ftop the Progrefs of thefe Crimes, and the prefent Moderation and Tendernefs of this holy Tribunal.* Thefe Letters he wrote, as *Ludovicus a Paramo* obferves, when as yet he acted as Inquifitor only by the Authority of the Abbot of *Cifteaux*, and thefe Letters *Paramus* produces to prove, that *Dominick* af- *l.* 2. *t.* 12. fumed this Office, *from a Refolution to punifh Hereticks with fuch Severity, as that c.* 2. *n.* 5. *by the Fear of Punifhment he might deter others from the like Wickednefs.* He was born in *Spain* in the Village *Calaroga* in the Diocefe of *Ofma*. His Mother, before fhe conceived him, is faid to have dreamed, that fhe was with Child of a Whelp, carrying in his Mouth a lighted Torch ; and that after he was born, he put the World in an Uproar by his fierce Barkings, and fet it on Fire by the Torch that he carried in his Mouth. His Followers interpret this Dream of his Doctrine, by which he enlightned the whole World ; whereas others, if Dreams prefage any thing, think that the Torch was an Emblem of that Fire and Faggot, by which an infinite Multitude of Men were burnt to Afhes.

In the Beginning the Inquifitors had no proper Tribunal ; they only enquired after Hereticks, their Number, Strength, and Riches. After they had detected them, they informed the Bifhops, who then had the fole Power of Judging in Ecclefiaftical Affairs, and fometimes urged them, that they fhould anathematize, and otherwife punifh the Hereticks they had difcovered to them. Sometimes they ftirred up Princes to take Arms againft Hereticks ;
fometimes

fometimes the People. Such of them as engaged in this Work they figned with the Crofs, and encouraged them in their Expeditions againſt Hereticks. Farther than this, *Dominick*, who was of a bloody fierce Temper, that he might the more effectually extirpate all Herefy, invented a Method, how, under the Appearance of Mercy and Tenderneſs, he might exercife the moſt outragious Cruelty, *viz.* the laying fome certain Puniſhments, by way of wholfome Penance, upon fuch as were converted to the *Roman* Faith, that being thus converted, they might be freed from Excommunication. For what could carry a greater Appearance of Mercy, than to abfolve and receive into Communion, thofe Hereticks that returned to the Church, and voluntarily fubjected themfelves to a wholfome Penance? But the Truth is, that this was the Height of Cruelty: For they fubmitted to fuch Penances, not from Conviction and Choice, but for fear of a more terrible Puniſhment. For the Fire and Faggot and other Puniſhments were ready prepared for fuch as were not converted; and all that refufed to fubmit to thefe Penances, were pronounced excommunicate, convict, and obftinate Hereticks, and as fuch turned over to be puniſhed by the Secular Court. Befides, thefe wholfome Penances were attended with the greateſt Miferies to the Penitents; for either they were condemned to perpetual Imprifonment, there to wear out a wretched Life with the Bread and Water of Affliction, or were marked on their Back and Breaſt with Croffes, that by thefe Marks of Infamy, they might be expofed to the Reproaches and Abufes of all Men; and were withal publickly whipped before the People, either in the open Street, or in the Church, and commanded many other Things, under the fpecious Name of Penance; that by this Severity, which the Penitents were forced voluntarily to fubmit to, that there might be an Appearance of Mercy in their Cafe, all others might be deterred from Herefy.

CHAP. XI.

Of the Wars againſt RAYMOND, *Father and Son, Earls of* THOLOUSE.

IN the mean while the Pope, being intent on the Extirpation of Hereticks, excited all the Princes, that they ſhould not yield them any Refuge in their Dominions, but oppreſs them with all their Force. His principal Care was to expel them from the Country of *Tholoufe*, where the *Albigenfes* were very numerous. He was perpetually preffing *Raymond* Earl of *Tholoufe* to baniſh them from his Dominions; and when he could not prevail with him, either to drive out fo large a Number of Men, or to perfecute them, he ordered him to be excommunicated as a Favourer of Hereticks. He alfo fent his Legate, with Letters to many of the Prelates, commanding them to make Inquifition againſt

I   the

the heretical *Albigenfes* in *France*, and to deftroy them, and convert their Favourers. He also wrote to *Philip* King of *France*, that he fhould take Arms
againft thofe Hereticks, and ufe his utmoft Force to fupprefs them ; that by
endeavouring to prevent the Progrefs of their Herefy, he might be under
no Sufpicion of being tainted with it himfelf. With the Pope's Legate there
came alfo twelve Abbots of the *Ciftercian* Order, preaching the Crofs againft
the *Albigenfes*, and promifing, by the Authority of *Innocent*, a plenary Remiffion of all Sins, to all who took on them the Crufade. To thefe *Dominick*
joined himfelf, and, as we have related, invented in that Expedition the Inquifition. The *Roman* Pontiffs had appointed this kind of War, which they called
Holy, againft the *Infidels* and *Saracens*, for the Recovery of the Holy Land ;
and becaufe all who lifted themfelves in that Service wore the Sign of the Crofs
near their Shoulders, they were called Crofs-bearers. They ordered it alfo to
be proclaimed, that all who would enter into that Holy War, or pioufly contribute any Money for the Pay of the Soldiers, being confeffed and penitent,
according to the Rules and Methods fixed by the Divines, fhould obtain a full
Indulgence and Remiffion of their Sins, and be abfolved from the Sentences
of Interdict, Sufpenfion, and Excommunication, and efpecially from thofe they
had incurred by firing or breaking into Churches, or by laying violent Hands
on Ecclefiafticks, and from all other Sentences, except the Crime was fo enormous, that they could not receive Abfolution but immediately from the Apoftolick See. They were allowed alfo, in the Time of a General Interdict, to
be prefent at Divine Services, and to receive the Ecclefiaftical Sacraments,
in thofe Places where they were celebrated, by a fpecial Indulgence from the
Apoftolick See, if they had been abfolved before from their refpective Sentences, as may be feen in the Bull of *Innocent* the Fourth, which begins,
Malitia hujus temporis ; that by the Hopes of this Immunity, Men might
be excited to undertake thefe Expeditions. Accordingly Multitudes came together, and chearfully engaged in them, upon the Belief that they could in
fo eafy a manner atone for their Sins. But now the Popes turned thefe Expeditions againft Chriftians themfelves, whom they loaded with the infamous
Name of Hereticks, only becaufe they were Enemies to their See, and the
exorbitant Power of it. Some of thefe Crofs-bearers *Dominick* fent into the
Country of *Tholoufe* againft the *Albigenfes*, to overcome thofe Hereticks by the
material Sword, whom he could not cut off by the Sword of the Word of
God.

[For this Fraternity *Dominick* framed certain Conftitutions, by which they
were to preferve and govern themfelves. The firft was, that fuch who entered into this Warfare, fhould take a folemn Oath, that they would endeavour with all their Might to recover, defend, and protect the Rights of the
Church againft all who fhould pretend to ufurp them ; and that in Defence of the Ecclefiaftical Effects they would expofe themfelves and their
own Eftates, and take up Arms, as often as they fhould be called on to do it
by the Prelate of the War, who was then *Dominick*, and afterwards the Mafters General of the *Dominican* Order. *Dominick* further exacted an Oath from
the

Bzovius,
a. 1204.
§ 11.

the Wives of thefe Crofs-bearers, if any of them were married, that they would not perfwade their Hufbands to forfake this War for the Support of the Ecclefiaftical Immunity ; and promifed them eternal Life for fo holy a Service. And to diftinguifh them from other Laicks, he ordered that both the Men and their Wives fhould wear Garments of white and black Colours, tho' they differed as to their Make. They alfo repeated in the canonical Hours the Lord's Prayer, and the Salutation of the Angel fo many Times, as was cuftomary in any other common Wars. It was ordained alfo, that none fhould be admitted to this facred Warfare, without a previous rigorous Examination of his Life, Manners and Faith, whether he had paid his Debts, forgiven his Enemies, made his Will, that he might be more ready for the Battle, and obtained Leave from his Wife before a Notary and proper Witneffes. The Wives of thofe who were flain in the Expedition promifed they would never marry again. This kind of Warfare was at that Time very acceptable, fo that many eagerly entered into it, that by the Slaughter of Hereticks, and the Plunder of their Goods, they might march away to Heaven.]

But becaufe even thefe Crofs-bearers did not fight againft them with that continued Zeal and Fury, that the Pope and *Dominick* would have had them, the *Dominicans* excited larger Numbers to engage in this Warfare, by the Hopes of a plenary Indulgence. The Text which their Preachers ufed to chufe for this Purpofe, was from *Pfal.* xciv. 16. *Who will rife up for me againft the Evil doers? Or who will ftand up for me againft the Workers of Iniquity?* And as they directed their whole Sermons to their own cruel Purpofe, they generally thus concluded: *You fee, moft dear Brethren, how great the Wickednefs of the Hereticks is, and how much Mifchief they do in the World. You fee alfo how tenderly, and by how many pious Methods the Church labours to reclaim them. But with them they all prove ineffectual, and they fly to the Secular Power for their Defence. Therefore our holy Mother the Church, tho' with Reluctance and Grief, calls together againft them the Chriftian Army. If then you have any Zeal for the Faith, if you are touched with any Concern for the Honour of God, if you would reap the Benefit of this great Indulgence, come and receive the Sign of the Crofs, and join your felves to the Army of the crucified Saviour.* There was indeed this Difference between thofe who took up the Crofs againft the *Saracens*, and thofe who did it againft the Hereticks, that the former wore it on their Backs, and the latter on their Breafts. And that their Zeal might by no Means grow cool, there were certain Synodical Decrees made by the Authority of the Pope, by which the Presbyters were enjoined continually to excite and warm it. *Let the Prefbyters continually and affectionately exhort their Parifhioners that they arm themfelves againft the heretical Albigenfes. Let them alfo enjoin, under the Pain of Excommunication, thofe who have taken the Crofs, and not profecuted their Vow, that they retake the Crofs and wear it.*

Raymond Earl of *Tholoufe* not being in the leaft diverted from his Purpofe by the Sentence of the Legate, who having confulted with *Dominick*, had forbid him, as a Favourer of Hereticks, the Communion of holy Things, and of the Faithful, was excommunicated by a Bull of *Innocent* himfelf, as a Defender of
Hereticks,

Uffer. de
Suc. cap.
5. §. 5.

Uffer. ibid.
c.10. §.23.

Raynold.
a. 1208.
§ 15. &c
Bzovius,
a. 1208.
§. 3, 4.

Hereticks, and all his Subjects abfolved from their Oath of Allegiance ; and Power was given to any Catholick Man, tho' without Prejudice to the Right of the fupreme Lord, not only to act againft his Perfon, but to feize and detain his Country ; under this Pretence chiefly, that it might be effectually purged from Herefy by the Prudence of the one, as it had been grievoufly wounded and defiled by the Wickednefs of the other.

The Earl, frighten'd by this Sentence, and efpecially by the terrible Expedition of the Crofs-bearers againft him, promifed Obedience, and fought to be reconciled to the Church ; but could not obtain it without delivering up to the Legate feven Caftles in his Territories for Security of Performance, and unlefs the Magiftrates of *Avignón*, *Nimes*, and *Agde*, had interceded for him, and bound themfelves by an Oath, that if the Earl fhould difobey the Commands of the Legate, they would renounce their Allegiance to him. It was farther added, that the County of *Venaifcin* fhould return to the Obedience of the Church of *Rome*. The Manner of the Reconciliation of the Earl of *Tholoufe*, was, according to *Bzovius*, thus : *The Earl was brought before the Gates of the Church of St.* Agde, *in the Town of that Name. There were prefent more than twenty Archbifhops and Bifhops, who were met for this Purpofe. The Earl fwore upon the holy Body of our Lord* Jefus Chrift, *and the Relicks of the Saints, which were expofed with great Reverence before the Gates of the Church, and held by feveral Prelates, that he would obey the Commands of the holy Roman Church. When he had thus bound himfelf by an Oath, the Legate order'd one of the facred Veftments to be thrown over his Neck, and drawing him thereby, brought him into the Church, and having fcourged him with a Whip, abfolved him. Nor muft it be omitted, that when the faid Earl was brought into the Church, and received his Abfolution as he was fcourging, he was fo grievoufly torn by the Stripes, that he could not go out by the fame Place thro' which he entered, but was forced to pafs quite naked as he was thro' the lower Gate of the Church. He was alfo ferved in the fame manner at the Sepulchre of St.* Peter *the Martyr at* New Caftres, *whom the Earl had caufed to be flain.*

However, the vaft Army of the Crofs-bearers was not idle after the Reconciliation of the Earl of *Tholoufe*, but every where attacked the Hereticks, took their Cities, filled all Places with Slaughter and Blood, and burnt many whom they had taken Captives. For in the Year 1209. *Biterre* was taken by them, and all, without any Regard of Age, cruelly put to the Sword, and the City it felf deftroy'd by the Flames. *Cæfarius* tells us, that when the City was taken, the Crofs-bearers knew there were feveral Catholicks mixed with the Hereticks ; and when they were in Doubt how to act, left the Catholicks fhould be flain, or the Hereticks feign themfelves Catholicks, *Arnold* Abbot of *Cifteaux* made Anfwer, *Slay them all, for the Lord knows who are his ;* whereupon the Soldiers flew them all without Exception.

Carcaffone alfo was deftroyed, and by the common Confent of the Prelates and Barons, *Simon* Earl of *Montfort*, of the Baftard Race of *Robert* King of *France*, [whom *Petavius* in his *Ration. Temp.* calls a Man as truly religious as valiant,] was made Governor of the whole Country, both of what was already conquered, and what was to be conquered for the future. The fame Year he

K   took

Marginal notes:
95.

§. 6.

Bzovius, *a.* 1209.

§. 1. Raynaldus, *a.* 1209. §. 22.

§. 23, 24.

took several Cities, and reduced them to his own Obedience. He cruelly treated his captive Hereticks, and put them to Death by the most horrible Punishments. *In the City* Castres *two were condemned to the Flames, and when a certain Person declared he would abjure his Heresy, the Cross-bearers were divided amongst themselves. Some contended that he ought not to be put to Death; others said 'twas plain he had been an Heretick, and that his Abjuration was not sincere, but proceeded only from his Fear of immediate Death. Earl* Montfort *consented that he should be burnt; alledging, that if his Conversion was real, the Fire would expiate his Sins; if otherwise, that he would receive a just Reward of his Perfidiousness.* In other Places also they raged with the like Cruelty. One *Robert*, who had been of the Sect of the *Albigenses*, and afterwards joined himself to the *Dominicans*, supported by the Authority of the Princes and Magistrates, burnt all who persisted in their Heresy; so that within two or three Months he caused fifty Persons, without Distinction of Sex, either to be buried alive or burnt; from whence he gained the Name of *the Hammer of the Hereticks.* *Raynold* affirms, that it ought not to be doubted but that Pope *Innocent* appointed him to this Office. At *Paris*, one *Bernard*, with nine others, of whom four were Priests, the Followers of *Almerick*, were apprehended; and being all had into a Field, were degraded before the whole Clergy and People, and burnt in the Presence of the King.

The Year following there was undertaken a new Expedition of the Cross-bearers against the *Albigenses.* They seized on *Alby*, and there put many to Death. They took *la Vaur* by Force, and burnt in it great Numbers of the *Albigenses.* They hanged *Aymerick* the Governor of the City, who was of a very noble Family. They beheaded eighty of lesser Degree, and did not spare the very Women. They threw *Girarda, Aymerick's* Sister, and the chief Lady of that People, into an open Pit, and cover'd her with Stones. Afterwards they conquered *Carcum*, and put to Death sixty Men. They also seized on *Pulchra Vallis*, a large City near *Tholouse*, and burnt in it 400 *Albigenses*, and hanged 50 more. They took *Castres de Termis*, and in it *Raymond de Termis*, whom they put in Prison, where he dy'd, and burnt in one large Fire his Wife, Sister, and Virgin Daughter, with some other noble Ladies, when they could not perswade them, by Promises or Threats, to embrace the Faith of the Church of *Rome.*

The Earl of *Tholouse*, terrified with these Successes of *Simon Montfort*, and fearing for himself and Country, raised a great Army, and had Forces sent him from the Kings of *England* and *Aragon*, to whom he was related. For he married *Joan*, Sister of the King of *England*, who had been formerly Queen of *Sicily*, and had by her a Son named *Raymond*. After her Death he married *Eleanor*, the Sister of *Peter* King of *Aragon*. But this Army was defeated with a great Slaughter by the Cross-bearers under the Command of Earl *Montfort*, and the Earl of *Tholouse* driven from his Dominions. About the Beginning of the Year 1215. in a Council of certain Archbishops and Bishops near *Montpellier*, held by the Pope's Legate, *Montfort* was declared Lord of all the Countries he had conquered, and the Archbishop of *Ambrun* was sent.

§. 25.

a. 1207.
§. 3.

a. 1210.
§. 10.
Bzovius,
a. 1209.
§. 11.

a. 1211.
§. 9.

fent to the Pope, to get him to ratify the Council's Sentence, and *Lewis*, eldeft Son of *Philip* the *French* King, confirmed him in the Poffeffion.

During thefe Tranfactions Pope *Innocent* III. in the Year of our Lord 1215. called the famous *Lateran* Council, where *Dominick* was prefent, in which there were many Decrees againft Hereticks, which were afterwards inferted in the Decretals of *Gregory*, *Tit. de Hæret. cap.* 13. To this Council fled the Earl of *Tholoufe*, with his Son *Raymond*, being difpoffeffed of his Dominions by *Montfort*. *Guido*, the Brother of Earl *Montfort*, appeared againft him, and after many Debates, Earl *Raymond* is declared, *to be for ever excluded from his Dominions, which he had govern'd ill, and ordered to remain in fome convenient Place out of his own Lands, in order to his giving fuitable Proofs of his Repentance. Four hundred Marks of Silver were affigned him yearly out of his Revenues, as long as he behaved himfelf with an humble Obedience.* But as all bore *Teftimony* to his Wife, *that fhe was a good Catholick Lady*, fhe was left in Poffeffion *of the Lands of her Dowry, provided fhe caufed the Commands of the Church to be obferved, and fuffered none to difturb the Affairs of Peace or Faith.* However, all that the Crofs-bearers had taken was adjudged to *Montfort* ; *and as to the reft, which they had not feized on,* the Church decreed *it fhould be kept by proper Perfons, to preferve the Peace, and the Faith, that there might be fome Provifion for the only Son of the Earl of* Tholoufe, *according as he fhould deferve it in Part or Whole, after his coming to Age.*

Upon this Decree of the Synod *Raymond* went into *Spain*, and his Son *Raymond* into *Provence*, where, with the Help of many auxiliary Forces, he made War on *Montfort*. He recovered fome Part of his Dominions, and even the City of *Tholoufe* it felf. Whilft *Montfort* was endeavouring to retake it with a large Army, he was killed by the Blow of a Stone, and thereby the City delivered from the Siege. Thus *Raymond* recover'd by Arms his Father's Earldom, who died in the Year 1221. and was fucceeded by this his Son, who could not obtain, with all his Endeavours, a Chriftian Burial for his Father.

As Things thus took a different Turn, fometimes according to the Pope's Wifh, at other Times contrary to it, he preffed the Inquifition as the moft effectual Remedy for the Extirpation of Hereticks. *Bzovius* relates, that at[a. 1215.] this Time many Hereticks were burnt in *Germany*, *France*, and *Italy*, and that[§. 7.] in this Year no lefs than 80 Perfons were apprehended at once in the City of *Strafbourg*, of whom but a very few were declared innocent. *If any of thefe denied their Herefy, Friar* Conrade *of Marpurg, an Apoftolical Inquifitor of the Order of* Predicants, *put them to the Trial of the Fire Ordeal, and as many of them as were burnt by the Iron, he delivered over to the Secular Power to be burnt as Hereticks ; fo that all who were accufed, and put to this Trial, a few excepted, were condemned to the Flames.*

About that Time Pope *Honorius* fent a Refcript to the Bifhop of *Boulogne*, Bzovius, anathematizing all Hereticks, and Violaters of the Ecclefiaftical Immunity,[a. 1218.] in thefe Words : *We excommunicate all Hereticks of both Sexes, of whatfoever Sect,*[§. 11.] *with their Favourers, Receivers, and Defenders ; and moreover, all thofe who caufe any Edicts or Cuftoms, contrary to the Liberty of the Church, to be obferved, unlefs*

*they remove them from their publick Records within two Months after the Publica-
tion of this Sentence. Also we excommunicate the Makers, and the Writers of those
Statutes, and moreover all Governors, Consuls, Rulers, and Counsellors of Places,
where such Statutes and Customs shall be published or kept, and all those who shall
presume to pass Judgment, or to publish such Judgments, as shall be made according
to them.*

Raynald.
a. 1221.
§. 41.

In the mean while, after *Raymond* had recovered his Father's Dominions,
the Inquisition was banished from the Country of *Tholouse.* But Pope *Honorius* III. left no Stone unturned to render the Earl obnoxious. He took Care to
let him know by his Legate, that he should be stripp'd of his Dominions as his
Father was, unless he returned to his Duty ; and by Letters bearing Date the
8th of the Calends of *November,* he confirmed the Sentence of the Legate, by
which he deprived him of all his Right in every Country that had ever been

Bzovius,
a. 1221.
§. 8.
* de pœni-
tentia.

subject to his Father ; and to give this Sentence its full Force, he commanded
the *Dominicans,* and gave them full Power to proclaim an holy War, to be
called the * Penance War, against the Hereticks. A vast Number met together at the Sound of this horrid Trumpet, and entred into this holy Society,
as they believed it, wearing over a white Garment a black Cloak, and receiving the Sacrament for the Defence of the Catholick Faith.

Raynald.
a. 1223.
§. 41.

And that the Pope might more effectually subdue the Earl of *Tholouse,* he
sent his Letters to King *Lewis,* who had succeeded his Father *Philip,* in which
he exhorts him to take Arms against the *Albigenses* in this manner. *'Tis the
Command of God, If thou shalt hear say in one of thy Cities, which the Lord
thy God hath given thee to dwell there, saying, Let us go and serve other
Gods, which ye have not known, thou shalt smite the Inhabitants of that City
with the Edge of the Sword, and shalt burn with Fire the City. Altho' you are
under many Obligations already to God, for the great Benefits received from him, from
whom comes every good Gift, and every perfect Gift, yet you ought to reckon your self
more especially obliged couragiously to exert your self for him against the Subverters of
the Faith, by whom he is blasphemed, and manfully to defend the Catholick Purity,
which many in those Parts, adhering to the Doctrine of Devils, are known to have
thrown out.*

Usser. de
Succes. c.
10. §. 46.
& seq.

During this there met a Synod at *Paris,* by the Pope's Command, about the
Affair of the *Albigenses,* at which the Pope's Legate was present, with two
Archbishops and twenty Bishops, where *Amalric,* Son of *Simon Montfort,* demanded the Restitution of the Lands of *Raymond* Earl of *Tholouse,* which had
been adjudged to him and his Father by the Pope and *French* King. *Raymond* defended himself before the Legate, affirming his Country to be free from
Heresy. He entreated the Legate to come to the several Cities of his Dominions,
to enquire of all Persons the Articles of their Belief, that if he found any holding Opinions contrary to the Catholick Faith, he might punish them according
to the Rigour of Justice : Or if he should find any City rebelling against him,
he would use his utmost Power to compel it to make proper Satisfaction. For
himself he offered, that if he had offended in any thing, which he doth not remember to have done, he would give full Satisfaction to God and Holy Church, as
became

became a faithful Chriftian, and if the Legate pleafed, would fubmit to an Examination of his own Faith: But this the Legate contemn'd ; nor could the Catholick Earl (they are the Words of *Matthew Paris*) find any Favour, unlefs he would abjure his Patrimony, and renounce it for himfelf and his Heirs. So that an Expedition of the Crofs-Bearers was again refolved on, againft Earl *Raymond*, in which *Lewis* the *French* King engaged, by the Perfuafions of *Honorius* III. and many Earls and Prelates, for Fear of the Pope, who had rather have been abfent, as thinking it unworthy to opprefs a faithful Man and good Chriftian. And as *Raymond* held feveral cautionary Lands of the King of *England*, *Honorius* fent him prohibitory Letters, to prevent his making War on the *French* King, or fending Affiftance to *Raymond*, for the Defence of them, in thefe Words:

Make no War, either by your felf, or your Brother, or any other Perfon, on Raynald. *the faid King, fo long as he is engaged in the Affair of the Faith, and Service of* a. 1226. *Jefus Chrift ; leaft by your obftructing the Matter, which God forbid, the King,* §. 24. *with his Prelates and Barons of* France, *fhould be forced to turn their Arms from the Extirpation of Hereticks to their own Defence. As for us, fince we could not excufe fuch a Conduct, and Inftance of great Indevotion, we could not impart to you our paternal Favour, which otherwife, in all proper Seafons, fhould never be wanting to you. And as we are not only ready to do you Juftice, but even Favour, as far as God enables us, we have taken Care, that whatever becomes of Hereticks and their Lands, your Rights, and thofe of other Catholicks, fhall be fafe, according to the Decrees of the forefaid Council.*

So that the *French* King undertook the Expedition, and with a large Army, fat down firft before *Avignon*. But the City was valiantly defended, and E. *Raymond* did much Damage to the Befiegers, killing many of them. A great Part of the Army alfo, with the King himfelf, died of the Difentery and other Diftempers. The Pope's Legate concealed the King's Death for fome Time, leaft the whole Army fhould be forced to break up with Difgrace from the Seige of a fingle City, without being able to take it. At length, when the City was not to be conquered by Force, the Legate had recourfe to Fraud, fetting on Conferences for Peace, and giving Hoftages for Security. And when he could not perfuade the Deputies of the City to yield it up to him, he defired that they would admit him, with the Prelates who were with him, into the City, pretending that he would examine into the Faith of the Inhabitants ; and affirming with an Oath, that he put off the Siege of the City for no other Caufe, but to feek the Welfare of their Souls. He added, that the Cry of their Infidelity had afcended to the Pope ; and that he would enquire whether they had done altogether according to the Cry which was come up unto him. The Citizens trufting to the Legate, and fufpecting nothing of Fraud, agreed under the forementioned Condition, and the Security of an Oath on both Sides, that he, with the Prelates and their Servants, fhould enter the City. But the *French*, as it had been privately agreed, perfidioufly followed them, and violently rufhed through the Gates as they were opened, and in Defiance of their Oath, took the Citizens, bound them in Chains, plundered

dered the City, killed many of the Inhabitants; and having thus, by Treachery, obtained the Victory, broke down the Towers and Walls of that noble
City. Thus *Matthew Paris* relates this Story.

After *Avignon* was thus treacherously taken, they bent all their Forces
against *Tholouse*. That City sustained the Siege for a long while, E. *Raymond* omitting nothing that became the most valiant Commander: But at
length it was forced to surrender. As for *Raymond*, after several Conferences, he
was forced to go to *Paris*, where he obtain'd Peace upon these Conditions; That

Raynald.
a. 1228.
§. 3.
Bzovius,
§. 28.

as *Tholouse*, and the Bishoprick of *Tholouse* was given to him only for his Life,
he should not leave them to any one of his Heirs; that none of them, or his
Daughters, should, after him, claim any Right, excepting those only who descended from his only Daughter *Joan*, and the Brother of King *Lewis*, Lord *Alphonsus*: That he should abjure his Heresy, and promise to be ever after in
Subjection to the See of *Rome*: That he should expel all Hereticks, nor by
any Means defend them: That he should take the Cross, and at his own Expence war five Years against the *Saracens*, and other Enemies of the Faith and
Church: That he should pay 20000 Marks of Silver, and yield up to the
King and Church, all the Country beyond the Bishoprick of *Tholouse* to the
East, on this Side and the other Side the *Rhone*. After this he surrender'd

Usser. de
Succes. cap.
10. §. 58.

himself at the *Louvre*, to the King's Guards, till his Daughter, and five of his
best fortified Castles were delivered up to his Messengers, and the Walls of
Tholouse entirely demolished. When all this was done, in the Presence of two
Cardinals of the Church of *Rome*, one Legate in *France*, and the other in *England*, he was led to the high Altar, in a Linen Garment, and with naked Feet,
and absolved from the Sentence of Excommunication. *Bernard*, in his *Croni-
con* of the *Roman* Pontiffs, relating this History, says, as *Bzovius* tells us;
*How holy a Sight it was, to see so great a Man, who for a long while could resist so
many and great Nations, led naked in his Shirt and Trouses, and with naked Feet,
to the Altar.*

CHAP. XII.

Several COUNCILS *held, and the Laws of the Emperor* FREDERICK II.
by which the Office of the INQUISITION *was greatly promoted.*

Bzovius,
a. 1228.
§. 6.

THE Earl of *Tholouse* being thus subdued, severer Laws were enacted
against Hereticks. *Raymond* himself made many Laws against them;
ordered all the Hereticks in his Country to be apprehended; and that the Inhabitants of every City or Castle should pay one Mark for every Heretick,
to the Person who took him. *Lewis* also, the *French* King, put forth a Con-

2   stitution

ftitution againft Hereticks, in which he commands the immediate Punifhment of all who fhould be adjudged Hereticks by the Bifhop, or any other Ecclefiaftical Perfon. He deprives all their Favourers of the Benefit of the Laws ; commands their Goods to be confifcated, and never to be reftored to them or their Pofterity ; and that the *Ballive* fhould pay two Marks of Silver to any one that apprehended an Heretick.

And now the Pope laboured with all his Might, to confer a greater Power on the Inquifitors, and to eftablifh for them a Tribunal, in which they might fit, and pronounce Sentence of Herefy and Hereticks, as Judges delegated from himfelf, and reprefenting his Perfon. But to this there were in the Beginning great Obftacles, the People not eafily admitting that new Tribunal, rightly judging that great Numbers would be deftroyed by the Informations of the Inquifitors. So that they were very ill looked on by all, even before they had obtained the Power of Judging : For the Magiftrates and wifer Part of the People, forefaw what muft happen, upon their being invefted with fuch an Authority ; and were far from thinking it fafe, that their Fortunes and Lives, and thofe of their Fellow-Citizens, fhould be expofed to the Pleafure of the Popes Emiffaries, and that they fhould be made entirely obnoxious to their Tyranny.

But upon the Conqueft of the *Albigenfes*, and the taking their Countries and Cities, the Pope caufed the Inquifition to proceed with greater Succefs. For in *France*, as *Pegna* obferves in *John Calderin's* Treatife about the Form of Proceeding againft Hereticks ; *There were held feveral Councils at diverfe Times and Places, of the French Archbifhops, about the Method of Proceeding againft, and punifhing Hereticks. In the Year of our Lord,* 1229. *there was a Council at* Tholoufe, *where many Statutes were made ; which were publifh'd there by* Romanus, *Cardinal Deacon of St.* Angelus, *Legate of the Apoftolick See. In the Year* 1235. *another Council was held at* Narbonne, *of the* French *Prelates, in which this Affair was more fully difcuffed than at* Tholoufe. *Afterwards, An.* 1246. *there was another Provincial Council at* Biterre, *when thefe Things were more particularly fettled, than in the two former. The Acts of thefe Councils were not difcovered for a long while, but found fome Time fince in the* Vatican *Library, and in an old MSS. Parchment, which was brought to* Rome *from the Inquifition at* Florence. *Pegna* adds, that he would foon publifh thefe Councils, with his Comments on them ; and fays they are very ufeful, and fuited to the Office of the Inquifitors of heretical Pravity. But I could never yet learn whether they have feen the Light.

Thefe were the Tranfactions in *France*. In *Rome*, about the Year 1230. *Raymond* of *Pegnaforte*, who was a *Dominican*, compiled, by the Command of Pope *Gregory* IX. the Books of *Decretals*, into which he collected all the Laws of the Councils and Popes againft Hereticks. Afterwards *Boniface* VIII. ordered a Sixth Book of the *Decretals* to be wrote. After this were added the *Clementines* and the *Extravagantes*, made on various Occafions, that the Inquifitors might want nothing for the full Exercife of their Office : And as the *Valdenfes* had ftolen into *Arragon* and *Navarre*, chiefly from the neighbouring

bouring *Languedock*, there was a Synod held at *Tarracona*, about the Year 1240. in which there were many Things enacted concerning Hereticks and their Punishments.

Even the Emperor *Frederick* II. himself, put forth many Laws against Hereticks, their Accomplices and Favourers, at *Padua*, by which he greatly promoted the Inquisition. In the first, which begins *Commissi nobis*, he ordains, that those Hereticks who were committed by the Church to the secular Court, should be put to Death without Mercy : That Converts through Fear of Death, should be imprisoned : That Hereticks, with their Abettors, where-ever they were found, should be kept in Custody till they were punished according to the Sentence of the Church : That Persons convict of Heresy, who had fled to other Places, should be taken up : That such as were relapsed should be punished with Death : That Hereticks and their Favourers, should be deprived of the Benefit of Appeal ; that their Posterity, to the second Generations, should be incapable of all Benefices and Offices ; but that their Heirs should be indemnified if they discovered their Parents Wickedness. And lastly, he takes under his imperial and special Protection, the predicant Friars, deputed for the Faith against Hereticks, in all the Parts of the Empire, and all others who were sent for, and should come for the Judgment of Hereticks, commanding the Magistrates severely to punish all convict Hereticks, after Condemnation, by the Ecclesiastical Sentence. In his second Edict, which begins, *Inconsutilem tunicam*, after expressing great Abhorrence of the Crime of Heresy, he commands all impenitent Hereticks to be burn'd with Fire, and the Favourers of the *Patarenes* to be banished. In his third, beginning *Patarenorum receptatores*, he deprives the Children of Hereticks of their Honours, unless any of them should discover one of the Sect of the *Patarenes*; and puts Hereticks themselves under the Ban, confiscating their Estates. In his forth, beginning *Catharos*, he condemns all suspected Persons as Hereticks, if they do not purge themselves within a Year ; commands his Officials to exterminate Hereticks from all Places subject to them ; orders that the Lands of the Barons shall be seized by the Catholicks, if they do not purge them from Hereticks, within a Year after proper Admonition, and ordains many Punishments against the Favourers of Hereticks, and the most severe ones against all who apostatise from the Faith : But as the Office of the Inquisition was very much promoted by these Laws, 'tis worth while to give them entire.

The first is this :

FREDERICK, *by the Grace of God, Emperor of the* Romans, *and always August, King of* Jerusalem, *and* Sicily, *to his beloved Princes, the venerable Archbishops, Bishops, and other Prelates of the Church ; to the Dukes, Marquisses, Earls, Barons, Governors, Scultets, Burgraves, Advocates, Judges, Ministers, Officials, and all other his faithful Subjects, throughout the whole Empire, to whom these Letters shall come, Greeting and all Happiness.*

I

The Care of the Imperial Government, committed to us from Heaven, and over which we preside, by the Gift of God, and the Height of our Dignity, demand the material Sword, which is given to us separately from the Priesthood, against the Enemies of the Faith, and for the Extirpation of heretical Pravity, that we should pursue, with Judgment and Justice, those Vipers and perfidious Children, who insult the Lord and his Church, as though they would tare out the very Bowels of their Mother. We shall not suffer these Wretches to live, who infect the World by their seducing Doctrines, and being themselves corrupted, more grievously taint the Flock of the Faithful. We therefore appoint and ordain, that Hereticks, of whatsoever Name, throughout our Empire, being condemned by the Church, and delivered over to the secular Power, shall be punished according to their Deserts. If any of them, after their being apprehended, shall return to the Unity of the Faith, through the Fear of Death, let them suffer perpetual Imprisonment, and do Penance according to the Canons. Farther, whatsoever Hereticks shall be found in the Cities, Towns, or other Places of the Empire, by the Inquisitors appointed by the Apostolick See, or other orthodox Persons zealous for the Faith ; let those who have Jurisdiction there, seize their Persons, at the Instance of the Inquisitors and other Catholicks, and keep them in strict Custody, till being condemned by the Censure of the Church, they perish by an accursed Death, for their denying the Sacraments of Faith, and Life. We condemn also to the same Punishment, all whom the Craft of the deceitful Enemy shall employ as Advocates, unlawfully to defend the Error of these Hereticks, especially since those who are defiled with such Wickedness, are equal in Guilt ; unless they desist upon proper Admonition, and wisely consult the Preservation of their Lives. We subject also to the same just Punishment, those, who being convicted of Heresy in any one Place, fly to another, that they may more safely pour out the Poison of their heretical Pravity ; unless in this Instance, they have a Testimony in their Favour from those who have been converted to the Faith from the same Error, or from those who have convinced them of their Heresy, which in this Case we allow may lawfully be done. We condemn also to Death, all such Hereticks, who being brought to Trial, shall abjure their Heresy when in extreme Danger of Life, if afterwards convicted of having dissembled and taken a false Oath, and of having willingly relapsed into the same Error, that thereby their vile Dissimulation may be more destructive to themselves, and their Falsehood meet with its deserved Punishment. We farther deprive Hereticks, their Receivers and Favourers, of all Benefit of Proclamation and Appeal ; being willing that every Seed of this heretical Stain should, by all Means, be extirpated out of our Empire, in which the true Faith ought ever to be preserved. Moreover, as we have received greater Favours from the Divine Mercy, and are exalted to an higher Dignity than the Children of Men, we ought to pay the more solemn Services of Gratitude. If then we manifest our Displeasure against those who contemn us, and condemn Traytors in their Persons, and by stripping their Children of their Inheritance, how justly shall we be more incensed against those who blaspheme the Name of God, and revile the Catholick Faith, and deprive, by our Imperial Authority, all Hereticks, their Receivers, Abettors and Advocates, and their Heirs and Posterity, even to the second Generation, of their temporal Estates, publick Offices and Honours, that they may continually mourn at the Remembrance of their Fathers Crimes,

L   *and*

and certainly know that God is a jealous God, punishing the Iniquities of the Fathers upon their Children. Not that we would exclude from our Mercy those, who keeping themselves free from the Heresy of their Fathers, shall discover their secret Perfidiousness: For whatever Punishment their Guilt may receive, we would not subject their innocent Children to it. We hereby also declare our Pleasure, that we appoint the Friars Predicant of the Order of Predicants, to take Care of the Faith against Hereticks, in all Parts of our Empire. We also take under our special Imperial Protection, all others whatsoever, that shall come to judge Hereticks, and grant them Leave to go, stay or return, except those who are under the Ban of the Empire; and Will that none shall injure them; but that they shall have the Assistance and Recommendation of all the Faithful in the Empire. We farther command all, and singular of you, that wheresoever, and to whomsoever of you they shall come, ye receive them kindly, and keep their Persons safe from all the Attempts of Hereticks, who may lay in wait for them, and grant them your Advice, safe Conduct and Assistance in the Execution of Affairs, so acceptable before God. And as to all Hereticks they shall discover to you in their Jurisdiction, let them be apprehended, and kept in safe Custody, till being ecclesiastically condemned, they shall suffer the deserved Punishment; as knowing that in so doing, their Obedience will be pleasing to God, and acceptable to us, viz. in assisting, with their utmost Endeavours, the said Friars to root out of all the Parts of our Empire, this new unheard of, and infamous heretical Pravity. And if any one shall be negligent and remiss in this Matter, let him know that he shall be unprofitable before God, and justly incur our highest Displeasure. Dated at Padua, Feb. 22.

The second Constitution of the Emperor *Frederick.*

FREDERICK, *by the Grace of God,* &c. *The Hereticks are endeavouring to rent the seamless Coat of our God, and raging with deceitful Words, which declare their schismatical Intention, strive to divide the Unity of the indivisible Faith it self, and to separate the Sheep from the Care of* Peter, *to whom they were committed, by the good Shepherd, to be fed. These are the ravenous Wolves within, who put on the Meekness of the Sheep, that they may the better enter into the Lord's Sheepfold. These are the worst Angels: These are Sons of Naughtiness, of the Father of Wickedness, and Author of Deceit, appointed to deceive simple Souls: These are Adders who deceive the Doves: These are Serpents, which crawl in privately, and under the Sweetness of Honey, vomit out Poison: So that whilst they pretend to administer the Food of Life, they sting with their Tail, and mingle the most bitter Poison into the Cup of Death. These Sects are not now known by their ancient Names; either that they may conceal themselves, or what is yet more execrable, not content to be called by a Name from amongst themselves, as the* Arians *were from* Arius, *and the* Nestorians *from* Nestorius; *they call themselves* Patarenes, *after the Example of the Martyrs, who suffered Martyrdom for the Catholick Faith, as though they themselves were exposed to Sufferings. These miserable* Patarenes, *who do not believe the eternal Trinity, by their complicated Wickedness offend against Three,* viz. God, *their Neighbours and Themselves. Against God, because they do not acknowledge the Son and the true Faith. They deceive their Neighbours; whilst*

under

under the Pretence of spiritual Food, they minister the Delights of heretical Pravity. But their Cruelty to themselves is yet more savage ; since, besides the Loss of their immortal Souls, they expose their Bodies to a cruel Death ; being prodigal of their Lives, and fearless of Destruction, which by acknowledging the true Faith they might escape, and which is horrible to express, their Survivors are not terrified by their Example. Against such Enemies to God and Man we cannot contain our Indignation, nor refuse to punish them with the Sword of just Vengeance ; but shall pursue them with so much the greater Vigour, as they appear to spread wider the Crimes of their Superstition, to the more evident Injury of the Christian Faith, and of the Church of Rome, *which is adjudged to be the Head of all other Churches ; insomuch that they have propagated their Falsehood from the Borders of* Italy, *and the Parts of* Lombardy, *where we are certainly informed their Wickedness 'doth more especially abound, even to our Kingdom of* Sicily. *This being most highly offensive to us, we ordain in the first Place, that the Crime of Heresy, and of every condemned Sect, whatever be the Name of it, shall be reckoned amongst the publick Crimes, as the ancient Laws declare. Yea, let such know that they shall be deemed guilty of High Treason it self. For as the Crime of Rebellion reaches to the Loss of the Life and Goods of the Persons condemned, and after they are dead, makes their Memory infamous ; let the same be observed as to the aforesaid Crime, of which the* Patarenes *are guilty. And that the Wickedness of those who walk in Darkness, because they are not Followers of God, may be discover'd, we Will, that if there be none to acccuse them, strict Enquiry be made by our Officials after such who commit these Crimes, as well as after other Malefactors ; and that all who are informed against, if there be but the least Suspicion, be examined by the Ecclesiasticks and Prelates: And if they shall find them to err in any one Point from the Catholick Faith, we, by this our present Edict, condemn the* Patarenes, *and all other Hereticks, of every Kind and Name, to suffer Death, committing them to the Punishment of the Flames, that they may be burn'd alive in publick View ; if after being pastorally admonished to forsake the dark Snares of the Devil, they will not acknowledge the God of Light. Nor are we displeased that herein we gratify them, since we are assured they can reap no other Fruit of their Error but Punishment only. For such, let no one dare to interceed with us ; if any shall presume to do it, let him know he shall justly incur our Indignation. Dated at* Padua, Feb. 22.

The third Law is this :

We condemn the Receivers, Accomplices, and Abettors of the Patarenes, *to Forfeiture of their Goods and perpetual Banishment ; who by their Care to save others from Punishment, have no Fear or Regard for themselves. Let not their Children be in any wise admitted to Honours, but always accounted infamous ; nor let them be allowed as Witnesses in any Causes, in which infamous Persons are refused. But if the Children of those who favour the* Patarenes *shall discover any one of them, so that he shall be convicted, let them, as the Reward of their Acknowledgment of the Faith, be entirely restored by our imperial Favour, to their forfeited Honour and Estate.*

The

The fourth Constitution of the Emperor *Frederick*.

We condemn to perpetual Infamy, withdraw our Protection from, and put under our Ban, * the Puritans, Patarenes, Speromists, Leonists, Arnaldists, Circumcised, Passagines, Josepines, Garatenses, Albanenses, Francisci, Begardi, Commissi, Valdenses, Romanuli, Communelli, Varini, Ortuleni, *those of the black Water, and all other Hereticks of both Sexes, and of whatsoever Name ; and ordain that their Goods shall be confiscated in such Manner, that their Children may never inherit them, since 'tis much more heinous to offend the eternal, than the temporal Majesty. But if any come under a bare Suspicion, unless by a proper Purgation they shall demonstrate their Innocence, at the Command of the Church, according to the Degree of their Suspicion, and the Quality of their Person, let them be accounted infamous by all, and as under our Ban : And if they remain such by the Space of one Year, we condemn them as Hereticks. We ordain also, by this our perpetual Edict, that our Officers and Consuls, or Rectors, whatever be their Offices, shall take a publick Oath for the Defence of the Faith ; and that they will, bona fide, study to their utmost, to exterminate from all the Lands subject to their Jurisdiction, all Hereticks specified by the Church ; so that whosoever shall at any Time henceforward be admitted into any Office, either perpetual or temporary, he shall be obliged to confirm this Edict by an Oath ; otherwise let them not be owned as our Officers or Consuls, or any Thing like it. We pronounce all their Sentences null and void. But if any temporal Lord, having been cited and admonished by the Church, shall have neglected to purge his Dominions from heretical Pravity, after a Year elapsed from the Time of his Admonition, let his Country be seized by the Catholicks, and let them possess it without Opposition, and preserve it in the Purity of the Faith; by the Extirpation of Hereticks ; saving the Right of the principal Lord, provided that he gives no Impediment or Obstruction. But let those who have no principal Lord be subject to the same Law. Furthermore, we put under our Ban, those who believe, receive, defend, and favour Hereticks ; ordaining, that if any such Person shall refuse to give Satisfaction within a Year after his Excommunication, he shall be, ipso jure, infamous, and not admitted to any Kind of publick Offices, or the like, nor to chuse any Persons to them, nor to be a Witness. Let him also be* † *Intestable ; and let him not have the Power of making a Will,*

---

* Certain Hereticks, whose Opinions are now almost equally unknown as the Reason of their Names.

† *Intestabilis* or *intestatus*. Let him be as a condemned and infamous Person. Some of the Councils had decreed, that every Man should distribute a certain Part of his Goods, the Tyth for Instance, to pious Uses, for the Redemption of his Soul ; and whosoever did not this, was esteemed a wicked Wretch, that had no Care for his Salvation. On this Account the Priests were commanded to exhort dying Persons to wash away their Sins by sacramental Confession, and to dispose of some Part of their Effects in Favour of the Church or Poor, for the Salvation of their Souls. This grew so into Use, that the Absolution and Viaticum were denied to such as did not obey the Priests Orders in this Matter, as profligate Wretches, unmindful of their Salvation ; insomuch that they made no Difference between a Person who died without making any such Disposition of his Effects, and one that slew himself, but accounted them both equally infamous. *Du Fresne in voce.* And therefore I think the Meaning of the Word *Intestabilis*, in this imperial Constitution, is, That he shall be deprived of the Liberty of making any such Disposition of his Effects to pious Uses, by Will, either to save his Soul, or prevent his being infamous.

nor of receiving any *Thing by Succeffion or Inheritance. Furthermore, let no one an-fwer for him in any Affair, but let him be obliged to anfwer others. If he fhould be a Judge, let his Sentence be of no Effect, nor any Caufes be heard before him. If an Advocate, let him never be admitted to plead in any ones Defence. If a No-tary, let no Inftruments made by him be valid. Moreover we add, that an Here-tick may be convicted by an Heretick ; and that the Houfes of the* Patarenes, *their Abettors and Favourers, either where they have taught, or where they have laid Hands on others, fhall be deftroy'd, never to be rebuilt.* Dated at Padua, Feb. 22.

Paulus Servita tells us, in his Hiftory of the *Venetian* Inquifition, that thefe Laws were made in the Year of our Lord 1244. *Bzovius* and *Raynald* refer them to the Year 1225. But whatever was the Year of their Publication, 'tis certain that the Inquifition was greatly promoted by them ; and that they were approved and confirmed, by fome of the Popes Bulls, in which they were inferted.

C H A P. XIII.

The INQUISITION *introduced into* Aragon, France, Tholoufa *and* Italy.

IN the Year of our Lord 1231. in the Month of *February*, fome of the Patarenes were difcovered in the City of *Rome :* Some of them who were impenitent were burn'd alive ; others of them were fent to the Church of *Monte Cafino*, and to *Cava*, to be there kept till they recanted. The Pope and *Roman* Senate made alfo fevere Laws againft Hereticks ; and becaufe the *Milaneze* was moft infected with Herefy, *Frederick*, by an imperial Edict, commanded *all convicted of that Crime to be delivered over to the Flames, or their blafphemous Tongues to be cut out, if the keeping them alive would prove a Terror to others* ; which *Raynald* affirms *to be a fevere, but moft juft Edict.*

Raynald. a. 1231. §. 13. §. 14, 15.

This very Year Pope *Gregory* IX. gave a famous Inftance of his Tyranny and Injuftice. *Ezelinus*, Lord of *Padua*, and Vaffal of the Emperor *Frede-rick*, conftantly adhered to his Mafter, and faithfully took the Emperors Part againft the Faction of the Pope. On this the Pope endeavoured to ren-der him infamous by the Charge of Herefy ; that under this fpecious Pre-tence he might expel him his Dominions : But as he failed in this, he ftirred up his Children againft him this very Year, that being delivered by them into his Power, he might punifh him as he pleafed. In order to this, he fent Letters to *Ezeline*, befeeching him to take better Meafures, and admonifhed him to renounce his Errors. A Copy of thefe Letters he fent to his two Sons, young *Ezeline* and *Alterick*, who pretended to abhor their Father's Wickednefs, and promifed *Gregory* of their own Accord, as *Raynald* relates, that they would deliver

§. 10, &c.

deliver their miserable Father into the Hands of the Censors of the Faith, if he persisted obstinately in his Wickedness, that they might not lose the Inheritance of their Ancestors. Upon this the Pope gave them to understand, that he had deferred coming to Extremities against their Father for their Sake, whom he believed still to continue in the true Worship of God, that they might not be involved in his Misfortune ; for, says he, the Crime of Heresy, like that of High Treason, disinherits the Children. Then he beseeches and commands them, that they would use all possible Means to deter their Father from Heresy, and the Protection of Hereticks, and that if he despised their Admonitions, they would consult their own Safety, by sending him, as they had promised, before the Pope's Tribunal. *Nor is it to be wonder'd at,* adds *Raynald, that this Advice should be given to the Sons against their own Father, since the Cause of the divine Being, of whom all Paternity is named, is to be preferred to all human Affections.*

Bzovius, a. 1232. §. 8. The Year following, 1232. the Inquisition was brought into *Aragon.* The Bishop of *Hyesca* in *Aragon* was reported to err in Matters of Faith. Upon this *Gregory* committed the Office of making Inquisition against him to Friar - *Peter Caderite,* of the *Predicant* Order, and commanded *James* King of the *Aragons,* that he should not suffer him, or those whose Advice or Counsel he should think fit to make use of, to be injured by any Means whatsoever. And

§. 9. that he might entirely extirpate Heresy out of the Province of *Tarracon,* he gave Commission to the Archbishop of *Tarracon* and his Suffragans, to constitute Inquisitors against heretical Pravity of the Order of *Predicants,* by a Bull, in these Words : *Since the Evening of the World is now declining,* &c. *we admonish and beseech your Brotherhood, and strictly command you by our written Apostolick Words, as you regard the divine Judgment, that with diligent Care you make Enquiry against Hereticks, and render them infamous, by the Assistance of the Friars Predicants, and others whom you shall judge fit for this Business ; and that you proceed against all who are culpable and infamous, according to our Statutes lately published against Hereticks, unless they will from the Heart absolutely obey the Commands of the Church ; which Statutes we send you inclosed in our Bull ; and that ye also proceed against the Receivers, Abettors, and Favourers of Hereticks, according to the same Statutes. But if any will quite abjure the heretical Plague, and return to the Ecclesiastical Unity, grant them the Benefit of Absolution according to the Form of the Church, and enjoin them the usual Penance.* Amongst the Inquisitors appointed by them, Friar *Raymond Peciafortius Barninonensis* was particularly famous, who wrote a Formulary, of the Manner of proceeding against Hereticks, beginning, *I believe that Hereticks,* &c. which was of so great Authority, that *Gregory* enjoined *William* Archbishop Elect of *Tarracon* to follow it in every thing. *Bzovius* gives us this Formulary entire, in his Annals, under the Year 1235. §. 5.

a. 1234. §. 8. In *France* there were not wanting some, who stirred up the Remains of the *Albigenses,* so that, as *Bzovius* says, they very grievously oppressed the Inquisitors and other Persons, appointed by the Apostolick See for the Direction and Defence of the Catholick Faith [*]. *Gregory* IX. excited *Lewis* the King

[*] *i. e.* Perhaps they strove to prevent so intolerable a Yoke being put on their Necks.

against

aginft them, and advifed him to join with the Archbifhop of *Vienne*, fome Perfon famous for his Wifdom and Juftice, who might know what pertained to the
Ecclefiaftick Right, what to the Royal, and what to the Rights of others.
He alfo exhorted *Blanche* the Queen to perfwade her Son to perfect fo righteous a Work. The fame Author tells us, that the fame Year, after great §. 24.
ftruggling, the Inquifition was brought into *Tholoufe*, upon the firft Day of
the Feftival of *Dominick*, but not without a great Tumult of the People, raifed
by a feditious Sermon of a filly Monk, upon Occafion of the Death of a
certain Matron of *Tholoufe*, who lived near the Convent of the *Predicants*, and
had been hereticated before fhe died. " When this came to be publick, Friar
" *William Arnaldi*, an Inquifitor, condemned her for an Heretick, and left
" her to the fecular Court. After this the Prior of the Friars *Predicants*,
" *Fu Pontius*, of *Agde*, explaining thofe Words of *Ecclefiaftic*. xlviii. Elias
" *the Prophet rofe as Fire, and his Word burnt like a Torch*, to a vaft Company
" that had met together about Nine, and adapting his Words to the Feftival
" and the prefent Bufinefs, turned himfelf, and bowed and bent to the *Eaft*
" and *Weft*, to the *North* and *South*, and cried out towards every Part with as
" loud a Voice as he could, repeating it oftentimes, *In the Name of God, and*
" *his Servant St.* Dominick, *I do from this Hour renounce all Faith with Here-*
" *ticks, their Favourers, and Believers*. Then he bawled out again : *I adjure*
" *the Catholicks, in the Name of God, that laying afide all Fear, they would give*
" *their Teftimony to the Truth :* And thus left off. About feven Days after this
" Meeting many came in, by whofe Means the Inquifitors found out a Way
" to the Receffes of Darknefs. Many of them abjured their Herefy, fome dif-
" covered others, and promifed that at a proper Opportunity they would de-
" tect more." However, the Inquifitors were the Year following ejected from
Tholoufe. But that they were reftored there again, we learn from *Luke Wad-* Bzovius,
ding, who in his Hiftory of the Friars Minors, relates, that in the Year 1238. *a.* 1235.
there were at *Tholoufe* Friar *William Arnaldi* of the *Predicant* Order, and *Sera-* §. 4.
phinus de S. Tiberio of the Minors, Inquifitors of Hereticks. The fame Author
gives us alfo the Epiftle of *Gregory* IX. to the Deacon of the Order of Friars
Minors in *Navarre*, and to Mafter *Peter de Leedegaria*, a Predicant Friar, living
at *Pampilona*, in which, begins, *Rumor*, &c. in which, amongft other Things,
there is this : *Since therefore, according to the Office enjoined us, we are bound*
to root out all Offences from the Kingdom of God, and as much as in us lies to oppofe
fuch Beafts, we deliver into your Hands the Sword of the Word of God, which, ac-
cording to the Words of the Prophet, Jer. xlviii. 10. *ye ought not to keep back from*
Blood ; but, infpired with a Zeal for the Catholick Faith, like Phineas, *make dili-* Exod-
gent Inquifition concerning thefe peftilent Wretches, their Believers, Receivers, and xxxii. 33.
Abettors, and proceed againft thofe who by fuch Inquifition fhall be found guilty,
according to the canonical Sanctions, and our Statutes, which we have lately pub-
lifhed to confound heretical Pravity, calling in againft them, if Need be, the Affiftance
of the fecular Arm. Given at the Lateran, 8 *Cal.* Maii, *An.* 12.

It can't be doubted that the Office of the delegated Inquifition was in thefe Bzovius,
Times introduced into *Italy*, becaufe the Inhabitants of *Placentia* drove out *a.* 1234.
        2   from §. 25.

from their City Friar *Rowland* the Inquifitor in the Year 1234. The Year following the Pope committed the Office of the Inquifition to the Prior of St. *Mary ad gradus*, and to Friar *Radulph*, a Predicant at *Viterbo*, commiffioning them to enquire out all Hereticks coming from other Cities, and to abfolve from Cenfures fuch who abjured their Herefy, and reconciled themfelves to the Church. Upon this Affair he gave Letters to both of them at *Peroufe* the fecond of the Ides of *Auguft*, and ninth Year of his Pontificate. But two Years after, 13 Cal. of *June*, and the eleventh of his Pontificate, at *Viterbo*, he fent Letters to the Provincial of *Lombardy*, a Predicant, by which he invefted him with the Power of making Inquifitors. The Letters begin thus : *Ille humani*, &c. I think it worth while to give you them entire, becaufe they very diftinctly reprefent the Office given to the Inquifitors. After beginning with the ufual Complaint of the Rife of Herefy, he

enjoins the Inquifitors their Office in thefe Words : *We therefore being willing to prevent the Danger of fo many Souls, entreat, admonifh, and befeech your Wifdom, and ftrictly command you by thefe Apoftolick Writings, as you have any Regard for the Divine Judgment, that you appoint fome of the Brethren committed to your Care, Men learned in the Law of the Lord, and fuch as you know to be fit for this Purpofe, according to the Limitations of your Order, to be Preachers General to the Clergy and People affembled, where they can conveniently do it ; and in order the more effectually to execute their Office, let them take into their Affiftance fome difcreet Perfons, and carefully enquire out Hereticks, and fuch as are defamed for Herefy. And if they find out either any really culpable, or fuch who are defamed, let them proceed againft them according to our Statutes, lately publifhed againft Hereticks, unlefs upon Examination they will abfolutely obey the Commands of the Church. Let them alfo proceed againft the Receivers, Defenders, and Abettors of Hereticks, according to the fame Statutes. But if any will abjure their heretical Defilement, and return to the Ecclefiaftical Unity, let them have the Favour of Abfolution according to the Form of the Church, and be enjoined the ufual Penance. But let them be more efpecially careful, that fuch who appear to return, don't commit Impiety under the fpecious Pretence of Piety, and the Angel of* Satan *thus transform himfelf into an Angel of Light. Therefore let them perufe the Statutes which we have thought fit to publifh concerning this Affair, that they may beware of their Subtlety, according to the Difcretion given them of the Lord. And that they may more freely and effectually execute the Office committed to them in all the Premiffes, we, confiding in the Mercy of Almighty God, and the Authority of the bleffed Apoftles* Peter *and* Paul, *remit for three Years the Penance enjoined them, to all who fhall attend their Preaching for twenty Days in their feveral Stations, and likewife to thofe who fhall give them Affiftance, Counfel or Favour, in their Endeavours to fubdue Hereticks, their Abettors, Receivers, and Defenders, in their fortified Places and Caftles. And as for thofe who fhall happen to die in the Profecution of this Affair, we grant a plenary Pardon of all their Sins for which they are contrite in their Hearts, and which they confefs with their Mouths. And that nothing may be wanting to the faid Friars in their profecuting the forefaid Bufinefs, we grant them, by the Tenour of thefe Prefents, full Power of involving, under the Ecclefiaftical Cenfure, all*

I   *who*

who contradict and rebel against them. We also grant them the Power to restrain, under the same Censure, from the Office of Preaching, which by no means belong to them, the questuary Predicants, whose Business it is simply to ask only charitable Supports, and to sell an Indulgence, if they should happen to have one.

In the same Year 1235. 17 Cal. *June*, Pope *Gregory* commanded the Bishop of *Huesca*, the Prior of *Barcelona*, and Friar *William Barbarano*, a Predicant, that they should not suffer the Office by any Means to relax, but should make Inquisition against Hereticks in the Province of *Tarracon*, and proceed according to the Canons. He also appointed Friar *Robert*, a Predicant, Inquisitor General against Hereticks in the whole Kingdom of *France*, and commanded him so to proceed in the Causes committed to him, as that the Innocent should not perish, and that Iniquity should not remain unpunished. The Bull of this Commission is extant, dated at *Perouse*, 10 Cal. of *September*, and 9th Year of his Pontificate ; in which he prescribed the Form of Penance to such as abjured their Heresy, and ordained many other Things against Hereticks, and commanded the Provincial of the *Teutonick* Order of Predicants, that he should chuse fit Persons out of all *Germany*, to preach in every Place the Word of the Cross against the Hereticks and *Saracens*.

CHAP. XIV.

Concerning the first Hindrances to the Progress of the INQUISITION.

ALtho' the Pope perpetually pressed the Inquisition, yet it was with great Difficulty admitted. The Novelty of the Tribunal, by which the Laity were excluded wholly from all Judgment against Hereticks, greatly offended Men. They were indeed willing to leave to the Ecclesiasticks the Affair of Doctrine, to judge what was orthodox and what heretical. But they contended that the Judgment of their Persons belonged to them ; *viz.* to determine whether any Person professed any Opinion, condemned by the common Judgment of the Clergy, and so became an Heretick ; and especially they believed that it belonged to their Tribunal to pronounce Sentence against the guilty. Whereas they now found themselves wholly excluded from all Share in it by this new Tribunal, which the Pope was endeavouring every where to erect. All the Power left to the secular Magistrate was only to put to Death those who were condemned for Hereticks by the Ecclesiasticks, whereby he became a mere Slave to the Inquisitors, as being obliged to execute their Sentence with a blind Obedience, without any Cognizance of the Crime. This was the Case even of some, who otherwise were zealous Defenders of the Papal Authority. Amongst others, *Lewis* King of *France* made a Law, by which he commanded, that his Subjects, when cited before the Ecclesiastical Tribunals, should not appear to plead their Cause ; and that if they were censured for Contumacy, the Goods of those who had passed the Censure should

Raynald.
a. 1236.
§. 31, *&c.*

              M   be

be feized by the Civil Magiftrates, till it was recalled. The Pope thought this Law unjuft, and injurious to the prelatical Authority. And therefore, that their Power might not be wholly fuppreffed by this Law, he fent Letters to the King, in which he fet before him the Examples of *Charles* the Great, *Theodofius*, and *Valentine* the Emperors, who had greatly enlarged the Power of the Bifhops, and yet had not obfcured the Glory of their own Majefty, but rather increafed it, and admonifhed him to repeal thofe Laws, which were contrary to the Ecclefiaftical Liberty. He then put him in Mind of the Sentence pronounced by *Honorius*, by which the Makers of fuch Laws expofed themfelves to Anathema's, unlefs they repealed them within two Months. The King, who was foliciting the Title of the obedient Son of the Church, yielded to the Papal Severity, and was entreated by *Gregory*, that he would finifh the Work of cutting off all the Remains of Herefy in the Province of *Tholoufe*, and compel Earl *Raymond* to perform his Promife.

§. 39, &c.   The Earl had bound himfelf by an Oath to extirpate Herefy, and to lead an Army into the Holy Land, when he was at *Paris*, and had made Peace with the *French* King and the Church. But as there happen'd a Tumult at *Tholoufe* againft the Cenfors of the Faith, raifed by thofe who were faid to be infected with Herefy, and as there was not an immediate Stop put to it upon its firft Beginning, the Earl feem'd to have broke his Promife, and to cherifh Hereticks, becaufe he did not reftrain their Fury. Upon this the Pope feverely rebuked him, and, amongft other Things, fays : *That he had often hinder'd the Inquifition againft Hereticks, by commanding to be obferved in their Favour certain Forms, injurious to the Statutes of the Pope himfelf, and contrary to the Laws relating to the Inquifition of Hereticks ; that he had fuffered many Perfons condemned as Hereticks to dwell publickly in his Country ; that he had given Protection to others, who from other Places had fled to him ; that his Counfellors and Servants were fufpected and defamed of Herefy, &c. So that he had not been afraid to declare himfelf a Favourer, Receiver, and Defender of Hereticks, and their Abettors ; and that tho' he had been admonifhed on thefe Accounts, he had not been careful to amend.* The Pope gave frefh Inftructions to his Legate on this Affair, and ordered him to renew the *Tholoufe* Statutes, to reject all the Edicts and Laws, which infringed the Ecclefiaftical Liberty, to remove from the publick Counfels all fufpected or defamed of Herefy. And by other Letters he was order'd to caufe all the Houfes of the *Tholoufe* Hereticks to be demolifhed.

Raynald.   He alfo moft earneftly entreated the *French* King, that he would ufe the
a. 1236.   Power committed to him by God, to compel the Earl and Confuls of *Tholoufe* to
§. 45.   amend the aforefaid Crimes, and do his utmoft to extirpate Herefy. Then he admonifhed him to force the Earl to go to *Jerufalem* the next *March*, and fend his own Brother *Alphonfus*, to whom *Raymond*'s Daughter had been betrothed, to adminifter the Affairs of the Earldom of *Tholoufe*.

But the Tribunal of the Inquifition was not only hateful to the People by reafon of its Novelty, but becaufe the Inquifitors themfelves render'd it hateful by
Du Cange their exceffive Cruelty. Amongft thefe, one Friar *Robert* was not the leaft.
in voce In- He was furnamed *Bulgarus*, becaufe he had cruelly perfecuted and deliver'd
quifitio.
                                                                        over.

over to the Fire the *Valdenses*, then called *Bulgarians* ; or, according to others, becaufe he himfelf had been a *Bulgarian* or *Valdenfian*, and upon his forfaking them, had enter'd into the Order of the *Dominicans*.   He was Inquifitor of the Faith in the *Netherlands*, and *France*, a Man of an auftere Temper, fupported by the Royal Authority of *Lewis*, who commanded him to burn many who were infeted with Herefy.   But when afterwards the faid Friar, according to *Mat.Paris*, under the Year 1236. abufed the Authority given him, and tranf-greffed the Bounds of Modefty and Juftice, growing haughty, powerful and terrible, condemning to the fame Punifhment the Innocent as well as Guilty, he was put out of his Office by the Pope's Order, and fhut up in perpetual Imprifonment.   Afterwards *Fulco* exercifed the fame Severity in *Languedoc*, upon Account of whofe exceffive Cruelty, *Philip* the Friar fent in the Year 1301. certain Perfons to enquire into his Mifmanagement, and ordered that for the future thofe who were fufpeted of Herefy fhould be put in the Royal Prifons at *Tholoufe*, and that the King's Subjets fhould not be detained by the Inquifitor's Decree, without the Bifhop's Advice firft had, and the Affiftance of the Royal Senefchal.   It would have been well if thefe two Perfons only had exceeded the Bounds of juft Judgment ; but in Reality this was the Fault of moft of them.   And therefore, that the Minds of Men might not be too much exafperated, they added fome of the Order of the Friars Minors to the Predicants, by their Gentlenefs to temper the others Rigour.   This was atu-ally done in the Year 1238.

And indeed this Tribunal of the Inquifition was the fitteft Method in the World for Perfons to opprefs their Enemies, under the Pretence that they were infeted with Herefy, and was abufed to this Purpofe by political Men as well as Ecclefiafticks, if it be true what *Raynald* writes of the Emperor *Frede-rick*, that he was greedy of Revenge, and ufed by various Pretences and Sub-ornation of Crimes, to rage againft thofe, whom he inwardly hated.   To this Purpofe he pretended great Zeal to cut off Hereticks, and appointed that in all the Provinces and Places of Note there fhould be a Judge, together with a Prelate, to take Cognizance of the Examination of Perfons by Torture ; and for this pious Precaution, as it appeared, he was commended by Pope *Gregory*.   But he improved this to gratify his Revenge, caufing many inno-cent Catholicks, who had incurred his Difpleafure, to be accufed of Herefy, and burnt alive, to the great Grief and Offence of all ; infomuch that *Gre-gory* gravely admonifhed him, that he fhould endeavour to extirpate Hereticks, and not deftroy the Catholicks.

However, the *Roman* Pontiffs did much more infolently abufe their Power. For they were not afraid to brand with the Name of Herefy, and to proceed againft as Hereticks, Kings and Princes, and even the Emperor himfelf, if they would not own their unbounded Power, and do every thing according to their Beck.   Of this we have a famous Inftance in the Emperor *Frederick :* He had made very fevere Laws againft Hereticks, greatly increafed the Authority of the Inquifition, and in the Year 1236. having found fome Perfons at *Palence* infeted with Herefy, he ordered eternal Marks of Infamy to be imprinted on their

M 2

Marginal notes:
Raynald. *a.* 1238. §. 60.

Du Cange, *ibid.*

a. 1233. §. 33, 34.

Apud Gregor. *Ep.* 243.

Ep. 244.

Raynald. *a.* 1236. §. 50.

their Faces with a red hot Iron. And yet he could not efcape the Pontiff's
a. 1239. Thunder : For in the Year 1239. Pope *Gregory* pronounced the Sentence of
§.2, &c. Excommunication againft him, and abfolved all his Subjeds from the Obligation of any Duty or Oath they were under to him. *Frederick* gave an abundant Anfwer, and purged himfelf of the Crimes objected to him in this Sentence, in which there was no mention of Herefy. But the Pope fent Letters
to all the Prelates, and to the Chriftian Kings and Princes, in which he
charged him with various Herefies; and, amidft others, with this : *That
he conftantly affirmed, that he could not be excommunicated by him as the Vicar of
Chrift* ; *thus affirming that the Power of Binding and Loofing was not in the
Church, delivered by our Lord to* Peter *and his Succeffors. Whilft he thus afferts
Herefy, his own Argument concludes againft himfelf, fhewing by Confequence that he
hath wrong Sentiments concerning the other Articles of the orthodox Faith, as he endeavours to take away that Privilege of Power granted by the Word of God to the
Church, upon which the Faith is founded.*

Neither did the Pope reft till he had put in Execution the Sentence he had
a. 1245. pronounced againft the Emperor *Frederick.* For in the Year 1245. *Innocent*
§. 1, &c. calls a Council in *France,* and therein condemns and excommunicates him, de-
§. 45. prives him of his Empire, and abfolves his Subjects from their Oath of Fidelity, and by his Apoftolick Authority firmly and ftrictly forbids all Perfons to
obey him any more as Emperor or King, and decrees that whofoever fhould
from henceforward yield him Counfel, or Aid, or Favour, as Emperor or
King, fhould be *ipfo facto* excommunicated ; and that the Electors of the Empire might freely proceed to the Choice of another Emperor, to fucceed him in
his Place.

a. 1246. *Innocent* IV. procured *Henry* Landgrave of *Thuringheim* to be created King of
§. 3. §. 17. the *Romans,* that by his Affiftance he might drive *Frederick* from the Empire.
Frederick, to purge himfelf of the Crime of Herefy, fent Letters to feveral
Chriftian Princes, in which he defended himfelf againft the Charge. He alfo
commanded the Archbifhop of *Palermo,* the Bifhops of *Pavia, Monte Caffino,*
and *Cava,* the Abbots of *Cafanova, Roland,* and *Nicholas* a Predicant, diligently
to enquire and examine him concerning his Sentiments as to the Syftem of Chriftian Faith, and other Articles and Myfteries of Religion. This being done,
and an Inftrument drawn up, he appointed them his Procurators, that they
fhould make Oath before the *Roman* Pontiff, that *Frederick* having been examined, rightly agreed with all Chriftians in every Article of Faith, and was at
the fartheft Diftance from Herefy. They had a very unwelcome Reception,
as being the Procurators of a Man expelled the Company of the Faithful, and
for this Wickednefs were faid to deferve Punifhment rather than Audience. But
when they affirmed themfelves to be the Meffengers of a pure Chriftian Man,
the Affair was ordered to be examined by three Cardinals of the *Roman* Church,
who pronounced that Purgation trifling and void, inafmuch as they had no
Authority to take his Examination. On this he commanded *Frederick,* that
if he would regularly purge himfelf, and fubmit to a right Examination, he
fhould repair to the Apoftolick See, without the Noife and Terror of Arms,
attended

attended only by a fmall Retinue; and proper Security fhould be given, that no Injury and Difturbance fhould be offered to him or his.

After the Imperial Power was thus infulted, no one will wonder that the like Procefs fhould be carried on againft *Ezeline*, Lord of *Padua*, and zealoufly at-tach'd to the Emperor's Party. For in the Year 1248. the fame Pope *Inno-* a. 1248. *cent*, as we learn from his Letters to the Prelates of the *Milaneze*, the Mar-§. 25, 26. quifate of *Trevifo* and *Emilia* *, pronounced the Ecclefiaftical Cenfures againft him on the Day of the Feftival of the holy Sacrament. He had appointed Inquifitors of the Faith againft him before, becaufe he had been afperfed with the Report of Herefy. In order to refute the Charge, he fent Meffengers to *Rome*, who bound themfelves by a folemn Oath, in the Name of *Cæfar*, to declare that his Sentiments were right concerning the Catholick Faith. But as that Purgation was not allowed of by the Bifhop of *Sabine*, who was ap-pointed to take the Report of the Meffengers, nor by the Pope himfelf; be-caufe, as he pretended, the Importance of the Affair required the guilty Perfon to be prefent; he fixed him the Calends of *Auguft* for the Day in which he was to clear himfelf; and according to the Papal Manner provided for his Security; hereby demonftrating, that he muft entertain no Hopes of Re-conciliation, unlefs he would in all Things fubject himfelf to the Beck and Pleafure of the Pope, and own him as fupreme Judge in all Caufes what-foever.

But as *Ezeline* did not appear, the Pope, in the Year 1251. deputed the Raynald. Bifhop of *Trevifo*, and the Prior of the Predicants at *Mantua*, to let him know a. 1251. that he fhould be fubject to all the Punifhments ordain'd againft Hereticks, §. 36, 37. unlefs he appeared before the holy See within the next Calends of *Auguft*, and fubmitted himfelf to receive his Commands: That if he refufed to ap-pear, they fhould publickly declare, that he was to be avoided by all, as one defiled with Herefy, that his Body might be feized on, his Goods plundered; and that an Army of Crofs-Bearers fhould be fent againft him and his Fol-lowers. This Procefs lafted fome Time before the Pope pronounced the long intended Sentence. At length, in the Year 1254. on the Day of the Feftival a. 1254. of the Sacrament, *Ezeline* was condemn'd for Herefy, and fubjected by the §. 35, 36. Pope's Sentence, to all the Punifhments of Hereticks. *Innocent* publifh'd a moft bitter Sentence againft him, in which he charged him with the moft hor-rid Crimes. He commanded alfo all the Prelates, that they fhould publifh the Condemnation of *Ezeline*, for Herefy; and punifh all who adhered to him, with the Punifhments ordain'd againft the Followers of Hereticks. There are extant alfo the Pope's Letters upon the fame Subject, to *Alberic* his Brother; by which he gave him all his Brother's Effects, whom he had condemned to the Punifhments of Hereticks, and confirmed the Sentence of *William*, King of the *Romans*, by which he condemned him for Rebellion, and deprived him of all his Lands that were fubject to the Empire.

---

* Containing the Dutchies of *Parma*, *Modena*, *Mirandola*, and Part of *Mantua*.

§. 27.   *Raymond*, also Earl of *Tholouse*, quite oppressed with the several Misfortunes
we have before related, submitted his Neck to the Papal Yoke : For he signified to the Pope, that he desired that heretical Pravity might be quite destroy'd, and wholly extirpated out of his Dominions.   The Pope highly extolled him for so pious a Zeal ; and to oblige him, as he says, commanded
the Bishop of *Agen*, to make Inquisition after, and punish the Hereticks of
Tholouse. *William de Podo Laurentii*, as *Raynald* cites him, relates, that *Raymond* order'd about eighty Persons, who either confessed, or were convicted
of Heresy, in Judgment before him, to be burned with Fire in the City of
Agen, in the Place called *Berlaigas*.   But he did not long survive it, dying
a. 1249.   in the Year 1249. and was the last Earl of *Tholouse* of that Line.   After his
§. 8, 9.   Death, the Earldom went to his Son-in law, the Earl of *Poictiers*, and he
dying without Issue, it devolved to the Kings of *France*.

Bzovius,   The Office of the Inquisition was more than ten Years before this brought
a. 1247.   into *Lombardy*.   *Innocent* IV. *An.* 1247. willing to establish it, commanded
§. 4, & 6.   Friar *John Vicentinus*, a Predicant, that he should constantly oppose the Hereticks in *Lombardy*, and gave him Power to absolve those who would abjure
their Heresy, and return to the Church, and of granting Indulgencies to such
who would attend upon his Sermons ; and forbid that any of the Superiors of
the same Order, the Provincial, or Master General, should hinder him in the
Office of the Inquisition, or remove him from it.

a. 1248.   From the neighbouring Province of *Tholouse* the purer Doctrine had spread
§. 3.   it self into the Province of *Narbonne* and *Aragon :* Wherefore *Innocent* IV. in a
Letter, sent to *Raymond Penniafortius*, Master of the Predicants, and to the Provincial of *Spain*, commands that they should depute, by the Pope's own Authority, some of the Friars of his Order in the Kingdom of *Aragon*, to be Inquisitors of heretical Pravity, in the Province of *Narbonne*, in that District only
that was subject to *James*, King of *Aragon* ; and enjoin them, that they
should effectually proceed against Hereticks, their Abettors, &c. fearing no
one in this Affair, but God, according to the Form published by *Gregory*, and
renewed by himself.

But *Luke Wadding* relates, That in the Year 1232. Inquisitors were appointed in *Aragon*, by the Command of Pope *Gregory* IX. the King desiring
them of the Pope, at the Instigation of *Raymond Penniafortius*, his Confessor.
Not long after a Synod was held at *Tarracon*, which made many Decrees
against Hereticks ; and an Inquisition was there set up, after the Manner
of that at *Tholouse*, which was carried on with the greatest Rigour against
the Hereticks which arose in that Time, and which lasted more than an
whole Age.   For in the Life of *Nicholas Eymerick*, a Predicant Monk, and
Author of the Directory of the Inquisitors, 'tis related, that *Eymerick* flourished in the Times of *Urban* V. and *Gregory* XI. Popes, and of *Peter* IV. King
of *Aragon :* That he was created Inquisitor General about the Year of our
Lord 1358. and succeeded *Nicholas Rosell*, *An.* 1356. and made a Cardinal :
That he died the 4th of *January*, *An.* 1393. having strenuously kept up the
Office of the Inquisition against Hereticks, 44 Years successively.   Upon his

.   I   Death

Death the Inquifition remained in Force in that Kingdom; but gradually funk of it felf, upon the entire Extinction of the *Valdenfes.*

[About this Time alfo, the Inquifition was introduced into *Burgundy.* For *Des Loix,* about the Year 1223. the Friars Predicants, of the Order of *Dominick,* were *p.* 129,&c. received in *Befancon :* For whereas fome of the *Valdenfes* had retired into the Country of *Burgundy, John* Earl of *Burgundy,* at the Inftigation 'of the *Dominicans,* obtained a Bull from Pope *Innocent* IV. beginning, *Zelo mogno zelantes,* dated *An.* 1247. 12 Cal. *Sep.* by which the Inquifition was erected in the Territories of *Befancon.* The fame Pope had, in the preceding Year, by a Bull, dated 12 Cal. *Dec.* beginning, *Ille humani generis,* &c. admonifhed the Prior and Convent of the Friars Predicants at *Bifancon,* that they fhould appoint Inquifitors in that Country; and after an Exhortation to the whole Order, fhould make Inquifition againft Hereticks. But this Tribunal by degrees came alfo to nothing; becaufe, when the *Valdenfes* were extinguifhed, there were no others for the Inquifition to proceed againft. But in thefe laft Ages it was reftored again.]

C H A P. XV.

The more happy and fpeedy Progress *of the* Inquisition.

THUS far the Pope had laboured hard in promoting the Affair of the Inquifition. But as there were perpetual Quarrels between the Popes and the Emperor, the Pope's Succefs was not anfwerable to his Wifhes, as being more intent upon promoting War, than enquiring into, and judging of Herefies. But after the Death of the Emperor *Frederick,* the Affairs of *Germany* being in great Diforder, and *Italy* without any Prince; Pope *Innocent* IV. feeing all Things become fubject to his Power, in the *Milaneze* and other Parts of *Italy,* determined to extirpate all Herefies, which had greatly encreafed in the preceding War : And becaufe the *Dominican* and *Francifcan* Friars had greatly affifted the Pope againft Hereticks, and were animated with a fiery Zeal, he committed this Affair to them, rather than to any others whatfoever. He therefore erected a Tribunal, folely for the Bufinefs of the Faith; and gave to the Inquifitors perpetual Power to adminifter Judgment in his Name in this Caufe.

His firft and principal Care was to purge *Italy* from Herefy, which was neareft to himfelf, and moftly fubject to his Power; and therefore he erected feveral Tribunals of the Inquifition therein. In the Year 1251. he created *Vivianus Bergomenfis,* and *Peter* of *Verona,* both Friars Predicant, Inquifitors of the Faith in *Milan,* and gave them thefe Letters, in which he taxes even the Emperor *Frederick,* as a Favourer of Herefy. *Innocent,* &c. *Whilft that* Raynald. *perfidious Tyrant lived, we could not fo freely proceed againft this Plague, efpecially* a. 1251. in §. 34, 35.

in Italy, *through his Oppofition* ; *who, inftead of putting any Check to it, rather encouraged it. When he became evidently fufpected of this, he was condemn'd by us in the Council of* Lyons, *as well as on Account of his many other enormous Exceffes : And therefore we ftrictly command and enjoin your Difcretion, by thefe our apoftolick Writings, as you expect the Remiffion of your Sins, that ye profecute this Affair of the Faith, which lies principally upon our Heart, with all your Powers and with fervent Minds ; and that ye go perfonally to* Cremona *; fince we have thought proper to depute for the fame Bufinefs other difcreet Perfons in the other Cities and Places of* Lombardy *; and that after having called a Council in that Diocefe, ye do carefully and effectually labour to extirpate heretical Pravity out of that City and its Diftrict ; and that if you find any Perfons culpable upon this Account, or infected, or defamed, unlefs upon Examination they will abfolutely obey the Commands of the Church, ye proceed againft them, their Receivers, Abettors and Favourers, by the apoftolick Authority, according to the canonical Sanctions, laying afide all Fear of Men ; and that if there be need, ye call into your Affiftance the fecular Arm. Dated the Ides of* June, *and eighth Year of our Pontificate.*

This *Peter* of *Verona* appointed, that amongft other Statutes of the Republick of *Milan*, many alfo fhould be made and obferved againft heretical Pravity. But as he was going from *Como* to *Milan*, *An*. 1252. to extirpate Herefy, a certain Believer of Hereticks attack'd him in his Journey, and difpatch'd him with many Wounds. He was canoniz'd after his Death by *Alexander* IV. and is worfhipped as a Martyr by the *Dominicans*, whom next to *Dominick* they efteem as the Patron and Prince of the holy Office of the Inquifition ; fince he was the firft who confecrated it by his Blood. The Minifters alfo of the Inquifition, which they call in *Italy*, Crofs-Bearers, are from him called Co-Brothers of *Peter* the Martyr ; and in the very Enfigns of this Office he is painted as a Martyr, and Protector of this facred Tribunal, with a filken Crofs, of a red Colour, interwoven with Gold, as the Emblem of his Martyrdom.

But leaft the Pope fhould feem wholly to deprive the Bifhops of the Power of Judging, concerning the Faith, which hitherto had been wholly lodged with them, he appointed that a Bifhop, with the Inquifitor, fhould be Judges in this Tribunal : But the Bifhop was admitted only for Forms fake. The whole Power of Judging lay wholly in the Inquifitor. And that there might be fome fhew of Authority left to the civil Magiftrates, who by the laft Laws of *Frederick* had the Power of pronouncing Sentence upon Hereticks, he allowed them to appoint Minifters of the Inquifition, but fuch only as were nominated by the Inquifitors ; and to depute one of their Number, nominated alfo by the Inquifitor, to vifit with him the Territory committed to him ; and of claiming the third Part of the confifcated Goods ; together with fome other Things of the like Nature, by which the fecular Magiftrate feemed indeed to be admitted as a Companion of the Inquifitors, but was in reality render'd their Slave and Tool : For he was obliged, at the Command of the Inquifitor, to apprehend any one, and to imprifon him, wherever the Inquifitors pleafed. He was alfo under an Oath to expel from

his

his Family, and not to admit into any Office, any that should be adjudged Hereticks by the Inquisitors Sentence ; and if any of his Number assisted the Inquisitors, they were put under an Oath of Secrecy. From all which 'tis manifest, that the Magistrates were not the Companions of the Inquisitors in that Tribunal, but only their Slaves and Tools. The Pope also ordained, that all Persons should pay towards the Charges of the Jails, Imprisonments, and Support of those who were confined.

By this Means the Office of making Inquisition against Hereticks, was in Wadding, diverse Places of *Italy* committed both to the Minors and Predicant Friars. *a.* 1254. But least their mutual Power, and the neighbouring Jurisdiction of the Places § 7. should create Confusion, or raise Disputes about their respective Bounds, the Pope recalled all the Commissions that had been granted in the Affair of the Faith ; and divided, in an exact Proportion, to each Order, the several Parts of *Italy*. The Friars Minors he appointed in the City of *Rome*, throughout *Tuscany*, in the Patrimony of St. *Peter*, the Dutchy of *Spoletto*, *Campania*, *Maretamo* and *Romania*. To the Predicants he assigned *Lombardy*, *Romaniola*, the Marquisate of *Tarvisino*, and *Genova*. The Bull in which he commits the Office of the Inquisition to the Predicants, is in *Bzovius*, *An.* 1254. §. 4. and that to the Minors, in *Luke Wadding*, *An.* 1254. §. 7. After this, the Pope prescribed thirty one Articles to the Magistrates, Judges and People of the three Countries, which he had subjected to the Jurisdiction of the Predicants, which he commanded to be exactly observed, and register'd amongst the publick Records ; and gave Power to the Inquisitors to put under Excommunication and Interdict, all who refused to observe them. Armed with this Power, they sometimes very insolently abused it, and attempted to introduce into other Countries what the Pope had order'd only for those that he had put under their particular Jurisdiction. Upon this Account, in the Year 1255. Bzovius, there was a great Quarrel between *Anselm*, a Predicant Friar in the *Milaneze*, *a.* 1256. and the Magistrate of *Genova*. The Friar endeavoured, that some Constitu- §. 7. tions made against Hereticks, both by the Apostolick See, and the Imperial Power, should be published, and reposited amongst the Laws of the City. But *Philip Turrianus*, Prefect of the City, refused it, either because he favoured Hereticks, or despised the Commands of the Inquisitor. Upon this the Friar, supported by the Apostolick Authority, proceeded against *Philip* as suspected of Heresy ; and because he refused to obey and appear, excommunicated him, and all his Companions in the Government, as Accomplices in the Crime ; and interdicted the City from all holy Services. *Philip*, under that Censure, appealed to the Apostolick See ; and sent Ambassadors to the Pope, to entreat a Suspension of the Censures, and to wait for the Determination of the whole Affair. The Pope suspended the Curses *Hist. Con-* *Anselm* had pronounced to a certain Day ; but before that Day came, *Philip* *cil. Trid.* obeyed the Commands of *Anselm*, register'd according to his Order all *p.* 485. those Constitutions amongst the City Laws, and proceeded as they directed against all Contraveners.

Thus

Thus the Civil Magiftrate was fometime forced to yield to the Papal Authority : And this undoubtedly was the Reafon, that the Laws of *Frederick*
againft Hereticks, were, as Friar *Bernard* of *Como* relates in his Light of the
Inquifitors, printed at *Rome*, *An.* 1584. regifter'd in the Records of the City
Como, and accepted by the whole Council of that City, *Sept.* 10, 1255.
Neverthelefs, upon Account of the exceffive Cruelty of the Inquifitors, and
the Greatnefs of the Expence, the People were violently fet againft this Tri-
bunal ; and fome of the Popes could fcarce extricate themfelves out of thefe
Difficulties, till at length the People admitted it more eafily, being eafed of the
Expenfes they had born to fupport the Inquifition, and becaufe the Epifcopal
Authority in that Tribunal was greatly enlarged.

Sometimes however they broke out into open Violence, which was with
great Difficulty appeafed. Thus it happen'd in the Country of *Parma*, as
Honorius IV. relates it, in his Letter to the Bifhop of that City *, extant in
Bzovius. Thefe Difficulties were indeed overcome by the Authority of the
Pope, and Rigour of Punifhments ; but contrary to the Inclinations and Endeavours of the People, who curfed the Cruelty of the Inquifitors. From
fome Countries where the Inquifition had been brought in, it was driven out
again ; becaufe it affumed the Cognizance of thofe Affairs which did not
belong to it ; fo that the People could no longer bear the intolerable Yoke.
In thefe latter Ages, *viz. An.* 1518. the moft violent Tumults were raifed
in *Brefcia*, againft the Inquifitors, who exercifed the moft outragious Cruelties againft fome Perfons accufed of Magick, which were very difficultly
appeafed, and not till the Ecclefiaftical Tribunal and Proceffes were abolifhed, and other Judges appointed in their Room. Upon the Death of *Paul*
IV. the Prifons of the Inquifition were broke open by the Mob at *Rome* ;
and the whole Building, with all its Records, burnt to the Ground. At
Mantua, *An.* 1568. there was, on the fame Account, a violent Sedition,
which brought the City it felf into the extreameft Danger.

As there occurred to thefe new Judges many Cafes, not determined by the
Laws, fo that fometimes they were in doubt how to proceed ; they referred
them to the Pope, by whom they were deputed, who by his Refcripts, gave
them proper Directions, and declared how they were to pronounce ·in like
Cafes. There are extant many fuch Anfwers of *Innocent* IV. *Alexander* IV.
Urban IV. and *Clement* IV. to the Inquifitors, inftructing them in the Affair
of their Office againft Hereticks. And although thefe Refcripts were
fent only to the *Italian* Inquifitors, yet we muft not think, as *Pegna* remarks,
that thefe Decrees were to be obferved in *Italy* only : " For the *Roman* Pon-
" tiffs tranfmitted their Refcripts to the Inquifitors of *Italy* ; becaufe at that
" Time there were many of them againft the prevailing Herefies of the
" *Patarenes*, *Puritans*, *Leonifts*, and other Hereticks, who chiefly infected
" the Parts of *Italy* ; the Herefies of the *Valdenfes*, or poor Men of *Lyons*,
" being almoft buried and extinguifhed, the Apoftolick See having a little

Marginal notes:
κ. 1285.
§. 12.

Hift. Inq.
Venet.
c. 8. *ibid.*

Ia Eymer.
Direct. In-
quif. p. 3.
tom. 158.

---

* *See* Hift. Inquifit. *Book* 3. *Cap.* 10.

" before

" before fuppreffed them in *Languedoc, Dauphiny,* and *Provence,* by the
" Preaching of many famous Men, and efpecially of St. *Dominick.* And
" therefore the Refcripts fent by the Popes to thofe Inquifitors, they ordered
" to be obferved by the Inquifitors of other Provinces, where there were any.
" They were fent firft to thofe of *Italy,* becaufe they efpecially needed that
" Provifion, and thofe Conftitutions." One may alfo read in the Bulls the *Direct. Inq.*
fame Laws often repeated, without any Alteration, by different Popes. For, *Par. 2.*
as the fame *Pegna* obferves, " it feems to have been an ancient Cuftom, when *Comment.*
" the Matter required it, that every Pope, in the Beginning of his Pontifi- *22.*
" cate, fhould publifh Laws againft Hereticks, and Rebels againft the
" Church, to deter them from fo great a Crime by the Severity of Punifh-
" ments and Penalties, and thus reduce them to the Bofom of the Church.
" Sometimes they publifhed the Laws received by their Predeceffors, with-
" out altering a Word, unlefs the Occafion required otherwife.

This Tribunal was merely Ecclefiaftical, the Civil Magiftrate having no
Share in the Judgment. The Inquifitor, with the Bifhop, pronounced Sentence of Herefy againft the Perfon apprehended. They appointed wholfome
Penances to the Penitent, and delivered over the Impenitent and Obftinate
to the Secular Court, who without any farther Deliberation condemned them
to the Fire.

C H A P. XVI.

The INQUISITION *introduced into feveral Places.*

AFter this manner, Tribunals of the Inquifition were erected in other *Bzovius,*
Places befides *Italy.* Firft in the County of *Tholoufe.* For *Innocent* IV. *a.* 1251.
commanded the Provincial of the Predicant Order in *Provence,* to endeavour, *§. 8. n. 9.*
with all his Might, to extirpate Hereticks from that County, and the Country
of *Poicteau,* and gave him plenary Power to excommunicate, abfolve, and
reconcile.

In the Year 1255. *Alexander* IV. at the Requeft of *Lewis,* appointed Inqui- *Raynald.*
fitors of the Faith in *France,* and conftituted the Prior of the Predicant Friars *a.* 1255.
at *Paris,* Inquifitor over all that Kingdom, and County of *Tholoufe,* with the *§. 33, 34.*
moft ample Powers, and exhorted him to advife with grave and prudent Men *Bzovius,*
in pronouncing Sentences. Thefe Things are faid to have been done at the *§. 8. n. 15.* *a.* 1255.
Defire of *Lewis* the *French* King. *Raynald* adds: *The Kings afterwards for a*
long Time trod in the Steps of this moft holy Prince, in defending the Cenfors of the
Faith all over the Kingdom of France ; *till fome degenerating from his Piety, abo-*
lifhed the facred Tribunals, which had been appointed by the Defire of this religi-
ous King, and thus unhappily gave the Reins to all Impiety. How terrible a Fire
hath been raifed from hence, which at firft might have been extinguifhed by the

Blood

Blood of a few, France *is a Witness, which hath been thus long torn to Pieces by the Sword of Hereticks. So that all pious Men wish and pray, that another Prince may rise up equal in Piety to St.* Lewis, *who may restore the Tribunals of the holy Faith in* France. I cannot help remarking, that from these Words we may learn, not only what the Popes and their Devotees principally regard, *viz.* to restore the Inquisition wherever 'tis lost, but who and what Sort of Persons are their Saints, to whom they give such high Encomiums in their Writings ; not Men remarkable for their Sanctity of Life, nor for governing their Actions according to the Rule of the Christian Doctrine, but Persons who have been the most zealous Promoters of the Papal Authority, who have most advanced the Power of the Church, and heaped upon the Ecclesiasticks the most ample Possessions and Riches. *Philip de Comines* hath a pleasant Story of this kind, in his Commentaries of the *Neapolitan* War, Book 1. John Galeacius, *first Duke of* Milan *of that Name, had governed with great Cruelty and Pride, but had been very liberal in his Donations. I saw his Sepulchre in the* Carthusians *Church at* Papia, *and as I was looking on it, one of them spoke to me of his Virtue, and extolled his Piety. Why, said I, do you thus praise him as a Saint ? You see there are drawn the Ensigns of many People, whom he subdued without any Right. Oh, says he, 'tis our Custom to call them Saints, that have been our Benefactors.* Hence we may easily learn who are in their Account wicked and impious Men : Not such whose Manners are contrary to the Precepts of *Jesus Christ,* but who oppose the exorbitant Power of the Pope, and the intolerable Yoke of the Ecclesiasticks ; who assert the just Liberties of Mankind, and scorn to be the vile Slaves of the Pope. These they point out to us as wicked Wretches, and accuse of the worst of Crimes, and the most horrid Vices ; from whence it appears of it self, what Credit is to be given to those Histories, which are written only by Monks, those sworn Slaves to the Pope. But to return :

Raynald.
a. 1281.
§. 18.

When the Inquisition was once brought into *France,* the Pope carefully endeavour'd to preserve it, and to cherish and enlarge, by all Measures, the Jurisdiction of that Tribunal. Such who were defamed for Heresy, and afraid of being brought before the Tribunal of the Inquisition, fled to the Churches, for the Benefit of the Ecclesiastical Immunity, and could not be brought from thence by Force before the Inquisitors. The Pope seeing that by this Means

a. 1228.
§. 23, 28.

many would escape the Judgment of the Inquisition, decreed that this Privilege should not be allow'd them. Farther, to prevent the *Roman* Catholick Faith and Worship from being lost in those Provinces of *France,* where lived many of the *Valdenses;* he transmitted to the Magistrates and Prefects of those Places the Laws made by the Emperor *Frederick* against Hereticks, that they might proceed against those who were infamous on this Account. About this Time also, the Office of the Inquisition was brought into the Kingdoms of *Castile* and *Leon,* altho' there is scarce any mention of the *Castile* Inquisition in the Acts of those Times. However, *Lewis a Paramo* proves its Introduction from the Letters of Pope *Clement* IV. dated at *Viterbo,* Calend. *Feb.* 1267. by which Power is given to the Provincial of the Predicant Friars in *Spain,* which then comprehended *Castile, Andalusia, Portugal,* and *Navarre,* to nominate two of

the

the aforesaid Order, to make Inquisition against heretical Pravity ; which Letters are preserved at *Barcelona* in the Archives of .St. *Catherine* the Martyr. Another Bull of Pope *Clement* VI. is also kept there, expedited the 4th of the Ides of *April,* 1350. directed to Father *Nicholas Rossellis,* Provincial of *Aragon,* by which he appoints, that the Inquisitors he had made in his Province should not be subject to those who were chose by the Provincial of *Castile:* From whence *Paramus* rightly gathers, that there had arisen some Controversy between the Inquisitors of *Castile* and *Aragon* concerning their Jurisdiction, and that it had been ended by the Authority of the Pope.

About this Time many Hereticks from the Countries of *Italy,* to escape the Wadding. Hands of the Inquisitors deputed thither, transported themselves into the Isle of *a.* 1285. *Sardinia.* And therefore, that they might not escape Punishment, nor infect §. 9. the *Sardinians,* Pope *Honorius, An.* 1585. commissioned the Minorites, the In-Raynald. quisitors of *Tuscany,* to exercise the Office of the Inquisition also in that Island. *a.* 1285. Likewise, *An.* 1288. the Pope commanded, that the Minister of *Provence* should, §. 75. by the Apostolick Authority, appoint one of his Brethren, a wife and learned *a.* 1288. Man, Inquisitor in the County of *Venaisin* in *Dauphiny,* and the neighbouring §. 14. Places, who should execute this Office according to the Laws formerly prescribed by *Clement* IV. And, that there might be no Impediment to the Exercise of it, he two Years afterwards, *An.* 1290. commands the Governor of the *a.* 1290. *Venaisin,* by Letters given to him, that the Expences of the Inquisitors should §. 6. be defray'd. *Let him procure, at their Requisition, or any one of them, that the moderate Expences made or to be made by them, necessary to the Support of the Office of the Inquisition, be granted to them without any farther Obstacle or Delay, according to the Pleasure of the Apostolick See ; and that all and singular the Goods, movable and immovable, which shall be confiscated by the Sentence of the said Inquisitors, be applied to the Produce of the same District, towards the Necessities of the Court.* Then he adds : *For we intend that such Expences be defray'd by these Effects ; and know, that it will be very disagreeable to our Inclinations, that the said Office receive any Detriment upon Account of the Charges attending it.*

In the same Year 1290. the Inquisition was erected in *Syria* and *Palestine,* be-*a.* 1290. cause some Hereticks and *Jews* had crept in there, who promised themselves §. 2. Safety from the Disorders of the Wars. The Pope sent a large Bull to *Nicholas* Patriarch of *Jerusalem,* Legate of the Apostolick See, and commanded him to depute Inquisitors of heretical Pravity in all the Countries where his Legateship reached, by Advice of the Provincials of the Predicants in those. Parts, or their Vicegerents. The Inquisition lasted some Years in this Country, and was strenuously supported by the Minorites.

In the Year 1291. the Inquisition was brought into *Servia,* and the. Pope Wadding. wrote Letters to *Stephen* King of that Country. This same Year there was a *a.* 1291. great Quarrel in *Italy* between the Inquisitors of the Orders of the Minorites §. 11, 14. and Predicants. One Friar *Pagan,* a Predicant, Inquisitor in *Lombardy,* and Friar *Vivian* of the same Order, fiercely opposed the Inquisitor in the Marquisate of *Treviso.* This proceeded to such an Height, that many Disturbances were raised in the City of *Verona,* insomuch that the Pope found it necessary to
cite

cite them both before himself. After hearing what they alledged in their Defence, he determined that they had been guilty of great Excesses; and therefore removed them for ever from the Office of the Inquisition, and added other Punishments, which he wrote an Account of to the Bishop, Governor, and Citizens of *Verona*.

a. 1292.
§. 3.
Bzovius,
a. 1292.
§. 5.

The following Year 1292. the Inquisition was erected in the Cities of *Vienne* and *Albona*, after the same manner as it had been appointed in those of *Arles*, *Aix*, and *Ambrun*. The same Year *James* King of *Aragon* greatly promoted the Inquisition in all his Kingdoms. For by a Law made the 10th of the Cal. of *May* he commands all the Officials of all his Kingdoms, already made, or hereafter to be made, that at the Notification or Injunction of the Friars Predicants, who now are, or hereafter shall be Inquisitors of heretical Pravity, they do, fulfil, and execute, whatsoever they shall command to be done, by themselves or their Deputies, on the Part of the Pope, or the King himself, whether it be to apprehend, or imprison Mens Persons, or any other Thing relating to the Affair of the Inquisition. And he commands them to do this as often as, and wheresoever they shall be required by them, or any one of them.

And that there might be no Place of Refuge left for Hereticks, Tribunals of the Inquisition were erected up and down in various Countries : In *Germany*, *Austria*, *Hungary*, *Poland*, *Dalmatia*, *Bosnia*, *Ragusia*, *Croatia*, *Istria*, *Walachia* in *Lower Germany*, and other Places, to which the Power of the Pope could extend it self. The *Austrian* Inquisition was at first very terrible; for *Paramus*

l. 2. *t.* 3.
c. 4. *n.* 17.

relates from *Trithemius*, that in the City of *Crema* many thousand Hereticks were apprehended and burnt by the Inquisitors.

C H A P. XVII.

Of the INQUISITION *at* Venice.

THE Inquisition at *Venice* was under a different Management. The greatest Part of the Christian World being in Arms, upon Account of the fierce Contentions between the Pope, and *Frederick* the Emperor, *Lombardy* being torn in Pieces by its own Quarrels, and the Marquisate of *Treviso* and *Romaniola* divided between the Followers of the Pope and Emperor, there arose amongst them various Opinions, different from the *Roman* Faith. And because many Persons had fled to *Venice*, to live there securely and quietly, the Magistrates of that City, to prevent it from being polluted with foreign Doctrines, as many Cities of *Italy* were, chose certain Men, honest, prudent, and zealous for the Catholick Faith, who should observe and enquire out Hereticks. Full Power was also given to the Patriarch of *Grado*, and other *Venetian* Bishops, to judge of those Opinions ; and it was decreed, that whosoever was pronounced an
Heretick

Heretick by any one of the Bifhops, fhould be condemned to the Fire, by the Duke and Senators, or at leaft the major Part of them*. And leaft their fhould be any Hindrance to this Affair, by the Death of a fingle Bifhop, it was afterwards decreed, that fuch alfo fhould be condemned to the Fire, who were pronounced Hereticks by the Bifhops Vicars, upon the Demife of the Bifhop †. In this Procefs, the fecular Judges appointed by the Commonwealth, made Inquifition againft Hereticks. The Bifhop judged concerning their Faith, whether it was agreeable to the *Roman* Faith, or heretical. Then the Duke and Senators pronounced Sentence, not as meer Executors of the Bifhop's, but as Judges, properly fo called : But *Nicholas* IV. a minor Friar, being exalted to the Pontificate, in order to execute the Purpofes of his Predeceffors, and exalt the Friars of his own Order, did not ceafe his Endeavours, till he had got the Office of the Inquifition received by a publick Decree at *Venice* ; but under this Limitation, to prevent Scandal, that the Duke alone fhould have Power to affift the Inquifitors in the Execution of their Office ; that a Treafury fhould be appointed, and an Adminiftrator fet over it, who fhould difburfe the neceffary Sums for the Office, and fhould receive and keep all the Profits accruing from it, to the Treafury. This was done in the Year 1289. The Pope acquiefced in this Decree; and thus the Office of the Inquifition at *Venice* confifted of Secular and Ecclefiaftical Perfons, and doth fo to this Day ; three Inquifitors affifting at it in the Name of the Prince. The Ecclefiafticks have been indeed endeavouring to bring it entirely into their own Hands, but could never prevail with the *Venetian* Senate to agree to it. In the Year 1301. Friar *Anthony*, an Inquifitor, would feign have perfuaded Duke *Peter Gradenigo*, to have bound himfelf by an Oath, to obferve the Pontifical and Imperial Laws againft Hereticks. But the Duke anfwered, by a publick Refcript, that he was no ways obliged to take a new Oath ; becaufe when he was raifed to the high Office of Duke, he confirmed by an Oath the *Concordate* with *Nicholas* IV. and therefore infifted that he was no ways bound, by any Pontifical or Imperial Laws, not agreeing with this *Concordate*. Upon this Anfwer, the Inquifitor defifted from his Attempt.

From thefe Things 'tis evident, that the *Venetian* Inquifition is very different from what it is in other Countries, where Ecclefiafticks, intirely devoted to the Pope of *Rome*, have the whole Management of it. For whereas in other Places the Cognizance of Herefy belongs only to the Ecclefiafticks ; and whereas all who bear any Part in that Judgment, as Affeffors, Counfellors, Notaries, or Witneffes, take an Oath of Secrecy to the Inquifitors, whereby the Magiftrate is no more than the blind Executor of the Inquifitor's Sentence ; the *Venetian* Senate, by a wife Diftinction, confiders three Things feparately in this Affair : The Judgment concerning the Doctrine for which any Perfon is to be pronounced an Heretick : The Judgment

---

* This happened *An. Dom.* 1249. Father *Paul* Hift. Inquif.
† *An. Dom.* 1275. Ibid.

of the Fact, *viz.* who embraces and professes that Doctrine: And lastly, the pronouncing the Sentence. The first is acknowledged to belong to the Ecclesiastical Court; the two latter they contend belong to the Secular, and was always formerly administred by Seculars, during the *Roman* Empire. And though sometimes, by the Indulgence of Princes, the two last were allowed to the Ecclesiasticks, yet the Senate of *Venice* never gave up that Authority, but always order'd their Deputies, and in other Cities of their Territories, the Magistrate, to be present at all Actions of the Inquisitors. And so great is their Caution, that if any one hath any Commerce with the Court of *Rome*, he cannot assist at forming the Processes. The proper Business of these Assistants is, only to be present; and if any Thing doubtful occurs, to inform the Prince; and therefore they make no Promise of Secrecy to the Inquisitors, but are obliged to let the Prince know what is done in the Inquisition. Yea, although one of the Clergy, of the same Order with the Inquisitor himself, be accused before the Inquisition, the Civil Magistrate must be present, nor suffer the Inquisitor to proceed, unless he be with him, even after the Injunction made. And although the Inquisitor will communicate the whole Process to him, he must nevertheless be present at it: And if the Ecclesiasticks should form the Process whilst the Civil Magistrate is absent, he will command it to be resumed before him, even although the Process be carried on without the *Venetian* Territories. The Senate hath especially taken Care that neither the Process, nor the Persons taken up shall be sent out of their Dominions, unless by the Advice and Consent of the Prince. That this Method is observed in the Inquisition at *Venice*, Father *Paul* proves by a plain Example, in his History of the *Venetian* Inquisition. *An.* 1596. One *Lewis Petruccius Senensis*, was thrown into Prison at *Padua*. And whereas, according to the usual Custom of the Inquisition, the *Roman* Inquisitor ought to have sent to *Padua*, the Facts and Proofs which he had against him; he on the contrary demanded that the Prisoner should be sent to him; and urged this Matter at *Rome* to the *Venetian* Ambassador, and at *Venice* by the Pope's Nuncio: But the Senate made Answer, That it was not proper that that laudable Institution of the Republick should be altered, which orders the Prisoners to be tried in those Places where they are taken up and confined; but that it was just, and agreeable to the receiv'd Custom, that whatever Crimes the Prisoner was accused of should be transmitted to the Inquisitor at *Padua*, that so he might suffer the just Punishment of his Crime. And they thought this so evident and manifest a Piece of Justice, that no Body could oppose it. This Affair was controverted on both Sides by many Letters for five whole Years, *Petruccius* being all the while kept in Prison. But at length the *Romans* finding they could not get the Prisoner into their Possession, wrote, *An.* 1601. to the Inquisitor at *Padua*, to dismiss his Prisoner *Petruccius*; which created no small Suspicion what Sort of Crime it must be, which they had rather should go unpunished than discover it to the Inquisitor at *Padua*.

The

The *Venetian* Senate hath alfo been particularly careful that the Inquifitors fhall not have the Power of prohibiting Books, becaufe they may eafily abufe it to the Detriment of the Commonwealth ; for they oftentimes forbid, or adulterate good Books, and ufeful to the Publick ; fometimes they prohibit Books which have no Relation to their Affairs ; and fometimes becaufe they arrogate to themfelves the Cenfure of all Books, they hinder the Civil Magiftrate from prohibiting and condemning Books highly injurious to the Government.

From thefe Things and others, which might be mentioned from Father *Paul*, but which for Brevity I omit, 'tis evident that the *Venetian* Inquifition is not fo abfolutely fubject to the Pope as the other *Italian* Inquifitions are ; and that it is not entirely committed to Ecclefiafticks, but that the Civil Magiftrate hath a principal Share in the Management of it.

[*Thuanus* relates the fame of the *Venetian* Inquifition, *viz.* That the Senate, *An.* 1548. renewed the Edict that had been firft made, *An.* 1521. feveral Perfons fufpected as to their Religion, of being Sorcerers, and in a League with the Devil, being put to the fevereft Torture, at the Defire of the Pope's Legate in *Brefcia* ; but with this Caution, that Judgment fhould not be committed only to the Inquifitors and Bifhops, but that there fhould be always prefent the Governors of the Places, and fome Lawyers, who fhould know and fee the Depofitions ; that none in their Territories, under the Pretence of Religion, might, through Injuftice and Covetoufnefs, be oppreffed ; which Caution they obferved afterwards, when the Doctrine of *Luther* took deeper Footing, and do maintain even to this Day.] *Hift. lib.* 5.

C H A P. XVIII.

The Inquisition *againft the* Apostolicks, Templars, *and others,* &c.

ABOUT the Year of our Lord 1300. there was great Cruelty exercifed upon certain Perfons called Apoftolicks, in *Italy.* They feem to have been the Offspring of the *Albigenfes* : Their Rife is thus defcribed by *Eymericus.* In the Times of *Honorius* IV. *Boniface* VIII. *Nicholas* IV. and *Clement* V. about the Year of our Lord 1260. there appeared *Geraldus Sagarelli*, in the Bifhoprick of *Parma*, and *Dulcinus* in that of *Novara.* They gathered a Congregation, which they called Apoftles, who lived in Subjection to none ; but affirmed that they peculiarly imitated the Apoftles, and took on them a certain new Habit of Religion. *An.* 1285. *March*, Ides 5, they were condemn'd by the Letters Patents of *Honorius* IV. beginning, *Olim felicis recordationis*, and afterwards by *Nicholas* IV. *An.* 1290. *Direct.* *Inquif. p: 2 qu. 12.*

O   At

At length, after their Doctrine had prevailed near forty Years in *Lombardy*, *Sagarelli* was condemned as an Arch-heretick by the Bishop of *Parma*, and Friar *Manfred* the Inquisitor, a Predicant, in the Time of *Boniface* VIII. and burnt *July* the 18th, *A. D.* 1300. *Dulcinus*, with six thousand of his Followers of both Sexes, inhabited the *Alps*, who run into all manner of Luxury, as *Pegna* says, and gained many Proselytes for the Space of two or three Years; and that with such Success, as determined *Clement* V. to send amongst them Inquisitors of the Predicant Order, to put a Stop to so great an Evil, either by recovering *Dulcinus* and his Accomplices from their Error, or by acquainting him whether these Things were so or not, as he had been credibly inform'd, after they had made a strict and diligent Enquiry. Upon their Return they reported to the Pontiff what they had seen and heard, who upon being acquainted with their horrid Wickednesses and Impurities, published a Crusado against so heinous an Impiety, and promised large and liberal Indulgences to all who should engage in so pious a War against such wicked Men. An Army was accordingly gathered, and sent against them with an Apostolick Legate; who coming into the Places where these false Apostles dwelt, and unexpectedly attacking them, they were wholly oppressed by this Catholick Army of Cross-bearers, partly by Hunger and Cold, and partly by Arms. *Dulcinus* himself was taken, and eight Years after the Punishment of *Geraldus*, was, as an Arch-heretick, with *Margaret* his heretical Wife, his Partner in Wickedness and Error, publickly torn in Pieces, and afterwards burnt. The Opinions which *Eymerick* attributes to them agree for the most Part with those which are ascribed to *Peter Lucensis*, a *Spaniard*, excepting that abominable Principle of promiscuous Lust, of which there is not the least mention in the Sentence of the said *Peter*. From whence we may certainly conclude, that this is a mere Calumny upon these Apostolicks, as well as upon the *Valdenses*.

Direct. p. 2. Comm. 37.

The Sentence of this Peter Lucensis *is as follows.*

Tho' Inq. fol. 183. " *Peter Lucensis*, of the City of *Lugo*, in the Province of *Gallicia*, beyond' " *Compostella*, the Son of *Vivian* of the City of *Lugo*, as legally appears by his " judicial Confession, hath acknowledged, that twenty Years since he began " to observe that Order and Life which is called the Life of the Apostles in the " Poverty of the Gospel; and hath observed it with all his Power, as far as " his Frailty would allow him, ever since he was first informed by *Richard* " *Lombard* of *Alexandria*, who observed the said Life and Order, altho' the " said *Peter* had heard it reported and did believe that the Church of *Rome* had " condemned and disallowed the Order of those Apostles, and did believe that " such Apostles were condemned and persecuted by the Prelates and Reli- " gious, and Inquisitors of heretical Pravity, especially in *Lombardy*, and al- " tho' he had oftentimes and by many heard it said, that they were excommu- " nicated, who observed the said Order and Life of those called Apostles, all " which Things notwithstanding he did believe the said Order of the Apostles

" to

" to be good, and that they who obferved the faid Order and Life might be
" faved by obferving it, if they did not commit other Sins contrary to the
" Commands of God. Being afked, if he believed that the Pope and Pre-
" lates of the *Roman* Church, and the Religious and Inquifitors, did Evil, and
" finned in perfecuting that Order, and thofe who obferved and adhered to
" the faid Order ; he, after many Words, anfwered finally, that he believed
" they did Evil and finned in this, that they perfecuted that Good. Being
" afked, if the Sentence of Excommunication pronounced by the Church of
" *Rome*, or its Authority, againft thofe who obferved the faid Order, did
" bind them ; he anfwered, that it did not, faying, that he had heard it faid,
" that the Sentence of Excommunication unlawfully or unjuftly pronounced by
" any one, did not excommunicate another, but condemned the Perfon him-
" felf, and he brought and applied to that Purpofe fome Authorities from St.
" *Paul* and the Gofpel, and concluded, that he did not think himfelf to be ex-
" communicated for holding the faid Order, notwithftanding any Sentence,
" altho' he had heard it faid oftentimes, and by many, that *Gerard Sagarelli*,
" who was the firft Inventor of the faid Order of Apoftles, and *Dulcinus*, who
" held the faid Order, and many others of the faid Order, were condemned by
" the Inquifitors and Prelates of the *Roman* Church, and left to the fecular
" Arm and burnt. *Item*, Being queftion'd, if he believed thofe to be faved
" who fuffered Death for the faid condemned Order, he would not at firft an-
" fwer directly that he believed them either to be faved or damned. But after
" many Days, being afked and re-examined upon this, he anfwered, that he
" did believe that the faid *Gerard* was unjuftly condemned, faying, that one
" Chriftian, efpecially if he be a learned Clerk, and underftands the Scripture,
" ought not to deliver another Chriftian to Death. *Item*, He expounded ma-
" ny Things out of the holy Scripture before the Inquifitor, according to his
" own Underftanding, to reproach the State of the Church, in which were
" contained many erroneous Things ; and amongft other Things, he faid and
" expounded, that when Poverty was changed from the Church by St. *Silvefter*,
" then Sanctity of Life was taken from the Church, and the Devil enter'd into
" the Companions of St. *Silvefter* into this World. *Item*, That there was a
" double Poverty, the one perfect, which the Apoftles held, and all thofe who
" follow and imitate them, hereby meaning himfelf, and thofe like him, *viz.*
" to have nothing of one's own, or in common. *Item*, There is an im-
" perfect Poverty, fuch as that of the Religious who live according to the
" Rule of St. *Auftin* and St. *Benedict*, who have Poffeffions and Riches in com-
" mon, and that fuch Religious are not perfect in Poverty, becaufe they have
" Houfes to abide in, and all Neceffaries to eat and drink in common. *Item*,
" He faid that there is a double Church, *viz.* the Spiritual and the Carnal ;
" that the Spiritual Church is in thofe Men who live in perfect Poverty, and
" in Humility, and fpiritual Obedience to God, fuch as they are who imitate
" the Life of the Apoftles and Chrift : That the carnal Church is of thofe
" who live carnally, and in the Delights of the Flefh, and in Riches and in
" Honours, and in Pomp and Glory, fuch as are the Bifhops and Prelates of

" the

" the Church of *Rome*, who don't renounce the Things that they poffefs, nor
" give the Goods of the Church to their Parents, Kinsfolk, and Friends. This
" Church he fays is that carnal Church of which *John* fpeaks in the *Revelations*,
" which he calls *Babylon* the great Whore. *Item*, It is that Beaft of which
" *John* there fpeaks, which hath feven Heads and ten Horns, becaufe fhe hath
" feven mortal Sins, and keeps not the ten Commandments. *Item*, It is that
" Woman of which *John* there fpeaks, which had the Golden Cup in her Hand,
" full of the Abomination of Sins. *Item*, He expounds the double State of
" the Church, where, amongft other Things, he fays, that there can be no
" Sanctity where there is not true Poverty. So that from the Time that the
" State of Poverty of Chrift and his Apoftles was changed under Pope *Silvefter*,
" Sanctity was taken away.

" Afterwards the aforefaid *Peter* being judicially required that he would
" fwear to fpeak the Truth, fhowed himfelf very backward to fwear, faying
" that he was afraid for his Confcience, and faying to the Inquifitor, that he
" fhould fee and beware of finning by making him fwear, becaufe God had
" forbidden Swearing in the Gofpel. *Item*, After fome Days the aforefaid *Peter*
" being judicially required that he fhould take an Oath to fpeak the Truth,
" would not, and wholly refufed to fwear, faying that he repented that he had
" fworn before the Inquifitor, and believed that he finned by fwearing, faying
" that his Confcience was confirmed that he ought not to fwear, and in this
" Obftinacy he continued for a Month and more, faying that St. *James* in his
" canonical Epiftle, and *Chrift* in the Gofpel, had forbidden us to fwear, and
" he read the Words of St. *James* in his canonical Epiftle, and the Words of
" the Gofpel. And when it was faid and expounded to him that the Apoftle
" *Paul* fwore, and the Angel, and that the Catholick Church had determined
" that it was lawful to fwear for Affirmation of the Truth, and that it was
" the Decree of the Church, that whofoever, thro' a damnable Superftition,
" fhould refufe an Oath, and will not fwear, fhall for this alone be adjudged
" Hereticks, and fuffer the juft Punifhment of fuch, notwithftanding the afore-
" faid, he the faid *Peter* abfolutely refufed to fwear, faying that the making
" fuch a Statute or Order feemed to him erroneous. Being interrogated, if
" he believed that the Pope, the Vicar of *Chrift*, could make any Statute or
" Order, by which he and other Chriftians fhould be obliged, fince the Pope
" hath the Power of Binding and Loofing on Earth, he anfwered that he
" heard a certain learned Paftor fay, that fome mifunderftood thefe Words of
" the Gofpel, *Whatfoever ye fhall bind on Earth*, &c. becaufe they were fo to
" be underftood, that as the Pontiff or Prieft in the Old Teftament was to
" judge between Leprofy and Leprofy, fo the Pope and Bifhops have no
" other Power but to difcern between Sin and Sin, *i. e.* between thofe who
" are to be bound, and thofe who are to be loofed, becaufe otherwife
" they take upon them the Pride of the *Pharifees*, becaufe they mortify Souls
" they ought not to mortify, and enliven Souls they ought not to enliven.

" Some Days after this he oftentimes obftinately refufed to fwear, tho' at
" length, with great Difficulty, he confented to fwear the 7th of the Calends of
" *November*.

" *November*. Afterwards on the 4th of the Nones of *November*, the said *Pe-*
" *ter*, being judicially interrogated if he believed that the Lord the Pope could
" forbid, under the Pain of Excommunication, any Person to hold the said
" Order of those that call themselves Apoftles, which the before-named *Ge-*
" *rard Segarelli* is said to have begun. *Item*, If he believed that they who acted
" contrary to the forefaid Inhibition of our Lord the Pope under Pain of Ex-
" communication, did incur the Sentence of Excommunication ; he answered,
" that St. *Gregory* fays, that if any one excommunicates another unjuftly, he
" doth not excommunicate that Person, but condemns himself.

" Being interrogated, if he believed that the Pope, by reprobating and
" condemning the Order of those that call themselves Apoftles, and excom-
" municating them who will not forsake it, doth unjuftly ; he answered, that
" he did believe that the Pope did unjuftly and againft God in so doing, be-
" caufe they who call themselves Apoftles were approved of God the Father,
" and that God had done several Miracles for them, as he heard say, and be-
" lieves to be true ; and said, that he believed that the Inquifitors, and Reli-
" gious and others who perfecute those who hold the said Order of the Apoftles,
" do fin ; and to prove this, alledged Words and Examples, according to his
" own Underftanding, and would not swear, saying he had sworn too much
" already. Finally, the forefaid *Peter* being judicially required to abjure the
" Sect and Order of those falfe Apoftles, refused to do it, saying, that if he
" fhould swear, he fhould act againft his Confcience, and perhaps not obferve
" what he had sworn to, and so fhould fin ; and perfifted in his firft Opinion,
" that God had absolutely prohibited swearing.

However, at laft they made him folemnly abjure.

In the mean while, the Inquifition raged with no lefs Cruelty againft the *Al-* Tbol. Lig.
bigenfes and *Valdenfes* in the Kingdom of *France*, efpecially in the County of *Tho-*
loufe. The Penitent were condemned either to wear Croffes, or to perpetual
Imprifonment, and the Impenitent burnt without Mercy.

 At the same Time the Order of the Templars was fuppreffed by the Command of Pope *Clement* V. *Philip* the Fair, King of *France*, had accufed this
Order of various Herefies and Wickedneffes before *Clement*. And as it seemed
very hard utterly to abolifh so famous and rich an Order, and which had done
fuch excellent Service for the Defence of the Faith, their Caufe was debated in
feveral National Councils. At laft *Clement* held a General Council at *Vienna*,
where the Affair being throughly examined, they were condemned for various
Herefies and abominable Crimes ; which whether they were true, or whether the People envied them for their immenfe Riches, or whether King
Philip thirfted after them, 'tis not eafily to be determined.

 After they had been thus condemned in the Council of *Vienna*, all that were Bzovius,
in *France* were apprehended at once, as it were by a Signal, and before the *a* 1, 11,
third Year on the 13th of *October* put to the Torture. Moft or all of them, §. 8.
either thro' the Love of Life, or Confcioufnefs of their Wickednefs, confeffed
the

the Crimes they were accused of. Many were condemned and burnt alive. Amongſt theſe, *John Mola*, a *Burgundian*, chief Maſter of the Order, when after his Sentence he was carrying to Puniſhment, declared, in the moſt pathetick Manner, his own and his Order's Innocence, even tho' he was promiſed Life and Impunity, if he would openly and humbly aſk Pardon, and retract every thing that he had confeſſed againſt that Order before, begging Forgive-

§. 9. neſs for his falſe Confeſſion. The next Year Letters were ſent by the Pope, in which he commiſſion'd the Archbiſhops of *Compoſtella* and *Toledo* to make Inquiſition againſt the Templars in *Caſtile*, joining with them *Eymerick* the Inquiſitor, a Predicant, and other Prelates. In *Aragon* the ſame Affair was committed to the Biſhops *Reymond Valentinus*, and *Somenus Cæſar Auguſtanus*. The ſame was done in all the other Provinces of the Chriſtian World, with this Expedient, that as this Inquiſition was made concerning the moſt weighty Affairs, they ſhould be cognizable only in Provincial Councils. Many of them were put in Irons, and impriſoned in *Aragon* and *Caſtile*. At *Salamanca* there was held a Council of the Fathers, where there being a Debate concerning the Petitioners in Bonds, and their Cauſe throughly underſtood, they were pronounced Innocent by the common Suffrage of the Fathers. Nevertheleſs the Determination of the whole Affair was referred to the Pope, and the Council of *Vienna*. On this the Biſhops and Inquiſitors of the Faith, from *Spain, Italy, France, England, Germany*, and other Kingdoms and Provinces, put the Informations into Publick Writing, and propoſing them at the firſt Seſſion of the Fathers at the Council of *Vienna*, demanded a Re-hearing of the whole Cauſe of the Templars, and at length the Fathers decreed that that Order ſhould be ſuppreſſed ; and by their Advice Pope *Clement* publiſh'd an Edict

a. 1312. the 6th Nones of *May, An.* 1312. by which he ſuppreſſes and diſſolves the Or-
§. 2, 3. der of the Templars, not by a definitive Sentence, but by an Apoſtolick Proviſion or Ordination, and reſerves all their Effects to the Diſpoſal and Appointment of the Apoſtolick See. When this Edict came to the ſeveral Provinces, the Effects of the Templars were every where ſeized, and they themſelves ſeverely puniſhed.

Raynald. In the ſame Council large Power was given to the Inquiſitors of heretical Pra-
a. 1312. vity and the Biſhops, of proceeding againſt Hereticks. One *Walter*, a *Lol-*
§. 21.
Bzovius, *lard* in the City of *Crema*, and Dutchy of *Auſtria*, had many Followers, who,
a. 1307. according to ſome, had their Riſe from *Dulcinus*, who at the Command of Pope
§. 9. *Clement* were burnt by the Inquiſitors, in that City and other Places. Their
a. 1315. Number was large in *Bohemia, Auſtria*, and the neighbouring Countries. Some
§. 11. affirm they were 80000. Many of them were burnt in ſeveral Places of *Auſtria*, who all of them perſevered in their Opinions with great Chearfulneſs to their Death. And therefore, to extinguiſh both the old Hereticks, and the new ones that might poſſibly ariſe, ample Power was given by the *Vienna* Council to the Inquiſitors and Biſhops, to proceed againſt thoſe who were defiled with that Impurity, and Priſons were order'd to be built to ſecure them in Chains.

In

In *Bohemia* the Office of the Inquisition was committed to *Peregrine Oppo-* Raynald.
lienfis and *Nicholas Hippodines,* Predicants; and to *Coldas* and *Herman,* Mino- *a.* 1319.
rites; who were commanded to manifeft an holy Ardour againft the Guilty. §. 43:
The Pope exhorted *John* King of *Bohemia, Uladiflaus* Duke of *Cracow, Bolef-* Bzovius,
laus Duke of *Wratiflaw,* and the Marquis of *Mifnia,* that they fhould not fuf- §. 37.
fer Religion to decay and be obfcured by new Errors, but that they fhould
affift the Cenfors of the holy Faith.   Fourteen Men and Women were burnt
in *Bohemia. Walter,* the Principal of the Sect of the *Lollards,* was burnt at *Co-
lonne, An.* 1322.

About the fame Time Pope *John,* by a Letter, Nº 190. renewed the Con- Bzovius,
ftitutions of *Clement* IV. and other his Predeceffors, againft the *Jews,* and *a.* 1319.
confirmed by feverer Laws the Power given to the Inquifitors againft them, §. 9.
and commanded the Book of the *Talmud* to be burnt, and fuch who were
convicted of their execrable Blafphemies to be punifhed.

Nor did he fhew lefs Severity againft the *Valdenfes,* reviving about that Time §. 10.
in *France:* For he ordered that many of them, who were convicted of Errors by the Inquifitors, who were Predicant Friars, fhould be delivered to
the Princes to be punifhed according to the Ecclefiaftical Law.   There is
extant in the *Vatican* Library a large Volume of the Tranfactions of thefe Predicant Friars againft Hereticks in the Kingdom of *France,* this Year of our
Lord 1319.

C H A P. XIX.

The INQUISITION *againft the* BEGUINS.

THE fame *John* XXII. condemned the *Beguins* of Herefy, and commanded the Inquifitors of Heretical Pravity to proceed againft them,
and to deliver over to the Secular Court all who continued obftinate in their
Error, to be punifhed with Death.

Thefe *Beguins* were Monks of the Order of St. *Francis:* They are feveral
Times called, *of the third Rule of St.* Francis.   His Rule was, that the Friars
of his Order fhould have no particular Property of their own, neither Houfe,
nor any thing, but fhould live by begging: This he called Evangelick Poverty.   This Rule was confirmed and approved by feveral Popes.   But
as many believed the Obfervance of it to be above all human Strength, many
Doubts arofe concerning it;   fome contending that they were to renounce the
Property of all Things in particular, but not in common, and that it was no ways
contrary to the *Francifcan* Poverty to have the Poffeffion of Things in common,
fo that they poffeffed nothing in particular.   But *Nicholas* III. condemned this *sext. De-*
Opinion by a Conftitution, beginning, *Exiit qui feminat.*   However, tho' all *eret. de*
Property was taken from thefe Friars, as well in common as in fpeeial, yet were *verb. fign.*
they *cap. 3.*

I

they not deprived of the Use of what they had. For *Martin* IV. published a Bull, *Feb.* Cal. 10. 1282. by which he ordained that the Property, the Right and Dominion of every Thing which the Friars had by Donation or Legacy, should be in the Church of *Rome* ; but that the Friars should have the Use. He also allowed the Ministers and Keepers of the Order, the Faculty of naming Administrators, Stewards, Syndicks, who in the Name of the Church of *Rome*, and for the Advantage of the Friars, may receive and demand Alms and Legacies, and sue for the Recovery and Preservation of them. *Clement* V. confirmed the same in the Council of *Vienna*, by a Constitution, beginning, *Exivi de paradizo*, extant among the *Clementines.* However, *Clement* allow'd, that when it appeared very likely, even from Experience, that they could not otherwise secure the Necessaries of Life, they might have Granaries or Storehouses, in which they might reposit and keep whatever they could get by begging. He left, indeed, the Ministers and Keepers to judge of such Necessity, and gave it in special Charge to their Consciences.

Against this, those who were called *Beguins* protested, declaring they were of the third Rule of St. *Francis.* They contended that the *Franciscans* ought in no Case to have Granaries or Storehouses, because this was contrary to the Perfection of the *Franciscan* Poverty ; that the Pope had not Authority to dispense with the Rule of *Francis*, and that if he did, his Decrees were of no Force, and might justly be disregarded. One of them who lived at this Time, *Peter John Olivus*, who wrote a Postill on the Apocalypse, applied to the Pope and Church of *Rome* the Things spoken of the Beast, and the Whore of *Babylon*, of which frequent Mention is made in the Collection of the Sentences of the *Tholouse* Inquisition.

John XXII. succeeded *Clement*, who, by several Constitutions, condemn'd the Tenet of the *Beguins*, and allowed the *Franciscans*, that by the Judgment of the Heads of the Order they might lay up and preserve Corn, Bread and Wine in Granaries and Storehouses. The *Beguins* believed that such a Concession derogated from the Sublimity and Perfection of their Rule and Poverty, and therefore warmly opposed it ; and in order to defend their own Rule, dared to deny the Authority of the Pope : Upon this Account they were declared Hereticks, and Commandment was given to the Inquisitors of heretical Pravity, to bring them before their Tribunal, and to proceed against them as Hereticks. This was a bloody Decree, beginning, *Gloriosam Ecclesiam*, in which the Pope gave the Inquisitors these special Commands : *Call before you, by the Ecclesiastical Censure, all and singular received by them to their Sect, especially such as are professed ; examine them concerning the Faith, and enquire carefully and diligently, by your selves or others, without Noise and the Form of Judgment, concerning the Errors of the aforesaid, and search after their Complices and Abettors ; and if there be need, order them to be taken up and confined, making Use, when there is Occasion, of the Assistance of the secular Arm. Compel Gainsayers and rebellious Persons, by the Ecclesiastical Censure ; and by a like Censure oblige such Witnesses as you shall think proper to examine upon the Premises, to give their Testimony to the Truth, without allowing to them the Liberty of Appeal.*

Appeal. Furthermore we will, and by our Apoſtolick Authority decree, that any one of you may proſecute the Affair or Article, though begun by another, even although he who begun it, ſhould be under no canonical Impediment ; and that from the Date of theſe Preſents, you, and every one of you, ſhall have perpetual Power and Juriſdiction in all and ſingular the Premiſes, even though not begun, preſent, and future ; that ye may be able to proceed againſt the aforeſaid with that Vigour and Firmneſs in the Premiſes, though not begun, preſent and future, as though your, and every one of your Juriſdiction, in all and ſingular the Premiſes, had been perpetuated by Citation or other lawful Manner ; notwithſtanding the Edicts concerning the two Days Journey, made in a general Council, and of Pope Boniface VIII. our Predeceſſor of bleſſed Memory, by which, as well the Judges as the Conſervators, deputed by the aforeſaid See, are prohibited from proceeding themſelves, or putting others in their Room, without the Cities and Dioceſes in which they were deputed, and from forcing any Perſons more than one Days Journey from the Bounds of ſuch Dioceſe ; and any other Conſtitutions to the contrary notwithſtanding. This Decree was dated from *Avignon, Feb.* Cal. 10. 1318. Soon after four Friars Minors, about the Year 1318. were condemned and burnt as Hereticks at *Marſeilles* by the Inquiſitor of heretical Pravity, who was himſelf a Friar Minor, becauſe, as they ſay, they were reſolved to adhere and keep to the Purity, Truth and Poverty of the Rule of St. *Francis,* and becauſe they would not conſent to make the Rule leſs ſtrict, nor receive the Diſpenſation of the Lord Pope *John* XXII. made concerning it, nor obey him nor others in this Affair. Others of the ſame Order aſſert, that theſe four were unjuſtly condemned, and affirm them to be glorious Martyrs, and that the Pope, if he conſented to their Condemnation, was an Heretick, and forfeited his Power. Upon this, the three next Years, *viz.* from the Year 1318. or thereabouts, they were all condemned for Hereticks by the Judgment of the Prelates and Inquiſitors of heretical Pravity in the Province of *Narbonne, Beziers, Lodun* in the Dioceſe of *Agde,* and at *Lunelle,* and the Dioceſe of *Magalone,* who believed that the aforeſaid four Friars Minors were holy Martyrs, and who believed and held and thought as they did concerning Evangelical Poverty, and the Power of the Pope, *viz.* that he loſt it, and was become an Heretick. Many however privately gathered up the burnt Bones and Aſhes of theſe four Friars, who had been condemned as Hereticks, and kept them for Reliques, and kiſſed and worſhipped them as the Reliques of Saints ; yea, ſome marked their Names and the Days in which they ſuffered in the Calendars. This Account of *Eymerick* agrees well with what we read of the *Beguins* in the Sentences of the *Tholouſe* Inquiſition. Amongſt other Things, we read *Fol.* 155. in the Sentence of *Peter Moreſius de Bello Podio,* that *he believed, that* John XXII. *who was then Pope, and whom he calls the Boar of the Foreſt, had deſtroyed the Incloſure of the Church, and done more harm to the Church of God, than all former Hereticks had done.* In the 156th *fol.* 'tis aſcribed to *Bernard de na Jacina,* that *he ſaid twice or thrice, when he was ſpeaking about the Pope's Power to diſpenſe with the Rule of* St. Francis : *Do you believe that if the Pope bound the Tail of an Aſs upon Earth, the Tail of an Aſs would be bound in Heaven ?*

P   Thus,

Thus, from a Controversy originally of no Moment, rose up at length, thro' the Warmth of Men's Minds, a dismal Tragedy ; and after the Pope's Authority began to be called in question, a severe Persecution was raised against the *Beguins*. In the Book of Sentences of the *Tholouse* Inquisition there are several Sentences pronounced against the *Beguins*, by which they are declared Hereticks, and delivered over as such to the secular Court. One of these Sentences I will transcribe at large.

" *Peter Dominicus* being examined, hath judicially confessed all the Er-
" rors of the *Beguins*. *Item*, He believes and asserts that the Lord Pope can-
" not grant to the Friars Minors the Power of having Repositories and Gra-
" naries to keep Corn or Wine. *Item*, That he neither can nor could
" make or cause to be made such a Constitution or Declaration, and that it
" ought not to be obeyed if made, because contrary to the Vow of the Friars
" Minors. *Item*, That he can't grant to the Friars Minors, according to
" God, to carry great Habits, large or died. *Item*, That he cannot, by
" his Plenitude of Power, make it lawful for a Friar Minor to become a Friar
" of another Religion or Order, where he may have Possessions, or any
" thing in common, and that a Friar Minor ought not to obey the Pope in
" this, and that the Pope would sin in granting such a Dispensation. *Item*,
" That the Pope can't give Leave, that a Friar Minor, when made a Bishop,
" may become Lord of the Temporalties of his Bishoprick, or handle Money
" with his Hand, because he ought to dispense and administer all moveable
" Effects by another to the Poor. *Item*, He believes and asserts, that the
" Gospel of *Christ* is the Rule of St. *Francis* in Chastity, Poverty, and Obedi-
" ence, and that the Pope can't dispense with these three, or any one of them ;
" and that if he should grant a Dispensation, he would act contrary to the
" Life of *Christ*, and against the Gospel. *Item*, That the Pope can't dis-
" pense in any Case, under the Vow of Virginity or Chastity,
" whether that Vow be single or solemn, may marry ; and that if he should
" actually dispense, he would herein sin, and not do according to the Power
" given him of God, which Power he says is for the Nourishment of Virtue,
" and to be a Remedy against Sin. *Item*, That if the Pope should dispense in
" the foresaid Case that such Person should marry, it would not be Marriage,
" but Fornication or Adultery and Sin, and that the Children so born would
" be adulterous and illegitimate. *Item*, That the Pope can't make any De-
" cretal or Constitution which may dispense with the Vow of Virginity, or
" Chastity or Poverty, in any Case whatsoever, altho' some very great Good
" might hereby happen to the Community, such as the restoring Peace to any
" Kingdom or Province ; and that if the Pope should make such Decretal or
" Constitution, it ought not to be obeyed, neither would he obey it. *Item*,
" He asserts that he believes and holds that the four Friars Minors who were
" condemned as Hereticks about four Years ago at *Marseilles*, by the
" Judgment of the Inquisitor of heretical Pravity, after mature Advice ;
" and also that the *Beguins* or Friars of the third Order of Penitents, or
" third

" third Rule of St. *Francis*, who were condemned as Hereticks by the Judg-
" ment of the Prelates and Inquisitor of heretical Pravity of *Carcasson*, for
" three, two, and one Year paft, in the Province of *Narbonne*, and in divers
" Places and Cities, were and are Catholicks at the Time of their Condem-
" nation, and were Martyrs, and suffered for supporting the Gospel Truth.
" *Item*, That all those who condemned them, *viz.* the Prelates and Inquisi-
" tors, and all who consented to the Condemnation of the aforesaid, and even
" the Lord the Pope, if he consented to it, did err, and are become Here-
" ticks, and will be damned unless they repent. *Item*, That our Lord Pope
" *John* XXII. is a wicked Man and an Heretick, and is without the Church
" of God for this Reason, because he persecuted the poor *Beguins* of the
" third Rule of St. *Francis*. *Item*, That he hath lost totally the Power of his
" Jurisdiction of Binding and Loosing, and that he doth not think him to
" be Pope, nor that he is subject to him, because he condemns, or con-
" sents to the Condemnation of the *Beguins*, as Hereticks. *Item*, That all
" those who agree and believe that the Pope did well in persecuting the afore-
" said *Beguins*, are wicked Men and Hereticks. *Item*, That he would not
" confess his Sins to any Bishop or Prelate, who consented in the Condemna-
" tion of the aforesaid *Beguins*; and that if he should confess to any one of
" them, he doth not believe that they can absolve him from his Sins.
" *Item*, That he would not receive any Sacrament from any Prelate, who
" obstinately opposes the Deed of the aforesaid *Beguins*, saying, that every
" such Bishop hath lost the Power of conferring the Sacraments. *Item*, That
" all are Hereticks who obstinately believe and hold contrary to those Things
" which he hath confessed, and asserts that he believes and holds. *Item*, That
" all who believe and hold the Things which he believes and holds, and are
" under the Commands of God by keeping them, are faithful, and the
" Church of God. *Item*, That it is much greater Perfection for these *Be-*
" *guins* to live by Begging, than to live by Labour, or the Work of their
" Hands, altho' the said *Beguins* do not labour in preaching the Gospel.
" *Item*, That he would not obey the Pope, if he should command him not to
" beg, or otherwise to live by his own Labour ; and that he would not part
" with the Habit of the *Beguins*, which he wears, at the Command of the Pope.
" *Item*, That he believes and holds and asserts, that the Pope can't destroy or
" abolish any Order formerly confirmed by the *Roman* Church. *Item*, He af-
" serts that he believes and holds, that the whole Doctrine and Scripture of
" Friar *Peter John Olivi*, of the Order of Friars Minor, is true and catholick,
" according to the Understanding which he had therein, as he believes, that
" the Doctrine of St. *John* the Evangelist is faithful and catholick, according to
" the Understanding which he had therein; and adds, that he believes that as
" *John* the Evangelist is in *Paradise*, so he believes that the aforesaid Friar *Peter*
" *John* is in *Paradise*, altho' St. *John* hath the greater Glory. *Item*, He asserts,
" That if the Pope should condemn the Doctrine or Scripture of the aforesaid
" *Peter John*, he should not think it to be condemned, tho' he should con-
" demn it by a thousand Bulls, and altho' he should condemn it with the

P 2 " Advice

" Advice of the Cardinals, and all the Prelates, and even of a whole General
" Council. *Item,* That he would not believe the Pope, saying to him, that
" the Doctrine of the said Friar *Peter John* contains Errors and Heresies,
" nor obey the Pope if he should command him to recal what he had said
" on this Head ; and that if for this he should excommunicate him, he
" should not therefore think himself to be excommunicated. *Item,* He af-
" serts that he believes and holds those Things to be true, which Friar *Pe-*
" *ter John* wrote, in a Posthil upon the Revelations, of *Babylon* the great Whore
" sitting upon the Beast, by which he understands and expounds it to be the
" Church of *Rome,* which he says is *Babylon* the great Whore and the carnal
" Church. *Item,* He says, that the said *Roman* Church, under the Name of
" *Babylon,* is to be damned, and rejected, and exterminated by *Christ,* in
" that sixth State of the Church, which now is ; and says, that the spiritual
" Church is to be begun and restored by the Rejection of the carnal Church,
" even as the old Synagogue of the *Jews* was rejected by *Christ,* when the Go-
" spel of *Christ* and the primitive Church began. Therefore we the aforesaid
" Inquisitors, *&c.* leave him, as relapsed, to the Arm and Judgment of the
" Secular Court, *&c.* But we will and command that if the aforesaid *Peter Do-*
" *minici* shall humbly ask, and truly repent, he shall receive the Sacrament
" of Penance and the Eucharist. *

Bzovius,   But this Affair did not end here. Friar *Berengarius,* in a Council of many
a. 1322. Divines and Lawyers, summon'd by the Bishop and Inquisitor at *Narbonne,* de-
§. 1. fended the Cause of the *Beguins.* Friar *John Bemmius,* a Predicant and Inquisitor, pronounced this heretical, and ordered *Berengarius* to recant. He refused,
and appealing to the Apostolick See, went to *Avignion,* and gave the Pope an
Account of the whole Affair, who kept *Berengarius* in honourable Custody,
and proposed it afterwards to all the Academies, and the most learned Men
all over the World, as a Question fit to be debated, Whether it was not to be
esteemed heretical, obstinately to affirm, that our Lord *Jesus Christ,* and his
Apostles had nothing in special or in common ? After the Question was proposed, that all might give their Opinion with greater Freedom, he suspended
In Decre- the Anathema published by *Nicholas* IV. against the Interpreters of this Sense,
tal. Exiit. and of the Rule of St. *Francis,* and gave to all free Power to dispute, write,
and give their Sense concerning the Thesis.

* Besides the Tenets charged upon the aforesaid *Beguins,* there are others imputed to them of a
very flagitious Nature ; *viz.* that to kiss Women and embrace them, provided they did not consummate the carnal Sin, was greatly meritorious, and an Argument of Fortitude and Abstinence,
and of a strong and acceptable Love of God, and the truest Proof that each Party was resolutely
virtuous ; and that whatever Lies any Man told a Woman to gain her Consent to his Desires, was
not Heresy, so that he believed in his Heart that the carnal Act was Sin ; even tho' to gain her Consent he should tell her, that the carnal Act was meritorious, and for the Safety of her Soul, yet that
it would not be Sin, if he held the contrary in his Heart. And agreeable to this was their Practice,
putting themselves naked in Bed with naked Women, kissing and embracing them in a very lewd
manner, boasting of their Continence and Resolution, because they abstained from the last carnal
Act. These, and many Things of the like kind, are to be found in the Sentence of one *William*
Ruffi, in the Book of the Sentences of the *Tholouse* Inquisition, *fol.* 196. *b.*

                    The

The Friars Minors met at *Peroufe*, from all the Provinces of the Chriftian World, about the next *Whitfontide*. There was prefent *Michael Cæfenas*, General of the Order, and other Provincial Minifters. Being admonifhed by fome Cardinals, that they fhould give their Opinion in this Affair agreeable to the Senfe of the Fathers, they replied thus : *Adhering firmly and wholly to the Determination of the holy* Roman *Church, we fay and confefs with one Heart and Mind, that to fay and affert, that* Chrift, *fhewing the Way of Perfection, and his Apoftles following the fame Way of Perfection, and giving an Example to others who are willing to live perfectly, had nothing by Right of Property and Domain, no proper Right, whether fpecial or in common, is not heretical, but found, catholick, and faith-*xxiv. q. 1. *ful: Efpecially as the holy* Roman *Catholick Church, which is proved never to have*ªrecta,&c. *deviated or erred from the Path of Apoftolick Tradition, fays this exprefly, affirms,*pudenda *and manifeftly determines it.* Extra de verb. fignif. Exiit. l. 6.

When this Refcript of the Chapter was feen, by which the Opinion of the *Beguins* was approved, the Pope publifhed an Edict concerning the Ufe of Things diftinct from Property, beginning, *Ad conditorem Canonum.* But whn Friar *Bonagratia Bergomenfis*, made by the Chapter Procurator of the Order, protefted againft the Pope, and appealed to a future Pontiff, or Oecumenical Council, which Appeal was judged to be infolent ; the Pope by a Decree, beginning, *Cum inter nonnullos viros fcholafticos*, declared it to be heretical to affert, that our Saviour and his Apoftles had no Right to ufe or confume the Things which the facred Scriptures teftify they had, nor any Right to fell or give them, or procure other Things by them.

But as *Cæfenas* did not acquiefce in this Sentence of the Pope, but oppofed Bzovius, the Papal Conftitutions, being affifted by the Friars *Bonagratia Bergomenfis,*a. 1329. *Peter Corbarius*, and *William Ockam*, an *Englifhman*, in the Year 1329. May,§. 5, &c; Cal. 12. he was declared by the Pope to be a Favourer of Hereticks, an open Heretick, an Arch-heretick, and a Schifmatick, and degraded from all Offices, Dignities, and Honours whatfoever, and deprived of the Ecclefiaftical Privilege, and declared incapable of any, and fubjected to all the Punifhments and Sentences, Spiritual and Temporal, to which the Favourers of Hereticks, Arch-hereticks, and Schifmaticks, are liable, by Divine or Ecclefiaftical Law. The Friars Minors being gathered together in a General Chapter at *Paris*, after they had pronounced *Cæfenas* entirely degraded, and put *Gerard Odonis* into his Place, publifhed this Sentence of the Pope, and declared that both he and his Companions had incurred the Penalties of Excommunication and Privation, as notorious and manifeft Apoftates, which by the Statutes of the Order are well known to be inflicted on thofe Friars who withdraw themfelves, and apoftatize from the Obedience of the Order. This Sentence of the Order being fent to the Pope, he again pronounced *Cæfenas* guilty of various Crimes and Herefies, and condemned him, *December*, Cal. 16. of the fame Year. *Corbarius*, terrified with this dreadful Sentence, confeffed his Errors, and after having read his Confeffion and Abjuration of his Errors, and fworn to obey the Apoftolick Commands, he obtained the Benefit of Abfolution from all Sentences, either of the Law or Men.

Cæfenas

a. 1330.
§. 6.
 Cæsenas however not terrified by thefe Denunciations, afferted notwith-ftanding, that he was General of his Order, and a Catholick, and lived fafe from the Papal Violence with his Followers, under the Government of *Lewis* of *Bavaria.* Upon which the Pope renewed his Curfes againft them, and cited them by a peremptory publick Edict, to appear perfonally be-fore him, before the Feaft of the Afcenfion of our Lord, to hear their Sentence. But as they defended themfelves againft the Accufations and Pro-

a. 1331.
§. 1, &c.
cefs of the Pope, by the Apologies they publifh'd, *Gerard Odonis*, Gene-ral of the Minorite Order, fententially condemned them as Favourers of Hereticks, Hereticks and Arch-hereticks, and not only deprived them of the Privileges, Graces, Benefits, Habit, Company and Favour of the Order, but condemn'd them to perpetual Imprifonment. He commanded alfo all and fingular the Keepers and Guardians of Convents, in Virtue of their falutary Obedience, that they fhould publickly declare them in full Con-vent every Week deprived and excommunicate, and fententially condemn-ed. And finally, Pope *John* publifh'd againft them the thirty eighth, and

a. 1335.
§. 4.
the two hundred fifty ninth Sanctions. His Succeffor *Benedict* XII. in the Year 1335. and firft of his Pontificate, renewed the Curfes that *John* XXII. had pronounced againft the *Fratricelli* or *Beguins,* and their Complices, and thus render'd them more heavy.

C H A P. XX.

The PROCESS *againft* Matthew Galeacius, *Vifcount* Milan, *and others.*

Raynald.
a. 1320.
§. 13.
a. 1322.
§. 5, &c.
Bzovius,
a. 1322.
a. 1324.
§. 14.
 DUring this Quarrel with the *Beguins*, Sentence of Excommunication was pronounced againft *Matthew Galeacius*, Vifcount *Milan*, and againft his Sons and Followers. Hereby all the Cities and Lands, fubject to their Government (as is declared in the Sentence againft *Caftruccius Gerius*) and of his Party were put under an Ecclefiaftical Interdict, and many heavy Sen-tences publifh'd againft all Perfons who adhered to them, favoured, obeyed or affifted them ; and that folemn Indulgence, which was always granted to thofe who affifted in the Recovery of the Holy Land, was openly preach'd againft them. The City it felf was deprived of its Charter and all its Pri-vileges and Immunities whatfoever ; and all the Citizens and Inhabitants fa-vouring the faid condemned *Matthew*, given up to be feiz'd by the Faith-ful, to be made their Slaves by full Right, their Effects granted to any one that could lay hold of them, and their Debtors upon any Account freed from all their Debts, whatever Inftrument or Oath they were bound by. Farther, all who fent or bought, or carried Provifions, or any other Things ufeful in Life, to the City of *Milan,* or who received Pay from them, were fententi-ally

ally excommunicated. *Matthew* defpifed thefe Papal Cenfures, and continued more than three Years under Excommunication. To revenge this Contempt of his Cenfures, *John* XXII. profecuted him for Herefy, as contemning the Authority of the Church, and her facred Rites; and commanded
Aycard, Archbifhop of *Milan*, and the Inquifitors of heretical Pravity in
Lombardy, to proceed with all Vigour upon the faid Crime of Herefy;
who after feveral Citations, at laft pronounced the definitive Sentence
againft him; in which, amongft other Crimes this is imputed to him:
*That he held erroneous Opinions about the Sacraments, and the Power of the Keys
and Church; and had fuch an abfolute Contempt of them, that he fuffer'd himfelf
to lie under feveral Sentences of Excommunication pronounced againft him both by Men
and the Law: He caufed alfo the Ecclefiaftical Interdict, which the faid City of*
Milan *was put under, for the Crimes of* Matthew, *to be feveral Times violated,
by ordering the Bodies of dead Laicks to be buried in the Churches, and Church
Yards, with tolling the Bells, even though the Minifters of fuch Churches were
againft it. He alfo caufed the like to be done in thofe Lands and Places, which were
held by his Sons, though put under the like Interdict.* At length they pronounce
Sentence againft him in thefe Words: *For thefe and many other Reafons, moving us jufty and reafonably thereunto, invoking the Name of Chrift, and fitting on our
Tribunal, we pronounce the definitive Sentence; and by thefe Writings do fentence,
decree and adjudge the aforefaid* Matthew, *Vifcount* Milan, *abfent through Contumacy, the divine Prefence making up that Abfence, a manifeft Heretick: And we
condemn the faid* Matthew *as an Heretick; and by the fame Sentence confifcate, and
declare to be confifcated, all his Effects, moveable and immoveable, Rights, Jurifdi-
ctions, and all other Things belonging to him, where-ever they are, and by whatfoever Name they are called. We alfo deprive, and declare to be deprived, the faid*
Matthew *of his military Belt, Offices, publick Dignities and Honours whatfoever,
and fubject him to the Sentence of Excommunication, perpetual Infamy, and all other
Penalties appointed, ordained or promulgated againft Hereticks; and order his Perfon
to be feiz'd by the Faithful. Moreover we deprive, or rather declare to be already
deprived, the Sons and Grandfons of the aforefaid* Matthew, *of their Prelatures,
Dignities, and other Ecclefiaftical Benefices, either with Cure or without, and of all
publick Offices and Honours whatfoever, which they are known to poffefs, and declare
them to be for ever hereafter unworthy and incapable of holding Prelatures, Dignities, or other Ecclefiaftical Benefices, either with Cure or without, and all publick
Offices and Honours whatfoever.* This Sentence was pronounced *March* 14,
1322.

The Pope alfo commanded the Archbifhop and Inquifitors, that they fhould
proceed againft all who adhered to Vifcount *Matthew* and his Sons, as againft
Favourers of Hereticks condemn'd by the Church, and punifh according to the
Ecclefiaftical Law, all who were convicted of being of his Party, and of the
other Crimes. The Bifhop of *Parma* and two Abbots publifh'd thefe Sentences, and commanded the Anathemas to be every where proclaim'd; and order'd *Raymond Cardonus* to gather an Army to chaftife the Rebels. Several
Cities were taken, and the Vifcount routed. The Senate and People of *Mi-*

2   *lan*

lan not enduring thus every Day to be condemn'd, and forbid divine Services, sent twelve Men to the Legate, to beg Peace and Absolution. *Matthew* quite broke by these Evils and others that threaten'd him, resigned the Principality to his Son *Galeacius*, and order'd himself to be carried into the principal Church, where he complain'd that he was unjustly accused of Heresy; and protesting by an Oath that he was without any Crime deprived of divine Services, he appeal'd to God, the righteous Judge, that he was condemn'd most unrighteously by the factious Legate, and forced to abandon his Country. Thus departing from the City, and making the same Profession the Day after in the Church of St. *John Baptist* at *Monza*, he fell into a Fever, and died some Days after with Grief and Sorrow. His Sons buried him in a private mean Place, concealing for some Time his Death, least his Body should have been burn'd, according to the Order of the Cardinal Legate and Inquisitors, *October* 30. They used the most exquisite Diligence to find it out, but could not discover it, though they pronounced many Anathemas against those who knew where it was laid, and would not reveal it.

Bzovius, *a.* 1327. §. 7. The like Sentence was pronounced not many Years after by the same Pope, against *Marsilius Paduanus*, and *John Jardunus*, Assertors of the Imperial Authority against the unjust Usurpations of the Pope, who pronounced them Hereticks, and manifest Arch-hereticks, and commanded all who followed their Doctrine, to be universally accounted as Hereticks. He farther enjoin'd all the Faithful that they should not presume to receive, defend, maintain, or afford, by themselves, or any other or others, publickly or privately, directly or indirectly, any Assistance, Counsel or Favour to them, or any of them, but that they should rather avoid them as manifest Hereticks. Finally, he orders the Faithful to seize on them, that they might prosecute them with a Zeal becoming the Faith; and to take them where-ever they could find them; and when taken, to deliver them to the Church, that they might undergo the deserv'd Punishment.

CHAP. XXI.

The INQUISITION *introduced into* Poland, *and restored in* France.

AS nothing was more serviceable to enlarge the Papal Jurisdiction than the Office of the Inquisition, the Popes were continually endeavouring to promote it; and to establish it in those Kingdoms and Countries, that hitherto had been free from so grievous a Yoke, that there might not be any Place of Shelter or Refuge in the whole Christian World to such as Bzovius, should in the least contradict their Decrees. *An.* 1327. Pope *John* XXII. by *a.* 1327. Letters to the King and Prelates of *Poland*, and to the Provincial of the Pre-§. 18, &c. dicant Friars of the same Kingdom, appointed the Inquisition in *Poland*, which

in

in the Year following, 1436. *Uladiflaus Jagello,* King of *Poland,* confirmed and enlarged, by a Royal Edict, granting them the moft ample Power, and commanding all the Magiftrates to give them all Manner of Affiftance in the Execution of their Office.

At this Time the Inquifition began to decline in *France* ; but as there was a pretty large Number of the *Valdenfes* remaining in *Daupheny,* and their Religion began to fpread wider, *Gregory* applied himfelf to *Charles* King of *France.* He put him in Mind of the Examples of his Predeceffors in deftroying Hereticks, and admonifhed him to fupprefs the Nobles of *Daupheny,* who took the Hereticks under their Protection ; and that he fhould fupport the Authority of the Inquifitors, not only by feverer Edicts, but by fending fome Royal Officer to their Affiftance. King *Charles* yielded to the Pope's Defires ; and after the Manner of his Anceftors, by a Royal Edict, commanded that Hereticks fhould fuffer the fevereft Punifhments ; and that the Magiftrates in *Daupheny* fhould affift and aid the Officers of the Holy Inquifition. *Antonius Maffanus,* Apoftolick Inter-nuncio, acted in this Affair with fuch Zeal, that the Prifons were fcarce fufficient to hold the Criminals ; nor was their Provifion enough for their Support. *Gregory* having been confulted in this Matter, order'd, That as the great Number of Hereticks was owing to the Negligence of the Prelates, the Revenues of the Churches fhould be applied to that Ufe ; and commanded new and ftronger Jails to be built at *Arles, Ambrune, Vienne,* and *Avignon,* and granted Indulgences to the Faithful who fhould contribute to the Work.

From *France,* thofe who were called **Turelupini,* went into *Savoy:* And therefore the Pope commanded *Amedæus,* Count of *Savoy,* to condemn them to the Flames, and affift the Inquifitors. *Bzovius* adds, *It came to pafs, that this favage and brutal Sect was condemn'd, burn'd, and wholly extirpated this Year.* And again : *Many of thefe Hereticks were burn'd in* France *at the Pope's Command.* But this horrid Cruelty could not laft long, and proved at laft fatal to the Judges themfelves. For in *Savoy* the Inquifitors were killed, by thofe unqueftionably who were afraid that the like Cruelty would be practifed towards themfelves ; which when the Pope heard of, he endeavour'd to render the Murderers hateful to Count *Amedæus,* putting him in Mind, that he had given a moft excellent Example of defending the Faith by his Victories over the *Turks,* and recovering *Callipoli* from them ; and that therefore he hoped he would not fuffer the Blood of thofe Orthodox Prelates, who were flain out of a real Hatred to Piety, to be fhed with Impunity.

Raynald.
a. 1375.
§. 26, -7.

Bzovius,
a. 1372.
§. 7.
Raynald.
a. 137⁵.
§. 27.

---

* Some of the Followers of the *Valdenfes* ; fo called, according to Popifh Writers, becaufe they inhabited only thofe Places which were expofed to Wolves. *Du Frefne in Voce.*

C H A P. XXII.

Of WICKLEFF, HUSS, *and the* INQUISITION *against the* HUSSITES.

Bzovius,
a. 1377.
§. 8, &c.

ABOUT these Times *John Wickleff* arose in *England*, and not only opposed several of the Errors of the Church of *Rome*, but especially the exorbitant Power of the *Roman* Pontiff, vindicating the Rights of the secular Magistrates, and teaching that the Clergy were not exempted from their Jurisdiction and Obedience. The Pope, by his Letters to the University of *Oxford, commanded them by Virtue of their holy Obedience, and under the Penalty of being deprived of all Favours, Indulgencies, and Privileges, that had been granted them by the Apostolick See, that they should not suffer any one to defend* Wickleff's *Propositions, but should order* Wickleff *himself to be seiz'd, and send him in safe Custody to the Archbishop of* Canterbury, *and the Bishop of* London, *or one of them.* He also by Letters commanded the said Archbishop of *Canterbury* and Bishop of *London*, that *they should order* Wickleff *to be apprehended by the Papal Authority, and commit him to Jail, and put him in Irons under safe Custody, till farther Orders from himself upon this Affair.* And after mention of these Things out of his former Letters, he farther commands, *That if the aforesaid* John, *apprehending his being seized and imprisoned, should abscond, so that they could not apprehend and confine him ; that then they should take Care peremptorily to admonish and cite him, in the Pope's Name, by a publick Edict, to be set up in one of the Colleges of* Oxford, *then in the Diocese of* Lincoln, *and all other publick Places, to appear and answer personally to his Propositions before the Pope, where-ever he should be, within the Space of three Months, to be computed from the Day of this Citation ;* adding, *That whether the said* John *should appear or not, within the said Term, they should proceed against him upon the Premises, even to the Condemnation he had deserved, according as his Crimes should require, and as they saw fit for the Honour of God, and the Preservation of the Faith.* And in other Letters he commands them, *That they should endeavour to take* Wickleff's *Confession, and transmit it to him by a faithful Messenger, sealed with their own Seals, without shewing it to any one, and keep him in Irons till they should receive his farther Commands.* He sent also other Letters to *Edward* King of *England*, by which he requires and earnestly beseeches him, *That he would grant his Favour, Protection and Help to the Archbishops and Bishops, and others, employ'd in prosecuting this Affair.* All these Letters bare Date *June*, Cal. 11. 1377.

Raynald.
a. 1388.
§. 12.
a. 1396.
§. 9, &c.
Bzovius,
§. 6.
Raynald.
§. 17.

After the Death of *Wickleff*, *Richard* King of *England*, commanded by a solemn Edict, all his Writings to be burn'd, together with those of *Nicholas Hereford*, and *John Aston*. In the Year 1396. the Pope wrote to the King, and begged him to assist the Prelates of the Church in the Cause of God, of the King himself, and the Kingdom against the *Lollards*, and earnestly besought him that he would condemn those whom the Prelates should declare Hereticks. The same Year *Thomas Arundel*, Archbishop of *Canterbury*, and

I

Apo-

Apoftolick Legate, held a Provincial Synod at *London*, to extirpate the He-refy of *Wickleff*; in which were condemned eighteen of his Articles. After this the Archbifhop ufed great Severity againft thofe who maintained them, many of whom he condemned to the Flames. To fuch as abjured he appointed an wholefome Penance, that in the Time of publick Prayers, and in the open Market, they fhould go in Proceffion, only with their Shirts on them, carry-ing in one Hand a burning Taper, and in the other a Crucifix, and that they fhould fall thrice on their Knees, and every Time devoutly kifs it.

Soon after arofe *John Hufs* in *Bohemia*, and began publickly to reprove the diffolute Lives of all the Orders. Whilft he inveigh'd only againft the Seculars, all the Divines applauded him ; but when once he began openly to reproach them for their corrupt Manners and Vices, they abhorred and detefted him, and ufed their utmoft Endeavours to deftroy him. At that Time, *An.* 1400. *Jerome* of *Prague* returned from *England*, and brought with him *Wickleff's* Writings, which *Hufs* approved. And fince many others approved of them, out of Deference to the Doctrine and Authority of *Hufs*, and defended the Articles of *Wickleff*; thofe Articles were again examined and condemned, *May* 24, 1408. by forty Mafters, and an infinite Number of Batchelors, who prohibited, under the Penalty of the Bann, any Perfon to teach them. *Hufs* was very defirous to render all this ineffectual ; and therefore, as the Fo-reigners were divided into three Claffes of Votes, and the *Bohemians* made the fourth, according to the Inftitution of the School, he fo order'd it, that the *Bohemians* fhould be equal in Number of Votes to the other three : Upon which they left *Prague* with Indignation, and went into *Mifnia*, and there condemn-ed again *Wickleff's* Books, and adjudged them to the Flames. Above 200 Vo-lumes were burn'd, according to *Æneas Sylvius*, fairly written out, and adorn-ed with golden Boffes and curious Binding.

Not long after this, *Hufs* offer'd certain Thefes to be publickly difputed, by which he oppofed the Indulgencies which *John* XXIII. had granted to thofe who fhould engage in the Cruciad, which he had ordered againft the King of *Naples*. *Jerome* of *Prague*, alfo fhewed their Vanity. At length, after many Proceffes formed againft the Memory of *Wickleff*, and againft *Hufs*, the Council of *Conftance* affembled, and ordered *Hufs* to appear before them, and give an Account of his Doctrine ; and to prevent his not coming, *Sigifmond* the Emperor gave him Letters of fafe Conduct for his coming there, ftay-ing, and departure thence. In this Synod the Doctrine of *Wickleff* and *Hufs* was condemned : Several learned Men were deputed to examine both their Doctrines, who when they had read their Books, pronounced that they had found forty five pernicious Articles in *Wickleff*, and thirty in *Hufs* ; which tho' they were not all of them equally impious, fome being worfe than others, yet all contained deadly Poifon, and were altogether, or at leaft, in fome Part, con-trary to the wholfome Doctrine of the Church : Upon this the Synod not on-ly condemn'd the Books, but pronounced Sentence againft *Wickleff*, though dead, by which they declared him an Heretick, excommunicated him, and ordered his Bones, if they could be found, to be taken out of their Grave and

Q 2   burn'd.

burn'd. They alfo not only condemn'd *John Hufs*, who came to the Council with Letters of fafe Conduct from the Emperor ; but in Violation of the
publick Faith, order'd him to be burn'd alive. The Emperor, that he might
have fome Pretence thus to violate his Faith, made a Decree, that Inquifition might be made by a proper Judge of heretical Pravity, notwithftanding
the fafe Conducts granted by Emperors and Kings, &c. The Words of the
Decree are, *Although they fhould confide in their fafe Conduct, and thus come to
the Place of Judgment, and would not otherwife have come ; and that he who
fhould make fuch a Promife, was not oblig'd by it as to any one, becaufe he promifed what was not in his Power.* Afterwards alfo *Jerome* of *Prague*, terrified with the dreadful Punifhment of *Hufs*, renounced at firft, through humane Infirmity, the Doctrine of *Wickleff* and *Hufs* ; but foon recovered his
Courage, and boldly afferted and defended it before the whole Synod ; upon
which they condemned him as a Relapfe, and ordered him to be burn'd.

But fince many of the Papifts endeavour to wipe off this Infamy of having
violated the Faith, I fhall take this Occafion briefly to fhew that the publick
Faith was violated in the Cafe of *Hufs*, by Command of the Synod. They deny that the Synod gave their Faith to *Hufs*, and that 'twas only the Emperor ; fo that the Synod, which was the legal Judge of the Faith,
might pronounce Judgment concerning *Hufs*'s Doctrine, although the Emperor had given him Letters of fafe Conduct ; becaufe the Affair of Herefy
is wholly Ecclefiaftical, and not within the Bounds of the fecular Power. But
the Charge is not, that the Synod violated the Faith by condemning *Hufs*
of Herefy, but becaufe they caufed him to be burn'd. The Power of the
Synod, according to the Papifts themfelves, extends no farther than to their
judging of the Faith, and pronouncing by their Sentence any one an Heretick and Obftinate, and throwing him out of the Bofom of the Church ; after Sentence they immediately deliver him over to the fecular Power, that
he may inflict on him the Punifhments appointed by the Civil Laws. In
this Manner the Synod proceeded in the Caufe of *Hufs*. After they had declared him an Heretick, and degraded him in the Council, they added this
Decree to their Sentence : *This holy Synod of* Conftance, *confidering,* N. B.
that the Church of God cannot proceed farther, decrees that John Hufs *fhall be
left to the fecular Judgment, and given up to the fecular Court.* Thus far therefore the Church performed her Duty : All the reft belonged to the fecular
Jurifdiction. But here the Emperor had taken Care for *Hufs* his Security, by
giving him Letters of fafe Conduct, and therefore could not condemn him to
be burn'd without violating his Faith : And therefore the Synod, to remove
this Scruple from the Emperor, pronounced by their Decree, that he who
bound himfelf by fuch a Promife was in no Manner obliged by it as to any
one, becaufe he promifed what was not properly in his Power to grant. So
that the Synod did not properly violate the Faith given by themfelves, but
pronounced by their Decree, that Emperors, Kings and Princes were in no
Manner obliged by their Promifes of fafe Conduct, and that therefore they
might with a fafe Confcience break them, even when granted by publick

Letters,

Letters, at the Beck of the Council: And this is so manifest from the Decree of the Council of *Constance*, that *Simanca*, a *Spaniard*, proves from thence, that Faith is not to be kept with Hereticks: *Therefore*, says he, *Hereticks* are *justly burn'd with righteous Flames, by the most grave Determination of the Council of* Constance, *even though they had received the Promise of Safety.* And farther, *Bzovius* relates, that Pope *Martin* endeavouring to disſuade *Alexander*, General of *Lithuania*, from giving any Aſſiſtance to the *Bohemians*, thus, amongst other Things, writes to him in his Letter: *But if you have been any Ways engaged by Promise to undertake their Defence, know, that you could not give your Faith to Hereticks, who are Violators of the holy Faith, and that you will ſin mortally if you keep it, becaus̄e a Believer can have no Communion with an Infidel.* What can be clearer? I ſhall add nothing farther in so evident a Matter. It is enough that I have ſhewn that the Faith was violated by the Council of *Constance*, the Papiſts themſelves being Judges, and indeed approving it.

De Catho!. Doct. tit. 46. §. 52. a. 1422. §. 3.

Wickleff. Huſs, and *Jerome*, and their Doctrine, being thus condemned, *Martin* V. ſent Letters to the Archbiſhops, Biſhops, and the Inquiſitors of heretical Pravity every where, beginning, *Inter cunctas Paſtoralis curæ*, in which he tells them, *That in the Kingdom of* Bohemia, *the Marquiſate of* Moravia, *and the neighbouring Places*, John Wickleff, John Huſs, *and* Jerome *of* Prague, *Arch-hereticks, had riſen up, and that the Council of* Conſtance *had condemned their Writings and Books. But whereas some of their Followers were in Poſſeſſion of them; he commands, that all ſuch Perſons, and all who approved their Doctrines, and were their Abettors, ſhould be delivered over as Hereticks to the ſecular Courts: That ſuch who received them, if it were only through common Affection, or the like Cauſes, ſhould be ſtrictly prohibited: That the Impenitent ſhould be ſeverely puniſhed. He commands Princes to baniſh them their Dominions. He orders manifeſt Hereticks, though not condemned, to be puniſhed, and even ſuſpected ones, if they would not canonically purge themſelves. He farther commands the Princes to obey the Inquiſitors. He orders ſuſpected Perſons to be interrogated upon the Articles of* Wickleff *and* Huſs, *which he afterwards ſubjoins with the Interrogatories, and to be cited for this Purpose. He commands this Bull to be publiſh'd, and that all* Sundays *and* Feſtivals *it ſhould be publickly declared, that all Hereticks and their Abettors were excommunicated. That all who held the Errors of the aforeſaid Arch-hereticks, and their Abettors, even though confeſſed, ſhould be puniſhed, if they refuſed to make a publick Abjuration, or to undergo the Penance enjoined them. Finally, he repeals every Thing contrary hereto.*

By this Decree the Inquiſition was reſtored and eſtabliſhed in the Kingdom of *Bohemia*, whereby many were condemn'd of Hereſy, and put to Death by various Puniſhments: Some were burn'd alive, others thrown into the River, ty'd Hands and Feet, and so drowned; and others deſtroy'd by different Methods of Cruelty.

CHAP.

CHAP. XXIII.

Of the INQUISITION *in* VALENCE, FLANDERS, *and* ARTOIS.

Bzovius,
a. 1419.
§. 20.
Hitherto the Kingdom of *Valence* had no particular Inquisitor of the Faith. The Inquisitor at *Rofes* in *Catalonia* exercifed the Holy Office in that Kingdom by his Vicars and Commiffaries, fo that they could not make fo large a Progrefs in converting the *Jews* and *Moors*, of whom great Numbers lived there. And therefore Pope *Martin*, at the Requeft of King *Alphonfus*, by Letters dated at *Florence*, *Apr.* Cal. 6. 1419. decreed, that the Office of the Inquifition in the Kingdom of *Valence*, fhould, for the future, be governed and adminifter'd, without any Impediment, not by Commiffaries and Vicars, but by an Inquifitor deputed by the Prior, to whom that Affair belongs, who is to refide there perfonally himfelf, and act as Principal.

Boxhorm.
Hift. Belg.
p. 42, &c.
J. Le Clerc
Dom. de
Beauvoir.
About the Year 1460. the Inquifition raged cruelly in *Flanders* and *Artois*, againft certain Perfons, who were falfly accufed of Magick, and being in League with the Devil, who, to render the *Valdenfes* odious, were called *Valdenfes*, and the Place in which they were faid to have their nightly Meetings, *Valdefia*. At *Doway*, *Arras*, and other Places, many of them were thrown into Prifon at feveral Times, at the Demand of *Peter Bruffard*, Inquifitor, where being overcome with Torments, they confeffed every thing they were charged with, and, amongft other Things, that they had given themfelves to the Devil, adored him, and known him carnally, and other incredible Things of the fame kind. When they were condemned to the Fire, they protefted themfelves innocent, and publickly declared with a loud Voice that they never were in *Valdefia*, as they called the Place of this nightly Meeting of Witches and Devils ; but that they were deceived by their Judges, who by fair Promifes of faving their Lives and Eftates, if they would confefs the Crimes objected to them, drew from them a falfe Confeffion of Crimes they were never guilty of. Others faid, that they extorted a falfe Confeffion from them by Torments, finally befeeching the By-ftanders to pray for them to God, to whom they committed their Souls in the Midft of the Flames. But their Innocence afterwards appeared ; for in the Year 1491. thefe miferable Creatures, with others thrown into Prifon on the fame Account, were declared innocent by the Sentence of the Parliament of *Paris*, and had their Effects reftored to them, and their unrighteous Judges were feverely fined.

C H A P. XXIV.

Of the SPANISH INQUISITION.

IN the preceding Chapters we have feen how the Inquifition was brought into feveral Kingdoms of *Spain,* but as yet it had not been fixed in *Caftile* and *Leon,* or was there grown into Difufe. *Ferdinand* and *Ifabel* having united the feveral Kingdoms of *Spain* by their Inter-marriage, after having obtained fignal Victories over the *Moors,* order'd Tribunals of the Inquifition to be erected throughout all their Kingdoms. It is not eafy to be determined whether they did this out of their blind Zeal for Religion, or that they might poffefs their Kingdoms in greater Peace and Security, after having expelled the *Mahometan* and *Jewifh* Superftitions out of them, or, as fome believe, becaufe they affected the univerfal Monarchy of *Europe,* and therefore, by fome notable Undertaking, to fhew their great Zeal for the *Roman* Religion, endeavour'd to fecure the Good-Will and Favour of the Pope. However, as the Inquifition had flourifhed for many Years in *Italy, France, Germany, Poland,* and *Aragon,* they introduced the Inquifition into all their Kingdoms by Authority of Pope *Sixtus,* with greater Pomp, Magnificence and Power, that they might not be exceeded by any Nation, but might rather exceed all others, in their Endeavours to maintain the *Roman* Faith againft all Oppofition. The Pretence was this:

That by the Licentioufnefs of former Times great Corruptions had arifen [Bzovius, *a.* 1478. §. 14.] in the Kingdom, *Moors, Jews,* and *Chriftians* promifcuoufly converfing, and having all Sort of Commerce with each other; That by fuch Commerce and Familiarity fome Chriftians might be eafily infected, and others forfake the Chriftian Worfhip which they had received, after having renounced their native Superftition, being weak in the Faith, and having none to forbid them. The Infection was faid to have fpread moft at *Seville,* where many, after being privately put to the Queftion, fuffered the moft grievous Punifhments. The Occafion was this: *Alphonfus Hojeda,* Prior of the Convent of St. *Paul* [Param. *l. z. t. z. c. 3. n. z.*] at *Seville,* a Predicant, had for many Years, in his Sermons to the People, bitterly inveighed againft thofe, who, leaving the Profeffion of Chriftianity, apoftatized to *Judaifm.* This Man was informed by a certain Citizen of the Family of the *Gufmans,* that on a *Thurfday,* during the Feftival of the Sacrament, the firft Vigil of the Night, feveral *Jews* and Apoftates had got together in fome Houfes, and there performed the *Jewifh* Ceremonies, and uttered execrable Blafphemies and Reproaches againft our Saviour. All thefe Things *Gufman* faw with his Eyes in a private Part of a Houfe, where he concealed himfelf with a Girl. The Prior perfuaded *Gufman* to write all thefe Things down, and fign them with his Name, and then immediately went and difcover'd all to the King and Queen at *Cordova.* They ordered that the Affair fhould be enquired into. Upon this the Prior put fix of this Number into

Irons

Irons in the Convent of St. *Paul*, afterwards several more of them, and at last severely punished all of them, according to the Nature of their Offence. They who were the most guilty were burnt, after long Imprisonment and Torture; such as were less guilty, had their Families render'd infamons; great Numbers had their Estates confiscated, and were condemned to eternal Darkness and Chains. A large red Cross, with Cross Rays, upon a yellow Garment, which they call *San Benito*, different from the rest, was put on most of them, as an Example to others, and by the Severity of the Punishment, to be a Terror to them. All these Things seemed at first grievous to the Provincials, but especially that the Children should suffer for the Parents Crimes, that People should be render'd guilty by a private Accuser, and condemned without being confronted with the Informer, contrary to the ancient Custom, when Offences against Religion were punished with Death. But what they looked on as the worst was, that the Inquisitors took away all Liberty of free Conversation, having their Spies in Cities, Towns, and Villages, which they thought to be the lowest Slavery. Amongst many different Judgments, some were against Death, tho' all thought very severe Punishments should be inflicted. Amongst these was *Ferdinand Pulgarius*, a Man of a sharp and ready Wit, who wrote the History of King *Ferdinand*. Others thought they ought not to have the Benefit of Life and the common Air; that they ought to be punished with Forfeiture of Goods, and with Infamy, without any Regard to their Children; that this was wisely provided for by the Laws, that Parents should be render'd more cautious, by their Affection for their Children; that dropping of Actions would be prevented, by allowing private Witnesses; and that by this Means none would be punished but such as were plainly convicted, or confessed: That the ancient Customs of the Church were often changed, as Affairs and Times required; and that greater Licentiousness ought to be restrained with greater Severity. Judges were chosen out of every Province, to whose Pleasure the Fortunes, Reputations, and Lives of all Persons were committed.

These Transactions at *Seville* were soon known all over *Spain*, upon which divers Intimations were given to their Catholick Majesties, that most of the *Jews* lately converted to the Faith, whose Parents had been perswaded to believe by the Sermons of St. *Vincentius Ferrerius*, used secretly in their Houses the *Jewish* Rites, and taught Christians the old Law: That therefore they earnestly besought their Majesties, out of their Catholick Piety, to put a Stop to these growing Evils, least the poisonous Contagion should every Day spread farther; for otherwise, unless a Remedy was immediately applied, great Inconveniences would accrew to the Church of God. Amongst these the Chief were *Peter Gonzalez a Mendoza*, Archbishop of *Seville*, Friar *Thomas a Turrecremata*, a Predicant, the Prior of the Convent of the Holy Cross at *Segovia*, and their Majesties Confessor. By his Instigation principally *Ferdinand* and *Elizabeth* placed *Gonzalez Mendoza*, Archbishop of *Seville*, over all Causes of the Paith, joining in Commission with him Friar *Thomas a Turrecramata*, to recover the Office of the Inquisition, which in Process of Time had very

2   much

much declined in that Kingdom, to its former Vigour and Severity. They determined that the Office of the Inquisition ought to be reformed. Upon this their Catholick Majesties earnestly desired the Pope, that they might have Power of creating Inquisitors in the Kingdom of *Castile* and *Leon*. *Sixtus* IV. granted it to them; and altho' the Apostolical Letters of this Grant are not extant, yet the same *Sixtus* makes mention of them in two other Bulls, which *are preserved in the Books of Apostolical Bulls, by the General Inquisitor at *Madrid, fol.* 1. and 2.

Paramus; *l.* 2. *t.* 2. *c.* 3. *n.* 8.

By Authority of this Bull they appointed only two Inquisitors at *Seville*, Friar *Michael a Morillo*, and Friar *John a S. Martino*, the first Doctor, the other Batchelor of Divinity, both Predicants. *An.* 1482. the Pope confirmed these two, who were chosen Inquisitors by their Majesties, upon this Condition, that they should proceed in Causes of Faith in Conjunction with the Ordinaries of Places, according to the Order of the Law. But because the Pope apprehended that the Inquisitors, which were settled either by the General or the Provincials of the *Dominican* Order in the Provinces, were sufficient to manage the Affairs of the Faith, he deprived their Majesties of the Power of making Inquisitors in other Places. *An.* 1482. the same *Sixtus* IV. at the Request of their said Majesties, appointed by his Bull, bearing Date the 3d of the Ides of *February*, seven *Dominicans* Censors of the Faith, who might have Cognizance of Matters relating to the Faith in the Kingdoms of *Castile* and *Leon*, because the two Inquisitors at *Seville* were not sufficient. These, by the Pope's Command, made a severe Inquisition against all who were secretly guilty of *Judaism*.

Within the Time fixed for Persons voluntarily to confess their Sins, with the Hopes of Pardon, about 17000 of both Sexes appeared, who had their Lives granted them. Many however refused to obey either the Papal Letters, or Royal Edicts, but persisted in their Heresy; for which they were seized upon the Testimony of credible Witnesses, and, thro' the Violence of their Torments, confessing their Crimes, were thrown into the Fire; of which some are reported to have bewailed their Sins, and acknowledged Christ, whilst others persisted in their Errors, calling on the Name of *Moses*. Within a few Years two thousand of them of both Sexes were burnt. Others, professing Repentance, were condemned to perpetual Imprisonment, others wore Crosses; the Bones of others who were dead were taken out of their Graves and burnt to Ashes, their Effects confiscated, and their Children deprived of their Honours and Offices. Most of the *Jews* being terrified with this Cruelty, left their Country and Houses, and in this great Distress of their Affairs, fled from the Kingdoms of their Catholick Majesties. Many went into *Portugal*, many into *Navarre*, others into *Italy*, others into *France* and other Countries, where they thought they could be safe; all whose Goods and Effects, moveable and immoveable, if they had any, their Catholick Majesties distributed towards the War, which was then made against the *Moors* and other Barbarians. These Things amounted to a prodigious Sum. In *Andalusia* and *Granada* alone, those who fled with their Wives and Children left five thousand naked and

Bzovius; *a.* 1481. §. 11. Raynald; *Epit.*

R   empty

empty Houses. Others, according to *Paramus,* affirm, that their Number was much greater ; this is certain, that in the City and Diocese of *Seville* only, there were above 100000 Persons alive or dead, present or absent, who were condemned for Contumacy, or reconciled to the Church.

And thus the different Opinions concerning the Year of appointing the Inquisition in *Spain* may be easily reconciled. The general Opinion is, that 'twas brought in in the Year 1483 or 1484. *Ribadineira,* in the Life of *Ignatius Loyola,* says, that it was fixed in the Kingdoms of *Castile* and *Leon, An.* 1481. and in *Aragon, Valencia,* and *Catalonia, An.* 1483. *Bzovius* refers the Erection of it in the Kingdom of *Castile* to the Year 1478. and says that four Years after it passed into *Aragon.* They all agree, if we consider, that the Inquisition was first introduced, *An.* 1478. but that the first Inquisitor General, and the supreme Council of the Inquisition was not fixed till the Year 1483.

Lib. 2. cap. 28.

The Method of this Tribunal, as now in use, is this : The King proposes to the Pope the supreme Inquisitor of all his Kingdoms, whom the Pope confirms in his Office. The Inquisitor thus confirmed by the Pope, is Head and Chief of the Inquisition in the whole Kingdom, and hath given him by his Holiness full Power in all Cases relating to Heresy. It belongs to his Office to name particular Inquisitors, in every Place where there is any Tribunal of the Inquisition, who nevertheless cannot act unless approved by the King ; to send Visitors to the Provinces of the Inquisitors, to grant Dispensations to Penitents and their Children, and to deliberate concerning other very weighty Affairs. In the Royal City the King appoints the supreme Council of the Inquisition, over which the supreme Inquisitor of the Kingdom presides. He hath joined with him five Counsellors, who have the Title of Apostolical Inquisitors, who are chose by the Inquisitor General upon the King's Nomination. One of these must always be a *Dominican,* according to the Constitution of *Philip* III. dated *Dec.* 16, 1618. Besides these, there is an Advocate Fiscal, two Secretaries, and one of the King's, one Receiver, two Relators, several Qualificators, and Counsellors. There are also Officials deputed by the President, with the King's Advice. The supreme Authority is in this Council of the Inquisition. They deliberate upon all Affairs with the Inquisitor General, determine the greater Cases, make new Laws according to the Exigency of Affairs, determine Differences amongst particular Inquisitors, punish the Offences of the Servants, receive Appeals from inferior Tribunals, and from them there is no Appeal but to the King. In other Tribunals there are two or three Inquisitors : They have particular Places assigned them, *Toledo, Cuenca, Valladolid, Calahorre, Seville, Cordoue, Granada, Ellerena,* and in the *Aragons, Valencia, Saragossa,* and *Barcelona.*

Carena, lib. 3.

These are called Provincial Inquisitors. They cannot imprison any Priest, Knight, or Nobleman, nor hold any Publick Acts of Faith, without consulting the supreme Council of the Inquisition. Sometimes this supreme Council deputes one of their own Counsellors to them, in order to give the greater Solemnity to the Acts of Faith.

Carena, tit. 3. §. 8, &c.

Thefe

Thefe Provincial Inquifitors give all of them an Account of their Provin_cial Tribunal once every Year to the fupreme Council, and efpecially of the Caufes that have been determined within that Year, and of the State and Num_ber of their Prifoners in actual Cuftody. They give alfo every Month an Ac_count of all Monies which they have received, either from the Revenues of the Holy Office, or pecuniary Punifhments and Fines.

This Council meets every Day, except Holy-days, in the Palace-Royal, on *Mondays, Wednefdays,* and *Fridays* in the Morning, and on *Tuefdays, Thurf_days,* and *Saturdays* after Vefpers : In thefe three laft Days two Counfellors of the fupreme Council of *Caftile* meet with them, who are alfo Counfellors of the fupreme Council of the Inquifition.

This Tribunal is now arifen to fuch an Height in *Spain,* that the King of *ibid.* §. 12. *Caftile,* before his Coronation, fubjects himfelf and all his Dominions, by a fpecial Oath, to the moft holy Tribunal of this moft fevere Inquifition.

This Office is not, as formerly, committed to the *Predicant* or *Dominican* Pegna *in* Friars. They began to employ in it the fecular Clergy, who were fkilful in *Direct.* the Decrees and Laws, till at laft the whole Power gradually devolved on them, *Par. 3.* fo that now the *Dominican* Friars have no Part in it; tho' the Inquifitors often- *Comm.* 34 times ufe their Affiftance, in judging of Propofitions, and they are employed as Counfellors in the Holy Office.

The firft Inquifitor General in the Kingdoms of *Spain,* was Friar *Thomas Tur_recremata,* a Predicant, Prior of the Monaftery of the Holy Crofs at *Segovia,* who was in high Efteem with their Majefties, as having often expiated their Sins by Penance. *Paramus* relates, that he was created Inquifitor General of the Kingdoms of *Caftile* and *Leon* by *Sixtus* IV. *An.* 1483. and that the Pope gave him Power by his Letters of making fuch Inquifitors as he thought pro_per, and of recalling thofe who had been Inquifitors there before, and order_ed him to make ufe of the new Method appointed in managing Caufes of the Faith, which was much more proper than the old one. Afterwards the fame Pope made the Provinces of *Aragon, Valencia, Catalonia* and *Sicily,* fubject to the fupreme Inquifitor of *Caftile* and *Leon,* by his Bull, expedited the fame Year 1483. This Bull *Innocent* VIII. who fucceeded *Sixtus* in the Pontificate, confirmed, as far as it related to *Caftile* and *Leon, An.* 1485. and the next Year, as it related to *Aragon, Valencia,* and *Catalonia. Alexander* VI. did the fame. *Innocent's* Bull runs thus:

Innocent *Bifhop, Servant of the Servants of God, to our beloved Son* Thomas Turrecremata, *of the Order of Predicant Friars, and Profeffor of Divinity, Health and Apoftolical Benediction.* Sixtus IV. *our Predeceffor of happy Memory, in order to extirpate the Herefies, which through the Inftigation of the great Enemy of Mankind, had arifen in the Kingdoms of* Caftile, Leon, *and* Aragon, *and other Kingdoms and Dominions fubject to our moft dear Son in Chrift, King* Ferdinand, *and to our moft dear Daughter in Chrift,* Queen Elizabeth, *as we have been in_formed, to our great Grief, by diverfe Letters inftituted and deputed Thee Inquifitor General of heretical Pravity, in all the Kingdoms, Dominions, and Countries aforefaid, as in the faid Letters is more fully contained, the Tenor of which is hereby to be fully*

R 2 *underftood,*

understood, as though they were inserted in these present, Word for Word. We therefore desiring, according to the Duty incumbent on us, that in our Time also the Office of the Inquisition may, as it ought, proceed in a due Manner, do by our Apostolick Authority, and by our own certain Knowledge, by Virtue of these present, approve and confirm such Institution and Deputation, and all and singular the Letters for that End, and decree that they shall remain in full Strength; and we do now afresh make, constitute and depute Thee to be Inquisitor in the Kingdoms and Dominions aforesaid, with the same Powers which the said Sixtus, our Predecessor, had before granted you: We do also renew the aforesaid Letters in all and every Thing; and grant unto you full, free and universal Power to take and substitute other Ecclesiastical Persons, fit, learned, and fearing God, provided they be Masters in Divinity, Doctors of the Civil or Canon Law, Licenciates, Canons of Cathedral Churches, or otherways in Possession of Ecclesiastical Dignities, as often, and whensoever you shall know there is need; as also to remove any, and put others alike qualified in their room, who shall enjoy the like Jurisdiction, Power and Authority of Proceeding with the Ordinary in the said Affair, that any other Persons do. And because 'tis just, that those who labour in so holy an Office, Affair, and necessary Work, should not be deprived of their Rights, by the same Authority we grant to all and singular Ecclesiastical Persons, who shall be engaged in this Work, and so long as they shall labour in it, the Fruits, Returns and Profits of all Ecclesiastical Benefices, with or without Cure, which they have, or hereafter shall have, of what Kind soever, in any Churches or Places, freely to enjoy them in the same full Manner (all the Dues and Customs of such Benefices maintained) as they would have enjoyed them if they had personally resided in the said Churches or Places; and that they shall not be obliged in the mean Time to reside in them, nor forced to it by any Person or Authority whatsoever; notwithstanding ye have not made your first personal usual Residence in such Churches or Places, any Apostolical, Provincial, Synodical, or other general Edicts to the contrary, or any special Constitutions, Appointments, Statutes or Customs of those Churches where such Benefices may be, strengthened by Oath, Apostolical Confirmation, or any other Security whatsoever; and although the said Persons may have hitherto, or hereafter shall happen to sware by themselves, or their Procurator, that they will serve in such Benefices, and not obtain Letters Apostolical, to dispense with them, nor make Use of such Letters obtained by other or others, or granted to others upon any Account whatsoever, and all other Things to the contrary notwithstanding, mentioned by the said Sixtus our Predecessor, in his said Letters Apostolical, and all other Things to the contrary notwithstanding whatsoever. Given at Rome *at* St. Peter's, *in the Year of the Incarnation of our Lord* 1484, (or 1485.) Feb. Ides 3. *and second Year of our Pontificate.*

In the Year 1484. as we may collect from the first Instruction of *Seville,* there was held by the Papal Authority, and at the Desire of their Catholick Majesties, a famous Assembly of Men, most learned in both Laws, and in Divinity, at *Seville,* Friar *Thomas de Turrecremata,* Inquisitor General of all *Spain,* being President, in which the Method of Proceeding against heretical Pravity was agreed on, and several Laws and Constitutions made and settled, which the Inquisitors use to this Day. This Order was afterwards

in-

inlarged by other Inftructions. In the fame Affembly it was provided that *Hifp. Infr.* the Inquifitors fhould publifh an Edict in their Diocefes, by which it was or- *1. cap. 3.* dered, that whofoever, within forty, fifty, or more Days, as they fhould judge proper, fhould voluntarily and fully confefs their Errors and Herefies before the Inquifitors, and fhould difcover other Hereticks, fhould be admitted to wholfome Penance, and reconciled to the Church, without fuffering Death, Irons, or the Forfeiture and Confifcation of their Effects. The Ob- *a.* 1478. fervation of *Bzovius* is here remarkable. *From this Beginning the Inquifition grew* §. 14. *up into fuch an Authority and Power, as makes it the moft terrible to bad Men throughout the whole Chriftian World ; given by God for the unfpeakable Benefit of the whole Commonwealth, and as a prefent Remedy againft thofe threatning Evils with which other Provinces are afflicted : For no human Wifdom could ever have provided againft fuch fatal Dangers.* Neither muft I omit what *Simancas* fays : *De Cath. Spain was always moft zealous for the Chriftian Religion, and ever moft fincerely Inftit. tit. reverenced the Catholick Faith, after it once receiv'd it ; and bare the greateft Ha-* 46. §. 41. *tred to Hereticks. All in Spain who have Cognizance of the Affairs of Faith, obferve the Duty of their Office with that Fidelity, that Integrity and Vigilance, that no one dares whifper any Thing againft the holy Statutes of the Church. In other Places Vafæus Men are reftrained from acting impioufly, but in Spain they are not permitted to Cronic. fpeak but according to Piety. In other Places Errors are extirpated when they arife ; Hifp. tom. but in Spain the very Seeds of Herefy are deftroy'd before they fpring up.* 1. c. 9.

[*Ludovicus a Paramo* relates, that in the Year 1485. there were famous Acts *lib. 2. tit.* of the Inquifition, by the Inquifitors of heretical Pravity, in the Town of *Gua-* 2. cap. 4. *dalup,* held in a Pulpit and on a very large Scaffold, erected before the Doors of *n. 2. p.* the Church, in the Church Yard, over againft the Market Place, in which Acts 138, 139, of the Inquifition, which were feven or eight, Friar *Didachus Marchena,* an heretical Monk, and fifty two for judaifing, of both Sexes, were deliver'd over to the Fire ; forty fix Bodies of Hereticks were dug out of their Graves, and adjudged to the Flames ; the Images of twenty five abfent Perfons were burn'd ; fixteen condemned to perpetual Punifhment, befides innumerable others fent to the Gallies ; and others condemned to ware confecrated courfe Habits, as a Mark of perpetual Penance and Infamy. When thefe Acts were finifh'd, and the Fathers Inquifitors were departing from *Guadalup,* they publifh'd an Edict by the Common Cryer, that within one Month all Perfons, of every Sex and Age, infected with the *Jewifh* Superftition, fhould leave that Town, under the Penalty of being punifhed as relapfed : And they made it a perpetual Law, that for the Honour of the Virgin Mother of God, and her facred Convent and People, no converted Perfon, or of the Race of the *Jews,* fhould from henceforth ever dwell there. Upon Occafion of this Edict, Care was taken in the firft general Chapter, that was afterwards celebrated in the Convent of St. *Jerome,* the Prior of which, Friar *Numinis ab Arevolo,* with other Inquifitors, held thofe Acts, that no one of the faid Race fhould ever be admitted to the facred Order of St. *Jerome.* What *Paramus* adds farther is ridiculous : That when the aforefaid Inquifitor of the holy Office eagerly defired fome Sign from the bleffed Virgin *Mary,* of *Guadalup,* in thofe Days of the Inquifition, to exalt the Faith, and for the Confufion of Herefies and Errors, there were fo many evident Miracles wrought by pioufly invocating the holy Virgin, that Doctor *Francis Sanctius de la Fuente,* one of the faid Fathers, who had undertaken the Care of writing thofe Things, was quite tired out with writing them, through the Multitude of the Miracles. For there were fixty Miracles counted up for the Confirmation of the Faith, the Approbation of the Office of the holy Inquifition, the Edification of many, and the Difplay of the Divine Power.

lib. 2. tit.
2. cap. 8.
n. 13. p.
179, &c.
The fame Perfon relates, that Pope *Sixtus* IV. at the Defire of *Ferdinand* and *Ifabell,* extended the fupreme Power of the Inquifition, which he had granted to *Thomas a Turrecremata,* in the Kingdom of *Caftile,* to *Aragon, Catalonia, Valencia,* and *Sicily.* However, great Oppofition was made to this Tribunal in *Aragon,* many declaring that this new Form of the Inquifition was contrary to the Prerogatives and Liberties of the Kingdom, and was in it felf too fevere and unrighteous ; that the Depofitions of the Witneffes were not fhewn to the Criminals ; and that Perfons Eftates were confifcated becaufe of fome heretical Mark ; which Things they affirmed were not only contrary to the Ufage of the Kingdom, but to every Rule of Juftice. And that they might more eafily obtain the Abrogation of the Inquifition, they fent a large Sum of Money to the Courts of the Pope, and of the King. However, they obtained nothing ; fo that at laft the People broke out into an open Tumult, which *Raynald* and *Ozovius* principally attribute] to the new Converts, who from the *Jewifh* Superftition and Race were converted

Raynald.
a. 1485.
§. 21, 22.
Bzovius,
a. 1485.
§. 10, 11.
to Chriftianity. Many of the principal Men joined themfelves to them, who complained that new Laws were introduced contrary to the Liberties of *Aragon.* During this Sedition *Peter Arbuefius,* the Inquifitor, was killed at *Saragoffa,* as he was faying his Prayers before the High Altar. The Murder was imputed to the *Jews.* [The Murderers, as *Paramus* relates, were not long after all taken up by the Inquifitors, delivered over to the fecular Arm, and fuffered moft dreadful Punifhments.] But all Attempts for the Liberty of *Aragon* were in vain ; and fo far was this Tribunal of the Inquifition in Matters of Religion from being abolifhed, that upon the Death of thofe who oppofed it, it was much more ftrongly confirmed than ever. For *Ferdinand* and *Ifabel,* to give the greater Authority to the Tribunal of the Inquifition, gave the Royal Palace at *Saragoffa* to the Judges of the Faith, and by many Provifions confirmed the Tribunal of the Faith.

Bzovius,
a. 1491.
§. 3.
They alfo endeavoured to propagate the Office of the Inquifition in all their Kingdoms. Pope *Innocent* VIII. publifhed a Decree, *An.* 1491. againft thofe who fhould hinder any from appealing to the Apoftolick See. When that Conftitution was publifhed, it happen'd that the Bifhops of *Segovia* and *Calahorre* in *Spain,* their Parents, Kindred, and fome other illuftrious Ecclefiaftical Perfons, powerful for their Riches and Intereft, were accufed of Herefy before the Inquifitor General of *Aragon, Valencia,* and *Catalonia.* They appealed to Pope *Innocent,* that they might not be tried in the ordinary Court, but that their Caufe might be determined at the Court of *Rome.* Friar *Thomas Turrecremata*

recremata was at that Time Inquifitor General. The King and Queen thought that that Appeal was made to efcape Juftice, and would occafion great Scandal and Danger, and therefore intimated to the Pope what was neceffary to preferve the Faith, and befought him that he would not fuffer any Perfons, by frivolous Pretences, to bring the ordinary Jurifdiction of the Holy Office into Contempt. The Pope was not ignorant that the Caufes of the Bifhops, when guilty of Herefy, belonged to the Apoftolick See, but however did not cite them to *Rome*, but appointed the Bifhop of *Tournay* his Nuncio or Commiffary in *Spain*, who fhould examine the Caufe jointly with the Inquifitor, and report the whole Affair upon the Judiciary Procefs to the Apoftolick See, and wait for the Determination of his Holinefs thereupon, but ordered that the Inquifitor fhould proceed upon all others, who were not Bifhops, accufed of Herefy, according to his Office. *This was granted,* fays *Surita, at that Time to the Piety of their Majefties, whofe only and principal Care was to put a Stop to Impiety.* Paramus adds, " That when it was afterwards found by Experience, *c.* 4. *v.* 148 " and the Event of Things, that great Inconveniences arofe from that Me- " thod of Proceeding, the Pope ordered that the Inquifitor General fhould deter- " mine in all Caufes of Appeal, which is obferved to this Day, the Pope ne- " ver fuffering fuch Affairs to be brought before the Apoftolick See upon any " Appeal whatfoever.

　　In the mean Time, *Ferdinand* had made great Slaughter of the *Moors*, and at laft entirely fubdued them in the Kingdom of *Granada*, having reduced the City of *Granada* it felf into his Power. And therefore, to purge their King- Simanc. doms entirely of the *Jewifh* Superftition, *Ferdinand* and *Ifabel*, by a Law, *tit.* 35. drove the *Jews* out of *Spain*; to whom, however, after a long Confultation §. 7. of the Wife Men, was granted the Space of four Years, within which they were either to be converted to the Catholick Faith, or fell all their Effects, and depart from *Spain*, with all their Goods and Chattels they had purchafed with Money. For, as *Paramus* fays, they were not allowed to carry Money out of *Spain*, either Silver or Gold, becaufe it had been prohibited by Law long before for the publick Good. This Edict was render'd more fevere by a new Conftitution of *Thomas Turrecremata*, Inquifitor General of the Faith, in Bzovius, the Month of *April*, who forbid all the Pious to have any Commerce with that *a.* 1494. Nation, and prohibited them, under a grievous Penalty, not to affift them §. 39. with Provifion, or any other Thing, after the Period of Time that he had fet them. The fame *Thomas* had before perfwaded the King and Queen, that they fhould not, for the Sake of a large Sum of Money, difpenfe with the Confifcation of their Effects at the earneft Prayers of the *Jews*. And he prevailed *Aphor. In-* on them not to do it, as *Antonius de Soufa* relates it. But *Paramus* tells us, that *quif. l.* 4. he went up to the Palace, and hid under his Habit a Crucifix, and thus fpoke *c.* 22. §. 3. to the King and Queen with great Freedom: *I underftand the King's Affair.* lib. 2. tit. *Behold the Image of our crucified Saviour, whom that moft wretched* Judas *fold to* 2. cap. 3. *his Enemies for thirty Pieces of Silver, and betray'd him to his Perfecutors. If ye* n. 16. *approve that Deed, fell him for a greater Price. As to my felf, I renounce all Power. Let nothing be imputed to me. You muft give an Account of the Bargain to*
　　　　　　　　　　　　　　　　　　　　　　　　　　　　　　　　　　God.

God. After this, he laid down the Crucifix before them, and departed. When the Time was elapsed, they who persisted in their Religion were forced to depart, with their Wives, Children, Servants, Families, and Effects, and forbid ever to return into *Spain,* where if they were ever after found, they were to be immediately punished with Death and Confiscation of Goods. It was also provided by the Pragmatick Laws, that 'no *Jew* should ever enter *Spain* upon any Pretence whatsoever, under the same Penalty of Death, and Confiscation of Goods, if ever found there; and that it should signify nothing, tho' they declared they were willing to be converted to the Faith, unless they should make publick Protestation of it upon their first Entrance into the Kingdom. And if any Christian was convicted of harbouring the *Jews,* all his Effects were to be forfeited. *Pragm.* 5. at *Granada,* 1492. and *Pragm.* 6. *ibid.* 1499. *John Picus,* Earl of *Mirandola,* gives a fine Account of this Expulsion, in his Book against Astrologers, *lib.* 5 *cap.* 12. The Number of those who were thus banished from *Spain* were four hundred thousand *Jews,* according to *Reuchlin* and others. *Mariana* says, 'tis not easy to reduce them to

any certain Number. Most Writers affirm, there were 170000 Families that departed; others say there were 800000 Persons, a prodigious Number, almost exceeding Belief. Some of them, who were a little more dilatory in gathering together their Effects, and would not turn Christians, were sold for Slaves; and of those who left their Country, *Surita* tells us many died of the Fatigues of Travelling, or the Plague.

The *Jews,* thus driven from *Spain,* fled for the most part into *Portugal,* and obtained from King *John,* under certain Conditions, that they might live there for a certain Season. The Conditions were chiefly these, That every one should pay to the King eight Pieces of Gold, and leave *Portugal* within a limited Time, and forfeit their Liberty if they exceeded it; and that the King should grant them free Liberty to sail away. Whilst the King lived, *Bzovius* tells us he took great Care to perform his Promise to the *Jews.* He commanded his Officers in the Ports, that they should agree with the Masters of Ships, for transporting the *Jews* where they pleas'd for a reasonable Price; and farther order'd, that no one should injure them. But it happen'd far otherwise: For the Merchants and Masters, who had receiv'd the *Jews* on board their Ships, used them very cruelly at Sea. Not contented with the Price they had agreed for, they used all the Methods they could invent to extort more from them, and besides this, even forced their Wives and Daughters. These horrid Abuses terrifying the *Jews* that yet remained in *Portugal,* and not being able through Poverty to purchase within the Time the Necessaries for their Voyage, suffer'd it to elapse, and thus lost their Liberty; and he who wanted a *Jew* Servant, begged him of the King. In the mean while King *John* died.

His Successor *Emanuel,* finding that the *Jews* could not help staying longer in *Portugal* than the Time fixed them by *John,* gave them all their Liberty. Some Time after this he was advised by the King and Queen of *Castile* by
Letters, not to suffer that wicked Nation, hated by God and Man, to abide in *Portugal.* After mature Deliberation of the Affair, he commanded all the

Jews and *Moors* in *Portugal*, who would not profess the Christian Religion, to depart the Kingdom, and set them a Day, after which, if any of them were found there, they should forfeit their Liberty. The *Moors* immediately passed over into *Africa*. And as the *Jews* were preparing to depart, the King commanded that all their Children, who were not above fourteen Years old, should be taken from their Parents, and educated in the Christian Religion. It was a most affecting Thing, to see Children snatched from the Embraces of their Mothers, and Fathers embracing their Children violently torn from them, and even beat with Clubs, to hear the dreadful Cries they made, and every Place filled with the Lamentations and Yells of Women. Many through Indignation threw their Sons into Pits, and others killed them with their own Hands. What added to their Misery was, that those who would have gone over to *Africa* to avoid these Evils, were not suffered ; for the King deferred giving them the Liberty of sailing Day after Day. And although at first he assigned them three Ports, where they might go on board, he afterwards forbid their sailing from any other but that of *Lisbon*. This brought a vast Number of the *Jews* to that City. But in the mean while the appointed Day was past, so that such of them as could not get off were necessarily made Slaves. Most of them being overcome with these Calamities, chose rather either sincerely or feignedly, to make Profession of Christianity, than to live in such Miseries, and being baptized, recovered their Liberty and Children. No Violence however was offered to the *Moors*, least the *Saracens* in *Asia* and *Africa* should make Reprisals on the Christians in those Countries.

The Papists usually ascribe this Action of the King's to a pious Mind, and his Zeal to propagate the Christian Religion, and provide for the Salvation of Children, and yet in the mean while condemn it as wicked and unjust, and contrary to the Laws and Constitution of the Gospel ; since it is not lawful to compel any one against his Will to the Christian Worship, or to take Children from their Parents, unless the Parents forfeit their Right in them by their Crimes.

In the Year 1500, *Francis Ximenes*, Archbishop of *Toledo*, by the Pope's Persuasion, took great Pains to convert the *Moors* of *Granada* to the Christian Faith. He first of all gained over their chief Priests, which they call *Alfaquins*, by Gifts and Favours. A great Number followed their Example. However others vigorously opposed *Ximenes*, and endeavoured to deter the *Moors* from Christianity. *Ximenes* *ordered these to be put in Irons in Prison, and to be very cruelly used.* Of this Number was one *Zegri*, who was the most powerful amongst them, upon account of the Nobility of his Birth, and his excellent Qualifications of Mind and Body. *Ximenes* *laying aside almost all Humanity, determined to punish him most severely.* He delivered him to one *Peter Lyon, his Chaplain, a Man of a truly Lyon-like Mind,* who soon brought him to *Ximenes* his Beck, and made him in a few Days desire to be carried before the *Alfaquin* of the Christians. Bound and dirty as he was, he came before *Ximenes*, and declared he would be a Christian, for that he had had a Vision from *Ala* (as the *Moors* call God) that Night, admonishing him to it. *But*

truly,

Side notes:
Raynald.
a. 1496.
§. 26, &c.
Bzovius,
a. 1497.
§. 27.

Bzovius,
a. 1500.
§. 16.

truly, says he, laughing, *I am a Fool to seek for Arguments any where else, but from thy fierce Lyon, to whose keeping, if any of us are committed, they will immediately become Christians.* Upon this he declared himself a Christian, and was baptized, and experienced *Ximenes* his Bounty. He was afterwards of great Service, not only in promoting Christianity amongst his Country-men, but to the Common-wealth. *Ximenes* glorying in this Succeſs, commanded all the Alcorans, and all other Books whatſoever that had any Thing in them of the *Mahometan* Superſtition, to be brought publickly together. There were about 5000 Volumes, which were all openly burnt in one Heap to a ſingle Book, except ſome few relating to Medicine, which for the Honour of ſo uſeful an Art, were ſaved from the Flames, and laid up in the *Complutenſian* Library. *Bzovius* adds, *There were however many who thought it unjuſt, and altogether contrary to the Nature of Chriſtianity, to compel any one by Force, and ſuch like Arts, to profeſs the Faith of Chriſt, the entire Tendency of which is Gentleneſs, and which requires eſpecially a ready and ſincere Mind. Beſides that in the Councils of* Toledo, *which are reckoned ſacred by all Chriſtians, 'tis determined in the moſt ſolemn Manner, that no one ſhould be forced to believe in Chriſt. But he followed his own Judgment, and in the Midſt of Danger ſhewed the Conſtancy of his Mind, and declared in this important Caſe the invincible Reſolution of his Soul. For in all human Affairs every great Undertaking is ſure to raiſe Envy, which oftentimes overthrows the nobleſt Deſigns, and by a thouſand Difficulties renders them impracticable.*

One of *Ximenes*'s Family, called *Salzedus,* came with two Servants to the *Albaizinum.* This is a Place in the City of *Granada,* craggy, and hanging over the reſt of the City, and ſeparated from it by its own Walls. When they were come here, firſt there aroſe reproachful Words between them and the Inhabitants, at laſt they came to Blows, and the two Companions of *Salzedus* were killed by the Multitude. *Salzedus* fled for it, and with great Difficulty eſcaped. However the Tumult encreaſed, ſo that the whole City was in an Uproar. Their Deſign was to pull down the Houſe of *Ximenes.* The Tumult laſted ten Days, and was at laſt ſuppreſſed by the Garriſon. The *Albaizinenſes* were condemned for High Treaſon, and had the Choice given them of Death or Baptiſm, upon which to a Man they embraced Chriſtianity. The Archbiſhop of *Granada* took Care to have them daily inſtructed in the Chriſtian Myſteries. He alſo ordered ſome Leſſons out of the Old and New Teſtament to be read to the new Converts in the *Mooriſh* Language, and permitted the printing of ſome Books, in which ſome Parts of the Service of the Maſs, and ſome Paſſages of the Goſpel were tranſlated into *Arabick.* But *Ximenes* would not ſuffer it, ſaying, *It was a Sin to throw Pearl before Swine.* He allowed indeed the Uſe of ſome Books written by pious Men in the vulgar Tongue; but ſaid, *That the Old and New Teſtament, in which there were many Things that required a learned and attentive Reader, and a chaſte and pious Mind, ſhould be kept in thoſe three Languages only, which God, not without the greateſt Myſtery, ordered to be placed over his moſt dear Son's Head, when he ſuffered the Death of the Croſs;* and affirmed, *That then Chriſtianity*

would suffer the greateſt Miſchief, when the Bible ſhould be tranſlated into the vul-
gar Tongues.

This Tumult ſpread beyond the Kingdom of *Granada*. *Ximenes*, by the
Permiſſion of the Inquiſitors, endeavoured to force certain *Moors* called *Elches*,
who had embraced Chriſtianity, and afterwards rejected it, to become Chriſtians again, and commanded their Children to be violently taken from them
and baptized. This was the Beginning of Troubles, which afterwards grew
to ſuch an height, that the *Moors* formed a Conſpiracy, and rebelled in many Places. But as their Forces were inferior to the *Spaniards*, they were
ſubdued, and forced to turn Chriſtians. The King granted, that as many
as would ſhould go over to *Africa*, and provided them with Ships to tranſport them at the Port of *Aſtopa*, demanding from every one that went over
ten Pieces of Gold only, as the Price of their Liberty. They who would
not leave their Country, he ordered to become ſincere Chriſtians. This
Agreement being made, many went into *Africa*, *though moſt of them remained
in* Spain, *pretending themſelves to be Chriſtians, but not a jot better than thoſe who
left it, being of a very obſtinate and wicked Diſpoſition.*

An. 1501. *Ferdinand*, King of *Caſtile*, at the Inſtigation of Pope *Alexander*, Bzovius,
took great Pains in catechiſing the *Moors*, and preventing their Apoſtacy. *a.* 1501.
He publiſhed an Edict in *Caſtile*, againſt the *Moors* in that Province, and ſ. 13.
eſpecially againſt thoſe of *Andaluſia*, *Granada*, and *Aragon*, commonly called
Mudegiares, who lived and traded promiſcuouſly with the Pious, that unleſs
they would become Chriſtians, they ſhould depart his Dominions within a
certain Day.

Upon the Death of *Ferdinand*, *Charles* ſucceeded him. The new Converts Param. *l.*2.
offered him 800000 Pieces of Gold, if he would command, that the Witneſſes *tit.* 2. *cap.*
at the Tribunal of the Inquiſition ſhould be always made publick. The ſ. *n.* 4.
young King, who was about eighteen Years old, had a great Mind to the
Money. But Cardinal *Ximenes*, Inquiſitor General, ſhewed him the great
Danger of ſuch a Method, and that the Church would receive great Injury
by it, and by putting him in mind of his Grandfather *Ferdinand*, prevailed
with the King to refuſe the Offer.

C H A P. XXV.

Of the INQUISITION *in* Portugal.

W E have related in the former Chapter, how that the *Jews* being
drove out of *Spain*, were received under certain Conditions by the
King of *Portugal*. However, not many Years after, he erected the Tribunal of the Inquiſition in his Kingdom, after the Model of that in *Spain*.
Bzovius ſpeaks of this Affair, deſcribing the Death of King *John* III. " How *a.* 1557.
" great ſ. 56, 57.

" great his Zeal was to maintain the Faith in its ancient Splendor, his intro-
" ducing the facred Tribunal of the Inquifitors of Herefy into *Portugal*, is
" an abundant Proof, bravely over-coming thofe Difficulties and Obftru-
" ctions, which the Devil had cunningly raifed in the City, to prevent or
" retard his Majefty's Endeavours. For he learnt Experience from others,
" and grew wife by the Misfortunes of many Kingdoms, which from the
" moft flourifhing State were brought to Ruin and Deftruction by monftrous
" and deadly Herefies. And it is very worthy Obfervation, that the Year in
" which the Tribunal of the holy Inquifition againft heretical Pravity was
" brought into *Portugal*, the Kingdom laboured under the moft dreadful
" Barrennefs and Famine. But when the Tribunal was once erected, the
" following Year was remarkable for an incredible Plenty, commonly called
" the Year of St. *Blafe*, becaufe, before his Feftival, which was on the third
" of the Nones of *February*, the Seed could not be fown in the Ground for
" want of Rain, whereas afterwards Provifion was fo very cheap, that a
" Bufhel of Corn fold for Two-pence."

By what Means King *John* III. brought this Tribunal into *Portugal*, he no
where tells us. Only he gives us a Bull of *Paul* III. beginning, *Illius vices in
terris*. By which he approves of the Abfolution and Indulgencies granted by
his Predeceffor *Clement* VII. to fuch as were already converted, in order to
draw over the Hereticks and Unbelievers of the Kingdoms of *Portugal* and
Algarve, to the true Faith. In this Bull it is related, that *Clement* VII. deputed *Didacus de Silva*, a Minim Friar, Profeffor of St. *Francis de Paula*, to
be his and the Apoftolick Sees Commiffary, and Inquifitor over the new
Chriftians, returning to the *Jewifh* Rites they had forfaken, and all others
embracing Errors and Herefies, in the Kingdom and Dominions aforefaid,
with full Power to make Inquifition againft all who were guilty, or fufpected
of thefe Crimes, and to imprifon, corrrect and punifh them ; and that afterwards, for certain reafonable Caufes, he fufpends, by other Letters, during
his Pleafure, the aforefaid, and all other his Letters whatfoever, and all
Faculties and Commiffions granted in the Premiffes by the faid Letters, to the
faid *Didacus*, and all Ordinaries of Places whatfoever, and by Friar *Mark* Bifhop
of *Senogaglia*, Nuncio of the Apoftolick See to the King of *Portugal*, acquaints
Didacus and the aforefaid Ordinaries, and the other Inquifitors in thofe Parts, of
thefe laft Letters. Afterwards there is a long Detail of the Favours granted by
Clement VII. his Predeceffor, to the new Converts, or the Defcendants of the
Jewifh Converts, all which he approves and confirms, decreeing that all
fuch Perfons, though imprifoned, and their Crimes notorioufly proved in
their Trials, and they themfelves condemned as Hereticks, fhall be forgiven
all the Punifhments they were condemned to as fuch before the Date of the
faid Letters ; that they fhall not be obliged to confefs, abjure or renounce ;
that they fhall be freed from their Goals, Banifhments and Banns ; that they
fhall enjoy all Privileges and Favours, which are enjoyed by any other of the
Faithful of Chrift, their Children, and Grand-children, and that they fhall
not be under any Mark of Incapacity and Infamy ; he makes void, cancels,

a. 1535.
§. 33.

2   blots

blots out, and annuls all Proceſſes and Sentences pronounced againſt them, and other Tranſactions, though after the Date of the foreſaid Letters; he reſtores to them and their Heirs all their confiſcated Effects, if not already brought into the Treaſury; orders that no Inquiſition ſhall be made concerning any Crimes favouring of Hereſy, Apoſtacy and Blaſphemy committed by them any Ways, even to the Day of the Date of theſe preſent; that they ſhall not be accuſed of them, or moleſted for them, and that no Prejudice ſhall accrue to them or their Children upon account of them; that they ſhall not be looked on as reconciled and abſolved, and of Conſequence not be accounted as relapſed, if they ſhall afterwards fall into any of the aforeſaid Errors. It is his Pleaſure however that ſuch as are in Priſon, or out on Bail, who have been condemned or convicted of Hereſy, or Apoſtacy from the Faith, or Blaſphemy favouring of Hereſy, or have made their Confeſſion, ſhall be obliged publickly to abjure them, before ſome proper Perſon choſen by them; and that having made ſuch Abjuration, they ſhall be releaſed without any publick Penance enjoin'd them, according to the Form of the aforeſaid Letters, duly ſealed. Dated at *Rome, Octob.* 12, 1535. This Decree abundantly ſhews, that the Inquiſition was brought into *Portugal* before this Year, and that the Courſe of it had been for ſome time ſuſpended. But we cannot gather from it, when and by what Means it was firſt introduced, and what was the Cauſe of its Suſpenſion. This we muſt learn from other Authors.

Lewis Paramus relates, whom many others follow, "That one *Sahavedra* of "*Corduba* (*Mendoza* calls him *John Perez de Sahavedra,* by which Name "*Paramus* calls his Father, and one of his Brethren) a Forger of Apoſtoli- "cal Writings, Briefs or Letters, appointed himſelf Cardinal Legate, *A. D.* "1539. by forged Letters or Bulls, and declared that he was ſent by the "chief Pontiff to erect the ſacred Tribunal of the Inquiſition in this King- "dom, which, ſays *Paramus,* the Kings of *Portugal* refuſed to receive. "But that afterwards conſidering the great Advantage that would ariſe "from the Appointment of the aforeſaid *Sahavedra,* they demanded "it from the Pope. *Mendoza* differs ſomewhat from *Paramus,* and atteſts "that Cardinal *Taveira, An.* 1539. perſuaded the moſt ſerene King of *Por-* "*tugal John* III. to erect the ſacred Tribunal of the Inquiſition in his King- "doms, after the Model of that in the Kingdom of *Caſtile,* which, as he "ſays, the aforenamed King endeavoured to obtain, *An.* 1535. However "both theſe Authors agree in this, that *Sahavedra* erected the Tribunal of "the Inquiſition in *Portugal,* and was Inquiſitor General there ſix Months, "and that at laſt he was diſcovered and racked in *Caſtile,* and condemned "to the Gallies. *Paramus* alſo adds, that *Sahavedra* left this Account of "himſelf, written by his own Hand." This ſhort Account is taken from the larger one of *Paramus,* by *Anthony de Souſa,* a Predicant, Maſter of Divinity, Counſellor of the King, and of the ſupream Tribunal of the holy Inquiſition, in his Hiſtory of the *Portugal* Inquiſition prefixed to his Apho- riſms of the Inquiſitors, where he endeavours to refute the Account of *Pa-*

De Orig. Inquiſ. l. b. 2. tit. 2. cap. 15. num. 6.

Paramus, and gives this different one himself of the Original of the Inquisition in *Portugal.*

The *Jews*, as we have before observed from *Bzovius*, were admitted by *John* II. King of *Portugal*, under certain Conditions, into his Dominion. " *Ema-* " *nuel* succeeded King *John* II. who in the Year of our Lord 1497. commanded " by a publick Edict, all the *Jews* to depart out of the Kingdoms of *Portugal*, " under the Penalty of forfeiting their Liberty, as his Predecessor had before " him ; and although they incurred the Penalty, yet such was the King's " Clemency, that it was not inflicted. Many of them indeed departed ; but " others, either dreading the bad Treatment they apprehended they should re- " ceive from the Officers, Mariners, and others, who were to transport them in " their Ships, or else hoping to receive great Advantage from the Fruitful- " ness of the Country where they dwelt, desired to become Christians, but " upon this Condition ; That they should not be liable to any Inquisition " concerning the Faith, till after twenty Years : And upon this Condition " they were baptized. But as these *Jews* did not profess the Catholick Faith " truly and heartily, but feignedly and externally, they remained as much " *Jews* as they were before ; and so much the more dangerous, because con- " cealed. Thus they brought up their Children in their old Errors of Ju- " daism, as daily Experience demonstrates they do, many of them, to this " Day.

" King *Emanuel* was succeeded by *John* III. *An.* 1521. who observing that " Judaism spread greatly in his Time ; that the *Jews* publickly professed their " Errors, and taught them others ; that his domestick Servants, not only such " as proceded from them, but those who were ancient Christians, were in- " fected with the Poison of their Doctrine, contemned the Sacraments of the " Church, did not receive them in the Article of Death, treated with great " Irreverence holy Images, and especially some of the Virgin Mother of God, " the Lady of Angels (they are the Words of *Sousa*) considering these Things " in his Mind, he desired of Pope *Clement* VII. the holy Tribunal of the In- " quisition in his Kingdom. And although this Pope, for a long while, and " oftentimes refused it, through the vigorous Endeavours of the *Jews*, who " to their utmost opposed the royal Petition (for the *Jews* always hated this " holy Tribunal, as others do to this Day, for what Reason they best know) " yet at length, with Difficulty he granted it in Form of Law, *Jan.* Cal. 16, " 1531.

" Immediately after this Grant, *An.* 1533. they obtained from the same " *Clement* VII. a general Forgiveness of all Crimes committed against the " Catholick Faith, which however had not then its Effect. But when *Cle-* " *ment* was dead, they obtained in the Year 1534. from *Paul* III. his Succes- " for, by their importunate Prayers, continu'd Negotiations, and the Help " of those, who by their strenuous Solicitations with the upright Pontiff, " were best able to assist and defend them ; that the Inquisitors of *Portugal* " should be suspended, as to the Form they had made Use of to that Time ; " and in the Year following, 1535. they procured the general Indulgence,

" which

" which had been granted before by *Clement*, the same that we have related
" before from *Bzovius*. But the Effect of this was, that this Indulgence did
" not lead them to an Amendment of their Crimes ; but as the Event proved,
" was abused to a greater Indulgence of the Jewish Superstitions ; so that Ju-
" daism spread more and more, as the Pope himself declared in his Letters,
" dated *July* 15, 1547. in which he revoked, by Reason of their Perverseness,
" several Privileges that he had granted them.

" In the mean while King *John* III. perceiv'd that the Faith was more and
" more endangered, and as the Pope seemed to be negligent in the Affair,
" he applied the Remedy of the Inquisition in the Manner as then appeared
" most suitable to the Case ; and sent Letters to the said Pope, worthy of
" the holy Zeal which inflamed him ; in which he acquainted him, That he
" had, with the greatest Earnestness, solicited this Matter for fifteen Years,
" before his Predecessor *Clement* VII. and himself. With these Letters, and
" the Reasons contained in them, the Pontiff was prevailed with, and grant-
" ed the Inquisition, *A. D.* 1536. From this Time the sacred Tribunal of the
" Inquisition, and the Office of Inquisitor General hath been transmitted down,
" even to our own Times, in this Kingdom, by an uninterrupted Suc-
" cession."

And the more to confirm this Account, he gives us a List of the Inquisitors
General in the Kingdom of *Portugal*, of which the first was Friar *Didacus de
Sylva*, Bishop of *Ceuta*, and Confessor to King *John* III. whether of the Order
of Minims of St. *Francis de Paola*, or of the Minors of St. *Francis* of *Assise*, Writers do not agree, even to the Eleventh, now nominated by the Catholick
King, and to be confirmed by *Urban* VIII. to which he subjoins a List of the
Deputies. or Counsellors of the supreme general Inquisition, created by the several Inquisitors General. After this follow the Accounts of the Tribunals of
the Inquisition, erected in the several Cities of the Kingdom of *Portugal*, and
of the Names of the Inquisitors appointed for the several Tribunals. The
Inquisition at *Evora* was erected by *Didacus de Silva*, first Inquisitor General,
A. D. 1537. of which the first Inquisitor was *John de Mello*, Doctor of the Papal Law, and afterwards Bishop of *Algarva*, and at last Archbishop of *Evora*,
appointed by *Didicus*, the former Year one of the four Counsellors of the supreme general Inquisition. The *Lisbon* Inquisition was erected by Cardinal
Henry, second Inquisitor General, *A. D.* 1539. over which he appointed for
first Inquisitor, *John de Mello*, who had been made first Inquisitor at *Evora*,
by *Didacus de Sylva*. The same Cardinal also fixed the Inquisition at *Coimbra*, *An.* 1541. and placed in it two Commissary Inquisitors, *viz.* Friar *Bernard* of the Cross, a Predicant, Bishop of St. *Thomas*, and Rector of the University of *Coimbra*, and *Gomezius Alphonsus*, Batchelor of the Canon Law,
and Prior of the collegiate Church of *Aveiro*. —— And finally the Inquisition
was set up at *Goa*, in the *Indies*. *Francis Xaverius*, signified by Letters to
King *John* III. *November* 10, 1545. " That the Jewish Wickedness spread
" every Day more and more in the Parts of the *East Indies*, subject to the
" Kingdom of *Portugal* ; and therefore he earnestly besought the said King
" that

" that to cure fo great an Evil he would take Care to fend the Office of
" the Inquifition into thofe Countries.   Upon this Cardinal *Henry*, then In-
" quifitor General in the Kingdom of *Portugal*, erected the Tribunal of the
" holy Inquifition in the City of *Goa*, the *Metropolis* of that Province, and
" fent into thofe Parts Inquifitors, Officials, and other neceffary Minifters,
" who fhould take diligent Care of the Affairs of the Faith.   The firft In-
" quifitor was *Alexius Diaz Falcano*, fent by Cardinal *Henry*, *March* 15. *A.*
" 1560. who came to *Goa* the End of that Year, and began to execute the
" Office of Inquifitor *.

After having at large related thefe Things, *Soufa* thus concludes, " From
" thefe Things, and from the Apoftolick Bulls, of which the Originals are
" preferved in the royal Archives, and in the Rolls of the holy Inquifition ; as
" alfo from the Books of the particular Inquifitors of this Kingdom, 'tis evident,
" that the above mentioned Authors are miftaken in their Account, that *Sa-*
" *havedra* erected the holy Tribunal of the Inquifition in *Portugal*, or was the
" Caufe of its Erection.   For before this the firft Apoftolick Brief for its
" Inftitution was publifh'd, 1531. and the fecond, *A.* 1536. whereas *Sa-*
" *havedra*, according to thofe Authors, was not till three Years after, *viz.*
" *A.* 1539. which *Paramus* ought to have obferved." But *Paramus* alfo farther affirms, That before the Year 1539. the Inquifition was in *Portugal,*
and tells us, that the fame *Didacus de Sylva* was Inquifitor ; and that this Inquifition was no better than an Image of the genuine Inquifition ; and that the
Inquifition, after the Manner of *Spain*, was brought in by the Fraud of *Sa-*
havedra. Soufa adds alfo other very probable Arguments to fhew the Relation of *Paramus* to be contradictory, and ends his Account with this ; " That
" 'tis not to be believ'd, that an Impoftor, pretending to the Authority of a

---

* [*John Peter Maffeius*, Hift. Indic. *l.* 16. *p.* 758, 759. gives a more diftinct Account of the
Original of the Inquifition at *Goa*.   About the fame Time there was an horrible Wickednefs committed at *Lortnum*.   In the principal Church of that City, there was put up a Cheft, to receive
the Charity of pious Perfons: They who had the Keeping of it, found in it fome vile Papers, containing horrible Curfes and Reproaches againft Chrift, the Author of the Salvation of Mankind.
Befides, *Confalvus Sylverta*, a Jefuit, a Man noble by his Birth, but much nobler for his Virtue
and Learning, who then preached in the fame City, and afterwards was flain for the Caufe of
Chrift, at *Monomotapa* in *Æthiopia*, was reviled.   This moft impious, wicked and audacious
Crime was fufpected by many plain Tokens, to be committed by the falfe Brethren of the Circumcifion, of which Dregs feveral from *Europe* were by Stealth admitted for Money, by the Wardens
of the Ports, or Mafters of Ships, and brought into the *Indies*, under the Difguife of Merchants.   There they confpired the Prejudice and Deftruction of the Chriftian Name, with the
Ægyptians who were generally *Jews*, and of whom there was a great Number in thofe Places,
and with Perfons of other Nations and Sects.   Upon this Occafion the King began to introduce
the facred Inquifition into thofe Countries, which is there exercifed to this Day at *Goa*, by proper
and approved Perfons, fkilful in the Divine Law, to the great Advantage of the Chriftian Religion.   All thefe Things are taken Word for Word out of *Maffeius*, by *Paramus, l.* 2. *t.* 2.
c. xviii.]

This Infertion the learned Author ordered to be added, *p.* 89. but as he forgot to mark the Word
after which it fhould be put, I have added it, I think, in the proper Place, and in a marginal Note,
that I might not fpoil his Connection.

" Car-

" Cardinal, and Legate a Latere fent to erect the Inquifition, could ftay fix
" Months in this Kingdom, without being difcovered. For at that Time
" the Ambaffadors of King *John* III. were at the Court of *Rome* to folicite
" the Affair of the Inquifition, to whom the King would undoubtedly have
" fignified the Coming of fuch a Nuncio, and they would have certified him
" of the Truth of it, as they had fix Months to do it in, which yet was ne-
" ver done. At the fame time he wonders, as he well may do, at *Paramus*,
" that he did not more accurately trace out the Original of that Inquifition,
" of which he intended to treat, even though he himfelf is a Minifter in
" it to this Day, and muft know the Minifters of that Time, becaufe there
" could be no Difficulty in looking over the Bulls of its Inftitution or
" Foundation, in which we have an Account of it to the prefent Time in
" a continued Series without any Intermiffion."

He thinks *Paramus* was a little too credulous, becaufe, though he confeffes,
" That *Sahavedra* was a wicked Man, accuftomed to Frauds, and a Cheat, and
" that fuch an Event feems very improbable, and contrary to his Underftand-
" ing ; yet neverthelefs believes that it happened juft as he relates it, and thinks
" it abfolutely certain, upon the fole Authority of *Sahavedra*, who thus wrote
" concerning himfelf : " And he therefore thus refutes *Paramus*, who could
not perfuade himfelf to think that *Sahavedra* would dare to faften fuch a Crime
upon himfelf. " As though a Knave, a Cheat, and an infamous Fellow,
" would not think it the greateft Honour to be had in univerfal Remem-
" brance for fo famous an Undertaking, or refufe to affert that this was the
" Caufe of his Punifhment and Condemnation to the Gallies, that hereby he
" might conceal the real Crimes that brought him to this deferved Punifhment."

After the Inquifition had been introduced into *Portugal*, three general In- Soufa, A-
dulgences were granted to the whole Nation of the Defcendants from the He-*phor. In-*
brew Converts, in the whole Kingdom and Dominions, fubject to it, and *quf. l. 4.*
which were publifhed all over the Kingdom. The firft was granted by *Cle-* *c. 15.*
ment VII. by a Bull expedited, *Ap.* 7th. *An.* 1533. which had not its Effect.
Afterwards *Paul* III. who fucceeded *Clement* in the Popedom, confirmed the
general Indulgence which he had given, and granted it anew, *Octob.* 12, 1535.
and afterwards, *A. D.* 1536. fent Letters to erect the holy Tribunal of the
Inquifition, of which I have given an Extract out of *Bzovius.* The fecond
was given by the fame *Paul* III. *May* 11, 1547. For whereas the Inquifitors, as they fay, had before proceeded with great Moderation in Favour
of the new Converts, the Good of the Church required that they fhould
proceed againft Judaifers according to the Rigour of the Law. And therefore the Pope reduced the Method of Procefs in the Inquifition, according
to the Form of Law. But leaft the new Converts and their Children fhould
become fubject to a rigorous Inquifition for their paft Errors, he granted a
general Pardon. This was publifhed *June* 10, 1548. The third was granted by *Clement* VIII. *Aug.* 23, 1604. and publifhed in *Portugal, Jan.* 16, 1605.
The Caufes of it, as we may gather from the Bull it felf, were three. Firft,
That the Inquifitors ordered the Punifhments againft Hereticks to be execu-

T   ted

ted without Remiffion. Secondly, Leaft the Defcendants of the *Hebrews*, finding themfelves precluded from obtaining Pardon, fhould grow worfe, and add Sins to Sins. Thirdly, Becaufe upon the Grant of fuch a general Pardon, it was undoubtedly to be hoped, that in a little while, they who had departed the Kingdom, would return to it, and retain the Catholick Worfhip and Faith under Obedience to King *Philip*, who, as *Soufa* fays, greatly defires it, and earneftly feeks it.

He who carefully confiders the Reafons of thefe Pardons, will eafily difcern, that under the Name of Pardon they introduced a greater Cruelty and Rigour. This is too evident by the fecond Indulgence. They wanted a more fevere Inquifition againft the new Chriftians ; and therefore that they might have fome Pretence for it, and do it without any Appearance of Wickednefs, they abrogated the former Inquifition, that fo they might introduce a new one much worfe than the former. This *Soufa* very plainly intimates, who defends this Indulgence upon this Account, that *we fee the Difpofition of the Law is juftly altered and changed, becaufe of new Emergences that arife, and becaufe we want a new Remedy.*

Even thefe Indulgences themfelves, though they feem very large, yet are limited with many Reftrictions. " They are indeed granted to all the *Jewifh* " new Converts to the Faith, of both Sexes, in the Kingdom of *Portugal*, and " Dominions thereof, and to their Children, Grandchildren, and Defcendants " living in the fame, whither Natural or Foreigners, prefent or abfent, and " to thofe alfo who have departed out of the faid Kingdoms or Dominions to " other Places, even though put under the Bann. *Clem.* VII. *Paulus* III. and " *Clem.* VIII. However, thofe who are abfent, have no Benefit from thefe Par- " dons, if they have not retained the Habit and Name of Chriftians, but have " openly apoftatifed from the Chriftian Faith. *Clem.* VII. *Paulus* III. and " *Clem.* VIII.

" All Crimes of Herefy, Apoftacy from the Faith, Blafphemy, and all " other Offences whatfoever, however heinous and qualified, are forgiven to " the aforefaid Perfons.

" They are abfolved from every Sentence of Excommunication, Sufpen- " fion and Interdict, and from all other Ecclefiaftical Cenfures, although they " have been under them for 40 Years and upward, and though the Apofto- " lick See fhould have been confulted upon account of them, and from thofe " alfo contained in *Bulla Cœnæ*.

" They are abfolved from all the aforefaid in the Civil, Criminal and Li- " tigious Courts, and in the Court of their Confcience and Mind. But from " other Crimes, not favouring of heretical Pravity, they are abfolved in the " Court of Confcience only.

" They are reftored to the Condition they were in, at the Time they were " baptized, are freed from every Mark of Infamy, contracted by themfelves " or their Kindred, as though they had never departed from the Catholick " Faith. They are reftored alfo to every Dignity, Degree, Office, Bene- " fice, or Order, in which they were before, and are moreover qualified " to obtain all fuch Dignities. But *Clement* VIII. did not grant this Qualifi- " cation.   2.   " All

" All their confiscated Effects, and all the Profits arising from them are
" to be returned to them, though they should be in Possession of others, pro-
" vided they be not brought into the Treasury.

" All Persons in Prison, or otherwise in Custody, banished, or under the
" Bann, even though under Sentence for the aforesaid Crimes, are to be
" wholly freed from Prison, Custody, Banishment, and the Bann.

" All Processes, Informations, Proofs, Cautions, Surety-ships, and Obli-
" gations, of every kind, though confirmed with an Oath, are to be made
" void. As also all Injunctions against them for the Crime of Heresy, Apo-
" stacy, Blasphemy, or other Things favouring of Heresy, so that they
" shall not hereafter in any manner be accused, or molested upon account
" of them: Neither shall any Proof, no, not the least, be ever after taken
" against them for the aforesaid Crimes.

" No publick Penances are to be enjoined them, and they are to be freed
" from those already laid on you.

" Those who are at present relapsed, and kept in Prison for the Crime
" of relapsing into Heresy or Apostacy, are not to be delivered over to the
" secular Court to be punished with Death, but to be dismissed with such Pe-
" nalties as the Inquisitors shall think fit to lay on them. *Clement* VIII. grant-
" ed them no such Immunity.

" Such who shall make use of this Favour, though they relapse into Here-
" sy or Apostacy, shall not be accounted as relapsed, unless they have ju-
" dicially abjured."

The Restrictions by which these Indulgences are circumscribed and limited,
re various. " Such who shall fall into any Heresy, or persist in their old Er-
" rors, after the Day of the Publication of this general Indulgence, shall not
" enjoy the Immunities granted by *Clement* VII.

" None but such as are contrite in Heart, and after Confession in the Sa-
" crament of Penance, are absolved by a Confessor chosen by themselves,
" but approved by the Ordinary, shall obtain Absolution in the Court of
" Conscience.

" None shall be delivered from the Penances enjoined them by the Inquisi-
" tors, unless they have fulfilled them when out of Prison.

" Such shall not be dispensed with for their Irregularity, who in Contempt
" of the Keys, have celebrated Masses, or been otherwise present at them,
" when they have been under Censures.

" Those who have abjured, are bound to perform the Penances enjoined
" them, who, upon a previous Abjuration, have been delivered out of
" Prison.

" They are not exempted from abjuring before the Inquisitors, who being
" in Prison, or out upon Bail, have been convicted, or confessed ; nor are
" they freed from their Relapse, if they shall afterwards relapse into Heresy
" or Apostacy.

" According to the Bull of *Clement* VII. it was necessary to obtain the In-
" dulgence granted by the said Bull, even in the external Court, that they

T 2   should

" fhould confefs their Crimes before the Nuncio, Inquifitors, Minifters depu-
" ted by them, or Confeffor chofen by them to whom the Indulgence was
" granted, and that their Names and Sirnames fhould be written in a Book.
" This Condition was taken away by *Paul* III. and *Clement* VIII. as to the
" Temporal, Criminal, Civil, and Litigious Court, by which the aforefaid
" Perfons are exempted from Confeffion, Abjuration, Renouncing, Punifh-
" ment, and every other Attendance whatfoever.

" They fhall not enjoy the aforefaid Immunities, who, at the Time of the
" Publication of thefe Letters, have no manner of Houfe or Habitation in
" the Kingdom and Dominions of *Portugal*, and fhall not return into the faid
" Kingdom or fome of its Dominions, within the Term prefcribed them by
" thefe Letters.

" The Sentences already pronounced againft the aforefaid Perfons, and
" committed to Execution, are not to be annulled."

Befides thefe three, no other Indulgences have been granted to the new
Chriftians in *Portugal*, and the *Portuguefe* Divines ufe many Arguments to
prove that no other ought hereafter to be given them, alledging, amongft
Ibid. c. 21. other Things, " That the chief Pontiffs and the Inquifitors General in the
n. 9. " Kingdom of *Portugal*, have often ufed this Method of Cure without any
" Succefs. For from the Time of the doubled Indulgence, they are the Words
" of *Soufa*, they were not cured by Mildnefs. When afterwards, from the Year
" 1535, to the Year 1548, fome Punifhments were inflicted on them, but not ac-
" cording to the full Rigour of the Law, their Wickednefs ftill encreafed. When
" after this, to the Year 1606. the Law took Force in its full Severity, there yet
" appeared no Sign of Repentance in them. And when again they had the
" Eafe of a general Indulgence, and fome Favours were conferred on them,
" their Wickednefs grew to fuch an height, that they feemed almoft incurable."
*So that fince neither Mercy nor Juftice hath any Effect upon them, greater Extre-
mities muft be ufed, and they ought to be treated according to the fevere Sanctions
of the facred Canons ; and becaufe they ftill remain addicted to the Jewifh Errors,
the moft terrible Punifhments are to be inflicted on them. For where the Procefs
of the Inquifition hath not been interrupted by fo many Indulgences, as in Spain,
Judaifm is almoft extinguifhed.*

Ibid. c. 22. *Sebaftian*, King of *Portugal*, upon Occafion of his unfortunate and fatal Ex-
n. 4, 5. pedition into *Africa*, granted to the Defcendants of the *Jews*, for a large Sum
of Money, that their Effects fhould not be confifcated for ten Years, much
againft the Advice of his Uncle *Philip* II. King of *Spain:* This Indulgence
he granted them by the Authority of *Gregory* XIII. by his Bull expedited, *Octob.* 6, 1579. But afterwards upon the Rout of the King's Army
by the *Saracens*, Cardinal *Henry*, the King's great Uncle, fucceeded him in
the royal Dignity, who immediately, *Decem.* 19, of the fame Year, recalled
the faid Grant, with the Pope's Confent, alledging this Reafon in the Decree of Revocation, *That after the moft mature Confultation of learned Men,
they all agreed that he was bound to make fuch Revocation, becaufe the Good of the
Faith greatly required it.* After *Philip* King of *Portugal* obtained the Crown,
the ·

the new Chriftians offered him a large Sum of Money, and befought him, that he would procure in their Favour a general Indulgence from the Pope. But he contemned their Prayers, though he was at that Time at War with *France* and *England*, his Divines fuggefting to him, *That God was greatly offended with fuch Money, and that he could expect no profperous Succefs from it.*

The following Years the new Chriftians in *Portugal* endeavoured by many Entreaties to procure the Abolition, or at leaft Mitigation of the Inquifition. For after that King *Alphonfus* was expelled his Kingdom, and fucceeded by his Brother *Peter*, he endeavoured to gain the Affections of his Subjects by Indulgence and Kindnefs, the better to eftablifh his new Power, which gave fome Hopes to the new Chriftians of being releafed from the Inquifition. Upon this they deputed certain Perfons, who on the 9th of *June, An.* 1676. prefented, in the Name of the whole Nation, their humble Petition to his Highnefs, in which they reprefent to him, that they had before offered their humble Petition to him, for Leave humbly to defire of the Pope fome Mitigation of the Inquifition ; putting him in mind, that after mature Advice of many Divines, and Doctors of the Law, he had condefcended to their Requeft. They add, that for this End they had fent their Ambaffador extraordinary to *Rome*, and that the Office of the Inquifition, and College of Bifhops, had alfo fent thither Deputies, who were both Inquifitors, furnifhed with the Letters of his Highnefs. But that they were certified by Letters from *Rome*, that his Ambaffador had not only refufed to procure them any Affiftance, but joined his Endeavours with thofe of the Inquifitors Deputies, to prevent their Affair from being ever brought on the Carpet, becaufe they did not care that the leaft Alteration fhould ever be made in the Laws of the Inquifition. They therefore requefted from his Highnefs an authentick royal Inftrument, to certify the Pope, and the fupreme Congregation of the Inquifition at *Rome*, that it was not his Highnefs's Intention, that the Decifion of their Caufe fhould be fufpended, but that it was his Defire that they fhould have Juftice. The fame Day alfo they prefented an humble Petition to the King's Confeffor, to befeech him, that he would difpofe his Highnefs to grant their Requeft.

But as all this proved in vain, they prefented an humble Petition to the Pope, *Jan.* 10, 1680. in which they acquaint him, that they were fent and deputed by the new Chriftians in the Kingdom of *Portugal*, and efpecially by thofe who were detained in the Prifon of the Inquifition, who were about 500 in Number, of all Sexes and Conditions, fome of them having been there twelve, others fourteen, and none of them lefs than feven Years, and almoft deftroyed by Naftinefs and Filth. They farther relate the various Miferies of the new Chriftians, and how their Affair hath been prevented from being expedited by the Artifices of the Inquifitors. They therefore befeech the Pope that he would gracioufly regard and pity that miferable People, and renew his Commands to the Inquifitors to haften their Affair : And the more to move him, they give him Specimens, which they affirm they can prove by proper Witneffes, by which it plainly appears that the Inqui-

I

fitors,

fitors, notwithstanding the Pope's Prohibition, continually proceed in the Administration of their Office, and Oppression of the Miserable.

The same Year, *March* 11. they presented another humble Supplication to the Pope, in which they acquaint him, that after their having presented their former Petition, they had received Letters from *Lisbon*, by which they are informed how many Things were transacted at Court, in Favour of the Inquisitors, and such, which in the present State of Things, were greatly contrary to their Expectations. They also give a large Account of what had happen'd upon Account of the Revolution in the Kingdom ; that the Papers and Writings, which they had delivered to the Pope, as also the Writings of the Courts and Halls, were in the Possession of the *Portugueze* Inquisitors, who publickly talk'd of them, and permitted every one to read them, by which they prejudiced others against them : And therefore beseech the Pope, that he would regard them, and put an End to their Miseries.

Finally, in the same Year, *August* 6. they presented a third Petition, in which they tell him, that they had humbly petitioned the Apostolick Nuncio at *Lisbon*, who had referred them to the Archbishop of that See : That in Obedience to his Rescript, they went to the Archbishop. That he had a Conference with the Inquisitor General ; and that after a long Consultation nothing was concluded on. That the Archbishop indeed declared, he knew of a Remedy, and could point it out ; but that he would not contend with the Inquisitor about it, till he was suspended and deposed from his Office by him, who had the legal Authority to suspend and depose him. And that therefore, since they could not find Relief from his Nuncio, they apply themselves to the Pope, and most earnestly beseech him that he would expedite their Affair.

From these Accounts 'tis plain that these Deputies had some Hopes given them of Favour ; but that they were deluded with empty Words and flattering Promises : For they still groan as before, under the cruel Yoke of the Inquisition, without any Mitigation of their Punishments ; and to this Day are liable to all the Penalties ordain'd against Hereticks.

CHAP. XXVI.

Of the ATTEMPT *to bring the* INQUISITION *into the Kingdom of* NAPLES.

Param:
l. 2. *tit.* 2.
cap. 10.

AFTER *Ferdinand* and *Elizabeth* had brought the Inquisition into all the Kingdoms of *Spain*, they would feign have introduced it into others, that were under their Dominion. For as many of the *Jewish* Race had fled out of *Spain* for Fear of the Inquisition, into the Kingdom of *Naples*, and as that Kingdom had been again brought into Subjection to *Ferdinand*, *Didacus Deza*

Deza at that Time General Inquifitor of *Spain*, fent thither in the Year 1504.
Peter Balforatus, Archbifhop of *Meffina*, with the Power of Inquifitor. *Fer-*
dinand gave him Letters to the Governor, Nobles, and Univerfity of *Naples*,
that they fhould give him all Affiftance and Favour. He tells them that a
great Number of Hereticks, having fled from the Kingdoms of *Spain*, through
Fear of the holy Office of the Inquifition, had fheltered themfelves there as in
a Place of Safety, who had been burn'd in Effigy becaufe of their Abfence ;
and that therefore, to purge that Kingdom from the Crime of Herefy, he had
appointed *Peter Balforatus*, Inquifitor of heretical Pravity : He therefore commands them to receive him as fuch, to give him in all Things the Affiftance of
the fecular Arm, and not to fuffer him, or any of his Family to be molefted.
But as there arofe many Difficulties and Difcouragements, he could not finifh
his Undertaking.

In the Year 1547. *Charles* V. being Emperor, *Peter* of *Toledo*, Viceroy of
Naples, endeavour'd to introduce the Inquifition there, by the Command of
Charles. But as he apprehended this would be a difficult Thing, he put thofe
into the publick Offices, who he thought would be moft forward to promote
it.   After this he publickly declared, That it would greatly tend to the Efta- *Hift. Con.*
blifhment of Divine Worfhip, would be ferviceable to the Commonwealth, *Trid. l. 3.*
and be highly grateful to the Emperor ; if after the Example of the *Spa- p. 313,*
niards* and *Sicilians* they would receive the holy Office. But the *Neopolitans* 314.
were fo moved with the Novelty of the Thing, that they publickly declared *Hift. lib. 21* Thuan.
that they would rather loofe their Lives than fubmit to the Inquifition ; and
cry'd out, that the Extirpation of Herefies belonged to the Pope and the Ecclefiaftical Judges, and not to the Temporal Prince. When Pope *Paul* III.
underftood this, he declared by his Apoftolick Bull, That the Inquifition
againft Hereticks belonged to him and his Judges, and not to any other. The
King indeed would have had the Inquifition at *Naples* to be fubject to the fupreme Council of the *Spanifh* Inquifition, as were thofe of *Sicily, Sardinia,*
and the *Indies* ; whereas the Court of *Rome* would have had it fubject to them,
becaufe not only the Ecclefiaftical but Secular Government of the Kingdom
of *Naples* is under the Pope. However the Viceroy, that he might not feem
to yield to popular Fury, appointed Inquifitors and Officials of the holy Office ; with which the *Neapolitans* were fo enraged, that on a certain Day,
when two Perfons were leading to Prifon, and crying out they were taken up
by the Inquifition, they broke into open Sedition, ran immediately to Arms,
and bound themfelves by mutual Oaths, infomuch that there was a Civil War,
between the Citizens of *Naples*, and the *Spanifh* Garrifon, in which many on
both Sides were flain. At length the *Spaniards*, who held the Fortreffes, prevailing, and beating down their Houfes with their great Guns, the Tumult
was appeafed, and the Principal were punifh'd, Part with Death, and Part
with Banifhment. However, the Viceroy gave over the Attempt of introdu- *Paulus*
cing the Inquifition, not fo much for Fear of a new Tumult, as at the Intercef- *Serv. de*
fion of the Pope and Cardinals, who oppofed the Inquifition, as not being *Inquif. l. v.*
fubject to their Court. And becaufe the *Spaniards* are determined to bring in *net.*
                                                                                        the

the Inquifition to *Naples* fubject to their fupreme Council, and the Court of *Rome* is equally determined to oppofe thefe Attempts of the *Spaniards* ; hence it is that the Kingdom of *Naples* is to this Day free from this intolerable Yoke: And therefore, if any Matters of Faith are to be judged there, it is done either by the Bifhop, or fome other Prelate appointed by the Court of *Rome*, who neverthelefs dares not begin the Affair without Leave firft obtained from the Viceroy.

<hr/>

CHAP. XXVII.

Of the INQUISITION *in* SICILY, SARDINIA *and* MILAN.

lib. 2. t. 2.
cap. 11.
n. 8.

THE Inquifition had been long before brought into *Sicily.* *Paramus* gives us a Privilege of King *Alphonfus*, in the Year 1452. in which Mention is made of Friar *Henry Lugardi*, a Predicant of *Palermo*, and Inquifitor of heretical Pravity in that Kingdom ; by which he confirmed the Privilege given to him by the forefaid Inquifitor, which *Frederick* the Emperor had granted to the Inquifition in *Sicily*, at *Palermo*, in the Year 1224. By this Privilege *Frederick* is faid to have ordained, *That one third Part only of the confifcated Goods fhould be appropriated to the Treafury; a third Part referved to the Apoftolick See, and the other third, without any Contradiction, affigned to the Inquifitors, that the fpiritual Husbandman may not be defrauded of his Reward, nor fo wholfome an Inquifition come to nothing through want of Neceffaries to fupport it.* From whence *Paramus* infers, that the Inquifition was brought into *Sicily*, *An.* 1224. But this Privilege is liable to juft Sufpicion, unlefs there be an Error as to the Year. For I have fhewn before, that the Inquifitors had no Tribunals granted them any where at that Time ; and I fhall hereafter prove, that the Diftribution of the forfeited Effects into three Parts, did not take Place till feveral Years after. But whatever becomes of this Privilege, 'tis certain that the Inquifition was eftablifh'd in *Sicily, An.* 1452. and whether this Privilege of *Frederick* was genuine or forged, it was confirmed by King *Alphonfus*. It was afterwards confirmed by *Ferdinand* and *Elizabeth*, *An.* 1477. at *Seville*, who took the Title of King and Queen of *Sicily*, though *John*, King of *Aragon*, and Father of *Ferdinand*, was yet alive. This Inquifition the Emperor *Charles* V. favoured with many Privileges ; the Patents for which, *Paramus* gives us in a long Catalogue.

In the Year 1535. an Official was fent by the Inquifitors, to the Town of St. *Mark*, to apprehend certain Hereticks ; but he was affaulted by *Matthew Garruba*, and a large Company with him, who killed many of his Attendants, and gave the Official himfelf many Wounds, and left him half dead on the Ground. The Nobles alfo of *Palermo*, and the other Inhabitants of the Kingdom forced the Inquifitor by Threats, to depart, and made him go on Board

a

a Ship that was ready to fail from the Port ; and burn'd down the Office of the Inquifition, with all the Papers in it ; fo that the Inquifition was interrupted and fufpended during the Space of ten whole Years. After this the Emperor, by Decree of his Council, renewed it, *An.* 1543. and ordered it to be reftored to all its former Privileges, which were confirmed by *Philip* II. *An.* 1546. The Confequence of this was, that the Nobles, Barons, and moft illuftrious Perfons of the Kingdom, who before hated every Thing belonging to the Inquifition, and the very Name of its Minifters, now defired to become its Officials and Familiars ; and by their own Liberality caufed to be built convenient Prifons for the Guilty, which could not be done before by Reafon of the fmall Revenues and Returns of the holy Office. When ever there are any Edicts publifh'd, or Acts of Faith celebrated, they affift at them in great State, and accompany the Inquifitors in their Progrefs through the Ifle, entertain them generoufly, and fecure them from every Infult ; fo that no Sedition of the People can poffibly overthrow it. For in the Year 1562. as the Inquifitor *Horofius* was publifhing an Edict of the Faith at *Palermo*, and was hinder'd by the Tumult of the People, the Sedition was eafily appeas'd by the Appearance of the Nobles and Barons, who were Familiars ; fo that the following Day the Edict was publifh'd with univerfal Applaufe, and without the leaft Oppofition. And when afterwards there arofe fome Differences between the Viceroy and fecular Judges on one Hand, and the Inquifitors on the other, about their Jurifdiction, *Philip* II. with the Advice of two Counfellors of the Supreme General Council of the Inquifition, *An.* 1580. confirmed all the Prerogatives of the Inquifition ; and in the Year following decreed, that the Counfellors of the holy Office, and the Familiars thereof, fhould, in all Caufes, Civil and Criminal, enjoy the Pre-eminences and Court of the holy Office, as Perfons of the fame Rank with the Penfionary Officials. After this he commanded the Viceroys, by his Royal Letters, *September* 18, 1587. that they fhould pay all that Honour and Obfervance to it, which fo holy a Service was worthy of. But in the Year 1592. Count *Alva*, Viceroy of that Kingdom, declared by a publick Edict, that the Prerogatives of the Nobles, Familiars of the Court of the holy Office, were fufpended ; and from thence they have had no great Affection for the Inquifition, nor any longer difcharge the Function of Familiars.

The fame Princes brought the Inquifition into *Majorca, Minorca,* and *Sardinia* ; but not without fo great a Tumult of the People, as could hardly be fuppreffed. *cap.* 11 & 12.

In the Dutchy of *Milan*, after it had flourifh'd there for many Years, King *Philip* II. by the Perfuafion of *Pius* IV. would have formed it after the Model of the *Spanifh* Inquifition. [During the Council of *Trent, Philip* mov'd *Pius* IV. that the Inquifition at *Milan* fhould be under the fame Regulation as it was in *Spain*, and that he would place at the Head of it a *Spanifh* Prelate ; alledging that in regard of the Nearnefs of the Places infected, it was neceffary to ufe the moft exquifite Diligence for the Service of God and the Defence of Religion. It was foon known that the *cap.* 30. *Hift. Con. Trid. l. 8. p. 882.*

U   Mat-

Matter had been debated in a *Confiſtory*; and that notwithſtanding ſome Car-
dinals oppoſed it, the Pope ſeemed inclin'd to grant it, at the Inſtance of
Cardinal *Carpi*, who aſſured him, that it was neceſſary to keep the City of
Milan in Devotion towards the Apoſtolick See. This he did from a ſecret
Hope, cheriſh'd by the *Spaniſh* Ambaſſador, that by this Means he would ſecure the Favour of the King of *Spain* to make him Pope. Hereupon the Cities of that State, ſent *Sforza Marone* to his Holineſs, *Cæſar Taverna*, and
Principiale Biſoſto to the Catholick King, and *Sforza Brivio* to the Council of
Trent. This laſt they commiſſioned to beſeech the Prelates and Cardinals of
thoſe Places to have Compaſſion on their Country, which being already render'd miſerable by exceſſive Impoſitions, would be wholly ruined by this
which was worſe than all the other; many Citizens already preparing to
abandon their Country, well knowing that that Office did not always proceed
in *Spain*, to heal the Conſcience, but very often to empty the Purſe; and for
other ſecular Ends alſo. And if the Inquiſitors, under the King's own Eyes,
do ſo rigidly dominere over their own Countrymen, what will they not do to
the Citizens of *Milan*, who are ſo far diſtant from any Remedy, and have a
much leſs Intereſt in their Affections. *Brivio* alſo declared at *Trent*, how
generally the Citizens were perplexed with this ill News, and beſought the
Aſſiſtance of the Prelates. This Relation gave greater Uneaſineſs to the
Prelates, who had more to fear from the Inquiſition, than it did to the Seculars. The Prelates alſo of *Naples* were afraid, that if this Yoke were put
on the *Milaneze*, they could not keep it off from themſelves, as they had
done for ſome Years before. And therefore the Prelates of the *Milaneze* met
together, and reſolved to write Letters to the Pope, and Cardinal *Borromeo*,
ſubſcribed by them all, ſignifying how great a Prejudice it would be to him,
to whom it belonged as Archbiſhop, to preſide in that Office. They put
the Pope in Mind, that there were not the ſame Cauſes and Reſpects as there
were in *Spain*, to put ſo rigorous an Inquiſition amongſt them; which beſides
the evident Ruin it would bring on that State, would be a great Prejudice
to the holy See. For that he could not refuſe to eſtabliſh it in *Naples* alſo,
which would give Occaſion to other Princes of *Italy* to deſire it in their Dominions; and ſince the Juriſdiction of the Inquiſition extended over the Prelates, the holy See could not expect much Obedience from them, becauſe they
would be forced to ſeek the Favour of ſecular Princes, to whom by this Means
they would become ſubject: So that if there ſhould be any Occaſion for a new
Council, the Pope would find but few of the Prelates faithful to him, and ſubject to his Commands. Neither ought he to believe what the *Spaniards* might
poſſibly alledge, that the Inquiſition in *Milan* ſhould be ſubject to that at
Rome, ſince it appears by Experience, how they proceeded in the Cauſe of
the Archbiſhop of *Toledo*, always refuſing to tranſmit the Proceſſes to *Rome*,
though it had been often demanded from them, as is practiſed alſo by the Inquiſitors of the Kingdom of *Sicily*, who depend on *Spain*. The Prelates not
content with theſe and other Reaſons, alledg'd to the Pope and Cardinals,
and others in whom they had any Intereſt at *Rome*, did farther propoſe, that
                                                                    ſome-

fomething might be inferted in the Decrees of the Council in Favour of the Bifhops, either to exempt them from that Jurifdiction, or fecure them; and that the Manner of forming Proceffes in that Affair might be determined, which though it could not be accomplifhed in the next Seffion, might in that immediately following. Cardinal *Morone*, at that Time Prefident of the Council, gave them fome Hopes of Satisfaction. This Accident gave the Council much Trouble, becaufe of the great Number interefted in it. In the mean while this Attempt to introduce the Inquifition was looked on with fuch Indignation at *Milan*, that the City broke out into an open Sedition; where the univerfal Cry was, that it was infufferable Tyranny to impofe on a free City the Yoke of the Inquifition, which was introduced into *Spain*, to root out the *Moors*, and the wicked Nation of the *Jews*; efpecially fince, according to the moft ancient Practice of the Apoftolick See, Inquifitors had been deputed into that Province. Upon this the Duke of *Seffa*, underftanding what general Offence it gave, and fearing from fome Reports which had been brought him, leaft the Citizens of *Milan* fhould take Example from the *Low Countries*, who univerfally agreed to take up Arms to fhake off the Yoke of the Inquifition, which was endeavoured to be put on them, and knowing it was not a proper Time to prefs this Affair; ftopped the Ambaffadors that had been deputed to the King, and promifed that he would take Care that the Senate fhould have Satisfaction. And thus ended this Affair.]

l. 11. c. 30. Param.

CHAP. XXVIII.

The Return of the INQUISITION *into* Germany *and* France, *at the Time of the* REFORMATION.

WHEN *Luther* bravely attempted the Reformation of the Church, and feverely cenfured the various and intolerable Abufes of the Church of *Rome*, perfevering with great Conftancy in the Work he had undertaken, in Spite of Threatnings, Anathema's, and the Papal Thunders; and whereas *Suinglius*, *Oecolampadius*, and others in *Suifferland*, and elfewhere, oppofed the growing Superftition, and propagated the Reformation with great Succefs in many Places and Countries; the Pope, to put a Stop to the Courfe of their Preaching did not only continually ftir up the Emperor, the Kings and Princes againft *Luther*, and all who oppofed the Doctrines of the Church of *Rome*, but reftored alfo the Inquifition in many Places, which had grown into Decay in feveral Countries, either through the Cruelty of the Inquifitors, or the Want of Hereticks to proceed againft, and commanded it to proceed with great Severity and Rigour againft what they called the new Herefies. So that now the Authority of the Inquifitors was encreafed in *Germany*, and many were condemned for Herefy by the Sentence of that holy Tribunal, and being delivered over to the fecular Magiftrate were burn'd to Death.

U 2

From

From *Germany* that bloody Tribunal was soon brought into the neighbouring Kingdom of *France*, where it had drop'd of it self, for want of Herefies to proceed against. *Antonius a Prato*, Presbyter Cardinal, by the Title of St. *Anaſtaſia*, Archbiſhop of *Sens*, Primate and Chancellor of *France*, held a provincial Council, in *February*, 1528. in which, after he had condemned the Doctrine of *Luther*, *Melan& on*, *Suinglius*, *Oecolampadius* and their Followers, he publiſh'd a general Decree, by which he declares and renews all the ancient Canons of the Lateran Council against Hereticks, their Favourers and Defenders, Perfons ſuſpect of Herefy, and relapſed, as they are extant in the Decretals, and fometimes guards them by annexing a Puniſhment. He moreover ordains, *That the Suffragans, if they ſuſpect any Places of Herefy, ſhall immediately go themſelves, or ſend other fit Perſons, and oblige thoſe of the Neighbourhood, by an Oath, to diſcover ſuch Hereticks, who keep unlawful Conventicles. He alſo ſtrictly commands them, That they ſhould proceed with all Diligence and Care in this Affair, and proceed ſummarily and openly in the Buſineſs of ſuch heretical Pravity. And if they be remiſs or negligent in purging out this Leaven, let them know that they ſhall incur the Puniſhments ordained by the Sacred General Lateran Council. Let them alſo tremble at the Puniſhments publiſhed againſt the Inquiſitors, who offend in their Office, by the Sacred Council of* Vienne. *Let the Suffragans alſo diligently obſerve the Conſtitutions of* Urban V. Clement V. *and* Boniface VIII. He beſeeches moreover. the King, *That he would immediately drive out all Hereticks from every Part of his Dominions.* Laſtly, he ordains, *That the Rulers and Conſuls of Cities ſhall take a corporal Oath, according to the Sacred General Lateran Council ; that they will, according to their Office, aſſiſt, with all their Might, and lend their helping Hands, faithfully and effectually, to the Church in this Affair of Hereſy, when it ſhall be demanded of them. And whereas the Biſhops and Inquiſitors, whilſt they proceed in this Matter, may poſſibly require Aſſiſtance from ſecular Judges under Excommunication, he declares they ſhall not incur Excommunication by ſo doing.* To theſe Things he adds, in the Concluſion, after having recounted various Errors that had been condemn'd, an Exhortation to Chriſtian Princes, that they ſhould labour to extirpate Hereticks ; and ſets before them the Examples of *Conſtantine, Valentinian, Theodoſius,* and others, who by their vigorous Endeavours againſt Hereticks, found Favour with God, and obtained immortal Honour amongſt Men. And on the other hand, puts them in Mind of *Licinius, Julian, Valens,* and others, who experienced the Revenges of the Divine Anger, and received the juſt Rewards of their Wickedneſs ; becauſe, far from reſiſting heretical Errors, they ſupported and propagated them. *He earneſtly beſeeches and exhorts in the Lord, the Chriſtian Princes, that as they would conſult their Safety, as they would preſerve unhurt their Rights of Sovereignty, and as they deſire to preſerve in Peace and Tranquility the Nations ſubject to them, they would powerfully defend the Catholick Faith, and endeavour to their utmoſt to ſuppreſs the Enemies of it. This will be eaſy, when the antient Edicts of Chriſtian Princes againſt Hereticks, their Books and Favourers, are reſtored. When once theſe are put in Execution with an wholeſome Severity, there*

will

will be no Remains *of* Hereticks, *none of their Books or Writings in their Provinces.*
Their mischievous Sermons will then be at an End, there will be no more clandestine
Conventicles, in which Hereticks are wont to introduce strange Customs, abhorrent
from Christian Piety. This is what we desire with all our Soul, and ask in our con-
stant Prayers from the Lord, hoping that a Stop will be put to these Things, whilst
Christian Princes bravely suppress Hereticks, and we add our pious Labours to pre-
vent the Wolves from destroying the Sheep committed to our Care. And thus at length
the Lord will grant us that Peace and Tranquility in this Life, which is so much
desired and sought after by the Faithful, and after this Life shall be at an End con-
summate Happiness. But inasmuch as we know, that it is not sufficient to answer
these Ends, merely to exhort the Faithful, unless the Rebellious are suppressed by pro-
per Severity, we have decreed to provide a proper Antidote for this purpose. And
therefore by that Authority with which we are invested, we by these Writings put un-
der the Sentence of Excommunication, all Persons whatsoever in our Province,
who shall presume rashly to assert, teach or write such impious Tenets, as al-
so all such who by any Means shall assist, counsel or favour them. I cannot certainly
affirm whither the Inquisition, which for many Years had been dropped in
France, was by Means of this Synod restored there. This is certain, that the
Laws used in the Tribunal of the Inquisition were renewed by the Decree of
this Synod, and that there is express Mention of the Inquisitors in it ; and by
other Things it appears that about this Time the Inquisition was again brought
into *France*. For *Francis* I. chose Inquisitors of the Faith from the Predicant
Friars. For in the Orders of that Prince, *fol.* 408. there is a Writ bearing
Date *May* 30, 1536. by which he appoints *Matthew Orry*, D. D. a Predicant
Friar, Inquisitor of the Faith. *Ribadineira* also relates in the Life of *Ignatius* Du Cange
Loyola, Book II. Chap. II. and XIV. [and *John Peter Maffeius*, in his Life *in voce In-*
of the same *Loyola*, *l.* 1. *c.* 20. *p.* 315.] that about this Time he was accused *quisitio.*
before *Michael Orry*, a *Dominican* Divine, and Inquisitor of the Faith at *Pa-*
ris, and by him acquitted. There is also extant in the second Volume a like
Writ of King *Francis*, *fol.* 247. dated *April* 10, 1540. by which Authority is
granted to *Joseph Corregie*, a Doctor of the same Order, to execute the Office of Inquisitor of the Faith throughout the whole Kingdom. In the third
Volume, *fol.* 482. there is a royal Statute, bearing Date *July* 23, 1543. by
which Power is granted to the Ecclesiastical Judges and Inquisitors of the
Faith, to make Inquisition against *Lutherans* and Hereticks, provided that
Laicks, and such who had not received holy Orders, should be referred to the
ordinary Judges. There is also another Statute of *Henry* II. dated at St.
Germain en Laye, *June* 22, 1550. by which the Edict of *Francis* I. is recalled,
and *Matthew Orry*, Inquisitor of the Faith, delivered from the Trouble of
communicating to the supreme Courts, the Baillives and Senefchals, such
Actions as he brought against Hereticks, provided he communicated them
to the ordinary Diocefans or their Vicars. At the same Time that Power
was confirmed to him, by which he was authorized to recover to a found
Mind, either by Instruction or Admonition, such as erred from the Faith, of
grant-

granting Pardon and Mercy to the Penitent, and of punifhing and correcting the Obftinate. This Statute was inferted into the Acts of Parliament, with this Condition added, That the faid Inquifitors, in all privileged Cafes, fhould fhare the Procefs with the Royal Judges. [Father *Paul*, in his Hiftory of the Council of *Trent*, *B.* 5. *p.* 484, and 487. mentions *Anthony Demohares*, Inquifitor of the Faith ; and *p.* 494. fpeaks of other Inquifitors in *France*. And *Thuanus*, in his Hiftory, *B.* 8. *p.* 377. fays, that in the Year 1551. 19th Cal. *Febr.* there was a royal Law rehearfed in the Senate, concerning the Power and Office of *Matthew Orry*, Inquifitor of heretical Pravity.]

How long the Inquifition continued in *France*, and how and when it ended, I can't exactly affirm. I am apt to think, that when Liberty of Religion was granted by the Royal Edicts to Diffenters from the Church of *Rome*, that Tribunal immediately ceafed of it felf.

C H A P. XXIX.

Six CARDINALS *appointed at* Rome INQUISITORS *Generals.*

IN *Italy* the Pope took all poffible Meafures, that the Inquifition fhould difcharge its Office with the greateft Rigour. For when, in the Year 1530. the Vicar General of the Order of preaching Friars, fignified to *Clement* VII. that the *Lutheran* Herefy prevailed in *Italy*, to the great Detriment of the *Bullarium* Catholick Faith, this Pope publifhed a Bull, beginning, *Cum ficut ex relatione.* And leaft this Herefy fhould fpread like that of *Arius*, he commanded the Inquifitors to proceed againft all, even the Regulars of every Order ; but that they fhould abfolve the Penitent, difpenfe with them upon account of their Irregularity ; and grant Indulgences to the Crofs-Bearers appointed for the Service of the holy Inquifition. He commands the Bifhops, that in this Affair they fhould favour the Inquifition, any Thing to the contrary notwithftanding.

Paramus, And that the Inquifition might proceed without any Impediment, he ap-*l.* 2. *c.* 2. pointed a new Council of Cardinals Inquifitors Generals. Before this the In-*c.* 1. *n.* 9, quifitors were often forced to go to *Rome* to confult the Pope upon more dif-10, 11. ficult Affairs ; and therefore leaft the Office of the Inquifition fhould be interrupted by the Abfence of the Inquifitors, *Urban* IV. in the Year 1263. created by a Refcript, beginning, *Cupientes, John Caetanus Urfinus*, Cardinal of St. *Nicholas in carcere Tulliano*, General and Protector of all the Inquifitors, that there might be no need of their going to the Pope in Matters of Difficulty, but that they might confult the Cardinal by Letters, who was himfelf to confult with the Pope in all Cafes of Importance. Among other Things he thus commands : *Whatever great and dangerous Impediments have arifen in the before mentioned Affair, let them be fignified to our beloved Son,* John, *Cardinal Deacon*

I

of St. Nicholas in carcere Tulliano, *whom we have appointed to take Care of this Matter. And as to any other Difficulties that may hereafter arife, either for want of Affiftants, or from any other Caufe whatfoever, you may have Recourfe perfonally to the faid Cardinal if there be Need, and fafely confult him by your Letters or Meffengers, that we being fufficiently inftructed concerning the Premiffes, may provide fufficient Remedies againft thefe Difficulties.* This Cardinal, when raifed to the Papacy, and called *Nicholas* III. honoured Cardinal *Latinus Romanus,* his Nephew by his Brother, brought up amongft the Friars Predicants, with the fame Office of Inquifitor General. After his Death, in the Time of *Celeftine* V. the Office was vacant, and fo continued till the Papacy of *Clement* VI. who conferred it on *William* of *Tholoufe,* Cardinal of St. *Stephen* in Mount *Cælius.* He burnt fome Hereticks, and did feveral Things for the Inquifition. But becaufe this Dignity was not as yet fixed to the College of Cardinals, nor another primary Inquifitor immediately created by the Pope upon the Death of the former, as the Neceffities of the Church of *Rome* required, the Inquifitors were again involved in the fame Difficulties as before ; efpecially at the Time when the Doctrine of *Luther,* which had fpread it felf through all *Germany,* began to appear in *Italy* alfo. And therefore the Cardinals *John Peter Caraffa,* and *John Alvarez Toledo,* perfuaded Pope *Paul* III. to confer the Office of Inquifitor General upon fome certain Cardinals.

Upon this, in the Year 1542. Pope *Paul* III. by a Conftitution beginning, *Licet ab initio,* deputed fix Cardinals, Inquifitors General of heretical Pravity, in all Chriftian Nations whatfoever, as well on one Side as the other of the *Alps* ; and gave them Authority to proceed without the Ordinaries, againft all Hereticks, and fufpected of Herefy, and their Accomplices and Abettors, of whatfoever State, Degree, Order, Condition and Pre-eminence, and to punifh them, and confifcate their Goods : To depute a Procurator Fifcal, Notaries, and other Officials, neceffary to the aforefaid Affair : To degrade and deliver over to the Secular Court by any Prelate deputed by them, the Secular and Regular Clergy in holy Orders : To curb Oppofers, to call in the Affiftance of the fecular Arm, and to do every Thing elfe that fhould be neceffary : To fubftitute every where Inquifitors, with the fame, or a limited Power : To take Cognizance of Appeals from other Inquifitors to them : To cite, forbid, and abfolve, in the Court, and out of it, fimply or conditionally, from all Ecclefiaftical Sentences, Cenfures, and Punifhments, all that fhould appeal to them. In this Manner he ordains all Judgments to proceed, and annuls every. Thing to the contrary ; adding withal a penal Sanction, that if any one fhall break this Decree, or prefume to dare to contradict it, let him know that he fhall incur the Indignation of Almighty God, and of St. *Peter* and *Paul* his Apoftles.

Pius IV. afterwards enlarged the Power of thefe Cardinals, general Inquifitors of heretical Pravity. For in the Year 1564. *April, Id.* 7. by a Conftitution which begins, *Romanus Pontifex,* he gave them Authority to proceed in a certain Form, againft all manner of Perfons, whither Bifhops, Arch-

[margin: Bullar. Bzovius, a. 1442. §. 7.]

[margin: Bullar. Bzovius, a. 1564. §. 15.]

Archbifhops, Patriarchs, or Cardinals, that were Hereticks, their Abetters, and fufpected of Herefy, and of referring it to the Pope in a fecret Confiftory, in order to his pronouncing Sentence. In this manner he ordains Judgment to proceed, annuls every Thing to the contrary, and adds the ordinary penal Sanction.

Agreeable hereto in the Year 1563. the Pope commanded the Cardinals Inquifitors General to proceed at *Rome* againft *Odettus*. [*Coligni* Cardinal *de Chaftillion*, St. *Main* Archbifhop of *Aix*, *John de Muntluc* Bifhop of *Valence*, *John Anthony Caracciolus* Bifhop of *Troyes*, *John Barbanfon* Bifhop of *Apam*, and *Charles Gilaz* Bifhop of *Chartres* ;] and at length, in a private Confiftory, he pronounced Sentence upon each of them, by which he pronounces, judges and declares them to be Hereticks, Schifmaticks, Blafphemers, degraded from all Honour and Profit of the Cardinalate, Archiepifcopal, or Epifcopal Power, and Privilege of the Clergy, from the Day of their having committed their Crimes ; deprived, and for ever incapable of all Offices, Honours, Dignities and Prelatures, and decrees that they fhall be lawfully punifhed as Hereticks, and as unfruitful Branches cut off from the Church, and orders the Faithful of Chrift to apprehend and detain their Perfons, and deliver them over to the Minifters of Juftice, in order to their fuffering the deferved Punifhments. [But the *French* King did not acquiefce in that Sentence. Before the pronouncing of it, the Cardinal of *Lorain* advertifed the Pope, that the Maxims which prevailed in *France*, were very different from thofe amongft the *Romans*. That in this Kingdom it was very ill taken, that the Caufes of the Bifhops fhould, in the firft Inftance, be judged of at *Rome*. But when the Pope notwithftanding pronounced Sentence, the King commanded his Ambaffador *Henry Clutin Orifelle*, that he fhould put the Pope in mind of former Examples, and of the Liberties and Immunities of the *Gallican* Church, and of the Authority of the King in Ecclefiaftical Caufes, and defire him, that at prefent he would not be the Author of fo many Novelties. *Orifelle* executed his Commiffion with Diligence and Vigour, and after many Treaties with the Pontiff about it, obtained that the Affair of the Bifhops fhould be dropped.]

Pius V. that there might be an univerfal Obedience paid to the Decrees of the Cardinals Inquifitors General, and that none might be able to withdraw from their Authority, commanded the Princes, Judges, and Minifters of Juftice, that they fhould fubmit to and obey the Commands of thefe Cardinals in Matters relating to the Office of the holy Inquifition, in a Conftitution put forth, *Ann.* 1566. which, as being fhort, I fhall give entire.

Our moft holy Lord, Pius V. *by the Divine Providence, Pope, hath appointed, decreed, ordained and commanded, that Matters of Faith be preferred to all other Things whatfoever, fince Faith is the Subftance and Foundation of the Chriftian Religion ; and therefore, that all and every Perfon of this noble City, and its Diftrict, the Governor, Senator, Vicar, and Auditor of the Apoftolick Chamber, and all Legates, Vice-Legates, Governors of Provinces and Countries, mediately and*
im-

Bzovius, a. 1563. §. 3. Hift. Con. Trid. l. 7. p 808. l.8.p.908, 927.

Bullar.

immediately subject to his Holiness, and the holy Roman Church, and their Deputies, the Officials, Barisells *, and other Officers in those Places, and also all other Ordinaries of Places, and other Magistrates and Officials, and all Persons of whatsoever State and Condition in all and singular Countries, Towns and Cities throughout the whole Christian Commonwealth, do submit to and obey the said Cardinals Inquisitors, and their Orders and Commands in all Things concerning the holy Office of the Inquisition, under the Penalty of Excommunication, and the Displeasure of his Holiness, and of such other Punishments as shall be inflicted and executed at the Pleasure of his Holiness, and the most Illustrious and most Reverend Lords the Cardinals Inquisitors General.

He beseeches also in the Name of God, That the Kings, Dukes, Earls, Barons, and all other secular Princes, would favour the said Cardinals Inquisitors and their Officials, and afford them their Assistance, and cause the several Magistrates subject to them, to aid them in all Things concerning the said Office: And that they would without Delay, send all Persons imprisoned for any Crimes, or heinous Offences, if they should be accused before the said Office of the Inquisition, to the same Cardinals and Prisons of the Inquisition, suspending all Process for other lesser Crimes, that they might be kept therein, till through Cognisance and Trial should be made of the Crime of Heresy ; and after this to remit them to the civil Officers, to proceed against them for other Faults.

Supported by these Constitutions and Papal Decrees, the Cardinals Inquisitors extended their Power more and more. *Paulus Servita,* in his Time, complains, that whereas formerly the Pope sent his Inquisitors to the Princes with Apostolick Briefs, requiring them to protect and defend them by their Favour, as is even yet done in the Confirmation of a new Bishop ; yet that now the Council of the Inquisition at *Rome* gave their Inquisitors such Orders, as tho' they sent them into their own Dominions and Territories, and will not suffer any Contradiction to their Commands.   *Hist. Inq. cap. 3.*

At length *Sixtus* V. *An.* 1588. by a Constitution beginning, *Immensa Æterni Dei, &c.* appointed 15 Congregations of the Cardinals of the holy *Roman* Church, and assigned to each of them their proper Business. He approves the first Congregation held in the City for Inquisition of heretical Pravity, and confirms their Authority over all Prelates and Inquisitors, in Matters of Heresy, whether manifest or suspect, and the Privileges of their Ministers, and exhorts the Princes to support it, but so, that no Innovation should be introduced into the Office of the Inquisition, erected in the Kingdom of *Spain,* without consulting the Pope.

To these Cardinals Inquisitors General were added, for the quicker Dispatch and Determination of criminal Causes, a Commissary General of the holy   *Carena. p. 1. t. 2. §. 4, 5, 6, 7.*

---

* *Bariselli.* I cannot find any particular Account of these Officers. *Barisa is genus poculi,* a sort of a Cup ; and *Barillagium* is the Tribute paid for Wine Vessels ; and *Barillarius* is that Officer who had the Care of the Royal Wines. Whither the *Barisells* might not be some Officers to receive the Customs, or rather some Officers who had the Care of the Royal Provision, I am not able to determine.

Office, who is always a *Dominican*, and an Affeffor General. [Befides thefe there is prefent the Mafter of the facred Palace, who alfo always ufed to be of the *Dominican* Order. But becaufe his Power is very large, efpeci-ally in the Prohibition of Books, it is worth while to defcribe that Office a lit-tle more diftinctly. The Mafter therefore of the facred Palace, when there is a Confiftory, ordinarily reads in the Pope's Palace fomething in Divinity.

Det Loix They fay this Office was appointed by the Pope at the Advice of *Domi-*
Ante Spec, *nick.* For feeing daily, that when the Cardinals were engaged with the Pope,
Inq c.2,3. their Clergy and Attendance fpent their Time in idle Walks and Trifles, he went to the Pope, and faid, It was a Shame that thofe Minifters, who profeffed all Virtue, fhould do fuch fcandalous Things, and defile thofe holy Walls with the moft unbecoming Scurrilities. That he thought it would be ve-ry ufeful, that whilft the Cardinals were attending him upon the Affairs of the univerfal Church, fome learned Man fhould publickly interpret certain Places of the facred Scripture. *Honorius* was pleafed with the Motion, and appointed *Dominick* himfelf to the Office, who had advifed it. So that *Domi-nick* himfelf was the firft Mafter of the holy Palace, and it was appointed that fome Body fhould be always chofen to that Office out of the Predicant Or-der, and called Mafter of the facred Palace ; and he hath thefe Prerogatives. *Firft,* That he always dwells in the very Apoftolick Palace, with his Atten-dance and Houfhold, and hath a Salary for his Support affigned him by the Popes. *Secondly,* He fits in the Pope's Chapel near his Holinefs's Feet, and preceeds all the Divines and Mafters in Place, Advice and Refolution. *Third-ly,* Without his Licence no Book can be printed at *Rome* ; nor any Oration or Sermon pronounced before the Pope, without his Revifing and Appro-bation. *Fourthly,* In all Conferences and Difputations, his Definition, Refolu-tion and Sentence prevails, and no one can reply after him. *Laftly,* He is al-ways prefent in the Congregation of the moft holy Inquifition, with the Pope and Cardinals. He hath alfo the Title of the moft Reverend, and is the firft of the Predicant Order, after the Mafter General ; and to conclude, he is chofen into the Office by the Election and Nomination of the Pope, and not by Vote.

Thefe fupreme Inquifitors have alfo an Advocate Fifcal, feveral Coun-fellors, Prelates and Regulars, *viz.* the General of the *Dominican* Order, and the Affiftant of the Commiffary of the holy Office ; as alfo one of the Religi-ous of the *Francifcan* Order. They have alfo feveral Qualificator Divines, who qualify Propofitions in any Cafes that occur.] Whatever the Majority of the Cardinals decree, *Pius* IV. by a Conftitution beginning, *Cum nos per noftrum, &c.* ordered fhould be looked on as the Decree of the whole Congregation ; yea, that what the major Part of the Inquifitors prefent fhould appoint, fhould be efteem-ed as done by all, though fome were abfent ; that by the abfent Cardinals were to be underftood not fuch as were abfent from *Rome,* becaufe it might be very difficult to know this, but fuch Cardinals as were abfent from this Congregation.

§. 14.   Thefe fupreme Inquifitors meet twice a Week, *viz.* on *Wednefdays* for-merly in the Houfe of the oldeft Cardinal fupreme Inquifitor, but now in

St.

St. *Mary's* Church, *fupra Minervam*, except the Pope commands otherwife; and on *Thurfdays* in the Prefence of the Pope. Thefe Congregations are held every Week, excepting only the holy Week, which preceeds *Eafter*. [However *John de Loix* relates, that there are held three Congregations of the holy Office every Week.

Speculum Inq. Bizant p 92.

The firft is on *Monday*, in the Houfe of the holy Office, in which the Commiffary General of the Inquifition, who is always a Predicant, and his Attendants dwell. Here are prefent the Counfellors of the holy Inquifition, the Fifcal, and other Officials, where the Proceffes, Votes and Sentences of all of them are reported and regiftred. The Mafter General of the Predicants takes here the firft Place, the next the Mafter of the holy Palace, who is always a *Dominican*, out of Refpeft to St. *Dominick*, the Author and firft Mafter of this Office; then two or three Layers, next the Vicar General of the Predicants in the Abfence of the General, next the Commiffary General of the holy Office, who is always a Predicant; next the Affeffor of the holy Office; next the Procurator General of the collegiate Friars Minors; next the Provincial Inquifitors, when they are at *Rome*; next the Affiftant of the Commiffary General; next the Abbreviator of the Proceffes; next the Fifcal. We muft remark here, that the Mafter General of the Predicants, and the Mafter of the facred Palace, are alfo Counfellors to the Inquifition, for this Reafon, becaufe they are promoted to their feveral Offices.

The fecond Congregation is held on *Wednefday*, when the Cardinals meet in the Houfe of the oldeft, or the Dean of the Congregation, who have decifive Votes; although regularly they confirm what hath been determined on *Mondays* by the Counfellors and Commiffary.

The third Congregation is always held on *Thurfday* in the Prefence of the Pope, nor is it ever omitted, except on *Thurfday* in the Feftival Week of the holy Sacrament, and fometimes in the Feftival of *Corpus Chrifti*. In this Congregation his Holinefs decides or confirms the Votes of the Counfellors and Cardinals. The Cardinals only fit, all others ftanding. The Pope makes a Prayer when the Congregation comes in, as the oldeft Cardinal doth on *Wednefdays*, and the firft Counfellor on *Mondays*. The Provincial Inquifitors, who fupport their Authority, tranfmit by Letter their Difficulties to thefe Cardinals.]

Thefe Things, fays *Paramus*, *l. 2. t. 2. c. 1. n. 13.* were not thus ordered in the Beginning. For at the firft the other Cardinals, the Pope's Vicar, and the Mafter of the facred Palace, were joined with Cardinal *Caraffa*, and managed the Affairs of the Inquifition. But afterwards when *Caraffa* was elefted Pope on *May*, Cal. *5.* 1556. the aforefaid Congregations were held on certain Days in his Prefence; which Cuftom continued in the Reign of *Pius* V. *Gregory* XIII. and *Sixtus* V. but was difufed in the Time of *Pius* IV. who being taken up with Affairs of very great Confequence, could not be prefent with that Congregation.

In the mean while, as the Popes were conferring all this Authority on the Inquifition, and the fupreme Council of the Inquifition by their Bulls, feveral Books were publifhed at *Rome* for the Inftruftion of the Inquifitors. *An.* 1584.

X 2

there

there was printed at *Rome the Formulary of the Inquifition*, and the fame Year, *the Light of the Inquifition*, by Friar *Bernard* of *Como*, with Annotations, by *Francis Pegna*. In the Year following came out *the DireEtory of the Inquifitors*, by *Nicholas Eymerick* of the Friars Predicants, Inquifitor General of *Aragon*, with the Commentaries of *Pegna*. To this were fubjoined the Bulls and Refcripts of the Popes to the Inquifitors and others concerning Matters of Faith, by the Command of the Cardinals Inquifitors General throughout the whole Chriftian World.

CHAP. XXX.

Of the INQUISITION *in* Spain *againft* HERETICKS.

THE Tribunal of the Inquifition in *Spain*, at firft erected to difcover *Jews* and *Moors*, now began to proceed againft Hereticks, and exercifed the fame Cruelty againft thefe, as they had hitherto againft the others. *Charles* V. King of *Spain*, who with great Difficulty had brought the Inquifition into the *Netherlands* againft the *Lutherans* and *Reformed*, recommended it to his Son *Philip* in his Will. We have the Claufe of the Will given us by *Cæfar Carena*, from *Lewis Paramus*, in his Treatife of the Office of the moft holy Inquifition, *Prælud.* §. 62. in which the Emperor thus fpeaks: *Out of Regard to my Duty to Almighty God, and from my great AffeEtion to the moft ferene Prince* Philip II. *my deareft Son, and from the ftrong and earneft Defire I have, that he may be fafe under the ProteEtion of Virtue, rather than the Greatnefs of his Riches, I charge him with the greateft AffeEtion of Soul, that he take efpecial Care of all Things relating to the Honour and Glory of God, as becomes the moft Catholick King, and a Prince zealous for the divine Commands ; and that he be always obedient to the Commands of our holy Mother the Church. And, amongft other Things, this I principally and moft ardently recommend to him, highly to honour and conftantly fupport the Office of the holy Inquifition, as conftituted by God againft heretical Pravity, with its Minifters and Officials, becaufe by this fingle Remedy the moft grievous Offences againft God can be remedied. Alfo I command him, that he would be careful to preferve to all Churches and ecclefiaftical Perfons their Immunities.* And again in his Codicil to his Will he thus enjoins his Son. *I ardently defire, and with the greateft poffible Earneftnefs befeech him, and command him by his Regards to me his moft affeEtionate Father, that in this Matter, in which the Welfare of all* Spain *is concerned, he be moft zealoufly careful, to punifh all infeEted with Herefy with the Severity due to their Crimes, and that to this Intent, he confer the greateft Honours on the Office of the holy Inquifition, by the Care of which the Catholick Faith will be encreafed in his Kingdoms, and the Chriftian Religion preferved.*

Philip gave full Proof of his Zeal to execute his Father's Commands. For as *Famianus Strada* teftifies of him, when he was requefted by many to grant

De Bel.
Bel. Dec. 1.
l. 3.

Liberty

Liberty of Religion in the *Low Countries*, he proftrated himſelf before a Crucifix, and uttered theſe Words: *I beſeech the Divine Majeſty, that I may always continue in this Mind; that I may never ſuffer my ſelf to be, or to be called the Lord of theſe any where, who deny Thee the Lord.* Nor is this any Wonder: For the Popiſh Divines endeavour'd to perſuade the King of *Spain,* that the Inquiſition was the only Security of their Kingdom. Thus *Leonardus Vellius,* a Divine of the Jeſuits College at *Cremona,* teſtifies in his Letter to *Cæſar Carena,* prefixed to his Treatiſe of the Office of the moſt holy Inquiſition, where he ſays: *Since the Kings of* Spain *came to that Government, which now almoſt extends over the World, we read of no Sect profeſſing it ſelf an Enemy to the Pope, and the Catholick Religion, which did not at the ſame Time declare War againſt them. So that the Catholick Kings, and the Catholick Religion, have one common Intereſt and Cauſe. And if Pope* Paul V. *uſed to acknowledge, that by Means of the Inquiſition, the Pontiffs preſerved their Triple Crown; I doubt not but that the wiſeſt Kings have been taught by long Experience, that the Hereticks are dangerous Enemies to the* Auſtrian *Power, and are abundantly perſuaded, that their Sceptre and Kingdom can only be ſupported by the Miniſters of that ſacred Office.* No one can wonder, that under this Perſuaſion the *Spaniſh* Kings have been violent Promoters of the Inquiſition; and that they have inflicted the moſt cruel Puniſh-ments upon the miſerable Hereticks. *Philip* II. not only in the *Low Countries,* Hiſt. Com. but alſo in *Spain,* ſhew'd himſelf the Patron of it; and that the moſt outra-Trid. l. 5. gious Cruelty was acceptable to him. He gave ſome horrid Specimens of it p. 486. in the Year 1559. in two Cities of *Spain,* when he came thither from the *Low Countries:* " Immediately on his Arrival, as *Thuanus* relates, he began to " chaſtiſe the Sectaries. And whereas before this, one or more, juſt as it " happen'd, were deliver'd to the Executioner, after Condemnation for He-" reſy, all that were condemned throughout the whole Kingdom, were kept " againſt his coming, and carried together to *Seville,* and *Valladolid,* where " they were brought forth in publick Pomp to their Puniſhment. The firſt " Act of Faith was at *Seville,* the 8th of the Calends of *October;* in which " *John Pontius* of *Leon,* Son of *Rhoderick Pontius,* Earl of *Villalon,* was led " before the others, as in Triumph, and burn'd for an obſtinate heretical " *Lutheran.* *John Conſalvus,* a Preacher, as he had been his Companion in " Life, was forced to bear him Company in his Death; after whom follow-" ed *Iſabella Vænia, Maria Viroeſia, Cornelia,* and *Bohorquia;* a Spectacle full " of Pity and Indignation, which was encreas'd, becauſe *Bohorquia,* the " youngeſt of all of them, being ſcarce twenty, ſuffer'd Death with the " greateſt Conſtancy. And becauſe the heretical Aſſemblies had pray'd in " the Houſe of *Vænia,* it was concluded in her Sentence, and order'd to be " levelled with the Ground. After theſe came forth *Ferdinand a Fano Johan-" nis,* and *Julian Ferdinand,* commonly called the *Little,* from his ſmall Sta-" ture, and *John* of *Leon,* who had been a Shoemaker at *Mexico* in *New* " *Spain,* and was afterwards admitted into the College of St. *Iſadore,* in which " his Companions ſtudied, as they boaſted, the purer Doctrine privately. " Their Number was encreas'd by *Frances Chaveſia,* a Nun of the Convent
" of

" of St. *Elizabeth*, who had been inftructed by *John Ægidius*, a Preacher at *Se-*
" *ville*, and fuffer'd Death with great Conftancy. From the fame School came
" out *Chriftopher Lofada*, a Phyfician, and *Chriftopher Arellianus*, a Monk of St.
" *Ifidore*, and *Garfias Arias*, who firft kindled thofe Sparks of the fame Religion
" amongft the Friars of St. *Ifidore*, by his conftant Admonitions and Sermons, by
" which the great Pile was afterwards fet on Fire, and the Convent it felf, and
" good Part of that moft opulent City was almoft confumed. He was a Man of
" uncommon Learning, but of an inconftant wavering Temper ; and being ex-
" ceeding fubtle in difputing, he refuted the very Doctrines he had perfuaded
" his Followers to receive, tho' he brought them into Danger on that Account
" from the Inquifitors. Having by thefe Arts expofed many, whom he had
" deceived, to evident Hazard, and render'd himfelf guilty of the deteftible
" Crime of breach of Faith ; he was admonifhed by *John Ægidius*, *Conftantine*
" *Pontius*, and *Varquius*, that he had not dealt fincerely with his Friends, and
" thofe who were in the fame Sentiments with himfelf ; to which he replied,
" That he forefaw, that in a little Time, they would be forc'd to behold the
" Bulls brought forth for a lofty Spectacle ; meaning thereby the Theatre of
" the Inquifitors. *Conftantine* anfwer'd, You, if it pleafe God, fhall not behold
" the Games from on high, but be your felf amongft the Combatants. Nor
" was *Conftantine* deceived in his Prediction. For afterwards *Arias* was called
" on ; and whether Age had made him bolder, or whether by a fuddain Al-
" teration his Timoroufnefs changed into Courage, he feverely rebuked the
" Affeffors of the Inquifitory Tribunal, affirming they were more fit for the
" vile Office of Mule Keepers, than impudently to take upon themfelves to
" judge concerning the Faith, which they were fcandaloufly ignorant of. He
" farther declared, That he bitterly repented, that he had knowingly and wil-
" lingly oppofed, in their Prefence, that Truth he now maintained, againft
" the pious Defenders of it, and that from his Soul he fhould repent of it whilft
" he liv'd. So at laft being led in Triumph, he was burn'd alive, and con-
" firmed *Conftantine*'s Prophecy. There remained *Ægidius* and *Conftantine*, who
" clofed the Scene, but Death prevented their being alive at the Shew. *Ægidius*
" having been defigned by the Emperor, *Philip*'s Father, for Bifhop of *Droffen*,
" upon the Fame of his Piety and Learning, being fummoned, publickly re-
" canted his Error, wrought on either by Craft, or the Perfuafion of *Sotus*,
" a *Dominican* ; and hereupon was fufpended for a while from preaching, and
" the facred Office, and died fome Time before this Act. The Inquifitors
" thought he had been too gently dealt with, and therefore proceeded againft
" his Body, and condemned him dead to Death, and placed his Effigies in
" Straw on high for a Spectacle. *Conftantine*, who had been a long while the
" Emperor's Confeffor, and had always accompanied him in his Retirement,
" after his Abdication from his Empire and Kingdoms, and was prefent with
" him at his Death, was brought before this Tribunal, and died a little before
" the Act, in a nafty Prifon. But that the Theatre might not want him, his
" Effigies was carried about in a preaching Pofture. And thus this Shew,
" terrible in it felf, which drew Tears from moft who were prefent ; when

" thefe

" thefe Images were brought on the Scene, excited Laughter in many, and
" at length Indignation. They proceeded with the fame Severity the follow-
" ing *October*, at *Valladolid*, againft others condemned for the fame Crime,
" where King *Philip* himfelf being prefent, twenty eight of the chief Nobi-
" lity of the Country were tied to Stakes and burn'd." *Bartholomew Caranza*,
Archbifhop of *Toledo*, was alfo accufed ; who for his Learning, Probity of
Life, and moft holy Converfation, was highly worthy of that Dignity, Bzovius,
and caft into Prifon, and ftripp'd of all his large Revenues. His Caufe was *a*. 1559.
brought before *Pius* V. at *Rome*, and *Gregory* XIII. pronounced Sentence *§* 85.
in it.

Philip, not content to exercife his Cruelty by Land, eftablifhed the Inqui-Param.
fition alfo in the Ships. For in the Year 1571. a large Fleet was drawn *l. 2. tit. 2.*
together under the Command of *John* of *Auftria*, and manned with Soldiers *cap.* 14.
lifted out of various Nations. King *Philip*, to prevent any Corruption of the
Faith, by fuch a Mixture of various Nations and Religions, after having confulted Pope *Pius* V. deputed one of the Inquifitors of *Spain*, fixed on by the Inquifitor General, to difcharge the Office of Inquifitor ; giving him Power
to prefide in all Tribunals, and to celebrate Acts of Faith, in all Places and
Cities they failed to. This Erection of the Inquifition by Sea, *Pius* V. confirmed by a Bull fent to the General Inquifitor of *Spain*, beginning, Our late
moft dear Son in Chrift. *Jerome Manrique* exercifed the Jurifdiction granted
him, and held a publick Act of Faith in the City of *Meffina*, in which many
underwent divers Punifhments.

He alfo eftablifhed it beyond *Europe*, not only in the *Canary* Iflands, but
in the new World of *America* ; conftituting two Tribunals of it, one in the
City of *Lima*, in the Province of *Peru* ; the other in the Province and City of
Mexico. The Inquifition at *Mexico* was erected in the Year 1571. and in a *cap.* 21.
fhort Space gave large Proofs of its Cruelty. *Paramus* relates, that in the
Year 1574. the third after its Erection, the firft Act of Faith was celebrated
with a new and admirable Pomp, in the Marquiffes Market Place, where they
built a large Theatre, which covered almoft the whole *Area* of the Market
Place, and was clofe to the great Church, where were prefent, the Viceroy,
the Senate, the Chapter, and the Religious. The Viceroy, the Senate, and
a vaft Number of others, went with a large Guard, in folemn Proceffion,
to the Market Place, where were about eighty Penitents ; and the Act lafted from fix in the Morning to five in the Evening. Two Hereticks, one
an *Englifhman*, the other a *Frenchman*, were releafed. Some for Judaifing,
fome for Polygamy, and others for Sorceries, were reconciled. The Solemnity of this Act was fuch, that they who had feen that ftately one at *Valladolid*, held in the Year 1559. declared, That this was nothing inferior to it
in Majefty, excepting only that they wanted thofe royal Perfonages here,
which were prefent there. From this Time they celebrated yearly folemn
Acts of the Faith, where they brought *Portuguefe Jews*, Perfons guilty of
inceftuous and wicked Marriages, and many convicted of Sorcery and Witchcraft.

C H A P.

CHAP. XXXI.

Of the INQUISITION *in the* Low Countries.

THE Inquifition was introduced into the *Low Countries* in the Year 1522,
and *Francis Hulftus*, and *Nicolas Egmondanus*, a *Carmelite* Friar, were ap-
Epift. lib. pointed Inquifitors, of whom *Erafmus* thus writes to *John Carondilet*, Archbifhop
31. of *Palermo*, in the Year 1524. *And now the Sword is given to two violent*
Haters of good Learning, Hulftus, *and* Egmondanus, &c. *If they have a Spite
against any Man, they throw him into Prifon ; here the Matter is tranfacted between a few, and the Innocent fuffers barbarous Ufage, that they may not lofe any
Thing of their Authority ; and when they find they have done entirely wrong, they
cry out, We muft take Care of the Faith.* In the fame Year he writes to *Bili-*
Epift. lib. *baldus Pirkheimerus. There* (viz. in the Country of *Erafmus*) *reigns* Egmon-
30. danus, *a furious Perfon, armed with the Sword, who hates me twice more than he*
doth Luther. *His Collegue is* Francis Hulft, *a great Enemy of Learning. They
firft throw Men into Prifon, and then feek out for Crimes to accufe them of. Thefe
Things the Emperor is ignorant of, though it would be worth his while to know them.*
A great many were miferably ufed, and barbaroufly flain through their
Cruelty.

But in the Year 1549. *Charles*, created Emperor, endeavour'd to bring
the Inquifition more openly into the *Netherlands*, after the Manner of
that in *Spain*, by an Edict againft Herefy and Hereticks ; in which he commands all who had the Adminiftration of Juftice, and their Officials, when
required by the Inquifitors, and at the joint Requeft of the Ordinaries or Bifhops, to proceed againft any one in the Affair of Herefy, to give them their
utmoft Affiftance and Countenance, and to help them in the Execution of their
Office, and in apprehending and detaining thofe, whom they fhould difcover
to be infected with heretical Pravity, according to the Inftructions which the
aforefaid Inquifitors had received from him. In the Conclufion 'tis added,
that they fhould proceed againft Tranfgreffors by Execution, whatever Privileges had been before granted contrary to this Decree. This Edict occafioned great Difturbances, efpecially at *Antwerp*, where when it was known
for certain, and that is was foon to be publifh'd, a great Number of Mer-
Wefen- chants determin'd to go into other Places. As this would occafion great
bec. de Lofs to the City, and ruin their Trade, the Magiftrates called together the
ftat. rel. chief Merchants, and Citizens, and enquired what Lofs the City had already
in Belg. fuftained through Fear of the Inquifition, and what farther Damage it might
p. 20. fuffer if the Inquifition fhould be actually introduced. This was fairly drawn
out in Writing ; and the Magiftrates prefented it to Queen *Mary*, Sifter of
Charles V. then Governefs of the *Netherlands*, and largely fhewed, by many
Arguments taken from the Edict, the Inftructions of the Inquifitors, and the
Privileges of *Brabant*, how many Evils threatned the City and the whole

Country ; and befought her that fhe would intercede with the Emperor, her Brother, that fo rich and flourifhing a City might not be ruin'd by the Inquifition, from which, as well as from all Ecclefiaftical Jurifdiction, it had hitherto been free, and ought ever to remain fo according to their Privileges. The feveral Orders of *Brabant* join'd themfelves to the *Antwerpians*, and by their Reafons and Prayers, the Queen was fo moved, that fhe went to her Brother at *Augsburg*, and obtain'd another Edict, allowing the Ecclefiaftical Judges a Power of demanding fome Perfon from the fupreme Courts of the Emperor, to be join'd with them, when they proceeded againft any one for the Crime of Herefy. As to the reft of the former Decree, there was no Abatement. It was received with great Difficulty and Reluctance, and publifhed at *Antwerp* with this Proteftation, That this Edict fhould derogate nothing from their Privileges and Statutes.

But notwithftanding this Declaration of the Magiftrates, the Inhabitants could not be eafy, fuch was their Dread of the Cruelty of the Inquifitors ; efpecially becaufe they faw, that thofe who were privately commiffioned by the Pope and the Emperor to be Inquifitors, acted as fuch themfelves, as well as by their Commiffaries, in feveral Provinces and Cities. For feveral were condemn'd for Herefy by them, in many Cities, and either beheaded, hanged, or burn'd, or tied up in Sacks and drowned. The States, in vain, humbly befought the King to be delivered from fo grievous a Bondage. He was deaf to all their Prayers, and determined to lofe his Dominions, rather than fuffer them to be infected with Herefy. This occafioned ftill greater Difturbances ; and as the Cruelty of the Inquifitors every Day encreafed, they broke out at length into an open Revolt. The common People threw down the Images from the Temples, and committed other Violences ; on which the King, that he might have fome Shew of Juftice to conquer the *Low Countries*, and make Laws according to his abfolute Will, demanded the Judgment of the fupreme Office of the Inquifition in *Spain*, concerning thefe Revolters. After they had feen the feveral Informations and Proofs tranfmitted to them by the inferior Inquifitors ; they declared all the Inhabitants of the *Low Countries*, thofe only excepted whofe Names were fent to them, Hereticks and Favourers of Hereticks, and guilty of High Treafon, either for what they had done, or omitted to do. The King having received this Anfwer, fent the Duke of *Alva*, with a great Army into the *Netherlands* ; who, as he was a cruel and bloody Man, enter'd the Country with his Forces, and meeting no Refiftance, acted every where with the moft outragious Fury. One might have feen throughout all their Cities, old Men and young, Women and Girls, without any Diftinction of Dignity, Age or Sex, fuffering by the Sword, Gallows, Fire, and other Punifhments ; till at length the miferable Nation, warmed with the Remembrance of their former Freedom, took Courage and Arms, and after they had recovered their Liberty, drove out the Inquifition from the whole Country.

FINIS LIBRI PRIMI.

Y

THE

THE
HISTORY
OF THE
INQUISITION.

BOOK II.

CHAP. I.

Of the MINISTERS *of the* INQUISITION *in General.*

THUS far we have described the Original of the Inquisition, and its Propagation into several Kingdoms and Countries. There are three Things yet remaining to be treated of. *First,* The Ministers of the Inquisition, as well the Inquisitors themselves, as others who serve them in the holy Office, together with their Duties and Offices. *Secondly,* The Crimes subject to the Cognizance of this Tribunal; by what ways Guilt may be contracted; and what Punishments are annexed to the several Offences. *Thirdly,* What is the Manner of Process observed before the Tribunal of the Inquisition. These shall be dispatch'd in three several Books.

As to the first of these we need not repeat what hath been already said in the former Book concerning the Cardinals, Inquisitors General in all Christian Countries, and of the supreme Council of the Inquisition in the Kingdoms of *Spain* and *Portugal.* I shall speak only of the Inquisitors and those who serve them. For although the Erection of those Councils hath introduced no small Change in the Office of the Inquisition, yet it respects rather the Manner of Process, than the Officers of the Inquisition; which therefore I shall afterwards endeavour to explain according to the best Assistance I can gather from those Authors who have written of the Affair.

The Offices in the *Spanish* and *Portugal* Inquisition are somewhat different from what they were anciently, and from those of the *Italian* Inquisition to this Day. And becáuse thefe two Inquifitions are now the principal and moft famous ohes, wherein they differ from other Inquifitiöns, I fhall carefully de_ fcribe, and give an Account of the feveral Offices in them, as they are de_ livered by the *Spanifh* Doctors.

Simàncàs gives us this Account of the Minifters of the *Spanifh* Inquifition. De Catbol. " In every Province of *Spain* there ought to be two or three Inquifitors, one^{left. tit.} " Judge of the forfeited Effeĉts, one Executor, three Notaries, two for^{41. §. 3.} " Secrecy, and the third for Sequeftrations, one Keeper of the Prifon, one " Meffenger, one Door-keper, and one Phyfician. Befides thefe, Affeffors, " skilful Counfellors, Familiars and others are neceffary." In *Italy* they call them Crofs-bearers, of pretty near the fame Office with the *Spanifh* Famili- ars. Befides thefe, there is a Promoter Fifcal, a Receiver of the for- feited Effeĉts; and finally, Vifitors of the Inquifitors. Of thefe in their Order.

CHAP. II.

Of the INQUISITORS.

IN the Church of *Rome* there are two Sorts of Judges in the Affair of the Eymerié. Faith: The Ordinaries, fuch as the Pope, and Bifhops of Places, who Dire&. when ordained or confecrated, are believ'd to receive, by divine Right,^{p. 3. q. 1.} Power and Jurifdiĉtion over Hereticks: And Delegates, to whom the Office of judging Hereticks is particularly given by the Pope, who are called Inquifi- tors by the Laws. Apoftolick Inquifitors are therefore Judges delegated by the Pope, who is believed to be the fupreme Judge of the Faith, who grants them full Jurifdiĉtion againft all Hereticks and Apoftates. And they are de- legated for all Caufes.

No one can be thus deputed to this Office who is not forty Years old. *We or-* Clement, *dain by the Approbation of this holy Council, that no Perfon under forty Years old, fhall* cap. Nolem *from this Time be admitted to the Office of the Inquifition.* But becaufe Knowledge and tes. de hæ Prudence fometimes fupply the Defeĉt of Age, 'tis determined by a gene- ret. ral Decree of the Pope, that a Perfon of thirty Years old may be Apoftolick Inquifitor in *Spain* and *Portugal.* Even in this Age the Congregation of Cardi- Carena, nals created *Baptift a Martinengo,* Inquifitor at *Cremòna,* who was very little P. 1. t. 5. above thirty. 'Tis alfo the Cuftom to chufe Inquifitors for Cities, not out of n. 18. q. 3. the Citizens, but from Foreigners.

Thefe Inquifitors receive Power to execute this Office from the Pope, who fometimes immediately appoints them by Word of Mouth, fometimes by his Apoftolick Letters. Thus in the Letters of *Clement,* beginning, *Licet ex om- nibus mundi partibus,* written to the Inquifitors; we read, *That the Office of the Inquifition againft Hereticks may be more effeĉtually difcharged, we command your*

Difcre-

Difcretion by our Apoftolick Writings, enjoining you, by the Remiffion of your Sins, to execute the aforefaid Office, which we commit to you by our Apoftolick Authority, in the Love of God, and without any Fears of Men, putting on the Spirit of Strength from on high. Sometimes he commits it to a Cardinal or Legate.

Heretofore the Pope ordinarily granted it to the Mafter, and Provincial Priors of the Predicants; to the General and Provincials of the Minorites, that they fhould take Care to provide Inquifitors of the Friars of their Order, for the Places affigned to them, as we find it in their Privileges, and as appears from many Refcripts of the Popes, particularly *Innocent, Clement* and *Alexander* IV. which begin, *Licet ex omnibus. We firmly charge and command your Difcretion, by thefe Apoftolick Writings, that with the Advice of fome difcreet Friars of your Order, you chufe eight of the faid Order, fit for your Province, to perform this Work of the Lord ; and that you ftrictly charge them, in Virtue of their holy Obedience, by the Apoftolick Authority, that they execute the Office of the Inquifition,* &c. And they give this Reafon, becaufe they are prefumed to have greater Knowledge of their own Friars, and can therefore more eafily judge who are the moft proper to be advanced to fo high an Office. But at this Time the Apoftolick Inquifitors throughout *Italy* are not chofen by the Prelates of the aforefaid Orders, but either immediately by the Pope, or by a Brief, as the Inquifior at *Milan* and *Genoua* are chofen ; or by Letters Patents from the Cardinals, Inquifitors General over the whole Chriftian World. In *Spain* the Prefident of the Inquifition appoints the Inquifitors.

And as the Power of the Inquifitor depends on the Pope, fo no one can be removed from this Office, but by the Pope alone, and thofe to whom his Holinefs commits this Power. Formerly he granted the Power to the General and Provincial Mafters of the Orders, as appears from thefe Letters of *Innocent.*

Innocent, Bifhop, Servant of the Servants of God, to our venerable Brother John, *Bifhop, formerly Mafter of* Bofino, *and to our beloved Sons the Friars of the Order of Predicants, Health and Apoftolick Benediction. Being continually refrefhed with the fweet Savour of your Order, we defervedly bear an efpecial Favour towards it, with full Defire wifhing its Advancement, and endeavouring with our moft diligent Care to procure for it Peace and other Bleffings, by which it may obtain through the Lord the defired Encreafe. For this Reafon we have yielded to your Requeft, that you, Brother* John, *Bifhop and Mafter, and your Succeffors, the Friars of your Order, who are or fhall be deputed by the Apoftolick See to preach the Crofs, or to inquire againft heretical Pravity, or any other fuch Affairs, may lawfully and freely fet afide, or recall, quite remove and enjoin them to forbear, and fubftitute others in their Room, as fhall feem expedient to you, and exercife the Ecclefiaftical Cenfure againft all Contraveners. And by Authority of thefe prefent, we grant, that every Provincial Prior of the fame Order may act in like Manner in his Province, as to the Friars of the faid Order, to whom this Affair may happen to be committed by the fame See. Dated at* Lyons, *June Id. 5. and third of our Pontificate.*

But now the Cardinals, Inquifitors General in Chriftendom, remove and change, and tranflate them from one Place to another, as they think convenient.   The

Margin notes:
§. 9.

Bzovius,
a. 1245.
§. 12. n.
10.

The Popes were greatly defirous that this Office fhould be free from all Eymer.
Obftruction ; and therefore, as one very obvious Difficulty might arife direct.
from the Prelates of the feveral Religions, if fuch as were created regular In- part 3.
quifitors fhould be forced to obey their Prelates in their Office, therefore the qu. 11.
Popes exempted them as to this Affair from their Jurifdiction, as appears
from a Bull of *Clement* IV. beginning *Catholicæ Fidei*. *Although the Mafter and
Minifter Generals, and other Priors and Provincials, and the Keepers or Guardians of any Places of your Orders, under pretence of any Privileges or Indulgences of
the fame See, granted, or hereafter to be granted to the faid Orders, fhall enjoin,
or any ways command you, or any one or more of you, to fuperfede this Affair for a
Time, or as to any certain Articles or Perfons ; we ftrictly prohibit all and fingular
of you, by our Apoftolick Authority, from prefuming to obey, or in any manner to regard them in this Matter. For by the Tenor of thefe prefent, we recall all fuch
Privileges and Indulgences relating to this Article, and decree that all Sentences of
Excommunication, Interdict and Sufpenfion, that may be pronounced againft you, or
any of you upon this Occafion, fhall be altogether null and void.* So that in the Of- Q. 12.
fice of the Inquifition they are by no Means fubject to their Superiors, but only to the Pope ; infomuch that if an Inquifitor fhould unjuftly profecute any
one for Herefy, the Perfon apprehended can't appeal to the Superior of that
Religion, but only to the Pope.   Nor is the Inquifitor in any manner bound to
obey the Superior of his Religion, interrogating him on any Affairs relating to
his Office, but the Pope alone, whom he immediately reprefents.

And leaft the Superiors of Orders fhould claim to themfelves any Power
over the Inquifitors, by reafon of their Inquifitorial Office, *Urban* IV. wrote
to the Inquifitors in Privilege of the Catholick Faith. *For if the aforefaid See
hath fometimes committed by their Letters, under a certain Form, to fome Prelates of
your Order, a Power to chufe certain Friars of their Orders to exercife the Office of
the Inquifition againft heretical Pravity, and to remove and fubftitute others in their
Room, as they fhould think convenient ; as this was granted them only, becaufe it was
prefumed that they had a fuller Knowledge of the Fitnefs of fuch Friars, fo hereby no
Faculty, Jurifdiction or Power is given them over any fuch Affair committed, and
to be committed to you immediately by the aforefaid See.*

This is in Force only when the Inquifitors are of any particular Order,
whither Predicants or Friars Minor. It is now of no Ufe in *Spain* ; for, as
Simancas tells us, 'tis found by Experience, that 'tis much more ufeful and r't. 41.
proper, that the Inquifitors fhould be Layers, and not Divines.   §. 3.

In like Manner the Popes ordered, that in Favour of the Faith the Office
of the Inquifitors fhould be perpetual, fo that it was not to ceafe at the
Death of the Pope who conferred it, although the Jurifdiction delegated to
them might not have been made ufe of. Thus 'tis ordained by *Clement*
IV. and is to be found in the *Sext. Decret*. *Leaft any Perfons fhould be
in doubt, whither the Office of the Inquifition of heretical Pravity, committed by
the Apoftolick See under certain Limitations to your Care, expires at the Death of
the Pope who granted it, we by this prefent Edict declare, that the faid Office fhall
laft, in Favour of the Faith, after the Deceafe of him who conferred it, not only
with*

with refpect to Affairs begun during the Life of the Granter, but as to thofe which are untouched, and not begun, and what is more, even as to fuch as may not àrife

Simanc. *till afterwards.* For this Reafon the Office of particular Inquifitors continues de C*tbol.* in *Spain*, after the Death of the Inquifitor General, although they fhould be Inftit. tit. delegated by him ; and the rather, becaufe they are chofen under this Form: 34. §. 14. *We conftitute you our Vicegerents till we fhall fpecially recall the Commiffion.* In which Cafe the Jurifdiction of the delegated Judge continues after the Demife of him who deputed him. Cap. *Si delegatus,* de Offic. deleg. *l.* 6.

This Office is accounted of fo great Dignity in the Church of *Rome*, that the Title of *moft Reverend* is given to the Inquifitors equally as to Bifhops, and becaufe they are delegated by the Pope to their Jurifdiction, they are advanced to the principal Part of the Epifcopal Office, and are therefore thought

Caren.*p.*1. to deferve the Honour of an equal Title of Dignity with the Bifhops themt. 5. *n.*57. felves. From whence alfo they infer, that the Inquifitors ought to take place of the Vicar General of the Bifhop, not only in Caufes of Herefy, but in other Acts and Caufes that do not belong to the holy Office.

Simanc. In *Spain* oftentimes feveral Inquifitors are deputed together, and whenever tit. 34. this happens, they take Care not to create two who are akin, in the fame §. 21. Province, nor fuffer them to have any Official for their Servant, or of their Houfhold.

§. 15.   " If any Thing hard or difficult happens in any Province, the Inquifitors " muft refer it to the Council.

§. 16.   " The Inquifitors fit on their Tribunal fix Hours every Day, and if any " Thing comes before them that belongs to the Inquifitors of another Pro- " vince, they refer it to them, and the Meffengers are to be paid the Ex- " pences of the Journey by the Inquifitors to whom they are fent. 4 *Inftruct.* " *Tolet. cap.* 28. & 3 *Inftruct. Valdolit. cap.* 9.

§. 17.   " Farther, the Inquifitors are diligently to read thofe Books in which the " Teftimonies againft Hereticks are contained, that from hence they may " know the Names and Offences of the guilty Perfons, and underftand di- " ftinctly their feveral Crimes. And of this Matter the Vifitors are particu- " larly to enquire, and report it to the Inquifitor General, if the Inquifitors " fhould happen to be negligent herein. 5 *Inftruct. Hifpal. cap.* 3.

§. 18.   " The Inquifitors muft take fpecial Care to agree with and be friendly to " each other. If any Difference fhould arife againft them, they muft con- " ceal it, and refer it to the Inquifitor General, that after he underftands the " Matter he may compromife it, and judge between them. 1 *Inftruct. Hifpal.* " *cap.* 26."

Carena, The Office of the Inquifition ceafes upon the Inquifitors Advancement to any p. 1. t. 5. Dignity. If the Inquifitor, for Inftance, is made a Bifhop, thefe Dignities n. 102. are incompatible, becaufe both require perfonal Refidence, and therefore the Office of the Inquifitor ceafes.

Richer. [If the Inquifitors are negligent or remifs in their Office, the Synod of *Si-* Hift. Con. *nigaglia*, held *An.* 1423. hath decreed, That they fhall hereby incur the Pe-*l.* 3. *s.* §. nalty of Sufpenfion from entring into the Church for the Space of four Years. §. 1. *p.* The

The fame Synod commands, *That in Provincial or Synodical Councils, a proper Remedy shall be provided, besides the forementioned Penalty, against such negligent Persons, according to the Degree of such Fault or Negligence, all Privileges, Exemptions, Customs and Statutes whatsoever to the contrary notwithstanding.* But I am persuaded that few offend against this Decree, or incur the Penalty of Suspension by Negligence or Lenity ; since all Compassion is banished from this Tribunal, and since all who are promoted to this Office of Inquisitor immediately divest themselves, I will not say of all Pity only, but even of Humanity it self.]

If the Inquisitors offend, by unjustly extorting Money, it was anciently provided, in *Clement. de hæret. cap. Nolentes.* that they should be punished by the Prelates of their Order. *Which said Prelates are bound to remove from their Offices such Inquisitors and Commissaries as are found guilty, and when removed, otherwise to punish and correct them according to their Desert.* But now as the Prelates of the several Orders neither appoint or remove Inquisitors, so neither do they punish them ; but the Affair is referred to the Cardinals Inquisitors General in Christendom. In *Spain* the President of the Inquisition, whom they call Inquisitor Major, punishes the delinquent Inquisitors, which was expresly granted him by a Bull of *Leo* X. But however notwithstanding, this, the Pope can, as often as he pleases, call, cite, and punish the Inquisitors of all Kingdoms at the Court of *Rome* ; for he is the Judge of all, and the Inquisitors are delegated by him, and because it appertains to him to take Cognisance of their Causes, and punish their Offences. And if any others take Cognisance of these Affairs, they do it by a Power derived from the Pope, which he can resume as often as he thinks fit, and bring the whole Affair before himself.

When any Inquisitor is to be punished for his Offence, they take Care not to lessen Mens Opinion of the Dignity and Authority of the holy Office by his Condemnation or Punishment, which they say is more dangerous than to suffer an Offender to go unpunish'd ; unless it be such an Offence as gives Scandal, and therefore must not be passed over with Impunity. And they alledge this Reason ; That the Apostolick Inquisitors are both dreaded and hated by many, and especially by wicked Men ; and therefore if they should be easily or publickly punished, the foolish and mad People would soon be drawn by their Crimes to hate and dishonour the holy Office. So that when there is a Necessity to punish the Inquisitors, it must be done with Caution, to prevent greater Inconveniences.

However, from these Laws it is very plain, that the Tribunal of the Inquisition is not so very holy and blameless, as they would have them believe in *Spain* and *Portugal* ; but the Inquisitors punish innocent Men sometimes very unjustly, throwing them into Prison, and treating them in a very barbarous and unworthy Manner. Of this we have a fresh Instance in the Inquisition at *Goa*, in relation to Father *Ephraim*, a *Capucine*, whom out of mere Hatred and Revenge they seized, by Craft and Subtlety, and carried away to *Goa*, and there shut him up in the Prison of the Inquisition. The

Pegna, *in part.* 3.

Direct. *Com.* 61.

Tavern. *Travels.* *D.* 1. *C.* 1;

Story

Story is this: Father *Ephraim* having had an Invitation from some *English* Merchants, built a Church in the City of *Madrespatan*, which was near to the City of St. *Thomas*. To this Place several of the *Portuguese* came from St. *Thomas*'s, to have the Benefit of *Ephraim*'s Instruction. By this he incurred the Hatred of the *Portuguese*; and upon some Disturbance that was raised, Father *Ephraim* was called to St. *Thomas* to appease it, where he was seized by the Officers of the Inquisition, and carried to *Goa*, bound Hands and Feet, and at Night coming from on Board the Ship, hurried into the Prison of the Inquisition. All Men wondered that this *Capucine* should be brought Prisoner before the Tribunal of the Inquisition as an Heretick, who was known to be a Person of great Probity and Zeal for the *Roman* Religion. Many were concerned for his Delivery, and especially Friar *Zenon* of the same Order, who tried every Method to effect it. When the News of his Imprisonment came to *Europe*, Persons were very differently affected. His Brother the Lord *Chateau des Bois*, solicited the *Portugal* Ambassador at *Paris*, till he prevailed with him to send Letters to his *Portuguese* Majesty, to desire his peremptory Orders to the Inquisitors at *Goa*, to dismiss *Ephraim* from his Prison. The Pope also himself sent Letters to *Goa*, commanding him to be set free, under the Penalty of Excommunication. The King also of *Golconda*, who had a Friendship for him, because he had given him some Knowledge of the Mathematicks, commanded the City of St. *Thomas* to be besieged, and to be put to Fire and Sword, unless *Ephraim* was immediately restored to his Liberty. The Inquisitors not being able to surmount all these Difficulties, sent him Word that the Prison Gates were open, and that he might have his Liberty when he pleased. But he would not leave his Jail, till he was brought out by a solemn Procession of the Ecclesiasticks of *Goa*. And although there are many Instances of the like Injustice, yet they very seldom publickly punish'd the Injustice and Cruelty of the Inquisitors, least their Authority, which they would have always accounted sacred, should be contemned.

C H A P. III.

Of the VICARS *and* ASSISTANTS *of the* INQUISITION.

Eymer.41. WHEN the Inquisition was first appointed and delegated, there were no Cardinals Inquisitors General over Christendom, whom they could consult by Letter, and from whom receive an Answer in Cases of Difficulty, after their having first advised with the Pope. And therefore particular Inquisitors were often forced to go to *Rome*, during whose Absence the Affairs of the Faith were at a stand. To prevent this Inconvenience, the Inquisitor may in such a Case appoint a Vicar General over the whole Province,

43. Pegna, *in* Eymer. p. 436.

vince,

vince, with a Power of proceeding to the definitive Sentences of the Impenitent and Relapfed. *Urban* IV. in order to remove this Difficulty, *A. D.* 1263. created by a Refcript, beginning, *Cupientes*, the Cardinal of St. *Nicholas in carcere Tulliano*, Inquifitor General, or, as it were, Protector of the Inquifitors, whom particular Inquifitors might confult, either in Perfon, or by propofing their Doubts to him by Letters. But now all thefe Inconveniences are over, fince the Appointment of the Cardinals Inquifitors General over Chriftendom, whom they may confult by Letters, and to whom all Princes are fubject in this Affair. This is plain from the Bull of *Pius* V. publifhed 1566. In *Spain* the Inquifitors of particular Cities confult the Inquifitor General of thofe Kingdoms, or Prefident of the Inquifition; and he with thofe of other Provinces advifes with the Cardinals Inquifitors General.

'Tis however now the conftant daily Practice of all Inquifitors to have their Vicars General, who, in their Abfence, may manage the Affairs of the Inquifition. Thefe are ordinarily appointed by the Inquifitors themfelves; for the Inquifitor hath Power of conftituting his Vicar or Commiffary, by the Bull of *Clement* VII. fent to *Paulus Bugitella*, which begins, *Cum ficut*, in which we read: *Moreover we decree that you may have Authority to appoint your Vicars or Commiffaries, Perfons whom you fhall judge to be circumfpect, fit, and proper, provided they are full thirty Years of Age.* ^[marg: Qu. 13.]

This Power doth not extend only to the appointing one or two Vicars or Commiffaries, but feveral, if the Diocefe or Province be large, and contains feveral Cities. For as the Inquifitor cannot be perfonally prefent at all of them, 'tis neceffary he fhould appoint Commiffaries in them. He muft create at leaft in every City one, a Man prudent and learned, an old Chriftian, pious, and fit for Bufinefs, a religious Perfon of his own, or fome other Order, or a fecular Clergyman, *viz.* one poffeffed of fome Preferment in the principal Church of that City, or a Canonift, whom he verily believes will take Care of the Matters of the Faith diligently, and according to the Canonical Sanctions. ^[marg: Pegna, Com. 63.]

This Vicar General may be conftituted with fuch full Powers by the Inquifitor, as to be able to receive Denunciations, Informations or Accufations from and againft any Perfons whatfoever, and of proceeding, and of citing, arrefting, and putting in Irons as well the Witneffes as the Guilty, of receiving their Confeffions or Depofitions, and of proving them, of examining and compelling to give Evidence, and of putting to the Queftion and Torture to force the Truth from them, jointly with the Lord Bifhop or his Vicar; as alfo of imprifoning them by way of Punifhment rather than Safety, of calling together and advifing with fkilful Men at his Pleafure; and in general of doing every Thing, which the Inquifitor himfelf, if prefent, could do. Only the Inquifitor ufually referves to himfelf the definitive Sentence of all Impenitents and Relapfed, although he may alfo commit even this to his Vicar. In the *Seville* Inftruction, *A. D.* 1484. *cap.* 17. 'tis provided, *That the Inquifitors fhall themfelves receive and examine Witneffes, and not commit the Examination to a Notary, or any other Perfon; unlefs the Witnefs be fo ill, as that he can't appear before the Inquifitor, and it be not reputable for the Inquifitor to go to the Witnefs* ^[marg: Eymer. P. 3. 37.] ^[marg: 58. Pegna, P. 434.]

Z

nefs

ness to receive his Depofition, or except he be otherwise hindred. In fuch a Cafe the Inquifitor may commit the Examination of the Witnefs to the ordinary Ecclefiaftical Judge of the Place, or to fome cautious and honeft Perfon, who underftands how to examine with the Notary, and who fhall report the Manner in which the Witnefs

P. 41.
gave his Depofition. But the Power of pronouncing definitive Sentences is very feldom given to the Commiffary or Vicar, without firft confulting the Inquifitor, who in Decency is bound to defend the Proceffes of his Commiffaries. He cannot however grant fuch Commiffary a Power of fubftituting a Vicar for himfelf. Sometimes they appoint two Commiffaries, who fhall equally and jointly proceed againft the Guilty.

The Inquifitor only can depofe the Vicar thus appointed by himfelf, and 'tis not in the Power of the Prelates of the Religious.

Sometimes the Pope himfelf appoints the Commiffary, fo that there are two forts of Commiffaries, fome appointed by the Inquifitor, others by the Pope. Their Power is unequal. The Commiffary appointed by the Inquifitor, neither takes Place of the Ordinary, nor poffeffes all the other Privileges, which the Inquifitor doth. Whereas he who is particularly appointed by the Papal Authority, is in all Things equal to the Inquifitor himfelf.

Caren.
p. 1. t. 7.
n. 15, 16.
'Tis a Queftion amongft the Doctors, Whither upon the Death of the Inquifitor, the Jurifdiction of the Vicar ceafes. But though this was controverted heretofore, there feems to be no Doubt remaining about it now. For the Congregation of Cardinals Inquifitors General hath decreed, that the Vicars General of the Inquifitors fhall be nominated or chofen by the Inquifitors, and then confirmed by their Congregation. Whilft this Decree is in Force, the Vicars have their Jurifdiction properly from the Congregation ; and therefore as Acts derive their Validity from the Perfon confirming them, the Jurifdiction of the Vicars fhall not expire upon the Death or Removal of the Inquifitors. And thus *Carena* tells us it was obferved in the City *Pavia*, in which after the two Inquifitors that were dead, the Vicars General of the holy Office managed all the Affairs of the Inquifition.

P. 1. t. 11.
v. 5, 7.
As to what regards the Vicars appointed in the feveral Cities, which they call Foraneous Vicars, they have feldom any Thing elfe granted to them, but only the Management of an offenfive Procefs, as to which they are often to inform the Inquifitor of the Tranfactions in reference to it. So that they can imprifon no Perfon, unlefs the Affair be firft communicated to the Inquifitor, or except there be a very great and unavoidable Neceffity. For Inftance, if the Matter relate to a formal Heretick, and there fhould be Danger in a Delay, that he might endeavour to efcape by Flight.

Eymer.
p. 3. qu.
20.
If the Inquifitor needs an Affiftant in his Office, the Priors of the Orders are commanded by a Bull of *Clement* IV. beginning, *Ne Catholicæ Fidei negotium*, that to remove all Difficulty, they fhall take Care to affign to the feveral Friars chofen for Inquifitors, their feveral Affiftants, *viz.* Friars of their Order, careful and difcreet Perfons, fit for the faid Bufinefs, and who are worthy to be joined with thofe whom they are to affift. And as often as the Inquifitors fhall defire it, let them provide others of the fame Order befides

thofe.

thofe already provided. *Gregory* XI. by a Bull beginning, *Catholicæ Fidei negotium*, gives the Inquifitors free Power of going to the Court of *Rome*, and abiding there, and of taking an Affiftant without the Licence of his Order, and of changing fuch an Affiftant, and of taking another out of his Province, and of keeping him with him as often as he fhall judge fit, any Prohibition of Prelates or Chapters to the contrary notwithftanding.

CHAP. IV.

Of ASSESSORS *and* COUNSELLORS *neceffary to the Office of the* INQUISITION.

THE Inquifitors were originally religious Friars, fkilful only in Divini- Eymer.
ty, but ignorant of the Laws. And therefore becaufe they might be *p.3.qu.77.*
eafily deceived in a judiciary Procefs, and fo abfolve fuch as fhould be con- Pegna,
demned, and condemn fuch as fhould be abfolved, they were commanded to *Com. 126.*
call in fkilful Perfons, fuch as Divines, Canonifts and Layers, to confult
them, and if there was need to compel them to give their Advice in Virtue
of their Obedience ; as we find it, *cap. Ut commiffi.* §. *Advocandi.* de hæret.
lib. 6. *That you alfo call in as Occafion requires, any fkilful Perfons to affift you, and
give you proper Advice in paffing fuch Sentences, and enjoin them by Virtue of their
Obedience, that in this Matter they humbly obey you.* And thus we often find it
in the Book of the *Tholoufe* Inquifition, in the Sentences pronounced : *We the
aforefaid Bifhop and Inquifitor, with the Advice and Counfel of many good Men
fkilful as well in the Canon as Civil Law, and of many prudent religious
Perfons,* &c. I do not find that their Number is precifely determined by
any certain Law. *Carena* fays, that in the Congregation at *Cremona*, there P. 1. tit. 8.
are regularly prefent, four Regular Divines, four Secular Clergymen, Ca- *n. 12.*
nonifts, and four Lay Counfellors ; and becaufe the Inquifitor there is always
a Mafter in Divinity, they don't need fo many other Qualificators, as the In- *Ibid. n.35.*
quifitors of *Spain* do, who are Layers.

'Tis to be wonder'd at, that the Office of making Inquifition againft Hereticks, and of judging them, fhould be committed to Perfons entirely ignorant of the Law. But if we confider the modern Inquifitors, and compare
them with the more ancient ones, and judge of their Ignorance by what we
find of the Ignorance of the other, it muft be owned that they know nothing
either of Law, or of Divinity, or of any Theological Points. The Au- *a. 22i*
thor of the Hiftory of the Inquifition at *Goa*, was in doubt, whither the Baptifm of the Breath * could be reconciled with thofe Words of our Lord, *John*
iii. 5. *Except a Man be born again of the Water and the Spirit, he cannot enter into the Kingdom of Heaven.* The Inquifitor who examined him as to his Faith,
was aftonifhed at the citing of this Place, and asked where the Paffage was

---

* *Baptifmus Flaminis* is the Baptifm of the Holy Ghoft, founded on *Acts* i. 5. and, I fuppofe, fo
called from *Joh.* xx. 22. *He breathed on them, and faith unto them, Receive ye the Holy Ghoft.*

to be found. * He was equally ignorant of the Canon of the Council of *Trent*, about the Worſhip of Images. So that he concludes, that the Ignorance of the Inquiſitors, in Matters of Faith, exceeds all Belief. Father *Ephraim* alſo affirmed, That nothing was ſo troubleſome to him in the Priſon of the Inquiſition, as the Ignorance of the Inquiſitor and his Aſſeſſors, when they examined him, which was ſo very great, as that he verily believed not one of them had ever read the holy Scriptures. And therefore as the Inquiſitors are thus ignorant themſelves, they greatly want the Advice, not only of Perſons ſkilful in both Laws, or as they call them, of Canoniſts and Layers, but of Divines alſo. They are generally called Aſſeſſors and Counſellors.

They have their diſtinct Parts. They are not all indifferently conſulted in all Affairs, but each of them as to thoſe which they are preſumed to underſtand. The Divines are called in to examine Propoſitions, and explain their Quality. The Layers are conſulted about the Puniſhment or Abſolution of Offenders, and other Merits of Cauſes. The Inquiſitors generally conſult and deliberate with theſe ſkilful Perſons together, and not apart, as is provided in certain Letters of the *Spaniſh* Counſel.

When therefore any Queſtion happens in the Cognizance of the Cauſes of Hereſy at the Tribunal of the Faith, relating to the Quality of Propoſitions, ſpoken by Hereticks, or Perſons ſuſpected of Hereſy, the Deciſion of that

Tit. 54. Affair belongs to the Divines, from whence they are called *Qualificators*. *Simancas* diſtinctly deſcribes to us their Office.

§. 2. " The Anſwers of the Divines, containing the Quality of Propoſitions, are " to be inſerted in the Acts of the Judiciary Proceſs, ſubſcribed by them, " equally with the Sayings and Witneſſes of Perſons ſkilful in other Mat- " ters.

§. 6. " A Propoſition is either heretical, *viz.* when it is contrary to Scripture, " or the Church, or the Decrees of a general Council, rightly aſſembled, as to " Matters of Faith, or the Determination of the Apoſtolick See, or the com- " mon Opinion of the Doctors of the Church.

" Or it favours of Hereſy, when it hath an heretical Senſe in the moſt ob- " vious Signification, and firſt View of the Words, although if piouſly under- " ſtood, it may bear a Catholick Senſe. As for Inſtance, this Propoſition: " *'Tis ridiculous to carry the Sacrament of the Euchariſt in a ſolemn Proceſſion thro'* " *the publick Streets.* For this Propoſition manifeſtly favours of the Hereſy of " the *Lutherans*, and Sacramentaries.

§. 9. " Or it is erroneous, when any Thing is aſſerted againſt a Truth not " plainly determined by the Church, or againſt a Catholick Verity, not

---

* Dr. *Geddes* gives us a worſe Account of their Stupidity and Ignorance. The Writer of the *Repertorium*, printed at *Venice*, *An.* 1588. to ſhew his critical Learning, ſaith, the Word *Hæreticus*, according to ſome, is compounded of *Erro* and *Recto*, becauſe an Heretick errs from what is right. According to others, it is derived from *Erciſcor*, which ſignifies to divide ; and, according to ſome, it comes from *Adhæreo*, becauſe it is one's adhering obſtinately to an Error that makes him an Heretick. And with the ſame Stock of Learning it was that another Inquiſitor proved, from St. *Paul's* Words, *Hæreticum devita*, that Chriſtians were commanded to deprive Hereticks of their Lives. *Geddes Tracts, Vol.* I. *p.* 425.

" known.

" known to all, or at leaſt not to him who pronounced the erroneous Propo-
" ſition. But as to this Propoſition the Doctors greatly differ.

" Or it ſounds ill, and offends pious Ears, *viz.* ſuch as gives Scandal and §. 10, 11.
" Occaſion of Ruin to pious Hearers or Readers. When any are offended
" at ſuch Propoſitions, the Aſſertor of them is forced by the Inquiſitors pub-
" lickly to declare their true Senſe, that ſo the Scandal given may ceaſe. But
" if ſuch a Perſon be otherwiſe ſuſpected, he is to be called and interrogated
" by the Judges ; and if he gives a probable Senſe of the Words, he is not
" to be compelled to a publick Explanation, provided no one hath been ſcan-
" dalized. He is however to be admoniſhed not to ſpeak ſuch Things
" again for the future.

" Or it is raſh, *viz.* when atteſted without any grave Authority or juſt §. 12.
" Reaſon, inſolently and boldly, contrary to Eccleſiaſtical Modeſty. As if
" any one ſhould ſay, *The Day of Judgment will be within a Month.* Some-
" times however ſuch Propoſitions are not accounted raſh, when they
" are modeſtly aſſerted, or have ſome Probability, or pious Tendency to
" edify the Hearers or Readers. Of this ſort are many Things, which
" Men, given to Meditation, may probably imagine to have been done.

" Or it is ſcandalous, in which the Scandal may be obſerved, though other-§. 13.
" wiſe not heretical. As if any one ſhould reckon up the Inconveniences of
" holy Confeſſion, or tell the Abuſes of the Church of *Rome* before the com-
" mon People ; or if any one ſhould ſay, *That an evil Prelate is truly a Thief*
" *and a Robber* ; *The Univerſities and Colleges are introduced by human Vanity* ;
" *Pulſe and Fiſh blow up the Belly, and incline Men to Venery.*

" Or it is ſchiſmatical, when tending to introduce Diviſion into the Church. §. 14, &c.
" Or ſeditious, when it becomes the Cauſe or Occaſion of Sedition in the Church.
" Or blaſphemous, when injurious to God and his Saints. Or favouring Here-
" ticks, when it any ways favours the Perſons or Errors of Hereticks. This
" for Inſtance, *Hereticks are not to be puniſhed.* Or it is injurious, when it de-
" tracts from, or is injurious to the State of any one of the Faithful, ſome il-
" luſtrious Perſon or Dignity. Such are thoſe Things which mad and impious
" Men blab out againſt the Cardinals and Monks.

" The ſame Propoſition may alſo have ſeveral Qualities. It may be er-§. 19,
" roneous, and heretical, and ſchiſmatical, and ſeditious, raſh, and injurious,
" and thus have one, two, or more Qualities.

" Although doubtful Queſtions concerning the Faith, are to be determined§. 20.
" by the chief Pontiff or a general Council, yet as a doctrinal Matter, 'tis
" uſual for learned and prudent Men to explain and determine what Propoſi-
" tion hath this or the other Quality. And this properly is the Buſineſs of the
" Divines. However ſometimes the Layers can eaſily determine ſuch Mat-
" ters from the Decrees of the Popes, Councils and holy Fathers.

" And whereas many who can't deny that they uttered ſuch Propoſitions,
" yet will ſo endeavour to interpret them, as to prevent their being criminal, .
" therefore there muſt be careful Obſervation made as to the Nature of ſuch
" Interpretations. If they are juſt and probable, and do wholly, or for the
                                                                    " moſt

" moſt part, clear them of the Crimes objected to them, they are to be ad-
" mitted. But if they are abſurd, incredible, or unlikely, and don't agree
" with what goes before, or comes after, nor with the Nature of juſt ſpeak-
" ing, nor with the Circumſtances of Perſons, Times, and Places, they are
" to be rejected ; eſpecially when under the Pretence of an Interpretation
" the true Senſe of a Propoſition is deſtroyed and corrupted.

Part 1.   " *John Royas* affirms, That the adjudging of Propoſitions partly be-
§.400,&c.. " longs to the Canoniſts, and gives us a ſhort Account of the Office
" of the ſeveral Aſſeſſors, and in what Matters they are to be conſulted.
" If there be a Doubt whether any Aſſertion be expreſly condemned as he-
" retical, the Cogniſance of it belongs to thoſe who are ſkilful in the Canon
" Law ; becauſe Hereſies condemned are to be found in the *Decretals*, the *Sex-*
" *tum*, the *Clementines*, *Extravagants*, and *General Councils*. But if ſuch an Aſ-
" ſertion is not expreſly determined, it belongs to the Interpreters of holy
" Writ. But it belongs to the Divines to determine concerning the indiſtinctly
Inſt. Mad. " and abſolutely received Uſe and Manner of every Propoſition, and from their
a. 1561. " Aſſertions in judging Cauſes of Faith, there muſt be no receding, which al-
cap. 1. " ſo is more fully decreed by the Counſellors of the ſupreme General Council
" of the Inquiſition. But the proper Duty and Office of the Inquiſitors of he-
" retical Pravity, is to obſerve the judiciary Order againſt Hereticks, preſent
" or abſent, in their Apprehenſion, Accuſations, Publications of Witneſſes,
" and in their Sentences, whether definitive or interlocutory, with the Advice
" of ſuch Lawyers as are called Counſellors. Of all theſe Things, the Pro-
" feſſors of the ſacred Writings are wholly ignorant. Under theſe Counſel-
" lors Lay Perſons married, who are ſkilful in the Canon and Civil Law,
" are comprehended." This *Carena* confirms by his own Example, who
p. 1. *t.* 8. ſays of himſelf, *I who am a Judge, a Conſervator of the Rights of the holy Office,*
n. 7. *Counſellor and Advocate Fiſcal, am married.* But he thinks this is not the Manner
in the Kingdom of *Portugal*, becauſe there the Counſellors have a deciſive Vote,
and ſubſcribe to the Sentences.

Pegna,   However, the Inquiſitors are not bound neceſſarily to follow the Advice
Com. 117. of the Counſellors ; but after they have heard their Opinion, they are free to
determine what they think proper, though contrary to, or different from
the others Advice ; becauſe their Votes are not deciſive, but only by way
of Advice. This alſo is plain from hence, becauſe, as *Camillus Campegius*
In Zanch. ſays, " It may happen, that by the Intreaties of others, they may give
cap. 15. " wrong Advice, not to ſay unjuſt. For the Love of Chriſt is grown ſo
" cold, that few are to be found who have God only before their Eyes, in
" the Advices they give. For they who defend the Guilty, do ſo perpetual-
" ly tire even the Doctors themſelves with their Entreaties, that for the moſt
" Part they turn them aſide from Juſtice. Add to this, that the Inquiſitors
" in *Italy* are ſo poor, that they cannot maintain certain and fixed Counſel-
" lors, nor afford them even a ſmall Salary : So that little Care is taken of the
" Affairs of this holy Office."

Far-

Farther, the *Madrid* Inftruction, in the Year 1561. hath determined the fame. Cap. 66. *In all Cafes, in which the Inquifitors and Ordinary, or any of them, differ in Opinion, either in the Determination of a Caufe, or any other Act, or in an Interlocutory Sentence, the Caufe muft be referred to the Council. But if the Inquifitors and Ordinary agree, their Decree muft be executed, though the Counfellors differ, and fhould be more in Number.* There is alfo a Letter of the Counfel in Poffeffion of the Inquifitors of *Corduba* ; by which it is decreed, That if the Inquifitors and Ordinary Judge do agree, their Sentence is to be preferred, although the Advice of all the Counfellors differ from it.   For the Jurifdiction properly belongs to the Inquifitors and Ordinary Judge ; and when they have heard the Opinion of the Learned, and thoroughly confidered the Procefs of the Caufes, and fully weighed all Circumftances, they can much better determine, and with greater Certainty.   But as to the Inquifitors of *Valladolid,* unlefs the Majority of them agree in the fame Sentence, the Caufe muft be referred to the Council, although the aforenamed Judges fhould be unanimous.   In *Portugal* the Counfellors have a decifive Vote, and fubfcribe their Names together with the Inquifitors in the Determination of Caufes, and the Sentences ; and they are chofen under the fame Conditions as the Inquifitors are, excepting only that of being forty Years old, which is required by the common Law.

But although this Power is granted to the Inquifitors, yet 'tis fafer to follow the Advice of the Skilful.   To this End they ought fully to communicate the whole Procefs of Criminals to them.   Per cap. *Statuta.* §. *Jubemus,* lib. 6. *When the Bifhop proceeds before the Inquifitors, or whether the Bifhops or Inquifitors proceed, if there can be conveniently had a Number of Witneffes, let their Names be declared to certain other wife and honeft Perfons, whom we order to be called to this Service, and to whom the whole Procefs under Confideration muft be ferioufly opened, and fully explained, and by whofe Advice they muft proceed to Sentence or Condemnation.   And thus, notwithftanding the Names of the Witneffes be not declared to the Perfons accufed, let all Credit be given to the Depofition of the faid Witneffes, and the Judge proceed upon fuch Information.* 'Tis however a received Cuftom amongft the Inquifitors, never to tell the Names of the Witneffes to the Counfellors.   'Tis however the Duty of the Inquifitor to remark the Qualities of the Witneffes ; as whether they be religious, fkilful, grave, and approved, or whether lefs approved, common Perfons, poor, young, unfkilful, and the like ; that their Qualities being thus known, the Skilful may more eafily underftand what Credit is to be given to what they feverally fay, and what not.   If there be Reafon to fear that the Witneffes are Enemies to the Criminal, the Inquifitors may in fuch a Cafe declare the Names both of the Witneffes and Criminals ; becaufe poffibly the Counfellors may know them both ; and whether they are, or have been Enemies.   But to prevent any rafh Publication of this Matter, they may bind them by Oath, or under the Sentence of Excommunication, to keep it a Secret ; becaufe Secrecy, as they fay, is the principal Nerve of the Caufes of the holy Office.   Cap. eod. *More effectually to prevent any Danger to the Accufers and Witneffes, and for the more*

Simanc.
tit. 41.
§. 14.

Souza,
l. 1. c. 14.
§. 14.

Pegna,
part 3.
com. 128.

caufe

cautious Proceeding in the Affair of the Inquifition, by Authority of this prefent Conftitution, we permit, That the Bifhop or Inquifitors may enjoin Secrecy to thofe, whom they entruft with the Knowledge of fuch Procefs ; and if they think fit, publifh againft them the Sentence of Excommunication, which they, ipfo facto, incur, by difcovering the Secret, if they fhall reveal the Secrets of the Council, or Proceffes, committed to them in Secrecy, by the Bifhop or Inquifitors, to any Perfon, without their Leave. The Counfellors alfo generally fwear that they will keep Secrecy, and not reveal the Affairs treated of in the Congregation, under the Penalty of Excommunication, to be *ipfo facto* incurred, from which they cannot be abfolved, but by the Cardinals, fupreme Inquifitors. They likewife fwear under the fame Penalty, that they will not fpeak of, or debate, either by Word or Writing, or any other Way, of thofe Things which concern the Caufes of the holy Office, unlefs it be with the Counfellors, and other Officials of the faid Office. And although they fhould not exprefly fware ; yet there are many Laws that oblige them to keep it, enjoining them not to difcover the Caufes of Faith, becaufe of the great Danger that may arife from it. And if they fhould make fuch Difcovery, though not fworn to Secrecy, they may be punifhed by the Inquifitors without the ufual Way of Proceeding. But if they have malicioufly done it, and efpecially to thofe who may obftruct the Affair of the Faith, or otherwife hinder the Caufe, they may be punifhed as Obftructors of the holy Office, more or lefs, according to the Nature of the Offence, by which the Meafure of the Punifhment is to be regulated.

Carena, p. 1. t. 8. n. 65.

If Bifhops or Inquifitors difcover the Secrets of the holy Office, they would indeed incur no Cenfure, but be guilty of mortal Sin ; unlefs they alfo fhould have taken an Oath of Secrecy in the Congregation of their Counfellors, according as the Congregation of the Cardinal, fupreme Inquifitors, hath decreed they ought to do. For they alfo take themfelves the like Oath of Secrecy.

In Zanch. cap. 15.

Camillus Campegius contends, " That the whole entire Procefs, with the " Names and Circumftances, is not to be publifhed to the Counfellors ; becaufe " they have their Factions and Paffions, fince they are Fellow Citizens, or " otherwife allied to the Criminals, their Friends and Relations, whereby " the Safety of the Witneffes will not be fufficiently provided for, according " to the Decree of the Canon. Nor doth it fignify, though the Inquifitor or " Bifhop fhould enjoin them to Secrecy under the Sentence of Excommuni- " cation, to be *ipfo facto* incurred upon their difclofing the Secrets : For they " would think this as a very great Injury done them. Befides, this would be " a Snare laid for their Souls ; for they would foon fall under Excommunica- " tion, through the importunate Inftances of inquifitive Perfons. Nor will " this derogate any Thing from the Procefs of the Faith, or the Depofition " of the Witneffes : Yea, rather the imminent Danger apprehended by the " Judges, is a fufficient Reafon for not making a Difcovery to the Counfellors, " any more than to the Criminals. So that 'tis fafer to obferve the ancient " Cuftom, and not to difcover the Witneffes Names to the Counfellors. The " fame *Campegius* fays, undoubtedly, for the better keeping the Secret, that

I   " there

" there is no need of calling in many, and that a few of the better Sort is
" abundantly fufficient."

'Tis enquired by the Canonifts, whether the Inquifitors are obliged to call *p. 1. t. 8.* for the Vote of the Counfellors before Sentence; fo that without it the Sen- *n. 55, 56.* tence fhall be void. *Carena* doth not think them oblig'd to it; and fays, that in the Inquifition at *Cremona*, he hath oftentimes feen Caufes determined by the Bifhops and Inquifitors together, without afking the Votes of the Counfellors; and adds, that they ought not fo to truft to their Counfellors, as to think themfelves excufed from reconfidering the Procefs and Books, and examining the Caufe; becaufe as they are Judges, it is their Duty to examine the Merits of the Procefs. " Hence it is that if the Inquifitors of heretical Royas, " Pravity err in determining the Caufes of the Faith, whether from their own *p. 1. §. 424.* " or their Counfellors Judgment, they are worthy of Punifhment, and the " Votes of their Counfellors will not excufe them, becaufe they ought to " have examined whether their Advice was proper or not. But if the " Queftion is too difficult and hard, either through the Nature of the Fact, " or the various Opinions of the Doctors, the Inquifitors are in fome Mea- " fure excufed through their Ignorance of an obfcure Law. However, *§. 433.* " the Advice of the Counfellors, though wrong, hath this wonderful Effect, " that though the Inquifitors are faulty, yet their Error is not to be imputed " to Corruption. But to avoid all Blame, in all difficult and doubtful Cafes; " fuch as the Seifure of noble and religious Perfons, and the Releafe of Cri- " minals; the Affair, with all the Merits and Votes, is to be laid before " their Superiors, who are to be confulted, before it is put in Execution." *Inftruct. Granat. a.* 1499. *cap.* 13. *Inftruct. Hifpal. a.* 1500. & *Inftruct. Ma-dril. a.* 1561. *c.* 5. *and* 66.

Although thefe Counfellors or Afteffors of the holy Office may lawfully be Carena, chofen by the Inquifitors, and are in Fact deputed by them in feveral Cities, *p. 1. t. 8.* as at *Pavia*, and the other Cities of that Territory; yet at *Cremona* and *Mi- n. 3, 4, 5, lan*, the Counfellors, Advocate Fifcal, and Chancellor, are chofen by the Cardinals, Inquifitors General at the Nomination of the Inquifitors. So that thefe Counfellors depend on that Congregation, and cannot be removed but by it; becaufe the Act is his who confirms it.

The Father and Son muft not be chofen together Counfellors of the holy *n. 31:* Office. However, the Congregation of the fupreme Inquifitors General, for the Merits of *Francis Caucius* a Lawyer, deputed *John Baptift* a Lawyer, his Son, as a Counfellor of the holy Office, or rather as an Afliftant to his Father, who had been a Counfellor of the faid Office above thirty Years; but upon this Condition, That they fhould not be prefent together in the Congregations; be-caufe the Counfellors Votes ought to be altogether free.

The proper Place of thefe Congregations is the Hall of the holy Office. *n. 38.* *Carena* fays, that he heard from fome worthy Perfons, that there are Letters of the Inquifitors General upon this Affair, commanding that fuch Congrega-tions, when held before the Bifhop, fhall meet in the Epifcopal Palace. But when the Bifhop will not, or cannot be prefent, they fhall meet in the holy

Office;

Office ; and that the Vicar General of the Bifhop muft be there. And though he himfelf did not fee thofe Letters, yet he fays this is exactly the Method in the Inquifition at *Cremona*.

n. 44, 45. In voting they obferve this Order in the Congregation at *Rome*. The junior Counfellors vote firft, that they may not be afraid to differ from the Opinion of the Elder. In the Congregation at *Cremona* 'tis quite contrary, where the more Worthy vote firft.

n. 48. The Method of voting is this : When the Merits of the Procefs are propofed, the Counfellor firft examines, whether the Intention of the Fifcal is fully proved, and how. Then he confiders, whether the Intention of the Fifcal is drawn from the Proofs and Exceptions of the Matter ; and after having confidered thefe Things, he gives his Vote.

C H A P. V.

Of the PROMOTOR FISCAL.

Simanc. *tit.* 53. § 1, 2. " THEY ufually call that Official of the Inquifition the Promotor Fifcal, " who acts the Part of the Accufer. He muft be an honeft, dili-" gent and induftrious Perfon, fkilful in the Law. He is prohibited from " exercifing this Fifcal Office in the Province where he was born, that he " may not be thought to act out of Favour or Hatred.

§. 3, &c. " It belongs to this Office to examine the Depofitions of the Witneffes, to " give Information of Criminals to the Inquifitors, or Notice of them to the " Judges, and to demand their Apprehenfion and Imprifonment ; and finally, Carena, *p.* t. t. 9. *n.* 15. " when apprehended and admonifhed to accufe them." In the holy Office in *Spain*, the Fifcals do not form their Accufation againft the Criminal, till the Way is clear for the Inquifitors to proceed againft him. " And although " the Criminals, upon Admonition, fhould confefs all their Herefies, yet the " Promotor Fifcal muft accufe them of the fame Things, that Judgment " may be formed from the Accufer, Criminal and Judge. The Charge is, " to be drawn up and prefented to the Judges by the Promotor, to which he " is to add an Oath, that none of the Heads of it proceed from a malicious " Defign ; but only that he may the better profecute his Suit, and that he " intends to prove them all.

§. 7. " If the Judges fhall allow any Time to receieve the Proofs, he muft " produce the Witneffes againft the Criminal, and demand their Examina-" tion ; and that their Depofitions be allowed and publifhed. If after this " other Witneffes fhall appear to prove other Herefies, this alfo fhall be ad-" ded to the Accufation, and the Promotor Fifcal fhall accufe the Criminal " of thefe. He muft alfo take particular Care to obferve all the Confeffions, " Sayings and Anfwers, of the Criminals, that he may be able to gather what
" relates

" relates particularly to their Cafe, and what to other Hereticks. And when §. 10.
" the Depofitions of the Witneffes are written down and allow'd ; and when the
" Judges and Counfellors debate about the Sentence to be paffed, the Promotor
" Fifcal muft be abfent. But he may be prefent when the Procefs of the Caufe
" is reported, and from Fact or Law alledge what he thinks convenient." In
the *Cremona* Inquifition the Fifcal is not prefent at the Examination of the Carena,
Witneffes, unlefs the Inquifitor calls for him. He is however prefent at the p. 1. t. 9.
Examination of the Witneffes, by Way of Defence, and at the rehearing of ". 41.
the Witneffes, and muft be prefent in the Congregations when they vote in
the Caufe, and always at the Torture, together with the Inquifitor, who fits
between the Vicar General on the Right, and the Advocate Fifcal on the Left.

" Heretofore the Promotor Fifcal was bound to defend the Caufes of the §. 11.
Treafury before the Judge of the forfeited Effects, which is to this Day in
Ufe in fome Provinces. But generally fpeaking, this Affair belongs now to
the Advocate of the Treafury.

" Befides this, in *Spain* they chufe a Perfon for Procurator General of the tit. 52.
" holy Inquifition there, that he may manage the Affair of this moft holy §. 6. 2 In-
" Office at the Court of *Rome*, who is to have a proper Salary paid him out of ftruct. Hif-
" the forfeited Effects. Into this Office a fkilful and honeft Man muft be pal. cap. 2,
" chofen.

C H A P. VI.

Of the NOTARIES *of the* INQUISITION.

THE Office of the Regifters, whom they alfo call Notaries and Secreta- Simanc.
ries, is to write down the Injunctions, Accufations, and all the Plead- tit. 41.
ings of the Caufes. The Judge ought not only to take Care that the Notary § 7.
writes down the Depofitions of the Witneffes, or the Anfwers of the Crimi- Campeg.
nals, but alfo that he diligently explains, and particularly remarks, during *in* Zanch.
the Procefs, the feveral Circumftances relating to the Witnefs, the Infor- c. 9.
mer, and the Perfon againft whom Inquifition is made, *viz.* Whether the Colour of his Face changes ; whether he trembles or hefitates in fpeaking ; whether he frequently endeavours to interrupt the Interrogatories, by hauking or
fpitting ; or whether his Voice trembles, and the like. All thefe Circumftances the Judge ought to take Care to have particularly fpecified in the
Procefs, that it may not be faid, that the Perfon inquired againft is put to
the Torture without Proofs.

Whatfoever the Notary writes down from the Mouth of the Criminals, or Pegnæ-
Witneffes, muft be in the fame Language in which the Witnefs or Criminal prax. *Inq.*
fpeaks, without altering, adding, diminifhing, tranfpofing or inverting any l 2. c 20.
of the Words. If the Criminal or Witnefs doth not underftand *Latin* ; and n. 12, &c.

if the Notary or Inquifitor doth not underftand the Language of the one or
other, the Inquifitor muft have a fkilful Interpreter. For it may happen that a *Frenchman*, a *Spaniard*, an *Englifhman*, or a *German* may be exa-
min'd before an *Italian* Inquifitor. The Depofitions of the Witneffes and the
Confeffions of the Criminals, are to be written down by the Notaries, in the
fame Words in which they are deliver'd. And when there are feveral Witneffes, 'tis not fufficient that the Notary, when he hath particularly wrote
down the Depofitions of the firft Witnefs, fays, that the fecond or third fays
entirely the fame as the firft ; but he muft write down the particular Words of
the feveral Witneffes, becaufe oftentimes the Cafe before this Tribunal is the
Proof of formal Herefy. *Clement* VIII. in a general Congregation of the Inquifition, *November* 9, 1600. hath particularly commanded the Inquifition
not to omit any of the Interrogatories which are made by the Judge, in the
Examination of the Witneffes and Criminals, but to write them down at large.
[Yea, fo favourable are they to this Affair of the Faith, that though the Notaries fhould make one falfe Libel, yet all their others are valid, whilft they
are kept in Office ; although when the Author is condemned, the Book is commonly condemned too. *Ibid.*]

Ex Glof.
in cap.
Fraterni-
tatis.

   " Thefe Notaries are to be chofen of the Laity ; but in Caufes of Herefy, the
" Clergy and Monks, and alfo others in holy Orders may difcharge this Office.
" And although in *Spain* they ufually take them from amongft the Laity, yet

fit. 41.
§. 7.

" *Simancas* fays, that poffibly it would be better, that they fhould be chofen
" from the Clergy, becaufe they would want lefs than thofe who have Wives and
" Children ; for the Salary is fcarce fufficient for one. They are alfo obliged
" to regifter in a certain Book, all the Commands of the Inquifitors, given
" to the Executors and Receivers, againft Hereticks, and their Effects ;
" that if any Queftion fhould arife concerning thefe Things, they may be
" able, from thofe Regifters, to determine it. Befides, they muft be con-
" tent with their Salary, and receive nothing for their writing, except the
" Notary of the forfeited Effects, who may demand his lawful Dues, becaufe
" he hath no Salary. They muft alfo travel at their own Expences within
" their proper Province, to ratify the Depofitions of the Witneffes, the Proof
" of the Defences, and the Exceptions againft the Witneffes, as it is contain'd
" in a certain Decree of the Council." *C. ut Officium. §. ad confcribendum.* de
hæret. *lib.* 6. 2 *Inftruct. Hifpal. c.* 13. and 4 *Inftruct. Tolet. c.* 18.

Pegna, *in*
direct. par.
3. *com.* 20.

   Heretofore the *Roman* Pontiffs made feveral Provifions to fupport Perfons
to regifter the Acts of the Inquifition, becaufe the Inquifitors were poor, and
could not maintain a certain Notary, who fhould be appropriated to this Bufinefs ; fometimes difpenfing with the Clergy and Religious, who were Notaries
before, that they might exercife the Office of Notaries in the Caufe of the
Faith ; fometimes allowing that two proper Perfons fhould regifter the
Tranfactions, to whom full Credit fhould be given. This was decreed by the
Council of *Biterre.* Cap. IV. *Take Oaths from thofe, who being thus cited before you,
fhall appear within the Time of Grace affigned, that they fhall fpeak as far as they
know, the whole Truth, and nothing but the Truth, concerning the Fact of heretical*

2

Pravity,

Pravity, either relating to themselves, or others, the living or dead: and after having interrogated them carefully concerning all and singular the Matters worthy of Enquiry, either by yourselves, or by the Writers, see that their Confessions and Depositions be faithfully written down, and placed in the Acts of the Inquisition; either by some pub-lick Person, if you can get one, or by any other that is proper and sworn, to whom let another fit and sworn Person be added, that thus such Writings, whither by a publick Hand, or by two fit Persons, as we have mentioned, being thus reposited and written in the Acts, and recited to him who confesses and deposes before the Inquisitor and No-tary, or the said two proper Persons, may obtain full Confirmation and Validity. At that Time the Inquisitors themselves could not make Notaries, but were obli- Eymer, ged to take the publick Notaries of the Bishops, or of the temporal Lords of *p. 3. qu.* those Places, in which the Office of the Inquisition was committed to them, [18.] who were to make the Processes, and to execute other Things pertaining to the Affair of the Faith. Or they might desire the Pope to create for them two or three Persons for Notaries of their own Nomination. As to those who had been Notaries, the Inquisitor could compel them to execute that Office, although they were become Religious, by a Bull of *Urban* IV. beginning, *Licet ex omnibus. §. ad conscribendas.* But now by a Rescript of *Pius* IV. be- Pegna, ginning, *Pastoralis officii cura,* given *An.* 1561. Cal. 6th *September,* it is provi- *Com.* 67. ded, that the Inquisitors and their Commissaries, in all Causes of Faith, may, when they think it necessary, by the Apostolick Authority, chuse, assume, and create Notaries, one or more, either all Clergymen, or Regulars of any Order. However a Religious or Clergyman is not immediately created a Notary, when he is commanded by the Inquisitor to write the Acts of the sa-cred Office; but that all Things may be valid, he must create this Religious a Notary before some other Notary, before proper Witnesses, Pen and Ink being regularly delivered to him, and a solemn Oath administred to him, with the customary Words, *Be thou a Notary and Faithful:* And of all these Things *Com.* 68. the Notary, who is present at this Creation, must draw up a publick Instru-ment. And although when they are first created Notaries, they take an Oath *ad Zanchi* to do all Things faithfully, yet nevertheless as often as the Inquisitors send for *c. 9.* any Notaries afresh, to write down the Acts of the holy Office, they must take a new Oath of them faithfully to execute their Office, and to preserve the Secrets, which is peculiar in this Cause of Faith. So that if a Notary, or any other Minister of the Inquisition discovers the Secret committed to him, he may not only be punished, but condemned as guilty of Perjury, and fall into some Suspicion of favouring Heresy. [When the Notaries are thus created, the Prelates of the Orders can't remove or change them, since they are created by the delegated Authority of the Apostolick See; nor can the Delegates of the Apostolick See excommunicate them, by the Bull of *Ur-ban* IV. beginning, *Ne Inquisitionis.*]

" In *Spain,* even now, the Inquisitors may, if there be Occasion, create Simanc. " another Notary, and pay him a just Salary, as is provided for by one of *§. 8.* " the Letters of the Council. If he be sworn to Secrecy, he is obliged " to give Security to the Promotor Fiscal, and to the other Parties concerned, " and

" and to deliver in a written Account, of the Time of Condemnation, and
" Commiffion of the Crime. For they will not fuffer the whole Procefs to be
" fhewn, leaft Suits fhould arife from Suits, and the Secrets of the whole Caufe
" fhould be difcovered. For the Confequence of this would be, that the
" Names of the Witneffes would be known by all, whereby their Safety would
" be endangered, and many Exceptions would be urged againft them by Slan-
" derers. Provifion was made againft thefe Inconveniences, by a certain Let-
" ter of the Inquifitor General. Farther, all thefe Notaries muft attend the
" Tribunal of the Inquifitors fix Hours every Day. If any one offends in
" his Office, he is to be punifhed according to the Nature of his Crime by a
" Fine, Sufpenfion of Office, Deprivation, or Banifhment, to be moderated
" at the Pleafure of the Inquifitor General and Council. *Epift. dat. Granat.*
" *Sept.* 4, 1499. and 4 *Inftruct. Tolet. cap.* 28, and 13.

§. 9.

" The Writings of the holy Inquifition are to be kept under three Keys,
" which are to be in the Hands of the Promotor Fifcal, and Notaries, nor
" muft they be read or fhewn to any one, but in the Prefence of all. Befides
" thefe written Acts are to be carefully kept in the publick Hall of the Inqui-
" fitors, that they may be prefent, as often as there is need, nor may the
" Notaries fhew them to any one, nor remove them into another Place ; and
" if they are convicted of doing the contrary, they are to be removed from
" their Office, without Hope of Pardon. However, the Inquifitors, when
" required by the Royal Judges, or by thofe who have any Intereft and Con-
" cern in the Affair, muft command the Notaries to give a Copy of the Pa-
" pers, but fo as that the Secrets of the Office, which muft be kept concealed,
" may not thereby be difcovered, according to the Caution given by a Letter
" of the Council. But a Copy of the Acts, which are ufually read in pub-
" lick, may be given, *viz.* of the Confeffions, Sentences, and other Things
" of the like Kind, but of nothing more. 3 *Inftruct. Valdolit.* c. 7. & 4 *Inftruct.*
" *Tolet.* c. 13.

Brunus,
l. 4. c. 3.
§. 11.
Carena,
p. 1. t.12.
n. 7.
v. 9.

" Thefe Notaries have their Subftitutes, who ferve them as Coadjutors in
" writing, or taking Notes.

" As to the Salaries of the Notary, if they are certain, the Inquifitors of
" the holy Office ufually determine how much they are ; if uncertain, they
" can't exceed the Tax of the fupreme Inquifitors.

" In the Inquifition of *Cremona* there is one Notary, chofen by the fupreme
" Inquifitors at the Nomination of the Inquifitor, who hath a certain Salary
" of fixty Pieces of Gold ; which is afterwards ufually increafed by Order of
" the faid Inquifitors to thofe that have deferved well ; and one other regular
" Notary chofen by the Inquifitor himfelf. In the Diocefe the Inquifitor ufu-
" ally deputes one Notary, to be prefent with the other publick Vicars.

CHAP.

C H A P. VII.

Of the JUDGE *and* RECEIVER *of the confifcated Effects.*

" HE who is chofen Judge of the confifcated Effects, muft be an honeft Simanc.
"   Man, and skilful in the Law, not of *Jewifh* Extract, nor of the *tit.* 41.
" *Mahometan,* nor of an heretical one, but one who may be capable of dif-§. 4.
" charging the Office of Affeffor. His Office is, to judge between the Trea-
" fury and private Perfons, in Caufes relating to the Effects of Hereticks.
" But he may alfo take Cognizance between private Perfons, when their Caufe
" hath any Connection with the other. An Appeal lies from his Sentence to
" the Senate, but not to any other Judges. But if the Difpute is between the
" Treafury and the Church Defendant, or between Ecclefiaftical Perfons, or
" concerning the Revenues of Benefices, the Inquifitors are to take Cogni-
" zance of it, as is more fully contained in one of the Refolutions of the Se-
" nate. The Inquifitor General, by Advice of the Senate, chufes this Judge
" and all the other Minifters.

" He is generally called in *Spain* the Receiver, whom in *Italy* they call the Simanc.
" Treafurer of the holy Office. He receives the confifcated Effects, and by *tit.* 43.
" Command of the King is Procurator of the Treafury, demands, defends, §. 1, &c.
" and fells the confifcated Goods, and pays the Salaries and other Expences of
" the holy Office. He who is chofen to the Office, muft be an honeft and
" wealthy Perfon, capable of making up and reporting his Accounts, and
" muft give proper Sureties to pay all his Deficiencies. He is to be chofen
" by the Inquifitors, according to *Carena, p.* 1. *t.* 13. *n.* 1.

" It belongs to the Office of the Receiver to be prefent at the Sequeftration
" of Goods, which can't be done but by the previous Command of the Inqui-
" fitors. It muft be performed by the Executor, in Prefence of the Receiver,
" and Notary of the Sequeftrations, and fome other Notary ; and all the
" Goods of the Criminals, which are found in their Poffeffion, or are in the
" Hands of others, are to be written down feverally in a Catalogue or Invento-
" ry, two Copies of which are to be made out, each Notary to have one.
" 2 *Inftruct. Hifpal. cap.* 8. All the Effects are to be deliver'd to the Sequeftra-
" tor, with an Inventory fubfcribed by the Executor, and the faid Sequeftra-
" tor and the Notaries, one Copy of which is to be kept by the Notary of the
" Sequeftrations. The Sequeftrator is to be chofen by the Executor and Re-
" ceiver, who muft be a fufficient Citizen, not of kin to the Heretick, nor
" of an evil Race. But when the Procefs is formed againft any Perfon dead,
" his Effects muft not be delivered to the Sequeftrator, but taken an Account
" of, and fealed up, and left with the Poffeffors under good Securities. If any
" other Perfons Effects are with thofe of the Hereticks, they muft be imme-
" diately delivered to the Owners. Debts alfo muft be paid out of the Effects
" delivered in to the Sequeftrator, without waiting for the Iffue of the whole
                                                                    " Caufe-

" Caufe. Finally, if the Criminal be abfolved, all his Effects muft be imme-
" diately delivered to him. 4 *Inftruct. Tolet. cap.* 22. As to perifhable Effects,
" and which may grow worfe by keeping, and fuch alfo as are too chargeable
" to keep, *viz.* Cattle and Slaves, the Receiver muft fell them by Command
" of the Inquifitors, without whofe Permiffion nothing can be done.

" When the neceffary Expences are deducted, the Surplus Money which
" remains out of the Sale of the Effects, is to be depofited with the Seque-
" ftrator, of which the Receiver muft touch nothing till the Criminal is con-
" demned. As to other Things which may be kept, they are to be hired
" out at reafonable Prices by the Receiver and Sequeftrator. But thefe and
" other the confifcated Effects, muft not be fold but by Auction, and then
" go to the beft Bidder. The fame is to be obferved as to the Effects which
" are hired out. 2 *Inftruct. Hifpal. cap.* 9. In thefe Sales the Receiver muft
" ufe great Fidelity and Diligence, and though he promifes after the Rate of
" two or three *per Cent.* for the Recovery of any Effects, yet when they are
" recovered, he muft allow only one.

" When the Heretick is condemned, the Sequeftrator muft immediately
" deliver all the Effects to the Receiver before two Notaries, nor can he re-
" ceive or fell any Thing but in their Prefence. But the Judge of the con-
" fifcated Effects may at the Inftances of the Receiver give Notice by the
" Criers of the future Auction. If any one thinks himfelf to be concerned in
" it, he may, when he knows the Effects are to be fold, come to the Judge
" and demand his own, and fue for his Right. If no one comes, the immo-
" vable Effects are to be fold, and to be put up to Sale by Auction the thir-
" tieth Day, after the publick Notices, and other cuftomary Things of the
" City, before the Receiver and other Parties concern'd." 4 *Inftruct. Tolet.*
Cap. 24.

" As to thofe Effects which are difputed, they muft not be fold by the
" Receiver, till the Suit is finifhed. As to Effects that are pawned, the Re-
" ceivers may fell them, not fo as to prejudice the Right of the Creditors ;
" but if the Effects amount to more than the Debt, they muft be fold, and
" the former Creditors firft paid, and the Remainder carried into the Trea-
" fury. 4 *Inftruct. Tolet. Cap.* 23. However, the Sale of the forfeited Effects
" is not to be deferred upon Account of Actions, that do not appear to have
" any juft Foundation, but fuch Effects are to be fold, and fuch a Sum muft be
" depofited in the Sequeftrator's Hands, that is equal to the Value of the
" Debt fued for, and the Charges of the Suit. Farther, if there be any Ef-
" fects which are to be in common between the Treafury and others,
" they muft be divided, if it can be done conveniently : If it cannot, and it
" appears better to fell them entire and without Divifion, the Treafury
" hath the Privilege to order all of them to be fold by the Receiver, al-
" though the leaft Part belongs to it, but muft receive no more than
" its proper Debt, and pay the Remainder to the other Creditors." 4 *Inft.*
Tolet. Cap. 23.

" The

" The Receivers muſt omit none of theſe Things ; if they do they incur
" the Sentence of Excommunication, and are to be fined 100 Pieces of Gold,
" and make good all Loſſes to the Treaſury. *eod. cap. 23.*

" The Receivers of one Province muſt not ſeize on the Effects of Here-
" ticks which belong to other Receivers, but give them more certain No-
" tice of ſuch Effects; otherwiſe they are deprived of their Office, and pay
" the Loſs, and double more. 2 *Inſtruct. cap.* 2.

" All the Monies received by the Sequeſtrator, and the Money that ariſes
" from the Sale of the Effects, the Receivers muſt depoſit within three Days
" after into the publick Cheſt, which muſt be locked up with three Keys,
" which the holy Senate hath ordered under Excommunication, and a Fine.

" The Receivers of the Treaſury can't forgive any Monies to Debtors,
" and if any are forgiven by them they are reclaimed ; nor can they make any
" Bargain or Compoſition with them. 4 *Inſtruct. c.* 23.

CHAP. VIII.

Of the EXECUTOR *and* OFFICIALS *of the* INQUISITION.

" THE Executor is he who executes the Commands of the Inquiſitors. Simanc.
" His Office is principally to apprehend and keep in Cuſtody Crimi-*tit.* 41.
" nals, whom he is obliged to purſue, if they are at a Diſtance, and to put§. 5.
" in Irons, and to be content with his appointed Salary. But if it be needful for
" the Familiars to attend him, they muſt have a Salary appointed by the
" Inquiſitors, to be paid by the Receiver out of the Treaſury. And as he is
" a mere Executor of a Command, he muſt carefully keep within his Bounds,
" and punctually execute the Order of the Judges. Theſe they alſo call Ap-
" paritors and Purſevants. 4 *Inſtruct. Tolet. cap.* 26."

Their Office is the ſame with theirs who are otherwiſe called Officials, Bzovius;
concerning whom *Innocent* IV. hath ordained theſe Things, by a Conſtitu-*a.* 1252.
tion, beginning, *Ad extirpanda,* as they are all placed in Order, in a Book§. 3.
entitled, *The Manner of proceeding againſt Hereticks,* aſcribed to *John Cal-*
derine.

Let the Governor or Ruler be obliged, within three Days after his Entrance into his
Government, to appoint twelve honeſt and Catholick Men, and two Notaries, and
two Servitors, or as many as ſhall be neceſſary, whom the Dioceſan, if preſent, and
willing to be concerned, and two Friars Predicants, and two Minorites deputed to
this Service by their Priors, if there ſhould be there Convents of the ſaid Order, ſhall
think proper to be choſen. Such Perſons, when appointed and choſen, may and ought
to take up heretical Men and Women, to ſeize on their Effects, and to cauſe them to
be ſeized on by others, and to cauſe that theſe Things be fully done, as well in the City,

as

as in his whole Jurisdiction and District, and to bring them, and cause them to be brought into the Power of the Diocesan, or his Vicars.

Let their Office continue only during *six Months, after which let the Governor be obliged to substitute so many other Officials according to the prescribed Form, who may execute the foresaid Office according to the said Form for the six Months next following.*

But let them not be compelled to any other Office or Employment, *that doth or may in any manner hinder the said Office, nor let any Statute made, or to be made, hinder by any Means their Office.*

Let full Credit be given to these aforesaid Officials concerning *all Things which are known to belong to their Office, without requiring from them any special Oath, or admitting any Proof to the contrary, when two or more of them shall be present. Farther, when these Officials are chosen, let them swear to execute all these Things faithfully, and according to their Power, and to speak nothing but the Truth concerning all these Things, so that they may be more fully obey'd in all Things appertaining to their Office, and let the said twelve and their Servitors, and the before appointed Notaries, together, or separately, have full Power of commanding, upon Pain of Punishment and the Ban, all Things appertaining to their Office, and let the Governor or Ruler be obliged to confirm and ratify all their Commands which they shall give relating to their Office, and punish those who don't observe them.*

Farther, let the Governor be obliged to send with their Officials, *one of his Soldiers, or some other Assistant, if the Diocesan, or his Vicar, or the Inquisitors deputed by the Apostolick See, or the said Officials shall demand it; and let such Soldier faithfully execute their Office with them. Let every one also, if he be present, or required, whither in the City Jurisdiction or District, be obliged to grant to these Officials, or their Companions, Counsel and Assistance, when they will apprehend, seize the Effects of, or make Inquiry concerning any heretical Man or Woman, or enter into any House or Place, or Passage, to take Hereticks, under the Punishment of 25 Imperial Pounds, or the Ban. Let every corporate Town be obliged to it under the Penalty of an 100 Pounds and Ban, and a Village under the Penalty of fifty, to be paid every time in ready Money.*

Alexander IV. *An.* 1255. wrote to the Inquisitors of Liguria *, and *Insubria* †, *That the aforesaid Officials may command any City, Borough or Village, under the Penalty and Ban of 1200 Marks of Silver and more, at the Pleasure of the Governor of such Place, that they shall present, within a competent Time fixed, to the Governor, or Diocesan, or his Vicar, or the Inquisitors of Hereticks, all heretical Men and Women, which the said Officials shall signify to them. And the Governor of such Place shall be obliged to exact this Punishment from all who do not observe this Order.*

Innocent IV. adds in the same Bull, *That if any Loss shall at any Time happen to the said Officials in their Persons and Effects, in executing their Office, they shall be indemnified with full Restitution by such City or Place, and that the said Officials, or*

---

* Containing the Towns of *Genova, Nizza, Vintimilia, Albenga, Polenza, Alba, Aste, Aich, Tortona,* and *Voghera.*

† Containing *Milan, Lodi, Crema* and *Monza.*

their

their Heirs, fhall not at any time be fued for any Thing they have done, or belonging to their Office, any farther than as the faid Diocefan and Friars think fit.

And if the aforefaid Diocefan or Friars fhall think fit to remove any one of the faid Officials for being unskilful or improper, or for any Engagement, or Excefs, the Governor or chief Officer fhall be obliged to remove him at their Command and Appointment, and to fubftitute another in his Place, according to the prefcribed Form.

But if any one of them fhall, contrary to his Oath, or Duty of his Office, be found to have favoured Herefy ; befides the Mark of perpetual Infamy which he fhall incur as a Favourer of Hereticks, let him be punifhed by the Governor or chief Officer, at the Pleafure of the Diocefan of the Place and the faid Friars.

CHAP. IX.

Of the FAMILIARS, *or* ATTENDANTS.

I*Nnocent* III. granted large Indulgences and Privileges to thofe, who fhould accompany or affift the Inquifitor in his making Inquifition againft and punifhing Hereticks, that this newly appointed Office might have the more happy Succefs. Hence the Soldiers, who were Affiftants and Helpers to the Inquifitor, were commonly called Familiars *, as belonging to the Inquifitor's Family. In fome Provinces of *Italy* they are called Crofs-bearers, and in others the Scholars of St. *Peter* the Martyr, and they ware a Crofs before them upon the outfide Garment.

† Anciently certain Perfons were appointed, whofe Office it was to ufe all Diligence in fearching out Hereticks, and to this Purpofe they applied the Decree of the Council of *Biterre, cap.* 34. *In all Parifhes, as well within Cities as without them, let one Prieft, or two or three of the Laity of good Reputation, or more if need be, be bound by Oath to remove and change, as often as it fhall feem good to* Pegnā, prox. Inq. c. 5. §. 3.

---

* The Familiars are the Bailiffs of the Inquifition, which, tho' a vile Office in all other Criminal Courts, is efteemed fo honourable in this of the Inquifition, that there is not a Nobleman in the Kingdom of *Portugal* that is not in it, and fuch are commonly employed by the Inquifitors to apprehend People. Neither is it any wonder that Perfons of the higheft Quality defire to be thus employed, fince the fame plenary Indulgence is granted by the Pope to every fingle Exercife of this Office, as was granted by the *Lateran* Council to thofe who fuccoured the Holy Land. Dr. *Geddes Tracts, Vol.* I. p. 425, 426.

† When the Familiar is fent for to apprehend any Perfon, he hath the following Order put in to his Hand. *By the Command of the Reverend Father N. an Inquifitor of heretical Pravity, let N. be apprehended and committed to the Prifons of this holy Office, and not be releafed out of them, but by the exprefs Order of the faid Reverend Inquifitor.* And if feveral Perfons are to be taken up at the fame time, the Familiars are commanded fo to order Things, that they may know nothing of one another's being apprehended. And at this the Familiars are fo expert, that a Father and his three Sons, and three Daughters, who lived together in the fame Houfe, were all carried Prifoners to the Inquifition, without knowing any Thing of one another's being there until feven Years afterwards, when they that were alive came forth in *an Act of Faith. Geddes, Vol.* I. *p.* 429.

you, (the Inquisitors) *who diligently, faithfully and frequently may search out Hereticks in Villages, and find them when out of their Houses, their subterraneous Shelters, Huts and Fastnesses, and all other their hiding Places, all which let them cause to be stopped up or destroyed.* " The Familiars or Cross-bearers are now in their " Room ; and they are then especially in Service, when the Bishops or In-" quisitors have Dioceses bordering upon and near to the Lands of Hereticks, " or Persons suspected of Heresy, so that a mutual Commerce can scarce be " avoided amongst them. For as then they may more reasonably be afraid, " lest those who are subject to them, and belong to their Jurisdiction, should " be infected and corrupted by Hereticks, they ought to use the strictest Di-" ligence to know with whom Hereticks lodge, and into whose Houses they " are received ; and whither any subject to them go to the neighbouring " Towns of Hereticks, and for what Cause, and whither they have brought " from thence the Poison of heretical Pravity by Doctrines they have heard " or read." So careful are they upon every Occasion, that there shall not be the least Dispute about any of the Doctrines of their Church.

§. 4, 5.

But now the Familiars always accompany the Inquisitors in *Spain,* even though they are free from the Danger which *Pegna* was so very solicitous about. *Simancas* describes to us their Offices and Immunities.

Tit. 41.
§. 15.

" The Familiars or Attendants are necessary to accompany the Inquisitors, " and to defend them, if Need be, from the Insults of Hereticks ; and to fol-" low the Executor when going to apprehend Criminals ; and to do other " Things which the Judges shall think proper to fulfil the Duty of the holy " Office of the Inquisition. The Familiars are allowed to use Arms, but " must not abuse them. Such as are to be chosen, must be good, peaceable, " and married Men, as it is provided by a certain Letter of the Council ; and " no more must be admitted but what the Necessity of the Office requires. " *Clement.* 2. §. *ult. de hæret.*

§. 16.

" And because the Familiars have no Salaries, and no one is bound to serve " for nothing, 'tis necessary that certain Privileges should be granted them, in " which Matter there have been several Alterations by the Royal Commands, " they having sometimes had Immunities allowed them, and at other Times " been deprived of them, because of their Excesses, and unruly Multitude. " At length, by the King's Command, certain of the Royal Council and the " Senate of the holy Inquisition met together, and published a Constitution, " by which certain Immunities are granted to the Familiars, their Number " fixed, and the Manner prescribed, in which the Differences and Contentions " that may arise between the Inquisitors and royal Judges, upon account of " the Familiars, are to be suppressed and determined. 4 *Instruct. Toled. c.* 5. " *Constitut. Royal,* published *March* 19, 1553.

§. 17.

" And first as to the Number of Inquisitors, 'tis appointed, that in the City " of *Toledo* there shall be 50 Familiars chosen by the Inquisitors, as many at " *Seville,* and 50 in *Granada,* and no more ; 40 in *Corduba, Cuenca,* and *Val-* " *ladolid* ; at *Calahorre* and *Ilerena* 25 ; in the City of *Murcia* 30 ; in every " Town where there were 3000 Burgesses, six, in all others of 500 Burgesses,

" four ;

" four ; in other leſſer Towns two only in each. But in every Sea-port or
" Frontier Town four may be choſen. If more are choſen they have no
" Privilege.

" By the ſame Conſtitution 'tis provided, that in every Province there §. 18.
" ſhould be given in to the Conſiſtories of the ſeveral Cities a Liſt of the Fa-
" miliars, that the Governors and Magiſtrates may know them, and ſee that
" they don't exceed the Number ; and that if they are quarrelſome, or unworthy
" their Office, they may report it to the Inquiſitor General and Council ;
" which is alſo to be done when any one is put into the Room of another Fa-
" miliar. 'Tis farther appointed, that in all Civil Cauſes the Familiars ſhall be
" cited before the ſecular Judges as much as if they were not Familiars.

" But in Criminal Cauſes the Familiars are exempted from the Juriſdiction §. 19.
" of the ſecular Judges, and are to be puniſhed by the Inquiſitors, except in
" the Caſe of Treaſon, and the Crime againſt Nature, Rebellion and open
" Sedition. Likewiſe the Familiars are to be puniſhed by lay Judges, if they
" offend againſt Letters of Safety granted by the Prince, if they obſtinately
" oppoſe the Royal Commands, if they betray and raviſh Women, if they
" are publick Thieves, Breakers open of Churches, Monaſteries, or other
" Houſes, or if they ſet them on fire, or commit any other greater and more
" heinous Crimes than theſe, or if they inſolently and obſtinately contemn the
" royal Judges, or if they reſiſt them, or if being themſelves in ſecular Offices
" they commit any Offence therein.

" Farther, the ſecular Judges may take up the Familiars for thoſe Crimes, §. 20.
" the Cogniſance of which belongs to the Inquiſitors, but muſt immediately
" ſend them to their proper Judges, with a ſummary Proof of their Offences,
" at the Coſt of the criminal Familiar. 'Tis likewiſe provided by the ſame
" Conſtitution, that as often as the Familiars offend in any City or Place
" where no Inquiſitors reſide, they ſhall be ſo often obliged to ſhew to the
" Judges of the Place, where the Familiar hath committed his Offence, a
" Copy of the Sentence pronounced by the Inquiſitors againſt him, with a
" publick Teſtimony that he hath ſatisfied the Sentence pronounced againſt him
" for his Crime.

" But if any Difference ariſes between the Inquiſitors and ſecular Judges §. 21.
" concerning the Cognizance of any Offence committed by a Familiar, the
" Cauſe muſt be referred to the Royal Court, with a ſummary Proof of the
" Crime, that upon hearing the Caſe by two royal Counſellors, and two others
" of the Senate of the holy Inquiſition, the Cauſe may be remitted to thoſe
" Judges to whom the Cognizance of it ſhall appear to belong, ſimply, with-
" out Noiſe and Form of Judgment. And from this Sentence there muſt be
" no Appeal. Farther, if theſe ſupreme Judges ſhall diſagree to whom to ſend
" the Priſoner, and three of them ſhould not be of the ſame Opinion, the
" King muſt be conſulted. In the mean while the Familiar muſt be kept in
" Cuſtody by that Judge who took him up ; but his Trial muſt be deferred
" till he is ſent to his proper Judge, to whom, upon a Declaration made, he
" muſt be immediately reſtored, though he ſhould happen to have been
                                                                    " put

" put in Chains by another Judge. Thus far the royal Conftitution, dated
" the 10th, and confirmed the 19th of *March*, 1553.

We read of a famous Cafe of this Nature, concerning Jurifdiction between the
Inquifitors and fecular Judge in *Nicholas Rodrigues Fermofino*, which is added to
his Treatifes of Judgments, *&c.* This *Fermofino* was in the Office of Counfellor of the Treafury, in the Inquifition of *Valladolid*, and created Inquifitor,
and by King *Philip* IV. made Judge of the confifcated Effects of the faid Inquifition. The Cafe was this: The Magiftrates of *Valladolid* order'd rough
Walls to be built, to prevent Travellers coming into the City for Fear of
the Plague. *Antonius Moreno*, Governor of the Houfe of Penance, in that
City, and his Aunt *Mariana de Pareda*, formerly Wife of a certain Secretary of the Inquifition at *Ilerena*, obftructed this Building. And therefore
Jerom Antony de Torefillas, Mayor of the City, took both of them out of the
Houfe of Penance, *An.* 1648. 3d Cal. of *Auguft*, and put them in the common Jail, and laid them in Irons. The Inquifition demanded of him three
Times, that he would releafe the Prifoners, and fend them back to the Tribunal of the Inquifition, as their competent Judge, with all the original
Acts and Procefs. The Mayor firft faid he would reftore them, but afterwards declared that he would not deliver them over, but under this Condition,
that the Tribunal fhould proceed to no other Procefs. The Inquifition was
not fatisfy'd with this, and the Affair was greatly contefted on both Sides.
The Inquifition fent their Orders to the Mayor, and the Mayor, by his Anfwers, oppofed the Orders and Commands of the Inquifition. At laft, the
Difpute ran fo high, that the Inquifition, after a declaratory Injunction, laid
him under Excommunication and the Anathema; and becaufe he continu'd
to exercife every Act of Jurifdiction, they put him under a general local Interdict. But this made no Impreffion on him; for he anfwer'd, That the
Tribunal of the Inquifition had no Jurifdiction over him; and that whilft
the Difpute was to whom the Cognizance of the Prifoners belonged, their
Excommunication could not touch him, efpecially as he had appealed from
all Cenfures of the Inquifition. At length the Inquifition prepared to publifh
the Order for Ceffation of divine Services. But the Royal Court, to put an
End to this troublefome Difference, commanded the Mayor to difmifs his Prifoners; and the Tribunal of the Inquifition, to deftroy all the Acts and Procefs againft the Mayor, to grant him Abfolution, and remove the Interdict.
But the Inquifition was not fatisfy'd in this; but by *Fermofino*, their Fifcal
Advocate, prayed the King, That the Mayor might be feverely punifhed,
adding this Reafon, leaft a Way fhould be opened to infinite Contentions
and Extorfions of the like Nature; efpecially fince the other Judges will
every Day, confidering thefe Things went unpunifhed, urge many frivolous
Reafons for not acknowledging any of the Cenfures of this Tribunal, in Contempt of Juftice.

CHAP.

CHAP. X.

Of the CROSS-BEARERS.

BESIDES thefe Familiars, there is another Sort of them, called Crofs-*Campeg.* Bearers, inftituted by *Dominick*, to whom he gave fuch Conftitutions and *in Zanch.* Laws for their Direction, as obliges them vigoroufly to profecute Hereticks,*cap. 9.* and when there is Need, to endeavour, with the greateft Violence, their*f. 141.* Deftruction. " They make a Vow between the Hands of the Inquifitors to *cap. 1.* " defend the Catholick Faith, though with the Lofs of Fortune and Life ; " and may be compelled to perform their Vow. The Popes have honoured " this Fraternity with many Graces, Indulgencies and Favours," which may be feen at large in *Campegius*. *Bernard Comenfis* gives us the Main of them in his *Light of the Inquifitors.*

" Their Indulgence is, (1.) Their having a plenary Remiffion of all their *In voce* " Sins. This was granted by *Alexander* IV. in a Privilege beginning, *Præ Indulgen-* " *cunctis*, and by *Gregory* IX. and *Clement* IV. and alfo by the *Extravagants* *tia cruce* " *de bæret.* Cap. *Excommun.* §. *Catholici vero.* But upon this Condition,*rum.* " that they vigoroufly profecute their Vow in aid of the Inquifition, even to " Death. (2.) Every fuch Crofs-Bearer may be abfolved by the Inquifition, " from every Sentence of Excommunication, Sufpenfion and Interdict of a " Canon ; and from thofe efpecially which he may have incurred for the " burning of Churches, or laying violent Hands on Ecclefiaftical Perfons, " and from all other Sentences generally promulgated by the Apoftolick See. " (3.) The Inquifition may difpenfe with thefe Crofs Bearers, if of the Cler- " gy, for all Irregularities they may have contracted by celebrating divine " Service, when under any canonical Sentence. (4.) All their Vows may be " commuted for by the Inquifitors ; thofe only excepted of the holy Land, " and which are perpetual. (5.) The Inquifitors may allow them to be pre- " fent at Divine Services, and to receive the Ecclefiaftical Sacraments in fuch " Places where, by the Apoftolick Indulgence, they are allow'd to be ad- " miniftred, in the Time of a general Interdict. All thefe Things appear by " a Privilege granted by *Innocent* IV. which begins, *Malitia hujus temporis."* Thefe Privileges were confirmed by *Pius* V. by his Conftitution, beginning, *Sacrofanctæ Romanæ & univerfali Ecclefiæ,* dated *October* 13, 1570. fo far as they are not repugnant to the Decrees of the Council of *Trent.*

From thefe Privileges it appears, that when the Faithful are to take the *Campeg.* Crofs, their Vow muft be made only before the Inquifitors or their Vicars ; and*cap. 37.* that they receive no Advantage from them, unlefs they have the Inquifitors*fol. 167.* Leave. Thefe Things and the like, *Campegius* thinks, fhould be preach'd to*zeyo.* the Crofs-Bearers, leaft they fhould pretend Ignorance. " For he faith, That " he difcovered many Errors and Abufes of thefe Crofs-Bearers, in a City, " within his Province of the Inquifition ; for he found a large Number of them, " who

I

" who did not enter into this Warfare by the Door, nor receive the Crofs
" from any Inquifitor or Vicar; but that the very Laicks, the Minifters of
" this fame Fraternity, whom they call Officials or Maffaries *, wrote the
" Names of others that came to them in the Book of the Crofs-Bearers; and
" thus unjuftly invaded the Province of the Inquifition. He adds moreover,
" *Not being able to bear this, I made a Sermon on the Crofs, in the Cathedral, ac-*
" *cording to the ancient Stile of the Inquifitors, granting the ufual Indulgence to*
" *the Auditors; and publickly admonifhed them of their publick Error, and parti-*
" *cularly explain'd what they ought hereafter to do; who upon difcovery of the*
" *Truth, fubmitted, after many Difputes, and the Advice of Advocates. For they*
" *would have had, even againft my Will, that fome of thefe fhould have affifted*
" *at the Examinations, as though it belonged to them of right. Whereas I declared,*
" *That the Inquifitor was the Head and Captain of the Crofs-Bearers, and there-*
" *fore would not have them prefide over the Inquifitors, but according to Equity*
" *be fubjeEt to it.*

Lucerna
Inquif.

" The Office of thofe Crofs-Bearers is to provide the Inquifitors with
" Neceffaries; fo that they are excommunicated if they refufe to give Money
" to the Inquifitor, when he afks and wants it for the Service of the Office of
" the Inquifition; becaufe private Perfons, who have bound themfelves by
" Oath or Vow, are even by Omiffion faid to be Favourers, *viz.* if they
" do not manifeft, or perform what they have promifed by Vow.

The Ceremonies they ufe when they take the Crofs on them, are accurately defcribed by *Campegius.*

The InftruEtion of Campegius *concerning the Manner of Signing with
the Crofs.*

Tr. tr.
tom. xi.
p. 2. fol.
269. verfo.

" WHoever from his AffeEtion to the Catholick Faith, will take the Crofs,
" let him be diligently inftruEted by the Inquifitor, or his Vicar,
" concerning the Bond of his Vow, and the Weight of his Obligation. Let it
" be efpecially declared to him that he fhall be bound not only to part with all
" his outward Eftate, but even to give up his Life for the moft holy Faith, at
" the Command of the Inquifitor or his Vicar; and that having once taken
" the Crofs by Vow, he fhall not lay it down without the fpecial Difpen-
" fation of the Pope. If he be found ready to obferve all thefe Things, the
" Inquifitor or his Vicar may admit him to the Vow of the Crofs. And
" becaufe the Croffes given are firft to be bleffed, therefore we appoint this
" Form of BenediEtion.

> Verf. *Our Help is in the Name of the Lord.*
> Anfw. *Who made the Heavens.*
> Verf. *Lord fhew us thy Mercy;*
> Anfw. *And grant us thy Salvation.*

* A Sort of Houfe-keepers, who looked after the Goods and Furniture of the Monafteries.

Verf.

Verf. *The Lord be with you,*
Anfw. *And with thy Spirit.*

Let us pray.

Almighty and everlafting God, who haft confecrated the Sign of the Crofs with the precious Blood of thy Son, and by the fame Crofs and Death of thy Son Jefus Chrift haft redeemed the World, and by the Virtue of the fame venerable Crofs, haft deliver'd Mankind from the Tyranny of the old Enemy ; we humbly befeech thee, that thou wilt vouchfafe to bl † efs this Crofs, and grant unto it an heavenly Virtue and Grace, that whofoever fhall bear it on him may merit a Plenitude of heavenly Grace, and to have Chrift for his Protector, againft all the Enemies of his Soul and Body, who with thee lives and reigns, World without End. Amen.

" The Crofs thus bleffed, he who is to be figned with it, kneeling before
" the Inquifitor or his Vicar, thus reverently declares his Vow.

I N. Vow to God, and the bleffed Mary, and the bleffed Peter the Martyr, that I will receive and carry the Crofs, to the Honour of Jefus Chrift our Lord, the Advancement of the Catholick Faith, and to the Extirpation of Hereticks and their Favourers, throughout all the Diocefe of F. And I promife to expofe my temporal Subftance, and my proper Life, for the Defence of the Faith, when there fhall be need, and I fhall be fo required to do ; and that I will be obedient to the Reverend Father Inquifitor, his Succeffors or Vicars, in all Things appertaining to the Office of the Inquifition.

" This done, the Inquifitor or his Vicar gives him a red Crofs bleffed,
" faying," Receive the Sign of the Crofs of our Lord Jefus Chrift, in the Name of the † Father, and the † Son, and the Holy † Ghoft, as the Figure and Memorial of the Crofs, Paffion and Death of Jefus Chrift our Saviour, for the Salvation of thy Soul and Body, and the Defence of the Catholick Faith, that the Favour of the Divine Goodnefs may bring you to the heavenly Kingdom. Amen.

A Prayer to be faid over him that takes the Crofs.

Verf. *Lord fhew us thy Mercy ;*
Anfw. *And grant us thy Salvation.*
Verf. *The Lord be with you,*
Anfw. *And with thy Spirit.*
Verf. *Lord hear my Prayer ;*
Anfw. *And let my Cry come up unto thee.*

Lec

Let us pray.

GRant the Right-hand of thy heavenly *Aid,* O *Lord, to thy Servant, whom, for the Glory of thy Name, thou wouldst have mark'd with the Sign of the most holy Cross, and be a Defender of the holy Faith against perfidious Hereticks, that he may seek thee with his whole Heart, manfully defend the Catholick Faith, and may attain what he worthily seeks after ; so that when he hath finished his Warfare, he may merit to be a Co-heir of the Kingdom of thy Son, through the same Lord Jesus. Christ, &c.*

The Manner and Form of absolving these Cross-Bearers in the Article of Death.

fol. 270.   THE *Lord Jesus Christ, who said to his Disciples,* Whatsoever Things ye shall bind on Earth, shall be bound in Heaven ; and whatsoever Things ye shall loose on Earth shall be loosed in Heaven, *of which Number, though unworthy, he hath made me one ; he absolveth thee, by my Ministry, from all thy. Sins, whatsoever thou hast committed, in Thought, Word, or Deed ; and as far as 'tis permitted to my Weakness, by the Authority of the same, our Lord Jesus Christ, and of the blessed Apostles,* Peter *and* Paul, *as also of our Lord Pope* Urban III. *and according to the Privileges which the* Roman *Pontiffs have granted to the Office of the Inquisition, and by Virtue of the Privilege of Pope* Innocent IV. *of which this is the Tenor ;* That you, and such faithful Persons, who have taken the Cross for the Sake of this Vow, may receive a large Recompense of Reward ; we give you that Indulgence and that Privilege, which are given by a general Council to such who go for the Recovery of the Holy. Land, *by Virtue of this Indulgence and Privilege, which* Clement IV. *and* Clement VII. *or any other* Roman *Pontiffs have vouchsafed to all Cross-Bearers, who persevere to the End of Life, in the Vow of the Cross which they have taken, and give their Assistance to the Inquisitors, for the Defence of the Catholick Faith, by which is granted to them, in the Article of Death,. plenary Indulgence and Remission of all Sins :* I absolve thee from every Sentence of Excommunication, Suspension and Interdict, and restore thee to the Sacraments of the holy Roman Church,. *By the same Authority* I absolve thee from all and singular thy Sins, *for which thou art contrite in Heart, and which thou hast confessed with thy Mouth ;* and I grant thee full Remission of thy Sins, *as far as 'tis agreeable to the Divine Majesty, that thou mayest be absolved before the Tribunal of our Lord Jesus Christ, and receive eternal Life, and live for ever.* Amen.   *In the Name of the* † *Father,. and the* † *Son, and the Holy* † *Ghost.* Amen.

Param.   These Cross-Bearers were heretofore of great Use to the Inquisitors. But
l. 2. *t.* 3.   in Process of Time, as there was no need of Arms to subdue Hereticks,
c. 3. *n.* 7.   the Name of this Warfare grew into disuse ; and with the Change of some of their Constitutions, they were called, Of the Penance of St. *Dominick,* in honour
nour

nour of their Founder. This Religion is the Third of thofe inftituted by *Dominick,* the Conftitutions of which have been confirmed by the *Roman* Pontiffs.

CHAP. XI.

Of the VISITORS *of the* INQUISITORS.

" A S the Offices of the Inquifitors and other Minifters were perpetual, Simanc:
" A " it was neceffary, that fometimes they fhould give an Account of *tit* 41.
" their Behaviour. Therefore there was a Magiftrate created to vifit the §. 27, 28,
" Inquifitors, and all the other Minifters, who was called the Vifitor. His
" Office was to vifit all the Provinces of the Inquifitors, and report to the
" Inquifitor General and Council whatever was proper to be amended. He
" was ftrictly to keep to his Inftructions, not to be the Gueft of thofe he vifited,
" nor to receive any Thing from them himfelf, or by others. If one was not
" fufficient they might chufe more." *Simancas* adds, That his great Uncle, *Fran-*
cis Simancas, Archdeacon of *Cordova,* enjoy'd this Office without any Colleague.
But now they appoint Vifitors privately, as often as it is any where neceffary. 4 *Inftruz.*
" All the Minifters of the holy Inquifition are obliged to fwear before the *Tolet c.* 3,
" Inquifitors and Bifhop, or his Vicar, that they will faithfully difcharge the §. 30.
" Truft committed to them. The Inquifitors, Counfellors, and others alfo §. 31,
" fwear, that they will faithfully conceal all Secrets, which if any one dares
" to difcover, he is to be deprived of his Office, and to fuffer other Punifh-
" ments, according to the Nature of his Crime.
" 'Tis alfo part of their Inftructions, that the Inquifitors, and all other §. 35.
" Minifters, fhall ferve in their Offices, by themfelves, and not by their Sub- §. 36.
" ftitutes; the Minifters are not to abfent themfelves without Leave of the In-
" quifitors, which muft not extend to above twenty Days. If any one is long-
" er abfent, or goes without Leave, he muft be deprived of his Salary, his
" Abfence is to be noted, and his Salary not paid by the Receiver, without
" firft infpecting the Book of Defaults, according to feveral Letters of the
" Council.
" Farther, no one muft be a Minifter of this holy Office in any Province §. 38.
" where the Inquifitor is either kin to him, or his Lord. 'Tis alfo prohi-
" bited for any Minifter to intermeddle in any Negociation, either by him-
" felf or others. He who contravenes this Order is to be deprived of his
" Office, and fined 20000 Peices. He who doth not difcover this is be ex-
" communicated. 4 *Inftruct. Tolet.* Cap. 12. and at the End of all the written
" Inftructions, and the printed ones, *fol.* 21.
" If any leffer Crime be committed by thofe Minifters, they may be punifh- *'.* 35,
" ed by the Inquifitors. If their Offence be more grievous, it muft be re-

" ported

§. 40.

" ported to the Inquifitor General and Council, that if the Cafe requires it,
" they may be deprived of their Office.   1 *Inftruct. Hifpal. c.* 27.   'Tis al-
" fo prohibited by the fame Inftructions for any one to be in two Offices, or
" enjoy two Salaries.   4 *Inftruct. Tolet. cap.* 18.

CHAP. XII.

Concerning the Duty or Power of every MAGISTRATE.

Tit. 36.
§. 1.

§. 2.

T
HUS far we have treated of the Minifters which belong to the Inquifition of Hereticks.   The Civil Magiftrate hath no Part in this Affair ;
for he is entirely excluded from all Cognizance of the Crime of Herefy. Thus
Simancas teaches: " The Cognizance of Herefy folely belongs to the Eccle-
" fiaftical Judge, becaufe this is a Crime committed againft the Faith and
" Religion ; for as to thofe Crimes which the fecular Adminiftration knows
" nothing of, and which are declared fuch by the Chriftian Religion, fuch as
" Herefy, Schifm, and others of the like fort, the Ecclefiaftical Judge only
" hath Cognizance of them.   And therefore to whatfoever Branch of the fe-
" cular Judgment the Cognizance of fuch Crimes may at any time happen, it
" muft be immediately referred to the Ecclefiaftical Judges.
        " It is more largely forbidden by the royal Laws at this Day in *Spain,*
" that no one of the fecular Judges, of whatfoever Dignity and Power, fhall
" by any Means prefume to take Cognizance even of thofe civil or criminal
" Caufes which belong to the Inquifitors, and the Judges of forfeited Effects ;
" no not under Pretence of relieving Perfons oppreffed by Violence, which,
" in other Cafes, would be a moft wholefome and prefent Remedy to redrefs
" the Grievances of the Ecclefiaftical Judges.   However, if any will appeal
" in the before-mentioned Caufes, they muft apply to the Council of the holy
" General Inquifition.   This royal Command was dated at *Burgos, March* 7,
" 1508. and renewed 1553."
        However, they ftand in need of the Arms and Power of the Magiftrate,
for the Punifhment of Hereticks, and that they may execute the Sentences
pronounced againft them.   For 'tis not lawful for Ecclefiaftical Perfons to kill
any one.   Therefore they defire to have all Magiftrates obedient to their Beck
and Commands, and to have no Liberty of Confcience granted by them to Hereticks, but infift on their being ready and prepared to draw their Swords

Comment. againft Hereticks at the Pope's Command.   This is the Doctrine of *Maldo-*
on Mat. *net,* explaining the Parable of the Tares fown amongft the Wheat.   For after
xiii. 26. he hath faid that the *Calvinifts* and *Lutherans* are to be cut off as manifeft Hereticks, he adds thefe Things: *Not that I fpeak thus, as though I had not rather
have them converted than put to Death.   All that I intend is to admonifh Princes, or
because Princes may not read thefe Things, thofe who can advife them, that 'tis not
                                                                                        lawful*

lawful for them to grant Hereticks those Liberties of Conscience, as they are called, too much in use, in our Days, unless first of all the Church, or the Roman *Pontiff, who is the Head of the Church, the Person of Christ, and as it were the Father of the Family, shall judge, that the Tares cannot be plucked up unless the Wheat also be destroyed; and that 'tis for the Advantage of the Church to permit both to grow together till the Harvest. In this Matter Princes, who are but the Servants of the Father of the Family, are not to judge, but the Father of the Family himself, i. e. the Governor of the Church. Nor should Princes ask the Father of the Family, that he would suffer both to grow till the Harvest, but whether it be his Pleasure that they should go and pluck up the Tares. They ought to be so affected and prepared, as to need rather to be restrained than incited by the Father of the Family.*

But becauſe there is but ſeldom ſuch a Readineſs in Kings and Princes to extirpate Hereticks, the Eccleſiaſticks are inceſſantly egging them on till they have prevailed on them to yield to them all Things. Farther, they affirm that this is the Duty of the Pope and the other Biſhops, as we read in *Conrad Brunus,* in his Book of Hereticks and Schiſmaticks. *It belongs to the Duty of* l. 3. c. 8. *the* Roman *Pontiff and the other Biſhops, diligently to admoniſh the Emperor, and* §. 1. *other Kings and Princes, under whoſe Government there ariſe Hereſies and Schiſms, as often as there is Need; firſt, that they preſerve the true and Catholick Religion and Faith, and obſerve the Commands of God; and ſecondly, that they every where ſuppreſs and extinguiſh heretical Impiety, by the Diſcipline and Rigour of the ſecular Power, which the Sacerdotal Office cannot do by their Doctrine and eccleſiaſtical Cenſures. Thus Pope* Leo *implored the Aſſiſtance of the Emperor againſt Hereticks, in his* 55*th Letter to the Emperor* Martian, *and* 36*th to the Empreſs* Pulcheria, *and* 23*d to the Emperor* Theodoſius II. *It belongs alſo to the Care and Concern of the Pope, to take certain good and faithful Men in the Court of every Prince, who may enquire out Hereticks, and every Thing that belongs to the Defence of the Catholick Faith, and the Preſervation of Unity; and put the Prince in mind of whatſoever is neceſſary to Peace, and inform the Pope of all ſuch Tranſactions whatſoever; as we find it in the* 34*th and* 80*th Letters of* Leo *to Biſhop* Julian, *the* 55*th to the Emperor* Martian, *and* 73*d to the Emperor* Leo.

But not content with this, the Popes, by their Decrees, Bulls and Reſcripts, command all Magiſtrates whatſoever, to yield all Aſſiſtance to the Inquiſitors, ſeverely threatning them with the moſt grievous Puniſhments, if they are wanting to their Duty. All which Things are laid together in the Book concerning the Form of Proceeding againſt Hereticks, generally aſcribed to *John Calderine.*

" The Duty of every Magiſtrate or Governor is deſcribed perfectly enough Tr. tr.
" in the Conſtitutions of *Clement,* and in the Decretals, although the Emperor, Tom. xi.
" and the Popes *Gregory, Alexander* and *Innocent,* touch upon ſome of theſe Mat- P. 2. fol.
" ters. What the Magiſtrates and other Officers ought to do, is not put down in 412.
" the Order in which it is written, but in ſuch a Manner as renders it more eaſy to
" be remembred. *Clement* writes after this Manner to the Magiſtrates and Ru-
　　　　　　　　　　　　　　　　　　　　　　　　　　　　　" lers,

" lers, and Confuls, and Nobles *, and Councils, and Communities of Cities and
" other Places in *Italy: By thefe our Apoftolick Writings we command all of you, that ye*
" *feverally caufe to be written in the Regifters, the Conftitutions made by us, with the*
" *Additions, Modifications, and Declarations made by the faid* Alexander *our Pre-*
" *deceffor, and that they fhall never be erafed from thence ; and that ye proceed ac-*
" *cording to them, without any Omiffion, againft every Herefy that exalts it felf*
" *againft this holy Church.   Otherwife we command by our Letters our beloved Sons*
" *the Predicant and Minor Friars, Inquifitors of heretical Pravity, and every of*
" *them, deputed through* Italy *by Authority of the Apoftolick See, and hereafter to*
" *be deputed, that within a certain limited Time, they compel every one of you thus*
" *to do, under the Penalty of Excommunication againft your Perfons, and Interdiſt*
" *againft your Country, without any Benefit of Appeal.*

1.   " *We ordain, that the Magiftrate, Head Officer, or Governor, or Confuls, or*
" *whoever prefide over the City, or fhall be fubftituted in the Room of others, for a*
" *Time only, either now, or for the future in* Italy, *fhall fwear that he will precifely,*
" *and without any Delay, inviolably attend to and obferve, and caufe to be obferved*
" *the whole Time of his Government, by all as well in the Country as the City, and*
" *in all Places fubjeſt to his Jurifdiſtion, all and fingular the under written Conftitu-*
" *tions, and take an Oath from all that fhall fucceed them in the Power or Govern-*
" *ment, concerning thefe Things, that they will precifely obferve them.   And if any one*
" *refufes this, let him in no manner be owned for a Magiftrate, Head Officer, or Go-*
" *vernor, or Ruler ; and whatfoever he doth as Magiftrate or Head Officer, or Con-*
" *ful, or Ruler, let it have no Validity; and let no one be obliged or bound to attend*
" *on them, even though he fhall have taken an Oath to obey them.*

2.   " *We ordain alfo by a perpetual Ediſt, that the Magiftrate, or Confuls and Ru-*
" *lers, whatever be their Offices, fhall publickly fwear that they will defend the*
" *Faith, that they will ftudy in Sincerity, and with all their Might, to exterminate*
" *from the Places fubjeſt to their Jurifdiſtion, all Perfons marked out for Hereticks by*
" *the Church ; fo that whofoever for the future fhall be taken into any perpetual Ma-*
" *giftracy, fhall be altogether and wholly obliged to confirm this by Oath, otherwife let*
" *them not be acknowledged for Magiftrates, Confuls, or the like, and let all their*
" *Sentences be invalid and null by our Decree.*

3.   " *Alfo the fame Magiftrate, Head Officer, Conful, Ruler, and all others taken into*
" *the Government of any City or Place, fhall in the Beginning of their Government,*
" *in a publick Affembly, according to Cuftom, put under the Ban of fuch City and*
" *Place, as though it were for the worft of Crimes, all Hereticks of both Sex, and*
" *whatfoever be their Names, and they fhall be obliged to confirm fuch Ban pronounced*
" *by their Predeceffors.   Let them alfo command that no Heretick, Man or Woman,*
" *fhall any longer dwell, or ftay, or fubfift in fuch City, or any Place of the faid Ju-*
" *rifdiſtion or Diftriſt.*

---

* *Antianis.* They are in *Genoa* and other Towns of *Italy*, Patricians and Nobles, fuperior to others in Age, unto City and Honour, and are therefore themfelves Magiftrates. *Du Frefne in voce.*

" *Far-*

" Farther, we farther order and notify, that the Predicant Friars deputed against
" Hereticks for the Affair of the Faith, in the Parts of our Empire, and all others
" also who shall come to judge Hereticks, unless any of them be proscribed by the Em-
" pire, shall be received under the special Protection of our Empire, in going, staying
" and returning, and that they shall remain without Injury, under the Pro-
" tection and Recommendation of the Faithful of the Empire. We command every one
" of you, that ye receive them kindly, whensoever and to whomsoever of you they
" shall come, and that ye give them Counsel, safe Conduct and Assistance, in per-
" forming such acceptable Services before God. Whatsoever Hereticks also they shall
" discover to you in your Jurisdiction, let them be apprehended and kept in safe
" Custody, till by Judgment of Ecclesiastical Condemnation, they shall undergo the
" Punishment they deserve.

" Farther, let the Magistrate or Ruler, or he who hath the principal Government,
" be obliged to chuse one of his Assessors, and send him to the Diocesan if present, and
" the Inquisitors or Inquisitor, deputed by Authority of the Apostolick See, to go with
" them, as often as they please, within the Jurisdiction of such City, Place or Di-
" strict ; which Assessor shall force three or more Persons of good Report, according as
" the aforesaid Inquisitors or Inquisitor shall think fit, or the whole Neighbourhood, if
" they judge proper, to take an Oath, that if they know of any Hereticks there, or of
" their Effects, or of any Persons that keep private Conventicles, or differing in Life
" and Manners from the common Conversation of the Faithful, or of any Believers,
" Defenders, Receivers, or Favourers of Hereticks, they shall endeavour to discover
" them to the said Inquisitors or Inquisitor.

" Also the Magistrates, Consuls, Ruler, and all who are at the Head of Affairs,
" shall be obliged to purge from heretical Pravity the City or Place where they preside,
" and the whole Country or District subject to their Jurisdiction, according to the Laws
" published against heretical Pravity at Padua, by Frederick, heretofore Emperor
" of the Romans, then persisting in his Devotion to the Roman Church, and shall
" cause them to be registred in their Records, never to be rased out.

" But if the temporal Lord being required and admonished by the Church, shall
" neglect to purge his Dominions from heretical Pravity, for the Space of a Year, af-
" ter the Time of Admonition, we expose his Country to be seized by the Catholicks, who
" upon the Extermination of Hereticks, shall possess it without any Contradiction, and
" preserve it in the Purity of the Faith, reserving the Right of the principal Lord,
" provided he gives no Hindrance, nor creates any Obstacle to this Affair. Let the
" same Law be observed, with respect to such as have no principal Lords.

" Farther, let the Magistrate, Head Officer, Consul, or Ruler, or any other de-
" puted to such Government, be obliged to cause such Hereticks, when apprehended,
" to be carried, at the publick Expence, any where within the Jurisdiction or Di-
" strict of the Diocesan, Bishop, or City, or Place, wheresoever the Diocesan, or his
" Vicar, or Inquisitors, or Inquisitor aforesaid shall order them.

" Farther, let such Magistrate, Head Officer, Consul or Ruler, or others, be obliged
" to order such heretical Men or Women, when apprehended, to be kept at the com-
" mon Expence of such Place where they preside, by Catholick Men chosen to this Of-
" fice by the Diocesan, if present, or by the Inquisitors or Inquisitor, in some special
                                                              " Jcil,

I

" Jail, safe and secure, in which they shall be by themselves, separate from Robbers
" and Outlaws, till it shall be determined concerning them.

10.   " Farther, let such Magistrate, Head Officer, Consul or Ruler, or others such, be
" obliged to bring, with a sufficient and secure Guard, all Hereticks, of whatsoever
" Name, within twelve Days after they are taken, before the Diocesan, or his spi-
" ritual Vicar, or the Inquisitors of Hereticks, or Inquisitor, to form an Examina-
" tion of them and their Heresy.

11.   " Moreover, let the Magistrate, Head Officer, Consuls, or others such, be obliged
" to compel all Hereticks they have apprehended, without Loss of Members, or Dan-
" ger of Death, as real Thieves and Murtherers of Souls, and Stealers of the Sacra-
" ments of God, and the Christian Faith, expressly to confess their Errors, and accuse
" other Hereticks whom they know, and to discover their Effects, their Believers, Re-
" ceivers and Defenders, by the same Means as the Thieves and Robbers of temporal
" Things are compelled to accuse their Complices, and confess the Crimes they have
" committed. And when they are condemned for Heresy by the Diocesan or his Vicar,
" or by the Inquisitors or Inquisitor, the Governor, Head Officer, or any of the other
" above named, or his or their special Deputy, shall be obliged to receive them as soon
" as they are delivered over to them, and punish them with the deserved Pu-
" nishment.

12.   " Farthermore, the Magistrate, Head Officer, Consul or Ruler, or any other chief
" Officer of a City or Place, shall be obliged to write down in four Libels of the same
" Tenour, the Names of all those who shall be defamed or rendred infamous, or put un-
" der the Ban for Heresy, one of which shall be given to the Community of such City,
" or Place, another to the Diocesan, another to the Predicants, and another to the
" Minors. And they shall cause their Names to be solemnly called over in publick
" Assembly three times in a Year.

13.   " Farther, let the chief Magistrate of a City, or Ruler of any Place, under what
" Character soever, be obliged effectually to execute these Things, the pulling down
" the Houses of Hereticks, the causing them to be condemned, the delivering and di-
" viding their Effects, found and seized, of which we have spoken before, within
" ten Days after the Accusation or Injunction made, and to demand the Fines they are
" condemned to, to be paid down, and to divide their Effects, according to what is
" hereafter contained.

14.   " Moreover, let the chief Magistrate or Officers be obliged to appoint one of their
" Assessors, whomsoever the Diocesan, or his Vicar, and the said Inquisitors or In-
" quisitor of Hereticks shall chuse, faithfully to perform these Things, and to change
" them for any Time if they think proper. Nor let any Condemnations or Penalties,
" which shall be incurred on the Account of Heresy, be ever remitted by any Means,
" or upon any Account, neither by Word, Counsel, or at the Desire of the People.

15.   " Furthermore, let the chief Magistrate, Head Officer, Consul, or any other Per-
" son in Authority, be obliged to divide all the Effects of Hereticks and their Recei-
" vers, which shall be seized or found by the said Officials, and the Fines to which
" they shall be condemned for them, as also the Timbers, Stones, and Tiles of the
" Houses, and Castles, which shall be destroyed upon the Account of Heresy, and all
" the Effects, movable and immovable, which shall be confiscated upon the same Occa-

2

" sion,

" ston, in such manner, that the first Part shall be distributed for the common Use of
" such City or Place ; the second in Favour and for the Assistance of the Office, and
" be given to the Officials who shall have performed these Affairs ; and let the third
" Part be deposited in some safe Place, to be reserved by the said Diocesan and Inqui-
" sitors, or Inquisitor, as they think fit, and to be expended by their Advice in Favour
" of the Faith, and for the Extirpation of Hereticks, any Statute made, or to be made
" to the contrary notwithstanding.

" Farther, let the chief Magistrate or Ruler of any City or Place, be obliged faith- 16.
" fully to sell, with the Advice and Consent of the Inquisitors or Inquisitor, all Goods
" confiscated upon account of heretical Pravity, within three Months after such Con-
" fiscations : If he doth not do it, let him thereby incur the aforesaid Penalties ; and
" let the Inquisitors or Inquisitor nevertheless have free Liberty to sell them, with the
" Advice of the Diocesan, or of his Vicar, if he be absent, and of two Friars Predi-
" cants, and as many Friars Minor, whom the Prior and Guardian, if there be a
" Convent there of the said Orders, shall think proper to be chosen, and let the Buyers
" of such Effects freely and lawfully have and possess them, and let the real Property
" of them be transferred to them upon their buying them.

" But if any one shall otherwise attempt to destroy, diminish, or change any 17.
" Thing in these Statutes and Constitutions, without the special Authority of the Apo-
" stolick See, let the chief Magistrate, or Consul, or any other Officer, who shall be
" for any Time in such City, or their Deputies, declare him perpetually publickly in-
" famous, according to the prescribed Form, as a publick Defender and Favourer of
" Hereticks, and punish him with a Fine of Fifty Imperial Pounds of Money, which,
" if he cannot recover, let him put him under the Bann of common Malefactors, and
" never release him from it, but upon Payment of double such Sum.

" Moreover, let the chief Magistrate, or Head Officer, or Consul, or any other 18.
" Magistrate, of any City and Place, be obliged to destroy or erase wholly out of the
" Statutes and Records any Statutes made or to be made, that shall be found to con-
" tradict these Constitutions, or by any Manner of Means to oppose the mentioned Sta-
" tutes and Laws : And let them in the Beginning and Middle of their Government,
" cause these Statutes, Constitutions and Laws, to be solemnly rehearsed in publick As-
" sembly, and in all other Places without their City, as shall seem fit to the Dio-
" cesan, or the Inquisitors, or Inquisitor.

" Moreover, let all these Statutes, or before mentioned Constitutions, and Laws, and 19.
" any other that shall be made at any Time by Authority of the Apostolick See, against
" Hereticks and their Accomplices, be written down in Four Volumes, each of them ex-
" actly the same, and let one of them be placed in the Statute Office of every City or
" Place, the second deliver'd to the Diocesan, the third to the Friars Predicants, the
" fourth to the Friars Minors, to be carefully kept, that they may not suffer by any
" Forgery any Alteration in any Thing whatsoever.

" Farther, let the chief Magistrate or Head Officer, Consul, or any other Ma- 20.
" gistrate, be obliged, within twelve Days of his Government, to examine the
" chief Magistrate, Head Officer, Consul, or Ruler, whom he immediately
" succeeds, and his Assessors also, by three Catholick and faithful Men, to
" be chosen within three Days of the aforesaid Government, by the Friars Predi-
" cants and Minors, such as shall be appointed by their respective Prior and Guar-
" dian,

" dian, together with the Diocesan, or by the Inquisitors or Inquisitor of heretical
" Pravity, concerning all Things contained in the said Statutes, or Constitutions, and
" Laws, against Hereticks and their Complices, and to punish them if they have been
" faulty, for all and singular Matters which they have omitted, and force them to
" make Satisfaction out of their own Estates, notwithstanding they shall have been
" absolved from such Examination by any License of Counsel, or any other Person
" whatsoever. And the aforesaid three Persons shall sincerely swear that they will
" examine the before mentioned Persons concerning the before recited Matters.

Boniface VIII. touches upon all these Things, saying briefly, " That the
" Affair of the Inquisition against heretical Pravity may go on prosperously in our
" Times, to the Glory of God, and the Encrease of the Faith, we approve and com-
" mand to be observed certain Laws promulgated by Frederick, formerly Emperor of
" the Romans, then persisting in his Devotion to the Church of Rome, as far as
" they promote the Honour of God, and of his holy Church, and tend to the Extirpa-
" tion of Hereticks, and are not contrary to the canonical Statutes. Likewise we re-
" quire and admonish all chief Magistrates and temporal Lords, and the Governors
" of Provinces, Countries, Cities, and other Places, of whatsoever Dignities, Of-
" fices or Names, as they desire to be reputed and accounted faithful, that they do
" obey the Bishops of the Diocese, and the Inquisitors of heretical Pravity deputed, or
" hereafter to be deputed by the Apostolick See, for the Defence of the Faith, and that
" when required by them they do endeavour to search out, to apprehend and keep in
" safe Custody the Believers of Hereticks, their Favourers, Receivers and Defenders,
" and that they carry or cause to be carried, without Delay, the aforesaid pestilent
" Persons into the Power or Jail of the before mentioned Inquisitors, or to any Place
" where they or any of them shall command, within their Dominion, Power or Di-
" strict, where they shall be kept in strict and safe Custody by Catholick Men deputed
" by the aforesaid Bishops, or Inquisitors, or any one of their Deputies, till their
" Affair shall be determined by the Judgment of the Church: And that the aforesaid
" chief Magistrates, and temporal Lords or Governors, or their Officials or Deputies,
" do immediately receive such as are condemned for Heresy by the Bishop of the Dio-
" cese, or Inquisitor or Inquisitors, and when delivered to them, punish them with the
" deserved Punishment, notwithstanding the Appeals or Complaints of the aforesaid
" Children of Wickedness, since, according to the Appointment of our Predecessors,
" as well as by the Imperial Law, the Benefit of Appeal and Complaint is expressly
" denied to Hereticks, their Believers, Receivers, Favourers and Defenders.

21.　　" We also more strictly forbid the abovesaid chief Magistrates, temporal Lords and
" Governors, and their Officials, to take any manner of Cognizance, or to judge con-
" cerning this Crime, since it is meerly Ecclesiastical, or by their Leave and Com-
" mand to deliver out of Prison any Persons apprehended for the said Crimes, with-
" out the Leave and Command of the said Bishops or Inquisitors, or at least one of
" them, or to refuse to perform or fulfil Execution for such Crime appointed by the
" Diocesan, or Inquisitors or Inquisitor, as is agreeable to their Office, or that
" they otherwise presume directly or indirectly, to hinder any Judgment, Sentence, or
" Process of the Diocesan or Inquisitors.

22.　　" We moreover ordain, that the chief Magistrate, Head Officer, Governor or
" Consuls, or any other presiding over any City or Place, now or hereafter, shall,

" at

" at the Command of the Diocefan, or his Vicars, or the Inquifitors of heretical Pra-
" vity, fwear precifely to regard, inviolably to obferve, and caufe to be obferved by
" their Subjects, during the whole Time of their Government, in all the Countries
" fubject to their Jurifdiction and Government, the Conftitutions publifhed, and ap-
" proved by the Apoftolick See againft Hereticks, their Believers, Receivers, Fa-
" vourers and Defenders, their Children and Grandchildren : And whofoever refufes
" to fwear to obferve them is infamous, and fhall be deprived of the Honour and Office
" of his Government, as a Favourer of Hereticks, and fufpected concerning the Faith ;
" and let him not be accounted as a chief Magiftrate, Head Officer, Conful, or Go-
" vernor, or ever be raifed to any publick Dignity or Office. And let whatever he
" doth as chief Magiftrate, Conful, or Governor, have no Validity. But Clement,
in his Conftitutions, faith thus : " If any chief Magiftrate, Head Officer, or any
" of the before-named, fhall refufe and neglect to obferve thefe Conftitutions, and eve-
" ry Thing contained in them ; befides the, Mark of Perjury, and the Hazard
" of perpetual Infamy, let him forfeit two hundred Marks, which fhall be exacted of
" him without Remiffion, and converted to the publick Ufe of the Place where he go-
" verns ; and yet neverthelefs he fhall be deprived of the Honour and Office of his Go-
" vernment, as a perjured and infamous Perfon, and as a Favourer of Hereticks,
" and fufpected concerning the Faith, and never more be any where accounted as a
" chief Magiftrate, Head Officer, Conful, or Governor, nor ever after promoted to
" any publick Dignity or Office whatfoever. Boniface, in 6 Decret. fays thus : But
" if any one of the aforefaid chief Magiftrates, temporal Lords, Governors, or their
" Officials, or others, fhall act contrary to the aforefaid, or fhall prefume to oppofe him-
" felf in the aforefaid Affair of the Faith to the aforefaid Diocefan, Bifhop, or Inqui-
" fitors, or any ways to hinder him : As alfo every one who fhall knowingly give them Af-
" fiftance, Counfel, or Favour in the aforefaid, let him know that he fhall be pierced
" thro' with the Sword of Excommunication, which, if he endures for a Year with an
" obftinate Mind, he fhall from thence be condemned for an Heretick.

All thefe Conftitutions wholly fubject the fecular Magiftrate to the Inquifitors, who bid them draw their Sword at their Pleafure, and readily execute their Commands with a blind Obedience.

CHAP. XIII.

Of the Privileges of the INQUISITORS.

AS we have briefly defcribed the Offices of all the Minifters of the Inquifition, it remains now that we treat more fully and diftinctly of the Inquifitors, who are the Chief of all. We will therefore give an Account of
their Privileges and Power.

The Privileges of the Inquifitors are many and great, which the Popes of
Rome have granted them with a liberal Hand, that they may more chearfully

perform their Duty, and vigorouſly execute the Laws made againſt Hereticks.

Urban IV. by a Bull, beginning, *Ne Inquiſitionis negotium,* grants the Inquiſitors, *That no Delegate of the Apoſtolick See, or Sub-delegate under him, no Conſervator, or Executor deputed by the ſaid Apoſtolick See, or hereafter to be deputed, ſhall
be able to publiſh the Sentence of Excommunication, Suſpenſion or Interdict againſt
them, or their four Notaries or Writers faithfully obeying them in theſe Matters,
whilſt they ſhall be engaged in the Proſecution of this Affair, without the ſpecial Command of the aforeſaid See, making full and expreſs Mention of this Indulgence* ; and
he decrees *every Thing done contrary hereto to be null and void.* This Privilege is
granted them, that the Cauſes of Religion may not be forſaken or hindred by
the Excommunication of the Inquiſitors, and other Miniſters of the Office,
and Hereticks in the mean while go unpuniſhed by ſuch Hindrances of their
Judges.

He hath granted the ſame alſo by a ſpecial Privilege to the Inquiſitors of the
Orders of Predicants and Minors, that they may not be hindred by their Superiors in the Cauſes of Faith. *If it ſhould ſo happen that the Maſter and Miniſter General, and other Priors and Miniſters Provincial, and Keepers and Guardians of other Places of your Order, ſhall, under Pretence of certain Privileges or
Indulgences of the ſame Apoſtolick. See granted to the ſaid Orders, or hereafter to be
granted, enjoin, or in any manner command you, or any one or more of you, that
you ſuperſede this Affair for a Time, or as to certain Articles, or certain Perſons ;
we by our Apoſtolick Authority do ſtrictly prohibit you, and all and ſingular of you,
that ye do not preſume in this, or by any Means whatſoever, to obey and ſubmit to
them. For we, by the Tenor of theſe preſent, do revoke all ſuch Privileges or Indulgences, as far as relates to this Article, and do wholly pronounce null and void all Sentences of Excommunication, Interdict and Suſpenſion, if it ſhall ſo happen that they
have been pronounced againſt you, or any of you, upon this Occaſion. For if the aforeſaid See doth ſometimes give Commiſſion, under a certain Form, by its Letters to any
Prelates of your Orders, that they ſhall be able to take certain Friars of their Orders
to execute the Office of the Inquiſition againſt heretical Pravity, and to remove them
when they think expedient, and to ſubſtitute others, yet by this there is no Faculty,
Juriſdiction or Power granted them in this Affair, immediately committed, or to be
committed to you by the aforeſaid See, becauſe the only Reaſon why ſuch Commiſſion in
ſuch Part is granted them is, that they are preſumed to have a more full Knowledge of
the Fitneſs of the Friars of their own Order.*

'Tis alſo granted to the Inquiſitors in Favour of the Faith, that when they
cannot, without Loſs of Time, and Danger to the Affair, have Recourſe to
their Superiors, who, in ſuch Places may lawfully execute Juſtice, they may
require the temporal Lords, and their Officials, though excommunicated, to
afford them their Aſſiſtance and Favour, according to their Office, without
incurring themſelves the Penalty of Excommunication : per cap. *Præſidentes*
de hæret. l. 6. *Though they require ſuch excommunicated Perſons, they ſhall not therefore incur the Sentence of Excommunication.* Agreeable to this, although the Acts
of Tyrants are in Law void and null, yet in Favour of the Faith, if a Tyrant,

rant, or any other unjuſt Lord, by Command of the Inquiſitors, doth any Thing againſt Hereticks, 'tis valid.

The Inquiſitors only, and not the Ordinaries, can publiſh Edicts againſt Hereticks. Thus lately a certain Edict, publiſhed by Command of the Ordi-nary, during the Time of Lent, was revoked. But we ſhall ſpeak more of this in the fifteenth Chapter. Likewiſe the Inquiſitors only, and no others, can abſolve from Excommunication for Hereſy contracted, by Virtue of a Jubilee, or Letters of the Apoſtolick See, and even from the Sentence of Excommu-nication, which the Pope himſelf pronounces againſt them at the Feſtival of the Sacrament. Royas, *p* 2.§.425. §. 416.

The Inquiſitors can excommunicate, ſuſpend, and interdict. How grievous this their Excommunication is, ſhall be alſo related, Chap. XV. They can alſo command any Presbyter with Cure or without, to publiſh monitory Let-ters made by him, and denounce before the People the Perſons excommuni-cated by them. And if he refuſes to do it, they may puniſh ſuch Presbyter, not only with a Cenſure, but with ſome other Puniſhment. Pegna, Lucern. *Inq.* in voce E*x.* communi-catus. Lucern.

Perſons under Excommunication or Interdict by the Inquiſitor, can't be ab-ſolved by the Ordinary, or any other Perſon, without the Command of the Pope, except in the Article of Death. in voce In-quiſ. hær. prav.

The Inquiſitors may apprehend Hereticks, though they fly to Churches ; nor can the Biſhops hinder them from this under any Pretence. As *John* XXII. hath decreed by a Conſtitution, beginning, *Ex parte veſtra.* Ibid. in voce Ex-communi-catus.

The Inquiſitor may prohibit the ſecular Judge from proceeding againſt any Perſon upon Account of any Proceſſes made by the Inquiſitor himſelf, or up-on Occaſion of any Confeſſion made before ſuch Inquiſitor. See cap. *Tuam.* de ordi. cogni. Carena, *p.* 1. *t.* 5. *n.* 96. Lucern.

Whoſoever by himſelf or others ſhall kill, or beat, or ſtrike any one of the Inquiſitors or Officials of the holy Office, he is to be delivered over to the ſe-cular Court without any Charge of Irregularity, according to the Grant of Pope *Leo* X. dated at *Florence, Jan.* 28, 1515. The aforeſaid Grant is now extended to thoſe who damage the Effects of the Inquiſitors, or Officials, by the proper Motion of *Pius* V. dated at *Rome* 1569. in v.ce Index. Royas, *p.*2.§.419.

Likewiſe the Inquiſitors receive the entire Fruits of their Benefices, toge-ther with the daily Diſtributions, when abſent ; as appears in the Letters of *Paul* III. and *Pius* V. which are in the firſt Volume of the Letters of this In-quiſition in *Valentia, fol.* 308. 420.

The Penſions reſerved by the Apoſtolick Authority to the holy Office, are free from the Payment of the fifteenth, as the ſupreme Congregation of the holy Office hath declared, *Jan.* 4, 1622. for the Inquiſitor at *Pavia* againſt the Chapter of the Metropolitan Church at *Milan.* The Pope hath alſo often declared that the Benefices united to the Inquiſitions are free from Payment of the Tenths. Carena, *p.* 1. *t.* 5. *n.* 97.

They are alſo free from all real and perſonal Offices, and even from the Law of the Generality, by a ſpecial Royal Privilege, which is alſo extended to ſome of the Officials, as is more fully contained in the ſaid firſt Volume, *fol.* 288, 411.

Lodg-

424. Lodgings, Provifions, and other Neceffaries, are to be provided for the Inquifitors and their Officials at a juft Price, according to the Tenor of the Privilege of Queen *Joan*.

440. The Inquifitors may make Statutes againft Hereticks, and encreafe the Punifhments againft them.

They may alfo carry Witneffes above two Days Journey.

Eymer. Farther, *Urban* IV. hath granted another Privilege to the Inquifitors, that
p. 3. qu. they may abfolve themfelves and their Affiftants, and difpenfe with them-
13. felves as to their Irregularity. *That you may the more freely promote the Affair of the Faith, we grant you by the Authority of thefe prefent, that if it fhould happen that you, and the Friars of your Order, your Affiftants, fhould in any Cafes, by human Frailty, incur the Sentence of Excommunication and Irregularity, or remember that you have incured it ; fince you cannot eafily, on this Account, have Recourfe to your Priors, becaufe of the Office enjoin'd you, you may mutually abfolve one another upon thefe Accounts, according to the Form of the Church, and by our Authority may difpenfe with your felves, in Cafes in which the faid Priors can do it by Grant of the Apoftolick See.* They can likewife abfolve their Servants and Familiars from Excommunication for apprehending any one upon Account of their Office, as *Innocent* IV. fays in a Bull, beginning, *Devotionis veftræ.*

But there are three Cafes in which the Inquifitors cannot mutually abfolve themfelves. The firft is, when they have omitted to proceed againft any one they ought to have proceeded againft. The fecond, when they have falfely charged any one with Herefy, or faid that they have hindred the holy Office,
Clement. who in Reality have not. *But becaufe 'tis very heinous not to act for the Extirpa-
de bæret. tion of the aforefaid Pravity, when fuch infectious Wickednefs requires it ; 'tis
cap. Mul- alfo very heinous, and moft worthy of Condemnation, malicioufly to charge innocent
torvm. Perfons with fuch Pravity. We therefore command the aforefaid Bifhop and Inquifi-
§. Verum tor, and others fubftituted by them to execute the faid Office, in Virtue of their holy O-
quia. bedience, and under the Threatning of eternal Damnation, that they proceed fo difcreetly and readily againft Perfons fufpected or defamed for fuch Pravity, that they do not malicioufly or fraudulently, falfely charge any one with fo great a Crime, or with hindring them in the Execution of the Office of the Inquifition. But if through Hatred, Favour or Love, or with a View of any temporal Gain or Profit, the Bifhop or Superior fhall omit to proceed againft any one, contrary to Juftice and their Confcience, when they ought to proceed upon fuch Pravity ; or with the fame View fhall charge any one with fuch Pravity, or hindring the Office, and upon this Account fhall by any Means prefume to trouble him, befides other Punifhments to be inflicted on them according to the Quality of the Fault, fuch Bifhop or Superior fhall hereby incur the Sentence of Sufpenfion from his Office for three Years, and others the Sentence of Excommunication. From which Sentence of Excommunication thofe who incur it, fhall not obtain the Benefit of Abfolution from any one but the Pope himfelf, except in the Article of Death, and not then without Satisfaction made, any Privilege whatfoever to the contrary notwithftanding.* But the Inquifitors are not fubject to this Penalty, if they omit to proceed through Ignorance, but only when they know they ought to have proceeded, and have then omitted to proceed through Hatred, Favour,

Love,

Love, Money or Entreaty, contrary to Juſtice and their own Conſcience ; or, on the other Hand, have proceeded when they ought not. The third Caſe is when they have unlawfully extorted Money, under Pretence of their Office, or have confiſcated the Effects of the Church for the Offences of the Clergy. Clement. de hæret. cap. *Nolentes. We alſo do more ſtrictly enjoin all their Commiſſa-ries whatſoever, as well as thoſe of Biſhops and Chapters, during the Vacancy of the See, deputed for this Affair, that they ſhall not extort Money from any Perſons, by any unlawful Means whatſoever, under Pretence of the Office of the Inquiſition ; and that they ſhall not knowingly attempt to confiſcate to the Church the Churches Effects for any Offence of the Clergy. And if any act contrary to theſe Things, or any one of them, we decree that they ſhall be actually excommunicated, from which they ſhall not be ab-ſolved, unleſs in the Article of Death, till they have made full Satisfaction to thoſe from whom they have extorted Money : All Privileges, Agreements, or Remiſſions whatſoever to the contrary notwithſtanding.*

Amongſt the Privileges of the Inquiſitors 'tis not the leaſt, that the Inqui- Eymer. ſitor hath Power of granting an Indulgence of twenty or forty Days, as he 3. part. ſhall ſee fit, to all that are truly penitent, and confeſſed, and who attend on qu. 127. his Sermon made for the Faith, according to the Reſcript of *Innocent, Clement,* Com. 179. *Alexander,* and *Urban* IV. *Præ cunctis.* They can alſo releaſe from the Pe-nances enjoin'd them, for three Years, all the Companions and Friars of the Inquiſitor, and alſo his Notaries, who have laboured together with them in the Proſecution of this Affair, and who have, from their Hearts, perſonally afforded Aſſiſtance, Counſel and Favour againſt Hereticks, their Favourers, Receivers and Defenders. And if any of them ſhould happen to die in the Proſecution of this Buſineſs, they grant them full Pardon of all their Sins, for which they are contrite in Heart, and confeſs with their Mouth. *Gregory* IX. plainly de- Com. 178. clares thus, in his Reſcript, beginning, *Ille humani Generis,* in theſe Words. *Add to theſe Things, In order to their more freely and effectually executing the Office committed to them in all the Premiſſes, we confiding in the Mercy of Almighty God, and in the Authority of the bleſſed* Peter *and* Paul *his Apoſtles, do releaſe for three Years from the Penance enjoin'd them all who ſhall attend on their (the Inquiſitors) preaching, twenty Days in their ſeveral Stations ; and all thoſe who ſhall, from their Heart afford Aſſiſtance, Counſel and Favour to the ſubduing of Hereticks, and their Fa-vourers, Receivers and Defenders, in their fortified Places and Caſtles, or any other that rebel againſt the Church. And if any ſuch ſhould happen to die in the Proſecution of this Affair, we grant them full Pardon of all their Sins, for which they are contrite in their Heart, and which they confeſs with their Mouths.* Pegna tells us that the Croſs-bearers enjoy this Privilege to this Day, and they are the ſame with the Familiars in *Spain,* who are at the Beck of the Inquiſitors, and execute all Things they order them, to promote this holy Office, the Propagation of the Faith, and the Extirpation of heretical Pravity. But as there are extant the Lucern. Bulls of five Popes, who every one of them grant theſe three Years of Indul- Irq. in voc. gences, ſome infer from hence, that theſe Years of Indulgences are to be added Indulgen-together, and therefore that Indulgences of fifteen Years are granted to all who tia eorum qui, promote the Office of the Inquiſition, for every Time and Inſtance. And *Pegna,* who

I

who believed once that the Indulgences of the former Popes were only con-firmed by the Bulls of the latter, fays there is Reason to add them to one another.

But to the Inquifitors themfelves is granted a plenary Indulgence in Life and Death, by a Refcript of *Alexander* IV. beginning, *Firmiſſime teneat,* in which we read thus: *By the Mercy of Almighty God, and confiding in the Authority of his bleſſed Apoſtles,* Peter *and* Paul, *we grant unto you, being truly penitent, and con-feſſed, full Pardon of your Sins.* And by a Refcript of *Urban* IV. and *Clement* IV. beginning, *Præ cunEtis. And to you who labour in this Affair, we grant you that Pardon of Sins which was granted in a general Council, to thoſe who ſuccour the holy Land.* This Indulgence was granted by *Innocent* III. in the *Lateran* Coun-cil at *Rome, Anno* 1215. and runs thus: *In order to recover the holy Land,* &c. *we, trusting in the Mercy of Almighty God, and in the Authority of the bleſſed A-poſtles,* Peter *and* Paul, *by that Power of binding and loofing, which God hath con-ferred upon us, tho' unworthy, do grant to all who undertake this Labour in their own Perſons, and at their own proper Expence, full Pardon of all their Sins, for which they ſhall be truly contrite in Heart, and confeſs with their Mouths, and do pro-miſe them an Encreaſe of eternal Salvation at the Retribution of the Juſt. And as to thoſe who ſhall not go thither in their own Perſons, but only ſhall appoint proper Perſons, according to their Ability and Faculty, maintaining them at their own Ex-pences; and as to thoſe alſo who go thither in their own Perſons, tho' at the Expence of others, we grant them full Pardon of all their Sins. We alſo will and grant, that all ſhall be Partakers of the ſame Remiſſion, according to the Nature of their Aſ-ſiſtance, and the Affection of their Devotion, who ſhall agreeably miniſter of their Subſtance towards the Relief of the ſaid holy Land, or ſhall give proper Counſel or Ad-vice in the aforeſaid Matters. The holy and univerſal Synod alſo doth unanimouſly beſtow the Aſſiſtance of their Prayers and Bleſſings upon all in common, who piouſly proceed in this Work, that it may worthily profit them to Salvation.*

In verb. *Indulg.* §. *Item. Inquiſito-ros.*   This plenary Indulgence the Repertory of the Inquifition extends fo far, as that the Inquifitors ſhall not only obtain it once in their Lives, but by all perfect Acts whatfoever, that are celebrated againſt Hereticks, in Favour and to the Praife of the Faith.

CHAP. XIV.

Of the AMPLITUDE *of the* JURISDICTION *of the* INQUISITORS.

BEcaufe the Inquifitors are Judges delegated by the Pope in the Caufe of Faith, that all Herefy may be wholly extirpated according to the Pope's Pleafure, Power is given them in Favour of the Faith, of proceeding againſt all forts of Perfons whatfoever. Few only are excepted. The Inquifitor can't proceed againſt the Officials and Legates of the Apoftolick See, nor againſt Biſhops; but he may give Notice of their Crimes to the Apoftolick See. *Ex-trav.*

trav. de hæret. c. 3. and *cap. Inquifitores. de hæret. lib.* 6. *John* XXII. ordained the fame, when *Matthew de Pontiniano,* a Predicant, Inquifitor of heretical Bzovius, Pravity in the Kingdom of *Sicily,* pronounced Sentence of Excommunication *a.* 1316. againft *G. de Baleto,* Archdeacon of *Forli,* and Chaplain to the Pope. But *§. 9.* *Pius* IV. by an Extravagant, beginning, *Romanus Pontifex,* in the Year 1563. ordained, that the Cardinals Inquifitors General over all Chriftendom, might proceed againft Bifhops, and all other Prelates whatfoever, and admonifh and cite them, and require their perfonal Appearance within a certain Term, and that under grievous Penalties; that fo when the Procefs is formed, it may be reported to the moft holy Lord, and that the deferved and juft Punifhment may be publifhed againft them.

As to fuch Religious as were exempt, there was formerly a great Variety *Direct.* about the Power of proceeding againft them. For *Alexander* IV. by a cer- *Par.* 3. tain Refcript, beginning, *Ne commiffæ vobis, Anno* 1260. ordained, that the *Qu.* 28. Inquifitors fhould proceed, without Diftinction, againft all manner of reli- *Com.* 77. gious and exempt Perfons whatfoever. The fame alfo was ordained by others. But *Pius* II. about the Year 1460. granted to the Vicar of the Order of the Friars Minors, that he fhould make Inquifition, and punifh his own Friars fufpected concerning the Faith, or of Herefy. A few Years after *Sixtus* ordained by a golden Bull, beginning, *Sacri Prædicatorum* ; which may be feen in the Book of the Privileges of the Predicant Order, *fol.* 163. that the Predicants fhall not proceed againft the Friars Minors, nor the Minors againft the Predicants, in thofe Places where they exercife the Office of the Inquifition. A few Years after this, *Innocent* VIII. forbid all the Inquifitors to proceed in any Manner, or make Inquifition againft the Friars Minors, as appears from the Apoftolick Letters written about this Affair, contain'd in a Book entitled, *Fundamentum trium Ordinum beati Francifci.*

But whereas thefe Immunities were fometimes manifeftly dangerous to the Faith, the later Popes have fubjected all religious or otherwife exempted Perfons, in the Caufe of Faith, as formerly, to the Inquifitors of heretical Pravity. Thus *Clement* VII. by a Refcript, beginning, *Cum ficut* ; and *Pius* Simanc.' IV. by another beginning, *Paftoris æterni* ; for which Reafon it was declared *tit.* 34. by *Charles* V. Emperor in *Spain,* That the Soldiers of St. *James,* if they *§.* 32. fhould happen to be Hereticks, are not exempted from the ordinary Jurifdiction, nor from that of the Inquifitors. The fame Rule alfo is entirely to be obferved as to the Soldiers of St. *John,* and as to all others whatfoever.

In fome particular Religions, the Order is prefcribed, which muft be obferved in denouncing heretical or fufpected Friars ; whereby the Prior of the Convent muft make the Denunciation to the Provincial, the Provincial to the General, and the General to the Office of the Inquifition. But that this round about Way may be avoided, when this Method cannot be fo conveniently obferved, the Prior alone may make the Denunciation, or any other in his Room upon his Abfence, that the Caufe of Faith may not be delay'd.

E e But

But although the Inquisitors may thus proceed against all religious and exempt Persons, yet there are some religious against whom private Inquisitors are not easily allow'd to proceed, because of the Prerogative of their Dignity. Such are the Masters General of Orders, of the Predicants, Minors, and the like; and also the Masters General of the Military Religions. When such are to be proceeded against, the proper Way is, first to inform the Inquisitors General, who, upon taking Cognizance of the Cause, must decree what is necessary to be done, unless the Criminal attempts to escape, and their appears Danger in Delay.

Direct.
Par. 3.
Qu. 29.
per cap.
Accusatus.
§ Sacerdotes.
Extra. de haeret.
Qu. 31.

Farther, the Inquisitor hath Power to proceed against Priests. *Moreover, the Priests and others of the Clergy, who shall be found to hinder the Office of the Inquisition, either by instructing Hereticks and their 'Believers, when cited, to conceal the Truth, or speak Falsehood, or by endeavouring unlawfully to deliver them, may in such Cases, since 'tis certain they act in Favour of heretical Pravity, be restrained by the Inquisitors, and chastised with deserved Punishment, either by seizing their Persons, or otherwise, as the Fault of the Criminal shall require.*

And finally, they may proceed against all Laicks whatsoever, without Distinction, infected, suspected, or defamed of Heresy, of every Condition, not excepting Princes and Kings. In the latter Case they think it safer, when they proceed against Princes and Nobles that are Hereticks, or suspected of Heresy, to consult the Pope, according to whose Will, and Manner prescrib'd by him, they must proceed against them : Not for that they think any Deference is due to Nobility, which is forfeited by Heresy, but to prevent Scandal. For if the Inquisitors should publickly animadvert, on Nobles, Consuls, and Magistrates, they might easily be hinder'd, especially in suspected Places, and where the Inquisitors are poor and weak.

Moreover, they may proceed against all Persons whatsoever, of every Condition; and whatsoever Privileges they enjoy, if they any ways obstruct the Office of the Inquisition. Thus *Alexander* IV. commands in his Bull, beginning, *Cupientes. Let all Contraveners be punish'd by the Ecclesiastical Censure, without any Regard to their Appeal: Any Privileges or Indulgences whatsoever, granted by the said See, or hereafter to be granted, specially or generally, under whatsoever Expression or Form of Words, to any Persons of whatsoever Condition, Dignity, or Degree, Religion or Order, or to any Communities or Universities of Cities or Places, to the contrary notwithstanding. For by these or any other Privileges or Indulgences, we would not have an Affair of so great Piety obstructed.* The same Pope, in his Bull, beginning, *Ne commissum vobis,* commands, That if the Clergy and Religious do not assist the Inquisitors according to their Office and Power, they may be proceeded against according to the Canonical Sanctions, any Privileges to the contrary notwithstanding.

Cap. ut commissi de haeret. lib. 6.

The Inquisitors may also proceed against those, who have offended in their Province, and remove themselves to another; as also against those, who having offended any where else, are found in their Province. This is determined by the Council of *Narbonne,* cap. 19, 20, 21. *If there be any Criminal or Suspected Persons belonging to your Inquisition, you may freely proceed against them as if present,*

fent, though they are and have been abfent, if within a competent Time, perempto-
rily affigned by you to them, and publifhed in the Churches, they do not take Care
to appear, or lawfully excufe themfelves. For we judge that all belong to your In-
quifition, who have offended within the Bounds of the faid Inquifition, or who have,
or had any Dwelling there, when the Inquifition was began ; or who abide there up-
on Occafion of any publick or private Office, or fhall be found there, though they have
not any certain Dwelling, when cited by you, whether you laid them under any Secu-
rity or not, if you have begun to make any Inquifition againft them, or have com-
manded them to purge themfelves : For againft fuch you may and ought to proceed,
whether prefent or abfent ; unlefs any other Inquifitors have already began to proceed
againft them, upon Account of fome greater or leffer Fault, committed elfewhere, or
becaufe they have an Houfe, or for any other of the aforefaid Reafons. For fince the
Inquifition, of which God is the Author, is celebrated in different Places, and by
different Inquifitors, 'tis fafer and better that every Criminal, in whatfoever Places
he bath offended, fhould be fubject to one, viz. *to the Inquifitor of fuch Place, by*
whom he may have been firft apprehended, for any of the aforefaid Caufes, without
Fraud, and Danger of the Affair of Souls. Neverthelefs, let the other Inquifitors
make Inquifition as to every Thing they can difcover concerning him, and acquaint
thefe Inquifitors with it, to whom the faid Criminal is engaged. Thus will you fight
as it were as one Man, and fhall overcome. See alfo *Inftruct. Valadolit. A.* 1488.
Cap. 8.

In like Manner, when they want the Teftimony of other Perfons, they may *Direct.*
cite Witneffes from one Diocefe to another, notwithftanding the Conftitution *Par. 3.*
of the two Days Journey made in a General Council *.   But they fay this *Com. 123.*
muft be done with Prudence.   For Perfons of Diftinction are not eafily to be *Simanc.*
thus removed ; and therefore they muft be fo dealt with, that it may feem they *tit. 64.*
are rather entreated than compelled.   And leaft they fhould refufe to fubmit *§. 13.*
to the Power of the Inquifitors, they fay 'tis more decent and modeft for the
Judges to wait on them, or at leaft, to fend others to them to receive their Depofitions.   The fame muft be obferved as to all other illuftrious Perfons,
Nuns, and other honourable Women.   But then the Inquifitor muft determine what Decency and Modefty muft be ufed towards each of thefe, and
how the Caufes of Faith may receive the greateft Advantage, from the Dig-

---

* The Form of the Citation is thus :

To all and fingular Chriftians, as well Ecclefiafticks as Laicks of both Sexes, of whatfoever
Degree, Order, Condition, Pre-eminence, Dignity, or Authority, the higheft not excepted.
Know ye, That we, by the Series and Tenor of thefe Prefents, and by our Authority, and by that
of the Office we execute here, do Charge and Command, That within twelve Days after the
Publication hereof (the firft four of which, are to be as the firft, and the next four as the fecond,
and the laft four as a peremptory and third Canonical Admonition) all that do know or fufpect
any of Herefy, do come and inform againft them, upon Pain of the greater Excommunication
latæ Sententiæ, which fhall be *ipfo facto* incurred, and from which they cannot be abfolved by
any, but by our Lord the Pope, or by us.   And we do further Certify, That whofoever, defpifing the Penalty of this Excommunication, fhall forbear to inform us, fhall moreover be proceeded
againft as a *Favourer of Hereticks*. *Geddes* Tracts, *Vol.* I. *p.* 427, 428.

nity,

nity, Authority, Honourablenefs, and other Qualities of the Witneffes. We
have a famous Inftance how infolently the Inquifitors fometimes abufe this
Power, in *Joan*, Daughter of the Emperor *Charles* V. whom they cited before their Tribunal, to interrogate her concerning a certain Perfon, in fome
Matters relating to the Faith. The Emperor himfelf was fo afraid of this
Power, that he commanded his Daughter not to put off the Affair, but make
her Depofition without delay, to avoid the Sentence of Excommunication, as
well againft others as againft himfelf, if fhe believed him culpable in the
fmalleft Matter. Upon which the moft ferene *Joan* gave in immediately her
Depofition before *Fernand Valdez*, Archbifhop of *Seville*, at that Time Inquifitor General. But if the Bifhop or Inquifitor fends for Witneffes from any
other Diocefe, he is not obliged to fend the Procefs to the Bifhop of fuch
Diocefe ; nor can fuch Bifhop juftly demand it. On the contrary, he is obliged and bound to fend the Witneffes, after having read the Letters of the Bifhop who requires it, and fays he hath Need of this or the other Witnefs,
to give his Teftimony in the Caufe of Faith. The neceffary Witnefs
muft therefore be fent, and Care taken, if it can be done, that he may not
know that he is called to bear Witnefs againft any one in the Caufe of Faith,
leaft he fhould difcover the Affair, and fo obftruct it ; unlefs for other Reafons it ought to be done upon full Knowledge of the Probity and Fidelity of
the Witnefs.

　　In this Age the *Spanifh* Inquifition endeavoured, under a fpecious Pretence,
to extend its Jurifdiction over the Subjects of other Kings. According to the
Conventions and Treaties between the Kings of *England* and *Spain*, the *Englifh*,
who the *Spaniards* call Hereticks, were allow'd, upon the Account of Commerce and Trade, to dwell in the Countries of the Catholicks, upon this Condition, That they fhould not be molefted for any Matters relating to Religion
and Faith, unlefs they gave publick Offence ; in which Cafe they were to be
punifh'd in Proportion to the Scandal given, according to Law. *Antonius de
Soufa*, Counfellor of the Tribunal of the fupreme Inquifition in *Portugal*, enquires when the Inquifitors may proceed againft them, and gives many Limitations concerning fuch Hereticks, as they call them, whereby he fubjects
them entirely to the Power of the Inquifitors.

　　" And firft, he afferts, that the Condition that Hereticks fhall not be in-
" terrogated concerning the Faith, unlefs upon Account of Scandal, is of no
" Validity, if it is only fupported by the King's Authority ; but the Inqui-
" fitors have full Power to proceed againft them according to Law : Becaufe
" Lay Jurifdiction doth not extend to Matters Ecclefiaftical, and relating to
" the Faith. And therefore, unlefs that Condition be confirmed by the Pope,
" the Inquifitors may proceed againft any Perfon, as foon as ever it appears
" that he is an Heretick, whether he difcovers his Herefy in their Diftrict, or
" in any other ; becaufe an Heretick fins every where, and therefore may
" be taken and punifh'd any where. In this Cafe, if fuch Heretick hath re-
" ceived Inftruction, he may be compelled to keep the Faith ; if he hath not
" been inftructed, he may be oblig'd to receive it ; and if he refufes to accept
" it, he may be punifh'd as an Heretick. " But

Lud. Par.
de Orig.
S. Inquif.
l. 3. q. 5.
n. 23, &c.
& n. 40.

Apher Inq.
l. 1. c. 31.

" But if this Condition fhould be approv'd by the Pope, the Inquifitors
" may proceed againft Hereticks giving Scandal, and punifh them according
" to the Nature of it. And firft, he fays 'tis probable, that the Inquifitors
" may interrogate concerning the Faith, and oblige Hereticks that give
" Scandal, to receive Inftruction, or if inftructed, to forfake their Herefy :
" Becaufe the Condition ceafes by the Offence, and the Obftruction is remov'd,
" and the forefaid Hereticks remain within the Bounds of the Law. But that
" the Inquifitors may proceed thus far, they ought fully to prove that Here-
" ticks have given Scandal ; fince the giving this is the Condition that confers
" Jurifdiction. He thinks it however more probable, that when the Scandal is
" prov'd, the Inquifitors can punifh fuch Hereticks only for Scandal, and not
" for Herefy ; becaufe this feems to be excepted by Virtue of the Condition
" which the Pope hath approved. So that the Offence of Scandal gives no
" Jurifdiction over any other Offence that is excepted.

" As to Scandal, he faith, That any one who gives it, not only in *Spain*,
" but to any Catholick on the *Spanifh* Sea, may be punifhed as well as if he
" had given it by Land; but not if it was given in his own Country, or
" elfewhere without the Bounds of *Spain*.

" But if any of the aforefaid Hereticks fhall be accufed to the Inquifitors for
" any foreign heretical Act, before fuch Treaty of Commerce, and after-
" wards comes to *Spain*, notwithftanding fuch Treaty, he may be apprehend-
" ed, and obliged to receive the Faith. For the Inquifitors, by the preceed-
" ing Denunciation, have acquired a Power againft fuch Hereticks, which
" Power is not taken away by the Treaty of Commerce. If any one removes
" his Dwelling from *Spain* into *England*, to efcape the Judgment of the Inqui-
" fitors, although he fhould not be accufed before, but after the Treaty, of
" an heretical Act committed before it, he cannot enjoy any Benefit by it;
" becaufe he ought not to be countenanced in his Fraud.

" As to the Sorts of Scandal for which fuch an Heretick may be punifh'd,
" they are thefe, *viz.* If by Reafons, Perfuafions, or any other Way, he en-
" deavours to perfuade any Catholick to embrace his Sect, or any Error
" againft the Faith, or to turn him afide from the Catholick Doctrine, or
" Purity of Faith ; if he profanes the Sacraments, or doth any Injury to
" them, or to holy Images, if he doth not rife in Prefence of the Hoft, or
" covers his Head before it, with other Things of the like Nature.

" The Punifhment of fuch Perfons upon thefe Accounts is arbitrary, greater
" or lefs, according to the Nature of the Scandal. If it be very heinous, they
" may be turned over to the fecular Court. They may not be forced to
" make that Abjuration, which, according to Law, is enjoyn'd to Hereticks
" or fufpected Perfons ; becaufe even fufpected Perfons are not judged for He-
" refy only, nor do they return to the Catholick Faith. But they may be
" obliged to fwear, that as long as they remain in that Kingdom, or in any
" Places fubject to it, they will not commit any Fault whatfoever againft
" the Catholick Faith.

One may eafily infer from this Doctrine of *Soufa*, what the Subjects of *Great Britain*, and other Kingdoms and States muft expect, if all Things are to be done according to the Pleafure of the Inquifitors, and how little Safety they will find by fuch Treaties againft the Violence of the Inquifitors, unlefs they are protected by the Authority of their King, againft thefe their vile and unrighteous Practices. [Of this we have a noble Inftance given us by *Oliver Cromwel*, Protector of *England*. *Thomas Maynard*, Conful of the *Englifh* Nation at *Lisbon*, was thrown into the Prifon of the Inquifition, under Pretence that he had faid or done fomething againft the *Roman* Religion. *M. Meadows*, who was then Refident, and took Care of the *Englifh* Affairs at *Lisbon*, advifed *Cromwel* of the Affair ; and after having received an Exprefs from him, went to the King of *Portugal*, and in the Name of *Cromwel*, demanded the Liberty of Conful *Maynard*. The King told him, 'twas not in his Power, that the Conful was detained by the Inquifition, over which he had no Authority. The Refident fent this Anfwer to *Cromwel*, and having foon after received new Inftructions from him, had again Audience of the King, and told him, That fince his Majefty had declared he had no Power over the Inquifition, he was commanded by *Cromwel*, to declare War againft the Inquifition. This unexpected Declaration fo terrified the King and the Inquifition, that they immediately determined to free the Conful from Prifon ; and immediately opened the Prifon Doors, and gave him Leave to go out. The Conful refufed to accept a private Difmiffion, but in order to repair the Honour of his Character, demanded to be honourably brought forth by the Inquifition. The fame *Maynard* continu'd many Years after under the fame Character, in the Reigns of *Charles* and *James* II. and liv'd at *Lisbon* till he was about eighty Years old, without any Moleftation from the Inquifition. This Story was well known to all foreign Merchants, who lived at that Time, and many Years after at *Lisbon*.]

CHAP. XV.

Of the Power of the INQUISITORS.

Direct.
Par. 3.
Qu. 32.
cap. Abolendam.
§. Statuimus, de
hæret.

THAT the Inquifitor may difcharge his Duty without any Hindrance, Power is given him to compel the Governors of Cities to fware that they will defend the Church againft Hereticks. *We ordain moreover, that the Earls, Barons, Governors and Confuls of Cities and other Places, fhall take their corporal Oath at the Admonition of the Bifhop, and fwear that they will faithfully, effectually and fincerely affift the Church, according to their Office and utmoft Power, againft Hereticks and their Accomplices, when required by the Bifhops: And if they refufe to do this, let them be deprived of that Honour which they poffefs, and never be raifed to any other. Let them farther be excommunicated, and their*
Countries

Countries put under the Interdict of the Church. If any City shall think fit to op-pose these Injunctions, or neglect to punish those who do, at the Admonition of the Bi-shop, let their Commerce with other Cities be cut off, and let them know that they are deprived of the Episcopal Dignity. We ordain moreover, that the Chief Ma- Cap. ut *gistrate, Head Officer, Ruler or Confuls, or any others who preside over any City or* Officium. *other Place, either now, or who shall preside over it hereafter, shall, at the Command* §. Statut-*of the Diocefan, or his Vicars, or the Inquifitors of heretical Pravity, fware that* hæret. lib. *they will precifely regard, and inviolably obferve, and cause to be obferved by their* 6. *Subjects, during the whole Time of their Government, in the Countries subject to their Jurifdiction or Government, the Conftitutions promulgated and approved by the Apoftolick See, against Hereticks, their Believers, Receivers, Favourers and Defen-ders, and against their Children and Grand-children. And whofoever will not fware, and obferve them, let him be deprived of the Office and Honour of his Government, as infamous, and as a Favourer of Hereticks, and fufpected concerning the Faith; and let him no longer be accounted as a Chief Magiftrate, Head Officer, Conful or Ruler in any Place, nor ever after be advanced to any Dignity or publick Office. And whatever he doth as Chief Magiftrate, Ballive, Conful or Ruler, let it be null and void.*

To this there is another Oath annexed, *viz.* to extirpate with all their Qu. 33. Power, from their Countries, thofe who are noted for Hereticks by the Church, which the Inquifitor may compel all temporal Lords, having perpetual or temporal Jurifdiction, to take. *Let all fecular Powers, whatever be their Offices,* Cap. Ex-*be admonifhed and perfuaded, and, if it be neceffary, compelled by the Church, that* communi-*as they defire to be accounted and held as faithful, they publickly take an Oath for* itaque, *Defence of the Faith, that they will endeavour with all their Might, in good Faith* de hæret. *to root out of all Countries subject to their Jurifdiction, all Perfons declared Hereticks* §. Mone-*by the Church. And at the Time that any Perfon is advanced to any perpetual or* antur. *temporary Dignity, let him be obliged to confirm this Article by an Oath.* Thus also the Council of *Biterre*, cap. 32. *Let the Earls, Barons, Rulers, Confuls and Bal-* Par. 3. *lives of Cities, and other Places, fwear, that they will faithfully and effectually,* Com. 4; *when required by them, affift the Church against Hereticks and their Accomplices, according to their Office, and the utmoft of their Power; and that they will in good Faith endeavour with all their Might, to exterminate out of all Countries subject to their Jurifdiction, all Perfons declared Hereticks by the Church.* Thus also the Council of *Tholoufe. We forbid also the Prelates, Barons, Gentlemen, and all Per-* Cap 16. *fons of Eftates, to give the Stewardfhip and Management of their Lands to Here-ticks and their Believers. Neither let them prefume to have or keep in their Family or their Counfel, fuch Perfons, nor any defamed for Herefy, or who they believe to be fufpected of it.* And finally the Council of *Biterre* commands, that *Hereticks shall* Cap. 28; *not be entrufted with Stewardfhips, or Adminiftrations, nor fuffered to be in the Coun-fels or Families of the Great. Pegna* remarks here, that in the 6th Council of *Toledo*, held 686. there is a Paffage concerning the Kings of *Spain, That when* Cap. 3. *they come to the Kingdom, they shall not afcend the Royal Throne, till amongst other Stipulations by Oath, they have promifed that they will not fuffer any Perfons who are not Catholicks to remain in their Kingdom. This*, fays he, *I wifh was every where recalled into Ufe, and inviolably maintained.* The

Q. 33. The Inquifitors may alfo compel the temporal Lords to revoke all Statutes
Cap. *Sta-* that hinder the Office of the Inquifition. *Let not any Statute of any City, Caftle,*
tutum, de *Town, or other Place, by which the Affair of the Inquifition of heretical Pravity is*
hæret. l. 6. *directly or indirectly hindred, or any ways retarded, fo that ye cannot freely proceed*
therein, be of any Force whatfoever. And we decree, that the Lord, chief Magi-
ftrate, Head Officer, Confuls or Rulers of fuch City and Place, by whom the faid
City or Place is governed, under whatfoever Name, fhall be compelled by Ecclefiafti-
cal Cenfure, to difcover fuch Statute to the Diocefan of the Place, or his Vicars, or the
Inquifitor, or Inquifitors of heretical Pravity, without Delay. And if it fhall be found
fuch, let it be entirely repealed, or at leaft fo far moderated, that the Proceffes of the
Inquifition be not hindred thereby, or in any wife retarded.

P. 3. Farther, the fecular Magiftrates are exprefsly commanded to feize and keep
Com. 1. in Cuftody Hereticks at the Inquifitors Demand, and to carry them wherefo-
Cap. *Ut* ever they order. *That the Affair of the Inquifition againft Hereticks may go on*
Inquifiti- *profperoufly in our Times, to the Glory of God, and the Encreafe of the Faith, we*
onis, de *approve and order to be obferved certain Laws publifhed by* Frederick, *formerly Em-*
hæret. *peror of the* Romans, *then remaining in his Devotion to the Church of* Rome, *as*
lib. 6. *far as they promote the Honour of God, and his holy Church. We therefore require*
and admonifh all fecular Magiftrates and temporal Lords, and the Governors of Pro-
vinces, Lands, Cities, and other Places, by whatfoever Dignities, Offices or Names
they may be diftinguifhed, that as they defire to be efteemed and held as faithful, they
obey the Diocefan Bifhops, and Inquifitors of heretical Pravity, deputed, or hereafter
to be deputed by the Apoftolick See, in all Things relating to the Defence of the Faith;
and that when required by them, they endeavour to feize, and keep in fafe Cuftody
Hereticks, their Believers, Favourers, Receivers, and Defenders; and that without
Delay they carry or order to be carried the aforefaid Perfons into the Power or Jail
of the Bifhops, or the faid Inquifitors, or to any other Place which they or any of them
fhall command within the Power of the faid Lords, or the Diftrict of fuch Rulers,
where they fhall be kept in clofe and fafe Cuftody by Catholick Perfons, deputed by the
aforefaid Bifhops, or Inquifitors, or any one of them, till their Affair is determined
by the Judgment of the Church. The Law of the Emperor *Frederick* here referred to, begins, *Commiffi vobis;* the third Section of which is this: *Farthermore,*
whatfoever Hereticks fhall be found in Cities, Towns, or other Places of the Em-
pire, by the Inquifitors deputed by the Apoftolick See, and other Orthodox Perfons, zea-
lous for the Faith, let fuch as have Authority there, be obliged to apprehend them at
the Notice of the Inquifitors, and other Catholick Perfons, and when apprehended,
to keep them in ftrict Cuftody, till being condemned by Ecclefiaftical Cenfure, they pe-
rifh by an accurfed Death, who have condemned the Sacraments of Faith and Life.
Thus alfo *Innocent* IV. by a Refcript, beginning, *Ad extirpanda,* commands,
Let every Magiftrate or Ruler, caufe the faid Hereticks, when taken, to be carried,
at the Expence of the Place where he prefides, wherefoever the Diocefan or his Vicars
fhall order, within the Jurifdiction or Diftrict of fuch Diocefan, Bifhop, City, or
Place. And that thefe Words relate to the Inquifitors alfo, the Beginning and
whole Subftance of that Refcript fhews, which *Clement* IV. hath alfo declared
by another Refcript, beginning, *Ad extirpanda.*

And

And finally, the Emperor *Frederick* hath commanded by the fame Law, all Governors, as well Ecclefiaftical as Secular, kindly to receive the Inquifitors, and defend them againft the Incurfions of Hereticks, §. 10. *We hereby declare, that we take under our fpecial and Imperial Protection the preaching Friars of the Predicant Order, deputed for the Affair of the Faith againft Hereticks in the feveral Parts of our Empire ; as alfo all others fent for, and who come to judge Hereticks, unlefs any of them be profcribed by the Empire, where-ever they go, abide, or return ; and 'tis our Pleafure that they receive no Offence from any, but that they receive the Affiftance, and have the Recommendation of all the Faithful of the Empire. We therefore command you, and all of you, that wherefoever, and to whomfoever of you they come, ye receive them kindly, and preferve their Perfons free from the Incurfions of Hereticks that lie in wait for them, and that ye grant them all Counfel, fafe Conduct, and Affiftance, in their Execution of Affairs fo acceptable before God.*

The Inquifitors may alfo exact an Oath from the Magiftrates, for their obferving not only the Laws of the Emperor *Frederick* againft Hereticks, but all other Statutes as well Ecclefiaftical as Secular, as appears from two Refcripts of *Innocent* IV. beginning, *Orthodoxæ fidei*. The fame hath been particularly decreed by the Council of *Biterre*, cap. 31. *And that by the Help of the Lord Herefy may be the better and more fpeedily extirpated, and the Faith planted in the Earth, fee that the Statutes and Laws made concerning thefe Things by the Apoftolick See, and its Legates, and the Princes, be moft exactly obferved.* *Com. 3.*

As there are many Difficulties that daily arife in the Punifhment of Hereticks, and the Caufes of Faith, which are not fully and plainly determined by the Laws, for this Reafon, and to prevent the Neceffity of confulting the Pope in all doubtful Cafes, *Innocent* IV. by a Refcript, beginning, *Cum negotium* : and *Alexander* IV. by another, beginning, *Præ cunctis*, gave to the Inquifitors free Power of interpreting the Ecclefiaftical and Secular Statutes againft Hereticks, their Believers, Favourers, &c. as often as there appears in them any Thing ambiguous or obfcure. This is certainly a very large Power, which the *Seville* Inftructions have alfo granted to the Inquifitors. *Inft. 1. cap.* 28. *Direct. part. 3. qu. 85. com. 12.*

Simancas obferves here, " That fmaller Matters only, and fuch as 'tis impoffible to bring within the Laws, are left to the Determination of the " Inquifitors, and that they cannot of themfelves decide Matters of greater " Moment, which the Laws have not, but that they muft confult the Inqui- " fitor General and Senate about them. He adds, that even as to thofe " Things which are left to themfelves, they muft not judge according to their " own Will and Pleafure, but conformable to the Statutes and Laws ; nor " follow their own Confcience, unlefs it be entirely informed by the Laws." *Tit. 34. §. 34, 35.*

[*Paramus* is of the fame Mind with *Simancas*, altho', as he fays, " The Words " of the *Seville* Inftruction, *cap*. 28. feem to imply the contrary. For thus " they order. *It muft be left to the Pleafure and Prudence of the Inquifitors, to* " *proceed according to the Difpofition of the Law, in thofe Things which are not ex-* " *prefsly declared, and according to their own Confcience.* However, *Paramus* *Lib. 2. tit. 2. cap. 4. n. 3, 4, &c.*

" thinks,

"thinks, that if thefe Words are ftrictly examined, they will import no-
"thing more, than that thofe Caufes of the Faith, which are left to the Plea-
"fure of the Inquifitors, muft be judged and decided according to the San-
"ctions of the Laws. And thus the Judges muft fatisfy their Confcien-
"ces, becaufe the Words of the Inftructions, as of all other Statutes, re-
"ceive their Interpretation according to the common Law. Now, accord-
"ing to the Difpofition of the Law, the Judge muft form his Judgment,
"not according to his Confcience, but according to the Allegations and
"Proofs. *From which this is inferred, that tho' the Judge certainly knows in his*
"*Confcience, that the Perfon accufed is not guilty of the Crime, yet if he be convicted*
"*by Proofs againft him, the Judge ought, and without Sin may condemn him.* How-
"ever, *Paramus* believes it to be fafer, and more agreeable to Religion, for
"the Judge, in fuch a Cafe, to excufe himfelf from acting, and to defire of
"his Prince that the Caufe may be delegated to fome other, or he may thus
"delegate it to another himfelf.] But *Camillus Campegius* thinks, that all.
"Things, which the Laws have not fo clearly determined, are left to the In-
"quifitors Declaration or Interpretation; that whatever Things are obfcure
"and ambiguous, may be expounded and declared by the Inquifitor; and,
"that therefore whatever is not determined by the Law is committed to the
"Pleafure of the Judge." *Soufa* gives a yet larger Power to the Inquifitors,
"and allows not only that they can interpret what the Laws and Statutes have
"not, if any Thing doubtful occurs, but that " when there are feverally equal-
"ly probable Opinions in any Cafe, they may follow which they will, and
"when there is no Scandal, judge fometimes according to one, and fometimes
"to another. He adds, that 'tis more likely, that the Inquifitor cannot fol-
"low the lefs probable Opinion, unlefs it happens to be more eftablifhed.
"by Cuftom, and he knows that the Sentence will be repealed by the fu-
"pream Council."

In Zanch. *c.* 17.

Aphor. Inq. *l* 2. *c.* 1. §. 11, 12.

'Tis alfo further granted to the Inquifitors, ever fince the Beginning of the
delegated Inquifition, that for the Defence of their Perfon and Family, and
the better to apprehend Hereticks, their Receivers, Favourers, &c. they
may have their Officials, and an armed Attendance, and bear Arms themfelves. But becaufe it often happens, that Abufes creep in under the Pretence
of Privilege, unlefs fuch Privilege be wifely ufed, *Clement* V. in the Council
of *Vienne*, about the Year 1310. confirmed this Privilege to the Inquifitors,
but took away the Abufe that had crept in. Cap. *Nolentes* in Clement. §. *porro.*
Moreover, we ftrictly forbid the Inquifitors, in any manner to abufe their Privilege
of wearing Arms, and to have any other Officials but fuch as are neceffary to
help them in the Execution of their Office. And this Privilege is fo peculiar
to the Inquifitors in Favour of the Faith, and from the Hatred of heretical
Pravity, that their Officials, who in *Italy* are called *Crofs-bearers,* and in *Spain*
Familiars, and who are commanded by the Holy Office to denounce or apprehend Hereticks, or to wait on the Inquifitor whenever he commands it, may
carry Arms either by Night or by Day, any civil or municipal Law made, or
to be made, to the contrary notwithftanding. If indeed any one fhould make a
Law

Qu. 56.

Com. 105.

Law to prohibit the Officials of the Inquifitors to wear Arms, he might be *Qu.* 57. punifhed as an Hinderer of the Holy Office. If the Inquifitors own Servants are *c. ut offi-* not fufficient, he may call in the Aid of the fecular Arm. *Finally, that you and* *cium.* *every one of you may have immediate and inviolable Power of apprehending Perfons* *§. denique.* *concerning the aforefaid, we will, that in order to the more ufefully executing all thefe* *Things, you may, when there is Need, call in the Affiftance of the fecular Arm, and* *put all Contraveners under Ecclefiaftical Cenfure, without Benefit of Appeal.*

The Inquifitors may alfo punifh thofe, who prefume to injure them in Word Simanc. or Deed; and fo much the rather, becaufe they think that their Office *tit.* 34. ought to be efteemed more holy and venerable than that of all other Judges *§.* 28. whatfoever.

They may compel any Witnefs, even tho' a Perfon of Diftinction, to ap- pear before them, and to give Evidence in a Caufe of the Catholick Faith. But this is fo explained by *Campegius,* " As that the Inquifitor can only compel *In* Zanch " the Witnefs to give his Evidence, when it doth not expofe him to any *cap.* 13. *d* " imminent Danger ; if it doth, he cannot be compelled. The Judge may " alfo force them to appear, by forming a Procefs againft them, that they " 'refufe to appear and bear Witnefs, becaufe corrupted by the Criminal " with Money, which obliges them to be forth coming, leaft they fhould " be falfely condemned. If any refufe to appear, the Judge may cite them, " and proceed againft them ; and if they dont't then appear, he will treat " them as actually corrupted. He may farther punifh them for Contumacy " with Confifcation of their Effects." Thefe are the different Opinions of the Doctors, as alledged by *Campegius.*

Befides this the Inquifitors may compel the Witneffes to give Evidence, by Caren. threatning them with a Fine, or taking Pledges from them, by Excommuni- *part.* 3. cation and Torture. *Carena* tells us, that in the fupream Inquifition at *Rome,* a *tit.* 7. certain Perfon was forced by Torture to take the Oath which he refufed. *§. 1. n. 7.*

If the Advocates or Notaries give any Affiftance or Help to Hereticks, or their Favourers, the Inquifitors muft proceed againft them. *Since a fpecial In-* Direct. *junction is ufually more regarded than a general Command, we ftrictly forbid you Ad-* *Qu.* 39. *vocates and Notaries from granting in any Inftance your Help, Counfel or Favour to* *Hereticks, their Believers, Favourers or Defenders, and from giving them your Af-* *fiftance in Caufes or Facts, or to any who make any Difputes under their Examina-* *tion, and from drawing for them in any wife publick Inftruments or Writings ; which* *if any one fhall prefume to do, he fhall be fufpended from his Office, and be fubject to* *perpetual Infamy.* cap. *fi adverfus nos.* de hæret.

They have Power alfo to command thofe who have Proceffes, or any Cap. *ut* other Inftruments drawn againft Hereticks, to deliver them to them. *We grant* committi *you alfo the Power of caufing all Perfons to deliver to you the Books, or Regifters,* vobis. de *and other Writings in which the Inquifitions and Proceffes againft Hereticks, carried* hæict. l.6. *on by any by the Authority of the Apoftolick See, or its Legates, are contained.* A- lexander IV. ordained the fame by a Refcript, beginning, *Cupientes,* fent to Com. 88. the *Predicant* Friars, Inquifitors of heretical Pravity in *Lombardy,* and the Marquifate of *Genoa: Defiring that the Affair of the Inquifition againft heretical* *Pravity,*

Pravity, committed to your Care, may happily profper in your Hands, to the Glory of God, and Increafe of the Catholick Faith, we by Authority of thefe prefent, grant to you, and every one of you, the Power of compelling by the Ecclefiaftical Cenfure, either by your felves, or by others, whom you or any one of you fhall judge proper for this Bufinefs, all thofe who have, or have had any Writings or Inftruments of the Inquifition, or belonging to this Office, made hitherto by any, or to be made, againft Hereticks, their Believers, Receivers, Favourers or Defenders, to deliver them to you, or fome one of you, without any Difficulty or Danger of Delay, without allowing them any Benefit of Appeal.

From this Refcript they infer, that the Criminal, in a Caufe of Herefy, is obliged to deliver the proper Inftruments againft himfelf to the Fifcal, from which he may gather his Intention, and form his Accufation ; although regularly the contrary is determined by Law ; and not only againft himfelf, but againft every other Perfon the Fifcal proceeds againft ; which though it doth not take place in other Cafes, yet doth in Favour of the Faith. So that if *Titius* is apprehended for Herefy, and delivers an heretical Book, or the like, to *Sempronius*, *Sempronius* is to be compelled to produce it not only againft himfelf, but againft *Titius* too. And what in this Cafe is faid of Books and Writings, extends to all other Things which may help to find out the Truth, which are to be all given in, in Favour of the Faith.

Calder. *de modo pro- ced. cont. hæret. f.* 411. Excommunication alfo is a Branch of the Inquifitorial Power, which they have a very ample Power of inflicting, becaufe their Excommunication is more heavy than that of others, and that in a fourfold Refpect. Firft, becaufe whoever are excommunicated by them, muft be put under the Ban by a publick Edict and Proclamation. Secondly, their Effects muft be confifcated, and the Inquifitors may compel the Magiftrates and Governors to both. This appears from a certain Privilege of *Innocent* IV. beginning, *Cum Fratres Prædicatores* ; in which he writes to the Barons, and other Lords, and Governors, and Cities, faying, *We have thought it meet to befeech, exhort and admonifh all of you, and ftrictly charge you, by our Apoftolick Writings, and command that all thofe who fhall be excommunicated, and declared publickly to be excommunicated, by the faid Inquifitors, or others at their Command, for the Crime of Herefy, or for defending, receiving, or favouring Hereticks, be put under the publick Ban, and have all their Effects confifcated.* Thirdly, becaufe fuch who are excommunicated by the Inquifitors, and perfift with an obftinate Mind for the Space of a Year under Excommunication, muft be judged as Hereticks, and become fubject to the Punifhments publifhed againft Hereticks. As appears from the Law of the Emperor *Frederick*, beginning, *Patarenorum* ; and from many other Laws. Fourthly, becaufe they can excommunicate with the greater Excommunication all who partake with Perfons excommunicated by them, fuch as Hereticks, their Believers, Favourers, Receivers and Defenders, according to the Bulls of *Innocent* and *Alexander* IV. beginning, *Noverit univerfitas veftra. But if any fhall contemptuoufly refufe to avoid fuch Perfons, after being marked out by the Church, let them be excommunicated, and otherwife punifhed with due Severity.*

They

They have alſo Authority to excommunicate Lay Perſons diſputing concerning the Faith, publickly or privately ; as alſo all who do not diſcover Hereticks either by themſelves or ſome other Perſon, as appears from theſe Letters of the Popes.

Farther, the Power of the Inquiſitors was formerly very great, becauſe Cap. *ut*
they could reſerve to themſelves the Authority of encreaſing or leſſening the *commiſſi.*
enjoined Penances. *We alſo grant you Power, when you ſhall think it proper, to* de hæret:
mitigate or change, in Concert with the Prelates, to whoſe Juriſdiction they are ſub- lib. 6.
*ject, the Puniſhment of thoſe, who are ſhut up in Priſon or Jayl, if they humbly
obey your Commands.* The Inquiſitors may alſo encreaſe the Penances enjoined
to ſuch who are converted upon account of their Indevotion, Wickedneſs, or
Quarrelling, *i. e.* if they don't bear their Impriſonment with Patience, or
if there be any other Tokens, that they don't in all Things obey the Beck
of the Inquiſitors. This the Council of *Narbonne* hath ordered the Inquiſitors
to take Care of. Cap. 7. *This Reſtriction always carefully obſerved, that it ſhall
be lawful for you, or other Inquiſitors, or thoſe to whom the Church of* Rome *ſhall
think fit to commit this Affair, or thoſe to whoſe Office it belongs, at any time, and
for every reaſonable Cauſe, to add to, or take from the Penances enjoined them, according to your Will and Pleaſure.* Yea, this Power was given to the Inquiſitors
by the Council of *Biterre, Cap.* 22. even though there ſhould be no freſh Reaſon for it. *You ſhall always retain this Power, of ſending the aforeſaid Hereticks
to Jayl, without any new Cauſe, when you ſhall judge it expedient for the Affair of
the Faith.* Hence we find, that in the Book of the Sentences of the *Tholouſe*
Inquiſition, the Inquiſitors ordinarily reſerve this Power to themſelves. When
they ſhew Grace to condemned Perſons, and releaſe them from wearing their
Croſſes, and enjoin them other Penances in the room of this, ſuch as Pilgrimages, viſiting of Churches, and the like, they add ; *Reſerving to our ſelves* fol. 85.*b.*
*and Succeſſors in this Office, the Power of adding to, leſſening, and commuting in all
the aforeſaid, and of enjoining them to wear their Croſſes, if it ſhall ſeem good to us
and our Succeſſors, even without any freſh Cauſe.* When they bring them out of
Jayl, and change the Puniſhment of Impriſonment into that of wearing the
Croſs, or any others, they add ; *Reſerving to us, and every one of us, and our* fol. 100.*.*
*Succeſſors in the Office of the Inquiſition, full Power over the aforeſaid Perſons, and
every one of them, of bringing them back, and recalling to the aforeſaid Priſon, even
without any freſh Cauſe* ; *as alſo of encreaſing or leſſening, mitigating, or remitting in
the aforeſaid, if it ſhall ſeem convenient, to us, or any one of us, or our Succeſſors.*
Nor do they reſerve this Power to themſelves only, in conferring Graces, but
even in the pronouncing Sentences. Thus this Caution is ordinarily ſubjoined to
thoſe Sentences, by which Priſoners are condemned to wear Croſſes. *Reſerving to our ſelves and our Succeſſors in this Office, the Power of encreaſing, diminiſhing, mitigating, commuting, or even of remitting the aforeſaid Penance or Puniſhment.* But when they condemn any one to Impriſonment, they ſubjoin a larger Caution, and more fully expreſſed. *We reſerve to our ſelves, and to our
Succeſſors in this Office, full and free Power of mitigating, diminiſhing, encreaſing,
commuting, or even of remitting the aforeſaid Penance or Puniſhment* ; *as alſo of paſ-*

fing other Sentences upon any one or more of the aforefaid, if they fhall be found mali-cioufly to have fuppreffed any Things concerning the Fact of Herefy, or to have in-volved any innocent Perfon in the faid Crime of Herefy. Even though they fhould have forgot to have added this Caution to their Sentences, the Doctors how-ever think, that the Inquifitor hath and may exercife the Power of encreafing, diminifhing, remitting and commuting the enjoined Penances. *Per Cap.* Ut commiffi. *de hæret. lib.* 6.

Royas, *Affert.* 48. *part,* 2. But now this Power is not granted to the Inquifitors in *Spain.* For this kind of Difpenfation belongs at this Day there, only to the Inquifitor General, becaufe the Inquifitors and Ordinaries have already difcharged their Office. *Inftruct. Hifpal. cap.* 7. and *Tolet. cap.* 9. *Hift. Concil. Trid.* l. 6. p. 550.

CHAP. XVI.

Of the POWER *of the* INQUISITORS *in prohibiting* BOOKS.

THAT this may be more diftinctly explained, and that it may be known what and how great the Power is which is committed to the Inquifitors, concerning the Prohibition of Books ; I fhall give you an Ac-count of this Affair from the very Rife and Origin of it.

l. 8. c. 2. The firft of whom we read, who prohibited Books of Religion, was *Antio-chus Epiphanes,* whofe Servants are faid to *have rent in Pieces the Books of the Law, which they found, and to have burnt them with Fire ; and to have put to Death every one with whom was found the Book of the Teftament, or who confented to the Law,* 1 Maccab. i. 56, 57. *Dioclefian* was the next, that moft cruel Perfecutor of the Chriftian Faith ; of whom *Eufebius* relates, that by an Edict, he commanded *the facred Books to be burnt with Fire.* Yea, he adds in

Baron, *a.* 302. *n.* 22. the fame Chapter ; *We faw with our Eyes the facred Books of the divine Scriptures burnt in the publick Forum.* Farther, the Prefidents in every Province, City, Town and Village, took Care that the Chriftians fhould deliver up their fa-cred Books, and they compelled them to it by moft grievous Torments. Hence all thofe were called *Traditores,* Deliverers up of the Scripture, who terrified by fuch cruel Punifhments, delivered up the Books which they had.

Socrates, *Ec. Hift* l. 1. c. 6. The Chriftians themfelves afterwards brought into the Church this Cu-ftom of raging againft the Books of Hereticks, as they call them, as well as againft their Perfons, which was firft derived from the Heathens, when the Empire fell into the Hands of Chriftian Emperors. *Conftantine,* after the Conclufion of the Synod of *Nice,* commanded the Books of *Arius,* condemned by it, to be burnt under the Penalty of Death. *Theodofius* and *Valentinian* de-creed the fame concerning *Neftorius,* his Followers and Books, l. *damnato. c.*

de

de hæret. *Valentinian* and *Martian* concerning *Eutyches* and his Books. l. *quicun.*
§. *Nulli.* and *Omnes.* c. de hæret. *Juſtinian* ordained the cutting off the Hand
of thoſe who wrote out the Books of *Antimus,* condemned in the fifth Sy- l. 6. c. 6.
nod. And 'tis worth Obſervation what *Brunus* ſays concerning Hereticks §. 2.
and Schiſmaticks ; *That it appears to have been a moſt ancient Cuſtom of the*
Church, that when Hereſies were condemned, their Writings ſhould be deſtroyed,
from hence ; that of all the Hereſies, which for a long Time continued in the Church,
the Books containing them are now no where extant, and the Opinions of moſt of
them would have been altogether unknown, unleſs the Remembrance of them had
been preſerved in the Writings of the holy Fathers, who endeavoured to confute
them.

All theſe Laws againſt the Books of Hereticks were made by Emperors
who had the legiſlative Power in their Empire. [" But after the Year *Hiſt. Con.*
" 800, the Popes of *Rome* uſurped to themſelves many Branches of the ci- *Trid. l. 6.*
" vil Government, forbidding the Reading of Books, and commanding *P. 551.*
" them to be burnt, after they had condemned the Authors of them ; but till
" this very Age, there are but very few Books found, that are prohibited
" after this Manner : At leaſt, the univerſal Prohibition of reading Books,
" containing heretical Doctrine, or ſuſpected of Hereſy, under the Penalty
" of Excommunication, without any other preceding Sentence, had not yet
" grown into Practice."] But after that the Pope had arrogated to himſelf the
Judgment of the Faith, and order'd himſelf to be acknowledged the infallible Judge of all Controverſies of the Faith, he alſo aſſumed to himſelf all
Judgment concerning Books, and the Power of prohibiting them. From this
Claim of Power have ſprung thoſe expurgatory Indexes, by which, not only the Books of ſuch Authors as are condemned by the Church of *Rome* are
prohibited, but the Writings of all, even of the greateſt *Romaniſts* themſelves,
are ſubjected to a Cenſure ; and whatſoever is found in them contrary to the
Opinions of the *Roman* Church, or not altogether agreeable to them, is
marked with a †, and commanded to be blotted out ; and every Place
is ſo carefully noted, that no one can be ignorant, what Words are to be
eraſed. So that if the Popes Command, as contained in that Index, is to be
oberved ; we ſhall read no Books as written by the Authors, nor have their
Senſe, but only that of the Court of *Rome.* [" Pope *Martin* V. by his Bull *Hiſt. C:n.*
" excommunicated all Sects of Hereticks, but eſpecially the *Wickleſiſts* and *Trid. l. 6.*
" *Huſſites* ; but without any Mention of thoſe who read their Books, altho' *P. 551.*
" they were in the Hands of a great many. But *Leo* X. having condemned
" *Luther,* forbid alſo all his Books to be read under Pain of Excommuni-
" cation. The Popes after him, by the Bull, *In cæna,* condemned and ex-
" communicated all Hereticks, and therein devoted alſo to the ſame Curſes,
" all thoſe who read their Books. And in other Bulls, againſt Hereticks in
" general, did thunder out the ſame terrible Sentences againſt the Readers
" of thoſe Books. This occaſioned a very great Confuſion : For as the
" Names of the Hereticks who were condemned were not publiſhed, Per-
" ſons were to judge of the Books, rather from the Nature of the Do-
" ctrines

" &trines than the Names of the Authors. And as different Perfons judged
" differently concerning thefe, the Confciences of Men were troubled with
" innumerable Scruples. Thofe Inquifitors of heretical Pravity who were
" more diligent, made Catalogues of fuch Authors as they knew ; but as
" they had not compared them with each other, the fame Difficulty ftill
" remained.

But that no one might be at a Lofs for the future, what Books the Pope
had prohibited the reading of, by his Bull, it was neceffary to make an Index
of the prohibited Books. The *Roman* Authors differ amongft themfelves
who order'd the firft Index to be made.   Father *Paul.* tells us, that *Philip*,
King of *Spain*, firft endeavour'd to prevent this Confufion, by giving a
more convenient Form, and by a Law, made 1558. order'd, That the Catalogue of Books, prohibited by the Inquifitors of *Spain*, fhould be printed.
After his Example, *Paul* IV. commanded at *Rome*, That thofe who were at
the Head of the Office of the Inquifition, fhould make fuch an Index, and
print it, which was fhortly after done, *Anno* 1559. But *Gretfer* fays, that the
Index of prohibited Books was printed in *Italy*, by the Papal Authority, *An.*
1548. And a larger one, *An.* 1552. Another larger one yet, *An.* 1554. Another, *An.* 1559. by Pope *Paul* V. much larger than the others. But whether
the Pope, or *Philip* King of *Spain* firft ordered fuch an Index to be made, 'tis
certain that *Paul* IV. publifhed one, *An.* 1559. " In this they went many
" Steps farther than in former Ages, and laid the Foundations of maintain-
" ing and greatly enlarging the Authority of the Court of *Rome* ; depriving
" Men of that Knowledge which is neceffary to every one's defending him-
" felf from their unjuft Ufurpations : For till this Time the Prohibition of
" Books never extended to any but thofe of Hereticks ; neither were any Books
" forbidden to be read, unlefs the Author had been firft condemned.   But
" this Index was divided into three Parts. The firft contains the Names of
" thofe, all whofe Works, whatever be the Argument, even though pro-
" phane, are abfolutely forbidden. And in this Lift are placed, not only
" fuch who have profeffed a Doctrine contrary to the *Roman*, but many of
" thofe alfo, who have lived and died in the Communion of the Church of
" *Rome*. In the fecond are contained the Names of thofe Books which have
" been feverally condemn'd ; other Books of the fame Authors not being in
" the leaft prohibited. The third Part contains certain anonymous Writers,
" with the Addition of a general Claufe, by which all Books are prohibi-
" ted, which have not the Names of their Authors, from the Year 1519.
" Under this, many Authors and Books are condemned, which all learned
" Men in the Church of *Rome* have been converfant in, for one, two and
" three hundred Years paft, with the Knowledge of, and without any Con-
" tradiction from the Popes of *Rome*, during all that Time. Amongft the
" modern Books, fome were condemned that were printed in *Italy*, and even
" at *Rome*, with the Approbation of the Inquifition, and even by the Pope's
" own Bull. Such are the Annotations of *Erafmus* on the New *Teftament*,
" approved by *Leo* X. after he had read them over, by a Bull dated at

" *Rome*,

Hift. Con.
Trid. ibid.

De jure
prohib. lib.
l. I. *c.* 19.

Hift. Con.
Trid.
p. 552.

" *Rome*, *Sept.* 10, 1518. But above all this is remarkable, that under Colour of
" Faith and Religion, the Books of such Authors are prohibited and condemn-
" ed with the same Severity, in which the Authority of Princes, and the Civil
" Magistrate is defended against the unlawful Usurpations of the Ecclesiasticks;
" and in which the Power of Councils and Bishops is maintained against the
" unjust Encroachments of the Court of *Rome*: And finally, all those which
" plainly detect their Hypocrisy and Tyranny, by which, under the Disguise
" of Religion, they impose on the People, or persecute them. In a Word,
" Religion was never before made subservient, by such an admirable Myste-
" ry, to bereave Men of their Senses. Yea, this Inquisition went one Step
" farther, and made a Catalogue of sixty two Printers, prohibiting all the
" Books they had ever printed, or published, of whatsoever Author, Art,
" or Language, and that with an Addition of great Moment, by which they
" prohibited at once, all the Books that had been printed by any Printers,
" who had ever printed a single Book of Hereticks. So that there scarce re-
" mained any one Book to be read. And what added to this Severity of the
" Inquisitors was, that the Penalty pronounced against those who read the
" Books contained and prohibited in that Catalogue, was that of Excom-
" munication, *latæ sententiæ*, reserved to the Pope, the being deprived and
" made incapable of Offices and Benefices, perpetual Infamy, and other ar-
" bitrary Penalties. *Pius* IV. who succeeded *Paul*, revoked this severe Cen-
" sure, and referred this Index, with the whole Affair, to the Council of
" *Trent*.

" Amongst the Fathers at *Trent*, there was a great Difference of Opinions Hist. Conc.
" about the making this Index. For some thought that this of *Paul* IV. Trid. p.
" was sufficient, as being most perfect in it self; and that if any one should al- 553.
" low the Books prohibited in this Catalogue, he would declare that this
" Proceeding at *Rome* was imprudent, which would be to take away all Au-
" thority from the Index already published, and from the Decree now to be
" made; because it was a common Maxim, That new Laws lessen their own
" Value, more than they do that of the old ones. *Lewis Beccatellus*, Arch-
" bishop of *Ragusi*, said there was no Need of Books, because there was
" more than enough of them since the Invention of Printing; and that it was
" much better that many Books should be prohibited without Cause, than
" that one which deserved Prohibition should be allowed. Others thought
" that the Council should take this Affair of the Books into their Considerati-
" on, as if there had not been any Prohibition at all before; because that that
" which was made by the Inquisitors at *Rome*, was for that Name hateful to
" the *Ultramontanes*, and was so very severe, that no Body could observe it.
" That there was no juster Reason in the World for repealing a Law, than
" that it cannot be observed, or at least, not without great Difficulty; espe-
" cially if the Punishment annexed to the Breakers of it was too severe."
At Length, the Fathers, after several Debates, not being able to agree,
thought fit to refer the whole Affair to the Pope. Upon this, Pope *Pius*
IV. as *Clement* VIII. reports, in his Bull, *October* 17, 1595.] took the

Advice

Advice of certain Prelates of great Learning and Wifdom, and publifhed an Index of the prohibited Books, and certain Rules, by his Letters, in Form of a Brief. The fame *Pius*, in his Bull of *March* 24, 1564. fays, That the Index was prefented to him by Order of the Synod, that it fhould not be pub-lifhed before it was approved by him. Wherefore, after it had been ex-amined at his Command, by fome of the moft learned and approved Prelates, he approved it, together with the Rules put before it, commanding it to be received by all, and the Rules to be obferved ; adding this ftrict Charge : *We forbid all and fingular, as well Ecclefiaftical Perfons, fecular and regular, of whatfoever Degree, Order and Dignity, as Lay, of whatfoever Honour and Dignity, to read, or dare to have any Books, contrary to the Order of thefe Rules, or the Prohibition of the faid Index. And if any one fhall act contrary to thofe Rules, and that Prohibition, by reading, or having the Books of Hereticks, or the Writings of any Author condemned and prohibited for Herefy, or Sufpicion of falfe Doctrine, he fhall,* ipfo jure, *incur the Penalty of Excommunication ; and for this Reafon In-quifition and Procefs may be made againft him, as fufpected of Herefy ; befides other Penalties in this Cafe incurred, ordained by the Apoftolick Sea, and facred Ca-nons.* Thus by the Command of *Pius* IV. this Index of prohibited Books came forth, *An.* 1564. " But becaufe it was not received in fome Places " and Provinces, becaufe fome Books were prohibited by it, which learned " Men could not be deprived the reading of without great Inconvenience ; " and becaufe fome Things were obfcure, and needed Explication, they made " certain Rules, to provide, as well as they could, for the Advantage and " Studies of. learned Men, without any detriment to Truth and Religion." Hence *Sixtus* V. order'd it to be enlarged with many Rules ; but died before-he had brought it to Perfection. *Clement* VIII. commanded it to be retained,. and enlarged it, and thus encreafed and enlarged, he confirmed it, and the Rules prefixed to it ; and commanded it to be publifhed, *An.* 1595. The firft of thefe Rules is this : *All thofe Books, which either the Popes, or General Councils have condemned, before the Year* 1515. *are which are not in this Index, are to be looked on as really condemned here, even as they were condemned before.* By the fourth Rule, the common reading of the Holy Scripture is forbid, in thefe Words :

Since it is plain by Experience, that if the facred Writings are permitted every where, and without Difference, to be read in the Vulgar Tongue, Men, through their Rafhnefs, will receive more Harm than Good ; let the Bifhop or Inquifitor determine, with the Advice of the Parifh Prieft or Confeffor, to whom to permit the reading of the Bible, tranflated by Catholick Authors, in the Vulgar Tongue ; according as they fhall judge whether it be moft likely that fuch reading the Scripture may do harm, or tend to the Encreafe of Faith and Piety. Let them alfo have the fame Power as to all other Writings. But if any without fuch Leave, fhall pre-fume to read or have them, without firft fhewing the Bible to the Ordinaries, he fhall' not receive the Abfolution of his Sins. And as to all Bookfellers, who fhall fell the Bible tranflated into the Vulgar Tongue, without fuch Leave, or by any other Method fhall publifh them ; let them forfeit the Price of the Books, and let the Money be given to pious Ufes by the Bifhop ; and let them be fubject to other Punifhments at the Plea-
fure

fure of the faid Bifhop, according to the Nature of the Offence. As to Regulars they fhall not read or buy them, without Leave firft had from their Prelates. To this Rule there is added in the Index this Obfervation. *It muft be remarked, concerning this fourth Rule of the Index of Pope* Pius IV. *of bleffed Memory, that no new Power is given by this Impreffion or Edition to the Bifhops or Inquifitors, or the Superiors of the Regulars, to grant Licenfe of buying, reading and keeping the Bible publifhed in the Vulgar Tongue. Since hitherto, according to the Command and Ufe of the holy* Roman *and Univerfal Inquifition, this Power of granting fuch Licenfes to read and keep the Bible, and other Parts of the facred Scripture, as well of the New as the Old Teftament, publifhed in any Vulgar Language, is taken from them ; as alfo all Summaries, and hiftorical Abridgments of the faid Bible or Books of the holy Scripture, written in any Vulgar Language whatfoever. And this muft be inviolably obferved.*

In the tenth Rule there are feveral Things to be obferved about the printing of Books, *viz.* that no Books fhall be publifhed at *Rome*, unlefs firft examined by the Vicar of the Pope, and the Mafter of the holy Palace, or Perfons deputed by the Pope. And as to other Places, unlefs it be approved by the Bifhop, or fome one deputed by the Bifhop, or the Inquifitor of heretical Pravity, and fuch Approbation fubfcribed with their Hand. If any publifh Manufcript Books without Approbation, they are fubjeƈt to the fame Penalties as the Printers. The Shops of Bookfellers are order'd to be often fearched, and they themfelves are commanded to keep a Catalogue of all the Books they fell, and to keep no other, nor to deliver them upon any Account, without Leave of fuch as are deputed, under Penalty of lofing their Books, and other Punifhments to be inflicted at Pleafure of the Bifhops and Inquifitors. All Buyers, Readers, or Printers, are alfo punifhable at their Pleafure. If any one brings any Books into a City, he muft acquaint the faid Deputies with it, and not give or lend them to be read to any Perfon without fhewing the Books to them, and having their Leave.

Finally, in the Inftruction given to thofe who are intrufted with the Care of prohibiting, purging and printing Books, this Oath is ordered to be taken by Printers and Bookfellers. *Let Printers and Bookfellers promife upon Oath, before the Bifhop or Inquifitor, and at* Rome, *before the Mafter of the Holy Palace, that they will perform their Service in a Catholick, fincere and faithful Manner ; and that they will obey the Decrees and Rules of this Index, and the Edicts of the Bifhops and Inquifitors, as far as relates to their Arts, and will not knowingly fuffer any one to ferve under them, who is defiled with heretical Pravity.* Cap. de Impref. Libros. §. 6.

After this *Trent* Index was publifhed, *Philip* II. King of *Spain*, commanded another larger one to be printed at *Antwerp*, *An.* 1571. at the Houfe of *Chriftopher* Plantin, with this Title : *The expurgatory Index of Books, publifhed in this Age, either mixed with Errors contrary to found Doctrine, or with the Gall of unprofitable and offenfive Scandal, according to the Decree of the holy Council of* Trent, *drawn up in the* Netherlands, *by the Command of his Catholick Majefty,* Philip II. *and with the Advice and Affiftance of the Duke of* Alva, An. 1571. " This Book was printed by *Plantin*, the King's Printer, and at his Majefty's

" own

" own Charge, not with a Defign to be publifhed and difperfed, but to be
" given only to them, who were appointed to prefide over what they call the
" Expurgation of fufpected Books. There was added a moft fevere Com-
" mand of the King; That thefe Cenfors fhould keep this Index very pri-
" vately, and let no others know of it, nor communicate it to any one what-
" foever, nor give any Copy of it; but that they fhould moft carefully re-
" gard this only, to fearch out, expunge and reftore fuch fufpected Places of
" Books, as they fhould think proper to expunge. By this Means this
" Book lay concealed for fifteen Years, like certain Myfteries, in the Li-
" braries of thefe Cenfors. But by the fingular Direction of Divine Provi-
" dence, it happened, that about the Year 1586. this Index fell into the
" Hands of *Francis Junius*, who made it publick." *John Pappus* gives an
Account of this whole Affair, in his Preface to the new Edition of this In-
dex, which he publifhed at *Strasburg, An.* 1599.

Befides this, another *Expurgatory Index was publifhed in* Spain, *at the Command of* Gafpar Quiroga, *Cardinal and Archbifhop of* Toledo, *Inquifitor General of* Spain, *and with the Advice of the fupreme Senate of the holy general Inquifition,* and printed at *Madrid,* by *Alphonfus Gomez,* the King's Printer,
An. 1584. A Copy of this was, as it were, fnatched out of the Fire by
the *Englifh,* when they plundered *Cadiz,* and deftroy'd every Thing elfe
with Flames, and fent by King *James,* to the moft noble Lord *Mornæus,
Du Pleffis,* who caufed it to be printed a little after at *Saumur,* keeping the
Original himfelf, to prove the Edition authentick. After this, many other
Expurgatory Indexes of Books of all Sorts came out at *Rome* and *Naples.*
There was a much larger one, particularly printed in *Spain,* by Order of
Bernard de Sandoval, Archbifhop of *Toledo,* and Inquifitor General, and finally
the compleateft of all, by Command of *Anthony a Sotomayor,* fupreme Prefi-
dent and Inquifitor-General in the Kingdom of *Spain,* &c. and publifhed with
the Advice of the fupreme Senate of the General Inquifition, *An.* 1640,
which was reprinted at *Geneva, An.* 1667. according to the Copy printed at
Madrid, in the Printing-houfe of *Didacus Diaz.* To this there were many
Rules prefixed; and to the *Geneva* Edition was added the Index of the Decrees, which were made by the Mafter of the holy Palace, by Virtue of his
Office, or by the Command of the holy Congregation, or by the holy Congregations for the Indexes and holy Office, after the before-mentioned Index of
the Council of *Trent.*

As to what concerns the Rules prefixed to this Index; I fhall not give any
Summary of them, becaufe the Book it felf may be eafily had in the Shops.
The Rules of the former Indexes are explained and confirmed by thefe.
I fhall only tranfcribe out of the fifth Rule, fuch Things as are added to
explain more clearly the fourth Rule of the Index of *Trent,* in which the pro-
mifcuous Reading of Books is prohibited.

*All Bibles extant in the vulgar Tongue are prohibited, with all Parts of them, ei-
ther printed or Manufcript, with all Summaries and Abridgments, although hiftorical,
of the faid Bible, or Books of the holy Scripture, in the vulgar Language or Tongue;*
not

not including the little Claufes, Sentences, and Heads which are inferted in the Books of Catholick Writers, who cite and explain them.   This Caution is alfo to be obferved, that the Book of the Epiftles and Gofpels, as 'tis called, written in the vulgar Tongue, is comprehended in this Prohibition, although there be fometimes added fhort Expofitions in certain Parts and Gofpels; for it is almoft all written out of the facred Text, and therefore prohibited upon account of the Danger of Error, to which the ignorant common People are fubject, through a corrupted Underftanding, and other Inconveniences that have been found to arife by Experience.   And that all Scruples may be avoided, the Reader is to underftand which is the vulgar Tongue, and which not.   The Hebrew, Greek, Latin, Caldee, Syriack, Ethiopick, Perfick *and* Arabick *are not, being thofe original Languages, which are not now ufed in common Converfation.   All other Languages whatfoever are to be underftood to be vulgar.*   I have thought proper to add this Rule, Word for Word, that the Tyranny of the Papifts, in prohibiting the reading of the holy Scripture, which they endeavour to diffemble, conceal, and by various Pretexts to difguife, may clearly and evidently appear.

From thefe Things 'tis plain, that the Inquifitors, efpecially in *Spain,* have a very great Power in the Prohibition of Books; becaufe thefe expurgatory Indexes are made and publifhed by the Command of the Inquifition in the Kingdom of *Spain.*   How large this Power is, *Pegna* gives us a full Account. *Direct. Inq. Ey-mer. Com. 22. par. 2.*

" The Bifhops and Inquifitors may condemn and prohibit in their Diocefes all
" Books which contain Opinions, exprefsly condemned by the Church, al-
" though written by Authors not condemned by Name, becaufe Things
" once condemned may be forbidden with any new Condemnation.   Alfo all
" Books fufpected of Herefy, whatfoever be the Herefy they are fufpected of,
" though publifhed by Catholick Authors.   For fince they may proceed a-
" gainft all Perfons whatfoever, at leaft fo far as to make Inquifition even for
" fmall, tho' probable, Sufpicions of Herefy, he infers from hence, that they
" may much more proceed againft fufpected Books, and prohibit fuch as contain
" fufpected Propofitions.   For, fays he, Books are much more likely to do
" harm than Men, becaufe thofe who read them more firmly infift on the
" Things contained in them, than thofe who only hear the Converfations
" of others; and farther becaufe Hereticks by teaching can fcarce
" fpread their Doctrine over a fingle City, whereas Books may be carried
" from Place to Place, and infect not only a City, but Kingdoms and Pro-
" vinces.   Alfo all Books containing Propofitions fcandalous, dangerous, er-
" roneous, favouring of Herefy, and any ways differing from the Catholick
" Faith, and not agreeable to Chriftian Piety and good Manners.   This was
" provided for by *Paul* III, in a certain Refcript, beginning, *In Apoftolici*
" *culminis.*   The fame is to be faid of fuch Books as contain double, doubtful
" or dubious Propofitions, which contain a double Senfe, one heretical,
" the other Catholick.   Thefe may be prohibited by the Inquifitors, till fuch
" Propofitions are declared in a Catholick Senfe.   In the Index alfo of prohi-
" bited Books, at the End of the tenth Rule, Power is granted to the Bifhops
" and Inquifitors General, of prohibiting fuch Books as may be permitted
" in

" in thefe Rules, if they fhall think proper to do it in their Kingdoms, Pro-
" vinces or Diocefes."

Inquif.
Venet. cap.
29.
        The *Venetian* Senate, as they defend their own Authority againft the Inqui-
fition in other Cafes, fo they would never allow this important Affair to the
Power of the Inquifitors. For as Father *Paul* juftly obferves, they confider,
that the main Defign of the Ecclefiafticks, is to affume to themfelves a Power
to prohibit not only Books of Religion, but fuch as treat of any other Matters
whatfoever; and to deprive Princes of the Power of prohibiting in their own
Territories any Book, if they have approved it, whatever be the Subject it
treats of. The Confequence of which they fee would be this, that they cannot prohibit any Book from being brought into their Dominions, and publickly fold, if the Ecclefiafticks approve of it, though it be in it felf dangerous to the Commonwealth. For thefe Reafons they have vigoroufly endeavoured to referve this Power to themfelves, and not to fuffer it to be transferred to the Inquifitors. On this account great Differences arofe between the
Pope and the Senate, and in the Year 1595. there met the Cardinal Nuncio
and the Inquifition on the Pope's Part, and the principal Senators on the Senate's Part, who, after long and continued debating the Affair for four whole
Months, at length agreed, that the Power of prohibiting Books in the *Venetian* Territories, fhould belong to the Senate, and not to the Inquifitors. Of
this Agreement only fixty Copies were printed at the earneft Requeft of the *Romans*, for this Reafon, that it fhould become known but to a few. Whereas on
the other hand, innumerable Indexes of prohibited Books, in which the Power
of prohibiting them is afcribed only to the Ecclefiafticks, are every where to
be found; by which Artifice they defign, that this Agreement fhall be
known only to a few, and may be gradually wholly loft. For which Reafon Father *Paul* thinks, that the Senate ought particularly to guard againft
thefe Arts.

        And indeed the *Romanifts* have given Proofs enough, that they claim to
themfelves only the Prohibition and Approbation of Books, and would entirely deprive the Secular Powers of it, that they may not have the Power of
prohibiting Books, which they fee dangerous to their Government, and defigned to excite Sedition and Rebellion. We have a famous Inftance of this
in Cardinal *Baronius*, and on the other hand, we have as noble an Inftance of the
juft Vindication of the regal Majefty in the King of *Spain*, though himfelf fubject to the Yoak and Bondage of the Inquifition. *Baronius*, in the Beginning
of the Year 1605. publifhed his Eleventh Volume of Ecclefiaftical Annals, in
which he inferted a long Difcourfe of the Monarchy of *Sicily*, in which were
many Things contrary to the Honour of many of the Kings of *Aragon*, and
particularly againft King *Ferdinand*, and the other Anceftors of the King of *Sicily*, who then reigned, who alfo was King of *Spain*. This Book, as foon as it was
brought to *Naples* and *Milan*, was prohibited by the King's Minifters, as manifeftly injurious to their Sovereign. As foon as the Report of this Prohibition
came to *Rome*, *Baronius* called together a Counfel of Cardinals, upon the Vacancy of the See by the Death of *Clement* VIII. and bitterly inveighed againft

A. 1097.
§. 19,*&c.*

                                                                              the

the King's Minifters, who, by prohibiting his Book, had prefumed to lay hold of the Ecclefiaftical Authority. After this, *Paul* V. being created Pope, *June* 13th of the fame Year, the Cardinal wrote a long Letter to the King of *Spain*, in which, amongft other Things, he afferts, that it belonged only to the Pope, to approve or difapprove all manner of Books, and efpecially Ecclefiaftical ones ; and grievoufly complains that his Majefty's Minifters had prohibited his Book in *Italy*, to the great Reproach and Contempt of the Ecclefiaftical Authority. The King fent the Cardinal no Anfwer, but privately approved the Edict of his Minifters. In the Year 1607. the Cardinal publifhed his Twelfth Volume of Annals, and could not contain himfelf, but in an entire Digreffion reproached, and feverely inveighed againft this Action of the King's Minifters. *We therefore more ftrongly inculcate thefe Things, approved of by the antient Cuftom of* §. 1186. *the Church, and Authority of the Catholick Faith, becaufe in thefe moft unhappy* §. 29. *Times the King's Minifters have dared to do, what is dreadful to relate, and horri-* §. 84. *ble to act, viz. to cenfure Writings that have been approved by the Pope, fo that the Bookfellers are not fuffered to fell them, without Leave firft obtained from them, which fometimes they deny at Pleafure, prohibiting the Sale of them, and thereby manifeft to the World that they act contrary to Right and Juftice. What elfe is this, but what 'tis Impiety to fay, to wreft one of the Keys given by Chrift to* Peter, *viz. the Key of Knowledge, out of the Hands of his Succeffors, and to fuffer it to be ufurped by a Lay Hand, and Lay Princes.* The *Spanifh* Senate, according to Cuftom, proceeded flowly, and with mature Advice, and waited three whole Years. But in the Year 1610. the King publifhed an Edict, by which he condemned, and prohibited the faid Book, and treated the Cardinal in the fame manner as, he had done him and his Predeceffors. And to give that Decree the greater Authority, he commanded it to be publifhed in *Sicily*, by Order of Cardinal *Doria*, who confirmed it by fubfcribing it with his own Hand ; and which was printed, and every where difperfed about and fold. The Court of *Rome* was greatly difturbed at it, and efpecially becaufe 'twas put in Execution by the Cardinal's Command. However the *Spaniards* would never revoke the Decree.

Thus we fee that the King of *Spain* vindicated his Authority, and the Honour of his Anceftors, becaufe the Controverfy was about the Right of Empire. But this is the only Inftance of this Nature, and which the King could not pafs over without injuring his own Majefty. In all other Cafes the Power of prohibiting Books is left wholly to the Inquifitors, which, as we have feen, is very large in the Kingdom of *Spain*.

CHAP. XVII.

What the INQUISITORS *can do themselves, and what in Conjunction*
with the ORDINARIES.

BEcause the Judgment of Herefy is, as we have feen, committed to the
Ordinaries or Bifhops, and to the Delegates or Inquifitors, 'tis proper to
confider what each can feparately do, and what are thofe Acts in which both
muft neceffarily concur, in order to their being effectual and valid.

Eymer.   The Inquifitor without the Bifhop, and the Bifhop without the Inquifitor,
p. 3. q. 47. may cite and arreft, or apprehend and deliver any one to fafe Cuftody, and
put them in Irons, if they think proper, and make Inquifition againft fuch as
are accufed. But neither without the other can deliver any Perfons to hard or
clofe Imprifonment, which hath more of the Nature of Punifhment than of
Cuftody, or put them to the Torture, or force them in Irons by Hunger to
difcover the Truth, which is one fort of very grievous Torment, or proceed
Cap. *Mul-* to Sentence againft them. This appears from the *Clementines. Therefore to pro-*
torum. de *mote the Glory of God, and for the Encreafe of the fame Faith, and that the Affair of*
hæret.   *the Inquifition may go on more profperoufly, and that the fearching out of heretical Pra-*
vity may proceed more folemnly, diligently, and cautioufly, we decree that it fhall be
carried on as well by the Diocefan Bifhops, as by the Inquifitors deputed by the Apofto-
lick See, laying afide all carnal Love, Hatred and Fear, and every Regard to tem-
poral Intereft. So that every one of the aforenamed may without the other cite, ar-
reft or take up, or commit to fafe Cuftody, and alfo put Criminals into Irons, if they
fhall think proper. And this we lay upon their Confciences. They may alfo make In-
quifition againft them, as they fhall think it in this Cafe moft agreeable to God and
Juftice. But neither the Bifhop without the Inquifitor, nor the Inquifitor without the
Diocefan Bifhop, or his Official, or during the Vacancy of the Epifcopal See, fuch Per-
fon as fhall be deputed by the Chapter, if they can each of them refpectively obtain a
Copy, within eight Days after they have given Notice to each other, fhall be able to
commit any one to hard and clofe Imprifonment, which looks more like Punifhment than
Cuftody, or put them to the Torture, or proceed to Sentence againft them. And if any
one fhall prefume to do otherwife, it fhall be ipfo jure, null *and* void. In like manner the Inquifitor without the Bifhop cannot deprive, nor declare to be deprived of their Benefices and Ecclefiaftical Dignities heretical Clergymen, unlefs
it fhall legally appear that the Diocefans have conferred fuch Benefices know-
ingly upon fuch Perfons; *for we declare that their Confent in fuch Cafes fhall not*
Pegna: *be required, but rather that they fhould be punifhed by their Judge.* Decret. 6. de
Lucern. hæret. cap. Ut commiffi. §. ult. But whatfoever was the antient Law, 'tis now
Inq. in voce a very plain and clear Cafe, by the Refcript of *Pius* V. beginning, *Cum ex A-*
Inquifitor. poftolatus, *that the Benefices of the heretical Clergy, are vacant from the*
Day of their committing their Crime, and referved to the Difpofal of the A-
poftolick See. From whence it appears that the Inquifitor may declare them
deprived of them.   'Tis

'Tis controverted amongſt the Doctors, whether the Biſhop without the Inqui-_Direct._ ſitor, or the Inquiſitor without the Biſhop, can pronounce the Sentence of Ab-_p. 3. q. 48._ ſolution. 'Tis the Cuſtom in *Spain*, for the Inquiſitors to abſolve without _Com. 97._ the Biſhops. But if there is an Abjuration to be made, the Conſent of both _Caren._ is neceſſary, according to the Reſcript of *Innocent* IV. beginning, *Tunc potiſſime.* _p. 1. tit._ *But if any ſhall wholly abjure heretical Pravity, and will return to the Eccleſi-* _4. §. 11._ *aſtical Unity, let the Dioceſan be conſulted, and grant them the Benefit of Abſolution, according to the Form of the Church, and enjoin them the uſual Penance.* But if ſuch Abjuration or Purgation be made before one of them only, it is to be account- ed valid. From hence they draw this Inference ; That if any one ſhall have abjured, as an Heretick, or vehemently ſuſpected, before either one of the a- foreſaid, and ſhall afterward be found to have fallen into Hereſy, he may be delivered over to the ſecular Court as a Relapſe ; and that he cannot defend himſelf by urging the Nullity or Invalidity of the Abjuration, as having been made only before one of them.

The Biſhop and Inquiſitor may conſtitute each other their Vicegerents, in _Qu. 49._ thoſe Caſes in which neither can act ſeparately. *But if the Biſhop, or the Per-* _com. 92._ *ſon delegated by the Chapter during the Vacancy of the See, cannot for the aforeſaid* _Cap. Mul-_ *Reaſons, or will not perſonally meet with the Inquiſitor, or the Inquiſitor with either* _torum._ *of them ; the Biſhop, or his Delegate, or the Delegate of the Chapter, during the Vacancy of the See, may appoint the Inquiſitor in his Room, and the Inquiſitor or his Delegate may thus appoint the Biſhop, or ſignify their Advice and Conſent by Let- ters.* If they will not meet together, the one muſt require the other ; nor can either of them proceed till eight Days after they have thus mutually de- manded each others Attendance.

The Biſhop and the Inquiſitor may proceed by a delegated Authority, and _Qu. 5._ then they are equal. When the Biſhop proceeds by his ordinary Authority, and the Inquiſitor by a delegated one, the Inquiſitor is the greater. If the _Simanc._ Biſhop and Inquiſitor cite the ſame Perſon before them, to anſwer concerning _tit. 44._ the Faith, he muſt, when cited, appear before both, if the Times of the _§. 13._ Citation are different : if they are the ſame, he muſt appear before the In- quiſitor. For the Inquiſitors are ſpecially delegated for the Affairs of the Faith. But in this Caſe they may oblige each other. But in *Spain* the Inqui- _Direct._ ſitors are always preferred in theſe Cauſes, and the Biſhop cannot hinder the _p. 3. qu._ Proceſs of the Inquiſitor. _50._

When the Biſhop and Inquiſitor differ, they can't proceed to a definitive Sentence, but muſt refer the whole Cauſe drawn up to the Pope, or to the ſupream Tribunal of the Inquiſition. In *Spain* this muſt be done even, when they differ in Caſes of no great Importance. This is preſcribed by the *Ma-* *drid* Inſtruction, An. 1561. cap. 66. *In all Caſes where there ſhall happen a Dif-* _Com. 99._ *ference of Opinion between the Inquiſitors or Ordinary, or any one of them, in determi- ning a Cauſe, or in any other Act, or in an interlocutory Sentence, the Cauſe muſt be referred to the ſupream Senate of the Inquiſition. But if the Biſhop and Inquiſitors agree, although the Learned in the Law and the Counſellors differ, even though they may be more in Number, the Sentence of the Biſhop and Inquiſitors muſt be executed.*

However, in very important Cases, the Sentence of the Inquisitors, Ordinary and Counsellors, though they all agree, shall not be put in Execution, without consulting the Senate, according to Custom and Order.

Qu. 51.   When the Bishop and Inquisitor proceed separately, so that there are two Processes carried on for the same Fact, one by the Bishop, and the other by the Inquisitor, they ought to communicate their Processes to one another.

Cap. per hoc. §. Verum. de hæret. l. 6. *But that the said Affair of the Inquisition may proceed better, more effectually and profitably, we grant, that the Bishops and Inquisitors may make Inquisition concerning the same Fact, either together or apart. If they proceed separately, they shall be obliged mutually to communicate the Processes, that hereby the Truth may be the better found out. And unless in this Case the Inquisitors shall think fit to refer the pronouncing Sentence to the Diocesans, or the Diocesans to the Inquisitors, let them both join in passing it. If they cannot agree in pronouncing it, let them draw up a full Account of the Case, and refer it to the Apostolick See.*

Qu. 53. Ex. eo.   This Communication of the Processes is to be made only once, and that when the Process is finished. By an Extravagant of *Benedict.* XI. which says : *When they both proceed separately, they must at the End of the Process, when nothing remains but only to pronounce Sentence, communicate it to each other. One Case however we except,* viz. *if either of them cannot conveniently proceed, without seeing what the other hath done. In this Case let a Copy of the whole Proceedure be granted, though but one, to prevent any Fraud.*

Caren. p. 1. tit. 4. §. 21.   But in *Spain* and *Portugal* the Inquisitors only form the Processes, and apprehend Criminals in Causes of the Faith, and if the Bishops have any Informations against such Criminals, they must transmit them to the Inquisitors. But it is uncertain whether these *Spanish* Inquisitors claim this by any legal Custom and Prescription, or by the Pope's Privilege.

These are the Things to be observed, when the Ordinary and Inquisitor concur in the Judgment of the Faith. But because oftentimes in *Spain* several Inquisitors are deputed together, it will be proper to consider how far each of them may separately proceed.

Qu. 46. Com. 95.   As often therefore as it happens that two Inquisitors are constituted in the same Province, they may both together, or each of them separately, proceed against Hereticks throughout the whole Province committed to them, sit in Judgment in any Part of it, and when the Executor is absent create another, because they have entire Jurisdiction. However, a Criminal can be punished only by one of them. But if there be any special Inquisitor deputed against any Person by the Pope, the Inquisitors of Provinces and Dioceses, who, as general Judges, seem to have universal Jurisdiction, at least with respect to Persons, cannot proceed against him, though they have actually began the Process ; because their Jurisdiction is suspended by a special Commission granted by the Pope. He who is thus constituted special Inquisitor, may make use of every Thing that hath been done and discovered by the other Inquisitors, whom if it be necessary he may compel to deliver to him all the Processes, Writings, Inquisitions, Depositions of Witnesses, and all other Things they have discovered against any Criminal. Although 'tis reckoned more

hand-

handſome to do this by the Authority of their Superior, when this Power is not ſpecially given him in the Letters of his Commiſſion.

But although each of the Inquiſitors hath entire Juriſdiction, yet neither of Simanc. them can proceed without the other to the Publication of Teſtimonies, nor to *tit.* 34. grant a Copy of the Procſes to the Criminal. This Rule holds only when §. 37. both the Inquiſitors are preſent. For when either of them is abſent, the other can do every Thing that is needful, calling in the Aſſiſtance of skilful Perſons. 4 *Inſtruct. Tolet.* c. 1.

When the ſame Hereticks may be proceeded againſt by different Judges, *tit.* 44. that Inquiſitor who firſt began the Procſes, is to be preferred to the other in §. 19. the ſame Cauſe. For which Reaſon the Inquiſitors of other Provinces muſt ſend their Teſtimonies, and all Things they have diſcovered againſt the Criminals, to that Inquiſitor who firſt began the Procſes.

The elder Inquiſitor is to be preferred, although tranſlated from one Pro-*tit.* 34. vince to another, unleſs he may have been deprived of his Office, and after-§. 20. wards reſtored, or laid down the Office of his own Accord for any certain Time. This is fully contained in one of the Letters of the Inquiſitor General.

J. Royas hath fully explained this Matter, *viz.* how ſeveral Inquiſitors in one Part 1. Province, and how the Inquiſitors and Ordinary muſt act, and given in the §. 439. Reaſons why. " The Juriſdiction of the Inquiſitors is mutual and entire, " where one of them only preſides over the Juriſdiction for determining the " Cauſes of the Faith ; for a Colleague in any City or Territory hath no " Power in Cauſes already decided. 4 *Inſtruct. Tolet.* c. 1. But if they are all " preſent, neither of them without the other can proceed to apprehend Cri- " minals, to the Publication of Witneſſes, to the Torture, to enjoin canoni- " cal Purgation, or to pronounce any definitive Sentence. And as to the Or- " dinaries, ſuch of them as are Inquiſitors have a cumulative Juriſdiction, and " not a privative one, in theſe Articles only ; *viz.* in pronouncing Sentences " of Torture, and in other definitive Sentences, as well as in thoſe which ariſe 444. " from the Judgment it ſelf. But in all other Articles the Inquiſitors have priva- " tive and not cumulative Juriſdiction. For as to other civil and criminal Cauſes " not touching the Faith, the Inquiſitors may proceed without the Biſhop, be- " cauſe the Cogniſance of them belongs to them rather by the Royal than the " Apoſtolick Authority ; or elſe by daily Cuſtom, as particularly in the King- " doms of *Valencia, Aragon,* and Principality of *Catalonia,* which Cuſtom gives " them their Juriſdiction." *Royas* adds, " I am grieved and aſhamed to tell " how in our Times this Juriſdiction is almoſt deſtroyed, and rendred weak and " infirm by the Negligence of ſome, to the great Detriment of the Affairs " of the Faith:"

Finally, they obſerve, that 'tis much ſafer for the Biſhops to ſend to the Carena, Inquiſitors the Cauſes of Hereſy, and Suſpicions of Hereſy, becauſe Secrecy is *p.* 1. t. 4. the Strength of all the Cauſes of the Holy Office. This is inviolably obſer-*n.* 23, &c. ved before the Inquiſitors, but cannot be ſo well kept before the Biſhops. This the Inquiſitor *Cantera* atteſts, whilſt he was Vicar General of *Pampilona* ;

viz. that he could never procure Secrecy to be kept in that Ecclesiastical Court; and though he oftentimes punished the Notaries, it signified nothing at all. *Carena* also relates, that Cardinal *Camporeus*, Bishop of *Cremona*, and one of the supream Inquisitors, in all Causes in which Lay Persons had a Right to decide and give Judgment, did for fourteen Years always remit all Causes of Heresy, and Suspicion of Heresy, immediately to the Inquisitors; because he well knew, how great Inconveniences would arise, if the Ordinaries, who have neither secret nor safe Jayl and Ministers, should interest themselves in forming Processes.

CHAP. XVIII.

Of the JAYL *of the* INQUISITORS, *and* KEEPERS *of the* JAYL.

Direct.
p. 3.
Qu. 58.
com. 107·

JAYLS were formerly appointed to keep Men in Custody, and not to punish them. But by the Canon Law they may be used for Punishment. Cap. *Quamvis.* de pœnis. lib. 6. *Although it be well known that the Jayl is particularly designed to keep Criminals in Custody, and not to punish them, yet we do not disapprove that convict Persons should be delivered over to Prison to do Penance either for ever, or for a Time, as you shall judge most convenient, their Crimes, Persons, and other Circumstances, being carefully considered.* *Simancas* gives this Reason

Catbol. In-
*flit.tit.*16·
§. 15·

for it: *For since the sacred Canons, through the Ecclesiastical Lenity, cannot inflict the Punishment of Death, the Consequence is, that lest Crimes should go unpunished, they may inflict the Penalty of Perpetual Imprisonment for more grievous Offences, which is indeed very grievous, and equal to Death.* Heretofore the Bishop and Inquisitor might have their separate Jayls, to hold Persons in Custody, but not to punish them; for as they cannot condemn any one to Imprisonment without the Consent of both, 'tis therefore required that the Jayl for Punishment shall be common to both. But now they have not usually separate Prisons; the same that belongs to the Inquisitor, in which Criminals are kept in Custody, being common to the Bishop.

Here are two Things to be explained. First, what must be done before any Person can be thrown into Jayl. Secondly, what Method must be observed in keeping and placing the Prisoners.

Part 2.
Assert. 1.

As to the first, *Royas* gives this large Account of it. In all Causes, as well civil as criminal, Criminals must not be apprehended, without a summary Inquisition against them concerning their Crime first had. This is particularly to be observed in the Crime of Heresy. For though in other Crimes no one suffers much in his Reputation merely for his being thrown into Prison, yet to be taken up for the Crime of Heresy is greatly infamous, which must therefore be proceeded in with great Caution. For since the Reason of proceeding in the Crime of Heresy is much more important than in other Offences, there

is

is Need of a greater Inquifition, and of a fummary Cognifance, before Criminals are apprehended. So that no one is lightly to be fhut up in clofe Prifon for fmall Offences, for Propofitions that found ill, or that are fcandalous, or blafphemous, or others which do not contain real Herefy; but is to be confined either in fome Monaftery, or in his own Houfe or City.

The Inquifitors may indeed proceed in the Crime of Herefy againft any Perfon, efpecially if he be otherwife vile, upon a light and moderate Sufpicion, fo far as to afk fuch fufpected Perfon, what he thinks of the Faith. But in order to apprehend any one for Herefy, two credible Witneffes are required, although they fay that the Teftimony of a fingle one, if beyond all Exception, is fufficient, who depofes what he faw or heard; yea, if he be not beyond all Exception, yet is otherwife fit, provided he agrees with the Informer; for in this Cafe they fay there are two Witneffes, and confequently more than half Proof, which is fufficient for any ones being apprehended. But that one Witnefs above all Exception, is enough in this Cafe, they prove from the *Madrid* Inftruction, *An.* 1561. *Cap.* 4. which fays, *If the Teftimony be not fufficient for the apprehending*. This Inftruction is in the fingular Number, and therefore intimates, that one lawful Witnefs againft any one is fufficient for his being taken up; efpecially if the Perfon be fcandalous, and vile, and fufpected; as are all the new Converts of the Mahometan Sect in the Kingdom of *Valencia*; and as *Royas* fays, the *French* and *Germans* of the *Lutheran.* But if the Perfon accufed be noble, and of good Reputation and Fame, he is not to be apprehended upon a fingle Teftimony. However, this is left to the Pleafure of the Judge, after having confidered the Quality of the Perfon and his Offence; not that the Inquifitors of the Faith fhould appear eager to take up Criminals; for they are always to ufe great Circumfpection. This is efpecially neceffary in the receiving and examining Witneffes. They muft in the firft Place admonifh them, how horrible and dreadful a Wickednefs it is to give falfe Witnefs in any Caufes, and efpecially in the holy Office of the Inquifition, and that they fhould have God and his awful and tremendous Judgment before their Eyes, that they may not, for Prayer, or Price, or Entreaty, or any other wicked Affection, defame an innocent Perfon with fo great a Crime. Then the Witneffes are to be interrogated concerning the Place, and Time, what they faw or heard; whether the Perfon acted, or pronounced heretical Words, once or oftner; with what Obftinacy or Eagernefs he affirmed them; and what other Perfons were prefent; and for what Caufes, Reafons, and Occafions they were prefent; and concerning all other Circumftances neceffary to difcover the Truth or Falfehood.

Thefe Things premifed, the Witneffes received, and the Propofitions qualified, the Promotor Fifcal demands before the Inquifitors, that the Criminals be apprehended and imprifoned, that they may fuffer the deferved Punifhment.

When the Offence thus appears, and 'tis proper to apprehend the Criminal, the Inquifitor may then order him to be taken up. When they have determined

Pegna, *Com.* 107.

mined upon his being apprehended, they give out the Order to that Officer, who, according to the Custom of the holy Office, is to take up Criminals; and his Order is subscribed by the Inquisitors. If several Persons are to be taken up the same Day and Time, they give an Order for each Person, which is inserted in their respective Processes, that such Acts, which are of great Weight, may appear openly.

As to the second. All Criminals have not alike Places of Imprisonment, their Cells being either more terrible and dark, or more easy and chearful, according to the Quality of the Persons and their Offences. In Reality there is no Place in the Prison of the Inquisition, that can be called pleasant or chearful, the whole Jayl is so horrible and nasty.

These Jayls are called in *Spain* and *Portugal*, *Santa Casa*, i. e. the holy House. Every Thing it seems in this Office must be holy. The Prisons are so built, as the Author of the History of the Inquisition at *Goa* describes them, that they will hold a great Number of Persons. They consist of several Porticoes, every one of which is divided into several small Cells of a square Form, each Side being about ten Foot. There are two Rows of them, one being built over the other, and all of them vaulted. The upper ones are enlightned by Iron Grates, placed above the Height of a tall Man. The lower ones are under Ground, dark, without any Window, and narrower than the upper ones. The Walls are five Foot thick. Each Cell is fastned with two Doors, the inner one thick, and covered over with Iron, and in the lower Part of it there is an Iron Grate. In the upper Part of it is a little small Window, through which they reach to the Prisoner his Meat, Linnen, and other Necessaries, which is shut with two Iron Bolts. The outer Door is entire without any opening at all. They generally open it in the Morning, from six a Clock till eleven, in order to refresh the Air of the Prison.

In *Portugal* all the Prisoners, Men and Women, without any Regard to Birth or Dignity, are shaved the first or second Day of their Imprisonment. Every Prisoner hath two Pots of Water every Day, one to wash, and the other to drink, and a Besom to cleanse his Cell, and a Mat made of Rushes to lie upon, and a larger Vessel to ease Nature, with a Cover to put over it, which is changed once every four Days. The Provisions which are given to the Prisoners, are rated according to the Season, and the Dearness or Plenty of Eatables. But if any rich Person is imprisoned, and will live and eat beyond the ordinary Rate of Provisions, and according to his own Manner, he may be indulged, and have what is decent, and fit for him, his Servant, or Servants, if he hath any, with him in the Jayl. If there are any Provisions left, the Jayl-Keeper, and no other, must take them, and give them to the Poor. But *Reginald Consalvius* observes, *p.* 106. that this Indulgence is not allowed to Prisoners of all sorts, but to such only as are taken up for small Offences, who are to be condemned to a Fine. But if they find by the very Accusation that any Persons are to be punished with Forfeiture of all their Effects, they do not suffer them to live so plentifully, but order them a small Pension for their Subsistence, *viz.* about thirty Maravedis, of the Value of ten *Dutch* Stivers.

Stivers. This agrees with the Account of *Isaack Orobio*, who had a plentiful Fortune at *Seville*, and was neverthelefs ufed very hardly in the Prifon of the Inquifition there. Although his Eftate was very large, yet he was allowed a very fmall Penfion to provide himfelf Provifion. This was Flefh, which they made him fometimes drefs and prepare for himfelf, without allowing him the Help of any Servant. In this Manner are the richer Prifoners treated. As to the poorer, and fuch who have not enough to fupply themfelves in Jayl, their Allowance is fixed by the King, *viz.* the Half of a filver Piece of Money, called a Real *, every Day ; and out of this fmall Sum, the Buyer of their Provifion, whom they call the Difpenfer, and their Wafher muft be paid, and all other Expences that are neceffary for the common Supports of Life. Befides, this very royal Allowance for the Prifoners doth not come to them but through the Hands of feveral Perfons, and thofe none of the moft honeft ; firft by the Receiver, then the Difpenfer, then the Cook, then the Jayl-Keeper, who, according to his Office, diftributes the Provifion amongft the Prifoners. *Gonfalvius* adds, that he gave this particular Account of this Matter, becaufe all thefe Perfons live, and have their certain Profits out of this fmall Allowance of the King to the Prifoners, which coming to them through the crooked Hands of thefe Harpies, they cannot receive it till every one of them hath taken out more than a tenth Part of it.

The Author of the Hiftory of the Inquifition at *Goa* tells us, this Order is obferved in diftributing the Provifions. The Prifoners have Meat given them three times every Day ; and even thofe who have the Misfortune to be in this Cafe, and they have Money, are not treated much better than others, becaufe their Riches are employ'd to make Provifion for the Poorer. I was informed by *Ifaack Orobio*, that in *Spain* they fometimes give the Prifoners Coals, which they muft light, and then drefs their own Food. Sometimes they allow them a Candle. Thofe who are confined in the lower Cells generally fit in Darknefs, and are fometimes kept there for feveral Years, without any one's being fuffered to go or fpeak to them, except their Keepers, and they only at certain Hours, when they give them their Provifion. They are not allowed any Books of Devotion, but are fhut up in Darknefs and Solitude, that they may be broke with the Horrors of fo dreadful a Confinement, and by the Miferies of it forced to confefs Things which oftentimes they have never done.

And how dreadful the Miferies of this Prifon are, we have a famous In- p. 119. ftance given us by *Reginald Gonfalvius Montanus*. In the Age before the laft, a certain *Englifh* Ship put in at the Port of *Cadiz*, which the Familiars of the Inquifition, according to Cuftom, fearched upon the Account of Religion, before they fuffered any Perfon to come a-fhore. They feized on feveral

---

* Dr. *Geddes* tells us of one in the Inquifition at *Lisbon*, who was allowed no more than three Vintems a Day ; a Vintem is about an *Englifh* Penny Farthing.

Englifh

English Persons who were on board, observing in them certain Marks of
Evangelical Piety, and of their having received the best Instruction, and
threw them into Jayl. In that Ship there was a Child, ten or twelve Years,
at most, old, the Son of a very rich *English* Gentleman, to whom, as was
reported, the Ship and principal Part of her Loading belonged. Amongst
others they took up also this Child. The Pretence was, that he had in
his Hands the Psalms of *David* in *English.* But as *Gonsalvius* tells us, those
who knew their Avarice and cursed Arts, may well believe, without doing any Injury to the Holy Inquisition, that they had got the Scent of his
Father's Wealth, and that this was the true Cause of the Child's Imprisonment, and of all that Calamity that followed after it. However, the
Ship with all its Cargo was confiscated, and the Child, with the other
Prisoners, were carried to the Jayl of the Inquisition at *Seville,* where he
lay six or eight Months. Being kept in so strait Confinement for so long
a while, the Child, who had been brought up tenderly at home, fell into
a very dangerous Illness, through the Dampness of the Prison, and the
Badness of his Diet. When the Lords Inquisitors were informed of this,
they ordered him to be taken out of the Jayl, and carried, for the Recovery of his Health, to the Hospital, which they call the *Cardinal.* Here
they generally bring all who happen to fall ill in the Prison of the Inquisition, where, besides the Medicines, of which, according to the pious
Institution of the Hospital, there is Plenty, and a little better Care, upon
account of the Distemper, nothing is abated of the Severity of the former Jayl ; no Person besides the Physician, and the Servants of the Hospital, being allowed to visit the sick Person ; and as soon as ever he begins to grow better, before he is fully recovered, he is put again into
his former Jayl. The Child, who had contracted a very grievous Illness
from that long and barbarous Confinement, was carried into the Hospital, where he lost the Use of both his Legs ; nor was it ever known what
became of him afterwards. In the mean while 'twas wonderful, that the
Child, in so tender an Age, gave noble Proofs how firmly the Doctrine
of Piety was rooted in his Mind ; oftentimes, but especially Morning and
Evening, lifting up his Eyes to Heaven, and praying to him, from whom
he had been instructed by his Parents, to desire and hope for certain Help ;
which the Jayl-Keeper having often observed, said, He was already grown
a great little Heretick.

p. 121.   About the same Time a certain Person was taken up and thrown into
the same Jayl, who had voluntarily abjured the *Mahometan* Impiety, and
came but a little before from *Morocco,* a famous City of *Mauritania,* and
Capital of the Kingdom, into that Part of *Spain* which lies directly over
against it, with a Design to turn Christian. When he had observed that
the Christians were more vicious and corrupt than the *Moors* he had left,
he happened to say, that the *Mahometan* Law seem'd to him better than the
Christian. For this the good Fathers of the Faith laid hold of him, thurst
him into Jayl, and used him so cruelly, that he said publickly even when

in

in Confinement, that he never repented of his Chriftianity from the Day he was baptized, till after his having been in the Inquifition, where he was forced againſt his Will to behold all manner of Violences and Injuries whatſoever.

The Complaint of *Conſtantine*, the Preacher of *Seville*, was not leſs grievous concerning the Barbarities of this Priſon; who, although he had not as yet taſted of the Tortures, yet often bewailed his Miſery in this Jayl, and cried out: *O my God, were there no Scythians in the World, no Cannibals more fierce and cruel than Scythians, into whoſe Hands thou couldſt carry me, ſo that I might but eſcape the Paws of theſe Wretches.* *Olmedus* alſo, another Perſon famous for Piety and Learning, fell into the Inquifitors Hands at *Seville*, and thro' the Inhumanity of his Treatment, which had alſo proved fatal to *Conſtantine*, contraded a grievous Illneſs, and at laſt died in the Midſt of the Naſtineſs and Stench. He was uſed to ſay, *Throw me any where, O my God, ſo that I may but eſcape the Hands of theſe Wretckes.* *p.* 104.

The Author of the Hiſtory of *Goa* agrees in this Account, who frankly owns, that through the Cruelty and Length of his Impriſonment, he fell into Deſpair, and thereby often attempted to deſtroy himſelf; firſt by ſtarving himſelf, and becauſe that did not ſucceed, he feigned himſelf ſick; and when the Phyſician of the Inquifition found his Pulſe unequal, and that he was fevouriſh, he ordered him to be let Blood, which was done again five Days after. When the Doctor was gone, he unbound his Arm every Day, that ſo by the large Effuſion of Blood, he might continually grow weaker and weaker. In the mean while he eat very little, that by Hunger and Loſs of Blood, he might put an End to his miſerable Life. Whilſt he was in this ſad Condition, he had ſent him a Confeſſor of the *Franciſcan* Order, who, by various Arguments of Comfort, endeavoured to recover him from his Deſpair. They alſo gave him a Companion in his Jayl, which was ſome Comfort to him in his Confinement. But growing well again after about five Months, they took his Companion from him. The Loneſomeneſs of his Jayl brought on again his Melancholy and Deſpair, which made him invent another Method to deſtroy himſelf. He had a Piece of Gold Money, which he had concealed in his Cloaths, which he broke into two Parts; and making it ſharp, he opened with it a Vein in each Arm, and loſt ſo much Blood, that he fell into a Swoon, the Blood running about the Jayl. But ſome of the Servants happening to come before the uſual Time to bring him ſomething, found him in this Condition. The Inquifitor hereupon ordered him to be loaded with Irons upon his Arms and Hands, and ſtrictly watched. This Cruelty provoked him to that Degree, that he endeavoured to beat his Brains out againſt the Pavement and the Walls; and undoubtedly the Ligaments upon his Arms would have been torn off, had he continued any longer in that State. Upon this they took off his Chains, gave him good Words, encouraged him, and ſent him a Companion, by whoſe Converſation he was refreſhed, and bore his Miſery with a little more Eaſineſs of Mind. But after two Months they took him from him again, ſo that the Solitude of his Jayl was more diſtreſſing to him than before. *Cap.* 19, 20, 21.

The

Inquif.
Goan.
cap. 13.

The Prisoners, as soon as ever they are thrown into Jayl, are commanded to give an Account of their Name and Business. Then they enquire after their Wealth, and to induce them to give in an exact Account, the Inquisition promises them, that if they are innocent, all that they discover to them shall be faithfully kept for, and restored to them ; but that if they conceal any Thing, it shall be confiscated, though they should be found not guilty. And as in *Spain* and *Portugal* most Persons are fully persuaded of the Sanctity and Sincerity of this Tribunal, they willingly discover all their Possessions, even the most concealed Things of their Houses, being certainly persuaded, that when their Innocence shall appear, they shall soon recover their Liberty and Effects together. But these miserable Creatures are deceived ; for he that once falls into the Hands of these Judges, is stripped at once of all he was possessed of. For if any one denies his Crime, and is convicted by a sufficient Number of Witnesses, he is condemned as a negative Convict, and all his Effects confiscated. If to escape the Jayl, he confesses his Crime, he is guilty by his own Confession, and in the Judgment of all justly stripped of his Effects. When he is dismissed from Prison as a Convert and Penitent, he dares not defend his Innocence, unless he desires to be thrown again into Jayl, and condemned, and, as a feigned Penitent, to be delivered over to the secular Arm.

2. Part.
Assert. 2.

Of these Things *J. Royas* gives us an Account. " When any Criminal is " apprehended, and put into the Jayls of the Holy Office, his Effects must " be immediately sequestred, that they may not be conveyed away, or con- " cealed, and put into the Hands of some proper Person before the Notary " and Executor, who is to have the Custody and Care of them. Such Ef- " fects as cannot be kept, he who hath them in Custody, must sell by the " Inquisitors Command. This Sequestration is made only for real and formed " Heresy. From hence they infer, that this Sequestration or Description of " Effects is not to be made, when the Inquisitors proceed against Blasphe- " mers, or Fortune-Tellers, or those who marry again whilst their former " Wives are living, or against Clergymen in Orders, or professed Monks who " have contracted Matrimony, or against Persons who speak Propositions rash, " scandalous, injurious, or that found ill ; and in all other Causes, in which " there is not, *de jure*, any Confiscation of Effects, that which preceeds it, " *viz.* the Sequestration of such Effects, by Consequence ceases."

Inquif.
Goan. cap.
18.

When the Prisoner is brought before his Judge, he appears with his Head and Arms, and Feet naked. In this Condition he is brought out of Jayl by the Warder. When he comes to the Room of Audience, the Warder goes a little forward, and makes a profound Reverence, then withdraws, and the Prisoner enters by himself. At the farther End of the Audience Room there is placed a Crucifix, that reaches almost to the Cieling. In the Middle of the Hall is a Table about five Foot long, and four broad, with Seats all placed round it. At one End of the Table, that which is next to the Crucifix, sits the Notary of the Inquisition, at the other End the Inquisitor, and at his left Hand the Prisoner sitting upon a Bench. Upon the Table is a Missale, upon

which

which the Prifoner is commanded to lay his Hand, and to fwear that he will fpeak the Truth, and keep every Thing fecret. After they have fufficiently interrogated him, the Inquifitors ring a Bell for the Warder, who is com= manded to carry back his Prifoner to Jayl.

No one in the Prifon muft fo much as mutter, or make any Noife, but muft keep profound Silence. If any one bemoans himfelf, or bewails his Mis= fortune, or prays to God with an audible Voice, or fings a Pfalm or facred Hymn, the Jayl-Keepers, who continually watch in the Porches, and can hear even the leaft Sound, immediately come to him, and admonifh him that Silence muft be preferved in this Houfe. If the Prifoner doth not obey, the Keepers admonifh him again. If after this the Prifoner perfifts, the Keeper opens the Door, and prevents his Noife, by feverely beating him with a Stick, not only to chaftife him, but to deter others, who, becaufe the Cells are contiguous, and deep Silence is kept, can very eafily hear the Outcries and Sound of the Blows. I will add here a fhort Story that I had from feve= ral Perfons, which, if true, fhews us with what Severity they keep this Si= lence. A Prifoner in the Inquifition coughed. The Jaylors came to him, and admonifhed him to forbear coughing, becaufe it was unlawful to make any Noife in that Houfe. He anfwered, 'twas not in his Power. However, they admonifhed him a fecond time to forbear it, and becaufe he did not, they ftripped him naked, and cruelly beat him. This encreafed his Cough, for which they beat him fo often, that at laft he died through the Pain and Anguifh of the Stripes.

They infift fo feverely on keeping this Silence, that they may cut off every Degree of Comfort from the Afflicted, and efpecially for this Reafon, that the Prifoners may not know one another, either by finging, or any loud Voice. For it oftentimes happens, that after two or three Years Confine= ment in the Jayl of the Inquifition, a Man doth not know that his Friend, nor a Father that his Children and Wife are in the fame Prifon, till they all fee each other in the Act of Faith. And finally, that the Prifoners in the feveral Cells may not talk with one another, which, if ever found out, their Cells are immediately changed. *Gonfalv. p. 117.*

If any one falls ill in the Prifon, they fend to him a Surgeon and Phyfi= cian, who adminifter all proper Remedies to him to recover him to Health. If there be any Danger of his dying, they fend him a Confeffor, if he de= fires it. According to the Provifion of the *Madrid* Inftruction, *An.* 1561. cap. 71. *If any Criminal falls ill in Prifon, the Inquifitors muft take diligent Care that he may have Medicines, and all Things neceffary for his Safety, and the Advice of one Phyfician or more, to recover him. And if he defires a Confeffor, let them af= fign him one of known Probity, and who may be confided in, and let him be fworn to Secrecy. If the Penitent fays any thing to him in Confeffion, which he would have told out of the Jayl, let him not obey him in this by any Means, nor difcover any fuch Commands. But if he enjoins him any thing out of Confeffion, let him reveal that to the Inquifitors. Farther, let the Inquifitors admonifh and inftruct the Confeffor how he fhall behave towards the Penitent, particularly that he tell him, that fince he* *Direct. p. 2. com. 25.*

was

was imprifoned for Herefy, and accufed as guilty of it, he cannot be abfolved, unlejs he judicially declares his Herefy. Let other Things be left to the Judgment and Con-fcience of the Confeffor, who ought to be inftruEled that he may underftand what is fit to be done in fuch a Caufe.

If the Criminal doth not ask for a Confeffor, and the Phyfician believes the Diftemper to be dangerous, he muft be perfuaded by all Means to confefs; and if he judicially fatisfies the Inquifitors, he is to be reconciled to the Church before he dies, and being abfolved in Judgment, the Confeffor muft abfolve him Sacramentally. This is ordered by the fame Inftruction.

If he is well, and defires a Confeffor, fome are of Opinion he may not have one granted him, unlefs he hath confeffed judicially. Others think he may; and in this Cafe the Confeffor's Bufinefs is to exhort him to confefs his Errors, and to declare the whole Truth, as well of himfelf as of others, as he is bound *de jure*, to do. However, he muft add, that he muft not accufe himfelf or others falfely, through Wearinefs of his Imprifonment, the Hope of a more fpeedy Deliverance, or Fear of Torments. Such a Criminal the Confeffor cannot abfolve, before his Excommunication is firft taken off, and he is re-conciled to the Church. But in *Italy* the Prifoners are more eafily allowed a Confeffor than in *Spain*.

They are particularly careful not to put two or more in the fame Cell, un-lefs the Inquifitor for any fpecial Reafon fhall fo order, that they may not concert with one another to conceal the Truth, to make their Efcape, or to evade their Interrogatories. The principal Reafon indeed feems to be, that through the Irkfomenefs of their Imprifonment, they may confefs whatfoever the Inquifitors would have them. But if an Husband and his Wife are both imprifoned for the fame Offence, and there be no Fear that one fhould pre-vent the other from making a free Confeffion of the Crime, they may be put in the fame Cell.

Gonfalv.
p. 125.
The Inquifitors are obliged to vifit the Prifoners twice every Month, and to enquire whether they have Neceffaries allowed them, and whether they are well or not. In this Vifit they ufually ask him in thefe very Words, How he is? How he hath his Health? Whether he wants any Thing? Whether his Warder is civil to him? *i. e.* Whether he fpeaks to him in a reproachful and fevere Manner? Whether he gives him his appointed Provifion, and clean
Inquif.
Goan.
c. 12.
Linen? and the like. Thefe are exactly the Sentences and Words they ufe in thefe Vifits, to which they neither add any Thing, nor act agreeable; for they ufe them only for Forms fake, and when the Inquifitor hath fpoken them, he immediately goes away, fcarce ftaying for an Anfwer. And al-though any one of the Prifoners complains that he is not well ufed, 'tis of no Advantage to him, nor is he better treated for the future. If there be Oc-cafion or Neceffity, it will be convenient for them to vifit the Prifoners three or four times every Month, yea, as often as they think proper, *viz.* when the Criminal bears with Impatience the Misfortune and Infamy of his Imprifon-ment, in fuch Cafe the Inquifitor muft endeavour to comfort him very often, not only by himfelf, but by others, and to tell him, that if he makes a free Confeffion, his whole Affair fhall be quickly and kindly ended.   The

. The Inquifitors muft take Care not to talk with the Criminals, when they are examined or vifited, upon any other Affairs but fuch as relate to their Bufinefs. Nor muft the Inquifitor be alone when he vifits, or otherwife gives them Audience ; but muft have with him his Collegue, or at leaft a Notary, or fome other faithful Servant of the Holy Office. According to the *Madrid* Inftruction, *An.* 1561. *cap.* 17.

This alfo they are particularly careful of, that the Criminals may not be removed from one Cell to another, nor affociate with any other. If any Prifoners have been fhut up together at once in the fame Cell, when they are removed, they muft be removed together, that hereby they may be prevented from communicating any Thing that hath been tranfacted in the Prifon. This is more efpecially to be obferved, in cafe any of them recall their Confeffion, after they have been removed from one Cell and Company to another. But if a Criminal confeffes, and is truly converted, he may more eafily be removed from one Cell to another, becaufe the Inquifitor is in no Pain for fear of his retracting, but may oftentimes make ufe of him to draw out the Truth from other Prifoners, according to the Advice of *Eymerick*, in his Directory of the Inquifition, *p.* 3. *n.* 107. and *Pegna's* Commentary 23. *Things of this Nature,* fays he, *are to be learned rather from Experience than Art, or Precept, efpecially as there are fome Things which muft neither be revealed or taught, and are well known in themfelves to the Inquifitors.*

If Women are imprifoned, they muft each of them have, according to Pegna, their Quality, one honeft Woman at leaft for a Companion, who muft never *Prax. Inq.* be abfent from her, to prevent all Sufpicion of Evil. This Companion muft *l. 2. c. 15.* be antient, of a good Life, pious and faithful. Sometimes when Women are *n. 6.* to be imprifoned, they do not carry them to the Jayl of the Inquifitors, efpecially if they are Regulars, if the Jayls be within the Walls of the Monafteries, but to the Convents of the Nuns. When this happens, they command the Abbefs or Priorefs to admit no Body to difcourfe with the Prifoner without exprefs Leave of the Inquifitor, but diligently to obferve the Order given her. But when the Caufe is of Importance, and full of Danger, and fuch they efteem all that relate to the Faith, they think it fafer that Women fhould be imprifoned in the Jayls of the Inquifitors. But the Cardinals Inquifitors General are to, be confulted in this Affair, who, after mature Confideration, are to determine whether it be moft expedient that fuch Criminals fhould be kept in the Jayls of the Bifhops, or Inquifitors Regulars, efpecially if they are young and handfome, as is often the Cafe of thofe who are taken up for telling Peoples Fortunes about their Sweethearts.

'Tis farther the Cuftom and received Ufe of this holy Tribunal, that fuch who are imprifoned for Herefy, are not admitted to hear Mafs, and other Prayers which are faid within the Jayl, till their Caufe is determined. Their principal Pretence for this Cuftom is, that it may poffibly happen, when there is a great Number of Criminals, that the feveral Accomplices, Companions and Partakers of the Crime, may at leaft by Nods and Signs difcover to one another, how they may efcape Judgment, or conceal the Truth.

But

But the true and genuine Reafon is, that the Prifoner may have nothing to contemplate befides his prefent Misfortune, that fo being broken with the Miferies of his Confinement, he may confefs whatfoever the Inquifitors would have him. For this Reafon they deny them Books, and all other Things that would be any Relief to them in their tedious Imprifonment. If any one of the Prifoners whatfoever prays the Inquifitor when he vifits him, that he may have fome good Book, or the Holy Bible, he is anfwered, that the true Book is to difcover the Truth, and to exonerate his Confcience before that holy Tribunal ; and that this is the Book which he muft diligently ftudy, *viz.* to recover the Remembrance of every Thing faithfully, and declare it to their Lordfhips, who will immediately prefcribe a Remedy to his languifhing Soul. If the Prifoner in the fame or next Vifit is importunate about it, he will be commanded Silence, becaufe if he asks to pleafe himfelf, they may grant or deny him according to their Pleafure.

Simanc. tit. 41. §. 5.
 The keeping the Jayl antiently belonged to the Executors Office, and as often as he was abfent, he was obliged to provide another Keeper at his own Charge. But now the Jayl-Keeper is created by the Inquifitor General, and is different from the Executor.

Thofe who keep the Jayls for the Crime of Herefy, muft fwear before the Bifhop and Inquifitor, that they will faithfully keep their Prifoners, and obferve all other Things prefcribed them by *Clement.* I. de hæret. §. *Porro.*

Simanc. de Cathol. Inftit. tit. 16. §. 7, 8, 9.
 There muft be two Keepers to every Jayl, induftrious and faithful Men, one appointed by the Bifhop, the other by the Inquifitor. Each of them may have their proper Servant. Befides this, to every Cell there muft be two different Keys, each Keeper to have one, which they may give to their Servants, to fupply the Prifoners with Neceffaries. The Bifhop and Inquifitor have no Power to agree that there fhall be but one Keeper, becaufe it doth not feem fafe enough, neither is it allowed them by Law, nor appointed in their Caufe or Favour. *Clem.* 1. §. *Sane.* de hæret.

But now there is only one Jayl-Keeper appointed in every Province, chofen by the Inquifitor General, who is not allowed to give the Prifoners their Food. But the Inquifitors chufe fome proper Perfon to this Office, who is commonly called the Difpenfer. The Provifions they give the Criminals are generally prepared and dreffed in the Houfe of the Inquifition ; becaufe if they were to be prepared in the Houfes of the Criminals themfelves, or any where elfe, fomething might eafily be hid under them, that might furnifh them with the Means to conceal the Truth, or to elude or efcape Judgment. This however is to be left to the Prudence and Pleafure of the Inquifitors, whether and when the Criminals may without Danger prepare their Provifion in their own Houfes. But upon account of the Hazard attending it, the Inquifitors but feldom, and not without exquifite Care, gratify them in this Particular. If any Things are fent them by their Friends or Relations, or Domefticks, the Jayl-Keeper and Difpenfer never fuffer them to have it, without firft confulting the Inquifitors. *Inftruct. Tolet. c.* 26.

As

As these Keepers have it in their Power greatly to injure or serve their Prisoners, they must promise by an Oath, before the Bishop and Inquisitors,
that they will exercise a faithful Care and Concern in keeping them, and that
neither of them will speak to any of them but in Presence of the other, and
that they will not defraud them of their Provision, nor of those Things
which are brought to them. Their Servants also are obliged to take this
Oath.

But notwithstanding this Law, a great Part of the Provision appointed for
the Prisoners is with-held from them by their covetous Keepers ; and if they
are accused for this to the Inquisitors, they are much more gently punished, than
if they had used any Mercy towards them. *Reginald Gonsalve* relates, that in
his Time, *Gaspar Bennavidius* was Keeper of a Jayl. " He was a Man of mon-*p. 111;*
" strous Covetousnefs and Cruelty, who defrauded his miserable Prisoners of a *&c.*
" great Part of their Provision, which were ill dressed, and scarce the tenth
" Part of what was allowed them, and sold it secretly, for no great Price, at
" the *Triana*. Besides, he wholly kept from them the little Money allowed
" them to pay for the washing of their Linen, thus suffering them to abide
" many Days together in a nasty Condition, deceiving the Inquisitor and
" Treasurer, who put that Money to the Keepers Account, as though it had
" been expended every Week for the Use of the Prisoners, for whom it is ap-
" pointed. Neither was it very difficult to deceive them, because they took
" but little Pains to enquire out the Truth. If any one of the Prisoners
" complained, muttered, or opened his Mouth upon account of this intole-
" rable Usage, the cruel Wretch, who had divested himself of all Humanity,
" had a Remedy at hand. He brought the Prisoner immediately out of his
" Apartment, and put him down into a Place they call *Mazmorra*, a deep
" Cistern that had no Water in it. There he left him for several Days toge-
" ther, without any Thing to lie on, not so much as Straw. His Provision
" there was so very rotten, that it was more proper to destroy his Health
" by Sickness, than to preserve it, or support him in Life. All this he did
" without ever consulting the Inquisitors, and yet fraudulently and villanously
" pretended their Command to his Prisoner. If any one besought him to
" complain to the Inquisitors for so injurious a Treatment, for they could
" not do it by any other Person, and to desire an Audience, the cunning
" Wretch knowing that the whole Blame must lie upon himself, pretend-
" ed that he had asked, but could not obtain it. By such forged Answers,
" he kept the miserable Prisoner in that deep Pit twelve or fifteen Days,
" more or less, till he had fully gratified his Anger and Cruelty. After this
" he brought him out, and threw him into his former Jayl, perluading him
" that this Favour was owing to his Humanity and Care, having made Inter-
" cession for him with their Lordships. In short, his Thefts and Injuries with
" which he plagued his Prisoners, who were otherwise miserable enough,
" were so numerous, that some Persons of Interest with the Inquisitors at
" length accused him before them. Upon this he was imprisoned himself ;
" and being found guilty of many false Accusations, he received this Sen-
" tence :

" tence : That he fhould come out at a publick Act of the Faith, carrying
" a wax Candle in his Hand, be banifh'd five Years from the City, and for-
" feit the whole Sum of Money, which by Virtue of his Office he was to
" have received from the holy Tribunal.

p. 114.   " This very Man, whilft he was Keeper, had in his Family, an ancient
" Servant Maid, who obferving the Diftrefs of the Prifoners, labouring un-
" der intollerable Hunger and Naftinefs, through the Wickednefs and Bar-
" barity of her Mafter, was fo moved with pity towards them, being her felf
" well inclined to the Evangelical Piety, that fhe often fpoke to them through
" the Doors of their Cells, comforted them, and as well as fhe could ex-
" horted them to Patience, many Times putting them in Meat under their
" Doors, in Proportion to the mean and low Abilities of her Condition.
" And when fhe had nothing of her own, by which to fhew her Liberality
" to the Prifoners of Chrift, fhe ftole good Part of that Provifion from
" the wicked Thief her Mafter, which he had ftolen from the Prifoners, and
" reftored it to them. And that we may the more wonder at the Providence
" of God, who fo orders it that the worft of Parents fhall not have al-
" ways the worft of Children, but fometimes even the beft ; a little Daugh-
" ter of the Keeper himfelf was greatly affifting to the Maid in thefe pious
" Thefts. By Means of this Servant the Prifoners had Information of the
" State of the Affairs of their Brethren and fellow Prifoners, which much
" comforted them, and was oftentimes of great Service to their Caufe. But
" at length the Matter was difcover'd by the Lords Inquifitors, by whom
" fhe was thrown into Prifon for a Year, and underwent the fame Fate
" with the other Prifoners, and condemned to walk in the publick Proceffion,
" with a yellow Garment, and to receive two hundred Stripes, which was
" executed upon her the following Day through the Streets of the City, with
" the ufual Pomp and Cruelty. To all this was added Banifhment from
" the City and its Territories for ten Years. Her Title was, *The Favourefs*
" *and Aidrefs of Hereticks.* What excited the implacable Indignation of the
" Lords, the Fathers of the Faith, againft her, was, That they difcovered
" in her Examination, that fhe had revealed the Secrets of the moft holy
" Tribunal to fome of the Inhabitants of the City, particularly relating to
" the Provifion allotted to the Prifoners. From both thefe Examples, and
" from their different and unequal Punifhment, any one may fee, how much
" fafer it is to add to the Affliction of the Prifoners in their Jayl, than to
" comfort them by any Act of Humanity and Mercy whatfoever.

§. 11.   And in order that the Jayl of Hereticks may be kept fecret, no one of
the Officials, no not the Judge himfelf, as we fhall afterwards fee, can enter it alone, or fpeak with the Prifoners but before another of the Officials,
nor without the previous Order of the Inquifitors. All are obliged to fwear
that they will obferve this, that no one may fee or fpeak to the Prifoners befides the Perfon who gives them their Neceffaries, who muft be a faithful honeft Perfon, and is obliged to fware that he will not difcover the Secrets,
and muft be fearched to prevent his carrying any Orders or Letters to the
Prifoners.   This

This Command they will have obferved as moft facred, becaufe, as they fay, Secrecy is the Strength of the Inquifition, which might eafily be violated, unlefs this Order be punctually kept, and therefore they always moft feverely punifh thofe who tranfgrefs it. *Gonfalvius Montanus* gives us a very re- p. 108. markable Inftance of this. " A few Years ago, *viz.* before *Gonfalvius* wrote " this Account, one *Peter ab Herera*, a Man not altogether vile, but of fome " Humanity, and not very old, was appointed Keeper of the Tower of *Triana*, " which is the Prifon of the Inquifition. It happened, as it often doth in fuch " numerous and promifcuous Imprifonments, that amongft other Prifoners " committed to his Cuftody, there was a certain good Matron, with her two " Daughters, who were put in different Cells, and earneftly defired the Li- " berty of feeing one another, and comforting each other in fo great a Cala- " mity. They therefore earneftly entreated the Keeper, that he would fuffer " them to be together for one quarter of an Hour, that they might have the " Satisfaction of embracing each other. He being moved with Humanity " and Compaffion, allowed them to be together, and talk with one another " for half an Hour, and after they had indulged their mutual Affections, he " put them, as they were before, in their feparate Prifons. A few Days af- " ter this they were put with great Cruelty to the Torture; and the Keeper " being afraid, that through the Severity of their Torments, they fhould " difcover to the Lords the Fathers Inquifitors, his fmall Humanity in fuffer- " ing them to converfe together for half an Hour without the Inquifitors " Leave, thro' Terror, went himfelf to the holy Tribunal, of his own Ac- " cord confeffed his Sin, and prayed for Pardon, foolifhly believing, that " by fuch his Confeffion, he fhould prevent the Punifhment that threatned " him for this Action. But the Lords Inquifitors judged this to be fo heinous " a Crime, that they ordered him immediately to be thrown into Jayl, and " fuch was the Cruelty of his Treatment, and the Diforder of Mind that fol- " lowed on it, that he foon grew diftracted. However, his Diforder and " Madnefs did not fave him from a more grievous Punifhment. For after he " had lain a full Year in that curfed Prifon, they brought him out in the pub- " lick Proceffion, cloathed with the yellow Garment, and an Halter round " his Neck, as though he had been a common Thief, and condemned him " firft to receive two hundred Lafhes through the Streets of the City, and " then to the Gallies for fix Years. The Day after the Proceffion, as he " was carried from the *Triana* to be whipt with the ufual Solemnity, his Mad- " nefs, which ufually feized him every other Hour, came on him, and throw- " ing himfelf from the Afs on which, for the greater Shame, he was carried, " he flew upon the Inquifitory * *Alguazile*, and fnatching from him a Sword, " had certainly killed him, had he not been prevented by the Mob who at- " tended him, and fet him again upon the Afs, and guarded him till he had " received the two hundred Lafhes according to his Sentence. After this " the Lords Inquifitors ordered, that as he had behaved himfelf indecently

* An Officer that executes the Orders of the Inquifition.

K k

" towards

" towards the *Alguazile*, four Years more fhould be added to the fix for
" which he was at firft condemned to the Gallies."

Thefe Keepers are anfwerable for the fmalleft Fault, for they are to ufe
the fame Care in the Cuftody of their Prifoners, as Fathers ought to do in governing their Families ; fo that if they fuffer ony one to efcape from Jayl, they
are to be punifhed according to the Nature of their Offence. 'Tis therefore
their Bufinefs frequently to vifit and fearch the Cells of their Prifoners, to prevent any Thing from being clandeftinely carried in, by which they may deftroy
themfelves, dig through the Walls, and fo efcape. Their Care of the Women is to be peculiarly ftrict, fince the Sex is naturally frail, and more fubject than Men to yield to Paffion and Defpair, and fo are more likely to feek
an Occafion of deftroying themfelves. They muft, above all other Things,
take Care that they do not behave themfelves indecently towards their Women Prifoners. Thus the Congregation of Cardinals Inquifitors General,
condemned a Jayl Keeper to the Gallies for feven Years, and to perpetual
Banifhment from the Place where he committed his Offence, for having carnal Knowledge of a Woman that was Prifoner in the Holy Office ; as appears
from the Letters of Cardinal *Arigonius*, *Jan.* 13, 1610. directed to the Inquifitor of *Cremona*.

If the Inquifitor thinks it neceffary to prevent the Efcape of any Prifoners,
he may lay them in Irons. If the Poverty of the Inquifitors is fo great, or their
Jayls fo defective, as that they are not fit to hold in fafe Cuftody, either for
the Thinnefs of the Walls, or for want of Iron Bars to the Windows, or fufficient Bolts for the Doors, if the Magiftrate be required by the Inquifitor, he
muft take Care of the fafe Cuftody of the Prifoners, according to the Conftitution of *Alexander* IV. beginning, *Ad exftirpanda.*

What the feveral Duties of the Meffenger, Door-Keeper, and Phyfician
are, is plain enough from their very Names. They muft be honeft Men, and
not fufpected, and born of old Chriftians.

*Carena,
p.* 1. *t.* 15.
n. 114

*Simanc.
tit.* 41.
§. 10.

CHAP. XIX.

Of the Expences requifite in the Adminiftration of the INQUISITION
and Confifcation of Effects applied to this Ufe.

THESE Jayls cannot be built, nor Criminals be apprehended, nor maintained in Prifon, without Expence. It was therefore neceffary that
fome Law fhould determine how thefe Expences fhould be provided for. Befides the Inquifitors, and all other Servants of the Inquifition, muft have their
Salaries paid them. Originally this Burthen was laid on the Cities themfelves,
as may be collected from the Conftitution of *Innocent* IV. *Ad exftirpanda. Let
the chief Magiftrate or Governor be obliged, at the Expence of the Place where he
prefides,*

An. 1252.
§. 3.
Bzovius.

2

prefides, to caufe fuch Hereticks, when apprehended, to be carried wherefoever the Diocefan, or his Vicars, or the Inquifitors, or Inquifitor, fhall order them to be carried, within the Jurifdiction or Diftrict of fuch Diocefan Bifhop, or of fuch City or Place. The Officials fhall be allowed out of the Chamber of fuch City or Place, when they go without the faid City or Place, in Execution of their Office, every one of them eighteen Imperials in ready Money per diem, which the Magiftrate or Governor fhall give, or caufe to be given them, within three Days after their Return to fuch City or Place. They fhall alfo have the third Part of the Effects of Hereticks they feize on, and of the Fines to which they fhall be condemned, according as it is contained below, and with this Salary fhall be content. Neither fhall they be compelled by any Means to any other Office and Service, that may hinder them in the Exercife of this.

But as the Cities thought themfelves aggrieved by this Charge, and openly refufed to bear it, the confifcated Effects of Hereticks have been applied to thefe Ufes, and the Crofs-bearers have bound themfelves by Vow, that they will expend their own Eftates for the Defence of the Faith. But that it may be more diftinctly underftood how thefe Effects are applied to the Ufes of the Inquifition, I fhall endeavour to trace this whole Affair from the Beginning.

When the delegated Inquifition was firft conftituted, the Sentence concern- Direct. ing the Confifcation of Effects in the Dominions of the Church, was pro- p. 3. nounced by the Ecclefiaftical Judge; but in other Countries by fecular Prin- com. 148. ces, as appears plain from the Text in cap. *Vergentis.* de hæret. *But in the Countries fubject to our temporal Jurifdiction, we ordain that the Goods of Hereticks fhall be expofed to Sale; and in other Countries we command that it fhall be done by the fecular Powers and Princes, and if they appear negligent, we will and command that they fhall be compelled to do it by Ecclefiaftical Cenfure, without Benefit of Appeal.* But in a Courfe of Years it was, without any Difference, provided that the Declaratory Sentence concerning fuch Confifcation, fhould every where be paffed by the Ecclefiaftical Judge, who judges of the Crime; and farther, that the Execution of fuch Confifcation, viz. the Seizure of the Goods, fhould be made by the Ecclefiaftical Judge, viz. by the Bifhop or Inquifitor: *The Ex-* Cap. ut *ecution of fuch Confifcation, or the Seizure of the Effects themfelves fhall not be made* Inquifiti- *by Princes, or other temporal Lords, before the Sentence for fuch Crime fhall have* onis. *been publifhed by the Bifhop of the Place, or fome other Ecclefiaftical Perfon, who* §. Prohi- *hath Power in this Affair.* C. Cum fecundum leges. §. fin. de hæret. lib. 6. ibid. bemus.

Whether Hereticks repent or not, whether they are converted before they are delivered to the fecular Court, or afterwards, their Effects are *ipfo facto,* confifcated. *The Goods of Hereticks, who offend more grievoufly, horribly, and de-* C. Cum *teftably than others, we, with the Advice of our Brethren, decree to be,* ipfo jure, fecundum *confifcated.* Neither doth it fignify whether the Heretick hath perfifted in his leges. de Herefy for a longer or fhorter Time; becaufe Herefy is not judged of by hæret. l.6. the Length of Time.

But if any voluntarily return to the Church, before they are accufed or denounced, or if immediately after they are apprehended, they make a full and entire Confeffion of themfelves and others, whom they know to be Hereticks:

reticks : Such who thus return with a pure Heart, before the Depofitions of the Witneffes are publifhed, are, as feems equitable, kindly excufed from Imprifonment, and have alfo for the fame Reafon the Confifcation of their Ef-

fe&s remitted them. In *Italy* 'tis owing rather to Cuftom than to any Papal Conftitution, that the Effe&s of penitent Hereticks are not fold. But in *Spain*, the Effe&s of Hereticks, though penitent, are confifcated, not only by the Papal, but Royal Laws.

But as to the Seizure and Application of fuch confifcated Effe&s, the Civil

Law thus determines. *Whom alfo we perfue with the Publication of all their Effe&s.* However fuch Effe&s, publifhed becaufe of Herefy, were not condemned to the Treafury, if the Children of fuch Hereticks were Catholicks ; as is plain from the before-mentioned Law. *Neither do we permit their Children to become their Heirs, unlefs they forfake their Parents Wickednefs.* It is alfo farther explained, *L. Cognovimus*, C. de hæret. to whom the confifcated Effe&s of Hereticks fhall be applied, if their Children are not Catholicks, *viz.* to their next Relations and Kindred, if Orthodox and Catholick. But if none fuch are to be found, the Effe&s are all to be converted to the Treafury of the fecular Prince. And a little after, in Authent. §. *fi quis de prædi&is.* this Method of Succeffion is prefcribed, if the Fathers fhould be Catholicks, and their Children Hereticks. Becaufe heretical Children and Relations cannot fucceed Catholick Parents, if the Father be a Clergyman, the Church fhall inherit ; if a Layman, his Eftate fhall go to the Treafury. Many Ages after this, *Frederick* the Emperor, by a Law beginning, *Catharos.* thus ordained, about the Year 1220. *We condemn all Hereticks of both Sexes, and every Name, to perpetual Infamy, we deprive them of our Prote&ion, and put them under the Bann, ordering their Effe&s to be confifcated, and never more to return to them, fo that their Children fhall never come to the Poffeffion of them, fince 'tis much more heinous to offend the eternal than the temporal Majefty.*

But as the Crime of Herefy is merely Ecclefiaftical, they contend that the Ecclefiaftical Laws, which order all Things relating to the Punifhment of it, ought to prevail, and be every where obferved. And therefore fince the Confifcation of Effe&s is one of the Penalties ordained againft Hereticks, they affirm, that what hath been ordained by the Ecclefiaftical Papal Laws and Conftitutions, ought to be obferved by all that would approve their Obedience to the Church of *Rome*.

Pope *Innocent* III. in the Year of our Lord 1199 or 1200. and fecond Year of his Papacy, firft ordained at the *Lateran*, *April Cal.* 8. by a decretal Epiftle, beginning, *Vergentis in fenium*, directed to the Clergy, Confuls, and People of *Viterbo*, that the Effe&s of Hereticks fhould be confifcated, as had been determined by the Civil Laws, and that they fhould be applied to the Treafury of the Church in the Countries fubject to her, and in other Dominions of the Empire, to the Treafury of the fecular Judge. And this he commands to be obferved, although Hereticks fhould have Catholick Children, who by the Civil Law were allowed to fucceed to their Parents Eftates. The fame Confifcation of Effe&s, a few Years after, *viz. An.* 1215. was decreed in
the

the *Lateran* Council under *Innocent* III. *cap.* 3. and is contained, C. *Excommunicamus*, 1. §. *Damnati, vero.* but with this Difference obferved, between the Effects of heretical Laity and Clergy. *So that the Goods of fuch condemned Perfons, if they are Laicks, fhall be confifcated ; if of the Clergy, they fhall be applied to the Churches, from whom they have received their Stipends.*

Hence Pope *Innocent* IV. 1252. and ninth Year of his Pontificate, by a Conftitution made at *Peroufe*, the Ides of *May*, and beginning, *Ad exftirpanda* ; commanded the confifcated Goods of Hereticks to be divided into three Parts, and applied in the Manner as is prefcribed in thefe Words. *Moreover, the chief Magiftrate or Ruler fhall be obliged fo to divide the Effects of Hereticks, which fhall be feized and found by the faid Officials, and the Fines which fhall be exacted for them, as that one Part fhall go to the common Ufe of the City or Place, the fecond to the Officials who fhall be engaged in the Affair, in Favour and for the Affiftance of the Office : and the third fhall be depofited in fome fafe Place, to be referved and expended as the faid Diocefan and Inquifitors fhall think fit, and with their Advice, in Favour of the Faith, and the Extirpation of Hereticks, notwithftanding any Statute made, or to be made to the contrary.* This *Alexander* IV. confirmed *An.* 1259. by a Conftitution, beginning, *Ad exftirpanda.* But in the Year 1260. he granted by an Extravagant at *Genoa*, beginning, *Difcretioni veftræ*, to the Inquifitors in the *Roman* Province, and Adminiftration of St. *Francis*, that the Goods of Hereticks and others mentioned in it, fhould be fold, and the Money kept for the Ufes of the Church of *Rome. By Authority of thefe prefent, we grant full and free Power to your Difcretion, of which we have full Confidence in the Lord, of felling and dividing freely the Goods of Hereticks, their Favourers, Believers, Receivers, and Defenders, already publifhed, or confifcated, or hereafter to be publifhed and confifcated, as you fhall think the Affair of the Faith committed to you fhall require ; and of referving the Money arifing from thence to the Ufe of the Church of* Rome *; and alfo of compelling all who fhall oppofe you in this Matter, by Ecclefiaftical Cenfure, without allowing them the Benefit of Appeal.*

Clement IV. his Succeffor, *An.* 1265. by a Conftitution beginning, *Ad exftirpanda*, ordered the fame threefold Divifion, but makes more particular Mention of the Effects. *Moreover, the chief Magiftrate, Officer, Conful, or any other Ruler, fhall be obliged to divide in fuch a Manner all the Effects of Hereticks, and their Receivers, which fhall be feized or found by the faid Officials, and the Fines exacted for them ; as alfo all the Timber, Stones, and Tiling of the Houfes and Caftles that fhall be deftroyed on the Account of Herefy ; and alfo all the moveable and immoveable Effects that fhall be confifcated on the fame Account, as that one Part,* &c.

Boniface VIII. *An.* 1295. by a Conftitution of his to be found, Cap. *Cum fecundum leges.* de hæret. lib. 6. declared likewife, that the Effects of Hereticks were *ipfo jure* confifcated. But he prohibited the temporal Lords to lay hold of, or feize on them, before the lawful Ecclefiaftical Judges had pronounced concerning the Crime of Herefy. *Benedict.* XI. by an Extravagant beginning, *Ex eo. An.* 1303. orders ; *The faid Diocefans fhall not demand any Account of the Profits arifing from the Office of the Inquifition ; any Conftitution, Cuftom, or Command*

mand to the contrary notwithstanding. * *But you shall give it to our Chamber, or to any Person, whom we or the* Roman *Pontiffs our Successors shall appoint for this Purpose. And this we command to be generally observed.*

From these Constitutions they infer, that if any temporal Lord, in Favour of the Faith, actually doth these Things, or other Things equivalent, or greater, or of like Nature, to what the said Constitutions require, he ought to have a third Part of the confiscated Effects ; or more, if the Pope allows, and knowingly permits it. And therefore in *Spain* the Effects of such as are condemned for Heresy are rightly applied to the Royal Treasury ; because the King hath not only the Care of constituting the Senate, which manages in the Royal Palace all the Causes of the whole Kingdom of *Spain* relating to the Punishment of this Crime, and of which one of the principal Prelates is President ; but also liberally supplies the Inquisitors, which the said Prelate appoints by the Papal Authority, and sends throughout the whole Kingdom, to extirpate heretical Pravity, with all their Expences, and every Thing else necessary to their Office. But as in many Places the temporal Lords do not grant the Inquisitors their Expences, nor submit to those Burthens and Labours, which *Innocent, Alexander,* and *Clement.* IV.' have commanded, *Pegna* doth not understand by what Right they can appropriate to themselves the third Part of such confiscated Effects ; and therefore thinks that they ought all to be applied to promote and advance the Holy Office. Especially as the Inquisitors have now their proper Jayls, their necessary Attendance, and their own Notaries and Ministers, to the greatest Part of whom the temporal Lords give neither Subsistence or Salary ; and when desired, oftentimes refuse to do it. Yea, if the Inquisitor sometimes asks the Guards, Apparitors, or Soldiers of the secular Lord, to execute any Affairs of the Faith, to take up Hereticks, or carry them to Jayl, he will not suffer them to go, without first receiving the Satisfaction and agreed Price from the Inquisitors.

This *Camillus Campegius* especially urges with Reference to the Inquisitors of *Italy,* " Who, he says, are generally Mendicant Regulars, who scarce re-
In Zan-
chin. cap.
19. " ceive enough from their Monasteries to support them, or cloath themselves
" decently ; who in Justice ought to have their Provision and Cloathing, and
" other Necessaries, not from the Monasteries, but from the Office it self in
" which they serve. For that these Inquisitors are so entirely devoted to the
" Affairs of the Office, that they cannot serve Religion or the Monastery,
" which is such a Detriment to Religion as ought not to be suffered. Add to
" this that Religion, and the very Monasteries are greatly damaged upon
" Account of the said Office, because these Religious are hated, and are for
" this Reason deprived of much Alms, and exposed also to many Dangers of
" Life."

Hence he infers, that the Inquisitors may receive not only their Expences, but also a Salary or Fees. And as to the Objection that the confiscated Goods of Hereticks are appropriated to maintain the Inquisitors, he answers : " That such Confiscation seldom happens, since the Effects are restored to such " as return, few being found who are obstinate or relapsed, and these, gene-
" rally

" rally fpeaking, fo very poor, that they are not able to defray the Expen-
" ces of the Notaries, nor maintain themfelves whilft they are kept in Jayl.
" As to the other Objection, That the Inquifitors ought to be content with
" the Subfidy exacted from, or given them by the Crofs-bearers, he an-
" fwers, that this is far from being fufficient, becaufe either they cannot or
" will not give. Befides, many of them fubvert the very End of their Infti-
" tution, and are rather Mafters over the Inquifitor, than fubject to him, and
" fometimes do more harm than good to this Holy Office. 'Tis true, many
" of them are very jealous and zealous for the Faith, who, according to the
" Obligation of their Vow, willingly expofe their Life and Subftance for the
" Faith. But as they themfelves are poor, they want Affiftance inftead of
" being able to fupport others." He goes on, " Since this is really the Cafe,
" how can the Inquifitors fuftain the Burthens of their Office? How can they
" be able to repair or build Jayls? How can they fatisfy the Keepers, and
" other Officers? How can they provide Suftenance for the poor Prifoners,
" or Beds for them to lie on? How can the Inquifitors themfelves vifit their
" Diocefe or Province? Who fhall fupply them with Horfes and Ships?
" Who fhall give them, their Companions, Notaries, and Servants, the Char-
" ges of their Journey? For 'tis not decent or fafe that the Inquifitor fhould
" travel alone. The Duties of this Service are almoft infinite, which neither
" the Bifhops, Cities, or Princes, will fo much as touch with their Finger.
" Since therefore the *Italian* Inquifitors have no Benefice, or Incomes, or if
" they have, fuch as are not fufficient to maintain them, they may demand
" their Expences, Salary or Fees. This however the Inquifitors and other
" Officials who are Bifhops, as they are in *Spain*, cannot do. Nor fuch who
" receive their Expences from the Apoftolical Chamber, as is obferved at
" *Rome*, or who otherwife receive Affiftance or Support, to enable them to
" difcharge the Duties of the faid Office.
" At this Time the Inquifitors affirm, that the Church of *Rome* is the Trea- Zanchin.
" fury as far as relates to the confifcated Effects of Hereticks; and that fhe *c. 16.*
" hath ordered that one half of the faid Effects fhall be appropriated to her
" own Chamber, and that the other half fhall remain in the Office of the
" Inquifition for the neceffary Ufes thereof. - This Cuftom is now obferved."

Campegius, in his Additions, cites the Letters of *Innocent* IV. directed to the
Archbifhops and Bifhops, and Provincial of the Province. *We, treading in the
Steps of Pope* Gregory *our Predeceffor, of bleffed Memory, order that the moveable
Effects and Houfes of fuch who are imprifoned for Herefy, fhall be fold, if it can be
done without Prejudice of their Lords, or grievous Scandal ; and that the pecuniary
Penalties which fhall be laid by the faid Friars Inquifitors, on any Perfons, on Account of heretical Pravity, for the Advantage of the faid Affair, and after having
confidered the Quality of the Perfons, and Nature of their Offences, fhall be entirely
referved for building feparate and fufficient Prifons, and for fupplying the neceffary
Expences of the Prifoners, and of the faid Friars, and other Perfons, whom they
fhall think proper to make ufe of to carry on the faid Affair.* And in the Extravagant *Ex eo. de* hæret. §. *fin, The faid Diocefans fhall not demand any Account from*

you of the Profits arising from the Office of the Inquisition, any Constitution, Custom,
or Command to the contrary notwithstanding. But you shall send the Account to our
Chamber, or to such other Person as we or our Successors the Popes of Rome *shall*
appoint for this Purpose. This we command shall be generally observed.

In voce.
Bona ha-
ret.

And lastly, Friar *Bernard Comensis,* in his Light of the Inquisitors, hath
given us this short Account of the whole Affair. " The Effects of Hereticks,
" since they are *ipso jure* confiscated from the Day of the Crime committed,

4.
" shall not be sold or alienated by the said Hereticks. Yea, the Treasury or
" Inquisitors shall reclaim the said Effects, if sold or alienated, out of the
" Hands of the Possessors, without any Charge, through what Hands soever
" they may have passed ; unless the Price, or something equivalent to it, was
" amongst the Effects of the said Heretick thus alienating them.

5.
" The Ordinary or Diocesan shall have no Part of the Profits of the Goods
" of Hereticks, appropriated to the Office of the Inquisition, although he
" himself proceeds in the said Office ; but must discharge his Duty at his own
" proper Expences, and out of his own Returns, because he is the Ordinary,
" according to the Extravagant of *Benedict* XI. beginning, *Ex eo quod.* Nor
" are the Inquisitors obliged to give an Account to the said Diocesans of the
" Effects accrewing to the Office of the Inquisition. *Ibid.*

6.
" Whereas the Cross-bearers now generally provide, in Aid of the Office
" of the Inquisition, all the necessary Expences of the said Office, at the
" Pleasure of the Inquisitors, and appoint such Officials as are necessary to
" the said Office, and pay them, as the Inquisitors order them ; they have
" therefore now introduced a Custom, that the Confiscations made of the
" Effects of Hereticks by the Inquisitors, shall be applied to the Office of
" the Inquisition, and administred by the Inquisitors, or the said Cross-bearers,
" at the Pleasure of the Inquisitors, to expedite the Affairs of the said Of-
" fice, and in all Causes appertaining to it.

7.
" When the Effects of Hereticks are confiscated, such Confiscation reaches
" not only to such Effects as are found in the Territory where the Condem-
" nation is made, but to such as are found in any other Territory ; and the
" Execution shall be made by the Officials of that Place where the Goods
" are. For Instance, if a Man is born at *Bologne,* and hath a good Estate
" there, and yet builds himself an House at *Florence,* and is by the Inquisi-
" tor of *Florence* condemned there for Heresy ; in such Case the Inquisitor of
" *Bologne* shall seize upon all his Effects which he finds there, because the
" Purse of the Church of *Rome* equally extends to *Bologne* as to *Florence.* But
" 'tis not thus with the Part that comes to the Officials. See the Declara-
" tion of *Nicholaus* IV. *An.* 1291. *Oct.* 5.

" The moveable Effects of the Criminal, which are found in any other
" Territory, must go to the Treasury of such Place in which they are con-
" demned.

C H A P.

CHAP. XX.

Of the SALARIES *of the* INQUISITORS, *and other* OFFICERS.

'TIS very evident from what hath been already said, that the Method of paying the Inquisitors their Salaries, is not every where the same, but very different, according as the confiscated Effects are seized, either by the secular Lords or the Inquisitors.

Formerly, in *France*, the Expences and necessary Supports were given them out of the royal Treasury, by the *Ballives* *; who, in that Age, received the Returns of their several Districts, and had their Accounts audited in the Chamber of Accounts, as appears from those Accounts themselves. For some of them gave in an Account of the Expences of the Friars Inquisitors at Ascension Term, *Ann.* 1248. There is also extant in the Royal Chamber of Records, Register Book 36. Cap. 16. an Edict of *Philip* the Fair, by which they are commanded, not only to furnish the Inquisitors with necessary Provisions, but also to give them Assistance and Counsel in the Execution of the Office committed to them. *To the* Seneschall *of* Tholouse, *and* Carcassone, *greeting: Whereas Friar* William de Morreriis, *a Predicant, of whom we have received a favourable Account, is, as is reported, newly deputed by the Apostolick Authority, Inquisitor at* Tholouse, *we command you, that ye cause to be given and ministred to him our Jayls, situate in our Lands, for the Custody of Persons taken up for the Crime of Heresy ; as also Money for his Provision, and for executing his Office ; and that you grant him all Help, Favour and Counsel therein, as hath been hitherto granted to other Inquisitors, and as long as it shall be our Pleasure. Dated at* Vicenn. 1302.

James, King of *Aragon*, by a Law, beginning, *Quoniam fidei Catholicæ*, made *May* 23, 1292. thus commands : *Likewise also we Will and Command, that ye provide for the said Inquisitors, their Expences, and pay all their Charges they shall be at upon Account of the said Inquisition, as well for Horses as for other Matters, as they shall give in their Accounts of them, as often as you shall be required by them, or any one of them.*

In *Italy* and other Places, where the Inquisitors are poor, the Commonwealth must maintain them in the Places where they live, as is provided by many Rescripts of former Popes ; and particularly by a Rescript of *Innocent* IV. beginning, *Ad exstirpanda.* 'Tis also the Duty of the Cross-bearers to support the Inquisitors with their Estates, to which they have oblig'd themselves by Vow.

In *Spain* all these Things are determined by certain Laws. As to the Expences relating to the Criminal under Inquisition, the *Madrid* Instruction,

Marginal notes:
Du Cauge *in voce* Inquisitio.

Bzovius, *a.* 1292. §. 5.

Eymer. *p.* 3. *q.* 104. Com. 153.

Qu. 104. Com. 153.

---

* *Ballives*, are Judges to administer Justice in Provinces and greater Cities, and who also took Care of the Fines, Confiscations, Mortmains, and other Effects belonging to the King, in their respective Districts. *Du Fresne.*

L l

An.

An. 1561. *Cap.* 9. hath thus determined : *Let so much Money be taken out of the sequestred Effects of the Delinquent, as is necessary to carry him to Jayl, and six or eight Pieces of Gold more for his own Support ; nor shall any more Expences be allow'd him than are necessary for him, and the Cattle that are to carry him, and the Bed on which he is to sleep. If there be no ready Money in the sequestred Effects, such of them however as are less necessary shall be sold to bring in the said Quantity. The Executor of this Affair shall take Care to write down what he orders at the Bottom of the register'd Effects, and what remains shall be assigned over to the Dispensator of the Prisoners, in the Presence of the Attorney of the Sequestration. And the Inquisitors shall be certified as to the whole Affair.*

In many Inquisitions this exact Order is not observ'd, either through Poverty, or for other Reasons ; in which Case every one abides by the received Custom of his Inquisition.

In *Spain* there are fixed Salaries for the Inquisitors, and other Ministers of the holy Office, which are paid them at stated Times out of the forfeited Effects, according to the Quantity and Order describ'd by *Simancas.* *Cathol. Inst. tit.* 41. *n.* 33, 34.

§. 33.
" The Salaries must be paid to the Inquisitors and Officers by the Com-
" monwealth, which they serve with great Labour, but greater Profit.
" Every Inquisitor hath annually allow'd him 60000, which now is increas'd
" to an hundred thousand Pieces, every one of which is worth two of those
" Brass Pieces of Money, which they commonly call *Albi.* The Judges
" of the forfeited Effects have each of them 30000. The Promotor Fiscal
" as many. The Scribe or Notary the same. The Executor 60000. The
" Receiver as many. The Messenger 20000. The Door-keeper 10000.
" The Physician 5000. These Salaries may be increas'd at the Pleasure
" of the Inquisitor General, and are to be paid by the Receiver at the
" fixed Times, which if he neglects to do, he may be deprived of his Of-
" fice by the Inquisitors. 4 *Inst. Tolet.* c. 2. *Inst.* 3. *Valdolit.* c. 13.

§. 34.
" All these Salaries are paid out of the forfeited Effects. A third Part
" is to be paid in the Beginning of every fourth Month, and they then be-
" gin to be due, when the Judges and Ministers go from their Houses to
" manage the Affairs of this holy Inquisition. But if they die before the
" four Months compleat, their Salaries shall be paid and go to their Heirs.

§. 13.
" The Assessors and Counsellors have no Stipend, but must give their
" Advice *Gratis,* when the Inquisitors desire it, as some Lawyers affirm ;
" and though they may receive a Salary freely offer'd them, yet they can-
" not demand it, because all Christians are bound to support and defend
" the Affair of the Catholick Faith. However, these Assessors, who are
" the Eyes of the Judges in every Cause, even though it be spiritual, just-
" ly receive a Salary for their Service and Labour. For many Things are
" justly received, which it would be Injustice to demand.

Tit. 5.
§. 6, 7.
" Those Advocates who defend the Causes of the Poor have a Stipend
" out of the Treasury, which is usually very small, tho' honourable. But
" if the Criminals are not poor, the Advocates are paid out of their Effects.
'Tis

'Tis alſo provided in *Spain*, by many Conſtitutions, that Inquiſitors, who receive Gifts incur the Sentence of Excommunication, and are deprived of their Office, and fined double the Value of what they take. Simanc. This holds if they take Gifts from their Officials. 'Tis ordain'd al-de Cathol. ſo, by the ſame Inſtructions, That all the Officers ſhall be content with Inſt. t. 34. their Stipends, and receive no Gifts; not ſo much as any Thing to drink n. 45. or eat. And if any one is convicted of doing it, he is deprived of his Office, muſt pay double the Sum, incurs the Sentence of Excommunication, and is fined in 10000 Pieces. If any one of the Officers knows of any ſuch Thing, and doth not diſcover it to the Inquiſitors, he muſt ſuffer Puniſhment. The Words of the Inſtruction, *An.* 1484. Cap. 1.

> *and other their Officials, ſuch as Advocates, Fiſcals, Executors, Nota-*
> *Door-keepers, ſhall receive no Gifts or Money from any Perſons what-*
> *ſoever, which the ſaid Inquiſition doth or may lay hold of, nor from any other Per-*
> *them. And the Inquiſitor General ſhall command them not to re-*
> *under Pain of Excommunication, Deprivation of Offices, which*
> *holy Inquiſition, and returning double of what they take.*

But *Paramus* doth not interpret this Conſtitution, ſo as to make the In-Lib. 3. quiſitors, who are criminal in this Reſpect, actually incur Excommunica-q. 2. n. 68. tion, and Deprivation of Office, but only ſo as to make them liable to this Puniſhment from the Inquiſitor General. He alſo believes, if it be a ſmall Matter, the Inquiſitors may take it when voluntarily offer'd to them. But 'tis his Judgment that they would do better to take nothing at all, neither from the Criminals, which looks very ſuſpicious, nor from their Relations or Friends, or any other Perſons whatſoever.

Every Miniſter of the Inquiſition is alſo forbidden to concern himſelf in any Simanc. Traffick, either by himſelf or other Perſons: If any one doth, he is de-de Cathol. prived of his Office, and fin'd 20000 Pieces. If any one doth not diſcover Inſt. t. 41. this, he is excommunicated, 4 *Inſt. Tolet.* c. 12. n. 38.

The Inquiſitors, Miniſters, and Receivers, are alſo forbidden to buy any §. 29. Thing of the confiſcated Effects, although they are publickly ſold. If any one doth buy any of them, though openly and honeſtly, he nevertheleſs incurs the Sentence of Excommunication, and is fined in an 100 Pieces of Gold. *Ibid.* c. 23.

However, as the Author of the Hiſtory of the Inquiſition at *Goa* informs c. 13; us, the Inquiſitors know how to amaſs vaſt Riches, by two Methods. When the Effects of the Priſoners, after Confiſcation, are ſold by the Cryer, the Inquiſitors, notwithſtanding this Interdict, uſually ſend one of their Dòme-ſticks, who bid a low Price for ſuch Things as their Maſters want, being pretty   and by this Means they buy very valuable Things for half Price, or leſs. Beſides this, the Inquiſitors have a Right to demand the Payment of the Expences, and other neceſſary Charges they have been at, when, and in what Sums they pleaſe, whenever the Money ariſing from the Confiſcations is carried into the Royal Treafury ; without ever giving any Reason, or any ones daring to afk them' for what Purpofes they employ it.

Gonfalvius Montanus alfo tells us, in his Arts of the *Spanifh* Inquifition, *Cap.* 10. That the Inquifitors are fometimes prevailed with to ufe their Prifoners a little more kindly, by fome pretty Prefents made by their Friends and Relations. But this Matter muft be dextroufly managed, that fo the Inquifitor may not refufe the Offer. The firft Thing therefore is, to bribe one of his Servants, in which there is no Difficulty, provided it be done privately. When the In. quifitors themfelves are tampered with, they generally anfwer, That holy Tribunal is incorrupt, and fuffers no Manner of Gifts whatfoever to be received. But they have generally, amongft their Attendance, fome Child of their Brother or Sifter, or, at leaft, a Servant that they greatly efteem, and who is to be highly refpected, and who only fees the Inquifitor refufe the Prefents offered to him. This Servant comes to the Prifoners Friend, and privately points out to him the Relation of the Lord Inquifitor. This is giving him to underftand, unlefs the Perfon be a Stock, that though before he in vain attempted to corrupt the Integrity of this holy Tribunal, he may by this Conveyance prevail upon the Inquifitor, though he would refufe to accept the fame Prefent when more openly offered him.

The End of the FIRST VOLUME.

THE

HISTORY

OF THE

INQUISITION.

THE

HISTORY

OF THE

INQUISITION.

By *PHILIP a LIMBORCH,*

Profeffor of Divinity amongft the REMONSTRANTS.

Tranflated into *Englifh*

By *SAMUEL CHANDLER.*

VOL. II.

To which is prefixed,

A large INTRODUCTION concerning the Rife and Progrefs of PERSECUTION, and the real and pretended Caufes of it.

Their tender Mercies are Cruelty.
Their Throat is an open Sepulchre ; with their Tongues they have ufed
  Deceit ; the Poifon of Afps is under their Lips : Whofe Mouth is full
  of Curfing and Bitternefs.

LONDON:
Sold by J. GRAY, at the *Crofs-Keys* in the *Poultry.*

and Ecclefiaftical Offices. Some are Civil, which the Civil Laws have enacted, fuch as the depriving Men of the Privileges and Benefits of Law, pecuniary Mulcts, Banifhment, Death, and the Bann. Some are mixed, ordained both by the facred Canons, and the imperial Laws ; fuch as Confifcation of Goods, abfolving Subjects from their Allegiance, Infamy, and the Ecclefiaftical Interdict. I choofe rather to diftinguifh Punifhments only into Ecclefiaftical and Civil. By Ecclefiaftical, I mean thofe which are inflicted on any one confidered as a Member of the Church, and which are fuppofed to derive on him fome fpiritual Evil. By Civil, I underftand fuch Punifhments as refer to the Body or Eftate of any one, and are inflicted on him as a Member of Civil Society, whether they are appointed by the Civil or Canon Law, or by both.

Simancas gives a merry Reafon why they punifh Hereticks fo feverely, in-^{Cathol. In-} ftead of convincing them by Scripture of their Error and falfe Doctrine. *We* ^{flit. tit. 59.} *muft not contend with Hereticks by Scripture, becaufe by that our Victory will be un-*^{§. 11.} *certain and doubtful.* So that 'tis no wonder they fhould defend Doctrines, which have no Foundation in Scripture, by Force, and dreadful Punifhments, and extort that Confeffion by the Fear of Punifhment, which they can never perfuade the Mind of the Truth of, as being deftitute of the Weight of Reafon, and the clear Teftimony of Scripture. But 'tis time to return to our Subject.

The firft Punifhment ordained againft Hereticks by the Canon Law, is Ex-^{Cap. Cum.} communication. This was in ufe amongft the Chriftians in former Times.^{Chriftus.} For ever fince that Councils were held for the Extirpation of Herefy, the ^{Sicut ait,} Cuftom of excommunicating Hereticks was introduced. By this Excom-^{ad obolen-}^{dam.} munication Hereticks were driven from the Sacraments, deprived of the ^{Excommu-} common Suffrages of the Church, and expelled the Company of the Pious and ^{nicamus.} Faithful. Thus the Synod of *Vernon* determined in the Year 755. Chap. 9. ^{de hæret.} *That ye may underftand the Nature of this Excommunication, he muft not enter into* ^{Du Cange.} *the Church, nor eat and drink with any Chriftian ; let none receive his Gifts, nor of-* ^{In voce} *fer him a Kifs, nor join with him in Prayer, nor falute him.* ^{Excom.}

The Ceremony of Excommunication is thus : When the Bifhop pronounces ^{Brunus,} the Anathema, twelve Priefts muft ftand round him, and hold lighted Candles^{l. 5. c. 8.} in their Hands, which they muft throw down on the Ground, and tread under ^{§. 6.} their Feet at the Conclufion of the Anathema, or Excommunication. Then a Letter is fent about to the Parifhes, containing the Names of the excommunicated Perfons, and the Reafon of their Sentence.

Excommunication is either the greater or the lefs. Of both the Synod of *Nimes* hath thus decreed, *An.* 1284. The greater Excommunication is, *when the Prelate fays,* I excommunicate thee. *This Excommunication feparates a Perfon from the Communion of the faithful, and the Participation and Perception of the Sacraments.* The leffer Excommunication is, *when any one communicates with a Perfon under the greater Excommunication ; by thus partaking with him he is removed from the Perception of the Sacraments, fo that he ought not to receive the Eucharift or other Sacraments, till he is abfolved.* An Interdict is, *when the Prelate fays,* I interdict thee ; *or,* I put thee under the Ecclefiaftical Interdict ; *or,* I interdict or prohibit thee from entring the Church. *Such an interdicted Perfon, and he*

who

who is under the greater Excommunication muſt not enter the Church, nor ſtand near it, when divine Service is performing, as long as they are under the Sentence.

An Interdict is a general Excommunication, pronounced againſt a Province, a *Town*, or *City*, Cap. 17. *de verbor. Signif. Brunus* deſcribes it as applied to Eccleſiaſtical Affairs.

Brunus, *l.* 5, *c.* 16. § 10.
   " An Eccleſiaſtical Interdict is one of the principal Eccleſiaſtical Cenſures, " as it *forbids* a Perſon all divine Services, which is it ſelf the greateſt Puniſhment, as it deprives a Man of the Benefit of divine Services and Sacra-
" ments, and affects the Soul, even as a Civil Interdict doth the Body. It is
" pronounced ſometimes againſt a Perſon, *viz.* a Community or *Chapter.*
" Sometimes againſt a Place, *viz.* a Church or City. And there is this Dif-
" ference : When a Community is interdicted, the Clergy may perform di-
" vine Service with a loud Voice, the Gates being ſhut, and the Bells rung,
" provided the excommunicate and interdicted Perſons be excluded, which
" they can't do in an interdicted Place. Farther, when a Community is put
" under an Interdict, we are not to underſtand it of the Community as a Body,
" but of ſome particular interdicted Perſons ; becauſe the Matter of the Inter-
" dict is proportioned not to the Body, but the ſeveral Members. And yet an
" Interdict may be pronounced againſt the whole Community, as a Puniſhment
" of the Crime of the Governors of the Univerſity, or Body, in which
" caſe both the Guilty and Innocent are ſubject to the Eccleſiaſtical Interdict,
" eſpecially thoſe who were preſent, and knew the Faults of the Governors,
" without oppoſing them. In this Caſe the Truth is, that all the Citizens,
" even the Ignorant and Innocent, are included in the Interdict.

Q. Du Cange *in voce* Interdict.
The Form of the Interdict we have in the Council of *Limoges, An.* 1301. Seſſion the Second. *Unleſs they come to Terms of Peace, let all the Country of the* Limoſin *be put under a publick Excommunication, ſo that no Perſon, except a Clergyman, or poor Beggar, or Stranger, or Infant from two Years old and under, be permitted Burial, in the whole* Limoſin, *or permitted to be carried to Burial in any other Biſhoprick. Let divine Service be privately performed in all the Churches, and Baptiſm given to thoſe who deſire it. About the third Hour, let the Bells ring in the Churches, and all proſtrate pour out their Prayers, upon account of the Tribulation, and for Peace. Let Penance and the* Viaticum *be granted in the Article of Death. Let the Altars of all the Churches be ſtripped, as in* Eaſter Eve, *and the Croſſes and Ornaments be taken away, as a Token of Mourning and Sadneſs to all. Let the Altars be adorned at thoſe Maſſes only, which any of the Prieſts ſhall ſay, the Church Doors being ſhut ; and when the Maſſes are done, let them be ſtript again. Let no one marry during the Time of the Excommunication. Let no one give to another a Kiſs. Let no one of the Clergy or Laity, no Inhabitant, or Traveller, eat Fleſh or other Meat, than ſuch as is lawful to eat in Lent, in the whole Country of the* Limoſin. *Let no Layman or Clergyman be trimmed or ſhaved, till the cenſured Princes, the Heads of the People, abſolutely obey the holy Council.* Some Synods held at *Landaff,* recited in the *Engliſh* Councils, after the Eccleſiaſtical Laws of King *Alfred,* declare, that in the Time of the Interdicts the Altars were uncovered, the Croſſes and Relicts of the Saints laid upon the Ground, and the Bells turned upward.

There

There is another Form of the Interdict extant in a Manufcript of the Church of *Beauvis*, amongſt the Laws of *Charles* the Great. *In the Name of Chriſt, I Hildegarius, Biſhop of Beauvis, by the Authority of the Father, the Son, and the Holy Ghoſt, and by the Authority of St.* Peter, *Prince of the Apoſtles, and by our own Authority, do excommunicate and interdict this Church, and all the Chapels belonging to it, that no one may have Power from Almighty God, or from St.* Peter, *the Prince of the Apoſtles, from this Day to ſing or hear Maſs, or perform any divine Office, or receive the Tythe of Almighty God, without our ſpecial Leave. And whoever ſhall preſume, contrary to theſe Interdicts, either to ſing or hear Maſs, or to perform divine Service in any Place, or to receive the Tythe of Almighty God, let him be excommunicated and accurſed by the Authority of the omnipotent God the Father, the Son, and the Holy Ghoſt, and of St.* Peter, *and all the Saints, and ſeparated from the Society of Chriſtians, and from the Doors of our holy Mother Church, where there is Remiſſion of Sins, and let him be* Anathema Maranatha, *to the End of the World, with the Devils in Hell. So let it be, once, twice, thrice,* Amen. *Boniface* VIII. ordained, that notwithſtanding the Eccleſiaſtical Interdict, divine Service might be performed in the four Feſtivals, to which *Urban* VI. added the Feſtival of *Corpus Chriſti,* as may be found in the great *Belgick* Chronicle, *An.* 1389.

[Thus *Du Cange* deſcribes the Interdict. But the *Venetian* Divines, in their Treatiſe concerning the Interdict of Pope *Paul* V. *An.* 1606. *Propoſ.* 19. affirm that the Interdict is a new Cenſure in the Church ; and they thus prove it : Becauſe there is no mention of an Interdict, either as to the Word or Meaning, in the holy Scripture, or any one of the antient Fathers, or in the Collection of Canons by *Curcard* or *Gratian,* who wrote about the Year 1150. And therefore it did not begin till after his Time, becauſe *Alexander* III. firſt mentions it in the Decretals, in a certain Letter of his to the *Engliſh* Prelates, *An.* 1170. They add,

In the Beginning, when the Interdict took place, all divine Services were prohibited, except the Baptiſm of Children, and the Penance of the dying. *Alexander* III. Capit. *Non eſt nobis.* reſponſ. An. 1170. About the Year 1200. *Innocent* III. allowed of Preaching and the Sacrament of Confirmation. Capit. *reſponſo.* de Sent. Excom. About the Year 1230. *Gregory* IX. granted, that Maſs ſhould be celebrated once every Week, but without the ringing of the Bell, with a low Voice, and the Gates ſhut, in order to confecrate the moſt holy Sacrament for dying Penitents. Cap. *Permittimus.* de Sent. Excom. About the Year 1245. *Innocent* IV. permitted the Sacrament of Penance to be adminiſtred to the Croſs-bearers, and Strangers, and that two or three of the Clergy might celebrate divine Service with a low Voice. Cap. *Quod.* in Text. de Pœn. About the Year 1300. *Boniface* VIII. decreed that Penance ſhould not only be adminiſtred to the Sick, but to ſuch as were well, and every Day, and that divine Service ſhould be performed with a low Voice, the Gates ſhut, and without ringing the Bells, except on the Feaſts of the *Nativity, Eaſter, Whitſunday,* and the *Aſſumption of the Bleſſed Virgin,* when it ſhould be celebrated with open Gates, and the ringing of the Bells. *c. Alma Mater.* de Sent. Excom. in 6.

To

To this they fubjoin the Effects of an Interdict, to fhew that if this Cenfure be not ufed with fome Difference, it will deftroy the Church. It is worth while juft to recite thefe Effects in the Words of the aforementioned Place, *Alma Mater.* and from the Extravagant *Provide. Becaufe,* fays he, *by fuch fort of Statutes the Indevotion of the People is forgotten, Herefies fpring up, an infinite Number of Dangers arife to Souls, and the Church, without her Fault, lofes the Obedience due to her.* The Words of the Extravagant are thefe : *Prayers for the Dead, efpecially by the frequent Oblation of the falutary Hoft, are either entirely prevented, or greatly leffened ; young Perfons and Children more feldom partake of the Sacraments, and are thereby lefs inflamed and confirmed in the Faith, the Devotion of the Faithful grows cool, Herefies fpring up, and the Dangers of Souls are encreafed.* The Glofs upon the fame Chapter *Alma Mater* fays, That after the Removal of the Interdict from any Place, Perfons of thirty or forty Years old, who had never feen the Mafs celebrated, laughed at the Priefts as they were celebra-

Diftinct. 22. Qu. 3. Artic. 1. —ting it. *Sotus* a famous Doctor fays, *That though an Interdict on one hand tends to terrify the Excommunicate, yet on the other it endangers divine Service, efpecially if it lafts for any confiderable while ; for that not only the Laity lofe their Affection and Regard for divine Services from not being accuftomed to frequent them ; but even the Clergy themfelves grow more remifs and indolent in performing them : Upon which Account Religion it felf fuffers great Lofs, and the Manners of the People grow wild and favage.* Thus far the *Venetian* Divines.]

Pegna p. 2. Com. 22.

Hierolex in voce Proceffus.

Heretofore they ufed, three times a Year, folemnly to anathematife Hereticks of every Sect, *viz.* in the Day of *Cœna Domini,* the Afcenfion, when Chrift prayed for all the Faithful, and in the Feaft of the Dedication of the Churches of St. *Peter* and *Paul* ; to denote that the excommunicate Perfon was deprived of the Sacrament of the Supper, that he could not partake of the Prayers of the Church, and that he was expelled the Church, fo that he could not pray with the reft of the Faithful. To this Cuftom fucceeded the Procefs of the Bull, called *In cœna Domini,* which was read publickly, and with a loud Voice, every Year, on *Holy Thurfday,* in the Morning, by the laft Cardinal Deacon, in the Prefence of the Pope, and the reft of the Cardinals and Bifhops, by which all Hereticks are anathematized. When the reading of it is finifhed, the Pope takes a little lighted Torch, and throws it into the Street, as a Token of the Thunder fent againft the Excommunicate. The Ufe of this Bull doth not feem very antient ; for neither *Thomas,* nor *Eymericus,* nor other antient Writers mention it. But it feems to have begun in the Time of *Martin* V. about the Year 1420. when the *Bohemian* Doctrine was damned by the Council of *Conftance. Paul* II. and *Sixtus* IV. make mention of it in fome Refcripts, beginning, *Etfi dominici Gregis.* Afterwards *Leo* X. encreafed it againft *Luther,* as did *Paul* III. and the other *Roman* Pontiffs, till at length, *An.* 1616. it was brought into this Form by *Paul* V.

The paftoral Diligence and Care of the Roman *Pontiff is continually employed, according to the Duty of his Office, in procuring all Peace and Tranquility for the Chriftian Republick ; and efpecially fhines forth in maintaining and preferving the Unity and Integrity of the Catholick Faith, without which 'tis impoffible to pleafe God ;* viz.

that

that the Faithful of Chrift may not be as little Children, toffed, and carried about with every Wind of Doctrine, by the Wickednefs of Men who go about to deceive ; but may all meet in the Unity of the Faith, and Acknowledgment of the Son of God, and grow into a perfect Man, and may not hurt one another in the Fellowfhip and Communion of this Life, nor give Occafion of Offence to each other, but rather being joined in the Bond of Charity, as Members of one Body under Chrift the Head, and his Vicar upon Earth the Roman *Pontiff, the Succeffor of the moft bleffed* Peter, *from whom the Unity of the whole Church flows, may encreafe unto Edification, and may thus, with the Affiftance of divine Grace, fo enjoy the Quiet of the prefent Life, as that they may obtain the Bleffednefs of the future. For which Caufes the* Roman *Pontiffs, our Predeceffors, have, on this Day, celebrated for the anniverfary Commemoration of the Lord's Supper, been ufed folemnly to exercife the fpiritual Sword of Ecclefiaftical Difcipline, and the falutary Arms of Juftice by the Miniftry of the Chief Apoftolate, to the Glory of God, and the Salvation of Souls.*

We therefore to whom nothing is more defirable, than under God, to defend inviolable the Integrity of the Faith, the publick Peace and Juftice, following this antient and folemn Cuftom,

1. *Do excommunicate and anathematize, on the Part of Almighty God, the Father, Son, and holy Spirit, and alfo by Authority of the bleffed Apoftles* Peter *and* Paul, *and by our own, all* Huffites, Wickleffites, Lutherans, Zuinglians, Calvinifts, Hugonots, Anabaptifts, Trinitarians, *and Apoftates from the Chriftian Faith, and all and fingular other Hereticks, by whatever Name diftinguifhed, or to whatever Sect they belong, as alfo their Believers, Receivers, Favourers, and in general all their Defenders, and fuch who without our Authority, and the Authority of the Apoftolick See, do knowingly read, or retain, or print their Books containing Herefy, or treating of Religion, or who in any manner defend them, or upon any account, publickly or privately, upon any Pretence or Colour ; as alfo all Schifmaticks, and thofe who obftinately withdraw themfelves or depart from our Obedience, or that of the* Roman *Pontiff for the Time being.*

2. *Likewife we excommunicate and anathematife all and fingular Perfons, of every State, Degree, and Condition, and interdict all fuch Univerfities, Colleges, and Chapters, of whatfoever Name, who appeal from our Appointments and Commands, and thofe of the* Roman *Pontiffs for the Time being, to an univerfal future Council ; as alfo all thofe by whofe Affiftance, Counfel or Favour fuch Appeal fhall have been made.*

3. *Likewife we excommunicate and anathematife all Pirates, Corfaires and Robbers, who infeft our Sea, efpecially from* Monte Argentaro *to* Terracina, *and all their Favourers, Receivers and Defenders.*

4. *Likewife we excommunicate and anathematife all and fingular Perfons whatfoever, who, when the Ships of any Chriftians fhall be overfet by a Storm, or by any Means fuffer Shipwrack, fhall take away from them their Effects of any Kind, whether they find them in the faid Ships, or thrown into the Sea, or caft on the Shore, as well in our* Tufcan *and* Adriatick *Seas, as in other Regions and Shores of any other Sea whatfoever ; fo that they fhall not be excufed upon Account of any Privilege, Cuftom, or Poffeffion of Time immemorial, or any other Pretence whatfoever.*

5. *Like-*

5. *Likewife we excommunicate and anathematife all, who either lay or encreafe Taxes or Gabels in their Lands, except in fuch Cafes as are permitted them by Law, or by the fpecial Leave of the Apoftolick See, or who caufe fuch as are prohibited to be laid or encreafed.*

6. *Likewife we excommunicate and anathematife all Forgers of Apoftolick Letters, even in Form of Brief, and Supplications, concerning Grace or Juftice, figned by the Roman Pontiff, or the Vice-chancellors of the Holy Roman Church, or their Vicegerents, or by the Command of the faid Roman Pontiff: As alfo fuch who counterfeit Apoftolick Letters, even in Form of Brief; as alfo fuch who falfely fign any Supplications under the Name of the Roman Pontiff, or his Vice-chancellor, or their Vicegerents.*

7. *Likewife we excommunicate and anathematife all thofe who carry or fend over to the Saracens, Turks, and other Enemies and Adverfaries of the Chriftian Name, and fuch as are exprefsly, or by Name declared Hereticks by our Sentence, or that of this Holy See, Horfes, Arms, Iron, Bars of Iron, Tin, Steel, and all other Kinds of Metals, and warlike Inftruments, Timbers, Hemp, Ropes, made either of Hemp or any other Matter, and the Materials themfelves, and all other fuch fort of Things, by which they may injure Chriftians and Catholicks; and alfo all thofe who either by themfelves or others, give Information to the Turks and Enemies of the Chriftian Religion, or to Hereticks, of the Affairs concerning the State of the Chriftian Commonwealth, to the Prejudice and Deftruction of Chriftians, and the Detriment of the Catholick Religion, and all fuch who in this Affair any ways afford them Help, Counfel, and Favour, all Privileges whatfoever hitherto granted by us and the aforefaid See to any Perfons whatfoever, Princes, and Republicks, not making exprefs Mention of fuch Prohibition, to the contrary notwithftanding.*

8. *Likewife we excommunicate and anathematife, all who hinder or attack thofe who bring Provifions, or other Things neceffary for the Ufe of the Court of Rome; as alfo thofe who prohibit, hinder, and prevent fuch Things being brought or carried to the faid Court of Rome, or who defend thofe who do thefe Things, either by themfelves, or others, of whatfoever Order, Preheminence, Condition and State they may be, even though they fhould be rendred Illuftrious by the Pontifical or Regal, or any other Ecclefiaftical or worldly Dignity whatfoever.*

9. *Likewife we excommunicate and anathematife all thofe who, either themfelves, or by others, kill, mutilate, fpoil, apprehend or detain any Perfons coming to the Apoftolick See, or going from it; as alfo all thofe who not having the ordinary Jurifdiction, or that delegated by us and our Judges, fhall rafhly claim it to themfelves, and fhall prefume to commit fuch Things againft thofe who abide in the fame Court.*

10. *Likewife we excommunicate and anathematife all fuch who kill, mutilate, wound, detain, apprehend or rob fuch as are coming to Rome, or Pilgrims going to the City upon account of Devotion or Pilgrimage, and ftaying in it, or going from it, or who in thefe Things give them Affiftance, Counfel or Favour.*

11. *Likewife we excommunicate and anathematife all fuch who kill, mutilate, wound, ftrike, apprehend, imprifon, detain, or in an hoftile Manner purfue the Cardinals of the Holy Roman Church, the Patriarchs, Archbifhops, Bifhops, Legates or Nuncios of the Apoftolick See, or who eject them from their Diocefes, Territories,*

tories, Lands or Dominions ; as also those who command or confirm these Things, and grant their Assistance, Counsel or Favour in them.

12. *Likewise we excommunicate and anathematise all those, who kill, or any ways strike, or deprive of their Effects, either by themselves or others, any Ecclesiastical Persons whatsoever, or Seculars coming to the Court of* Rome *upon their Causes and Affairs, and prosecuting them in the said Court, or such who procure and manage their Affairs, Advocates, Procurators, and Agents, or Auditors and Judges in the aforesaid Causes and Affairs, deputed upon Occasion of the said Causes and Affairs ; as also all such who by themselves or others, directly or indirectly, shall dare to commit, perform or procure such Crimes, or shall grant Assistance, Counsel or Favour in them, of whatsoever Preheminence and Dignity they may be.*

13. *Likewise we excommunicate and anathematise all as well Ecclesiastical as Secular, of whatsoever Dignity, who, under the Pretence of a frivolous Appeal from the Burthen or future Execution of the Apostolick Letters, even in Form of Brief, concerning as well Grace as Justice, and of Citations, Inhibitions, Sequesters, Monitories, executorial Processes and other Decrees, proceeding, or which for a Time or otherwise may have proceeded from us, and the aforesaid See, or Legates, Nuncio's, Presidents, Auditors of our Palace, and of the Apostolick Chamber, Commissaries, and other Judges, and Apostolick Delegates, shall have Recourse to the Secular Courts, and Lay Power, and shall suffer such Appeals from it, though at the Instance of the Procurator or Advocates of the Treasury, and shall cause such Letters, Citations, Inhibitions, Sequesters, Monitories, and other the aforesaid to be taken and retained, or who hinder and prohibit, either simply, or without their Pleasure, Consent or Examination, these Things to be put in Execution, or the Attornies or Notaries employed in the Execution of such Letters and Processes from making such Instruments or Acts, or when made from delivering them to the Party concerned, or who apprehend, strike, wound, imprison, detain, banish from Cities, Places and Kingdoms, deprive of their Goods, terrify, extort Money from, or threaten by themselves, or any other or others, publickly or privately the said Parties or their Agents, Kindred, Relations, Acquaintance, Notaries, Executors, or Under-Executors of the said Letters, Citations, Monitories, and other the aforesaid, or who shall presume to forbid, ordain and command directly or indirectly any other Person whatsoever, either in general or particular, that they do not apply or have Recourse to the Court of* Rome *in pursuing the said Affairs, or obtaining Graces or Letters, or soliciting such Graces and Letters from the said See, or using them when obtained, or who shall themselves, or by their Notaries, or Attornies, or any other Ways dare to keep them.*

14. *Likewise we excommunicate and anathematise all and singular Persons whatsoever, who themselves or by others, by their own proper Authority, and in Fact, under the Pretence of any Apostolick Executions, or other Graces and Letters, remove Grants of Tythes, or other spiritual Causes, or annexed to spiritual, from our Auditors, and Commissaries, and other Ecclesiastical Judges, or who hinder the Course and Hearing of them, or Persons, Chapters, Convents, Colleges, who are willing to prosecute the said Causes, and who interpose themselves as Judges in the Cognisance of them, or who by Statute or otherwise compel the acting Parties who have, or do cause them to be tried, to revoke, or cause to be revoked Citations or Inhibitions, or other*

Letters decreed therein, and to cause, or consent that those Persons, against whom such Inhibitions have proceeded, shall be absolved from the Censures or Penalties contained in them ; or who in any manner obstruct them in the Execution of Apostolick Letters, or Executorials, or Processes, or aforesaid Decrees, or who give their Favour, Counsel, or Assent towards it, even though they should pretend it was to prevent Violence, or under any other Pretences whatsoever ; yea, though they should pretend that 'tis only till they have intreated, or caused Intreaty to be made for our Information, unless they legally prosecute such Supplications before us and the Apostolick See ; even though they who commit such Things should be Presidents of Chanceries, Councils, or Parliaments ; Chancellors, Vice-Chancellors, Judges, the Counsellors ordinary or extraordinary, of any secular Princes whatsoever, even though they are illustrious for the Imperial, Regal, Ducal, or any other Dignity whatsoever ; or whether they be Arch-Bishops, Bishops, Abbots, Commendatories or Vicars.

15. *Or who by Virtue of any pretended Office, or at the Instance of any Party or other Persons whatsoever, bring, or cause, or procure directly or indirectly, under any Colour whatsoever, to be brought, Ecclesiastical Persons, Chapters, Convents, Colleges of any Churches, before them to their Tribunal, Audience, Chancery, Judges, or Parliament, contrary to the Disposition of the Canon Law ; or who shall make, ordain, or publish Statutes, Ordinations, Constitutions, Pragmaticks, or any other Decrees whatsoever, in general or particular, upon any Account, or under any Colour whatsoever, and even under Pretence of any Custom or Privilege, or for any other Reason whatsoever, or who shall make use of them when made or ordained, by which the Ecclesiastical Liberty is taken away, or in any Degree hurt, or sunk, or otherwise by any Means restrained, or whereby our Rights, or those of the said See, or any other Churches, are any Ways directly or indirectly, tacitly or expressly prejudiced.*

16. *All such moreover, who, on this Account, in any manner directly or indirectly, hinder the Arch-Bishops, Bishops, and other superior and inferior Prelates, and all other ordinary Ecclesiastical Judges whatsoever, by imprisoning or molesting their Agents, Procurators, Familiars, or their Relations or Kindred, or others, so as to prevent their exercising their Ecclesiastical Jurisdictions against any Persons whatsoever, according to what the Canons and sacred Ecclesiastical Constitutions, and the Decrees of General Councils, and especially the Council of* Trent, *ordain ; and also those who after the Sentences and Decrees of their Ordinaries, or any Persons delegated by them, or who any other ways evading the Judgment of the Ecclesiastical Court apply themselves to Chanceries, or any other secular Courts, and who procure from them Probitions or penal Commands to be decreed and executed against the Ordinaries and their aforesaid Delegates ; and those also who decree and execute these Things, or give their Assistance, Counsel, Patronage or Favour therein.*

17. *Those also who seize on the Jurisdictions, Profits, Returns, and Incomes belonging to us and the Apostolick See, and to any Ecclesiastical Persons whatsoever, by reason of their Churches, Monasteries, and other Ecclesiastical Benefices, or who upon any Occasion or Cause sequester them, without the express Licence of the* Roman *Pontiff, or others who have a legal Power to do it.*

18. *Such also who lay any Imposts, Tythes, Taxes, Duties, and other Burthens upon the Clergy, Prelates, and other Ecclesiastical Persons, and upon their Effects, or those*

thofe of their Churches, Monafteries, and other Ecclefiaftical Benefices, or upon their Fruits, Returns, or fuch like Incomes, without the like fpecial and exprefs Leave of the Roman *Pontiff ; or who exact them by any other invented Methods whatfoever, or who receive them when laid, even from thofe who voluntarily give and grant them. Moreover all fuch who by themfelves or others, directly or indirectly prefume to do the aforefaid Things, or procure them to be done, or give their Affiftance, Counfel or Favour in them, of whatfoever Preheminence, Dignities, Order, Condition or State they may be, even though they fhine with the Imperial or Regal Dignity, or whether they are Princes, Dukes, Counts, Barons, or other Potentates whatfoever, or whether they be any ways Prefidents, Counfellors, and Senators, in Kingdoms, Provinces, Cities and Countries, or adorned with any, even with the Pontifical Dignity, renewing hereby the Decrees made concerning thefe Matters by the facred Canons, as well in the* Lateran *Council lately held, as in other general Councils, with alfo the Cenfures and Penalties contained therein.*

19. *Likewife we excommunicate and anathematife all Magiftrates and Judges, Notaries, Scribes, Executors, Sub-executors, who in any manner concern themfelves in capital or criminal Caufes, againft Ecclefiaftical Perfons, by proceffing, banning, apprehending them, or by pronouncing or executing Sentences againft them, without the fpecial fpecifick and exprefs Licenfe of this holy Apoftolick See, or who extend fuch Licenfe to Perfons and Cafes not expreffed, or who otherwife rafhly abufe it, even although fuch who do commit thefe Things fhould be Counfellors, Senators, Prefidents, Chancellors, Vice-Chancellors, or called by any other Name whatfoever.*

20. *Likewife we excommunicate and anathematife all thofe who by themfelves, or others, directly or indirectly, under any Title or Colour, fhall prefume to invade, deftroy, feize and detain, in whole or in part, this holy City, the Kingdom of* Sicily, *the Ifles of* Sardinia *and* Corfica, *the Countries on this Side* Faro, *the Patrimony of St.* Peter *in* Tufcany, *the Dutchy of* Spoleto, *the County of* Venaiffin, *and the Maritime Provinces of the Marquifate of* Ancona, Maffa, Treve, Romagna, Campania, *and their Countries and Places, and the Lands of the fpecial Commiffion of the* Arnulphs, *and our Cities of* Bologna, Faenza, Rimini, Benevento, Peroufe, Avignon, Civita Caftellana, Todi, Ferrara, Comachio, *and other Cities, Countries and Places, or Rights belonging to the* Roman *Church, and fubject mediately or immediately to the faid* Roman *Church ; as alfo prefume to ufurp, difturb, retain, or interrupt by any Methods the fupream Jurifdiction in them actually belonging to us, and the faid* Roman *Church ; as alfo their Adherents, Favourers, and Defenders, or who any ways grant them Affiftance, Counfel or Favour.*

It being our Will that thefe our prefent Proceffes, and all and every Thing contained in thefe Letters, fhall laft, and have their entire Effects, as long as there fhall be any fuch Proceffes made by us, or the Roman *Pontiff for the Time being.*

Furthermore, no one fhall be abfolved from the aforefaid Sentences by any other Perfon but the Roman *Pontiff, except in the Article of Death, nor even then, unlefs he fhall give Security to ftand to the Commands of the Church, and make Satisfaction ; notwithftanding any Pretences of Faculties or Indulgencies, granted and renewed, or to be granted or renewed by us, or the faid See, and the Decrees of any Council, by Word or Letters, or any other Writing, general or fpecial, to any Ecclefiaftical Perfons what-*

foever,

foever, Seculars, and the Regulars of all Orders, even of the Mendicant and Military ones, even to such as enjoy the Episcopal, or any other greater Dignity, and to the Orders themselves, and their Monasteries, Convents, and Houses, and Chapters, Colleges, Confraternities, Congregations, Hospitals, and holy Places; as also to any of the Laity, tho' Illustrious for the Imperial, Regal, or any other worldly Excellency.

But if any Persons, contrary to the Tenor of these Presents, shall actually presume to grant the Benefit of Absolution to such who are entangled in this Excommunication and Anathema, we put them under Excommunication, intending to proceed more severely against them, spiritually and temporally, as we shall know to be most convenient.

Declaring and protesting, that no Manner of Absolution, even to be made solemnly by us, shall comprehend, or be of any Benefit to the aforesaid excommunicate Persons, contained under these Presents, unless they shall first abstain from the Premisses, with the Purpose of not committing such Things for the future; or to those who have made any Statutes, as aforesaid, against the Ecclesiastical Liberty, unless first they shall publickly revoke such Statutes, Ordinations, Constitutions, Pragmaticks and Decrees, and shall erase and blot them out from their Archives, Records, or Books in which they are found to be registred, and shall certify us concerning such Revocation; moreover, that by such Absolution, or by any other contrary Acts, tacit or expressed, or by our Patience and Forbearance, or that of our Successors, continued for any Time whatsoever, no Prejudice can or ought to affect the Apostolick See, and the Holy Roman Church, in all and singular the Premisses, and in any of its Rights, where and whensoever pursued or to be pursued.

All Privileges, Indulgences, Grants and Letters Apostolick, general or special, to the aforesaid, or to any one of them, or to any others of any Order, State, or Condition, Dignity or Preheminence, altho' as before they may enjoy the Pontifical, Imperial, Regal, or any Ecclesiastical and worldly Dignity; or to their Kingdoms, Provinces, Cities, or Places, granted by the aforesaid See, upon any Account, even by way of Contract, or Reward, and under any other Form and Tenor, and with any Clauses, even the Derogatories of Derogatories, even tho' they contain that they may not be excommunicated, anathematised, or interdicted, by Letters Apostolick not making full and express Mention, Word for Word, of such Privileges, Indulgences, and Grants, and of their Orders, Places, proper Names, Surnames and Dignities; as also all Customs, even Immemorial, and Prescriptions the longest that can be, and all other Observances whatsoever, written or not written, by Virtue of which they may be able to help or defend themselves, so as to exclude themselves from being concerned in these our Processes and Sentences, to the contrary notwithstanding.

All which Things, as to this Affair, and the Tenors of all of them, as tho' they were inserted here to a Word, without the Omission of any Thing, taking them as expressed in these Presents, we entirely take away, and wholly revoke, and all other Things whatsoever to the contrary.

And that these our present Processes may more easily come to the publick Knowledge of all, we will cause the Papers or Parchments containing these Processes, to be fixed up in the City, on the Gates of the Church of St. John Lateran, and the Cathedral
Church

Church of the Prince of the Apostles, that they whom such Processes concern, may be able to pretend no Excuse, or alledge Ignorance, that they had not seen them or known them ; since it is not probable, that that should remain unknown, which is thus openly published to all. Moreover, that these Processes, and present Letters, and all and singular the Matters contained in them may become yet more known, by being published in most Cities and Places, we by these Writings, order, and in Virtue of their holy Obedience, strictly enjoin and command, all and singular, Patriarchs, Primates, Arch-Bishops, Bishops and Ordinaries of Places, and Prelates constituted every where, that either by themselves, or any other or others, they solemnly publish, and propose, shew, and declare to the Minds of the Faithful of Christ, these our present Letters, after they have received them, or had the Knowledge of them, once every Year, or oftener, if they think fit, in their Churches, when the greatest Number of People shall be met together for divine Worship.

Moreover, let the Patriarchs, Arch-Bishops, Bishops, and other Ordinaries of Places, and Prelates of Churches, and also all Rectors, and others having the Cure of Souls, and Presbyters, Seculars, and the Regulars of every Order, deputed by any Authority to hear Confession of Sins, have by them a Transcript of these present Letters, and study diligently to read and understand them : It being our Will, that altogether the same Credit shall in Judgment, and out of it, be every where given to the Transcripts of these Presents, even when printed, subscribed with the Hand of a publick Notary, and marked with the Seal of the ordinary Judge of the Roman *Court, or any other Person constituted in Ecclesiastical Dignity, as would be given to these Presents, if they were themselves exhibited and shewn. Let therefore no Man dare to infringe, or by any rash Endeavour to contradict this Page of our Excommunication, Anathematization, Interdict, Innovation, Innodation, Declaration, Protestation, Sublation, Revocation, Commission, Command and Will. If any one shall presume to attempt this, let him know that he shall incur the Indignation of Almighty God, and his blessed Apostles,* Peter *and* Paul. *Given at St.* Peter's *in* Rome, *in the Year of the Incarnation of our Lord* MDCXVI. Apr. 22. *and Twelfth Year of our Pontificate.*

M. DATARIUS.

J. Bulgarius.

The Place † of the Seal.
Registered in the Secretary of Briefs.
S. de Ursinis.]

This Excommunication infers other Punishments. For if an Heretick excommunicated hath any spiritual Jurisdiction, he forfeits it, nor can he validly perform those Acts which require Jurisdiction, because as this is given by the Church, the Church may resume it. Hence all Things that are done by a Priest or Bishop, without Permission, are null, for the want of Jurisdiction. All Absolutions, Censures, Sentences, Punishments, done by him, are void. Thus it is said, that an excommunicated Person can't excommunicate, and that they are not to be looked on as excommunicate, who are excommunicated by Hereticks. Yet they so far retain the Powers belonging to their

their Order, that they may validly do an Act which doth not require Jurif. diction, tho' not lawfully, becaufe they fin in doing it ; and they give this Reafon, becaufe the Power of any Order confifts in an indelible Character. Hence they infer, that he who hath once legally received this Power, muft al- ways keep it, and that therefore he may validly do an act, which doth not re- quire Jurifdiction, provided the due Matter, Form and Intention be prefer- ved, becaufe fuch a Power hath its Force from the Inftitution of Chrift, which the Church cannot take away.

Eymer, *poft. 3 Qu. 113. Pegna, Com 161* Finally, Hereticks are deprived of all Ecclefiaftical Benefices and Dignities. But there is this Difference between Hereticks, and their Favourers, Recei- vers and Defenders. Hereticks are *ipfo jure*, deprived of their Ecclefiaftical Benefices from the Day of their committing their Crime, by a Refcript of *Pius* V. beginning, *Cum ex Apoftolatus*, in which he referves all Benefices of what- foever fort, and where-ever they are, vacant for the Crime of Herefy com- mitted by any one, to the Nomination and Appointment of the Apoftolick See ; whereas the Receivers, Favourers and Defenders of Hereticks are not *ipfo jure*, deprived of their Benefices, but muft be deprived by Sentence. Cap. *Excom*. 1. §. *Credentes*. de hæret.

Qu. 114. Com. 163, 164. This is extended to their Pofterity, to the fecond Generation by the Fa- ther's Side, and the firft by the Mother's. Cap. *Quicunq*; §. *Heret*. de hæret. l. 6. and Cap. *Statutum* de hæret. lib. 6. So that if the Father be an Here- tick, his Son and Daughter, and Grandfon by his Son, is judged incapable, but the Grandfon by the Daughter is not incapable, becaufe he is *reckoned* of his own Father's Family. If the Mother be an Heretick, the Son or Daugh- ter only in the firft Degree is incapable, and no farther. The Sons of thofe alfo fufpected of Herefy are incapable. But when the Receivers and Abettors of Hereticks and the like are dead, there can be no Procefs againft them, becaufe their Crime is extinguifhed by Death. As for thofe Children who accufe their heretical Parents to the Judges of the Faith, the Punifhments appointed by Law don't affect them.

Amongft the Ecclefiaftical Punifhments is alfo reckoned, that no Offering is to be made for thofe who die in Herefy, nor are they to receive Chriftian Burial. Cap. *Sicut ait B. Leo* de hæret. And this *Innocent* IV. efpecially or- dained by a perpetual Conftitution, induced thereto by that folemn Sentence, *Brovius, a. 1247. §. 4. n. 15.* *The Bodies of excommunicated Perfons ought not to be buried in the facred Places of the Faithful, becaufe as the Church had no Communion with them when alive, fhe will have no Communion with them when dead.*

C H A P.

C H A P. II.

Of the Civil Punishments of HERETICKS.

POlitical Punishments appointed by the Canon and Civil Laws against Hereticks, are various.

The first is what is commonly called, the Confiscation of their Goods. Cap. *Vergentis in Senium.* de hæret. *We ordain that the Goods of Hereticks be confiscated in all Countries subject to our temporal Jurisdiction, and in other Places also by the Powers and secular Princes of them ; and if they should prove negligent in this Affair, we will and command that they be compelled to it, by an Ecclesiastical Censure, without Benefit of Appeal.*

[" This Confiscation of Effects, *Lewis a Paramo* derives from the Example L. 1. t. 2.
" of God, who, not contented with the Sentence of Death pronounced against c. 7. p. 45.
" our first Parents, drove Man from the Place of his Delights, stript of all
" his Goods, wounded in Naturals, and spoil'd of those Gifts that had been
" freely granted him, his original Integrity especially being irreparably lost,
" and adjudged him to hard and continual Labours, and out of his Hatred to
" so great a Wickedness, commanded the very Earth to bring forth Briars
" and Thorns. This Example, he saith, the most holy Tribunal of the In-
" quisition follows, confiscating by a just Proscription the Goods of Hereticks,
" and depriving them of all their Effects and Fortunes. Neither ought this
" Instance to be accounted Foreign from the Case. For altho' the Confisca-
" tion of Effects doth not regularly take place as to all other Crimes, tho'
" very heinous, nevertheless God, the first of the Inquisitors, that in this de-
" testable Crime of Heresy he might give an Example to other delegated In-
" quisitors, deprived our Parents of all their Effects, of the Possession of their
" earthly Paradise, the Use of all the Fruits of it, and their Dominion over
" all the Creatures ; for they did not only after this not obey our first Pa-
" rents, but became Enemies to them. He also deprived their Children and
" Successors of these Goods, &c. and this irrevocably. Nor can any one ever
" more come to such a Place."] Moreover, the Goods of Hereticks are declared *ipso jure,* confiscate, in the Chap. *Cum secundum leges.* de hæret. l. 6. *We decree by the Advice of our Brethren, that the Goods of Hereticks, who offend more grievously, horribly and detestably than the before mentioned, be* ipso jure, *confiscate.*

This Law is of great Use in the Tribunal of the Inquisition, and extreamly hard and severe upon the Criminals, their Relations and Heirs. For hence Simanc. it is, that because the Goods of Hereticks are *ipso jure* confiscate, they be-m. y. come forfeited from the very Day of their Crime, so that all Donations by §. 21, &c. Hereticks, altho' secretly made, are null and void. Even Portions given to Daughters, to support the Burthens of Matrimony, tho' it be the Duty of a Father to portion them out, or given to such as have taken on them the holy,

holy Vow of a Monaſtick Life, are to be revoked and confiſcate. *Zanchinus* gives this Reaſon, *Cap.* 27. Becauſe his Goods are confiſcate from the very Day of his committing the Crime, and therefore he can have no right of Ad- miniſtration. But as for the Goods of ſuch, who can't purge themſelves, or are condemned for Contumacy, they are not forfeited but from the Day they are preſumed to be Hereticks, not from the Day that the Witneſſes declare them to have been Hereticks.

§. 9, &c.   If any one gives a Legacy upon account of Death, and falls into Hereſy, and his Goods become confiſcate, the Legacy ſhall be recovered as void, and belongs to the Treaſury equally with all the other Goods of the Heretick. If an Husband bequeaths any Thing to his Wife, and his Memory be con- demned for Hereſy after his Death, ſuch Donation ſhall be revoked, altho' his Legacies to others ſhall ſtand good. If any Thing be owing to an Heretick by a conditional Contract, it belongs to the Treaſury under that Condition, who muſt perform it, if they conveniently can. All the Goods of a Wife condemned for Hereſy and Impiety are forfeited, whether they be her Dowry, or any other Things beſides, which ſhe brought to her Husband, or ſuch Donations as the *Spaniards* call *Arrhæ* * ; or ſuch Profits as belong to Wives by the Royal Laws. But the Husband hath all his Actions good againſt the Treaſury. In like manner the Goods of an heretical Son gotten in

Zanch. War are confiſcated, becauſe that is the Son's private Property, in which the
c. 27. Father hath no Right. If he ſhall happen to have ſold any of his Goods, and the Money be in his Poſſeſſion, or any Thing equivalent, let it be reſtored to the orthodox Buyer, but if it be conſumed, it ſhall not be reſtored.

Hence it is, that in every Sentence, the Time of the Perſon's falling into Hereſy is particularly expreſſed, and theſe or the like Words inſerted in it,

c. 41. *And by this our Sentence we declare, That all and ſingular his Goods were brought into our Treaſury from the ſaid Time of committing the Crime, and we do ſolemnly de- clare all and every of them to be confiſcated to the Treaſury of the Church of* Rome, *and our Office of the Inquiſition.*

A Perſon however muſt be declared an Heretick by the Judge, before his
l. 4. c. 11. Goods are actually confiſcate. For as *Brunus* ſays, " The Law hath taken
§. 3.   " Care, that if any one falls into an Hereſy already condemned, he ſhall nei-
" ther be accounted or puniſhed as an Heretick, unleſs the Judge ſhall have
" pronounced by his Sentence, that he is under the principal Condemnation.
" So that the Hereticks do, *ipſo jure*, loſe all Property in their Eſtates, yet
" they can't be confiſcated till after the declaratory Sentence is pronounced.
" But however, this muſt be underſtood of ſuch a Crime as hath not been
" certified to the Judge, either by Confeſſion, or legal Proof, or the Evidence
" of the Thing it ſelf. For in notorious Crimes, which need no Declaration,
" there ſeems no need of a declaratory Sentence, according to *Dominick* ;
" who thought it ſufficient, that if an Heretick did not appear to purge him-
" ſelf, by the Time fixed by the Judge, nor produce his Vindication, an

* *Arrhæ* are the Preſents given to any Women upon their being betrothed.

" Execution

" Execution might be granted againſt him, even without a declaratory Sen-
" tence, altho' there are ſome who inſiſt upon the Neceſſity of a declaratory
" Sentence even in notorious Crimes, and think that no Execution can be
" granted without it."

This Confiſcation of Goods is ſo rigidly inſiſted on, that there is no poſſible
way of evading it, no not by the Alienation of a Man's Effects. The Treaſury of the Inquiſition devours all. Thus we read, that amongſt other Conditions of Peace preſcribed to *Raymond* Earl of *Tholouſe*, theſe were ſome.

N. 11. *Likewiſe we ordain, that whereas we have underſtood that the Believers of* Bzovius,
Hereticks, who intend to become perfect Hereticks, according to their deteſtable Life, a. 1228.
ſell before-hand their Poſſeſſions and Inheritances, to defraud the Treaſury, or give or §. 6.
*convey them, or by other Means alienate them, thoſe Contracts ſhall be all void, and
the aforeſaid Goods ſhall be confiſcated, if all Circumſtances of the ſaid Contracts and
Contractors conſidered, it ſhall appear to us that they were fraudulently made.*

N. 12. *Furthermore, whereas we have underſtood that certain Hereticks remove
to other Hereticks, under the Pretence of Merchandize or Travelling, that by ſuch Abſence they may defraud the Treaſury, and convey away their Goods, we ordain, that the
Biſhop of the Place ſhall admoniſh and require their Relations, or ſuch who have their
Goods in Poſſeſſion, to aſſign ſome juſt and reaſonable Cauſe of their continued Abſence,
and if they do not aſſign ſuch Cauſe within a Year, to be computed from the Time of the Admonition given by ſuch Biſhop, that then, if ſuch abſent Perſons are otherwiſe ſuſpected,
they ſhall be preſumed Hereticks, and all their Goods confiſcated. But if they, or their
Heirs, or thoſe who poſſeſs their Goods, ſhall aſſign any juſt or probable Cauſe of ſuch
their Abſence beyond the aforeſaid Time, either after or before the Confiſcation of their
Goods, that then ſuch Goods may be lawfully left in their Poſſeſſion, or reſtored to
them.*

The ſame Things as are preſcribed in theſe Conditions to the Earl of *Tholouſe*, are obſerved in *Italy*, by the Pope's Command, that by no Pretence of
Alienation there may be any Poſſibility of eſcaping the Confiſcation of Goods,
or Forfeiture of Dominion. *Lucas Waddingus* relates in his Annals, that Friar a. 1260)
Andrew, Inquiſitor in *Tuſcany*, proceeded to ſeize a certain powerful Heretick, §. 5, &c.
called *Capellus de Chia*. The Pope commanded, that all the Faithful, both
Eccleſiaſtical and Secular, ſhould grant their Aſſiſtance, that they ſhould
muſter an Army againſt him, and proceed in an hoſtile Manner to waſte and
deſtroy his Lands. *Capellus*, knowing himſelf proſcribed, made a pretended Sale
of the Caſtle of *Caſal*. *Peter James Surdus*, a Citizen of *Rome*, obtained from the
Senators of the City an Order, that the Inhabitants of *Viterbo*, who had taken Arms in Obedience to the Church and the Inquiſitors, ſhould not attack it,
falſely pretending that it belonged to him. The Pope chid him ſeverely, adding theſe amongſt other Words. *We therefore will, and by theſe Preſents ſtrictly
command you, that as ſoon as ever you receive them, and as you regard the divine Favour and ours, you deſiſt from ſo impious and pernicious an Undertaking, as the Defence of the ſaid Caſtle, and that you don't enter it by any Means whatſoever ; but
that you do procure, that the Inhibition given thro' your Inſtigation by the aforeſaid
Senators of* Viterbo, *be totally revoked. Otherwiſe we will have you to know, and cer-*

tainly to underſtand, that we ſhall proceed againſt you, by Authority of the
Lord, both ſpiritually and temporally, as a Defender and Favourer of Hereticks.
Anagni, 2 May, and ſixth Year of our Pontificate. Moreover he exhorts the
Inhabitants of *Viterbo,* that notwithſtanding the contrary Orders of the Sena-
tors of the City, they ſhould proceed in an hoſtile Manner, to waſte the Lands
of the aforeſaid *Capellus de Chia.*

But in our own Time the *Spaniſh* Inquiſitors are endeavouring to extend their
Power and Juriſdiction further, and under the Pretence of Confiſcation of Goods,
to ſeize on theirs alſo, who have any Commerce with the *Spaniards,* though
they live in other Countries not ſubject to them, and have ſeparated from the
Communion of the Church of *Rome,* becauſe they have in their Poſſeſſion
ſome of the Effects of thoſe who are in the Priſon of the Inquiſition, or condemned by the Inquiſitors, according to the daily Practice of Traders and
Merchants. Of this the Inquiſition of *Madrid* gave a remarkable Inſtance a-
few Years ago. *Feb.* 1687. Many Perſons were thrown into the Inquiſition at
Madrid, accuſed of be ng concealed *Jews.* Amongſt theſe were *Diego* and *Anthony Diaz,* and *Don Damianus de Lucena.* About the End of *Auguſt* 1688.
Sentence was pronounced againſt them, by which all their Effects were confiſcated, and they themſelves ſent to *Toledo,* there to perform wholeſome Penance. Theſe Perſons traded with *Peter Poulle,* a Merchant of *Amſterdam,*
who was neither a *Jew* nor a *Spaniard,* but a Chriſtian, and a *Dutchman,* who
had in his Hands ſeveral of the Effects of theſe *Spaniards.* The Inquiſition, in
order to poſſeſs themſelves of thoſe Effects, which were not ſubject to their
Power, diſcovered by private Enquiry, that this *Dutch* Merchant traded with
ſeveral *Spaniſh* Merchants, and that he had a great many Effects in their
Hands, and therefore ordered them all to be ſeized by the Receiver of the forfeited Goods, till they had the Value of thoſe Effects, which the *Amſterdam*
Merchant had in his Cuſtody ; and gave this Reaſon for the forcible Seizure,
that the impriſoned Perſons had a Claim upon the Eſtate of the *Dutchman,* and
that their Claim was devolved upon the Inquiſition, and that therefore they had
the ſame Right as the Priſoners themſelves to attach the others Effects, where-
ever they could be found in *Spain :* However, this Endeavour was in vain, becauſe no Confiſcation can be juſt, of ſuch Effects which are in the Poſſeſſion of
another Perſon, who lives out of the Territories of the Judge, and is not ſubject to his Juriſdiction ; and therefore the Lords of the united Provinces, at
the Information and Requeſt of the *Amſterdam* Merchant, obtained that thoſe
Effects ſhould be reſtored to him.

This Puniſhment of Confiſcation is inflicted upon all who are convict of
Hereſy, or confeſs, whether they repent, or perſiſt in their Hereſy, becauſe they
are declared to incur the Puniſhment, *ipſo jure,* as ſoon as they fall into Hereſy.

Pegna,
Com. 148.
in 3 *Part.*
Direct.
But if any return of their own Accord to the Church, before they are accuſed or denounced, or immediately after their being ſeized give a full and
genuine Confeſſion of themſelves, and of all others whom they know to be Hereticks, and who return with a pure Heart, before the Depoſitions of the Witneſſes are made publick, as they may be graciouſly ſaved from Impriſonment,

                                                                    ſo

fo for the fame Reafon it feems equitable, not to confifcate their Goods. In *Italy* 'tis rather owing to Cuftom, than to any Right given by the Popes, not to confifcate the Eftates of penitent Hereticks. But in *Spain* this Confifcation Simancas of the Effects of Hereticks takes place, even tho' they are penitent, by the *tit.* 42. Papal Authority, and the Laws of their own Kings ; for there they believe §. 17. &, that the Inquifition ought not to reftore the forfeited Goods even of Penitents, *t.* 47. to the Damage of the Treafury, when once it hath a Right to confifcate §. 15. them.

But if any return to the Church within the Time fixed by the Inquifitors, §. 17. the Catholick Kings have ordained, that they may recover and difpofe of their own Effects, as tho' they had never fallen into Herefy, except they attempt to alienate their immoveable Effects ; for this they are prohibited to do, without a Decree of the Prince, left they fhould difpofe of all their Effects, and fly over to the Enemies of the Catholick Religion. 2 *Inftruct.* Cap. 5.

In the Conditions of Peace prefcribed to *Raymond* Earl of *Tholoufe*, it is farther provided, *That the Goods of fuch as are heretically cloathed, fhall be confifcated,* Bzovius, *even tho' they have of their own Accord forfaken the Manners of the Hereticks, unlefs a.* 1228. *they can produce Letters teftimonial of their Reconciliation, or can make it appear, and* §. 6: *prove it by other Catholick and reputable Perfons. And altho' there be good Proof of their Reconciliation, yet they are fubject to the fame Punifhment, unlefs they wear Croffes according to the Admonition of their Bifhop, or if they lay them afide by their own Authority, or if they are found to conceal them within their Garments, when they ought to wear them upon the Outfide of their Cloaths, hanging down upon the Forepart of their Breafts.*

But whereas the Children of the condemned Perfons are by this Punifhment reduced to the extreameft Want, being thus ftripped of every Thing that belonged to their Fathers, to make it appear that they don't wholly abandon the Pegna *in* Care of them, 'tis order'd, that the Inquifitors, out of the Dictates of Mercy, *Direct.* may make fome Provifion for the poor Children of condemned Hereticks, ac-*p.* 103. cording to their refpective Sexes and Ages. Lufty Boys they order out to fome mechanick Trade. The Girls they put to Service to fome honeft Matrons of the City, that they may be inftructed in the Faith. As for thofe who can't work, either thro' their Age, or bad Health, their Pity reaches no farther than to give them a mere Suftenance out of their Fathers Effects, fometimes intreating the Ecclefiaftical and Secular Princes to exercife a little Liberality towards them ; which they efpecially ought to do, who receive thefe forfeited Effects. In relation to which 'tis thus provided in *the* Seville *Inftruct.* c. 22. a. 1484. *In like manner they have decreed, that if there be any unmarried Sons or Daughters of Perfons delivered over to the fecular Court, or condemned to perpetual Imprifonment for their Crimes, the Inquifitors fhall provide and order, that the aforefaid Orphans fhall be recommended to fome honeft Perfons, and Catholick Chriftians, to be bred up, and diet with them, and to be inftructed in the Catholick Faith ; and let them draw up an humble Petition for the aforefaid Orphans, in Reference to their Condition, what they want, and whether they are good Chriftians, efpecially for the poor Girls, that they may either marry, or profefs.* In our own Time they

leave

leave nothing for the Children of Hereticks, tho' they prove Catholicks, no not so much as seems due to them by the Law of Nature.

The next Punishment that follows this Confiscation of Goods, is the disinheriting the Children, insomuch that tho' they are Catholicks, they can never inherit the Estates of their Fathers who died in Heresy. Cap. *Vergentis in senium* de hæret. *Neither ought any Pretence of Compassion to prevent this severe Censure of disinheriting even their orthodox Children, since in many Cases the Judgment of God so proceeds, as that the Children are temporally punished for their Fathers, and because, according to the Canonical Sanctions, Crimes are revenged not only upon the*

Cap 28. Authors *of them, but upon their Posterity.* Zanchinus adds, that the Children of
§ 2 part Hereticks are incapable of succeeding to any of their Kin, or to other *Per-*
2. Asert. *sons,* whither *they die* with a *Will* or *intestate.* John Royas adds, that the Chil-
44. dren of Hereticks, tho' born before the Commission of the Crime, are comprehended under the canonical Penalties and Prohibitions, and says this is the common Opinion of the Doctors. The Reason is, because Heresy is a spiritual Crime, and doth not derive its Original from the Flesh ; and therefore it signifies nothing whether the Children be of the infected Root or not. But if a Son accuses his heretical Father, as his Reward, he is freed from the Penalties ordained against the Children of Hereticks, according to the Law of the Emperor *Frederick. We don't exclude from the Bounds of our Mercy such who, far from following the Heresy of their Fathers, shall discover their Wickedness ; so that to whatever Punishment the Fathers Guilt is subject, let their innocent Children be freed from it.*

The third Punishment is, their being rendred infamous. Cap. *Excommunicamus.* 1 §. *Credentes.* de hæret. There, amongst other Things, 'tis said, *Let him be* ipso jure, *infamous ; let him not be admitted to any publick Offices, or Counsels, nor to chuse any into them, or to bear Witness ; let him also be Intestable *, so that he can have no Power to make a Will, or to inherit by Virtue of one. Farthermore, let no one be forced to answer him upon any Affair, but let him be forced to answer others. If he should happen to be a Judge, let his Sentence be void, and no Cause be referred to his Hearing. If he be an Advocate, let him not be admitted to plead. If a Notary, let no Instruments, drawn by him, be valid, but condemned with their condemned Author. And in all like Cases we command the same to be observed.*

Direct.p.3. The fourth Punishment is, that they are deprived of all Dominion, natu-
Qu. 116. ral, civil, and that which is introduced by the Law of Nations. First, they
tom. 165. are deprived of that natural Power they have over their Children. Cap. *Qui-*
Simanc. *cunq;* §. ult. de hæret. l. 6. Being thus deprived of the natural Power of Parents,
tit. 46. they lose all Authority over their Children, who, becoming as it were Strangers
§. 74. and Foreigners from their Fathers Family, are under no Obligation to obey them as before. This Crime of Heresy in the Father, even before 'tis declared by the Church, frees the Son from his Father's Power, according to the Gloss in Cap. *Quicunq;* §. ult. verbo *desierint,* de hæret. l. 6.

Farther, they are deprived of that civil Power which they have over their
Direct.p.3. Servants, and of that political Power, which they have over any others sub-
Qu. 119. ject to them. *Cap. ult. Extrav. de hæret.* So that Slaves, Freed-men and Ser-
Rom. 168.

* See Marginal Note, *Vol.* I. *Pag.* 76.

vants

vants are *ipſo faĉto*, freed from Servitude, and every Inſtance of Duty, the Moment their Maſter falls into Hereſy. In *Spain*, if the Slaves are Believers, or profeſs the Chriſtian Religion, when their Maſter falls into Hereſy, they recover their Freedom, according to the *Seville Inſtruĉtion*, An. 1484. cap. 24. *Our Lords the King and Queen, out of their Goodneſs and Clemency, will and ordain, that the Servants of all Hereticks ſhall be made free, provided that if whilſt they lived with them they were Chriſtians.* But if they had not profeſſed the Chriſtian Religion, they are forfeited with the other Effeĉts. And tho' ſuch Slaves ſhould have been made free by their Maſters, yet if it was after their becoming Hereticks, 'tis for that Reaſon null and void.

Subjeĉts, when the Prince or Magiſtrate is an Heretick, are freed from their Obedience. Thus it hath often happened, that Kings pronounced Hereticks by the Pope, have, with all their Poſterity, been deprived of all their Dignities, Juriſdiĉtions and Rights, their Subjeĉts abſolved from their Oaths of Allegiance and Fidelity, and their Dominions given as a Prey to others.

And finally, they are deprived of that Power, which is introduced by the Law of Nations, whereby they loſe all Property in every Thing they have. Cap. *cum ſecundum leges.* de hæret. l. 6. inſomuch, that every one is at once wholly freed $_{\mathcal{Q}u.\ 119;}$ from every Obligation he can be under to Perſons fallen into manifeſt Here-$^{com.\ 168.}$ ſy. Cap. *abſolutos*, de hæret. *Let all know that they are freed from the Debt of Fidelity, Dominion, and all Service, to manifeſt Hereticks, how ſtrong ſoever the Obligations may be which they are under.* Theſe Things are thus inferred : " Firſt, if an $^{Simanc.}$
" Heretick depoſites any of his Effeĉts with any Perſon, ſuch Perſon is not $^{t.\ 46.}$
" obliged to reſtore them to the Heretick, after his Hereſy is manifeſt, but $^{§.\ 73.}$
" to the Treaſury. Farther, a Catholick Wife is not obliged to any Du-
" ty to her heretical Huſband, becauſe by the Huſband's Hereſy ſhe is freed
" from her Duty. In like manner a Catholick Huſband is freed from all Du-
" ty to his Wife, if ſhe be an Heretick. Neverthelefs they can't marry with
" others, becauſe the Band of Matrimony is not diſſolved. An Huſband can't $^{Royas, p. 2.}$
" be forced to cohabit with his Wife if ſhe is fallen into Hereſy, even tho' $^{Aſſert\ 40.}$
" ſhe is reconciled ; nor is he bound to maintain her, becauſe her Dowry is $^{§\ 315.}$
" confiſcated by Hereſy ; and as ſhe is ſtripped of her Dowry by her own
" Fault, the Huſband is not obliged to maintain an unindowed Wife. *Zan-*$^{c.\ 18.\ §.2.}$
" *chinus Ugolinus* explains this Matter more largely. The very Children,
" Brothers and Siſters of Hereticks, ought to forſake them. Yea, the very
" Band of Matrimony with ſuch is diſſolved. For if any one departs from the
" Orthodox Faith, and falls into Hereſy, his Wife is not obliged to cohabit
" with him, but may ſeek to be ſeparated from him by the Judgment of the
" Church, ſuch Separation of the Bed being as reaſonable upon account of
" ſpiritual Fornication, as for carnal. And if any Heretick ſhall, after his
" Fall, return to the Unity of the Church, the other married Perſon ſhall be
" obliged to return to him, if they were not before parted by the Sentence of
" the Church. But if they were parted by Sentence, it ſhall be at the Op-
" tion of the other Party who continued in the Faith, whether to return, or
" *become Religious* ; becauſe ſuch Party can't *remain* in the World, and take
" another

" another during the Life of the Party converted, becaufe made whole by
" Penance.

Simanc.
ibid.
" Moreover, the Governors of Forts and Caftles, of People or Cities, are
" not obliged to reftore them to their heretical Lord, nor to keep them in
" his Name. Finally, all Vaffals whatfoever are *ipfo jure*, freed from every
" Obligation to their Lords, tho' fuch Obligations fhall have been con-
" firmed by an Oath."

Hence proceeds the Maxim, that Faith is not to be kept with Hereticks,
which fome are not afraid openly to teach; altho' thofe who are more wife
in *Germany*, *France*, and the *Low Countries*, endeavour to wipe off this Spot
from their Church. But the *Spaniards*, tho' they can't be daily charged with
this Perfidioufnefs, becaufe they have none whom they call Hereticks living
amongft them, yet affert it in plain and open Words, without diffembling,
and are not afhamed to defend and confirm it by the Practice of the
Council of *Conftance*. See amongft others, *Simancas Cathol. Inftit. Tit.* 46. §. 52,
53, 54.

Tit. 46.
§. 52.
This then is one Part of the Punifhment of Hereticks, and what tends to
render them more odious, that Faith is not to be kept with them. For if it is
not to be kept with Tyrants, Pirates, and other publick Robbers, becaufe
they kill the Body, much lefs is it to be kept with obftinate Hereticks, who
deftroy the Soul. And therefore certain Hereticks were moft juftly burnt by
the grave Decree of the Council of *Conftance*, tho' they had the Promife of Security. St. *Thomas* alfo is of Opinion, that an intractable Heretick is to be betrayed to his Judges, notwithftanding a Catholick may have given his Faith,
and bound himfelf by an Oath to the contrary. Add to this, that the Catho-
§. 53.
licks ought to have no Commerce, nor enter into Peace with Hereticks ; and
therefore notwithftanding the Faith given to them, and confirmed by an
Oath, it is not to be kept, becaufe againft the publick Good, the Salvation of
Souls, and contrary to the Laws of God and Man. But if Faith be given to
Hereticks by a Prince, or any publick Power, 'tis to be exactly preferved,
§. 54.
excepting only in thofe Things which the infpired or natural Law forbids the
Performance of.

To the fame Purpofe fpeaks *Brunus*, altho' many now endeavour to difguife
Brunus,
l. 3. *c.* 15.
this Villany. No Peace can, at this Day, be confirmed with Hereticks, who
fpread their impious Doctrine amongft the Chriftian People by their wicked
§. 8.
Preaching, if made on this Condition, that they muft not be offended. Yea,
fo much the more to be abhorred and abominated is Peace made with Hereticks and Schifmaticks upon this Condition, that fuch as offend them fhall be
condemned for Breach of the Peace. For how can Peace be broken by offending
them, with whom no Chriftian Man ought to have Communion, and whom
they ought not to bid God fpeed? Such may fafely be offended, who by the
Civil Laws are put under the Imperial Bann, who are permitted to have no Liberty of meeting or abiding on the *Roman* Ground, or indeed in any Place,
wherein they may injure the very Elements themfelves, and finally, who by
all Laws human and divine, deferve to be extinguifhed.

The

. The fame Perfon teaches, that no Covenants, Conventions or Laws are C. 16 17, firm, that permit Hereticks to have or reform Churches, or to poffefs or ad- 18. minifter their Revenues ; or by which the Proceffes of Churches againft He- reticks or Schifmaticks, that are or may be moved in Judgment, are wholly put off, or fufpended for a Time, or for ever ; or finally, by which Hereticks and Schifmaticks are permitted to exercife any Jurifdiction or Adminiftration, either by themfelves or with Catholicks, or to enjoy any publick Offices.

Moreover, all Places of Refuge, which are open to Malefactors and the worft of Villains, are denied to Hereticks, as tho' they were the very Off- fcouring of the Earth, and had put off the very human Nature at the fame time they did the *Roman* Religion. Thus *Simancas :* " An Heretick flying to *tit.* 46. " a Church, fhall not be protected by the Sanctity of the Place, *i. e.* the Im- §. 65. " munity of the Churches. And therefore *Gundemir*, King of the *Goths*, who " granted this Immunity to the Churches of *Spain* more than 900 Years ago, *Tit.* 46. " excepted three Sorts of Men from it, *viz.* Thieves, Traytors and Here- §. 65. " ticks, as *Peter Medina* relates in his Life.

" *Simancas* adds, That altho' in almoft all Crimes nobler Perfons are fubject §. 67. " to one fort of Punifhment, and the meaner to another, yet in the Crime of " Herefy the fame Punifhment is appointed for all, without Refpect of Per- " fons. So that a noble Perfon falling into Herefy is infamous and vile, and " muft fuffer the Punifhment due to the meaneft. For there is no Difference in " Matters of Faith and Religion between the Great and the Small; the No- " ble and Ignoble. The Law of *Honorius* and *Theodofius* fays, They are all §. 68. " equal to one another, who are equal in the Pravity of Doctrine. And ano- " ther Law fays, They who are alike defiled, and made equal by their " Wickednefs, are equally fubject to the fame Punifhment, *l.* 49. *tit.* 4. *lib.* 16. " C. Theod. and *l.* 1. *tit.* 27. *lib.* 9.

Finally, they teach, that heretical Kings are to be deprived of their King- doms for Herefy. Thus *Simancas :* " 'Tis enquired whither the Kingdom §. 75. " of an heretical King, who hath no Superior, can be confifcated ? The Rea- " fon of the Doubt arifes from this, becaufe the Goods of Hereticks are for- " feited to the fuperior Lord. And therefore *Alphonfus Caftrenfis* is of Opi- " nion, That fuch Kingdom belongs to the Catholick Son of an heretical " King, in the fame Manner as it would if the Heretick were dead. But if " the Son and next of Kin be alfo Hereticks, a Catholick Kingdom may " chufe themfelves an Orthodox King. But if the Kingdom be heretical, the " Election of a Catholick King belongs to the chief Pontiff." This Opinion. is not difpleafing to *Simancas*, tho' he adds, that it may juftly be feized on by the Catholicks.

The fifth Punifhment is Imprifonment. For altho' by the Civil Law the Brunus, Prifon is only to detain Men, yet by the Canon Law it may be ufed as a Pu- *l.* 5. *c.* 12, nifhment. C. *Qyamvis* de pœnis, lib. 6. So that an Heretick either confef- fed or convict, may either be delivered to the fecular Court, or condemned to perpetual Imprifonment. In which Cafe the condemned Perfon fhall be punifhed at the Option of the Judge.

The

Brunus,   The fixth Punifhment is the Bann and Diffidation *. Authent. *Gararos.* c.
l 5. *c.* 14. de hæret.   The Bann is that Sentence, by which any Perfon is caſt out of the
Commonwealth, ſo that he can't enjoy the publick Protection, or diſcharge
any publick Offices, or receive any Benefit of Law, and hath ſome Likeneſs
with Excommunication.   For as by Excommunication a Perfon is caſt out
from the Converſe of the Faithful, ſo by the Bann he is excluded from the
common Good. Diffidation declares Hereticks to be Enemies of their Country
Direct.   and the Empire. Its Effect is this: When any one is declared an Heretick
3 *part.*   by the Sentence of the Judge, any Man, by his own private Authority, may
com. 36. ſeize, plunder and kill him, as an Enemy or Robber, even tho' he be a Clergyman.   He may be capitally puniſhed as a Deſerter, and attacked with Impunity where-ever he is found.   That Hereticks may thus be ſeized on, and
plundered by the private Authority of any Man, *Innocent* IV. openly determines by a Reſcript, beginning, *Ad extirpanda*, in which, amongſt other
Things, there are theſe.   *Alſo the ſame Governor or Ruler of any City or Place, in
the Beginning of his Government, ſhall hold a publick Aſſembly as uſual, and put under the Bann of that City or Place all Hereticks of both Sexes, and of whatſoever
Name or Degree, even as he would the vileſt Offenders, and ſhall be bound to confirm
the Bann they were put under by his Predeceſſors ; eſpecially that no Heretick, Man
or Woman, may any longer inhabit, abide, or dwell in the City, in any Part of its
Juriſdiction, or Diſtrict of the ſame.   And whoſoever ſhall diſcover him or her, he
may freely and ſafely apprehend and ſeize them, and lawfully ſtrip him or them of all their
Effects, which they who take them ſhall have full Right to, unleſs they happen to be*
De hæret. in Office.   And this Plunder of Hereticks *Brunus* tells us is by divine Right.
l. 5. *c.* 5. *Hereticks, by divine Right, may be ſtripped of all their Effects, as unworthy their*
§ 2, 4, 7. *Poſſeſſions.   For the Juſt ſhall devour the Labours of the Wicked ; and therefore Catholicks may claim the Places of Hereticks.   Theſe Things are permitted againſt Hereticks, becauſe Religion and the Chriſtian Faith is endangered by their Impiety.* Auſtin
Epiſt. 48.

Brun. *l.* 5.   " But if an whole City or Community favours and defends Hereſies, or
c. 16.   " nouriſhes Schiſm againſt the Catholick Church, let it be out-lawed, and
§. 13.   " put under the Imperial Bann.   The Conſequence of this will be, that a City
            " thus banned and out-lawed will become an Enemy of the Empire, and all
            " its Citizens, as Enemies, may be with Impunity hurt in their Perſons and
            " Goods, and be all of them expelled, by the Prince, from ſuch Cities where
            " they dwell. Such a City may be alſo ſubject to ſuch a Puniſhment as is pro-
            " portionable to Death it ſelf ; *i. e.* by the Civil Law it may be eraſed
            " from its very Foundations, and by the Canon Law burnt to Aſhes.
            " This Puniſhment the Canoniſts derive from *Deut.* xiii. where the *Iſraelites*
            " are commanded to burn that City which ſhould ſerve other Gods, and de-
            " ſtroy it utterly, and all that is therein, and the Cattle thereof, with the
            " Edge of the Sword.   And there are ſome who think this is allowed to every

---

* *Diffidare* is properly to withdraw by Letters or Writing, that Protection, which one owes to
another, or hath promiſed him.

" one, and that the Church hath granted Authority to all to extirminate He-
" reticks; tho' others are of Opinion this can't be done but by the Authority
" and Command of their Superiors; which Opinion, according to *Brunus*, is
" the fafeft, if not more agreeable to Law, as *Dominick* apprehended it was.
" But the moft neceffary Thing of all is, that no Injury be done to heretical
" Univerfities or Communities, before they are pronounced guilty of this
" Crime by a declaratory Sentence."

But if Hereticks are apprehended, 'tis not lawful for any one to undertake
their Defence *. All Advocates or Notaries, who give Affiftance or Favour
to Hereticks or their Abettors, or who plead for them when under Examination, or draw any Inftruments for them, are pronounced infamous, and fufpended from their Office †. Hence they infer, " That no one muft defend,
" or be an Advocate for any who are known to be Hereticks. As often in-
" deed as this is doubtful, and it is not yet certain whether the Words or Deeds
" objected againft any Perfon as heretical, do favour of manifeft Herefy; or
" whilft the Charge of Herefy is not confirmed by Witneffes, or other legal Pegna *in*
" Proofs, any one may be Advocate for him, and plead in his Defence; *i.e.* if *Direct.*
" the Inquifitors allow him, and provided he take an Oath before-hand to make *l.* 104.
" a juft Defence, and to defift from it as foon as ever it fhall be known that the
" Perfon he defends is an Heretick. And this is always the Method obferved."

The laft Punifhment of Hereticks is that of Death, and that not the common one, but the moft terrible that can be inflicted; *viz.* to be burnt alive.
This they infer from 2 *Kings* xxiii. where *Ozias* commanded the Bones of the
heretical Priefts to be burnt; and from the Words of our Lord, *John* xv. 6.
If a Man abide not in me, he is caft forth as a Branch, and is withered, and Men *l.* 5. *c.* 13:
gather them, and caft them into the Fire, and they are burned. Here *Brunus* obferves, §. 14.
fome think that this Punifhment was introduced only by Cuftom, and can be
proved by no other Right, whither divine or human. This is his Opinion, for,
fays he, *this Punifhment can't be inferred from that Paffage of the Gofpel, of throwing the Branch into the Fire. For this fpeaks of the eternal Fire of Hell, and not of
the temporary Punifhment of Fire. Nor do the Civil Laws prove this Punifhment.
For tho' they fix that Punifhment againft Hereticks, which we call Death, yet
they don't exprefs this kind of Death,* viz. *the Punifhment of Fire; which undoubtedly the Lawgivers would have done, if they had determined to appoint it againft Hereticks; especially as the Punifhment is fo terrible, that they exprefsly mention it, when
ever they think the Heinoufnefs of the Crime deferves it; as may be made appear from
other Conftitutions, where this Punifhment is particularly fpecified.* [However, Ludovicus a Paramo finds out this Punifhment of Fire in many Places of the New
Teftament. " *James* and *John* thought that the *Samaritans*, who would not
" receive our Lord, fhould be deftroyed with Fire from Heaven, according to
" St. *Luke*. Cap. 9. See here now the Punifhment of Hereticks, *viz.* Fire. For
" the *Samaritans* were the Hereticks of thofe Times, *Mat.* xxi. and xxii.
" *Mark* xii. and *Luke* xx. Chrift adds three Parables. One of the two Sons.

* Cap. *Si adverfus nos terra confurgeret.* de hæret. † See cap. *Excommunicamus.* §. *Credentes.*
& cap. 2. §. 1. *de hæret.* lib. 6.

" Another of the Vineyard let out to the Husbandmen. The third of the
" Nuptial Feaſt prepared for thoſe who were invited. By theſe he plainly
" ſhews, that the Kingdom was to be taken away from the heretical *Jews*, and
" their City to be burnt with Fire. See here now the very Confiſcation of Ef-
" fects, and Fire with which Hereticks are puniſhed." Nor is this Reaſoning
to be wondered at in a Man, who every where in the Old and New Teſtament,
and even in Paradiſe it ſelf, finds out an Inquiſition againſt Hereticks, and endeavours to prove by many Arguments, that God himſelf exerciſed the Office
of Inquiſitor of heretical Pravity againſt *Adam* in Paradiſe, *lib.* 1. *tit.* 2.] The
firſt who ordained this Puniſhment of burning Hereticks, after it had been
ſome time in Uſe in the Church of *Rome*, was *Frederick* II. by a Law
which begins, *Inconſutilem.* §. 4. which ſays: *By the Tenor of this preſent Law,
we decree, that the Patarenes, and all other Hereticks whatſoever, being condemned,
ſhall ſuffer that Death which they affect, and that being committed to the Flames, they
ſhall be burnt alive in the View of all Men.* This Law many Popes have confirmed, and therefore the Puniſhment of Fire hath been ordinarily inflicted upon impenitent Hereticks, as is the Cuſtom of the Church of *Rome* to this Day.
Panormitanus ſays *, *that Hereticks ought to be puniſhed with Fire, and burnt, and
that in this the Divine, Canon, Civil, and Common Law agree.* *Simancas* alſo †
not only endeavours to prove by many Arguments, that Hereticks ought to
be burnt, becauſe Heathens and Hereticks thus puniſhed the Catholicks, as
Euſebius, Ruffinus, Socrates and others teſtify ; but contends that 'tis the moſt antient Puniſhment, as appears from the Acts of the Council of *Chalcedon* ; becauſe
the Biſhop of *Alexandria* is there reported to have ſaid, If *Eutiches* pretends to
be wiſer in his Opinions than the Church, he is not only worthy of Puniſhment, but to be burnt ; and becauſe, as *Nicephorus, Eccleſ. Hiſt.* Book 18.
Chap. 4. relates, they ordered *Anatolius* the Heretick to be burnt alive.

De Cathol *Simancas* alſo infers this Puniſhment from a certain Law of *Theodoſius*, ſay-
Inſtit. tit. ing, that *Theodoſius* publiſhed a Conſtitution, in which are theſe Things. *Far-*
46. §. 48. *thermore we command, that whoſoever ſhall bring over a Servant or Freeman unwillingly, or by Perſuaſion, to the wicked Sect, or Ceremony from the Chriſtian Worſhip, ſhall loſe both his Fortune and his Head.* And a little after, *Let him farther
know, that his Goods ſhall be forfeited, and afterwards he himſelf put to Death, who
ſhall pervert any one from the Faith by falſe Doctrine.* *Simancas* adds, *A Law truly
worthy of a* Spaniſh *Emperor.* Vid. Cod. Theodoſ. *Tit.* de Judæis L. prima.&
lib. 16. tit. 6. l. 55.

§ 53.   So that Hereticks muſt be puniſhed with Fire, and if that can't be done,
they muſt at leaſt be baniſhed and expelled, and their Effects forfeited, agreeable to the Laws of the old *Gothick* Kings in *Spain*, by which the Goods of Hereticks were confiſcated, and they themſelves deprived of Honour and Dignities,
and baniſhed for ever.

With this Puniſhment of Fire only Hereticks relapſed, obſtinate and impenitent are puniſhed, who, after Sentence, are delivered over to the ſecular

* In cap. *ad Abolendam.* de hæret. lib. 6. ſuper gloſſ. in verb *Audientia*, allegans Hoſtienſem
poſt Joan. Andr.   † Cathol. Inſtitut. tit. 46. §. 47. & ſeq.

Judge,

Judge, who was bound immediately to condemn them, and fend them to the Fire. The Obftinate were to be burnt alive; others to be firft ftrangled, and then burnt. *5 Inftruct. Hifpal. cap. 9. Simanc. Ibid. §. 49.*

Sometimes this Punifhment of Burning is heightned by another kind of Cruelty. In *Spain* and the *Netherlands,* left they fhould fpeak to the Spectators when brought to the Stake, and pioufly teftify their Conftancy, they were gagged with an Iron Inftrument, fo that in the Midft of their Torments they could utter only an inarticulate Sound. Thus alfo *Simancas* pronounces, *That obftinate Hereticks fhould be burnt alive, and be brought to the Stake* tit. 48. §.6. *gagged, that they mayn't offend the little ones.* This Muzzle or Gagg the *Spaniards* in their Language call *Mordaza.* And if they could invent any Thing more terrible, they would not fail to ufe it againft Hereticks. This *Carena* tit. 13. teftifies, affirming that the Cuftom of punifhing Hereticks with Fire is moft §. 1. Num: reafonable, *becaufe Burning is the moft terrible Death, and therefore the moft grie-* 7. *vous of all Crimes ought to be punifhed with it ; fo that if any Punifhment more terrible than this could be found out, it ought to be inflicted on Hereticks ; and alfo becaufe by this Means the Heretick and his Crime is more fpeedily blotted out from the Remembrance of Mankind.*

Thus we fee that there is no kind of Punifhment that can poffibly be invented, but is enacted againft Hereticks, and that greater Gentlenefs is ufed towards Thieves, Traytors and Rebels, thofe Enemies of Mankind, than towards miferable Hereticks ; who endeavouring to worfhip God with a pure Confcience, and regulate their Lives by the Gofpel Rule, yet oppofe fome Doctrines of the Church of *Rome,* which they are perfuaded are contrary to the Gofpel ; and that it is a much more grievous Offence in that Church, to oppofe certain Opinions by the clear Light of the Word of God, and to reject certain Pharifaical Superftitions, than openly to contemn the divine Commands by an impious and profane Life, and vilely to difhonour the moft holy Name of God.

C H A P. III.
Of Open and Secret HERETICKS.

HEreticks are divided into feveral Claffes in the Church of *Rome,* and this is very neceffary for the Inftruction of the Inquifitors, that they may always certainly know what Sentence to pronounce upon each. However, every Thing is not fo fully determined, but that there yet remain great Controverfies amongft the Doctors and Inquifitors themfelves, fo that one of them often judges more favourably than another ; and therefore 'tis of great Concern by what Inquifitor any Perfon is to be judged ; for he who happens to be condemned as an Heretick by a fevere one, might have obtained a milder Sentence, had he been tried by a Judge of more favourable Sentiments and Opinions.

First of all Hereticks are divided into Open and Secret. " An open He- Eymer, " retick is one, who publickly avows fomething contrary to the Catholick P. 2. qu. E 2   " Faith, 33.

" Faith, or who profeffes an heretical Error contrary to the Faith, or who
" defends an Error of his own, or one of other Hereticks, or who is con-
" victed before the Judges of the Faith of heretical Pravity, or confeffes it
" himfelf ; or finally who is condemned for it by their Sentence.

Simanc.
tit. 52. §. 3. " A fecret or concealed Heretick is one who errs in his Mind concerning
" the Faith, and purpofes to be obftinate in his Will, but yet hath not fhewn
" it outwardly by Word or Deed. He who is a concealed Heretick in this
" Senfe, is generally called an Heretick purely intellectual : and the common
" Opinion of the Doctors is, that fuch a one doth not incur the Sentence of
" Excommunication, and is not fubject to the Judgment of the Church for
" his Herefy, becaufe the Church hath no Power over purely internal Acts,
" and cannot by its Jurifdiction direct, prohibit or punifh them ; and be-
" caufe Excommunication doth not belong to the Court of Confcience, but to
" that of external Judgment.

Part. 1.
§. 240,
&c. " *John Royas* however affirms, that the Canonifts differ from this general
" Opinion of the Divines, and determine that an altogether concealed Here-
" tick is excommunicated, becaufe there is no Need of the Service of Men in
" Penalties which are *ipfo jure*, contracted. For as a Man falls into Herefy
" by a mere Act of his Will, fo for the fame Reafon, becaufe he by his Will
" alone believes heretical Errors, he actually falls into Excommunication ;
" efpecially becaufe Excommunication neceffarily draws along with it imme-
" diate Execution, and cleaves to Herefy as a Leprofy to a Leper, and a
" Shadow to a Man. He adds : If any one contracts Herefy in his Mind and
" Underftanding, believing God was not incarnate, or that holy *Mary* was not
" a Virgin, and doth not proceed to the external Act, by openly declaring it
" to himfelf or another, but contains his Error and aforefaid Herefy entirely
" in his Heart, but afterwards, through the Influence of better Counfels, for-
" fakes and repents of it, and then comes, as hath been often done, to the In-
" quifitors of heretical Pravity, confeffing that he received and believed the
" faid Errors, defiring from them Abfolution and wholefome Penance, is not
" fuch an one an Heretick, even though altogether and entirely concealed and
" mental, and by Confequence excommunicated, and therefore to be abfol-
" ved ? And whereas 'tis objected, that the Church doth not judge of fecret
" Things, he adds, this is meant only of that Court; which confifts of the
" Actor, the Criminal, the Judge and Witneffes ; whereas the Crime of He-
" refy, tho' altogether concealed, requires nothing external, becaufe 'tis a
" mental Offence, and is committed by the mere Thought of the Mind, and
§. 215. " therefore the Church may well judge of this without the Judgment of a
" Court, and by a Parity of Reafon of Excommunication which cleaves to
" Herefy. Befides the Church forbids the inward Acts of the Mind, and
" declares a Perfon an Heretick, tho' fecret or mental, and therefore it judges
" of fecret Things, and therefore why not of Excommunication, which ad-
" heres to Herefy. This is a Decifion of great Moment. For an excom-
" municate Perfon needs Reconciliation, and tho' the Reconciliation granted
" to a Penitent be favourable, yet as 'tis the Abfolution of Excommunication,
" fuch Reconciliation is attended with Forfeiture of Goods and perpetual Im-
" prifonment.   " But

" But a Perſon may be called a concealed Heretick in another Senſe, *viz.* Simanc.
" who by Word or Writing hath brought forth that Hereſy which he hath *tit.* 52.
" conceived in his Heart, tho' with Secrecy and Craft; ſo that 'tis called
" concealed Hereſy, becauſe 'tis not notorious, and can't be proved. Such a
" one incurs the Sentence of Excommunication, and is liable to the other
" Puniſhments of Hereticks, becauſe he hath declared his Hereſy, tho' pri-
" vately; and if he confeſſes his Hereſy before the Inquiſitor, and repents,
" he is to be privately abſolved. Thus in *the* Seville *Inſtructions,* 1 Cap. 5. §. 11.
" where we have the general Form of publick Abjuration laid down, with
" this Exception : *Unleſs the Crime be ſo ſecret, that the Penitent only knows it,*
" *and it can't be diſcovered by another, in ſuch Caſe he is to be ſecretly reconciled and*
" *abſolved* ;" which they thus explain, When an Heretick hath declared or
written down his intellectual Hereſy, and yet no one hath heard or read it,
tho' others underſtand this of an Hereſy purely mental.

Altho' an Heretick be thus concealed, yet if he infects or perverts others, §. 12.
he is immediately to be diſcovered to his Judges without any preceeding Admonition. But yet they don't affirm that a concealed Heretick is obliged to
betray himſelf, when he is asked by the Judge in a general Inqu.ſition, Whether he knows any Heretick. In like manner, when an Heretick purely mental confeſſes his intellectual Hereſy in the ſacred Court of Penance, he doth
not incur Excommunication by this external Act, becauſe ſuch an Action is §. 9.
good and pious, and not liable to human Judgment.

CHAP. IV.
Of Affirmative and Negative HERETICKS.

HEreticks are farther diſtinguiſhed into Affirmative and Negative. Affir- Eymer.
mative are ſuch, who err in their Mind in Matters of Faith, and who *part.* 2.
ſhew by Word or Deed, that they are thus obſtinate in their Will, and open- *q.* 34.
ly confeſs it before the Inquiſitor. Negative Hereticks are thoſe, who, according to the Laws of the Inquiſition, are rightly and juſtly convicted of ſome
Hereſy before a Judge of the Faith, by ſome lawful Witneſſes, whom either
they cannot or will not refute, but yet who will not confeſs, conſtantly per-
ſiſting in the Negative, and that they profeſs the Catholick Faith, and deteſt
heretical Pravity. They except indeed againſt Facts committed many Years
before, which are preſumed to be forgotten. But even this is not to be preſumed in Facts of Importance and Weight, according to the *Seville* Inſtructions, *An.* 1484. *cap.* 13. Such are, If any hath wilfully preached up heretical Propoſitions, or broken the Images of the Saints. Neither is this to be
underſtood of Perſons of good Memories, but only of light Facts, and of Perſons naturally dull and forgetful. Who are to be eſteemed ſuch, and what Time
is to be ſuppoſed ſufficient to ſuch Forgetfulneſs, is entirely left to the Eccleſiaſtical Judges, after they have weighed the Circumſtances of Perſons and Things.

He alſo is eſteemed by many a negative Heretick, and, as it were, diminute, confeſſed, and obſtinate, who doth not diſcover either all the Hereſies of
which.

which he is convicted, or the whole Time of his Offence, or all his Accomplices, if the Things are so fresh, as that he can't be supposed to have forgotten them. Amongst these sort of Negatives are also reckoned by some, such who confess before the Inquisitor heretical Facts or Words, but who deny any Pravity of Intention, altho' others, as we shall soon see, call them Impenitent.

Cathol. In- *stit. tit. 6.* *§. 19.* What their Punishment ought to be, the Doctors differ. *Simancas* says, That he who confesses heretical Words, but denies the Pravity of Intention, may be condemned as Impenitent, except the Matter be doubtful. In such Case he ought to be purged, or abjure, because of his being suspected, or put to the Torture, which is generally the Custom.

De haret. *part. 1.* But because this Case often happens in *Spain*, because of their new Converts from the *Jews* and *Moors*, *John Royas* handles this Matter largely, of which I shall here give you the Substance; from whence we shall know what sort of Christians they are, which the *Spanish* Kings have converted to their Church by the Fear of Punishment from amongst the *Jews* and *Moors*.

n. 1, &c. We know by Experience, how many there are who are detained for heretical Pravity in the Prisons of the Office of the holy Inquisition, who ingenuously confess heretical Deeds and Words, but who absolutely deny all rash Belief, and

3. Pravity of Intention. Thus a Man may confess that he hath said, as often happens in examining Causes of Faith, that every one may be saved in his own Sect and Opinion, a *Jew* by the *Jewish* Law, a *Saracen* by

4. the *Mahometan*, and a *Lutheran* in the *Lutheran* Sect. For the guilty Person sometimes confesses in his Discourse, that he pronounced the aforesaid Words inadvertently, and thro' the Error of his Tongue, and being asked by the Inquisitors of heretical Pravity, Whether he believes such Things, he says he never did, but that he ever held what the holy *Roman* Church preaches and

7. teaches. Thus he denies the Intention, and only confesses the Words, which without doubt are heretical. Another Instance is of one who confesses that he said simple Fornication is not a mortal Sin, and yet denies all rash Belief and Error of Understanding, asserting that, speaking for Wantonness sake, he pronounced the aforesaid Words to some Wenches, which are in Reality heretical Words.

An Instance of an heretical Fact shall be in him, who being baptized, is afterwards circumcised, and observes the Fast called *Ramadan*, and the Passover,

10. after the *Mahometan* Manner, and makes the *Zalah*, i. e. his *Adoration or Prayer* in his own Home or in the Mosques, washing first his Body, and especially his Privities, bending his Knees, bowing down, and lifting up his Head, and who feeds on Fleshes killed from the * *Keblah*. The new Converts in the Kingdoms of *Valencia*, *Aragon* and *Granada*, publickly observe many other sacrile-

15. gious and impious Rites. Another Example is of him, who especially if he be of the *Jewish* Race, observes the Sabbath by refraining from all Labour, and

33. observes the other Festivals of the *Jews*, and who confesses such Facts and Words, but affirms that he said or did them inadvertently and ignorantly, and that he is ready to submit to the Correction of the Church. 'Tis queried,

* The *Mahometans* call that Part of the World, where *Mecca* is situated, by the Name of *Kebla*, towards which they are obliged to turn themselves when they say their Prayers. *Mecca* is situated towards the South.

whether

whether fuch a one is to be accounted an Heretick, even tho' not convicted by lawful Witneffes.

On the negative Side 'tis urged, that Herefy fuppofes an Error in the Un- 40. derftanding, and Obftinacy in the Will in adhereing to thofe Things which are contrary to the Determination of the Church. Hence they infer that that 64. of *Innocent* is reafonable and true, who faid, That if any one believes what the Cap. *Fir-* Church believes, but thro' the Influence of natural Reafon falfely fuppofes that *miter de* the Father is either greater than the Son, or before him, or that the three *fumma* Perfons are three Things diftinct from each other, he is not an Heretick, and *n. 6.* doth not offend, becaufe he believes this is the Churches Belief, and fuppofes his own Opinion to be the Faith of the Church. Therefore he thinks 'tis but 66, 67. reafonable, that in the Defences of the Criminals, regard ought to be had to their Simplicity and Imprudence, fo that the Punifhment may be mitigated, and that the Judges, efpecially the Inquifitors of heretical Pravity, according to their Office, fhould be very folicitous and diligent in examining and fearching into their Defences, becaufe of the partial and maimed Defence of the Crimi- §. 69. nals, tho' the Party doth not feek it, or even refufe it. But he adds, that 'tis. *antiently* decided by the *Rota* 875 in C. *Accufatus de herefi*, in tit. *de hæret.* that if any one be accufed of Herefy, and legally convicted by Witneffes or other- wife, and yet denies that he faid or believed fuch heretical Things, yet that he ought neverthelefs to be condemned as a negative and impenitent Heretick, and delivered over to the fecular Arm, altho' he afferts that he believes, and hath believed as the Church believes.

However, the Doctors generally maintain the Affirmative, becaufe the §. 276. Nature of Facts demonftrate the Intention, Mind and Will of the Doers. For Inftance, If any one fhould do a properly *Jewifh* Action, fuch as obferving §. 184; the Sabbath, and other *Jewifh* Rites, from thence is inferred the Intention and Will of *Judaifing*. If the Intention doth not appear, in a doubtful Cafe, 'tis pre- fumed that this was done with the Intention of *Judaifing*, when the Act or Com- miffion is certain, either from the Perfon's Confeffion, or by Witneffes, and efpe- cially if the Perfon be fufpected. He therefore who confeffes an heretical Action, and denies the Intention, which is the Quality affecting fuch an Action to make it punifhable or not, may poffibly be condemned as a negative Heretick ; at leaft may be tortured to difcover his Intention, as the Doctors are generally of Opinion, and as is the ufual Practice. But if the Fact be plainly heretical, fuch as a Perfon's going over, or returning to the *Jewifh* or Pagan Rites, 'tis fufficient to his being condemned as an Heretick, that he be convicted of the Fact, altho' there be no certainty as to his *Belief.* They alfo make a Diffe- *part. 1.* rence between an heretical Word and Fact, and *Royas* gives the Reafon of this §. 400. Difference. There is this Difference between one who confeffes an heretical Fact, and one who confeffes an heretical Word, and denies the evil Intention ; that he who confeffes the Fact is to be delivered over efpecially if he be a fufpected Perfon, and the Fact hath been repeated ; whereas he who confeffes an he- retical Word, is to be tortured to difcover his Intention. The Reafon of the Difference is, becaufe there is a greater Affection of the Soul, and Delibera- tion of the Mind in Facts than in Words. To this they add, that there are §. 317. other

other Sins, such as Covetousnefs, Intemperance, Luft, &c. to which Men are naturally prone. Others to which Nature doth not lead Men, yea rather to which the Appetite and Pleasure of Men is repugnant; such as, in the Time of a Faft not to eat till Night, or pray, or not to eat Swines Flesh, not to drink Wine, or to obferve the evil Ceremonies of the *Mahometans* or *Jews*. As to the former, Men are carried into them by their own Wills. As to the latter, the Will is undoubtedly governed in its Choice by the Underftanding, and therefore it may be concluded that they proceed from an evil Intention and

§. 346. *Belief.* So that if feveral Witneffes depofe in general, that fuch a one hath a good Reputation, their Teftimony deferves no Credit to prove fuch a one to be a Catholick, if he be convicted by two Witneffes, to have particularly faid

§. 358. or done fomething repugnant to the Catholick Faith. This is the Cafe when the Action is forbidden. But if it be of an indifferent Nature, which may be either good or evil, they fay there ought to be no Prefumption of a Crime, but that the ambiguous Deeds or Words ought to be interpreted on the more

§. 366. charitable Side. If, for Inftance, any one fays, The *Lutherans* are more noble, *i. e.* in the Catholick Senfe, the Peers and Nobles in *France* are *Lutherans* more than the common People, 'tis not heretical. If it be underftood of the Nobility of their Virtues and Morals, 'tis fufpicious; if of the Nobili-

§. 373. ty of Religion, 'tis heretical. But this they fay muft only be underftood as to the full Proof of an Offence, and not as to any Prefumption for which a Perfon may be tortured, efpecially if he be fufpected. For in a doubtful Cafe Herefy is to be prefum'd, and if the Proofs appear too plain, he is to be put to the Torture (becaufe the Salvation of his Soul is concerned) that he may confefs under Torture, and be reconciled, and receive his Penance, that if he be capable of Correction

§. 378. his Spirit may be faved, according to St. *Paul.* Farther, 'tis ufual in this Office of the Inquifition, that in expounding the Words of any Propofition, the Nature and Condition of the Speakers be attended to; particularly whether the Words were fpoken by a Countryman, of poor Capacity, in a blundring Way, and without Deceit and evil Belief; or by a learned Perfon, of an acute Underftanding, and in a fubtle Manner; for then they are to be underftood to be deceitful. All thefe Things are to be confidered by the Qualificator Divines, whom the Inquifitors call and confult, and to whofe Opinions the In-

§. 384. quifitors ought wholly to affent. Finally, they affirm, that if the Mind and
§. 577. Intention is not to be proved by the external Actions, it can never be proved,
§. 590. and fo the Crime of Herefy can never be punifhed. From hence *Royas* concludes, that he who confeffes an heretical Action or Word, but denies the wicked Intention, denies that which is the principal Form and Subftance, and is therefore to be delivered over as a diminute, impenitent and negative Heretick. The fame is to be affirmed of him, who being fully convict of feveral

§. 595. Errors, confeffes fome, but denies others; becaufe he is deficient in a fubftantial Part. 'Tis not fo with one who confeffes all his Errors, tho' not the feveral Times which are proved by legal Witneffes.

From this long Account, of which this is only the fummary, one may infer, that 'tis the common Opinion of the *Spanifh* Doctors, that fuch who confefs an heretical Word or Action, but deny the Intention, are to be put to the Torture

ture to make them confefs fuch Intention ; but that fuch who confefs an heretical Deed, and deny the Intention, are to be fent back as negative Hereticks, and delivered over to the fecular Court. Yea, as to doubtful Words,
it is to be prefumed there is Herefy ; not fo indeed as to be full Proof, but fo
far as to be a juft Reafon for the Torture.

Royas affirms the fame of fuch who retract the Confeffion they have made *Part. 1.*
when under Examination. " He who confeffes his heretical Errors when under *Affert. 25.*
" Profecution, and afterwards retracts his Confeffion, is to be delivered over as
" a Negative, unlefs the Miftake plainly appears. For by Confeffion the Of-
" fence is fully proved, and by retracting it, the guilty Perfon becomes obfti-
" nate, impenitent and negative. And therefore unlefs the Miftake appears, he is
" to be delivered over even though there be no other Proof of the Crime, and
" although his Confeffion was made and confirmed under Torture. For
" this is the fame Thing as a free and fpontaneous Confeffion, although
" afterwards revoked, if the Miftake doth not plainly appear."

C H A P. V.

Of HERETICKS *Impenitent and Penitent.*

OTHER Hereticks are called Obftinate, or Impenitent, others Peni- *Eymer.*
tent. An impenitent one is he, who being legally convict of Herefy *part. 2.*
before a Judge of the Faith, or having confeffed it, will not obey his Judge, *q. 40.*
when he commands him to forfake his Error and abjure it, and give competent Satisfaction, but obftinately perfeveres in fuch Error.

Simancas diftinguifhes between an obftinate Heretick and an impenitent *Tit. 48.*
one.

" Whofoever believes any Propofition to be true, and knows the contrary *§. 7.*
" Opinion to be the Catholick one, is for this Reafon only a confummate ob-
" ftinate Heretick.

" There are others whofe Obftinacy is not fully manifeft, but who are ac- *§. 9, &c.*
" counted as confummate obftinate by the Prefumption of the Law. Every one
" for Inftance, who being capable of Reafon, denies any Propofition of the Ca-
" tholick Faith, publickly known amongft all the Faithful ; efpecially if he
" appears to be a skilful and wife Perfon ; becaufe he is prefumed to know
" what all know, and what all Chriftians are bound explicitely to know. -
" 2. He who afferts any Herefy, having before taught the contrary Catholick *§. 10.*
" Truth, even tho' he errs in fuch Propofitions, which he was not bound ex-
" plicitely to know. But however this doth not hold, when 'tis propable there *§. 11.*
" may have been Forgetfulnefs, either through Length of Time, Decay of Me-
" mory, or Foolifhnefs. 3. He who for a long while perfifts in an Error, the *§. 12.*
" contrary Catholick Truth of which he was not bound explicitely to know ;
" becaufe

§. 13:

" becaufe his perfifting in Error is his own Fault, which he is bound to for-
" fake under Neceffity of Salvation, and becaufe he is negligent in his Search
" after Truth, in which the Chriftian Salvation confifts. 4. He who hinders
" the Preaching, Defence and Doctrine of the Catholick Faith, and contemns
" the Cenfures of the Church ; and alfo he who fwears he will never depart
" from his Error.

§. 15.

" And although any Perfon fhould err thro' probable Ignorance, yet if after
" legal Admonition he doth not immediately repent, he is to be accounted
" obftinate ; becaufe he is then as truly an Heretick, as if he had willingly

§. 17.

" erred from the Beginning. A legal Admonition is to be judged of accord-
" ing to the Nature of the Herefy. In Herefies plainly condemned, that is a
" legal Admonition, if it be fhewn to the erroneous Perfon, that the holy
" Scripture, or the Determination of the Catholick Church be contrary to his
" Herefies. But if the Herefy be not condemned by Name, evident Argu-
" ments fhall be efteem'd as a juft Admonition ; in a Word, whatever is a

§. 6.

" probable Caufe to recover the Erroneous from his Error." *Obftinate Here-*
ticks, according to *Simancas, are to be burnt alive, and delivered over to the*
Fire with their Mouths gagged, and their Tongues tied, that they may not offend

p 3. *t.*14.
§. 13.
n. 92.

the little ones. For in this, fays *Carena, 'tis the only kind of Piety, to be cruel,*
whilft he is Impenitent.

" An impenitent Heretick is one, who will not repent of his Error, as to
" which every impenitent Perfon is alfo obftinate. So that if his Herefy be
" plainly proved, and he will not confefs his Error with a pure Heart, nor
" readily abjure his Herefy, and fubmit to the Penance enjoined him, he is
" to be left to the fecular Judge as obftinate and impenitent, although he pro-
" tefts a thoufand times over that he was and is a Catholick, and is refolved

§. 27.

" to live and die in the Chriftian Faith. So that the Impenitent is the fame
" that others call Negative ; and if fuch a one be convicted to have faid or
" written any Herefy, it fignifies nothing, though it be proved that he was
" a Catholick before, or after, and every time elfe, unlefs he will return to
" the Church, and fubmit to his Penance."

But *Simancas* gives a different Account, *viz.* That a Perfon may always retract his Confeffion before the Tribunal of the Inquifition, and that his laft
Confeffion only is to ftand, from whence 'tis to be concluded, whether he
be a penitent or impenitent Heretick. If he perfifts in his Confeffion, and
fubmits himfelf to the Church, he is penitent. If he retracts his Confeffion,

Tit. 13.
§. 14.

he is accounted and punifhed as an Impenitent. His Words are plain. " In the
" Procefs of the holy Inquifition, the guilty Perfon may retract his Confef-
" fion when and how he pleafes ; and although he gives no probable or fuffi-
" cient Reafon, his Retractation is to be admitted ; and his laft Confeffion is
" to ftand, whether it be for or againft him ; for by this 'tis to be determi-
" ned, whether the Criminal be penitent or impenitent. And this is the
" Courfe of the Law."

If it fhould happen that any one fhould confefs through Fear of Punifhment,
yet he muft not affert his Innocence, upon Pain of being again delivered to
the

the Inquisition, and punished as Impenitent. So that 'tis not lawful so much as to mutter any Thing against the Judgments of this holy Tribunal, tho' they are unjust. This *Simancas* plainly teaches. " He who is reconciled to §. 25. " the Church, and says he never was an Heretick, but that he confessed " Things he never committed, through Fear of false Witnesses, is to be pu- " nished as an Impenitent, unless he repent. This is upon Supposition that §. 26. " he hath not satisfied the Penance enjoined him ; for if he hath performed it, " he is rather Rash than Impenitent. Now rash Persons are to be punished " according to the Pleasure of the Judges, and sometimes to be scourged and " threatned with more grievous Punishments, if they afterwards fall into the " same Rashness." *Zanchinus* treats more distinctly of such Persons. " If *de haret.* " any one, after having confessed his Error, and receiv'd Sentence of Penance, *cap.* 23. " retracts his Confession, and says that he confessed through Fear of Charges, " or some greater Punishment, he appears by this his Retractation not to have " been really but feignedly converted, and is therefore to be punished as an " Heretick ; and if he hath abjured in his first Confession, he may be looked " on only as a feigned Relapse ; but if he persist in his Denial, he may be con- " demned as an obstinate Heretick."

In the mean while, that they may not appear to be the Defenders of any unjust Sentence, they allow innocent Persons, who, wearied with Imprison- ment, and through Fear of Death, have confessed Crimes they never com- mitted, to have their Cause reheard before the Inquisitors, but with such a Limitation, as is enough to deter the most innocent Person in the World, which *Simancas* thus describes to us. " An innocent Person, who, through *Tit.* 13. " Fear of Witnesses, and wearied out with Imprisonment, confesses he hath §. 27, 28. " been an Heretick, if he can prove his Innocence, ought not to neglect his " Reputation, but to have the Cause heard over again by the Inquisitors. But " if he can't refute the Witnesses, nor justly retract his Confession, he ought " to confess that Sin to his Parish Priest, and do nothing more, lest something " worse should happen to him ;" *i. e.* lest he should be dismissed as an Im- penitent, and delivered over to the secular Court.

Besides these, there is another Kind of Impenitents, *viz.* such who have professed their Heresy, but don't observe the Penance enjoin'd by the Inqui- sitor. Such are thought to be but feign'd Converts, and therefore Impeni- tent. Thus *Simancas.* " Those who don't satisfy the Penance enjoin'd them, *Tit.* 48. " ought to be punished as impenitent, perjured, and feigned Converts. They §. 29. " are Impenitent, because they don't perform Penance ; perjured, because " they violate the Oath, by which they promised they would obey the Com- " mands of the Church ; feigned Converts, because they neither perform " true Penance, nor remain in due Obedience to the Church." Friar *Bernard in voc.* *Comensis*, in his Light of the Inquisition, calls these Impenitent. But *Pegna Imprani-* says, there is Need of mature Deliberation, and manifold Distinctions in this *tens. n. 3.* Matter.

However, *Simancas* doth not rank them with other Impenitents, because he adds, " That such Impenitents are not immediately to be left to the secu- §. 31. " lat

" lar Court, but they muſt be dealt with by Law till the pronouncing the
" definitive Sentence.   Neither are they to be rooted up out of the Catholick
" Church, till they have been once and again, and ſeveral times admoniſhed
" about the Salvation of their Souls, by learned, pious, and religious Men."

Eymer.   Penitents are thoſe, who, admoniſhed by the Eccleſiaſtical Judge, abjure
p. 2. q. 40. their Error, and give ſuitable Satisfaction at the Pleaſure of the Biſhop and
Inquiſitor.   Of theſe there are two Sorts : Some come of their own accord, or
within the Time of Grace, without being cited, or called by Name, or having
any particular Inquiſition made after them ; whereas others return after being
apprehended, cited, and inquiſited, and oftentimes after many Admonitions.
The firſt are treated with greater Mildneſs, and are ſometimes enjoin'd a ſecret Penance, but muſt however abjure their Errors, and be bound under the
Forfeiture of all their Effects to the Inquiſition, to accompliſh the Penance enjoined them.   Theſe Things we have in the Council of *Biterre,* cap. 5. *To ſuch*
who confeſs within the Time of Grace, voluntarily and fully, and declare they will
return to the Eccleſiaſtical Unity, grant them the Benefit of Abſolution, according to
the Form of the Church; viz. cauſing them to abjure every Hereſy that exalts it
ſelf againſt the holy Roman *Church, and the Orthodox Faith, under every Name*
whatſoever, and to ſwear that they will alſo preſerve and defend the Catholick Faith,
which the ſaid holy Roman *Church holds and preaches, and that they will proſecute to*
their utmoſt Hereticks of every Kind, convicted as well as condemned, their Be-
lievers, Receivers, Defenders and Abettors, by ſeeking after, accuſing and ſeizing
them, or at leaſt, by faithfully diſcovering them to the Inquiſitors, or other faithful
Perſons, who have better Inclination and Ability to apprehend them: And that in
whatſoever Reſpect they are or ſhall be found to have offended in the ſame Crime, they
ſhall abide by the Commands of the Inquiſitors and Church, and receive and fulfil the
Penance which at any time they ſhall enjoin them, and ſhall ſolemnly bind themſelves
thus to receive and fulfil it, under Penalty of forfeiting all their Effects to the Inquiſition
and Church.

fol. 416.
verſo.   In the ſame Council, towards the End, there is very ſtrict Command, concerning the giving this pecuniary Caution.   *As to ſuch who return of themſelves,*
without being accuſed by others, let the Inquiſitor take diligent Care, that they give
Money Security, after they have ſworn to ſtand preciſely by the Commands of the Church,
and to obſerve and obey them.   Afterwards let a private Penance be enjoined them at
the Pleaſure of the Inquiſitor, and thus returning, let them be abſolved and diſpenſed
with.   Clement IV. in his Bull, *Licet ex omnibus,* commands the Inquiſitors to
look to it very carefully, that they be not deceived by a feigned Converſion.
But if any of the aforeſaid Perſons will wholly abjure their heretical Pravity, and re-
turn to the Eccleſiaſtical Unity, grant them the Benefit of Abſolution according to the
Form of the Church, and enjoin them the uſual Penance, being particularly careful,
that they do not fraudulently return by a feigned Converſion, and thus deceiving you, or
rather themſelves, wear the Wolf under the Appearance of the Lamb.

As to thoſe who do not voluntarily return, the Penance enjoin'd them is
more ſevere, for they are accounted convict, and in ſome Meaſure forced. There
is no particular Account to be given of their Penances, which are left to the
Plea-

Pleasure of the Inquisitors. The Manner they are herein to observe, we have in the Council of *Narbonne*, cap. 5. in these Words. *This we strictly enjoin in this Manner, because we would not have you enjoin all the Penances aforesaid every where, or subject all Persons to all of them, but that you should cautiously and wisely dispense them according to the Discretion given you by the Lord ; according to the Nature of the Offences, Persons, Places, Times, and other Circumstances, so that whether you punish or pardon, the Life of Offenders may be amended ; or at least that it may appear who walks in Darkness and who in Light, and who is truly penitent, and who a pretended Convert, that from hence there may be no Scandal to true Catholicks, nor under Pretence of Scandal, nor any other Way, as far as lies in your Power, by which Heresy may either be defended or nourished.*

But if there be a great Number of Penitents, the Council of *Taracon* hath decreed, that a prudent Judge may use somewhat of Moderation. *Likewise if* Bzov. *the Number of Hereticks, or their Believers be large, and they are ready to abjure* a. 1242. *their Heresy, a prudent Judge may inflict Canonical Punishments on them, whether* §. 4. *greater or less, according to the Provision of the Apostolick See, and thus avoid the Punishment of Intrusion* *. *Or if the Number be not so very large, a prudent Judge may use Moderation according to his Discretion, as to the Believers in Hereticks, after having considered Circumstances. Provided always, that perfect Hereticks, or those who dogmatically affirm their Heresies, or Believers of them being relapsed into such Belief, after having abjured or renounced Heresy, shall be perpetually imprisoned, after having fully abjured their Heresy, and Absolution from Excommunication, that there they may save their Souls, and may not corrupt others.*

Finally, also the Council of *Narbonne* hath provided, c. 18. that none recovered from Heresy, if they had been greatly culpable, should be admitted to any Religion ; in these Words : *And least such Persons should corrupt the Simplicity of Religion, let none of the aforesaid Criminals enter into any Religion whatsoever, without the Leave of the Lord Pope, or his Legate. And if any such shall have entered without their or your Leave, after the Inquisition against them hath been begun, or even before, without having confessed, and being canonically absolved, recal them.* Lastly, 'tis required that such as are reconciled, shall confess the same Crimes to their own Parish Priest, after they have been judicially absolved by the Inquisitors ; which is also provided by the *Madrid* Instruction : *After* a. 1561. *the Penitent shall have been judicially absolved, let the Priest sacramentally absolve him.* cap. 71.

But they will by no Means allow such to be received, who, after a long Time, and frequent Admonitions and Exhortations, scarce seem capable of Conversion, and especially if they appear so, at that Instant of Time, when they are to be deliver'd over to the secular Court ; because the Fear of Death seems rather to induce them to seek Mercy, than the Love of Truth. Nor such who by Commands, Threatnings, Punishments, Rewards, sworn Promises, or any other the like Ways, endeavour to persuade any to Heresy, or obstinately to defend any Heresy they may have embraced. Nor finally such, who have persuaded, or endeavoured to persuade, Kings, Princes, the Queen, or

---

* *Intrusio* is a Person's thrusting himself into the Possession of something to which he hath no legal Right.

the Sons and Daughters of Kings, to embrace Herefy. *Simancas* gives the
Cathol. Reafon : " Becaufe fuch a one is to be left to the fecular Judge without Mer-
Inftit. tit. " cy, as having added High Treafon to Herefy, by endeavouring to deftroy,
47. §. 68, " with the moft aggravated Crime, the Soul of the Prince, and thereby in
&c. " Confequence of the whole Common-wealth. Kings alfo themfelves may ea-
" fily be perverted by Means of fuch Women ; and if fuch are guilty of
" High Treafon, who violate their Chaftity, much more thofe who caufe their
" Souls to commit Adultery."

Tr. tr.   As to the Heirs of penitent Hereticks, there is a Decree of the Council of
fol. 417. *Biterre,* determining what they are obliged to. *You ought to require a fuitable*
Satisfaction from the Heirs of fuch, who having confeffed and being reconciled, have
died without Penance, that fo great a Crime, publickly confeffed in Judgment, may
not go unpunifhed in any. Let the fame be done to thofe who having received Pe-
nance, have died without performing it, or delay'd to do it, or who have obliged
themfelves to fulfil it, under Forfeiture of their Effects, or who have been command-
ed to tranfport themfelves. Alexander IV. in his Confultations agrees with this,
faying, *Moreover, fome, as you add, have bound themfelves to the Inquifitors, un-*
der Forfeiture of all their Effects, to receive Penance from them, and fulfil it for
their heretical Offences, who, after being enjoined it, have died without performing
it, or rather having neglected it wholly, or in part. 'Tis therefore asked, Whether
the Inquifitors themfelves, or thofe who fucceed them, may force the Heirs or the
Poffeffors of the Goods of fuch deceafed Perfons, to make Satisfaction for them?
To which we anfwer, That if by fuch Penance, any Obligation profitable to Salva-
tion, fhall have been laid, for which the temporal Effects are to be anfwerable, the In-
quifitors may force the Heirs to fulfil it, or fuch other Perfons to whom the Effects
may come under fuch Obligation. But they can by no Means be forced to undergo thofe perfonal Punifhments that Hereticks themfelves muft fuffer if they
return. Hence *Guido Fulcodius,* in his Confultations, anfwers, *That he believes*
fuch as are abfolved by the Inquifitors, and die before they have performed their Pe-
nance, are referved for Purgatory, and that nothing farther is to be laid upon their
Heirs. Alexander IV. alfo anfwers: *There are others alfo who have confeffed*
in Judgment their Herefy, before the Inquifitors of heretical Pravity, and died be-
fore they have been enjoined Penance. We anfwer, That inafmuch as they did not die
Hereticks, but rather incorporated into the Unity of the Church, we do not fee that Sa-
tisfaction for a Crime extinct is to be required from them after Death, or from their
Heirs who fucceed to their Eftate. But in the Cafe where Heirs are not admitted
to inherit for the Fault of their Predeceffors, if Death fhould happen between the Sentence declared, and the Confifcation of their Effects, fuch Confifcation muft take
place after Death, notwithftanding it did not whilft the Criminals lived.

cap. 28. 2.   *Zanchinus* explains thefe Things more diftinctly and briefly. " A three-
" fold Punifhment defcends to the Children of a Perfon condemned as an He-
" retick. The firft is the Forfeiture of Effects, becaufe they are abfolutely
" deprived of paternal Succeffion. The fecond is, their Incapacity to fucceed
" any of their Relations, or other Perfons whatfoever, either by Will or
" without one. The third, their Inability to enjoy any Ecclefiaftical Bene-
" fice,

" fice, or even publick Office. As to other Punifhments inflicted on Here- Cap.28. 3.
" ticks, their Children are exempted from them. As to the Children of
" fuch who return, and are received to Mercy, though once Hereticks, and
" theirs who have been fufpected, but died with Purgation enjoined them, or
" not, thefe Punifhments are not to be inflicted on them. The third Punifh-
" ment only is to be laid on the Children of Perfons fufpected of Herefy, be-
" caufe of their favouring, defending and receiving it, if their Parents die
" fuch. But if they die after being received to Mercy, and Penance enjoin'd
" them, even this Punifhment doth not pafs to their Children, whether they
" have accomplifhed their Penance or not.

   " As to the penitential Punifhments, fome are of fuch a Nature, as that
" they may be fulfilled by others ; particularly pecuniary ones ; fuch as the
" building a Church or Hofpital, the giving Portions to poor Girls, the pay-
" ing a Fine, the returning of Ufury. If any one dies before the Accom-
" plifhment of fuch Penance, his Children and Heirs are obliged to fulfil it.
" Others are perfonal, fuch as to pray, faft, hear Divinity, to hear Mafs
" every Day, to abjure their Error, and be confeffed every Week. Thefe
" cannot pafs to the Children or Heirs, but are referved for Purgatory."

   Pegna agrees with this Account. " The Heirs of fufpected Perfons, Fa- Direct. Inq.
" vourers of Hereticks, *&c.* cannot be compelled to perform the perfonal quif. p. 3.
" Penance enjoined a fufpected Perfon, but not accomplifhed by him. But Q: 120.
com. 169.
" they may be compelled to accomplifh the Penance enjoined him when
" living out of his Effects. If therefore it was enjoined him to build a Church Cap. Accufatus §.
" or Hofpital, to return Ufury, and the like, and his Eftate was bound to fi vero. de
" accomplifh this Penance, to whatfoever Succeffor or particular Perfon fuch hæret. l. 6.
" Eftate fhall devolve after his Death, it muft come to him under fuch Obli-
" gation." The fame is provided for alfo by the Council of *Biterre.* Let the Cap. 19.
*fame take place with refpect to thofe, who die without fulfilling the Penance enjoined
them, if they have delayed it, or bound their Eftate for Performance of it.*

CHAP. VI.

Of Arch HERETICKS.

A Mongft Hereticks there are fome Arch Hereticks, fuch who have in- Direct.
vented and broached Herefies, or taught them others when invented, part. 2.
and fo become themfelves the Mafters of Error. Thefe are ufually called qu. 39,40.
Dogmatifts or Dogmatifers, and antiently perfect Hereticks. If fuch as thefe
will be converted, the Council of *Biterre* hath thus determined concerning them.
Cap. 16. *Let perfect Hereticks, or convicted ones, be fecretly examined before certain
difcreet and faithful Men, perfuading them, according to their Duty, to Converfion,
and to fuch as are willing to turn approve themfelves favourable and kind, becaufe by*
fuch

such much Light will be spread, and great Advantage will accrue ; and mitigate their Penances according to the Nature of their Conversion and Merit, or shew them Regard, as you shall think proper and convenient. Thus also the Council of *Tarracon:* But *let perfect Hereticks, and Dogmatisers, if they will be converted, after Absolution and Abjuration, be shut up in perpetual Imprisonment.* Hence in the Sentence of *Pe-*

Lib. Sent. Inquis. Tho-los. fol. 40. *ter Auterius,* a Doctor of the *Albigenses,* we read: *Saving however, and retain-ing, that if thou wilt turn from this Sect and Heresy, and be converted, and return to the Ecclesiastical Unity, thy Life shall be saved: reserving however to our selves full and free Power of enjoining thee a Punishment and wholesome Penance for the Things thou hast done in thy former Sect and Heresy.*

The Reasons they assign, why they receive to Penance penitent Arch He-reticks, or Dogmatists, are these. Because, if they are converted, and preach to those they have deceived, they may easily convert many of them. Add to this, that as they best understand the Errors and Deceits of Deceivers, which they themselves have taught, they can more easily refute them by Wri-ting or Talking. And finally, because Dogmatists, truly converted, and openly penitent, are as it were a clear Mirror of Repentance and Humility, into which Sinners may look and be converted, and be preserved in their Duty. This is especially to be observed, when an Arch Heretick is of great Authori-ty, for his Doctrine and Dignity, and who therefore, it may be hoped, will convert many by his Authority. And thus *Berengarius* was heretofore recei-ved. However, the Doctors now think, that considering the most miserable Condition of these Times, in which Hereticks dare every Thing that is im-pious, all Arch Hereticks are to be delivered over, without Mercy, to the se-

tit. 47. §. 54. §. 71. §. 63. cular Court, because, as *Simancas* says, *They deserve to die not one Death only, but many* ; and therefore he is for punishing them *not as other Hereticks, but with severer Punishments, without any Compassion.* He farther says, *That the Masters of the* Lutheran *Heresy are by no Means to be spared* ; *as being tainted with many Vices and Crimes,* viz. *Enemies to the Church, Haters of the Saints, Violators of the divine Law, sacrilegious Persons, Corrupters of good Works, and therefore of all good Manners, and Subverters of Nations. And therefore* he adds, *they must not be for-given, who commit such wicked, abominable, and heinous Crimes.* Thus also, ac-cording to *Pegna,* " No Arch Heretick, though he should give Proofs of a " real Conversion, ought to escape the Punishment of Death. But because " the Church is kind and merciful, there is no Papal Law by which 'tis pro-" vided, that Dogmatists shall, without Distinction, be delivered over to the " secular Court. Yea, the contrary may be gathered from Cap. *ad abolendum.* " de hæret. But then especially are Arch Hereticks to be received, when " they come, without any Inquisition after them, or being cited or called by " Name, but of their own Accord, to confess their Sin, and implore Mercy. " But when they are received, he will have very heavy Penances enjoined " them, which ought not to be mitigated, but after a long Season, and the ' most evident Signs of true Repentance, Conversion and Humility.

C H A P,

CHAP. VII.

Of the Believers of HERETICKS *and of* SCHISMATICKS.

FUrthermore, there are some who are Believers, others who are Receivers, *Direct.* some Defenders, and others Favourers of Hereticks. The Believers of He-*p. 2. q. 50.* reticks are, some of them, they who believe their Errors and Heresies. Such are excommunicate. Others are judged to believe the Errors of Hereticks, from their Words or Actions. By their Words, *viz.* by their own Confession, when they say they believe such an one's Errors. Or by the Evidence of the Fact, *viz.* by publickly preaching or defending their Errors. Or by legally produ-cing Witnesses, by whom they are convicted of divulging such Errors. As to Facts : In the Beginning of the delegated Inquisition, it was much doubted by what Facts any Persons could be judged to be Believers of Hereticks. But the Council of *Narbonne* hath determined it. Cap. 29. *Amongst those Faults by which they may be judged to be Believers of Hereticks, these, to prevent your farther Doubt, we firmly think to be such, viz. if they have done Reverence to Hereticks, or, as be-lieving them, have implored their Prayers, declared them to be good Men, and have thus as it were adored them. If without any Design to betray or seize them, or any other excusable and commendable Cause, they have been present at their Consolation, when they falsely and deceitfully pretend, that they save him by the Imposition of Hands, whom they comfort, though hereby they make him an Heretick. Or at their Service, when they ima-gine that their Principal, holding an open Book in his Hand, gives them Remission of their Sins, as in a general Confession. Or at the Supper of the* Valdenses, *when, on the Day of the Supper, the Table is set, and the Bread placed on it, and he believes, according to their damnable Sect, that when one of the* Valdenses *blesses it, and breaks it, and gives it to those present, he makes the Body of Christ. If they confess their Sins to the said* Valdenses, *as a Person uses, and ought to confess to his proper Priest. If they knowingly and damnably receive from Hereticks or the* Valdenses *Peace, or Bread blessed by them, sent or given them by any one whatsoever. If they have believed that they may be saved in their Sect, or that they are good and holy Men, or the Friends or Messengers of God, or of good Conversation and Life. Or that their Persecutors sin. Or if they have so far praised them, or by any other Sign or Word have pro-fessed that they give them Credit or Belief, in a Case of Law or otherwise. If they have willingly and oftentimes received them, heard them, visited them, gave them, or sent to them Provision or other Things; or have learnt Prayers, Epistles or Gospels from them. These Things and the like, although they will not prove singly, yet will be of great Service; especially as St.* John *hath said in his Epistle,* If any one comes to you, and brings not this Doctrine, receive him not into your House, nor bid him God speed; for he who bids him God speed, partakes of his evil Works. *But we would have all these Things to be so understood, as to intend that such who shall be found thus culpable, did know the Persons by whom these Things were done to be Here-ticks and* Valdenses; *and that holy Church doth declare them separated from the Unity of the Catholick Faith for their own Errors, and their damnable Sects, and doth ex-communicate, persecute, and damn them. Nor is he lightly to be believed, who says he was ignorant of it.*

Qu. 34.   By this Decree any Facts are made Signs, by which a Person may be judged to be a Believer of Hereticks. But because no Inference can be made concerning any Man's Faith with equal Certainty and Strength from every one of these Facts, the Popish Doctors make use of a Distinction. For, say they, there are some Facts in which the Error is manifestly expressed, which cannot by any Means be taken in a good Meaning ; *viz.* to do Reverence to them according to their Custom, and to receive the Communion from them after their Manner. These Things demonstrate a Person to be an Heretick, and he may be proceeded against as such. For they say the Plea can hardly be allowed, that he did these Things for the sake of some temporal Profit, and not out of any real Error of Mind. There are other Things which occasion violent Suspicions: As when any one defamed for, or suspected of Heresy, seeks Consolation from Hereticks, according to their Manner at the Time of Death. If any one doth this, the Law presumes him an Heretick, and against this Presumption no Proof can be regularly admitted. Other Things there are, in which there is no Appearance of any heretical Rite, such as to visit Hereticks, give them Food, accompany them, defend their Persons, and the like. These Things demonstrate no Man to be an Heretick, but only render him suspected of Heresy.

Amongst others Signs by which the *Valdenses* may be known, is the Refusal of an Oath, when they are compelled to it by the Inquisitors ; because they hold every Oath in every Case to be unlawful. Thus we read, *If any* Cap. Ex- *of them, thro' a damnable Obstinacy, refuse the Solemnity of an Oath, and will not* com itaq; *sware, from this alone they are to be accounted Hereticks.*

Extra de   There are other Believers of Hereticks, concerning whom 'tis not evident hæret §. that they believe their Errors, but who appear to believe the Words, Commands, *Adjicimus.* and Works of Hereticks. Such are they who commit those Facts in which there is no Appearance of any infidel Rite ; who go and come at their Command, hear, tho' seldom, their Sermons, carry their Letters here and there, wait on them, receive their Books without burning them, carry them Provision, afford them safe Conduct, visit them, and do other Things in which there is nothing of any heretical Custom.

Such are neither looked on nor treated as Hereticks, though they bring themselves under Suspicion greater or less, in Proportion, as the Appearances are greater or less. Wherefore they deal with them as with suspected Persons, of whom afterwards. 'Tis here enquired, whether a Person, who hath heard the Sermons of Hereticks, once or twice, ought to be accounted for a Believer of Hereticks. The common Opinion is, that he ought not to be accounted such for once or twice hearing the Sermons of Hereticks, unless he hath done it oftener. However, they distinguish. If any Catholick, living in the Country of Hereticks, goes once or twice to their Sermons, he is not to be judged to be a Believer of them. But if in Catholick Countries he knows.
                                                                                    that

that Hereticks hold private Conventicles, if he goes to them but once, he will incur the Suspicion of believing them, unless he discovers it to the Bishop or Inquisitor. Because in this latter Case he is judged to approve what he might have prevented, if he had made a Discovery to the Ecclesiastical Judges, as he ought to have done.

Schismaticks have a very near Agreement with Hereticks, and they are thus distinguished by *Simancas.*

" Schismaticks are either consummate Hereticks, or near akin to Here-*tit.* 58. " ticks, *viz.* who only depart from the Unity of the Church, and the Obe-§ 4, 5. " dience of the chief Pontiff. These differ but little from Hereticks. For " they believe that there may be Salvation and true Sacraments without the " true Church, and many other schismatical Things. These are to be pu- " nished with almost the same Punishments as Hereticks themselves.

" Others are without Blame, and have a just Excuse ; *viz.* they who, thro'§. 9. " probable or insuperable Ignorance, believe a Person to be Pope who is not " rightly elected ; which sometimes happens upon a doubtful Election, when " two or more contend for the Pontificate. One of these may, with a good " Faith, be owned for true Pope, though not justly elected." After *Siman- cas* hath thus explained the Matter, he pronounces a cruel Sentence against the modern Hereticks, *i. e.* against all in this Age, who live without the Com- munion of the Church of *Rome,* in *Germany, France,* the *Netherlands,* and some other Northern Countries.

" The modern Hereticks are not united. There are many Schisms amongst§. 12. " them, so that in one House you may find several Beliefs, the Husband, " Wife, Children, and Family, all believing differently.

" Against these impious Fanaticks, who endeavour to defile all divine " Things, the Laws rise up with revenging Fire. These pestiferous Here-§. 14. " ticks are driven out of *Spain,* who rejecting all that antient Discipline, " which the holy Spirit taught, which so many Ages, the Consent of so ma- " ny Nations, so many great Men, famous for their Piety and Learning, have " delivered down to us, instead of retaining the true Method of governing " the Christian Commonwealth, throw all Things into Disorder, and more " than *Babylonish* Confusion."

The Punishments of Schismaticks are Privation of Ecclesiastical Power, Carena; Excommunication, Incapacity for all Offices for the future, and finally Death,*P.* 2. *t.* 3. And the Doctors observe, that when Schismaticks are impenitent, the secular§. 12. Judges may in such Case punish them, if Clergymen, without degrading them. They add, that all Lords and Magistrates, as well Ecclesiastical as Secular,*n.* 49. who fall into or raise Schism, ought to be punished likewise with Death ; ac- cording to the Bull of *Paul* IV. beginning, *Cum ex Apostolatus officio,* in which the Pope commands that all such Schismaticks shall be punished, even for the first Offence, as the very Relapsed themselves. But if they repent, the In-§. 13. quisitors, after a formal Abjuration of their Schism, and their Suspicion of Heresy, according to the Degrees of it, usually punish them with other Pu-

nishments

nifhments at Pleafure; either by Fines, Banifhment, Imprifonment, Confinement, Gallies, and Death, according to the Nature and Aggravation of their Fault.

CHAP. VIII.

Of the Receivers and Defenders of HERETICKS.

Direct.
part. 2.
qu. 51.

THE Council of *Tarracon* hath determined thofe to be Receivers of Hereticks, who have twice, or more, knowingly received Hereticks in their Houfe, or any other Place. A Receptacle is an Houfe or Lodging, where Hereticks have met together twice or more to preach or read, or where they have frequently lodged. But fuch offend more grievoufly who know their Errors, and that the Church doth perfecute them, and neverthelefs receive and conceal them from the Hands of the Church, even though they have done this but once; and by this Reception they render themfelves fufpect of Herefy, more or lefs, according to the Difference of Circumftances. And therefore, as fufpected Perfons, they are obliged to abjure. Their Punifhment is Excommunication, and if after this they perfift in their Crime, they are put under the Bann, banifhed for ever, and fuffer Confifcation of all their Goods. But if any one receives an heretical Relation, his Crime is lefs, and he is more gently punifhed. And in this they confider the Degrees of Kindred, that fuch who are neareft akin to the received Heretick, may be more gently dealt with than thofe who are farther off.

Qu. 52.

The Defenders of Hereticks, according to the Definition of the Council of *Tarracon*, are fuch who knowingly defend Hereticks by Word or Deed, or any Method in their own Lands, or any where elfe, whereby the Church is prevented from executing its Office in the Extirpation of heretical Pravity. Now there are different Ways of defending. An Heretick may be defended with Arms, or without them, or by giving him Notice for his Efcape. He may alfo be defended, when under Trial, or when he is not. They may alfo be faid to be Defenders of Hereticks by Confequence, who hinder in any Manner the Office of the Inquifition. Befides this, there is another Cafe by which a Man may be faid to be a Defender of Hereticks, when he puts another Perfon or himfelf in the Room of the Heretick to be apprehended. Concerning which, *Innocent* IV. fent this Refcript. Ad extirpanda. *If at any Time, any Men or Women not Hereticks, fhall, with their Confent, be taken and put in the Place of Hereticks, or themfelves perfonate Hereticks, let them fuffer perpetual Imprifonment, and at the fame time let the Hereticks themfelves be compelled to return and deliver up themfelves. And as for thofe who contrived the Deceit, let them, according to the aforefaid Law, fuffer Confifcation of their Goods, and perpetual Banifhment.* In the fame Bull there are other Sorts of Punifhments appointed

pointed againſt the Defenders of Hereticks. *Whoſoever ſhall dare to reſcue an heretical Man or Woman, when taken, from him or thoſe who have apprehended them, or to prevent their being taken, or to hinder any one's Entrance into any Houſe or Tower, in order to ſeize or ſearch for them, let ſuch an one, according to the Padua Law of* Frederick *the Emperor, ſuffer Confiſcation of Goods, and perpetual Baniſhment, and let the Houſe from which they were excluded be raſed to the Ground, and never rebuilt* ; *and let the Effects found there be his who can ſeize them, as if Hereticks had been actually found there.* Moreover, he makes their Sons infamous, and excludes them from all Honours, unleſs they diſcover Hereticks. But if they diſcover them, they are delivered from theſe Penalties. *Pius* V. alſo by a certain Reſcript, beginning, *Si de protegendis*, ordained the moſt ſevere Puniſhments againſt the Defenders of Hereticks, which they incur in many Caſes therein mentioned.

C H A P. IX.

Of the Favourers of HERETICKS.

THE Favourers of Hereticks, as the Name ſhews, are thoſe who ſhew2. 53. Favour to Hereticks, and are in all Things equal to the Defenders of them. They are either Magiſtrates or private Perſons, and they may all favour Hereticks by Omiſſion or Negligence, by Deed or Aſſiſtance, and finally by Counſel or Words. The Magiſtrates Office is to extirpate Hereticks, and expel them from his Kingdoms and Dominions, and to give all Counſel and Favour to the Inquiſitors of heretical Pravity, for the puniſhing and reſtraining of Hereticks, and the Suppreſſion of all riſing Hereſies, becauſe the Inquiſitors without the Magiſtrates Help are weak, and cannot drive away Hereticks ; and therefore they muſt bend all their Endeavours to this, that the Wickedneſs of Hereticks may not encreaſe under their Government, and the Security and Religion of the Catholicks be not diminiſhed or diſturbed. The Favourers therefore of Hereticks are ſuch : Firſt, who omit to do thoſe Things concerning Hereticks, or Perſons ſuſpected and defamed for Hereſy, or thoſe who believe, receive, defend, and favour them, which they are obliged to do by Office, when required to do it by the Inquiſitors or Biſhops, or one of them, *viz.* if they do not take them up, keep them in ſafe Cuſtody, ſend them to the appointed Place, or if they don't readily puniſh them, when condemned and delivered over to them. For they are obliged to all theſe Things. Cap. *Ut Inquiſitionis*, de hæret. lib. 6. and eſpecially by a Reſcript of *Inno-*Souza, *cent* IV. and *Clement.* IV. beginning, *Ad extirpanda.* In like Manner the Pre-lib. 1. lates or Inquiſitors, who neglect to make ſafe Priſons, to ſet over them faith-c. 25. §. 4. ful Keepers, to apprehend, torture, or puniſh Hereticks, or to keep them in ſafe Cuſtody, in order to favour Hereticks, are judged to be themſelves Favourers

vourers of them ; but not if thefe Omiffions proceed from Negligence; or any other Caufe. Secondly, the Magiftrate is a Favourer of Hereticks by Commiffion. If, when taken, he delivers them from Jayl without the Leave or Command of the Bifhop and Inquifitor, or one of them ; or if he doth directly or indirectly hinder their Procefs, Judgment, or Sentence, or do other Things like them. As appears from the Chapter before mentioned, *Ut Inquifitionis.* §. *prohibemus.* All thefe are *ipfo jure,* excommunicated, as Favourers of Hereticks ; and if they obftinately remain under this Excommunication for the Space of a Year, are to be punifhed as Hereticks. The Council of *Tholoufe* hath appointed other Punifhments for them. Chap. 3, 4. *We likewife ordain, that whofoever fhall knowingly permit any Heretick to dwell in his Jurifdiction, either for Money, or any other Caufe whatfoever, and fhall confefs, or be convicted of this, he fhall lofe his Eftate for ever, and his Body fhall be in the Power of his Lord, to do with it as he ought to do. And if he be not convicted of having done this knowingly, and his Negligence be not proved to be fcandalous, and yet Hereticks are frequently found in his Country ; or if he be defamed upon this Account, let him fuffer the legal Punifhments.* See alfo the Bull of *Paul* IV. beginning, *Cum ex Apoftolatus officio. Bzovius* alfo relates, in his Account of the Year 1215. §. 10. that by the Command of the Apoftolical Legate the Walls of *Narbonne* were thrown down ; and alfo of *Tholoufe,* the greateft Part of them, becaufe they had been the Receptacles of Hereticks. The fame Council of *Tholoufe* determines what fhall be the Punifhment of inferior Magiftrates, in their feveral Diftricts, if they are found negligent in apprehending Hereticks. Cap. 6. *As to the Ballive of any Place as to which there is any Prefumption, who is always Refident, unlefs he be found very diligent and careful againft Hereticks, let him forfeit all his Effects, and never more be fuffered to be a Ballive there, or any where elfe.*

Private Perfons are faid to be Favourers of Hereticks, when out of their own Rafhnefs they free from Prifon Hereticks, or Perfons apprehended for Herefy, or give any Affiftance, Council or Favour towards their Deliverance, or fo accompany them, when freed, as not to feize them ; or refift thofe who would apprehend them, or prefume directly or indirectly to hinder Procefs, Judgment, or Sentence, in a Caufe of Faith, or give Council, Affiftance or Favour to fuch Hindrance. Private Perfons indeed are not faid to be Favourers of Hereticks by mere Omiffion, *viz.* for not apprehending or not taking them into Cuftody, as not being obliged to it. Neverthelefs they will be Favourers, if they fhall omit to difcover and apprehend them, when obliged to it by Office : Such, for Inftance, are the Crofs-bearers, who in *Spain* are called *Familiars* ; or if when called on by the Magiftrate, to affift in apprehending Hereticks, they refufe to do it without Reafon, and when they have nothing to prevent them.

Laftly, both Magiftrates and private Perfons may be faid to be Favourers of Hereticks, by omitting to difcover them, becaufe all Perfons are obliged under Pain of Excommunication, to difcover all Hereticks, even concealed ones, to the Bifhops and Inquifitors, and, if it be neceffary, to accufe them.

So

So *Gregory* IX. ordained in one of his Extravagants againſt the *Patarenes*, beginning, *Excommunicamus*, inſerted amongſt the Apoſtolical Letters for the
Office of the Inquiſition. *Likewiſe if any Perſon knows any Hereticks, or ſuch
who hold private Conventicles, or who differ in their Life and Manners from the Converſation of the Faithful, let him endeavour to diſcover them to his Confeſſor, or ſome
one elſe, who he believes may give Notice to the Prelate, otherwiſe let him be excommunicated.* And this Obligation of informing againſt Hereticks is ſo ſtrict,
that it takes place notwithſtanding any Oath, Covenant, or Promiſe to the
contrary. But if the Wife only ſhould happen to know that her Husband eats
Fleſh on forbidden Days, and knows him to be ſo furious, as that probably he
would murther or abuſe her, if ſhe informed againſt him, ſome think her
Fear may excuſe her from the Suſpicion of Hereſy. But we ſhall ſpeak more
fully of the Obligation to inform in the following Book.

The Council of *Narbonne* hath determined the ſeveral Ways, by which any
one may be ſaid to be a Favourer of Hereticks. Cap. 14, 15, 16. *We account
thoſe equally Favourers of Hereticks, who obſtruct the Extirpation or Correction of
Hereticks or their Believers, and thoſe who don't give that Aſſiſtance to it, which
they can't omit without a manifeſt Fault. But ſuch Perſons may be more or leſs guilty
in theſe Matters, from a careful Conſideration of Circumſtances. He, for Inſtance,
greatly favours Hereticks or their Believers who conceals them, when he may, and
ought to diſcover them. He favours them more, who by concealing them, or otherwiſe maliciouſly endeavours to prevent their Examination or Impriſonment, or Puniſhment. He moſt of all, who releaſes thoſe who are apprehended or impriſoned, without the Churches Leave ; or if ſuch Things are done by his Counſel, Help, Command or Care. But he is above all others to be accounted guilty of this Crime, who
having temporal Juriſdiction, defers to perſecute theſe aforeſaid peſtiferous Hereticks,
or Perſons declared to be Rebels againſt the Church, or to extirminate them out of his
Country or Province, or to animadvert againſt them without Delay. Such a one is
juſtly to be ſuſpected of being joined in wicked Society with them, who neglects to put a
Stop to ſo great a Wickedneſs, after having received the proper Information by the
Church or otherwiſe ; ſince he both may do it, and is bound to it ; eſpecially if he is
under the Obligation of an Oath to do it. But neither are they free from this Crime,
who, when they have the Opportunity of Time and Place, and Leave to apprehend
Hereticks, or the aforeſaid Rebels, and to aſſiſt thoſe who are to take them up, wicked-
ly neglect it ; eſpecially if required by thoſe who apprehend them, or are willing to do it.
And ſince there are many, and almoſt unſearchable Methods of doing Harm, by which
Hereticks, their Believers and Favourers endeavour to deſtroy the Vineyard of the
Lord of Sabaoth, which ought to be prudently and vigorouſly oppoſed, let your Piety
take Care, according to the Grace given you of the Lord, to find out theſe Evils, and
apply the wholeſome Remedy ; and let your Prudence make up what can't ſo eaſily be
committed to Writing.*

Laſtly, Friar *Ivonetus* deſcribes the Marks and Signs, by which Perſons
may be known to be Favourers of Hereticks. There is extant a Volume of his,
the Fragment of which is in a Parchment Book of the *Vatican* Library, inti-
tled, *How the Favourers of Hereticks may be diſcovered.* And he there reckons up
five

five Signs in thefe Words. *The Favourers of Hereticks may eafily be known by thefe five very probable Marks. Firft, Whoever privately vifit them, whilft in Cuftody, and whifper with them, and gives them Victuals, are fufpected of being their Difciples and Favourers. Secondly, Whoever greatly lament their Apprehenfion or Death, feem to have been their fpiritual Friends whilft they lived ; for 'tis fcarce credible that any Perfon can be a long while intimate with an Heretick, and not know his Secrets. Thirdly, Such who complain that they are unjuftly condemned, after they have been openly convicted, or have confeffed their Herefy, it appears that they approve their Sect, and think the Church hath erred in condemning them. Fourthly, Such who look with a bitter Countenance upon thofe who perfecute Hereticks, or preach vigoroufly againft Herefy ; for he who diligently obferves, may fee by their Eyes and Nofe, and Afpect, that they do not look with a favourable Countenance, and are therefore greatly to be fufpected, that they hate thofe againft whom their Heart appears to be fo bitter, as their Countenance betrays, and love thofe for whofe Deftruction they fo much grieve. Fifthly, If any are found to have by Stealth gathered together in the Night the Bones of Hereticks burnt, as Reliques, 'tis not to be doubted but that they reverence them as Saints, whofe Bones they lay up as a kind of Sanctuary, and are therefore equally Hereticks with them. Becaufe no one accounts an Heretick for a Saint, but he who believes his Sect to be holy, and is equally an Heretick with him. Thefe Things give great Prefumption of Herefy againft him, altho' it be not fufficient Proof to condemn him, unlefs there concur other Arguments, by which it manifeftly appears they did the aforefaid Things in Favour of Herefy.*

C. Excom-
munica-
mus.
§. Creden-
tes.
Ibid. de
haret.

The Favourers of Herefy are *ipfo jure,* excommunicated. If they are mere Favourers, but not publickly excommunicated, they don't incur any other Penalties. But if they are publickly declared excommunicate, and don't give Satisfaction within a Year, they fuffer other Penalties, which are largely defcribed.

CHAP. X.

Of the Hinderers of the Office of the INQUISITION.

THE Hinderers of the Office of the Inquifition come neareft to the Favourers of Hereticks, and are ufually reckoned amongft them.

That this Office may be vigoroufly exercifed, and that no Hereticks may efcape the Rigour of it, all are ftrictly commanded, of whatfoever Dignity or Condition, efpecially Arch Bifhops, Bifhops, and other Prelates, to favour the Bufinefs of the Inquifition, and yield all Countenance and Help to the Inquifitors. Thus *Alexander* IV. in his Bull, beginning, *Orthodoxæ fidei Chriftianæ,* commands all Arch Bifhops, Bifhops, and other Prelates. *Since therefore there are certain Predicant Friars appointed by the Apoftolick See, Inquifitors againft Hereticks in the aforefaid Provinces, that they may carry on the Bufinefs of the*

f. 410.
Tr. tr.

Faith

Faith, with a fervent Mind, and conſtant Heart, through many Tribulations and Perſecutions, we admoniſh and exhort all of you in our Lord Jeſus Chriſt, ſtrictly commanding you by theſe Apoſtolical Writings, in Virtue of your Obedience, and enjoining you, that you favourably aſſiſt theſe Inquiſitors in carrying on the ſaid Affair ; and that laying aſide the Fear of Man, you effectually give them your Counſel and Help : Knowing, that thoſe who hitherto have done, and ſhall do theſe Things, ſhall always obtain the ſpecial Favour of the Apoſtolick See, and find us favourable and kind in all their Occaſions. But as for thoſe whom we ſhall know to be Contemners, beſides the divine Judgment that hangs over them, they ſhall not eſcape the Eccleſiaſtical Vengeance.

The ſame Pope, in the Bull beginning, *Ne commiſſum vobis,* ſays, That if the Clergy and Religious ſhall not aſſiſt the Inquiſitors, according to their Duty and Ability, they ſhall be proceeded againſt according to the Canonical Sanctions, notwithſtanding any Privileges. And in the *Decretals* V. in the Chapter *Excommunicamus,* at the End, the Biſhops are commanded, under the Penalty of Depoſition, to perform all theſe Things.

But *Innocent* IV. in his Bull to the Provincial of *Lombardy,* beginning, *Tunc potiſſime,* hath threatned with all imaginable Curſes, and the moſt terrible Deſtruction, Magiſtrates, unleſs they promote the Affair of the Inquiſition, and much more if they preſume by any Means to hinder it. *Inaſmuch* Bzovius, *as we deſire above all Things to promote this wholeſome Affair, we intend, with the* a. 1252. *Help of God, wholly to remove all manner of Obſtructions from it. And therefore* ſ. 4. *if it ſhould ſo happen, which however we do not believe, that any City or Community, any Princes or Nobles, or others in Power, ſhall preſume to oppoſe this Buſineſs, or by any Means to obſtruct it, ſo that thoſe who are deputed by us for this Affair cannot freely proceed therein ; yea, unleſs they cheriſh it, and ſtudiouſly aſſiſt it, we ſhall ſeverely reach forth againſt them the Sword of the Eccleſiaſtical Power, to ſuppreſs ſo audacious and pernicious Inſolence, and wholly to confound it ; and we will call in againſt them the Kings and Princes, and other Faithful of Chriſt, who have taken on them the Sign of the Croſs, whether for the Succour of the holy Land, or otherwiſe for Chriſt's Service, as alſo the reſt of the Catholicks, that Heaven and Earth may be moved up together againſt this deteſtable Raſhneſs ; ſince 'tis no leſs expedient, but rather more ſo to defend the Faith in Places near us, than in thoſe which are farther diſtant.* The ſame Things are almoſt to a Word extant in the Bull of *Urban* IV. beginning, *Licet ex omnibus mundi partibus.* Publiſhed *An.* 1262. *April* 19th.

Perſons are ſaid to hinder the Office of the Inquiſition, either directly or Direct. indirectly. Directly, ſuch who deliver from Priſon by their own Raſhneſs Inq. p. 2. Perſons taken up for the Crime of Hereſy, or who deſtroy the Proceſſes of the qu. 54. Inquiſition, or who wound the Witneſſes in a Cauſe of Faith for their Teſtimony. Or if a temporal Lord ordains, that no one ought to take Cognizance of the Crime of Hereſy but himſelf, and that no one ſhall be accuſed, or give Teſtimony but before himſelf. As alſo all ſuch, who uſe only Threatnings Carena, and terrifying Words ; and who directly hinder Proceſs, Judgment, and Sen- p 2. t. 4. tence in a Cauſe of Faith, or give Counſel, Help and Favour in doing thus. n. 23.

They are said indirectly to obstruct, who use any Insinuation or other Means, from whence consequentially any Impediment may arise to the Office of the Inquisition. Such for Example, who order that no one shall bear Arms, unless of the Houshold of the temporal Lord, and that no one shall apprehend, or cause to be apprehended any Person, but the temporal Lord. For from thence it follows, that those who belong to the Inquisitors can't wear Arms, nor take up any Person. These are less criminal than the former ; but are all excommunicated ; and if they lie under that Excommunication for a whole Year, they must, in order to their Reconciliation, abjure such Impediment and Favouring, otherwise they are delivered over as impenitent Hereticks to the secular Arm.

The Power of proceeding against such Persons, was given to the Inquisitors by *Urban* IV. and other Popes, in a Rescript to the Inquisitors of heretical Pravity, beginning, *Præ cunctis,* where, amongst other Things, there are these. *But if, what we do not believe, there should happen to be any, of what Condition soever, who shall oppose this Affair committed to you, or shall presume in any wise to obstruct it, so that you cannot freely proceed in it ; yea, unless, when required, they shall support it, and, according to their Office and Ability, give it their Assistance ; proceed without Fear, in Dependance upon the said Authority, according to the Canonical Sanctions, against such Persons as against Favourers and Defenders of Hereticks.* See also Chapter *Ut Inquisitionis.* §. *Prohibemus.* lib. 6.

Nor are there wanting Examples of an Inquisition actually made, not only against private Persons, but also against Magistrates, yea, whole Cities and Communities, on the Account of their hindring the Inquisition. *Bzovius* relates a memorable Instance, which happened in the Territory of *Parma,* about the Year 1285. from a Letter of *Honorius* IV. brought to the Bishop of *Parma,* in which there are these Things. " Friar *Florius* a Predicant, Inquisitor of heretical Pravity in the Parts of *Lombardy,* deputed
" by the Apostolick See, condemned a certain Woman, relapsed into Here-
" sy, after Abjuration, who being delivered to the secular Court, was burnt.
" But some Persons, who were met together in the Place where the said
" Woman was burnt, and a great Number of others, who flocked from the
" different Parts of the City, ran in a violent Manner to the Place of the
" Friars of the said Order, and forcibly enter'd the said Place, and broke
" open the Church Doors, destroyed the Houses with Stones, and presumed
" to enter by Violence the little Chapels of the said Place, and unjustly plun-
" dered the said Friars of their Books, Garments and Effects, and beat and
" wounded several of them, one of whom, after a few Days, died of the
" Wounds he had received ; so that the Friars were forced to leave the Place.

" And because the Governor and Magistrate neglected to proceed to the
" Punishment of that Crime, according to their Office, they were cited by
" the Bishop of *Ostia* personally to appear before him at a certain Place and
" Time. They appeared ; but because there was no proper Syndick for
" the aforesaid Community, who appeared before him, according to the
" Form

" Form of the faid Citation, he publifhed the Sentence of Excommunica-
" tion againft them, and put the City under an Interdict. After this the Go-
" vernor and Magiftrate defired that the Sentence of Excommunication and
" Interdict fhould be taken off, and promifed that they would obey the Plea-
" fure of the Church ; and that they would give fufficient Security upon
" Oath, and Sureties, to ftand to the Law for all the aforefaid Enormities,
" Offences and Injuries. This Security was accepted, and upon the Ap-
" pearance of the proper Sureties for the aforefaid Community, each Perfon
" being bound in a thoufand Marks of Silver, that they fhould obey the
" Commands of the Church, the Sentence was remitted, and they themfelves
" fummoned to appear within the Space of one Month before Pope *Martin* IV.
" by themfelves, or their Syndicks, or their Procurators, fufficiently inftructed
" for this Purpofe, in order to obey the Pope's Command for thefe Exceffes,
" and to receive what in Juftice was to be exacted of them. They appeared
" within the faid Term before the Pope, but there was no farther Procefs
" made upon the faid Affair. So that *Honorius* IV. commanded the Bifhop
" of *Parma* to cite them again before him, to obey his Orders, and to re-
" ceive what in Reafon fhould be appointed them. What was the Event of
" this Procefs, and what was the Punifhment inflicted upon the Magiftrate,
" *Bzovius* doth not relate."

We have another Inftance in the Book of the Sentences of the *Tholoufe* In- *Fol.* 138.
quifition. Certain Perfons were thrown into the Prifon of the Inquifition at
Cordes, in the Territories of *Tholoufe*. The Magiftrate and People rofe up
againft the Bifhop of *Viviers*, and the Inquifitors, and by feveral Methods obftructed the Office of the Inquifition. The Sentence of Excommunication
was pronounced againft them. At length the Magiftrates and principal Perfons threw themfelves in a very humble Manner before the Inquifitors at a general Sermon of the Faith, fubmiffively confeffing their Fault, and begging
Pardon for their Offence. They fubmitted themfelves purely and entirely to
the Will and Order of the Inquifitors, declaring that they were ready to make
Satisfaction, and to receive and do Penance, fuch as they fhould think fit to
enjoin them. They pray to be abfolved from the Sentences of Excommunication, and promife that they would be devoted, and perfevere in their Devotion and Reverence and Obedience to the Inquifitors, their Succeffors, and the
Office of the Inquifition all the Days of their Life. This fo humble a Supplication, moved the Minds of the Inquifitors to Mercy, fo that tho' the Magiftrates and People had grievoufly offended againft the Bifhop of *Viviers*, the
Inquifitors and their Office, and were therefore worthy of the fevereft Punifhments, yet in Confideration of their Humiliation and Supplication, they abfolve them from the Sentences of Excommunication ; but under this Penance,
that they fhall build a Chapel in their City, with Ornaments, and all other
Requifites, to perform divine Service, and fhould farther erect three Images
over the Door of the Chapel, one of the Bifhop of *Viviers*, and the other two
of two Inquifitors. And finally, they referve to themfelves the Difpofal of
certain particular Perfons of the faid Community, to the Number of fix or

eight,

eight, whom they would call by Name that Day or the following, whom, as the principal Offenders, they would enjoin wholesome Penance; and they oblige the whole University, and every Person thereof, that they and every one of them shall satisfy the Bishop and Church of *Viviers*, as also the Office of the Inquisition and the Inquisitors, and all Persons belonging to them, and pay the Expences they have been at upon account of the said Affair.

In the same Book of Sentences there are two other Instances of Inquisition made against private Persons for hindring the Office of the Inquisition.

The first is that of Friar *Bernard Deliciosi*, who was accused, that, as the principal Director, he had prosecuted the Complaints of the Cities of *Carcasson*, *Viviers*, and *Cordes*, having procured for this Purpose a large Sum of Money from the said Places, and by the Sale of his Books, and by Borrowing; that he had spoken very freely of the Processes and Sentences of the Inquisitors published against certain Persons for Heresy, in the most publick Conversations and elsewhere, even in the secular Courts; that he had justified Persons apprehended and condemned for Heresy, and said, That *though they were true Catholicks, they were forced by the Violence of their Tortures to confess themselves and others guilty of Heresy, and that they were unjustly condemned*; and hereby excited the Magistrates and People to oppose the Bishop and Inquisitors: That he also publickly asserted at *Tholouse, That St.* Peter *and St.* Paul *could not defend themselves from Heresy if they were alive, and had Inquisition made against them in the Manner practised by the Inquisitors*, and that he thus informed the King of *France* against the said Inquisitors: That he falsely ascribed to the Inquisitors an Instrument drawn up against the City of *Carcassone* upon the Affair of Heresy, and made this an Argument of exciting the People, that they might see what these Predicants would be able to do against particular Persons, who could make so false and pernicious an Instrument against a whole Community: That by this Means he hindred the Office of the Inquisition, raised a Sedition and Rebellion, and did many other Things, by which the Exercise of the Office of the Inquisition was obstructed: That moreover, after having taken the Advice of many Persons, at several Times, and in different Places, he had been deputed by the Magistrates of *Carcassone*, to the Lord *Ferrand de Majoricis*, and had offered to him the Borough of *Carcassone* in these Words. "My Lord, you may know that the Magistrates of *Carcassone*, upon " account of the Disturbances raised by the Inquisitors, and because the King " of *France* will not take Care to protect them from the Actions of the Inqui- " sitors according to their Desire, are willing to receive you for their Lord " and Defender, and will receive you, if, and whensoever you will please to " come, and deliver up to you the Borough of *Carcassone*, &c." And that the Lord *Ferrand* answered, that he would willingly accept what they offered him by the said Friar. And finally, he was accused of Magick, and that he had by him, and read a certain conjuring Book: That hereby he incurred the Sentence of Excommunication, and with an obstinate Mind continued under it for fifteen Years, and at the same time celebrated divine Services: That at length, after daily Contumacy, and long Processes form'd against him, he

had.

had fully confeſſed all, and humbly deſired to be abſolved from his Sentences of Excommunication.　Upon this he was abſolved from the ſaid Sentence,
but immediately pronounced, degraded, condemned to perpetual Impriſonment, and to do perpetual Penance in Irons, and with the Bread of Sorrow,
and Water of Affliction.　Moreover, the Inquiſitors reſerve to themſelves
the Mitigation of the aforeſaid Penance, according as they ſhould think expedient, and he himſelf ſhould deſerve it by Patience and Humility, and the
Sacrifice of a contrite Heart.　But Pope *John* XXII. revoked this Reſerva-*fol.* 135.
tion of mitigating the Puniſhment, and commanded that the whole Sentence
and Penance pronounced againſt him, ſhould be rigorouſly and entirely executed.

　The ſecond Inſtance is that of *William Garrici*, who, beſides his being preſent at the Heretication of a certain Perſon, and adoring Hereticks after an
heretical Manner, is ſaid to have conſented, with others, in the Advice and
Endeavour, privately by the Aſſiſtance of one of the Servants of the ſaid
Inquiſition, to ſteal away and burn the Books of the Inquiſition at *Carcaſſone*,
in which were written the Confeſſions and Depoſitions in the Fact of Hereſy,
and to have hindred by ſeveral other Methods the Office of the Inquiſition.
For this Reaſon he was excommunicated, and continued under it ſeveral
Years, and was condemned to be impriſoned.　But at length, after many E-
vaſions, he acknowledged his Fault, and ſubmitted himſelf to the Pleaſure
of the Inquiſitors, humbly deſiring Favour and Mercy from them.　After he
had ſolemnly abjured, not only Hereſy, but alſo the favouring, receiving,
defending, and partaking with Hereticks, he was abſolved from his Excommunication, and had this Penance enjoined him ; That in the firſt general
Paſſage he ſhould perſonally tranſport himſelf, where he ſhould tarry during
the Pleaſure or Command of the Inquiſitors, or their Succeſſors.　Or if he
ſhould be legally prevented, that then he ſhould be obliged to ſend in his
Room, at his own Coſt and Expence, a ſufficient and proper Soldier for the
Defence of the holy Land.　That within the Space of thirty Days he ſhould
depart the Kingdom of *France*, to ſuch Place as the Inquiſitors ſhould appoint,
there to abide till the Time of his tranſporting himſelf, or after that Time,
if he ſends a Soldier in his Room.　After this Sentence was pronounced, read
and publiſhed by the Inquiſitors, Maſter *William Garrici*, upon his bent Knees,
and with his Hands held up together, in Token of great Humility, ſaid,
That he accepted the aforeſaid, giving and returning Thanks, firſt to the
Lord Jeſus Chriſt, and then to the Inquiſitors, for theſe Favours beſtowed
upon him.

　Other Magiſtrates are puniſhed with Sentences of Excommunication, their
Countries are put under Interdict, and given to the firſt Conqueror of them,
many Inſtances of which we have ſeen in the firſt Book of this Hiſtory.　And
becauſe this Office, in it ſelf hateful, is rendered much more ſo by the exceſſive Cruelty of the Inquiſitors, who have hereby raiſed the Anger and Indignation of all Mankind againſt them ; therefore Pope *Pius* V. to prevent
the leaſt Hurt or Injury from being offered them, and every Hindrance
　　　　　　　　　　　　　　　　　　　　　　　　　　　　　　　　that

that may be made to this Office, did, in the Year of our Lord 1569. publish a most severe Bull against all who should hurt the State, Effects and Persons of the sacred Office of the Inquisition of heretical Pravity, which it is well worth while to give here entire.

PIUS, *Bishop, Servant of the Servants of God, for the perpetual Remembrance of the Thing.*

IF we are possessed with a daily Care of protecting all other Ministers of the Church, which we have received into our Care and Patronage from the Lord; how much more necessary is it that we should be careful, that they who are employed in the sacred Office of the Inquisition of heretical Pravity, may remain free from all Dangers, under the Protection of the inviolable Authority of this See, and that all Offices for the Exaltation of the Catholick Faith may be discharged? Since therefore the Violence of such ungodly Persons grows every Day stronger, who by all evil Arts endeavour to subvert the aforesaid Office, and to disturb the Ministers of it in the Discharge of their Duty, we are driven by Necessity more severely to curb this their wicked and ungodly Insolence. We therefore ordain by this general Constitution, with the Advice of our Brethren, that whosoever, whether a private Person, or whole City, or People, or Lord, Earl, Marquis, Duke, or any other more illustrious Person, shall kill, wound, drive away, or terrify any one of the Inquisitors, Advocates, Procurators, Notaries, or other Ministers of the aforesaid Office, or of the Bishops who execute this Office in their Diocese or Province, or the Accuser, Denouncer, or Witness, at any time produced, or called out in a Cause of the Faith; and whosoever shall assault, invade, burn, or plunder the Churches, Houses, or other Things, whether publick or private, of the Office or its Ministers; or whosoever shall burn, take away, or destroy the Books, Letters, Authorities, Copies, Registers, Protocols, Draughts, Writings, or other Instruments, whether publick or private, wheresoever they are placed; or whosoever shall carry them away from the Fire, or plunder, or by any other Method; or who shall be present, though unarmed, at such Fire, Assault, or Plunder, with a Design to seize, burn, or conceal them; or who shall prohibit such Effects and Persons to be preserved and defended; or whosoever shall break open any Jayl, or other Place of Custody, whether publick or private, ; or shall take out and cause to escape any Prisoner; or shall forbid any one to be apprehended, or if apprehended, shall rescue, receive, or conceal him, or shall furnish him with an Opportunity of escaping, or shall command it, or who shall make any Assembly or Concourse, or for these Ends shall give any Persons his Assistance, or shall knowingly otherwise grant them Help, Counsel or Favour, publickly or privately in any of the aforesaid, even though no Person should be killed, no one wounded, no one delivered, escape, or rescued, nothing forced, nothing broken open, burnt or plundered, altho' no Damage should actually follow; he shall nevertheless by Authority of this present Canon be put under Anathema, become guilty of High Treason, and be deprived of Dominion, Dignity, Honour, Fee, and every other temporal and perpetual Benefice whatsoever, and left to the Pleasure of the secular Judge, who shall inflict on him the self same Punishments, which are by the
lawful

lawful Conftitutions ordained againft condemned Perfons, and fhall have all his Goods and Effects confifcated, as the Canonical Sanctions have ordered againft condemned Hereticks ; his Children fhall be liable to their Fathers Infamy, and incapable of all Inheritance, Succeffion, Gift, Legacy whatfoever, whether from Relations or Strangers, nor ever be advanced to any Honours whatfoever. Nor fhall any Perfon be able to purge himfelf, or to propofe or carry any Caufe, who fhall have committed fo heinous a Crime out of Contempt or Hatred of this Office, unlefs he can make the contrary to appear by very evident Proofs. The fame alfo that we have ordained of the aforefaid, and their Children, we declare fhall alfo take place with refpect to all the Clergy, and Presbyters, Seculars and Regulars of all Orders, even tho' exempt ; to all who have the Epifcopal, or any higher Dignity, or whatfoever Privileges they may enjoy ; fo that they, by Authority of thefe Prefents, fhall be deprived of all their Ecclefiaftical Benefices and Offices, degraded after the Manner of Hereticks, by the Ecclefiaftical Judge delivered over to the fecular Power, and fubjected, as though they were lay Perfons, to the aforefaid Punifhments. However, we referve to our felves and our Succeffors, the Caufes belonging to the Popes, that when the Matter is enquired into, and related to them, we may proceed againft them to Depofition and other the beforenamed Penalties, as the Heinoufnefs of the Crime fhall require. And whofoever fhall attempt to ask Pardon, or otherwife to intercede for fuch Perfons, let them know they fhall actually incur the fame Penalties, which by the facred Conftitutions are denounced againft the Favourers of Hereticks. But if any one who is confcious or acceffary to fuch Crimes, fhall, through a Regard to Religion, or moved with Repentance, difcover the Matter, before it is otherwife known, he fhall be freed from Punifhment. But 'tis our Defire, that this Method of granting all Abfolutions whatfoever from the aforefaid Crimes, as alfo of Reftorations and Reftitutions to Reputation and Honour, fhall be henceforth obferved, viz. that our Succeffors fhall grant none of them till fix Months at leaft after their Advancement to this fupream Dignity, nor without Petitions exprefsly made and verified to the fupream Office of the Inquifition eftablifhed here. Decreeing that all and every fuch Abfolutions, Reftorations and Reftitutions, which fhall henceforward be granted to Petitions not thus verified and exprefs, fhall be of no manner of Advantage to any one ; and that they ought not to derogate in any Part from thefe Prefents, unlefs the whole Tenor of them be inferted to a Word, and fuch Grace be granted from the certain Knowledge of the Roman *Pontiff, and figned with his own Hand ; and if it fhould happen that for any Reafon they be derogated from, fuch Derogations fhall be of no Strength and Validity whatfoever. We therefore command all and fingular the Patriarchs, Primates, Arch-Bifhops and Bifhops, and other Prelates of Churches conftituted throughout the whole World, that by themfelves, or another, or others, they procure thefe prefent Letters, or Copies of them, to be folemnly publifhed every one in their Provinces, Cities, Diocefes, and Places, and as far as they are able to be firmly obferved, by reftraining all Contradictors whatfoever by Ecclefiaftical Cenfures and Penalties without any Appeal, and by encreafing again and again fuch Cenfures and Penalties, and by calling in, if Need be, the Affiftance of the fecular Arm. All Conftitutions and Ordinations Apoftolick, and all other Things whatfoever to the contrary notwithftanding. 'Tis alfo our Will, that Copies of thefe Prefents fhall be printed and publifhed, and figned with the Hand of a*
publick

publick Notary, and with the Seal of every Ecclefiaftical Court or Prelate, and that they fhall every where have the fame Authority, as thefe Prefents would, if they were exhibited and fhewn. Moreover, we conjure all Princes of this World, to whom the Power of the fecular Sword is granted for the Punifhment of evil Men, by that Faith which they have promifed to defend, fo to interpofe and act their Parts, either by granting Affiftance to the aforefaid Minifters, or by punifhing the Crimes after the Sentence of the Church, that by their Help the Minifters of fo great an Office, may happily execute their Truft, to the Glory of the eternal God, and the Encreafe of Religion, whereby they will receive a moft ample Reward from God, in the Participation of eternal Bleffednefs, which he hath prepared for the Defenders of the aforefaid Faith. Let it therefore be lawful for no Man to infringe, or rafhly dare to contradict this Page of our Sanction, Legation, Statute, Decree, Command, Obteftation and Will. But if any one fhall prefume thus to do, let him know that he fhall incur the Indignation of Almighty God, and of his bleffed Apoftles Peter *and* Paul. *Given at St.* Peter's *in* Rome, *in the Year of the Incarnation of our Lord,* CIƆICLXIX. Ap. 1. *and Fourth Year of our Pontificate.*

p. 2. t. 13.
§. 24.   According to the Conftitution of this Bull, very grievous Punifhments are often inflicted on thofe who violate it. *Carena* relates from *Farinacius,* that a certain Prifoner in the holy Office was hanged for killing his Keeper, in order to make his Efcape. He adds, That at *Cremona, An.* 1614. a certain *Jew* was hanged for killing another *Jew* who had depofed againft him in the holy Office. And not only thus, but if the Wound is not mortal, but flight, he fays that he hath feen fuch Offenders fometimes condemned for ever to the Gallies, or at leaft for ten Years. This was executed upon a certain Perfon at *Cremona,* who had caned a Witnefs for depofing againft his Brother in the holy Office. His Sentence was publickly read to him in the great Epifcopal Hall at *Cremona, Carena* himfelf being prefent.

The fame *Carena* gives us a Cafe, by which it will appear, that fometimes thofe who terrify Witneffes, but yet don't obtain their End, have been difmiffed with a fevere Reprimand, and being put in mind of the before-mentioned Bull. A certain Sergeant of the holy Office had a Meffage from the Inquifitor to deliver to a certain Countryman's Wife: The Woman not being at home, the Sergeant would leave it with her Husband, upon which the Countryman gave him feveral hard Names, and follow'd him with Weapons, crying out, *Li fcirro becco torna in dietro a tor il tuo precetto.* The Pope confented that the Caufe fhould be tried before him, *July* 15, 1621. and the Sentence approved was, that the faid Countryman had incurred the Penalty of this Conftitution, and that he was to be condemned to the Gallies for five Years; with this Addition, That from the Goodnefs of the Pope he fhould be heard, if he defired the Grace of Commutation, upon Confideration of the Plainnefs of the Man, and his conjugal Affection.

However, *Carena* adds a Caution, that from thefe Inftances 'tis not lawful for the Inquifitors and Minifters of the holy Office, to make for themfelves a general Rule, *viz.* that fuch who terrify the Witneffes ought to be
punifhed,

punifhed, as above, and after the fame Manner as thofe who wound them ; for this is not left to the Pleafure of the Inquifitors or Ordinaries by the Matter of this Bull, but to the Cardinals, the fupream Inquifitors, to whom it belongs to declare, whether Criminals have incurred the Penalties of this Conftitution, or not.

He gives us another Inftance that happened at *Cremona*, *An.* 1592. A certain Perfon had accufed all the Witneffes examined againft him in the holy Office, and had caufed them to be imprifoned by the fecular Judge for fundry Crimes and Damages which they and their Cattle had occafioned in his Grounds. The major Part of the Congregation at *Cremona* thought, that although the Accufation could not be called formally that terrifying of which the Bull fpeaks, yet inafmuch as it appeared flanderous and deceitful, the Criminal fhould be obliged to free the imprifoned Witneffes from Jayl at his own Expence, and pay them, when delivered, all their Charges.

This takes place, not only when any Perfon is accufed as an Heretick, §. 17. " but in all and every Caufe whatfoever belonging to the holy Office ; be- " caufe every Caufe belonging to this Tribunal, is properly faid to be a Caufe " of the Faith, and to belong to it, and to infer fome Mark of the Faith, " either directly or indirectly. And in all Caufes of this holy Office there is " the fame Reafon for maintaining the Liberty of this Tribunal. Thus in " the Year 1635. a certain *Neopolitan* Soldier had refcued from the *Sbirri* a " certain Blafphemer, taken up in the Name of the holy Office, for which " he was condemned by Order of the fupream Tribunal of the City to all " the Penalties of this Conftitution. Altho' afterwards, through the Fa- " vour of the faid fupream Tribunal, the Punifhment of Death was exchanged " for that of the Gallies for ten Years. And this was publickly executed at " *Cremona*, in the Hall of the holy Office."

Yea, they extend this Affair fometimes fo far, that all manner of Offences committed againft any one that belongs to the Inquifitors, though they have no Relation to the Faith, are punifhed in the fame Manner, as though the Office of the Inquifition had been hindered by them, or the Inquifitor himfelf had received fome grievous Injury. *Reginald Gonfalvius* gives us a re- *p.* 191. markable Inftance of this which happened in the former Age at *Seville*. The Bifhop of *Terragone*, chief Inquifitor at *Seville*, went one Summer for his Diverfion to fome pleafant Gardens fituate by the Sea Side, with all his Inquifitory Family, and walked out, according to his Cuftom, with his Epifcopal Attendance. A Child of the Gardener, two or three Years old at moft, accidentally fat playing upon the Side of a Pond in the Garden, where my Lord Bifhop was taking his Pleafure. One of the Boys that attended his Lordfhip, fnatch'd out of the Hand of the Gardener's Child a Reed, with which he was playing, and made him cry. The Gardener hearing his Child, comes to the Place, and when he found out the Occafion of his crying, was angry, and bad the Inquifitor's Servant reftore the Reed to him. And upon his Refufal, and infolently contemning the Countryman, he fnatched it away, and as the Boy held it faft, the Gardener flightly hurt his Hand

by the ſharp Huſk of the Reed, in pulling it from him. The Wound was
far from being mortal, or from endangering the Loſs of any Part, and ſo
could not deſerve a ſevere Puniſhment. 'Twas no more than a Scratch of
the Skin, a mere childiſh Wound, as one may imagine by the Cauſe of it.
However, the Inquiſitor's Boy came to his Maſter, who was walking
near the Place, to complain about his Wound, upon which the Inquiſitor
orders the Gardener to be taken up, and thrown into the Inquiſitory Jayl,
and kept him there for nine Months in very heavy Irons, by which he received ſuch Damage in his Circumſtances, which were at beſt but mean, as the
poor Man could not eaſily recover; his Children and Wife, in the mean while,
being ready to periſh for Hunger. And all becauſe he did not pay Deference enough to the Inquiſitor's Boy, as a Member of the holy Tribunal. At
nine Months End they diſmiſſed him from Jayl, and would have perſuaded
him, that they dealt much more mercifully with him, than his Crime deſerved.

C H A P. XI.

Of Perſons ſuſpeſted of HERESY.

Direſt.
part. 2.
Qu. 55,
56.

Aſhough, in other Caſes, 'tis uſual to diſtinguiſh between a Suſpicion
and a Preſumption, a Suſpicion being no other than a Man's Opinion
concerning a Crime, ſeveral of which Suſpicions muſt concur to form a Preſumption of it, yet in the Cauſe of Hereſy they are taken for the ſame. A
Preſumption or Suſpicion therefore in this Affair is, a probable Gueſs of a
doubtful Matter, proceeding from the Nature of the Thing, or the Circum-
Simanc. ſtances of Affairs or Perſons. Preſumptions ariſe from a Perſon's Country
2. 50. §. 8, and Parents; but theſe are too general. Others ariſe from his Education,
&c. §. 17. and the Manners of thoſe with whom he converſes. This is the Reaſon that
the Inquiſitors, in their firſt Examinations, ſo diligently aſk the Criminals of
what Nation, Country, Family and Kindred they are, amongſt whom they
have been educated, who were their Maſters, Inſtructors, Companions and
Friends. For theſe Things, and a thouſand other ſuch are uſually conſidered in doubtful Caſes, that from hence they may draw more probable Proofs.
They alſo conſider the Sex. A Man may more eaſily be preſumed guilty
of Robbery. A Woman of Witchcraft. And farther, they conſider the
Age, Fortune, Difference of Condition, Nature of Mind, and Inclinations.

In the Cauſe of Hereſy Suſpicion is threefold; Light, Vehement and
Violent: A light Suſpicion is that which ariſes from the external Signs of
Actions and Words, by which ſuch a Gueſs may be made, as may imply,
not indeed frequently, but ſeldom, and by Accident, that he who ſays or
does ſuch Things is an Heretick. This is inferred by a ſmall Conſequence.
As

As if any one fhould argue thus : He is found to frequent private Conventicles, and in his Life and Manners departs from the common Converfation of
the Faithful ; therefore he is an Heretick, becaufe Hereticks themfelves are
found to do fuch Things frequently. Such are lightly fufpected of Herefy.
But the Inquifitors teach, that fuch Perfons ought not eafily to be proceeded
againft in a Caufe of fuch Importance. However, fometimes the very fpeaking to Hereticks hath not efcaped without Punifhment. Thus *Bzovius* relates, *An.* 1234. §. 14. *Acurfius*, the Son of *Aldobrandinus*, a Citizen of *Florence*, incurred the Canon, becaufe, whilft he dwelt in *France*, he converfed
with Hereticks. For 'twas, they thought, a Crime for any one fo much as
to falute them, contrary to the Apoftolick Inftitutions. But as he was afterwards abfolved by *Raymond Peniafortius*, Penitentiary of the Apoftolick
See, Pope *Gregory* enjoin'd the Prior, and Friar *Robert*, and the reft of the
Predicant Friars in *Paris*, that they fhould not any ways moleft him, or fuffer
or command him to be molefted.

A vehement Sufpicion, which is alfo called *Juris*, arifes from fuch external
Words and Deeds, which, when known, infer an Argument frequently con-
clufive ; and becaufe, as to moft, he who doth or fays fuch Things is an Heretick ; and is ufually taken for full Proof, if there be nothing proved to the
contrary. Such are thofe, who being called to anfwer concerning the Faith,
do not appear in the Time affigned them ; fuch who knowingly hinder the
Office of the Inquifition ; who knowingly give their Counfel and Affiftance
and Favour to fuch Hinderers ; who inftruct Hereticks when cited to conceal
the Truth, and fpeak falfely ; who are any ways excommunicated upon Account of the Faith ; who knowingly favour, defend, and receive Hereticks ;
who are infamous for Herefy, upon account of their Familiarity with fuch
whom they know to be Hereticks ; who knowingly accompany, vifit and receive Hereticks. He alfo who gives a Kifs to an Heretick is vehemently to
be fufpected of Herefy, according to the Judgment of the Synod of *Terragone*,
according to this Decree : *It is likewife enquired : Whether he who gave a Kifs
to one of the* Inzabbatati, *or an Heretick, when he believed and knew him to be
fuch a Perfon, or prayed with him, or concealed him, or heard preaching or reading
from him, and believed him to be a good Man, is to be judged of as a Believer of
his Errors? And we fay that he is not. However, let fuch an one be condemned as a
Favourer, or Concealer, and Benefactor, and vehemently fufpected to believe his Errors ; unlefs he fhould be fo learned or difcreet, as not to be able to pretend Ignorance.
And this we think proper to leave to the Pleafure of the prudent Judge.* Befides
thefe, fuch alfo are vehemently fufpected, who are judicially convicted of Perjury, or a Lye, in a Caufe of the Faith, and who have often done or faid any
thing againft the Faith, and the like, for all the particular Cafes cannot be enu-
merated. They who do fuch Things are faid to be vehemently fufpected.

Amongft thefe are reckoned alfo, fuch who knowingly give Ecclefiaftical *Direct.q.p.5.*
Burial to Hereticks, their Believers, Receivers, Defenders, and Favourers, *i. e.* qu. 40.
who bury them in the Church-yard, after a Chriftian Manner, with Pfalms com. 89.
and Prayers. For he who knowingly buries thofe, whom the Church perfecutes

cutes and condemns as Hereticks, or fufpected of Herefy, doth, whatever he may think in his Mind, feem by Fact to declare and profefs, either that the Church ought not to deprive fuch Perfons of Burial, or that it is lawful to pray for Hereticks and their Believers, &c. becaufe he buries them after the Manner of Catholicks. But whether this Sufpicion be only light, or vehement, skilful Men muft judge of according to the Quality of the Perfons. The Punifhment of fuch is Excommunication, from which they cannot be abfolved without proper Satisfaction, whether it be Abjuration or Canonical Purgation. Nor can they merit the Benefit of Abfolution, unlefs they unbury them with their own Hands, and throw out the Bodies of fuch condemned Perfons from their Graves. Cap. *Quicunq*; in princ. de hæret. lib. 6.

The fame Sufpicion arifes, if any one celebrates the Obfequies of fuch a Perfon after the Manner of Catholicks, when fuch Heretick or fufpected Perfon dies any where elfe, at *Geneva* for Inftance, or any other Place, where Men live and believe heretically. And finally, if any one fteals away and preferves the Afhes, Bones, Garments or the like, of burned Hereticks.

But if any one finds an Heretick, or a Believer or Favourer of Hereticks, or any fuch Perfon dead, in thofe Places in which he cannot eafily accufe them before the lawful Judges, then he may inter them, but not in holy Ground, that fo their unburied Bodies may not corrupt the Air ; nor fhall he hereby deferve any Punifhment, or contract any Sufpicion of Herefy. He muft however report the Affair to the Judges of the Faith, as foon as he can, that they may appoint what is needful to be done.

Tit. 49.
§. 1, 3.

There is alfo another Kind of fufpected Perfons, *viz.* thofe who have faid any Thing fcandalous or fufpected, as *Simancas* teaches us. *Tit.* 49. "No one " ought to preach, who is not examined and approved. But if any Preacher " thus examined and approved, fhall have faid any Thing fcandalous or " fufpected, the Inquifitors muft fummon him, and immediately compel him, " either publickly to retract it, or to explain it to the People in a pious and " catholick Senfe ; and he is moreover to be corrected and admonifhed, not " to dare to preach fuch Things for the future. But if he preaches any He- " refy, he muft be punifhed according to his Crime, and deprived of the Of-

part. 2.
affert. 33.

" fice of Preaching. *J. Royas* explains this more fully. Whofoever fhall " confefs, or be convicted of Propofitions rafh, injurious, fcandalous, or the " like, he muft be punifhed in an extraordinary Manner, and forced to ab- " jure, according to the Nature of the Sufpicion, whether it be light or vehe- " ment. 4 *Inftruct. Tolet.* cap. 8. *Inftruct. Madril.* An. 1561. c. 53. and 65. " For thefe and the like Crimes, which are not direct Herefies, Criminals " are feldom detained in the fecret Prifons of the holy Office, but in Mona- " fteries or private Places. 4 *Inftruct. Hifpal.* c. 4. 3 *Inftruct. Pinciana.* c. 10. " This is the Cafe, though the Crime be not fully proved ; but pecuniary " Punifhments inflicted for fuch Offences, muft be converted to the Ufe of " the holy Office."

But left the Popifh Doctors fhould be eafily rendered fufpected of Herefy, and deprived of their Office by the Inquifitors, they generally make ufe of a
certain

certain Proteſtation, that by this Means they may eſcape Cenſure, as *Siman-* *Siman-*
cas teaches. " Becauſe 'tis dangerous to diſpute about Matters of Faith and *Tit.* 55.
" Religion, even though the Truth be ſpoken, therefore learned Men, wiſe and §. 1.
" pious, when they treat of theſe Things, do with Prudence uſually make a
" ſolemn Proteſtation, that they would not by any Means deviate from the
" Catholick Faith, but in all Things, and always embrace the Doctrine of
" the Univerſal Church, and willingly ſubject themſelves to her Cenſure. After
" this they add a conditional Revocation, to this Senſe : That if it ſhall hap-
" pen that they have ſaid or written any Thing againſt the Catholick Faith,
" they do from henceforth retract it, and would have all underſtand that it was
" ſaid or written through Unſkilfulneſs or Imprudence, and not through Ma-
" lice or Obſtinacy." But leaſt any one ſhould eaſily eſcape the Cenſure of
the Inquiſitor by ſuch kind of Proteſtations, *Simancas* adds theſe Limitations. §. 6.
" That ſuch Proteſtation, though repeated a thouſand times, doth not ex- §. 8.
" cuſe, when any one willingly errs againſt the Catholick Faith ; or when
" through Ignorance he errs in thoſe Things, which he is explicitely re-
" quired to know, unleſs poſſibly he is able to prove his Ignorance, or ſome
" Cauſe of his Error. But it will be of great Advantage to him when he errs §. 9.
" in thoſe Things, which are ſo difficult, obſcure and doubtful, that may
" ſometimes eſcape the moſt learned Men. Becauſe ſuch an Error is ſuppo-
" ſed to ariſe more from Ignorance than Malice."

Suſpicion alſo ariſes, that a Perſon thinks ill of ſome Doctrine or Inſtitution, *par.* 3.
or Order of the Church, or ſome other Thing concerning which he muſt *com.* 23.
believe as the Church believes, *viz.* concerning the Power of the Pope, and *f.* 472.
Prelates, the holy Religions of the Monks, the Rites of the Sacraments, and
other Things, if he treat them unworthily, injuriouſly and diſgracefully ; or
if he defiles theſe excommunicatory Libels, which are commonly called *Ce-*
dulones, by drawing naſty Figures upon them. Such Perſons *Columna Marſi-*
lius, Arch-Biſhop of *Salerno,* in a certain Anſwer contends, do belong to the
holy Office, becauſe, by this Action, they ſeem to think wrong of the Power
of the Prelates, and to contemn the Cenſures of the Church, and to ſcoff at
and diſgrace the Church which uſes ſuch Cenſures. Farther, if any one per- *Lucern,*
ſiſts in his Excommunication for two Years, or for one, he is ſuſpected of He- *Inqu'ſ in*
reſy. For then 'tis preſumed that he thinks ill of the Sacraments, and *v. Suſpi-*
Church, and its Power, becauſe he deſpiſes its Excommunication. But if any *cion.*
one be excommunicated for Contumacy committed, in a Cauſe of Hereſy,
after a Year he is looked on as an Heretick, and may be puniſhed as ſuch.

Such alſo are ſuſpected who converſe with Hereticks, and from ſuch Converſation there ariſe Signs ſufficient to put ſuch an one to the Torture, as
Carena teaches, *p.* 2. *t.* 4. §. 7. *n.* 69.

A violent Suſpicion, which is alſo called *Juris* and *de Jure*, is a certain
Diſpoſition of the Law, preſuming ſomething, and determining upon ſuch
Preſumption, as though it were certain and known. Nor can any Proof to
the contrary be regularly and directly admitted againſt ſuch Preſumption ;
becauſe, as it proceeds from open and violent Marks, it is taken for a manifeſt

fest Truth. It arises from external Signs of Actions or Words, by which it may be concluded effectually, and almost always, that he who says or doth these Things is an Heretick. As if heretofore any one should adore Hereticks, or reverence them after their Manner; or receive the Consolation or Communion from them, or do the like Things belonging to their Custom. Cap. *Filii* & *Accusatus.* Extra. de hæret. lib. 6. Such are said to be violently suspected.

A Person lightly suspected, is enjoined Canonical Purgation, or even a light Abjuration. In this Case however the Proceeding must be cautious; because if any one falls into the like Suspicion after Abjuration, he must be more grievously punished. Cap. *Accusatus.* In princip. *A Person accused or suspected of Heresy, against whom there is arisen great and vehement Suspicion of this Crime, if in Judgment he abjures his Heresy, and afterwards falls into the same Suspicion, ought to be looked on as a Relapse by a certain Construction of Law,. although before his Abjuration the Crime of Heresy hath not been proved. But if such Suspicion shall be light and moderate, although on this Account he is to be more grievously punished, yet he is not to be punished as those who relapse into Heresy.*

. A Person vehemently suspected is not an Heretick, nor can he be punished as an Heretick. Extra. de præsumpt. c. *literas.* §. *Quocirca.* where 'tis expressly said, *Because for the mere Suspicion, though vehement, we would not have him condemned for so grievous a Crime.* But he must be commanded to abjure generally every Heresy, and especially that in which he offended, as a Person vehemently suspected. And this is no light Punishment. Because if he afterwards relapses either into his former Heresy, or any other, or associates with those whom he knows to be Hereticks, or affords them such Favour as is capable of no Excuse, he incurs the Penalty of the Relapsed. Cap. *Accusatus.* where we have these Words. *But as to the Person who offends in one Sort or Sect of Heresy, or errs in one Article of Faith or Sacrament of the Church, and afterwards shall abjure simply or generally his Heresy; if after this he offends by falling into another Sort or Sect of Heresy, or errs in any other Article or Sacrament, we will that he shall be judged as one relapsed into Heresy. He also, concerning whose Fall into Heresy before Abjuration, there hath been, or now is a Certainty, who, after such Abjuration, shall receive, accompany, visit, or associate himself with Hereticks, or shall make or send them Presents or Gifts, or grant them such Favour as cannot be excused, even though he doth not adore them, to use your Words, is deservedly to be judged as a Relapse; since 'tis not to be doubted that these Actions are the Consequence of the former Error be approved.* If he doth not consent immediately to abjure at the Command of his Judge, he is excommunicated; and if he continues under Excommunication for a Year, he must be condemned as an Heretick, and delivered over to the secular Arm; and may in the mean while be punished with some lesser Punishment, at the Pleasure of his Judge, as particularly with a Fine.

Simanc.
t. 46.   " But this only takes Place, when the Criminal is vehemently suspected,
§. 76.   " and upon account of his Age, or State of Health, or any other Cause, can-
          " not be tortured or purged. In such a Case he is carried out in publick,
                                                                    " cloathed

" cloathed with the penitential Habit, and is folemnly.to abjure, and to for-
" feit the third Part of his Effects, more or lefs, at the Pleafure of the Judge.
" But thefe Penalties muft be applied to the Expences of the Office of the
" holy Inquifition, nor can they be received as Payment of the Salary due to
" them, or their Minifters, as is more fully contain'd in a certain Command
" of the General Inquifition. 4 *Inftruct. Tolet.* cap. 8."

As to the Heirs of thofe who are fufpected of the Crime of Herefy, and §. 77.
who are Favourers, &c. of them, they muft not be condemned to pay thofe
pecuniary Penalties, if fuch fufpected Perfons die, whilft the Accufation is
depending ; becaufe Sufpicions, though vehement, are extinguifhed by the
Death of the Criminals. Cap. *Accufatus.* §. *Porro. Moreover, if any one, upon
account of the Reception, Defence, or favouring of fuch Hereticks, fhall have bound
his Eftate to perform that Penance which the Inquifitors would enjoin him, and fhall
die before fuch Penance be enjoin'd him, his Heirs fhall not be obliged to make
fuch Satisfaction for a Crime already extinguifh'd by Death.* Nor can they be com- Eymer.
pelled to perform a perfonal Penance enjoin'd to fuch fufpected Perfon, but *p.3.q.120.*
not actually perform'd by him. But they may be forced to perform the Pe- *com. 169.*
nance actually enjoined him, whilft alive, out of his Eftate. Cap. *Accufatus.*
§. *fi vero. But if any one hath tied his Eftate to the Inquifitors, to receive from them
and perform Penance, upon account of thofe Things in which he hath offended, by receiving Hereticks, or defending and favouring Hereticks, though he is not an actual Heretick himfelf, and fhall die after fuch Injunction of Penance, without having performed
it ; if by fuch Penance any Burthen, profitable to Salvation, be laid upon, and to be
exacted from his temporal Eftate, his Heirs may be compelled by the Inquifitors to fulfil
it, or any other to whom fuch Eftate with this Incumbrance on it may devolve.* So
that if it was enjoined him to build a Church or Hofpital, or to reftore Ufury,
and the like, and he hath bound his Eftate for accomplifhing the faid Penance, to whatfoever Succeffor, even though to any particular one, fuch E-
ftate fhall, after his Death, devolve, it always comes to him with fuch Incumbrance. This is alfo provided for by the Council of *Biterre,* cap. 19. *Let
the fame take place as to thofe, who die after having received Penance, but have delay'd to perform it ; or, as above-mentioned, have tied their Eftates to fulfil it.*

He who is violently fufpected, is to be condemned as one convicted of Herefy, and as an Heretick. Cap. *Excommunicamus.* 1. §. *Qui vero.* Extra. de
hæret. lib. 5. & Cap. *Cum contumacia.* & Cap. *Ut Officium.* For he either confeffes his Crime or not. If he confeffes, and will return, and abjure his Herefy, he muft be admitted to Penance. Cap. *Ad abolendam.* & Cap. *Excommu-
nicamns.* 2. §. fin. If he doth not confent to abjure, he muft be delivered over
to the fecular Court, and receive his deferved Punifhment. Cap. *Ad abolendam.*
§. 1. If he doth not confefs his Crime after he is convicted, and will not confent to abjure, he is to be condemned as an impenitent Heretick. Cap. *Ad
abolendam.* From thefe Things it appears, that although a light, a vehement, or violent Sufpicion, arife from different Caufes, yet it may happen
that a light Sufpicion may at length arife to a violent one, and the Beginning of a violent Sufpicion end in a light one. For Inftance, if one lightly
fufpected,

fufpected, and cited to anfwer concerning the Faith, doth not appear, he becomes vehemently fufpected, and is excommunicated.   And if he abides under that Excommunication for a Year, he is violently fufpected, and condemned as an Heretick.

<hr />

C H A P. XII.

Of Perfons defamed for HERESY.

<table>
<tr><td>

Direct.
p. 2. qu.
57.

</td><td>

WHO they are that are defamed for Herefy, we are taught by the
Council of *Tholoufe.* Cap. 16. *Such ought to be accounted defamed, who
are cried out againft by publick Report, or of whofe Defamation amongft good and
grave Perfons there is legal Proof before the Bifhop of the Place.* So that to the
perfect Proof of fuch Defamation or Infamy for Herefy, two good and grave
Witneffes fuffice.   But if they are vile and infamous, although they are not
to be defpifed on this Account, fo as to ftop proceeding to an Inquifition
from what they depofe, yet fuch Defamation is not fully proved by them.

</td></tr>
</table>

Lucern.
Inq. in
voce Infa-
mia.

They fay alfo, that 'tis not neceffary that the Witneffes fhould hear this
Infamy from the fame prudent and difcreet Perfons ; but 'tis fufficient, though
they hear it from different.   And they give this Reafon for it ; becaufe as they
are only to prove Infamy, 'tis fufficient if the Witneffes agree in and concerning this Matter.   Yea, they teach farther, that 'tis not neceffary that the
Witneffes fhould agree as to the Caufes of their own Knowledge.   So that
if the Witneffes fhould fay, they know this Infamy, becaufe they have heard
of it, they are not bound to prove they have heard it ; nor is it required that
one Witnefs fhould agree with the other as to Time and Place, and the Caufes of their Knowledge.   Becaufe the Queftion is not about thefe Things, but
only concerning the Fame and Infamy.   So that tho' they appear fingular in
what they fay, their Affertion fhall be abided by.

Ibid.

When once this Infamy is proved by Witneffes, they enquire, whether the
Perfon inquifited can prove himfelf to be of good Reputation, and thus put
a Stop to the Inquifition concerning the Truth of the Crime, and take away
the Proof of his bad Character.   Here the Popifh Doctors greatly differ.
Some fay, that the Proof concerning his good Character, ought not to be admitted, becaufe it feems to be elufive.   For if an hundred Perfons fhould fay
fuch an one hath a bad Character, and a thoufand that he is of a good one, the
Proof of the good one doth not difcharge him, becaufe he ftill remains infamous
in the Account of others, and the Inquifition is to be made in regard of them.
Others fay, that the Report of the greateft Number is to be ftood to.   O-
thers, that the Proof is to be admitted, but whether it affects the contrary
Proof depends upon confidering wherein the publick Report agrees, what is
the Quality of the Witneffes and Perfons, according to which the Judge is

to

to determine which of the Proofs is valid. Others say, that either the Witnesses on both Sides depose concerning the Person's Character, as to the same Place and Time, and then the most credible Witnesses are to be believed; or the Witnesses on both Sides are equally credible, and then the greatest Number must determine; or the Number of them is equal, and then the most probable Proof is to take Place, and that Proof is to be accounted the most probable, which adds Weight to the Cause by any like Presumption.

The Punishment of one thus defamed is Canonical Purgation, and some other ordinary Penalty. Cap. *Excommunicamus itaq;* Extra. de hæret. §. *Adjicimus,* when the Defamation is fully proved. But if it is not fully proved, the Person cannot be compelled to a Canonical Purgation, unless there be fuller Proof, and other Signs and Tokens concur with the Defamation. They say 'tis the same, if the Infamy arises from Rivals and Enemies. This is sufficient to give a Beginning to the Inquisition, but not to enjoin Canonical Purgation, unless what they say be probable. Sometimes also Persons are defamed for Heresy upon this Account, that they have lived in Places defamed or suspected of Heresy, and from thence have come amongst the Papists. In this Case the Synod of *Saltzbourg,* held two Ages ago, hath decreed: *The Parish Priests ought also to observe those who come from the Countries of* Constit. 6. *Hereticks, or Places suspected of Heresy, and to consider the Words and Deeds of all* cap. 2. *such, and to take Cognizance of their Life, Behaviour and Manners; and if there be any Ground of Suspicion, to acquaint the Ordinary with it.* Finally, the Council of *Tholouse* hath provided, That the Prelates, Barons, and all other Lords Cap. 16. of Countries, shall not have in their Families or Counsel, Persons defamed or suspected of Heresy, in these Words: *Neither let them presume to have or retain in their Family or Counsel, such Persons,* viz. Hereticks, or Believers of Hereticks, *or any other defamed of Heresy, or whom they believe to be suspected concerning it.* This they explain, not only of Persons condemned, and judicially and legally proved to be infamous and suspected, but of such Persons before they have received Sentence.

CHAP. XIII.

Of Persons Relapsed.

A Person is said to be relapsed, upon a double Account, either into Here- Direct. sy, or the favouring of Heresy. One relapsed into Heresy is he, who p 2. qu. 58. after he hath been convicted either by the Evidence of the Fact, or his own Confession, or by a legal Production of Witnesses, hath publickly abjured his Heresy, and is convicted of falling into it again. So that though a Person who falls into the same Error again and again, without any solemn Penance

nance intervening, or making an Abjuration or Canonical Purgation, may be truly faid to be a Relapfe, yet he cannot be punifh'd as fuch, fo as to be delivered over to the fecular Court, if fo be he will repent. Of thefe relap-

Carena, fed Perfons there are four Sorts. The firft, when any one falls into the fame
p. 2. t. 2. Herefy he hath abjured. Here the Doctors difpute, whether or no a Per-
§. 6. n. 36. fon who abjures as an Heretick before the Inquifitors Subdelegate, and after-wards falls into the fame or any other Herefy, is to be accounted as a Re-lapfe, if there be no Certainty of the Subdelegation of that Judge before whom he abjures. However, in the City of *Como,* a certain Woman, who had thus abjured, was given over as a Relapfe to the fecular Arm, and burnt, by the Advice of the whole College of Counfellors in that City, and of the Bi-fhop, and of *John Thomas Odefchalcus,* a Senator. It was determined alfo after

Cap. *Accu-* the fame Manner at *Mantua* in a like Cafe. The fecond, when any one falls
fatus. de into an Herefy which he abjured as vehemently fufpected, but not if he only
hæret 1.6 falls again into a vehement Sufpicion of Herefy. The third, when after a
Ibid. §. general Abjuration of Herefy, he falls into an Herefy different from the par-
Cum vero. ticular one he abjured. The fourth, when after having abjured as an Heretick,
§. Ille quo- he accompanies, vifits, &c. Hereticks, fends them Prefents, or grants them
que. Favour.

Carena, The Glofs on the aforefaid cited Chapter only excepts the Cafe of Hunger,
p 2. t. 2. which excufes, provided it be violent. But this Exception was not allowed by
§. 5. n. 31. the fupream Council of the *Spanifh* Inquifition, in which a certain Perfon was delivered over to the fecular Arm as a Relapfe, who having been reconciled as a *Moor,* returned afterwards to fome of that fort, and would have excufed himfelf by this Glofs, that he went to them upon account of Hunger.

p. 2. affert. So that in order to a Man's being accounted as a Relapfe, *J. Royas* fays
41.§. 332. 'tis neceffary, that it be proved that the Criminal did fall into Herefy, and is now fallen again into it. The Proof, as to the firft, muft be true or pre-fumptive, as to the fecond Legal: He therefore advifes, that the Promoter Fifcal fhould be cautious in accufing the Criminal of his firft Lapfe, that he may not be obliged only to exhibit the firft Sentence pronounced againft fuch a Relapfe, but that it may appear by the Confeffion of the Criminal, and the Inftrument of his Sentence, that he was fallen into Herefy, and hath ab-jured. But even then the Criminal is to be heard, defiring to alledge and
§. 335. prove his Innocence. The fame *Royas* fays, that in the Inquifition of *Valence,* there is an Apoftolick Indult, which provides, that Perfons relapfed, if *Moors,* and truly penitent, may be again reconciled to the Inquifitors, becaufe new
§. 348. Converts fhould be more mildly dealt with. But this muft not be extended to their Teachers commonly called *Alfaquins.*

Tr. tr. fol. But befides thefe, there are two other Ways, by which a Perfon is ac-
417. counted to be a Relapfe. Firft, When he is found to be perjured after Ab-juration, according to the Refcript of *Innocent* IV. *Sperabamus. Calling before you again as well thofe who have confeffed concerning heretical Pravity, as thofe who have not, whether they have been enjoined Penance by you on this Account or no, compel them to declare the Truth, as well concerning themfelves, as others fufpected of Herefy ;*

Herefy ; fo that if any of them be found to have fuppreffed the Truth in any Thing,
or as Dogs, to have returned to the Vomit, they fhall be altogether accounted unworthy
of all Favour. From whence the Author of the Book, *Concerning the Form*
of Proceeding againft Perfons inquifited for Herefy, of which *Calderine* is fuppofed
to be the Author, infers, that fuch Perfons are accounted Relapfed. Secondly, When after Abjuration and Purgation, the Criminal hath not performed
the Penance enjo ned him by the Inquifitors. To this Purpofe the Words of
the Council of *Biterre* are cited. *Whofoever fhall lapfe again after fuch* (general)
Abjuration, and they who do not obferve and do the Penances enjoined them, let them be
punifhed as Relapfed. Bernard Comenfis is of the fame Opinion. *If Hereticks do not* Lucern.
fulfil the Penance enjoined them after having abjured Herefy, Matthew *fays, they* Inquif. in
ought to be accounted as Relapfed, and he alledges the Text, Clem. 3. eod. tit. in fi. voce, pœna
ibi, & fatisfactionem habuerint. *He alfo cites* Cap. ad Abolendam. §. penult. ria.
Pegna notes, *That this Opinion, fimply taken, is not true, but that many Heads muft*
be diftinguifhed, that the Truth may be underftood, as we have taught in our Directory
of the Inquifitors, p. 3. q. 97. But between thefe and the former fort of relapfed Perfons, there is this Difference, that the former are to be left without
any Mercy to the fecular Arm ; but as to the latter, 'tis in the Inquifitors
Pleafure to deliver them to the fecular Judgment or not.

However, all who do not obferve the Penance enjoined them, are not pro-Simane.
mifcuoufly accounted Relapfed. This Penance is either altogether contrary tit. 47.
to Herefy, *viz.* if the Penitent be commanded to abjure, to preach againft §. 77.
his Errors, not to communicate with Hereticks, and the like. In this Cafe,
if he doth not obey, they fay he may be punifhed as a Relapfe. Or the
Penance tends to the Purgation of his Fault, *viz.* when Faftings, Prayers,
and other pious Works are enjoined the Penitent. In this Cafe he who doth
not perform every Thing, may be punifhed with an arbitrary Fine. But *Si-*
mancas is of a different Opinion, who thinks fuch Perfons to be obftinate, impenitent, or any Thing rather than Relapfed ; and that therefore Penance
ought to be again enjoined them at the Pleafure of the Judges, according to
the Nature of their Crime.

In like manner he who is condemned to perpetual Imprifonment, and efcapes Simane.
out of it, is generally accounted as a Relapfe, becaufe his Converfion feems to tit. 16.
have been feigned, and he himfelf to have fallen into his former Error. §. 24, 25.
Bernard Comenfis is of this Opinion. But *Simancas* rejects this Opinion as cruel Lucern.
and falfe, and fays, fuch a one is an Impenitent, but not a Relapfe. So that Inq. voce
whilft he continues his Efcape,and doth not fatisfy the Penance enjoined him, he Fugitivus.
may be condemned as an Impenitent. But if either he returns himfelf, or is
apprehended, and ready to fatisfy the Church, then he is to be enjoin'd a greater Penance upon account of his Efcape, but is to be kindly received into the
Bofom of the Church.

As to the Punifhment of the Relapfed, the Council of *Tarragone* hath formerly thus determined. *Some Perfons doubt, whether Perfons relapfed into the*
Belief of Hereticks, and dogmatifing Hereticks, ought to be left to the fecular Judgment,
if after they are apprehended they will repent. To us it feems that they ought not. But

in

in every such Case they are to be condemned to Imprisonment. Thus also *Guido Fulcodius,* in a certain Consultation, answers. *But if, which God forbid, such should relapse, they are not to be received without a publick Penance, which is elsewhere determined, unless it may possibly occasion any Scandal, and a greater Division, which we ought diligently to take Care of.* But the Council of *Narbonne,* cap. 11. thus determines. *As to those, who, after their Abjuration of Error and Purgation, shall be found to have fallen again into the Heresy they have abjured, leave them without farther hearing to the secular Judgment, to receive their due Punishment, since 'tis enough that such have once deceived the Church by a false Conversion.* There is only this Difference, that if they repent, they are not denied the Sa-

Carena, craments of Penance and the Eucharist. Cap. *Super eo.* de hæret. lib. 6. But
p. 2. t. 1. in *Spain* the Eucharist is generally denied to such Relapsed, upon account of
§. 6. n.41. the Danger which may happen by the Alteration which he receives, who is to be delivered over to the secular Arm, and he is only allowed the Sacrament of Penance. Hence they say, that relapsed Penitents are reincorporated into the Church, which is done by the Sacrament of Penance ; but that they are not reconciled to it, because the Sacrament of the Eucharist is necessary in order to it. But if they do not repent, they are delivered over to the secular Court as obstinate Hereticks. But *Simancas* observes, that there are some
tit. 57. " who think that relapsed Hereticks may sometimes obtain Pardon, *viz.* when
§. 8. " any one really relapsed, and not yet accused, nor convicted by any Witnesses,
" secretly accuses himself to the Inquisitors, voluntarily confesses his Errors,
" and with Tears asks Mercy, being ready to undergo any Penance, because
" as to him there can't be that evil Suspicion, by which relapsed Persons are
" presumed to be feignedly converted. But *Simancas* himself is of Opinion,
" that this can't be defended, unless it be helped out with a favourable Inter-
" pretation, because the Judge is the Keeper and Minister of the Laws, and
" not the Lord of them." We must not omit here, that Pope *Paul* IV. *Anno* 1555. by a Bull beginning, *Cum quorundam hominum,* commands, *that all and singular such should be accounted as relapsed into Heresy, and delivered over as such to the secular Court, even for the first Fault, who teach that God is not three in Persons, that the Lord Jesus is not consubstantial to the Father and the Holy Ghost ; or that he was not conceived of the Holy Ghost ; or that he did not undergo the Death of the Cross to reconcile us to the Father ; or that the Virgin* Mary *is not the* true Mother of God *; or did not preserve her Virginity entire,* viz. *before, when, and always after she brought him forth.*

A Relapse into the Favouring of Heresy, is one who hath abjured such Favouring, and afterwards relapses into it, as the Council of *Tarragone* defines it. But whether this is to be understood, if they relapse into the same Favouring, or into any other, and whether both, or the former only, are to be delivered over to the secular Court, and punished with Death, the Laws do not clearly determine. And therefore some think it the safest way, in such Case, to consult the chief Pontiff, or the Senate of the general *Roman* Inquisition.

The Council of *Tholouse* hath thus determined concerning Persons relapsed into the Favouring of Heresy, as this Decree is extant in the Book, *Concerning*
                                                                                    the

*the Method of Proceeding against Perfons inquifited for Herefy. As to thofe who*ᵀʳᵃᶜᵗ.
*were known to be Receivers, Defenders and Favourers, and have been reconciled, and*ᴰᵒᶜᵗᵒʳ.
*fworn to obey the Commands of the Church, and have fallen again into the Crime*ᵗᶜᵐ. 11,
*they have abjured, or obftinately refufe to receive and fulfil their Penances ; if being*ᴾ₄:²:. ᶠᵉ.
afterwards admonifhed, or not admonifhed, they will humbly acknowledge their Guilt 7
and amend, after receiving from them fuch and fo great Securities, befides the Caution.
of an Oath, as may reftrain them by the Fear of temporal Punifhment, enjoin them
fuch Penance as may be a Terror to others. But otherwife proceed againft them as far
as ye can by Law.

C H A P. XIV.

Of fuch who read and keep prohibited Books.

BEfides thefe there are others, whofe Crimes may be thought more properly to belong to another Court. But it fometimes happens that they
are faid to be fprinkled with the Plague of Herefy, becaufe they are fufpected
of it, and therefore muft be inquifited upon account of their Intention. A-
mongft thefe firft occur thofe who read and retain Books prohibited upon account of Herefy. Thefe are numbered amongft fufpected Perfons, and there
are feveral fevere Edicts of the *Roman* Pontiffs againft them.

Pius V. publifhed a Bull upon the Feftival of *Cœna Domini.* In the firft Compeg.
Chapter are excommunicated all Hereticks and Shifmaticks, of whatfoeverin Zanch.
Name or Sect, and all Favourers, Receivers, and Believers of Hereticks,ᶜ·³⁴·
and thofe who any wife knowingly read, keep in their Houfes, print, or in
any wife defend, for any Caufe, publickly or privately, under any Pretence
or Colour, and in general all who defend their Books, without the Authority
of the Apoftolick See. *Pius* IV. recalled all Licences of reading and keeping
fuch Books, by his Conftitution, which begins, *Cum pro munere,* March 24,
1564. By thefe Letters he commands, that all Perfons fhall deliver and
confign over all condemned Books to the Inquifitors of the Cities where fuch
Books are. In like manner thofe who retain them cannot be excufed, even
though they keep them locked up in a Cheft, fo that no one can fee or read
them, becaufe all fuch Excufes are cut off by this Sentence, and by the alledged Conftitution of *Pius* IV. Again, thofe who print them are excommunicated ; and alfo thofe who in any wife, or for any Caufe, publickly or privately defend heretical Books, *&c.* and the Abfolution of all fuch Perfons is
referved to the Pope.

And that all manner of Leave of reading even the leaft Thing in a Book Soufa A-
condemned for Herefy, may be cut off, they declare that they underftandᵖʰᵒʳ. In-
not only printed Books, but even Manufcripts and Parts of them, which�q ᵘⁱf. *l.* 1.
they thus expound. He who reads that Part of the Books of Hereticks ᶜ·²¹· §·8·
ₑₜ𝒸.

that

that are divided into Tomes, which doth not profeffedly contain Herefy, is not accounted to read a Book prohibited by the Bull *Cæna*, even tho' the other Tomes fhould be heretical. But if a Tome contains Herefy, or treats of Religion, and it be divided into feveral Books, he who reads one of the Books of fuch a Tome, is faid to read a Book prohibited by this Bull, even though the particular Book doth not contain Herefy, nor treat of Religion, and is bound up feparately from the others. Yea, 'tis enough to fay that a Perfon hath read a prohibited Book, if he only juft runs it over with his Eyes, adverting to the Things written in it, though he doth not mention one Word of it with his Mouth. And yet, which is ftrange, they add, that he who by Memory recites a prohibited Book, though he doth it with an evil Intention, is not accounted fo to read it, as to incur the Cenfure pronounced againft fuch who do; fo obfervant are they of the Letter of the Law; though at the fame time he incurs the Cenfure of the Bull, who reads a Book prohibited by it, though he doth not do it with an ill Defign, but out of pure Curiofity, or to confute the Errors of Hereticks. But to a Man's incurring the Penalty of Excommunication, 'tis neceffary that he fhould knowingly read it. So that Ignorance excufes, but not when 'tis grofs and affected, *viz.* when a Perfon pretends not to know that the Author of a Book was an Heretick, although he knew the Book treated of Religion, or that the Book treated of Religion, although he knew the Author to be an Heretick. He who keeps the aforefaid Books either in his own, or another's Houfe, whether he underftands the Book or not, whether it be the whole or a part, even fo much as a fingle Leaf, whether he keeps it to read, or only for Curiofity and Ornament's fake, or to exchange for other Books, or to wrap up what he fells with the Leaves of it, incurs the Excommunication of the Bull. Likewife he who caufes it to be printed, defends it, praifes it, fays 'tis not fit to be burnt or prohibited, or hinders its coming to the Inquifitors Hands.

Thefe are all fufpected concerning the Faith, and may be punifhed by the Inquifitors as fufpected. But if any one doth not deliver an heretical Book to the Inquifitors, but burns it by his own Authority, he is not fufpected of Herefy, though he falls into Excommunication; becaufe *Julius* III. by a Conftitution, beginning, *Cum meditatio cordis*, commands, that fuch Books fhall be really and effectually delivered up to the Inquifitors. When any one delivers up a Book to the Inquifitors, he muft be interrogated by them whence he had it. He who keeps an heretical Book, which hath not the Author's Name, is himfelf reputed the Author, unlefs he difcovers his Name, and whence he had the Book. If any bring the Books of Hereticks, prohibited either for Herefy, or falfe and fufpected Doctrine, to any Country of the Faithful, they are Favourers of Hereticks, incur Excommunication, have all their Goods confifcated, and if they are mean Perfons, are whipped; but if they are of the better Sort, they are banifhed at the Pleafure of the Inquifitors. But thefe are not the only Punifhments ufed. Tyranny prepares the Way for greater Cruelty. If there arifes a vehement Prefumption of Herefy, upon account of any one's reading, retaining, defending, or printing the Books

of

Margin notes:
22.
23.

28.

33.
34.

36.
30.

Carena,
p. 2. t. 10.
n. 46.
39.

41.

42.

of Hereticks, and other additional Circumstances, they can make use of the Torture to find out the Truth.

The Circumstances are such as these. If the Persons inquisited are learned. Carena, Secondly, If the Books contain Heresies. Thirdly, If they have kept and*p. 2. t. 10.* read them a considerable Time, and with Care, and have imported them*n. 44.* from distant Countries. These Things render the Person vehemently suspected, and he may be tortured concerning his Intention and Belief of heretical Propositions, and his Accomplices, from whom he had the Books, and may be forced to abjure upon account of the vehement Suspicion, and be banished at the Pleasure of the Inquisitors. Such who write out the Books of Here-Sousa 43. ticks, in order to print and publish them, and such who sell Paper and Ink for such Writing and Printing, if it be knowingly, are Favourers of Hereticks, and may be arbitrarily punished. Nor is he free from Punishment who Carena, reads and retains the Book of an Heretick, professedly containing Heresy,*n. 28, 29.* or treating of Religion, although he doth it with a Design to confute the Errors of it, and the holy Office is apprised of such Design. For Instance, if an House be searched, and prohibited Books are found in it, and at the same time such Writings as recite the Passages of such Books, and confute the Errors of them ; although such a Person is free from all Suspicion of Heresy, and must not therefore be tortured or made to abjure, yet he is to be punished, and falls into the Excommunication of the Bull *de Cœna*, because he keeps the said Books without Leave, and by his own Authority, but must therefore be absolved from it again.

This Interdict of reading prohibited Books is so universal, that it comprehends even the Clergy themselves, and as most contend, the Bishops and very Cardinals, who cannot read the said Books without the Pope's Licence ; because all Licences and Privileges were revoked by *Julius* III. in a Constitution, beginning, *Cum meditatio* ; and afterwards by a Constitution of *Paul* IV. beginning, *Cum futurum* ; and of *Pius* IV. *Cum pro munere* ; and by a Constitution of *Gregory* XV. published *Dec.* 30. 1623. beginning, *Apostolatus officium* ; and finally by a Constitution of *Urban* VIII. published *Ap.* 11. 1631. this Revocation was often confirmed. Hence it is that this Penalty is appointed against the Clergy who retain and read prohibited Books, that they are vehemently suspected, may be deprived of the active and passive Voice, suspended from divine Services, deprived of the Offices of Reading, Preaching, &c. and farther be enjoined Fastings, Pilgrimages, &c.

As to the Inquisitors, some will have them not to be comprehended in the 12, 13. Bull ; others, that they are as well as others, unless they have particular Leave from the Pope himself, or the Congregation of the Cardinals of the holy Office, who alone have the Power of giving this Licence, and not this unless it be in full Congregation, or at least not without the major Part of the 9. Cardinals be present. And even this their Power some so far restrain, as to contend that the College of Cardinals cannot grant it during the Vacancy of the See. But whatever the Power of the Cardinals Inquisitors General in this Sousa, l. 1. Case is, 'tis limited by an express Exception of the Books of *Charles Moli-c. 2 § naeus, §. 5.*

§. 64.

næus, the reading of which the Pope only can allow ; according to the Constitution of *Clement*. VIII. beginning, *Apoſtolicæ ſedis autoritati*, publiſhed *An.* 1602. But in *Portugal* the Inquiſitors General may, by the Conceſſion of *Paul* IV. to Cardinal *Henry*, *Dec.* 10. 1560. grant Leave to the Inquiſitors and other Perſons of approved Life and Religion, if they are proper, and ſkilful and learned in Divinity, and not at all ſuſpected, to read any prohibited Books whatſoever, for this Reaſon only, to enable them to oppoſe and refute Here-

§. 57.

ticks. The ſame Power that is granted to the Inquiſitors, is alſo underſtood to be granted to the Deputies of the Inquiſition in the Kingdom of *Portugal*. Becauſe, as they enjoy the Privileges of Inquiſitors, and have a deciſive Vote in Cauſes, and are Judges in Cauſes of Hereſy, and can puniſh Hereticks, as well as burn their Books, they may read the ſame prohibited Books, which the Inquiſitors themſelves are permitted to read. This they may with much greater Reaſon do, who are of the Council of the ſupream Senate of the Inquiſition.

CHAP. XV.

Of POLYGAMISTS.

Carena,
p. 2, t. 5.
§. 2.

POlygamiſts are thoſe who marry ſeveral Wives at once. The Tribunal of the Inquiſitors takes Cognizance of their Cauſe, becauſe they are ſuſpected of Hereſy, and are preſumed to think wrong concerning the Sacrament of Matrimony, and to hold it lawful to have ſeveral Wives at once.

§. 10.
n. 55.

When a Polygamiſt is in the Jayls of the holy Office, and he is known to be the ſelf ſame Perſon, either by his Confeſſion, or by Witneſſes, and when his Crime is proved, he is aſked, Whether he truly believes that it is, and hath been lawful for a Chriſtian Man, after the Evangelick Law, to marry ſeveral Wives at once ? If he anſwers affirmatively, he is taken for a formal Heretick, and is to be puniſhed as ſuch. But if he anſwers negatively, and like a Catholick, denying that he had any heretical Intention, but was rather enticed to a ſecond Matrimony by the Luſt and Concupiſcence of the Fleſh, he muſt be put to the Torture concerning his Intention, that the Judges of the Faith may certify themſelves what the Polygamiſt truly thinks concerning the Faith, becauſe the Crime of Hereſy is ſecret, and lies hid in the Mind. This is peculiar to this holy Office ; though, according to the Laws of it, they rightly apply the Torture. For ſince the Fact which the Criminal confeſſes, or of which he is convicted, may be committed without any Error of the Mind, but for ſome other Cauſe, for Inſtance, Concupiſcence, the Criminal is tortured concerning his Intention and Belief of thoſe Things which he hath done. And thus we ſee, that 'tis a ſmaller Crime in the Church of *Rome* to marry two Wives thro' Luſt and carnal Concu-

piſcence,

cupifcence, contrary to the Dictates of Confcience, than from fome Error of the Mind, and with a Confcience that doth not condemn the Fact.

Polygamifts are fufpected of Herefy. In *Spain* they are only lightly §. 11. fufpected, and therefore, according to the general Cuftom of *Spain*, they muft abjure only as lightly fufpected. But in the fupream Tribunal of the *Roman* Inquifition, they are vehemently fufpected, and muft abjure as fuch.

Yea, fuch who marry a fecond Wife, being ignorant that the firft is dead, n. 59. but yet bring Witneffes to prove that they had no Wife, although their actual Polygamy is not certain, yet they muft abjure as vehemently fufpected, and be condemned to the Gallies. *Carena* gives us an Inftance of a certain Perfon of *Bologna*, who had married his firft Wife there, and afterwards, having examined Witneffes, to prove he never had a Wife, married a fecond at *Naples*, being ignorant whether the firft was dead. This Man was brought before the Pope by the facred Congregation, *Octob*. 19. 1620. and being firft put to the Torture concerning his Intention, he was forced to abjure as vehemently fufpected, and condemned to the Gallies for five Years. Becaufe, though his actual Polygamy was not certainly proved, yet, as to himfelf, he had confummated the Crime.

But if any one, during the Life of his firft Wife, betroths another, he is only lightly fufpected, and muft therefore only abjure as fuch. And they give this Reafon of the Difference ; becaufe, in this Cafe, there is no actual Abufe of the Sacrament, but only an evil Difpofition of Mind to abufe it.

After Abjuration thefe Polygamifts are enjoined various falutary Penances by §. 13. the Inquifitors, fuch as Faftings, Prayers, and the like, after which, he who n. 61. hath married two Wives, is condemned to the Gallies for five Years ; and if he hath produced falfe Witneffes to prove the Death of his former Wife, for feven Years and more, at the Pleafure of the Inquifitors, and is commanded to return to his firft Wife. If they are of the ordinary fort of People they are generally beat, and half their Effects confifcated. And in fome Places they have an infamous fort of a Mitre put on their Heads, and are afterwards beaten. In *Spain* they are condemned to the Gallies for ten Years. If any one hath married thrice or more, he is more grievoufly punifhed, and condemned for a longer while to the Gallies. Thus at *Rome*, *May* 18. *An*. 1597. four Polygamifts were condemned to the Gallies in the Church of St. *Mary fupra Minervam*, by the fupream Tribunal of the *Roman* Inquifition, two of them for feven Years, who had married three Wives, and the other two for five Years, who had married two.

CHAP. XVI.

Of those who celebrate and administer the Sacrament of Penance, not being Priests.

Sousa, *l.* 1.
q. 32. *n.* 7. HE who celebrates Mass, not being in Presbyters Orders, is subject to the Judgment of the Inquisitors, and opposes in Fact the Catholick Verity, according to the Constitution of *Gregory* XIII. beginning, *Officii nostri*. The Evil of this Crime, according to *Sousa*, reaches to Idolatry, because those who thus celebrate, make the Faithful of Christ to adore Bread and Wine, as though it were the true Body and Blood of our Lord.

In like manner he who is no Priest, and yet hears Confessions, and gives Absolution, is said to abuse the Sacrament, and greatly to injure his Neighbour.

Carena,
p. 2. *t.* 11. Such are vehemently suspected of Heresy, because they think, at least as *§.* 1. to the very Fact, that other Persons besides Priests may be the Ministers of those Sacraments.

Such Criminals are to abjure as vehemently suspected, and are then delivered over to the secular Arm to be punished with Death; but are first degraded *§.* 6. *n.* 30. from their Orders if they are in any. Thus *An.* 1636. and the following, two of these Criminals were delivered over to the secular Court at *Naples*, and by Order of the holy Council first hanged, and then burnt.

§. 7. *Urban* VIII. commanded by a Letter of Cardinal *Mellinus*, to the Inquisitor General of *Portugal*, *March* 5. 1622. that Criminals confessing, or convicted of this Crime, should be absolutely delivered over to the secular Arm, and punished with Death. But in as much as before these Letters they were not punished with Death in *Spain*, according to the Constitutions of *Gregory* and *Clement*, so *Sousa* affirms, that he never saw this Punishment inflicted in Sousa, *l.* 1. the Kingdoms of *Spain*, after the said Letters of Cardinal *Mellinus*. But this *c.* 32. *n.* 13. was the Method of Punishment there generally made use of, *viz.* that if the pretended Priest was a Layman, or vile Person, he was beat, and sent to the Gallies, and enjoined some spiritual Penances. Or if he was a Person of Credit, or a Religious, he was sent to the Gallies. If of such Quality as that he could not be sent to the Gallies, he was banished; and, if in any Order, suspended from it the whole Time of his Banishment. If the Offence was attended with any aggravating Circumstances, they add other Punishments according to their Quality.

We have an Instance to this Purpose in the Book of Sentences of the *Tholouse* Inquisition, *fol.* 122. A certain Countryman called *Rolland*, believed he had a Power from the Lord to celebrate Mass, and to consecrate the true Body of Christ from common Bread, and the true Blood from Wine mixed with Oyl and Salt, in a wooden Bowl that had a Foot to it, which he used instead of a Chalice. And thus he every Day sacrificed secretly in his own
House,

House, upon a Coffer covered over with a Linnen Cloth, and often communicated of that Bread, believing it to be the true Body of Christ. After
four Years he was thrown into Prison, and was very difficultly prevailed with
to abjure his Error. But whilst he was in his Imprisonment, he was found to
have relapsed into the same Error, and to have repeated this Ceremony. But
before he was punished as a Relapse, he died in Jayl, without a Confession
of his Sins, and the Sacrament of the Eucharist. The Inquisitors commanded
his Body to be taken up and burnt.

Raynald gives us another Instance of one, who did not indeed celebrate or
administer the Sacrament of Penance as a Priest, though he really was none,
but who said he was a Bishop, though he had not the Pope's Bull, and as such
consecrated Priests. And because he was made an Example of extream
Cruelty, I will here relate the Matter exactly as I find it in his Annals.

"*James* the Priest, a false Minorite, born in the Dutchy of *Juliers*, forged
" the Pope's Bull, and declared in the *Netherlands* that he was a Bishop;
" and although he had not been ordained a Bishop, he consecrated Priests
" by a false Ceremony in several Dioceses of *Germany* and the *Low Countries*.
" At length he was convicted of his Wickedness, and the Magistrates of *Utrecht*
" thought fit, not to condemn him to the Flames, that he might be quickly
" consumed, but to be gradually burnt by boiling Water, that so they
" might conquer his Obstinacy, because he most impudently refused to
" acknowledge his Crime. But being gradually let down into the boiling
" Cauldron, and overcome with the Extremity of the Pain, he detested his
" Wickedness, and pray'd that he might receive a milder Punishment. His
" Judges being moved with Compassion, ordered him to be taken out of the
" boiling Cauldron, and then to be beheaded." *Heda* tells the same Story in
fewer Words, in the Life of *Florentius*, the fiftieth Bishop of *Utrecht*. "A cer-
" tain Person of the Profession of St. *Francis*, took upon him the Character
" of a Priest and Bishop, and of Suffragan to Bishop *Florentius*. And having
" for a long while performed all sacred Offices, it was at last discovered, that
" his Character and Letters were forged. Upon this he was deprived, and
" condemned to be put in boiling Water. But as soon as ever he was thrown
" into it, he moved, by his Cries, the Compassion of the Bishop, and was
" immediately taken out, and being beheaded, obtained the Favour of Bu-
" rial. Most of those who were consecrated by him, were reconsecrated by
" some other Bishop, whilst others returned to the World and married, all his
" Acts being null and void."

In the Records of the Chapter of St. *Saviour*'s at *Utrecht*, in the forecited
Book, *fol.* 105. & *seq.* this very Story is to be read, and the Sentence
against the said *James* is added; and because it gives us a just Account of
the Custom of that Age, I will here faithfully transcribe it, as I find it in
the said Book.

" In the Year of our Lord 1392. *Sept.* 30. one *James*, of the Order of the
" Friars Minor, a Presbyter, born in the Dutchy of *Juliers*, was verbally
" and actually degraded, in the Manner under-recited, in the City of *Utrecht*,

" upon a certain Scaffold built of Wood, in the Market-place of the City,
" which they call *Noede*, becaufe he affumed to himfelf, by certain falfe A-
" poftolick Letters which he had forged, the Title and Name of the Bifhop
" of *Laubatch*, and being for fome time taken as a Suffragan to the Bifhop of
" *Utrecht*, had prefumed to celebrate and exercife the leffer and greater Or-
" ders, and other Epifcopal Functions in the faid Bifhop's Diocefe, and for
" ten Years before that in the Diocefes of *Treves*, *Mayence*, and *Strasburg*. After
" his Degradation, he was delivered over as a Laick to the *Scultet* and *Sca-*
" *bines* * of *Utrecht*, who were prefent, and received him into their Court ; and
" by their Sentence, *Florentius*, Lord Bifhop of *Utrecht*, prefiding in the
" faid Place, the faid *James* was condemned to be burnt with Fire, in a Caul-
" dron, made ready for that Purpofe near the Scaffold. But he was at laft
" gracioufly taken out of the Cauldron, and beheaded in the fame Place.

" And therefore the aforefaid Lord *Florentius*, and the fix under-written
" Bifhops, more being met together, and each of them robed in their *Pon-*
" *tificalibus*, and feated on the aforefaid Scaffold, Mafter *Arnold Pot*, in their
" Stead, and at their Command, pronounced this Sentence againft the faid
" *James*.

In the Name of God, Amen. Florentius de Wevelichoven, *by the Grace of.*
God and the Apoftolick See, Bifhop of Utrecht, *and alfo by the fame Grace,*

Arnoldus, *Bifhop of* Capitolias.	Wenemarus, *Bifhop of* Sibula.
Hubert, *Bifhop of* Opinum.	Bertoldus, *Bifhop of* Lindavv.
Andrew, *Bifhop of* Mofcow.	*and,* James, *Bifhop of* Sarrepte.

Judges together in the under-written Affair. The Empire of Reafon prefiding in
the Mind of the Judge, Juftice fits upon the Tribunal in the Examination of Truth,
and the Righteoufnefs of the Judges, as a King upon the Throne, out of whofe Mouth
proceeds a two-edged Sword. By the terrible Afpect of which the Pleafure of a Man's
own Will is fcattered, and the criminal Appetite of the Wicked, without Refpect of
Perfons, is limited under the Rule of the Law. For this hath been taken Care of
by the Judge, from whofe Countenance right Judgment proceeds, that Judges fhould be
appointed in the World, who fhould love Righteoufnefs, judge the Children of Men,
and punifh Offenders, according to the Meafure of their Fault. Attending therefore
with great Grief of Heart to thy heinous Wickednefs, unheard of in all Ages, which
thou haft committed, who art the Head of Scandal, and Rock of Offence, and with
frequent Sighs and Groans recounting the moft unhappy Boldnefs of thy Rafhnefs,
which even difturbs the Heaven, and makes the very Earth to tremble, we are
forced, Juftice demanding it, to proceed againft thee, to that juft Punifhment and
Revenge which thou haft deferved. Having therefore called on the Name of Chrift,
fitting on our Tribunal, and having God only before our Eyes, and having taken the
Counfel of prudent and skilful Perfons ; whereas by thy Confeffion, and by other
Proof, it evidently and legally appears to us, that thou haft forged Apoftolical Let-

* The chief Magiftrates and Officers of the City.

ters,

ters, *and haſt impudently and damnably preſumed to uſurp and aſcribe to thy ſelf raſhly and fallaciouſly the Title of the Pontifical Dignity, and to confer on great Numbers of Perſons the greater and leſſer Orders, to perform Chriſms* †, *to conſecrate Churches, Chapels and Altars, to reconcile Perſons, and confirm them, by anointing them on the Forehead, and to exerciſe other Offices incumbent on the Miniſtry of the Pontifical Dignity, under a falſe and feigned Epiſcopal Title, in the Dioceſes of* Treves, May-ence, Straſburgh *and* Utrecht, *and in other Places, for the Space of ten Years and more, although thou waſt not a Biſhop, and in Fact art not, to the great Danger of thy own Soul, and the Souls of many others, and to the Injury and Contempt of the whole Catholick and Univerſal Church ; even although we* Florentius *Biſhop of* Utrecht, *out of the Motion of our Clemency, have thought fit to indulge thee for a long while with Space for Repentance, whilſt thou haſt been kept in Cuſtody in our Jayl, that thou mighteſt ſtudy to appeaſe the Anger of the moſt High, whom thou haſt grievouſly offended with thy horrible Impieties, and with devout and frequent Prayers and Tears mighteſt endeavour to obtain his Mercy. But thou being ignorant to return to a ſound Mind, and to bring forth thoſe Fruits meet for Repentance, which we have long expected, with an hardened Heart, and obſtinate Mind, haſt not been afraid, we ſpeak it with Grief, to deſpiſe the Space mercifully granted by us to thee for thy Repentance, even to this preſent Time, to the Loſs of thy own Salvation. Therefore we* Florentius, *and the other Biſhops above named, being ſpecially and preſentially called, and met together to this preſent Act, upon account of thoſe Things which we have ſeen, heard and known, and do know and underſtand, do perpetually degrade, depoſe and deprive thee, being legally cited to the ſaid Act, from all Eccle-ſiaſtical Orders, and the Prieſtly Office, as a Falſifier of Apoſtolick Letters, an A-buſer of the Eccleſiaſtical Sacraments, an Enemy of Souls, a Deſtroyer of the Faith-ful, and a Tranſgreſſor of the ſacred Canons, and we ſententially condemn thee thus actually to be degraded, and at length degraded, to be left to the ſecular Court, and then to be puniſhed without danger of Death.*

" After the aforeſaid Sentence pronounced on him, being preſent, the de-" graded Perſon was carried down, and cloathed with the ſacerdotal Veſt-" ments, carrying the Chalice, &c." After this follows a long Account of the Degradation in the ſaid Book. But as I ſhall profeſſedly treat of this Degradation in the following Book, I ſhall there together and at once give an Account of this whole Affair, and ſay nothing of it here, that I may not repeat the ſame Thing.

† *Criſmata conficere*, is to conſecrate the holy Oils which were uſed in the Church of *Rome*. Theſe were principally two. One that was made of Oil and Balſom, which is the principal Sort. Thoſe who were baptized were anointed with it on the Top of the Head , thoſe who were confirmed on the Forehead, as were alſo thoſe who were ordained. The other is Oil without any Mixture, conſecrated by the Biſhop, with which the *Catechumens* were anointed upon their Breaſt, Shoulders and Forehead, before their Baptiſm. Sick and poſſeſſed Perſons alſo were anointed with the ſame Oil.

C H A P.

CHAP. XVII.

Of SOLICITING CONFESSORS.

Souſ,*l* 1.
c 34 §.1.
Catena,
p. 2 *t.* 6.
§. 1.
 BY thefe are underſtood ſuch Confeſſors, who, in the Sacramental Confeſſion, ſol cite and provoke, or attempt to ſolicite and provoke Women to diſhonourable Actions. *Paul* IV. *An.* 1561. *Ap.* 16. publiſhed a Bull againſt ſuch Perſons, directed to the Arch-Biſhop of *Seville*, beginning, *Cum ficut fuper*, and *Pius* IV. another, *Ap.* 6. 1564. and the ſupream Inquiſitors General an Edict, approved by *Clement*. VIII. But thoſe Bulls, and that Decree ſeem only to take place in *Spain*, becauſe the Bulls were directed to the Arch-Biſhop of *Seville*, and the Decree of the ſacred Congregation expreſsly reſtrained to the Places of *Spain*. But in the Year 1612. in the Month of *April*, it was decreed by *Paul* V. that all the Inquiſitors ſhould be admoniſhed to command the Confeſſors, to abſtain from all and every ſort of Solicitation, and to proceed rigorouſly againſt all thoſe who did not. And finally, there is extant a Conſtitution of *Gregory* XV. publiſhed *Aug.* 30, 1622. beginning, *Univerſi dominici*, in which he confirms the Letters or Bull of *Paul* IV. and commands it to be firmly and inviolably obſerved, not only in the Kingdoms of *Spain*, but in all other Parts of the Chriſtian World. And becauſe the Words of that Bull about the Middle of it, *Whatſoever Perſons, and whoſoever they ſhall be which they ſolicite*, are general, from this Generality of the Words they conclude that they extend alſo to Confeſſors, who ſolicite Boys in the Sacramental Confeſſion.

 The Incontinence of the Prieſts gave Occaſion to theſe Edicts and Bulls, *viz.* becauſe, as the Words are in the Bull of *Paul* IV. *Certain Prieſts in the Kingdom of* Spain, *and in the Cities and Dioceſes thereof, having Cure of Souls, or exerciſing ſuch Cure for others, or otherwiſe deputed to bear the Confeſſions of Penitents, have broken out into ſo heinous an Iniquity, as to abuſe the Sacrament of Penance in the very Act of hearing Confeſſions, and thus are not afraid to injure this Sacrament it ſelf, and him who hath appointed it, the Lord God and our Saviour* Jeſus Chriſt, *by enticing and provoking, or trying and procuring to entice and provoke penitent Women to lewd Actions, whilſt they are hearing their Confeſſion.*

Confalv.
p. 185.
 When this Bull was firſt brought into *Spain*, all Perſons were commanded by a publick Edict, ſolemnly publiſhed throughout all the Churches of the Arch-Biſhoprick of *Seville*, that whoſoever knew or had heard of any Monks or Clergymen who had abuſed the Sacrament of Confeſſion to theſe Crimes, or had in any manner acted in this vile Manner at Confeſſion with their Daughter or Daughters, they ſhould diſcover him within thirty Days to the holy Tribunal ; and very grievous Cenſures were annexed to ſuch as ſhould neglect or contemn it. When the Decree was publiſhed, ſo large a Number of Women went to the Palace of the Inquiſitors in the City of *Seville* only, to make their Diſcoveries of theſe moſt wicked Confeſſors, that twenty Secretaries,
with

with as many Inquifitors, were not fufficient to take the Depofitions of the Witneffes. The Lords Inquifitors being thus overwhelmed with the Multitude of Affairs, affigned another thirty Days for the Witneffes ; and when this was not fufficient, they were forced to appoint the fame Number a third and a fourth time. For as to Women of Reputation, and others of higher Condition, every Time was not proper for them to apply to the Inquifitors. On one hand their Confcience forced them to a Difcovery through a fuperftitious Fear of the Cenfures and Excommunication ; and on the other hand, their Regard to their Hufbands, whom they were afraid to offend, by giving them any ill Sufpicion of their Chaftity, kept them at home ; and therefore veiling their Faces after the *Spanifh* Cuftom, they went to the Lords Inquifitors, when, and as privately as they could. Very few, however, with all their Prudence and Craft, could efcape the diligent Obfervation of their Husbands at the Time of Difcovery, and hereby poffeffed their Minds with the deepeft Jealoufy. However, after fo many had been informed againft before the Inquifitors, that holy Tribunal, contrary to all Mens Expectations, put a Stop to the Affair, and commanded all thofe Crimes which were proved by legal Evidence, to be buried in eternal Oblivion.

In the mean while this Crime, according to the Bulls and Edicts of the Popes, ought to be judged and punifhed before the Tribunal of the Inquifitors. Thefe Edicts are generally fo interpreted by the Doctors, as to comprehend §. ς. thofe who folicite by other Perfons, *viz.* when they folicite a Woman to be Procurefs. For the Words of the Bull are, *To be committed either by themfelves, or with others:* As alfo to comprehend all lewd Actions, whether compleat or not. As for Inftance, when a Prieft doth not folicite a Woman, but a Woman her Confeffor, and he not only yields to the Perfuafions of the Woman, *c.* 34. but at her Perfuafion doth any difhonourable Action in the Confeffion § 9. it felf.

It is required however, that the Solicitation be made in the Act of Sa- 30. cramental Confeffion, or immediately before or after it, *i. e.* that no Act intervene between the Solicitation and Confeffion. Hence they do not count it 33. an immediate Act, if a Woman coming to confefs is prevented by her Confeffor, and perfuaded to put off her Confeffion to another Time, and when fhe hath changed her Intention of Confeffing, is folicited by her Confeffor. Such a one however, is comprehended in the Conftitution of *Gregory*, becaufe he folicites under the Pretence of Confeffion. Nor is an Act immediate, if a 32. Woman defifts from her Purpofe of Confeffion after the Confeffion is actually begun, and fays to her Confeffor, fhe will not confefs any more, but talk with him, and the Solicitation immediately follows in a long Difcourfe, provided there be no Pretence of Confeffion, if the Solicitation be made by the Confeffionary ; or if when the Confeffion is ended, the Confeffor follows the Woman to her own Home, and there at any intervening Time folicites her.

'Tis therefore neceffary to conftitute an immediate Act, that it include Confeffion by fome depending Circumftance or other. *Soufa* enumerates fix 36, &c. Cafes, which include Confeffion. " Firft, If a Woman, not intending to fo-
" licite

" licite her Confeffor, but to make a full Confeffion, accufes her felf, by
" difcovering a luftful Mind towards the Confeffor himfelf, or towards any
" other Perfon, and the Confeffor fays, We will talk of this when your Con-
" feffion is ended, and then immediately folicites her. Secondly, If a Con-
" feffor perfuades a Woman to confefs to him with an Intention of foliciting
" her, and immediately after the Confeffion tempts her to difhonourable
" Actions. Thirdly, If immediately after Confeffion he fays to the Peni-
" tent, repeating the Sin confeffed by her, fince you have carnally lain with
" another Perfon, do me alfo the Favour and lay with me. Fourthly, if a
" Confeffor folicites a Boy, after he hath confeffed and abfolved him, by car-
" rying him immediately, after Confeffion, into his Houfe or Chamber, to
" give him a figned Copy of his Confeffion. Fifthly, If a Confeffor enjoins
" Penance to a Woman that hath confeffed to him, *viz.* to be whipped na-
" ked by the Confeffor himfelf, and when the Penance is to be done, he him-
" felf whips her with his own Hand or with a Scourge. Sixthly, If a Confeffor
" perfuades a Woman to fhew her Privy Parts to him, which, in her Confef-
" fion, fhe declared to be affected with a certain Difeafe."

'Tis the fame with thofe, who, tho' they do not folicite in the very Act of
Confeffion, yet do it in the Place appointed to hear Confeffion, according to
the Conftitution of the General Inquifition, before *Paul* V. *July* 10.
1614.

Women thus folicited are admitted to prove this Offence, *viz.* if the Woman be of an approved Life, and the Confeffor be given to the Sins of the
Flefh ; but not if the Woman be fcandalous, and a Whore ; and if they do
not appear voluntarily before the Inquifitors, but are forced by their Confeffors, upon their Refufal to abfolve them, unlefs they difcover the evil Confeffor. Hence it comes to pafs, that the Depofition of feveral Women is not
fufficient for the Conviction of a Confeffor. Thus *Carena* reports, that by
Order of the facred Congregation of the fupream *Roman* Inquifition, a Parifh
Prieft at *Naples* was not accounted as convicted, though feveral Women depofed that he had folicited them, moft of whom he had attempted by Touches
and Signs, and one by Words. He was only tortured by Order of the fame
Congregation, and, confeffing nothing, fufpended for a Year from his Cure.

However, the Depofition of a Woman only is not fufficient Proof for the
Apprehenfion or Torture of the Confeffor, unlefs he himfelf hath a bad Character, becaufe they never proceed to torture, unlefs the Crime be half proved. So that as they teach, fince two Women are not enough to make a full
Proof, one cannot be fufficient for the half Proof.

But if the Crime be half proved, the Confeffor may be tortured, to make
him confefs the Act. If he confeffes it, or is fully convicted of it, and denies
an heretical Intention, he is to be tortured as to his Intention, *viz.* to difcover whether he believed, that it was lawful to abufe the Sacrament of Penance to lafcivious Actions, and to ufe the Sacrament as a Means to obtain
fuch Purpofes.

Carena,
§. 9.

n. 59.

§. 12.

§. 14.

In

In *Spain* thefe foliciting Confeffors are only lightly fufpected, becaufe the §. 15. *Spaniards* confider it rather as proceeding from Luft than an Intention to abufe the Sacrament of Penance. But in *Italy* they are vehemently fufpected ; and therefore whereas in *Spain* they abjure only as lightly fufpected, in *Italy* they abjure as vehemently. So *Carena* gives an Inftance of a certain Con- *n. 75.* feffor in one of the Cities belonging to the Territories of *Cremona*, who abju- red as lighty fufpected for this Crime of Soliciting, but was forced to abjure again as vehemently fufpected at *Cremona*, by Order of the fupream Tribunal of the City of *Rome*.

Befides falutary Penances, fuch as Faftings, Prayers, and the like, fuch §. 18. Confeffors are ufually condemned to the Gallies for five or feven Years, to perpetual Imprifonment ; yea, fometimes at the Pleafure only of the Cardi- nals fupream Inquifitors, they may be delivered over to the fecular Arm, as the Conftitution of *Gregory* XV. plainly directs. They are alfo to be fufpended for ever from hearing Confeffions, to be deprived of their Benefices, Digni- ties, active and paffive Vote, at the Pleafure of the Inquifitors. Such Con- feffors as are Regulars, may alfo be enjoined to be in the laft and loweft Place amongft the Regulars of their Monafteries. Sometimes the Inquifitors muft command, that the Sentence againft a Regular Confeffor fhall be read pub- lickly in the next general Chapter of their Religion, as a Terror and Exam- ple to others.

[Yea fometimes, according to the Heinoufnefs of the Offence, a more grievous Punifhment is inflicted. *John Stock*, Notary of the Apoftolick *Rota*, relates, in a Letter written at *Rome*, *October.* 8, 1564. to *J. Hensberg*, a Di- vine of *Cologn*, a remarkable Inftance of this. *Thefe Wretches of ours are not fo holy as they appear. They walk in the Likenefs of Sheep, but within are ravening Wolves, and their pretended Sanctity is a double Iniquity. They are under the Influence of a ftrong Ambition. The Venetians ordered one of them to be burnt alive, by Command of the Pope. He had been Father Confeffor to fome Nuns in the Dominions of* Venice, *and had got twelve of them with Child, amongft whom the Abbefs and two others had Children in one Year. As he was confeffing them, he agreed with them about the Place, Manner, and Time of lying with them. All were filled with Admiration and Aftonifhment, taking the Man for a perfect Saint, he had fo great a Shew of Sanctity in his very Face.* Epift. ad Belgas, Cent. 1. Ep. 66. p. 345. and Ep. 63. p. 316.]

In *Portugal* alfo the Crime of Sodomy belongs to the Tribunal of the In- *Soufa;* quifition, by the Decree of *Gregory* XIII. *Aug.* 13. *An.* 1574. by which 'tis *Aphor.* granted to the Inquifitor of *Portugal*, to proceed in the Crime of Sodomy, *Inquif.* as in the Crime of Herefy, obferving the fame Manner and Form. By §. 29, 30. the Laws of the Kingdom of *Portugal*, Sodomites are punifhed with Death, and Confifcation of all their Effects, and their Children and Grandchildren become infamous. After the natural Death of a Sodomite, if the Crime §. 31. hath not been proved, they cannot proceed againft him, neither as to the Crime, nor Confifcation of Effects, although the Crime can be proved by legal Witneffes. Becaufe Crimes, which are not particularly excepted, of

which *Sodomy* is one, are extinguifhed by the Death of the Delinquent.
§. 31.   Nor do they proceed againft a dead Sodomite, nor confifcate his Effects, or
l. 2. *c.* 26. although he hath been convicted or confeffed when he was alive. If fuch a
§. 30.   one takes Sanctuary in a Church, he can't be taken out of it.

If we compare thefe Things with the Punifhments of Hereticks, as related
in the fecond Chapter of this Book, it will appear, that the Crime of Sodomy in the Kingdom of *Portugal* is efteemed a much fmaller one than that
of Herefy, becaufe Sodomites enjoy Privileges which are denied to Hereticks.
And yet it may happen, that a truly pious Man, who fears God, and is
moft careful of his eternal Salvation, may be accounted an Heretick by the
Portuguefe Inquifitors, whereas a Sodomite cannot but be the vileft of Men.
But 'tis not at all ftrange, that by the Laws of that Tribunal, *Barabbas*
fhould be releafed, and Chrift crucified.

CHAP. XVIII.

Of one that is infordefcent in Excommunication.

Carena,   A Man is faid to be infordefcent in Excommunication, who, after he
p. 2. *t.* 8.   hath been by Name declared Excommunicate, perfifts in that Ex-
§. 2.   communication for a Year. The Nature of this Crime requires Obftinacy
of Mind, including the Contempt of the Keys. This they infer, when the
excommunicated Perfon hath had Knowledge of the Excommunication, and
taken no Care to obtain Abfolution. For if within a Year he endeavours to
obtain Abfolution, though he fhould not actually receive it ; or if there be
any real Hindrance that prevents his Appearance, he is not judged guilty
of Contempt.

§. 3:   He who thus perfifts in his Excommunication, is accounted as confeffed
and convicted of the Crime for which he was excommunicated ; nor is he to
be any farther heard, unlefs he can demonftrate his Innocence with new
Proofs. If the Crime for which he was excommunicated be of the Number
of thofe, which do, *ipfo jure,* infer Privation, he muft be deprived of his
Benefice for Infordefcence. But if it be fuch a Crime for which the Delinquent is to be deprived of his Benefice, but not *ipfo jure,* in fuch a Cafe he is
alfo to be deprived for Infordefcence.

§. 5. *n.*39.   He who thus perfifts in Excommunication, is violently fufpected of Herefy.
For if there be only a light Sufpicion of Herefy againft any Perfon, and if
when cited he is obftinate, the Sufpicion then begins to be vehement. If
through Contumacy he continues in Excommunication for a Year, the vehement Prefumption becomes violent, and thus he may be taken for an Heretick, and punifhed as fuch. Becaufe, from thus perfifting, there arifes a
Prefumption of the Law, and *de jure,* by which the Crime of Herefy is fufficiently proved.   But

But that such a one may be condemned as an Heretick, he must not fail to *n.* 21. be cited, in order to purge himself from the Suspicion of Heresy, because he continued for a Year in Excommunication.

If such an excommunicated Person appears when the Year is elapsed, and *n.* 23. desires to prove his Innocence, before he is declared an Heretick, he must *24.* be admitted to Trial. Yea, as some affirm, he must be heard even after he is declared an Heretick, and his Effigies burnt.

If when he appears, and doth not prove any legal Impediment, but only *§* 8. his Innocence as to the Heresy for Suspicion of which he was cited, altho' he is to be absolved from the Heresy, yet he is to be tortured to discover his Intention, upon account of a vehement Suspicion of his Contempt of the Keys of the Church, and must abjure as one vehemently suspected. If neither a legal Impediment nor his Innocence appear, he is to be dealt with as one vehemently suspected of Heresy, and of the Contempt of the Keys.

If he proves nothing, and is impenitent, or relapsed, he is to be left to the secular Court. If he is penitent he must abjure, according to some, as vehemently suspected; according to others, formally. Besides, wholesome Penances are to be enjoined him, and he may be condemned, according to the Nature of his Crime, to more grievous Punishments, and especially pecuniary ones.

CHAP. XIX.

Of BLASPHEMERS.

THere are two Sorts of Blasphemers. Some who do not utter heretical *Eymer.* Blasphemies, who do not belong to our History; and others who *p.* 2. *Q.* 41. throw out Blasphemies that are heretical, and who are therefore subject to the Judgment of the Inquisitors. *J. Royas* argues concerning them in this man-*Royas,* ner. " 'Tis very often a Matter of Doubt in the Court of the Inquisition, *p.* 2. " what Blasphemies may be said to be heretical, to make the Cognisance of *affert.* 12. " them belong to the Inquisitors. But, according to the common Custom, *§.* 170. " and agreeable to Law and Reason, these Words are heretical, *I deny God*, " *I do not believe in God.* In *Spanish, Discreo de Dios, reniego de Dios, o reniego* " *de la fe, o de la cruz, o Crisma a que teng o en la trente, o reniego de la pu* " *ridad de nuestra senora*, i. e. *I do not believe in God, I deny God, or I deny* " *the Faith, or the Cross, or the Chrism, which I have received in my Forehead,* " *or I deny the Virginity of our Lady.* These Words are said to be heretical " Blasphemies, and the Inquisitors have Cognisance of them, because they " have an Infidel Signification, and Denial of the Faith, and are directly " opposed to a Confession of the Faith. But other Blasphemies, *viz. Pese a*

" *Dios,*

" *Dios, por vida de Dios, voto a Dios, malgrado aya Dios, o despecho de Dios,*
" and the like, *i. e. let it trouble God, by the Life of God, I vow to God, God's*
" *Curse on you,* or *God spite you,* are not heretical, because not opposed to a
" Confession of the Faith, although they are absolutely Blasphemies. The

Carena,
p. 2. t. 7.
§. 8.

" Punishment of these belongs to the ordinary Judges." In *Italy* also 'tis
" not reckoned Blasphemy : if any one says, *Al corpo di Dio, o dira vel pu-*
" *tana di Dio becco* ; *vel al dispetto di Christophero,* or *putana della virgine Gio-*
" *vanna*; i. e. *Body of God,* or *he will say,* &c. *or in spite of St.* Christopher ;
or the Whore of the Virgin Joan.

'Tis disputed amongst the Doctors whether this be Blasphemy, *Al dispetto,
che non vo dir di dio,* or, *putana, che no vo dir della V. M. In spite, not meaning*
God ; *or Whore, not meaning the Virgin* Mary ; which some deny, and
others affirm. But these are accounted heretical Blasphemies : *Dio partesano,*
& putana della Virgine, i. e. *The Whore of the Virgin,* altho' the Word
Mary is not pronounced ; as is also this ; *Dio becco diavolo,* if pronounced
by any one who is accustomed to utter heinous Blasphemies against God.

§. 173.

According to *Royas,* " Heretical Blasphemy, though spoken conditional-
" ly, is to be punished by the Inquisitors of the Faith ; as for Instance,
" *I do not believe in God unless I will strike you.* Because this conditional
" Blasphemy contains in it a pure affirmative Impliciteness, *viz.* that if he
" could not kill him without not believing in God, he was prepared wil-

§. 179.

" lingly to do so. They also proceed very severely against an execrable
" Custom that hath crept into the Kingdoms of *Arragon* and *Valencia, viz.*
" of swearing by the Members of God, which is greatly blasphemous ; and
" by the Members of Christ, which is great Irreverence, and from both
" these there arises great Suspicion of Heresy." To these may be added
that execrable Species of Blasphemy, related by *Arnold Albertinus,* in his
Book *de Agnos. Assert. hæret. Qu.* 6. §. 21.

These Blasphemies, according to the Quality of the Words and Persons,
and the Circumstances of Times and Places, are esteemed more or less wicked,
and horrible. *Pegna* " thinks those are to be reckoned amongst the greatest,
" which are uttered against the most holy *Mary,* Virgin Mother of God.
" And altho' Blasphemers regularly think differen ly in their Mind from
" what they say, yet they belong to the Judgment of the Inquisitors, be-
" cause by blaspheming they are thought to put on the Person of one who
" thinks agreeable to what he himself had spoken ; and since by the exter-
" nal Act they give some Token of Infidelity, therefore certain Blasphe-
" mies are subject to the Jurisdiction of the Judges of the Faith, that they
" may understand, whether Blasphemers do really think as they speak."

Heretical Blasphemers are punished in this Manner by the Inquisitors. If
the Blasphemy be very heinous, and the Blasphemer a mean Person, he is
made to wear an infamous Mitre, hath his Tongue tied, and pinched with an
Iron or Wooden Gag, is carried forth as a publick Spectacle without his
Cloak, whipt with Scourges, and banished. But if he be a Person of better
Condition, or Noble, he is brought forth without the Mitre, thrust for a
Time

Time into a Monaſtery, and puniſhed with a Fine. In ſmaller Blaſphemies they are dealt with more gently at the Pleaſure of the Inquiſitors, *viz.* the Blaſphemer is condemned to ſtand, during divine Service, upon ſome Holyday or other, with his Head naked, without his Cloak, and Shoes, his Feet naked, a Cord tied round him, and holding a burning Wax-Taper in his Hands. Sometimes alſo they ſqueeze his Tongue with a Piece of Wood. After divine Service is over his Sentence is read, by which he is enjoined Faſtings and a Fine.

This Puniſhment however doth not take place as to a Clergyman, as *Ca-* p. 2. t. 7. *rena* obſerves. For if a Clergyman was to appear without his Shoes, and §. 17. with an Halter about his Neck, and thus ſtand at the Gates of the Church n. 88. before the People, the Clerical Order, and the Miniſtry of the Clergy would ſuffer Diſgrace, and it would become the Wonder and evil Example to the Laity, if the blaſpheming Clergy were thus expoſed. He adds, that he never ſaw this Puniſhment inflicted by this Tribunal on noble Perſons, who, altho' they are not to be more mildly puniſhed for their Nobility, yet may be excuſed from ſuch Puniſhments which do of themſelves render Perſons infamous, and receive other Puniſhments in the room of them.

And becauſe ſuch who accuſtom themſelves to blaſpheme, though they do it in Paſſion, are vehemently ſuſpected of Hereſy, they are forced to abjure as thus ſuſpected. Thus *Diana* relates, that in the Inquiſition in *Sicily*, two Reſol mo- Blaſphemers were made publickly to abjure, as vehemently ſuſpected, Dec. ral. Par. 4. 16. 1633. in the Preſence of the Judge himſelf. But in ſmaller Blaſphe- tract. 7. mies, becauſe they are but lightly ſuſpected, they only abjure as ſuch. reſol. 8.

But in theſe Caſes the Inquiſitors moſtly act according to their own Pleaſure, who have an ample Power of judging according to the Nature and Heinouſneſs of the Crimes. *Gonſalvius* tells us of a certain Perſon who had p. 195. a Quarrel with a Clergyman of *Ecya*, a City in *Spain*, who accidently ſaid, in the Hearing of others, that he could not believe that God would come down into the Hands of ſo profligate an Adulterer. The Vicar of the Ordinary fined him for the Speech. But the Clergyman not contented with this Revenge, afterwards accuſed him of Blaſphemy at the Tribunal of the Inquiſitors at *Seville*. Nor did the Fine to which he was before condemned by the Ordinary, prevent his being taken up by Command of the Inquiſitors, impriſoned for a whole Year, brought out in Triumph without Cloak or Hat, carrying a Wax-Candle in his Hand, his Tongue gagged with a wooden Gag, thus to puniſh his Blaſphemy ; and being forced to abjure as lightly ſuſpected, he was fined a ſecond time.

CHAP.

CHAP. XX.

Of DIVINERS, FORTUNE-TELLERS, *and* ASTROLOGERS.

Eymer.
p L. qu 42.
Com. 67.

FOrtune-Tellers and Diviners are diftinguifhed. For there are fome who act merely by the Art of Divination, fuch as tell Fortunes, by looking into the Palms of the Hand, and judiciary Aftrologers. Others who exercife Divination by Lots, with the Addition of fome heretical Word or Fact: As if any one in telling Fortunes about Sweethearts fhould deny God and the Sacraments of the Church; or fhould mingle any of the Sacraments of the Church with his Fortune-telling, or thofe Things which the Divines call Sacramental; as if he fhould baptize Images, rebaptize a Child, or only anoint him with holy Oil, or incenfe the Head of a Perfon dead, or do any of the like Things to divine future Things, or ufe a Candle and holy Water to difcover ftolen Goods. All thefe Things render the Doer fufpected; for unlefs he had believed fuch Sacraments or Sacramentals had fome Virtue to effect fuch evil Operations, he would not have ufed them for this Purpofe. So that the Inquifitors take diligent Care to interrogate them concerning their Belief, and if they deny the Intention they are tortured; and if they do not confefs, they may be made to abjure as vehemently fufpected. They may alfo be punifhed with Excommunication, Sufpenfion of Dignities, Whipping, Banifhment, Imprifonment in Monafteries, and other Punifhments, according to the Quality of the Perfons. They may alfo be publickly brought forth wearing the infamous Mitre, or be difgracefully tied to a Ladder near the Gates of the Church, and be banifhed from the Diocefe.

Carens.
p. 2.*s.* 12.
§. 12.

As to Judiciary Aftrologers, their Art is generally condemned as fuperftitious. But there is one Species of it, which the Doctors pronounce erroneous and heretical, *viz.* that which profeffes to foretel the Myfteries of our Faith by the Stars. In like manner they are condemned as rafh Aftrologers, who pretend they are able to foretel by the Stars certain Things concerning the State of the Church, Life or Death, or the Affumption of the chief Pontiff. Pope *Urban* VIII. by a Conftitution, beginning, *Infcrutabilis*, publifhed *Ap.* 1. 1631. hath appointed, that Judiciary Aftrologers, who make Judgments concerning the State of the Chriftian Republick, or Apoftolick See, or the Life of the *Roman* Pontiff, or his Kindred, or who, when made, keep them in their own Poffeffion, or fhew them to others, or fpeak of them by Words, befides the Punifhment of Excommunication which they fhall, *ipfo jure*, incur, fhall be punifhed with Death as guilty of High-Treafon, Confifcation of Effects, and that if they are of the Clergy, they fhall be punifhed with Deprivation of their Benefices and Offices.

We have alfo Inftances of very grievous Punifhments inflicted on thefe judiciary Aftrologers, one of which may be feen in *Bzovius*, under the Year 1327. *Bzovius* his Words are, " *Francis Afculanus* was thrown into Jayl at *Florence*,
" and

" and burnt, being by Name convicted of Blafphemies, Herefy and judici-
" ary Aftrology, as alfo of other damned Arts, and was condemned by the
" Inquifitors of the Faith." After this he fubjoins a Catalogue of the
Crimes objected to him, from which it appears that moft of them were taken
from Judicial Aftrology.

***

CHAP. XXI.

Of WITCHES.

WITH thefe Fortune-Tellers are properly joined Witches or Hags,
which in *Italy* they commonly call *Strigiæ*, from their Refemblance to
the Scritch-Owl, a Night and troublefome Bird, becaufe they are reported
to deal in their Witchcraft principally at Night, and to fuck the Blood of
Infants. Others call them Sorcereffes, Charmers, and the like. They are Bernard.
faid to have been a Sect of People, principally Women, who arofe in *Italy* in *Comenſis de*
the Year 1400. They gather together in certain Places near Towns and *Strigiis.*
Villages, at particular Times, and efpecially the Night preceding *Friday*,
when the Devil appears to them in a vifible human Shape. When they enter into this Gang, they firft, and before all Things, do, by the Devil's
Command, deny their holy Faith and Baptifm, the Lord God, and the
bleffed Virgin *Mary*, and after this trample under their Feet on the Ground,
a Crofs made by one of the Witches. After this they promife Allegiance between the Hands of the Devil, taking him for their Lord, and promife Obedience to him in all Things. As a Token of all this, they put their left Hand
behind their Back, and touch the Devil's Hand, and offer him fomewhat as
a Mark of their Subjection. From henceforth they are faid to believe the Devil to be their true Lord and God; and as often as they go to their nightly
Affemblies, which they call the Play of good Fellowfhip, they worfhip the
Devil appearing in human Shape, and by bowing their Head profoundly
down, adore him as their true God. 'Tis reported of them, that they go
to this Affembly or Play, truly and corporally, when awake and in their
perfect Senfes: If the Place be near they go on Foot; if diftant, they are
carried by the Devil through the Air.

Many Authors have written largely of thefe Witches or Hags, *James Sprez-
ger, Sylvefter de Prierio, Bartholomew Spineus*, and others, who warmly contend that they are all corporally carried to thefe Night-Plays or Dances.
Francis Ponzinibius is the only one amongft the Papifts of former Ages, who
oppofes their common Opinion, and affirms that they are not corporally carried, but only deluded by Dreams and Phantafms.

They who contend for their being carried corporally, ufe thefe Arguments:
Becaufe all thefe Perfons, whether Men or Women, confefs as with one Mouth
and

and Tongue, that they every where obferve uniformly the fame Manner in
every Thing, in the Denial of their Faith, Baptifm, God, the bleffed Virgin, trampling on the Crofs, and Promife of Obedience, by turning the left
Hand behind their Back, and that this appears by the Confeffions of all of
them made before the Inquifitors, every where throughout _Italy_, and by the
written Proceffes formed againft them. That this Conformity argues they
are not deluded by Dreams, becaufe thefe would vary as to Time and Place,
according to the Variety of Caufes, and the Quality of Perfons.

They add, That thefe Perfons have been feen and known by feveral Ca-
tholick People, as they have been going to, or returning from thefe Affem-
blies. Yea, that fome who have been carried by the Devil to fome diftant
Place, have, God fo ordering it, been let down, and then found themfelves
at a great Diftance from their own Country. And farther, when thefe
Witches confefs before the Inquifitors, and are converted to the Bofom of the
Church, abjuring their Herefy and Apoftacy, they never after return to their
Play; which could not be, if thefe Things were prefented to them only in
Dreams or Imaginations, becaufe Dreams are not in the Power of Men. To
which they add as a Conclufion, That many of thefe Perfons have for many
Years paft been delivered over by the Inquifitors of heretical Pravity to the
fecular Arm, and burnt; which would never have been done, nor fuffered
by the Popes, unlefs thefe Things did really happen, and they were found to
be in this Herefy and Apoftacy.

And although it may fometimes happen that thefe Things may appear to
them only in Dreams and Fancy, and that they are not really carried to this
Play, being found at Home at the fame time they thought themfelves prefent at it, they think it doth not at all follow from hence, that they are never
corporally carried through the Air. And indeed although they never fhould
have been fo carried, yet becaufe after they have been thus deluded by
Dreams, they do not only firmly believe that they did thefe Things when
they are awake, and in their Senfes, but do confirm and approve them, and
ftrongly believe that they have denied the Catholick Faith, adored the Devil as God, and do take him for their God, and that by doing fo, they do not
fin, but do well, and perfevere in all thefe Things before the Inquifitors,
they therefore think them truly Hereticks, Idolaters and Apoftates; becaufe
thofe who believe thefe Things do depart from the Faith.

I have no Inclination to fpend any great Time or Labour in examining and
refuting thefe Things, and enquiring what Truth there is in fuch Accounts,
and whether fome Parts of them may not be admitted as true, whilft others
ought to be rejected as fabulous; nor how far credulous, fearful and fuperftitious Perfons may be deluded by vain Imaginations and Dreams, and what
may be truly performed by Devils. Others have done this abundantly, and
the doing it is foreign to my Hiftory. And therefore I refer my Reader to
Theol. l. 3. _Simon Epifcopius_, who hath very learnedly and folidly treated of this Matter.
§. 5 c 1.
f. 143, &c. I fhall only fay in a few Words, that this Contract with the Devil, which is
afcribed to the Witches, is fo horrible, that one would think it could never

enter

enter into the Mind of any Perſon whatſoever. Moſt of the Things they are ſaid to do, deſerve no Belief, becauſe they don't ſeem poſſible to be done. Their Confeſſions are often extorted by the Violence of their Torture, and conceived in ſuch Words, that any conſiderate Perſon may ſee they are formed by the Inquiſitors themſelves, *viz.* to encreaſe the Honour of the bleſſed *Mary*, and of the Sacraments, as though the Devil had a particular Spight to the Worſhip of them.' And this is ſo evident and manifeſt, that many of the Papiſts themſelves are perſuaded, that moſt of thoſe are innocent, whom, on this Account, they have ſeen condemned to the Fire. Yea, a certain Popiſh Divine publiſhed an entire Book, entitled, *Cautionis criminalis*, in which he tells us that many innocent Perſons were burnt ; and this he affirms, not only from the Reports of others, but ſays that he accompanied ſeveral Women who were lead to Death, of whoſe Innocence no one now makes any doubt.

But to diſmiſs this Argument, I will now ſhew by what Method the Tribunal of the Inquiſition proceeds againſt them.

They prove that it belongs to the Inquiſitors of heretical Pravity to take Cognizance of the Sect of Witches, to proceed againſt them, and puniſh them as other Hereticks, becauſe they are themſelves Hereticks, Idolaters and Apoſtates. 'Tis alſo appointed by many Sanctions of the *Roman* Pontiffs, and particularly by that of *Innocent* VIII. writing to the Inquiſitors of *Germany.* Innocent, *Biſhop, Servant of the Servants of God, for the future Remembrance of the Thing. As we deſire, with our ſtrongeſt Affection, according to the Duty and Care of our Paſtoral Office, that the Catholick Faith may every where encreaſe and flouriſh, eſpecially in our Times, and that all heretical Pravity may be driven away far from the Borders of the Faithful, we willingly declare, and grant a new thoſe Things, by which this our pious Deſire may obtain its wiſhed for Effect ; that all Errors being extirpated by the Miniſtry of our Operation, as by the weeding Hook of a careful Workman, a Zeal and Obſervance of the ſame Faith may be more ſtrongly impreſſed on the Hearts of the Faithful. We have indeed lately heard, to our great Grief, that in ſome Parts of* Upper Germany, *as alſo in the Provinces, Cities, Places and Dioceſes of* Mayence, Cologne, Treves, Saltzburg, *and* Bremen, *many Perſons of both Sexes, unmindful of their own Salvation, and deviating from the Catholick Faith, abuſe themſelves with he and ſhe Devils, and by their Incantations, Charms, and Conjurations, and by other horrid Superſtitions, Sorceries, and Exceſſes, Crimes and Offences, do cauſe, and procure to periſh, blaſt, and be deſtroyed, the Conceptions of Women, the young ones of Animals, the Fruits of the Earth, the Grapes of Vineyards, and Fruits of Trees ; moreover, Men, Women, Beaſts, Cattle, Sheep, and other Animals of divers Sorts, as alſo Vineyards, Orchards, Meadows, Paſtures, Grain, Corn, and other Pulſe of the Earth, and do affect and torture Men, Women, Beaſts, Cattle, Sheep, with cruel Pains and Torments, inwardly and outwardly, and do hinder the ſaid Men from begetting Children, and the Women from conceiving them ; Husbands from rendring due Benevolence to their Wives ; and Wives from performing conjugal Actions towards their Husbands ; and farther, do with an impious Mouth deny the Faith it ſelf, which*

Pegna, ad lib. de Strig. Ber. Comenſis.

they took on them when they received holy Baptism, and at the Instigation of the Enemy of Mankind, are not afraid to commit and perpetrate many other Enormities, Excesses and Crimes, to the Hazard of their own Souls, the Offence of the divine Majesty, and to the evil Example and Scandal of many. And a little after, *We therefore, as in Duty bound, being compelled hereto by our Zeal for the Faith, being willing, by seasonable Remedies, to provide against and remove all Impediments, by which the Execution of the Office of the Inquisitors may be in any manner retarded, and that the Infection of heretical Pravity, and other such like Excesses, may not spread their Poison to the Destruction of other Innocents, and that the Provinces, Cities, Dioceses, and Countries, and other the aforesaid Places, in the Parts of Upper Germany, may not want the necessary Office of the Inquisition, do by the Tenor of these present, by our Apostolick Authority appoint, &c. that it shall be lawful for the said Inquisitors to execute the Office of such Inquisition in these Cases, and that they ought to be admitted to correct, imprison and punish the aforesaid Persons concerning the aforesaid Excesses and Crimes, in all and every Thing, as though such Provinces, Cities, Dioceses, Countries, and Places, Persons, and Excesses, were by Name, and specifically expressed in these Letters.*

These Letters were confirmed as to the greater Part of them, and sent to Master *George de Casali,* here*t*ofore Inquisitor at *Cremona,* by *Julius* II. and were afterwards extended to all the Inquisitors of the Congregation of *Lombardy,* of the Order of Predican s, by these Letters of *Alexander* VI.

Alexander, Pope, to our beloved Son Angelus de Verona, *of the Order of Predicants, Doctor of Divinity, Inquisitor of heretical Pravity in the Province of* Lombardy, *and to his Successors. Beloved Son, Health and Apostolical Benediction.*

Having received Advice that divers Persons of both Sexes, in the Province of Lombardy, *make use of divers Incantations and diabolical Superstitions, and by their Witchcrafts and numerous Observations perpetrate many horrid Crimes, destroy Men, Cattle and Fields, bring in divers Errors, and cause many Scandals to arise. We have decreed, according to the Ministry of the pastoral Office, committed to us from on high, to check such Wickednesses, and to prevent, as far as with the Help of God we can, the aforesaid Scandals and Errors, for this Reason give in Charge, and command you, as also your Successors, to be appointed throughout* Lombardy, *concerning whom in these and other Things, we have full Confidence in the Lord, that you of your selves, associating however such worthy Persons as you shall think fit to chose, shall diligently make Inquisition against the said Persons of both Sexes, and punish and check them according to Justice. And that you may the better execute this Commission, we grant you full and entire Power against them, all Apostolick Constitutions and Ordinations, as also Grants and ordinary Concessions made possibly for a time, and all other Things whatsoever to the contrary notwithstanding.*

Although it be more safe and decent in Processes against Witches for the Inquisitors to proceed, as in Causes of Hereticks, and to form their Processes with the Assistance of the Diocesans, according to the Disposition of the Law, *Cap.* per hoc. *de hæret. lib.* 6. Extrav. ex eo. *de hæret. Clement.* I. *de hæret.* yet neverthelefs 'tis manifest from these Constitutions, that they may,

if

if they will, proceed by themfelves, and that what they do or decree when they proceed alone, either in condemning or abfolving, is valid.

Here 'tis enquired, whether Witches, if they have confeffed the Murthers of Children or Men, or any other Crimes to which the Punifhment of Death is annexed by the Civil Laws, may be delivered over to the fecular Court by the Inquifitors and other Judges, although they repent? Some think, that notwithftanding their Repentance, they ought not to be perpetually impri-foned as other Hereticks, but put to Death. But the greater Number are of Opinion, that fuch of them who are willing with a pure Heart to return to the Bofom of the Church, are to be received. Becaufe the Caufe of Herefy hath nothing to do with murthering Children, or other Crimes committed by Witches, the Cognifance of which doth not at all belong to the Inquifitors. And therefore they believe the Judges of the Faith would do unjuftly, if they fhould deny to thefe Wretches, when willing to repent, the Benefit of Mercy and Abfolution.

But if thefe Witches are firft taken up by the fecular Judges for the Mur-ther of Infants, or any other fecular Crime, and when they are interrogated confefs Herefy, or any Thing that favours of Herefy, of which the fecular Judges have no Cognifance, and, upon account of this Confeffion, are deli-vered over to the Inquifitors, in this Cafe when the Judgment concerning Herefy is finifhed, they teach that the Witch muft be turned back to the fe-cular Judge, that he may finifh the Procefs begun for other Crimes by the Civil Laws. For in fuch a Cafe the Perfon is not fo properly faid to be left to the fecular Court, as to be reftored to his former Judge, who upon account of the fecular Crime, hath legal Jurifdiction over fuch Witch. And this Obfer-vation is, as they fay, according to the Conftitution of *Pius* V. whofe Words are thefe. *Moreover, let them, without any Delay, tranfmit all Perfons whatfoever im-prifoned for any Offences, or by any Means whatfoever accufed or denounced of any hei-nous Crimes, before the faid Office of the Inquifition, fufpending the Cognifance of all other inferior Crimes, to the faid Cardinals and Prifons of the Inquifition, and there let them be kept till the full Cognifance and Difpatch of the Crime of Herefy, and afterwards let them be fent back to the faid Officials to expedite the Affair of their other Crimes.*

Yea farther, the Ecclefiaftical Judges, if they have any legal Evidence, that one of thefe Witches, imprifoned by the fecular Judge, is an Heretick, or fufpected of Herefy, may compel the fecular Magiftrate to deliver her over to them to be judged for the Caufe of Herefy, and alfo to exhibit the Proceffes and any other Writings, in order to their Underftanding, whether there be any Thing contained in them relating to the Faith, and which may help the Judgment of the Inquifitors. If the Magiftrate refufes it, they may compel him to all this by the Ecclefiaftical Cenfure, *viz.* Excommunication, Sufpenfion and Interdict. Whereas the fecular Magiftrate cannot compel the Judge of the Faith to deliver up to him Criminals of either Sex, who have committed fecular Offences, in order to punifh them according to the Civil Laws, becaufe he hath no Jurifdiction over the Ecclefiaftical Judge. But when the Ecclefiaftical Judge hath punifhed Offenders in his Tribunal,

then

then the secular Judge may punish the same Persons for Crimes cognisable in his Court.

They say there are two Ways of discovering these Witches. The first is the Confession, and Accusation of their Companions. For as these Women know one another when they are met at their Assemblies, they are able to detect each other. But that such Accusations may gain Credit, 'tis necessary that several of them separately, each making a Confession without the other's Knowledge, do agree in the several Circumstances of the Accusation, *viz.* as to the same Person, Time and Place, and that they do. severally affirm the same Th ng before the Person accused, one after the other separately, without the other's knowing of it. And yet at the same time they confess themselves, that this sort of Proof is very uncertain, because it may happen that the Devil may sometimes assume another Person's Shape, and appear in these Assemblies under that Form, in order to render her infamous, though at the same time she may be entirely innocent, and far from being concerned in such a Crime. For which reason they make use of another Way, *viz.* Conjectures and Presumptions to detect and discover them. And of these they have several, *viz.* their bewitching Children, causing Distempers and other Harms to Men and Women, to Cattle, and the Fruits of the Earth, the Grapes of Vineyards, and the Fruits of Trees. When therefore skilful Physicians by any Conjectures or Circumstances judge, that a Damage of this sort doth not happen from any natural Defect, nor from any natural intrinsick Cause, but from something external, and yet not from any venemous Infection ; or when they see any Disease to be incurable, so that the sick Person cannot be relieved by any Medicines or Remedies, but rather grows every Day worse and worse, this they think is a sufficient Proof that 'tis the Effect of Witchcraft. In like manner, when any Men or Women, who are ignorant of the Art of Physick, prevent the Effects of such Witchcrafts, and heal D.seases, they say 'tis a Sign that these Things are done by the Co-operation of the Devil.

To this they add another Sign, which is greatly uncertain. When, say they, any Person, whether in a Quarrel or not, threatens another, and says, Because you have done to me so and so, I will do something to you that shall make you know whether you have done well by me or not ; or I will make you repent it ; or you shall see the ill Effects of it, or any Thing to the like Purpose. If the Thing comes to pass, 'tis a Sign that such an Effect is produced by the Assistance of the Devil, especially if it can't be known how such an Effect could otherwise follow. And therefore when such Threatnings are attended with their Effects, 'tis a very great Presumption and Reason to conclude, that the Person who utters such Threatnings is a Witch, and dedicated. to the Devil by a Denial of the Faith. This is a sufficient Proof to proceed to Torture.

But certainly if such Signs be sufficient to put Persons to the Torture, what Innocence can be safe ? 'Tis easy to extort a Confession from such who are most innocent, by the Cruelty of these Tortures, with which they punish without End or Measure, those whom they suspect, as the very Plagues of

human

human Nature, even of Crimes they have never thought of, and of which they have never heard so much as the Description. And therefore 'tis not to be wondered at, that the Inquisitors, within the Space of 150 Years, should have burnt 30000 Witches, as *Ludovicus a Paramo* says they have ; adding : *De Orig.* " The Inquisitors have most severely prosecuted these most outragious Furies, *Inq. l. 2.* " who have thrown off all Humanity, especially in the Kingdom of *Sicily,* *t. 3. c. 4.* " where, when I my self, a few Years past, executed the Office of Inquisi-*p. 296.* " tor, many of this kind of Apostate Witches were discovered and pu-" nished."

But as by this Method of Proceeding many notorious and manifest Acts of Injustice were commited, a certain Instruction was put into the Hands of the Inquisitors in *Italy,* which *Carena* hath published, in which 'tis affirmed : " That it hath for a long time been observed in the Congregation of the " Universal Inquisition at *Rome,* that scarce any Process hath been ever " found to be rightly and juridically formed ; that it hath been generally " found necessary to censure most of the Judges, and oftentimes to punish " them for illegal Vexations, Inquisitions, Imprisonments, as also for several " evil and impertinent Methods used in forming Processes, interrogating " Criminals, inflicting excessive Tortures ; insomuch that sometimes unjust " and unrighteous Sentences have been pronounced, even of Death, or de-" livering Persons over to the secular Arm. And it hath been found in " Fact, that many Judges have been too easy and ready to believe a Wo-" man to be a Witch for a light Proof, or rather none at all, upon which " Account have omitted nothing, no not unlawful Methods, to extort " such a Confession from these Women, notwithstanding there have been so " many Improbabilities, Differences and Contrarieties, that one would think " there could be little or no Debate about the Matter."

This *Carena* confirms by several Instances. In the City of *Logronno* in *Spain,* many Persons were condemned for Witchcraft, and yet afterwards 'twas discovered that there were many Deceits in the Affair of their Condemnation, upon which Account the Effects of the condemned Persons were not confiscated, nor their Sentences fixed upon the Churches, but they were reconciled, and moreover declared capable of any Office of the Inquisition: He gives another Instance of four Women, accused before the Ordinary by some others who had been condemned to Death, and hanged, who appealed to the Royal Council, to whom the Presumptions against them appeared so very slight, that upon finding Sureties they were dismissed, and never called into Question afterwards. He reports in the same Place the Words of *Ferrerius,* who calls those Judges, *Assassines, Judges that have no Fear of God, and less Love for Truth.* For this Reason certain Rules are prescribed to the Inquisitors, that they may proceed in this Affair with more Caution.

And first, before they begin the Process, there must be some Certainty as to the Reality of the Crime, whether the Offence be of that sort which leaves the proper Traces behind it. For it hath been observed, that some Judges have ordered certain Women to be punished with Death, for confessing

feffing a Crime which had never been committed. Thus *Ferrerius* reports, that a Woman confeffed, that in the Night fhe took a certain Infant from the Breafts of its Mother, and carried it into the Affembly of the Witches, where it was killed by her and her Companions. But upon examining the Mother of the Infant, fhe declared that no fuch Accident had ever happened to it. Now the Reality of the Offence is proved by the Judgment of skilful Phyficians, if they do clearly determine that the Difeafe is not natural, but poffibly and probably a Witchcraft, and there be legal Proofs that the Witchcraft is committed by the Woman. After this the Inquifitor may proceed to Imprifonment, firft taking Advice of the Counfellors. After Imprifonment he fearches her Houfe with a Notary, to fee what Things they can find in the Coffers and Beds, both for the Affiftance of the Perfon inqui-fited, as whether there be Crowns*, Divine Services, Books of Devotion and the like; and for the Affiftance alfo of the Fifcal; as whether there be any Images of Wax run through with Needles, Powders, Ointments, Papers with Croffes, Books containing Witchcrafts, Bones under Ground, Poyfons, Bones of dead Perfons, and all extraordinary Things found under the Threfhold, and in the Beds. This Search muft be made by the Minifters of the holy Office, in the Prefence of the Notary before the Inquifitor. None of the Family of the Perfon accufed of Witchcraft muft be prefent. And here they advife that all unufual Things found in Beds are not to be looked on as a Token of Witchcraft; for fome fuch Things may naturally happen; and therefore fuch Things can caufe but a very light Sufpicion, unlefs what they find in the faid Places are in themfelves, and, according to the common Ufe of Witches, fit to perform magical Operations. As for Inftance, if half of an human Skull is found in the Bed or on the Pillow of the Witch, and another half exactly anfwering to the former, is found in her Cheft, a very confiderable Sufpicion would from hence arife againft fuch Perfon, as the prudent Judge fhall determine, and certainly greater than if no fuch half Skull had been found at all. Thefe and other Things, too tedious to mention, the Inqufitor is commanded to take prudent Notice of, leaft he fhould proceed againft any Perfon as a Witch, rafhly, and without juft Caufe.

C H A P. XXII.

Of JEWS, *and fuch as return to* Jewifh *Rites.*

THE Nation of the *Jews*, after the Deftruction of the City and Temple of *Jerufalem*, were brought into miferable Bondage and Captivity, and difperfed throughout the whole World. But being impatient of their

* Confecrated Bread made like a Crown, or in a round Form.

Miferies,

Miseries, they have often taken up Arms, and endeavoured to assert their Liberties. But having been subdued by most grievous Slaughters, they have at length laid down their Fierceness, and are forced to bear the Yoke. The Christians, partly through Fear of the Rage of the *Jews*, and partly through an intemperate Zeal for Christianity, have endeavoured either wholly to destroy by various Miseries this disperfed People, or to tire them out by the Grievousness and Length of their Miseries, and thus to compel them to profess the Christian Faith. Upon this account various Edicts have at different Times proceeded against the *Jews*. Some have proscribed them in the Countries where they have lived, others have deprived them of their Liberties, and reduced them to Slavery ; others have stripped them of those Advantages and Privileges which their other Subjects have enjoyed, that by these Means they might at length be wholly extinguished, or wearied out by the Miseries they endured for their *Judaism*, renounce it, and embrace the Christian Religion. Very severe Edicts have been made against them, especially in *Spain*, where a very large Number of them dwelt, and were thought to endanger the Safety of the Kingdom.

In the Sixth Council of *Toledo* this Decree was published against the *Jews*. Simanc.*tit.* *We the holy Council, with the Consent of the most Christian Prince, and his No-*35. §. 9. *bles, and most Illustrious Persons, publish this Sentence, pleasing to God, that who-soever shall enjoy the Kingdom for Time to come, shall not ascend the Royal Throne, before he hath promised upon the holy Sacraments, that he will suffer no Persons but Catholicks to dwell in his Kingdom. And if any one, after his Accession to the King-dom, shall rashly violate this Promise, let him be* Anathema Maranatha *before the eternal God, and become Fewel for the everlasting Fire, and also all such who agree with him,* Can. 3. Baronius, under the Year 638, says this was principally decreed out of Hatred to the *Jews*, and bestows great Praises on it, and from hence concludes, *'Tis not without Reason that the Kings of* Spain *have had the Title of Catholick bestowed on them, being worthy of so high a Title, because they not only swear that they will be Catholick themselves, but that they will not suffer any one that is not a Catholick to dwell in their large Dominions.* But notwithstanding this Decree, a great many *Jews* remained in *Spain*, and soon encreased to such a Number, that they began to appear formidable to the Kings, and they were accused, whether right or wrong, of a Design to raise a Rebellion. Upon which account another Edict was made against them in the Seventeenth Council of *Toledo*, Can. 8. *Since the Perfidiousness of the* Jews *hath not only defiled the Coat of sacred Christian Baptism which they have received, but also attempted to conspire against the King and Kingdom ; let them be deprived of all their Effects, and those perfidious Wretches themselves, their Wives and Chil-dren, and the rest of their Posterity, throughout all the Provinces of* Spain, *be sub-ject to perpetual Slavery, and remain every where dispersed ; and let such who have made Slaves of them, by no Means permit them to celebrate their Ceremonies.* Yet still the Posterity of the *Jews* greatly multiplied in *Spain*.

In the mean while the *Romanists* contend that the *Jews* ought not to be compelled by Force to embrace the Christian Religion against their Will, because

Religion

Religion ought to be voluntary, yea sometimes they have been protected by the Papal Authority against the Injuries of some intemperately zealous Christians.

Bzovius,
A. 1200.
§. 13.

Thus Pope *Innocent* III. published a Constitution for not oppressing the *Jews*, in which there are these Things. *We ordain that no Christian shall by Violence compel them (the* Jews*) against their Inclination and Will to come to Baptism. But if any of them shall, of their own accord, come over to the Christians upon account of the Faith, after he shall have discovered his Intention, let him become a Christian without any Reproach. Such a one cannot be supposed to have the true Faith of Christianity, who is known to come to Christian Baptism not voluntarily but unwillingly. Farther, let no Christian without the Order of the secular Power, wickedly hurt their Persons, or presume by Violence to take away their Effects, or to change the good Customs which they have hitherto. used in the Countries where they dwell. Moreover, let no one disturb them with Sticks or Stones in the Celebration of their Festivals ; nor let any one strive to exact or extort from them undue Services, nor any but those which they have. been accustomed to yield in Times past. And that we may prevent the Wickedness and Covetousness of evil Men, we decree that no one shall dare to mangle or lessen the Burial-place of the* Jews*, or with a View to get Money, to dig up their Bodies when buried. But if any one, which God forbid, knowing the Tenor of this Decree, shall attempt to contradict it, and shall not make Amends for his Presumption by condign Satisfaction, his Crime shall be avenged by the Punishment of Excommunication. It is our Pleasure however that such only shall enjoy the Defence of this our Protection, who shall not presume to attempt any Thing to the Subversion of the Christian Faith.*

§. 27.

The Papists also farther contend, that although they oblige the *Jews* in *Spain* and *Portugal* to depart thence, unless they embrace the Christian Religion, yet they do by no Means force them to become Christians ; and therefore *Osorius* and *Mariana* blame King *Emanuel*, who kept the younger Children of the *Jews* against their Parents Will, and compelled the *Jews* by a severe Bondage to receive Baptism ; and they say that this Action is neither agreeable to Law or Religion. The Words of *Bzovius*, by which he blames this Action, under the Year 1497. are not to be omitted here. *What is this ? Wouldst thou force rebellious Minds, not bound by any Obligations of Religion, to believe those Things, which they do so vehemently despise and reject ? What, do you assume this to yourself, to restain the Liberty of the Will, and throw Chains upon such unbridled Minds ? This is an Impossibility, nor doth the most holy Deity of Christ approve it. What he desires is a voluntary Sacrifice, and not such a one as is forced from Men by an unlawful Violence ; nor doth he command that the Mind should be compelled, but that the Will should be allured and invited to the Study of true Religion. Besides, how can any one arrogate that to himself, which the holy Spirit only can effect in their Minds, who do not go on to oppose his Goodness to the End of Life ? For 'tis he only who illuminates their Minds, and allures and invites them, and brings those who do not reject so great a Gift with an obstinate and ungrateful Heart, to confess and have Communion with Christ. Finally, who doth not see how unworthy 'tis to commit to Men of different Persuasions in Religion so many Mysteries, so*
many

many *facred Things, fo great an Affair of divine Matters, and thus inconfiderately to afford an Occafion of Wickednefs to thofe who defpife the Difcipline of Chrift, and by this Means moft unworthily to proftitute Religion it felf under a Pretence of Religion?* Can any one believe that thefe People fpeak ferioufly, who by fo many Methods cruelly diftrefs the *Jews*, that they may force them, thus broken by Miferies, of which they fee no End, to embrace the Chriftian Religion? For 'tis owing to this that fo many amongft the new Converts are found to be *Jews* in their Hearts. Hence 'tis that they themfelves always fufpect the new Chriftians, *viz.* fuch who are converted from the *Jews* and *Saracens*, and defire that their Pofterity may be always feparated from the Pofterity of the old Chriftians.

Sometimes alfo they have openly perfecuted the *Jews*, and compelled them to become Chriftians. *Sethus Calvifius* relates from *Cedrenus*, under the Year 722. that *Leo* the Emperor forced the *Jews* to embrace Chriftianity; but that they afterwards either renounced their Baptifm, or fhut themfelves up in their Houfes, and burnt themfelves with all their Families.

But what fhall we fay to thefe Perfons, who, though they teach that the *Jews* are not to be compelled to the Faith, yet plead for forcing, and actually force thofe who in their Judgment err concerning fome Principles of Religion, whom they call by the infamous Name of Hereticks, to renounce their Errors, or rather the very Truth it felf, by all manner of Methods, and every kind of Cruelties. *Conrad Brunus* refolves this Queftion, reciting a De- de Heret. cree of one of the Councils of *Toledo* concerning the *Jews*. *As to the* Jews, *the* & fchif- *holy Synod commands, that no one of them fhall be henceforwards compelled: For the* mat. l. 3. *Lord fheweth Mercy on whom he will have Mercy, and whom he will he hardens ;* c. 3. §. 18. *for fuch are not to be faved againft their Confent, but willingly, that the Form of* Cap. de *Juftice may be compleat. For as every one obeying the Serpent by his own free* Difp. *Will perifhes, fo every one who is called by the Grace of God, believing thro' the Converfion of his own Mind, is faved. So that Perfons are to be perfuaded, that by their own free Will and Power they may be converted, and are not rather to be compelled.* " Since this is determined concerning the *Jews*, why is it, fays *Bru-* " *nus*, that we compel Hereticks to return to the Unity of the Catholick " Church, and do not rather leave them to their Will? There is a Reafon " to force the one, and not the others, as the fame Council of *Toledo* de- " clares; becaufe Hereticks have been once Partakers of the Divine Sacra- " ments, and received the Grace of Baptifm, and been anointed with Oil, " and partaken of the Lord's Body; and therefore they are to be compelled " to hold the Faith they once received, that the Name of the Lord may " not be blafphemed, and the Faith which they have received become vile " and contemptible."

Bellarmine explains this Matter more fully in Anfwer to the Objection, de Laicis, that Faith is free. He diftinguifhes Freedom, and fays, *'tis capable of a double* c. 22. *Senfe. The firft is a Freedom from Obligation, as when we fay 'tis a Matter of Freedom to vow Chaftity, to enter into Religion, but 'tis not Matter of Freedom to break one's Vow, or to go out of Religion. And in this Senfe Faith is a Matter of Free-*

dom as to those who have never received it, as to any Obligation of human Law, though not as to the Divine, and therefore such Men ought not to be compelled. God will punish them. But as to such who have professed Faith in Baptism, Faith is not free from Obligation either of the divine or human Law, and therefore they compel Men to preserve it. Again, Liberty is so taken as to distinguish it from Necessity, and in this Sense 'tis free whether a Man will believe or no, &c. But that I may by the way refute this Foundation of Popish Persecution, I would observe that neither *Bellarmine* nor any of the Popish Crew will ever be able to shew, that by receiving Baptism, there is any Obligation whatsoever to human Laws contracted. The Vow is made to God, and the Person baptized obliges himself by Baptism to God only, and not to any Man, and therefore he receives Baptism in the Name of the Father, Son and Holy Ghost ; and as our Saviour commands this Form of Baptism to be observed, he evidently shews that a Person hereby becomes devoted only to God ; nor doth the baptized Person make any, either express or tacit Promise, by which he lays himself under Obligation to any Man. He professes himself a Disciple of Jesus Christ, binds himself to observe his Commands, and acquires a Right to those spiritual Blessings which God seals his Title to by Baptism. So that here is nothing to be found by which a Person binds himself to any Man, or renders himself obnoxious to human Punishment if he departs from the Faith, and from an holy Life. All Things in this Transaction are divine and spiritual. 'Tis from God he expects the Remission of Sins and eternal Life, if he observes those Things to which he binds himself in Baptism. If he breaks his baptismal Vow by Apostacy and Profaneness of Life, he will experience the divine Punishment. So that herein there is no Change made as to any human Obligation ; nor is he by Baptism more bound to any Man whatsoever than he was before. It may be said perhaps, that by Baptism he is made a Member of the Church. He is so ; but doth not on this Account come under any human Obligation, and cannot therefore be obnoxious to the Decrees of any Man, but to those only of God ; which if he departs from, he immediately ceases to be a Member of the Church, and therefore the Church may declare that he is no longer a Member of her Body, and that therefore he hath no Hopes remaining of the Remission of Sins, and eternal Life. And the Church may pronounce just the same of those who have never been baptized, nor professed the Christian Faith. And therefore I conclude, that if any one falls from the Faith into an Heresy truly such, he doth not depart from any Obligation he is under to the Church, or to any Man, but from that which he is under to God, whose Word only he is bound to obey as the sole Rule of his Faith ; and that therefore he is to be punished by God only with a spiritual and eternal Punishment, and not by any Man with a corporal Punishment. This by the way.

To return therefore to our Purpose. The Inquisition was not introduced to compel the *Jews* to the Christian Religion ; because, say they, as they are not baptized, and have not professed the Faith of Christ, they cannot be said to be Hereticks or Apostates, and therefore are not subject to the Jurisdiction.

rifdiction of the Inquifitors. For the Church doth not judge of thofe that are without, and the Jurifdiction of the Inquifitors is only granted them againft heretical Pravity and Apoftacy. The Inquifition indeed in *Spain* is introduced againft thofe, who being converted from the *Jews* or *Mahometans,* to the Chriftian Religion, return again to *Judaifm* or *Mahometanifm,* and give fuch Marks of that Apoftacy as are capable to convict them. Such a one, as well as a Chriftian, that goes over to the *Jewifh* Rites, may be punifhed by the Inquifitors as any other Heretick or Apoftate. And in order to prove this Crime, they admit the Teftimony of *Jews* ; and when it is legally proved, they are by the royal Laws of *Spain* delivered over, as Relapfed and Impenitent, to the Fire.

Befides this there are other Cafes in which the *Jews* are fubject to the Inquifition, concerning which *Zanchinus de hæreticis,* and *Campegius* difcourfe, *Addit. ad* and which I fhall here mention. " Becaufe the Church doth not judge of *Zanchin.* " thofe who are without, fome, without making any Difference, believe, *c. 36.* " that the Inquifitors can't proceed againft the *Jews,* nor punifh them. O-
" thers indeed grant, that the *Jews* are not againft their Wills to be com-
" pelled to receive the Chriftian Faith, or Baptifm, but yet that in certain
" Cafes they are fubject to the Inquifitors. And to prove it they ufe this Di-
" ftinction. A *Jew* either offends by Contempt of the Orthodox Faith, or
" hindring the Office of the Inquifition. Or elfe as to their own Faith, or
" otherwife not relating to the Premiffes. In the two latter Cafes this is
" nothing to the Inquifitor. But if he offends as to the Contempt of the
" Faith, by reproaching the Churches or Altars, or even the facred Orna-
" ments of the Church, and the like, or hinders the Inquifitor in the Di-
" fpatch of his Office, the Inquifitor may proceed againft him, becaufe the
" Nature of his Offence is fuch as fubjects it to the Court of the Church.
" The Penalties by which fuch a *Jew* may be punifhed, are various. Chri-
" ftians may be forbid to have any thing to do with him, and this is a
" moft grievous Punifhment to live amongft Men, and to be abfolutely de-
" prived of their Affiftance. He may alfo be fined, and receive other cor-
" poral Punifhment, *viz.* Imprifonment or Whipping."

There are yet other Cafes, in which the *Jews* are fubject to the Inquifitor, *Campeg.* if they relapfe into *Judaifm,* or if any one fimply forfakes Chriftianity for *in Zanch.* *Judaifm,* or if a *Jew* perfuades a Chriftian to the *Jewifh* Rites. All which *c. 36.* are mentioned in the Extravagant of *Gregory* X. to the Inquifitors of the Predicant and Minor Orders, in the Year 1271. *With Grief of Heart we have heard and relate, that not only certain Perfons converted from the Error of* Jewifh *Darknefs to the Light of the Chriftian Faith, are known to return to their former Wickednefs ; but that many Chriftians denying the Truth of the Catholick Faith, have damnably gone over to the* Jewifh *Rites. This is fo much the more reprobate, as hereby the moft holy Name of Chrift is by a kind of friendly Enmity more fecurely blafphemed. Since therefore it becomes us to obviate by fit and fpeedy Remedies this damnable Plague, by thefe Apoftolick Writings, we command all of you, that within the Times appointed you by Authority of the Apoftolick See, to make In-*

quifition

quisition against Hereticks, you do diligently and carefully enquire out the Truth concerning the Premisses, as well with respect to Christians as to Jews, and that you endeavour to proceed against those, whom you shall find hitherto to have committed these Things, or who shall commit them for the future, as against Hereticks, the Favourers also, Receivers, and Defenders of Hereticks. And as to those Jews, *who have perswaded Christians of either Sex to embrace their execrable Rites, and whom you shall find hereafter endeavouring to perswade them, let them undergo the deserved Punishment. Compel all Contradictors by the Ecclesiastical Censure, without allowing them any Appeal; calling, if there be Need, to your Assistance in this Affair, the secular Arm.*

There are also extant the like Records, in the Acts of the Inquisition at *Ferrara,* written in Parchment, which *Campegius* gives us, two of which I shall here only transcribe. The one is a Letter of *Latinus D'Ursinis,* Cardinal Legate of *Romagliona* and *Tuscany,* to the Inquisitor of *Ferrara, A.D.* 1280. and second of the Pontificate of *Nicholas* III. *Our Beloved in Christ,* Boniface *of* Ferrara, *heretofore a Jew, but now, through the Grace of Christ, converted to the Catholick Faith, hath declared to us, that the* Jews *dwelling at* Ferrara, *being stirred up against him by a malignant Spirit, endeavour to oppress him with grievous Persecutions, and invent wicked Things to his Destruction; on which Account he cannot dwell in the aforesaid City without Fear of Danger. Wherefore he hath humbly besought us, that we would take Care to provide him with proper Assistance in this Difficulty. Since therefore 'tis very unworthy, that such who forsaking the Error of* Jewish *Blindness, have returned to the Light of the Christian Faith, should suffer Persecution and Injuries from those who remain in Darkness it self, we command your Discretion, by the Authority we are invested with, that you receive under your Protection the said* Boniface, *and all others, who are converted to the Catholick Faith, in the City and Diocese of* Ferrara, *or who shall be hereafter converted; and that you take Care to protect and defend them from the aforesaid* Jews, *by restraining the said* Jews *from their Insolencies and Blasphemies against the Orthodox Faith, as to you shall seem convenient. Calling in, if Need be, in this Affair, the Assistance of the secular Arm.*

The other is the Answer of several Divines of *Padua,* Bologna, *and* Ferrara, to eight Articles proposed by the said Inquisitor of *Ferrara,* which, as 'tis abridged by *Campegius,* I shall here faithfully transcribe.

First, 'tis asked, *Whether a* Jew *baptized, and converted to the Christian Faith, becomes subject to the Office of the Inquisitor if he apostatises from the Truth of the said Faith to* Judaism, *and denies the Christian Faith which he hath received, and may by him be compelled and condemned as other Hereticks, if he contemptuously refuses to hold the Faith he hath received.*

The Answer of the wise Men of Padua, *A.D.* 1281. *to this Question is, That such a one is subject to the Office of the Inquisition, and that he may be proceeded against as well as any other Heretick. Those of* Ferrara *said the same, viz. that the Inquisitor can, and ought to proceed against baptized* Jews, *who have afterwards returned to* Judaism.

Secondly,

· *Secondly, Whether the Inquifitor may proceed againft thofe by whofe Help; Will, Counfel, or Affent, fuch or fuch a Chriftian apoftatifes, and denies the Faith of Chrift; which he hath once received ; and alfo againft his Favourers, Receivers, and Defenders, whether they are* Jews, *or of any other Condition and State.*

Thofe of Padua *replied, That the Inquifitor may and ought to proceed againft fuch; as againft Favourers, Receivers, and Defenders of Hereticks. Becaufe, although* Jews *are tolerated by the Church in their Rites, yet by the Nature of their Crime, which they commit againft the Church, they are to be reftrained by Ecclefiaftical Severity, and becaufe he ought to forfeit his Privilege who abufes the Power intrufted with him.* Thofe of Bologna *fay the fame, viz. That fuch are to be feverely punifhed. Yet they advife that fuch fhould not be proceeded againft with the laft Extremity, not to the fhedding their Blood, nor to their being delivered over, or left to the fecular Arm. But that they may and ought to be punifhed with a Fine, Banifhment, Imprifonment, and alfo with an indirect Excommunication, and the like, as the Nature of their Offences require. Again, fuch ought to be proceeded againft, as Favourers, Receivers and Defenders of Hereticks, who give Counfel, Affiftance and Favour to fuch an Apoftate, by keeping him in their Houfe, feeding him, giving him Money, and accompanying him out of the City, fo that what is done may not come to the Knowledge of Chriftians, or by admitting him to Judaife in a Synagogue, and the like. But thefe are to be punifhed lefs than the former, becaufe thefe feem to be Favourers only ; but the former, properly fpeaking, Makers of Hereticks. From thefe alfo the Truth may be forced by moderate Torture, if they will not themfelves confefs it, fince there are Witneffes or violent Sufpicions againft them, that they have committed thefe or the like Things to the Prejudice of the Chriftian Faith. The Doctors of* Ferrara *fubfcribed to this Decifion.*

Thirdly, Whether an Inquifitor, having violent Prefumption againft fuch Perfons, that they do not fpeak the Truth, whilft he is making Inquifition againft them in the aforefaid and like Crimes, may force it from them by Torture, fo as not to fhed their Blood, by the fecular Executor or Judge, and proceed againft them to Canonical Punifhments, if they are convicted, or confefs. They of Padua *anfwered in the Affirmative, to which thofe of* Bologna *agreed. The Truth, fay they, may be forced from them, if they will not confefs it, by Punifhments not extending to the fhedding their Blood, by the fecular Judge, at the Command of the Inquifitor, when there are legal Witneffes, or violent Prefumptions that they have committed the aforefaid or like Things.* Campegius adds here, Obferve, I befeech you, the Scruple of the Antients, as to the Punifhments of Torture, becaufe they would not have them ufed by the Ecclefiaftical Judge, but by the fecular one at the Command of the Ecclefiaftical. But now this Scruple is entirely removed by *Cle. Multorum.* de hæret. §. *Duro tamen. Thofe of* Ferrara *gave the fame Advice, viz. that the Inquifitors may and ought to proceed againft fuch, by whofe Help, Counfel, or Affent, any one hath apoftatifed.*

Thofe of Padua *moreover fay, that the Truth may alfo be extorted by the fame Punifhments, if they deny that which is proved by feveral Witneffes, although the Witneffes who prove it fay, that the aforefaid Crimes were committed by the Help, Counfel and Affiftance of the* Jews *of fuch a City, and yet doth not feverally exprefs their*

their Names. And moreover, by such sort of Proofs they may be proceeded against without the Confessions of any others of them.

Fourthly, Concerning the Synagogue 'tis enquired, What must be done with such a one, wherein, by the Help, Will and Counsel of the Jews *who dwell in the Country, any Christians have been washed by the* Jews, *to the Prejudice of holy Baptism, and have denied the Faith by their Persuasions. Those of* Padua *answer, that it must needs be entirely destroyed, or deprived of the Privileges of Christians, which Sentence is approved by those of* Bologna *and* Ferrara.

As to a Person who offends in the said Cases within the Bounds of the Inquisition, where he lives, and hath an House within the said Bounds, in which he has been used to dwell with his Family; those of Padua *say, 'tis sufficient, that an Edict of Citation be sent to the said House, if the Person hath transported himself to foreign and unknown Parts; and if he doth not appear within the proper Terms assigned him, he must be proceeded against, and his Effects found therein be disposed of according to Law.*

In another Instance the Paduans *answer thus ; That an Infant Child of a baptized* Jew, *left with its Mother, who continues in* Jewish *Blindness, must, whilst the Father is absent in remote and unknown Parts, be taken from her in Favour of the Faith, by the Church or Ordinary of the Place, or the Christian Prince, to whose Government 'tis subject, and brought up amongst faithful and unsuspected People, and baptized, unless the Child it self appears to be against it.*

As to another Instance, of a certain Person, against whom it was proved by several legal Witnesses, that being in a Jewish *Synagogue, and about to read the Law solemnly before other* Jews, *according to their Manner, it was objected to him by one present, that he was not worthy to read the Law, for that in such a Country he had been baptized; and he himself owned and confessed that he had been there baptized, but that he was returned to* Judaism, *and had performed the Penance which the* Jews *had appointed him for his Sin in being baptized, and that he would live and die from henceforwards as a* Jew *; those of* Padua *and* Bologna *say, that the Truth concerning these Things may be extorted from him by Punishments not reaching to the Effusion of Blood, by the secular Judge, at the Command of the Inquisitors.*

As to two other Persons, viz. a Man and a Woman, who declare themselves, and act publickly as Jews, *and yet it may be legally proved against them by Witnesses, that the Parents of each were Christians, and they themselves were baptized, viz. in this Manner. For the Father of this Man, who declares himself, and acts as a* Jew, *was himself first a* Jew, *but afterwards baptized, and so made a Christian, and married a Christian Woman for his Wife, by whom he had this Son, and caused him to be baptized, so that he lived many Years as a Christian. A long while after his Father returned to* Judaism, *and caused this Son, of whom we speak, to be circumcised, so that he afterwards always lived as a* Jew, *and what is more, caused his Mother, who was truly a Christian, to* Judaise, *who was at length buried in the Burial Place of the* Jews. *And as to the Woman who publickly declares her self, and acts as a* Jewess, *she also is proved to have been first a Christian after the aforesaid Manner. For her Mother was first known to be a* Jewess, *but was afterwards made a Christian, and married a Christian Man, upon whose Death she re-*
turned

turned to Judaifm, *and married a* Jew *for her Husband. Of both thefe they of* Bologna *fay, that they muft proceed againft them as againft Hereticks, and that the Truth muft be extorted from them by Punifhments, if they will not confefs it. But if they will neither thus confefs the Truth, nor return to the Faith which they firft received in Baptifm, they may, after Confifcation of their Effects, either be fhut up in perpetual Imprifonment, or left to the fecular Arm.*

In Teftimony of which Thing the Lords Advifers of Padua, Bologna *and* Ferrara, *have figned their diftinct Opinions with their own proper Seals.*

Simancas *alfo adds thefe Cafes, of which fome do not much differ from the* *Tit.* 35. Cafes mentioned in the above Writing of *Ferrara.*

" If a *Jew, Mahometan,* or any other Perfon receives, defends or favours
" Hereticks, or hinders the Inquifitors, or obftructs their Office, or fhould
" keep in his Poffeffion the Books of Hereticks, he may be punifhed by the
" Inquifitors. Alfo by one of the Extravagant Conftitutions of *Nicholas* IV.
" Power is granted to the Inquifitors of taking Cognizance of the Crimes of
" *Jews,* as often as they offend againft the Old Teftament, or induce any
" Chriftian to *Judaifm,* or circumcife him, or compel him to deny the Ca-
" tholick Faith."

Pope *John* XXII. alfo, as *Bzovius* relates under the Year 1319. §. 9. by a Letter N°. 190. renewed the Conftitutions of *Clement.* IV. and other his Predeceffors, and by feverer Laws encreafed the Power given to the Inquifitors againft them ; commanding that they fhould gather together and burn all the Books of the *Talmud,* and punifh thofe who were convicted of execrable Blafphemies. In the Month of *December* following, by the Command of *Bzou. Inquifit. fol.* 156. Friar *Bernard Guido,* Inquifitor of heretical Pravity, the Books of the *Jews* called the *Talmud,* were as many of them as could be found in the Poffeffion of the *Jews,* burnt at *Tholoufe,* after it had been declared by fworn Examiners, skilful in the *Hebrew* Tongue, that they contained Errors and Blafphemies againft the Lord Jefus Chrift, and his moft holy Mother the Virgin *Mary.*

In the Kingdom of *Valencia* the Inquifitors may proceed againft the *Jews,* Royas, *p.* 1. or *Saracens,* or other unbaptized Infidels dogmatifing amongft Chriftians, efpe- cially againft the *Alfaquins,* or thofe who hinder the Office of the Inquifition, §. 552. or circumcife Boys, or are Receivers of Hereticks, or who compel any one to deny the Faith, or perfuade them to ufe their Rites or publick Ceremonies. But yet others think that a *Jew,* who fays to a Chriftian, *La fede voftra e fede di* * *Cazzi,* i. e. Your Faith is the Faith of a ———— or who throws Naftinefs upon the Crofs which is carried in the Litanies, ought not to be punifhed by the Inquifitors, but by the fecular Judge.

And finally, *Gregory* XIII. *An.* 1581. publifhed a Conftitution, beginning, *Comp. Bul. par* 2. *p.* 178. *Antiqua Judæorum improbitas,* by which he granted Power to the Inquifitors of heretical Pravity, freely to proceed againft the *Jews* in the following Cafes. " If they deny Matters of Faith common to them and Chriftians. If " they invoke Devils, or facrifice to them. If they teach any Chriftian

* *Cazzi* is an obfcene Word.

" thefe

" thefe Things, or bring them to them. If they fpeak heretical Blafphe-
" mies. If they pervert a Chriftian from the Faith. If they hinder Infidels
" from coming over to the Faith of Chrift. If they knowingly receive an
" Heretick, or give him Affiftance. If they keep heretical Books, or Tal-
" mudical, or any other *Jewifh* Books any ways condemned. If they deride
" the falutary Hoft, or the Crofs, or the like Things, or Chriftians. If they
" keep Chriftian Nurfes, or fhall compel them from the Day in which
" they have received the Sacrament of the Eucharift, to throw their Milk
" into the Jakes."

But efpecially in the Kingdom of *Spain* and *Portugal* the Inquifition is in-
troduced to detect and punifh thofe who, being *Jews*, have embraced the
Chriftian Religion, and witneffed their Profeffion by the folemn receiving of
Baptifm, and have afterwards turn'd again to *Judaifm.*

Pegna,
Com. 25.
in 3. part.
Eymerick There are feveral Signs by which it may be collected, that a Perfon is re-
volted to *Judaifm.* Anciently the converted *Jews* themfelves allowed, that it
might be known by certain Marks which of them were not fincerely converted to Chrift, but cherifhed *Judaifm* in their Heart in a certain Ordinance
made in the Name of the King of *Spain*, about the Year 653. *Leg. del Fuero
Jurgo. lib.* 12. as follows.

To our moft clement and ferene Lord, King Rocefuind. *All we* Hebrews *of the
City of* Toledo *and* Spain, *your Glory, who have under-written our Names, or put
our Marks. We well and juftly remember that we were compelled to think it our
Duty to write our Opinion in the Name of King Chintillan, of holy Memory, for
preferving the Catholick Faith, even as we have done. But becaufe the Perfidioufnefs of our Obftinacy, and the Antiquity of our Error that we have derived from
our Fathers, hath fo poffeffed us, that we have neither truly believed in Jefus Chrift
the Lord, nor fincerely kept the Catholick Faith: We now therefore willingly and
readily promife your Glory by this our Ordinance, as well for our felves, as for our
Wives and Children, that we will never hereafter mix in any* Jewifh *Obfervations or
inceftuous Cuftoms. And as we are baptized, we will never more in any fort be
joined with the* Jews *in an execrable Society; nor will we, according to our Cuftom,
ever be joined with them by Nearnefs of Blood, even to the fixth Degree, by an inceftuous Pollution in Matrimony or Fornication. We will not enter into Marriages
with our Race in any fort, neither our felves or our Children, or any of our Pofterity, but as to both Sexes we will henceforwards marry only with Chriftians. We
will not work the Circumcifion of the Flefh. We will not celebrate the Paffover
and Sabbaths, and other Holy-days, according to the Rite of* Jewifh *Obfervation.
We will not obferve the Difference or Cuftom of Meats, nor do any of all thofe
Things, which the Ufe and abominable Cuftom and Converfation of the* Jews *doth.
But we believe with a fincere Faith, grateful Mind, and entire Devotion in Chrift,
the Son of the living God, according to the Evangelick and Apoftolical Tradition, and
him we confefs and adore. We do alfo truly hold and fincerely embrace all the
Cuftoms of the holy Chriftian Religion, as well as to Holy-days as to Marriages and
Foods, and all other Obfervations, without referving to our felves any Object of Oppofition, or fallacious Argument, by which we will do again thofe Things which we*
have

have denied to do, or not sincerely fulfil those Things which we have promised to ob-
serve. And as to Swines Flesh we promise to observe, that if we cannot possibly eat
it through Custom, yet that we will, without Contempt or Horror, take and eat
Things that are dressed with it. And if in all these Things which are above men-
tioned, we shall be found Transgressors in any the least Point, or shall presume to act
contrary to the Christian Faith, or shall delay to fulfil in Word and Deed what we
have promised agreeable to the Catholick Religion : We swear by the same Father,
Son and Holy Spirit, who is one in Trinity, and the true God, that whosoever of us
shall be found a Transgressor of all or any one of these Things, he shall perish with new
Flames or Stones. Or if Goodness shall reserve him for Life to your Glory, he shall
lose his Liberty, and forfeit all his Substance, and shall be for ever a Slave to any
Person you shall appoint. And whatsoever you shall command to be done as to him or
his Effects, you shall not only have free Power to do it by the Power of your King-
dom, but by the Engagement of this our Ordinance. This Ordinance was made
March 21. *in the happy Sixth Year of the Reign of your Glory, in the Name of*
God, at Toledo.

But *Pegna* is of Opinion, that a more certain Suspicion of secret *Judaism*
arises from other observed Rites of the *Jews, viz.* from too intimate conversing with them, by frequenting the Places in which they dwell, and especially the Synagogues, by the Observations of the Sabbaths, and many o her
Things, than from their Abstinence from Swines Flesh, which may be either unpleasant to the Taste, or nauseous to the Stomach. This Consideration particularly affects the new Converts, who, through Custom, cannot be
supposed easily to relish Swines Flesh, or other Meats forbidden them before
their Conversion. But this doth not hold as to their Children and Grandchildren, and other Descendants, who can't be supposed to abstain from
these Things for any other Reason, but their Reverence and Approbation
of this accursed Sect, because the Reason of Custom cannot be pleaded in
their Behalf, though it may as to those who are themselves converted.

Amongst other Signs of secret *Judaism*, the Name that a Person takes is
accounted one. For they say 'tis customary amongst the *Hebrews* frequently
to give the same Name to those who come over or return to their Sect, which
they had before they were baptized. If therefore any Person, after Baptism,
in which he put off his old *Jewish* Name, and took the Name of some Saint,
according to the Custom of Christians, shall take it again, or some other
Name familiar and usual amongst the *Jews* ; it will be a Presumption that he
approves *Judaism.*

In how many, and in what Cases the *Jews* and other Infidels are subject
to the Power of the Inquisitors, *Gregory* XIII. hath largely declared, *An.*
1581. by a Rescript, beginning, *Antiqua Judæorum*, which shall be hereafter
mentioned.

As to the Punishments of such offending *Jews*, their Crimes are distin-Carena,
guished into three Sorts. Some of them are common to them and Christians.[p] 2. t.14.
Others are against the Christian or rather Popish Faith. And lastly, others[q] 18.
against their own Faith, which are not to be treated of here.

As

As to Crimes of the firſt ſort, reſpecting them as well as Chriſtians, ſuch are declared Hereticks who deny God to be Almighty. If they confeſs that they ſaid and believed this, they are compelled to abjure as for formal Hereſy. If they confeſs they ſaid it, but deny that they believed it, they muſt be tortured as to their Intention, and be made to abjure as well as Chriſtians, according to the Degree of the Suſpicion, whether light or vehement.

As to Crimes of the ſecond ſort, they are tortured only to get out the Truth, and diſcover their Accomplices. For in theſe Things they are not truly Hereticks; but becauſe they grievouſly offend againſt the Chriſtian or Popiſh Faith, they are uſually puniſhed in a very ſevere Manner; and in this Caſe they are not compelled to abjure, becauſe the Church doth not compel them to the Faith.

The Puniſhments which the Inquiſitors inflict upon the *Jews* who offend in the aforeſaid Caſes, are various, and lighter or heavier, according to the Nature or Degree of the Crimes, *viz.* Privation of all Converſation with Chriſtians, Fines, perpetual Impriſonment, Whipping, and alſo to be delivered over into the Power of the ſecular Arm.

Finis Libri Tertii.

T H E

THE

HISTORY

OF THE

INQUISITION.

VOL. II.

BOOK IV.

Of the Manner of Proceeding before the Tribunal of the INQUISITION.

CHAP. I.

How the INQUISITOR *begins his Office.*

IT now remains that we give an Account of what relates to the Execution of the Inquisitorial Office. This will be a more difficult Task,
becaufe, altho' the Inquifitors are bound to certain Laws, yet many
Things are left to their Pleafure. Befides, the very Application of
the Laws to particular Cafes, which come before the Inquifitors; and alfo
the Method of proceeding and drawing a Confeffion from the Prifoners, depends very much on their Will. Hence it comes to pafs, that altho' all
the Inquifitors are directed by certain general Laws, fo that one and the
fame general Method of Proceeding is obferved by all, yet, as to many Circumftances, the Method is very various and different, which befides cannot
be fo fully explained, becaufe the Inquifitors learn many Things rather by
Ufe and Practice, than by Inftruction and Precepts; efpecially confidering
that they oblige all Perfons by Oath, whom they difmifs from the Prifon of
the Inquifition, to Silence; that the Secrets of the Inquifition, as tho' they

P 2   were

were the facred Mysteries of *Ceres*, may not by any Means be revealed. I
have determined therefore faithfully to give my Reader whatfoever the Popifh Doctors and the Inquifitors themfelves have with great Labour gathered
together from the Laws, Papal Bulls, and their Inftructions, concerning the
Method of Proceeding, and to illuftrate the Whole by fuch Examples as
offer themfelves to me. And that I may omit nothing, I will trace this
Matter from the very Beginning, *viz.* from the very firft Moment in which
the Inquifitor begins his Office, down to the Acts of Faith, in which the
Sentences are pronounced upon all the Prifoners, and actually put in Execution.

Direct.
Inq. part
3. n. 1.

When the Inquifitor is firft conftituted by the Pope, he muft prefent
himfelf to the King, or temporal Lord of thofe Territories, in which the
Inquifitor is deputed by the Apoftolick See, and exhibit his Apoftolick

2.
Commiffion. Then he muft demand his Protection for himfelf, his Colleague,
Notary, Servants and their Effects, and his Orders to his Officials to.
obey the Inquifitor in apprehending Hereticks, their Believers, Receivers,
Defenders, Favourers, and fuch as are defamed for Herefy, and that they do
all and fingular Matters that belong to their Office in making Execution,
againft the aforefaid, to extirpate heretical Pravity, and to extol the Catholick Faith, whenfoever, and as often as they are required by the Inquifitor,
or in his Name.

4.
When he hath obtained thefe Letters, he muft likewife exhibit his Apoftolick Commiffion to the Arch-Bifhop and Metropolitan of the Province to
which he is deputed ; as alfo to all the Bifhops and their Vicars, to whofe

5.
Dioceffes he is fent. After this he muft fhew the Letters which he hath obtained from the King or temporal Lord of the Place, to his Officials, and
require of them, according to the Law of the Emperor *Frederick*, that at the
Defire of the Inquifitor, or other Catholick Men, they will apprehend Hereticks, and when taken, ftrictly keep them, till being condemned by the

6.
Ecclefiaftical Cenfure, they perifh with an accurfed Death. Finally, he takes
an Oath from thefe Officials for their defending the Church againft heretical
Pravity, and that they will obey the Inquifitor with all their Might, for

8.
which End he fummons them before him by Letters. If they appear, he

10.
propofes the Form of the Oath to them. If they confent to take it, they
muft do it publickly in the Church, or in fome other Place appointed for
that Purpofe, upon their bended Knees, and their Hands upon the Book
of the Gofpels. If the Officials defire Time to confider, and refufe after
the Expiration of it to take the Oath, the Inquifitor, a few Days after,
muft cite them before him, and demand of them to take the Oath, under the
Penalty of Excommunication. If they appear within the fixed Term, and
confent to fwear, the fame Form of the Oath is fhewn them. If they do
not appear, after the faid Time is elapfed, they are declared excommunicate, and the Excommunication is ordered to be publifhed in the Cathedral
Church. After the denouncing the Excommunication, they are abfolved
from the Sentence of it if they will take the Oath, and enjoined fome hard
arbitrary

arbitrary wholefome Penance, as fhall be moft conducive to the Honour of the Faith. When their Abfolution is given, they are denounced free from Excommunication. However, they cannot be abfolved, unlefs they firft take this Oath, at the Command of the Inquifitor. *I fwear that I will obey the Commands of the Church.* Or thus : *I fwear that I will ftand to and obey thy Commands.*

But if they abide under this Sentence of Excommunication two or three Months, the Proceffes are aggravated, and they are commanded to be denounced publickly excommunicated in the aforefaid Churches, with lighted Candles thrown on the Ground, or put out in Water, and the Bells rung once or oftener in a Week or Day. If without being terrified by this Excommunication, they refufe to take the Oath, they are not only excommunicated, but all who have any manner of Converfe with them, who eat, drink or talk with them. If neverthelefs they perfevere in their Contumacy, their Lands are put under an Ecclefiaftical Interdict. If after this they will not take the Oath, they are deprived of the Honour and Office of Government, as infamous, Favourers of Hereticks, and fufpected of the Faith, and are condemned to be never hereafter admitted to any publick Office or Dignity ; and whatfoever they do after this is null, according to the Chap. *Ad abolendam.* §. *Statuimus.* Extra. de hæret. and Chap. *Ut officium.* §. *Statuimus.* lib. 6. And this Sentence is commanded to be publifhed by thofe who have the Cure of Souls in the Cathedral and other Churches. If the City or Place acquiefces in the Sentence, and deprives fuch Perfons of their Offices ; others are chofe in their Room, who, before they are admitted to the Difcharge of their Office, are bound to take the Oath which the others have refufed. But if the City doth not fubmit to the Sentence, but fupports their Officials, tho' deprived of their Offices by the Inquifitor, he may cut it off from all Communication with other Cities, and deprive it of the Epifcopal Dignity. But they think it better to acquaint the Pope with the Contumacy of fuch a City, that he may order in what Manner to proceed againft it.

At this Day the Inquifitors in *Spain,* when they enter upon their Province or City, where they never were before, muft in the firft place fhew their Letters of Delegation, by which they are created Inquifitors, to the Chapter of the greater Church, and Confiftory of the City, that it may appear that they are Judges of the Caufes of Herefy. 1 *Inftruct. Hifpal. cap.* 1. And fuch who have offended therein muft be profcribed by the Inquifitors, and apprehended and punifhed by the Royal Hand.

But if the Officials, terrified by the more grievous Denunciation of the Inquifitor, take the Oath, they are freed from their Excommunication, but receive an heavy Penance, which is always encreafed according as their Contumacy is longer or more aggravated. In their firft Penance they are enjoin'd to ftand in the Gate of the Church, or on the Steps before the Altar, on feveral *Sundays,* or Holy-days, whilft the greater Mafs is faying, and there is a large Concourfe of People, without Hat or Shoes, and to hold in their Hands a Wax Taper of a certain Weight, and to offer it to the
Prieft

(margin notes:) 27. 33. Simanc. t. 44. § 1. Pegna, *in direct.* p. 45. n.

Priest when the Mass is ended. Or they must do this always, or at some certain Time, when it happens that the Inquisitor makes a general Sermon for the Faith. Other milder Punishments may be also thought of; for Instance, some larger Almsgiving, the building some holy Place, and the like. But if they persist longer in their Contumacy, there is somewhat added by way of Penance, which directly turns to the Honour of the Christian Faith.

n. 24.

n. 37.

During these Transactions, whether the Oath be taken or not, the Inquisitor may and must appoint in every Bishoprick one Commissary of forty Years old, a religious or secular Clergyman, a wise and prudent Person, famous for Knowledge and good Manners, and zealous for the holy Faith, with a Power of receiving Denunciations and Informations or Accusations from or against any Persons whatsoever, and of proceeding, and doing other Things, which the Inquisitor himself, if present, could do.

C H A P. II.

Of the Promulgation of the EDICT *of* FAITH.

47.

THE Commissaries thus appointed or not, the Inquisitor appoints a general Sermon, according to the Prescript of the Council of *Biterre.* Cap. 1. *And then calling together the Clergy and People, and propounding to them the Word of God, declare the Command that is given you, and the Cause of your coming, reading the Letters, by Authority of which you are to proceed, even as you know you ought to do.* And that there may be no Hindrance to the Offices of the Church, he must not appoint this Sermon on a solemn Festival, but on the common *Sunday,* excepting *Lent,* or the *Advent;* and must take Care that the Rectors of the Churches have these Letters of Indiction on *Sunday,* that the *Sunday* after they may appoint the general Sermon to be the *Sunday* following. And that the Solemnity of that Day may be the greater, all other Sermons on it must be suspended; and it must be notified to all the Heads of Religious Houses, and Indulgencies of forty Days promised to all who come to the Sermon. When the *Sunday* before that, on which the general Sermon is to be made, comes, the Inquisitor must admonish the Heads of Religious Houses, that two or four of each Religion be present at the said Sermon.

50.

51.

On the *Sunday* appointed, the Inquisitor makes the general Sermon to the People, in which he speaks concerning the Faith, commends it, and exhorts the People to the Defence of it, and the Extirpation of heretical Pravity. When the Sermon is ended, he admonishes the People, that 'tis their Duty to discover it to the Inquisitor, if they have known any Person that hath spoken or done any thing against the Faith, or who holds any Error. After

ter this Admonition he commands monitory Letters to be read from the Pulpit by his Notary, or some other Clergyman, by which all Persons, of what- *n.* 52. soever Condition or State, Clergy or Laity, are commanded, under Pain of *n.* 53. Excommunication, to discover to the Inquisitor within six or twelve Days next following, any Heretick or Person suspected of Heresy that they know. These monitory Letters are an Edict of the Faith, and usually read out of the Pulpit. I will here add, as what will give a Light to whatsoever I shall say of the Inquisition, a Copy of it, not only of that which is published in *Spain,* but also of that which at this Day is published in *Italy,* translated from the *Italian.*

A General EDICT *of the Inquisition at* Cremona.

WE Peter Camporeus, *by divine Mercy, Cardinal Presbyter of St.* Thomas *in* Parione, *Bishop of* Cremona, *Earl,* &c. *and we* Vincentius Peter Serravallensis, *Predicant, D. D. and Inquisitor General of* Cremona, *and of the Diocese thereof, especially delegated by the holy Apostolick See against heretical Pravity.*

Desiring, according as the holy Office conferred on us requires us, that the most holy Catholick Faith, without which no one can please God, may be preserved pure and free from all heretical Contagion, we by the Apostolick Authority granted us, do command all and singular Persons under our Jurisdiction, of whatsoever Condition, State, Degree, or Dignity, as well Ecclesiastical as secular, whatsoever it be, by Virtue of their holy Obedience, and under Penalty of Excommunication, latæ sententiæ, *and other Penalties which the sacred Canons, Decrees, Constitutions, and Bulls of the chief Pontiffs ordain, that within twelve Days ensuing, the four first of which we assign for the first Term, the four next immediately following for the second, and the other remaining four for the third, last and peremptory Term, they do juridically discover and notify to the holy Office, or the Ordinary, all and singular Persons whom they know, or of whom they have had Notice, or shall have Notice for the future.*

If any Persons are Hereticks, or suspected, or defamed for Heresy, or Believers, Favourers, Receivers or Defenders of them ; or who have, or do adhere to the Rites of the Jews, Mahometans, Saracens *or* Gentiles, *or who have apostatised from the holy Christian Faith, or who have or do in any manner, expresly or tacitly invocate the Devil, or have done, or do him honour, or who have had any Part, or have, or do concern themselves in any magical Trick, Necromancy, Incantations, or other like superstitious Acts, especially with the Abuse of any sacred Thing.*

If any Persons not being Priests, have with an impious Boldness, or do usurp to themselves the Celebration of Mass, or have, or do presume to administer the Sacrament of Penance to the Faithful of Christ.

If any have, or do abuse the Sacrament of Penance, contrary to the Apostolical Decrees and Constitutions.

If any have, or do hold secret Conventicles in the Matter of Religion.

If any utter heretical Blasphemies against God, or his Saints, and especially against the most blessed Virgin Mary.

If any do, or have hindred the Office of the holy Inquisition, or do, or have injured any Witness, Accuser, or Minister of it.

If any have, or do keep Books or Writings containing Heresies, or the Books of Hereticks, which treat of Religion, without Authority of the holy Apostolick See, or who have or do read, print, or cause them to be printed, or defend them, under any Pretence or Colour, or Books of Necromancy, Magick, or containing sorcerous Incantations and the like Superstitions, especially if with the Abuse of sacred Things.

Declaring, that tho' we do expresly specify as above the Cases which ought to be discovered, we do not exclude other Cases relating to the holy Office, which are always contained in the sacred Canons, Decrees, Constitutions, and Bulls of the chief Pontiffs.

And that no one can be absolved from the aforesaid Excommunication and Penalties, which the Disobedient incur, but by us or the supream Tribunal of the Inquisition at Rome, *nor shall be absolved, unless he shall first give Satisfaction, by juridically revealing the said Hereticks, or as above, those suspected of Heresy.*

And because much of the Service of God, and the private and publick Good, in these Particulars, greatly depends upon the Endeavours of the Confessors, we command all the reverend Confessors, that in the Administration of the Sacrament of Penance, they use all that Diligence in interrogating those who confess to them, concerning all the aforesaid Heads, which they shall think respectively necessary, both as to those who are principal Offenders, and those who are Partakers of, and any ways conscious to those Offences. And we command the said Confessors, under the said Penalty of Excommunication, latæ *sententiæ, and as above, that they do not presume to absolve those whom they shall find to have offended, or to be Partakers, or conscious, as above, in the aforesaid Particulars, because they have incurred those Censures which are reserved by the holy See, to its Delegates.*

Admonishing, that such Persons do not satisfy, nor are understood to satisfy these our Commands, who pretend to discover Delinquents by Papers or Letters without the Name or Sirname of the Authors, or by any other uncertain Method, because they may be absolutely secure, that they shall not be discovered, according to the Custom of this holy Office, and do not lay themselves under a Necessity of proving what they declare.

And that this our present general Edict may be known to all, and no one pretend Ignorance, we command all the reverend Arch-Presbyters, Curates and Rectors of Churches, subject to our Jurisdiction, or their Vicars, in Virtue of their holy Obedience, under Pain of Excommunication, that the first Holyday after they receive it, they shall be absolutely obliged to publish, read, or cause it to be read, at length, before the People, when they shall be met together in largest Numbers in their said Churches, and when published, cause it to be fixed up upon the principal Gate of the said Churches, or some other publick Place, where it may be seen and read of all ; and this also we enjoin all the Priors of Monasteries.

Farther, 'tis our Pleasure, that under the same Penalties they shall be obliged to read it again before the said People, twice at least in a Year, viz. *upon one Sunday in* Lent, *and one in* Advent.

And

And that they may obey this our Commandment as they ought, they muſt have a Copy from the ſacred Congregation it ſelf, always fixed upon the Sacriſties of their Churches.

According to the Deſire which we have, that this our Juriſdiction may be preſerved in that Purity of the Faith in which it now is, adhering to the above-mentioned E-dict, and other Commands of the ſacred Congregation, we command, under Pain of Excommunication, and other arbitrary Penalties.

That no Currier, Sailor, Muletier, or others, preſume to carry Books either in-to or out of any City, or other Places ſubject to us, no not as he paſſes by, if he hath not a Catalogue of the Books ſubſcribed by the Inquiſitor, or other Perſon to whom it belongs, living in thoſe Places from whence they come, or thro' which they paſs, un-der Penalty of loſing the Books, and other Puniſhments, according to our Pleaſure.

Under the ſame Penalties and Loſs of the Books, we command, that no Perſon, who-ſoever he be, do receive ſuch Books when imported, or any ways brought in to this our Juriſdiction, nor open Boxes, Bales or Bundles, in which ſuch Books are, nor carry them away from the Cuſtom-Houſe, without our Leave, or that of our Vicars, and till they have firſt given a Catalogue to the holy Office, or ſhewed them to it, if they have imported them without Licence.

That no Merchant preſume to receive or ſend Books, under Pretence of Goods packed up in Bundles, Bales or Boxes, without due Licence, under Pain of Excom-munication, Forfeiture of the Books and Goods in which they are packed up. And what is here ſaid concerning the importing or receiving Books, is alſo to be underſtood of all Sorts of News Papers, Pictures and Almanacks, and ſuch like Papers.

All the aforeſaid Things we likewiſe command the Jews, under the Penalty of fifty Pieces of Gold, the Forfeiture of Books and Goods as above, and others, to be re-ſpectively inflicted according to our Pleaſure.

We command all Bookſellers in this our Juriſdiction, under the ſame Penalty of Ex-communication, and other arbitrary Puniſhments, that they don't preſume to ſell Books bought of the Jews, whether within or without the City.

Printers alſo ſhall not, under the ſame Penalties and other arbitrary ones, print any thing without our Licence, except the Edicts and other like Matters of the E-piſcopal and ſecular Court, which are not to the Prejudice of the holy Office.

The Impoſt-Gatherers, Cuſtom-Houſe Officers, and Officers of Ports, ſhall not per-mit any Books to be imported or exported without a written Catalogue as above. And when any are brought to the Place of their Office without ſuch written Catalogue, let them detain the Books, and be obliged to ſhew them to us or our Vicars. And this we command, under Pain of Excommunication, and other arbitrary Puniſhments.

And to give Credit to theſe Things, we have written this Edict, and ſigned it with our own proper Hand.

Dated at the Holy Office at Cremona, October 26, 1639.

> P. *Cardinal* Camporeus *Biſhop of* Cremona.
> F. Vincent Peter, *Inquiſitor of* Cremona.
> Jerom Calcinous, *Chancellor.*

VOL. II.   Q   The

The Form of an EDICT of FAITH used in *Spain.*

Param:
l. 3. q. 5.
§. 43.

WE the Inquisitors of heretical Pravity and Apostacy, by that Apostolick Authority we possess, especially delegated on this Account to us in the Dioceses of N. or N. &c. to all and singular, as well Clergy as Laity, Regulars as Seculars, of every State, Condition, Quality, Degree, Order, Religion, Dignity or Pre-eminence, exempt, or not exempt, to all and every one of you, to whom this our general Edict shall be known, Salvation in our Lord *Jesus* Christ, who is the true Salvation, and to our Commands, which are more truly *Apostolick* Words, firm Obedience, Submission and Observance. We make known to you, that the Licentiate or Doctor N. Promoter and Advocate Fiscal of this holy Office, hath appeared before us, and declared that it hath been long since known to us, and is very certain, that in many Places of this District and Territory, there hath not been held a general Visitation and Inquisition; and that for this Reason many Offences committed and perpetrated against our most holy Catholick Faith, which it is fit and right should be punished and chastised, have not come to our Knowledge and Notice, the Consequence of which hath been grievous Offence to God, and great Damage and Prejudice to the Christian Religion. For which Reasons we have commanded and appointed the aforesaid Inquisition, and general Visitation to be made and executed, and have caused the publick Edicts to be published and read, designing that all who shall be found guilty of these Wickednesses and Crimes shall be chastised, that so our Catholick Faith may every Day more flourish, and be exalted high, and greatly encrease. Assenting therefore to his most just Petition, and earnest Request; even as we ought, and desiring to use the best Remedy in those Things which relate to the Honour of God, and our blessed Lord; we have commanded and ordained this present Command, and publick and general Edict to be made and published amongst all and singular, and every one of you, for the same mentioned Cause and Reason, that if you know, understand, or have seen, or previously found out, that any living Man or Woman, present or absent, or already dead, hath made, published, said or spoken any or more Opinions or Words heretical, suspected, erroneous, rash, ill-sounding, favouring of Scandal, or any heretical Blasphemy against God, and his holy Catholick Faith, and against that which our holy Mother the Church of Rome embraces, teaches, preaches, and holds, you declare, speak and manifest it to us.

And first, if you know, or have heard that any Men or Women have kept or observed any Sabbath, according to the Rites, Ceremonies, and Observance of the Law of Moses, and on the said Days have put on a clean and fresh Shirt or Shift, and other Garments, or better, handsomer and Holyday Cloaths; or have laid clean Napkins on the Table, and clean Sheets on the Bed, in Honour of the said Sabbath; or have not blown up, nor kindled their Fire; or have abstained from all other Work on the said Sabbath, and begun to keep them from Friday Evening; or have washed their Meat; or drawn out and taken away the Sewet from that Flesh they were about to eat, soaking it in Water to suck and draw out the Blood; or have cut the Nerve or Gland out of the Leg or Thigh of a Sheep or Goat, or any other Animal; or have killed Animals by sticking them, and as it were muttering out certain and deter-

minate

minate Words, trying first of all their Knife upon their Nail, to see whether it be sharp, or notched, or blunt, afterward covering the Ground with the Blood ; or who have eat Flesh in Lent, and other Days forbidden by the holy Mother Church, with-out any Necessity to urge or require it, certainly thinking and believing that they may lawfully eat them, and without Sin ; or who have kept the greater and solemn Fast, which they call the Fast of Remission and Indulgence, going that Day without Shoes, and with their Feet naked ; or have prayed after the Manner of the Jews, *and at Night have asked Pardon one of another ; or Fathers have laid their Hands on their Childrens Heads, without pronouncing any Words, or giving them any Blessing ; or saying, Be ye blessed by God and us, according as the Law of* Moses *directs, and the Tradition thereof.*

Or who have kept the Fast of Queen Esther, *or the Fast commonly called* Rama-dan, *upon account of the Loss and Destruction of the Holy Land and House, or other Fasts of the* Jews, *within the Week, viz. by abstaining from Meat* Monday *or* Thursday, *till the Evening, when the Stars begin to shine, and from Flesh during those Nights, cutting their Nails and Ends of their Hair ; keeping all those Things, or burning them ; reciting* Jewish *Prayers ; lifting up, or bowing down their Heads ; turning their Face to the Wall ; and before these Things washing their Hands in Water or Earth ; putting on Garments of Sackcloth, with twisted Fringes, hanging down at the End of the Girdle, made with little Threads or Thongs of Leather, and formed into Tossels.*

Or who have celebrated the Passover of unleavened Bread, beginning this sort of Food with Lettice, Parsley, or other green Herbs ; or have observed the Passover of Tabernacles, by fixing up green Boughs, or rich Tapestry ; Feasting, and ac-cepting each others Invitations to eat and drink together ; or the Passover of Candles ; lighting up Candles gradually, and one after another, till they come to the Tenth, after which they extinguish them, and recite Jewish *Prayers on such Days. Or if they say Grace after the Manner of the* Jews, *drinking Wine made at home, and celebrate what they call the* Baraka, *i. e. receiving with one Hand a Cup or Vessel of Wine, and pronouncing over it certain Words ; after which they give a Draught of Wine to all that sit down. Or if they eat Flesh killed or slain by the Hands of the* Jews ; *or sit at their Table ; or taste their Meats ; or recite the Psalms of* David *without the* Gloria Patri ; *or if they expect the Messiah promised in the Law ; or have said that the Messiah promised in the Law is not yet come, but is to come ; and that they yet expect him to deliver them from that Bondage, which they say they are under, and to lead them into the Land of Promise. Or if any Wo-man, after Child-bearing, delays going to the Temple forty Days, according to the Rite of the Law of* Moses, *and is purified, according to the Ceremony thereof. Or if they circumcise new-born Infants, and give them* Jewish *Names, calling them thereby. Or if they have shaved, or caused to be shaved the Chrism, or the Parts of those newly baptized, which have been anointed with Oil and Chrism ; or if they have taken a Bason full of Water the seventh Night after the Birth of a Child, throw-ing into it Gold, Silver, Jewels, Wheat, Barley, and the like ; to wash the new-born Infant with the said Water, pronouncing certain Words ; or have recommended their Children either to* Witches *or* Magicians. *Or if any have been married after*

the

the Jewish *Manner, or have celebrated the* Ruaia *when they go a Journey; or if they have born* Jewish *Names; or if at any time they have baked leavened Bread, and taken out the Leaven from it, and thrown it into the Fire after the Manner and Rule of a Sacrifice; or if any one about to die, turns to the Wall to breathe out his Spirit; or if they wash any dead Corpse with warm Water, shaving the Hairs under his Armpit, and the other hairy Parts of his Body, covering the dead Body with new Linnen Breeches, and a Shrowd, with a Veil thrown over it, putting a Pillow under the Head, and some new or Virgin Earth; or putting into the Mouth a Piece of Money, or a Jewel, or any Thing else. Or have wash'd with Water the House of a dead Person out of the Pitchers and Tubs of the House, and other Houses of the Neighbours, after the* Jewish *Ceremony; eating on the Ground behind the Doors, Fish and Olives, not Flesh; in token of Mourning for the Deceased; not going out of their House for a whole Year, according to the Observation of the said Law; or if they bury them in new and Virgin Earth, or in the Burial-Place of the* Jews; *or if any return and become converted to* Judaism; *or if any one shall say that the Law of* Moses *is equally holy with that which is given by our Lord and Saviour Jesus Christ.*

Or if ye know or have heard that any Men or Women have said and affirmed that the Sect of Mahomet *is good, and that there is no other by which any one can enter into Heaven, and ascend into Paradise; and that Jesus Christ is not God, but a Prophet; nor born of our Lady the Virgin* Mary, *a Virgin before, in and after his Birth; or hath done any of the Rites and Ceremonies of the* Mahometan *Sect, with an Intention to observe and keep them. For Instance, If they eat Flesh on* Fridays *as tho' they were Holydays, or on other Days forbidden by our holy Mother Church, affirming it to be no Sin, putting on the said* Fridays *new and clean Shirts and Shifts, and other Holiday Garments or Cloaths; or if they have killed Birds, or cut off the Heads of Cattle, or any Thing else, by sticking it with a Knife, leaving the Epiglottis to the Head, and turning the Face to the* Alkibla, *i. e. towards the East, saying,* Vizmila, *binding the Feet of Cattle; or if they abstain from eating of Birds, whose Heads are not cut off by the Hands of Women, and the Women will not cut off their Heads, because 'tis prohibited them in the* Mahometan *Sect. Or if they circumcise their Sons giving them Names of the said Sect, or calling them by the Names of the* Moors *and* Saracens; *they who name them so, or they who have caused themselves to be called by Names belonging to the* Agarenes, *or when they are so called, giving a Sign of Joy; or who have said that there are no other in Heaven but God and* Mahomet *his Messenger and Legate; or who have sworn by* Alquibla, *or* Alayminsula, *i. e. according to them by all that is sacred; or who have kept the Fast of* Ramadam, *by observing the Passover thereof, and giving Alms the same Day to the Poor, and abstaining from all Meat and Drink from Morning to Evening, till the rising of the Star, and then indulge to Flesh and other Meats; or who have celebrated* Zohor, *rising before Day-break, and stuffing themselves with Meat before 'tis light, after this washing their Mouths, and returning to Bed; or have celebrated* Guadoc, *washing their Arms from the Wrist to the Elbow, their Cheeks, Mouths, Noses, Ears, Legs, and Privy Parts; or after having done these Things have celebrated* Zala, *turning their Face towards* Alquibla, *being on a* Spartan Carpet,*

Carpet, or Tapestry, raising up and bowing down the Neck, pronouncing certain and determinate Arabick *Words, and reciting the Prayer which they call* Allanda lu ley and colhua and guohat, *and the like* Arabick *Prayers; eating no Swines Flesh, nor drinking Wine according to the Rule and Observation of the* Saracen *Sect; or who have celebrated the Passover of the Lamb or Ram, and killed him, making and celebrating first of all* Guadoc *; or if any have married after the* Mahometan *Manner, and sung the* Arabian *Songs of* Moors, *or have celebrated* Zambras *; or* Leleylas, *with prohibited and forbidden musical Instruments, observing the five Precepts and Commands of* Mahomet.

Or if any one hath tied up for himself or his Children, or other Persons, Lianeas, *i. e. one Hand in Memory of the five Precepts ; or hath washed the Dead, buried the Corpse wrapped up in new Linnen, putting it into new, pure, or Virgin Earth ; or who have ordered these Things in their hollow Sepulchres, putting a Stone at the Head of it, and putting into the Sepulchres green Boughs,* Milk, Honey, *and other Meats ; or who have cried out, and called upon* Mahomet *in all their Events and Actions, saying, that he is a Prophet, the Messenger of God, and that the first Temple of God was in* Mecca, *where they believe* Mahomet *was buried; or who have said that they did not receive Baptism with the Intention and Faith of the holy Mother the Catholick Church; or who have said that their Fathers who died in the* Mahometan *or* Jewish *Sect, and that a* Saracen *or* Jew, *each tenacious of his own Sect, may be saved; or if any Person hath fled over to the* Turks, *or* Infidels, *and denied the Catholick Faith, and departed from it ; or gone to other Parts and Places without these Kingdoms, to profess the* Jewish *or* Mahometan *Sect ; or have done, held, or said any other Rites or Ceremonies of the* Saracens.

Or if you know, or have heard that any Men or Women have said, held, or believed the false and condemned Sect of Martin Luther *and his Followers to be true, holy, and approved ; or have believed or approved his other Opinions, by asserting that Confession to a Priest is not necessary ; that 'tis sufficient to confess to God only ; that the Pope and Priests have not Power to absolve Sins ; that in the Host there is not truly contained the Body of our Lord* Jesus Christ *; that Saints are not to be invocated ; that Images are to be taken out of Churches ; that there is no Purgatory ; that the Dead are not to be prayed for ; that good Works are not necessary ; that Faith only with Baptism is sufficient to Salvation ; that any one may bear another's Confession, and give the Communion under both Kinds of Bread and Wine ; that the Pope hath no Power to confer Indulgences, Graces, Indults, and Bulls ; that the Clergy, Religious, Monks, and Nuns, may contract Matrimony ; or who have said that the Religious, Monks, Monasteries, and Ceremonies of Religion ought to be taken away ; or have said that God hath not instituted the Religions, and that a Marriage State is more perfect than the Religious State of the Clergy and Monks ; and that there are no Holidays besides the Lord's Days ; that 'tis no Sin to eat Flesh on* Fridays, Vigils *and* Lent *; because eating Flesh is not forbidden and limited to certain Days ; or who have believed any one or more of the Opinions of* M. Luther *or his Followers ; or fled over to other Provinces to profess* Lutheranism.

Or if you know, or have heard that any Men or Woman, living or dead, have said or affirmed that the Sect of the Illuminated, *or* Relicts *is approved ; particularly that*

that mental Prayer is of divine Appointment ; and that all other Duties are fulfilled in it ; and that Prayer is a Sacrament under Accidents ; and that mental Prayer is of great Weight and Efficacy, and vocal Prayer of but small Moment ; that the Servants of God are not to be distracted by bodily Exercises ; that the Prelate, Father, or Superior are not to be obeyed, if they command Things that call Persons off from Contemplation and mental Prayer ; or if by Words they have derogated from the Sacrament of Matrimony ; and said that no one can get the Secret of Virtue, unless he become the Disciple of those Masters who teach the aforesaid perverse Doctrine ; and that no one can be saved, who is not taught by such Masters, and generally confessed to them ; and that certain secret and inward Ardors, Tremors, Extasies, Shiverings and Faintings, which they undergo, are Signs of a vehement Love towards God ; and that from hence it may be certainly discerned that they are in a State of Grace, and have the holy Spirit within them ; and that being thus perfect, they want no other Helps, and ought not to be obliged to laborious Acts ; and that when they attain to a certain prefixed Term of Perfection, the divine Essence, and the Mysteries of the Trinity may be beheld in this Life, and are actually beheld ; and that the Holy Spirit doth immediately govern those who thus live ; and that the internal Motion and Inspiration of the Holy Ghost is only to be followed in what they do, or refuse to do ; or who say that when the most Holy Host, in the Sacrifice of the Mass, is held out to View, the necessary Rite and Ceremony, during the Elevation, is to shut the Eyes ; or that any Persons have said and affirmed, that when they are come to a certain determinate Point of Perfection, 'tis a Sin to look on the Images of the Saints, to be present at Sermons, pious Conferences, and other Exercises of the said Sect, and absurd Doctrine.

Or if ye know or have heard of any other Heresies, and especially these. That there is no Paradise, nor heavenly Glory for the Good, nor Hell for the Wicked, but that the Soul perishes together with the Body, with other heretical Blasphemies, such as, I do not believe, but disbelieve, defy and deny our Lord God, the Virgin Purity of our Lady, the Virgin Mary, or the He and She Saints of Heaven. Or who have, or have had familiar Spirits, calling upon them, making Circles, and asking them concerning certain Matters, or waiting for their Answers. Or whether they have been Fortune-Tellers or Gypsies ; or have made a tacit or express Covenant with the Devil, mixing sacred Things with profane, in Confirmation of it ; attributing to the Creature that which belongs to the Creator only ; or that any Person, being a Clergyman, or in holy Orders, or a professed Religious, hath contracted Matrimony ; or that any one, not being invested with the sacerdotal Character, hath said or celebrated Mass, or administred any Sacrament of our holy Mother the Church. Or that any Confessor, or Priests being Confessors, or Religious or Seculars, of whatsoever State or Dignity, hath enticed the Daughters of Penance in the Act of Confession, or immediately after it, by provoking or inducing them, by Deeds or Words, to filthy, carnal and immodest Acts. Or if any Person whatsoever hath married twice, or oftener, the former Wife or Husband being living. Or that any one hath said or asserted that simple Fornication, Usury or excessive Interest or Perjury, are not mortal Sins ; or that it is better to live in a State of Concubinage than in lawful Wedlock ; or hath disgracefully used and done Despite to the Images of Saints and Crosses ; or that any

Man

Man or Woman hath not believed the Articles of the Catholick Faith; or called any of them into Queſtion; or hath ſtaid and continued for a Year or longer under Excommunication; or hath deſpiſed the Cenſures of our holy Mother the Church, by ſaying or doing any Thing againſt them.

Or if ye know, or have heard of any Perſons, Men or Women, that under Pretence of Aſtrological Science, or Looks or Aſpeƈts of the Stars, or by the Lines and Tokens of the Hands, or any ſuch Things, do by this Knowledge, Faculty, or any other Way, anſwer or foretel future Things depending on the Liberty and Free-will of Man, or accidental Things that may come to paſs, or Things already paſt that are ſecret and free, ſaying and affirming that there is a certain Art, Science, and certain Rules whereby to know theſe Things, in order to perſuade People to ſeek after and conſult the aforeſaid Diviners concerning the ſaid Matters, when, on the contrary, the ſaid Science is falſe, vain and ſuperſtitious, and turns to the great Damage and Prejudice of Religion and the Chriſtian Faith.

Likewiſe if ye know, or have heard that any Men or Women have had, or have Books of the Seƈt and Opinion of Martin Luther, *or other Hereticks, or the Alcoran of* Mahomet, *and other Books of the ſaid Seƈt, or Bibles in the* Spaniſh *Tongue, or any other Books or Writings condemned and prohibited by the Cenſures, Catalogues and Ediƈts of the holy Office of the Inquiſition; or any Men or Women who have not fulfilled that to which they were obliged; or who have omitted to deteƈt, diſcover and ſay what they know in theſe Affairs; or who have ſaid to, or perſuaded other Perſons not to declare theſe Things, and give Information to the Inquiſitors; or who have ſuborned or corrupted Witneſſes to give Evidence againſt thoſe who have depoſed in the Court of the holy Office; or that any Men or Women have depoſed and given falſe Witneſs againſt others to their Damage and Infamy; or who have cheriſhed, received, concealed and hid Hereticks, by giving them Favour and Aſſiſtance, in order to conceal and preſerve their Perſons and Effeƈts; or who have been any Hindrance by themſelves, or by the Interpoſition of other Perſons, to the free and right Adminiſtration of the holy Office of the Inquiſition, their Miniſters and Officials, and Family; or who have taken down, or cauſed to be taken down the Habits or* Sanbenito's *from thoſe Places, in which they were put up by the holy Office, or have put up others in their Room; or that thoſe who have been reconciled and enjoin'd Penance by the Office of the holy Inquiſition, have not fulfilled the fixed Times of their Impriſonment, or the Penance enjoin'd them; or if they refuſed publickly to wear the Habit of Reconciliation; or that any Perſons reconciled publickly or privately, being enjoined the Yoke of Penance by the holy Office, have ſaid or affirmed, that what they confeſſed before the holy Office, either of themſelves or others, was falſe, that they did, and ſaid it thro' the Influence of Fear, or for any other Reaſon; or have revealed the Secret committed and commended to them by the holy Office; or that any Perſons have ſaid that thoſe who were delivered over by the holy Office of the Inquiſition, were condemned without any previous Fault, or ſuffered as Martyrs; or that any Men or Women reconciled, or the Children or Grandchildren of Perſons condemned for the Crime of Hereſy, have adminiſtred, or do adminiſter publick and honourable Offices, which are prohibited them by divine Law, and by the Laws and Pragmaticks of theſe Kingdoms, and the Inſtitutions of the holy Office; or have been promoted to ſacred Orders; or have any Eccleſiaſtical or Secular Gift or Dignity ; or the Enfigns of fuch Dignity ; or have worn prohibited Things, fuch as Arms, Silk, Gold, Silver, Blood-ftone, Jewels, Corrals, fine Cloth ; or have got on Horfeback, or rid as Horfemen ; or that there are any Proceffes, Acts, Denunciations, Informations or Proofs concerning the Crimes contained in this Edict, in the Hands of any Notary, Attorney, or any other Perfon whatfoever.*

By Virtue of thefe Prefents therefore we admonifh, exhort and require, and command you, and every one of you, in Virtue of your holy Obedience, and under the Penalty of Excommunication, latæ fententiæ, after three Canonical Admonitions, that if you have known, done, feen or heard any Man or Woman, or Perfons, to have committed, faid, held, or affirmed any of the Things aforefaid and declared, or other Things, whatfoever they be, againft our holy Catholick Faith, and againft what our holy Mother the Catholick Church of Rome *holds, teaches and preaches, as well concerning Perfons living, prefent or abfent, as dead, you do, without mentioning it to any other Perfon, for thus 'tis convenient and becoming, come and appear perfonally before us, to declare and manifeft it within fix Days immediately following the Day of the Publication of this our Edict, altho' you may by any Means have had a Part in, or Knowledge of this Matter ; giving you previous Admonition, which we now do, that after the faid Term is lapfed, and Obedience not paid to the aforefaid, befides that you incur the faid Cenfures and Penalties, we fhall proceed againft them who fhall have been found contumacious, difobedient, and rebellious, as againft Perfons who fraudulently cover and conceal thefe Things, and who have wrong Sentiments concerning Matters of the holy Catholick Faith, and the Ecclefiaftical Cenfures. And becaufe the Abfolution of the Crime and Offence of Herefy is fpecially referved to us, we forbid and prohibit, under the aforefaid Penalty, all Confeffors whatfoever, Clergy or Religious, that they do not abfolve any Man or Woman intangled in, or guilty of this Crime, or who have not faid or difcovered to the holy Office whatfoever they have known of thefe Things, or heard others fay. Yea, who have not fent it to us, that the Truth being known and found out, evil Men may be punifhed, and good and faithful Chriftians may be known and honoured, and our holy Catholick Faith may be happily fpread. And that all the aforefaid Matters may come to the Knowledge of all, and no one may excufe himfelf by pretending Ignorance, we command them to be publifhed this Day.*

Pegna 3.
part. com
12.
Simanc.
tit. 44.
§. 2. In many Places, but efpecially in *Spain*, 'tis the Cuftom, that when the Sermon of the Catholick Faith is ended, all promife upon Oath, before the Crucifix and Gofpels, that they will give Favour, Help and Counfel to the holy Inquifition, and the Minifters of it ; and that they will by no Means directly or indirectly hinder them. This Oath the Magiftrates of Cities muft particularly take, which muft be regiftred amongft the Acts by the Notaries of the Inquifition, 1 *Inftruct. Hyfpal. cap.* 1, 2. This Oath the Inquifitor may force them to take, and will do it when he thinks fit. In all other Cafes he muft follow the received Cuftom of the City, where he is, to prevent Innovations, and that there may be no Hindrance in this Caufe.

The Form of the Oath they are obliged to take is this. *We the Viceroy, or Pretor, &c. of fuch a Province, or City, or Place ; and fuch Confuls or Jurats of fuch a City, &c. at the Requeft and Admonition of the Reverend Lord Inquifitor, Doctor or Licentiate N. as true, faithful and obedient to the holy*

Church

Church of God, do promise and swear by these holy four Gospels placed before us, and by us corporally touched, that we will hold, and cause to be held, observe, and order to be observed, the Faith of our Lord Jesus Christ, and of the holy Roman Church, and defend it to our utmost against all Persons; also that we will prosecute and apprehend, or cause to be apprehended, whensoever we can, Hereticks, their Believers, Favourers and Receivers, and their Defenders, and those who are defamed or suspected of Heresy, and we will accuse and denounce them to the Church or Inquisitors, when we know them to be any where, or any one of them, especially when we shall be required hereto. Likewise that we will not grant Ballives, Saionies, or any publick Offices, of any Name whatsoever, to any one of the aforesaid pernicious Persons, or to such as are suspected or defamed of Heresy, nor to any other Person who shall have been judged unworthy of it upon account of Heresy, or otherwise prohibited by the Inquisitors or the Law, from enjoying publick Offices; nor will we permit them to enjoy the aforesaid, or to hold publick Offices. Likewise that we will receive none of the aforesaid Persons, nor entertain them knowingly in our Family, Conversation, Service or Counsel. And if the contrary should happen, thro' Ignorance, we will immediately expel them, after it shall come to our Knowledge by the Church, or Inquisitors of heretical Pravity, or their Commissaries: And that in these Things and all others which belong to the Office of the Inquisition of heretical Pravity, we will be obedient to God, and the Church of Rome, and the Inquisitors of the said heretical Pravity, according to our Duty and Ability. So help us God, and these holy Gospels of God, upon which we swear, and which we touch with our own Hands.*

This Form of Swearing was drawn from the Constitution of the Emperor *Frederick* II. published at *Padua, Feb.* 22. 1239. *Indict.* 12. and is annexed to it, with four other Constitutions of the same Day, of which mention is made in the first Book, which were afterwards inserted in the Rescripts of several Popes.

After the Sentence of Excommunication is read, the Inquisitor explains it *Direct.* more distinctly, and reduces it to several Heads. Then he publishes an In-*p. 3. n. 54,* dulgence of forty Days to all who come to his Sermon, and promises, in the 55. Name of the Pope, Indulgences for three Years, to all who give him Counsel or Favour in his Office of reducing Hereticks. He also adds three other Years of Indulgences to those who discover to him any Heretick, or Person defamed for Heresy, or suspected, or who in any other Case bear true Witness before him in a Cause of Faith, according to the Privilege of *Urban* IV.

Finally, he assigns a Time of Grace to all Hereticks, and their Favou-   56. rers, and Persons suspected of Heresy, *viz.* the entire Month following, and promises, that if within that Space they come to him freely, or not admonish'd, by Name, and don't wait till they are denounced, accused or apprehended, and voluntarily discover their Guilt, and ask Pardon, they shall obtain large Pardon and Mercy, *viz.* Freedom from Death, Imprisonment, Banishment, and Confiscation of Effects, according to the Determination of the Council of *Biterre,* cap. 2. *Farther, do you command that all, who know themselves or others to have offended in the Crime of heretical Pravity, do appear before*

* *Ballivæ* and *Saioniæ* are a sort of Messengers attending on Princes and Magistrates.

R   *you*

you to speak the Truth, assigning them a competent Term, which you usually call the Time of Grace, who otherwise would not have had such Grace shewn them. And such who appear within this Term, and are penitent, and speak the whole Truth of themselves and others, let them be free from the Punishment of Death, Imprisonment, Ba- **Pegna,** *nishment, and Confiscation of Effects.* However, this Power of granting Par- **Com. 12.** don is allowed the Inquisitors only when they are sent to a City or Diocese, in which the Inquisition is first erected. *Instruct. Hispal. A.* 1484. cap. 1, 2, 3. but not when upon the Death or Removal of an Inquisitor, another is put into his Place. In *Spain* also the Letters Patent of such Grace must be inserted in the Edict.

CHAP. III.

Of the Obligation to denounce every HERETICK *to the* INQUISITORS.

THE Publication of the Edict of Faith is repeated every Year, and all are obliged, under Penalty of Excommunication, to be present at the publishing of it, and at the general Sermon concerning the Faith, unless they are prevented by Sickness, Age, or any other Hindrance, and can make a legal Excuse.

The Oath which all Persons, not only private, but Magistrates, are compelled by the Inquisitors to take, obliges them not to obstruct the Office of the Inquisition, either directly or indirectly. Such are believed to obstruct it indirectly, who do not reveal the Truth they know, *i. e.* do not accuse to the Inquisitor every one they know to be an Heretick, or suspected of Heresy. So that in *Spain* they are doubly obliged to accuse to the Inquisitor, every Heretick, first under Penalty of Excommunication, which they incur if they are wanting in their Duty; and secondly, by their own Oath.

In order therefore to excite all Persons to turn Accusers, the Popish Doctors lay the greatest Stress they can upon this Obligation to accuse. **In Zan-** *Camillus Campegius,* after laying together the Testimonies of several Doctors, **chin.** teaches, that every one is obliged to accuse and testify, and that according **9. 13. d.** to *Cajetan,* he is bound to it as necessary to Salvation; if there be no other way of preventing the general Danger but by this Method, and then concludes in these Words: *These Things ought so to excite every faithful and Catholick Person, as to engage them willingly to accuse or denounce and bear Witness, for the common Good of the Christian Religion, without the Admonition, Citation or Punishment of the Judge. Tho' this ought to be observed in all Cases, yet it ought to be done with greater Ardency in the Affair of the Christian Faith, since hereby we not only avoid the most severe Punishments, but secure incomparable Rewards, thro' the Bounty of the supream God, and the Favour of his holy Church.*

Nor

Nor is there any Regard to Kindred in this Affair. For the Brother is bound under the fame Penalty to accufe his Brother, yea, the Wife her Huf-band, and the Husband his Wife, if guilty, or fufpected of Herefy. *Pegna Direct.* however thinks, that the Wife is to be excufed, if fhe doth not accufe her *part. 2.* Hufband for eating Flefh on prohibited Days ; if the Hufband be a terrible *com. 78.* Fellow, and fhe is afraid of ill Ufage from him. In all other Cafes he thinks the Wife is obliged to accufe her Hufband.

[*Ludovicus a Paramo* tells us, that *Lewis de Carvajal,* altho' Governor and *l. 2. t. 2.* Captain General of the Province of *Tampico* and *Pamico,* was forced to walk *c. 21.* out in publick Penance, becaufe he did not denounce four Women, who *n. 16,* were fecretly *Jews,* and to whom he was Uncle ; and that tho' a little be-fore he' had the honourable Title of Prefident, he was forced to hear his ignominious Sentence publickly, was for ever deprived of all Offices under the King, reduced to the loweft Mifery, and thro' Grief and Wearinefs of his Life, foon went the Way of all Flefh.]

'Tis difputed amongft the Popifh Doctors, whether a Son be obliged to *Simanc.* accufe his Father, who is a fecret Heretick, or at leaft to difcover him to *de Cathol.* the Judges. The general Opinion is, that he is obliged to it. But others *Inft. tit.* think differently, becaufe there is no Law, natural, divine, or human, that *29. §. 35:* lays fuch a Burthen on the Shoulders of Children. And yet even fuch who *&c.* are of this Opinion, confefs the Son may do it, efpecially if the Father be incorrigible. Yea, think fuch a Son ought to be commended who conquers his natural Love, and overcomes this moft ftrong Affection, from an ardent Love to divine Religion. He muft however try every Method before he ac-cufes his Father to the Judge. But yet they teach, that there are two Cafes in which the Son is obliged to betray his heretical Father to the Judges. The firft, when the Son is legally interrogated by the Apoftolick Inquifitors ; the fecond, when the Father's Herefy is dangerous to the Common-wealth.

Pegna however affirms, that the Son ought to accufe and denounce before *In Eymer;* the Inquifitors, his Father, whom he knows to be an Heretick. The Re-*part. 2.* ward of fuch Accufation is, that the Son who thus acts, is freed from the *com. 15.* Penalties ordained againft the Children of Hereticks, according to the Law of the Emperor *Frederick. Nor do we think proper to exclude from the Bounds of Mercy fuch, who not following the Herefy of their Fathers, fhall difcover their fecret Wickednefs ; fo that in what manner foever the Father's Guilt be punifhed, let not the Innocence of their Children be fubject to the aforefaid Punifhment. Carena* adds, that not only an heretical Father, but even one only fufpected of Herefy, muft be accufed by the Son to the Inquifitors, becaufe the fame Reafons hold good as to Hereticks, and thofe fufpected of Herefy.

An Heretick alfo reformed, according to *Royas,* ought neceffarily to be *part. 2.* accufed before the Inquifitors of the Faith ; becaufe they often feign them-*Affert. 3.* felves to be corrected and amended, and in the mean while infect with their Doctrine unwary Catholicks. And altho' fuch Hereticks fhould be really reformed, 'tis neverthelefs ufeful and neceffary to accufe them, that the In-quifitors of the Faith may interrogate them from what Mafters they learnt

their

their Errors ; what Difciples they taught before their Converfion ; or if any of their Friends and Acquaintance have been corrupted by their perverfe Doctrine. He faith this may be gathered from the *Madrid* Inftruction, *A.* 1561. *c.* 53. *in fin.*

And from this Obligation to accufe, no one is freed, of whatfoever Order and Dignity they may be. For the Edict of Faith obliges all. So that they will have neither Princes nor Kings themfelves exempted. *Ludovicus a Paramo* proves this by a famous Inftance. *Joan* the Daughter of the Emperor *Charles* V. was cited by the Inquifitors to be interrogated before them, againft a certain Perfon concerning fome Things relating to the Faith. She confulted her Father, who advifed her to make her Depofition without any Delay, leaft fhe fhould incur Excommunication, not only againft others, but even againft himfelf, if fhe knew him to be blameable in the leaft Matter. *Joan* obeyed this Command of her Father, and immediately depofed before *Ferdinand Valdez*, Arch-Bifhop of *Seville*, at that Time Bifhop and Inquifitor General.

CHAP. IV.

Of fuch who voluntarily appear, and the Grace fhewn them.

" 'TIS the prefent Cuftom in *Spain* for one of the Inquifitors in thefe " Acts, to vifit the Province, and to propofe general Edicts where- " ever he goes, by which he commands, under Penalty of Excommunica- " tion, that whofoever knows of any Thing done or faid againft the Catho- " lick Faith and Evangelick Law, he muft immediately difcover it to the " Inquifitor. Whatever is reported, muft be fecretly written down by the " Notary of the Inquifitors. The other of the Inquifitors remains in the Ci- " ty in which their Refidence is fixed, and muft prefide, in ordering the " Acts of Caufes. But if there be no Occafion for his Refidence there, that " he may not fit idle, he muft vifit in the fame Manner the other Part of " the Province, 5 *Inftruct. Hifpal.* cap. 2.

" This Vifitation and general Inquifition the Inquifitors muft make, each " in his Turn, thro' all the Cities and Corporations of their Province ; and " if they are negligent in this Affair, they muft be deprived of their Office. " In this Vifitation the Inquifitors may compel all thofe whom they judge

" proper, to fwear and bear Witnefs, and muft take particular Care not to " be entertained by thofe who are related and akin to Hereticks, *Jews*, and " *Mahometans*, which muft alfo be obferved by their Minifters. Nor muft " they receive any Gratuity from the Perfons where they lodge, becaufe they " are to be content with their Salaries, and becaufe fometimes an intimate " Friendfhip is contracted by this Means, 8 *Inftruct. Tolet.* c. 19."

Whilft

Whilst one of them is visiting the Province, the other Inquisitor stays at *Direct.* home, that all who come voluntarily may have Access to him. If they come *part.* 3. within the appointed Term, and accuse themselves, he treats them more *§. 58.* gently. He must not however admit them after the Manner of Sacramental Confession, but after the Manner of Confession in a judicial Court; so that they must declare their Crime before the Inquisitor, and the Notary take down their Confession.

After such Confession, every one of them is interrogated by the Inquisi- *Pegna,* tor, whether he hath adhered to such Errors, or only been in doubt con- *prax. Inq.* cerning them? For how long Space of Time he hath continued in them? *l. 2. c 4.* From whom, and how he learnt them? Whether he hath had and read any he- *n. 6, &c.* retical or suspected Books? What they were, from whom he had them, and what he hath done with them? Other Questions are added concerning his Accomplices in Heresies, that he may tell the Names of all those Hereticks, or Persons suspected of Heresy, whom he knows. He is farther asked, Whether he hath ever been inquisited, processed, or accused or denounced in any Tribunal, or before any Judge, on account of the aforesaid Errors, or other Things relating to Heresy? He is also admonished simply to tell the whole Truth which he knows, as well of himself as of others; because, if he is afterwards found deceitfully to have concealed any Thing, he is judged as one whose Confession is imperfect, and as impenitent, and feignedly converted. Finally, he is interrogated, Whether he repents of these Errors and Heresies into which he hath fallen? And whether he is ready to abjure, curse and detest them, and all other Heresies whatsoever, that exalt themselves against the holy Apostolick and *Roman* Church, and to live for the future catholickly, according to the Faith of the Church of *Rome*, and devoutly to fulfil the salutary Penance enjoined him?

If the Inquisitor finds that he was before admonished, yet he is to be dealt with *n. 60.* more gently, because he appeared voluntarily. For such are said voluntarily to *Lucern.* return to Favour, who come within the Time of Grace, altho' they have *Inq. in* been admonished. For they don't appear to be forced, since they are *voc. re-* apprehended by no one. Yea, 'tis the same if they come after the Time *dire.* of Grace, whilst their Cause is entire, because they were not personally required, nor the Proofs against them received.

However, at their first Appearance, the Inquisitors must not write down, *n. 12.* that they appeared voluntarily; because such Appearance, after Accusation, altho' the Person may not have been verbally cited, is not presumed to be voluntary, nor made with a candid and pure Will, but is rather thro' Terror, and unwilling, thro' Fear and Dread of the Proofs, to avoid the ordinary Punishments. However, it may be minuted down, that such a one appeared not cited or called.

If the Crime be entirely concealed, the Inquisitor may absolve him secretly; *n. 61.* enjoining him wholesome Penance. But if it be not secret, and the Person *n. 62.* confesses that he hath not only believed wrong, but hath revealed his erroneous Belief to others, and infected them, the Inquisitor must proceed against him.

him, according to the Canonical Sanctions, but yet in a milder Manner, because he came of himself, without being called on, and within the Time of Grace.

Carena, *annot. in* Pegnam. *Ibid.* If those who thus voluntarily confess, say, that they have done any external Action against the Faith, without any Error of the Understanding, altho' some sort of Proof may have preceded, they must not be proved to be Hereticks; for those who are ready to be corrected, must by no Means be reckoned amongst Hereticks. From these Things they infer, that if any one confesses that he hath done certain *Jewish* Ceremonies, or those of any other Sect, upon the account of some Profit to himself, he is not to be accounted an Heretick. This sometimes is the Case of Captives, who, without any other Intention, but that of their being better freed from their Captivity, externally deny the Faith. *San Vincente* the Inquisitor tells us, That he saw a certain Person who wanted to satisfy his lustful Desires upon a Woman, who was one of the newly converted *Saracens*. She promised to lie carnally with him, if he would first perform a Ceremony of their Sect, called *Gaodoc*. He, tho' an old Christian, in order to gratify his lewd Inclinations, did it, but immediately went and voluntarily confessed it, adding that he had no other evil Intention. After consulting the supream Senate, he was absolved, *An.* 1618. A Case may however happen, when a Person who makes a voluntary Confession, may be obliged to abjure vehemently. A certain new Christian of the *Saracens* being driven from *Spain*, was afterwards taken by the Christians. He immediately accused himself, that whilst he was amongst the *Moors*, he did some Ceremonies and Acts of the *Mahometan* Sect, denying an evil Intention therein. But as some of these Things seemed to the Inquisitor entirely voluntary, *viz.* his marrying an Infidel *Moorish* Woman for his Wife, without any Violence, or any other Advantage, he examined his Fellow-Captives; and when it was proved that he made his Confession thro' Fear of Proof, it was determined that he should abjure as vehement, which Determination pleased the supream Council. But when this very Criminal had been kept in Custody a few Days, in order to his confessing the whole Truth, he made the Confession desired, and was reconciled in Form.

However, such as come voluntarily, are far from escaping all Punishment, but are either treated kindly at the Pleasure of the Inquisitor, according to the Quality of their Persons and Crimes, or else condemned to pay a Fine, or give Alms, or some such Works of Charity. But if they wait till they are accused, denounced, cited or apprehended, or suffer the Time of Grace to slip over, they are pronounced unworthy of it.

And in this Case many foolishly deceive themselves with a false Opinion, believing, that because Favour is promised to such who appear voluntarily, they shall be free from all Punishment; because they are only saved from the more terrible ones, it being left to the Pleasure of the Inquisitors to inflict some penitential Punishment on them, according to the Nature of their Gonsalv. *p.* 193. Crime, as will appear from the following Instance. " There was at the " City of *Cadiz*, a certain Foreigner, who yet had lived in *Spain* for twenty
" Years,

" Years, who, according to a common Superſtition, dwelt in a Deſart in a
" certain Chapel, upon the Account of Religion. Hearing in his Chapel of
" the great Number of thoſe who were taken up every Day at *Seville* by the
" Inquiſitors, for what they call the *Lutheran* Hereſies ; having heard alſo
" of the Decree of the Inquiſitors, by which he was commanded, under the
" Terrors of Excommunication, immediately to diſcover to the Inquiſition
" whatſoever he knew of thoſe Things, either as to others or himſelf ; the
" poor ſtupid Hermit comes to *Seville*, goes to the Inquiſitors and accuſes him-
" ſelf, becauſe he thought the ſaid Inquiſitors would uſe ſingular Clemency
" towards thoſe who thus betrayed themſelves. His Crime was, That where-
" as, being about twenty Years before this at *Genoa*, and hearing a certain
" Brother of his diſputing about a Man's Juſtification by Faith in Chriſt ; of
" Purgatory, and other Things of the like Nature, he did not wholly condemn
" them, tho' he never thought of them afterwards. He therefore acknow-
" ledged his Crime, and came to ask Mercy. When the Lords Inquiſitors
" had received his Confeſſion, they commanded the poor Hermit to Jayl,
" where, after a long Confinement, he was brought out in publick Procef-
" fion, and was ſentenced to wear the Sanbenito, to three Years Impriſon-
" ment, and the Forfeiture of his Effects."

Sometimes alſo they uſe a certain Stratagem to draw Perſons to a volun- *Ib. 262.*
tary Appearance before the Inquiſitors. " When they have apprehended
" any remarkable Perſon, who hath been the Teacher of others, or who
" they know hath been reſorted to by many others, upon account of his
" Doctrine and Learning, as being a Teacher and Preacher of great Re-
" pute ; 'tis uſual with them to cauſe a Report to be ſpread amongſt the
" People, by their Familiars, that being grievouſly tortured, he had diſco-
" vered ſeveral of thoſe that had adhered to him, ſuborning ſome Perſons
" out of the neighbouring Priſons, to aſſert that they heard his Cries amidſt
" his Tortures, in order to give the greater Credit to the Report. Theſe
" Reports are ſpread for this Reaſon, that ſuch who have attended on his In-
" ſtructions, or have been any ways familiar with him, may in time go to
" the holy Tribunal, confeſs their Fault, and implore Mercy, before they
" are ſent for, or apprehended. By this Means they impoſe on many, who,
" if they had waited for their Summons, had never been ſummoned at all.
" Or if it ſhould have happened that they had been ſummoned, would not
" have been dealt with more ſeverely than they generally are who truſt to
" the Inquiſitors Promiſes.

C H A P.

CHAP. V.

Of the three Methods of beginning the Proceſs before the Tribunal of the INQUISITION.

Direct.
p. 3. n.63.

IF any appear within the Term aſſigned to diſcover Hereticks, *&c.* to re-veal to the Inquiſitor certain Matters relating to the Faith, ſuch * De-nunciations muſt be received judicially. If ſo great a Number appear, that the Denunciation of all cannot be taken judicially, the Inquiſitor muſt provide himſelf with a diſtinct Book in every Dioceſe, to write down in it all the De-nunciations brought to him, the Names of the Denouncers and Witneſſes, and the Town and Place where they dwell ; which Book he keeps privately to himſelf, that the Names of the Denouncers may not be diſcovered, and they thereby come into any Danger.

6ʃ.

When the Time of Grace is elapſed, the Inquiſitor muſt carefully examine the Informations, *viz.* which have the greater Appearance of Truth, and which Crimes are more heinous and prejudicial to the Faith. Where this appears he begins to make Inquiſition, by citing the Informer, giving him his Oath, and taking the beſt Information from him that he can. If he finds no Appearance of Truth, he over-rules it, but however muſt not cancel the Information out of his Book, becauſe what may not be diſcovered at one time, may at another. If he finds an Appearance of Truth, he makes farther Inquiſition.

Simanc.
t.19.§.16.

Now there are three Ways of Proceeding and beginning the Proceſs. Firſt, by Accuſation, which muſt be preceded by † Inſcription. Secondly, by Denun-ciation, which muſt be preceded by a charitative Admonition. But 'tis now the Cuſtom in *Spain,* that Hereticks, altho' concealed, muſt be immediately diſco-vered to the Judges, without any brotherly Correction. So that thoſe who, under pretence of brotherly Correction, do not diſcover ſecret Hereticks to the In-quiſitors, and thoſe who adviſe them not to do it, are puniſhed as Concealers of Hereticks, and as Hinderers of the Office of the holy Inquiſition. Thirdly,

Pegna in
Direct.
p. 3.
Com. 16.

by Inquiſition, which muſt be preceded by notorious Suſpicion. This Inqui-ſition is either General or Special. The General is whenſoever the Inquiſitors viſit their Province, or when being newly created, they go to the Provinces decreed to them, and begin to exerciſe their Inquiſitory Office. For then they publiſh general Edicts, to enquire out ſecret and uncertain Hereticks, for the Exerciſe of which there is no Need of preceding Infamy. But the In-quiſitors are obliged, *ex officio,* thus to act at certain ſtated Times.

---

* There is this Difference between a Denunciation and an Accuſation. A Denunciation doth not diſable the Perſon that makes it to be a Witneſs, as an Accuſation doth.
† Inſcription is a certain Inſtrument, by which the Accuſer, if he fails in his Proof, binds him-ſelf to undergo the ſame Puniſhment, which the accuſed Perſon muſt, if the Crime he is accuſed of be fully proved.

In

In feveral Inquifitions 'tis cuftomary to publifh fuch Edicts for the Difcove-Pegna, *Prax. Inq. l. 1. c. 1=. §. 2. n. 5.* ry of Hereticks every Year, the fecond *Sunday* in *Lent*, in the Cathedral Church during the Celebration of Mafs, and therefore on that Day there is no Sermon, that all may more attentively regard the Things contained in that Edict of the Faith. This Method of Inquifition is prefcribed by the Coun-cil of *Tholoufe*, cap. 2. *We ordain that the Arch-Bifhops fhall oblige by Oath one Prieft, and two or three, or more, if Need be, of the Laity, of good Reputation, in every Parifh, as well in Cities as out of them, who may diligently, faithfully and frequently inquire out Hereticks in the faid Parifhes, by fearching every Houfe, and under-ground Rooms that are remarkably fufpicious, and all Buildings leaning upon and joining to fuch Buildings, and any other hiding Places, all which we command to be deftroyed ; and that if they find any Hereticks, their Believers, Favourers and Receivers, or Defenders, they fhall take fpecial Care that they do not efcape ; and they fhall difcover them to the Arch-Bifhop or Bifhop, or Lords of fuch Pla-ces, or to their Ballives, with all Speed, that they may fuffer the deferved Punifh-ment. Let alfo fuch Abbots as are exempt do the fame in fuch Places which are not fubject by Diocefan Right to the Ordinaries. Let alfo all Lords of Places be careful to inquire out Hereticks in their Villages, Houfes and Woods, and to deftroy fuch ad-joining Buildings and under-ground hiding Places.*

A fpecial Inquifition is a certain Right of proceeding by Office to Con-demnation and Punifhment againft certain Perfons inquifited by Name, defa-med for particular Crimes, to which the Judge cannot proceed without pre-ceding Infamy, which fupplies the Place of an Accufer. However, in the Crime of Herefy, the Inquifitor may act upon Signs and probable Sufpicions, where there is no preceding Infamy, and even where he is not fure of the Bo-dy of the Offence, becaufe Herefy is a Crime that leaves no Traces after it. But in this Cafe he muft proceed cautioufly, and very privately, that no Per-fon's Reputation and Honour may be injured.

But of thefe three Methods of Proceeding, the firft, by way of Accufa-§. 3. n. 6. tion, is not ufed ; the fecond, by Formation, altho' common and ufual, yet feems rather to be the Beginning than the Completion of the whole Pro-cefs ; becaufe upon Information given againft thofe who are guilty of High Treafon againft the Divine Majefty, to the Judges of the Faith, they begin to inquire and to proceed, and in this whole Affair the Inquifition claims to it felf what is otherwife done chiefly by Witneffes. And therefore the Judges are called Inquifitors, and the Tribunal and Minifters are faid to be of the Office of the moft holy Inquifition, from this third Method of Proceeding by Inquifition.

CHAP. VI.

How the Proce∫*s begins by way of* INQUISITION.

WHEN the Proce∫s is made by Inquisition, he who goes to the Inqui∫i-tor ∫ays, that he doth not appear as an Accu∫er or Denouncer, but only relates to him that there is ∫uch a Report, and that it hath frequently come to the Ears of the Inqui∫itor from grave and reputable Per∫ons, that ∫uch a one hath done or ∫aid ∫ome Things again∫t the Faith, and the publick Report plainly di∫covers the common In∫inuation. And by this Means the Proce∫s is carried on.

Direct.   Then the Inqui∫itor cau∫es certain Witne∫∫es to be cited, e∫pecially grave and
p. 3. n.79. reputable Per∫ons, and in the Pre∫ence of a Notary, and two Religious, or otherwi∫e reputable Per∫ons, inquires of them only concerning the Report. Whether 'tis the common Report of ∫uch a one, that he did or ∫aid ∫uch Things again∫t the Faith ? How they know there was ∫uch a Report ? How long ∫uch Report hath been ? Whether they know ∫uch Per∫on to be defamed ? Whether they know whence the Report aro∫e ? Whether from ill di∫po∫ed Per∫ons or others ? And the like.

This is the Command of *Innocent,* Cap. *Qualiter & quando, de Accu∫at.* Hence we may gather how Infamy is proved. For the Witne∫s mu∫t ∫ay, that the Per∫on under Con∫ideration is defamed of ∫uch a Crime. And when 'tis inquired of him, in who∫e Account he is infamous, he mu∫t an∫wer with ∫uch and ∫uch ; and unle∫s he a∫∫igns them, he doth not appear to give a good Rea∫on of what he ∫ays. Be∫ides, it can't be known whether they are ∫erious or ill di∫po∫ed People.

Brunus de   When the Report is thus proved, the Inqui∫itor proceeds to inquire out
hæret. the Truth of the Affair. For this Purpo∫e he cau∫es the Witne∫∫es to be ci-
l. 4. c. 7. ted, and e∫pecially ∫uch as have been intimate with the Per∫on accu∫ed, and
§. 10. other reputable Men, and zealous for the Faith ; and after giving them their Oath, he inquires of them, not concerning the Report, but the Thing it ∫elf, in Pre∫ence of the Notaries, and two religious or reputable Per∫ons. After this he proceeds to draw out a Confe∫∫ion from the Criminal him∫elf. And fir∫t he goes to the Place of the Inqui∫ition, where, when the Crimi-nal appears before him, he tells him that he is excited and moved by the Fame and frequent Reports, that he the Criminal appearing and ∫tanding before him, hath taught, written, or publickly declared certain Things again∫t the Truth of the Catholick Faith, or that he hath believed and fa-voured ∫uch who teach the∫e Things, or received or defended them. That therefore he, according to his Office, cannot di∫∫emble that there is ∫uch a Report ; however, that he will not condemn him, till the∫e Crimes are legal-ly and plainly proved before him.

If

If the Criminal be not defamed of the Crimes laid in the Articles of the Inquifition, and he makes this Exception, the Promoter Fifcal and the Denouncer muft necefſarily prove the Defamation.

If this cannot be done, the Criminal is abfolved from all farther Concern Brun. *de* in Judgment. He may alfo prove himſelf to be a Perfon of good Report. *hæret. l. 4.* For Inſtance, if he is accufed of being defamed for defending the Doctrine *c. S. §. 11.* of an Heretick, by fome Writing that he publiſhed, he may prove that he confuted fuch Doctrine by writing againſt it ; or if he be accufed of harbouring an Heretick, in fome Houſe belonging to him, he may prove that he hath no Home in that Place, nor ever had ſince fuch Perfon hath been taken for an Heretick. He may likewiſe object, that fuch evil Report was raiſed of him by loofe and infamous Perfons, Enemies, Confpirators, and the like.

But if the Inquiſitor proceeds and inquiſits not at the Promotion, Denuncia- §. 12. tion or Inſtance of another, but *ex mero officio*, the Criminal is not to be heard when he excepts, that he is not defamed of the Crime objected to him ; nor is the Judge obliged to regard fuch Infamy ; for there is no Perfon who can oblige him to do it, unlefs the Criminal appeals. In this Cafe the Judge muſt inform his Superior of the Infamy of the Appellant. If alfo any one departs from the common Converfation of the Faithful in divine Worſhip, he is not to be heard, if he alledges that he is not defamed. For Inquiſition may be made againſt him without Infamy.

This is the Method of private Inquiſition, according to *Eymerick* and Tr. *tr. fol.* *Brunus. Peter*, Biſhop of *Elvas*, gives it in a fomewhat different Manner, in his 420. firſt Confultation. " Let this Manner be obferved as to a private Inquiſi-
" tion. Firſt, let the Parfon of the Place or Country be fent for, and car-
" ried to a fecret Place, and be required upon Oath to declare the Truth.
" When this is done, he muſt be asked if there is a Report that any Per-
" fon is an Heretick, or fufpected of the Faith in his Diſtrict, or a Fa-
" vourer or Receiver of them ; and if he fays there is, he muſt be asked,
" Whether the Report be general ? If he can form any probable Conjectures
" from him, the Inquiſitor commands him to name fome good and reputable
" Perfons, Men and Women, and makes alfo Inquiry of them upon Oath. If
" they agree, and it appears that they proceed not thro' Hatred, Envy or
" Revenge, he enjoins them Secrecy, and tells them he will keep the Mat-
" ter fecret himfelf, and that they need not fear. After this the defamed
" Heretick muſt be called to a private Place, in the Prefence of fome
" few Friars, and a Notary of a good Character, and be told ; You are ac-
" cufed and named to me as an Heretick, or a Favourer or Receiver. But
" I am willing to proceed with you in a way of Peace and Secrecy, and
" therefore defire you will abjure every wicked Herefy, and give fufficient
" Security that you will not return to them. The Inquiſitor muſt be care-
" ful not to difcover the Accufers to the Perfons accufed. He muſt alfo fay,
" If you will fwear, and do what I defire you, I am ready to grant you my
" Letters Teſtimonial, that you are of the Number of the Faithful. But if
" you will not do it, I will declare before the People that you are an Here-

" tick,

"ſtick, or a Believer of them, nor can I ever receive you without publick
" Penance ; the Conſequence of which is, that you muſt return and do Pe-
"nance, or your Effects will be confiſcated, you will be accounted infa-
" mous, be avoided by all, and deprived of all common Privileges. But in
" this Affair great Caution is to be uſed. In like Manner let the Inquiſitor
" be careful not to grant his Letters too generally, and eſpecially not to thoſe
" who have been otherwiſe apprehended, becauſe he ought not to do thus, un-
" leſs they do publick Penance.

CHAP. VII.

How the PROCESS *begins by Accuſation.*

WHEN the Accuſer reports to the Inquiſitor any Crime committed by
another, and the Accuſation hath the Appearance of Truth, they
proceed in this Manner, according to the Inſtruction of *Eymerick*, which hath
been long obſerved. Firſt the Inquiſitor inquires, whether the Accuſer will
accuſe, and proceed in the Affair by way of Accuſation, or not ? If he ſays
he will proceed by way of Accuſation, he is to be admoniſhed by the Inquiſitor, that he renders himſelf liable to the Puniſhment of Retaliation, unleſs his
Proof be good. But this Method of Proceeding the Inquiſitor muſt not eaſily allow, becauſe 'tis not cuſtomary in a Cauſe of the Faith, and becauſe 'tis
very dangerous, and greatly difficult to the Accuſer. But if the Accuſer per-
ſiſts, he muſt give his Accuſation in Writing, which muſt be written by the
Notary, in order to begin the Proceſs. But others contend, that in the Crime
of Hereſy 'tis not neceſſary that a Perſon ſhould oblige himſelf to the Law of
Retaliation. And as they now ſeldom admit the Perſon of an Accuſer, they
have conſtituted a publick Miniſter, whom they call the Fiſcal, who ſuſtains
the Perſon of the Accuſer, and accuſes the Criminals, who doth not oblige
himſelf to the Puniſhment of Retaliation, nor any others which falſe Accuſers uſually ſuffer.

Formerly, when the Proceſs was carried on at the Inſtance of the Accuſer,
after the Accuſation was made before the Inquiſitor, the Inquiſitor commanded the Accuſer to produce the Names of his Witneſſes, who being cited by the
Inquiſitor, are ſtrictly examined upon Oath. If what they depoſe doth nothing concern the Fact, the Inquiſitor muſt adviſe the Accuſer, to withdraw
the Word Accuſation, and put in the Room of it Denunciation, that ſo the
Inquiſitor may proceed *Ex officio*, and not at the Inſtance of the Party, becauſe ſo very dangerous to the Accuſer. But if the Proof of the Witneſſes
be full, the Inquiſitor produces them, and giving them their Oaths upon the
four Goſpels to declare the Truth, which he can oblige them to take if they
refuſe it, ſtrictly examines them in a judicial Manner before the Notary and
two religious Perſons, or otherwiſe reputable. Then he interrogates them

Direct.
part. 3.

67.

Pegna,
Com. 14.

71.

con-

concerning fundry Things, as, Whether they know fuch a one? As to the Occafion and Time of their knowing him? Concerning his Character? Whether they have feen, or heard him fay, or do any Thing againft the Faith, and what that was? Where they faw him, how often, and who prefent? In what manner he faid thofe Things, whether in Jeft, or by way of Recital, or whether with a deliberate Mind, and by way of Affertion? And finally, whether they depofe thefe Things thro' Hatred or Rancour? Or whether they omit any Thing thro' Love or Favour? The Anfwers of the Witneffes to all thefe Queftions are taken down by the Notary. Thefe Interrogatories of the Witneffes may be oftentimes repeated at the Pleafure of the Inquifitors, that what was omitted in the former Interrogatories may be fupplied.

CHAP. VIII.

How the PROCESS *begins by Denunciation.*

BUT if the Accufer fays, as is commonly the Cafe, that he will not accufe, but denounce; and that he doth this thro' Fear of incurring the Penalty of Excommunication, ordered by the Inquifitor for difcovering Things pertaining to the Faith within the prefcribed Term, then the Inquifitor prepares himfelf to make Inquifition. And becaufe this is the ordinary and moft generally ufed Method of the Inquifition, I will defcribe it more largely and diftinctly, that hereby the whole Method of making Inquifition may be more fully underftood. Eymer. p. 3. n. 62.

When the Denouncer, who is alfo called the appearing Witnefs, comes to the Bifhops or Inquifitors, before the Notary takes his Denunciation in a juridical Manner, he is ufually afked, what he hath to propofe? that they may know, whether what he is determined to denounce belongs to the holy Office. Becaufe fometimes Country ignorant People, or thofe who are troubled with Scruples, bring fuch Matters before them, the Cognifance of which doth not belong to the Inquifitors. When they find that the Crime brought before them is cognifable by the holy Office, they make the Denouncer fwear that he will relate the Truth. After this the Notary receives the whole Denunciation before the Bifhop or Inquifitor, or their Vicar, taking down the Denunciation, or the Report of the Denouncer in the firft Perfon. And that there may no Doubt arife as to the Validity of the Oath, to fpoil the Credit of the Denunciation, as the Inquifitor doth not only take an Oath from the Denouncer, or Witnefs voluntarily appearing, but alfo from the Witnefs who is cited, upon the holy Scriptures touched with their Hands, fo 'tis farther requifite, that the Notary fhould write at length, that fuch a one *took his Oath touching the Scriptures*, and not only write down, *touching* with an *&c.* that there may be no Difficulty in defending fuch Acts upon account of this Defect. Pegna, Prax. Inq. l. 2. c. 1.

The

The Oath being taken, the Denouncer is interrogated concerning various Things by the Inquisitor. " First, if he be not a well known Person, he is " interrogated concerning his own Name, Surname, Country, Employment, " and Place of Abode. Then, how long he hath known *N.* against whom " he denounces? Likewise how he came to know him? Again, whether he " observed that the aforesaid *N.* was suspected of Matters relating to the " Faith from his Words, or his Actions? Likewise, how often he had seen the " said *N.* do or say those Things for which he thought him an Heretick, or " suspected of Heresy? Likewise, at what Time, and in the Presence of " whom the aforesaid *N.* did or said those Things of which he is denounced? " Likewise, whether the aforesaid *N.* hath had any Accomplices in the afore-" said Crimes, or any Writings belonging to the Offences denounced? Like-" wise, to what End and Purpose the aforesaid Things were done or said by " the aforesaid *N.* whether seriously, or in Jest? If it appears that there was " a long Interval of Time between the Commission of the Crimes denounced, " and the making the Denunciation, the Inquisitor interrogates the Denoun-" cer, why he deferred so long to come to the holy Office, and did not depose " before, especially if he knew, that he incurred the Penalty of Excommuni-" cation by such Omission." They account this Interrogatory necessary for two Reasons. First, because the Delay of Denouncing may give a just Pre-sumption of Calumny in the Denouncer. Secondly, that it, may be known, whether he hath been compelled by his Confessor to denounce, upon his Re-fusal to absolve him without denouncing, in which Case greater Credit is gi-ven to the Denouncer. " He is moreover asked, whether he knows any " Thing farther of *N.* which concerns the holy Office, or of any other Per-" son? Likewise, whether he hath at any time had any Cause of Hatred or " Enmity with the aforesaid *N.* and whence it proceeded? With what Zeal, " and with what Intention he comes to the holy Office, and to make Denun-" ciation? Whether he hath denounced thro' any Passion of Mind, ill Will, " Hatred, or Subornation? And he is admonished ingenuously to tell the " Truth." He is especially interrogated how he came by his Knowledge, because on that principally the Truth and Weight of the Testimony depends. From the Denunciation, and the Answers to these Interrogatories they form other Questions, that there may be nothing wanting in the Inquisition. And whatsoever the Denouncer answers to these Interrogatories, the Notary writes down.

The Denunciation thus received, three Things are usually observed before the Denouncer goes from Audience. First, the whole Denunciation, as writ-ten down, must be read over to the Denouncer, that he may add, take away, or alter as he pleases. Secondly, the Denouncer must subscribe to his Depo-sition ; or if he can't write, he must at least put under it the Sign of the Cross. Thirdly, the Denouncer must take an Oath of Secrecy. All these Things are exactly written down by the Notary.

If thro' Straitness of Time, or a late unseasonable Hour, or the Length of the Denouncer's Account, the whole Denunciation cannot be taken at once,

the

the Depofition muft be broke off, and it muft be minuted down, that the Examination was difmiffed thro' the Latenefs of the Hour, and that the Denouncer was ordered to return foon to the holy Office. And this he muft fubfcribe. When he comes again to continue his Denunciation, he muft again take his Oath before the Inquifitor and Notary, touching the holy Scriptures, that he will fpeak the Truth, and be admonifhed to report what he omitted in his former Appearance, fuch a Day of the Month in this holy Office. But if it can be done, tho' with fome Inconvenience to the Judge, they fay Care muft be taken not to interrupt the Depofitions of the Denouncers, or Witneffes who are cited.

Sometimes the Denouncers bring with them their Denunciation written down by themfelves, which they give to the Inquifitor. When this is done, the Inquifitor receives it in the Place of Audience, and gives it to the Notary to infert in the Procefs. The Notary alfo further inferts in the Acts, that N. delivered his Denunciation in Writing to the faid Inquifitor, containing fo many Leaves, beginning thus, *&c.* and ending thus, *&c.* and the Inquifitor commands the Denouncer to fubfcribe his Name.

When the Denouncers are not prefent themfelves, and denounce any ones *Cap.* 3. Herefy, not in Perfon, but by private Letters, fuch a Denunciation may be alfo received by the Inquifitor, if the Writer of the Letters be a Perfon of Credit, dwelling in remote Places, or fick, or prevented by any legal Impediment, fo that he cannot eafily come himfelf to the Inquifitor ; or if he be detained upon account of any peculiar Quality, fuch as Nuns, or other honourable Women, who muft not eafily be drawn by others into any publick Caufe. But the Inquifitors may fupply the Defect in this manner of denouncing by this Method, either by going himfelf with the Notary to the Denouncer, and examining him in the Manner already defcribed ; or by fending his Colleague or Vicar to him with the Denunciation Letters, concerning which he examines the Denouncer in the ufual Manner, to know whether they are his, and with what Defign and Reafon written. Or if the Inquifitor hath already in fuch Places a Vicar or Commiffary appointed, he may write to him, and fend him the private Letters of Denunciation, to examine the Denouncer upon Oath after the ufual Manner. As to the Denunciation made *Annot.* by a Nun, fhe is obliged to denounce before her Confeffor, who demands Caren. Leave and Faculty from the Inquifitor to receive the Denunciation, which as *n.* 4. fpecially deputed he takes, firft giving her her Oath, making her fubfcribe, and enjoining her Secrefy. And he muft thoroughly interrogate and fearch her. But in this Cafe, the Confeffor muft receive from the Nun a Command of making Denunciation to the Inquifitor out of Confeffion. The Form which they obferve in taking this Denunciation is as follows. *Such a one was difmiffed from her Confeffor, who would not abfolve her, unlefs fhe denounced to the holy Office. Upon which fhe appeared before me* N. *efpecially deputed by the moft Reverend Father Inquifitor, the Day* .... *Month* ...... *Year* ...... *and being given her Oath, which fhe took touching the moft holy Gofpels, fhe denounced, for the exonerating her Confcience, as fhe declared, after the following Manner, viz.* &c.

CHAP.

CHAP. IX.

Of the Witneſſes, and who are admitted as Witneſſes before the Tri-
bunal of the INQUISITION.

AFTER the Denouncer hath diſcharged his Duty by legally denouncing,
he hath no farther Concern, but the whole Affair is left to the Inquiſitor
to make Inquiſition concerning the Offence of the Offender, from the Witneſſes named by the Denouncer. Before therefore we proceed to the Examination of the Witneſſes, we muſt premiſe ſome Things concerning the Witneſſes themſelves, *viz.* as to their Perſon and Number.

All Perſons may be Witneſſes as well in Civil as Criminal Cauſes that are not
expreſsly prohibited. In the Affair of the Inquiſition, in Favour of the Faith,
all Perſons, even ſuch as are not allowed in other Tribunals, are admitted as
Witneſſes, Enemies only excepted. But here they diſtinguiſh between the
Accuſer or Denouncer, and the Witneſs. For although an Enemy can never
be a Witneſs, he may be an Accuſer or Denouncer, and his Denunciation
muſt not be neglected by the Inquiſitor, according to *Campegius.*

Campeg.
in Zanch.
c. 13. *d.*

"In the Crime of Hereſy any one may be an Accuſer, even an Enemy.
"For as the Judge doth not condemn according to the Petition of the Accu-
"ſer, but the Proofs of the Witneſſes, there can be little Danger if an Ene-
"my be admitted to accuſe. He adds, that he hath often found in the Ex-
"erciſe of this ſacred Office, that Enemies have made, not a falſe but true
"Denunciation, which he hath known to happen by heavenly Counſel and the
"juſt Judgment of God. For this blind World can't as yet underſtand the
"Wickedneſs and Pravity of this Crime; and therefore we ſee that Mor-
"tals are more ready to accuſe and puniſh Thieves and Murtherers, than to
"correct and condemn Hereticks. Yea, when Inquiſition is made againſt
"any one for Hereſy, or he is taken up, all run together, and pray, and be-
"ſeech, excuſe, and endeavour to defend him, and ſay that they are wicked
"and very vile Perſons, who would mark the poor Man for an Heretick. Be-
"ſides, they call the Officers very cruel, if they ſtrive to reduce an
"Heretick to the Light of Truth, by Impriſonment, Bonds, and Fetters,
"or finally by Tortures, and think they do God great Service, if they ſtrive,
"tho' unjuſtly, to free him from Impriſonment and Bonds, and to deliver him
"out of the Hands of the Inquiſitors. They would rather he was diſmiſſed,
"as they ſay, only with holy Water. If we anſwer and put them in mind of
"the Crime of High Treaſon againſt earthly Majeſty, they reply, this is
"quite another Thing, that the Caſes very much differ, and the like. As
"tho' 'twas a leſs Thing to offend the great God than an earthly Prince.
"Theſe Things are rather to be lamented than rehearſed. Let us therefore
"pray the Lord to open the Eyes of thoſe blind Perſons, and to preſerve his
"holy Faith, and to defend and protect the Miniſters of this Office. For it
"   "happens,

" happens, as we faid before, thro' the Difpofal of God, bringing this Good
" out of another's Wickednefs, that one Man fhall not difcover another whom
" he knew to be an Heretick, during their Friendfhip. But upon the ari-
" fing of fome Enmity between them afterwards, he immediately goes to the
" Inquifitor, and now denounces againft the Perfon whom he hath long known
" to be an Heretick, and fays that he doth it thro' a Zeal for the Faith, and
" with a Regard to Charity, altho' poffibly he is induced to it by the Influ-
" ence of Hatred. Therefore the Inquifitor ought diligently to attend to the
" Quality of the Deponents or Denouncers, and very exactly and cautioufly
" make Inquifition concerning the Truth of the Things attefted and faid, and
" well to remark the Words of the Chapter, *In Fidei favorem*, de hæret.
" lib. 6. *viz.* Whether or no thofe who thus teftify may be prefumed not to
" fpeak Falfehood, from likely Conjectures, and the Number of the Witnef-
" fes, or the Quality of the Perfons, as well thofe who depofe, as thofe who
" are depofed againft, and from other Circumftances."

But 'tis quite otherwife as to Witneffes themfelves, for an Enemy is not admitted as a Witnefs. Not that every fort of Enmity prevents a Perfon from
being a Witnefs, but mortal Enmity only. Thus the Council of *Biterre* determines, *Cap.* 13. and that of *Narbonne*, Cap. 25. *Such Exceptions only
fhall wholly deftroy the Credit of the Witneffes, which feem to proceed not
from a Zeal for Juftice, but from the Inftigation of Malice,* viz. *Confpiracies and mortal Enmities. For although other Crimes weaken, they do not fet
afide the Evidence, efpecially if the Witneffes have amended their Fault.*
So that, according to this Decree, feveral Crimes do indeed leffen the Simane.
Credit of the Evidence, but do not wholly render the Perfons incapable of be- *t.* 64.
ing Witneffes. In like manner every fort of Enmity doth indeed fomewhat §. 79, 80.
weaken the Weight of the Evidence, but don't entirely overthrow it,
unlefs it be mortal Enmity.

The Caufes by which we are to judge of mortal Enmity are various, and de- Pegn. *in*
termined by the *Spanifh* Law. If any one hath killed, or endeavoured, or *p.* 3. *com.*
even threatned to kill the Kinfman of that Perfon againft whom he would 116.
bear Witnefs, if he hath laid Snares for his Life, or accufed him of a Crime,
which, if proved, would be punifhed with Death, Lofs of a Member, Banifhment, or the Forfeiture of all, or the greateft Part of his Eftate. To
thefe *Pegna* adds fome other Things, which, however, are not determined by *ibid.*
that Law, *viz.* if any one depofes againft him in a criminal Caufe; or if the
Party accufed hath at any time put his Accufer in Chains; or even if he hath
fpoken very reproachfully of him, *viz.* if he hath called him Cuckold, or his
Wife a Whore; or called a fober Man a Drunkard, &c. In thefe Cafes,
however, he fays the Circumftances of the Perfons, reproaching each other,
fhould be confidered; as whether they are vile and infamous Perfons, who
have little Regard to their Honour, and are given to reproachful Language,
and fo eafily forget what they fay; or whether they are noble, and well
born: Befides this, the Cuftom of the Provinces and Cities are alfo to be regarded. Farther, he fays that mortal Enmity may arife from one Man's

keeping another's Wife, contrary to his Confent and Demand, or his Sifter,
or any other Women related to him, the very Attempt upon whofe Chaftity
is an Injury to him. Or if any one goes to Law with another concerning
his Condition, to prove him only a Freedman, not Free-born, or about his
Eftate, or greateft Part of it, or for a large Sum of Money, or for robbing
him of, or deftroying a Thing of great Value, or when any one injures another
in his Perfon or Effects. Farther, he cannot be a Witnefs, if having been an
Enemy a long while he is newly reconciled, or who defcends from a mortal E-
nemy ; nor one who lives with another's Enemies, or contracts Friendfhip
with them. Finally, nor they who are of a Family or Faction contrary to
another Family or Faction. However, if the Witneffes are Perfons of tried
Virtue and Probity, they would not be liable to fuch a bad Sufpicion. This Sufpicion alfo ceafes, when the Enmity is procured by Fraud and Deceit, and
with this View, to prevent any one's being a Witnefs ; or when there hath
been a long and well-grounded Reconciliation between the Perfons who were
Enemies, as to which, 'tis left to the Pleafure of the Judge to determine. And
becaufe the Names of the Witneffes are not difcovered to the Perfon accufed,
as fhall be fully fhewn hereafter, becaufe of the Danger that might accrue
to them, the Inquifitors are ordered to enquire concerning the Enmity of the
Witneffes, and to fearch out if there are any Caufes, from which it may be
probably gathered that there is mortal Enmity between the Criminal and
them, the whole of which is left to the Prudence and Pleafure of the Inquifitor.
But if an Enemy be reconciled, he may be a Witnefs, provided the Reconciliation be not new, but of long ftanding. Whether it be one or the other,
the Inquifitor is to determine.

Lucern.   Here they enquire, whether Credit is to be given to a Witnefs, who fays
Inq. in voc. he is the Enemy of that Perfon againft whom he is interrogated ? And they
Teftes.   ufually anfwer with this Diftinction. Either the Witnefs fays he is his Enemy
§. 5.   before he fwore, or was produced as a Witnefs ; and thus he is prefumed to have
faid it fraudulently, and muft therefore be received ; but if it doth not appear that he faid it fraudulently, he muft not be received, efpecially if it be
mortal Enmity. But if it be not, or there be any Doubt about it, the Judge
muft not defift for the bear Affirmation of fuch Witnefs, but muft enquire
into the Nature of the Enmity, becaufe, as was faid before, every fort of Enmity doth not difable a Perfon to be a Witnefs. But if he declares himfelf a
mortal Enemy, he muft not be received. But if the Enmity is not mortal, he
muft be allowed, and the Judge muft determine what Credit is to be given to
him. Or he declares himfelf an Enemy after he is fworn, but before he depofes, and then he is not to be credited ; or after he hath fworn and made
Depofition ; and if he declares himfelf an Enemy immediately after he hath
finifhed his Depofition, he is credited as to the general Interrogatories ; but
if he declares himfelf an Enemy fome Diftance of Time after, he is not
regarded, but his former Depofition muft be abided by.

Pegna in   But except thefe mortal Enmities, almoft all kind of Perfons may be ad-
p. 3. com. mitted as Witneffes by the Inquifitor. Firft, Perfons excommunicated, and
113.   guilty

guilty of the fame Crime, Cap. *In Fidei favorem,* de hæret. lib. 6. *We grant
in Favour of the Faith, that in the Affair of the Inquifition of heretical Pravity,
Perfons excommunicated, and Partakers, and Perfons guilty of the fame Crime, fhall be
admitted to bear Witnefs, efpecially when there is a Deficiency of other Proofs againft
Hereticks, their Believers, Favourers, Receivers, and Defenders, if it may be
prefumed from probable Conjectures, and the Number of Witneffes, or Quality of the
Perfons, as well thofe who depofe, as thofe who are depofed againft, that fuch Witneffes do not fpeak falfely.* In this the Council of *Biterre* agrees, Cap. 12. *Altho' in
this Crime all Criminals and infamous Perfons, and thofe who are Partakers of their
Guilt, may be admitted as Accufers and Witneffes.* The Decree of *Alexander* IV.
is to the fame Purpofe, *An.* 1261. *Feb.* 1. beginning, *Confuluit nos.*

Next to Perfons excommunicated are joined Hereticks, *Jews,* and Infidels, Pegna, *ib.*
who, in the Crime of Herefy, are admitted as Witneffes againft Hereticks. *com.* 117.
But becaufe 'tis provided by the Laws, that Hereticks fhall not be admitted
as Witneffes, an Heretick is not allowed as a Witnefs for one of the Faithful. But if an Heretick, whether in Prifon or elfewhere, charges one of the Faithful, or one who is efteemed as fuch, with the Crime of Herefy, or as a Partaker of his Crime, tho' this doth not amount to half Proof, fo as to occafion
his being apprehended, yet it is Difcovery enough to proceed to a fecret Inquifition againft him. But, as was faid, the Teftimony of an Heretick againft an
Heretick, is admitted, but not for an Heretick. They affirm the fame of a
Jew and an Infidel, who, when they are admitted as Witneffes, muft not
fwear upon the Gofpels as Chriftians do, but according to their own Laws.

In like manner the Teftimony of a Wife, Sons and Daughters, or Domefticks, againft Perfons accufed of Herefy, is allowed, but by no Means in
their Favour and Behalf. *C. Filii,* de hæret. lib. 6. The Reafon *Simancas* *Tit.* 64:
gives, why Kindred are admitted as Witneffes againft Kindred, is, becaufe §. 47.
they can't poffibly be fufpected. Yea, fome add, that when other Proofs Carena,
are wanting, the Judge may compel not only a Brother, but even a Wife, or *p.* 3. *t.* 5.
Son, to witnefs againft a Father. Servants alfo may be tortured againft their *n.* 21.
Mafters.

Even perjured Perfons, who having taken an Oath before the Inquifitors to fpeak the Truth, have forfworn themfelves by concealing it,
and would afterwards correct themfelves, and fwear back again againft
themfelves and others, are to be admitted, if it plainly appears that they
act not from Levity of Mind, nor the Inftigation of Enmity, nor from being
corrupted by Money, but from their Zeal for the Orthodox Faith, and
that on this Account they would difcover in Favour of the Faith what they
had concealed before, according as *Alexander* IV. hath decreed, and as may
be found in the VI. of the Decretals. And altho' perjured Perfons are not
allowed as Witneffes even after Repentance, yet 'tis quite different in a Caufe
of the Faith; and the Doctors obferve, that fuch a one's fecond Depofition
muft be ftood to, when hereby he difcovers the Crime of Herefy. But if
when he takes his fecond Oath, he denies what he depofed concerning Herefy when he took his firft, the firft Depofition muft be ftood to, and not

T 2

the

the fecond ; for which they give this Reafon, becaufe he may have fpoken with the Criminal, and fo is prefumed to be corrupted and fuborned, and therefore his firft Depofition ftands firm.

Carena, p. 3. t. 5. §. 12. Farther, infamous Perfons may be admitted as Witneffes in this Tribunal, fuch as Whores and Bawds, when they teftify of Things done in the Bawdy-Houfe. Such alfo as are under the Ban, whom the Inquifitors may cite before their Tribunal, and grant a fafe Conduct, that they may be examined as Witneffes in the Tribunal of the Inquifition, altho' the fecular Prince hath put them under the Ban, becaufe the Inquifitor is greater than any fupream, fecular Judge, and may proceed in Caufes of the Faith freely, and without any Impediment whatfoever of Law or Fact. Ufurers alfo, Baftards, common Blafphemers, common Gamefters, Perfons quite drunk, and not only exhilarated by Wine, Stage-Players, and Prize Fighters, Apoftates from Religion, Perfons baftinadoed, Bankrupts, Traitors, Backbiters and Spendthrifts. But they add, that thefe are not Witneffes above all Exception, and that they amount only to half Proof ; that they may be admitted to prove Herefy, and the fubftantial Circumftances that prove it, fuch as Familiarity with Hereticks, fecret Conventicles, and the like, but not the external Circumftances neceffary to it, Baptifm for Inftance, which is pre-requifite in the Cafe of Herefy. Befides the Number of Witneffes may make good their Incapacity, though every one fingly fhould be incapable of being a Witnefs, yea if the Number be large, 'tis fufficient to inflict the ordinary Punifhment. This Number they fix, and fay that four are fufficient to condemn the Criminal to the ordinary Punifhment. Others leave it to the Inquifitor to determine the Number.

Lucern. Inq.in voce Teftes. §. 12. Here 'tis to be obferved, that a Witnefs, whatfoever he is, faying one Thing out of the Trial, is not allowed to fay the contrary in the Trial, fo that they ftand to what he firft fays, unlefs 'tis to be prefumed that he fpoke fraudulently. As if a Witnefs of mean Fortune fhould fay in the Prefence of fome great Perfon fomewhat in his Favour, and afterwards fhould fay upon Oath the contrary, what he firft fays muft not ftand good, becaufe 'tis prefumed he faid it to pleafe the Party, but what he afterwards fays at the Trial muft be allowed, becaufe 'tis fuppofed he fpeaks Truth through Fear of his Oath. 'Tis otherwife where there is no fuch Prefumption.

CHAP.

CHAP. X.

Of the Number of the WITNESSES.

AS to the Number of the Witnesses, 'tis generally believed that two Wit- _{Eymer.} nesses are sufficient fully to prove Herefy, and to condemn any one^{P. 3. qu.} for Herefy. But 'tis neceffary they fhould be worthy of Credit, and, as ^{71. coot.} they fay, above all Exception. Hence it is, that tho' excommunicated Per-^{120.}_{Simane.} fons, and thofe guilty of the fame Crimes, are not abfolutely rejected from^{tit. 64.} being Witneffes againft Hereticks, their Defenders, Receivers, and all other^{§. 36.} fufpected Perfons, yet full Credit is not to be given to them, unlefs it appears that they fpeak Truth, from probable Conjectures, the Number and Qua-lity of the Perfons, and other Circumftances. C. *In Fidei favorem*, de hæret. lib. 6.

The Informer or Denouncer is now alfo reckoned amongft the Witneffes. _{Simanc.} For altho' no Man can be Accufer and Witnefs in the fame Caufe, yet he who^{t. 19. §. 17.} difcovers an Heretick to the Judges is a legal Witnefs. For, as they fay,^{&. t. 64.} fuch a Witnefs is not influenced by any private Advantage, but by a Zeal for^{§. 55.} the moft holy Religion, and for the publick Benefit of the Catholick Church, and with a View to the Amendment of the Heretick. Nor can he have any private Intereft to difcover an Heretick, but only as being of the Number of the Chriftian People, in which Cafe they affirm the Teftimony of the Infor-mer to be compleat.

Several fingle and entirely different Witneffes have no more Weight than_{§. 63.} one Witnefs.

There are fome who fay that a Man may be proved to be an Heretick by_{§. 68.} fingle Witneffes, as if one fhould witnefs againft him for one Herefy, another for another, and others likewife for other Herefies. In fuch a Cafe they af-fert it will be proved in general, that the Man is an Heretick. But as par-_{§. 70.} ticular Herefy can't be proved by fingle and feparate Witneffes, fo neither can it be proved that any one is an Heretick in general by the fame Witneffes; for by the fame way it might be proved that a Man was a Catamite in gene-_{§. 73.} ral, upon which Occafion *Simancas* gives us a pleafant Story. A certain Per-fon, a Year ago, cried out, and faid, it was proved in general by fingle Wit-neffes, that fuch a one was a Catamite. I remember, fays he, I anfwered, if this wicked Crime is proved in general, let the Punifhment likewife be in-flicted in general. Let the Individual be fafe, and, if you pleafe, let the Cata-mite in general be burnt.

Yet there are two Cafes, in which Herefy may be proved by fingle Wit-_{§. 75.} neffes. The firft is, when the Witneffes teftify of the fame Species of Here-fy, but are different as to the Place and Time. For they agree in the Proof of the fame Herefy, whereas the Place and Time are quite foreign Things, and are not neceffary Circumftances to the Proof of Herefy. The fecond is, _{§. 77.} when.

when single Witnesses aim at the same End, are many in Number, and worthy of Credit.

Direct. But *Pegna* says, if there are many single Witnesses, and one deposes as to
part. 3. the Fact, another as to the common Fame, one as to what he saw, another
q 71. com. as to what he heard, the Criminal cannot be condemned, no not altho' the
120. common Fame, legally proved, strengthens the Testimony of the single
Witness. However, the Inquisitor may at Pleasure enjoin such Criminals
Purgation, or any other Penance. If several Witnesses testify separately of
different Heresies, and a different Time and Place, this will not prove a
Man an Heretick ; no, nor is it full Proof if they testify of the same Heresy, but differ as to Time and Place. But if any one is convicted by more
than two proper Witnesses, and will not confess, some say they must wait for
some time, and see if they can find out Witnesses agreeing in all Things ;
but first the Criminal is to be tortured, that if it can be they may draw the
Truth from his Mouth. If he confesses nothing he may be most justly
compelled to abjure as one vehemently suspected, or to undergo canonical
Purgation, because, in this Case, he cannot be thought to have purged away
the Evidence by Torture, since the Proofs against him are many and
strong.

Part. 3. However, in such a Case, 'tis left to the Inquisitors Pleasure to proceed as
com. 121. they think fit, as 'tis expressly commanded in the Constitutions of the Bishop
of *Albano*, Legate of the Apostolick See, who, 'tis probable, was appointed Legate, and published by the Pope's Commission many Constitutions,
relating to the Punishment of Hereticks, and the Order of proceeding against
them, about the Time when the poor Men of *Lions*, or the *Albigenses* and
other Hereticks infested the Countries of *France* and *Lombardy*. These Constitutions are very useful to private Inquisitors, to enable them to determine
rightly and profitably Causes and Controversies of the Faith, and are extant in an old Parchment Manuscript in the *Vatican* Library, and in a very
old one at *Florence*. Amongst other Things in it 'tis thus determined. *But when*
the Witnesses or Informers differ in what they depose, but yet agree in the Substance
and Nature of the Thing, we leave it to the Pleasure of the Inquisitors so to proceed, as,
in the Sight of God, they shall think fit, especially if common Fame, and the Fitness and
Credit of the Deposers agree and make against him, who is to undergo the Inquisition.

C H A P. XI.

Of the Examination of the WITNESSES.

Pegna, AFter having thus spoken of the Witnesses themselves, I now come to
Prax. Inq. their Examination. When therefore the Witnesses named by the In-
l. 2. c. 5. former are found out, the Inquisitor orders them to be cited by his spiritual
Messenger,

Meffenger, to the Office of the Inquifition, where, when they come, they are legally examined. Firft, they take an Oath upon the Scriptures to fpeak the Truth. After this he is asked by the Inquifitor, whether he knows, or can guefs the Caufe of his Citation and prefent Examination? If he fays yes, he is interrogated how he knew it? If he fays no, he is interrogated, whether he hath known, or doth now know any one or more Hereticks, or Perfons fufpected of Herefy, or at leaft is able to name any fuch? Whether he knows *N*? What was the Occafion of his Acquaintance with him? How long he hath known him? Whether he hath been ufed to converfe with him? Whether he hath heard at any time any Thing from the faid *N*. concerning the Catholick Religion? Whether ever he was in fuch a Place with the faid *N*. and whether the faid *N*. did or faid there fuch and fuch heretical Things, or favouring of Herefy? Who were prefent when *N*. did or faid the aforefaid Things? How often he faw them faid or done, and on what Occafion, and how? Whether the faid *N*. fpoke the aforefaid Things in Jeft, or without thinking, or thro' a Slip of his Tongue, or as relating the Herefies of fome other Perfon or Perfons? Whether he faid any Thing which ought not to have been faid thro' Hatred or Love, or omitted and concealed fomewhat that ought to have been explained? He is farther admonifhed to tell the fingle Truth, becaufe, if he is detected of fpeaking falfely, he will be made to fuffer the Penalties, not only of Perjury, but of favouring Herefy, and that therefore he ought to tell the Truth, and beware of Lies. Becaufe, if it appears to the holy Office, by Witneffes worthy of Credit, that the Witnefs himfelf is confcious to the Things concerning which he is interrogated, and conceals and hides them, he may be confined, and compelled to give Security, and to oblige himfelf not to depart from that City and Place where he is examined, and under a Penalty, fixed by the Inquifitor, to make his Appearance as often as and wherefoever the Inquifitor fhall command him. When the Truth cannot be found out from the Mouth of the Witnefs and thefe general Interrogatories, the *Italian* Inquifitors come to particular Interrogatories concerning the Place and Perfon denounced, that fo the Truth may be difcovered, after which the Witnefs is difmiffed, being firft injoined Secrecy upon Oath, and figning what he hath faid. All thefe Things are taken down by a Notary, and inferted into the Acts of the Procefs. *Simancas* gives a fhort Account of this Matter, *Tit.* 44. §. 11.

Carena, Annot. Ibid.

" When the Witneffes come to the Inquifitors, to teftify againft Here-
" ticks or fufpected Perfons, they are to be exhorted and admonifhed, that
" they don't dare to give falfe Witnefs thro' Hatred, Enmity, or other evil
" Affection. And befides, it muft be declared to them, how heinous a
" Wickednefs all falfe Witneffes commit, but efpecially thofe who defame
" innocent Perfons with the Crime of Herefy. But if they affirm that they
" are moved only by a Zeal for the Catholick Faith, their Teftimonies are
" to be written down."

'Tis the Cuftom in fome Inquifitions, that before the Criminal is apprehended, the Witneffes named by the Denouncer fhould, after two or three

Days,

Days, be cited again, and interrogated upon Oath, laying their Hand on the Scriptures, whether they have any farther Truth to communicate befides what they depofed in their former Examination. And whatfoever is the Anfwer, the Notary takes it from his Mouth.

If there be Reafon to apprehend from the Circumftances of the Witnefs, that he will difcover the Caufe, he is enjoined Silence, under the Penalty of Excommunication, *latæ fententiæ*, after a fingle Admonition, and other Penalties, at the Pleafure of the holy Office. Sometimes alfo, for juft Reafons, they take Care and command the Witnefs or Witnefes not to depart from the Palace or Houfe of the Inquifitor, without the exprefs Leave of the Inquifitor, written under his Hand.

After the fame Manner all other Witnefes named by the Informer in his Information, are examined.

But if the Informer be alfo a Partaker and Partner in the Crime, and when informing againft his heretical Companions, depofes nothing againft himfelf, and any Thing appears againft him from the Examination of the Witnefes or Accomplices, he is cited by the Inquifitor, and proceeded againft as a Criminal, but punifhed in a milder Manner, becaufe of his having informed againft others.

In the Examination of Witnefes, in many Places, there muft be five Perfons prefent. The firft is the Judge, *i. e.* the Inquifitor or his Commiffary, whofe Bufinefs is to examine the Witnefes and Perfons accufed, by forming Articles and Interrogatories upon them. The fecond is the Witnefs. Every one of thefe muft firft fwear to fpeak the Truth, otherwife their Depofition will be invalid, according to the Precept of the Council of *Biterre*, Cap. 4. *Give to all thofe, who being cited before you, appear within the Time affigned them, their Oath, to tell the entire and whole Truth concerning the Fact of heretical Pravity, which they know of themfelves, or of others, living or dead.* The Form of the Oath is commonly this: *I fwear by God and the Crofs, and the four moft holy Gofpels, now touched with my Hands, that I will fpeak the Truth. If I do, fo help me God ; if I do not, fo God condemn me.* The third Perfon is the Writer, who writes down the Interrogatories of the Inquifitor, and the Anfwers of the Perfon accufed, and the Witnefs. He muft be a publick Perfon, *viz.* a Notary that hath Authority, either a Layman or Clergyman, or a Religious. But when the Inquifitor cannot have fuch a publick Perfon, or Notary, he may chufe two proper Perfons, Secular, or Ecclefiaftical, who jointly have the Power and Authority of one publick Perfon, and thefe two act by the Apoftolick Authority in Writing. The fourth and fifth Perfons are two who affift the Inquifitor, and are Witnefes to the whole Examination, and they muft be two difcreet Men, religious, or otherwife reputable. But when the Inquifitor cannot conveniently have thefe two Perfons prefent at the whole Examination of the Witnefs or Perfon informed againft, he muft, at leaft, have them at the End of the Depofition, when the Depofition is read over by the Notary to the Witnefs that depofes, or the Informer, in the Prefence of the Inquifitor, and the two aforefaid difcreet Perfons, and then the Witnefs is asked if he ftands

to

Eymer.
p. 3.

81.
82.

83.

84.

to and perseveres in that Deposition. If he doth, 'tis written in the Acts, how that in the Presence of such Persons the Deposition was read to him, and he stood to it, and persevered in it. And this *Eymerick* thinks is sufficient. But as *Pegna* tells us, *Comment.* 112. the Processes are now carried on in the holy Tribunal generally without the Presence or Intervention of these Persons, and the supream Senate of the *Roman* and general Inquisition allows the Processes thus formed. And indeed these two Persons are of no Use. The Pretence for their being present is, that there may be no Suspicion of foul Play, when the Things transacted are seen by so many Eyes, and open to so many Senses; and that they may know the Witnesses in the Stead of the absent Criminal, as *Simancas* declares, *tit.* 64. §. 8. & 21. But how doth it make any thing to the Defence of the Criminal, that his Accusers are known to Persons that he himself knows nothing of, and who are forbidden to discover any Thing to him?

The Witnesses must be examined by the Inquisitors themselves, nor must their Examination be committed by any Means to any one else, unless the Witnesses are justly hindred, and the Judges cannot easily go to them, or ought not. In this Case the Inquisitors may commit the Examination of the Witnesses to the Bishop's Vicar, or other Ecclesiastical Judge, or to some skilful and prudent Man, who, with a Notary or Secretary to write down the Depositions in the Cause, must diligently examine the Witnesses, and send the Manner and Constancy, and other Circumstances of the Witnesses and their Depositions to the Inquisitors. 1 *Instruct. Hispal. cap.* 17. and 4 *Instruct. Tolet. c.* 14.

[side note: Simanc: *tit.* 68. §. 11.]

CHAP. XII.

How the CRIMINALS, *when informed against, are sent to* Jayl.

WHEN the skilful Men or Counsellors are called together to give proper Advice, either as to the Quality of the Propositions, or the Weight of the Proofs and Discoveries, or as to the Process or giving Sentence, or any doubtful Article of the Cause, that nothing may appear in the whole Affair but a burning and serious Zeal for the divine Glory, they make solemn Prayers to the Holy Ghost, which are usually said over in all the Congregations. The Inquisitor and Counsellors say them on their bended Knees. The Form is this:

We are here present, O God, the Holy Ghost, we are here detained with the Greatness of Sin, but gathered together specially in thy Name. Come to us, be present with us, vouchsafe to enter into our Hearts, teach us what we should do, where we should walk, and shew us what we ought to perform, that we may be able to please thee, assisting us in all Things. Be thou the Health, the Suggestor and Maker of our

[side note: Pegna, *prax. Inq.* l. 2. c. 9.]

Judg-

Judgments, who alone with God the Father and his Son, possessest a glorious Name. Suffer us not to be Perverters of Justice, O thou who lovest the strictest Equity. Let not Ignorance draw us to the left, let not Favour bend us, nor Regard to Office or Person corrupt us, but join us to thy self effectually by the Gift of thy only Grace, that we may be one in thee, and in nothing deviate from the Truth; and as we are gathered together in thy Name, so let us in all Things preserve Justice moderated by Piety, that our Sentence here may in nothing differ from thee, and that hereafter we may obtain everlasting Rewards for our good Deeds. When the Prayer is ended, all answer *Amen.*

This Prayer, in the Time of *Carena*, was recited in the Inquisition at *Cremona*, by Cardinal *Camporeus*, Bishop of that City, the Inquisitor on his right Hand at a Corner of the Table, and the Vicar General at his left at another Corner, and the other Counsellors in their Order, all on their Knees. But if a single Bishop only is present, then the Bishop and Inquisitor sit at the Head of the Table, their Seats being equal, in all the Inquisitions in *Italy.* But the Bishop sits by Virtue of his Episcopal Dignity in the Seat placed on the right Hand, and the Inquisitor in the other.

Pegna,
ibid. c. 7. These Prayers being over, the Inquisitor consults whether the Cognisance of the Crimes which are denounced and proved by the Witnesses, belongs to the holy Office. If there be any Doubt of this, he must call in the Qualificator Divines, who must give their Opinion written and subscribed with their own Hand, that it may be inserted in the Process, as the Foundation of the Jurisdiction of the Inquisitor. If the Crimes are small, or the Propositions only sounding ill, scandalous or blasphemous, or which do not include formal Heresy, no one upon account of these is immediately ordered to secret Imprisonment, but must rather be confined in some Monastery, or in his own House, or City. If these Things were omitted, the Inquisitors might possibly usurp to A not. ad.
cap. 7. themselves Causes belonging to other Tribunals. Thus *Carena* relates, that on the first of *August*, *Anno* 1630. two *Portuguese* Women at *Placentia* received the Eucharist twice; and being interrogated why they did it, they answered, because they apprehended, that as often as they communicated, they obtained the Jubilee of a Part, as they call it. On this they were kept in the Prisons of the Inquisition, and their Effects sequestred. But when the Lords Inquisitors found that the Cause did not belong to the Tribunal of the Faith, they dismissed them from Jayl, and caused their Effects to be restored to them. This Consultation with the Counsellors is recommended by the *Madrid* Instruction, *An.* 1561. cap. 3. *When the Inquisitors have seen the Information together, if they are present, let them consult as to the taking them up, which would appear more just if done with the Advice of the Counsellors of the Inquisition, if it conveniently can be, and it appears to the Inquisitors convenient and necessary; and whatsoever is determined, let it be inserted in the Acts.*

Carena,
lib. 3. tit.
2. §. 6. No one can be taken up without half full Proof at least, or such Evidence as is sufficient to put to the Torture, because the Imprisonment made by the Inquisitors always renders the Prisoners infamous. But if the Person be otherwise suspected, for Instance, if he be of the *Moorish* Race, and hath been denounced.

denounced before the Inquifitors, upon account of fome Ceremonies of that Nation, he may poffibly be imprifoned upon the Affirmation of one Witnefs, even
tho' liable to fome Exception, according to *Carena*, becaufe the Prefumption a-
rifing from his Birth, joined to the Depofition of fuch a Witnefs, would amount
to an half Proof.   And he gives an Inftance, that in the fupream Council of the
Spanifh Inquifition, two Men were taken up for Herefy, at the Information of one
Woman, under eighteen Years old, becaufe they were both of *Moorifh* Extract,
and becaufe the Ceremonies witneffed to by the Woman were *Mahometan*. And
thus the Prefumption was againft them, becaufe they were of that Race. *Zan-* Zanch.
chinus enumerates more particularly feveral Caufes for which Perfons may be c. 10. §. 1.
imprifoned.

   " If Inquifition be made againft any one, he is imprifoned, if, tho' the Crime
 ' be fo fmall as that Bail may be taken for it, he doth not give the neceffary
 " Bail.   Or if Inquifition be made againft him for fome deteftable and grie-
 " vous Crime, and there are Proofs againft him, or if he himfelf hath confeffed
 " fuch a Crime as renders him liable to the Punifhment of an Heretick."

   The Confultations which are held on thefe Affairs, are ufually called De- Simanc.
liberations concerning the Citation of the Criminal, and this Citation is verbal *tit.* 44.
or real.   Verbal Citation is that which is made by Letters or a Meffenger, §. 12.
which is ufed when the Queftion is about a leffer Crime, or if the Criminal be
but flightly fufpected.   For if it be an heinous Crime, and fully proved, there
is need of a real Citation, that the Criminal may not efcape.   This verbal
Citation muft not contain in it the Caufe for which the Criminal is cited, and
therefore 'tis not neceffary to infert in it the Place, Time, or Offence, but he
is commanded in general to come before the Inquifitors, becaufe they want
to know of him certain Matters.   Clement. §. *de hæret*.   But this Method of
Citation is not to be frequently ufed, according to the *Toledo* Inftruction 4.
An. 1561. becaufe if fuch a one be examined, 'tis often found, that being
free, and in Poffeffion of his Liberty, he will not eafily confefs himfelf to be a
Criminal.   And fuch Citations and Examinations do rather tend to warn the
denounced Criminals to take Care of themfelves, and conceal their Crime, than
to produce any other good Effect.   They therefore think it fafer to wait, till
new Proofs and fufficient Difcoveries arife.   In the mean while they employ a
careful Spy, one friendly and faithful to the holy Office, to confider and
fearch into fuch a one's Life, Manners, and Converfation.

   A real Citation, or the actual apprehending any one, is ufually decreed after
this twofold Manner.   In fome Inquifitions, that the Profecution may appear
to be according to Jurifdiction, as comprehending in it the Accufer, Criminal
and Judge, the Procurator Fifcal, who is acquainted with every Thing in the
Procefs that lies againft the denounced Criminal, exhibits an Inftrument, demanding that the denounced Criminal may be taken up, and duly punifhed,
and in that Inftrument he inferts and exhibits the Depofitions againft him, and
the Qualification of the Propofitions, that it may appear that he may legally
be apprehended.   This Demand of the Fifcal is ufually inferted in the Procefs
of the Perfon to be taken up.   But in other Inquifitions 'tis ufual for the In-

                                                                        quifitors,

quifitors, after confidering the Acts, to confult about apprehending the Perfon, without any Inftance of the Fifcal, and to command what they refolve
on to be put in Execution.　And this Decree for the Apprehenfion is alfo
ufually inferted in the Procefs, with the Day, Month and Year.　But if the
Party accufed be fome illuftrious Perfon, or in any Poft of great Authority,
the Senate of the *Spanifh* Inquifition muft be confulted before he is to be apprehended, to whom that their Deliberations may be right, they muft fend a
Summary of the Proofs, and the Information of the Crimes.　This is gathered from the *Madrid* Inftruction, An. 1561. cap. 5.　*If the Inquifitors agree
as to the Apprehenfion, let them command what they have decreed to be executed.
But if it be a Matter of great Moment, by reafon of the Quality of the Perfons, or
for other Caufes, let them firft confult the Senate before they put their Decree in Execution.　But if they don't agree in their Judgments, let the Matter be referred to the
Senate, that they may confider what is proper to be done.*　But this very great and
exquifite Caution muft not be obferved, when there is any Fear of the Efcape
of the Perfon accufed, or if he is a manifeft Heretick.　For in fuch Cafe they
think it would be imprudent and dangerous to wait for the Anfwer of a Superior.

After 'tis determined that the Criminal fhall be fent to Jayl, the Inquifitor
fubfcribes an Order for his Apprehenfion, and gives it to the Executor, who
is to take up the Criminal.　The Form of the Order is this: *By Command of
the Reverend Father* N. *an Inquifitor of heretical Pravity, let* N. *be apprehended
and committed to the Prifons of the holy Office, and not be releafed but by the exprefs
Order of the faid Lord Inquifitor.*　If feveral Criminals are to be taken up at the
fame time, a feparate Order for each Perfon muft be given to the Executor,
that if it fhould be neceffary to acquaint any Perfon, who is not one of the
Minifters or Officials of the holy Office, with the apprehending of one or
another Criminal, he may know nothing of the taking up of the reft.　This
Order muft be inferted in the Criminals Procefs by the Notary, in the very
Words in which 'tis given to the Executor.　If the Inquifitors have an armed
Attendance of their own, they give this Order to their own Executor.　If
they have not fuch an armed Attendance, but find it neceffary to call in the
Help of the fecular Judge, the Inquifitor muft take Care, that fuch Orders
be given to a trufty Executor, and who knows how faithfully to keep the Secret he is intrufted with, becaufe, if the Perfon to be apprehended fhould receive any private Information, he would eafily efcape.

In a City, where any noble Perfons, Doctors, or Religious, or others of illuftrious Birth or Dignity are to be fent to Jayl, the Commiffary of the Inquifition, or fome other Officer, ufually goes to the Houfes of fuch Perfons,
and takes them in a Coach and carries them to Jayl.　But if there is no Fear
of their Efcape, they are commanded to come to the holy Office by a fpecial
Meffenger.

When the Criminal is apprehended, he muft be well guarded, and if there
be Need, put in Irons, and thus carried by the Executor to the Jayls of the
Inquifition, and delivered into the Hands of the Jayl-Keeper.　The Keeper
muft

muft take him into his Cuftody, and ufe him according to the Laws made about Prifoners. If any one is to be brought from very diftant Places, they don't think it fafe for him to lodge in Inns, or private Houfes, becaufe by this Means he might eafily make his Efcape ; and therefore the Executor is ufually charged, to go to the Bifhops of the Place, if there be any, or to the fecular Judges, that the Criminal may be placed and kept in their Jayls. And this the Inquifitor fignifies by his Letters given to the Executor to the Magiftrates, through whofe Territories the Criminal is to be carried, and exhorts them to give the neceffary and convenient Affiftance to the Executor. And that no one may dare to oppofe him, and that the Criminal may be kept in fure and fafe Cuftody, they defire he may be attended with a proper Guard. But this Caution is not neceffary in the Cities of *Spain.* For as foon as ever the Executor fhews, that he is to apprehend any one by Command of the holy Office, no one dares oppofe him. And if any one fhould, the Mob would immediately run together to lend an helping Hand to the holy Office, and fo over-power him, that unlefs he would undergo the fevereft Treatment, he would, of his own Accord, offer himfelf to be taken up by the Executor. All thefe Things are largely fettled by the *Toledo* Inftruction, *An.* 1561. *Cap.* 10, 12, & 13.

CHAP. XIII.

Of the Examination of the PRISONERS.

WHEN the Criminal is put in Jayl, he is brought before the Inquifi- *Inquif. de* tor. The Place where he appears before the Inquifitor, is called by *Goa. cap* 8. the *Portugueze* the Table of the holy Office. At the farther End of it there is placed a Crucifix, raifed up almoft as high as the Cieling. In the Middle of the Room there is a Table. At that End which is neareft the Crucifix fits the Secretary or Notary of the Inquifition. The Criminal is brought *c.* 18. in by the Beadle, with his Head, Arms and Feet naked, and is followed by one of the Keepers. When they come to the Chamber of Audience, the Beadle enters firft, makes a profound Reverence before the Inquifitor, and then withdraws. After this the Criminal enters alone, who is ordered to fit down on a Bench at the other End of the Table over againft the Secretary. The Inquifitor fits on his right Hand. On the Table near the Criminal lies a Miffal, or Book of the Gofpels, and he is ordered to lay his Hand on one of them, and to fwear that he will declare the Truth, and keep Secrecy.

After taking this Oath of declaring the Truth both of himfelf and others, *Pegna,* the Inquifitor interrogates him of divers Matters. As, whether he knows why *prax. Inq.* he was taken up, or hath been informed of it by any one or more Perfons ? *l. 2. c.* 14. Where, when, and how he was apprehended? If he fays that he knows nothing of it, he is asked, whether he can't guefs at the Reafon ? Whether he
knows

knows in what Prifons he is detained? and upon what Account Men are imprifoned there? If he fays he can't guefs at the Caufe of his Imprifonment, but
knows that he is in the Prifons of the holy Office, where Hereticks and Perfons fufpected of Herefy are confined, he is told, that fince he knows Perfons
are confined there for their Profanation of Religion, he ought to conclude
that he alfo is confined for the fame Reafon, and muft therefore declare what
he believes to be the Caufe of his own Apprehenfion and Confinement in the
Prifons of the holy Office. If he fays he cannot imagine what it fhould be,
before he is asked any other Queftions, he receives a gentle Admonition, and
is put in mind of the Lenity of the holy Office towards thofe who confefs
without forcing, and of the Rigour of Juftice ufed towards thofe who are obftinate. They alfo compare other Tribunals with the holy Office, and re-
mind him, that in others the Confeffion of the Crime draws after it immediate Execution and Punifhment; but that in the Court of the Inquifition,
thofe who confefs, and are penitent, are treated with greater Gentlenefs. After this he is admonifhed in Writing, and told, that the Minifters of the holy Office never take up any one, or are ufed to apprehend any one without a
juft Caufe, and that therefore they earneftly befeech him, and command and
enjoin him exactly to recollect and diligently to confider his Actions, to examine his Confcience, and purge it from all thofe Offences and Errors it labours under, and for which he is informed againft.

After this he is asked, what Race he comes of? Who were his Parents
and Anceftors? that hereby he may declare all his Family. Whether any
one of them was at any time taken up by the holy Office, and enjoined Penance? This they are efpecially asked who defcend from *Jews, Mahometans,*
and Sectaries. Where he was brought up? In what Places he hath dwelt?
Whether he ever changed his Country? Why he did fo, and went into another Place? With whom he converfed in the aforefaid Places, who were his
Friends, and with whom he was intimate? Whether he ever converfed with
any of his Acquaintance about Matters of Religion, or heard them fpeak a-
bout Religion? In what Place, and when, and how often, and of what
Things or Matters they converfed? They particularly ask thefe Queftions of
Perfons whom they imagine to be crafty and cunning, and not eafily
brought to declare the Truth, that from their Kindred, Country, Education, Employment, Time paft, Acquaintance, Friendfhip, Behaviour and
Words, the Inquifitor may draw ftrong Arguments of Sufpicion. Thefe
Queftions are efpecially asked, when fuch Criminals are examined, who have
dwelt in the Countries of Schifmaticks, Hereticks, and other infidel and erroneous Perfons, becaufe, when they have dwelt a long while amongft fuch
Perfons, they are believed the more eafily to have followed their Practices.

He is moreover asked, of what Profeffion he is, and what Employment
of Life he follows? Whether he be rich or poor? What Returns he hath,
and what the Expences of his Living? Then he is commanded to give an Account of his Life, and to declare what he hath done from his Childhood,
even to this Time. And that he may declare all this, he is asked, in what
Places

Places or Cities he ftudied, and what Studies he followed? Who were his Mafters? whofe Names he muft tell. What Arts he learnt? What Books he hath had and read? and whether he hath now any Books treating of Religion, and what? Whether ever he hath been examined and cited, or fued, or proceffed before any other Tribunal, or the Tribunal of the holy Inquifition, and for what Caufes; and whether he was abfolved or condemned, by what Judge, and in what Year? Whether ever he was excommunicated, and for what Caufe? Whether he was afterwards abfolved or condemned, and for what Reafon? Whether he hath every Year facramentally confeffed his Sins, how often, and in what Church? Then he is commanded to give the Names of his Confeffors, and of thofe from whom he hath received the Eucharift, and efpecially for the ten Years laft paft, and more. What Orations or holy Prayers he recites? Whether he hath any Enemies? whofe Names he muft tell, and the Reafons of their Enmity.

If the Criminal is perfuaded by thefe, or by more or lefs fuch Interrogatories, openly to confefs the Truth, his Caufe is finifhed, becaufe 'tis immediately known what will be the Iffue of it.

But if after all thefe Interrogatories the Prifoner perfifts in the Negative, and fays he doth not know why he is cited or fent to Prifon, the Inquifitor replies, that fince it appears from his own Words, that he will not difcover the Truth, and that there is no Proof of his having fuch Enmities with any Perfons, or that there are no fuch Caufes of Hatred as he alledges, by which others could, or ought to be induced flanderoufly, and falfely to inform againft him, that therefore there arifes the ftronger Sufpicion, that the Depofitions againft him in the holy Office are true. And therefore he is befeeched and adjured by the Bowels of Mercy of Chrift Jefus, to confider better and better, and ingenuoufly to confefs the Truth, and to declare whether he hath erred in Words or Deeds in the aforefaid Matter relating to the Faith, and the holy Office, or rendred himfelf fufpected to others. All thefe Things are provided for by the *Toledo* Inftructions, *An.* 1561. *cap.* 13, 14, 15, 16.

All thefe Interrogatories propofed to the Criminals, and their Anfwers and Sayings, as propofed and fpoken, are faithfully and at large to be written down by the Notary; and if the Criminal can write, he fubfcribes it; if he can't, he puts the Sign of the Crofs.

If by fuch general Interrogatories the Inquifitor can't draw from the Prifoner a Confeffion of the Crime of which he is accufed, he comes to particular Interrogatories, which relate to the Matter it felf, or the Crimes or Herefies for which the Criminal was denounced. For Inftance, if he was accufed for denying Purgatory, then one, two, or three Days after his firft Examination, he is again interrogated by the Inquifitor, whether he hath any Thing, and what, to fay befides what he faid in his other Examination? Whether he hath thought better of the Matter, and can recollect the Caufe of his Imprifonment, and former Examination, or hath at leaft any Sufpicion who could accufe him to the holy Office, and of what Matters? Whether he hath heard any one difcourfing of Paradife, Purgatory, and Hell? What he heard con-

Cap. 15.

concerning that Matter? Who they were that he heard speaking or disputing of those Things? Whether he ever discoursed of them? What he hath believed, and doth now believe about Purgatory? If he answers, that his Faith concerning it hath been right, and denies any ill Belief, but that he believes as holy Mother Church believes and teaches, he is order'd to say what the holy *Roman* Mother Church doth think and believe concerning this Article.

When he hath given in his Answer he is admonished to consider well and tell the Truth, and to beware of lying, because the contrary is proved by Witnesses against him, *viz.* that speaking of Purgatory, he said such and such Things; and then they recite the Words which the Denouncer and Witness have deposed were spoken by him. And thus he is successively in the same or another Examination interrogated in the same manner concerning the several Articles for which he is denounced: As, whether he said, that simple Fornication is no Sin, that 'tis lawful to invocate Devils, and offer Sacrifices to them, and the like. All these Things the Notary receives, as in the first Examination, and the Prisoner subscribes them.

If the Prisoner's Answers don't agree with his former Answers, he is examined again and again, and, as shall hereafter be shewn, they proceed to farther Remedies. And whatever the Popish Doctors may write, [they who have been in the Prison of the Inquisition with one Mouth, complain] that they are left in Uncertainty for a long while, what are the Crimes of which they are accused; and that the Inquisitors would willingly draw from their own Mouths a Confession of Crimes to which they are not conscious. And this is cunningly invented for this Reason, that if any Person should have happened to have spoken any thing not agreeable to the *Roman* Faith, and of which possibly he is not accused, he may discover those Things also, because he is uncertain of what Crime he is accused, on Account of that horrid Silence which is there observed; or that he may accuse himself falsely of certain Things to free himself from that dreadful Jayl. So that they all affirm their Accusations are not discovered to them till after a long Confinement, that so being broken and tired out with a continued and horrible Imprisonment, they may confess of themselves Things that never came into their Minds.

If the Prisoner knows the Reason of his being apprehended, and openly confesses every Thing of which he hath been accused to the Inquisitor, he is commended, and encouraged to hope for a speedy Deliverance. If he confesses some Things, but can't guess at others, he is commended for taking up the Purpose of accusing himself, and exhorted by the Bowels of Mercy of Jesus Christ, to proceed, and ingenuously to confess every Thing else of which he is accused, that so he may experience that Kindness and Mercy, which this Tribunal uses towards those, who manifest a real Repentance of their Crimes by a sincere and voluntary Confession. If the Case doth not relate to formal Heresy, but to some certain kind of Fortune-telling, or heretical Word, and the Prisoner confesses the Act or Word, but denies the heretical Intention, the Inquisitors use all their Endeavours to draw from him also a Confession. And first they enquire, whether that Fact or Word was committed once, or oftener?

Annot. 1b.

oftener? If oftener, they don't eafily believe the Criminal, affirming his good Intention and Belief; becaufe the oftener an heretical Propofition was uttered, there arifes a greater Sufpicion, that both his Intention and Faith were bad.

Carena alfo advifes the Inquifitors to ufe great Caution in the Examination of Priefts guilty of Solicitation, that they may not make the Confeffors by their Interrogatories reveal thofe Things which fall under the Seal of Secrefy. He tells us of a Cafe that happened in a certain Inquifition, that when the Procefs was fent to the facred Congregation, and their Eminencies the Fathers had confidered it, they commanded every Thing to be erafed out of it, which in the leaft favoured of the Breach of the Seal.

During the firft ten Days of the Imprifonment, thefe Admonitions are ufu-Cap. 16. ally repeated three times by the Inquifitor. But 'tis in the Inquifitor's Plea-fure to admonifh and examine them oftener, efpecially when they think the Prifoners refufe to difcover the Truth out of Wickednefs, or don't remember thofe Things of which they are denounced. In the fupream Inquifition at *Rome* Criminals are brought into Court to Audience, examined, and admo-nifhed, not only thrice, but five times, and fometimes feven, and fometimes thrice within ten Days. Others, efpecially young Perfons accufed of heinous Crimes, are examined and admonifhed thrice only. From whence they draw thefe Rules. 1. When the Perfon accufed is taken up, the Inquifitor muft examine and interrogate him frequently concerning thofe Things which he denies, but which are proved, or of which there are vehement Sufpicions that he is guilty, till he will fay nothing more, either by confeffing or deny-ing, and his Caufe is therefore concluded. 2. It is then proper to admonifh and interrogate the Criminal feveral times, when he either denies the Crimes objected to him, or partly denies, and partly confeffes them, or if there a-rife new Evidence and Proofs. 3. 'Tis left to the Pleafure of the Inquifitors, how often the Criminal fhall be brought up, admonifhed, and examined, and in a doubtful Cafe 'tis fafeft often to admonifh and examine him. 4. Altho' 'tis not determined by any particular Law, and three Admonitions ought to be made within the firft ten Days after Imprifonment, yet 'tis fafe, that foon after the Criminals are fent to Jayl, they fhould be brought to Audience, admonifhed and interrogated, and that other Examinations fhould be made a few Days after, whilft their Memories are frefh. But their Practice is di-rectly contrary to this Advice, for the Prifoners are detained in the Jayls of the Inquifition feveral Years, and 'tis very often an whole Year, before they are again examined, after the three firft Admonitions.

CHAP. XIV.

What Arts the INQUISITORS *use to draw a Confession from the Prisoners.*

Pegna,
prax. l. 2.
c. 19.

THESE Examinations and Admonitions are repeated by the Inquisitors, as often as they think fit, for they are not bound to any certain Number. But in these Examinations the Inquisitors use the greatest Artifice, to draw from the Prisoners Confessions of those Crimes of which they are accused. And altho' they say that the Inquisition makes use rather of Prudence than Art, yet they suggest several Orders and Artifices which must be used, and which they generally use in making Inquisition.

First, they observe this exactly, that as often as the Criminals are judicially interrogated, they must so often touch the holy Scriptures, swearing that they will declare the Truth, so that an Oath always precedes the Deposition. The same also is observed as to the Witnesses. Yea, if the Examination should be broke off, and what follows should be only a Continuation of the former, they must first take an Oath before they are suffered to proceed. Besides, the Inquisitors always admonish and exhort the Criminals, to confess simply, fully and truly, whatsoever they have done against the Catholick Faith, and especially to take Care that they don't bear false Witness either against themselves, or any others. They must not give them Occasion to be-

Cap. 20.

have indecently or rudely, or to utter Reproaches; neither must they promise them Impunity or entire Deliverance, whilst they are endeavouring to draw a Confession from their Mouths, least they should prove Liars, by promising what possibly they may not be able to perform, or least the Criminals, under this Hope should confess Things which perhaps they never committed.

They must not be negligent and slothful in omitting such Interrogatories, as belong to the Cause it self, and the Articles brought into Judgment; nor must they be too troublesome and imprudent, by putting impertinent Interrogatories, which don't relate to the Cause. But if the Criminal gives Occasion to ask other Questions by his Answer to such Interrogatories as are founded upon legal Proofs, if they are not altogether trifling and foreign to the Cause, he may be interrogated upon them, because he himself gave Occasion for them in his Answer. And thus sometimes, as they say, it happens in this Tribunal, that from the Answers of the Criminals they begin to make great Discoveries.

But particular Care must be taken, that the Witnesses who depose against the Criminal, may not be discovered by the Interrogatories, in Favour of the Faith, least the Criminals should conspire against them, whereby few would be found to denounce Hereticks, or suspected Persons, or to give Testimony against them. If the Criminal begins to confess, and freely to declare the Truth, the Inquisitor must not hinder, disturb, or interrupt him, nor break off his Confession, tho' other Affairs call for him, or the Time be elapsed; be-

cause

caufe, they fay, 'tis often found, that thofe whofe Confeffions have been once interrupted, will not afterwards confefs any more, or will retract what they have begun to confefs.

If there arifes any Thing doubtful, worthy of Confideration, from the *Cap.* 18. Criminals Anfwers, which 'tis proper to know how the Denouncer and Witneffes underftood it, they are to be called again and re-examined. For Inftance, whether the Prifoner fpoke what he faid in jeft, or earneft? Or as repeating the Words of other Perfons, or afferting it as his own Mind and Opinion? But here the Inquifitor muft be cautious, that he doth not by re-examining the Depofition or Witneffes difcover any Thing, from whence the Depofer or Witneffes may gather what the Criminal hath confeffed; but muft fo interrogate him, as tho' 'twas only for his own Information.

Thefe are the principal Cautions which they are commanded to obferve in the Examination of Criminals, all which the Inquifitors do very carefully and exactly keep to, as far as they find any of them of any Service to draw Confeffions from the Prifoners own Mouths, but which they eafily omit, when they think proper, and it will ferve their Turn, efpecially when they would be of any Ufe and Affiftance to the Criminals. That they may draw from them a Confeffion, they are at firft kind, and pretend the fincereft Affection, and 'tis recommended to the Inquifitors to treat the Criminals tenderly, whilft they are heard, interrogated and examined, and to remember that they themfelves are Men, who might have fallen into the fame or like Crimes, unlefs they had been guarded by the Grace of God, and not to fuffer the Criminals, altho' common and mean Perfons, to ftand whilft they are hearing, but to command them to fit down. If in their Confeffion, or in the Beginning or Progrefs of their Examination they are fo moved with Grief, or affected with Repentance, as to fhed Tears, or to implore the Mercy of the Judges, and ask Pardon for their Offence upon their bended Knees, or holding up their Hands, or beating their Breafts, all thefe Circumftances muft be inferted by the Notary in the Acts of the Procefs.

But if the Prifoners don't confefs thofe Things of which they are accufed, as it may often happen, either becaufe the Accufations are falfe, or becaufe they don't remember Things, efpecially if at the Diftance of feveral Years, and what was faid was not in the leaft premeditated, but inadvertently and in common Difcourfe, they make ufe of a quite different Method of Inquifition, and try every Art to catch and infnare thefe miferable Criminals, already tired out by their vile Imprifonment, Arts not always wholly agreeable to the Admonitions juft now mentioned. This is well defcribed by *Eymerick,* ¹*Direct.* and therefore I fhall give it here, that the Manner of proceeding againft the *Inq.part.*3. Prifoners in the Jayl of the Inquifition, may be more diftinctly and fully underftood. -

According therefore to the Directory of *Eymerick,* the Inquifitors don't in- *n.* 86. terrogate all Perfons of the fame Things, nor in the fame Order, but begin and carry on their Inquifition, either from what the Accufers and Denouncers fay, or from the Anfwers of the Witneffes, or from what

they

they learn by Experience, or from what their own Judgment dictates to them ; so that they often vary the Manner of their Examination, leaft if the Criminals fhould forefee the ordinary Manner and general Rule, they fhould take the proper Precaution and Care to evade it.

n. 87.

If any openly confefs their Errors, and perfift in them, and defire to defend them, they are convicted by learned Men of the Crime of Herefy ; for 'tis fhewn that their Opinions are condemned by the Church of *Rome*, and are therefore heretical, and becaufe they obftinately defend their Opinions before the Inquifitors, they are judged to be Hereticks.

Com. 22.

But if they will not declare their Errors, but rather cover them by ambiguous Anfwers, the Inquifitor ufes various Arts to difcover them. For as far as it can be done he openly interrogates them, and propofes a fingle Thing in each Interrogatory, and not feveral together, and compels the Criminal to anfwer directly to each of them. If he gives obfcure and doubtful Anfwers, he is commanded to explain them, before he proceeds farther. If he will difpute, the Inquifitor enters into no Difpute with him, but only interrogates and examines him. Sometimes he fpeaks kindly to him, pretends that he pities his Misfortune, advifes him to fpeak the Truth, which he gives him to underftand he is acquainted with, and intimates to him fome Hope of Favour and Freedom if he confeffes, becaufe the holy Office of the Inquifition ufes to fhew Mercy to fuch who voluntarily confefs their Crimes, how grievous and heinous foever they may be, and in a friendly Manner fpeaks to him thus.

100.
Com. 23.

" Don't be afraid openly to confefs, if you did happen to believe thefe fort of
" Perfons, who taught fuch and fuch Things, to be good Men. You be-
" lieved them, and willingly heard them, and gave them fomewhat of your
" Subftance, or received them fometimes into your Houfe, or made Con-
" feffion to them, becaufe you were a fimple Man, and loved them, thinking
" them to be good Men, and knowing no Evil of them. The fame Thing
" might have happened to Perfons much wifer than you, and fo they might
" have been deceived. I have Pity on you, and fee your own Simplicity hath
" deceived you, and tho' you are in fome meafure faulty, yet they are more
" fo who have inftructed you. Tell me therefore the Truth, for you fee I
" know the whole Matter, that I may immediately free you, and fhew you
" Favour." After this he interrogates him, not fo much concerning the Fact, as the Circumftances of it, that the Perfon may believe he knows the Fact already.

101.

If the Inquifitor knows that he who denies the Fact is convicted by Witneffes, he reads over to him what they have depofed, fuppreffing their Names,

102.

fo as that he may know he is convicted by them, but may not underftand who they are. If he knows he is not convicted by Witneffes, and the Depofitions againft him have from the Proofs an Appearance of Truth, the Inquifitor takes up the Procefs, looks it over, and fays, 'tis evident you don't fpeak the Truth, but that 'tis as I fay. Tell me therefore the plain Truth. This the Inquifitor doth, that the Criminal may believe that he is already convicted, and that it appears fo in the Procefs. Or he hath a Paper in his Hand, and pretends

tends to read out of it Things that are not contained in it, and then with an
Air of Admiration cries out, How can you deny it? Is it not fully evident to
me? But here they take Care not to come to such Particulars, from which
the Criminal might easily gather, that the Cause is not so well known to the
Inquisitor as he pretends. He only mentions what he is certain of, and as to
other Things speaks only in the general. Sometimes the Inquisitor pretends   103.
he must go to some other Place, and shall not return for a long while, and
says that he pities the Prisoner, would expedite his Affair, and so persuades
him to confess; otherwise he must remain in the Jayl in Irons till his Return,
and he doth not know when that will be, that by this Means the Prisoner may,
thro' Dread of that direful and wearisom Imprisonment, be persuaded to confess. And indeed in the Book of the Sentences of the *Tholouse* Inquisition, there
are Instances of several, who have been continued in Jayl several Years, before Sentence pronounced against them. And even to this Day the Prisoners
are kept many Years in the Prison of the Inquisition, which in *Spain*, and
especially in *Portugal* is very dismal, as hath been related, Book 2. Chap. 18.
that they may at length confess. Sometimes the Inquisitor multiplies his In-   104.
terrogatories, and teases his Prisoner, that he may confess this or the other
Thing, or may be caught contradicting himself. When this happens, the
Prisoner is shewn the Contradictions in his Answers, and admonished to declare the Truth, or that otherwise he will be put to the Question and Tortures. And if he will not confess, he is, as will be afterwards shewn, by the
Advice of the Learned, actually made to undergo them, that by Torments
they may draw forth the Truth.

If neither by this Means he can draw out a Confession from the Priso-   106.
ner, he treats him more kindly in his Food and Drink, and procures certain
Persons, no ways suspected concerning the Faith, to go to him, and frequently to converse with him of several Things, not at all relating to his Cause,
and at length to persuade him to have Confidence in them, and to advise him
to confess the Truth, promising that the Inquisitor shall be favourable to
him, and that they will be Mediators in his Behalf. At length the Inquisi-   'Pegna,
tor comes along with them, and promises to shew him Favour if he will con-   *Comm.* 23,
fess the Truth, for all is gracious that is done for the Conversion of Hereticks,
and even their Penances are Graces, and Remedies. If the Person accused
by this Means prays for Favour, and confesses his Error, the Inquisitor answers, you shall have much greater Favour than you asked, but promises it
only in general Terms, for he thinks he fulfils his Promise, in shewing the
least Kindness to him afterwards. And when they promise to shew Favour;
'tis understood only of those Punishments, which are left to their own Power;
viz. several penitential Punishments, because they can't remit those which are
appointed by the Law. They farther teach, that notwithstanding the Promise of such Grace, they may inflict penitential and arbitrary Punishments;
because, if after a long time, continual Admonitions, and sometimes after
the Torture, Criminals confess their Offence upon the Promise of such Grace,
the Inquisitors may legally and justly inflict more grievous penitential Punishments,

ments, if they omit the leffer ; for if one or another be rémitted, they think they abundantly fatisfy their Promife.

And by thefe flattering Affurances they fometimes overcome the Minds of more unwary Perfons, and when they have obtained the defigned. End, immediately forget them all. Of this *Gonfalvius* gives us a remarkable Inftance.

Pag. 82, &c. " In the firft Fire that was blown up at *Seville*, *An.* 1558, or 1559,
" amongft many others who were taken up, there was a certain pious Ma-
" tron, with her two Virgin Daughters, and her Niece by her Sifter who
" was married. As they endured thofe Tortures of all Kinds, with a truly
" manlike Conftancy, by which they endeavoured to make them perfidi-.
" oufly betray their Brethren in Chrift, and efpecially to accufe one another,
" the Inquifitor at length commanded one of the Daughters to be fent for to
" Audience. There he difcourfed with her alone for a confiderable time, in
" order to comfort her, as indeed fhe needed it. When the Difcourfe was end-
" ed, the Girl was remanded to her Prifon. Some Days after he acted the
" fame Part again, caufing her to be brought before him feveral Days to-
" wards the Evening, detaining her for a confiderable while, fometimes tel-
" ling her how much he was grieved for her Afflictions, and then intermixing
" familiarly enough other pleafant and agreeable Things. All this, as
" the Event fhewed, had only this Tendency, that after he had perfuaded
" the poor fimple Girl, that he was really, and with a fatherly Affection
" concerned for her Calamity, and would confult as a Father what might be
" for her Benefit and Salvation, and that of her Mother and Sifters, fhe might
" wholly throw her felf into his Protection. After fome Days fp ent in fuch
" familiar Difcourfes, during which he pretended to mourn with her over her
" Calamity, and to fhew himfelf affected with her Miferies, and to give her
" all the Proofs of his good Will, in order, as far as he could, to remove
" them, when he knew he had deceived the Girl, he begins to perfuade her
" to difcover what fhe knew of her felf, her Mother, Sifters, and Aunts, who
" were not yet apprehended, promifing upon Oath, that if fhe would faith-
" fully difcover to him all that fhe knew of that Affair, he would find out a
" Method to relieve her from all her Misfortunes, and to fend them all back
" again to their Houfes. The Girl, who had no very great Penetration,
" being thus allured by the Promifes and Perfuafions of the Father of the
" Faith, begins to tell him fome Things relating to the holy Doctrine fhe had
" been taught, and about which they ufed to confer with one another. When
" the Inquifitor had now got hold of the Thread, he dextroufly endeavoured
" to find his Way throughout the whole Labyrith, oftentimes calling the
" Girl to Audience, that what fhe had depofed might be taken down in a le-
" gal Manner, always perfuading her, this would be the only juft Means to
" put an End to all her Evils. In the laft Audience he renews to her all his Pro-
" mifes, by which he had before affured her of her Liberty, and the like.
" But when the poor Girl expected the Performance of them, the faid Inqui-
" fitor, with his Followers, finding the Succefs of his Craftinefs, by which
" he had in part drawn out of the Girl, what before they could not extort
" from

" from her by Torments, determined to put her to the Torture again, to force
" out of her what they thought she had yet concealed. Accordingly she
" was made to suffer the moſt cruel Part of it, even the Rack, and the See *Cap.*
" Torture by Water, till at laſt they had ſqueezed out of her as with a Preſs, 29.
" both the Hereſies and Accuſations of Perſons they had been hunting af-*Book* 4.
" ter. For, thro' the Extremity of her Torture, ſhe accuſed her Mother
" and Siſters, and ſeveral others, who were afterwards taken up and tortured,
" and burnt alive in the ſame Fire with the Girl."

But if they don't ſucceed neither with this Way, the Inquiſitor permits ſome 107.
Perſon or other, who is not unacceptable to the Priſoner, to go to him, and converſe with him, and if it be needful to feign himſelf ſtill one of his own Sect,
but that he abjured thro' Fear, and diſcovered the Truth to the Inquiſitor.
When he finds that the Priſoner confides in him, he comes to him again late
in the Evening, keeps on a Diſcourſe with him, at length pretending 'tis too
late to go away, and that therefore he will ſtay with him all Night in the
Priſon, that they may converſe together, and the Priſoner may be perſuaded
by the other's Diſcourſe, to confeſs to one another what they have committed.
In the mean while there are Perſons ſtanding at a proper Place without the
Jayl, to hear and to take Notice of their Words, who, when there is need,
are attended by a Notary.

This *Eymerick* taught was to be done in his Time. But now the Perſon, Gonſalv.
who thus treacherouſly draws out any Thing according to his Deſire from his *p.* 95.
Fellow Priſoners, prays the Jayl-keeper, when, according to Cuſtom, he is
viſiting his Priſoners, to deſire that he may have an Audience. For this is
the Method the Priſoners take. And when he goes out of his Jayl to give an
Account of his Office, he diſcovers not only what he heard from any of the
Priſoners, but alſo how they received the Doctrine propoſed to them, whether with a chearful or angry Countenance, and the like, if they refuſed to
give them an Anſwer, and what they themſelves think of them. And the
Accuſations of ſuch a Wretch they look on as the beſt and moſt unexceptionable Evidence, altho' the Perſon be otherwiſe one of no manner of Worth,
Credit or Regard.

Theſe ſort of Perſons they call Flies, and, as *Gonſalvius* tells us, they may
be known and found out by this one Thing, that for the moſt part they
thruſt themſelves into ſuch ſort of Converſations, without any one's asking
them, and begin very impertinently ſuch Diſcourſes concerning Doctrine.
And therefore he adviſes, that if the Priſoners act prudently, they will let
them talk themſelves weary, without giving them any Anſwer.

They who have been lately in the Priſon of the Inquiſition in *Spain* and
Portugal, tell us of another Method they make uſe of to draw a Confeſſion from
the Priſoners, *viz.* The Inquiſitor ſuborns a certain Perſon, to go and ſpeak to
the Priſoner, and to tell him he comes of himſelf, and of his own Accord,
and to exhort him to tell the Inquiſitor the Truth, becauſe he is a merciful
Man, and ſuch fine Tales. This is now particularly the Cuſtom in *Spain* and
Portugal, as to thoſe they call the new Chriſtians. If the Priſoner affirms
himſelf

himself to be a Catholick, and denies that he is a *Jew*, and is not convicted by a sufficient Number of Witnesses, they suborn one to perswade him to confess. If he protests himself innocent, the other replies, that he also hath been in Jayl, and that his protesting his Innocence signified nothing. What, had you rather dwell for ever in Jayl, and render your Life miserable, by being ever parted from your Wife and Children, than redeem your Freedom, by confessing the Crime? By this and other like Things the Prisoners are oftentimes perswaded to confess not only real but fictitious Crimes. And when their Constancy is thus almost overcome, the Inquisitor commands them to be brought before him, that they may make him a Confession of their Faults.

Pag 95. Here *Gonsalvius* justly wonders, how Men can be of so devilish a Temper, as voluntarily to hire themselves out to such Offices, and at so great an Expence to themselves, who, in order to obtain their Desire, don't refuse to be Prisoners with others, even for two or three Months together, in a vile narrow Jayl, but bear willingly what the Prisoners themselves bear with the greatest Uneasiness, all the Inconveniencies of it, Hunger, Nastiness and Stench; and what is more wonderful, go out of one Jayl into another, and then into a third, twice, thrice, four times, always experiencing the same Inconveniencies, and passing their whole Lives in such a Circle of Delights.

After these Examinations, if the Prisoner confesses nothing, he is carried back to Jayl, and there kept sometimes for a whole Year, before he is again brought up to the Inquisitor. In the mean while, if he desires an Audience, to confess certain Matters, he may gently rap at the Door of his Jayl. The Keeper being acquainted herewith by his Officers, immediately comes to him, and is desired by him to ask the Favour of the Inquisitor of being brought before him.

If the Criminal will not answer to the Interrogatories judicially put to him, or answers uncertainly and doubtfully, as, I don't know, I don't remember, I have forgot; or when he answers as to the main Fact, but refuses to answer concerning the principal Circumstances of the Crime, if the Circumstances are such, which 'tis probable he may remember, he may be put to the Torture to make him precisely answer affirmatively or negatively: Because Criminals are not apprehended for the Crime of Heresy without legal Proofs, *i. e.* more than half full Proof. 'Tis the same Case if they pretend Madness. Sometimes also they are humbled by Imprisonment and Fasting.

Pegna, prax. l. 2. c. 21. n. 5. And to shew that they deal more mildly in their Tribunal than in others, they add, that in other Tribunals, when the Criminal is accused of any certain Fact, he hath not Time allowed him to deliberate whether he will confess, or be tried, but is immediately compelled to answer. But that in this Tribunal, where Criminals are dealt with more mildly and gently, they not only give them Time to answer when they ask it, but oftentimes admonish, and even invite them, to think better of the Matter, and carefully to recall to their Remembrance their Actions and Words, that they may answer truly,
and

and that for this Reafon they are often examined and interrogated. But in Truth this Pretence of Mercy is ufed only for this End, that the Criminal, who if convicted by two agreeing Witneffes, and ftill perfifting in the Negative, is fure to be condemned as a Negative without Mercy, and delivered over to the fecular Court, may, through Fear of this horrible Punifhment, confefs the Crime he is accufed of, and fo be reconciled as a Penitent, by certain Penances laid on him by way of Punifhment, or delivered over as impenitent to the fecular Court, and burnt alive. But if he revokes his Confeffion when made, and be not legally and fully convicted by Witneffes, he is moft cruelly tortured, becaufe by his own Confeffion he hath given Proof againft himfelf fufficient for the Torture. If he is overcome by the Torture, and renews his Confeffion, he is punifhed as an Heretick ; if he overcomes the Torture, he is enjoined falutary Penances at the Pleafure of the Inquifitor, as one fufpected of Herefy.

As often as the Criminals or Witneffes are examined, either in their firft Pegna, or after Audiences, when the Examination is ended, before they go from *c. 22.* Audience, the Inquifitors order the Notary clearly and diftinctly, to read over to them their Depofitions, that fo the Criminals or Witneffes may add, diminifh, correct or change what they pleafe, that, if there be any Miftake, it may be rectified, which otherwife fcarce could be. For if after the Criminal or Witnefs goes from Audience, or if at any Diftance of Time after, they would amend or alter what they have faid, it would not be allowed them. And therefore the Notary, at the End of the Examination, writes down, that the Depofition was read over to the Criminals or Witneffes, and adds whatever either of them added, diminifhed, altered or amended.

If, befides the Depofition of the Informer, and the Witneffes named by *Cap. 22.* him, they have any other Matters, the Inquifitors inquire farther, that the Evidence may be more fully confirmed. This they particularly obferve, when the Witneffes or Criminal name any other Perfons in their Examination on one Side or the other. If fuch Perfons are prefent, the Inquifitor orders them to be called and interrogated. If they are abfent, and it be not fafe or eafy to come at them, he writes to the Inquifitor or Bifhop, in whofe Diocefe they are, that he fhould cite and interrogate them privately, and find out the Truth, and to tranfmit the Matter to him faithfully and fecretly as he difcovers it. Thus 'tis determined by the Council of *Narbonne,* Cap. 22. *Yet fo, that the other Inquifitors may neverthelefs inquire out what they are able to difcover, and write to thofe Inquifitors in what Things fuch Perfon is culpable.*

CHAP. XV.

How the Prisoners are allowed an ADVOCATE, PROCURATOR
and GUARDIAN.

WHEN the Procefs hath gone thus far, and all the Informations and
Proofs relating to the Caufe, are taken in a fummary Manner, and
the Criminal fully examined, if he confeffes his Crime, there is no room for
a Defence, nor do they proceed to the re-examining of the Witneffes. But
if he perfifts in the Negative, and demands the Depofitions to be given him,
whether he is prefumed to be innocent or obftinate, he is admitted to his
Defence, and all Matters are prepared to form the Procefs. And therefore
becaufe the Criminal muft be convicted by Witneffes, the Witneffes muft be
re-examined. And that the Criminal may not feem to be denied his Defence,
he hath an Advocate and Procurator allowed him. He is not however at
Liberty to chufe the one or other as he pleafes, nor is it lawful for any Advocate to defend an Heretick under Pain of Infamy. Cap. *Si adverfus nos.*
de hæret. The Inquifitors appoint him his Advocate, and he is bound to
them by Oath. The Criminal may alfo fometimes, if he demands it, have
a fecond Advocate. The Qualifications neceffary in fuch an Advocate are
Direct. thefe : That he be a good Man, not fufpected as to his Honefty, fkilful in the
p. 3. com. Canon and Civil Law, zealous for the Faith, and not in the leaft tinctu-
28. red with Herefy, and he is allowed to the Criminal, according to the prefent
Cuftom in *Spain*, after he hath received three Admonitions, freely to confefs the Truth. The Manner to be obferved in thefe Things, and how the
Advocate muft act in defending the Criminal, is provided by one of the *Madrid* Inftructions, *A.* 1561. *c.* 23. *The Inquifitor or Inquifitors fhall admonifh the
Criminal how much it concerns him to confefs the Truth, after which they fhall nominate him an Advocate or Advocates, appointed by the holy Office for this Purpofe, in
order to his Defence ; and in the Prefence of every one of the Inquifitors, the Criminal fhall confer with his Advocate, and, as he counfels, fhall anfwer to his Accufation by Word or Writing. But before the Advocate undertakes his Defence, he fhall
fware that he will truly and faithfully defend him, and obferve Secrefy in every
Thing he fhall hear or fee, even altho' he took his Oath when he was firft appointed
by the holy Office to this Employment. The Bufinefs of the Advocate is to admonifh
the Criminal to confefs the Truth, and to ask Pardon for his Fault, if he be guilty of
any. The Anfwer fhall be notified or intimated to the Fifcal.*

De Cathol. The fourth Inftruction of *Toledo*, *cap.* 4. as *Simancas* relates it, gives a fome-
Inftit. what fuller Account of this Matter. The Advocate muft not defend any
tit. 5. §. 1, Criminals, unlefs he be allowed it by the Inquifitor. He muft fwear, that
3. he will faithfully defend the Caufe, and ufe only juft Exceptions, and that as
foon as ever he knows the Caufe to be unjuft, he will inform firft the Criminal
of it, and then the Inquifitors, and immediately throw it up. After this he
muft

muſt ſwear to obſerve Secreſy, and not to make any Diſcoveries to any one. The Form of the Oath adminiſtred to the Advocate, is this. *I* N. *Doctor of both Laws, being here before you, Reverend Fathers, Inquiſitors of the holy Inquiſition againſt heretical Pravity, touching theſe moſt holy Goſpels of God now before me, do ſwear, and promiſe, that I will ſincerely and faithfully, without any Cavilling or Fraud, defend N. whoſe Defence was committed to me, now impriſoned as a Criminal, and under Inquiſition, in the Jayls of this holy Office, for ſuch Cauſes as appear in the Acts of the ſaid holy Office, and that I will maintain his Cauſe, and that I will not inſtruct this my ſaid Principal to conceal the Truth in his Trial, and that as far as I ſhall know this my ſaid Principal to be guilty, convicted of the Crime, or criminal, in the Matter or Matters for which he is inquiſited, I will throw up his Defence: And moreover, as ſoon as I ſhall have Knowledge in the Management of this Cauſe of any Accomplice, or Perſon culpable in this Cauſe, I promiſe and engage to diſcover it immediately to the ſaid Office, under Penalty of Perjury and Excommunication, from which I cannot be abſolved, but by this holy Office. So help me God, and theſe holy Goſpels of God.* This Oath is written down by the Notary, and inſerted in the Acts of the Proceſs. The Advocates receive §. 6, 7, 8. their Stipend from the Treaſury, when they defend the Cauſes of the Poor, which is uſually very ſmall, but honourable. But if the Criminals are not poor, the Advocates receive their Pay out of their Effects. *Inſtruct.* 1. *c.* 16. Whatever the Advocates alledge, in the Preſence of the Criminal, is taken, as if it had been alledged by the Criminal himſelf, unleſs the Advocate hath been miſtaken, and the Priſoner contradicts it within three Days. But in the Cauſe of Hereſy, if after three Days it ſhall appear that the Advocates have been miſtaken, or imprudent, it ſhall not prejudice the Criminal, becauſe it ſeems, in this Judgment, they act with Simplicity and the higheſt Equity, and reject the Rigour of the Law. If the Criminal ſays the Crimes objected to him are forged, his Advocate adviſes him either to challenge the falſe Witneſſes, or to find out ſome juſt Exception and Defence, and ſays he is prepared to defend his Cauſe as far as juſt.

The Criminal alſo had formerly allowed him a Procurator. But theſe Pro-Pegna, curators are now ſeldom allowed, becauſe the Advocates are ſufficient, and *com.* 28. exerciſe the Office of Procurators. Yea, they ſay that the Inquiſitors appear more truly to be the Procurators of the Criminals, ſince by Office they are to take Care of the Criminals Defences. Concerning theſe we thus read in the *Madrid* Inſtruction, *An.* 1561. *c.* 35. *Altho' the Inſtruction provides that Procurators ſhall be allowed the Criminals, yet they ought not to be granted them, becauſe Experience teaches that many Inconveniencies ariſe from thence ; and becauſe of the little Advantage which the Criminals obtain by it, they ſhall not be any longer allowed them : Altho' ſometimes when the Caſe is urgent, 'tis allowed the Advocate to defend the Criminals.*

If the Criminals are under twenty-five Years of Age, they are allowed Curators (a ſort of Guardians) by whoſe Authority they are defended, leaſt, thro' Unſkilfulneſs or Youth, they ſhould conceal, or ſay any Thing, which if ſpoken or concealed, might be of Advantage to them. The ſame In-

ſtruction

ſtruction thus provides, cap. 25. *If the Criminal be not of the Age of* 25 *before he anſwers to his Accuſation, let him be allowed a Curator, by whoſe Authority the Confeſſions made ſhall be ratified, and the whole Proceſs formed.   But let not ſuch Curator be of the Officials of the holy Office, but he may be either his Advocate, or, any other grave, faithful and conſcientious Perſon.* He muſt alſo take an Oath. before the Inquiſitor, laying his Hand upon the Goſpels, *not to defend the Priſoner falſely, not to inſtruct him to conceal the Truth in Judgment ; but to protect. him according to the Form of the ſacred Canons, and the Manner of the holy Office ; and that as ſoon as ever he ſhall know him to be an Heretick, and obſtinate, he will deſiſt from the Proſecution of his Cauſe and his Defence.   But in caſe he will. reconcile himſelf to holy Mother Church, that he will aſſiſt him ; and that if it ſhall happen that he knows any Perſon or Perſons in the Proſecution of ſuch Cauſe,. to be an Accomplice, or culpable, he will diſcover him or them, and that he will. not diſcourſe of his Proceſs, nor of any Thing contained in it, much leſs of the. Merits of ſuch Cauſe, directly or indirectly, with any Perſon except his Principal, or his Procurator or Advocate, under Pain of Perjury and Excommunication,* latæ ſententiæ, *from which he cannot be abſolved but by this holy Office, nor even by, this, unleſs he expreſſes the Cauſe that induced him thus to falſify his Oath.*

CHAP. XVI.

How the Priſoners are interrogated by the INQUISITOR, *whether they allow the Witneſſes to be rightly examined, and re-heard.*

THE Advocate being thus granted, and ſometimes, if the Criminal demands it, the Procurator alſo, the Inquiſitor uſually asks the Criminal whether he allows the Witneſſes examined againſt him, to be well and truly examined, and legally re-heard.   If he anſwers, that he would have the Witneſſes heard over again, and examined with his Interrogatories, and thus convict them of Falſhood, the Inquiſitor orders him a Copy of the Articles formed by the Procurator of the Exchequer, to the End that he may form his Interrogatories, and allows him three Days to give them in. If he anſwers, that he will conſider, and conſult his Advocate or Procurator, the Copy of the Articles formed by the Promotor of the Exchequer is given him, to aſſiſt him the better how to reſolve.   If he refers himſelf to the Diſpoſition of the Law, 'tis the ſame Thing as if he had anſwered, he would have the Witneſſes re-examined. Becauſe, according to Law, the Proof of Witneſſes received in a ſummary Manner is not regular, unleſs they be fully re-produced when the Party is cited, and re-examined upon the Interrogatories of the Criminals, that they may thus confirm their Evidence and Depoſitions.   If he anſwers, that he refers himſelf to the Pleaſure of the Inquiſitor, the Inquiſitor muſt not accept it, leaſt it ſhould be afterwards objected to him that he hindered the Criminal from

making

making a legal Defence, and therefore he refers him to his Advocate or Procurator. If he anfwers, that he allows the Witneffes, who have depofed a-
gainft him, to be well and truly examined, and legally re-heard, but faves
to himfelf the Liberty of making Exceptions againft Perfons and their Depofitions in drawing out his Defences, this is wrote down by the Notary in the
Acts. But altho' the Criminal fhould thus allow the Witneffes as legally
examined, the Inquifitors muft however take Care, that they be formally
re-examined, efpecially when there is any Fear of their Death, or long Abfence. In fuch a Cafe the Witneffes muft be admitted, before the Trial commences. *Simancas* more fully defcribes this Matter : " In the Caufe of He- §. 15, 22.
" refy, in which Inquifition is made by Virtue of the Judges Office, the Wit-
" neffes are to be admitted before the Commencement of the Trial. The Pro-
" motor of the Exchequer ought however to be careful, and to infift, that the
" Witneffes repeat what they have faid, and give in again their Evidence, be-
" fore fome Religious Perfons, leaft poffibly they fhould die before the Trial
" commences. And the Judges ought not to deny this, leaft the Proofs
" fhould fail, but when-ever there is a juft and probable Caufe, the Witnef-
" fes muft be produced again, and their Evidence confirmed. Now 'tis a §. 23.
" juft Caufe for re-hearing the Witneffes before the Trial, if they labour
" under any dangerous Diftemper ; or if they are to be long abfent, or if the *Tit.* 44.
" Criminal himfelf be abfent, or if prefent not yet apprehended, nor put in §. 23.
" Jayl ; or if the Witneffes are to be delivered over to the fecular Court.".

CHAP. XVII.

How the PROMOTOR FISCAL *exhibits the Bill of Accufation.*

AFTER the Inquifitor hath received, as hath been faid, Information Pegna,
　　 againft the Criminal denounced to him, the Procurator Fifcal, in c. 29.
fome Inquifitions, prefents in Court, in Prefence of the Criminal, a Bill of
Indictment, containing the Heads of the Offences, of which the Criminal is
accufed, and prefents it to the Inquifitor. The Form of this Bill is not every
where the fame. *Eymerick* gives this in his Directory of the Inquifitors.

I N. Fifcal *of the Office of the moft holy Inquifition, do before you the Reverend Inquifitor, delegated Judge in Caufes of the Faith againft heretical Pravity,
criminally accufe* N. *who being baptized a Chriftian, and accounted as fuch among ft
all Perfons, hath departed from the Catholick Faith, and hath impioufly gone over
to the deadly Herefy of the* Manichees, *and other Hereticks, particularly fuch a
one, and fuch a one ; preaching, writing, compofing, and firmly afferting many heretical, erroneous, fcandalous, and greatly fufpected Opinions, in Approbation and
Praife of the aforefaid Herefy, and Hereticks, whom he follows as his Mafters.
Simancas* gives us another in thefe Words.

I accufe

I *accufe* N. *who being baptized a Chriftian, believes and teaches many Herefies, and efpecially this and that*, after mentioning which, the Promotor Fifcal concludes, with demanding that *N.* may be punifhed as an obftinate Heretick, and fuffer the moft grievous Punifhments of Herefy.

Lewis a Paramo gives us a larger Form of this Bill of Indictment, in his Hiftory of the Inquifition, *Lib.* 3. *Qu.* 9. *n.* 21.

Very Illuftrious and moft Reverend Lords ;

I *Doctor or Licentiate* N. *and Advocate Fifcal of this holy Inquifition, that I may act better, according to Law, as I ought to do, appear before your moft reverend Lordfhips, and having performed all the Solemnities required, and neceffary by Law, do criminally accufe* N. *of the Town or City of* N. *the Diocefe of* N. *and Kingdom of* N. *and by fpecifying the Fact fay, that when the aforefaid* N. *was a Chriftian, and wafhed with the Waters of Baptifm, and marked with the Character of Chrift, and by common Eftimation reputed as fuch, and called fo in the Opinion of all, or being found fuch, and in Poffeffion, or as tho' he had been a Chriftian, enjoying alfo the Exemptions and Immunities of Chriftians, and ufing their Privileges as he ought to do, yet neglecting the Fear of Chrift, our Saviour, and defpifing the Rigour of Juftice of this Office of the holy Inquifition, hath faid and done, fome Thing heretical, and many other Things as an Heretick, by which 'tis prefumed, and ought to be prefumed, that the aforefaid* N. *hath loft that Faith, and that Belief or Virtue of Believing, which was given him in the moft holy Sacraments of Baptifm and Confirmation ; and that he hath given undoubted Faith to thofe Errors, which thofe falfe and impious Perfons* Martin Luther, Calvin, Mahomet, *and other Arch Hereticks have advanced, and I do efpecially accufe him, becaufe he was perfuaded, that any Perfon in thofe Errors might obtain eternal Glory.*

And, in the firft Place, about two Years ago, as, I fuppofe, the aforefaid N. *when he was in a certain Place of the City or Town of* N. *did, in the Prefence of the venerable and difcreet Perfons,* N. *fay and pronounce certain heretical Words, or fufpected of Herefy, or did fuch a Thing as favoured of Herefy, plainly manifefting that he thought fo, viz. that Faith alone, without Works, was fufficient to Salvation, and to obtain eternal Glory ; or that* Mahomet *was the Meffenger of the true God, and that the Laws given by him are fufficient for any one to be faved by, and he may be faved by them. On this account one of the By-ftanders, perfectly hearing what he faid, fharply reproved him ; but he, on the contrary, produced, and fuddenly alledged feveral Places of the holy Scripture, to defend his impious and heretical Opinion, and changing and defpifing the true Senfe and right Underftanding, interpreted the alledged Places according to his own Will, and contrary to the vulgate Edition of the Church of* Rome, *and the canonically received Opinion, tenacioufly adhered to his Error. And not content with thefe Things, he produced many other Arguments, by which he might maintain and confirm his Herefy, which he doth firmly hold, believe and defend, from whence 'tis clearly inferred, that he is, without doubt, an Heretick.*

Befides, the aforefaid N. *endeavouring every Day to fpread his Error, not content with his own Fall, hath, with the greateft Diligence and earneft Care, in this or that Place, the third Day of the fourth Month* N. *taught others according to his own*
Mind

Mind his poisonous Opinions, acting herein as a Master, and thus dogmatizing, hath deceived his Hearers, and caused them to deviate from the Catholick Truth, so that in very many Discourses he hath endeavoured to persuade all into the Belief of his Errors.

To these Things I add, that by this suspected Doctrine, contrary to the Faith, and by his Deed or Word which was not right, he hath given manifest Occasion of Ruin to other Standers by, remarkable for their Probity of Manners, Religion, and good Life, who, by this Offence, have deviated from the Catholick Faith, and believed his Opinions.

Farther, the aforesaid N. comes to be accused, because, little regarding his spiritual Profit, and his Conscience, he doth not know how to sign himself with the Sign of the Cross, and what is worse, doth not know the Apostles Creed, the Lord's Prayer, the Salutation of the Angel, and other Things of the like Nature.

Add to this something not less grievous, and affording great Suspicion, viz. that there was found in his House a Book, or certain Volume, or Paper, containing the Opinions and wicked Errors of Luther, Bucer, *or other Hereticks, or the Law published by* Mahomet, *all which Things secretly kept by him, and prohibited by publick Edicts, and the Ecclesiastical Censures, afford no light Suspicion of his depraved Heart.*

Farther, that having been otherwise received to Mercy, because he had confessed his Errors, and being withal reconciled, and united to the Bosom of holy Mother Church, who, according to her motherly Tenderness, doth not reject those who fly to her, or having vehemently abjured, promising he would not assent to such Errors, under the Penalty of being a Relapse, he hath fallen into them again. All which Things he did, and willingly performed, pretendedly, feignedly, and with an evil Intention, only craftily to escape Punishment, which appears to be plainly proved, since, like the Dog to the Vomit, he hath returned to the same, and the like Errors, as is certain, by sufficient Evidence. Hereby he is become liable to the Punishment of the Relapsed, which therefore by Law I demand may be inflicted on him, and therefore I exhort your Lordship or Lordships, that he may be cut off as a Member, now almost dead, and incapable of the Influences of the Head of the Church, viz. Christ, and may be thrown out, separated and excluded from the Conversation of the Faithful, that there may be no Occasion to others to waver in the Faith, and the whole Mass may not be corrupted: And because the Church, of whose Mercy he is unworthy, hath nothing farther to do with him, let him be thrust out from her as an unfruitful and barren Tree, and finally delivered over to the secular Judge.

Farthermore, I accuse him, that being born of the Saracen Race, *and it being therefore prohibited and forbidden him by your Lordships, to have any Correspondence with them, or to eat in their Houses, yet in Contempt of that Command, he hath spoken to them openly, and in suspected Places hath secretly insinuated himself into their Discourses.*

Farthermore, I accuse him of having used scandalous Words and new Opinions in his publick Sermons, not edifying enough the People, yea, he hath rashly given them an handle of erring against the received Doctrine of the holy Fathers, and the Determinations of the School-men. What, hath he not taught all these Things, being mo-

·*ved by Vanity, proud, haughty, and full of Arrogance? Carefully endeavouring to d:part from the Catholick and universally received Truth, that he might appear to be singular by the Singularity of his Opinions and Tenets, · and might be known among all as one by himself, and the Author of such Things. Wherefore I stedfastly·demand that he may be made to recant what he preached, and publickly·to change his Mind, at least in those Things that are scandalous, and found ill, and immediately declare in what Sense he understands other doubtful Matters which are capable of different Interpretations, that from henceforward no one may be scandalized, and that he may be deprived of the Office of Preaching without any Delay.*

Finally, since it may be presumed, or is presumed from many Things said by him, ·and inconsiderately uttered, that the aforesaid Criminal hath possibly asserted or said other Things contrary to the Catholick Faith, and hath believed many other Errors, as an Heretick and Apostate, tho' I do not now accuse him of them, yet I intend, in ·the Progress of the Cause, to accuse him. Possibly also he knows other Accomplices infected with Heresies, and defiled with this or the other, in the Dominions of our Lord the King, and will not inform against them, least they should be punished. These ·also, lastly, as far as by Law I can, I denounce and accuse that they may be pu-·nished in the same Manner.

Wherefore, I beseech your Lordships, that crediting all the aforesaid Matters, or ·so much of them as is sufficient, the aforesaid N. may, by your Sentence, be declared and condemned as a relapsed, impenitent, negative, feigned, pretended, confessing, obstinate, perjured, incorrigible Heretick, and that the Punishments appointed by the common Law, and the pragmatick Laws, and the Instructions of this ·holy Office, and any others any ways incurred by·him, may be inflicted on him ; ·and that finally, according to Custom, he may be delivered over to the secular Arm. To this must be added, that the said Criminal is under Excommunication, and ob-·noxious to the same, by which all his Goods, moveable and immoveable, any ways ·appertaining to him, as also all Deeds and Rights are to be applied and confiscated to our Lord the King, and finally, that all his Contracts are to be absolutely and entirely annulled, and finally, that all his Children and Grandchildren, descending from him in the Male Line, even to the second Generation, ·be declared unfit, unworthy, and in-·capable of any Offices or Dignities whatsoever.

But if all those Things proposed by me, and considerately said before this most solemn Tribunal, shall·not be so proved by Witnesses as to cause him to be immediately ·punished as an Heretick, they are however enough to put him to the Torture, by which he may be made openly to discover the aforesaid Matters, and to·acknowledge the Errors of which he is accused.'

Finally, I call God to Witness, and this holy Cross, that I have not formed this ·Accusation out of Hatred, or any other evil Affection of Mind, but with this View only, that Crimes may be punished, and the Good of the Common-wealth ·consulted, and that herein I may be successful, I implore this your holy Office.

Licentiate or Doctor *N.*

In

In the fupream Court of the general Inquifition at *Rome*, the Procurator of the Exchequer gives in the Points and Articles containing the Offences inftead of this Bill of Indictment.

But the Promoter of the Exchequer muft give in Writing the Accufation to the Judge, in Prefence of the Perfon he accufes, and read himfelf the Bill of Accufation, and immediately fwear that he hath not put in the Accufation malicioufly, but to difcharge his Office, and becaufe he intends to prove the Crimes objected. "But 'tis fufficient, as *Brunus* fays, that any Bill *l.* 4. *c.* 7. " be put in, which, tho' the exact Form of Law is not obferved, contains the §. 11, 12. " naked Intention of the Petitioner. Yea, a Bill is valid in this Procefs, al- " tho' it contains no Demand, or a trifling one, fo that the Intention of the " Petitioner is known by the Declaration."

Here *Gonfalvius* obferves, that when the Accufation is put in, in Writing, *p.* 25. it ordinarily contains very many pretended Crimes, which the Criminal never thought of, and for which no one inform'd againft him before the Inquifitors ; and that for thefe Reafons. Firft, That the miferable Wretch may be confounded with the Multitude and Heinoufnefs of the Crimes charged on him, and being almoft out of his Wits, may not know where he is, where to turn himfelf, or what to anfwer. Secondly, That they may try whether he admits any Thing of the Crimes objected to him, or at leaft by difcourfing with him upon any one of them, may draw him into a Snare. And that this is Truth, and not feigned out of Hatred to the Inquifition, plainly appears from the Hiftory of the Inquifition at *Goa*, the Author of which was a Papift, and *c.* 22. fays, that when the Heads of his Accufation were read to him by the Procurator of the Exchequer, this was one Article, amongft others, that he was accufed, and fufficiently convicted, that he had fpoken very irreverently of the Pope, and againft his Authority. To which Accufation he anfwered, that he did not remember that he had fpoken of the Pope in the Manner fet forth in the Accufation ; but that if they would relate to him the whole Difcourfe, he would fincerely and faithfully confefs whatfoever he had faid. When, after *c.* 23. this, he was brought before the Inquifitor again, and the Promoter of the Exchequer repeated the fame Accufation, they would not open to him the whole Series and Connection of the Difcourfe, nor was this Accufation afterwards repeated, nor any Mention made of it in his Procefs, when his Sentence was publickly read at the Act of Faith. From hence he infers, that this Accufation was falfe, and only brought againft him to fee if they could fifh any Thing out of him.

A Copy of the Accufation is ufually given to the Criminal, to which he *Simanc.* muft anfwer Article by Article, and his Reply muft be immediately written *tit.* 44. down by the Secretary before the Inquifitors. But if he continues to deny §. 22. every Thing, he hath an Advocate allowed him, who generally doth nothing more, than deny the Matters contained in the Accufation, and affirms that the Criminal is and always was a Catholick, and that this is plain from his many pious and good Works, and that his Character hath been always very good and unblemifhed amongft all Perfons. Then they come to a Conclufion, and a certain Term is fixed by the Judges to prove the Matters alledged on each Side, within which the Promotor of the Exchequer produces his Witnesses again, and the Criminal proves his Defences.

CHAP. XVIII.

How the Interrogatories given in by the CRIMINALS *are formed and exhibited.*

IN Order to prepare his Defence, the Criminal also puts in his Interrogatories, and desires of the Inquisitor that the Witnesses may be interrogated upon them. But if they are impertinent, or deceitful, or tending to discover the Informers, or to intangle and puzzle the Witness, or to conceal the Truth, or to discover such Circumstances by which he might come to the Knowledge of the Informer or Witnesses, the Inquisitor hath Power to set them aside.

But as *Simancas* tells us, this is not the Method in the *Spanish* Inquisitions, where the Criminals are not allowed to put Interrogatories to the Witnesses of the Promotor of the Exchequer, but the Judge is obliged by Office diligently to examine into the Credit, Life and Manners of the Witnesses. But the contrary is observed in all the Inquisitions in *Italy*, as *Carena* informs us, and that it ought to be thus, he proves by this Reason. *That by not giving the Names of the Witnesses, the Defence of the Criminals at this Tribunal is imperfect and maimed enough, without introducing any other Novelty ; but that the Defences of the Criminal would be necessarily much more imperfect and maimed, if the Witnesses against him should not be suffered to be interrogated by him.*

In *Italy* 'tis usual for the Criminals Advocate, to demand that the Witnesses may be examined and interrogated, concerning their Country, Age, Condition, State, Employment. As, whether he is rich or poor, Clergyman or Layman, a Religious, Regular or Secular, married or unmarried, a Father or a Son ? Whether he be a Citizen or Inhabitant of that City where the Cause is carried on ? When he came to the Place ? Whether he always lived in it ? Whether he lives at his own or other Person's Charge ? Whether in no Trial or Case he never deposed upon Oath Things which were not true, either for or against any Person ? Whether he was ever excommunicated, and on what Account, and in what Place ? Whether he, or his Parents, were not declared infamous, interdicted, excommunicated, and incapable to bear Witness ? Whether he confessed his Sins this Year at *Easter*, to what Confessor, and in what Church ? Likewise whether he hath taken the Sacrament of the Eucharist, from what Priest, and whom present ? Whether he was ever under Inquisition, accused or processed, for any Crime or Crimes, what they were ? Whether he was absolved or condemned, and by what Judge ? Whether any Thing was said, promised, forgiven, or granted

to

Cathol.
Instit.
*t.*64.*n.*10.

p. 3. *t.* 7.
§. 11.

Pegna,
l. 2. *c.* 31.

to him on this Account, that he fhould bear Witnefs againſt any one, or that he fhould fay in his Examination any Thing general or particular, and whether he doth or hath expeＦted any Advantage, and what, by his Depofition? Whether he hath or doth know *N.* what was the firſt Time, Place, and Occafion of his knowing him? Whether he hath often converfed with him, and concerning what Matters, and whether when he firſt knew him, the faid *N.* was accounted a good and Catholick Chriſtian, a Man of a good Confcience, and fearing God? Then they proceed to the Articles, and interrogate the Witneſſes concerning the Year, Month, Day, Place and Hour, where and when the aforefaid *N.* difcovered Herefy? Whether he fpoke it as the Sentiment of his Mind, deliberately and ferioufly, or only as repeating another's Words? What the precife Words were which he fpoke? And the like with regard to the other Articles.

C H A P. XIX.

Of the re-examining the Witnesses, *and the Puniſhment of falſe* Witnesses.

THE Witneſſes cited by the Judges muſt be carefully examined and in-　Simanc. terrogated. And firſt they are aſked, Whether they know why they *t.* 44. are fummoned? If they fay they do know or guefs that they are fummoned §. 25. in the fame Caufe in which they have already given Witnefs before the fame Judge, tney are aſked, if they remember what they depofed in the faid Caufe? And whether it be true? And whether they will add, take away, change or correＦt any Thing? Whatfoever they anfwer muſt be faithfully written down by the Notary. Then they are examined again without feeing their former Depofitions, that the Truth or Falfhood may more evidently appear from their Confiſtency or Inconfiſtency. Finally, this Confirmation of their Teftimony muſt be made before the Judges and Secretary, and two religious and difcreet Perfons. For as the Party concerned is not allowed to be prefent, two Perfons of Reputation muſt be prefent in his Stead.

If the latter Depofitions do not agree with the former, the former muſt be §. 24. read over to the Witneſſes, and they interrogated what is the Meaning of this Difference in what they fay, and gently admonifhed to perfiſt in the Truth. Laſtly, whatfoever they fay muſt be written down, and if they contradiＦt themfelves, or faulter, they muſt be fent into Cuſtody, and if the Cafe requires it, be tortured and punifhed.

When a Witnefs fwears that he will conceal his Evidence, and is afterwards *tit.* 64. convicted of difcovering it before the Publication of it, he may be condemned §. 83. by the Judges at their Pleafure, either to do publick Penance, or to pay a　　　Fine,

Fine, or to Banifhment, or the Pillory, or to be whipped, and, if the Nature of the Crime requires it, to the Gallies.

If the Witneffes are evidently caught in a Falfhood, they may be punifhed by the Inquifitor, according to their Merits. He is accounted a falfe Witnefs who tells a Lie, by depofing a Falfhood, and who fupprefles or conceals the Truth. And if the Inquifitor finds any Witnefs to be manifeflly falfe, *Direct.* he, together with the Bifhop, may punifh him. Thus 'tis provided by a *p. 3. com.* certain Refcript of *Leo* X. *An.* 1520. in which there are many Rules for the *122.* Obfervation of the Inquifitors of the Kingdom of *Arragon,* and, amongft others, this which I have mentioned. *And that if any Witnefs fhall depofe a Falfhood in the faid Office of the Inquifition, he fhall be punifhed by the Ecclefiaftical Judges, the Ordinaries of the Diocefe in which fuch Falfhood fhall be committed, and by the Inquifitors of the faid Pravity, deputed together, for the Time being, in the fame Diocefe, fo that the one fhall not be able to proceed without the other.*

Direct.   *Eymerick* mentions a Cafe, which happened at *Tholoufe, An.* 1312. that a *p. 3. § 73.* Father accufed his Son of the Crime of heretical Pravity, and afterwards re-*com. 122.* tracted it. His Sentence may be feen in the Book of the Sentences of the *Tholoufe* Inquifition, *fol.* 42. The Doctors however think, that as there is no Law extant concerning this Matter, fuch a one ought not to be delivered to the fecular Court, but that his Life ought in Mercy to be granted to him. But *Leo* X. by a Bull directed to Cardinal *Adrian,* Inquifitor General of *Spain, An.* 1518. granted full Power of condemning to whatever Punifhments the Inquifitor fhould think proper, and of delivering or turning over to the fecular Court, without any Fear of any Ecclefiaftical Punifhment or Cenfure, or Mark of Irregularity, *all and fingular Perfons of every State, Degree, Order, Dignity and Condition, who, in the Crime of Herefy, fhall be legally proved to have knowingly given falfe Witnefs, or to have induced any other to do fo, or to conceal the Truth, or to have killed any one for giving true Evidence, or falfe Evidence not proved fo, or to have maimed him in any Member, or to have deprived him, or caufed him to be deprived of all, or the greateft Part of his Effects*; which they believe ought to be done in this Cafe only, when the Witneffes have charged any one with formal Herefy, and the Criminal is delivered over to the fecular Court, and punifhed with Death, as a Negative and Impenitent, upon account of their Evidence. But when any falfe Witnefs voluntarily accufes himfelf, and asks for Mercy before the Perfon he gave Evidence againft is delivered over to the fecular Court, and put to Death, they think he ought to be fpared, and his Life given him, but that he ought to fuffer fome very grievous Penance. Thus they acted in that Inftance of *Tholoufe,* with *Pontius Arnaldi,* a falfe Witnefs againft his Son, in the Crime of Herefy, acknowledging his Fault, and craving the Mercy of the Inquifitor, who was condemned to perpetual Imprifonment, in which, during Life, he was to do wholefome Penance, with the Bread of Grief, and the Water of Affliction; and befides this, to ftand publickly, fo as to be openly feen and known by all By-ftanders, upon an high Ladder, before the Door of the Cathedral Church of St. *Stephen,* the fame Day, and the following, from the Beginning of the Morning till the

ninth

ninth Hour, in an open Place, without any Covering on his Head, in his Shirt, or Girdle, wearing two red Tongues, a Span and a half long, and three Fingers broad, before on his Breast, and two hanging down between his Shoulders, and his Hands tied together; and to be placed also in the same Manner, and to stand before the Gates of the Church of St. *Saturninus* the Lord's Day following, and the Lord's Day after before the Gate of the gilded Church; and to wear always upon every outward Garment the said Tongues, and never to go in or out of his Prison without the said Tongues hanging down or appearing, and to mend them when ever they were torn, and to make new ones whenever the old ones should be worn out; and the Moment he came down from the Ladder, to be carried and shut up, without Delay, in the Jayl near the Castle of *Narbonne*, there to remain for ever. The same Sentence was pronounced against *John de Salvetate*, a false Witness, *fol.* 83, 84.

Sentence is pronounced openly against false Witnesses, because they are brought into publick View, and their heinous Wickedness is declared before the People, and their Design and Villany is discovered in expres Words, and the Reason given and made known to all why they are thus punished. But if such false Witnesses have done but little Mischief, they receive a lesser Punishment; for they are brought forth, wearing an infamous Mitre, with returning Hereticks, and other Penitents at the publick Act of the Faith, or publick Procession, when their Crimes are read openly, and they themselves bastinadoed or whipped, banished, or sent to the Gallies, or punished with some other extraordinary Punishment.

However, such false Witnesses are seldom punished in a manner proportioned to the Heinousness of their Crime, for this Reason undoubtedly, that they may not deter Persons too much from giving Evidence. The Author of the History of the Inquisition at *Goa*, gives us a memorable Instance of *Joseph Pereira de Meneles*, accused to the Inquisition as a Sodomite, by a certain Enemy of his, who pretended himself to be reconciled. This Person had bribed five of *Pereira*'s Servants, who all, with one Mouth, testified, that they saw their Master committing this Crime with such a Servant. *Pereira* denied the Crime, but the Servant, who was young, thro' Fear of being put to Death, confessed it, tho' never committed. *Pereira*, as a convicted Person, was condemned to be burnt. When he was brought forth in Procession at the Act of Faith, he continued to protest his Innocence. Upon which the Judges remanded him to Prison, and ordered him to be kept to the next Act of Faith, in order, if possible, to find out more exactly the Truth. In the mean while the Witnesses were often interrogated, and being each of them separately asked, whether or no the Moon shone that Night in which they saw *Pereira* committing that detestable Crime, their Answers were found contradictory, and the Falshood of the Accusation discovered; and being put to the Question, they confessed their Crime, and declared their Master innocent. But what was the Punishment inflicted upon the Author of so villanous a Crime? Trifling, in Comparison of the Heinousness of the Offence. *Pereira*'s Enemy,

Enemy, who had bribed his Servants, was condemned to a nine Years Banishment in *Africa*, and the suborned Witnesses to the Gallies for five. *Carena*
also relates from *Diana*, that in the Inquisition in *Sicily*, a certain Regular,
who was a false Witness, and who had suborned others to give false Evidence
in the holy Office, was condemned to the Gallies for ten Years, and the Women, his Accomplices, to be whipped, and to six Years Banishment.

From these slight Punishments, which, if compared with the Heinousness
of the Offence, bear no Proportion with it, 'tis evident that the Inquisitors are
not willing to deter any one from giving Evidence. And indeed here is a great
Inequality between the Offence and Punishment. If any one grievously wounds
a Witness, who hath born Witness against him, altho' he hath not killed him,
he is punished with Death ; and if the Wound be slight, he is condemned for
ever, or at least for ten Years, to the Gallies. Whereas he who gives false
Witness, and suborns and bribes others to fix by false Evidence a Crime upon
another, which being proved by the Agreement of the Witnesses, the Criminal must suffer the cruel Punishment of being burnt, is only banished, and the
false Witnesses condemned to nothing more than the Gallies for ten or five
Years, or to be bastinadoed, and banished for six. Now who doth not see,
that the Inquisitors are careful only to provide for the Security of the Witnesses, and had rather condemn Persons loaded with false Accusations, than deter
any one by the Severity of Punishment from giving a false Evidence, which,
in this Case, ought especially to be regarded, because the Witnesses are not
discovered to the Criminal.

Hoofdii,   A much more exemplary Punishment was inflicted upon a Woman, con-
Hist. Belg. victed of giving false Evidence, at the *Hague*, by the Command of the Court
l. 2.   of *Holland, An.* 1561. *William Bardesius*, Prætor of *Amsterdam*, and M. *Henry Theodorus*, Consul of the same City, were at mortal Enmity with each other,
upon Account of some political Differences. The Consul burnt with a Desire
of Revenge, and that he might have a specious Pretence for destroying his E-
nemy, determined to accuse him of the Anabaptistical Heresy, at that Time
universally hated for the late Disturbances which had been raised on that Account at *Munster* and *Amsterdam*. He joined with him in this Design, *Florentius
Egberti*, Parish-Priest of the Old Church, and Commissary of *Ruardus Tapperus* the Inquisitor, that the Fraud being thus covered over with an Ecclesiastical Varnish, might be carried on with greater Success. They could not find
out a more proper Instrument to execute this vile Design, than a certain old
Woman named *Sophy*, nick-named *Yellow Sophy*, upon account of the execrable
Colour of her Body, a Widow, burthened with a great many Children, who
made it her Business to betray the Reformed, who held their private Meetings,
not being allowed the Use of the publick Churches, and maintained her wretched Family with the accursed Wages she earned, by informing against them.
This Woman, with two others of the same Stamp, and two Men, one of
which was a Notary, they prevailed with, by a little Money, and large Promises, to bear false Witness against the Prætor. Their several Evidences,
which were suggested to them by the Consul and the Parson, they confirmed

b*y*

by Oath, in which they declared that the Prætor, who with his Wife, were both re-baptized, had a Meeting of the Anabaptiſts in his Houſe, and that his Wife was preſent at the Meeting. This Evidence the Parſon ſent in Writing to *Ruardus Tapperus*, Inquiſitor of *Lovain*. But altho' this Matter was carried on very privately, the Prætor was too quick not to ſmell it out ; and therefore to prevent his being deſtroyed ſuddenly, and without being able to make his Defence, he goes immediately to *Bruſſels*, and applies himſelf to *Mary* Queen Dowager of *Hungary*, then Governeſs, and in whom he had a very conſiderable Intereſt, and managed his Cauſe with ſo much Dexterity and Succeſs, that the Senator *Cornelius Monk*, and with him the Secretary of the ſupream Council of *Mechlin*, were ſent to *Amſterdam* to enquire into the Affair. And they found it no difficult Matter, upon examining the Witneſſes, to detect the Falſhood and Perjury. But as it was neceſſary to proceed ſlowly to make a full Diſcovery, the Cauſe was committed to the Court of *Holland*, who deputed ſome of their Members to make Inquiſition concerning it. The two Women were impriſoned at the *Hague*, and being interrogated about the Prætor's Anabaptiſm, and the Circumſtances of it, they ſaid that he was re-baptized in a Chapel that lay near his Garden, and that they ſaw it thro' the Window ſtanding upon a Bench. Upon this two of the Senators were ſent to inſpect the Place, and found the Window ſo very high, that tho' they ſtood upon the Bench, they could not reach it with their Hand, ſo that 'twas impoſſible the Women could look thro' it, to ſee what was tranſacted within. And thus the Falſhood was diſcovered. The Authority of the City, and the Favour of the Eccleſiaſticks, for ſome time protected the Conſul and the Parſon. But the Crime was too enormous to eſcape unpuniſhed, and therefore both of them were apprehended by Order of the Court of *Holland*, May 3, 1557. the Parſon, as he was ſtanding before the Altar, and in ſo haſty a manner, that they would not ſuffer him to go home, and change his Garments. After this they were both carried to the *Hague*. The Notary and the other Evidence had the ſame Fate. And though it was difficult to cover over a Falſhood, proved by ſo many Perſons, who agreed in their Confeſſions, yet it was a long while, yea, ſeveral Years before the whole was openly diſcovered. But at laſt the falſe Witneſſes ſeeing no Poſſibility of eſcaping, asked Pardon for their Offence of the Royal Clemency, and publickly confeſſed their Falſhood and Perjury. One of the Witneſſes was publickly whipped. The Notary deprived of his Office, and baniſhed. The Parſon openly confeſſed that the Accuſations he had written againſt the Prætor and his Wife, to *Ruardus Tapperus*, were raſh, impertinent, and without due Information, and ſaid he repented of it, and was therefore commanded to depart from *Amſterdam*, and deprived of the Office of Commiſſary of the Inquiſition. One of the Women died in Jayl, and as to *Sopby*, ſhe had, May 3, 1561. her Tongue firſt cut out, was then hanged, had her Body burnt, and publickly expoſed. But before ſhe was carried to Execution, ſhe ingenuouſly confeſſed, in the Preſence of three Senators, that every Thing ſhe had depoſed and given in Evidence upon Oath, and in her Examinations in Court, againſt the Prætor of *Am-*
　　　　　　　　　　　　　　　　　　　　　　　　ſterdam,

fterdam, was falfe and forged, and that fhe was perfuaded to this Villany by the Solicitations, Promifes and Gifts of M. *Henry Theodore*, Conful of *Amfter-dam*, and of M. *Florentius*, Parfon of the Old Church in that City, and being brought to the Place of Punifhment, fhe publickly declared the fame before all the Spectators. Conful *Henry* however denied every Thing, and becaufe he could not be convicted by any Thing under his own Hand, he deftroyed the Evidence of the Witneffes againft him, by pleading that they were perjured, and by this Means efcaped with his Life. He was however kept Prifoner for a long while, but at laft difmiffed, upon giving Security and Bail. This was the Punifhment inflicted by the fecular Judge. If the Inquifitors would pro-ceed with the fame Rigour againft falfe Witneffes, fo many miferable and in-nocent Creatures would not be deftroyed by falfe Informations and Evidence. But they had rather entice Perfons with hope of Impunity, and when the Falfhood of the Evidences appears fo plain, as not to be palliated, they chufe to inflict on them a flight Punifhment, rather than deter them from becoming Evidences, by a Punifhment juft and proportioned to their Crime.

CHAP. XX.

How the PRISONER *hath a Copy of the Evidence, without the Names of the* WITNESSES.

Pegna, p. 47.

THE Witneffes having been re-examined, a Copy of the Proofs brought againft the Criminals is ufually given to them, that they may the fooner determine, whether they will give up the Caufe, or ftand Trial, and in this Cafe the following Things are obferved in this Court. Firft, that the Depo-fitions be literally given to the Criminal as made by the Witneffes, that he may fully underftand what every Witnefs hath depofed againft him, fo that 'tis not fufficient to give them him in fhort. Secondly, The Depofitions are not to be confounded or mixed, but each of them to be diftinctly and fepa-rately from others given him in Writing, that the Criminal may the better un-derftand them, and feverally anfwer them, and thus be able the better to defend himfelf. Thirdly, The Names of the Witneffes are not to be given him, nor their Surnames, nor any Circumftances by which he may difcover who they are, becaufe fuch Difcovery might occafion great Danger either to the Witneffes or the Inquifition, upon account of the Power of the Perfons ac-cufed, by reafon of their Family, Riches, or Malice. The fupream Senate determined the fame, with refpect to the Anfwers of the Witneffes to the In-terrogatories of the Criminals, ordering they fhould not be given them, if the Witneffes were in Danger of being difcovered hereby. For the fame Reafon they add the Year and Month, but not the particular Day when the Witneffes affirm the Crime to be committed. Thus alfo the Place is added

in

in general, but not the particular Houfe or Room where. All thefe Things they carefully avoid, that the Criminal may not by any Means difcover who are the Witneffes or Informers againft him. This they will in no wife fuffer. For as they generally fay, Secrecy is the very Sinew of the Inquifition. Hence 'tis eafy to infer, that many of thofe Interrogatories which are formed by the Advocates of the Criminals, are not allowed, becaufe they muft relate to fuch Circumftances, which, if known to them, would eafily difcover to them the Witneffes. However the Advocates, bound to the Inquifition by Oath, muft form them, that they may feem to do fomething for the Criminals, when in Reality they do nothing, and deceive the miferable Prifoners, with the vain Hopes, what they will do in their Defence, when nothing at all is done for them; for whilft the Witneffes or Informers are concealed from them, they are deprived of the beft and moft neceffary Means of their Defence. However, this is ftrictly prohibited by feveral Edicts of the Popes, and Inftructions of the Inquifitors.

Thus *Innocent* IV. exprefsly decreed in a Bull publifhed *An.* 1253. *'Tis our Pleafure that the Names both of the Accufers and Witneffes of heretical Pravity, fhall by no Means be difcovered, becaufe of the Scandal or Danger that may follow upon fuch Difcovery, and yet neverthelefs let the Depofitions of fuch Witneffes be entirely credited.* The Council of *Biterre* hath decreed the fame, Cap. 10. *But beware of this, according to the wife Pleafure of the Apoftolick See, that the Names of the Witneffes be not difcovered by any Sign or Word.* Formerly *Boniface* VIII. *c. Statuta.* §. *Jubemus, de hæret. l.* 6. granted that the Names of the Witneffes and Accufers might be difcovered, when there was no Danger. *When there is no Danger in the aforefaid Cafe, let the Names of the Witneffes and Accufers be made known, according as is ufual in other Trials. But in all thefe Things we command both the Bifhop and Inquifitors to act with a pure and cautious Intention, and not to fupprefs the Names of the Accufers or Witneffes, by pretending Danger where there is none ; nor on the other hand, to fay there is no Danger, when in Reality there is. And let them charge this upon their Confciences.* And this was fometimes obferved, as *Fol.* 131. appears from the Sentences of the *Tholoufe* Inquifition, in the Sentence of *William Cavalerius* of *Cordua,* who having revoked the Confeffion that had been drawn from him by Torture, is faid to have been convicted by Witneffes. *And the Depofitions againft him being difcovered to him, and read to him plainly, and in his own Language, and the Names of the Witneffes depofing againft him expreffed,* &c. But now they think there is always Danger in this Difcovery, and therefore they never publifh the Names or Perfons of the Witneffes, becaufe they believe, after fuch Difcovery, they fhall never find any Perfons willing to become Informers againft Hereticks. There is alfo extant an Apoftolick Brief of *Pius* IV. concerning this Affair, beginning, *Cum ficut.*

In *Spain* alfo 'tis commanded not to difcover the Witneffes Names, by the *Seville* Inftruction, *An.* 1484. c. 16. *In like manner, becaufe it appears, and is certain, upon legal Information, that if the Names and Perfons of the Witneffes, who depofe in the faid Crime of Herefy, be difcovered, they may incurr great Damage and Hazard, as to their Perfons and Effects ; for Experience hath demonftrated.*

and doth demonstrate that some Witnesses have been killed, or wounded, and evil treated by Hereticks on the aforesaid Account, and considering especially that there is a great Number of Hereticks in the Kingdoms of Castile *and* Aragon, *their Lordships have decreed, that the Inquisitors may refuse to discover the Names or Persons of the Witnesses who have deposed against* Hereticks, *because of the grievous Damage and Hazard aforesaid, that the Witnesses are exposed to when their Names are declar'd.*

The same Provision is made by the *Madrid* Instruction, *An.* 1561. *c.* 72. *Altho' in other Tribunals the Judges always bring the Witnesses and Criminals Face to Face, in order to discover whether the Offences are real ; this ought not to be allowed, neither is it usually practised in Trials before the Inquisition ; because, besides, that hereby Secresy is broken, which is ever enjoined with respect to the Witnesses, 'tis known by Experience, that when ever this is practised, it is attended with no good Effect, but rather with Inconveniencies.* And in the Instruction of *Seville,* An. 1484. c. 16. *When the Proof is made, and the Witnesses re-examined, the Inquisitors must shew their Evidence and Depositions, but suppress and keep secret their Names, and those Circumstances by which the Criminal accused may come to the Knowledge of the Witnesses.* But in the *Madrid* Instruction. *An.* 1561. *cap.* 32. 'tis commanded, that when the Depositions are published, the Month and Year, which the Witnesses swear to, must be added, but not the Day ; and in like Manner the Place and Time when the Offence was committed.

<table>
<tr><td>De Cathol.
Inst.
t. 61.
§. 26, &c.</td><td>And this is the Custom at this Time in Spain, as appears from Simancas.
" After this the Evidence of the Witnesses must be shewn, and a Copy of it
" granted to the Criminal, those Circumstances only omitted, by which he
" might easily understand who they are, that have given Evidence against</td></tr>
</table>

" him. Hence it is that they don't let him know neither the Hour or Day
" in which the Witnesses say the Crimes were committed, unless possibly the
" Criminal should demand it to make his Defence. Likewise another Copy
" of the Depositions must be written out by the Secretaries, and examined
" and corrected by the Inquisitors, and another Copy be inserted in the Acts
" of the Process. Besides, the Copy of the Evidence must be given to the
" Criminal in such a Manner, as that he may plainly understand, whether the ·
" Witnesses depose of what they have heard from others, or of those Things
" they have seen themselves." 1 *Instruct. Hispal.* c. 16.

§. 27.   " In this Publication of the Evidence, the Names of the Witnesses must
" not be discovered to the Criminal.

§. 28.   " Hence it is, that in the Crime of Heresy, the Criminal must not be ci-
" ted, when the Evidence is ratified, least he should know the Witnesses,
" even altho' in all other Crimes the Criminals are to be cited to see the Wit-

§. 29.   " nesses. Thus also in all other Crimes the Names of the Witnesses are given
" to the Criminals, that they may refute them, and shew their own Innocence ;
" and this ought always to be done, even altho' the Process be carried on by
" Inquisition, least by concealing the Names, Occasion should be given to
" wicked Persons of defaming others, and by denying them the Means of
" their Defence, of giving false Evidence against them. For no Man ought
" to

" to be denied the Means of defending himself. This ought more especially §. 30.
" to take place in Inquisitions and Visitations carried on against Judges and
" their Ministers. For they are placed as a Mark to be shot at, and are not
" capable of pleasing all, because they are bound by Office daily to repri-
" mand many engaged in Law-Suits to imprison them, banish them, fine,
" condemn, and sometimes punish them with Death."

But if any one now should presume, without a manifest Necessity, and un- *Com* 124.
less there is no manner of Danger, rashly to discover the Names of the Wit- *in part.* 5.
nesses, Accusers, or Informers, he would act, according to *Pegna*'s Mind, very *Direct.*
imprudently, and, for what he knows, fall into mortal Sin ; because he would
act against so many Decrees of Popes, and against the received Custom of
the holy Office, which, though not supported by any Law, yet being a commendable, approved, and legally prescribed Custom, hath the Force of a
Law.

And tho' the Criminal insists, and demands, that he be allowed to make
his Defence, according to the Course of the Law, and by Consequence that
the Names of the Witnesses be shewn him as well as their Depositions, he is
not to be heard. Those who are called new Christians in *Spain*, never could
obtain it, tho' they used their utmost Endeavours for it. *Ludovicus a Para-l. 2. K.2.*
mo tells us, that in the Reign of *Charles*, who succeeded his Grandfather *Fer-c. 5. n. 4.*
dinand, the new Converts offered 800000 Pieces of Gold to the King, if he
would order the Witnesses to be made known in the Tribunal of the Inquisition.
And when the young King, who was but 18 Years old, was greatly tempted by
so vast a Sum of Money, Cardinal *Ximenes*, Inquisitor General, by setting before him the great Danger of such Witnesses, and the Damage that would
hereby accrue to the Church, wrought upon him to despise that Offer.

But when the Person accused cannot particularly defend himself upon account of the suppressing the Names of the Witnesses, but can only conjecture
in general, not being able to make any tolerable Guess, 'tis recommended
to the Prudence of the Inquisitor, to take such proper Measures, as that
he may know, whether the said Deponents and Witnesses are the mortal E-
nemies of the Persons accused or not.

Eymerick, in the third Part of his Directory of the Inquisitors, describes to
us six Ways of giving a Copy of the Process to Persons accused of Heresy, sup-
pressing the Names of the Accusers, by which 'tis evident, that this one
Thing is determined by the Inquisitors, *viz.* to condemn the Prisoners as
guilty, right or wrong, by using various Arts and Impostures, and especially
by denying them the principal Means of their Defence.

The first Method is, to exhibit the Names of the Informers, not in the 119 & *seq*
Copy of the Process, but in a separate Paper, nor in the Order in which they
depose ; but in such a Manner as that he who is the first Informer in the
Copy, shall be the sixth or seventh in the separate Paper ; that by thus
changing the Order of the Names, the Person accused may not know what
every one deposes.

The

The second is, to give a Copy of the Proceſs to the Perſon accuſed, and in another Paper the Names of the Deponents, mixing with them the Names of ſome other Perſons, who have never depoſed againſt him in that Affair, that ſo he may object againſt this and the other, and yet never know who hath depoſed againſt him. But theſe ways are greatly diſapproved of, and but ſeldom practiſed, becauſe they can't be of much Service to him that is accuſed, becauſe he can't hereby know who depoſed this and the other Thing againſt him; and may be greatly hurtful to the Accuſers; becauſe the Paper it ſelf makes it certain that the Criminal is accuſed by ſome one of them, and being uncertain by whom, he may form a Reſolution againſt thoſe who have never depoſed againſt him, or whoſe Depoſitions againſt him are true, or who have depoſed in his Favour. And thus he may lay Snares for them, and bring them into very great Danger, which they carefully provide againſt.

The third Way is, that the Perſon accuſed is interrogated when he is examined, at the End of his Confeſſion, and before the Copy of the Proceſs is granted him, whether he remembers that he hath any mortal Enemies, who, laying aſide the Fear of God, may charge him falſely with heretical Pravity; ſo that without farther thinking, and before he ſees the Depoſitions of the Witneſſes, he may anſwer either that he doth not remember that he hath any ſuch Enemies, or that if he doth call any ſuch to mind, he may name them as they occur to him.

Campeg. *in* Zanch. *c.* 13.

If he ſays he hath no ſuch Enemies, the Inquiſitor may charge him to think well upon the Matter, and allow him a convenient Space of Time to conſider of it, and to write down their Names if he remembers any, and thus deſcribed; to exhibit them to the Judge with the Notary and Witneſſes. The Judge muſt cauſe all theſe Things to be inſerted in the Acts, *viz.* that ſuch a one, *&c.* appeared ſuch a Day, *&c.* before the Inquiſitor, *&c.* and gave in a certain written Paper, containing as underwritten, which muſt be inſerted at length. After which the Judge gives him his Oath, and asks him whether that be his Writing, and written with his own Hand? Likewiſe, whether he affirms that all and ſingular the Matters contained in it are true? Likewiſe, whether all and ſingular the Perſons, there deſcribed by Name, are his mortal Enemies? Likewiſe, concerning the Time, Riſe, Cauſe or Occaſion of the Enmity? Likewiſe, whether beſides the before-named, he hath any other Enemies, and whom, and what the Cauſe and Time of the Enmity? Again, whether after ſuch Enmity contracted or ariſen, he hath ever made uſe of them as Evidences for him in any Civil or Criminal Cauſe? To theſe other Interrogatories may be added at Pleaſure, as the prudent Judge ſhall think proper, from the Anſwers given to the Premiſes, and other reaſonable Circumſtances; which being well conſidered, and diligently examined, it will be eaſy to diſcover whether the Enmity pretended be real or not. But even here they are particularly cautious, that whilſt they are thinking of Methods to find out the Enmity of the Witneſſes, the Criminals may not come to the Knowledge of them. Theſe Things almoſt agree with the Words of the Biſhop of *Albano,* in which he preſcribes what the Inquiſitors muſt do in ſuch a

Caſe.

Cafe. *Moreover, let the Inquifitors inquire from the Perfon againft whom they are to proceed, whether he hath any mortal Enemies, or certainly fufpected to be fo, who, thro' Hatred, might fwear againft him, and let him put down their Names in Writing, whom he fays he hath Reafon legally to fufpect ; and let them proceed and receive other Witneffes againft him, and yet neverthelefs they may receive fuch fufpected Witneffes if they judge it proper.* And a little after he adds, *And altho' the Witneffes, who are faid to be fufpected, or found to be Enemies, are not to be believed, unlefs there be any Thing that may legally fupport their Evidence.*

The fourth is, that the Perfon accufed, in the End of his Confeffion, before he is allowed to make his Defence, fhould be interrogated concerning thofe Witneffes who have depofed the moft heinous Things againft him, as tho' they were accufed themfelves, after this Manner. Do you know fuch a one, naming one of the moft confiderable Witneffes? If he faith he doth not, he can't reject him in his Defence as a mortal Enemy, having declared upon Oath he did not know him. If he anfwers, that he doth know him, he is interrogated, whether he knows, or hath heard that he hath faid or done any Thing againft the Faith? Then he is asked, whether he is his Friend or Enemy, and prefuming that he will anfwer, His Friend, that his Evidence for him may be admitted, he can't after he hath faid fo, reject him as a mortal Enemy. *Eymerick* is for ufing thefe two Methods but feldom, becaufe, tho' not at all dangerous to the Deponents, they are prejudicial to the Accufed. But yet he approves that the latter fhould be ufed againft cavilling and cunning Perfons, and fays that he himfelf hath fometimes, tho' feldom, taken this Method againft fuch Perfons, whereby, as the Apoftle fays, *being cunning, he caught them by Guile.*

Camillus Campegius adds, if he anfwers, that he doth not know that he hath *In Zanchi* faid any Thing againft the Faith, the Inquifitor muft not omit to ask him, *c. 13.* whether he be his Friend or Enemy? If he anfwers, his Friend, but that he would not be filent even on this Account, but would come in Evidence againft him, if he knew that he had offended againft the Faith, he can't object againft him any more in this Caufe as a mortal Enemy. For this is to be remarked, that he who once allows a Witnefs, can never after reject him.

The fame *Campegius* adds another Way, viz. the Inquifitor asks the accufed Perfon in his firft Examination, what he thinks to be the Reafon of his being apprehended or imprifoned? Likewife, who he fufpects to be his Accufers? And if he particularly names any, he is asked, why he fufpects them rather than others? To which Queftion perhaps he will anfwer, by affigning, as the Reafon or Caufe, Hatred, a Law-Suit, or Quarrel, or fome like Matter. After this the Inquifitor asks him again, whether he hath any other Enemies, and who they are, and of the Time, and Occafion of their Enmity, as above. He asks him again, who were prefent, when the Perfons he rejects as Enemies, affaulted or wounded him, and the like, and by whom he can be informed of the Reality of fuch mortal Enmity. After this the Inquifitor diligently confiders his Anfwers and Affertions, and receives Informations from religious Perfons concerning the Credit of the Witneffes, in order to find out.

out the Truth, and if he finds that the Witneffes are juftly charged with mortal Enmity, he muft confult the Laws, Doctors and Counfellors, and then act as he fees fit.

The fifth is, to give the Perfon accufed a Copy of the Procefs, fuppreffing the Names of the Deponents, fo that when he fees the Depofitions, he may conjecture who it was that depofed fo and fo againft him. On this fometimes he names feveral as his mortal Enemies, affigning the Reafons of it, and producing his Witneffes. If he gueffes at any, the Inquifitor enquires the Caufes of the Enmity ; if they are not fufficient, he rejects them ; if they are, he examines the Witneffes privately, who, upon not giving legal Proof are rejected. This is performed with the Advice of the Learned. And this Method is generally obferved.

The fixth is, that when the Perfon accufed fays, upon giving him a Copy of the Procefs, that he hath many mortal Enemies, names them, and affigns the Reafons of fuch Enmity, the Diocefan and Inquifitor hold a Council of Divines and Lawyers, caufe the whole Procefs to be read over by the Notary, difcover to them the Names of the Witneffes and Deponents, and oblige them by Oath, or under Penalty of Excommunication, not only to give found Advice, but alfo to obferve perfect Secrefy. After this 'tis debated amongft them, whether they fully know the Perfon accufed, and the Witneffes, and whether there is mortal Enmity between them? If they fully know them, their Counfel and Advice is ftood to, and whofoever are adjudged by them to be mortal Enemies, are rejected from giving Evidence ; and thofe who are adjudged not to be fo, are admitted. If the Counfellors do not fully know the Perfon accufed and the Witneffes, two, three or four Perfons of Reputation, well acquainted with the Criminal, are chofen by their Advice, out of the City, where the accufed Perfon dwelt. One of thefe at leaft, or two, muft be Parifh-Priefts, and another, if it can conveniently be, a Religious, and the others Layicks, reputable Men, zealous for the Truth. Thefe are fecretly called together by the Bifhop and Inquifitor, and being obliged to fpeak the Truth by Oath, or under Penalty of Excommunication, are interrogated, concerning the mortal Enmity or Friendfhip of the Perfon accufed, and the Witneffes. The Bifhop and Inquifitor entirely acquiefce in their Judgment, fo that after they have well and carefully confidered the Matter amongft themfelves, they reject from being Evidences fuch as thefe Perfons fay and prove to be the Accufeds mortal Enemies, and admit thefe which they fay are not. This is the ufual Method, and feems to agree with the Determination of the Council of *Biterre,* Cap. 10. *But let Care be taken of this, as the Apoftolick See hath carefully determined, that the Names of the Witneffes be not difcovered by any Act or Word. But if the Perfon, under Inquifition, infifts on it, and fays that poffibly he may have Enemies, or that fome Perfons have confpired againft him, let the Names of fuch Enemies or Confpirators, and the Occafion and Truth of fuch Enmities and Confpiracies be fo drawn out of him, as that the Safety of the Witneffes, and the Perfons alfo to be convicted, may be provided for.*

· And

And in order the more effectually to prevent all Danger to the Witnesses, which may arise from their being known, *Camillus Campegius* advises, not only to suppress their Names, but even all Circumstances that may tend to point out or discover them. For he says he hath oftentimes seen that the granting such a Copy hath given Rise to Enmities, Hatreds, Wounds and Death ; and sometimes, that those under Inquisition, falsely imagining a Person to have deposed against them, who hath not, nor said or did any Thing against them, have notwithstanding, thro' such a false Persuasion, contrived not only greatly to injure him, but even his Destruction. Thus it happened at *Ferrara*, and at other Places, as he says he was credibly informed. And therefore he advises the Inquisitors, to proceed very cautiously in this Affair, and so to defend the Catholick Faith, as to secure the Lives of the Witnesses. For he says there are few to be found, who are willing to inform or depose in this Cause of Hereticks, and that if the Safety of the Witnesses should be endangered by the World, he imagines there would not be so much as a single Informer.

When any just Exceptions are objected against the Witnesses, the Criminal is admitted to prove them. But his Witnesses are so cautiously examined, as if possible to prevent their knowing who the Witnesses against the Criminal are. And, in order to this, they are interrogated not only concerning the Enmity or Conspiracy of the real Witnesses against the Criminal, but of others also who are not Evidences against him.

But here I cannot omit, what *J. Royas* says, " That by suppressing the *Part 2.* " Names of the Witnesses, Criminals are deprived of the full Means of making *Assert. 4.* " their Defence, and by Consequence it must be very imperfect and maimed. " For which way can the accused Person, kept secretly in Jayl, and depri- " ved of the Comfort and Assistance of his Friends and Relations, and Pro- " curators, either object the Defects of the Evidence, or the just Exceptions " against the Witnesses, if he is ignorant of their Names, if they should hap- " pen to be his Enemies, or Criminals themselves, or infamous, or excom- " municated, or otherwise uncapable ? For, in so heinous a Crime, punish- " ed with all Kinds of Punishments, *viz.* Excommunication, Forfeiture " of Estate, the Delivery of the Person to the secular Arm, his own and " his Family's perpetual Infamy, stronger Proofs are necessary than in other " Crimes. Nor can it be rash to assert, that the Witnesses, whose Names " are not discovered, cannot be, as to the Criminal, above Exception ; be- " cause he cannot object any Thing against them, when he doth not know " them. They only are said to be beyond all Exception, who cannot be re- " jected as Witnesses by any just Exception made against them ; and there- " fore, as in this Case, one solemn Usage of the Law is over-ruled by sup- " pressing their Names, there is no Room to urge against them Crimes, De- " fects, and Objections. But afterwards, as I considered the Words of the " Extravagant of *Innocent* VI. *That full Credit shall be nevertheless given to what* " *such Witnesses say,* I am, upon this Account, ready to recant. However, " in my poor Opinion, I should not dare to condemn any one if there were

" two

" two legal Witneſſes only, in ſo grievous a Crime, upon ſo maimed and im-
" perfect a Defence by the Criminal, but ſhould follow the Opinion of *Haſti-*
" *enſis*, as the more equitable, who determines, that two Witneſſes only are
" not ſufficient to prove the Crime of Hereſy, but that three or more are re-
" quiſite, unleſs the Perſon accuſed be one of an ill Character or Reputation,
" and there be other Circumſtances concurring againſt him, in which Caſe
" the common Opinions of the Doctors may be followed.

" However, 'tis the Judgment of moſt, that the Cuſtom obſerved in re-
" producing the Witneſſes, and examining them in full Judgment before the
" Inquiſitor and two religious Perſons, according to *Cap. ut officium,* §. *verum.*
" de hæret. l. 6. & *Inſtruct. Tolet.* c. 14. abundantly ſupplies the other Defect
" of not exhibiting the Names of the Witneſſes, when their Evidence is given
" in. But in my Judgment they are greatly miſtaken ; becauſe this Omiſſion
" is in an eſſential Point of Law, and the Cuſtom of examining before theſe
" religious Perſons is, as Experience teaches, of little or no Effect. For 'tis
" too common with the Generality to perſiſt in what they affirm or deny,
" whether true or falſe, and they think it Advantage enough to have their
" own Wills".

Since therefore they are ſo exceeding cautious not to diſcover by any
Means the Informers or Witneſſes to the Criminals, 'tis evident they are not
brought before, or confronted with one another, that they may be heard
againſt, and what they ſay and anſwer be oppoſed to each other. *Carena*
teaches us, that Perſons are ſeldom confronted in the holy Office, and that
'tis never done in the ſupream Tribunal of the City, unleſs the Cauſe be fully known, and the Cardinals ſupream Inquiſitors interpoſe by their Decree, who uſually determine, whether or no any Danger may accrue to
the Witneſſes and Criminal by being confronted. But becauſe ſometimes
it happens in the holy Office, that the Criminal muſt neceſſarily be ſeen
and pointed out by the Witneſſes, this is done not by openly confronting
them, but by making the Witneſſes look through the Crevices of the Door
of ſome faſtened Room, where the Criminal is put, in Company of ſome other
Perſons alike in their Dreſs, Stature, and Face. This *Carena* ſays was
practiſed formerly in the Inquiſition at *Cremona*, according to the Command
of the ſacred Congregation, where a certain Regular, who had contracted
Matrimony, was thus viewed and pointed out, notwithſtanding his Confeſſion, that the Sentence of the Nullity of his Marriage might be more ſafely
pronounced.

P. 3. *t.* 7.
§. 6.

CHAP.

C H A P. XXI.

How the Articles and Witnesses for the CRIMINAL *are produced and examined.*

WHEN the Criminal hath received a Copy of the Evidence and Proofs Pegna, against him, if he insists on his Defence, a certain Term is granted *l. z. c.* 48. him to exhibit the Articles by which he would prove his Innocence. This Term is not fixed to any precise Day, but left to the Pleasure of the Judge, who can grant him more or fewer Days, as he thinks fit. And because the Defence of the Criminal consists of three Parts, *viz.* in denying the Fact, or disabling the Witnesses, or proving his good Life and Behaviour, his being a good Christian or Catholick, the Articles to be proved are disposed into Method, according to the aforesaid Division. But yet the prudent and Catholick Procurator or Advocate must consider his Oath, and both insert in the Articles the Things which he believes to be true, just as they have been suggested to him by the Criminal, he is to defend, and continually admonish him simply to confess the Truth.

At the End of the Articles produced by the Criminal, the Names of the *c.* 49. Witnesses by which he would prove his Innocence, are put down, and the particular Article upon which he would have each Witness examined, specified. For as it can't easily happen that any single Witness should know all the Matters contained in all the Articles, therefore to prevent the Inquisitor, or he to whom the Inquisitor commits the Examination, the Trouble of being forced to guess who knows the Contents of such and such an Article, or of examining all the Witnesses upon every Article, 'tis particulary shewn, that such a Witness must be examined upon such and such an Article, and so of the rest. By some he endeavours to prove, that the Person who he imagines hath deposed against him, is his mortal Enemy ; by others, that he hath lived a good Life, and so on.

If after the Articles have been produced and admitted, the Criminal will add one or more additional Articles to them, the Inquisitor may admit them as well as the first, because 'tis not expressly prohibited by Law. In forming these Articles, a skilful Advocate or Procurator must consider those Things, which may either remove or extenuate the Crime, *i. e.* prove the Falshood of the Accusation, or extenuate the Guilt by proper Circumstances ; as, whether the Person was mad or drunk when he said it, of which more hereafter.

After the Criminal hath once produced and named his Witnesses, the Inquisitor may, if he sees fit, and knows there is no Fraud or Deceit, allow the Criminal to name others afterwards, and admit them.

Cap. 50.   When the Witnesses thus produced by the Criminal have deposed before the Inquisitor, a Copy of their Depositions is given to the Procurator of the Exchequer, who, in his Turn, exhibits his Interrogatories upon them, that the Witnesses brought by the Prisoner in his Defence, may be examined upon them.   And here, just as the Criminals Advocate doth, he asks abundance of Questions about the Witnesses Person, Condition of Life, and whether they know the Criminal, or are any ways a-kin to him ? and the like. Besides this he is asked, How he came to put himself upon this present Examination ? Whether any Body desired him to do it ? And who ? With what Words ? And what he the said Witness answered ? Whether the Articles upon which he was to be examined, were shewn him ? Or whether he hath been otherwise instructed what to depose ? Whether any Thing hath been given, promised, or forgiven him, and what ? Whether he expects any Advantage by his present Deposition, or by the Delivery of the Prisoner out of the Jayl of the holy Office, and what ? To these he adds others suitable to the Affair, and thus running over every Article produced by the Criminal, he demands that his Witnesses be interrogated upon each of them.

Cap. 52.   The Procurator of the Exchequer of the supream Senate of the general *Roman* Inquisition, usually demands at the End of his Interrogatories, that the Inquisitor, who is to examine the Witnesses, will form other proper Interrogatories, as the Matter shall require, and the Answers of the Witnesses shall make necessary.   For it often happens, that as the Witnesses are examining, such Things are said by them, as give Occasion to new Interrogatories, so necessary and suitable to the Case as tends very much to discover the Truth.

'Tis sometimes the Custom, as *Pegna* tells us, for the Procurator of the Exchequer of the holy Inquisition, at the End of his Interrogatories, to put such an Interrogatory as this against a Criminal to his Witness. Whether he knows, or hath heard it said, that the said *N.* in the said City of *N.* was accounted as one suspected of Heresy, and a Man of an ill Character, Opinion and Fame, in Matters relating to the holy Catholick Faith ? If he answers Yes, he is asked how he came to know this, and must name the Errors and Heresies, who were Witnesses with him, at what Time, what the particular Place, all which he must particularly relate. If he answers No, he is interrogated, How 'tis possible that the said *N.* should be accounted as one suspected of Heresy, and otherwise of evil Life, Condition and Fame, in Matters appertaining to the holy Catholick Faith, and yet he the said Witness should be ignorant of it ? *Pegna* adds, that the second Part of this Interrogatory seems to him very dangerous, and proper only to invalidate the Evidence of the Witness for the Criminal. For if such Witness should answer, 'tis possible that *N.* may have been suspected of Heresy, and yet that he might be ignorant of it, his Evidence would be weakned. And altho' some Doctors greatly admire such an Interrogatory, and say that 'tis a most excellent and admirable one, and what will invalidate the Depositions of almost all Witnesses for the Criminal, yet he is rather of Opinion, that if such an Interrogatory should be

put

put by the Procurator of the Exchequer, it ought not to be allowed by the Inquifitor ; leaft if an ignorant Witnefs, which almoft all the common and vulgar People are, fhould anfwer, it was poffible, and really is fo, the fame Procurator of the Exchequer, after the Procefs is ended, and the Proofs ex-amined, fhould by fuch a Caution fhake the Credit of all the Proofs urged in Behalf of the Criminals.

If there is any Reafon to doubt of the Faithfulnefs, Conftancy or Silence of any one of the Witneffes, *viz.* that, if difmiffed after his Examination was ended, he would confer with any other Witneffes to be examined, he is ufu-ally kept in the holy Office till after their Examination. But if he be an ho-neft Man, of good Condition and Reputation, and in no Danger of difcover-ing any Thing he hath acknowledged, he is immediately difmiffed after his Examination.

No Copy of the Depofitions is or ought to be given before the Examina-tion is finifhed. But if after the Examination of fome, the Criminal declares that he renounces any farther Examination, a Copy may be given him.

Altho', after the Publication of the Evidence, Witneffes are not to be ad-Simanc. mitted upon the fame Articles, or others contrary to them, yet in the Caufe*tit.* 64. of Herefy they are always to be allowed, whether it be for or againft the§. 50. Criminal ; becaufe, as this Publication is done in private, there can be no Sufpicion of the Witneffes being corrupted in thefe Caufes.

It often happens that the Witneffes to be re-produced, or otherwife examined, Pegna, are abfent from the Place in which the Action is carried on againft the Crimi-*Cap.* 54. nal, and therefore there muft be a Commiffion to examine them, or their Ex-amination muft be committed to fome proper Perfon. And altho' in Cri-minal Caufes fuch Commiffion for examining diftant Perfons is not allowed, the Judge himfelf being to interrogate the Witneffes, and to confider with what Steadinefs, Trembling, or Countenance they fpeak, yet fuch Commif-fion is granted in the Crime of Herefy, and efpecially when the Witneffes are in remote Places, and in other Diocefes, and can't come to the Inquifitors without great Expence.

With thefe Letters of Commiffion there muft alfo be fent to the Judge or Inquifitor, to whom the Examination of Witneffes in Behalf of the Criminal is committed, Articles and Interrogatories, upon which the faid Witneffes muft be examined, in the fame Manner as if they were examined by the In-quifitor before whom the Caufe is tried. But the Inquifitor or Bifhop, who delegates the Examination to another, muft not allow the Party to give Articles for the Witneffes, before the Judge to whom they direct the Ex-amination, but they are to be given to the Judge of the Caufe. When the Examination is ended, the Judge, who receives thefe remiffory Letters, muft take Care to tranfmit to the Inquifitor who delegates him, an authentick Copy of the original Procefs, faithfully extracted, compared with the Original, and fubfcrib'd by the Judge and Notary. But if it can be done without Dan-ger of lofing it, the original Copy it felf muft be fent to him, and the dele-gated Judge keep the authentick Copy by him.

If whilst the Caufe is depending there arife new Proofs againft the Criminal, or he commits a new Offence, or if there appears any Thing favourable in his Behalf; if, for Inftance, the Informer or Witnefs, upon recollecting himfelf, comes to depofe any Circumftance that may extenuate the Crime; or if any other comes to difcover any Thing that may make the Criminal's Innocence appear, they are to he received. This is efpecially to be obferved, in cafe any Difcovery can be made of a Confpiracy againft the Criminal, or of the Subornation of the Witnefs or Witneffes to give Evidence againft him.

CHAP. XXII.

Of the Defence of the CRIMINALS.

Cap. 57. — AFTER the Parties have prepared their Proofs, *Pegna* fays, a Copy of the defenfive Procefs muft be delivered to the Criminal. But *Carena* obferves, that for the Space of twenty Years, during which he acted in the Inquifition at *Cremona*, he never faw a Copy of the defenfive Procefs given to the Criminals in that Court, and he advifes all the Inquifitors, to act in the fame Manner; becaufe fometimes the Criminal produces in his Defence Witneffes of a tender Confcience, who rather make againft him, and for this Reafon Inconveniencies may arife from the Grant of this Procefs. And this he fays is the Practice of the *Spanifh* Inquifition. But whatever the Copy is which is granted him, he hath a Term fixed him for making his Defence, within which, if he thinks fit, he gives in his Informations as to Fact and Law, to prove his Innocence.

Simanc. — Obftinate Hereticks are denied a Defence, but Criminals, not yet con-
Cath. Inft. victed, are allowed to make the beft they can. The firft and principal
c. 17. — Defence of thofe who are innocent, is to deny the Crimes which are falfely objected to them. Such a one muft conftantly perfift in his Denial of them, that he may not unjuftly condemn, and give falfe Evidence againft himfelf. Such a one however can't prove directly by Witneffes that he did not fay or do fuch a Thing; but when the Place and Time of the Crime, faid to be committed, is affigned, he may prove that he was not then and there prefent, and that therefore he did not fay or do any Thing of which he is accufed. And when he hath proved this by feveral reputable Witneffes, he is to be abfolved.

Another kind of Defence is, if he can refute the Witneffes, *i. e.* if he can prove they are his Enemies, or fuborned with Money by his Enemies, or have confpired againft him.

But 'tis not an eafy Matter to fet afide the Witneffes in a Caufe of the Faith, becaufe, as we have faid, in favour of this, infamous Perfons, fuch as are privy to and Accomplices in the Crime, excommunicated Perfons, and
thofe

thofe guilty of any other Crimes whatfoever, are here admitted as Witneffes, especially when other Proofs are wanting. Nothing legally fets afide any one *Eymer.* from being a Witnefs but Enmity only, and that neither unlefs it be mortal. *Dir.eft.* Leffer Enmities will fomewhat weaken the Evidence of the Witneffes, but not *p. 3, n. 118.* abfolutely fet them afide. This is determined by the Councils of *Biterre*, cap. 12, 13. and *Narbonne*, cap. 24, 25. *Altho' in this Crime all Criminals, infamous Perfons, and Accomplices in the Crime, are to be admitted as Accufers and Witneffes, fuch Exceptions only fhall wholly deftroy the Credit of the Witneffes, which can be made appear to proceed not from a Zeal for Juftice, but the Inftigation of Malice, fuch as Confpiracies and mortal Enmities. Altho' other Crimes weaken, they don't deftroy the Evidence, efpecially if the Witneffes have repented of their Crime.*

Befides this Exception againft the Witneffes, there is another kind of De- *Simanc.* fence, which the Advocates make ufe of to wipe off and break the Force of *Cath. Inf.* the Accufation, *viz.* to prove that the Criminal is, and always was a Catho- *t 44. §. 22.* lick, and that this evidently appears from a great Number of pious and good Works that he hath done, and that he always had an entire good Reputation amongft all Perfons. But *Royas* fhews that all this is trifling, and of no Weight. *de bæret.* *Altho' feveral Witneffes depofe in general that fuch a one is of good Reputation, their p.1.n.346. Evidence fignifies nothing to prove him to be a Catholick, if he be convifted by two Witneffes to have faid or done any Thing in particular againft the Catholick Faith.*

If the Criminal confeffes his Offence, the Caufe is finifhed. If he confeffes it, but with the Addition of fome Circumftance, that either takes away, or leffens the Crime, the Procurator of the Exchequer receives the Confeffion of the Offence, and puts it upon him to prove the Circumftance added. Now there are various Circumftances to be urged in Abatement, which the Advocates ufe in defending Criminals. As if Herefy was fpoken by a Madman, an *Simanc.* Infant, or a decrepit old Man, except fuch aged Perfon hath his Judgment *Cath. Inf.* entire. Likewife if it be pronounced in a Dream, or by one fo drunk as to *t. 17.* be quite out of his Senfes ; or if by one, who, without any ill Defign, relates the Herefies of others ; or who, by a Slip of his Tongue, drops any Thing heretical, and immediately retracts it. Or if any one errs againft any Article of the Catholick Faith without Obftinacy, which he is not obliged explicitly to know, and efpecially if drawn into this Error by one whom he was obliged to believe. Very great Simplicity alfo may excufe ; alfo a Joak or Jeft, if thoughtlefsly pronounced, and in hafte, upon a particular Occafion, and without Deliberation, may fometimes excufe from Herefy, tho' fuch Perfons may be punifhed as rafh and evil Speakers. Add to this, any one's faying or doing any Thing heretical, thro' Fear of Death or Tortures. Such a one indeed grievoufly offends, but yet is not an Heretick. For, as *Brunus* fays, as a *l. 1. c. 4.* forced Confeffion of the true Faith doth not make a Catholick, fo neither is *§. 10.* the afferting a forced Error to be imputed for Herefy. Finally, fuch Things as are uttered thro' any vehement Commotion of Mind, fuch as Love, Jealoufy, Anger, fuddain Grief, and the like. There is alfo a kind of Defence taken from the Command of a Superior. As when a Servant by his Mafter's Command breaks Images, or commits any fuch Thing, he is to be

more

more gently punifhed. *Brunus* adds, that an Heretick may objeɛt, that the Caufe hath been already judged, and the Affair determined, which is allowed, whether Cognizance hath been taken of the Crime either by Accufation or Inquifition.

There is alfo another kind of Defence, *viz.* when any Perfon confeffes fome heretical Word, or Faɛt, but denies the evil Intention, and thus fhews himfelf to be clear of Herefy, becaufe Herefy confifts properly in the Mind. When this Defence is urged, the Criminals are tortured to difcover their Intention, and to make them fully and entirely confefs. But this they limit in certain Cafes, and don't proceed to the Torture to find out the Intention, if there be no confiderable Proof of the Crime befides the Criminal's Confeffion, and when there is juft Ground to conclude by the Circumftances of the Faɛt and other Prefumptions, that the Criminal offended with a quite different View, and not thro' an heretical Mind. *Carena* relates a memorable Inftance of this decided before the Tribunal of the holy Office at *Granada,* by *Francis Marin de Rodezno,* Inquifitor at *Granada.*

In the Year 1640. *Apr.* 5. on *Thurfday* in the Week before *Eafter,* there was a Writing fixed upon the Gates of the Senate-houfe at *Granada.* In this Paper the Law of *Mofes* was greatly extolled, and the Seɛt of *Calvin* commended, and the moft holy Faith of Chrift accurfed with the moft terrible Imprecations. The Virginity and Chaftity of the Mother of God was denied in fo very obfcene a Manner, as would fcarce become a common Whore proftituting her felf in a Bawdy-houfe. He alfo, with a Shew of Compaffion, advifed all Perfons, that they would not thoughtlefsly fuffer themfelves to be drawn away by a falfe Religion. And finally he threatned, that he would caufe to be deftroyed all thofe Regards of Worfhip and Piety, which the City of *Granada* payed to a marble Image of the Virgin, ereɛted as a Token of Viɛtory, and placed in an open Field over-againft the Gate of *Elvira,* at the Entrance into the City, and commonly called, *Our Lady of Triumph.* This Writing was feen by two Men after the Dead of Night was over, by Twilight, and as the Paper and Charaɛter was very extraordinary, it eafily excited their Curiofity, and altho' they were ignorant of the Contents, they took it down from the Gates. But after they had read it, and perceived the Wickednefs and Blafphemy of it, they carried it the next Day to the facred Tribunal of the Inquifition. The Report of this Wickednefs immediately took Air, and the Enormity and Greatnefs of the Crime alarmed the whole City of *Granada.*

One Friar *Francis Alexander* was appointed by the Senate of *Granada,* to take Care of the Worfhip of the faid *Lady of Triumph,* who, upon this Account, was, after the *Spanifh* Cuftom, called, *The Hermit,* and whofe Habit was very agreeable to his Office. He pretended to his Neighbours that he was injured above all others by this Offence done againft the Mother of God, and in his private Converfation in the City oftentimes inveighed againft the Heinoufnefs of the Crime, and at laft depofed in a legal Manner what he had Reafon to fufpeɛt, and what he himfelf had obferved in that facred Night. But as nothing came of the moft diligent Inquifitions that had been made

into

into the Affair, there arose at laſt great Suſpicions and Preſumptions againſt the Hermit himſelf, after his own Depoſitions had been privately, and at Leiſure conſidered. His Depoſitions were found inconſiſtent and contradicto- ry, tho' he made them voluntarily and freely, without any one's asking or calling upon him, and in ſome of them he was openly convicted of Falſhood. Several times he repeated ſeveral of the very Expreſſions of the ſaid Paper, ſo expreſsly and particularly, as could not poſſibly be done by any one who was not the Author of it, or at leaſt privy to it ; whereas he himſelf confeſſed, after he had been informed againſt before the Tribunal, that he had neither ſeen nor read it. And when a certain Perſon ſaid before him, that it was com- monly reported thro' the City that he was the Author of the Paper, when the Suſpicion was inſinuated, he immediately turned pale, and dextrouſly ſhifted the Diſcourſe to ſomething elſe, without mentioning a Word of the Affair, tho' his Countenance was obſerved to fall. The Circumſtances of the Perſon added to the Suſpicion, as he was a Man of an ill Life and Behaviour, remarkable for Hypocriſy, and guilty of many Crimes. And finally the common People were univerſally perſuaded, and all affirmed, as with one Voice, that no one elſe could be guilty of ſo heinous a Crime.

Upon this the Hermit was ordered to Jayl, and after three Admonitions made on three ſeveral Days, and upon comparing other Writings of his with the Letters of this Paper, finding that they were exactly ſimilar and perfect- ly alike, and that therefore the Hand and Author muſt be the ſame, he was cited by the Fiſcal of the Inquiſition, and arraigned for the Crime, and im- mediately ingenuouſly confeſſed it, and began to give an Account of the paſt Courſe and Manner of his Life, ſaying that he was a Religious of a certain very venerable Religion and Fraternity, a Lay Brother, and Profeſſed ; but that on the Account of certain Differences and Quarrels therein he fled, and had forſaken his Religion ſeveral Years. But inaſmuch as he had not loſt his Regard to Piety and Religion, tho' he had changed his Habit, he travelled to *Jeruſalem*, and there viſited the holy Places, where, thro' a peculiar ſtrong Affection to the Mother of God, he had received certain Marks on his Arms as a conſtant Monument of his Devotion. From *Jeruſalem* he came to the lower *Pannonia*, and in the City of *Vienna* built and dedicated a Temple to *our La- dy of Conception*. After this he returned back to the City of *Granada*, where he had conſecrated his Life to *our Lady of Triumph*, and the Care of her Wor- ſhip. And that when he had found that there was nothing done towards finiſh- ing her Temple, and that the Devotion of the Faithful grew cool, he was excited by theſe Motives to endeavour to encreaſe the Worſhip and Venera- tion of that ſacred Place, and that with this View he fixed up the Paper filled with Reproaches and outrageous Affronts againſt the Mother of God, and particularly directed againſt *our Lady of Triumph*. And that he might pre- vent himſelf from being ſuſpected of the Crime, and throw it upon one of the *Jewiſh* Race, who are more liable to Suſpicion, he wrote in the Paper an high Encomium of the Law of *Moſes*, and an Abjuration of Chriſtianity. And fi- nally, that no *Portugueze* might be thought guilty of this Wickedneſs, and that.

that that Nation might not come hereby into Difcredit, he added a very great Commendation of the *Calviniftick* Sect, to which, as he now thinks, he was moved by the Inftigat on of the Devil.   For he thought that by this Means he fhould more eafily bring the People into a more fervent Devotion, in order to expiate the Wickednefs of that Paper, and perfuade them to celebrate the moft venerable, pompous, and magnificent Ceremonies in Honour of the Virgin, to finifh her Church, and to encreafe the Veneration and Worfhip paid her, and finally to render that facred Place famous for its being reforted to by great Multitudes from that City and the neighbouring Towns.   And therefore that he was fo far from fixing up the aforefaid Paper out of an he-retical Mind, and from believing the Errors contained in it, that he did it with a quite contrary Defign, and always intended hereby to encreafe the Ho-nour and Worfhip of the Virgin, as became a Man faithful to the Mother of God, a Chriftian, and alfo a Catholick, and one born of pious and Catholick Parents.

When they had heard his Confeffion, and examined and finifhed his Caufe, they did not think proper to put him to the Torture, for difcovering his Com-panions or Accomplices, and whether or no he acted with an heretical Inten-tion ; becaufe many Circumftances and Prefumptions concurred, which not only gave Reafon to think, but notorioufly proved that the Criminal had no heretical Intention, but that his only Defign was to caufe greater Veneration to be paid to *our Lady of Triumph*, that he himfelf might be held in greater Efteem, and fo obtain more liberal Alms.   Nor did they think proper to de-liver him over to the fecular Arm, becaufe he had fixed up the Paper to bring the greater Honour to the Virgin, and becaufe as foon as ever his Accufation was read over, he ingenuoufly confefs'd his Crime ; and finally, becaufe he had implored Mercy with many Tears and Signs of Repentance, and, during the Time of his Imprifonment, had undergone many voluntary Penances, macerating his Body by Whipping, Faftings, and other Chaftifements, and was a Monk of a moft venerable Religion, which had produced many Saints, whofe Merits were fufficient to fupply and excufe the Errors of others, at leaft fo far as to fave them from Punifhment.   It was therefore decreed, that the Criminal fhould come forth at a publick Act of the Faith, if there was any one near at hand ; or if not, that he fhould appear in fome publick Church with the Marks of a Blafphemer, with his Tongue in a Gag, that he fhould, as one vehemently fufpected, be condemned to the Gallies for ten Years, and without any Stipend fuffer perpetual Banifhment from the City, the whole Kingdom of *Granada*, the Royal Court, and five Leagues around it ; and that he fhould be expofed in the Habit in which he was apprehend-ed, and whilft his Sentence was reading with the Merits of the Caufe, fhould lift up his right Hand, faftened into an Iron Collar, and efcape Whipping, becaufe he was a Religious.

Thus we fee that this Hermit came off with a leffer Punifhment, becaufe by a pious Fraud he intended to promote the Glory of *our Lady of Triumph*. But if they believe that any Thing is done to the Prejudice of the *Roman* Religion,

Religion, altho' the Criminal fhould deny his Intention, he will find his Judges to be cruel, and void of Mercy, and that they will put him to the Torture at Pleafure, that by the Severity of his Torments they may force from him a Confeffion of his Intention.

<hr>

CHAP. XXIII.

How the INQUISITOR *may be rejected.*

THERE are other Exceptions againft the Judge himfelf, and thofe are *Direct.* principally two, the firft is the Refufal of the Inquifitor. This Refufal *P. 3. n. 120.* is fometimes reafonable and juft, fometimes frivolous and void. But in this Tribunal many Caufes, which are fufficient to fet afide other Judges, are not admitted, but only thefe, Enmities, Confpiracy againft the Criminals, or fomething like it, as a grievous Contention, whence Enmity may eafily arife. Leffer Caufes are never allowed. Or if the Inquifitor hath dealt hardly by the Criminal, contrary to the common Courfe of the Law. If the Inquifitor apprehends that the accufed Perfon will refufe him upon this latter Account, he may give a full Deputation to fome other Perfon before he is acquainted with his being rejected, after which fuch Rejection is void, and the Deputation made ftands good. If fuch Rejection be prefented to the Inquifitor, he may amend his Miftake, and reduce the Procefs to the Condition it was in, before the Injury complained of ; and thus the Grievance being removed, the Reafon of Sufpicion ceafes, and the Refufal of the Inquifitor becomes void.

If he rejects him as an Enemy, or as a Friend of his Enemy or Accufer, *Com. 30.* *Eymerick* is of Opinion, that the Matter muft be left to Arbitrators to determine it. But now the Reafon of fuch Refufal muft be remitted to the fupream Senate of the Inquifition, that the Affair being fummarily taken Cognifance of, the Inquifitor refufed may be rejected, or prohibited to judge in that Caufe, or on the contrary may be commanded to proceed. This is determined by the *Madrid* Inftruction, *An.* 1561. *c.* 52. *If any one of the Inquifitors fhall be refufed by any Criminal, if fuch Inquifitor hath a Colleague on the Spot, he muft then abftain from the Cognifance of fuch Caufe, and certify the Senate of the Matter, and in the mean while let his Colleague proceed. If he hath no Colleague, let him in like manner certify the Senate, and not proceed in the Caufe, 'till the Senate fhall decree what ought to be done, after having feen and examined the Reafons of the Sufpicion. The fame muft be done when all the Inquifitors are rejected.*

C H A P. XXIV.

Of the APPEAL *from the* INQUISITOR.

*n.*121,&c.
com. 31.

ANother Exception againſt the Judge is, to appeal from the Inquiſitor. For altho' the Emperor *Frederick*, in l. *Commiſſi nobis*, §. 7. decrees, *That all Benefit of Proclamation and Appeal ſhall be wholly denied to Hereticks, their Receivers and Favourers*, yet ſometimes ſuch Appeal is allowed to the Perſon accuſed. However, Hereticks are allowed no Appeal from a definitive Sentence, becauſe no one is definitively condemned for Hereſy, unleſs one that hath confeſſed it, or who hath been legally convicted, according to the Laws of the Inquiſition ; and from ſuch definitive Sentences there can be no Appeal, in Favour of the Faith, and out of Hatred to Hereticks, leaſt Judgment ſhould be protracted. Cap. *Ut Inquiſitionis*, de hæret. l. 6. But an interlocutory Sentence is a quite different Thing, and from this Criminals are allowed to appeal, when they think they have been unjuſtly dealt with.

De Cathol.
Inſt. tit.6.
§ 3.

Simancas confirms the ſame. " Hereticks can't appeal from a definitive " Sentence, tho' they may from all interlocutory Sentences, if it doth not yet " appear that the Criminals are Hereticks. So that if a Criminal be condemn-" ed to the Torture, or to Purgation, or to be baſtinadoed, or to a Fine, " he may appeal, becauſe it doth not appear that he is an Heretick, but only " ſuſpected ; nor doth he appeal from the Law, but from the Judges, who " have pronounced Sentence according to their Pleaſure."

This Appeal muſt conſiſt of two Parts. The Grievance which the Criminal affirms he lies under, and the Plea by which ſuch Grievance is proved.

Notab. 18,
19.

But here *Bernard Comenſis*, in his *Light of the Inquiſitors*, obſerves, Voc. *Appellatio*. " That he who offers a probable Reaſon, muſt be prepared to " prove it, to name the Witneſſes by which he intends to prove it, and to " have them ready ; becauſe otherwiſe thoſe who make theſe Exceptions, " would have it in their Power to act fraudulently, which would be the Caſe " of all who would not have their Exceptions rejected, to give needleſs Trou-

Notab. 20.

" ble to the Accuſer. He adds, that when ſuch an Appeal from an interlo-" cutory Sentence is put in, with the Reaſon ſpecified, and a Proteſtation for

Notab. 15.

" the Aſſigning of other Reaſons, ſuch an Appeal cannot be afterwards ſup-" ported by ſuch Reaſons in Reſerve, becauſe the very Proteſtation it ſelf of " aſſigning them, would be of no Strength or Obligation. Nor can it be " ſuppos'd that any one would have the Judge pay any Regard to ſuch Appeal, " unleſs it appears to the Judge that the Appeal is valid. So that if he doth " not believe it to be good, he need not pay any Regard to it".

Some Grievances are capable of being remedied. As if the Inquiſitor ſhould not admit the accuſed Perſon to make his Defence, or hath ſingly, and by himſelf, without the Biſhop or Vicar commanded him to be put to the Queſtion. Other Grievances are irreparable, as if he hath actually made him undergo the Torture. And therefore when the accuſed Perſon alledges the

Grievances,

Grievances, and again and again demands * Letters of Appeal; the Inquisitor, after such an Appeal is exhibited to him, must, within thirty Days, examine the Reasons of such an Appeal, and if after having taken the Advice of
proper Persons, he finds that he hath unjustly aggrieved the accused Person,
he must, at the Term assigned, amend what hath been amiss, remedy the
Grievances complained of, and bring the Process to its former State, and then
proceed as before. For when the Grievance is removed, the Appeal is
void.

As to irreparable Grievances, there must be a very cautious Procedure, nor
must any one be put to the Torture without legal Proofs. This is taken Care
of by the *Madrid* Instruction, *An.* 1561. c. 50. *The Inquisitors ought especially to
consider, whether the Sentence of putting the Criminal to the Torture be justly pronounced, and upon legal Proofs proceeding. And when they doubt of this, let them
grant to the Criminal his Appeal when he demands it, because putting him to the Torture is doing him an irreparable Injury, and because an Appeal from the interlocutory
Sentence of the Judge is allowed in the Cause of Heresy. But if they have no such
Doubt, but rather think the Proofs resulting from the Process are legal, then let them
proceed to the Torture without Delay; because an Appeal, in such Case, would be
deemed frivolous. But in a doubtful Case the Appeal must always be allowed, and
the Inquisitors must farther consider the Matter, nor pronounce Sentence of Torture,
nor proceed to the Execution of it, till the Cause is finished, and the Defences of the
Criminal received.* For if there have been such Grievances as these, the Process can't be reduced to its former State.

If the Inquisitor believes that he hath not proceeded unjustly, he assigns, within thirty Days, to the accused Person a certain Term, specifying particularly the
Place, Day, and Hour, for his having given him, and receiving from the Inquisitor such Letters of Appeal, as the Inquisitor shall determine to give him. If he
finds the Causes of the Appeal to be false or frivolous, or void, and that the Appellant only endeavours to escape Judgment, the Inquisitor gives him what
they call negative Letters, or Letters of Refutation, in which he refutes all
the Reasons alledged in Support of such Grievances, and says, that he doth
not admit, nor intend to admit the Appeal put in, and that he pays no Regard to it, nor ever intends it. This is the Answer he gives to him who appeals unjustly, which he commands to be inserted directly and immediately
after the Appeal presented to him, and then delivers it to the Notary who
presented it. But if he finds the Grievances to be real, and unjustly laid on
him, and to be irreparable; or if he is in doubt concerning these Things, he
gives the Appellant what they call affirmative Letters, or Letters of *Reverence*, in which he says he hath proceeded justly; and after running thro' the
several Causes of the Appeal, and answering them, at length concludes, that
he hath given no Cause of Appeal. But that nevertheless for the *Reverence*
he bears to the Apostolick See, which is appealed to, he allows the Appeal,

* *Apostoli.* Those *Apostoli* were dimissory Letters, granted by Ecclesiastical Officials and Judges,
to those who appealed to the Pope at *Rome.*

and remits the whole Affair to the Pope, and affigns to the Appellant a certain Term, within which he muft appear at the Court of *Rome* before the Pope, with the Proceffes inclofed and fealed up, to be delivered to him by the Inquifitor, upon giving good Security, or under a fafe and ftrict Guard. This is the Anfwer he gives to him, who appeals for affirmative Letters, which he commands to be immediately inferted after the Appeal put in, and thus delivers it to the Notary who prefented it.

If the Inquifitor gives the Appellant negative Letters, he continues his Procefs againft him, to let him know, that he doth not ceafe to be his Judge, till he is prohibited to proceed by that Judge to whom the Appeal is made. But yet from the Hour of the Appeal, he can do nothing new againft the Appellant, till he hath delivered to him the negative Letters. But if he grants him affirmative or reverential Letters, he immediately ceafes to be his Judge, and can take no farther Cognizance of the Caufe, unlefs it be remitted to him by the Pope. He may however proceed againft the Appellant in any other Caufe, *viz.* if after having given him fuch Letters of Reverence, he is informed againft before the Inquifitor for other Herefies and Crimes.

But now the inferior Inquifitors are not allowed to ufe this Power. In *Spain* the *Madrid* Inftruction, *An.* 1561. *c.* 51. gives this Caution in the Affair. *If the Inquifitors think that an Appeal is to be allowed in any Cafe, in the criminal Caufes of fuch Criminals as are imprifoned, they muft fend the Proceffes to the Senate of the Inquifition, without certifying the Criminals themfelves of it, and with fuch Caution and Secrefy, that no one without the Prifon may know it; becaufe, if the Senate fhould think otherwife in any particular Caufe, it may give Order, and take the neceffary Care about it.* But in other Provinces, and efpecially in *Italy*, where the Appeal is admitted, the Inquifitors confult the Senate of the general *Roman* Inquifition for the whole Chriftian Common-wealth, the Caufe being briefly and fummarily reported to them; and if the Senate thinks fit that the Criminals fhould be fent to *Rome*, it muft be done, and the Inquifitors muft fend them there under good Security and fafe Cuftody.

C H A P. XXV.

How they proceed againft fuch who make their Efcape.

Direct.
P. 3. *n.* 130.
Com. 33. T HUS have we given an Account of the Method of proceeding againft a Criminal actually in Jayl. But if he abfent, or hath made his Efcape, the Procefs is formed againft him after this manner. When any one is informed againft before the Inquifitor for being infected with Herefy, and fuch Perfon is not prefent in the Place where the Inquifitor lives, but dwells in fome other Place, within the Bounds of the Inquifitor's Jurifdiction, he is faid to be abfent, but not a Fugitive. When there is any Apprehenfion of

his

his Efcape, tho' they determine that they may omit the making any verbal Citation, and proceed immediately to apprehend him, yet fometimes fuch abfent
Perfon is fummoned to appear on a certain Day and Place, to anfwer to fuch
Matters whereof he is accufed. But becaufe by fuch a Citation the Criminal may
be induced to meditate his Efcape, others advife, that no particular Caufe fhould
be mention'd in this Citation, but that he fhould be only commanded in general to appear before the Inquifitors, to inform them of certain Matters. Likewife the Inquifitor writes to the Rector of the Church, to which the Criminal
is fubject, commanding him to fummon the Criminal before him to anfwer concerning the Faith, and to declare the Truth of himfelf and others as to the
Crime of Herefy.

Com. 131.

 This feems to be taken from the Council of *Biterre,* c. 3. *Let the Clergy and*   132.
Laity of that Place, which the Citation belongs to, be called together by fome Eccle-
fiaftical Perfon, to whom you fhall commit this Affair by your Letters Patents, who, in
Token of his having received the Command, muft add his Seal to the faid Letters, and
write back by his own Letters Patents, figned with his Seal, how, before whom, and
when he difcharged the Order given him.

 If the abfent Perfon be wholly out of the Jurifdiction of the Inquifitor, the
Inquifitor examines the Witneffes privately, that it may not come to the
Knowledge of the abfent accufed Perfon that Inquifition is made againft him.
Then the Inquifitor farther inquires, whether he will return into his Jurifdiction; if 'tis probable he will, he waits a Year or more for his Return. If
'tis probable he will not, but that he hath changed his Place of abode, 'tis at
the Pleafure of the Inquifitor either to require the Inquifitor or Diocefan,
whofe Jurifdiction the Criminal is under, to fend him to him, or elfe to tranfmit him the whole Procefs, that he may do what he thinks proper. In *Portugal*
Perfons accufed are never turned over to another Place, but punifhed in the
Diftrict where they are taken, whether the Crimes and Informations againft
the Criminals are fent by the Inquifitors of other Diftricts.

 But when any one knows that Inquifition is made againft him, or is actually   133.
imprifoned, and yet makes his Efcape, to avoid the Hands of the Inquifitors,
he is faid to be a Fugitive. In this Cafe the Inquifitor firft inquires diligently,
and without Noife, to what Place he is fled, and where he hath concealed
himfelf; and if he finds out the Place, orders him to be taken up, and
fent back to him. If it be within his own Jurifdiction, he may require the
temporal Lord to apprehend him, and conduct him within his Diftrict. Yea,
he may require the fame from any other Lord, whilft he hath him in Poffeffion.
If he be without his Jurifdiction, he may neverthelefs proceed againft him,
and require the Inquifitor, in whofe Jurifdiction he is, to caufe him to be taken up, and fent back to him, or fend him his Procefs, that he may do what
Juftice fhall require. Thus the Council of *Tholoufe* heretofore ordered, *cap.* 8.
We ordain alfo, that any one may make Inquifition, and apprehend Hereticks in ano-
ther's Province, and let the Ballives of fuch Places be obliged to grant them Af-
fiftance and Favour; fo that the Ballive of the King may do thus in the Dominions
of the Earl of Tholoufe *and others, and the Earl of* Tholoufe *and others in the*
                       Dominions

Dominions of the King. The firft Inftruction of *Seville, An.* 1484. *c.* 21. hath ordained Punifhments againft fuch temporal Lords, as do not obey the In-quifitors. *Becaufe the moft ferene Kings have commanded, and Reafon requires it, that Inquifition fhould be equally made for the Crime of Herefy, as well in the Lands of Nobles, as in their own; therefore the Inquifitors who now are, or hereaf-ter fhall be, muft ordain in their Diocefes, that they may freely proceed to make In-quifition in the faid Countries. But if the Nobles fhall not obey the Commands of the Inquifitors, they muft proceed againft them for Rebellion and Contumacy, and inflict on them all the Cenfures and Punifhments appointed by the Law.* But when Criminals are fent from one Place to another, it muft be at their own Expence if they have Effects, according to the Decree of the *Madrid* Inftruction, *An.* 1561. *c.* 9. The fame is alfo obferved in *Portugal.*

135. If the Inquifitor cannot find out the Place to which the Criminal is fled, he cites him perfonally in the Cathedral Church of that Diocefe to whom he be-longs, and in the Parifh Church of that City, where he dwelt before his E-fcape, and finally in his own proper Houfe in which he commonly lived, per-fonally to appear within a certain Term before the Inquifitor, to anfwer con-cerning the Faith and Articles of Faith, under this Penalty, that if he doth not appear within the Term affigned him, he fhall be excommunicated with the greater Excommunication.

Thus the Council of *Biterre* prefcribes, cap. 14. *As to thofe who are abfent thro' Contumacy, caufe them to be folemnly cited in their Parifh or Cathedral Church, and in the Places where they dwell, or have been ufed to dwell. And having thus put forth legal Edicts againft them, and after having waited a proper Time, and ha-ving carefully confidered and difcuffed the Acts, and having receiv'd the Advice of fuch Prelates, in fuch Matters, as you have thought fit to confult them about, under their Seal, proceed to their Condemnation, according to the Exigency of the Crimes, the Prefence of God and his Gofpels fupplying their Abfence. And if any of them are afterwards willing to return and obey, receive from them, and in general from all fuch who have been guilty of Contumacy and Difobedience, or of whofe Efcape you have Reafon to be apprehenfive, good Security and Bail, or caufe them to be confined, if you think it more expedient.*

But in the firft Council of the Prelates, probably at *Tholoufe,* 'tis thus de-creed of fuch abfent Perfons. *But if there are any Perfons criminal, or fufpected, belonging to your Inquifition, who are not prefent, or have not been fo, and who do not take Care to appear or excufe themfelves, within a competent Term peremptorily by you affigned them, and publifhed in the Churches, proceed, without Doubt, againft them, as againft Impenitents. And 'tis our Senfe, that all fuch Perfons belong to your Inquifition, who either have offended within the Bounds of the faid Inquifition, or have a Dwelling there, or had when the Inquifition was firft made; or who have refided there upon account of any Office publick or private; or who having no fixed Abode, fhall be found there when cited by you, whether they have any Security or not, if you have begun to make Inquifition againft them, or have enjoined them their Pur-gation. For againft fuch Impenitents, or Abfenters, you may and ought to proceed; excepting only, if other Inquifitors have begun to proceed againft them, upon ac-*
count

count of some greater or lesser Crime committed elsewhere, or by Reason of their dwelling under their Jurisdiction, or for any of the aforesaid Causes. For as the In-quisition is carried on, under God, in different Places, and by different Inquisitors, 'tis more wholesome and safe, that every Criminal in the Place where he hath offended, should stand accountable to that Inquisitor wholly and only, by whom he was first be-gun with, for any of the aforesaid Causes, without Deceit, and Danger of the Affair and of Souls. But so however, that the other Inquisitors shall inquire out whatever they can know concerning him, and write an Account hereof to those Inquisitors to whom the said Criminal stands accountable. For thus you shall all fight as one Man, and overcome.

But that such Escape may not go unpunished, in the Person who being in Custody for Heresy, breaks out of Jayl, 'tis a Matter of Custom rather than Law, especially in *Spain*, that if he who makes his Escape, be of any consi-derable Reputation, and apprehended again, for Instance, a Nobleman, Doctor, religious Person, or otherwise a Citizen of Account, he shall be kept in stricter Custody, and punished more severely. But if he is a mean Person, he is publickly whipped, and his Cause is to remain, and be carried on in the State it was before, but he is not to be treated for his Escape as one con-victed of Heresy ; because the breaking out of Jayl, or an Escape, hath no-thing common with Heresy, and 'tis rather to be presumed that he fled be-cause tired out with his Imprisonment, or thro' Fear of false Witnesses, or the Severity of his Torments, rather than from any Error of his Understanding. However, *Zanchinus* says, that a Prisoner who escapes, or attempts to break Prison, ought to be esteemed as a Convict, and condemned as an Heretick. *Simancas* on the other hand says, this cannot be proved by common Law, and tho' it be more plainly ordained by the royal Laws, yet in his Judg-ment 'tis extreamly severe. 'Tis usual also with the Inquisitors, as soon as ever they understand the Criminals have escaped, to write to the neigh-bouring Inquisitors or Bishops, or other Persons whom they judge proper, to find out whether the Person escaped hath fled to their City, that they may take Care to apprehend him, adding in their Letter his Name, Surname, Country, Stature, Colour, and other Circumstances, by which the fugitive Criminal may be easily known.

But if such Fugitive shall be found guilty of Heresy, not only by Witnes-fes, but by his own Confession, and hath declared himself ready to abjure it, and yet escapes before his Abjuration, especially if he be a religious Person, who hath himself preached Heresies, he is cited personally to appear before the Inquisitor at a certain Place, and within a certain Day, to abjure his He-resy, and threatned with Excommunication unless he obeys. And if with an obstinate Mind he lies under the Sentence of Excommunication for a Year, and doth not make his Abjuration, he is to be judged as an obstinate Here-tick, and delivered over to the secular Court. If being thus cited they never-thelefs refuse to appear, but suffer themselves to continue under Excommuni-cation, they are declared publickly to be excommunicated in all those Churches and Places in which they have been cited, and all are commanded under

Pegna in Direct. p. 3. com. 35.

c. 10. § 3.

tit. 16. §. 23.

n. 136.

under the Penalty of Excommunication, to avoid them as excommunicated Perfons, and to difcover them to the Inquifition, if they know where they have concealed themfelves. Thus the Council of *Tholoufe* hath decreed, *cap. 2. And if they find any Hereticks, their Believers, Favourers, and Receivers, or Abettors, let them take due Care that they don't efcape, and be fure to difcover them to the Archbifhop, or Bifhop, or Lords of the Places, or their Ballives, with all Speed, that they may receive their due Punifhment.* *Conrad Brunus* gives a fuller Account of this Matter. " He is guilty of Contumacy, who being cited before a Judge by " three Edicts, or by one peremptory one, once for all, will not appear be- " fore the Judge by whom he is cited, and that in full Procefs. He may be " proceeded againft either of thefe ways. He may be either pronounced " guilty of Contumacy, or elfe legal Proofs may be taken to make out " his Crime. In the former Cafe the Perfon cited, and guilty of Obftinacy, is " excommunicated, and if he lies under it with an obftinate Mind a whole " Year, he is condemned as an Heretick, *&c.* In the other Cafe, the Crime " of Herefy is to be proved againft him, by Witneffes, Writings, compa- " ring of Letters and Likenefs of Hand, and other Evidences, which being " proved, he fhall be condemned, together with the Books and Writings con- " taining fuch Errors and Herefies. Moreover, an abfent Heretick fhall be " declared and pronounced an Heretick, and be excluded from Ecclefiaftical " Communion, and deprived of all Ecclefiaftical Dignities and Orders.

CHAP. XXVI.

How the PROCESS *is ended in the* INQUISITION.

AFter the Procefs is thus begun and carried on, it remains that we now explain how it is finifhed.

When all the Defences are exhibited, the Criminal preffes to have his Caufe difpatched. This may and muft be done either by the imprifoned Criminal himfelf, or by his Procurator or Advocate, and that either by fpeaking, or by prefenting a fhort Petition.

Simanc. *t.44.§.26.* " After this the Judges with their Affeffors and Counfellors, having examined " the Proofs, fhall confider, and fhall proceed according to the Merits of the " Caufes to pafs Sentences, or to * Interlocutories, and abfolve the Innocent, " and leave the Obftinate to the fecular Judge, and condemn fuch as are " fufpected, according to the Nature of their Crimes, Perfons and Proofs, " either to the Queftion, or Abjuration, or Purgation, or Imprifonment, " or Banifhment, or to a Fine ; or fhall injoin them to purge and redeem their " Fault by Faftings, Prayers and Alms.

* *Interlocutio* is not a definitive Sentence, but the Determination of fome fmaller Matter in a Caufe, till the principal Caufe is fully difcuffed.

" The

" The Judges muft alfo be very careful, generally to interrogate the Cri-§. 27.
" minals concerning their Accomplices, and of all others from whom they
" have learnt Herefies, and who they know to be, or to have been Hereticks.
" And if they difcover any Thing of thefe Matters, it muft be written down
" in the Books of the Inquifition.
" 'Tis farther provided in a certain Chapter of the third Inftruction, that §. 30.
" all the Inquifitors of *Spain* fhall obferve the fame Order in proceeding a-
" gainft Hereticks and fufpected Perfons, and as this had not been ufual, we
" drew up, fays *Simancas,* eighty Heads, by which the Form of Proceeding
" might be always uniform and confiftent with it felf, which Heads are to be
" obferved by all Inquifitors, according as 'tis ordered by the general Edict
" of the Inquifitor, printed in the Year 1561.
" Finally, There are feveral Heads of Inftruction which provide, that §. 31.
" thefe Caufes fhall be carried on with as much Brevity as poffible, and not
" be deferred or fufpended thro' any Expectation of future Proofs, becaufe
" probably there may never happen any fuch, and in the mean while the Cri-
" minal will be oppreffed, and his Effects be diffipated and wafted. 3 *Inftruct.*
" *Valdolit.* cap. 2, 3. 4 *Inftruct. Tolet.* c. 6. 5 *Inftruct. Hifpal.* c. 6.
" For which Reafons this one Thing is to be confider'd and avoided, tho' §. 32.
" many Inquifitors have often practifed it, *viz.* the deferring and fufpending
" the Caufes of many Perfons which have been a long while concluded, that
" they may punifh feveral Criminals together. The Confequence of this is,
" that fuch Criminals, who have fully confeffed their Errors, are made un-
" righteoufly to fuffer the Punifhment of remaining in Jayl, and of pining
" away thro' Naftinefs, Infection and long Confinement, and which is much
" more grievous and dangerous, occafions them to retract the Confeffions
" they have rightly made, and never more to think of them, and fometimes
" to defpair and die. 'Tis therefore much more agreeable to Piety and Mer-
" cy, immediately to reconcile fuch to the Church, who have made a full
" Confeffion, which may be done with Solemnity enough upon fome Holy-
" day within the Church, unlefs there be fome juft Reafon to the con-
" trary."
When the Opinions of the Counfellors are heard, and the Sentence given,
the Criminal is fummoned to come and hear his Sentence. 'Tis not determined by any particular Law by what Officer he is to be cited, and therefore the Cuftom of each Inquifition is to be obferved. Without fuch Citation
there can be no Sentence. This *Pegna* gives us a large Account of in his
Notes upon *the Light of the Inquifitors.*
" The judiciary Method is to be fully obferved in almoft all Caufes, other- In voce
" wife the Procefs is rendred void. But this is particular in the Caufes of he-Ordo juris.
" retical Pravity, that in order to their being more quickly difpatched, and
" that fuch heinous Offences may be more fpeedily punifhed, the full
" judiciary Method need not be obferved. So that they proceed herein
" fimply, and plainly, and without the Noife and Appearance of Judgment.
" Neither is there any Room here for the Conteftation of the Suit, which

" confifts in debating on the principal Matter on one Side, and the other be-
" fore the Judge, and the putting in Anfwers either by denying or con-
" feffing.

 " But if any Thing be omitted, which is effential to fuch Trials, fuch as
" the Citation, the Term, and the receiving the Witneffes after Citation, and
" if the Sentences be not given in Writing, in proper Place and Time,
" with the ufual Solemnities, all is void. And this is true alfo in the Crime
" of Herefy; for by omitting any Acts which are effential, the Procefs even
" in Caufes of the Faith would be deftroyed.

 Simancas hath given us a brief Account of the Manner of pronouncing Sentences, which I fhall here infert, becaufe it fully reprefents to us the Method
which is ufually obferved in thefe Cafes.

Simanc.
t. §0. §.1.
 " All the Judges are obliged to read the Sentences out of a little Book or
" Brief, and muft do it themfelves, and not by others, unlefs they are illuftrious
" Perfons, or in fome Poft of great Dignity. And therefore when the Inqui-
" fitors have a Caufe before them of more than ordinary Confequence, they
" may pronounce Sentence by others, which muft be done before the Clergy
" and People, for Inftruction, Warning and Terror. And this was for-
" merly the Cuftom in *Spain.*

§. 2.
 " The Form of a Sentence of Condemnation is this. Firft the Nature of
" the Doctrine or Opinions afferted by the Criminal himfelf is declared; af-
" ter this the diligent Inquiry that hath been made into his Crimes, the Ci-
" tations, Admonitions, Confeffions, legal Proofs, the Times given for Re-
" pentance, his Mind hardned in his Errors, his obftinate perfifting in them,
" and all other Things, which may tend to fhew that the Procefs which
" hath been carried on and obferved againft him hath been juft, are enume-
" rated. All which Particulars being laid down in their Order, then fol-
" lows the Sentence it felf, formed as the Nature of the Crime requires, ac-
" cording to the Ecclefiaftical Rules, containing the Condemnation of the
" Opinions, Authors, Books and other Matters.

§. 3.
 " Befides, in the Sentence of Condemnation, the Time muft be declared
" from which the Criminal fell into Herefy, that by a bare Infpection the
" Judge of the forfeited Effects may know from what Day his Effects are to
" be confifcated, which is provided by a certain Letter of the Inquifitor Ge-
" neral, for this Reafon, that there may be no Need of looking over the
" whole Procefs on this Account, in which there are feveral Things which
" ought to be kept fecret. It is alfo provided by another Letter of the Se-
" nate, that when the Judges and the Learned are deliberating about the
" Sentence to be pronounced, they fhall fix the Time of the Herefy. This
" Letter is printed amongft the Inftructions, and dated from *Granada, An.*
" 1499.

§. 5.
 " The Sentence, by which Perfons lapfed into Herefy, are re-incorpora-
" ted into the Church, is in this Form. They are declared to have been He-
" reticks or Apoftates, and to have incurred the Penalties eftablifhed by
" Law. But inafmuch as they fay they will return to the Church with a
                  " pure

" pure Heart, and Faith unfeigned, the Judges abfolve them from Excom-
" munication, and reconcile them to the Church, if it be true what they fay,
" that they are unfeignedly and truly converted. 1 *Inftruct. Hifpal.* c. 10.

" But in a Sentence of Condemnation the Criminal muft be declared an ob- §. 6.
" ftinate Heretick, and his Effects be confifcated, and his Opinions and Wri-
" tings muft be condemned and anathematifed, and he muft be moreover de-
" prived of all Ecclefiaftical Herefies, publick Offices, and Honours what-
" foever, and finally be deliver'd over to the fecular Court, to receive his due
" Punifhment.

" But if any one, after Sentence of Reconciliation, fhall be convicted of §. 8.
" having concealed any Herefies or Hereticks, or to have boafted that he
" was innocent, and unjuftly condemned, he muft be examined again as an
" Impenitent ; nor will the Sentence by which he was reconciled to the Church,
" be of any Service to him, becaufe it appears by this very Thing, that it
" was pronounced upon a feigned Confeffion and pretended Converfion. Be-
" fides, if any new Proof arifes againft the Convert, his Caufe muft be tried
" over again, notwithftanding the Sentence of Re-incorporation or Abfolu-
" tion, or Purgation, or Queftion pronounced before in the fame Caufe.
" 1 *Inftruct. Hifpal.* c. 13. 3 *Inftruct. Valdolit.* c. 3.

" When the Inquifitors differ, and the Caufe is determined by the Senate of §. 10.
" the holy Inquifition, all muft fubfcribe to the Sentence, even they who
" were of the contrary or different Opinion. If there fhould happen to be in
" any Province three Inquifitors, and one agrees with the Bifhop or his Vicar,
" and the two others differ from them, the Caufe muft be remitted to the
" Senate. But if two agree with the ordinary Judge, the Sentence muft be
" immediately pronounced, without any Mention made of the Difference
" about pronouncing fuch Sentence. All thefe Things are more fully contain-
" ed in feveral Letters of the Senate.

" It is alfo the Cuftom, that when the Sentences againft Hereticks are pub- § 11.
" lickly pronounced, to read thofe laft of all, by which the Obftinate and
" Impenitent are condemned ; and after they have read over a fummary
" Account of the Acts of the Procefs, to make a Paufe, and admonifh the
" Hereticks before all the People, that they would at length be converted,
" becaufe as yet the Time of Mercy is not out. If they fay they will be
" converted, they are to be carried back to Jayl, and admitted to Penance
" if converted. But if they perfift in their Obftinacy and Impenitence, their
" Sentence muft be read, after which they muft be immediately feized on
" by the fecular Judge, and being condemned to the Flames, be directly
" burnt. *Lutherans* are dealt with in a different Manner, becaufe they are
" the worft, and the moft pernicious of all Hereticks, and very feldom truly
" converted ; on which Accounts they are treated with greater Severity.

" In this Order the Sentences were pronounced in *Spain* againft Hereticks §. 12.
" defcending from *Jews* and *Moors*, becaufe they could hurt only themfelves,
" or thofe of the fame Race with themfelves ; for during the Space of 800
" Years, none of the noble or antient Chriftians were infected by them. But
" after

" after that the pernicious Hereticks of our Time are found to have infected
" not only antient, but even some noble Christians with their Impiety, they
" are not admitted to be reconciled at the last Moment when Sentence is to
" be pronounced, because then they ask Pardon rather thro' Fear of immedi-
" ate Death, than willingly and from the Heart, and being thus but feigned
" Converts, may do a great deal of Mischief.

C H A P. XXVII.

How the PROCESS *is ended by Absolution.*

HAving said these Things in general, it now remains, that we distinctly
explain how every Process is finished.

The first Manner of ending a Process in Causes of the Faith, is by Absolution, when the Criminal is not found guilty. And this may happen two
ways, either because he was really found innocent, the Informers and Witnesses being found guilty of Falshood, or because the Accusation against him
was not fully proved.

If he is found innocent after the first Manner, especially if the Witnesses
have retracted their Depositions, then he may be pronounced innocent. And
l.2.t.3. in this Case, as *Paramus* tells us, the accused Person, whose Innocence ap-
c.1.n.12. pears, rides upon an Horse, amidst the Applause of the People, crowned with
Laurel and Palm-Branches, after the Manner of a Triumph.

Direct. If he is not found guilty, after the second Manner, because he is not con-
p.3.n.141. victed neither by his own Confession, nor the Evidence of Fact, nor by the
legal producing of Witnesses, and is not otherwise found to be suspected, nor
publickly defamed for the aforesaid Crime, he is absolved by the Bishop and
Inquisitor together, or by either of them separately.

Rom. 121. For that the Prisoner cannot be condemned in such a Case, is expresly determined by the Council of *Biterre,* c. 11. and by that of *Narbonne,* c. 23.
*But proceed to the Condemnation of no Person, without his own Confession, or clear
and open Proofs ; for 'tis better to suffer a Crime to go unpunished,. than to condemn
the Innocent.*

In such a Sentence of Absolution there is no mention made of the Heresies
or Crimes, for which such Person is accused or informed against, because
they are not proved. This hath been provided for by the *Madrid* Instruction,
An. 1561. *c.* 62. whether it be pronounced upon a Person dead or alive. *When
he who defends the Memory and Reputation of a Person deceased, hath legally maintained his Cause, and the deceased Person is to be absolved from any farther Trial, his
Sentence shall be pronounced in the publick Act, because the Edicts were published
against him. However, in this Case, the Statue of such deceased Person who is absolved in the publick Act, shall not be brought forth, nor shall the particular Errors*

of

of which he was accused, be recited, because they are not proved. The same must be observed with respect to those, who are personally apprehended, and accused, and absolved from farther Trial, if they shall demand it.

Not that they are wont to pronounce such Criminal free from Heresy, but only to declare that nothing is legally done against him, on Account of which he may, or ought to be pronounced an Heretick, or any ways be suspected of heretical Pravity ; and that therefore he is wholly released from his present Trial, Inquisition and Judgment. But they carefully avoid putting into his Sentence that he was innocent, or not guilty, that if so be he should afterwards be informed against, and the Crime legally proved, he may be condemned notwithstanding the aforesaid Sentence of Absolution. But if it should happen that any one is pronounced wholly innocent, and is afterwards accused of the same Crime, their Doctrine is, that notwithstanding his Sentence of Absolution, he may be again judged and condemned ; because, in this Crime no Sentences whatsoever can ever be accounted as an adjudged Case, in Favour of the Faith. This *Pius* V. hath determined by a certain Rescript, which I shall here give intire.

Of our own proper Motion, &c.

Pope Pius V.

AMongst *the manifold Cares which continually imploy our Mind, this, as it ought to be, is the Principal, that the Church of God committed to us from on high, may safely carry on its Warfare, and as a Ship in a calm Sea, when the tempestuous Waves and Storms are all assuaged, may securely sail, and come to the desired Port of Safety, by purging out of it, yea as far as we can, by wholly exterminating all Heresies, and the evil Principles of erroneous Opinions. Since therefore, even when in a lower Station we managed the Affairs of the most holy Office of the* Roman *and Universal Inquisition against heretical Pravity, we have at length by long Use, and that Experience which leads into the true Understanding of Things, known, that many Persons accused, and processed in the aforesaid most holy Office, or elsewhere, before the Ordinaries of Places, and the Inquisitors of heretical Pravity, and against whom Inquisition hath been made on the Account of heretical Pravity, have, by causing false Witnesses to be examined in their Defence, and by the Assistance of the Endeavours and Evidence of Compurgators, not at all informed of their Life and Doctrine, and by deluding and deceiving with divers other unlawful Methods, and the Invention of deceitful Excuses and Wickednesses, the aforesaid holy Office of the most holy Inquisition, and the other Judges, and even the* Roman *Pontiffs themselves, obtained and extorted many definitive Sentences of Absolution from the aforesaid Processes and Inquisitors, as tho' they were innocent, and also upon a preceding canonical Purgation of their attested, good, and Catholick Faith, Life and Doctrine, declaratory Sentences or Decrees from the said most holy Office, and other Ordinaries of Places, or Delegates, and even from the* Roman *Pontiffs our Predecessors ; which Sentences and Decrees the aforesaid* Roman *Pontiffs have confirmed, partly by injoining perpetual Silence, and prohibiting the said most holy Office, or other Inquisitors, from proceeding to any farther Matters, and partly by removing Causes only before the* Roman *Pontiff, to whose Protection the said Office was subject, and by other Derogatories*

rogatories of Derogatories, and by most effectual Clauses, even such as made the Pro-cesses void, and by other Decrees even in Form of Grace, by several of their own proper Motions, and by several Letters expedited under the Seal or Fisher's Ring, is-suing in consistory, or consistorially; from whence it came to pass that the afore-said inquisited Criminals, under the Veil and Protection of the aforesaid declaratory Sentences, and Letters Apostolick, and especially confiding in the Strength of the in-hibitory Clause made against the Inquisitors, have by secretly and sometimes openly persevering in their old Errors against the Catholick Faith, never truly returned to the Bosom of the Church, but by conversing securely with others, and as tho' they were Catholicks, have corrupted and infected the Minds of others, and have been enabled easily to seduce them into their heretical Opinions, to the no small Scandal and Pre-judice of the whole Christian Common-wealth, and to the Destruction and Loss of the Souls of the aforesaid accused Persons: We therefore, being willing to obviate so per-nicious and infectious a Scandal, and to consult and provide for the Salvation of the said Souls, and to remove all Doubt and Altercation from Lawyers, and all Impedi-ments and Hindrances, by which the holy Inquisition of heretical Pravity, may by any Manner or Means be obstructed or hindred, from a like Motion, and of our certain Knowledge, and by the Fulness of our Apostolick Power, reducing, in the first Place, all and singular such Letters Apostolick whatsoever, under any Form of Words whatsoever, even in the aforesaid, or any other Causes of Heresy, even such as were issued out of proper Motion, &c. and also consistorially, &c. or any other way how-soever, as likewise the above-mentioned Schedules of proper Motions, and any others, to Law and Justice, and the Bounds of Law, and wholly and perpetually revoking the Inhibitions by the Fiscal of the abovesaid holy Office of the Inquisition, and other ordinary and delegated Judges, against the aforesaid Letters, and also the Deroga-tories of Derogatories, and all other Clauses whatsoever that open their Mouth, and as far as they are contrary to the Disposition of Jurisdiction, or the Style of the said Office, do, by this our perpetual and universal Constitution, to be in Force for ever, declare, decree, appoint and ordain, by our Apostolick Authority, that all and sin-gular Sentences of Absolution whatsoever, even upon the Head of asserted Innocence, or declaratory Sentences, under any Form of Words, even tho' canonical Purgation may have preceded, and tho' such Sentences be definitive, and all Decrees pronounced in Favour of the said Criminals and accused Persons, by the aforesaid most holy Office, and other ordinary and delegated Judges, and even by the Roman Pontiffs, or here-after to be pronounced even by us, and our Successors the Roman Pontiffs, for the Time being, never have, and for the future never shall be esteemed as an adjudged Case; but that all the aforesaid Sentences and Decrees whatsoever, even tho' by Let-ters Apostolick, or in Form of Grace, or several times repeated, or tho' issuing from, confirmed, or to be confirmed by several Roman Pontiffs, together with the aforesaid, or any others whatsoever, even Derogatories of Derogatories, and even such as make void, and all other Clauses and Decrees, as also Inhibitions, and even canonical Sanctions, (the Tenors of all and singular of which, and of the other Premisses, and such as follow them, we order to be looked upon as expressed, and wholly inserted, as tho' they were inserted Word for Word in these Presents) to the contrary notwithstanding, we do, by the same Apostolick Authority, will and command, that it shall and may be lawful for our aforesaid holy Office of the holy Inquisition, and our beloved Sons,

who

who now are, or shall be, for the Time being, Cardinals of the holy Roman *Church, Inquisitors of heretical Pravity, and deputed for the said Office, now, or for the Time being, against the said accused Criminals under Inquisition, even tho' they have been, or are Bishops, Arch Bishops, Patriarchs, Primates, Cardinals of the said holy* Roman *Church, Legates a latere, Counts, Barons, Marquisses, Dukes, Kings and Emperors, to make again Inquisition and Process, as well concerning the old as new Witnesses, in the same Articles received, or to be received, and other Arguments, Proofs and Evidences, according to the Privileges in any manner granted and given, or hereafter respectively to be given and granted to the same Cardinals Inquisitors by us, or any of our Predecessors, and Successors, the* Roman *Pontiffs for the Time being, and the Apostolick See, even in and thro' all Matters, as tho' the aforesaid Sentences, Decrees, and Letters Apostolick, and even canonical Purgations had never been made in Favour of the aforesaid accused Criminals under Inquisition, whether Bishops, Arch-Bishops, Patriarchs, Primates, Cardinals, Legates, Counts, Barons, Marquisses, Dukes, Kings, and Emperors, especially when there arise new Proofs of the same, or another Species of Heresy, even respecting the Time past, or where it appears by certain Proofs, that the Criminal under Inquisition had been formerly absolved by unlawful Methods: Granting also to the said Cardinals Inquisitors, and deputed Persons, now or hereafter, for the said most holy Office of the Inquisition, full, free, ample, and absolute Faculty, Power and Authority, of revising such Causes, tho' decided by Authority of the Oecumenical Universal Council of* Trent, *and of re-assuming them in the State and Terms in which they shall any ways be found to have been previous to the aforesaid Sentences, and Decrees, and even canonical Purgations, and of bringing them to their proper Conclusions, even as it is, and may be, and usually hath been done by the said Cardinals Inquisitors, according to their Privileges in all other depending and undecided Causes, &c. An.* 1567. *and first Year of our Pontificate.*

In the same Manner also they are absolved who are accused of receiving, defending, or otherwise favouring Hereticks or heretical Pravity, when nothing is legally granted against them.

C H A P. XXVIII.

How the PROCESS *against a Person defamed for Heresy is ended by Canonical Purgation.*

WHEN the Person accused is only found to be defamed for Heresy, *n.* 142. in any Village, City, or Province, and is not convicted either by *com.* 38. his own Confession, or the Evidence of the Fact, or by the legal producing of Witnesses, or any other legal Proofs, and Infamy only is precisely against him, he is not absolved, but he is injoined canonical Purgation by the Bishop and Inquisitor together, and not separately.

"There

Simanc.
c. 56 § 1. " There is frequent Mention made of canonical Purgation, in the Papal Law, and tho' in all other Crimes 'tis grown into Difuse, yet in the Crime of Herefy 'tis now practifed, and is very common in the facred Court of the Inquifitors. For which Reafon *Godofred* praifes *Spain* in thefe Words. Perfons fufpected of Herefy are punifhed in the moft religious Kingdoms of *Spain*, triumphing efpecially in thefe Times, and worthy of fingular Praife, becaufe it fuffers not only no real Herefy, but even no Sufpicion of Herefy to remain even a Moment without a fuitable Cenfure."

In the Caufe of Canonical Purgation they proceed accord ng to this Manner and Cuftom. The Inquifitors, Bifhop, or his Vicar and Affeffors, or the learned Council meet together, and after difcuffing the Proofs, condemn the Criminal to purge himfelf by certain Witneffes. The Number of thefe Witneffes is arbitrary, and not precifely determined. Sometimes two Abbots were deputed. Cap. *in Juventute* de purgat. Canon. Sometimes there have been fourteen Compurgators. Eod. tit. Cap. *Inter follicitudines.* In the fame *Lucern. Inquif.* in voce *Purgatio Canonica.* Place there are twelve named, and in the Chapter *Ex tuarum*, feven or five are prefcribed. The Judge is to confider the Nature of the Perfon, Crime and Infamy, and then to order the Number of the Compurgators to be greater or lefs. For as to Perfons of greater Power, or of more Note, or who labour under greater Infamy, more are required, than from other mean and unknown Perfons, who can't fo eafily procure a large Number of Compurgators, to purge themfelves, becaufe all Compurgators muft come in voluntarily, and can't be compelled as other Witneffes. But yet ordinarily the Number is determined, that every Criminal fhall purge himfelf with about feven Witneffes, with this Addition, that if he fails in one, two, three or more, he fhall be looked on as fully convicted of the Crime.

Simanc. t. 56. §. 15. " Formerly, he who was defective in only one Expurgator, was condemned as a Convict, becaufe he was not purged by all. But when that was found to be very dangerous, and, as it might be faid, that he was purged by all who was purged by the greater Part, it was agreed on, that at the fame time when the Number of Purgators were agreed on, it fhould be determined, that if any one failed either of one, two or three, or more of them, he fhould be efteem'd as an Heretick Convict. For both thefe Things are entirely at the Pleafure of the Judge."

Thefe Witneffes muft be of the fame Order as the accufed or defamed Perfon himfelf, *i. e.* if he be a Religious they muft be religious ; if of the fecular Clergy, they muft be of the fecular Clergy ; if a Soldier, they muft be Soldiers. But here they take the Word Order in general, but don't extend it to any particular Divifions under it. So that if a Bifhop is to be purged, Abbots and religious Presbyters may be admitted with Bifhops in the Purgation. And fo in the others. But if fuch Compurgators are not to be found, t. 56. §. 11. there muft be chofen fome other good Men, Citizens or others. The Compurgators muft be Catholick Men, of an approved Life and good Reputation, who have not only been acquainted with his prefent, but with his former Converfation and Life, and who probably will not conceal the Truth, or

fay

say a Falshood, thro' Affection, Hatred, Fear, Money, or Entreaty. This Sentence is to be declared to the Criminal, who may appeal from it, and after his Appeal the Cause must be referred to the Council, except the Appeal appears to be frivolous. In such a Case the Inquisitors must not allow it, as it is in general appointed by *Clement* IV. and in particular by a certain Letter of the Council of the holy Inquisition.

If there be no Appeal from the Sentence, or if the Sentence be confirm'd after the Appeal, or if it be rejected as frivolous by the Inquisitors, the Criminal, in order to purge himself, must name so many good Men, for expurgatory Witnesses, as are mentioned in the Sentence of the Inquisitors. These Witnesses must be separately cited before the Inquisitors, and asked these three Things. 1. Whether they know the Criminal, and how long? 2. Whether the Criminal, or his Relations, or Kindred, have given and promised any Thing to them the said Witnesses, that they should favour the Criminal? 3. Whether they have offered themselves to purge the Criminal? After this they are all called to the Place where the Inquisitors give Audience, and the Criminal is brought to the Tribunal, and interrogated by the Inquisitors, whether he knows those Men, and whether they are the Persons which he hath named for his expurgatory Witnesses? He usually answers that he knows them, and that they are the same which he nominated. These Things are done before the Inquisitors only, and a Secretary or Notary, who commits every Thing to Writing; nor must any one be permitted to be present at this Purgation, no, not the Vicar of the ordinary Bishop, as is contained in a certain Letter of the Council of the Inquisition. However, the Ordinary or his Vicar must not be excluded when the Sentence of Purgation is given. Then the Inquisitor turns himself to the Expurgators, and speaks to them in this manner. *Know ye, Brethren, that the Criminal* N. *is accused and suspected of this and that Crime, on which account he is obliged to purge himself from this Suspicion, and you are named as Witnesses of his Innocence. And you* N. *answer by* p. 514> *God and the holy Gospels, whether thou hast committed those Crimes?* Having thus been sworn upon the Cross and the holy Gospels of God, to declare the Truth, the Inquisitors say to him, *Thou* N. *hast been accused of such and such a Crime,* specifying those Crimes only which favour of Heresy, *of which thou art vehemently suspected upon Consideration of the Merits of the Process, and therefore we demand of you, upon the Oath you have taken, whether you have committed, or done or believed these Crimes, or any one of them?* And when he hath given his Answer in the Presence of his Compurgators, he is carried back to Prison. Then the Inquisitor interrogates the Purgators, whether they have rightly understood all these Things? Who answer that they have. After this the Witnesses withdraw, and being each separately called in, the Inquisitor demands of them, upon a solemn Oath, whether they believe *N.* hath sworn true or false? And whatever they answer, must be faithfully written down by the Notary. All these Matters are almost to a Word contained in one of the *Seville* Instructions, *An.* 1500. *Cap.* 4. Formerly also, if a Person was publickly defamed for Heresy, he was injoined canonical Purgation publickly,

VOL. II.   E e   that

that he might publickly satisfy thofe by Purgation, whom he had publickly offended by the ungrateful Smell of Infamy, and he was therefore purged in that Place where he was known to be defamed. And if he had been defamed in feveral Places, he was obliged publickly to profefs in all of them the Catholick Faith, and to deteft the Herefy for which he was there defamed. The Form of the Oath, by which defamed Perfons were formerly obliged to purge themfelves, was prefcribed by the Council of *Tarracone. I* N. *fwear by Almighty God, and by thefe holy Gofpels of God, which are now in my Hands, before you the Lord* N. *Arch-Bifhop, or Bifhop, and before you who are here prefent, that I neither am, nor was one of the* Inzabbatati, Valdenfes, *poor Men of* Lyons, *nor an Heretick of any Sect of Herefy condemned by the Church, and that I do not believe, nor ever have believed their Errors, nor ever will, the whole Time of my Life. Yea, I profefs and proteft that I do believe, and always will for the future, believe the Catholick Faith, which the holy* Roman *and* Apoftolick *Church publickly holds, teaches and preaches, and which you my Lord Arch-Bifhop or Bifhop, and the other Prelates of the univerfal Church do hold, and publickly preach and teach.* The Form of the Oath, prefcribed to the Compurgators, is this : *I* N. *fwear by God, and by thefe four holy Gofpels of God, which I hold in my Hands, that I firmly believe, that fuch a one hath not been one of the* Inzabbatati, Valdenfes, *or poor Men of* Lyons, *nor an Heretick, nor a Believer of their Errors, and I firmly believe that in this Matter he hath fworn the Truth.* Having performed the Purgation injoined him, the Criminal muft be abfolved, and declared to be a Perfon of good Reputation, nor can he be afterwards proceeded againft upon the preceding Proofs. And thus the Infamy is removed, or the Effect of the Infamy of the Fact.

If he fails in his Purgation, *i. e.* if he can't procure fuch and fo many Purgers as he is injoined, he is efteem'd as a Convict, and condemned as an Heretick.

<small>Lucern. Inquif. Puig. Can.</small> But others ufe this Diftinction. If he can't procure fo many Witneffes, becaufe they don't believe he hath fworn the Truth, in fuch a Cafe he is accounted as a Convict, and deficient in his canonical Purgation. But if he can't procure them becaufe he is poor, or a Foreigner, and fo doth not know fo many Perfons in the whole Town, in this Cafe the Judge may relieve him at his Pleafure, upon confidering the Quality of the Perfon, Crime, and Infamy. So that if he can't procure fo many of the Clergy to be his Compurgators, they may admit Laicks, or Women for want of Men. And if for the fame Reafon they can't procure fo many of the Laity, they may believe his Oath alone. And inafmuch as one who is defective in his Purgation, is accounted as a Convict, they infer from hence, that if at any other Time he had fallen into Herefy, he ought now to be accounted as a Relapfe for the Defect of his Purgation, and, as fuch, to be delivered over to the fecular Court.

But if he refufes to purge himfelf he is excommunicated, and if with an hardned Mind he lies under this Excommunication for a Year, he is condemned as an Heretick. If after his Purgation he falls into the Herefy from
which

which he is purged, he is accounted a Relapfe, and as fuch is to be deliver'd over to the fecular Court. Cap. *Excommunicamus* 1. §. *Adjicimus.* Verfic. *Vel. fi poft purgationem,* &c. And Cap. *Ad abolendam,* §. *Illos quoque,* de hæret. This is particularly the Decree of the Council of *Narbonne,* Cap. 11. *And as to thofe who, after Abjuration or Purgation of their Error, fhall be found to have returned to the Error they have abjured, leave them to the fecular Judgment without any farther Hearing, to receive their due Punifhment. For 'tis enough that they have once deceived the Church by a falfe Converfion, efpecially where there is a very great Number of them,* &c. *Altho' if they are penitent, Penance is by no Means to be denied them.* But this properly takes place when any one is vehemently defamed for Herefy. An Infamy is faid to be vehement, when any one hath been oftentimes, or in many Places marked with Infamy, amongft good Men, or hath on this account been excluded their Company, and when there arife any Signs or Sufpicions increafing the Infamy of the Herefy, or if after any grievous Offence committed, *viz.* the deftroying the Images of the Saints, the burning of Churches, the Profanation of the Sacraments, and the like, any one is immediately looked upon as infamous. But if he falls into any other Herefy, from which he had not purged himfelf before, he is not accounted as a Relapfe.

If he humbles himfelf in his Purgation, and will fubmit to Penance, Simanc. he is to be admitted, and not deliver'd over to the fecular Court, unlefs he *t.* 56. happens to be a Relapfe ; for if a convicted Heretick is received when peni- §. 16. tent, much more is this Benefit of the Church to be granted to him who is convicted only by a kind of Prefumption and feigned Proof.

'Tis a Cuftom amongft many Inquifitors, that a Criminal vehemently §. 17. fufpected fhall be firft tortured, and afterwards forced to purge himfelf if he confeffes nothing. After this, when he is purged, he is obliged alfo to abjure, and after his Abjuration punifhed with other arbitrary Punifhments. But §. 18. others think it very unjuft, that any one fhould be condemned to feveral Punifhments for a fingle Crime, and inafmuch as every one of thefe Punifhments §. 20. is fufficient to purge away any Sufpicions, 'tis, without doubt, needlefs and unjuft, that a fufpected Criminal fhould be made to undergo many.

But as this Purgation depends wholly on the Pleafure of other Perfons, it Pegna, is a very deceitful and uncertain Thing, and therefore fhould not eafily be in- *in Direct.* joined Criminals by the Inquifitors. Thus the *Madrid* Inftruction, *An.* 1561. *p. 2. com.* cap. 47. *Canonical Purgation is, thro' the Wickednefs of Men, a very dangerous* 14. *Remedy, efpecially in thefe Times, and therefore 'tis not much ufed, and muft therefore be feldom practifed, and with great Caution.* Hence *Simancas* judges, that *tit.* 56. thofe who are born of *Jewifh* or *Moorifh* Parents, muft not be compelled to §. 1. this Purgation, becaufe it would be the fame Thing as to throw them directly into the Fire. For who doth not think ill of them, or at leaft doubt of their Innocence? And therefore he thinks it would be better to compel them by Abjuration, Torments, or arbitrary Punifhments. But if they are at any time condemned to this Purgation, and they can't procure fuch Compurgators as are required, others are to be admitted, tho' not altogether fo

fit,

fit, that he may not be wholly deprived of the Means of his Defence. And finally, he again and again admonishes the Inquisitors not rashly or easily to condemn any one to canonical Purgation, for this Reason, amongst others, that 'tis enough to sink the Criminal, if the Witnesses answer, that they don't know, or doubt, whether he swore true or false. And indeed who would not be doubtful in this Case, who knows that no one is condemned to Purgation who is not vehemently suspected. And therefore, in his Opinion they only are to be injoined Purgation, whose Reputation is of high Concern to the Christian People, *viz.* Bishops, Priests, Preachers, and others of the same Kind.

CHAP. XXIX.

How the PROCESS *is ended by Torture.*

WHEN the Person accused is not found guilty either by his own Confession, or the Evidence of the Fact, or legally producing the Witnesses, and when there is no such Evidence to support the Suspicion, as is necessary to his being condemned to abjure Heresy, he is condemned by an interlocutory Sentence to the Question and Torture, that if he confesses nothing when interrogated by Torture, he may be esteemed as free and innocent, and that if he confesses his Errors he may be converted and live. *For the same End,* says *Simancas,* Paul *delivered the* Corinthian *to Satan for the Destruction of his Flesh, that his Spirit might be saved.*

Cathal Instit. l. 65. §. 11. p. 2. Assert 31. §. 295, 296.

Royas however says, that *Ulpian* spoke well, when he affirmed, that Credit should not always be given to the Question, for 'tis a very frail and dangerous Thing, and oftentimes keeps the Truth from appearing. Some are fearful, who had rather lie and speak Falshood instead of Truth, than endure Torments. And yet in the Crime of Heresy, *Royas* would have the Judges peculiarly disposed, and ready to put Men to the Torture, because 'tis a Crime concealed in its Nature, and there is oftentimes great want of Proof. *Simancas* adds, that in secret Crimes a Judge ought to be more ready to inflict Torture than in others, and especially in Heresy, which lies hid in the Heart, and is more concealed than other Crimes. Add to this, that an Heretick's confessing, will be greatly profitable to himself and the whole Commonwealth.

tit. 65. §. 51.

The Cases, in which they proceed to the Torture in the Process of the Inquisition, are various. This however is a received Thing, that they are never to proceed to Torture, unless there be a Defect of other Proofs, and they think that the Truth can't otherwise be found out. Hence they do not proceed to the Torture, till after the Criminal hath a Copy of his Process, and he hath answered to all the Articles, and exhibited his Defences, and yet

cant'

can't make his Innocence appear plainly to the Judge, when at the same time he can't be fully convicted by Witnesses, or the Evidence of the Thing.

'Tis however difputed amongst the Doctors, whether the Proofs are to be given to the Criminal when the Procefs is carried on *Ex mero officio.* Some affirm it, fome deny it. Thefe different Opinions *Camillus Campegius* thus reconciles. Some Things precede all Inquifition, and are the Original of the Inquifition it felf, *viz.* fuch Things as excite the Judge himfelf to make Inquifition, or which any ways give Information of the Crime committed. Thefe Things are called Informations, which are received in Court, by which the Judge is certified of the Defamation. And he thinks the Doctors are to be underftood of thefe Things when they affirm, that a Judge proceeding *merely by Office*, and not at the Inftance of any one elfe, is not obliged to give a Copy of the Proofs. But if the Criminal denies that he is defamed of fuch a Crime, the Judge ought to inquire concerning the Fame and Infamy, and upon Knowledge of this muft begin to proceed to Inquifition concerning the Offence. Not that he is obliged to afcertain the Criminal of the Infamy it felf, becaufe 'tis fufficient that the Judge knows him to be defamed. So that if in this Cafe the Criminal demands a Copy, the Judge is not obliged to give it him. But if the Judge proceeds at the Inftance of another, he is obliged to give him a Copy of the Infamy it felf if he demands it. The Reafon of the Difference is this, that when any one proceeds *ex mero officio*, 'tis fufficient that the Infamy appears to the Judge, fo that there is no need of a formal Trial, becaufe there is no Adverfary to try the Caufe with; but the Trial is, as it were, between the Infamy it felf, which is in the Place of an Accufer, and the Anfwer of the Perfon under Inquifition. Add to this, that an Inquifition may be carried on, *ex mero officio*, without any preceding Infamy.

He adds farther, that a Copy of the Proofs is not to be given, when the Criminal is found contradicting himfelf, faultering or trembling. For fuch Contradiction, Faultring, or Trembling, when other external Proofs are wanting, may determine the Judge to proceed to Torture upon any one of them. But others fay that every Variation is not enough to order to the Torture. *Bernard Comenfis* writes to the fame Purpofe.

" In the Crime of Herefy the Judge or Inquifitor proceeds merely by Virtue of his Office, becaufe he doth not proceed upon the Accufation of an " Accufer, but upon Depofitions taken by Virtue of his Office, and therefore 'tis not neceffary that he fhould deliver the Criminal a Copy of the " Proofs and Articles. But *Pegna* teaches the contrary in his Annotations " upon the Word, *Tradere Copiam*.

If the Perfon to be put to the Queftion is caught contradicting himfelf, and there are at the fame time other Proofs fufficient for the Torture, both thefe Things muft be added in his Sentence. But if both of them don't concur, but only one of them, *i. e.* if he is caught in Contradiction without other Proofs, or if there are other Proofs, but no fuch Inconfiftency, let it be put in his Sentence juft as it appears. 'Tis

'Tis farther to be obferved, that the Judge muft take Care that it be diligently and diftinctly inferted at large by the Notary in the Acts, whether the Perfon interrogated anfwered with Refolution, or in a trembling Manner, what Signs he difcovered in his Face, whether Palenefs, or Tears, or Laughter, or Sweat, or Trembling ; becaufe, in Cafe of an Appeal, the fuperior Judge, who can't look on the Criminals and Witneffes perfonally, but only as they are defcribed in Writing, can't come to the Knowledge of thefe Particulars, unlefs they are defcribed at large by the firft Judge ; nor can the Judge appealed to prefume that there hath been any Inconfiftency, becaufe he knew, that if there had, it ought to have been expreffed in the Acts tranfmitted to him. And this is the more neceffary, left the Judge himfelf, upon Examination, fhould be proved to have ordered the Criminal to be tortured without Proof. This Inconfiftency muft be declared in Prefence of the inconfiftent Witnefs, when the Judge intends to punifh him on this Account.

And this is what *Campegius* particularly recommends to the Vicars or Commiffaries of the Inquifitor, or the other Deputies of the holy Offices, that they let the Inquifitor know how far Perfons, under Examination, are to be credited, which principally depends on their Looks. He thinks the fame ought to be diligently obferved, whether the Inquifitor himfelf, or his Vicar, makes the Examination, with refpect to thofe fkilful Perfons, whofe Advice they take, who alfo ought to know thefe Things.

But it depends wholly on the Pleafure of the Judge, whether or no the Perfon accufed fhall be tortured or not, upon Account of fuch Inconfiftency, Faultering, Contradiction, Trembling, Sweat, &c.

If there are Proofs fufficient for Inquifition and Arreft, but not for the Torture, a prudent Judge may collect fufficient Proofs for the Torture from fuch Inconfiftency, and the like.

But yet there is a Cafe given, in which a Perfon may be tortured, without any Proofs and Copy given, *viz.* when the Perfon under Inquifition is prefent, and will not anfwer. For then he is to be tortured not to extort a Confeffion, but an affirmative or negative Anfwer. Likewife if a Perfon under Inquifition doth not appear within the due Term, and is thereupon declared guilty of Contumacy, and afterwards comes to purge himfelf from fuch Contumacy, he may, without any other Proofs, be tortured upon Account of it.

Addit. in Zanch. c. 11. The fame Perfons give us the Opinion of *Gand*, who alledging feveral Reafons, concludes, that a common Report amounts by the Canon Law to an half full Proof, and is equal to the Evidence of one Witnefs, and that for this Reafon fuch common Report is fufficient to order to the Torture ; and this he attefts hath been ufually practifed by all the Affeffors, altho' the Judges generally act one way or the other, according to their different Opinions.

When the Fame is either vehement, or great, or flight, the Quality of the Perfons and Fact is to be confidered. For if the Fact be great, and the
Perfon

Perfon of great Worth, 'tis neceffary that this Fame fhould be either of
the whole City, or at leaft the greater Part of it. But if the Fact is incon-
fiderable, and reftrained to a certain Number of Perfons, who moft probably are acquainted with it, the Evidence of the major Part of them is enough
to prove the Fame. As if a Bifhop, living with his Canons, fhould be defamed for Fornication, fuch Infamy will be fufficiently proved by the major
Part of thofe Canons. But if the Fact be very fmall, and the Perfon mean,
the major Part of his Neighbourhood is enough.

Of all thefe Things *Pegna* gives us a diftinct Account. In this Caufe, *Direct.*
the Crime is faid to appear fo far as to inflict the Torture, when there is an *P. 3. com.*
half full Proof, or Proof fufficient for the Torture. Of thefe Proofs there *110.*
are feveral. Firft, Inconfiftency, not indeed of any kind, but fuch only as *Lucern.*
regards the main Subftance of the Crime, and in a Matter which it can't *voce Tor-*
be prefumed fhould be forgotten in fo little a while, which is left to the Judge *tura.*
to determine ; and when the Criminal himfelf doth not appear to be very ftu-
pid and forgetful. Secondly, when any one is found defamed for Herefy,
and 'tis farther proved that there is a Witnefs againft him who can teftify
from his own Knowledge, or that there is one or more vehement or violent
Proofs. Thirdly, If there is one Witnefs againft him who can teftify from
his own Knowledge, and at the fame Time there is one or more vehement or
violent Proofs againft him. Or if it be found that there are againft him feveral vehement or violent Proofs of Herefy, without any Infamy, or Witnefs
from his own Knowledge. But when thefe Proofs are vehement, or fufficient
for the Torture, is left to the Judge to determine.

However, the Inquifitors do fometimes fhamefully abufe this Liberty,
and rafhly proceed to the Torture of innocent Perfons, as will evidently appear by one Inftance, not to mention more, given us by *Gonfalvius.* " At *p. 181.*
" the fame time almoft they apprehended in the Inquifition at *Seville*, a noble
" Lady, *Joan Boborquia*, the Wife of *Francis Varquius*, a very eminent Man,
" and Lord of *Higuera*, and Daughter of *Peter Garfia Xerefius*, a wealthy
" Citizen of *Seville.* The Occafion of her Imprifonment was, that her Sifter,
" *Mary Boborquia*, a young Lady of eminent Piety, who was afterwards
" burnt for her pious Confeffion, had declared in her Torture, that fhe had
" feveral times converfed with her Sifter concerning her own Doctrine. When
" fhe was firft imprifoned, fhe was about fix Months gone with Child,
" upon which Account fhe was not fo ftraitly confined, nor ufed with that
" Cruelty which the other Prifoners were treated with, out of Regard to
" the Infant fhe carried in her. Eight Days after her Delivery they took the
" Child from her, and on the fifteenth fhut her clofe up, and made her under-
" go the Fate of the other Prifoners, and began to manage her Caufe with
" their ufual Arts and Rigour. In fo dreadful a Calamity fhe had only this
" Comfort, that a certain pious young Woman, who was afterwards burnt
" for her Religion by the Inquifitors, was allowed her for her Companion.
" This young Creature was, on a certain Day, carried out to her Torture,
" and being returned from it into her Jayl, fhe was fo fhaken, and had all
" her

" her Limbs fo miferably disjointed, that when fhe laid upon her Bed of
" Rufhes, it rather encreafed her Mifery than gave her Reft, fo that fhe
" could not turn her felf without the moft exceffive Pain.   In this Condition,
" as *Boborquia* had it not in her Power to fhew her any, or but very little
" outward Kindnefs, fhe endeavoured to comfort her Mind with great Ten-
" dernefs.   The Girl had fcarce began to recover from her Torture, when
" *Boborquia* was carried out to the fame Exercife, and was tortured with fuch
" diabolical Cruelty upon the Rack, that the Rope pierced and cut into the
" very Bones of her Arms, Thighs, and Legs, and in this Manner fhe was
" brought back to Prifon, juft ready to expire, the Blood immediately
" running out of her Mouth in great Plenty.   Undoubtedly they had burft
" her Bowels, infomuch that the eighth Day after her Torture fhe died.
" And when after all they could not procure fufficient Evidence to condemn
" her, tho' fought after and procured by all their Inquifitorial Arts, yet as
" the accufed Perfon was born in that Place, where they were obliged to
" give fome Account of the Affair to the People, and indeed could not by
" any Means diffemble it, in the firft Act of Triumph appointed after her
" Death, they commanded her Sentence to be pronounced in thefe Words.
" Becaufe this Lady died in Prifon, without Doubt fuppreffing the Caufes of
" it, and was found to be innocent upon infpecting and diligently examining
" her Caufe, therefore the holy Tribunal pronounces her free from all Char-
" ges brought againft her by the Fifcal, and abfolving her from any farther
" Procefs, doth reftore her both as to her Innocence and Reputation, and
" commands all her Effects which had been confifcated, to be reftored to
" thofe to whom they of Right belonged, *&c.*   And thus after they had
" murthered her by Torture with favage Cruelty, they pronounced her in-
" nocent."

Simanc.
t. 65.
§. 53.
　　　　When the Sentence is pronounced by which the Criminal is condemned to
the Torture, according to the Manner of the Inquifitorial Law and Proceffes, 'tis immediately to be notified to the Promotor of the Exchequer, that
he may either appeal from it, or demand the Execution of it, as it is contained in the Letters of the Inquifition.

Pegna, in
p. 3. *com.*
110.
　　　　Formerly the Torture was inflicted by Lay Judges upon Hereticks or
fufpected Perfons, according to the Conftitution of *Innocent* IV.   But becaufe
by this Means fecret Matters were oftentimes divulged, and great Inconveniencies to the Faith arofe from hence, they afterwards thought it more
convenient and wholefome, that the whole Cognifance and full Difcuffion of
thefe Crimes, which are merely Ecclefiaftical, fhould be confined to the Inquifitors.   And as this could not oftentimes be done without the Queftion,
'twas therefore provided, that the Inquifitors and Bifhops might torture Criminals for thefe Offences.   And upon this Account they had this Privilege
granted them, that if at any time they fhould happen to contract any Irregularity, they fhould mutually difpenfe with each other.   As appears
from the Refcript of *Urban* IV. beginning, *Ut negotium.*   And this is the Law
now in Practice.

The

The Bifhop and Inquifitor therefore meet together, and by an interlocutory Sentence, pronounce that the accufed Perfon is to be put to the Torture fuch a Day and fuch an Hour. Thus the *Madrid* Inftruction, *An.* 1561. *c.* 48. commands. *Let the Inquifitors and Ordinary meet together to pronounce Sentence of Torture, and in the fame Manner be prefent at the Execution of it, by reafon of the various Cafes that may happen under the Torture.* For neither the Bifhop without the Inquifitor, nor the Inquifitor without the Bifhop, or his Vicar, can put any one to the Torture. But if the Bifhop or his Vicar, upon Summons fent them, either refufes or neglects to be prefent within eight Days, the Inquifitor may proceed alone to the Torture ; or if one be not within Reach of the other, if he be abfent a great way off, then the other may proceed by himfelf. But what Place may be faid to be a great way off, is left at the Pleafure of the Judge to determine. However, the Bifhop and Inquifitor may depute each other, or fignify their Confent by Letters, which muft be done within eight Days after they are fummoned. In the Inqui-Carena, fition at *Cremona*, the Advocate of the Exchequer is prefent at the Torture,*p.* 1. *t.* 9. and the Inquifitor there fits in the Middle between the Vicar General on his*num.* 41. right Hand, and the Advocate on his left.

As to the Perfons who may be tortured, altho' in all other Caufes andPegna, Crimes fome Perfons are excepted, fuch as Doctors, Soldiers, Officers, No-*Ibid.* blemen, and their Sons, yet in this moft grievous and horrible Crime of He-*p.* 642, refy, there is no Privilege to defend any one, but all may be put to the 643. Torture, even Clergymen, Monks, and other Religious. But to prevent Excommunication, by grievoufly torturing or hurting them, and on Account of the Dignity with which they are invefted, they torture them more gently and mildly, unlefs the Heinoufnefs of the Crime, and the Strength of the E-vidence requires otherwife. As to fuch who are freed from being tortured for other Crimes upon Account of their Youth, or old Age, or being with Child, they are not to be tortured for Herefy. Perfons under twenty-five may be tortured for Sufpicion of Herefy, but not if they are under fourteen, but they may be terrified and beat. Neither is there any Exception of Place, altho' by antient Cuftom or municipal Laws the Torture is not otherwife to be inflicted there. Thus in the Kingdom of *Aragon* no Judge can order any Criminal to the Torture, but yet in Favour of the Faith any Perfons, even tho' privileged, may be tortured for Sufpicions of Herefy.

After the Sentence of Torture is pronounced, the Officers prepare them-felves to inflict it. "The Place of Torture in the *Spanish* Inquifition is gene-Gonfalv. "rally an under-ground and very dark Room, to which one enters thro' fe-*p.* 65, 66. "veral Doors. There is a Tribunal erected in it, in which the Inquifitor, "Infpector, and Secretary fit. When the Candles are lighted, and the Per-"fon to be tortured brought in, the Executioner, who was waiting for the "other, makes an aftonifhing and dreadful Appearance. He is covered "all over with a black Linen Garment down to his Feet, and tied clofe to his "Body. His Head and Face are all hid with a long black Cowl, only two "little Holes being left in it for him to fee thro'. All this is intended to

"ftrike the miferable Wretch with greater Terror in Mind and Body, when
"he fees himfelf going to be tortured by the Hands of one who thus looks
"like the very Devil.

Whilft the Officers are getting Things ready for the Torture, the Bifhop
and Inquifitor by themfelves, and other good Men zealous for the Faith,
endeavour to perfuade the Perfon to be tortured, freely to confefs the Truth,
and if he will not, they order the Officers to ftrip him, who do it in an In-

Simanc.
t. 65.
§. 50.
ftant. Clergymen however muft not be tortured by a Lay Officer or Torturer, unlefs they can't find any Clergymen who know how to do it, or are
willing, becaufe it would be in vain for the Judges to order any Clergyman
or Monk to the Torture, if there was no Body to inflict it; and therefore in
fuch a Cafe 'tis ufual to torture them by Lay Officers.

Whilft the Perfon to be tortured is ftripping, he is perfuaded to confefs the
Truth. If he refufes it, he is taken afide by certain good Men, and perfuaded to confefs, and told by them, that if he confeffes, he will not be put to
Death, but only be made to fwear that he will not return to the Herefy he
hath abjured. The Inquifitor and Bifhop promife the fame, unlefs the Perfon be a Relapfe.

If he is neither perfuaded by Threatnings or Promifes to confefs his Crime,
he is tortured either more lightly or grievoufly, according as his Crime requires, and frequently interrogated during the Torture, upon thofe Articles
for which he is put to it, beginning with the leffer ones, becaufe they think he
will fooner confefs the leffer Matters than the greater.

Royas, *p.* 2.
Affert. 20.
§ 226.
"The Criminals are with great Care and Diligence to be admonifhed by
"the Inquifitors, and efpecially when they are under Torture, that they
"fhould not by any Means bear falfe Witnefs againft themfelves or others,
"thro' Fear of Punifhments or Torments, but fpeak the Truth only. Nor
"may the Inquifitors promife Pardon or Forgivenefs of the Offence, to com-
"pel the Criminals to confefs Crimes which they have not committed, out of
"their great Zeal to inquire out the Truth. And fuch a falfe Confeffion the
"accufed Perfon may fafely revoke."

Simane.
t. 65.
§ 54.55.
The Inquifitors themfelves muft interrogate the Criminals during their
Torture, nor can they commit this Bufinefs to others, unlefs they are engaged in other important Affairs, in which Cafe they may depute certain
good and fkilful Men for the Purpofe. 1 *Inftruct. Hifpal.* c. 18. Altho' in
other Nations Criminals are publickly tortured, yet in *Spain* 'tis forbidden
by the Royal Law, for any to be prefent whilft they are torturing, befides
the Judges, Secretaries and Torturers. The Inquifitors muft alfo chufe proper Torturers, born of antient Chriftians, who muft be bound by Oath, by
no Means to difcover their Secrets, nor to blab out any Thing that is faid.

§. 56.
The Judges alfo ufually proteft, that if the Criminal fhould happen to die
under his Torture, or by reafon of it, or fhould fuffer the Lofs of any of his
Limbs, 'tis not to be imputed to them, but to the Criminal himfelf, who

§. 59.
will not plainly confefs the Truth before he is tortured. An Heretick may
not only be interrogated concerning himfelf, but in general alfo concerning
his

his Companions and Accomplices in his Crime, his Teachers and his Disciples, for he ought to discover them, tho' he be not interrogated; but when he is interrogated concerning them, he is much more obliged to discover them than his Accomplices in any other the most grievous Crimes. A Person also § 6ͻ. suspected of Heresy, and fully convicted, may be tortured upon another Account, *i. e.* to discover his Companions and Accomplices in the Crime. This must be done when he boggles, or 'tis half fully proved at least that he was actually present with them, or hath such Companions and Accomplices in his Crime; for in this Case he is not tortured as a Criminal, but as a Witness. But he who makes full Confession of himself, is not tortured upon a different Account; whereas if he be a Negative, he may be tortured upon another Account, to discover his Accomplices and other Hereticks, tho' he be fully convicted himself, and it be half fully proved that he hath such Accompli- ces. *Instruct. Madrid.* An. 1561. c. 45. The Reason of the Difference in these Royas, Cases is this, because he who confesses against himself, would certainly much *p.* 2. rather confess against other Hereticks if he knew them. But 'tis otherwise *Assert.* 34. when the Criminal is a Negative.

Whilst these Things are doing, the Notary writes every Thing down in the Process, as what Tortures were inflicted, concerning what Matters the Cri- minal was interrogated, and what he answered. If by these Tortures they can't draw from him a Confession, they shew him other kind of Tortures, and tell him he must undergo all of them, unless he confesses the Truth. If neither by this Means they can extort the Truth, they may to terrify him and engage him to confess, assign the second or third Day to continue, not to repeat the Torture, till he hath undergone all those Kinds of them to which he is condemned.

The Degrees of Torture formerly used were five, which were inflicted in their Turn, and are described by *Julius Clarus.* _Know therefore, says he, that_ Pract. _there are five Degrees of Torture, viz. First, the being threatned to be tortured._ crim. § fin. _Secondly, being carried to the Place of Torture. Thirdly, by stripping and binding._ qu. 64. _Fourthly, the being hoisted up on the Rack. Fifthly, Squassation._ Verhc.

Nunc de

This Stripping is performed without any Regard to Humanity or Honour, gradibus. not only to Men, but to Women and Virgins, tho' the most virtuous and Gonsalv. chast, of whom they have sometimes many in their Prisons. For they cause *p.* 67. them to be stripped, even to their very Shifts, which they afterwards take off, forgive the Expression, even to their *Pudenda,* and then put on them strait Linen Drawers, and then make their Arms naked quite up to their Shoulders. As to Squassation, 'tis thus performed: The Prisoner hath his Hands *p.* 7ͻ. bound behind his Back, and Weights tied to his Feet, and then he is drawn up on high, till his Head reaches the very Pully. He is kept hanging in this Manner for some time, that by the Greatness of the Weight hanging at his Feet, all his Joints and Limbs may be dreadfully stretched, and on a sudden he is let down with a Jirk, by the slacking the Rope, but kept from coming quite to the Ground, by which terrible Shake, his Arms and Legs are all disjointed, whereby he is put to the most exquisite Pain; the Shock which

he

he receives by the sudden Stop of his Fall, and the Weight at his Feet stretching his whole Body more intensely and cruelly.

In the next Paragraph, *Et Audivi*, he gives a more distinct Explication of this Matter, and reckons up three Degrees of Torture. *The first is to terrify, which comprehends not only Threatnings to Torture, but the being carried to the Place of Torments, the being stripped and bound ; unless such Binding should happen to be too severe and hard, and perform'd with a Twist, as is the Custom of most Judges. Thus it was practised upon a certain Physician of* Olezo, *who suffered more by being bound, than others in the very Torture. And therefore such Binding may be equalled to the Torture it self. The second Degree is, to put to the Torture, or to interrogate by Torture. This is done by hoisting a Person up, and keeping him hanging for a considerable Time. The third is to torture by Squassation, which is performed amongst us by one Jirk of the Rope. But if the Senate commands that the Person be well or severely thus tortured, they give two Jirks of the Rope.* Antonius Drogus, *in his Annotations to this Place, says, That you may have the perfect modern Practice, observe, that when the Senate orders, let him be interrogated by Torture, the Person is lifted or hoisted up, but not put to the Squassation. If the Senate orders, let him be tortured, he must then undergo the Squassation once, being first interrogated as he is hanging upon the Rope and Engine. If it orders, let him be well tortured, 'tis understood that he must suffer two Squassations. If it orders, let him be severely tortured, 'tis understood of three Squassations, at three different Times within an Hour. If it says very severely, 'tis understood that it must be done with Twisting,— and Weights at the Feet. In this Case the Senate generally expresses the Twisting, or any other particular Manner which they intend, and the Judge may proceed to every Severity not reaching to Death. But when it says, very severely even unto Death, then the Criminal's Life is in immediate Danger.*

The like Method of Torture was formerly practised in the Inquisition at *Tholouse*, as appears from several Places in the Book of Sentences. Thus *fol.* 67. at the End of the Sentence of *William Sicred*, jun. we read, *Nor would he judicially confess concerning the aforesaid, till he was put in Jayl, and hoisted up a little upon the Rope.* And in *fol.* 131. we read that *William Cavallerii*, after a considerable Time, revoked what he had before confessed, *saying, that he confessed nothing concerning Heresy, but what was forced from him. by the Violence of Torment.* And finally, *fol.* 132. in the Sentence of Friar *Bernard Deliciosi*, of the Order of Minors, amongst other Things, this was imputed to him as a Crime, *that he justified those who were apprehended for Heresy, and condemned for it, and ordered to perpetual Imprisonment and other Punishments, and that tho' they were true Catholicks, they had confessed Heresy of themselves and others, only thro' the Violence of their Torments, and were unjustly condemned.*

Cap. 23. The Author of the History of the Inquisition at *Goa* tells us, that the Torture now practised in the *Portuguese* Inquisition is exceeding cruel. *In the Months of* November *and* December, *I heard every Day in the Morning the Cries and Groans of those who were put to the Question, which is so very cruel, that I have seen several of both Sexes who have been ever after lame. In this Tribunal they regard neither Age nor Sex, nor Condition of Persons, but all without Distinction are tortured, when 'tis for the Interest of this Tribunal.* The

The Method of Torturing, and the Degree of Tortures now ufed in the *Spanish* Inquifition, will be well underftood from the Hiftory of *Ifaac Orobio*, a *Jew*, and Doctor of Phyfick, who was accufed to the Inquifition as a *Jew*, by a certain *Moor* his Servant, who had by his Order before this been whipped for thieving ; and four Years after this he was again accufed by a certain Enemy of his for another Fact, which would have proved him a *Jew*. But *Orobio* obftinately denied that he was one. I will here give the Account of his Torture, as I had it from his own Mouth. After three whole Years which he had been in Jayl, and feveral Examinations, and the Difcovery of the Crimes to him of which he was accufed, in order to his Confeffion, and his conftant Denial of them, he was at length carried out of his Jayl, and thro' feveral Turnings brought to the Place of Torture. This was towards the Evening. It was a large under-ground Room, arched, and the Walls covered with black Hangings. The Candlefticks were faftned to the Wall, and the whole Room enlightned with Candles placed in them. At one End of it there was an inclofed Place like a Clofet, where the Inquifitor and Notary fat at a Table, fo that the Place feemed to him as the very Manfion of Death, every Thing appearing fo terrible and awful. Here the Inquifitor again admonifhed him to confefs the Truth, before his Torments began. When he anfwered he had told the Truth, the Inquifitor gravely protefted, that fince he was fo obftinate as to fuffer the Torture, the holy Office would be innocent, if he fhould fhed his Blood, or even expire in his Torments. When he had faid this, they put a Linen Garment over his Body, and drew it fo very clofe on each Side, as almoft fqueezed him to Death. When he was almoft dying, they flackned at once the Sides of the Garment, and after he began to breathe again, the fudden Alteration put him to the moft grievous Anguifh and Pain. When he had overcome this Torture, the fame Admonition was repeated, that he would confefs the Truth in order to prevent farther Torment. And as he perfifted in his Denial, they tied his Thumbs fo very tite with fmall Cords, as made the Extremities of them greatly fwell, and caufed the Blood to fpurt out from under his Nails. After this he was placed with his Back againft a Wall, and fixed upon a little Bench. Into the Wall were faftned little Iron Pullies, thro' which there were Ropes drawn, and tied round his Body in feveral Places, and efpecially his Arms and Legs. The Executioner drawing thefe Ropes with great Violence, faftned his Body with them to the Wall, fo that his Hands and Feet, and efpecially his Fingers and Toes being bound fo ftraitly with them, put him to the moft exquifite Pain, and feemed to him juft as tho' he had been diffolving in Flames. In the Midft of thefe Torments the Torturer, of a fudden, drew the Bench from under him, fo that the miferable Wretch hung by the Cords without any Thing to fupport him, and by the Weight of his Body drew the Knots yet much clofer. After this a new kind of Torture fucceeded. There was an Inftrument like a fmall Ladder, made of two upright Pieces of Wood, and five crofs ones fharpned before. This the Torturer placed over againft him, and by a certain proper Motion ftruck it with great Violence againft both his Shins, fo that he received upon each of
them.

them at once five violent Strokes, which put him to such intolerable Anguish that he fainted away. After he came to himself, they inflicted on him the last Torture. The Torturer tied Ropes about *Orobio's* Wrists, and then put those Ropes about his own Back, which was covered with Leather, to prevent his hurting himself. Then falling backwards, and putting his Feet up against the Wall, he drew them with all his Might, till they cut thro' *Orobio's* Flesh even to the very Bones; and this Torture was repeated thrice, the Ropes being tied about his Arms about the Distance of two Fingers Breadth from the former Wound, and drawn with the same Violence. But it happen'd, that as the Ropes were drawing the second time, they slid into the first Wound, which caused so great an Effusion of Blood, that he seemed to be dying. Upon this the Physician and Surgeon, who are always ready, were sent for out of a neighbouring Apartment, to ask their Advice, whether the Torture could be continued without Danger of Death, least the Ecclesiastical Judges should be guilty of an Irregularity if the Criminal should die in his Torments. They, who were far from being Enemies to *Orobio,* answered, that he had Strength enough to endure the rest of the Torture, and hereby preserved him from having the Tortures he had already endured repeated on him, because his Sentence was, that he should suffer them all at one time, one after another. So that if at any time they are forced to leave off thro' Fear of Death, all the Tortures, even those already suffered, must be successively inflicted, to satisfy the Sentence. Upon this the Torture was repeated the third time, and then it ended. After this he was bound up in his own Cloaths, and carried back to his Prison, and was scarce healed of his Wounds in seventy Days. And inasmuch as he made no Confession under his Torture, he was condemned, not as one convicted, but suspected of *Judaism,* to wear for two whole Years the infamous Habit called *Sambenito,* and after that Term to perpetual Banishment from the Kingdom of *Seville.*

p. 19.   *Erneſtus Eremundus Friſius,* in his History of the Low Country Disturbances, gives us an Accouut from *Gonſalvius,* of another Kind of Torture. There is a Wooden Bench, which they call the Wooden Horse, made hollow like a Trough, so as to contain a Man lying on his Back at full Length, about the Middle of which there is a round Bar laid across, upon which the Back of the Person is placed, so that he lies upon the Bar instead of being let into the Bottom of the Trough, with his Feet much higher than his Head. As he is lying in this Posture, his Arms, Thighs and Shins are tied round with small Cords or Strings, which being drawn with Screws at proper Distances from each other, cut into the very Bones, so as to be no longer discerned*. Besides this, the Torturer throws over his Mouth and Nostrels a thin Cloath, so that he is scarce able to breathe thro' them, and in the mean

Gonſalv.   while a small Stream of Water like a Thread, not Drop by Drop, falls from
p. 76, 77. on high, upon the Mouth of the Person lying in this miserable Condition,

---

* These two Methods of Punishment seem to be taken from the two different Forms of the antient *Equleus.*

and

and fo eafily finks down the thin Cloth to the Bottom of his Throat, fo that there is no Poffibility of breathing, his Mouth being ftopped with Water, and his Noftrels with the Cloth, fo that the poor Wretch is in the fame Ago. ny, as Perfons ready to die, and breathing out their laft. When this Cloth is drawn out of his Throat, as it often is, that he may anfwer to the Que- ftions, it is all wet with Water and Blood, and is like pulling his Bowels thro' his Mouth. There is alfo another Kind of Torture peculiar to this Tribunal, which they call the Fire. They order a large Iron Chafin-difh full of lighted Char-coal, to be brought in, and held clofe to the Soles of the tortured Per- fon's Feet, greafed over with Lard, fo that the Heat of the Fire may more quickly pierce thro' them.

This is Inquifition by Torture, when there is only half full Proof of their Crime. However, at other Times Torments are fometimes inflicted upon Perfons condemned to Death, as a Punifhment preceding that of Death. Of this we have a remarkable Inftance in *William Lithgow*, an *Englifhman*, who, as he tells us in his Travels, was taken up as a Spy in *Mallagom*, a City of *Spain*, and was expofed to the moft cruel Torments upon the Wooden Horfe. But when nothing could be extorted from him, he was delivered to the In- quifition as an Heretick, becaufe his Journal abounded with Blafphemies againft the Pope and the Virgin *Mary*. When he confeffed himfelf a Pro- teftant before the Inquifitor, he was admonifhed to convert himfelf to the *Ro- man* Church, and was allowed eight Days to deliberate on it. In the mean while the Inquifitor and Jefuites came to him often, fometimes wheedling him, fometimes threatning and reproaching him, and fometimes arguing with him. At length they endeavour'd to overcome his Conftancy by kind Affu- rances and Promifes. But all in vain. And therefore as he was immovably fixed, he was condemned in the Beginning of *Lent*, to fuffer the Night fol- lowing eleven moft cruel Torments, and after *Eafter* to be carried privately to *Granada*, there to be burnt at Midnight, and his Afhes to be fcattered into the Air: When Night came on his Fetters were taken off, then he was ftripped naked, put upon his Knees, and his Hands lift up by Force; after which opening his Mouth with Iron Inftruments, they filled his Belly with Water till it came out of his Jaws. Then they tied a Rope hard about his Neck, and in this Condition rolled him feven times the whole Length of the Room, till he was almoft quite ftrangled. After this they tied a fmall Cord about both his great Toes, and hung him up thereby with his Head towards the Ground, and then cut the Rope about his Neck, letting him remain in this Condition, till all the Water difcharged it felf out of his Mouth; fo that he was laid on the Ground as juft dead, and had his Irons put on him again. But beyond all Expectation, and by a very fingular Accident, he was deliver'd out of Jayl, efcaped Death, and fortunately fail'd home to *England*. But this Method of Torturing doth not belong to this Place, where we are treat- ing only of the Inquifition of a Crime not yet fully proved.

If when the Perfon is decently tortured he confeffes nothing, he is allowed to go away free, and if he demands of his Judges that he be cleared by Sen- tence,

tence, they can't deny it him; and they pronounce, that having diligently examined the Merits of the Procefs, they find nothing of the Crime of which he was accufed legally proved againft him.   There is extant in this Cafe a Decree in the *Madrid* Inftruction, An. 1561. cap. 54. *If the Criminal over-comes the Torture, the Inquifitor muft then weigh and confider the Nature of the Proofs, and the Degree and Form, or Manner of the Torture, and the Difpofition or Nature and Age of the tortured Criminal.   All which Things confidered, if it ap-pears that he hath fufficiently purged himfelf of all Marks, let them abfolve him from any farther Procefs.   But if there be any Reafon and Caufe, upon confidering the aforefaid Circumftances, to think that the Torture was not inflicted with due Rigour, then let them inflict on him either a light or vehement Abjuration, or fome pecuniary Penalty.   Altho' this ought not to be done without great Confideration, and unlefs the Proofs are not thought fufficiently purged off.*

Pegna, in Direct. p. 122.

   But if, when under the Queftion, he confeffes, 'tis written in the Procefs, after which he is carried to another Place, where he hath no View of the Tortures, and there his Confeffion made during his Torments is read over to him, and he is interrogated feveral times till the Confeffion be made.   But here *Gonfalvius* obferves, that when the Prifoner is carried to Audience, they make him pafs by the Door of the Room where the Torture is inflicted, where the Executioner fhews himfelf on purpofe to be feen in that Shape of a Devil I have defcribed before, that as he paffes by, he may, by feeing him, be forced to feel, as it were, over again his paft Torments.   The Space of Time allowed between the Torture and the Ratification of the Con-feffion, is determined by the *Madrid* Inftruction, An. 1561. cap. 53. *Twenty-four Hours after the Torture the Criminal muft ratify his Confeffion, and if he re-tracts it, the Remedies provided by Law muft be made ufe of.   And at the time when the Torture is inflicted the Notary muft write down the Hour, as alfo the Time of the Ratification, left if fuch Ratification fhould be made the next Day, a Doubt may arife, whether it was after or before the twenty-four Hours.   If the Criminal ra-tifies his Confeffion made under Torture, and the Inquifitors are fatisfied of his good Confeffion and Converfion, they may admit him to Reconciliation, altho' his Confef-fion was made under Torture.   They muft however prudently take Care how they re-ceive fuch Perfons, and confider the Nature of the Herefies they have confeffed, and whether they have learnt them from others, or have taught them themfelves to others, upon Account of the Danger that may enfue hereby.*

p. 73.

   I am not able to fay what was the Space of Time between the Torture and the Ratification of the Confeffion made under it, formerly in the Inquifition at *Tholoufe*, nor whether the Criminal was difmiffed if he retracted his Con-feffion after the Torture was over.   There is one Inftance only of *William Cavallerii*, in the Book of the Sentences of the *Tholoufe* Inquifition, who be-ing in Court, and not under the Queftion or Torture, but in a different Place, and before different Officers, and three whole Days after the Torture was over, again confeffed the Things he had before confeffed under Torture, and perfevered in them feveral Times.   But afterwards he retracted all, faying, that he confeffed thro' the Violence of his Torments, who yet is faid to be
convicted

convicted by certain Witneffes, fome of them fingle, of certain heretical Facts. This Perfon was pronounced an Heretick by a definitive Sentence, and as fuch deliver'd over to the fecular Court. But upon this Condition, that if within fifteen Days, each five of which were affigned him as fo many Terms, he would confefs his Crimes, and with a pure Heart and Faith un-feigned return to the Ecclefiaftical Unity, abjure all Herefy, and fwear fim-ply to obey the Commands of the Church and Inquifitors, he fhould be ab-folved from Excommunication, and condemned to perpetual Imprifon-ment.

If there be very ftrong Evidence againft the Criminal, if new Proofs arife, *Simanc.* if the Crime objected to him be very heinous, and the Difcoveries againft *t. 65.* him undoubted, if he was not fufficiently tortured before, he may be tor- *§. 75.* tured again, but then only *when his Mind and Body is able to endure it.*

We read in the firft *Seville* Inftruction, c. 15. *That he who afterwards retracts §. 80. the Confeffion extorted from him by Torture, muft folemnly abjure thofe Errors of which he was defamed, and fuffer fome pecuniary Penalty at the Pleafure of his Judges, upon account of the Infamy and Sufpicion yet remaining againft him.* But for all this the Inquifitors oftentimes order the Queftion in this Cafe to be repeated.

Skilful Judges ufually enter a Proteft in the Acts of the Procefs, that they intend to carry on the Torture fome other Day, that they may be able to repeat it. But *Royas* fays, fome Criminals are fo crafty, that he hath of- *Par. 1.* ten actually feen them immediately confefs their Fault when put to the Tor- *Affert. 31.* ture, and after twenty four Hours retract their Confeffion when they fhould *§. 300.* confirm it, and when tortured again confefs again, and retract again, and re-peat the fame as often as they are tortured. In which Cafe, to prevent the Procefs from being never finifhed, he thinks they are to be punifhed with a very grievous arbitrary Penalty, becaufe of fo many Variations, which occa-fion Proofs and bad Prefumptions. For by the fame Reafon any one may be tortured again, he may be punifhed in an extraordinaty Manner.

If he doth not perfift in his firft Confeffion, and is not fufficiently tortured, he may be put to the Torture again, not by way of Repetition, but Conti-nuation of it ; but they do not agree how often it may be repeated, when the Confeffion extorted by it is retracted. Some affirm it may be repeated once only, others that it may be often. *Eymerick*'s Opinion is, that a Perfon fuf-ficiently tortured ought to be difmiffed freely, if he retracts what he con-feffed by Torture. But *Simancas* fays, that a Criminal muft not be condemned *n.65.§.67,* for a Confeffion drawn out by Torture, unlefs he afterwards perfeveres in it. *63, 69.* 'Tis the fame in Law, if it be extorted by Fear, or Dread of impending Tor-ments. The Confeffion is then faid to be extorted thro' Fear of Torments, when the Criminal is carried to the Place in which the Torture is inflicted, and there ftript of his Cloaths, or bound, or fo terrified by the Judge, as that he hath great Reafon to believe the Torture will be inflicted. For 'tis not enough if the Judge frightens him but flightly in any other Place, unlefs it be fuch a Fear as may affect a Perfon of Refolution. Hence the Light of the Inquifitors fays, *In voce* " Altho' the Judge fays to the Criminal, when he is out of the Place *of Tortura.*

" Torture, either confefs, or I will order you to the Torture, frightening
" him by this Means as much as he can, upon hearing of which he makes
" his Confeffion, in fuch a Cafe the Confeffion is not faid to be made thro'
" Fear of Torments, becaufe the Terror it felf is but flight.

But if he perfifts in his Confeffion, owns his Fault, and asks Pardon of
the Church, he is condemned as guilty of Herefy by his own Confeffion, but
as penitent. But if he obftinately perfifts in Herefy, he is condemned, and
delivered over to the fecular Arm to be punifhed with Death. If the accufed Perfon is found to have fallen into Herefy, or there is otherwife Evidence
proved againft him, upon account of which he is obliged to abjure, as lightly or vehemently fufpected of Herefy, he muft not be tortured on this Account; but if befides this he denies fome Things not fufficiently proved, and
there be Proofs fufficient to put him to the Queftion, and he accordingly is
tortured, but confeffes nothing, he is not to be abfolved, but is to be proceeded againft according to the Things proved, and muft be commanded to
abjure either as fufpected, or found guilty, as the Merits of the Procefs require. Or if he confeffes any Thing by Torture, he muft be forced alfo
to abjure it.

C H A P. XXX.

How the PROCESS *is ended againft a Perfon fufpected of Herefy, as
alfo againft one both fufpected and defamed.*

Direct.
p.3.n.161,
162.
com. 40.
WHEN a Perfon accufed of Herefy is found to be only flightly fufpected of it, he is confidered either as fufpected publickly or privately.
If he is publickly fufpected, this was formerly the Manner of his Abjuration. On the preceding Lord's Day the Inquifitor proclaims, that on fuch a
Day he will make a Sermon concerning the Faith, commanding all to be
prefent at it. When the Day comes, the Perfon to abjure is brought to the
Church, in which the Council hath determined that he fhall make his Abjuration. There he is placed upon a Scaffold, erected near the Altar, in the
Midft of the People, and is not allowed to fit, but ftands on it that all may
fee him, bare-headed, and with the Keepers ftanding round him. The Sermon being made on the Mafs, to the People and Clergy there prefent, the Inquifitor fays publickly, that the Perfon there placed on the Scaffold is fufpected, from fuch and fuch Appearances and Actions, of the Herefy that hath been
refuted in the publick Sermon, and that therefore 'tis fit that he fhould purge
himfelf from it, by abjuring it as one flightly fufpected. Having faid this,
a Book of the Gofpels is placed before him, on which laying his Hands he
abjures his Herefy. In this Oath he not only fwears that he holds that
Faith which the *Roman* Church believes, but alfo that he abjures every Herefy.

refy that extols it felf againft the holy *Roman* and Apoftolick Church, and particularly the Herefy of which he was flightly fufpected, naming that He: refy: And that if he fhall do any of the aforefaid things for the future, he willingly fubmits to the Penalties appointed by Law to one who thus ab_ jures, and is ready to undergo every Penance, as well for the things he hath faid and done, as for thofe concerning which he is defervedly fufpected of Herefy, which they fhall lay on him, and that with all his Power he will endeavour to fulfill it. After this Abjuration the Inquifitor fays to him, *Son, Thou haft purged away by this Abjuration, the Sufpicion, which, not without Caufe, we entertained of you. Henceforth take heed to your felf. that you don't fall into this abjured Herefy; for altho' if you repent, you would not be delivered over to the fe-cular Arm, becaufe you have abjured as one flightly fufpected only, and not vehement-ly, yet you would be much more feverely punifhed than if you had not abjured, and inftead of being flightly fufpected, would become vehemently fo, and made to abjure as fuch. And if you fhould fall again, you would fuffer the Punifhment due to re-lapfed Perfons, and be delivered over without Mercy to the fecular Court, to be punifhed with Death.*

If he hath not been publickly fufpected, he abjures privately after the fame Manner in the Epifcopal Palace, or Inquifitors Hall. 'Tis now the Cuftom for flightly fufpected Perfons to make all their Abjurations in pri-vate, whether the Fact be publick or not. Afterwards he is injoin'd Penance for what he hath committed, and upon Account of which he was thus fufpected.

If he is vehemently fufpected, he is placed in like Manner upon a Scaffold, *n.* 166. & and after he hath taken his Oath upon the Gofpels, his Abjuration is deli-*feq. com.* vered him in Writing to read before all the People if he can. If he can't 4ᵗ. read, the Notary, or fome Religious, or Clergyman reads it by Sentences, paufing between each till the other hath repeated it after him, and fo on till the whole Abjuration is gone thro'. In this Abjuration he fubmits him-felf to the Punifhments due to Relapfes, if he ever after falls into the He-refy he hath abjured. After the Abjuration is made, the Bifhop admonifhes him, that if ever hereafter he doth, or fays any Thing by which it can be proved, that he hath fallen into the Herefy he hath abjured, he will be de-livered over to the fecular Court without Mercy. Then he injoins him Pe-nance, and commands him to obferve it, adding this Threatning, that other-wife he will become a Relapfe, and may, and ought to be judged as an Im-penitent. However, fufpected Perfons, whether it be flightly or vehemently, are not condemned to wear Croffes, nor to perpetual Imprifonment, becaufe thefe are the Punifhments of penitent Hereticks; tho' fometimes they are ordered to wear for a while the *Sambenito*, according to the Nature of their Offence. Ordinarily they are injoin'd to ftand on certain holy Days in the Gates of fuch and fuch Churches, holding a burning Taper of fuch a Weight in their Hands, and to go a certain Pilgrimage; fometimes alfo they are im-prifoned for a while, and afterwards difpofed of as is thought proper.

Gon-

p. 192.	*Gonſalvius* gives us ſome Inſtances of theſe Puniſhments. " There was at
" *Seville* a certain poor Man, who daily maintained himſelf and his Family
" by the Sweat of his Brows. A certain Parſon detained his Wife from him
" by Violence, neither the Inquiſition nor any other Tribunal puniſhing this
" heinous Injury. As the poor Man was one Day talking about Purgatory
" with ſome other Perſons, of his own Circumſtances, he happened to ſay,
" rather out of ruſtick Simplicity, than any certain Deſign, that he truly had
" enough of Purgatory already, by the raſcally Parſon's violently detaining
" from him his Wife. This Speech was reported to the good Parſon, and
" gave him an Handle to double the poor Man's Injury, by accuſing him to
" the Inquiſitors, as having a falſe Opinion concerning Purgatory. And
" this the holy Tribunal thought more worthy of Puniſhment than the Par-
" ſon's Wickedneſs. The poor Wretch was taken up for this trifling Speech,
" kept in the Inquiſitors Jayl for two whole Years, and at length being
" brought in Proceſſion, was condemned to wear the *Sambenito* for three
" Years in a private Jayl ; and when they were expired, to be diſmiſſed, or
" kept longer in Priſon, as the Lords Inquiſitors ſhould think fit. Neither
" did they ſpare the poor Creature any thing of his little Subſtance, tho'
" they did his Wife to the Parſon, but adjudged all the Remains of what he
" had after his long Impriſonment to the Exchequer of the Inquiſition.

p. 195.	" In the ſame Proceſſion there was alſo brought forth a reputable Citizen
" of *Seville*, as being ſuſpected of *Lutheraniſm*, without his Cloak and his
" Hat, and carrying a Wax Taper in his Hand, after having exhauſted his
" Purſe of 100 Ducats towards the Expences of the holy Tribunal, and a
" Year's Impriſonment in the Jayl of the Inquiſition, and having abjured as
" one vehemently ſuſpected, only becauſe he was found to have ſaid, that
" thoſe immoderate Expences, and on theſe Accounts the *Spaniards* are pro-
" digiouſly extravagant, which were laid out in erecting thoſe large Paper
" or Linen Buildings, which the common People corruptly call Monuments,
" to the Honour of Chriſt now in Heaven upon *Holy Thurſday*, and alſo thoſe
" which were expended on the Feſtival of *Corpus Chriſti*, would be more ac-
" ceptable to God, if they were laid out upon poor Perſons, or in placing
p. 196.	" out to good Perſons poor Orphan Girls. Two young Students added to
" the Number in that Proceſſion. One becauſe he had written in his Pocket-
" Book ſome Verſes made by a nameleſs Author, ſo artificially, as that the
" ſame Words might be interpreted ſo as to contain the higheſt Commenda-
" tion of or Reflection upon *Luther*. Upon this Account only, after two
" Years Impriſonment, he was brought forth in Proceſſion, without his Hat
" and Cloak, carrying a Wax Taper, after which he was baniſhed for three
" Years from the whole Country of *Seville*, made to abjure as lightly ſuſpect-
" ed, and puniſhed with a Fine. The other underwent the ſame Cenſure,
" only for tranſcribing the Verſes for their artful Compoſition, excepting
" only that he commuted his Baniſhment for 100 Ducats towards the Ex-
" pences of the holy Tribunal."

If he is violently fufpected, altho' it may be that he is no Heretick, yet by the Conftruction of the Law he is accounted one, and judged as fuch. What this Judgment is, fhall be hereafter explained.

If he is found fufpected of Herefy, and alfo defamed, he is condemned firft to purge himfelf by his Compurgators, and after he hath thus purged himfelf as a defamed Perfon, he muft abjure as one fufpected of Herefy, whether it be lightly, vehemently, or violently, according to the Manner in which fuch Perfons are dealt with, and he is injoined Penance, heavier or lighter, according as his Sufpicion is greater or lefs. When the Sentence is pronounced, and committed to Execution, it may be difpenfed with, mitigated, or commuted, as the Affair, or the Amendment and Humility of the Penitent deferves it.

[What the Manner is of proceeding at this Day in the Inquifition general at *Rome*, againft Perfons fufpected of Herefy, we have a moft clear Inftance, in the Sentence pronounced againft *Galileus Galilei*, a famous Aftronomer, becaufe he taught, that the Sun ftood immovable in the Midft of the Univerfe, and that the Earth moved round it as about its proper Center. I have thought it worth while to tranfcribe it here intire, that it may appear, that Opinions purely Aftronomical, and that have nothing to do with Religion, and which can neither be of any Advantage or Diflervice to Piety, which foever fide of the Queftion is defended, are a fufficient Argument to the *Roman* Inquifitors, to render any one vehemently fufpected of Herefy, after the Prelates of that Church have once determined on one fide, and to injoin him a folemn Abjuration, which it felf is a very grievous Punifhment in the Inquifition. The Sentence is thus:

" We *Gafpar Borgia*, of the Title of *Sainéte Croix de Hierufalem.*

" Friar *Felix Centino d'Afcoli*, of the Title of St. *Anaftafia.*

" *Guido Bentivoglio*, of the Title of St. *Mary del Populo.*

" Friar *Defiderius Seaglia di Cremona*, of the Title of St. *Charles.*

" Friar *Antony Barberini*, called *Mefroy.*

" *Lewis Zacchia*, of the Title of St. *Peter*, in *Vinculis*, called St. *Sixto.*

" *Berlingerius Gypfius*, of the Title of St. *Auftin.*

" *Fabritius Verofpius*, called *Presbyter*, of the Title of St. *Lawrence*, *in pane*
" *& perna.*

" *Francifcus Barberini*, of St. *Laurence*, in *Damafo*, and

" *Martius Ginettus*, of the Title of St. *Maria Nuova*, Deacons, by the
" Mercy of God, Cardinals of the holy *Roman* Church, fpecially deputed
" by the holy Apoftolick See, to be Inquifitors againft heretical Pravity
" throughout the whole Chriftian Republick.

" Whereas you *Galileus*, Son of the late *Vincent Galileus* of *Florence*, aged
" Seventy, were informed againft in the Year 1615. in this holy Office,
" that you maintained as true a certain falfe Doctrine, held by many, *viz.*
" that the Sun was in the Center of the World, and immovable, and that
" the Earth moved even with a daily Motion. Likewife that you have had
" certain Scholars, whom you have taught the fame Doctrine. Likewife
" that

" that you have kept up a Correſpondence with certain *German* Mathemati-
" cians concerning the ſame. Likewiſe that you have publiſhed certain
" Letters concerning the ſolar Spots, in which you have explained the
" ſame Doctrine as true, and that you did anſwer the Objections, which in
" ſeveral Places were made againſt you, drawn from the holy Scripture, by
" gloſſing the ſaid Scripture according to your own Senſe, and finally, where-
" as there hath been ſhewn us a Copy of a Writing, under the Form of a
" Letter, which is reported to be written by you, to one who was formerly
" your Scholar, in which you followed the Hypotheſes of *Copernicus,* contain-
" ing certain Propoſitions contrary to the true Senſe and Authority of the
" holy Scripture.

" This holy Tribunal therefore being willing to provide againſt the Incon-
" veniencies and Dangers which have proceeded and increaſed upon this Ac-
" count to the Ruin of the holy Faith : By the Command of the ſaid *N.* and of
" the moſt eminent Lords the Lords Cardinals of this ſupream and univerſal In-
" quiſition, two Propoſitions concerning the Fixedneſs of the Sun, and the Mo-
" tion of the Earth have been thus qualified by the Qualificator Divines, *viz.*

" *That the Sun is in the Center of the World, and unmovable with a local*
" *Motion, is an abſurd Propoſition, falſe in Philoſophy, and formally heretical,*
" *becauſe 'tis expreſsly contrary to the holy Scripture.*
" *That the Earth is not the Center of the World, nor immovable, but moves*
" *even with a daily Motion, is likewiſe an abſurd Propoſition, and falſe in*
" *Philoſophy, and, theologically conſidered, at leaſt erroneous in the Faith.*

" But as it pleaſed us in the mean while to proceed kindly with you, it was
" decreed in the ſacred Congregation, held before our Lord *N. Feb.* 25. *An.*
" 1616. that the moſt eminent Lord Cardinal *Bellarmine* ſhould command
" you, that you ſhould entirely depart from the aforeſaid falſe Doctrine ;
" and in caſe you ſhould refuſe to obey him, you ſhould be commanded by
" the Commiſſary of the holy Office, to forſake the ſaid Doctrine, and that
" you ſhould not teach it to others, nor defend it, nor treat concerning it ;
" and that if you would not ſubmit to this Order you ſhould be put in Jayl ;
" and in Execution of the ſaid Decree, you were commanded by the ſaid
" Commiſſary of the holy Office, for the Time being, on the Day follow-
" ing in the Palace, before the aforeſaid moſt eminent Lord Cardinal *Bellar-*
" *mine,* after you had been kindly admoniſhed by the ſaid Lord Cardinal, in
" the Preſence of the Notary and Witneſſes, that you ſhould wholly deſiſt
" from the ſaid falſe Opinion ; and that it ſhould not be lawful for you
" for the future, to defend it, or by any Means to teach it, neither by Word
" nor Writings : And upon promiſing Obedience you were diſmiſſed.

" And that ſo pernicious a Doctrine might be wholly removed, and ſhould
" not ſpread any farther, to the great Damage of the Catholick Truth, there
" came forth a Decree from the ſacred Congregation, of an Index, in which the
" Books treating of the ſaid Doctrine were prohibited, which Doctrine was
" declared

" declared to be falfe, and altogether contrary to the holy and divine Scripture ;
" and whereas at length there appeared this Book publifhed at *Florence* the
" Year next enfuing, the Title of which fhewed that you were the Author of
" it, becaufe it ran thus, *Dialogo di Galileo Galilei delle duo maffime fifteme del*
" *mundo, Tolomeico & Copernicano :* And whereas the facred Congregation at
" the fame Time knew, that by the Impreffion of the aforefaid Book, the
" falfe Opinion concerning the Motion of the Earth, and the Fixednefs
" of the Sun, did daily gain Ground, the aforefaid Book was diligently con-
" fidered, and there plainly appeared therein a Difobedience to the aforefaid
" Command, of which you had Intimation, becaufe, in the faid Book, you de-
" fended the aforefaid Opinion already condemned, and declared to be fo in
" your own Prefence, inafmuch as you endeavour by various round about Me-
" thods in the faid Book, to perfuade Perfons, that you leave the faid Opinion
" as undecided, and yet greatly probable ; which is really likewife a very
" grievous Error, becaufe no Opinion can by any Means be probable, which
" hath been declared and determined to be contrary to the divine Scripture.

" Wherefore, by our Command, you are cited to this holy Office, in
" which being examined upon Oath, you have owned the faid Book as writ-
" ten and printed by you : Likewife you have confeffed, that about ten or
" twelve Years ago you began to write the faid Book, after you had received
" the above Command : Likewife that you defired Licence to publifh it,
" without fignifying to the Perfons who gave you fuch Licence, that you
" were commanded not to hold, defend, or by any Means to teach fuch Do-
" ctrine.

" You have likewife confeffed, that the aforefaid Book is fo composed in
" feveral Places, as that the Reader may think that the Arguments brought
" for the falfe Side of the Queftion are fo laid down, as by their Strength
" rather to convince the Underftanding, than to be eafily capable of being
" anfwered ; excufing your felf that you have ran into an Error, fo foreign
" as you have declared from your Intention, becaufe you have wrote by way
" of Dialogue, and upon Account of that natural Pleafure which every one
" takes in his own Subtleties, and in fhewing himfelf more fhrewd than the
" Generality of Men, in finding out ingenious Arguments that have the Ap-
" pearance of Truth, even tho' it be only in Favour of falfe Propo-
" fitions.

" And whereas there was affigned to you a convenient Term for your ma-
" king your Defence, you produced a Certificate under the Hand of the
" moft eminent Lord Cardinal *Bellarmine*, procured, as you faid, by you,
" that you might defend your felf from the Calumnies of your Enemies, who
" reported that you had abjured, and was punifhed by the holy Office, in
" which Teftimonial 'tis declared that you had not abjured, neither been
" punifhed, but only that you had been acquainted with the Declaration
" made by our Lord, and publifhed by the facred Congregation of the
" Index in which 'tis contained, that the Doctrine of the Earth's Mo-
" tion, and the Sun's Fixednefs is contrary to the holy Scripture, and there-
" fore

" fore ought neither to be defended or maintained. And in as much as there-
" in there is no Mention of two Particulars contained in the Command gi-
" ven you, *viz. Docere, to teach* ; and *quovis modo, by any Means* ; 'tis to
" be believed, that in a Courfe of fourteen or fixteen Years, thofe Particu-
" lars might have been forgotten by you, and that on this Account you con-
" cealed the Injunction you had been ferved with, when you demanded Li-
" cence to print your Book, and that you faid all this not to excufe your Error,
" but that it might be imputed to vain Ambition rather than to Malice. But
" this very Teftimonial produced in your Defence, hath made your Caufe
" rather worfe, for as much as therein it is faid, that the aforefaid Opinion is
" contrary to holy Scripture, and yet you have dared to treat of it, to de-
" fend it, and perfuade others 'tis probable. Neither can you receive any
" Advantage by the Licence you artfully and fraudulently procured, becaufe
" you did not fignify the Injunction you had received.

" And whereas it appears to us, that you have not declared to us the
" whole Truth concerning your Intention, we have judged that 'tis neceffary
" to proceed to a rigorous Examination of you, in which, without any Pre-
" judice to thofe Things which you have confeffed, and which have been
" produced againft you, concerning your faid Intention, you have anfwered
" in a Catholick Manner. And therefore upon feeing and maturely confi-
" dering the Merits of this your Caufe, together with your aforefaid Con-
" feffions and Excufes, and all other Things by Law to be feen and con-
" fidered, we have proceeded againft you to the underwritten definitive Sen-
" tence.

" Calling therefore upon the moft holy Name of our Lord Jefus Chrift,
" and his moft glorious Mother *Mary*, ever a Virgin, we do by this our de-
" finitive Sentence, which, fitting on our Tribunal, we pronounce in thefe
" Writings, with the Advice and Judgment of the Reverend Mafters, Do-
" ctors of Divinity, and both Laws, our Confultors, concerning the Caufe
" and Caufes now depending before us, between the magnificent *Carolus Sin-*
" *cerus*, Doctor of both Laws, and Procurator of the Exchequer of this holy
" Office, on one Part, and you *Galileus Galilei*, the Criminal here under In-
" quifition, by this prefent written Procefs, examined, and confeffed as above,
" on the other Part, fay, judge and declare that you the aforefaid *Galileus*
" have, upon account of thofe Things which are produced in the written
" Procefs, and which you have confeffed as above, render'd your felf vehe-
" mently fufpected of Herefy to this holy Office ; *i. e.* that you have believed
" and held a Doctrine falfe, and contrary to the facred and divine Scriptures,
" *viz.* that the Sun is the Center of the Orb of the Earth, and doth
" not move from the Eaft to the Weft, and that the Earth moves, and is
" not the Center of the World, and that this may be held and defended as a
" probable Opinion, after it hath been declared and determined to be con-
" trary to the facred Scripture ; and confequently that you have incurred all
" the Cenfures and Penalties appointed and promulgated by the facred Ca-
" nons, and other general and particular Conftitutions, againft fuch Offen-

" ders,

" ders ; from which 'tis our Pleasure that you should be absolved, provi-
" ded that you do first, with a sincere Heart, and Faith unfeigned, ab-
" jure, curse, and detest before us the aforesaid Errors and Heresies, and
" every other Error and Heresy, contrary to the Catholick and Apostolick
" *Roman* Church, in that Form which shall be exhibited to you by us.

" But least your grievous and pernicious Error and Transgression should go
" altogether unpunished, and that you your self may be render'd more cau-
" tious for the future, and that you may be an Example to others, that
" they may abstain from such Crimes, we decree that the Book of Dialogues
" of *Galileus Galilei,* shall be prohibited by a publick Edict, and we con-
" demn you formally to be imprisoned in this holy Office for a Time de-
" terminable at our Pleasure ; and we enjoin you, under the Title of a fa-
" lutary Penance, that for the three Years ensuing you repeat, once in a
" Week, the seven penitential Psalms ; reserving to our selves the Power of
" moderating, changing, or wholly, or in part removing the aforesaid Pe-
" nalties and Penances.

" And thus we say, pronounce, and by our Sentence declare, ordain,
" condemn and reserve in this, and every other better Manner and Form,
" which we can, and ought to do by Law.

Thus we the under-written Cardinals pronounce.

F. Cardinal *d' Afcoli.*
G. Cardinal *Bentivoglio.*
F. Cardinal *de Cremona.*
Fr. Cardinal *a Mefroy.*
B. Cardinal *Gypfius.*
F. Cardinal *Verofpius.*
M. Cardinal *Ginettus.*

The Abjuration of *Galileus.*

I Galileus, *Son of the late* Vincentius Galileus, *a* Florentine, *aged Seventy,
being here personally upon my Trial, and on my Knees before you, the most
Eminent and Reverend the Lords Cardinals, Inquisitors General of the universal
Christian Common-wealth, against heretical Pravity, having before my Eyes the
most holy Gospels, which I touch with my proper Hands, do swear that I always
have believed, and do now believe, and by the Help of God, hereafter will believe
all that, which the holy Catholick and Apostolick* Roman *Church doth hold, preach
and teach. But because, after I had been juridically enjoined and commanded by this
holy Office, that I should wholly forsake that false Opinion, which holds, that the
Sun is the Center, and immovable, and that I should not hold, defend, nor by any
Manner, neither by Word or Writing, teach the aforesaid false Doctrine, and after
it was notified to me that the aforesaid Doctrine was contrary to the holy Scripture,
I have written and printed a Book, in which I treat of the said Doctrine already
condemned, and produce Reasons of great Force in Favour of it, without giving any*

Anſwer to them, I am therefore judged by the holy Office as vehemently ſuſpected of Hereſy, viz. that I have held and believed that the Sun is the Center of the World, and immovable, and that the Earth is not the Center, but moves.

Being therefore willing to remove from the Minds of your Eminences, and of every Catholick Chriſtian, this vehement Suſpicion legally conceived againſt me, I do with a ſincere Heart and Faith unfeigned, abjure, curſe and deteſt the above-ſaid Errors and Hereſies, and in general every other Error and Sect contrary to the aforeſaid holy Church ; and I ſwear, that for the future, I will never more ſay or aſſert, either by Word or Writing, any Thing to give Occaſion for the like Suſpicion ; but that if I ſhall know any Heretick, or Perſon ſuſpected of Hereſy, I will inform againſt him to this holy Office, or to the Inquiſitor or Ordinary of the Place in which I ſhall be. Moreover, I ſwear and promiſe, that I will fulfill and wholly obſerve all the Penances which are, or ſhall be injoined me by this holy Office. But if, what God forbid, it ſhall happen that I ſhould act contrary by any Words of mine, to my Promiſes, Pro-teſtations and Oaths, I do ſubject my ſelf to all the Penalties and Puniſhments which have been ordained and publiſh'd againſt ſuch Offenders, by the ſacred Canons and other Conſtitutions general and particular. So help me God and his holy Goſpels, which I touch with my own proper Hands.

I the aboveſaid Galileus Galilei *have abjured, ſworn, promiſed and obliged. my ſelf as above, and in Teſtimony of theſe Things have ſubſcribed with my own proper Hand this preſent Writing of my Abjuration, and have repeated it Word for Word at* Rome, *in the Convent of* Minerva, *this 22d Day of* July, *An.* 1633.

I Galileus Galilei, *have abjured as above, with my own proper Hand.*

CHAP. XXXI.

How the PROCESS *againſt an Heretick confeſſed, and penitent, ends, and firſt of* ABJURATION.

Direct. p. 3.
n. 188.
ſim. 44.

IF any Heretick is informed againſt, and upon Oath confeſſes his Hereſy judicially before the Biſhop or Inquiſitor, but profeſſes, that upon In-formation of the Biſhop or Inquiſitor he will depart from it, return to the Boſom of the Church, and abjure that and every other Hereſy, he is not de-liver'd to the ſecular Arm, but differently puniſhed according to the Heinouſ-neſs of the Crime. For in the firſt Place all ſuch Perſons are compelled pub-lickly to abjure their Hereſy in the Church before all the People ; but they are not permitted to excuſe themſelves, or in any manner to teſtify their Innocence, leſt the People ſhould be offended by thinking him unjuſtly con-demned. Before the Perſon who is to abjure, there is placed the Book of the Goſpels, and then he puts off his Hat, falls on his Knees, and putting his Hands on the Book, reads, if he knows how to read, his Abjuration ; if he can't read, the Notary or ſome religious Perſon or Clergyman reads for him,

and

and making a Paufe, the Perfon abjuring repeats what is read; then the Notary goes on, and the Abjurer always repeats his Words, with a loud Voice, fo as to be heard by all, till the whole Abjuration is read over even to the End.

Formerly, before Perfons violently fufpected of Herefy abjured, the Bifhop or Inquifitor ufed thus to addrefs to him. *My Son, we violently fufpect you of Herefy, upon account of thofe Things 'tis declared you have committed, upon account of which you are by Law to be condemned as an Heretick. Therefore confider and attend to what I fay to you. If you will fo depart from the faid Herefy or Herefies, as to be willing now here publickly to abjure them, and patiently to undergo the Penance which we enjoin you, the Church and we, as the Vicars of Chrift, will receive you to Mercy. But we will enjoin you a Penance, which you may well bear, and abfolve you from the Sentence of Excommunication, which you were under, that you may be faved, and have Glory in the future World. But if you will not abjure, nor fubmit to Penance, we will immediately deliver you to the fecular Arm, and fo you will deftroy together both Body and Soul. Which therefore will you chufe, to abjure and be faved, or to refufe to abjure and to be damned?* If he fays, I will not abjure, and perfifts in it, he is delivered over to the fecular Court, as fhall be afterwards fhewn. But if he fays that he will abjure, the Abjuration is made according to the Forms prefcribed. But now the Bifhop ufes no fuch Difcourfe, but before the Criminal is brought upon the Scaffold, all Methods are diligently made ufe of for his Converfion, and if he be truly converted, he will abjure without any fuch foregoing Admonition.

This Abjuration is injoined all who return from Herefy, and even all fufpected upon any Account of Herefy; nor is any one, tho' otherwife privileged, and of great Dignity, excepted. Even Boys of fourteen, and Girls of twelve Years old, are compelled to it, according to the Decree of the Council of *Tholoufe,* An. 1229. cap. 11. *Let all Perfons, as well Men as Women, the Males from fourteen Years old and upwards, and the Females from twelve, abjure every Herefy extolling it felf againft the holy and Catholick Church of* Rome, *and the Orthodox Faith, under whatfoever Name it be ranked.* The Council of *Biterre* hath decreed the fame. And this perhaps is the fame which is cited in a Book concerning the Form of proceeding againft Hereticks. *And that by the Help of the Lord Herefy may be the better extirpated, and the Faith fooner planted in the Earth, caufe the Statutes and Laws publifhed on thefe Accounts by the Apoftolick See, and the Legates and Princes thereof, to be moft fully obferved. Farthermore, caufe all Perfons, Males and Females, the Males from fourteen, the Females from twelve Years old and upwards, to abjure every Herefy, and to fwear that they will keep the Faith, and defend the Catholick Church, and perfecute Hereticks, as is above more fully and largely contained, in Reference to them, in the Oath which thofe who are to be reconciled muft make, writing down the Names of all of them, as well in the Acts of the Inquifition, as their refpective Parifhes, and if any prefent fhalt not take fuch Oath within* 15 *Days after their Return, let them be accounted fufpected of Herefy. Take Care alfo that this univerfal Abjuration be performed as foon as you can, either by your felves, or your Notaries or Writers, or by*

Direct.p.3. com. 40.

H h 2 *other*

other Ecclefiaftical Perfons, whom you fhall think fit to entruft with the Affair, cau-fing alfo the Counts, Barons, Rulers and Confuls of Cities and other Places, to fwear, that when it fhall be required of them, they will faithfully and effectually affift the Church againft Hereticks and their Accomplices, according to their Office and Power, and bona fide, *endeavour to exterminate with all their Might, out of the Places fubject to their Jurifdiction, all fuch Perfons as fhall be marked for Hereticks by the Church. And whoever fhall relapfe after fuch Abjuration, and fhall not obferve and do the Penances injoined them, let them fuffer the Punifhment due to relapfed Perfons.*

But the Inftruction of *Valadolid,* made *An.* 1488. *c.* 12. fays thus: *Likewife they have appointed, that fuch who are not come to the Age of Difcretion, as well Males as Females, fhall not be obliged to abjure publickly, till after the faid Years of Difcretion, which is the twelfth Year of Women, and the fourteenth of Men. And in this Senfe is to be underftood the Statute of the* Seville *Inftructions, which regulates this Matter. And when they fhall have exceeded the aforefaid Years, let them ab-jure what they have offended in when they were of younger Years, if they have been capable of Deceit.* From whence it may be collected that Boys and Girls might abjure before this Age, tho' not publickly. Finally, the Council of *Nar-bonne* hath thus decreed, cap. 6. *Caufe all Perfons to confefs and abjure their Faults publickly in an Affembly of the Clergy and People, and to fwear according to what is more fully contained in the Apoftolick Commands, and in the Statutes of our Lord the Pope of* Rome, *unlefs where the Slightnefs of the Fault, and the Enormity (poffibly it fhould have been read the Smallnefs) of the Scandal, fhould be thought in Reafon to deferve an Abatement of this Rigour. And as to every one of them, let there be drawn up publick Inftruments containing the Crimes, Abjurations, Promi-fes and Penances of the faid Perfons, left the Truth, long concealed, but now fo won-derfully and mercifully difcovered, fhould farther perifh or difappear.*

If the Criminal knows how to write, he muft fubfcribe his Abjuration ; if he doth not know how to write, or can't, the Inquifitor and Notary muft fubfcribe for him. This is prefcribed by the Inquifitors of *Spain,* by the *Madrid* In-ftruction, *An.* 1561. c. 42. *Let the Abjuration which the Criminals make, be put at the End of the Sentence, and the Pronunciation of it, which the Criminals fhall fubfcribe, if they know how to write, putting their Names to it ; but if they know not how to write, then one of the Inquifitors and the Notary fhall fubfcribe for them.*

When the Abjuration is made, becaufe every Heretick is excommunicated, they are abfolved from Excommunication upon this Condition, *viz.* if they return to the Unity of the Catholick Faith with a true Heart and Faith un-feigned, and obferve the Commands injoined them ; which is exprefsly ad-ded, that if they fhould not obferve them, it may appear that they were not abfolved.

Thofe who commit heretical and apoftate Facts, muft be thus reconciled ac-cording to the Practice received in the Tribunal of the Inquifition. If they voluntarily appear and fay, that they did not believe they ought to do fo, but retained the Faith in their Heart, then they abjure as vehemently fufpected, and have other falutary Penances injoined them. If they fay that they both

did

did fo, and believed that they ought to do fo, then they abjure as formally Hereticks or Apoftates, and are more grievoufly punifhed, efpecially if they have committed heretical or apoftate Actions voluntarily, or without being compelled by Fear, or by a flight Occafion of Fear. If they do not appear voluntarily, and yet confefs heretical and apoftate Actions, but deny the evil Intention, then they are to be tortured upon fuch Intention, that it may be known whether they have really believed fo or not; and if after the legal Torture they perfift in the negative, faying, they had no ill Intention, then they likewife abjure as vehemently fufpected. As to thofe who have committed fuch Things thro' grievous Fear, 'tis determined that 'tis likely they had no evil Intention. But if they confefs the evil Intention or Error of the Mind, then they are compelled to abjure as formal Hereticks or Apoftates, upon their being willing to return to the Unity of the Church, and are farther condemned as converted Hereticks to other Punifhments and Penances, which we fhall hereafter defcribe. But in order to their being more grievoufly or mildly punifhed, the Nature of that Fear they were under is confidered, and the Circumftances of the Perfon offending; as whether he was a Youth, or a Man, learned or unskilful, one of the Laity or Clergy, or Religious, and the like Things which ufually leffen or encreafe the Offences. There are alfo others who pronounce heretical Words which have no Excufe, *viz.* in Jeft, or Anger, or mere Simplicity, on which Offenders the Inquifitors may lay pecuniary Mulcts.

As to fuch Facts in which there appears nothing of an Infidel Right, and which therefore only render a Perfon fufpected, but don't demonftrate him to be an Heretick, no one is proceeded againft as an Heretick, or Believer of Hereticks, upon account of them, but only as a fufpected Perfon; becaufe fuch Facts are fometimes committed thro' carnal Affection, fometimes thro' the Entreaties of Friends, fometimes alfo thro' Corruption by Money. *Lucern. Inquif vre. Pœna pecun.*

The Form of Abjuration formerly ufed in the Inquifition of *Tholoufe*, oftentimes occurs in the Book of Sentences. Herein they abjure *every Herefy extolling it felf againft the Catholick Faith of our Lord Jefus Chrift, and the holy Roman Church, and all Belief of Hereticks of every condemned Sect whatfoever, by whatfoever Names they are called, and all favouring, receiving and defending of them, and Communication with them, under the Punifhment due by Law to thofe who relapfe into the Herefy they have judicially abjured.* They moreover promife and fwear, *that they will purfue, and reveal and difcover Hereticks, and their Believers and Favourers, and Receivers and Defenders, and who fly for Herefy, whenfoever and wherefoever they know them to be, or any one of them; and that they will obey and be obedient, that they will hold and keep, and defend the Catholick Faith of our Lord Jefus Chrift, which the holy Church of* Rome *preaches and obferves; and that they will obey and be obedient to the Commands of the Church, and the Inquifitors and their Succeffors, and that they will receive, and, according to their Power, fulfil and perfect the Penance injoined them, and that they will never fly nor abfent themfelves thro' Contumacy and Wilfulnefs.* This Form in another Place is a little alter'd. *fol. 100. 140.*

Iq

In Ecclefiaftical Hiftory we find two remarkable Forms of Abjuration prefcribed to certain famous Doctors by the Church of *Rome*. The one is that of *Berengarius*, the other that of *Jerom* of *Prague*.

Berengarius abjured in thefe Words. *I-*Berengarius, *an unworthy Deacon of the Church of St.* Maurice *of Angiers, acknowledging the true and Apoftolick Faith, do anathematife every Herefy, and particularly that for which I have hitherto been defamed ; which endeavours to prove, that the Bread and Wine placed upon the Altar are, after Confecration, only a Sacrament, and not the true Body and Blood of our Lord Jefus Chrift, and cannot be fenfibly, but only facramentally, handled or broken by the Hands of the Priefts, nor chewed to Pieces by the Teeth of the Faithful. But I confent to the holy Church of* Rome *and Apoftolick See, and with my Mouth and Heart confefs that I hold that Faith concerning the Sacrament of the Lord's Table, which our Lord and venerable Pope* Nicholas, *and this holy Synod, by Evangelick and Apoftolick Authority, hath delivered to be held and confirmed to me, viz. that the Bread and Wine placed on the Altar, are, after Confecration, not only a Sacrament, but also the true Body and Blood of our Lord Jefus Chrift, and is broken fenfibly, not only facramentally, but in Truth, by the Hands of the Priefts, and chewed by the Teeth of the Faithful, fwearing by the holy and confubftantial Trinity, and by thefe moft holy Gofpels of Chrift. And as to thofe, who fhall go contrary to this Faith, I pronounce them, with their Opinions and Followers, worthy of eternal Damnation. And if I my felf fhall at any time prefume to think or preach any Thing contrary to this, I fubject my felf to the Severity of the Canons. I have voluntarily fubfcribed to this, being read over and thro'.*

The Abjuration of *Jerom* of *Prague* is longer. *I* Jerom *of Prague, Mafter of the liberal Arts, acknowledging the true Catholick Church and Apoftolick Faith, do anathematife every Herefy, and efpecially that for which I have hitherto been defamed, and which in former Times* John Wycleff *and* John Hufs *have dogmatifed and held in their Works, Books, or Sermons to the Clergy and People, for which Reafon the aforefaid Perfons, with their Opinions and Errors, have been condemned as Hereticks by this Synod of* Conftance, *and their aforefaid Doctrine fententially damned, efpecially in fome Articles expreffed in the Sentences pronounced againft them by this holy Council. I confent alfo to the holy Church of* Rome, *and the Apoftolick See, and this holy Council, and with my Mouth and Heart profefs it, in and concerning all Things, and efpecially concerning the Keys, Sacraments, Orders, Offices and Ecclefiaftical Cenfures, Indulgencies, and Relicts of Saints, and Ecclefiaftical Liberty, as alfo concerning the Ceremonies, and all other Things pertaining to the Chriftian Religion, even as the Church of* Rome *and Apoftolick See, and this holy Council profefs ; and particularly that moft of the aforefaid Articles are notorioufly heretical, and long fince condemned by the holy Fathers ; fome of them blafphemous, others erroneous, others fcandalous, fome of them offenfive to pious Ears, and others of them rafh and feditious ; and the aforefaid Articles have been lately condemned as fuch by this holy Council, and it hath been forbidden all and fingular Catholicks, under Penalty of an Anathema, ever for the future to prefume to preach, dogmatife, or to hold the faid Articles, or any one of them.*

After

After these Things follows a long Abjuration of a certain triangular Figure used by him, and called the Shield of Faith, and then he goes on. *Besides, that it may appear to all what were the Reasons why I have been refuted to adhere to and favour the said late* John Huss, *I notify by these Presents, that where as I had often heard him in his Preachings and Schools, I believed him to be a good Man, and to go in nothing contrary to the Traditions of our holy Mother Church and the holy Doctors ; yea, as there were certain Articles lately offered to me in this City, laid down by him, and condemned by this holy Council, I did not at first View believe them to be his, at least in that Form: And when I had heard it affirmed by several famous Doctors and Masters in Divinity, that they were his, I desired, for my full Information, that they would shew me the Books of his own Hand-writing, in which the said Articles are said to be contained, which being shewn to me written with his own proper Hand, which I know as well as my own, I found all and singular the said Articles were written by him in that Form in which they were condemned. From whence I have found, and do find, that he and his Doctrine, with their Followers, have been deservedly condemned and rejected as heretical and mad, by the holy Council. And all these Things aforesaid I affirm purely, and without any Reserve, as one who is now fully and sufficiently informed of the aforesaid Sentences pronounced by this holy Council against the Doctrines of the said late* John Wycleff *and* John Huss, *and against their Persons ; to which Sentences I do, as a devoted Catholick, in and concerning all Things humbly consent and adhere.*

After this he abjured the Opinion, that Faith was to take place even in the future Life, and concludes thus. *Moreover I swear both by the holy Trinty, and by these most holy Gospels, that I will always, and without Doubt, remain in the Truth of the Catholick Church, and pronounce all those who shall oppose this Faith, together with their Opinions, worthy of eternal Damnation. And if I my self shall at any time, which God forbid, presume to think or preach any Thing to the contrary, I subject my self to the Severity of the Canons, and shall be found obnoxious to eternal Punishment. And this Confession and Writing of my own Profession I do voluntarily offer to this holy general Council, and have subscribed the same with my own proper Hand, and have written all these Things.* This Abjuration was made September 15, 1415.

Jerom of *Prague* seems to have been terrified by the Condemnation of *John Huss*, and to have fallen thro' the Infirmity of human Nature. But afterwards he took Courage, and with great Resolution revoked his Abjuration in the Synod, and was, *May* 30, 1416. pronounced, declared, and condemned by the Council of *Constance* as an Heretick, and relapsed into Heresy, excommunicated, and anathematised, and as such deliver'd over to the secular Arm ; and being brought to the Stake he suffer'd Death, and endured the severest Torments of the Fire, with a truly heroick Mind.

And in this Manner all Persons are forced to abjure, which the Church of *Rome* pronounces Hereticks, unless they are willing to be delivered over as impenitent Hereticks to the secular Arm or Court, but especially Doctors, whom they call Dogmatists, Dogmatisers, and Arch-hereticks. *Bzovius*, under the Year 1479. §. 9. gives us a famous Instance which hapned in *Spain*.

I

Peter-

Peter de Ofma, who read Theological Lectures at *Salamanca*, had publifh'd a Book, in which were feveral Things contained contrary to the Doctrines of the Church of *Rome*. The Arch-Bifhop of *Toledo*, then at *Alcala de Henarez*, where he generally refided, did, by Command of Pope *Sixtus*, after having confulted the moft learned Men, and well confidered the Matter for a long while, condemn his Opinions, and put the Author himfelf under the Infamy of an *Anathema*, unlefs he changed his Sentiments. The Sentence was pronounced *June* 23. Pope *Sixtus* confirmed the Sentence of the Arch-Bifhop by a Bull, and commanded him, that he fhould not omit to proceed againft the Followers of *Peter de Ofma*, as Hereticks, if they fhould refufe or wickedly defer to abjure this Herefy they are fallen into, or to imitate the faid *Peter* abjuring his Errors and repenting, as they had imitated him in his Error.

CHAP. XXXII.

Of the Punifhment and wholefome Penances injoined fuch as abjure.

SUCH who abjure, and after Abjuration are reconciled to the Church, are injoined various Punifhments, and, as they call them, wholefome Penances. They are impofed by the Inquifitors at Pleafure. Extra. de hæret. c. *Ad abolendam.* §. *Præfenti.* [And thus the Council of *Narbonne* hath decreed, *Cap.* 5. *This indeed we fo injoin, not that you fhould impofe every where, or upon all alike, all the fore-mentioned Penances, but that ye may, according to the Difcretion given you of the Lord, fo cautioufly and providently difpenfe them, according to the Nature of the Crimes and Perfons, Places and Times, and other Circumftances, that whether by punifhing or pardoning, the Life of Offenders may be amended, or at leaft that it may appear who walks in Darknefs, who in the Light; who is truly penitent, who feignedly converted; and that no Scandal may arife from hence to true Catholicks, and that Herefy may not be defended or nourifhed thro' Pretence of Scandal, or any other whatfoever.* But, as *Carena* advifes, in this Impofition of Punifhment the Inquifitors muft be careful *always to ufe Clemency and Mercy, not Cruelty and Severity.* But he adds, *This muft be underftood with a Grain of Salt,* viz. *that this Clemency muft not be fhewn to an impenitent Heretick; for after the Inquifitors have ufed all their Endeavours for his Converfion, they muft by no Means mitigate the Punifhments of Death, Infamy, and others threatned againft him by Law. For as to this, whilft he remains impenitent,* N. B. *the only Inftance of true Piety is to be cruel.*] They have alfo Power of commuting and mitigating them; becaufe this impofing of Penance is not a definitive Sentence, but rather an Injunction, and Command or Precept of Purgation. 'Tis otherwife, when the Inquifitor hath condemned any one as an Heretick, and impofes Penance on him as fuch, becaufe that is a Punifhment determined by the Law, and which

p. 3. *t.* 19. *dal,* §. 13.

2   therefore

therefore doth not depend on the Pleafure of the Inquifitor, and becaufe by fuch Condemnation he hath pronounced a definitive Sentence, and fo ceafes to be a Judge. *Zanchin. de hæret. cap.* 21. And thefe Penances in general are laid upon any Perfons.

Priefts and others of the Clergy are not ufually injoined publick Penance, Simanc. both becaufe of the Dignity of their Order, and that the Flock of the Faith-*t.* 47. ful may not be offended. But altho' this is to be obferved in fmaller Crimes, §. 74, 75. yet in more heinous ones the Priefts are to be compelled to undergo publick[76.] Penance, and the rather in the Crime of Herefy, becaufe fuch Offences in Priefts are more heinous than in the Laity. And not only Clergymen and Presbyters are obliged to this publick Penance, but alfo Bifhops, Cardinals and others, howfoever dignified; becaufe all Men are upon an equal Foot in Matters partaining to the Orthodox Faith. Add to this, that heretical Clergymen, returning to the Church, are, after Injunction of Penance, to be depofed, at leaft by a verbal Degradation, by which they are fufpended from the Exercife of their Orders: But of this hereafter.

[*Carena* obferves particularly concerning Regulars, that when they fall into *p.* 3. *t.* 19. Crimes relating to this Tribunal, they are ufually punifhed with fome pecu-§. 11. liar Punifhments. Thefe are the Privation of active and paffive Votes, of the Office of Preaching, and of hearing Confeffions, efpecially thofe of Women; that the Sentence of the Inquifitors muft be read twice a Year in a Chapter of the Religious and Prefence of the Criminal, that they take the laft Place in the Quire and Refectory, that they muft be whipped by their Religious in a Chapter and Prefence of the Notary of the holy Office; and others. But *Carena* adds, thefe Punifhments are to be injoined with great Moderation, Regard being always had to the Heinoufnefs of the Offence, and the Quality of the Offender; but yet in fuch a Manner, as that the Inquifitors ought to know, that fuch Punifhments are not impofed only on foliciting Confeffors, but even upon the Religious who offend otherwife. Hence it happened fome Years ago in our Congregation at *Cremona*, by Order of the facred Congregation, that a certain Regular, who had rafhly incurred the Conftitutions of *Paul* V. and *Gregory* XV. publifhed upon the Affair of the Conception; was condemned, publickly to revoke fome Propofitions that were rafh, fcandalous, and offenfive to pious Ears, in the fame Place where he had preached them; and was farther deprived of his active and paffive Vote, and the Office of Preaching and Lecturing, together with other wholefome Penances. Thus alfo in a folemn Act of the Faith celebrated in the Kingdom of *Sicily*, Friar *Marcellus de Pratis*, a Religious of the Order of the Minors, was condemned by that moft illuftrious Tribunal, becaufe he had rafhly feigned himfelf a Saint, impeccable, confirmed in Grace, and had pronounced other fcandalous and rafh Propofitions, to the Gallies for three Years, to be banifhed for two more into fuch a Convent of his own Religion as fhould be affigned him, with this Addition, that he fhould faft every *Friday* on Bread and Water, eat upon the Ground in the Refectory, walk without his Hat, and fit in the loweft Place in the Quire and Refectory, and be perpetually deprived of his active and passive Vote, and of the Faculty of hearing any Persons Confessions whatsoever.

l. 2 t. 2.   *Lewis a Paramo* gives us another remarkable Instance of one *Mary* of the
c. 15. Annunciation, Prioress of the Monastery of the Annunciation at *Lisbon*, a
n. 10. Maid of 32 Years old, who had pretended that the Wounds of Christ, by the
p. 233. special Grace and Privilege of God, were imprinted on her, and shewed 32 Wounds made on her Head, representing the Marks of those which were made by our Saviour's Crown of Thorns, and Blood sprinkled on her Hands like a Rose, the Middle of which was like a Triangle, and shewed the Holes of the Nails narrower on one Side than the other. The same were to be seen in her Feet. Her Side appeared as tho' it had been laid open by the Blow of a Lance. When all these Things were openly shewn, it was wonderful to see how they raised the Admiration and Devotion of serious and holy Men, and withal surprized and deceived them ; for she did not suffer those pretended Wounds to be seen otherwise than by Command of her Confessor. And that absent Persons might have a great Veneration for her, she affirmed, that on *Thursdays* she put into the Wounds a small Cloth, which received the Impression of five Wounds in Form of a Cross, that in the Middle being the largest. Upon which these Cloths were sent, with the greatest Veneration, thro' the infinite Devotion of the Faithful, to the Pope, and to almost all the most venerable and religious Persons of the whole World. And as *Paramus* then had the Administration of the Causes of Faith in the Kingdom of *Sicily,* he saw several of those Cloths, and the Picture of that Woman drawn to the Life, and a Book written by a Person of great Authority concerning her Life, Sanctity and Miracles. Yea, Pope *Gregory* XIII. himself determined to write Letters to that wretched Creature, to exhort her thereby to persist with Constancy in her
Ibid. t. 3. Course, and to perfect what she had begun. At last the Imposture was
c. 5. n.16. found out, that the Marks of the Wounds were not real, but made with red
p. 303. Lead, and that the Woman's Design was, when she had gained Authority and Credit enough, by her pretended Sanctity, to recover the Kingdom of *Portugal* to its former State, which had legally fallen under the Power of *Philip* II. Upon this the following Sentence was pronounced against her by the Inquisitors of *Lisbon, Decemb.* 8. *An.* 1588. First, she was commanded to pass the rest of her Life shut up in a Convent of another Order, that was assigned to her, without the City of *Lisbon.* Likewise, that from the Day of pronouncing the Sentence, she should not receive the Sacrament of the Eucharist for the Space of five Years, three *Easters*, and the Hour of Death excepted, or unless it were necessary to obtain any Jubilee, that should in the mean while be granted by the Pope. Likewise that on all *Wednesdays* and *Fridays* of the whole Year, when the religious Women of that Convent held a Chapter, she should be whipped, whilst the Psalm, *Have Mercy on me, O God,* was reciting. Likewise, that she should not sit down at Table at the Time of Refreshment, but should eat publickly on the Pavement, all being forbidden to

eat

eat any Thing fhe left. She was alfo obliged to throw her felf down at the Door of the Refectory, that the Nuns might tread on her as they came in and went out. Likewife, that fhe fhould perpetually obferve the Ecclefiaftical Faft, and never more be created an Abbefs, nor be chofen to any other Office in the Convent where fhe had dwelt, and that fhe fhould be always fub-ject to the loweft of them all. Likewife, that fhe fhould never be allowed to converfe with any Nun without Leave of the Abbefs. Likewife, that all the Rags marked with Drops of Blood, which fhe had given out her fpurious Re-licks, and her Effigies defcribing her, fhould be every where delivered to the hóly Inquifition; or if in any Place there was no Tribunal of the Inquifition, to the Prelate, or any other Perfon appointed. Likewife, that fhe fhould ne-ver cover her Head with the facred Veil, and that every *Wednefday* and *Friday* of the whole Year fhe fhould abftain from Meat, and live only on Bread and Water, and that as often as fhe came into the Refectory, fhe fhould pro-nounce her Crime with a loud Voice in the Prefence of all the Nuns.

He tells us in the fame Place, that *Michael Piedrola* took upon himfelf for many Years the Name of a Prophet, boafted of Dreams and Revelations, and affirmed they were revealed to him by a divine Voice. Being convicted of fo great a Crime, he abjured *de levi*, was for ever forbid the reading of the Bible, and other holy Books, deprived of Paper and Ink, prohibited from writing or receiving Letters, unlefs fuch only as related to his private Af-fairs, denied the Liberty of difputing about the holy Scripture, as well in Writing as in Difcourfe, and finally, commanded to be thrown into Jayl, and there pafs the Remainder of his Life.]

The common Punifhment of Hereticks is the Confifcation of all their Ef-fects; for altho' this Confifcation is kindly remitted to thofe who come of their own Accord, and voluntarily confefs before they are accufed, yet this Favour is never granted in *Spain*, to thofe who at length confefs after they are accufed and thrown into Prifon, or who perfift in their Opinion. And this Confifcation is made with fuch Rigour, that the Inquifition orders the Exche-quer to feize on not only the Effects of the Perfons condemned, but alfo all others adminiftred by them, altho' it evidently appears that they belong to others. The Inquifition at *Seville* gives a remarkable Inftance of this Kind, which *Gonfalvius* gives us a long Account of, with all its Circumftances.

" *Nicholas Burton*, an *Englifhman*, a Perfon remarkable for his Piety, was *p. 175,* " apprehended by the Inquifition of *Seville*, and afterwards burnt for his im- *&c.* " movable Perfeverance in the Confeffion of his Faith, and deteftation of " their Impiety. When he was firft feized, all his Effects and Merchandifes, " upon Account of which he came to *Spain*, were, according to the Cuftom " of the Inquifition, fequeftred. Amongft thefe were many other Merchan-" difes which were configned to him as Factor, according to the Cuftom of " Merchants, by another *Englifh* Merchant dwelling in *London*. This Mer-" chant, upon hearing that his Factor was imprifoned, and his Effects feized " on, fent one *John Frontom*, as his Attorney, into *Spain*, with proper In-" ftruments, to recover his Goods. His Attorney accordingly went to *Se-*

" *vile*,

" *ville*, and having laid before the holy Tribunal the Inftruments and all
" other neceffary Writings, demanded that the Goods fhould be delivered to
" him. The Lords anfwered, that the Affair muft be managed in Writing,
" and that he muft chufe himfelf an Advocate, undoubtedly to prolong the
" Suit, and out of their great Goodnefs appointed him one, to draw up for
" him his Petitions and all other Inftruments, which were to be offer'd to the
" holy Tribunal, for every one of which they exorbitantly took from him eight
" Reals, altho' he received no more Advantage from them, than if they had
" never been drawn at all. *Frontom* waited for three or four whole Months,
" twice every Day, *viz.* in the Morning, and after Dinner, at the Gates of
" the Inquifitor's Palace, praying and befeeching, on his bended Knees, the
" Lords Inquifitors, that his Affair might be expedited, and efpecially the
" Lord Bifhop of *Tarraco*, who was then chief Inquifitor at *Seville*, that he
" in Virtue of his fupream Authority would command his Effects to be re-
" ftored to him. But the Prey was too large and rich to be eafily recovered.
" After he had fpent four whole Months in fruitlefs Prayers and Intreaties, he
" was anfwered, that there was need of fome other Writings from *England*,
" more ample than thofe he had brought before, in order to the Recovery
" of the Effects. Upon this the *Englifhman* immediately returns to *London*,
" and procures the Inftruments of fuller Credit which they demanded, comes
" back with them to *Seville*, and laid them before the holy Tribunal. The
" Lords put off his Anfwer, pretending they were hindred by more impor-
" tant Affairs. They repeated this Anfwer to him every Day, and fo put
" him off for four whole Months longer. When his Money was almoft fpent,
" and he ftill continued earneftly to prefs the Difpatch of his Affair, they
" referred him to the Bifhop. The Bifhop, when confulted, faid he was
" but one, and that the expediting the Matter belonged alfo to the other
" Inquifitors ; and by thus fhifting the Fault from one to the other, there
" was no Appearance of an End of the Suit. But at length being overcome
" by his Importunity, they fixed on a certain Day to difpatch him. And
" the Difpatch was this : The Licentiate *Gafcus*, one of the Inquifitors, a
" Man well skilled in the Frauds of the Inquifition, commands him to come
" to him after Dinner. The *Englifhman* was pleafed with this Meffage, and
" went to him about Evening, believing that they began to think in good
" Earneft of reftoring him his Effects, and carrying him to Mr. *Burton* the
" Prifoner, in order to make up the Account, having heard the Inquifitors
" often fay, tho' he did not know their real Meaning, that it was neceffary
" that he and the Prifoner fhould confer together. When he came, they
" commanded the Jayl-Keeper to clap him up in fuch a particular Prifon,
" which they named to him. The poor *Englifhman* believed at firft, that he
" was to be brought to *Burton* to fettle the Account, but foon found him-
" felf a Prifoner in a dark Dungeon, contrary to his Expectation, and
" that he had quite miftaken the Matter. After three or four Days they
" brought him to an Audience, and when the *Englifhman* demanded that the
" Inquifitors fhould reftore his Effects to him, they well knowing that it
" would

" would agree perfectly with their ufual Arts, without any other Preface,
" command him to recite his *Ave Mary.* He fimply repeated it after this
" manner. *Hail,* Mary, *full of Grace, the Lord is with thee, bleffed art thou*
" *amongft Women, and bleffed is Jefus the Fruit of thy Womb.* Amen. All was
" taken down in Writing, and without mentioning a Word about the refto-
" ring his Effects, for there was no Need of it, they commanded him back
" to his Jayl, and commenced an Action againft him for an Heretick, be-
" caufe he had not repeated the *Ave Mary* according to the Manner of the
" Church of *Rome,* and had left off in a fufpected Place, and ought to have
" added, *Holy* Mary, *Mother of God, pray for us Sinners ;* by omitting which
" Conclufion, he plainly difcover'd that he did not approve the Interceffion of
" the Saints. And thus at laft upon this righteous Pretence he was detained
" a Prifoner many Days. After this he was brought forth in Proceffion
" wearing an Habit, all his Principal's Goods for which he had been fu ng be-
" ing confifcated, and he himfelf condemned to a Year's Imprifonment.

But as to fufpected Perfons, and thofe who voluntarily appear, 'tis not ufual
to punifh them with Confifcation of Effects, and therefore other Punifhments,
which they call wholefome Penances, are injoined them. The Punifhments
and Penances to which fuch Penitents are condemned, are various. Thofe
which *Dominick* ufed to injoin them, in order to their Reconciliation to the
Church, may be collected from his Forms, which are ftill extant. One of
them is in this Manner. *To all the Faithful of Chrift, to whom thefe prefent Letters* Bzovius,
fhall come, Friar Dominick, *Canon of* Ofma, *the leaft of Preachers, Salvation* An. 1:15.
in Chrift. *By Authority of the Lord Abbot of* Cifteaux, *Legate of the Apoftolick* §. 13.
See, who hath committed this Office to us, we have reconciled the Bearer of thefe,
Pontius Rogerius, *converted thro' the Grace of God from the Sect of the Hereticks ;*
commanding him by Virtue of the Oath he hath taken, to be led naked in his Breeches
by the Prieft on three Feftival Sundays, *and to be whipped from the Entrance into*)
the Town, *even to the Church. We alfo injoin him always to abftain from Flefh,*
Eggs and Cheefe, or from all Things derived from Flefh, excepting Eafter-Day,
Whitfontide *and* Chriftmas, *at which Seafons we command him to eat of them for*
the Denial of his former Error. Let him keep three Lents in a Year, abftaining
from Fifh. Let him always abftain from Fifh, Oil and Wine, and faft three Days
in a Week, unlefs bodily Infirmity, or the Labours of the Summer fhall require a
Difpenfation. Let him be cloathed with religious Veftments, both as to Form and
Colour, upon the Breafts of every one of which let ftrait fmall Croffes be fewed. Let
him hear Mafs every Day if it be convenient, and go to Vefpers at Church on Holy-
days. Let him confecrate to God other Hours, as well by Night as by Day, viz.
feven times wherefoever he is. Let him fay over his Pater-nofter *ten times in the*
Day, and at Midnight twenty times. Let him obferve Chaftity, and in the Morn-
ing fhew every Month to his Parfon that Paper at the Town of Ceri. *We alfo com-*
mand the Parfon diligently to obferve his Life. Let him carefully obferve all thefe
Things, until the Lord Legate fhall otherwife exprefs his Pleafure to us in this Mat-
ter. But if he fhall neglect to obferve them, we command that he be accounted as
perjured, an Heretick, and excommunicated, and feparated from the Converfation of

the Faithful. There is extant alfo another fhorter one of the fame *Dominick,* in thefe Words. *To all the Faithful of Chrift, to whom thefe prefent Letters fhall come,* Friar Dominick, *Canon of* Ofma, *an humble Preacher, Salvation and fincere Affection in the Lord. May all your Difcretions know by Authority of thefe Prefents, that we have granted Licence to* Raymond Will. Pelaganirio, *of* Haulteripe, *to fuffer to abide with him in his Houfe at* Tholoufe, William Ugotio, *cloathed, as he himfelf hath declared before us, in a certain heretical Habit, and converfing after the Manner of other Men, until the Lord Cardinal fhall give a farther more exprefs Command to us or him in this Affair. And let not this be any Occafion of Infamy or Damage to him the faid* Raymond William.

In the Council of *Tarraco,* thefe Forms of Penances are fixed. *Let Hereticks perfevering in their Error, be left to the Judgment of the fecular Court, and let convicted Hereticks, if they will be converted, and Dogmatifers, after Abfolution and Abjuration, be perpetually imprifoned.*

Let the Believers of Hereticks do folemn Penance, viz. after this manner, viz. that on the next enfuing Feftival of All-Saints, *and on the Lord's-Day of the* Advent, *on the Day of our Lord's Birth, Circumcifion,* Epiphany, St. Mary *in* February, St. Eulalia, St. Mary *in* March, *and all Sundays in Lent, they walk in Proceffion to the See, or Cathedral Church, without Shoes, in their Breeches and Shirt: Befides this, on* St. Mary's Day *in* February, *and on* Palm-Sunday, *they fhall be reconciled in the Parifh-Church, and in the Proceffion receive publick Difcipline by the Bifhop or Prieft of the Church. Likewife on* Wednefday, *at the Beginning of the Faft, they fhall come together to the See, and after the fame Manner, and according to Form of Law, appear without their Shoes in their Breeches and Shirt, and be excluded the Church, and be kept out of it during the whole Time of* Lent, *but fo as to be fuffered to come to the Gates of the Church to hear Service. And on the Feftival of* Cœna Domini, *let them appear without Shoes, in their Breeches and Shirt, before the Gates of the Church, and be publickly reconciled to the Church, according to the Canonical Inftitutions. And let them do this Penance on* Wednefday, *and of ftanding without the Church the whole Time of* Lent, *and on the Day of* Cœna Domini, *every Year whilft they live. But on* Lent Sundays, *after Reconciliation, let them go out of the Church, and ftand before the Gates of it till the Feftival of* Cœna Domini, *and always wear two Croffes before their Breafts, of a different Colour from their Cloaths, and fo wear them, that they may appear folemnly penitent, with this Exception only, that they fhall not be hindred from entring into the Church in* Lent *more than ten Years.*

The Penance of thofe who have relapfed into favouring of Herefy, fhall be in like manner folemn, as that laft mentioned of thofe believing in them, and upon all the aforefaid Days ; this excepted, that they fhall wear Croffes, and in like manner do Penance on Afh-Wednefday *and* Holy Thurfday *for ten Years.*

The Penance of thofe who are not relapfed into favouring, but are Favourers, and moft vehemently fufpected, fhall be in the fame Manner folemn upon the Feaft of All-Saints, *the* Nativity of Chrift, Epiphany, St. Mary *of* February, *and all* Sundays in Lent. *And let them do the other Penance for feven Years, ordered to be*
done

done on Wednefday *in* Lent, *ftanding without the Church during the Time of* Lent, *and being reconciled upon the Feftival of* Cœna, *as abovefaid.*

The Penance of thofe who are Favourers, and vehemently fufpected, fhall be folemn, in the fame Manner, upon the Feftival of All-Saints, Chriftmas, St. Mary *of* February, Palm-Sunday, *and they fhall do for five Years the other Penance of the* Wednefday *in* Lent, *and of ftanding without the Church during the whole Time of* Lent, *and being reconciled on the Feftival of* Cœna, *as abovefaid.*

The Penance of thofe who are Favourers, and fufpected, fhall be folemn, in the fame Manner, upon the Feaft of All-Saints, St. Mary *of* February, *and* Palm-Sunday, *and they fhall do for three Years the other Penance, on the* Wednefday *in* Lent, *and of ftanding without the Church during the whole Time of* Lent, *and of being reconciled on the Feftival of* Cœna Domini. *This however is to be underftood, that the Women fhall come cloathed, and fuffer Difcipline.*

This Penance all the aforefaid Perfons, who are Citizens, fhall do, upon the Feftivals and Days before prefcribed, in that City and Place where they are Citizens, and no where elfe, till the Feftival of Eafter. *Thofe who are Foreigners fhall do it in their Parifhes, and no where elfe; excepting on the* Wednefday, *in the Beginning of* Lent, *and on the Day of the Feftival of* Cœna, *in which all muft come to the* See *or the Place of their Church. But in the following Seafons of* Lent, *let all Citizens and Foreigners do the ten, feven, five, and three Years Penance which they ought to do on* Wednefday *at the Beginning of* Lent, *and on the Feftival of* Cœna Domini, *according to the different Nature of their Crimes, as is before determined, in the* See *of their City, and no where elfe, unlefs upon any juft and reafonable Caufe, and by the fpecial Licence of the Bifhop or his Vicar; and then in fuch Places where they fhall go by the Bifhop's Leave, they fhall do the fame Penance before the Bifhop of that Place, or his Vicar, carrying the Letters of the Bifhop or his Vicar, containing the Penance which they ought to do. And let him alfo, who doth the Penance, bring back the Letters of the Bifhop of that Place, to* N. *of fuch a Diocefe, containing a Teftimonial of the Penance being performed. But if it fhould happen, that by Accident, and not by Fraud and Deceit, they can't come on thofe two Days to the Cathedral Church, then after their Return let them undergo publick Difcipline, at the Pleafure of the Bifhop, at the* See *of* N. *according to the Manner of thofe two Days, upon two other Solemnities to be affigned them.*

From thefe Things it appears that the Punifhments to which fuch Penitents are ufually condemned, are many and different. For firft, there are fome which they ftrictly call wholefome Penances, fuch as Faftings, Prayers, Alms, the frequent Ufe of the Sacraments of Penance, and the Eucharift, and finally Pilgrimages to certain Places. Thus in the Book of the Senten- *fol.* 99. *b.* ces of the *Tholoufe* Inquifition fome are injoined, *That they fhall vifit every Year, whilft they live, the Church of St.* Stephen *at* Tholoufe, *in the Feftival of its Invention, and the Church of St.* Saturninus *at* Tholoufe, *on the Octave of* Eafter. *Likewife we injoin all and fingular of you the above mentioned Perfons, Pilgrimages to St.* Mary *de la Roche d'*Amateur, *and of* Le Puy *d'une vallee Verte, and fol.* 102. *a. of* Montpellier, *and of* Serignan, *and to St.* Guillaume *in the Defert, and St.* Geniez *in* Provence, St. Pierre *of* Montmaiour, St. Martha *of* Tarafcon,

St.

St. Mary Magdalene *at St.* Maximin, *St.* Anthony *of* Vienne, *St.* Martial *and St.* Leonard *in the* Limoufin, *St.* Dionyfius, *and St.* Lewis, *and to the Virgin* Mary *of* Chartrin *in* France, *St.* Severin *in* Burdeaux, *the Virgin* Mary *of* Soulac, *St.* Faith *of* Concq, *St.* Paul *at* Narbonne, *and St.* Vincent *of* Caftres.

This Pilgrimage the Penitent is injoined to make, with a black Habit, which he muft carry with the Inquifitors Letters, to that Place which he is to vifit in his Pilgrimage ; and he is farther required to bring back Letters te-ftimonial of the Predicant Friars, or others who dwell there in Witnefs of the Truth.

Sometimes they were injoined Pilgrimage, to go to War in the Holy Land againft the *Saracens*. Thus the Council of *Biterre* hath determined, that fuch *who have thus offended the Faith or Church, fhall alfo defend it for a Time, to be appointed at your Pleafure, either by themfelves or others more fit, on the other or this Side the Sea, againft the* Saracens, *or Hereticks and their Favou-rers, or fuch who otherwife rebel againft the Faith and the Church.* And after-wards, *as to thofe who fhall be injoined Pilgrimages, they fhall be obliged to fhew the faid Teftimonial Letters in each of their Pilgrimages to him, who prefides over the Church which they vifit, and to bring back the faid Letters to you, in Teftimony of their having made fuch Pilgrimage. As to thofe who go beyond Sea, let them, as foon as they can, after their Tranfportation, prefent themfelves, with your Letters, to the venerable Fathers the Patriarchs of* Jerufalem, *and* Acre, *or to any other Bi-fhop whatfoever, or to their Vicegerent, and let them bring back to you at their Re-turn the Letters of every fuch foreign Bifhop, in Witnefs of their having laudibly performed their Pilgrimage there.* An Inftance of fuch a kind of Sentence we have in the Book of Sentences of the *Tholoufe* Inquifition, pronounced againft

fol. 141. b. Mafter *William Garrici,* Profeffor of Laws at *Carcaffone,* who was condemned to go to the War in the Holy Land, or if he was legally prevented, to fend, at his own Charge and Expence, another proper Soldier to the Relief of the faid holy Land. And as for himfelf, he was within thirty Days to depart out of the Kingdom of *France,* and to ftay in the Place affigned him, till there fhould be a Tranfportation into *Afia*; to which was added the Punifh-ment of perpetual Imprifonment, if he refufed to fulfil this Penance.

Secondly, Some Penances are honorary, attended with Infamy to thofe who do them. Such are, walking in Proceffion without Shoes, in their Breeches and Shirt, and to receive therein publick Difcipline by the Bifhop or Prieft, to be expelled the Church, and to ftand before the Gates of the great Church upon folemn Days, in the Time of Mafs, with naked Feet, and wearing up-on their Cloak an Halter about their Neck. At this Time they only ftand before the Gates of the Church, with a lighted Candle in their Hand, during the Time of folemn Mafs on fome holy Day, as the Bell is ringing to Church.

Befides thefe, they now ufe the Punifhment of Banifhment, and Criminals are banifhed not only into fuch Places as are fubject to the Jurifdiction of the Inquifitor who banifhes them, but to Places fubject to other Inquifitors, be-

caufe

cause all Places are subject to the same chief Pontiff, by whom all the Inquisitors are delegated. To this may be added the Punishment of being thrust
into a Monastery, which, tho' now seldom inflicted, was much more in use
formerly. *Bzovius* gives us an Instance of it in the Year 1479. " This § 8.
" Year was condemned at *Mayence, John Rucard,* of the Upper *Wesel,*
" D. D. and compelled by the Inquisitor to recant certain Articles which he
" was reported publickly to have preached at *Worms.* All his Writings
" were before his Face thrown into the Fire and burnt, and he himself sent
" to do Penance to the Convent of *Austin* Friars in that Place, where he died
" in a little while of Grief." *Bzovius* also relates the Articles against him,
most of which were against the Papal Authority. The first of them deserves
to be mentioned: *That the Prelates of the Church have no Authority to ordain or
add any Thing to what Christ and his Apostles have ordained: Yea, that neither
Apostles nor the Popes have received such Power from Christ.*

There is also another Punishment of Beating or Whipping, when Criminals
are condemned to be whipped with Scourges or Rods. If they are religious
Persons, they are whipped in their own Monastery by other Religious, in the
Presence of the Notary of the holy Office. This Punishment, *Paramus* be- *l. 2. t. 3.*
ing Witness, *Laurentius Valla* suffered, who being condemned for Heresy at *c. 4. n. 31.*
Naples, was preserved from the Fire by the King's Favour, but upon this
Condition, that after he had publickly recanted and damned the Things he
had uttered, he should atone for his Crimes by Whipping. And accordingly
in the Convent of the Predicants, being led round the Cloysters with his
Hands tied, he was whipped upon his Shoulders and Back, by the Religious of
the House.

Sometimes they are condemned to Fines, according to the Rescript of *A-
lexander* IV. *Super exstirpatione* ; and this they are especially desirous of laying
upon rich and covetous Persons. *Alexander* IV. makes this Disposition in the
Affair. *As to the Money which may possibly arise from such Punishments, or from
the third Part of the Fines or Condemnations, to be exacted from such Persons and
Places, or from the Effects to be seized on by Occasion of Heresy or Hereticks,
according to the Tenour of our Constitutions, let it be deposited in the Hands of
three faithful and approved Men, to be chosen by you and the Diocesan, or his
Vicar in his Absence, and be faithfully kept by them, and let such Expences as
are necessary to the Prosecution of the Affair against Hereticks, be allowed you,
and every one of you, without any Difficulty, by the Advice of the Bishop himself,
and let a full and faithful Account be given to the said Diocesan of all such Expences.*

But here must be observed what *Zanchinus* teaches. " If the Inquisitor *Cap. 19.*
" condemns any one as an Heretick, he can't condemn him in a certain Sum
" of Money, for two Reasons. First, because as he condemns him for an
" Heretick, all his Effects are to be taken from him ; so that since his All
" is to be forfeited, 'tis idle to talk of taking from him a Part, or any
" Thing less than All. Secondly, because as he condemns him for Heresy,
" and as an Heretick, he cannot mitigate his Punishments by commuting for

" them with Money ; becaufe the Punifhments againft Hereticks are deter-'
" mined by Law, and therefore certain, for which Reafon 'tis not in the Power
" of the Judge or Inquifitor to convert or commute them into Money. But
" if the Inquifitor doth not condemn him as an Heretick, but will punifh him
" as difobedient or fufpected, or correct and purge him upon his Return, then
" he may lay a Fine on him, as he may from his own Motion injoin him other.
" Punifhments. But let him take Care, that when he intends to fine him, he
" doth not take away all from him, becaufe this is not lawful."

Sometimes, however it happens, that the Inquifitors do, either thro' Imprudence or Inadvertence, offend againft this Admonition of *Zanchinus*, as may

p. 180. be collected from an Inftance related by *Gonfalvius*. " In the Inquifition at
" *Seville*, they proceeded by an Inquifitory Cenfure againft a certain Citizen,
" upon Account of Religion. Amongft other Parts of his Punifhment, he
" forfeited all his Effects and Incomes, on which he had lived creditably
" enough before, and was ordered to be confined in a certain private Jayl,
" for ten Years, being thus ftripped of all he had. After he had been fome
" Days in the Prifon, in which, being reduced to extream Poverty, tho'
" otherwife far from being in mean Circumftances, he was fupported by the
" Contribu'ions of fome pious Perfons, one of the Notaries of the Inquifition
" comes to him, and brings him a Command in Writing from the holy Tri-
" bunal, by which he was ordered to pay the Sum of 130 Ducats for his Ex-
" pences and Provifion during his Imprifonment in the Inquifition. The An-
" fwer he returned to the Order was, that it was true, that having been
" plundered and ftripped entirely of all his Effects, by thefe felf fame Fa-
" thers of the Faith, he had nothing left to pay that Money. This Anfwer
" did not fatisfy their Lordfhips, who fent the Notary to him a fecond time,
" commanding him to pay, within a few Days, the Money they had de-
" manded, or that otherwife they would take him out of his private Prifon,.
" and throw him into the publick Jayl of the City. Unthinking Creatures,
" who did not take Care to pay themfelves their own Expences, before they
" brought the Man's Effects into the Exchequer."

Direct. However, Fines are not exacted for all forts of Crimes, but for fome par-
p. 2. *n* 19.ticular kind of them only. For the Popifh Doctors obferve, that thofe who
com. 7. offend concerning the Faith, may two ways offend the Church. Firft, by
only believing amifs, and alfo by publifhing Herefies. Secondly, when befides their ill Belief, they have added other Crimes, *viz.* if they have burnt
Churches, deftroyed Images, killed Catholicks, or committed the like
Things. If they offend in the firft Manner, and are returned, the Inquifitor
may, if he will, before they are abfolved from Excommunication, exact from
the Perfon returning, not only an Oath of obeying the Commands of the
Church, but alfo Security and Bail, under Penalty of a Fine of obeying fuch
Commands, and exact fuch Penalty if he doth not obey. *Alexander* IV. hath
exprefsly provided this in a Refcript beginning, *Super exftirpatione*. 'Tis,
however more honourable, not to take fuch Security, under Penalty of a
Fine, that they may not appear to do any thing rather out of Covetoufnefs,

than

than the Love of Religion, as the Council of *Narbonne* hath advifed, cap. 17. *You muft abſtain from and forbear ſuch pecuniary Penances and Exaſtions, becauſe of the Honour of your Order.* If they have offended in the ſecond Manner, they are not according to the Rigour of the Law, to be received and abſol-ved, before they have made good and repaired the Damage out of their own Eſtates. C. *Porro*, and C. *Parochianos*, de ſent. excom. *You muſt admoniſh and perſuade them, that they give due Satisfaſtion to thoſe they have injured.* And, *cauſe them to be ſtriſtly avoided as excommunicated Perſons, till they have made proper Satisfaſtion to the Perſons injured.* If they can't immediately give Satisfaſtion for the Damage they have done, either thro' Poverty or other Cauſes, they are to be abſolved, upon giving proper Security, *viz.* by laying ſomething down as a Pledge, or giving Sureties to make Satisfaſtion when they are able, or when they ſhall come to a larger Eſtate. 'Tis alſo now a Cuſtom ob-ſerved by all the Inquiſitors, tho' it be provided for by no Law, gently to ſtrike with a Rod ſuch as return when they abſolve them.

Such Perſons alſo are excluded from all publick Offices as infamous. Theſe publick Offices are, Offices of all ſorts, and of every Name, according to the various Rites and Cuſtoms of different Provinces. The Council of *Tholouſe* reckons even the Office of a Phyſician amongſt them. Cap. 14. *We ordain alſo, that whoſoever ſhall be defamed for Hereſy, or marked as ſuſpeſted, ſhall no longer be allowed the Profeſſion of a Phyſician.*

Farther alſo, Penitents, and thoſe reconciled, returning from Hereſy to the Church, and the Children and Grandchildren of condemned Perſons are not only excluded from bearing publick Offices, or having Benefices and Digni-ties, but from uſing Silver, Gold, or precious Garments and Ornaments, according to the Council of *Biterre*, c. 28. *Let them not hold Ballives or Admi-niſtrations, nor be in the Councils or Families of the Great, nor be allowed to praſtiſe as a Phyſician or Notary, nor be admitted to other publick Offices, or legal Aſtions, nor wear Gold-laced Cloaths, nor Silk, or the like Ornaments, or yellow Ribands, nor Shoe-ſtrings tagged and ſtriped with Gold or Silver, nor carved or painted Shoes ; and when it appears proper, let them be turned out of the City where they dwelt, and remain for ſome time in ſome other City or Province.* 'Tis alſo forbidden them to ride on Horſes with Trappings, as Nobles do, which Pro-hibition extends alſo to Mules. But in theſe Caſes they allow a Diſpenſation after ſome Time.

But the moſt uſual Puniſhment of all is, their wearing Croſſes upon their penitential Garments, which was not only formerly in Uſe, but is now fre-quently injoined Penitents in *Spain* and *Portugal.* And this is far from being a ſmall Puniſhment. Becauſe ſuch Perſons are expoſed to the Scoffs and Inſults of all, which they are obliged to ſwallow, tho' the moſt cruel in themſelves, and offered by the vileſt of Mankind, for by theſe Croſſes they are marked to all Perſons for Hereſy, or as it is now in *Spain* and *Portugal* for *Judaiſm.* And being thus marked, they are avoided by all, and are almoſt excluded from all human Society. We have an Inſtance of this in the Book of Sentences of the *Tholouſe* In-quiſition, in one *Arnald Yſarni* of *Villemaur*, who had thrown off his Croſſes, and being afterwards again apprehended, gave this Reaſon for doing it before the

In-

Inquifitor ; *becaufe by wearing his Croffes he could find no Perfons and Place, where he could get his Living, and that therefore he ftood for ten Years without them at the* Moyffac, *and got his Livelihood by going and coming with the Ships to* Bourdeaux.

But there is fome Difference in the Manner of wearing thefe Croffes, for they are not always fixed on the penitential Habits the fame way. For, in the firft place, the Council of *Tholoufe, An.* 1229. held againft Heretics, hath thus determined concerning them. *Alfo in Deteftation of their former Error, let them wear two Croffes for the future on the Top of their Garments, of a different Colour from their Cloaths, one on the right, and the other on the left ; and let not any one be excufed on Account of thefe Croffes, unlefs he can produce the Letters Teftimonial of his Bifhop, as to his Reconciliation.* Thefe Croffes were fo placed, as that they exactly anfwered the two Breafts, as appears by the Letters of *Dominick. Let them be cloathed with religious Garments, both as to Shape and Colour, on which let two fmall Croffes be fown directly upon each Breaft.* But afterwards that thefe Penitents might be more openly and fully expofed to the View of all Perfons, whether they ftood before or behind them, 'twas decreed that they fhould wear one before upon their Breafts, and the other behind between their Shoulders. Thus we read in the Acts of the Council of *Biterre, c.* 26. *In Deteftation of their former Error, let them wear upon their outward Garment, two Croffes of a yellow Colour, two Spans and a half long, and two wide, and having the Breadth of three Fingers in themfelves, one before on their Breaft, and the other behind between their Shoulders, not having that upper Garment, upon which they wear the Croffes, of a yellow Colour, neither fhall they put any Thing over it; either within Doors or without. And if they are convicted Hereticks, or condemned, let them wear a third Crofs of a competent Largenefs, or of the fame Colour, upon their Hat or Veil. And if they happen to be forfworn, or have caufed others to forfwear themfelves, let them wear upon the upper Part of the two Croffes, which they carry upon their Breaft, and between their Shoulders a Crofs-Arm or Bar of a Span long, or thereabouts. Thofe who are to tranfport themfelves muft wear the aforefaid Croffes, till they are got beyond Sea, but fhall not be obliged to wear them after that, till they fhall come to the Shore to go aboard, in order to their Return, but they fhall always wear them on the Sea-fhore, when at Sea, and in the Ifles.* This Garment was formerly of a black and bluifh Colour, like a Monk's Cloak, made without a Coul, and the Croffes put on them were ftrait, having one Arm long, and the other a-crofs, after this manner †. Sometimes according to the Heinoufnefs of the Offence, there were two Arms a-crofs, after this manner ‡. But now in *Spain* this Garment is of a yellow Colour, and the Croffes put on it are oblique, after the Manner of St. *Andrew's* Crofs, in this Form X, and are of a red Colour. [This Habit was ufed to be made always, and every where, of Woollen Cloth, but now 'tis made fhorter than formerly. For heretofore 'twas full as long as the Monks Cloaks, and remained fo all the while it was marked with Croffes. For as the Croffes themfelves were three Spans Length, it could not be otherwife but that the Sackcloth muft be long too. But afterwards, upon Account of the Croffes being taken away, and that the Sackcloth might differ from the Monk's Cloak, it was reduced to a fhorter Meafure. In fome Tribunals alfo of *Spain,* another

Direct.
p. 3.
tom. 42.
Param.
l. 1, t. 2.
c. 5. p. 42.

2   kind

kind of penitential Garment was in Ufe. For upon fuch Criminals as were not convict, but only vehemently fufpected of Herefy, they ufed to put a half penitential Garment, covering the Breaft only, which was marked only with one Line, of a red Colour, and not with two crofs ones, as the whole Sackcloth ufed to be marked with, that it might be hereby fhewn, that he was not truly and formally an Heretick, but vehemently fufpected of Herefy.} This Cloak the *Italians* call *Abitello*, the *Spaniards*, *Sant benito*, as tho' it was *Sacco benito*, *i.e.* the bleffed Sackcloth, becaufe it is fit for Penance, by which we are bleffed and faved. But *Simancas* fays, 'tis the Garment of St. *Benedict*. The wearing it is commanded, 4 *Inftruct. c.* 9. They pretend that the Foundation of this Habit is to be found in the facred Writings, becaufe thofe who fuffered formerly for their Impieties, were, befides other Penances, fometimes cloathed with Sackcloth, in order to implore the divine Mercy, and to render God propitious whom they had offended, as they fhew in the Example of *Achab*, 1 Kings xxi. 27.

But *Ludovicus a Paramo* carries its original higher, *viz.* that as God *l.* 1. *t.* 2. cloath'd our firft Parents with Garments of Skins, in Token of Confufion *c.* 4. 5. and perpetual Shame, fo the Inquifitors, at this Day, in Imitation of God, cloath fuch as are convicted of Herefy, with thefe bleffed Sackcloths, with oblique Croffes on them, to the proper Ignominy and Confufion of thofe who wear them. And he gives this Reafon why thefe ignominious Garments are called *bleffed Sackcloths*. Becaufe formerly Sinners were cloathed with bleffed Sackcloths, in Token of publick Penance, and was taken upon a voluntary Vow by the Penitents themfelves. But this Cuftom, in Procefs of Time, came into Difufe; and becaufe antiently thefe Sackcloths were bleffed in the Primitive Church, therefore they were called *bleffed Sackcloths*. And therefore the Inquifition, in Deteftation of the Crime of Herefy, hath renewed the Cuftom of publick Penance and bleffed Sackcloth. He gives alfo a very ridiculous Reafon, why the Croffes, which were formerly ftrait, are now made oblique, upon the penitential Garments. *Becaufe the Crofs is the external Sign, by which all the Worfhippers of Chrift profefs the Catholick Faith. Since therefore they who offend againft the Catholick Faith, deviate from the Rectitude of the Faith, the Inquifitors are ufed to cloath Penitents with thefe tranfverfe Marks, in Token of fuch Deviation, that it may appear to all by the Figure of the oblique Crofs, what is the inward State of him that wears it, what he hath been, and how he hath wandered from the Rectitude of the Faith and of the Chriftian Religion.*

Thefe Croffes are put on thofe, who have believed Herefies, and fometimes on thofe who have been Dogmatifers, but who immediately, upon their being found out and informed againft before the Bifhops and Inquifitors, depart from their Errors, and confent to abjure them. Such are more gently dealt with, and 'tis eafier to have a Difpenfation as to their Penance. For either they are to wear their Croffes only for a Time, or if they are injoined them for their whole Life, after they have worn them for fome Years, in another Sermon or Act of Faith, they leave them off again, or if they are in an ill State of Health, or if the Penitent be remarkably humble, and truly converted.

verted. But such a Dispensation is the more difficultly obtained, because the publick wearing these Crosses may make great Satisfaction in Behalf of those who carry them, yea, it may be greatly meritorious in them, because of the great Degree of Shame which such Persons endure, and may be, and is a considerable Warning to others.

He who throws off, or conceals this Garment, is to be punished as an Impenitent. Nor can the Inquisitors themselves, now in *Spain*, moderate the Time which they have fixed for the wearing it ; both because their Office is discharged after they have pronounced from the Tribunal, and because this Matter is reserved to the Inquisitor General and Council. 4 *Instruct.* c. 9.

§. 13.

This Habit of the Penitents, and Sackcloth of condemned Hereticks, is to be hung up in the Church of that Parish where they dwelt, that these sort of Ensigns may be a Monument to keep up the everlasting Remembrance of their Impiety ; for the Names of the Hereticks, and the Reasons of their Condemnation are to be inscribed and renewed on them. *Madrid Instruct.* An. 1561. c. 81. *viz.* after the Example of *Moses, who made broad Plates for a Covering of the Altar, of the Censers of the two hundred and fifty Men who had offered Incense to the Lord, that they might be a Memorial and a Sign to the Children of* Israel, *Numb.* xvi. 39, 40. If any one steals these Ensigns, 'tis the common Opinion, that he is to be punished at the Pleasure of the Judges, not as a Thief or sacrilegious Person, but as a Contemner of Religion and the Judges, and must therefore be whipped, or fined, or banished.

§. 14.

Finally, the most grievous Punishment is the being condemned to perpetual Imprisonment, there to do wholesome Penance with the Bread of Grief, and the Water of Affliction. This is usually enjoined on the Believers of Hereticks, and such as are difficultly brought to Repentance, or who have a long while denied the Truth during the Trial, or have perjured themselves. For because such Persons do not seem to be voluntarily and willingly converted, they will not allow them their Liberty, left being feignedly converted, as may be easily presumed, they should corrupt others. There is a Decree of the Council of *Tholouse* on this Affair, c. 10. *But as to those Hereticks, who thro' Fear of Death, or any other Cause, but not voluntarily, return to the Catholick Unity, let them be shut up in Prison to do Penance, by the Bishop of the Place, with such Caution, as that it may not be in their Power to corrupt others.* And the Coun-

cil of *Biterre. If any one of the Professed, or Consolati, will, thro' Fear of Punishment, return to the Faith, let him be committed to perpetual Imprisonment by the Bishop, left under the Shew of pretended Good the Church should be deceived.* Thus also the Emperor *Frederick* in L. *Commiss,* §. 2. Nor are those only who are very difficultly converted from Heresy, condemned to perpetual Imprisonment, but also certain other Persons, whose Crimes committed in the Cause of Faith are very remarkable, which the Council of *Narbonne,* held a few Years after that of *Tholouse,* particularly enumerates, in these Words, cap. 9. *But as to Hereticks, or their Believers, who have notwithstanding the aforesaid Immunity, suppressed the Truth concerning themselves or others, or have not come in within the Time of Grace, or who are otherwise unworthy, but yet are*
ready

ready abfolutely to obey the Commands of the Church, and to acknowledge that Truth *which they have fuppreffed or denied, altho' fuch are without Doubt, according to the Statutes of our Lord the Pope, to be thruft into perpetual Imprifonment ; yet in-afmuch as we have underftood that you have found in feveral Parts, fo great a Multitude of them, as that there is not only not Money enough, but neither Stones nor Mortar fufficient to build Jayls for them, our Advice is, that you defer their Imprifonment as you think: it convenient, till our Lord the Pope himfelf be more fully advifed concerning their Number, except poffibly any of them fhould be fo very wicked, as that there is too much Reafon to fear that they will be impenitent, or efcape, or relapfe, or corrupt and difturb others. Such Perfons are to be fent without farther Delay to a fecure and perpetual Jayl.* In our Times this antient Confinement or perpetual Imprifonment, is feldom or never ufed ; but the Bifhops and Inquifitors often change it for a Confinement in fome Monaftery.

But altho' in our Ages the perpetual Jayl is not made after the fame Man-*Direct.* ner in which it was formerly built, yet *Pegna* is of Opinion, that fome cer-*P. 3. com.* tain Houfe ought to be procured, and made ufe of as a perpetual Jayl, in [108.] which thofe who are to be fhut up fhould dwell ; becaufe otherwife he can't underftand how Penitents can perform the Penances enjoined them. The Order to be obferved in thefe Things is provided for by the *Madrid* Inftruction, *An.* 1561. c. 79, 80. *Thofe who are condemned to perpetual Jayl, fhall be configned to the Keeper of fuch perpetual Jayl, who muft be injoined to keep the Criminals, and to take Care that they fulfill the Pénances injoin'd them, and to inform the Inquifitors if they are negligent. Likewife let him take Care to affift them in their Neceffities, by procuring for them the proper Implements according to every one's particular Bufinefs or Trade, that they may hereby procure fomething for their own Support, and thus better bear their prefent Mifery and Poverty. Alfo the Inquifitors are to vifit their perpetual Jayl feveral times in a Year, to fee how they live, how they are treated, and what their Condition is. And becaufe in fome Inquifitions there is no perpetual Jayl, tho' the Thing be very neceffary, they muft procure fome Houfes for this Purpofe ; becaufe if there be no fuch Jayl, it can't be underftood how thofe who were reconciled, can fulfil their Penances, or thofe who are condemned to it be kept in Cuftody.* But this Cafe of obferving whether they fulfil the Penances injoined them, was formerly committed to fome Priefts, by the Council of *Narbonne,* c. 8. *Let the Care of obferving their Pénances be committed by you to their proper Priefts, fo that the Priefts themfelves having the Penances of their feveral Pärifhioners committed to them, and carefully infpecting how they obferve them, they may inform, without Delay, againft all Contemners, if any fuch there be to you, or to thofe whom you fhall appoint, that you may proceed againft them according to the Form hereafter defcribed.*

The Manner of this Imprifonment is determined by the Council of *Biterre,* c. 23, 24, 25. *Take Care that each of the Perfons to be immured, have, according to the Appointment of the Apoftolick See, feparate and private Cells, as far as it can be done in the feveral Cities of the Diocefes that are corrupted, that they may not pervert each other, either themfelves or others. But let not the exceeding Rigour of the Jayls deftroy them, but you fhall caufe thofe who are in Poffeffion of their Effects,*

to provide for them in *Neceſſaries, according to the Statutes of the Council of* Tholouſe, *which thus determines, c.* 10. " *Let the Perſons who are immured be pro-*
" *vided for in Neceſſaries, according to the Diſpoſition of the Prelate, by thoſe who*
" *are in Poſſeſſion of their Effects. But if they have no Effects, let them be provi-.*
" *ded for by the Prelate." But this Puniſhment or Penance of perpetual Impriſon-*
ment, ſhall never, from the Beginning of it, be remitted to any of the aforeſaid Cri-
minals, or commuted for another, unleſs it would either reſtore Hereticks, or unleſs be-
cauſe of his Abſence his Children or Parents would be in imminent Danger of Death, or
for any other Cauſe, which appears very juſt and reaſonable. Let alſo the Wife have
free Acceſs to her immured Huſband, and the Huſband to his Wife, that they may
not be denied to cohabit with each other, whether both be immured, or only one.
This Puniſhment of Immuration is very difficultly diſpenſed with, as the
Council of *Biterre* hath decreed, *c.* 24. and the Council of *Narbonne,* more
clearly, c. 19. *As to Perſons to be impriſoned, we have thought proper to add this ;*
that no one ſhall be excuſed from the Jayl, neither the Huſband for his Wife, though
ſhe be younger, nor the Wife for the Huſband, nor any one for his Children or Parents,
or other Kindred, or for Weakneſs or Age, or any other the like Cauſe, without the
ſpecial Leave of the Apoſtolick See. However, the Inquiſitors with the Ordinaries have now a Power of diſpenſing, excepting only that it is denied to the

Com. 108.Inquiſitors in *Spain,* by the private Sanctions of that Inquiſition ; ſo that the
Inquiſitor General only diſpenſes in this Caſe, even as he doth alſo with reſpect to the Habit marked with Croſſes. After how long a Time this Diſpenſation may be allowed, is left to the Pleaſure of the Inquiſitors, who, upon
conſidering the Humility and Repentance of the Penitents, may remit this
Puniſhment within a leſſer while, or commute it for another. But 'tis generally remitted at the Expiration of three Years. But if this Puniſhment of
the Jayl is injoined never to be remitted, 'tis generally diſpenſed with at the
End of eight Years. But the whole of this depends on the Inquiſitors
Pleaſure.

However, this Remiſſion muſt be granted with the Advice of the Dio-
ceſans, as is ordered, *lib.* 6. *decret. de hæret. As to thoſe who humbly obey your*
Commands, and are ſhut up in Priſon, or in Jayl, upon the Account of Hereſy, we
give you full Power, as you ſhall ſee fit, of mitigating or changing their Puniſhment,
in concert with the Biſhops, to whoſe Juriſdiction they are ſubject.

Theſe Remiſſions may alſo be obtained with Money, by which Perſons may
redeem themſelves from Jayl, and the Habits of their Guilt ; and this Me-

Gonſalv.
p. 166.thod of Redemption uſed to be very common in *Spain ;* becauſe, as the
" King granted certain Redemptions of theſe *Sambenito's* to the Court young
" Ladies and Gentlemen, he who received the Grant, diligently enquires
" where, and who the Perſons are that are ſubject to this Puniſhment, and
" who are moſt inclined and able to redeem it, with whom he afterwards
" agrees about the Price, as he beſt can, either for more or leſs, taking into
" the Account the Perſon that buys it off, and the *Sambenito* it ſelf. Such as
" are irremiſſible, the Price is dearer ; ſuch as are ordered to perpetual
" Impriſonment, 'tis cheaper. Such which are but for a Time, and de-
" pending

" pending on the Inquifitor's Pleafure, cheaper yet ; and fuch which depend
" on the Inquifitor's Pleafure only, cheapeft of all. The King alfo fometimes
" fhew'd the fame Liberality to fome others, who prayed to be affifted with
" the Money arifing from thefe Sambenito's, to redeem their Brethren or
" Kindred from *Turkifh* or *Moorifh* Captivity. But if any one defires thus to be
" freed from his Sambenito, 'tis neceffary before all Things, in order to ob-
" tain his Defire from the King, that he before-hand fecure the good Will of
" the Inquifitors and Secretaries. For otherwife, tho' the King himfelf fhould
" grant it, and the Money be paid down, they would ufe all their Endeavours
" to fruftrate it, and would cunningly and malicioufly throw in effectual Ob-
" ftacles, even by this fingle Expreffion, *viz.* that the King ought to be bet-
" ter informed of the Affair, and even the Pope himfelf, if he fhould have
" happened to grant the Abfolution. And if the Matter fhould come thus
" far, it would be eafy for them, before not over-fcrupulous, to invent this
" Anfwer, that the Perfon was not fo throughly purged from his Guilt, as to
" render it fafe for him to be fet at Liberty.

Befides this Condemnation to perpetual Imprifonment, fuch Perfons are
alfo injoined other Penances, *viz.* Sometimes to ftand in the Habit marked
with the Crofs at the Door of fuch a Church, fuch a Time, and fo long,
viz. on the four principal Feftivals of the glorious Virgin *Mary* of fuch a
Church, or on fuch and fuch Feftivals, at the Gates of fuch and fuch Churches.
Concerning this there is a Decree extant of the Council of *Biterre, c.* 26.
where, after commanding that Penitents fhould be prefent at divine Service
on *Sundays* and Feftivals, this is added, *That on the Mafs of every* Sunday *and*
Feftival, between the Epiftle and the Gofpel, they fhall publickly prefent themfelves
with Rods in their Hands, ftripped of their outward Garment, and with their Veil
or Hat off, to the Prieft celebrating Mafs in the Prefence of the People, and there,
after having received Difcipline, the Prieft fhall declare, that they fuffer this Difci-
pline for heretical Pravity. Sometimes before they are fhut up in Prifon, they
are publickly expofed, *viz.* being cloathed with the Habit of the Croffes,
they are placed upon an high Ladder in the Gate of fome Church, that they
may be plainly feen by all, where they muft ftand till Dinner-time, after
which they muft be carried, cloathed in the fame Habit, to the fame Place,
at the firft Ringing to Vefpers, and there ftand till Sun fet ; and thefe Spectacles are ufually repeated on feveral *Sundays* and Feftivals in feveral Churches,
which are particularly fpecified in their Sentence. However, there is no
mention made in the Book of the Sentences of the *Tholoufe* Inquifition, of
fuch a Spectacle, on the Account of Herefy, but of two only who were condemned for falfe Witnefs. But if they break Prifon, or do not otherwife fulfill the Penances injoined them, they are condemned as Impenitents, and as
under the Guilt of their former Crimes ; and if they fall again into the
Hands of the Inquifitors, they are delivered over as Impenitents to the fecular Court, unlefs they humbly ask Pardon, and profefs that they will obey
the Commands of the Inquifitors. Thus 'tis determined by the Council of
Tholoufe, Let all fuch Hereticks or Believers of them, who, after they have fworn

to obey the Commands of the Church, and either have, or have not obtained the Benefit of Abſolution, refuſing to obſerve and do the Penance of Impriſonment injoined them, either by not going into Jayl, or getting out of it after their Entrance, or any other Penance whatſoever, or thro' Contumacy, abſenting themſelves from receiving it, thus become Rebels, and thus openly manifeſt their Impenitency and feigned Con-verſion, be left by you, without any farther Audience at all, to the ſecular Judgment, to be puniſhed according to their Deſert, ſince 'tis ſufficient that they have once deceived the Church by a falſe Converſion.

Pegna,
p. 5-8.

They are now alſo condemned to the Puniſhment of the Gallies, becauſe the antient Practice of Immuration is at this Time ſeldom uſed. This is con-firmed by *Royas, p. 2. Aſſert.* 15. §. 202. " It was a Cuſtom very frequent " and uſual in the Court of the Inquiſition, that a Perſon condemned to a per-" petual Jayl, ſhould be diſpenſed with by the Inquiſitor General, after three " Years. But that if any one was condemned to perpetual and unredeemable " Impriſonment, if he appeared humble and truly penitent, he ſhould be diſ-" penſed with after eight Years. But now inſtead of perpetual Impriſonment, " Hereticks are condemned to the Gallies, provided they are not weak or aged. " Such Condemnation muſt not be for leſs than three Years, left the Exche-" quer ſhould receive more Damage than Benefit by the Expences. Thus " the ſupream and general Council of the Inquiſition hath decreed. Theſe " are the Puniſhments of Penitents.

Others will not depart from their Errors, but obſtinately perſiſt in them for a great while, and at length perhaps more thro' Fear of Death than the Love of Truth, depart from them, or pretend to do it, and abjure ; and therefore they don't give much Credit to their Abjurations. Such are ordina-rily condemned to perpetual and ſtrict Impriſonment, and to Iron Fetters and Chains, where they are daily allowed the Bread of Grief for Meat, and the Water of Affliction for their Drink. To this Purpoſe is the Decree of the Council of *Biterre, c.* 23. *Take Care however, that, according to the Appointment of the Apoſtolick See, ſeparate and ſecret Cells be appointed to ſuch as are to be immu-red, as it can be conveniently done in the ſeveral Cities of the corrupted Dioceſes, that they may neither be able to pervert themſelves or others.*

The Inquiſitors may alſo increaſe theſe Penances, if the converted Perſons want Devotion, or are malicious and quarrelſome, becauſe theſe Things ſhew that their Mind and Soul is far from being obedient to the Law of God, or the Commands injoined them. Hence it is that the Council of *Narbonne* gives this Caution to the Inquiſitors, *c.* 7. *This Reſtriction always carefully obſerved, that it may be lawful for you, or the other Inquiſitors, or thoſe to whom the Church of* Rome *ſhall think proper to commit this Affair, or he to whom it belongs by Office, according to your or their Pleaſure and Will, to add to, or take from the Penances injoined at any time for a reaſonable Cauſe.* The Council of *Biterre* gives this farther Caution, *c.* 22. *Always retaining to your ſelves this Power, that if you ſhall think it expedient for the Affair of the Faith, you may, without any new Cauſe, bring back again the aforeſaid Perſons to Jayl.* Hence alſo in the Book of the Sentences of the *Tholouſe* Inquiſition, the Inqui-

2   ſitors

fitors ordinarily referve this Power to themfelves. And if the Inquifitor, either thro' Forgetfulnefs, or other Caufes, hath not exprefsly referved this
Power to himfelf, he may neverthelefs increafe, change, remove, or leffen
thefe Penances. According to C. *Ut Commiffi,* de hæret. l. 6.

CHAP. XXXIII.

When and how far any one is to be admitted to PENANCE.

'TIS a very important and difficult Queftion amongft the Popifh Doctors,
and very intricate, at what Time, and how penitent Hereticks are to
be admitted. And that it may be more diftinctly underftood, I will here
give the Opinions of three celebrated Doctors in this Matter. The firft
is *Simancas,* who ufes many Diftinctions in the Solution of this Queftion.
" For either he is a concealed Heretick, difcovered by no one, and accufes *tit.* 47.
" himfelf to the Inquifitors, and plainly confeffes his Errors. Such a one, §. 27.
" without Doubt, is to be received, and ought not to be injoined publick
" Penance, but is to be fecretly abfolved. Or he hath been publickly an A- §. 28.
" poftate or Heretick in another Kingdom, and before any one gave Evi-
" dence againft him, he voluntarily returns to a found Mind, and asks Par-
" don and Abfolution from the Inquifitors. Such a one alfo is to be admitted,
" but he muft publickly abjure his Errors, and do wholefome Penance. But
" he muft not fuffer the Punifhment of Imprifonment, nor wear the Habit
" of Penitents. 1 *Inftruct.* c. 8.
" Or he comes to the Inquifitors thro' Fear of impending Proofs, and §. 29.
" difcovers his Confederates in Wickednefs, and fully confeffes his Errors ;
" and fuch a one alfo, tho' Witneffes come in againft him, is to be reconciled
" to the Church, but is more gently to be dealt with ; for he muft not be con-
" demned to perpetual Jayl, nor wear for any confiderable Time the peni-
" tential Habit. Or he is already apprehended, and thrown into Prifon, and §. 30.
" then confeffes his Herefies, and then his Confeffion is faid to be voluntary.
" He alfo who upon Admonition confeffes his Herefies, before the Evidence §. 31.
" of the Witneffes is fhewn him, is to be kindly received, and not condemned
" to perpetual Jayl, becaufe he confeffes before he is convicted by Witnef-
" fes, 1 *Inftruct.* c. 11. Or he confeffes after the Accufation is publifhed, and §. 32.
" is then to be admitted, but punifhed more feverely ; becaufe he would not
" confefs before he was informed, and made fully to underftand by the Accu-
" fation of what Herefies he was accufed. Or he confeffes after being con- §. 33.
" victed by the Witneffes, *i. e.* after the Publication of the Evidence. For
" altho' fuch a one doth not feem to return voluntarily, who is fcarce perfuaded
" at length to confefs his Errors, and beg Pardon, after being tired out with
" the Difmalnefs of his Jayl, after feveral Admonitions, after Accufation,

　　　　　　　　　　　　　　　　　　　　　　" the

" the Publication of the Evidence, fix hundred Perjuries, and feveral Months,

§. 44.   " yet inafmuch as being in Prifon he confeffes of his own Mind and Will his
" Errors, without being compelled by Violence, he is adjudged to confefs

§. 45, 46.   " voluntarily. Farther, they think that he alfo confeffes voluntarily,
" whofe Confeffion is violently, *i. e.* by Torture drawn from him. For al-
" tho' the firft Confeffion is drawn from him by Torment, yet is it not fuffi-
" cient to the Proof or Condemnation, unlefs he afterwards confirms it by
" a voluntary Confeffion. And therefore when the Criminal ratifies of his
" own Accord the extorted Confeffion, they fay he is not to be looked upon
" as acting herein unwillingly, nor his Confirmation as extorted by Force,
" but that 'tis altogether voluntary, and that therefore if the Confeffion be
" juft that fuch a one is to be admitted : And 'tis then accounted juft, when
" the Penitent teftifies it with Tears, Groans, and Humility.

§. 46.   " 'Tis alfo farther inquired, whether a Perfon is to be received to the Bofom
" of the Church after the definitive Sentence, even till he is delivered to the fe-
" cular Court. Here the Laws determine that Penitents may be admitted
" till the definitive Sentence, but that afterwards there is no Place for Pardon
" and Mercy.

p. 2.   The Opinion of *Royas* is different, who thus propofes and refolves it.
Affert. 15. " 'Tis no fmall Controverfy amongft the Profeffors of the Law, until what
" Term and Time converted Hereticks are to be received. Some fay, if
" they immediately and voluntarily return after the Difcovery of their Er-

§. 192.   " ror. Others, that Hereticks may return to the Faith after Sentence, and
" are then to be admitted, and may efcape the Punifhment of being turned
" over to the fecular Court. Others, that they may be received only till the
" pronouncing of the Sentence. Concerning which Matter the *Seville* In-
" ftruction treats, *c.* 12. and that of *Madrid, An.* 1561. *c.* 4. But if negative
" Hereticks are converted in a publick Act of the Faith, their Converfion
" is prefumed to be feigned and counterfeit, and that they are converted ra-
" ther thro' Fear of Death, than a Zeal for the Catholick Faith. For this
" Reafon fuch a kind of Converfion is very feldom or never to be admitted,
" unlefs very urgent Caufes arife, *viz.* if any one fhould confefs his Errors
" with many Tears and Signs, and not only thofe of which he is accufed,
" but others alfo, and farther difcover his Accomplices, efpecially if they
" are Perfons related to him, and beloved by him. By thefe and other Cir-
" cumftances, which depend wholly on the Pleafure of the Inquifitors, it may
" be examined whether the Converfion be real or feigned. Cap. *Ut officium,*
" §. *fi vero,* verfio, *Provifo folerter.*

§. 197.   " Altho' the Converfion of Hereticks and their Confeffion is to be waited
" for during the whole Procefs of the Trial, yet he who at the Beginning of
" the Trial confeffes before Accufation, is to be condemned to Imprifonment
" and the penitential Habit for a fhort Seafon ; but if he confeffes after Accu-
" fation, his Punifhment and Penance is to be encreafed. But he who con-
" feffes his Herefies after the Publication of the Evidence, is to be condemned
" to perpetual Prifon, becaufe 'tis prefumed that he confeffes thro' the Fear

" of Proofs, and therefore fuch a Converfion is not without its Sufpicion. *In-*
" *ftruct. Hifpal. An.* 1484. *c.* 14. In all the abovefaid Cafes the Effects are
" confifcated, according to the Cuftom generally obferved by all the Inquifi-
" tors. For 'tis in the Power of the Bifhop and Inquifitors to mitigate or
" change the Punifhment, even after the Sentence is paffed. Cap. *Ut Commiffi,*
" §. *nec non*, de hæret. 6. 1 *Inftruct. Hifpal. c.* 8, 11. This Determination
" takes place to this Day, before the pronouncing of Sentence, but after 'tis
" pronounced, the Inquifitor General only can difpenfe with and change it.
" 5 *Inftruct. Hifpal. c.* 7. and 4 *Inftruct. Tolet. c.* 7. But as to the Confifcation
" of Effects, this is never left to the Pleafure of the Inquifitors, but the com-
" mon Law is ever to be obferved, becaufe, from the Time of the Commif-
" fion of the Crime, the Effects of Hereticks are *ipfo jure*, confifcated. And
" therefore no one can deprive the Exchequer of this Right.

　　The third is that of *Camillus Campegius*, who feems rather to relate the O- *In Zan-*
pinions of others, than to propofe his own. " Some fay that in the Admif- *chin.*
" fion to Penance there is need of a Diftinction. For either the Judge finds *c.* 16.
" the Perfon to be fome fimple young Man or Woman, or elfe otherwife a
" Perfon of good Condition and Fame, who is fallen into the Crime of
" Herefy. Such ought not to be denied to recant even till the very Sen-
" tence, and efpecially if there is Reafon to hope that they will lead a better
" Life for the future. Or elfe the Perfon is one of an evil Condition and
" Fame, found in other Refpects criminal, or he hath long perfevered in this
" Crime, or hath been otherwife lightly fufpected of it, or one of whom there
" is no Reafon to hope there will be any future Amendment. The late Repen-
" tance of fuch a one ought not to be admitted. Thefe Circumftances and
" Cafes confidered, the Judge may fooner or later admit them to Abjuration
" and Penance.

　　" There are not wanting fome who determine that none are to be received
" who do not return voluntarily, and without Force ; and that they only re-
" turn voluntarily who ask Mercy within the Time of Grace, without being
" previoufly informed againft by an Accufer; or at leaft whilft the Caufe re-
" mains untried, they themfelves not being corporally taken up, nor con-
" victed by Proofs. For in thefe Cafes they don't appear to return voluntarily,
" but thro' Fear of being apprehended, and of the Proofs. But this Opi-
" nion is rejected by others as too fevere ; becaufe it would follow from hence,
" that fuch a one, willing to return, could not be more gently treated than
" an obftinate Perfon, inafmuch as he muft be condemned without Hope of
" Pardon equally with one obftinate. Befides, the Text, *Extra. de hæret. c.*
" *ad abolendam*, and C. *penult*, exprefsly fays, that Hereticks may be received
" after the Difcovery of their Error.

　　By comparing thefe Opinions together, it appears, that they are all of this
Mind, that in order to any one's being admitted to Repentance, he muft manifeft it before Sentence is pronounced. They efpecially require that he fignify it before Sentence given, or at leaft before Publication of it. But if he
remains impenitent, he is perfuaded not only before he is brought out in Procession,

ceffion, but even on the very Scaffold, and oftentimes, and moft earneftly admonifhed to forfake his Errors and abjure. The Method of doing it is this.
The Sentences of the Penitents and Converts, if any fuch there be, are read
firft, and laft of all thofe of the Impenitents, if there are any. But before
the pronouncing of them, they are admonifhed before all the People to repent, and at length to be converted, becaufe there is yet Room for Mercy.
If they fay they will be converted, they are carried back to Jayl, and admitted to Penance. If they perfevere obftinate and impenitent, the Sentence
is read, and they are delivered to the fecular Court, that being burnt in fight
of the People, they may fuffer the Punifhments due to their Impenitency.
But however, as to thofe who do not convert themfelves till they are actually
on the Scaffold, and the Sentence is going to be pronounced, the *Madrid* Inftruction, *An.* 1561. *c.* 44. advifes, that they are not to be admitted to Penance but upon the moft extraordinary Confiderations ; becaufe they appear
to be converted rather thro' Fear of inftant Death, than the Love of true
Repentance.

s. 204.   'Tis certainly the Opinion of *Eymerick*, that even fuch ought to be admitted to Repentance. But *Pegna*, tho' he thinks this Opinion of *Eymerick* to be
the fafer, yet determines that to be the more juft, which leaves to Criminals
Room for Mercy only, till they are brought forth from the Jayls of the Inquifitors, and that after this they are by no Means to be heard. *Zanchinus*
c. 16. §. 4. *Ugolinus* faith, that fuch a one is fo far to be received, as that he may efcape
the Punifhments of the Soul, *i. e.* the Punifhments of Hell ; and therefore
may be admitted to the Ecclefiaftical Sacraments, and abfolved from the Excommunication he was under, if he fhews Signs of true Repentance ; but
that he is by no means to be admitted to efcape corporal or temporal Punifhment, becaufe he came in too late who ftaid for his Sentence. *Extra. de*
hæret. c. Super eo. l. 6. Others fay this is wholly arbitrary, and depends merely on the Pleafure of the Judge, whereas others do not think it at all fafe,
that the Life of Penitents fhould depend on the Will of the Judges.

However, after Sentence pronounced, there is no farther Place for Pardon.
And yet there is one Inftance of *Stephana de Proaudo*, extant, in the Book
of the Sentences of the *Tholoufe* Inquifition, who, being judged an Heretick
the Day before, and left as an Heretick to the fecular Court (from whence it
appears that it was not then ufual for thofe who were left to the fecular Court
to be burnt the fame Day, on which the Sentence is pronounced, as is now
practifed in *Spain* and *Portugal*) feeing on the following Day, *viz. Monday*,
that the Fire in which fhe was to be burnt was made ready, faid, on that very Day that fhe was willing to be converted to the Catholick Faith, and to
return to the Ecclefiaftical Unity. And when 'twas doubted whether fhe
fpoke this feignedly or fincerely, or thro' Fear of Death, and was anfwered,
that the Time of Mercy was elapfed, and that fhe fhould think of the Salvation of her Soul, and fully difcover whatfoever fhe knew of her felf or
others concerning the Fact of Herefy, which fhe promifed to fay and
do, and that fhe would die in the Faith of the holy Church of *Rome* ; upon
                                                              this

this the Inquifitor and Vicars of the Bifhop of *Tholoufe* called a Council on the following *Tuefday*, and at length it was concluded, that on the follow-ing *Sunday* fhe fhould confefs the Faith of the Church of *Rome*, recant her Errors, and be carried back to Prifon, where it would be proved whether her Converfion was real or pretended ; and fo ftrictly kept, that fhe might not be able to infect others with her Errors. *Eymerick* alfo gives us an Inftance at *n. 104.* *Barcelona* in *Catalonia*, of three Hereticks impenitent, but not relapfed, who were delivered over to the fecular Arm. And when one of them, who was a Prieft, was put in the Fire, and one of his Sides fomewhat burnt, he cried to be taken out of it, becaufe he would abjure and repent. And he was ta-ken out accordingly. But he was afterwards found always to have continbed in his Herefy, and to have infected many, and would not be converted, and was therefore turn'd over again as impenitent and relapfed, to the fecular Arm, and burnt.

The Author of the Hiftory of the Inquifition at *Goa*, gives us another In- *Cap. 38.* ftance of a very rich new Chriftian, whofe Name was *Lewis Pezoa*, who, with his whole Family, had been accufed of fecret *Judaifm*, by fome of his Ene-mies, and who, with his Wife, two Sons and one Daughter, and fome other Relations that lived with him, were all thrown into the Jayl of the Inquifition. He denied the Crime of which he was accufed, and well refuted it, and de-manded that the Witneffes who had depofed againft him, might be difcove-red to him, that he might convict them of Falfhood. But he could obtain nothing, and was condemned as a Negative, to be delivered over to the Arm of the fecular Court ; which Sentence was made known to him fifteen Days be-fore it was pronounced. The Duke of *Cadaval*, an intimate Friend of the Duke *d'Aveira*, Inquifitor General, had made ftrict Enquiry how his Affair was like to turn. And underftanding by the Inquifitor General, that un-lefs he confeffed before his going out of Prifon, he could not efcape the Fire, becaufe he had been legally convicted, he continued to intreat the Inquifitor General, till he had obtained a Promife from him, that if he could perfuade *Pezoa* to confefs, even after Sentence pronounced, and his Proceffion in the Act of Faith, he fhould not die, tho' it was contrary to the Laws and Cuftom of an Act of Faith. Upon that folemn Day therefore, on which the Act of Faith was to be held, he went with fome of his own Friends, and fome that were *Pezoa's*, to the Gate of the Inquifition, to prevail with him, if poffible, to confefs. He came out in the Proceffion, wearing the infamous Samarre, and on his Head the Caroch, or infamous Mitre. His Friends, with many Tears, befought him in the Name of the Duke *de Cadaval*, and by all that was dear to him, that he would preferve his Life, and intimated to him, that if he would confefs and repent, the faid Duke had obtained his Life from the Inqui-fitor General, and would give him more than he had loft. But all in vain, *Pezoa* continually protefting himfelf innocent, and that the Crime it felf was falfly invented by his Enemies who fought his Deftruction. When the Pro-ceffion was ended, and the Act of Faith almoft finifhed, the Sentences of thofe who were condemned to certain Penances having been read, and on the Approach of Evening, the Sentences of those who were to be delivered over to the secular Court being begun to be read, his Friends repeated their Intreaties, by which at last they overcame his Constancy, so that desiring an Audience, and rising up, that he might be heard, he said, *Come then let us go and confess the Crimes I am falsly accused of, and thereby gratify the Desires of my Friends.* And having confessed his Crime, he was remanded to Jayl. Two Years after he was sent to *Evora,* and in the Act of Faith walked in Procession wearing the Samarre, on which was painted the Fire inverted, according to the usual Custom of the *Portuguese* Inquisition ; and after five Years more that he was detained in the Jayl of the Inquisition, he was condemned to the Gallies for five Years.

t. 47.
9. 73.

    Finally, *Simancas* proposes and resolves a Question concerning another Case, *viz.* " Whether an Heretick converted after a definitive Sentence, who says " that he will repent, and discover other Hereticks to the Judges, and is " upon that Account returned to the Inquisitors by the secular Judge, and " makes a full Confession before them, is to be left again to the said secular " Judge. This Question in the former Age was actually debated by the In-" quisitors of *Cuenca,* and after the supream Judges and skilful Men had been " consulted, they unanimously answered, that such a Penitent was not to be " left again to the secular Court ; both because he had made a true Confes-" sion before the Inquisitors, and therefore ought not to be delivered up by " them, and because the secular Judge seems to renounce his own Right, by " delivering to the Inquisitors the Heretick that had been turned over to " him."   Add to this, that 'tis neither consistent with Goodness nor Equity, that he who is now neither impenitent nor relapsed, should, upon any Account, be delivered over to the secular Power.

CHAP. XXXIV.

How the PROCESS *ends against a relapsed* PENITENT.

Direct.
p.3.n.197.
com. 45.

IF the accused Person is found a Relapse by his own Confession, but penitent, professing that he believes in a Catholick Manner, and is willing to return to the Unity of the Church, the Bishop and Inquisitor send to him two or three good Men, and especially Religious, or Clergymen, zealous for the Faith, neither suspected by, nor ungrateful to him, who, upon some convenient Hour go to him, and after discoursing with him in the first Place concerning the Contempt of the World, the Miseries of this present Life, and the Joys and Glories of Paradise, do afterwards, in the Name of the Bishop and Inquisitor, discover to him, that inasmuch as he is relapsed, he can't escape temporal Death ; and that therefore he ought to be careful of the Salvation of his Soul, and prepare himself for the Confession of his Sins, and the Reception

ception of the Sacrament of the Eucharift. And thefe Admonitions they repeat till he hath confeffed his Sins, and humbly defires that the Sacrament of the Eucharift may be given him, becaufe the Ecclefiaftical Sacraments are not to be denied to a relapfed Penitent, if he humbly defires them. Cap. *Su. per eo* de hæret. lib. 6. After having received thefe Sacraments, and by this Means being, in their Opinion, rightly prepared for Salvation, the Bifhop and Inquifitor order the Ballive of the Place, or the chief Magiftrate of the fecular Court, to be ready with his Attendants fuch a Day or Hour, in fuch a Street or Place, to receive from their Court fuch a Relapfe, which they will deliver to him ; and that on the fame Day, or the Day before he fhall make Proclamation by the Crier throughout the City, in all the ufual Places and Streets, that on fuch a Day, Hour and Place, the Inquifitor will make a Ser. mon for the Faith, and that he and the Bifhop will then condemn a certain Relapfe, by delivering him over to the fecular Court.

Here they differ, whether a condemned Perfon may be delivered over to the fecular Court, on *Sunday*, or a Holy-day. In many Cities of *Europe* 'tis a Cuftom, that the Inquifitors do not deliver over to the fecular Court Re. lapfes, or Impenitents, on a Holy-day, but on fome other ; and therefore the Criminal, two or three Days before he is burnt, is removed from the Houfes or Jayls of the Inquifitors, to the Jayls of the fecular Judges. But in *Spain* and *Portugal*, all Things relating to the Act of Faith are done on fome Fe-ftival, to ftrike the greater Terror into the People.

In like Manner they are not all agreed, whether when the Criminals are delivered over to the fecular Court, the Act of Faith ought to be celebrated within the Church, or without it. In *Spain* and *Portugal* fuch publick Acts of Faith are held without the Church, and, generally fpeaking, in a large and open Street or Market, and upon very high Scaffolds, that all the People may more eafily and clearly fee, which could not be done fo conveniently within the Church.

Matters being thus ordered, if the Perfon to be delivered over to the fe-*n.* 195. cular Court is in holy Orders, a Prieft, or of any other Degree, he is, before he is turned over, ftripped of the Prerogative of the whole Ecclefiaftical Or-der, or, as they call it, degraded, that being deprived of every Dignity that might exempt him from the fecular Power, he may be delivered over to it.

This Degradation is twofold, one verbal, the other actual. The verbal is, when the Bifhop pronounces Sentence againft a Clergyman, by which he deprives him of all Clerical Orders, or rather of the Miniftry or Execution of thofe Orders, which is more properly Depofition. The actual is, when the Clergyman is not only deprived by Sentence, but alfo deprived actually and perfonally, ftripped and defpoiled of his Ecclefiaftical Orders ; and this takes Place in the Crime of Herefy, when the Perfon is to be deliver'd over to the fecular Court. But if he is only to be perpetually imprifoned, they only make ufe of verbal Degradation.

In order to an actual Degradation, a certain Number of Judges was formerly required. In the Cafe of a Bifhop, twelve Bifhops were requifite ; of a Presbyter, fix Bifhops ; and of a Deacon, three. But becaufe in the Affair of Herefy, it would be difficult for fo many Bifhops to affemble, to degrade a Religious, already judged by the Judges of the Faith, the Bifhop, according to a Power granted by *Gregory* IX. calls together the Prelates, Abbots and Religious Men of his Diocefe, to be prefent on the Day appointed for this Ceremony. The Bifhop himfelf, cloathed in his *Pontificalibus*, affifted by the Prelates of his Diocefe, places before him the Perfon to be degraded, cloathed with all his Veftments, juft as if he was going to divine Service, and degrades him from his Order, beginning with the higheft, and fo gradually defcending to the loweft. And as in conferring Orders, the Bifhop ufes a Form of Words appointed by the Church for this Purpofe ; fo alfo in degrading, when he depofes him from the Cloak and the Gown, and other Degrees, he ufes Expreffions quite the contrary, by which he declares he deprives him of this Order.

So that the conferring of Orders, and the Degradation from them are performed in a Manner, and with Ceremonies directly contrary to each other. For when Orders are conferred, they begin from the loweft till they gradually rife to the higheft. Firft, they confer the Order of the Door-keeper. The Bifhop takes the Keys from the Altar, and delivering them to him when he appoints a Door-keeper, fays, *Do this as one who muft give an Account to God for the Things locked up by thefe Keys.* The Bifhop ordains the Reader with this Ceremony. The People being prefent at his Ordination, the Bifhop delivers him a Book, in which are written the Things belonging to his Function, faying, *Receive it, and be thou a Rehearfer of the Word of God, and if you faithfully and profitably fulfill your Office, have part with thofe, who from the Beginning have adminiftred well the Word of God.* The Bifhop ordains an Exorcift, by delivering to him a Book, in which the Exorcifms are contained, ufing this Form of Words, *Receive and commit to Memory, and have Power of laying Hands upon the Poffeffed, whether baptized, or Catechumens.* In the Ordination of an Acolythift, this Ceremony is obferved. After the Bifhop diligently admonifhes the Perfons to be ordained of their Office, he delivers to each of them Wax-lights, after this manner. *Receive the Candleftick with the Wax-light, and know that you are ingaged to light the Tapers of the Church, in the Name of the Lord.* Then he delivers to him the empty Flaggons, in which they ferve up Water and Wine at the Sacrifice, faying, *Receive the Flaggons to minifter Wine and Water for the Eucharift of the Blood of Chrift, in the Name of the Lord.* When the Bifhop ordains Sub-Deacons, he admonifhes them, that the Law of perpetual Continence is injoined this Order, and declares that no one is taken into the Order of Sub-Deacons, who is not voluntarily determined to fubmit to this Law. After this, when the folemn Prayer of the Litanies is faid, he enumerates and explains what are the Duties and Functions of the Sub-Deacons. When thefe Things are done, all thofe who are to be ordained, receive from the Bifhop the Chalice and facred Pattens ; and from
the.

the Hands of the Arch-Deacon, to let them know that the Sub-Deacon is to affist the Deacon's Office, the Flaggons full of Wine and Water, together with the Bafon, and Napkin with which they wipe their Hands ; and the Bifhop fays, *You fee what Miniftry is hereby committed to you, therefore I admonifh you, fo to behave your felves, as that ye may pleafe God.* Befides this, they ufe fome other Prayers. At laft after the Bifhop hath put the facred Veftments on the Sub-Deacon, at every one of which proper Words and Ceremonies are ufed, he delivers him the Book of the Epiftles, and fays, *Receive the Book of Epiftles, and receive Power to read them in the holy Church of God, as well for the Living as for the Dead.* In the Ordination of a Deacon the Bifhop ufes a greater Number of more folemn Prayers, and adds other Ornaments of facred Veftments. Befides this, he lays his Hand on him, and finally delivers him the Book of the Gofpels, with thefe Words. *Receive Power to read the Book of the Gofpel in the Church of God, as well for the Living as for the Dead, in the Name of the Lord.* The Bifhop ordains a Prieft with thefe Rites. In the firft place, he, with all the Priefts who are prefent, lay their Hands on him ; then fitting the Veft to his Shoulders, he brings it over on his Breaft in Form of a Crofs ; after this he anoints his Hands with holy Oil, and delivers him the Chalice with the Wine, and the Patten with the Hoft, faying, *Receive Power of offering Sacrifice to God, and of celebrating Maffes, as well for the Living as for the Dead.* At laft he lays his Hands again upon his Head, faying, *Receive the Holy Ghoft, whofe Sins you remit, they fhall be remitted to them, and whofefoever you retain, they are retained.*

Degradation is performed by Words and Ceremonies directly contrary. We have an Inftance of this in the Book of the Sentences of the *Tholoufe* Inquifi- *fol.* 137. tion, in one *John Philibert*, a Presbyter, who had joined himfelf to the *Valdenfes*, and whom by Order of the Pope, the Arch-Bifhop of *Tholoufe*, in the Room of the Bifhop of *Aux* his Diocefan, who was dead, degraded from all his Orders in the Prefence of the Abbots, and Prelates, or their Vicars, and delivered over to the fecular Court. For after he was fet before them in his Sacerdotal Veftment, they ftripped him of all his Ornaments, ufing certain Expreffions. The Chalice and Patten : *We take from you the Chalice and Patten, and ftrip and deprive you of the Office and Power of offering Sacrifice to God, and of celebrating any Mafs.* The Prieft's Veft : *We take from you the Prieft's Habit or Veft, fince you have defpifed to wear the eafy Yoke of the Lord reprefented by it, and to preferve the Veft of Innocence.* [To this Ceremony there is another *Lib. Cere-* immediately fubjoined, which was obferved in the Degradation of one *James, mat. fol.* a pretended Minorite. " After this the Bifhop immediately takes out the A- 105. " nointing, by flightly fcraping with a Piece of Glafs, fo as not to draw Blood, " thofe Places of the Hands which had been anointed, drawing the Glafs " from the right Hand Thumb to the left Hand Fore-finger, and then " again from the left Hand Thumb to the right Hand Fore-finger, as " is the Manner when the Bifhop anoints any Perfon for a Prieft." And thus by taking away all the Marks of the Priefthood, he is deprived of the Ornaments of the other Orders.] The Surplice : *We take from you the*

Surplice,

Surplice, the Ornament of the Diaconal Office, since you have not worn it as the Covering of Gladness, and the Garment of Salvation. The Book of the Gospels: We take from you the Book of the Gospels, and strip and deprive you of the Office and Power of reading in the Church of God. The Diaconal Vest: We take from you the Diaconal Vest, and strip and deprive you of the Power of exercising the Diaconal Office. The Chalice, Patten, Flaggon, Water, Bason and Napkin: We take from you the Chalice, Patten, Flaggon, Water, Bason, Napkin, the Instruments of the Sub-diaconal Office, and strip and deprive you of the Use of them. The Sub-Deacon's Tunick: We take from you the Tunick, the Ornament of the Sub-diaconal Office, since you have not used it to Righteousness and Salvation. The Maniple *: We take from you the Maniple, the Ornament of the Sub-diaconal Office, and we-strip and deprive you of the Ministry designed thereby. The Book of the Epistles: We take from you the Book of the Epistles, and divest and deprive you of the Power of reading them in the holy Church of God. The Candlestick: We take from you the Candlestick, and divest and deprive you of the Office of lighting the Tapers in the Church. The Flaggon: We take from you the Flaggon, that from henceforth you may not use it in serving up Wine and Water for the Eucharist of the Blood of Christ. The Book of Exorcisms: We take from you the Book of Exorcisms, and deprive and divest you of the Power of laying your Hands upon the Possessed, whether baptized, or Catechumens. The Book he received when made Reader: We take from you the Book you received with the Order of Reading, and divest and deprive you of the Power of reading it any more in the holy Church of God. The Keys: We take from you the Keys of the Church, and divest and deprive you of the Office and Power of keeping the Things locked up with those Keys, and of opening or shutting the Gates of the Church. By the Authority of Almighty God, Father, Son, and Holy Spirit, and also by the Power committed to us, as aforesaid, in this Affair, we take from you the Clerical Habit, and depose and also degrade you, from all Priestly, and every other Order, and divest and deprive you of every Clerical Honour, Benefice and Privilege. And therefore we farther pronounce and declare to the noble Person, the Lord Guiardo Guido, Seneschal of Tholouse, here present, that he shall receive you, thus degraded, into his Court. However, we earnestly require and beseech him, that he will so moderate the Sentence concerning you, as to prevent the Danger of Death, and maiming of Limbs. After these Things his Head is shaved, before the secular Court receives him. [This shaving the Head is performed in this manner. The Bishop begins to pull out some few of the Hairs of his Head with Nippers, after which the Barber finishes it with a Razor, so that there remains on it no Mark of his Tonsure or Clericate.]

Lib. Catenat. fol. 106.

After the Degradation is performed, Sentence is pronounced against him as a Relapse, and he as such, altho' penitent, is cast out of the Ecclesiastical Court, and delivered to the secular Arm. But they generally add this Clause to such Sentences, by which a Relapse, or impenitent Heretick, or any other, is delivered to the secular Arm. Nevertheless we effectually beseech the said secular Arm, that he will moderate his Sentence concerning you, so as to prevent the

---

* Manipulus. An Ecclesiastical Vestment, called also the Sudarium, which the Priests wear on the left Arm.

Effusion

Effufion of Blood, and Danger of Death ; according to Cap. *Novimus*, de verb.
fign. where, after 'tis commanded that a Clergyman degraded fhall be delivered to the fecular Court, 'tis added, *For whom neverthelefs the Church ought
effectually to intercede, that the Sentence may be moderated, fo as to prevent Danger
of Death* ; *viz.* leaft the Inquifitors, when they deliver Criminals to the fecular Judges, fhould feem to confent to the Effufion of Blood, and thereby
become irregular.

When this Sentence againft a Relapfe is concluded, the Bifhop and Inqui- *n.* 100.
fitor don't fhew it to the Criminal, left he fhould be enraged againft them ;
but they fend to him certain good Men, efpecially Religious or Clergymen,
not unacceptable to him, who difcover to him the Sentence to be pronounced againft him, and the Death to be inflicted on him, to confirm him in
the Faith, to exhort him to Patience, to accompany him after his Sentence,
to comfort him, and pray with him, and not to depart from him, till he
hath returned his Spirit to his Creator. But they muft diligently take Care,
that they do not fay or do any Thing by which the Death of the relapfed
Perfon may be haftned, *viz.* by exhorting him when condemned, to offer his
Head to the Executioner, or to go up the Ladder, or to fay to the Hangman
fo to direct his Sword, as to ftrike off his Head at one Blow, and not at feveral, or to fay or do, or perfuade to any Things of like kind, by which his
Death would be fooner effected, altho' the fame would have hapned, altho'
thefe Words or Actions had never been ; becaufe they contract Irregularity
by thefe Things. Who would not believe that thefe Men detefted with all
their Soul every Effufion of Blood, who fo effectually intercede for the Condemned, and are fo extreamly careful not to fay or do any Thing by which
their Death may be haftned? Here fome think, that fuch Penitents relapfed
ought to be allowed Ecclefiaftical Burial, as well as all other Catholicks. But
this is contrary to Law and Cuftom, becaufe their Bodies are burnt with Fire.
In this Refpect however they are dealt more favourably with than the Obftinate and Impenitent, inafmuch as thefe latter are burnt alive, whereas the
others are ftrangled before they are burnt, which, as *Simancas* fays, is more
human, and leads to Repentance. *Tit.* 47. §. 17.

C H A P. XXXV.

How the PROCESS *ends againft an impenitent* HERETICK, *and
impenitent* RELAPSE.

IF the accufed Perfon be an impenitent Heretick, but not relapfed, he is *Direct.*
kept in clofe Imprifonment, and put in Chains, that he may not efcape *p.* 3.
and infect others ; nor is any one allowed to come to him, or to fpeak with *n.* 101.
him, except the Keepers, who muft be good Men, and not fufpected con- *cap. 96.*
cerning the Faith, nor eafy to be deceived. In the mean while all Methods
muft be ufed for his Converfion, according to the Decree of the Council of
Baterre, c. 17. *Thofe who will not be converted, be flow, as you conveniently can, to
condemn.*

condemn them, admonishing them frequently by your selves and others to confess ; and if they are finally obstinate in their Wickedness, cause their Errors to be publickly declared, in Detestation of them, and leave them thus condemned to the secular Powers present, or their Ballives, according to the Apostolick Command. Herewith the *Madrid* Instruction, *An.* 1561. *c.* 43. agrees. *When the Criminal is negative, and hath been legally convicted of the Crime of Heresy of which he was accused, or continues obstinate, 'tis evident from the Law that he ought to be delivered to the secular Court. However, in such a Case, the Inquisitors ought greatly to endeavour his Conversion, that at least he may die in the Grace of God. And here they must do all they can consistent with Piety.* So that the Bishop and Inquisitor frequently, sometimes both together, sometimes apart, must cause him to be brought before them, to refute his Opinions, and persuade him into the Faith of the Church of *Rome.* If he doth not submit to their Information, ten or twelve Persons are sent to him to instruct him, learned Men, Clergymen of different Religions, and secular Lawyers, who frequently converse with him, to shew him that his Opinion is contrary to the sacred Scripture, and the Decrees of the Church of *Rome.* If he is not converted, he is not immediately delivered to the secular Arm, tho' he desires it, but is kept in Chains a long while, half a Year, or a whole one, in a hard and close Jayl, that by the Misery and Distress of his Imprisonment, his Constancy may be overcome. In the mean while he is frequently admonished, that if he persists he must be burnt, and after this Life burn in Hell Fire for ever. But if he is not moved by this Calamity, he is removed into a somewhat more comfortable Jayl, and used in a little kinder Manner. They also make use of Promises, that if he will turn, he shall experience the Mercy of the Judges. If they can neither prevail with him by this Means, they suffer his Wife and Children, especially his little ones, if he hath any, and his other Relations, to come to him, to break his Resolution and Constancy. But if after all these Methods used he persists in his Opinion, the Bishop and Inquisitor prepare to deliver him over to the secular Court. When therefore the Sermon concerning the Faith is held, the Inquisitor causes his Faults and Heresies to be read over by the Notary, or some other Clergyman, and then asks him whether he will depart from his Heresies and abjure them? If he consents to abjure, he is admitted ; and having made his Abjuration, he was condemned in the Times of *Eymerick* to perpetual Imprisonment, because he was believed to abjure rather thro' Fear of Death than the Love of Truth. And if he was a Clerick, he was degraded from his Orders, by a verbal Degradation only, *i. e.* he was deposed from the Function of his Ministry.

But if in this Condition he will not repent and abjure his Opinions, as is commonly the Case with such Persons, he is condemned as an obstinate Heretick, and as such delivered over to the secular Court. Cap. *ad abolendam,* §. *Præsenti,* Extrav. de hæret. And whilst the secular Court is performing its Duty, some good Men, and zealous for the Faith, may attend him, and persuade him to the Catholick Faith, and exhort him as yet to turn from his Errors. And 'tis the Opinion of *Eymerick,* that if even then he will be converted, he may be admitted to Repentance. But *Pegna* judges it more safe, not to receive him by any Means, altho' he promises a thousand times his Conversion; both because 'tis provided for by no Law, and because Experience shews us that Persons thus received, seldom or ever become good.

If an Heretick impenitent or relapsed be present, the Bishop and Inquisitor, in Presence of the Magistrate of the secular Court, Cap. *Excommunicamus*, 1, 2. *Extrav. de hæret.* declare him impenitent, or relapsed, cast him out from the Ecclesiastical Court, and leave him to the secular Arm, or to the Jurisdiction of the secular Court. And the secular Court, which is in that Place, receives him as one left to their Court and Arm. If he be absent and fugitive, he is by Sentence declared impenitent or relapsed, and cast out from the Ecclesiastical Court, and left to the secular Arm; and whenever the secular Court can lay hold of him, he is punished as one obnoxious to that Court, according to the Nature of his Crime, Cap. *ad abolendam*, §. *Præsenti*, Extrav. de hæret.

If the accused Person be an Heretick impenitent and relapsed, all Reme-*n. 105.* dies are to be made use of for his Conversion, and he is closely and carefully confined, and no one admitted to him. But he can't escape Death. And therefore they exhort him, inasmuch as he can't avoid the Punishment of Death, to consult at least the Salvation of his Soul, to confess and receive the Sacrament of the Eucharist. Behold the amazing Charity of these reverend Fathers, who when they deliver a penitent Criminal to Death, are so solicitous about the Salvation of his Soul! But whether he repents or not, he is delivered to the secular Court, with a very earnest Intreaty, so to mitigate their Sentence concerning him, as to prevent the Effusion of Blood, and Danger of Death.

C H A P. XXXVI.

How the PROCESS *ends against a Negative* HERETICK *convicted.*

IF the Person accused be found in Heresy either by the Evidence of the *Direct.* Fact, or the legal Production of Witnesses, and yet he doth not confess *p. 3.* it, but persists in the Negative, he is at this Day called a convicted Nega- *n. 207.* tive Heretick. Concerning these the Council of *Biterre* hath thus determined.*com. 43.* Cap. 6, 7, 8, 9. *As to those who are Criminals, and contemn to appear within the Time of Grace, or maliciously suppress the Truth, let each of them be cited by Name in their Turn; and if they will not confess the Truth found against them, read over to them the Heads of the Matters in which they are found criminal, and discover to them the Depositions of the Witnesses, and granting them competent Times, and allowing them the Liberty of defending themselves, receive candidly their legal Exceptions and Replications. And if they fail in their Defence, assign them a competent peremptory Time for their Sentence, and condemn them, unless they will of their own Accord confess the Crime proved against them. For they are not to be received to Mercy whilst they persist in their Denial, how much soever they submit themselves to the Will of the Church.* Thus also the Council of *Narbonne*, c. 26. *But if any*
one

one is not afraid obstinately to deny his Fault, upon account of which he may be judged a Believer of Hereticks, or an Heretick, and which is fully proved by Witnesses, or other Proofs, as long as he persists in this Denial, tho' otherwise he may pretend Conversion, he is, without Doubt, to be accounted an Heretick. For he is evidently impenitent, who will not confess his Sin. In *Spain* the same Opinion and Sentence is openly declared for by the first *Seville* Instruction, *An.* 1484. *cap.* 14. where also 'tis provided, that as often as such a Case should occur, the Inquisitors should diligently inquire into the Life and Marners of the Witnesses.

Pegna,
in Direct.
part. 3.
p. 565.

An Heretick is also judged to be impenitent, altho' he protests himself to be a Believer, not only when he is convicted of the Heresy he hath said, but also of any heretical Fact, by which he may be judged to be an Heretick, or Believer of Hereticks. This is to be understood of one, who denies the heretical Fact of which he is legally convicted ; and not of him who confesses such heretical Fact, but denies the evil Intention. And these are the Reasons alledged why such a one may be condemned as an impenitent Heretick. Because if the Heresy of such a Negative is fully and legally proved, it appears to the Church, that such a one is an Heretick, and therefore unless he confesses and detests his Errors, he is deservedly delivered to the secular Court, as an impenitent Heretick. Besides, he who doth not admit the Errors legally proved against him, doth not satisfy the Church, tho' he protests that he holds the right Faith, the Church first demanding Satisfaction for the Heresies proved, which he denies that he ever said. And therefore not being amended, he may be condemned as an Impenitent, because Pardon of Sin is granted to no one without Amendment. And finally, Confession is necessary to true Repentance, nor doth he deserve to obtain Pardon, who doth not acknowledge his Sin ; and therefore as a Negative doth not confess his Crime, he is accounted as Impenitent, and therefore is deservedly to be left to the secular Court. *Nor let any one affirm,* says *Pegna, that he is by this Means unjustly condemned, nor complain of the Ecclesiastical Judges, or of the Judgment of the Church which hath thus determined, and which doth not judge of any Thing that is secret. But if it should happen that any one is convicted by false Witnesses, let him bear it with Patience, and rejoyce that he suffers Death for the Truth.* But before such a Sentence can take place, 'tis, according to this Doctrine, required : First, that the Person be convicted either of true and formal Heresy, *viz.* saying there is no Purgatory, and not of a scandalous, rash or ill-founding Assertion, and the like ; or of Facts from which arise Heresy or Apostacy. And here there is Need of great Prudence. Secondly, 'tis required that the heretical Words, of which a Negative is convicted, be certain and clear, and not dubious or doubtful, capable of a double Sense, one heretical, the other catholick ; because as doubtful Expressions are to be interpreted in the best Sense, the Catholick Sense is to be received, and the heretical Sense rejected. Thirdly, that one guilty of an Heresy which he denies, be convicted by legal and proper Witnesses, above all Exception, and not by Enemies, or single Witnesses, or others unfit. Fourthly, that the heretical Fact or Saying, of which the Criminal is convicted, be lately done, and not an old Matter.

Matter, which the Criminal may be suppofed likely to have forgot; becaufe in a Matter done a great while ago, fuch Forgetfulnefs may be prefumed. Laftly, that a Negative be convicted by Witneffes to have afferted, that he doth fo believe himfelf, and that others ought to believe fo too.

Such a Negative is kept in hard Confinement, and laid in Irons, and is by the Bifhop, Inquifitor, and others oftentimes admonifhed to confefs the Truth, with the Hopes of Mercy if he doth, and the Threatning of being delivered to the fecular Court if he perfifts in the Negative. If he ftill perfifts in the Denial, the Bifhop and Inquifitor, either feparate, or together, privately examine the Witneffes themfelves, and by other good Men, and admonifh them to tell them the Truth privately, that the accufed Perfon may not die unjuftly. If the Witneffes perfift in the Affirmative, and the Party accufed in the Negative, they are examined with greater Care; not that the Witneffes are confronted with the Perfon they accufe, that they may be examined together. 'Tis only recommended to the Inquifitors to ufe Prudence in fearching out the Truth, left it fhould happen that an innocent Perfon, who can't fully defend himfelf, fhould be unjuftly condemned. Thus the *Madrid* Inftruction orders, *An.* 1561. *c.* 38. *That the Inquifitors fhould carefully confider in the Defences of the Criminals, that being confined in fecret Jayls, they can't fo conveniently defend themfelves, and that therefore they ought to fupply this Defect by their Diligence and Prudence, in inquiring particularly into the Life, Manners, Enmity or Confpiracy of the Witneffes.* If any one of the Witneffes faulters, or if there are other Signs againft him, they are taken notice of, that the Truth may be found out. If they are found falfe Witneffes, or if they retract their Evidence, the accufed Perfon is pronounced and difmiffed as innocent, and they themfelves condemned to perpetual Imprifonment, and oftentimes expofed as publick Spectacles upon Ladders before the Gates of certain Churches, and their Lives only mercifully fpared them. But if the Witneffes perfift, and the accufed Perfon perfifts alfo in the Negative, having been kept in Jayl for a competent Time, *viz.* a Year, he is at laft, by the Sentence of the Bifhop and Inquifitor, caft out of the Ecclefiaftical Court as obftinate and impenitent, and delivered over to the fecular Arm. So that if it fhould happen that he is accufed by falfe Witneffes, and is really innocent, the miferable Wretch, tho' falfly condemned, is delivered to the Power of the fecular Court, to be burnt alive; nor is it lawful for him, without the Commiffion of mortal Sin, as the Pegna, *Roman* Doctors think, to fave his Life, by falfly confeffing a Crime he hath *p.* 567. not committed. And therefore in this Cafe, tho' it may feem very hard to fuch a Negative to die when he is innocent, and for this Reafon he may poffibly believe it lawful for him to confefs the Crimes objected to him to fave his Life, yet this is not to be fuffered by any Means; and therefore 'tis the Duty of the Divines and Confeffors, who comfort fuch a Negative, and attend on him to his Punifhment, to perfuade him to difcover the Truth; but to caution him by all Means not to acknowledge a Crime he hath not committed, to avoid temporal Death; and to put him in Remembrance, that if he patiently endures this Injury and Punifhment, he will be crowned as a Martyr.

'Tis however evident, if the Practice of the *Portugal* Inquisition be confidered, that the Inquisitors are not so very solicitous about the eternal Salvation of those they condemn, as they are to consult their own Honour by the Criminals Confessions even of false Crimes. We have seen the Instance of *Lewis Pecoa*, given in Chapter xxxiii. who being led forth in solemn Procession at an Act of Faith, and being at last overcome by the continued Prayers and Tears of his Friends, said, *Come then, let us go and confess the Crimes I am falsly accused of, and thus satisfy the Desires of my Friends ;* and having made his Confession, he was saved from the Sentence of Death. The same History of the Inquisition at *Goa*, in the preceding Chapter, gives us another not less remarkable Instance, of a noble *Portuguese*, descended from the Race of the new Christians, who was accused of *Judaism.* But as he did most firmly deny the Crime objected to him, nothing was omitted that might persuade him to a Confession of it ; for he was not only promised his Life, but the Restitution of all his Effects, if he would confess, and threatned with a cruel Death if he persisted in the Negative. But when all this was to no purpose, the Inquisitor General, who had some Respect for him, endeavoured to overcome his Constancy by Wheedling and other Arguments ; but when he constantly refused to confess himself guilty of a Crime he had not committed, the Inquisitor General being at last provoked by his Firmness, said, *What then do you mean ? Do you think that we will suffer our selves to be charged with a Lye ?* And having said this he went off. These Words of this Judge, says the History, carry in them a very unbecoming Meaning, and raise Reflections dishonourable enough to the holy Office. For 'tis almost the same as if he had said, we will rather deliver you, tho' innocent, to the Fire, than suffer any one to believe that you were unjustly imprisoned by us. When the Act of Faith drew near, the Sentence of Death was pronounced against him, and a Confessor allowed him to prepare him for Death. But at last he sunk under the Fear of his approaching dreadful Punishment, and by confessing on the very Day of the Act of Faith the Crime falsly fastned on him, he escaped Death ; but all his Estate was confiscated, and he himself condemned for five Years to the Gallies.

P. 2. t. 1.
§. 10.   *Carena* observes, that it sometimes happens, that a Negative Heretick, given over by the Inquisitors to the secular Arm, cites and challenges them to the Valley of *Jehosaphat*, or the Tribunal of God. But if it appears to the Judge that he hath proceeded justly in the Condemnation of a negative Heretick, he ought not to be afraid of his Citation. But if the Judge should not be certain of the Justice of his Sentence, but perceived any Disturbance in his Mind when he pronounced it, then 'tis his Duty more maturely to inquire into all Circumstances, that the former Sentence may be either revoked or confirmed. In the mean while they say, that if such Citation and Appellation be made not thro' Hatred and Revenge, but with a good Design, that his Innocence may appear, and his Family be preserved from Infamy, it is lawful.

Because

Becaufe Negatives conftantly deny the Crime of Herefy, and profefs that they are, and always were Catholicks, and are willing to die in the Faith of the Catholick Church, they are firft ftrangled before they are burnt. But *Souza* fays, that Hereticks convict and negative, if after they are delivered to *l.* 3. *c.* 6. the fecular Judge, they do not confefs before him the Catholick Faith, are §. 11. burnt alive ; becaufe, as it appears that they are Hereticks, fo by being fi_ lent when they ought to anfwer, they are looked upon as obftinate. Thus it was actually judged by all the Judges of the Council of Supplication in the City of *Lisbon, An.* 1629. the fecond *Sunday* of *September,* and twelfth Day of that Month, when, in an Act of Faith then celebrated, three Men, *Hebrews* by Birth, and called new Chriftians, were delivered over by the Inquifitors to the fecular Court for *Judaifm,* of which they were convicted ; who, perfifting in the Negative, affirmed before the Inquifitors that they were Chriftians. And being brought before the fecular Judges, and interrogated concerning the Faith, would make no Anfwer ; upon which they were delivered over to the Officers to be burnt alive, and were accordingly burnt alive.

CHAP. XXXVII.

How the PROCESS *ends againft a Fugitive* HERETICK.

IF the accufed Perfon be a Fugitive, after he is waited for a competent *Direct.* Time, he is cited by the Bifhop or Inquifitor in the Cathedral Church of *P.* 3. *n.* 211. that Diocefe where he hath offended, and in other Churches of that Place where *com.* 49. he lived, and particularly from whence he made his Efcape, perfonally to ap- pear on a certain Day in fuch a Cathedral Church of fuch a Diocefe, there to hear, upon a certain Hour, his definitive Sentence before them, to which they add, whether he appears or not, that they will proceed againft him to a defini- tive Sentence, as Law and Juftice require. This Citation is fixed upon the Gates of the Cathedral Church. In this Citation fome Delay is granted, *viz.* of thirty Days, and that is peremptory, fo that this fingle one ferves for three, in which the Criminal is cited to all and fingular the Proceedings of his Trial.

If the Criminal doth not appear, his Contumacy is complained of in the feveral Terms of the Edict, and the Fifcal of the Inquifition puts in his Bill of Accufation, after which the Procefs is carried on according to Courfe of Law, obferving the Cuftom and Laws of the holy Office. When all this is finifhed, if the Crime really appears, Sentence is pronounced againft the Criminal whenever the Procefs is rightfully and legally determined. If he hath been informed againft for Herefy, he is declared an obftinate Heretick, and as fuch left to the fecular Arm. If informed againft as one fufpected of Herefy, and if excommunicated, becaufe he would not appear, and if remain- ing under the Sentence of Excommunication for a Year, he is not pronoun-

ced

ced an Heretick, but condemned as tho' he was one. But if upon the Expiration of the Year he appears, he is heard as far as relates to the excufing his Crime, and teftifying his Innocence ; but not in order to recover his Effects, unlefs he can make his Innocence, or fome other juft Impediment legally appear. If he is in facred Orders, he is firft degraded, by a verbal Degradation only, becaufe he cannot be actually degraded, inafmuch as he is abfent. But *Eymericus* thinks, that the Perfon, thus degraded, is not to be left to the fecular Arm, but that if he will repent, he may freely, and without the Queftion be admitted to Mercy and Abjuration.

Pegna, *in* Dirett. part. 3. cum. 91.

This whole Affair is prefcribed the Inquifitors of *Spain,* by a certain firft Inftruction, Cap. 19. *They have likewife decreed, that the Inquifitors may proceed againft Criminals in the faid Crime of Herefy, altho' abfent, by citing the aforefaid abfent Perfons by publick Edicts, which they fhall caufe to be publifhed and faftned to the Doors of the principal Church of the Place or Places where they dwelt. Now, the Inquifitors may form Proceffes againft Abfentees by one of thefe three ways. Firft, according as 'tis prefcribed,* Cap. cum contumacia, de hæret. lib. 6. viz. *by citing and admonifhing the Abfentees to appear to defend themfelves, and anfwer, according to Law, upon certain Articles relating to the Faith, and upon a certain Crime of Herefy,* &c. *under Pain of Excommunication, with their Admonitions in Form. But if he doth not appear, they fhall command the Promotor Fifcal to accufe him of Contumacy, and to demand Indictments or Bills more fully charged, by which he may be denounced. But if he continues in his Obftinacy for the Space of a Year, they may declare him an Heretick in Form of Law. And this Method of Procefs is the fafeft, and leaft fevere. The fecond way is this, That if it fhall appear to the Inquifitors, that the Offence ought to be fully proved againft any Abfentee, they may cite him by Edicts, as aforefaid, to come and anfwer and declare according to his Right, and to fhew his Innocence within 30 Days, divided into three Terms, every Term confifting of ten Days ; or they may allow them a longer Time, if they think proper, according to the Diftance or Remotenefs of the Places, in which 'tis or may be prefumed that the aforefaid cited Perfons dwell ; whom they ought to cite to all the Acts of the Procefs, even to the definitive Sentence inclufively ; in which Cafe, if the Criminal doth not appear, his Contumacy fhall be complained of in all the Terms of the Edict, and the Inquifitors may receive his Denunciation and Accufation from the Fifcal, and draw up his Procefs in Form. And when all this is done, if the Crime appears to be fufficiently proved, they may condemn the Abfentee, without waiting for him any longer. The third Method to be obferved in drawing up the Procefs againft the Abfentee, is this ; that if in the Management of the Procefs made in the Inquifition, there appears to be a Prefumption of Herefy againft the Abfentee, altho' the Crime doth not feem to be fully proved, yet the Inquifitors may order an Edict againft fuch Abfentee noted and fufpected of the Crime of Herefy, and command him to appear within a certain Time to free himfelf, and canonically to purge himfelf from the faid Error or Crime ; with this Addition, that if he doth not appear to receive and perform the aforefaid Canonical Purgation, or doth not free or purge himfelf, they will look on him as a Convict, and proceed to act according to Law. And this Form of Procefs is a little too fevere ; but ftill 'tis rightly founded upon Law, and prudent*

and

and learned Inquifitors may chufe a Method which they judge more fafe, and may be better ufed in Practice, according to the different Caufes that may arife.

And left the Sentence againft Fugitives may feem to be pronounced in vain, *Pegna,* 'tis ufually publifhed before all the People, and the Image, or, as they com- *Ibid.* monly call it, the Statue of the abfent Perfon is publickly produced, on *p. 574.* which there is a Superfcription fixed, containing the Name and Surname of the abfent obftinate Perfon who is condemned, which Statue is delivered to the fecular Power, on which he executes the Sentence and Penalty of Burn- ing, as he would do upon the abfent Perfon himfelf, if he were prefent, un- lefs he would turn, or upon a Perfon otherwife relapfed. Thus, as *Lewis l. 1. t. 2. a Paramo* tells us, the Statue of *Sigefmond Malatefta* was burnt at the Gates of *c. 1. n. 6.* St. *Peter* ; and the Statue of *Luther*, after he had been cited, and did not ap- pear, was alfo burnt, together with his Books, at the Command of *Leo* X, by the Bifhop of *Afcoli*, and *Silvefter Prieriates*.

When this Cuftom of burning the Statues of abfent Criminals began, is un- certain. *Pegna* believes it not to be very antient, becaufe neither *Eymerick*, who, with great Diligence, hath treated of every Thing relating to Practice in this Crime, nor any other of the Antients, who have written of the Order of proceeding againft Hereticks, have mentioned this Cuftom ; nor is there to be found any fingle Trace of it in the *Vatican* Copy, nor in that of the moft illuftrious Cardinal *Sirletto*, where there are many Things, and even the moft minute Things concerning the Method of judging and punifhing Hereticks. But yet he thinks it very commendable, and proper to ftrike Terror, and therefore altogether fit to be ufed.

CHAP. XXXVIII.

Of the Method of proceeding againft the Dead.

PRocefs is alfo carried on againft the Dead for the Crime of Herefy. Now *Direct.* it may happen feveral ways, that a Perfon may be judged an Heretick *p. 3.* after Death. *Firft*, If before his Death the Inquifition againft him was be- *Qu. 43.* gun, and his Crime appeared either by his own Confeffion, or the Evidence *com. 9:.* of the Fact, or the legal Proof of Witneffes, and the Criminal dies before the Procefs is ended, either confeffed and impenitent, or negative or relapfed. *Secondly*, If being in Jayl for Herefy he kills himfelf, for by thus deftroying himfelf, he feems to confefs the Crime. *Thirdly*, If, tho' when alive, his Herefy did not appear, and he was not accufed of it, yet, if after his Death, it at any time appears that he died an Heretick, either by the Depofitions and Atteftations of others, or by Facts, or Deeds, or Books compofed by him, or by any other legal Reafons. This Procefs is carried on againft the Dead before this Tribunal, chiefly for thefe three Ends ; That their Memory may be be condemned, that the Heirs of the Dead, or any other Poffeffors of their Effects, may be deprived of them by the Fifcal ; and finally, that the dead Bodies may be taken up, caft out of holy Ground and burnt, as 'tis determined by the firft Inftruction of *Seville, An.* 1484. *c.* 20.

This Action againft the Dead, when carried on in order to the Confifcation of their Effects, is faid to laft for 40 Years. Thus 'tis determined, *cap.* 2. §. 1. *de præfcript. l.* 6. That the Effects of deceafed Hereticks fhall be the Catholick Childrens and Heirs by Prefcription, at the End of forty Years, if fo be they have poffeffed them *bona fide.* The fame is determined by the Inftruction of *Seville, An.* 1484. *cap.* 20. Now the Children and Heirs of the Deceafed fhall then be faid to have poffeffed his Effects *bona fide,* when, at the Time of his Death, and for the whole Space of forty Years they have believed and underftood that the Perfon deceafed died a Catholick. But if within thefe forty Years they have at any time been informed that he died an Heretick, they fhall never plead Prefcription, becaufe from that time they began to be in *mala fide* ; and if therefore they have been thus in Poffeffion of them, *mala fide,* the Fifcal of the Office of the Inquifition fhall feize on fuch Effects even after forty Years.   As to what regards the Condemnation of the Memory of the Dead, fuch an Action is never hindred or determined by any Intervals of Time. For even when 40 Years and more are elapfed, the Inquifitors may, when ever 'tis difcovered and legally proved that any one died an Heretick, carry on an Action againft him to condemn his Memory, and declare him to have died excommunicated, and to forbid any one from praying for him, and to dig up his Bones, if poffible, that they may be burnt ; for he with whom 'tis not lawful to have any Communication when alive, 'tis neither lawful to have it with him when he is dead.   But altho' the Children efcape this Confifcation of their Eftates, if they have been in Poffeffion of them *bona fide* for forty Years, they incur however the other Penalties which the Laws have decreed to the Children of the Condemned, *viz.* Infamy and Incapacity for all publick Offices and Benefices.

Formerly a Father was prefumed to die in Herefy, when fick on his Bed, he defired Confolation from any one of the *Albigenfes* by Impofition of Hands. And therefore 'twas cuftomary for Children, to prevent their being excluded from their Patrimony, to object that their Parents were not in their Senfes when they defired that Confolation.   Hence arofe a Queftion, whether fuch an Excufe ought to be admitted.

'Tis decided, cap. *Filii,* de hæret. l. 6. *The Children or Heirs of thofe, who, when on their Death-beds have defired Hereticks to comfort them, that they might receive the Confolation from them by Impofition of Hands, according to their moft wicked Cuftom, and thus go the Way of all Flefh, ought not to be admitted to prove, that fuch deceafed Perfons received this Confolation, or more truly this Defolation, when they were not of a found Mind, or after they loft their Speech, fince, as 'tis faid, 'tis their Cuftom never to confole fuch a one who is not in his Senfes, and hath not his ordinary Memory, if whilft they lived they were defamed for Herefy, or fufpected, or if it legally appears that, being in their Senfes, they defired fuch Hereticks. In other Cafes the aforefaid Children or Heirs may be admitted to prove the Premifes,*

mifes, not by their *Wives, Children, Acquaintance*, or any that belong to them, *but* by other *Witneſſes worthy of Credit*, and eſpecially by Perſons zealous for the Faith.

Here there is a double Method of excuſing ſuch Perſons propoſed. *Firſt*, If it be proved that the deceaſed Perſon, when alive, was not ſuſpected or defamed of Hereſy, but lived in good Repute, and received the Sacraments of the Church after a Chriſtian Manner, at proper Times, and performed other Things which are uſually done by true and Catholick Chriſtians. *Secondly*, If it can be ſhewn that he was not of a ſound Mind, when he deſired the Conſolation of Hereticks, which muſt be done one of theſe two ways: Either by ſhewing, that he was at a certain Time mad, and that 'tis to be preſumed that he committed the Crime whilſt the Madneſs laſted, and during the Time of ſuch Madneſs; and in this Caſe the Fiſcal or Judge, if he proceeds *ex officio*, muſt prove, that the Offence was committed when the Perſon was himſelf: Or by ſhewing, that by the Violence of his Diſtemper he was diſturbed in Mind, and deprived of his Reaſon; for ſometimes Perſons are delirious in a Diſtemper, eſpecially in old Age, who in Health were in full Poſſeſſion of their Senſes and Reaſon. Theſe Proofs muſt not be made by their Wives, Children, or other Relations, but by Witneſſes above all Exception, and in the laſt Caſe ſkilful Phyſicians are principally to be regarded. If the Children fail in this Proof, their Excuſe is not to be admitted.

Farther, ſince a Criminal at the Article of Death ought to be ſacra- *Direct.* mentally abſolved, if he confeſſes, and is ready to obey the Commands of *p. 2.* the Church, according to the firſt Council of *Orange*, cap. 2. *As to Hereticks* *com. 2 ſ.* *who lie at the Point of Death, if they deſire to be Catholicks, let the Presbyters, if there be a. Biſhop to do it, ſign them with the Chriſm and Benediction*; hence it oftentimes happens, that Perſons dying have confeſſed Hereſy to a Prieſt, and received their Abſolution from him. And as no Action can be carried on againſt the Dead, unleſs it be preſumed that they died impenitent, there aroſe formerly a Queſtion in the Council of *Tarragona*, whether the Prieſt, who aſſerts that he abſolved any one from Hereſy, ought to be credited? This Queſtion was at that Time of great Importance, becauſe if the Prieſt affirming this Matter was to be believed, the Inquiſitors could not proceed againſt ſuch a one after his Death. The Matter was thus decided in the Council of *Tarragona*. *It is alſo inquired: What if any one ſhould confeſs to his Prieſt Hereſy, or favouring of Hereſy, before the Inquiſition began againſt him, and ſhould be afterwards called on by the Inquiſitors? In ſuch Caſe his Confeſſor muſt be believed; and if he be found to have rightly confeſſed by the Confeſſion of the Prieſt, altho' the Prieſt hath done ill in not ſending him to the Biſhop, yet the Perſon confeſſing may avoid temporal Puniſhment by ſuch Confeſſion, unleſs it be diſcovered that his Repentance was falſe, or that he relapſed after his Repentance, or was publickly defamed.*

The Council of *Narbonne* hath made this Determination in the Caſe, c. 28. *Whether or no the Confeſſor alone is to be believed concerning the Abſolution or Repentance of a dead or living Perſon, altho' it ſeems plain enough that he ought not, yet that nothing may be imputed to the Church, let the Anſwer of the Lord Pope be waited for.* But now this Queſtion is at an end, becauſe Confeſſors have no Power of

I nb.

absolving Hereticks. Such a Cafe may however happen, *viz.* when any one is abfolved by Virtue of any Jubilee, in which the Pope grants the Power of abfolving from fuch a Crime: Or when an Heretick abfolutely concealed, or mental, is abfolved, whofe Herefy is afterwards difcovered, and himfelf proceeded againft. A like Cafe may happen in an Heretick, who being about to die, repents, and becaufe there is no room to reconcile him to the Church, according to the ordinary Courfe of Law, is abfolved by fome private Prieft when at the Point of Death, and afterwards recovers; or if he doth not recover, is accufed after his Death to the holy Office.

In thefe and the like Cafes they fay, that if any one will make ufe of the Teftimony of a Confeffor, yet the Inquifitor ought not to neglect the Courfe of Law upon account of fuch a Witnefs. *Gregory* XIII. in a certain Bull of Jubilee, *An.* 1572. declared, That Perfons abfolved in the penitential Court, are to be looked on as abfolved only in that Court or Judgment, and that therefore they ought to make Satisfaction in the external or judicial Court. And therefore now no Perfon receives any Advantage by excepting that he received Penance in the internal Court. The Reafon is, becaufe penitential Punifhment injoined in the internal Court hath this Tendency, that hereby the Penitent may make Satisfaction to God and his Soul. Whereas temporal Punifhment regards the Punifhment of the Body, and is an Inftance of publick Juftice, whereby the Commonwealth is fatisfied, which hath been injured by the ill Example of Zanchin. the Offender. And as there is a double Punifhment, fo there is a twofold
c. 34. Judge. One which injoins Penance whereby the Criminal may be freed from eternal and fpiritual Punifhment, and this is the proper Prieft; the other he who injoins temporal Punifhment, and this is the Judge of the Place where the Offence is committed, or alfo the ordinary Judge of the Offender. Hence it follows, that as the Prieft is not the proper Judge of this Crime, but the Inquifitor and Bifhop, Abfolution given by a Prieft can't hinder the Procefs of the proper Judge.

However, no Action is to be carried on againft a dead Perfon, or rather his Memory is not to be condemned, unlefs the Proof be full, according as 'tis determined by the Inftruction of *Avila,* An. 1498. c. 4. *Nor let any dead Perfon be cited to a Trial, nor any Procefs be carried on againft his Memory or Reputation, unlefs there be full Proof that he may be thereby condemned.* When therefore there are any fuch preceding Proofs, the Fifcal inftantly demands, by putting in a Bill, that fuch a Criminal may be proceeded againft. This Accufation is exhibited to the Children or Heirs, or others whom it may concern, that the Memory of the Deceafed fhould not be condemned, and if there are any Defcendants of the dead Perfon, they are perfonally cited to defend his Memory, according to the *Madrid* Inftruction, *An.* 1561. *c.* 61. Thus alfo the Council of *Biterre* formerly ordained, *c.* 18. *Proceed in like manner to the Condemnation of Hereticks or their Believers, who have not been canonically reconciled before their Death, giving firft a Citation to their Heirs, or others, who, according to Law, ought to be cited, and allow them a proper Liberty of defending them.* And that no one may pretend Excufe or Igno-

rance,

rance, the Children or Heirs of the Deceafed, or any others whom it may concern, are alfo cited by publick Edicts to come and make a legal De_fence for him, and a legal Term is affigned them for their Appearance. After fuch Term is elapfed, if no one of the afore-cited Perfons appears, the Inquifitors appoint one to undertake the Defence, a pious and faithful Man, and fit for the Bufinefs, who is to propofe the legal Excufes and De_fences for the Deceafed. To this Perfon they communicate the Accufation and Evidence againft the Deceafed, and injoin him Secrefy, and to confer concerning the Affair only with the Advocates of the holy Office, that fo the Procefs may be carried on according to the due Order and Courfe of Law. But if any one appears, he is admitted to defend the Deceafed's Memory. Nor doth it fignify, if the Perfon appearing as Defendant in this Caufe, be noted for Herefy, or under Inquifition, or in Prifon ; becaufe as it may hap_pen, that both the Deceafed, and the Defendant under Inquifition, may be both freed from the Profecution carried on againft them, 'tis allowed him, that no Prejudice may be done to any one, and becaufe it may be for his own Advantage, to appear in Defence of the deceafed Criminal, according as the *Madrid* Inftruction hath determined in the afore-cited Place. And far-ther, the *Avila* Inftruction, *An.* 1498. *cap.* 4. determines, *That the Procefs against a dead Perfon fhall be fpeedily finifhed, and that the Inquifitors fhall not put off the Caufe for want of Proof, unlefs poffibly 'tis likely, that within a little while, other kind of Proofs may arife.* But when the Criminal is not convicted upon full Proof, he is immediately to be abfolved. And the afore-cited Inftruction gives this Reafon of the Decree ; becaufe unlefs it were thus, the Sons and Daugh-ters of the Deceafed under Profecution, if his Caufe fhould be put off, would not poffibly find any Perfons to marry with, and could not difpofe of the Ef-fects left by the Deceafed. But if after the Deceafed is abfolved there appear new Witneffes againft him, there may be a new Action commenced againft him, becaufe, in this Crime, in Favour of the Faith, Sentences pronounced are not to be taken as an adjudged Cafe. And the former Evidences alfo fhall retain their intire Force, and be added to thofe which arife anew, in order to make full Proof.

When all thefe Things have been duly obferved, if it appears that the De-ceafed is to be abfolved, the Sentence of Abfolution is publickly pronounced, becaufe as publick Edicts were fet forth againft him, at the Beginning of his Procefs, he is therefore to be publickly declared abfolved, that he may be reftored to his Reputation. But if his Memory is to be condemned, he is pro-nounced to have died in Herefy, his Memory is condemned, his Effects con-fifcated, his Bones dug up, and if they can be diftinguifhed from the other Bones of Catholicks, to be publickly burnt.

And thus we read that the Bones and dead Bodies of feveral Hereticks have been unburied and thrown away, or burnt. *Peter John*, of the Diocefe of *Biron*, followed and taught the Errors of *Joachim*, Abbot of St. *Flour*, and publifhed concerning this Affair feveral Books upon the Revelation of St. *John*, and the Gofpel of *Matthew*. Thefe Books were afterwards diligently

Bzovius, A. 1199.

§. 39.

O o examined

examined by many Doctors in Divinity by Authority of the Pope, and at a solemn Meeting at the Court of *Rome*, were condemned and burnt. *Peter* also himself, by Command of the same Prelate, was taken up out of holy Ground, and by the general Vote and Sentence declared an Heretick, tied to a Stake and burnt. There lived also, some Years ago, in *Italy*, in the *Bresciano*, a certain Person, of so great Integrity and Severity of Life, that some affirmed that, when alive, he was the Successor of *John Baptist* himself, and on this Account greatly reverenced him after his Death. The Inquisitor of the Faith having been informed by the Evidence of the Faithful, that he was tinctured with Heresy, and that he died out of the Communion of Believers, with the Advice of the Bishop, commanded his dead Body to be unburied, and thrown into the Fire. At *Faenza* in *Lombardy*, an Abbot buried a certain Heretick in the Church of St. *Hippolytus* the Martyr. *Innocent* commanded the Abbot and Monks to take up the Corps, and to observe the Interdict his Church was laid under on that Account. Master *Almericus* was also turned out of his Grave, and buried in a Field.

Idem.
An. 1233.
§. 11.

An. 1207.
§ 8.
An. 1209.
§. 11.

But that we may not look for more Examples than we need, we have a famous one of this sort of Condemnation, in the Synod of *Constance*, against *John Wickleff*, in the eighth Session. *Inasmuch as by the Authority of the Sentence, and Decree of the* Roman *Council, and by the Command of the Apostolick See, after the proper Delays, Process was carried on concerning the Condemnation of* John Wickleff *and his Memory, Edicts being set forth, and Denunciations to summon all, if any there be, who are willing to defend him or his Memory; having farthermore examined Witnesses concerning the final Impenitence and Obstinacy of the said* Wickleff, *by Commissaries deputed for this Purpose, and observed all Things to be observed, as the Order of Law requires in this Case, and his Impenitence and final Obstinacy being evidently proved by legal Witnesses, the Matter was legally believed and assented to. And therefore at the Instance of the Procurator of the Exchequer, and after putting forth an Edict for hearing of Sentence as on this Day, this holy Synod declares and determines, that the said* John Wickleff *was a notorious Heretick, and died obstinately in his Heresy, by anathematising him, and likewise condemning his Memory, and decrees that his Body and Bones, if they can be separated from the other Bodies of the Faithful, shall be taken up, and thrown out from the Burial of the Church, according to the canonical and legal Sanctions. And the Judges being interrogated whether they were content, answered, Content. And they approved all the aforesaid Matters.*

Brovius,
An. 1556.
§. 36.
E. Thuan.

Hist. Con.
Trid. l. 5.
p. 451.

There was a like Edict in *England* against the dead Bodies of *Bucer* and *Fagius*. For when Cardinal *Pool*, the Pope's Legate in *England*, went, after Queen *Mary*'s Inauguration, to the University of *Cambridge*, to restore all Affairs there, they began the Process of taking up the dead Bodies of *Bucer* and *Fagius*. The dead Persons were cited by a first and second Edict, and several Witnesses produced against them once and again. When no one appeared who would undertake their Defence, they were at last condemned for Contumacy, and on the said Day Sentence was pronounced before all the Orders of the University, and their dead Bodies were ordered to be dug up, and

       delivered

delivered to the Queen's Officers. After some few Days, whilst the Sentence was sent to *London*, an Order came from the Queen that the Punishment should be inflicted. Finally, on the sixth of *February* the Bodies were dug up, and a large Stake fixed into the Ground in a certain Part of the Market-place prepared for that Purpose, to which the Bodies were tied, and a large Pile of Wood placed round them to burn them. After this the Chests were set up on end with the dead Bodies in them *, and fastned on both Sides with Stakes, and bound to the Post with a long Iron Chain. After the Pile was set on Fire, they threw a great Number of the Books of the Protestants in-to it, which they had gathered together, which were soon consumed by the spreading Flames. Not long after this, *Brookes*, Bishop of *Glocester*, dealt in the same Manner at *Oxford*, with *Catharine*, the Wife of *Peter Martyr*, who dying about † four Years ago, was buried in *Christ-Church* near St. *Fridef-wide's* Relicts, who was held in great Veneration in that College. For be-ing ‖ convicted that she had embraced her Husband's Heresy, she was con-demned, her dead Body taken up, carried upon Shoulders, and thrown upon a Dunghill.

Besides this, the Statue of such deceased Person is now brought forth in publick, on which the Name of the Person, whose Memory is to be condemn-ed, is written in large Characters, and before which all the erroneous or he-retical Articles, and all the heretical Deeds or Works, which have been legally proved against the Deceased, are recited in the same Manner in which they were done, as tho' the Deceased himself was living and present. This Statue is delivered to the secular Court, which the secular Judge afterwards burns, as he would have burnt the Deceased, if he had been living, and died ob-stinate.

We have a very famous Instance of such a Sentence pronounced against a dead Person, in this Age, by the Inquisition at *Rome*, in *Mark Anthony de Do-minis*, as *Bzovius* relates it under the Year 1479. §. 12. and following. He left the Church of *Rome* and the Arch-Bishoprick of *Spalato*, and came into *England* in the Year 1616. and published Books containing the Reasons of his Departure, and also concerning the Ecclesiastical Republick. Those Books were condemned as heretical at *Rome*, and himself cited to appear and purge

---

* They were buried, as *Fox* tells us, in Chests.

† *Fox* says, two Years

‖ *Fox* assures us, that *Brookes*, Bishop of *Glocester*, *Nicholas Ormanet*, R. *Morwen*, President of *Christ-Church* College, *Cole* and *Wright*, coming to *Oxford* as the Cardinals Visitors, summoned before them all that had any Acquaintance with her or her Husband, and ministred an Oath to them, that they should not conceal any Thing that was demanded of them; and that being examined, their Answer was, that they knew not what Religion she was of, because they did not under-stand her Language. But that notwithstanding this, the Cardinal by his Letters ordered the Dean of *Fridefwide* to dig her up, which the Dean accordingly did that Evening, and buried her in a Dunghill After this, in Queen *Elizabeth's* Reign, she was, by Order of *Parker*, Arch Bishop of *Canterbury*, *Grindal*, Bishop of *London*, and others, the Queen's high Commissioners, taken up out of the Dunghill, and buried in her former Place, and her Bones mixed with those of *Fridef-wide*, that they might never afterwards know one from the other.

him-

himself within fix Months before the Congregation of the Universal Inquisition. As he did not appear, after having observed the usual Methods in that Office, he was pronounced an Heretick, excommunicated, deprived of all Dignities, Benefices and Offices whatsoever, and to have incurred all the other Penalties which are prescribed by the sacred Canons.

Some Years after he privately abjured his Heresies, and having published a Writing declaring his Intention to depart out of *England*, he was received into Favour by Pope *Gregory* XV. and had granted him an House, Provision, Money, and other Things necessary for himself and Family, yearly, according to his Archiepiscopal Character, and besides this, a noble Ecclesiastical Pension. This Bounty of the Pope many Persons beheld with envious Eyes. More than this, he was restored to his Honours, so that he was afterwards stated in the Habit and Ensigns of his Dignity, in the Sessions, and all other Things, as tho' he had never fallen from his Rank. These Honours, as *Bzovius* says, puffed him up with Pride, which he discovered in his Gate, Countenance, and Conversation, as tho' he had been called, not to receive Mercy, but to Triumph.

Not long after this he was informed against by certain Religious and others, before the Assembly of the Universal Inquisition, that he was not afraid privately to spread the Errors he had abjured, and that he commended a certain Agreement cried up by himself between the Catholicks and Hereticks, and threw out Words contrary to the Authority of the Councils, and especially that of *Trent*, and that tho' oftentimes admonished, he would not abstain from such Discourses. Upon this they examined Witnesses concerning the Matters denounced according to the Sanctions of the Law; and as he was particularly said to endeavour an Escape, and to gather up his Effects in order to return to his own Country, he was apprehended and put in Prison, not such as Hereticks are usually confined to, but in the Castle of *Adrian*, where the first Quality are usually imprisoned, some of his Domesticks being allowed to attend him.

Being thus taken into Custody, and his Writings, according to Custom, diligently examined, one was found amongst them concerning the Sacrament of Matrimony, in which there were several heretical Propositions. Upon this Friar *Desiderius Scalea*, a Predicant, Cardinal of *Cremona*, one of the general Inquisitors, whom the Pope had delegated to carry on the Inquisition, and to take Cognisance of the whole Cause, admitted other proper Witnesses, and such as were beyond all Exception; after which *Mark Anthony* himself being brought before him, confessed most of those Things which he had plainly abjured. He added, that he believed that the Church of *Rome* and the Protestants agreed in all fundamental Articles, and that as to other Things wherein they differed, they were not equally necessary; but that it might be allowed to the Protestants to abound in their own Sense, at least till these Things were more fully examined, because it might be doubted whether they were sufficiently discussed and determined by the Council of *Trent*; and that therefore such Articles might be subjected to a new Disputation between Catholicks and Proteftants, chofen on each Side for this Purpofe. For he believed that the Council, and efpecially that of *Trent*, had declared many Things as Matters of Faith, which did not at all belong to it ; particularly as to Juftification and Grace, as an inherent Quality, and the Efficacy of the Sacraments, *ex opere operato*, and many others. That the Articles which he called Fundamental, were fuch only as were neceffary to Salvation, and not fuch as were controverted between both Parties ; and that therefore he who denied them was not a Member cut off from the Church, but a living one, and joined to it in Faith and Charity. From whence he concluded, that notwithftanding this Difference, there might be a Union and Agreement between the Church of *Rome* and the Proteftants. All thefe Things he guarded by this Rule, that the holy Scripture, as far as clear and exprefs, was an adequate Rule of Faith, and in Defeft of this, fuch Tradition as was certain, and that therefore no Chriftian Man ought to believe, with a divine Faith, any Thing not expreffed in holy Scripture without any Obfcurity, and Difference of Catholick Explications ; or not delivered by the Apoftles or Apoftolick Men to the Church, without any Ambiguity whatfoever ; and that beyond this Rule every Man was free to follow his own Opinion.

When he had anfwered that he had faid and believed thefe Things, the Congregation of the Cardinals General Inquifitors thought proper to confult the Cenfors of Theological Propofitions, who, examining the Affair before the Cardinal of *Cremona*, unanimoufly pronounced the Propofitions heretical. And as there was farther a vehement Sufpicion that his Abjuration was feigned, he was interrogated, whether he would perfift in the faid Herefies ? He faid, No ; but that he repented of them, and was ready to deteft and abjure them, as far as they fhould be declared Herefies by the Apoftolick See. Whilft his Caufe was in this State, and during the Time allowed him to make his Defence, and for granting him his Procefs, as he was confulting his Advocate, he fell into a very grievous Diftemper, which fo encreafed on him, that the Phyficians defpaired of his Life, and the rather, on account of the Seafon of the Year, and the Greatnefs of his Age, being fixty-fix Years old. He abjured however before the Cardinal of *Cremona*, and other Officials of the Inquifition, the Herefies he had confeffed, and all others ; and having given Signs of Repentance, and received the Sacraments, and fent a Meffenger to the Pope, to give him Thanks, in thefe Words, *That by the Preffure of his Confinement, he had given him Opportunity ferioufly to think of the Salvation of his Soul, and to behold the Light, which he was too blind to difcern before, and that therefore he was indebted to him; that by the Mercy of God he died with a good Hope*, after thefe Things he departed this Life. His Bowels, in order to prevent any Refleftions, were taken out by the moft excellent Phyficians of feveral Nations, who having carefully infpefted his Inwards, all agreed that he died with a natural Illnefs.

His Corpfe was depofited till the Iffue of the Trial, and four of his Relations, who then happened to be at *Rome*, were by Name cited by a publick Edift, and all other Perfons whatfoever who thought themfelves any ways concerned, to defend the Memory of the aforesaid *Mark Anthony*. And when his four aforesaid Relations declared they would not defend it, and no other appeared to do it, the Tribunal of the Inquisition chose some proper Persons for this Purpose, who, upon carefully infpecting the Procefs, anfwered, that nothing appeared to them, whereby they could defend the faid Memory according to Law, fince from *Mark Anthony*'s own Confeffion, they moft clearly found that he died a relapfed Heretick. But that they might proceed to Sentence entirely, according to Law, they confulted with Divines and skilful Lawyers, and had the Matter propofed and carefully examined by them. At length they all agreed that the fame Punifhments fhould be executed upon the Memory, Body, and Effects of the Deceafed, which would have been executed upon himfelf had he been alive.

Having taken this Refolution, the twenty-firft Day of *December, An.* 1624. was appointed for the pronouncing Sentence. Early in the Morning of it, fo vaft a Multitude had got together to St. *Mary fupra Minervam*, where they generally give thefe religious Shews, that they were forced not only to fhut up, but to guard the Gates with armed Men, and the great *Area* before the Church was fo prodigioufly thronged, that there was fcarce Room for the Cardinals themfelves to pafs. The middle Ifle of the Church, from the firft to the fourth Pillar was boarded in, with Boards above the Height of a tall Man. At the upper and lower End of it there were Gates, guarded by *Switzers*. On each Side there were Scaffolds, running the whole Length of the Inclofure, in which were Seats for the Cardinals and other Prelates, and other Conveniencies, to receive the Courtiers and other Noblemen ftanding or fitting. On the right Hand coming in the facred Council prefided, on the left Hand were placed the inferior Officers of the holy Inquifition, the Governor of the City and his Officials. Before the Pulpit was to be feen the Picture of *Mark Anthony*, drawn in Colours, covered with a black common Garment, holding a Clergyman's Cap in his Hand, with his Name, Surname, and Archiepifcopal Dignity, which formerly he had born, infcribed upon it, together with a wooden Cheft bedaubed with Pitch, in which the dead Body was inclofed. The reft of the Church was filled with Citizens, and a great many Foreigners, the Number of whom was at that Time larger, becaufe the Jubilee that was at hand had brought them from all Parts to the City, that they might be prefent at the opening the facred Gates.

Things being thus difpofed, a certain Parfon mounted the Pulpit, and with a fhrill Voice, which rung thro' all the Parts of the fpacious Church, and in the vulgar Language, that the common People might underftand him, read over a Summary of the Procefs, and the Sentence by which the Cardinals Inquifitors General, fpecially deputed for the Affair by the Pope, pronounced *Mark Anthony*, as a Relapfe into Herefy, to have incurred all the Cenfures and Penalties appointed to relapfed Hereticks by the facred Canons, and Papal Conftitutions, and declared him to be deprived of all Honours, Prerogatives, and Ecclefiaftical Dignities, condemned his Memory, and caft him out of the Ecclefirftical Court, delivered over his dead Body and Effigies into
                                                                        the

the Power of the Governor of the City, that he might inflict on it the Punish-ment due, according to the Rule and Practice of the Church. And finally, they commanded his impious and heretical Writings to be publickly burnt, and de-clared all his Effects to be forfeited to the Exchequer of the holy Inquisition. After this Sentence was read, the Governor of the City and his Officers threw the Corps, Effigies, and aforefaid Writings into a Cart, and carried them into the *Campo Fiore,* a great Multitude of People following after. When they came there, the dead Body, which as yet in all its Members was whole and entire, was raifed out of the Cheft as far as the Bottom of the Breaft, and fhewn from on high to the vaft Concourfe of People that ftood round about, and was afterwards with the Effigies and Bundle of his Books, thrown into the Pile prepared for the Purpofe, and there burnt.

I was willing to give this long Story in all its Circumftances, not only be-caufe the Perfon himfelf was famous, and the Thing frefh in Memory, but chiefly becaufe all Things ufually practifed in the Procefs againft the Dead, were here exactly obferved, whereby the whole Scene of this Iniquity and Cruelty doth moft fully appear.

CHAP. XXXIX.

Of the Manner of proceeding againft Houfes.

IN order to beget in the common People a greater Abhorrence of the Crime of Herefy, they are ufed to pull down, and level with the Ground the Houfes or Dwellings, in which the Heretick or Arch-Heretick holds Conven-ticles and Congregations. Of this we have feveral Inftances in the Book of the Sentences of the *Tholoufe* Inquifition. This Demolition of Houfes, in Detefta-tion of the Crime of Herefy, was formerly appointed by the Council of *Tholoufe,* An. 1229. c. 5. *We decree that that Houfe, in which an Heretick fhall be found, fhall be deftroyed, and the Place it felf or Ground be confifcated.* And the Council of *Biterre,* c. 35. *Let the Houfes alfo in which living or dead Hereticks, whether convicted or condemned, are or fhall be found, if with the Knowledge and Confent of the Owners of fuch Houfes being of legal Age, be pulled down, and the Ef-fects of all who then inhabit there be confifcated, unlefs they are able manifeftly to prove their Innocence or juft Ignorance.* And not long after, *Innocent* IV. decreed this very Thing by a certain Writing, beginning, *Ad exftirpanda,* of which the Original is extant, in the Inquifition of *Bologna,* in thefe Words. *The Houfe al-fo, in which any Heretick, Man or Woman, fhall be found, fhall be deftroyed to the Ground, without any Hope of being ever rebuilt, unlefs the Owner of the Houfe fhall have procured the Difcovery of them there. And if the Owner of fuch Houfe fhall have any other Houfe contiguous to it, let all thofe Houfes be likewife demolifhed.* But *Alexander* IV. by a Conftitution beginning, *Fælicis recordationis,* declares, *That*

this

this must be understood of the Out-houses of such Dwelling, viz. that such House, with all other Buildings contiguous to it, i. e. the House it self, and Out-houses, whether an Heretick, Man or Woman, shall be found in the House it self, or the Out-houses, shall be destroyed; because the House, tho' divided into ever so many Dwellings, is nevertheless accounted to be one House.

If the Owner of the House is not condemned of Heresy, but Hereticks have committed such Things in an House that did not belong to them, without the Knowledge of the Owner, the House is to receive no Damage. But if he knew it, or ought to have known it, 'tis confiscated, and being confiscated, remains subject to the Pleasure of the Inquisitor. The Materials of such Houses go to the Exchequer, or are decreed to be applied to other pious Uses. The Ground on which such House stood must not be shut in, but must always be uninhabited, that as it was formerly a Receptacle of wicked *Lib. Sent.* Wretches, it may from henceforth become a Place of Naftiness, and made *fol. 2.* a Dunghill and Stench. Excommunication also is threatned against all those who shall presume to rebuild it, or to inhabit or inclose it, or shall knowingly give any Advice or Assistance to it. Sometimes also the Ground on which the House stood, is sprinkled over with Salt, to denote its Barrenness, at which Time certain Curses and Imprecations are uttered. And finally, that there may be a perpetual Monument of its Infamy and just Punishment, a solid Stone, or a marble Pillar four or five Foot high, is erected in this last Age, in the said Ground, with certain large Characters cut on it, containing the Name of the Owner of the House, shewing the Reason of its being destroyed, and signifying the Time, viz. under the Reign of what Pope, Emperor or King, the Matter was transacted. In the former Age there was a famous Monument erected on this Account in *Spain*, in the noble City of *Valladolid*, where *Austin Cazzalla*, altho' converted, and penitent, was, *An.* 1559. delivered as a Dogmatist to the secular Court, and his House pulled down, on the Ground of which there was a little Pillar erected, containing an Account of the Affair.

C H A P. XL.

How the Sentences are pronounced, and the condemned Persons delivered over to the secular Arm.

Direct.   THE Inquisitors are commanded to pronounce the Sentences against He-
p. 3. com.   reticks, and to leave the condemned Persons to the secular Powers pre-
4º.   sent, to be punished according to their Desert. C. *Excommunicamus*, 1. in princip. de hæret. C. *Ad Abolendam*, §. *Illos*, de hæret. and C. *Novimus*, de verb. signific. Altho' this Command requires the secular Judge to be present at the pronouncing Sentence, yet the Sentence of Condemnation against Hereticks,

reticks, pronounced when the fecular Judge is abfent, is valid, provided there be all other Things effential to it. For the Laws do not fo require the Prefence of the fecular Judge or his Officers, as tho' nothing profitable could be tranfacted without him, but only that they, as Servants, fhould put in Execution the Sentence pronounced; for every other Act is forbidden them in this Crime, which is merely Ecclefiaftical. Cap. *ut Inquifitionis,* §. *Prohibemus,* de hæret. l. 6. And if the Prefence of the fecular Judge was neceffary in pronouncing Sentence of Condemnation againft impenitent or relapfed Hereticks, he might eafily by this Means hinder the Office of the Inquifition, by denying his Prefence, either for no Reafon, or for a feigned and pretended one. So that when the Inquifitor and Bifhop have pronounced Sentence upon the Criminal, it fhall be valid, tho' the fecular Magiftrate cannot or will not be prefent; and it fhall be fufficient to intimate to him by fome legal Perfon in Writing when there is Need, and which is the fafeft Method, that fuch a Perfon is judged to be an obftinate Heretick, and impenitent or relapfed; and the fecular Magiftrate, tho' not prefent at the Sentence, fhall be obliged to give Credit to fuch an Intimation, and to put to Death the Heretick delivered over to him, unlefs he will be moft grievoufly punifhed as a Favourer of Hereticks, and Hinderer of the holy Office. Nor muft he have any Copy of the Procefs.

Alfo in the fame Chapter *Novimus,* 'tis commanded, that the Church fhall effectually intercede for him, who is to be delivered over to be punifhed by the fecular Court, that the Sentence concerning him may be fo moderated, as to prevent Danger of Death *. And altho' the Emperor *Frederick* provided by his Law, *Let no one prefume to intercede with us in Behalf of fuch, which if any* Pegna, *doth, he fhall defervedly incur our Indignation;* yet the Ecclefiaftical Judges may com 10. intercede in another Court for fuch a one; and altho' fuch Interceffion is for-*in part. 2.* bidden, which tends to favour the Heretick, or to the Hindrance of Juftice; *Direct.* yet fuch Interceffion is not, which tends to the avoiding Irregularity, and which is particularly injoined by the Law it felf. However, every Difficulty

---

* " Is there, fays Dr. *Geddes,* in his View of the Court of Inquifition in *Portugal, p.* 446. in " all Hiftory, an Inftance of fo grofs and confident a Mockery of God, and the World, as this of " the Inquifitors befeeching the civil Magiftrates, not to put the Hereticks they have condemned " and delivered to them, to Death? For were they in Earneft when they made this folemn Pe- " tition to the fecular Magiftrates, why do they bring their Prifoners out of the Inquifition, and " deliver them to thofe Magiftrates, in Coats painted over with Flames? Why do they teach " that Hereticks, above all other Malefactors, ought to be punifhed with Death? And why do " they never refent the fecular Magiftrates having fo little Regard to their earneft and joint Pe- " tition, as never to fail to burn all the Hereticks that are delivered to them by the Inquifition, " within an Hour or two after they have them in their Hands? And why in *Rome,* where tho " Supream, Civil, and Ecclefiaftical Authority are lodged in the fame Perfon, is this Petition of " the Inquifition, which is made there as well as in other Places, never granted? Thus far Dr. *Geddes.* And let me here add, that this Hypocrify and Diffimulation is the more vile and execrable, in that the Inquifitors are commanded by the Bulls of feveral Popes, to compel the fecular Magiftrate, under Penalty of Excommunication and other Ecclefiaftical Cenfures, within fix Days readily to execute the Sentences pronounced by the Inquifitors againft Hereticks, *i. e.* to burn them. *The tender Mercies of thefe Wretches are Cruelty.*

of this kind the cunning Induſtry of the Popes hath wholly taken away, who have provided, how both the Inquiſitors and Counſellors may more ſecurely avoid Irregularity. For *Paul* IV. confidering, at *Rome, April* 29, *An.* 1557. in the Congregations held before him on the Cauſe of Hereſy, that the greateſt Part of thoſe imployed in this Affair, were Clergymen ſecular and regular, being in Orders, in the Prieſthood, and the Epiſcopal, Archiepiſco-pal, or other higher Dignity, and even ſome Cardinals, and that it oftentimes happened, that, according to the Nature of the Cafes and Crimes before them, they gave Sentence againſt the Criminals, whereby was occaſioned the Loſs of a Limb, or the Effuſion of Blood, and ſometimes even natural Death; and being therefore willing to conſult their Safety, and the Eaſe of their Mind and Confcience, determined and decreed, that all the aforeſaid who ſhould aſſiſt him in judging not only, in Cauſes of Hereſy, but alſo in every other criminal Cauſe, which ſhould or might be managed before him, might give Sentence againſt Criminals, by which they ſhould be condemned to the Queſtions or Torture, or to any other condign Puniſhment, even to the Loſs of a Member, and to natural Death incluſively, without incurring any Cen-ſure or Irregularity. *Pius* V. afterwards confirmed the ſame Decree, and ex-tended it to all the Inquiſitors, their Vicars, Commiſſaries, and Counſellors, as *Umbertus Locatus* witneſſes in his Book *de opere Judiciali Inquiſitorum,* towards the End, tit. *de decretis.* So that as theſe Decrees now ſtand in Force, this Proteſtation doth not ſeem neceſſary, that the Inquiſitors hereby may avoid Irregularity, when Criminals for Hereſy are actually delivered over, or left to the ſecular Court. However, they will not ſuffer it to be omitted, be-cauſe 'tis ſupported by common Law, and the general Cuſtom of the Eccle-ſiaſtical Court; nor are ſeveral Remedies, which may be had more ſecurely to obtain the ſame End, to be rejected.

Nor can the ſecular Judges, after Criminals for Hereſy, relapſed or impe-nitent, are delivered over, or left to them to be put to Death, re-examine the Proceſs and Cauſe, and correct or alter it if needful, or pronounce the Sen-tence void.

However, *Simancas* relates from other Authors certain Inſtances of Perſons, who were unjuſtly condemned by the Inquiſitors for Hereſy, and whoſe Sen-tences were not executed by the ſecular Judges. He cites *Alciatus,* as aſſerting, " That the Lay Judge is not bound immediately to condemn a Criminal left " to him by the Inquiſitors, if he was not really defiled with the Crime of " Hereſy, altho' the Eccleſiaſtical Judge might have pronounced it ſo; and " thus he adds, it was ſaid, that the Lay Judge was not bound to execute the " Sentence of the Inquiſitor, by which he pronounced a certain Woman an " Heretick, who in Reality had only made ſome Love-Potions, and againſt " whom there were beſides Proofs of certain Witchcraft. *John Igneus* alſo " relates, that the ſame twice happened at *Milan,* where two Women, con-" demned for Hereſy by the Biſhop of *Parma* and the Inquiſitor, eſcaped " unpuniſhed, it being found that they ever thought right concerning the " Faith. He alſo adds, that a certain Woman at *Rouen* being condemned to
" the

" the Flames for Herefy, was abfolved by the fecular Judges, and thofe who
" had condemned her, condemned to pay Cofts." But *Simancas* believes thefe
Things and others of the fame kind, were either feigned out of Hatred to the
holy Inquifition, or elfe rafhly and unjuftly done by wicked and unskilful § 4. 5.
Judges, and thinks that the fecular Judge is bound in a Caufe of Herefy immediately, and, as they fay, with his Eyes fhut, to execute the Sentence of
the Ecclefiaftical Judge, without any Cognifance or Affurance of the Juftice
of it. And this is now moft exactly obferved in *Spain* and *Portugal*. In the
Accounts of the *Spanifh* Court, lately publifhed by a noble *French* Lady, who
attended the Queen out of *France*, there is an Inftance of a *Jewifh* Girl, fcarce
entred into her feventeenth Year, extreamly beautiful, who, in a publick Act
of Faith at *Madrid, An.* 1680. *June* 30. together with twenty others of her
Nation, of both Sexes, being condemned to the Stake, turned her felf to the
Queen, and prayed, that out of her Goodnefs and Clemency fhe might be delivered from the moft dreadful Punifhment of the Fire, in thefe Words:
*Great Queen, is not your Prefence able to bring me fome Comfort under my Mifery ? par. 2.
Confider my Youth, and that I am condemned for a Religion which I have fucked in pag. 52.
with my Mother's Milk.* The Queen turned away her Eyes, and declared fhe
pitied the miferable Creature, but did not dare to intercede for her with a fingle Word.

Nor muft the Inquifitor fhew to the Lay Judge the Procefs made by him;
but the fecular Magiftrate muft immediately, and without Delay, put in Execution the Sentence of the Ecclefiaftical Judge. If he omits to do it, or defers the Execution beyond the ufual Time, without a legal Caufe, the Inquifitor may compel him to execute it by Ecclefiaftical Cenfure. *Alexander* IV.
hath, in the fulleft Manner, given this Power to the Inquifitors by a Refcript,
beginning, *Ad audientiam.*

But in this Affair the Cuftom of Provinces is different. In *Spain*, as foon as
ever the Sentence of the Relapfed or Impenitent, or any others who are to be
delivered over to the fecular Court, is read, the fecular Judges receive them
immediately into their Court, and having pronounced the Sentence of Death
or Burning, carry them directly to the Place of Execution. In many Cities
of *Italy* the fecular Judges keep in their Jayls the Criminals left or delivered
over to them by the Inquifitors three or four Days before they put them to
Death; which feems to be done by Authority of *Innocent* IV. in a Bull beginning, *Ad exftirpanda*, where we thus read. *As to thofe who are condemned for
Herefy, by the Diocefan or his Vicar, or by the aforefaid Inquifitors, let the chief Magiftrate or Ruler, or his fpecial Meffenger, receive them when they are left to him,
and immediately, or within five Days at leaft, put in Execution the Conftitutions
made againft fuch Perfons.* And they may be compelled to this by the Punifhment of Excommunication, and other Ecclefiaftical Cenfures, by a Refcript
of *Innocent* VIII. beginning, *Dilectus Filius*, in thefe Words. *Injoin and command the faid fecular Officials, under the Penalty of Excommunication, and other
Ecclefiaftical Cenfures, that within fix Days, after they fhall be legally required,
they readily execute the Sentences pronounced by you againft fuch Hereticks, without*

feeing

seeing the said Processes carried on by you, and without allowing any Appeal. If the Inquisitor finds the secular Judge to be so negligent, as not to take Care to put to Death the Hereticks delivered to him after these five or six Days are elapsed, tho' there be nothing legally to hinder him, then the Inquisitor may command him to execute the Punishment of Burning, or of Death, upon the Hereticks left to him, since this is the Punishment usually inflicted on such ; nor will the Inquisitor hereby fall into Irregularity. But others think it a safer Method, that the Inquisitor should not in this Case mention by Name the Punishment of Burning, or Death, commanding the secular Judge to inflict it, because possibly he might become irregular ; to avoid which, he makes the usual Protestation, when he consigns over Hereticks to the secular Judge ; and therefore they think it safer, that he should in general command him, under Penalty of Excommunication, or other Censures, to put in Execution the Sentences pronounced by him. This manner of speaking is contained in a Rescript of *Alexander* IV. beginning, *Ad Audientiam* ; and of *Leo* X. beginning, *Honestis petentium votis :* Or that he should observe the Constitutions and Laws published against Hereticks, which Manner is not obscurely injoined by *Innocent* IV. in Extrav. *Ad exstirpanda*, §. *Damnati vero.* And these Methods they say are sufficient to avoid Irregularity.

How they proceed in the Dutchy of *Milan* in the Execution of the Sentence *p. 2. t. 2.* against Hereticks, *Carena* teaches us in these Words. " And that we may *§. 6. n.44.*" see how our Senate at *Milan* proceeds in executing the Sentences pronounced " by the Inquisitors against Hereticks, and how great the Zeal of the said " Tribunal is in Things concerning the Catholick Religion, I here subjoin " the following Rescript of the said Senate in this Affair. *Our Beloved: We* " *have seen what you have written to us concerning* Don Baptista Gaudentius, " *alias Friar* Seraphin *of* Ferrara, *who, as you have written to us, is guilty of* " *heretical Pravity. Wherefore when he is delivered to you, immediately put his* " *Condemnation in Execution.* Milan, Aug. 6. 1573. Directed to *The Wise* " J. C. *Judge of the Malefactors at* Cremona. And in Execution of this De- " cree the said Criminal was, on the 12th Day of the said Month, burnt " alive in the publick Place of Justice, as a relapsed and impenitent He- " retick.

CHAP. XLI.

Of an ACT of FAITH.

THE last Act of the Inquisition now remains, in which may be seen the Accomplishment of all the several Matters we have been explaining, and relating. 'Tis commonly called an Act of Faith. And 'tis worth while more particularly to describe this Solemnity, because 'tis celebrated with the greatest Pomp.

When

When the Inquifitor is determined to pronounce the Sentences of certain Criminals, he fixes on fome Lord's-day or Feftival to perform this Solemnity. But they take Care that it be not *Advent Sunday*, or in *Lent*, or a very folemn Day, fuch as the *Nativity of our Lord, Eafter*, and the like; becaufe 'tis not decent that the Sermons on thofe Days fhould be fufpended, but that every one fhould go to his own Parifh Church. A certain *Sunday* or Feftival therefore being appointed, the Parfons of all the Churches of that City or Place, in which this Solemnity is to be performed, do, by Command of the Bifhop and Inquifitor, when they have done preaching, publickly intimate to the Clergy and People, that the Inquifitor will, in fuch a Church, hold a general Sermon concerning the Faith; and they promife, in the Name of the Pope, the ufual Indulgence of 40 Days, to all who will come and fee and hear the Things which are there to be tranfacted. They take Care to give the fame Notice in the Houfes of thofe Religious, who commonly preach the Word of God, and that their Superiors fhould be told, that becaufe the Inquifitor will in fuch a Church make a general Sermon concerning the Faith, therefore he fufpends all other Sermons, that every Superior may fend four or two Friars, as he thinks fit, to be prefent at the Sermon, and the pronouncing the Sentences. This Solemnity was formerly called, *A general Sermon concerning the Faith*, but 'tis now called, *An Act of Faith*. And in this, great Numbers of Perfons, fometimes one or two hundred are brought forth in publick Proceffion to various Kinds of Penances and Punifhments, all wearing the moft horrible Habits. They chufe Feftivals for this Solemnity, becaufe then there is a greater Confluence of People gathered together to fee the Torments and Punifhments of the Criminals, that from hence they may learn to fear, and be kept from the Commiffion of Evil. Concerning this Rite, the *Madrid* Inftruction, *An.* 1561. *c.* 77. thus prefcribes. *When the Proceffes of* Param. *l.* 3. *the Criminals are concluded, and the Sentences fixed, the Inquifitors fhall af-* qu. 4. *fign fome Holyday, on which there fhall be a publick Act of the Faith:* n. 36. *Which Day they fhall fignify to the Chapters of the Church and Confiftory of the City; and where there is any Royal Council, it fhall be notified alfo to the Prefident and Members, who muft be all invited to attend the Act of Faith, according to the Cuftom of every Place. And let the Inquifitors take Care that thefe Things be done in fuch convenient Time, as that the Execution of the Sentences of thofe who are to be delivered over to the fecular Court may be done by Day, to prevent Inconveniences.* And indeed, as this Act of Faith is now celebrated in *Spain* and *Portugal*, the Solemnity is truly an horrible and tremendous Spectacle, in which every Thing is defignedly made ufe of that may ftrike Terror, for this Reafon, as they fay, that they may hereby give fome Reprefentation and Image of the future Judgment.

If any one, whether an impenitent or relapfed Heretick, is to be delivered to the fecular Court, the Bifhop and Inquifitor give Notice to the Ballive of the Place, or principal Magiftrate of the fecular Court, that he muft come fuch a Day and Hour with his Attendance to fuch a Street or Place, to receive

ceive a certain Heretick or relapfed Perfon out of their Court, whom they will deliver to him ; and that he muft give publick Notice the fame Day, or the Day before in the Morning, by the Crier, throughout the City, in all the ufual Places and Streets, that on fuch a Day and Hour, and in fuch a Place, the Inquifitor will make a Sermon for the Faith, and that the Bifhop and Inquifitor will condemn a certain Heretick or Relapfe, by delivering him to the fecular Court.

In moft of the Tribunals of the Inquifition, efpecially in *Spain*, 'tis a remarkable Cuftom they ufe, *viz.* on the Day before the Acts of Faith, folemnly to carry a Bufh to the Place of the Fire, with the Flames of which they are confumed, who deferve the Punifhment of being burnt. This is not without its Myfteries ; for the Burning and not confuming Bufh, fignifies the indefectible Splendor of the Church, which burns, and is not confumed ; and befides this, it fignifies Mercy towards the Penitent, and Severity towards the Froward and Obftinate. And farther, it reprefents how the Inquifitors defend the Vineyard of the Church, wounding with the Thorns of the Bufh, and burning up with Flames all who endeavour to bring Herefies into the Harveft of the Lord's Field. And finally, it points out the Obftinacy and Frowardnefs of Hereticks, which muft rather be broken and bent, like a rugged and ftubborn Bufh, and that as the Thorns and Prickles of the Bufh tear the Garments of thofe who pafs by, fo alfo do the Hereticks rend the feamlefs Coat of Chrift.

Befides, the Day before the Criminals are brought out of Jayl, to the publick Act of Faith, they part with their Hair and their Beard, by which the Inquifitors reprefent, that Hereticks return to that Condition in which they were born, *viz.* becoming the Children of Wrath.

All Things being thus prepared to celebrate this Act of Faith, all the Prifoners, on that very Day which is appointed for the Celebration of it, are cloathed with that Habit which they muft wear in the publick Proceffion. But the Cuftom in this Matter is not altogether the fame in all the Inquifitions. In that of *Goa,* the Jayl-Keepers, about Midnight, go into the Cells of the Prifoners, bring in a burning Lamp to each of them, and a black Garment ftriped with white Lines ; and alfo a Pair of Breeches, which reach down to their Ankles, both which they order them to put on. The black Habit is given them in Token of Grief and Repentance. About two a Clock the Keepers return, and carry the Prifoners into a long Gallery, where they are all placed in a certain Order againft the Wall, no one of them being permitted to fpeak a Word, or mutter, or move ; fo that they ftand immovable, like Statues, nor is there the leaft Motion of any one of their Members to be feen, except of their Eyes. All thefe are fuch as have confeffed their Fault, and have declared themfelves willing to return by Penance to the Bofom of the Church of *Rome.* To every one of thefe is given a Habit to put over their black Garment. Penitent Hereticks, or fuch as are vehemently fufpected, received the bleffed Sackcloth, commonly called the *Sambenito,* which, as we have before related, is of a Saffron Colour, and on which there is put the

1　　　　　Crofs

Margin notes:
Param. l 2. t 3 c 10 r. 70, &c.

lord c.11. n. 63.

Hift Inq. Goan. c. 16.

they were under, giving each of them a Blow by the Hands of thofe Priefts who attend him.

Farther, when the Inquifitors abfolve and reconcile Penitents at an Act of Faith, they make ufe of Rods, to admonifh them, that by Herefy they have fallen from the Favour of God into his Anger and Fury. Hence *Paramus* ad-vifes fuch Penitents to confider, with how great Indulgence they are treated, becaufe they are only whipped on their Shoulders, that they may go away, and being mindful of the divine Fury, may take heed not to relapfe for the future. The Rod alfo points out the judiciary Power which the Inquifitors ex-ercife over impious Hereticks, and thofe who are fufpected of Herefy, be-caufe a Rod is the Meafure by which any one's Deferts are meafured, and therefore Penitents are whipped with Rods according to the Nature of their Offence, whereby their Faults are weighed and meafured. Farther, the In-quifitors ufe Rods, becaufe, as a Rod at the Beginning is in its Nature flexi-ble, tender and foft, but at laft hard, blunt and ftiff, fo the Inquifitors are foft and tender, whilft Penitents, offending thro' Frailty and Ignorance, re-concile themfelves; but if Hereticks do afterwards fuffer themfelves to be overcome by Wickednefs, and fall again into the Crimes they have committed, then they whip them, and ftrike them feverely, even to the burning of the Fire. And finally they ufe Rods to eftablifh and fupport the Weak in the Faith, becaufe Rods are a very apt Inftrument to fupport and confirm the Lame and Weak.

The Penitents carry in their Hands extinguifhed Wax Tapers, whilft the Inquifitors reconcile them, to intimate, that the Light of the Faith hath been altogether extinguifhed in their Minds by the Sin of Herefy and Infide-lity. Thefe Tapers are made of Wax, whereby Hereticks profefs (*Rifum te-neatis*) that their Hearts have been fo melted, thro' the Heat of Concupi-fcence, as to receive various Sects; and that as Wax grows hard by Moifture, but melts by Drynefs and Warmth, fo they being hardned by the Moifture of carnal Delights, have remained in Infidelity, but are melted as Wax, and converted by the Drynefs and Heat of Tribulation and Penance injoined them. And finally, the Cotton of the Taper, and the Wax of which 'tis made, and the Fire with which 'tis lighted after Abfolution, fhadow forth, that the He-reticks have denied Faith, Hope and Charity. But when the Tapers are lighted after their Reconciliation, this fignifies, that they profefs they will demonftrate by the Light of good Works the Faith which they have reco-vered.

Farther, thofe who are reconciled are fprinkled with holy Water and Hyf-fop, in Token, that being brought out of the Power of Darknefs, and ha-ving turned the Eyes of their Minds to the true Light of the Faith, they are to remain free from all the Snares and Calumnies of the Devil, that they may ferve God with greater Freedom.

Farther, he who hath offended againft the Catholick Faith which he had profeffed, hath a Rope tied round his Neck, to fignify, that the inward Parts of fuch a Perfon being poffeffed by the Craftinefs of the Devil, have

been

been given to fuch Sins, of which his outward Parts being tied with Ropes, give a very evident Sign and Proof. And tho' they are reconciled after Abjuration of their Herefy, yet they walk with a Rope tied about their Necks, that they may come out as Witneffes againft themfelves, and may be Examples to others, that they may turn their Eyes to the inward Spots of the Mind.

During this Action, every one of the Prifoners eats the Bread and Figs in the Church, which were given them by the Officers of the Inquifition in Jayl.

When this Ceremony is performed, the Inquifitor goes back to his Place, after which the Sentences of thofe who are appointed to Death are read over, the Conclufion of which is, that the Inquifition can fhew them no Favour upon Account of their being relapfed, or impenitent, and that therefore it delivers them over to the Arm of the fecular Court, which they earneftly intreat fo to moderate their Punifhment, as to prevent the Effufion of Blood, and Danger of Death. When thofe laft Words are read, one of the Officers of the holy Office gives each of them a Blow on the Breaft, by which he fignifies that they are left by the Inquifition ; upon which one of the Officers of fecular Juftice comes to them and claims them. If any of them are in holy Orders, they are degraded, and deprived of all their Orders, before they are delivered to the fecular Arm. After this they read the Sentences againft the Dead. At laft thefe miferable Wretches are brought to the fecular Judge, to hear the Sentence of Death, and when they come before him, they are feverally asked, in what Religion they defire to die. Their Crime is never inquired into ; becaufe 'tis not the Office of the fecular Magiftrate, to ask, whether thofe, who are condemned by the Inquifition, are criminal. He is to pre-fuppofe them guilty, and his Duty is to inflict the Punifhment appointed by Law upon thofe who commit fuch Crimes of which they are pronounced guilty by the Inquifition. When they have anfwered this one fingle Queftion, they are foon after tied to a Stake, round about which there is placed a Pile of Wood. Thofe who anfwer that they will die Catholicks, are firft ftrangled ; but thofe who fay they will die *Jews* or Hereticks, are burnt alive*. As thefe are leading out to Punifhment, the reft are carried

back

---

* I cannot avoid here giving my Reader a more particular Account of this Execution from Dr. *Geddes*, who himfelf was once prefent at it. His Words are thefe : " The Prifoners are no " fooner in the Hands of the Civil Magiftrate, than they are loaded with Chains, before the " Eyes of the Inquifitors, and being carried firft to the fecular Jayl, are, within an Hour or two, " brought from thence, before the Lord Chief Juftice, who, without knowing any Thing of " their particular Crimes, or of the Evidence that was againft them, asks them one by one ; *In* " *what Religion they do intend to die ?* If they anfwer, That they will die in the Communion of " the Church of *Rome*, they are condemned by him, *To be carried forthwith to the Place of Execu-* " *tion, and there to be firft ftrangled, and afterwards burnt to Afhes.* But if they fay, *They will die* " *in the Proteftant*, or in any other Faith that is contrary to the *Roman*, they are then fentenced " by him, *To be carried forthwith to the Place of Execution, and there to be burnt alive.*

" As

Oath, by which the King obliges himſelf to protect the Catholick Faith, to the
Extirpation of Hereſies, and the Defence of the Inquiſition. The King ſtanding bare-headed, having on one Side of him the Conſtable of *Caſtile*, or one
of the Grandees of *Spain*, who holds up the Sword of State, ſwears that he
will keep the Oath, which is publickly read over to him, by one of the Members of the Royal Council; and remains in the ſame Poſture, till the ſupream
Inquiſitor goes back to his Place. After this one of the Secretaries of the Inquiſition goes into a Desk, reads over the like Oath, and takes it from the
Council, and the whole Aſſembly. Then all the ſeveral Sentences are read
over, and the Solemnity ſometimes laſts till nine a Clock in the Evening.

In *Rome* and throughout all *Italy*, as far as I could gather from any Authors, they do not obſerve ſuch ſolemn Proceſſions in Acts of Faith, or in the
Sermons concerning the Faith. But in what Manner the Sentences are there
pronounced, and how they are executed, may, in ſome meaſure, be gathered
from the two following Accounts.

Bzovius tells us, that in the Year 1498. there were diſcovered 230 Moors, §. 31.
who had abjured the Chriſtian Faith after their Expulſion from *Spain*. After
they had wandered about they came to *Rome*, where they were known,
informed againſt, thrown into Jayl, and at length being recovered to the
ſame Faith, were thus admitted into the Church by Pope *Alexander*. On
Sunday, *July* 29. as *J. Bruchard* writes, who ſaw it, an high and large Scaffold
was built before the Portico of the great Church of St. *Peter*'s at *Rome*,
between that and another Portico, which is above the Steps of the Aſcent
to the ſaid Church. Upon this Scaffold were placed the 230 *Moors* to be reconciled. All theſe Perſons being ſat down on the Floor of the Scaffold, in their
uſual Habit, and the moſt Reverend Fathers and Lords, the Lord *Peter*
Arch-Biſhop of *Regio*, Governor of the City, *John* of *Carthagena*, Ambaſſador
of the moſt ſerene the King and Queen of *Spain*, *Octavianus*, Biſhop of *Ma-
rano*, Referendary of our holy Lord the Pope, *Dominicus Jacobatius*, and
James Dragatius, Auditors of the Cauſes of the holy Apoſtolick Palace,
Maſter *Paul* of *Moneglia*, in the Country of *Genoua*, a Predicant, Maſter of
the ſacred Palace, and Maſter *John* of *Malcone*, of the Order of Minors,
Doctors of Divinity, Penitentiaries of our aforeſaid Lord the Pope, in the
ſaid Church, for the *Spaniſh* Nation, being ſeated as above in their proper
Places, and in their ordinary Habit; a certain Maſter in Divinity, a Predicant, made a Sermon concerning the Faith in the vulgar *Italian*, and againſt
the ſaid *Moors*, who were all of the *Spaniſh* Nation, and of whom one was a Profeſſed of the Order of St. *Francis*, whoſe Habit he publickly wore, whom,
and all the aforeſaid Perſons, he accuſed of all their Errors, which he knew
concerning the Faith, and reproved and inſtructed. After the Sermon was
ended, the *Moors* asked Pardon, and deſired Abſolution. Then the Maſter
of the holy Palace admoniſhed them in *Latin* faithfully to believe, and to
live well, and put them in Mind of the Penance which they had deſerved; which Admonition he expounded to them in *Spaniſh*. After this, as
they were on their Knees, this Penance was injoined them; that they ſhould

walk two and two to the Church of St. *Peter,* and there pray, in that Habit which fhould be injoined them for this Purpofe ; and in the fame Order fhould alfo go to the Church of the Convent of St. *Mary fupra Minervam,* where they fhould put off their Habit, and every one freely return to his own Place. When they had received this Habit and Penance, the aforefaid Mafters *Paul* and *John* abfolved them all, who, after Abfolution, went to the two Churches aforefaid, the Pope feeing the whole Ceremony in the new Rooms, and grant-ing them his Bleffing. The Habit which thefe *Moors* were injoined to wear, was of this Form. Upon their ordinary Garments there was a red or purple Cloath, hanging over their Shoulders upon their Breafts and Backs, quite down to their Hips, having on it a yellow Crofs four Fingers wide, and of the fame Length with the Cloath it felf. Every one of them went to the Al-tar of the aforefaid Church of St. *Mary ad Minervam,* and there laid down the aforefaid Cloath, which the Friars received, and hung up on high in the Church, to preferve the Memory of that Affair.

Bzovius, *Peter* of *Aranda,* Bifhop of *Calahorra,* Mafter of the Houfe of his Holi-
A. 1498.   nefs our Lord the Pope, was kept in Jayl, being defamed for *Mahometanifm*
§ 32. fin.   and Herefy. *Alexander* the Pope committed the Hearing and legal Determi-nation of his Caufe, to *Peter,* Arch-Bifhop of *Regio,* Governor of the City, *Peter* of *Venance,* Bifhop of *Cefena,* Auditor General of the Court of the Cau-fes of the Apoftolick Chamber, and *Egardus Durca,* Bifhop of *Slefwick,* one of the faid Auditors of the Caufes of the facred Apoftolick Chamber. When they had examined feveral Witneffes on Behalf of the Fifcal, and 101 on the Behalf of *Aranda,* who all of them depofed either in part or in whole, a-gainft the faid *Aranda,* after the Procefs was duly carried on againft him, at length the faid Lords Commiffaries did, on *Wednefday, Sept.* 14. report the Procefs and Depofitions of the Witneffes to our holy Lord the Pope, in a private Confiftory. *Alexander,* when he underftood the Affair, by the Ad-vice of the moft Reverend Lords the Cardinals, deprived *Aranda* of the E-pifcopal Dignity, and of all his Benefices and Offices, and depofed and de-graded him from all his Orders ; and being thus deprived, depofed, and de-graded, he was at laft thrown into Jayl in the Caftle of St. *Angelo. Brucardus in diariis hujus anni.*

How the Solemnity of a general Sermon or Act of Faith was formerly ob-ferved, plainly appears from the Book of the Sentences of the *Tholoufe* Inqui-fition. The People being called together into the Church, and after the preaching the Sermon concerning the Faith, the Act commenced by an Oath, which the Inquifitors gave to the Civil Magiftrates, by which they promifed their Affiftance to difcover and apprehend Hereticks, and to accufe and de-nounce them to the Inquifitors ; and finally conclude, *And in thefe and all other Things which belong to the Office of the Inquifition, we will be obedient to God, and the Church of* Rome, *and the Inquifitors.* This Oath, as appears by compa-ring the feveral Sermons together, was afterwards fomewhat enlarged, that the Magiftrates might not have the leaft Pretence for conniving at He-refy.

After

After this Oath the Sentence of Excommunication was pronounced againſt ſuch as ſhould hinder the Office of the Inquiſition, by which all were put under Excommunication, *Who have knowingly hindered the Office of the Inquiſition, or for the future ſhall hinder it by any Means, directly or indirectly, openly or ſecretly, either by concealing the Truth themſelves, or revoking what they have legally confeſſed, or by unlawfully perſuading others to conceal or revoke it ; and alſo whoſoever ſhall directly or indirectly, openly or privately, knowingly grant Counſel, Aſſiſtance or Favour hereto.* Thus runs the firſt Form of Excommunication in the ſecond Sermon in the Book of Sentences, which was in others differently enlarged, that no Perſon, ever ſo ſlightly ſuſpected, might eſcape the Hands of the Inquiſitors, and that the Magiſtrate might have no poſſible way of throwing any Hindrance to the Inquiſitors in their holy Office.

After this follows the Act of the Inquiſition, and that the Tribunal may appear ſomewhat merciful and kind, they uſually began the Act with pardoning or mitigating the Puniſhment to ſome few Perſons, condemning at the ſame time a great many to the ſame or heavier Puniſhments. From ſome they took their Croſſes, and injoined them ſome arbitrary Penance. Others were brought out of Jayl, and had Croſſes put on them, which was a leſſer Puniſhment. When theſe Favours were beſtowed, the Sentences were read over, by which Penances were injoined the Criminals.

The firſt Sentences were thoſe of the Croſs-Bearers, who were injoined to wear Croſſes on their Breaſt and Back, and if their Crimes were very heinous, they were condemned to wear two. If it happened that their Faults were ſlight, they were injoined arbitrary Penance without Croſſes. An Inſtance of which we have, *fol.* 81. Then follow the Sentences of thoſe who were to be immured, who were condemned to perpetual Impriſonment, there to do wholeſome Penance with the Bread of Grief, and Water of Affliction. If the Offences of any ſuch were very grievous, they were more cloſely and ſtraitly confined, and put in Irons.

Then follow the Sentences of the Impenitent and Relapſed, who are delivered over to the ſecular Court ; then the Sentences againſt the Dead, and againſt the Houſes in which any Perſons have committed Hereſy, and finally againſt the Fugitives. When the Sentence is pronounced, the Goſpels are placed before the Inquiſitors, as tho' nothing was decided without taking Counſel from God. This their uſual Form, which generally occurs in the Sentences, plainly ſhews. *Having God before our Eyes, and the Purity of the orthodox Faith, and having theſe holy Goſpels placed before us, that our Sentence may come from the Face of God, and our Eyes may behold Equity.*

The whole Act being finiſhed, the Inquiſitor performed three Things. Firſt, He granted forty Days Indulgencies to all who were preſent at Church at the aforeſaid Acts of Faith. *Secondly,* He proclaimed publickly, that all who had given Counſel, Aſſiſtance or Favour, towards any one's abjuring Hereſy, and returning to the Unity of the Church, *viz.* all ſuch as inform, bear Witneſs, adviſe, read the Crimes, Abjuration and Sentence, and the Officers who keep them in Cuſtody, ſhall obtain three Years Indulgencies from the Pope. *Thirdly,* He notifies to all, that whoſoever knows any Heretick,

Eymer. P. 3. n. 195.

retick, or Perfon defamed or fufpected of Herefy, and fhall denounce him to the Inquifitors, fhall alfo obtain from the Pope three Years Indulgencies. And this concludes the whole Act, and was formerly the Manner of holding a Sermon of the Faith.

Now let us fee how all Things are put in Execution at this time in *Spain* and *Portugal*, after the Act of Faith.

Direct.
p.3. n.164.
cont. 40.
Criminals penitent and reconciled, and brought out in publick Proceffion, are carried back to their former Jayls in the holy Office, the fame Day in which the Sentences are pronounced againft them, and the Day following are brought to an Audience of the Inquifitors, and are admonifhed of thofe Things which are injoined them by their Sentences, and how grievoufly they will be punifhed, unlefs they humbly do the Penances affign'd them. After this, they fend every one to the Place to which his Sentence ordered him. Thofe who are condemned to the Gallies, are fent to the Jayls of the fecular Judges. Some are whipped thro' the principal Streets of the City, and fometimes receive two hundred Lafhes. Others wear the infamous *Sambenito*, fome every Day, others muft appear in them only *Sundays* and Holydays. But in thefe Things every one obferves the Cuftom of his own Inquifition. In the Inquifition at *Goa* this is the Method. Before the Prifoners are difmiffed, they are carried from Jayl to fome other Houfe, where they are every Day inftructed in the Doctrines and Rites of the Church of *Rome*; and when they are difmiffed, every one hath a Writing given him, containing the Penances injoined them; to which is added a Command, that every one fhall exactly keep fecret every Thing he hath feen, faid or heard, and all the Tranfactions relating to him, whether at the Table, or in other Places of the holy Office. And to this Secrefy every Prifoner binds himfelf by a folemn Oath.

The Day after this Solemnity alfo, the Effigies of thofe condemned to Death, painted to the Life, are carried to the *Dominicans* Church, and there hung up to be viewed by all. The Cuftom in this Matter is defcribed by *Ludovicus a Paramo*. " There is another Monument of Infamy, which, tho' " vulgarly called by the *Spaniards*, *Sambenito*, yet is not a Garment, but a " Cloath affixed to the Walls of the Churches for perpetual Infamy in the " Parifhes where they lived. On this Cloath is written the Name and Sur- " name of the Criminal, and the Bufinefs he carried on is alfo expreffed. " If he difcovers any farther, they add another little Piece to the Cloath to " prevent Doubt, defcribing his Country, and oftentimes alfo the Parents and " Grandfathers of the condemned Perfon.

l. 1. t. 2.
c. 5. n. 9.
10, 11.

" In fome of thefe Cloaths may be read, who were the Parents of the Crimi- " nals, of what Race they were, whether they were married, or if married " Women, whofe Wives they were, whether lately recovered to the Chri- " ftian Religion from the *Jewifh* Law and *Mahometan* Sect. Finally, the " Caufe of their Penance is declared according to the Nature of their Crime, " *viz.* that he was an Arch-Heretick, a Dogmatift, a declared Heretick, " an heretical Apoftate, a feigned Penitent, negative and obftinate, an im- " penitent and relapfed Heretick, a *Lutheran*, Anabaptift, *Calvinift*, *Mar-* " *tianift* Heretick, even tho' they died before Condemnation. Befides this

I   " In-

" Infcription, there is alfo painted the Mark which is ufually put on living
" Penitents, as is above explained. In the antient Cloaths, which have not
" yet been repaired, one may fee an upright Crofs. Befides thefe already
" mentioned, other Things may be feen in them ; for in fome the Perfon and
" Crime is omitted, and this one Word only written without the Picture,
" *Combuftus, Burnt.* On the Cloaths of fuch as are reconciled, this Word on-
" ly without any Crofs or Mark, *Reconciliatus, Reconciled.* Sometimes the
" Date of the Year is wanting. Sometimes the Flames are painted without
" any Infcription, fo that the Criminal can't poffibly be known. Some
" Cloaths are to be feen, from the Ends of which the Threads hang out, in
" which probably there is nothing remarkable, and which feem to be made
" of the very End of the Piece. The Caufe of fo great a Variety in thefe
" Cloaths feems to be this, that formerly the Fathers of the holy Inquifition
" did not publifh Conftitutions concerning all thefe Matters, as they have
" now done. For after that the Inftructions of the Inquifitors were printed
" at *Madrid*, there is extant a peculiar Conftitution, in which the Manner of
" fixing up, and keeping in Repair thefe Cloaths of Infamy is prefcribed.
" 'Tis decreed in this manner, *Cap.* 81. *'Tis known, that the Monuments of*
" *Infamy of condemned Perfons, both living, whether prefent or abfent, or*
" *dead, muft be hung up on the Walls of the Churches of the Parifhes where*
" *they lived ; and that whether they are imprifoned, or deceafed, or fled.*
" *'Tis the fame as to reconciled Perfons, after having performed the Penan-*
" *ces injoined them, and the taking off their Habits, even altho' they were*
" *cloathed in them only for the Proceffion at the Act of Faith, and whilft*
" *their Sentences were read over.* This is inviolably obferved, and no one
" hath Power to make any Alteration herein ; but 'tis always recommended·
" to the Inquifitors, that they fhould take diligent Care to repair thefe Effi-
" gies, efpecially in the Provinces which they vifit, that the Infamy of He-
" reticks and their Pofterity may never be forgotten. The Time alfo of
" Condemnation muft be written on thefe Cloaths, and it muft be particularly
" fpecified, whether they offended as *Jews, Saracens, Lutherans,* and embra-
" ced the Herefies of their Followers and other impious Perfons. However,
" thefe Monuments of Infamy and Difgrace are not to be fixed up to render
" thofe infamous, who are reconciled during the Time of Indulgence and
" Grace. For as it was agreed with them, that they fhould not wear fuch in-
" famous Habits, nor be cloathed with them during the Time of their Re-
" conciliation, it would be contrary to Reafon and Juftice to hang them up ;
" becaufe it would be wholly to deftroy the Favour granted them. This
" Conftitution is obferved in all the Kingdoms and Dominions of the King of
" *Spain,* except in *Sicily* ; where, in the Year 1543. when the Licentiate *Cer-*
" *vera* was Inquifitor there, there was a very great Commotion at *Palermo,*
" when the People rofe againft the holy Inquifition, and tore off the infa-
" mous Cloaths from the Walls of the Church dedicated to St. *Dominick,* with
" fo great a Fury and Rage, that they could never, to this Day, fix them up
" again upon the Walls either of that, or any other Church.

C H A P.

C H A P. XLII.

An Enumeration of the several Instances of Injustice and Cruelty practised in the Tribunal of the Inquisition.

THUS far we have described the Method of Proceeding observed in the Inquisition, as far as we could learn it from the Writings of the Papists, and even the Inquisitors themselves ; and if we attentively consider it, and compare it with the usual Method of Proceeding in all other Courts, we shall find it to be a Series and Connection of Injustice and Cruelties, and subversive of all Laws both divine and humane.

The Papists usually recommend to their own People this Tribunal as an holy one, and call the Inquisition the holy Office. But if we consider it throughly, we shall find 'tis all Disguise, by which they endeavour to palliate and cover over the Villany and Injustice of this Court. I will not now undertake to shew that the Causes which are managed before this Tribunal, are not subject to humane Judgment, but belong to the Tribunal of God and his Son Christ. For God only, the supream Lord of all, who can save, and can destroy, can prescribe the Laws of Salvation and Damnation. He only, as Omniscient and Searcher of Hearts, can pronounce an infallible Judgment of every one's Faith, which lies concealed in his Mind, and which he may dissemble by Words or Actions, and hath admitted no Man as Partner with himself in this Power. From hence it evidently follows, that 'tis a sacrilegious Violation of the divine Majesty and Laws, in that the Pope of *Rome* arrogates to himself the Judgment of the Faith, prescribes Laws of Believing to the Faithful, erects the Tribunal of an Inquisition, sends every where Inquisitors as Judges delegated by him, who, in his Name, and by a Power granted by him, are to inquire into the Faith of all, and punish those who are not in all Things obedient to the Pope. Nor will I here examine that villanous Doctrine by which they teach, that Hereticks are to be deprived of all Power, so that Faith is not to be kept with them, Subjects are not bound by their Oath of Allegiance and Fidelity, that the Husband or Wife, for the Heresy of either, is freed from the Laws of Matrimony, and even Children from Obedience to their Parents. For 'tis fully evident that this Doctrine subverts all Laws divine and humane.

I will only in a few Words represent the principal Iniquities and Instances of Injustice of this Tribunal, in which, as to the Reason and Method of Proceeding in Favour of the Faith, it differs from the Laws and Customs of all other Courts ; whereby Things evidently unjust in other Tribunals, are in this accounted just. I shall not indeed mention all, but the Chief only, and most remarkable Instances, as Specimens of the rest.

I. The

I. The firft is, that the Inquifitors by publifhing an Edict of the Faith, oblige all under the Penalty of Excommunication, to inform before them of every one, whom they fufpect of Herefy for the flighteft Caufe; fo that not only a Relation is bound to accufe his Relation, a Brother his Brother, and by his Information to bring him into Danger of being burnt, the moft horrible of all Punifhments; but even a Wife her Husband, yea, what deftroys all the Laws of Nature, a Son, according to the Opinion of many Doctors, is bound to inform againft his Father, if a fecret Heretick. And tho' fome think the Son exempted from this Obligation, yet they fay he is to be commended when he accufes his Father, becaufe he prefers the Caufe of the Faith and Church to any carnal Relation. Yea, he is fometimes tempted by Rewards to give fuch an Information. For when the Effects of Hereticks are confifcated, fo that the Son can't be his Father's Heir, yet he recovers his Father's Effects as the Reward of informing againft him. What is this better than to folicite by Rewards wicked, ftubborn and rebellious Children, whom their Parents may have corrected for their diffolute Manners, to accufe their Parents of feigned Crimes, or at leaft to become Betrayers of them.

II. A fecond Inftance of Injuftice is, their condemning a Perfon, defamed only for Herefy, to make canonical Purgation, *i. e.* to purge himfelf with feven, more or lefs, Compurgators; fo that if he fails in one, two or three, he is accounted guilty. For thus the Life and Torture of any one depends on the Will and Pleafure of another, and 'tis enough to declare him to be an Heretick, if one of the Compurgators dares not fwear, that he believes to be true, what the defamed Perfon afferts upon his Oath. And altho' they confefs that canonical Purgation is a very deceitful Method, their Injuftice can't be excufed, becaufe notwithftanding this, they ufe it in their Court.

III. A third is, that in this Office, every one, tho' excluded by other Courts, is admitted for a Witnefs, a mortal Enemy only excepted.

IV. To this may be added a fourth, that the Names of the Witneffes are not fhewn to the Prifoner, nor is any Circumftance difcovered to him by which he can come to the Knowledge of the Witneffes. Who doth not fee, that the Defence of the Prifoners is maimed and imperfect, who, tho' accufed, as they think, of the moft heinous Crime, hath no Adverfary againft whom he can defend himfelf, but like blind and groping Perfons, muft endeavour to find him out, whilft, in the mean while, they are ordinarily accufed by, and make their Defence againft a different Perfon? 'Tis well known, that fuch is the Wickednefs of Mankind, that fome will readily endeavour the Deftruction of others by falfe Information and Witnefs, if they can conceal themfelves, efpecially if infamous and perjured Perfons, guilty of almoft
every

every Crime, be admitted as Witneffes, and folicited with Promifes and Re-wards. Befides, who can pretend to form a certain Judgment of mortal Enmity, which lies concealed in the Mind, and of which no Man can therefore be a certain Judge? The Caufes of fuch Enmity are no abfolute Difcovery of it. One may fee fome Perfons fo meek, and fo fully poffeffed with the Fear of God, as that tho' they are injured in the moft grievous Manner, they will not harbour Enmity in their Breaft; whilft others, tho' injured in a very trifling Manner, yea, giving a wrong Turn to an indifferent Action, fhall conceive an irreconcilable Hatred, and cherifh a mortal Enmity. Who can here judge of the Mind of either? When the Judge hath confidered the Caufe of the Enmity, if it doth not appear to him to be fufficient, he will pronounce the Man not to be at mortal Enmity, tho' at the fame time his Mind may burn with Anger and Revenge. And thus he becomes a proper Witnefs, becaufe he is of a worfe Difpofition than the Judge dares prefume him to be; whereby the miferable Wretch, who happens to have fuch an Enemy, perifhes by fuch an Evidence.

V. A fifth Inftance of Injuftice is, that if two unexceptionable Witneffes, who yet muft ever be liable to Exception, becaufe unknown to the Criminal, teftify of different Facts, yea, fometimes if there be one only, yea, if but a mere Report, they think it enough to order to the Torture. Hereby there is an End at once of the moft innocent Perfon in the World, and the Inquifitor hath it in his Power by this Means to make any one guilty by his own proper Confeffion. For how eafily doth it happen, and there are Inftances enough of this in the Court of the Inquifition, for a wicked Wretch, or an Enemy to charge an innocent Perfon with the Crime of Herefy, when he is certain that he is not obliged to prove his Information, and that his Name fhall not be difcovered. In the mean while the Perfon informed againft is condemned to the Torture, and without End and Meafure tormented with the moft cruel Torments, till he makes a Confeffion of a Crime that he hath never committed; which is fo evident, that Friar *Bernard Deliciofi* formerly faid, as appears in his Sentence, *That even St.* Peter *and St.* Paul *could not defend themfelves from Herefy, if they were now alive, if Inquifition was made againft them according to the Manner ufed by the Inquifitors.*

VI. The fixth is, that two unexceptionable Witneffes who agree, are fufficient for the Conviction and Condemnation of any Perfon. 'Tis well known that many Things might be objected againft the Credit of the Witneffes, if they were known, by which the Weight of their Evidence might be leffened; and that they might be oftentimes convicted of Falfhood by feveral Circumftances, by the Teftimony of others prefent, and by other Means. But who can defend himfelf againft Perfons he doth not know? All that he can do is to guefs and conjecture who the Accufers and Witneffes are. If he miftakes in this, all his Defence is in vain. If the Prifoner fhould happen to guefs right, yet the Witneffes are never difcovered to him, and he muft make his

Defence

Defence againſt them upon a bare Suſpicion. In the mean while the Inquiſitor is to judge, whether the Priſoner weakens or deſtroys the Credit of the Witneſs. If he cannot deſtroy the Evidence, altho' he be the moſt innocent Perſon, al. tho' he proteſts that he is a Catholick, and will die in the Faith of the Church of *Rome,* yet he can't eſcape being condemned as a convicted Heretick, and being delivered over to the ſecular Power to be burnt for Contumacy and Impenitency. Nor muſt he, unleſs he will commit a mortal Sin, redeem his Life by a falſe Confeſſion of a Crime he hath not committed. So that in this Caſe the miſerable Wretch, falſly accuſed, which they themſelves allow doth ſometimes happen, is condemned as an Heretick by the Laws of the Inqui. ſition, delivered over to the ſecular Court to be burnt, and yet is at the ſame time a true Catholick, and, as they themſelves ſay, ſhall obtain for this Wrong the Crown of Martyrdom. So that an innocent and juſt Perſon is condemned by the Laws of the Inquiſition, and he whom the Inquiſitors ſen. tence to Death, is a Perſon acceptable to God, and to be honoured with a Crown of Martyrdom. 'Tis a Scandal that any Tribunal ſhould be erected, againſt which ſo foul an Objection lies ; or that the Church, after Satisfaction is made to God, and the internal Court of the Church by Repentance, ſhould erect another external Court, where Satisfaction muſt be made by the Puniſh-ment of the Penitent.

VII. A ſeventh Inſtance is, that they would have Perſons informed againſt become their own Accuſers. For as ſoon as ever any one is thrown into Jayl, he is bound by an Oath to declare the Truth. Then he is asked the Reaſon of his Impriſonment, that he may accuſe himſelf, if he hath happened to do any thing that will render him guilty in the Court of the Inquiſition. Whereas the Method of all Courts requires that the Accuſation be ſhewn to the Cri-minal, and he himſelf be examined concerning the Fact he is accuſed of. But in the Inquiſition every Priſoner is left to gueſs at the Crime he is accuſed of. There are oftentimes Things ſpoken innocently and inadvertently, ſome-times Words are turned into a quite different Senſe, ſometimes the Crime it ſelf is evidently forged; and, in the mean while, if he can't accuſe himſelf, he miſerably pines away ſometimes for Years together in an execrable Jayl, that his Conſtancy may be broken by the Ted{iou}ſneſs of his Impriſonment. If he can't gueſs at the Crime, and waits till 'tis objected againſt him by the Promotor Fiſcal, he is looked on as guilty of Contumacy, ſtubborn, and perjured, and if then by Chance he remembers the Crime, and owns it, he is more grievouſly puniſhed, becauſe he would not voluntarily confeſs it. But if he doth not acknowledge it, he is tortured, tho' it be not fully proved; but if it be fully proved, he is condemned, according to the Laws of the In-quiſition, as a negative Convict. So that however he behave, he can't poſ-ſibly eſcape the cruel Hands of the Inquiſitors.

VIII. An eighth Inſtance is, that the Inquiſitors uſe various Arts to draw out a Confeſſion from the Priſoners, by making them deceitful Promiſes,

which, when they have got the Confeffion, they don't believe themfelves obliged to fulfil ; and to get them by artful and evafive Interrogatories to declare,
that the Informers and Witneffes are not their mortal Enemies ; that fo the
Prifoner being deftitute of all human Affiftance and Comfort, and feeing no End
to his Miferies, may, thro' the Art and Fraud of the Inquifitor, have no poffible
way left to defend himfelf. And yet in the mean while thefe Wretches affect
the Appearance of Juftice, and grant the Criminals an Advocate and Procurator to manage their Caufe. But in this the Prifoner is miferably deceived.

IX. And this is a ninth Specimen of their Injuftice, becaufe the Advocate
granted to him is given him only to betray him. For he may not choofe
fuch an Advocate as he himfelf approves of, nor is it lawful for the Advocate to defend the Prifoner, unlefs he would be accounted as a Favourer of
Herefy ; but the Inquifition it felf affigns him his Advocate, bound to them
by an Oath, whofe principal Bufinefs is to perfuade the Criminal to
confefs the Crime he is accufed of, not to ufe any Methods of Defence not practifed in the Court of the Inquifition, and immediately to
quit his Defence, if he can't defend him according to the Laws of the
Inquifition. Befides, the Defences they ufe are mere Trifles and Impoftures,
by which they miferably deceive the Prifoners, fo that tho' they feem to be
endeavouring to do a great deal, they in Reality do nothing at all ; but only
obferve a few Forms, that the Procefs in the mean while may be prepared
and finifhed, according to the Cuftom obferved in the Inquifition.

X. A tenth is, that when the Crimes cannot be proved againft the Prifoner,
he is not abfolved from the Crime of which he is accufed, but only from Profecution ; and all the Declaration that is made is, that the Crime againft him
is not proved by proper Witneffes ; and this Sentence is never taken for an
adjudged Cafe. So that he who is once informed againft to the Inquifition,
altho' he be innocent, and his Crime can't be proved according to the received Manner of the Inquifition, tho' indeed, according to that Manner, all
Crimes, of which there is but the leaft Sufpicion, may be eafily proved ; yet
he is never blotted out of the Inquifitors Book or Index, but his Name is
there preferved in perpetual Remembrance of his being a fufpected Perfon,
that if he fhould happen to be informed againft for Herefy at any other time,
thefe latter Informations added to the former may amount to a real Proof,
and that altho' he is difmiffed from Jayl by the Sentence of the Judge, he
may never be able to live in Safety, but that being always fufpected by the
Inquifitor, he may be arrefted for the fame Crime which ought to have been
forgotten, upon the frefh Information of fome vile and wicked Fellow.

XI. An eleventh, and that not the leaft Inftance of Injuftice, is, their
Readinefs to put Perfons to the Torture, and that to difcover a fecret Crime,
lying concealed in the Mind ; yea, that they will ufe the Torture fo much
the fooner, becaufe the Crime is more concealed than other Crimes. 'Tis
well

well known to all, that Torture is a very deceitful Method of difcovering the Truth, becaufe thofe who confefs the Truth, and who declare Falfhoods, have the very fame End to their Pain. And therefore Lawyers will never have the Torture made ufe of, unlefs when the Crime is fufficiently proved, and there wants nothing but the Criminal's own Confeffion. But as to fecret Crimes, to be ready to inflict the Torture is the higheft Injuftice, and neceffarily fubjects many innocent Perfons to the moft grievous Punifhment ; whilft being unable to refift the Cruelty of their Torments, they had rather make themfelves guilty, by a falfe Confeffion of a Crime they never fo much as thought of, to put an immediate End to their moft cruel Punifhment, than to endure any longer thofe moft dreadful Torments, of which they can fee no manner of End.

XII. The twelfth is, their putting Perfons to the Torture upon half full Proof of the Crime. This half full Proof is Faultering, Defamation, and one Witnefs of his own Knowledge, or when the Tokens are vehement and violent. All thefe Things are fubject to the Pleafure of the Judge. So that if any one falls into the Hands of a cruel Inquifitor, and faulters in his Anfwer, or is informed againft by one Witnefs, who declares he was prefent at the Action or Words he gives Information of, he can't poffibly efcape the Torture, nor confequently the Punifhment of the Crime he is accufed of, confidering the Violence of the Torments. Nor is this all, but as there may be fome Facts occafioned not fo much by Herefy concealed in the Mind, as by carnal Concupifcence or Rafhnefs, they will have fuch to be tortured for their Intention, and force them by Torments to confefs they had an heretical Intention in their Mind.

XIII. A thirteenth is, that when they prepare themfelves for the Torture, they gravely and ferioufly admonifh the Criminal, to fpeak nothing but the Truth, and to confefs nothing that is not agreeable to Truth to avoid the Tortures. By this Means they put on the Appearance of Sincerity, as tho' they fought nothing but the naked Truth, that when the Torture is finifhed they may be very fecure that the tortured Perfon hath confeffed a real Crime ; becaufe they have ferioufly and gravely admonifhed him to fay nothing contrary to Truth. In the mean while they fuppofe, that the Crime objected againft him is real, and endeavour to force from him a Confeffion by Torture, and threaten to double his Torments unlefs he confeffes ; fo that if he denies the Crime, his Torments are aggravated ; if he confeffes it his Torments are foon ended. Hence it appears, that their Defign is not honeftly to find out the Truth by Torture, but that they fuppofe the Crime is real, altho' according to the Laws of the Inquifition it be only half proved, and then extort a Confeffion of it.

XIV. A fourteenth is, that whereas in other Courts the Number is certainly fixed how often the Torture may be repeated, they have invented a Method

of

of torturing Perfons very often, without offending againſt the Law, which provides that the Tortures ſhall not be repeated above twice or thrice. If, for Inſtance, they make uſe of the leſſer Tortures, and the Priſoner confeſſes nothing, they afterwards make uſe of more grievous ones, then proceed to ſuch as are more cruel, till at different Intervals of Time they have gone thro' all the ſeveral Kinds of Tortures. And this they don't call a Repetition, but only a Continuation of the Torture ; ſo that if any one hath been ſeveral times tortured, but with a different kind of Torture each time, and hath thus at certain Diſtances gone thro' all the Kinds of Torture, according to the Opinion of theſe merciful Caſuiſts, he ought to be accounted as tortured only once.

XV. A fifteenth is, that when they deliver condemned Perſons to the ſecular Arm, they intercede for them, that their Puniſhment may be ſo moderated, as to prevent ſhedding of Blood, or Danger of Death. And in the mean while, if the Magiſtrate is not ready to burn the Hereticks, or delays the Puniſhment, they oblige him, under Penalty of Excommunication, to execute the Sentence. The ſuperſtitious Wretches are afraid they ſhould become irregular, by delivering a Criminal to the ſecular Magiſtrate without Interceſſion, and yet are not afraid of becoming irregular, by compelling the Magiſtrate under Penalty of Excommunication, to murther thoſe whom they have condemned. Can any thing be more evident, than that this is nothing more than acting a Part, and an Affectation to be thought by the People to have no Hand in the Murther of which they are really the Authors ?

XVI. The laſt Inſtance I ſhall mention appears in their ridiculous Proceſs againſt the Dead, whoſe Relations and Heirs they cite, to appear on ſuch a Day to defend, if they can and will, the Memory of the Dead. Whereas they themſelves have made it a Law, that if any one appears in Defence of an Heretick, he ſhall be accounted as a Favourer of Hereticks himſelf, and condemned as ſuch, and have no Advocate or Procurator to defend himſelf. So that they cite all Perſons to defend the Memory of the Dead, and yet deter all Perſons from ſuch Defence by a moſt grievous Puniſhment, appointed againſt the Favourers of Hereticks. So that all this is, like their Interceſſion for Criminals, mere Impoſture and Sham. Then they provide an Advocate to manage the Cauſe, bound to them under an Oath, and he publickly declares he can't defend the Memory of the Deceaſed. So that as no one undertakes his Defence, the Accuſations againſt him are reckoned juſt, the Proofs legal, and the Deceaſed is condemned for Hereſy. But what greater Inſtance of Injuſtice can there be, than to condemn a Perſon as convicted, whoſe Defence no one dares undertake, without running the Hazard of his Fortune and Life.

If any one conſiders theſe Things, which I have mentioned as Specimens only, he will find no Sanctity in the Court of the Inquiſition ; but muſt acknowledge, that in the whole Method of Proceeding there is nothing but Injuſtice,

Fraud, Impoftures, and the moft accurfed Hypocrify, by which the Inquifitors, under the feigned Pretence of Sanctity, endeavour to difguife the Villany of their Proceedings, that fo they may maintain their Dominion over the
miferable common People, and keep them all in Subjection to themfelves.
And tho' they do every Thing that is wicked and vile, yet they would have
all adore them for the venerable Character of Sanctity.

'Tis needlefs to mention here more Inftances of their Cruelty. I fhall fay
all in a few Words. The Miferies of the Jayl, in which the Prifoners are
generally confined by themfelves for feveral Years, fhut up in Darknefs, without being allowed any human Converfe, are fo great ; the Cruelty of their
Torments fo fevere, and their Punifhments fo exquifite, that they greatly exceed the Cruelty of all other Courts. For Perfons are not only burnt alive,
but their Mouths gagged, fo that they have not the Liberty to groan or
cry out in thofe moft horrible Tortures ; and by thus ftopping up their
Mouths, they are in fuch an Agony as that they are almoft ftrangled. But
their Cruelty towards the Penitent and converted is moft deteftable. For
whereas the Church ought, with open Arms, to embrace Penitents, in Imitation of the Shepherd who carried the loft Sheep on his Shoulders, and brought
it home to the Sheepfold, thefe Wretches injoin the moft grievous Punifhments on thofe whofe Lives they fpare, which with them are only wholefome
Penances. For they condemn them either to wear the infamous *Sambenito*, or
to Imprifonment, or the Gallies, whereby their very Life is oftentimes a Punifhment to them ; whilft others are denied the very Hopes of Life, efpecially the Relapfed, tho' they convert themfelves, who are condemned to Death
without Mercy. And yet the Sacraments are given to thofe who are reconciled to the Church when they defire it, and thus before they are put to Death
they become Members of the Church, put in a State of Salvation, and by the
Priefts themfelves moft certainly affured of an heavenly Crown. Can there be
any greater Cruelty, and more abhorrent from the Spirit of Chriftianity, than
to punifh with Death an erroneous Perfon who repents, detefts his Error, and
is now reconciled to the Church ? But the Ecclefiaftical Sanctions muft be fatisfied, and the Authority of the Church preferved intire, tho' the Laws of Jefus Chrift and the Commands of the Gofpel are trampled under Foot.

All thefe Iniquities are committed according to the very Laws of the Inquifition. Many Things are indeed in the Execution of this Office, left to the
Pleafure of the Inquifitors, which Power they often villanoufly abufe, as appears from their daily Practice, and innumerable Inftances ; for it was the
common Complaint of all Nations againft the Inquifition, what *Thuanus* tells
us was the Complaint of the *Neapolitans*: *That the perverfe and prepofterous* Hift. Lib. 3.
*Form of Trials increafed the Horror, becaufe it was contrary to natural Equity, and
to every legal Method in carrying on that Jurifdiction. Add to this the Inhumanity
of their Tortures, by which they violently extorted from the miferable and innocent Criminals, that they might deliver themfelves from their Torments, whatfoever
the delegated Judges would have them confefs, tho' generally contrary to Truth: And
for this Reafon 'twas juftly faid, that it was invented not for the fake of defending Religion,*

ligion, *which the primitive Church had provided for by a quite different Method,*
but that by this Means they might strip all Men of their Fortunes, and bring innocent
Persons into Danger of being destroyed. And that this was not said without Cause,
the *Netherlands* alone, not to seek for Instances elsewhere, are the most evident Demonstration.

Tom. 9.
p 860,
861. Ad-
vers Mo-
nach. Hisp.
    Erasmus gives us this Account of the Inquisition in his Time. *The Affair is*
carried on by Informers, deputed Persons, and Monks for Judges, without Honesty
or legal Form of Law. The three former pass Sentence in Jayl, two Monks are Wit-
nesses, and then the Stake is prepared. And afterwards : *But now sometimes the*
Monks spread a false Report, then they carry the poor Wretch, as a suspected Per-
son, to Jayl, there they dispute after their Manner, the Articles are taken down, and
the Fagots immediately got ready. The same Writer intimates, p. 858. *There is*
a great deal of Difference between an holy, and a false ensnaring Inquisition. A Fa-
ther inquires into the Life of his Son, that he may take Care of it. A Physician in-
quires into the Distemper of his Friend to cure him. So he who loves the House of
God inquires into the evil Errors that are in it, to heal them if he can ; or if he can-
not, to cut off the incurable Member when all Methods have been tried in vain, to
prevent the Evil from spreading wider. Again, another inquires in a very different
Manner only that he may betray. A Robber inquires that he may seize his Prey.
A scurrilous Person inquires that he may have an Opportunity of throwing Scandal.
An Enemy inquires, in order to destroy. A Tyrant inquires, that he may overthrow
the publick Liberty. The Devil also inquires, going about as a roaring Lion, seeking
whom he may devour. Such a kind of Inquisition every Christian Inquisitor ought
to detest. All who understand *Erasmus*'s Stile and Method of Writing, know,
that 'tis his Design to insinuate by this Caution, that the Inquisition is truly
such as he hath described it, and which therefore ought to be abhorred by every Christian Inquisitor.

l. 2. t. 3.
c. 4, 5.
    The Papists indeed glory, that the Inquisition is the most certain Remedy
to exstirpate Heresies. Especially *Ludovicus a Paramo* takes a great deal of
Pains to shew, that Heresies have in several Places been extinguished by Help
of the Inquisition, and at last concludes in these Words. *These are some of the*
fairest Fruits, which the most fertile Field of the holy Office hath produced to the
Church in all Kingdoms where it hath not been obstructed. But amongst all Provinces
and Countries the Kingdoms of Spain *do every Day receive the noblest Fruits. For*
as in these Countries the holy Office of the Inquisition is maintained with greater Se-
verity, and is in greater Honour and Esteem with the Nobles and Princes, so it flou-
rishes in greater Authority and Power, whereby the Judges of the Faith carry on
more diligent Inquisition against Heresies, and more effectually pull them up by the very
Roots. And because the Inquisition is so effectual a Method to exstirpate Heresies, he gathers from thence that it was ordained for this Purpose, by the
most wise Providence of God. But what is really unjust in it self, and carried on by unjust Methods, cannot have God for its Author, nor is Success
any Argument that the Inquisition is from God. The first Inquiry is, whether it be suitable to the Nature of the Christian Doctrine. If it be not, 'tis
then unjust and Anti-christian. Many Things are unrighteously undertaken
by

by Men, and accomplifhed by Violence and Cruelty, by which Innocence is oppreffed, which altho' God in his juft and wife Counfel permits, he is far from approving. Even in *Japan*, a cruel Perfecution hath extinguifhed the Chriftian Religion, as preached by the *Roman* Priefts; fo that the *Roman* Catholick Religion is equally extinguifhed there by the Violence of Perfecutions, as thofe Doctrines are in *Spain*, which are contrary to the Church of *Rome*, and which they render odious by the infamous Name of Herefy. And yet they will not allow that any juft Argument can be drawn from hence to prove, that that Perfecution was given by divine Providence, as a moft effectual Remedy for the Exftirpation of their Religion. If other Parties of Chriftians would ufe the fame Diligence and Cruelty of Inquifition againft them, I may venture to affirm, that they themfelves could not withftand it, but that within a few Years the Popifh Religion would be extinguifhed in all Proteftant Countries, and fcarce a fingle Perfon left who would dare to profefs it. But God forbid, that the Chriftian Religion fhould ever be propagated this way, which doth not confift in a feigned and hypocritical Profeffion, but in a fincere and undiffembled Faith. And therefore as no one ought to affume to himfelf the Power of Judging concerning it, but God the Searcher of Hearts, to him only let us leave it to pafs the true Judgment concerning every Man's Belief. Let us in the mean while deteft the Tyranny of the Papifts, and ftrive to reduce thofe who, in our Judgment, hold Errors, into the way of Truth, by the good Offices of Charity and Benevolence, without arrogating to our felves a Judgment over the Confciences of others. And out of a ferious Regard to the laft great Day of Judgment, let us approve our Confciences to God, and every one of us expecting from his Mercy an equitable and righteous Judgment, pray without ceafing, ARISE, O LORD, AND JUDGE THY CAUSE.

F I N I S.

Printed in Great Britain
by Amazon

45197110R00413